RECORD *of* SERVICE OF SOLICITORS AND ARTICLED CLERKS

WITH HIS MAJESTY'S FORCES

1914—1919

RECORD OF SERVICE

OF SOLICITORS AND ARTICLED CLERKS

WITH HIS MAJESTY'S FORCES

1914—1919

PRINTED BY
SPOTTISWOODE, BALLANTYNE & CO. LTD.
LONDON
1920

PREFACE

THE publication of this Record of the War Services rendered by the Solicitors and their Articled Clerks in the years 1914 *to* 1919 *is the fulfilment of one of the three objects of the Solicitors' War Memorial Fund. Although every effort has been made to render it complete and accurate it is known that there are many omissions which it has not been possible to supply and probably there are errors which have been overlooked.*

These imperfections it is hoped will be forgiven in the knowledge of the difficulties of the task and the belief that it has been gladly and lovingly discharged to the best of their ability by those to whom it was entrusted.

R · A · PINSENT,
Chairman of the Memorial Trustees.

4*th August,* 1920.

"These are they who for their Country and Freedom's sake jeoparded their lives unto the Death. Therefore they shall be mine, saith the Lord of Hosts, in that day when I make up my jewels."

RECORD OF SERVICE

OF

SOLICITORS AND ARTICLED CLERKS

GEORGE WYMAN ABBOTT.

Admitted Dec. 1909. Member of Wyman & Abbott, of Peterborough. Joined Nov. 1914 as 2nd Lieut. 1/1 Huntingdonshire Cyclist Batt., promoted Lieut. 1/7 Batt. The Royal Warwickshire Regt. Sept. 1916, and subsequently A/Capt., A/Major, A/Staff Capt., &c. Awarded the M.C. and Croce di Guerra (Italy). Served Home 1914 to June 1916, France June 1916 to Nov. 1917, and Italy Nov. 1917 to March 1919.

MAURICE ABBOTT.

Admitted Aug. 1897. Of 5 New Court, Lincoln's Inn, W.C. Served as Driver Royal Army Service Corps, attached to the 76th Field Ambulance, Royal Army Medical Corps.

RICHARD HUGHES ABELL.

Admitted April 1902. Practising at Worcester. Gazetted 2nd Lieut. 2/8 Batt. Worcestershire Regt. (T.F.) Sept. 1914, afterwards attaining the rank of Capt. Seconded to 1/1 South Midland Div. Cyclist Co. March 1915 and went to France, and subsequently seconded to 8th Corps Cyclist Batt. In Nov. 1918 appointed 3rd Corps Education Officer in Belgium.

LIONEL ABRAHAMS.

Admitted April 1912. Member of Wade-Gery & Brackenbury, St. Neots, Hunts. Joined Nov. 1916 as Lieut. T.F. Reserve General List. Served at Home.

ROBERT BERNARD ABRAHAMS.

Admitted July 1913. Member of Roberts, Abrahams & Co., of Basinghall Street, E.C. Joined University of London O.T.C. in July 1915. Appointed 2nd Lieut. to 3/4 Batt. Yorkshire Regt. Sept. 1915. Served in France. Killed Sept. 15, 1916, in the Battle of the Somme, and was buried near Martinhuich and High Wood.

CHARLES GERALD ACHESON-GRAY.

Articled to W. Ward-Higgs, of 29 Mincing Lane, E.C. Joined the Inns of Court O.T.C. and afterwards gazetted 2nd Lieut. 4th Batt. Dorsetshire Regt. Promoted Lieut.

WILLIAM FITZROY ACKLAND.

Admitted Dec. 1908. Member of Ackland, Son & Baily, of Saffron Walden, Essex. Mobilised Aug. 1914 as Major 8th Essex Regt., promoted A/Lieut.-Col. March 1919. Once mentioned in Dispatches. Awarded the T.D. Served at Home 1914 to 1916, France 1916 to 1918, Ireland, 1918 to 1919.

JOHN WILLIAM ACKROYD.

Admitted Oct. 1916. Member of Butler & Ackroyd, of Bradford, Yorks. Joined July 1, 1916, as Private Royal Army Service Corps (M.T.).

ALAN GORDON ACHESON ADAM.

Admitted Aug. 1910. Practised at Cranbrook & Malling, Kent. Mobilised Aug. 1914 as Lieut. 5th Batt. the Buffs. Promoted Capt. Nov. 1915. Once mentioned in Dispatches. Served in India & Mesopotamia. Killed in the Advance for the Relief of Kut-el-Amara, Jan. 21, 1916.

CHARLES CLEMENTS ADAM.

Articled to S. T. James, of 3 & 4 Clement's Inn, W.C. Served as Petty Officer Air Mechanic, Royal Naval Air Service.

ALFRED FRANCIS ADAMS.

Admitted May 1908. Of 5 Fenchurch Street, E.C. Served as 2nd Lieut. Machine Gun Corps.

APPELBE CHISHOLM ADAMS.

Admitted June 1906. Member of Stephenson, Harwood & Co., 31 Lombard Street, London E.C. 3. Joined January 1916, Ensign, First or Grenadier Regt. of Foot Guards. Promoted Lieut. Sept. 1916, A/Capt. May 1918. Served in France and Belgium 1916 to 1917, General Staff 1917 to 1919. Wounded July 27, 1917, at Boesinghe in Belgium.

ARTHUR JOSEPH ADAMS.

Admitted Dec. 1912. Practised at 25 Bedford Row, W.C., and Coventry. Enlisted August 1914 as a Private in Public Schools Batt. Obtained commission as Lieut. and attached to 3rd Batt. Royal Warwickshire Regt. Oct. 1914. After 12 months' training went to France, where he joined 2nd Batt. Went into action at Somme Battle July 2, 1916, and wounded severely in leg. Sent to France again April 1918, joined 1st Batt. Killed at Remy Aug. 30, 1918, during attack on Cambrai. Buried at Remy.

EDWARD CARINGTON ADAMS.

Articled to Hugh Adams, of 20 Essex Street, Strand, W.C. Joined Sept. 1914 as 2nd Lieut. 20th Batt. County of London Regt. (Blackheath & Woolwich). Served in France. Killed at Battle of Loos, Sept. 25, 1915.

GERALD DAY ADAMS.

Admitted Oct. 1908. Member of Harvey, Clarke & Adams, of Leicester. Joined Jan. 1915 2nd Lieut. Leicestershire Regt., Lieut. June 1916, Capt. and Adjutant July 1917 to Dec. 1917. Served in France, June 1915, Palestine, February 1918 to 1919. Gassed 1915, Malaria and Dysentery, Nov. 1918.

HENRY GORDON ADAMS.

Admitted Oct. 1910. Solicitor to the Town Clerk of Sheffield. Served as 2nd Lieut. Royal Field Artillery. Served in France. Killed in action Oct. 5, 1917.

KENNETH LEMESLE ADAMS.

Admitted Jan. 1912. Member of Adams & Son, of Wolverhampton. Joined Sept. 1914, as Private, 21st Batt. Royal Fusiliers. Gazetted 2nd Lieut.

Royal Engineers Nov. 1914, promoted 1st Lieut. Sept. 1915, Capt. Feb. 1918, Major Feb. 1918. Awarded the O.B.E. Served at Home Sept. 1914 to June 1915, Gallipoli June 1915 to Jan. 1916, Egypt Feb. 1916, Mesopotamia March 1916 to June 1916, India June 1916 to July 1919. Wounded Jan. 1916, Cape Hellas, Gallipoli.

LESLIE HORACE ADAMS.

Admitted Aug. 1912. With Blake, Reed, & Lapthorn, of Portsmouth. Mobilised Aug. 4, 1914, A.D.C. to G.O.C. Wessex Divisional Artillery, Aug. 1914 to Dec. 1914, promoted A/Major Dec. 1915. Commandant R.A. Depot, Bagdad, Nov. 1918 to March 1919. Served at Home, India, and Mesopotamia.

WILLIAM ADAMS.

Articled to Charles Alderson, of Morpeth, Northumberland. Joined July 16, 1917 as Private Northumberland Fusiliers, subsequently transferred to West Yorkshire Regiment and later to the Army Pay Corps. Left with rank of Corporal. Served at Home.

LEONARD HEDLEY ADCOCK.

Admitted July 1910. Practising at West Bromwich. Served as Corporal 18th Batt. Yorkshire Regt.

ARCHIBALD WILLIAM NORMAN ADDISON.

Admitted Dec. 1908. Member of Addison & Son, of Portsmouth. Served as Capt. 6th (Duke of Connaught's Own) Batt. Hampshire Regt. (T.) One of the Assistant Military Secretaries H.Q. Staff of the Army in India.

GERALD LACY ADDISON.

Admitted June 1900. Member of Linklaters & Paines, 2 Bond Court, Walbrook, E.C. Joined August 4, 1916, as Gunner Royal Garrison Artillery, promoted A/Bombardier, Sept. 1916, Full Bombardier Dec. 1916. Gazetted 2nd Lieut. July 1, 1917. Served at Home and in France.

GUY TEMPEST ADKIN.

Admitted Dec. 1908. Member of Adkin & Son, of 3 Salters' Hall Court, Cannon Street, E.C. 4. Joined May 27, 1916. Assistant Paymaster Royal Naval Reserve. Gazetted Paymaster-Lieut. Sept. 1918. Awarded M.B.E. (Military). Served June 1916 to July 1919 with H.M. Naval Base, Havre (Trawlers and Drifters).

CECIL GEORGE ADLER.

Admitted Aug. 1902. Practising at 2 Throgmorton Avenue, London, E.C. Joined Oct. 22, 1914, 2nd Lieut. Interpreter, promoted Lieut. Royal Army Ordnance Corps, Feb. 1915, and Capt. Nov. 1918. Served at Home, in France, Italy, and South Russia.

ARTHUR JOSEPH JOHN PAUL AGIUS.

Articled to A. G. Gibson, of 21 Leadenhall Street, E.C. 3. Mobilised Aug. 3, 1914, as Lieut. 3rd Batt. London Regt. (T.F.), promoted Temp. Capt. May 1915 and Substantive June 1916. Twice mentioned in Dispatches. Awarded the M.C. Served at Home Aug. 1914 to Sept. 1914, Malta Sept. 1914 to Jan. 1915, France Jan. 1915 to Jan. 1917, Home Jan. 1917 to March 1919.

FRANCIS BASIL AGLIONBY.

Admitted Aug. 1904. Member of Ellis, Richardson, Aglionby, & Hazel of Portland House, Basinghall Street, E.C. Joined Dec. 5, 1915, as Private 15th Batt. London Regt. (T.). Gazetted 2nd Lieut. Royal Garrison Artillery (T.), Aug. 1, 1917. Served in France July 1916 to March 1917, London A.A. Defences Nov. 1917, to Jan. 1919.

DENYS ALFRED LAFONE AINSLIE.

Articled to W. L. Ainslie, of 19 Surrey Street, W.C. Mobilised Aug. 1914 and transferred to 1st Batt. Devonshire Regt., promoted 1st Lieut. April 1915 (after death). Served in France. Killed in action at Givenchy lès La Bassée, Oct. 24, 1914.

ALBERT ROY HAMILTON AKASTER.

Admitted Feb. 1910. Member of Gill & Akaster, of Devonport. Enlisted as Gunner Royal Garrison Artillery and subsequently gazetted 2nd Lieut. in same Regt., promoted Lieut.

CEDRIC HARCOURT AKASTER.

Admitted March 1914. Practising at 7 Arundel Street, Strand, W.C. Enlisted as Private 30th Batt. Royal Fusiliers. Gazetted 2nd Lieut. 14th Batt. Royal Fusiliers Jan. 1916.

FRANCIS AKENHEAD.

Admitted Sept. 1907. Member of Morgan & Co., of Newport, Mon. Gazetted 2nd Lieut. 5th Batt. Manchester Regt. (T.), and attained the rank of Capt.

WILLIAM MASON AKERMAN.

Admitted May 1889. Practised at Hereford. Served as Lieut. Royal Army Service Corps.

JOHN HODSON ALCOCK.

Articled to J. E. Alcock, of Mansfield. Joined Jan. 11, 1915, as 2nd Lieut. 8th Batt. Lincolnshire Regt., promoted Lieut. July 1, 1917. Served in France. Taken prisoner at Loos Sept. 26, 1915. Prisoner of War in Germany till April 1918. Interned in Holland April to Nov. 1918.

THOMAS JONES ALCOCK.

Articled to F. J. Poole, of Sandbach. Joined July 1916 as Corporal Despatch Rider, Royal Engineers. Served in France.

ALAN STUART ALDERSON.

Admitted Oct. 1906. Member of Sidney, Son & Alderson, of Blyth. Mobilised July 29, 1914, as Capt. The Tynemouth Royal Garrison Artillery. Promoted Major June 1, 1916. Awarded the T.D. Served at Home 1914 to 1916, Ceylon 1916 to 1919.

HORACE WILFRED ALDRICH.

Admitted Nov. 1909. Practising at Brighton. Joined Feb. 9, 1917, as Private Inns of Court O.T.C. Gazetted 2nd Lieut. 304th Reserve Labour Company July 15, 1917, transferred to 3rd Batt. Devonshire Regt. Nov. 1917, promoted Lieut. Jan. 15, 1919. Served at Home and in France. While in France attached 10th Batt. The Duke of Cornwall's Light Infantry.

ERKINWALD BRAXTON MOORING ALDRIDGE.

Admitted Dec. 1908. Member of Mooring, Aldridge & Haydon, of Bournemouth. Joined as Private in Hon. Artillery Co. Dec. 6, 1915. Served in France 1916 to 1918.

GERALD ASHBURNER MOORING ALDRIDGE.

Practising at Bournemouth. Joined Aug. 1916, as Sub.-Lieut., Royal Naval Volunteer Reserve, subsequently promoted Lieut. Attached to H.M.M.L. Hydrophone Flotillas, Zeebrugge & Ostend Operations. C.O. of H.M.M.L. 260 Rhine Flotilla.

ALBERT GEORGE RICKARDS ALEXANDER.

Articled to James Millar, of 22 St. Thomas' Street, London Bridge, S.E. Enlisted as Private 8th Batt. Essex Regt.

AUBREY ALEXANDER.

Admitted Oct. 1908. Practised at Gray's Inn Chambers, High Holborn, W.C. Enlisted Sept. 1914, as Private 9th Batt. County of London Regt. (Queen Victoria Rifles). Gazetted 1st Lieut. 7th Batt. Middlesex Regt., attached 1/4 Batt. Royal Welch Fusiliers. Once mentioned in Dispatches. Served in France. Wounded German advance, March 1918. Died after bringing over a convoy of prisoners from France.

DONALD FOLEY ALEXANDER.

Articled to F. H. Trethowen, of Salisbury. Served as Private 14th Batt. County of London Regt. (London Scottish).

JAMES GRAHAM ALEXANDER.

Admitted Jan. 1906. Member of Grace, Smith & Co., of Liverpool. Enlisted Oct. 1914 as Private 4th Batt. Norfolk Regt. Transferred as Private to Inns of Court O.T.C. Jan. 29, 1915, subsequently gazetted 2nd Lieut. 7th Batt. Shropshire Light Infantry.

ROBERT MIDDLETON ALEXANDER.

Admitted June 1912. Of Hull. Served as Sergeant 10th Service Batt. East Yorkshire Regt. and subsequently gazetted 2nd Lieut. 13th Batt. East Yorkshire Regt., promoted Lieut.

WILLIAM LINDSAY ALEXANDER.

Articled to William Arthur Wightman, of Liverpool. Joined Royal Naval Volunteer Reserve as Signalman Sept. 4, 1916. Served at Home Signal Stations.

TREVOR RHYS ALLAWAY.

Articled to W. T Carless, of Hereford. Joined Jan. 6, 1912, as 2nd Lieut., 3rd Batt. South Wales Borderers, promoted Capt. May 1, 1915, and attached 2nd Welch Regt. Oct. 1914. Once mentioned in Dispatches. Awarded the M.C. Served in France 1914 and 1915, at Home 1915 to May 1916, and in Egypt May 1916 to June 1916. Accidentally killed by premature explosion of bomb at Grenade School, Zeitoun, Egypt, June 29, 1916.

FRANCIS PRIDEAUX ALLBUTT.

Articled to Nunn & Co., of Colwyn Bay. Mobilised Aug. 4, 1914, as Lance-Sergt. 5th Batt. Royal Welch Fusiliers, promoted to C.Q.M.S. April 1915.

Gazetted 2nd Lieut. 4th Batt. Royal Welch Fusiliers (T.F.) Dec. 1915. Joined Royal Flying Corps Jan. 1917, promoted Lieut. May 1917, Capt. Royal Air Force July 1918. Served in France.

ALBERT GEORGE ALLEN.

Articled to J. Ingram Dawson, of Barnard Castle. Joined Sept. 12, 1914, as Trooper Royal Horse Guards (Blue). Appointed Temp. 2nd Lieut. South Staffordshire Regt. March 2, 1915, promoted Temp. Capt. July 3, 1916, appointed Staff Capt. 51st Inf. Brigade Oct. 28, 1917, appointed Brigade Major 51st Inf. Brigade Sept. 7, 1918. Twice mentioned in Dispatches. Awarded the D.S.O. and M.C. Served at Home Sept. 1914 to July 1916, and in France July 1916 to May 1919. Wounded Battle of Somme July 10, 1916.

ALBERT VICTOR ALLEN.

Articled to W. W. Reed, of Dorchester. Served as Driver Royal Field Artillery.

CHARLES ROYLE ALLEN.

Admitted May 1899, practised as Ormerod & Allen, at Manchester. Rejoined 6th V.B. Manchester Regt. March 1915 and was sent to France July 1916, attached to the Royal Berkshire Regt., rank Capt. Awarded M.C. in Oct. 1917. Killed in action Sept. 27, 1918.

FREDERICK CLIFFORD BAWDEN ALLEN.

Articled to Frederick Allen, of Eastbourne. Served as Staff Sergt. 50th Gordon Highlanders, coming from British Columbia.

GERALD ELLISTON ALLEN.

Articled to H. E. Allen, of Wigan. Joined March 26, 1914, as 2nd Lieut. 5th Manchester Regt., promoted Lieut. March 1915, Capt. Aug. 1915, attached Royal Flying Corps Sept. 1917 to Aug. 1919. Served at Home, in Egypt, Gallipoli, France, and Canada. Wounded Aug. 8, 1915.

KENNETH FREDERICK ALLEN.

Articled to Frederick George Allen, of Portsmouth. Joined Sept. 9, 1914, as Second Lieut., Hants Royal Garrison Artillery (T.F.). Gazetted Lieut. July 9, 1915, and A/Capt. Sept. 1918. Once mentioned in Dispatches. Served at Home Sept. 1914 to Aug. 1916, and in France and Belgium until Jan. 1919.

RALPH ERIC HERBERT ALLEN.

Articled to the late Frederick Allen, of Eastbourne. Joined November 30, 1914, as Petty Officer Despatch Rider, Royal Navy Armoured Car Section, Air Mechanic Royal Naval Air Service Sept. 1915, Warrant Officer (Engineer) June 27, 1917, 2nd Lieut. Royal Air Force April 1, 1918, Flying Officer Sept. 12, 1919. Served in France 1915 and Coast Defence Stations. Wounded May 1915, Jan. 1916, and Aug. 1919.

RONALD WILBERFORCE ALLEN.

Admitted February 1913. Practising at 2 Walbrook, E.C. 4. Joined August 25, 1917, as Sub-Lieut., Royal Naval Volunteer Reserve. Served at Home Aug. 1917 to April 1919.

THOMAS FREITH ALLEN.

Articled to F. E. Hall, of Mexborough. Enlisted Feb. 6, 1916, as Private, 8th. Batt. York & Lancaster Regt., afterwards transferred to 1/6 West Yorkshire Regt. Served in France. Wounded on Jan. 7, 1917. Died from wounds Jan. 9, 1917.

FRANK LEONARD ALLWARD.

Admitted April 1906. Practising at 10 Gray's Inn Square, W.C. Joined the Middlesex Regt. Nov. 8, 1916, and afterwards transferred to the Army Pay Corps.

RICHARD ALMACK.

Admitted July 1909. One of the Assistant Solicitors to M. C. Tait, Solicitor, L. & N.W. Rly., Euston Station. Enlisted August 9, 1914, as Private, 1st Batt. Hon. Artillery Co. (Infantry). Gazetted 1st Lieut. Royal Engineers March 9, 1915. Gazetted Capt. Dec. 1, 1915. Served in Belgium and France from Sept. 1914 until May 1918, when invalided home.

ARTHUR JAMES ALMOND.

Admitted Nov. 1900. Member of Edwin Almond & Sons, of Manchester. Joined Inns of Court O.T.C. Dec. 1915. Gazetted 2nd Lieut. Dec. 1916, 1st Lieut. June 1918. Served in France Feb. 1917 to Dec. 1918.

WILLIAM EDMUND AMBROSE.

Admitted June 1907. Practising at Plymouth. Joined Royal Army Service Corps (M.T.) March 27, 1917. Commissioned as 2nd Lieut. May 22, 1917. Promoted Lieut. Nov. 22, 1918. Served at Home.

REGINALD AMOS.

Admitted Aug. 1905. Practised at Warrington. Served as 2nd Lieut. 10th Batt. King's Own Royal Lancaster Regt. from May 11, 1915, afterwards transferred to 12th Batt. Devonshire Regt. Promoted Lieut.

RICHARD FERRAND AMPHLETT.

Admitted June 1906. Member of Adams & Amphlett, of Wolverhampton. Joined June 1916, as 2nd Lieut., Worcestershire Regt. Served in France. Killed in action April 5, 1917.

ALBERT JOHN GORDON ANDERSON.

Admitted Oct. 1912. With Martineau & Reid, of 2 Raymond Buildings, Gray's Inn, W.C. Served as 2nd Lieut. 14th Batt. County of London Regt. (London Scottish) and attained the rank of Capt.

ANDREW STEWART ANDERSON.

Admitted July 1901. Member of Harrison, Burton, Alcock & Anderson, of Liverpool. Mobilised on outbreak of war as Capt. 10th Batt. King's Liverpool Regt. (Liverpool Scottish) (T.) and gazetted to his Majority Jan. 1905. Reported missing, believed killed, June 1915.

ARTHUR GEORGE ANDERSON.

Admitted July 1909. Member of Roberts, Riley, Creeke & Anderson, of Manchester. Enlisted April 1916, as Gunner, 3/1 Home Counties Brigade Royal Field Artillery (T.). Commissioned Dec. 16, 1916, as 2nd Lieut., Royal Field

Artillery and attached Royal Garrison Artillery, Sept. 1917. Promoted Lieut. June 1918, and A/Capt. and Adjutant Aug. 1918. Once mentioned in Dispatches. Served in France.

JOHN SLOANE ANDERSON.

Admitted Nov. 1911. Assistant Solicitor to Metropolitan Railway, Baker Street Station, N.W. Enlisted Aug. 28, 1914, as Private, 18th Batt. Royal Fusiliers. Gazetted 2nd Lieut. 9th Batt. The Queen's Royal West Surrey Regt. Feb. 22, 1915, 2nd Lieut. Royal Flying Corps Sept. 1915, promoted Lieut. Sept. 1916 and Capt. April 1, 1918. Served in France. Wounded Savy June 16, 1916, night bombing.

JOSEPH BAKER ANDERSON.

Admitted April 1900. Practising at Nottingham. Served as Sergeant 7th Batt. Notts & Derby Regt. (Sherwood Foresters) (T.).

KENNETH REINHARDT ANDERSON.

Articled to Alleyne Brown, of Southport. Served as 2nd Lieut. 7th Batt. King's Liverpool Regt. (T.) and attained the rank of Capt.

REGINALD ANDERSON.

Admitted Oct. 1908. Managing Clerk with Oxley & Coward, of Rotherham. Enlisted Nov. 1, 1915, as Private, 28th Batt. County of London Regt. (Artists Rifles). Gazetted 2nd Lieut. 5th Batt. York & Lancaster Regt. June 1916, promoted Lieut. July 12, 1917. Served in France 1916. Wounded Sept. 1, 1916.

GEORGE LYONS ANDREW.

Admitted Sept. 1905, practised at 52 Cheapside, E.C. Served as Lieut. 11th Batt. Cheshire Regt.

RICHARD HYNMAN ANDREW.

Admitted Jan. 1910. Managing Clerk with Andrew Wood, Purves & Sutton, of 8 & 9 Great James Street, Bedford Row, W.C. Joined Aug. 9, 1914, as Private, Hon. Artillery Co. (Infantry). Gazetted Temp. 2nd Lieut. Suffolk Regt. July 10, 1915, Temp. Lieut. (General List) July 10, 1916, Temp. Capt. (General List) Sept. 25, 1917 (Dep. Asst. Military Secretary), Temp. Lieut.-Col. (General List) Jan. 1, 1917 (Asst. Military Secretary). Mentioned in Dispatches three times. Awarded the M.C., the British Empire Order 4th Class, and the Order of the Nile 3rd Class. Served at Home Aug. 9 to Sept. 18, 1914, France Sept. 19, 1914 to June 1917, Egypt and Palestine June 1917 to Oct. 1919.

LANCELOT FREDERICK ANDREWES.

Admitted Feb. 1914. Practised at Hove. Served as Lieut. Royal Army Service Corps.

ARTHUR GEORGE ANDREWS.

Admitted May 1911. Practised at Enfield. Served as Lieut. " A " Battery Hon. Artillery Co.

ARTHUR NEWTON ANDREWS.

Admitted Nov. 1912. Private Secretary to Mr. E. A. Strauss, M.P. Joined Aug. 28, 1914, as 2nd Lieut., Oxford and Bucks Light Infantry, promoted to Captain 1915. Served at Home and in France. Invalided out March 1918.

FRANCIS NICHOLAS ANDREWS.

Articled to S. R. Andrews, of Bourne, Lincs. Joined Sept. 1914 as Private, Public Schools Batt. Gazetted 2nd Lieut. 15th Batt. Royal Irish Rifles, Dec. 10, 1914. Served in France. Died Oct. 11, 1915, at Villers Bocage (France) from sickness contracted during War.

GEORGE RODDAM ANGUS.

Articled to G. W. Hodgson, of Stanhope, Co. Durham. Joined Dec. 1914, as 2nd Lieut., 6th Batt. Durham Light Infantry. Promoted Temp. Lieut. in June 1915, Temp. Capt. April 1916. Reverted to 2nd Lieut. on returning to England in April 1916. Acting Capt. Nov. 1917. Awarded the M.C. Served at Home and in France and Belgium. Slightly wounded March 1916.

JOHN ARCHIBALD ANGUS.

Admitted Dec. 1913. Practised at Newcastle-on-Tyne. Served as 2nd Lieut. 3rd Batt. York and Lancaster Regt., and attained the rank of Capt. Awarded the M.C.

ALLAN YOUNG ANNAND.

Admitted Aug. 1913. On the Staff of the Public Trustee. Joined 28th Batt. County of London Regt. (Artists Rifles) as Private, Aug. 1914. Gazetted 2nd Lieut. 1st Batt. Highland Light Infantry, May 1915. Served in France and Mesopotamia. Wounded at Senn-a-gat March 1916. Killed in bombing action Jan. 9–10, 1917.

FRANK FOSTER ANNEAR.

Articled to W. P. Annear, of Cardiff. Served as Sergeant Royal Field Artillery (T). Gazetted 2nd Lieut. 3rd Batt. Royal Welch Fusiliers Dec. 1915.

JAMES BERTRAM ANNETT.

Admitted April 1913. Practising Morpeth, Northumberland. Joined June 1915 as Private, Inns of Court O.T.C. Gazetted 2nd Lieut. 7th Batt. Northumberland Fusiliers Oct. 11, 1915. Promoted Lieut. June 1, 1917. Once mentioned in Dispatches. Served in France.

ALFRED ANSTEY.

Admitted March 1900. Member of Houlditch, Anstey & Thompson, of Exeter. Served as Major with the 4th Batt. Devonshire Regt. in India.

HENRY CHARLES ANSTEY.

Admitted Nov. 1898. Member of Anstey & Co., of 30 Essex Street, W.C. Served as Capt. 3rd Batt. Royal Warwickshire Regt.

ERNEST FRANK ANTHONY.

Admitted March 1892. Member of Watts & Anthony, of Plymouth. Served as Capt. 5th Batt. Devonshire Regt.

HENRY ANTHONY BIRRELL ANTHONY.

Admitted Feb. 1884. Practised at Thame. Served as Lieut-Col. 1st (Reserve) Batt. Monmouthshire Regt.

JOHN RANDOLPH ANTHONY.

Admitted June 1900. Member of Garrard & Anthony of Worcester and Bromyard. Joined March 29, 1915, as 2nd Lieut. 3/8th Batt. Worcester Regt. (T). Promoted Lieut. Oct. 29, 1915, and transferred T.F. Reserve, Capt. Feb. 15, 1916, Law Officer Southern Command. Served at Home.

JOHN RICHARD ANTHONY.

Admitted July 1909, practised at Pwllheli. Mobilised Aug. 1914 with Territorials as Lieut. Promoted Capt. in 1915 and transferred Royal Flying Corps. Flight Commander in 1917. Killed in action May 26, 1917, and fell within the German line.

ALFRED JAMES APPLETON.

Admitted April 1908. Member of Appleton, Son & Snowdon, of Leeds. Joined Royal Army Service Corps as Private April 1916. Commissioned Temp. 2nd Lieut. May 22, 1916, Temp. Lieut. Nov. 22, 1917, A/Capt. Nov. 30, 1917, Temp. Capt. Oct. 1, 1918. Once mentioned in Dispatches. Awarded the M.C. Served in Mesopotamia Nov. 1916, to March 1919, and India March 1919 to June 1919.

CHARLES EGERTON APPLETON.

Admitted Dec. 1902. Member of Wright & Appleton, of Wigan. Joined March 19, 1918, as Private, Royal Army Service Corps, subsequently promoted to Sergeant. Served Mesopotamia.

JOSEPH ARCH.

Articled to M. K. Pridmore, of Coventry. Served as Lieut. 3rd Batt. Royal Warwickshire Regt.

CHARLES DOUGLAS WARD ARCHER.

Admitted Dec. 1898. Member of Murr, Rusby & Archer of 63 Lincoln's Inn Fields, W.C. Served as Capt. 23rd Division Royal Field Artillery.

CHARLES KENNETH ARCHER.

Admitted Oct. 1910. Practised at Newcastle-on-Tyne. Served as Lieut. 3rd King's African Rifles.

CLIFFORD WALTER ARCHER.

Admitted Nov. 1907. Solicitor's Office, Port of London Authority, Victoria Embankment, E.C. Enlisted Jan. 5, 1915, as Private, Royal Army Ordnance Corps. Gazetted Lieut. Royal Army Ordnance Dept. Jan. 28, 1916. Promoted A/Capt. July 1917, A/Major, April 1919. Twice mentioned in Dispatches. Served in France.

FULBERT RATCLIFFE ARCHER.

Admitted Oct. 1913. Of Wolverhampton. Served as 2nd Lieut. Royal Devonshire Yeomanry. Promoted Lieut.

GOODWYN LUDDINGTON ARCHER.

Admitted Sept. 1900. Member of Archer & Archer, of Ely & Lynn. Served as Major 1st Batt. Cambridgeshire Regt.

LEWIS KENDRAY ARCHER.

Admitted Feb. 1912. Practising at Bristol. Served as Private Royal Army Service Corps (M.T.).

RONALD HEDLEY ARCHER.

Admitted Feb. 1899. Member of Archer, Parkin & Archer, of Stockton-on-Tees. Joined Jan. 1916, as 2nd Lieut., Northumberland Fusiliers, promoted 1st Lieut. 1916. Served at Home and in France. Wounded and taken prisoner Dec. 1917 in Bullecourt Sector and escaped same day. Died on Dec. 27, 1917 from wounds in Hospital near Bapaume.

THOMAS HOLLINS ARDEN.

Admitted Dec. 1889. Member of Gamon, Farmer & Co., of Liverpool. Mobilised Aug. 5, 1914, as Lieut.-Col. commanding Lancashire and Cheshire Royal Garrison Artillery. Served at Home.

HERBERT THOMPSON ARGENT.

Admitted May 1906. Managing Clerk with Jones & Son, of Colchester. Embodied Aug. 5, 1914, as Lieut. 5th Batt. Essex Regt. (T.), promoted Capt. Aug. 26, 1914, Major June 1, 1916. Awarded the T.D. May 25, 1919. Served at Gallipoli. Very severely wounded at Suvla Bay, Aug. 17, 1915. Gazetted out on account of wounds, May 21, 1919.

EDWARD NORMAN GWYNN ARKELL.

Managing Clerk with Speechly, Mumford & Craig, 10 New Square, Lincoln's Inn, W.C. Joined Nov. 30, 1915, as Private, Inns of Court O.T.C. Gazetted 2nd Lieut. 5th Batt. Suffolk Regt. Aug. 10, 1917, went as Instructor to No. 24 (Tank Corps) Officer Cadet Batt., promoted Lieut. April 25, 1918, A/Capt. June 1, 1918. Served at Home and in France.

FRANK JOSEPH ARKELL.

Articled to R. E. Steel, of Cheltenham. Joined Sept 10, 1914, as Private, 5th Batt. Gloucestershire Regt. (Machine Gun Section). Killed at St. Quentin in Oct. 1917.

BENJAMIN ARKLE.

Articled to John Cameron of Liverpool. Served as Private, 10th Batt. King's Liverpool Regt. (Liverpool Scottish), subsequently gazetted 2nd Lieut. same Batt. and Regt., and attained the rank of Capt. Once mentioned in Dispatches. Awarded the M.C.

STEPHEN CECIL ARMITAGE.

Admitted Oct. 1911. Member of Ekin, Morris & Armitage, of Nottingham. Mobilised as Lieut. Army Service Corps, Aug. 5, 1914, promoted Capt. Oct. 12, 1914. Once mentioned in Dispatches. Served in France and at Home.

WILLIAM ARTHUR ARMITAGE.

Admitted April 1913. Managing Clerk with Barstow & Midgley, of Halifax. Enlisted Oct. 17, 1914, as Private, 15th Batt. West Yorkshire Regt. Gazetted 2nd Lieut. 1st Batt. West Yorkshire Regt. March 1, 1917, promoted Lieut. Sept. 1918 and transferred General List as Brigade Intelligence Officer, 18th Infantry Brigade. Appointed Administrative Staff Capt. with Army of Occupation (Rhine) Jan. 1919. Served in Egypt Dec. 1915 to Feb. 1916, France, Feb. 1916 to July 1916, France and Belgium, March 1917 to Nov. 1918, Army of the Rhine. Wounded July 1, 1916, Battle of Somme

WILLIAM JAMES ARMITAGE.

Admitted Oct. 1896. Practised at Sheffield. Served as Major 4th (Hallamshire) Batt. York and Lancaster Regt. (T.).

FORSTER MOORE ARMSTRONG.

Admitted Nov. 1902. Member of J. M. Moore & Armstrong, of South Shields. Mobilised Aug. 1914 as Capt. 4th Northumbrian Brigade, Royal Field Artillery, attached to Northumbrian D.A.C. as Adjutant Nov. 1914, promoted Major June 1, 1916, vacated Adjutant D.A.C. Feb. 1917. Once mentioned in Dispatches. Served at Home till April 21, 1915, and afterwards in France. Killed in action between Héninel and St. Martin's-sur-Cojuel, France, Sept. 25, 1917.

GEORGE JACKSON ARMSTRONG.

Admitted Nov. 1907. Managing Clerk with Messrs. Lidiard & Co., 7 Great James Street, Bedford Row, W.C. 1. Enlisted in the Rifle Brigade on Nov. 10, 1914. Commissioned 2nd Lieut. 11th Batt. West Yorkshire Regt. April 26, 1915, promoted Capt. July 7, 1916, Major April 26, 1918. Awarded the M.C. and Italian Cross of Merit (Croce di Guerra). Served at Home, Nov. 1914 to Aug. 1915, France and Belgium, Aug. 1915 to Nov. 1917, Italy, Nov. 1917 to April, 1919. Wounded at Contalmaison July 10, 1916, and at Ypres, March 11, 1917.

HERBERT ROWSE ARMSTRONG.

Admitted Feb. 1895. Member of Cheese & Armstrong, of Hay, Breconshire. Joined Oct. 20, 1914, as Capt., 1st Wessex Field Co., R.E., promoted Major—substantive rank—June 1916. Served in France May to Oct. 1918, otherwise at Home.

JOHN ARMSTRONG.

Admitted March 1908, practising at Manchester. Joined Aug. 29, 1914, as 2nd Lieut., 7th Batt. Cheshire Regt., promoted Lieut. Oct. 1914, Capt. June 30, 1916, General Staff Officer 3rd Grade Jan. 22, 1918. Twice mentioned in Dispatches. Awarded the Order of the Nile 4th Class. Served at Gallipoli July to August 1915, Egypt and Palestine Feb. 1916 to March 1919. Wounded at Suvla, Aug. 1915.

JOHN ARTHUR ARMSTRONG.

Admitted Nov. 1897. Practising at Eye, Suffolk. Joined May 5, 1917, as Driver in No. 2 Cadet Company, Royal Army Service Corps, Aldershot. Gazetted 2nd Lieut. Royal Army Service Corps July 29, 1917, promoted 1st Lieut. Jan. 29, 1919, graded Staff Lieut. whilst employed in Record Office and transferred to General List with effect from Feb. 8, 1918. Served at Home.

VINCENT ARMSTRONG.

Admitted Feb. 1913. Of Leicester. Served as Corporal, Royal Army Service Corps (M.T.).

RONALD HENRY ARNHOLZ.

Articled to H. P. Arnholz, of 3 & 4 Great Winchester Street, London, E.C. 1. Joined Sept. 21, 1914, as Private, Inns of Court O.T.C. Commissioned as 2nd Lieut. Hertfordshire Regt. March 25, 1915, and promoted Lieut. June 1,

1916. Served in Mesopotamia with Kut Relief Force, and subsequently in France. Killed in action Aug. 23, 1918.

ALFRED LEWIS ARNOLD.

Admitted March 1910. Member of Hicks, Arnold & Bender, 35 King Street, Covent Garden, W.C. Enlisted May 25, 1916, as Private, The Queen's Royal West Surrey Regt. Granted a commission as 2nd Lieut. in 24th Batt. London Regt. (Queen's), attached to 9th London Regt. (Queen Victoria Rifles). Killed in action at Ypres on Aug. 15, 1917.

EDWARD GLADWIN ARNOLD.

Articled to Sydney Morse, of 1 Kingsway, W.C. Joined 1914, as Lieut., 1st Wessex Brigade, R.F.A. Reported "missing" on March 21, 1918, and subsequently officially reported "believed killed" and "buried in a military cemetery abroad."

MONTIE PHILLIP ARNOLD.

Admitted June 1906. Member of Hicks, Arnold & Bender, 35 King Street, Covent Garden. Enlisted Sept. 1916 as Rifleman, 5th Batt. City of London Regt. (London Rifle Brigade). Gazetted 2nd Lieut. 1st Batt. London Regt., attached 39th Royal Fusiliers Feb. 1918, attached H.Q. D.E.T.A., E.E.F., Jerusalem, Sept. 1918, Staff Lieut. (graded G.G.), Assistant to Senior Judicial Officer, President of Court of First Instance for Kazas, Haifa, Acre, and Nazareth, and Staff Capt. (graded F.F.) Jan. 1919. Served at Home, Egypt, and Palestine.

ROBERT ANTHONY ARNOLD.

Admitted July 1895. Member of Arnold, Day and Tuff, of Rochester. Joined Sept. 8, 1914, as Lieut., Royal Army Service Corps, promoted Capt. Royal Engineers Oct. 20, 1914, Major June 1918. Once mentioned in Dispatches. Served in France and Flanders July 1916 to Feb. 1919.

WILLIAM NOEL ARNOLD.

Admitted Dec. 1909. Member of Arnold & Son, of Birmingham. Served as 2nd Lieut. Royal Field Artillery and subsequently promoted A/Lieut. Once mentioned in Dispatches. Awarded the M.C.

SPENCER LUMSDEN ARNOTT.

Admitted July 1892. Member of Arnott, Swan & Walker, of Newcastle-on-Tyne. Served as Lieut. 23rd (Service) Batt. Northumberland Fusiliers.

EDWARD HUGH ARUNDEL.

Articled to W. F. Challinor, of Leek. Joined Nov. 27, 1914, as A.B., Royal Naval Division. Gazetted 2nd Lieut. Tank Corps Feb. 27, 1917. Promoted Lieut. July 18. Served at Gallipoli Peninsula, May 1915, to the Evacuation, Imbros, Evacuation to May 1916, France, May 1916, to Aug. 1916, France, May 1917 to Oct. 1918. Wounded Oct. 3, 1918, at Estrèes near Peronne.

WILLIAM FAWELL ASCROFT.

Admitted Nov. 1901. Member of R. & W. Ascroft, of Preston. Joined April 20, 1915, as Capt., Loyal North Lancashire Regt, seconded for duty as R.T.O. (overseas) March 11, 1916, graded as Staff Capt. July 6, 1917, relinquished commission April 29, 1919, "on account of ill-health contracted on active service." Gazetted Brevet-Major Jan. 1, 1919. Served at Home and in France.

JOHN PRENTICE ASHBRIDGE.

Admitted Nov. 1902, practising at 88 Fenchurch Street, E.C. Served as Private 28th Batt. County of London Regt. (Artists Rifles) and subsequently gazetted 2nd Lieut. 18th Batt. County of London Regt. (London Irish Rifles). Promoted Lieut.

LAWRENCE ASHBRIDGE.

Admitted Oct. 1908. Member of Blair & W. B. Girling, of 1 Wool Exchange, Basinghall Street, E.C. 2. Enlisted Oct. 1, 1914, as Private, 10th Batt. Royal Fusiliers, gazetted 2nd Lieut. March 27, 1917, to East Yorkshire Regt., promoted Lieut. Sept. 1918, served in 8th and 1st Batt. East Yorkshire Regt. Served in France. Wounded Somme, July 15, 1916, and Aug. 26, 1918.

JOHN FRANCIS ASHBY.

Admitted Aug. 1909. Member of Ashby & Clothier, of Liverpool. Joined Aug. 15, 1914, as 2nd Lieut., 3rd (Special Reserve) Batt. The Cheshire Regt., subsequently promoted 1st Lieut. (attached 1st Cheshire Regt.). Invalided home from Ypres April, 1915. Resigned commission on grounds of ill-health occasioned by service Aug. 1916. Secretary Forging and Casting Dept., Ministry of Munitions, Sept. 1916 to June 1918.

WILLIAM ASHCROFT.

Admitted April 1907. Member of Dodds, Ashcroft & Cook, of Liverpool. Enlisted Sept. 1914 as Private, 17th Batt. King's Liverpool Regt. and rose to Sergeant. Received commission (early 1915) and transferred to 19th Batt. King's Liverpool Regt., subsequently promoted Lieut. Served in France 1915 to 1917 and 1918. Wounded April 9, 1917. Killed in action March 22, 1918.

HARRY SHERARD OSBORN ASHINGTON.

Articled to A. Brown, of Southport. Joined 1914 as 2nd Lieut., 7th Batt. East Yorkshire Regt. Went to the front July 1915, and a year later was wounded and brought home. Went back in Nov. 1916 and gazetted A/Capt. Killed in action Jan. 31, 1917.

ALBERT LEES ASHTON.

Admitted April 1915. Practising at Liverpool. Served as 2nd Lieut. 16th (Service) Batt. King's Liverpool Regt.

CHARLES ASHTON.

Articled to W. H. Tyrer, Town Clerk, Wigan, Lancs. Enlisted Jan. 1916, as Private, Royal Army Service Corps (M.T.). Served in France.

GEORGE FREDERICK ASHTON.

Admitted July 1903, practising at Runcorn, Cheshire. Joined Oct. 2, 1914, as Temp. Capt., 10th Batt. Northumberland Fusiliers, promoted Temp. Major Dec. 1916, transferred to Labour Corps. Oct. 1917. Awarded the M.C. Served in France. Wounded on the Somme on July 27, 1916.

HENRY OSWALD ASHTON.

Admitted Dec. 1912. Member of Bankes, Ashton & Co., of Bury St. Edmunds. Joined July 1916 as 2nd Lieut., 3/5th Batt. Suffolk Regt, promoted to 1st Lieut. and whilst in France attached to the 15th Batt. Royal Warwickshire Regt. Killed in action in France on Aug. 29, 1918.

JOHN ASHTON.

Admitted Jan. 1912. Managing Clerk with William E. Gregson, of Liverpool. Enlisted Feb. 28, 1917, as Private, Labour Corps, subsequently promoted Sergeant. Served in France (Forward Area) from March 1917 to Nov. 1919.

FRANCIS EDWARD ASHWORTH.

Admitted Oct. 1907. Of St. Annes-on-Sea. Enlisted Sept. 2, 1914, as Private, 1st City Batt. Manchester Regt., afterwards known as 16th (Service) Batt. Manchester Regt., transferred Feb. 20, 1917, to Royal Army Service Corps (M.T.). Served Nov. 1915 to Nov. 1917 in France and Belgium, and Dec. 1917 to March 1919 in Italy.

ROBERT SPENCER ASHWORTH.

Admitted Nov. 1909. Member of Rowley & Co., of Manchester. Joined Oct. 7, 1914, as 2nd Lieut., 5th Batt. Lancashire Fusiliers, promoted Lieut. 1915, Capt. 1916, Temp. Major 1917. Served at Home and in France.

THOMAS ASPDEN.

Admitted July 1905. Of Chorley, Lancs. Served as Private, 1st Batt. Loyal North Lancashire Regt.

THOMAS LESLIE ASTBURY.

Articled to R. J. Curtis, of Birmingham, and afterwards an Assistant Clerk to the Birmingham Board of Guardians. Enlisted Oct. 1914 as Private, 14th Batt. Royal Warwickshire Regt. (1st Birmingham Batt.), gazetted as 2nd Lieut. to South Staffordshire Regt. Aug. 9, 1915, and attained rank of Capt. Killed March 21, 1918, at Bullecourt, France.

NORMAN HENRY ASTE.

Admitted Oct. 1912. Member of John Holmes & Son, 34 Clement's Lane, Lombard Street, E.C. Mobilised Aug. 1914 as Lance-Corporal, Hon. Artillery Co., promoted Corporal on arrival in France Sept. 1914. Wounded slightly in Feb. 15 and returned to England. Received Commission as 2nd Lieut. of the Royal Garrison Artillery in April 1915. Killed in action near Albert Aug. 4, 1916.

FREDERIC MARRINER ASTON.

Admitted Dec. 1892. Formerly a member of Norman & Aston, of 23 Surrey Street, Strand. Served as Capt. Duke of Cornwall's Light Infantry. Killed in action in Flanders July 30, 1915.

WALTER VINCENT ASTON.

Articled to H. W. K. Rawlins, of Bournemouth. Joined 1914 as Private, Universities and Public Schools Batt. Royal Fusiliers, subsequently gazetted 2nd Lieut. Royal Fusiliers, and promoted Lieut.

ROLAND WALDEGRAVE ATCHLEY.

Admitted Dec. 1913. Practising at 50 Jermyn Street, S.W. 1. Joined June 1916 as Private, 28th Batt. County of London Regiment (Artists Rifles). Commission in Royal Flying Corps as Equipment Officer 3rd Class, Sept.

1916, rank 2nd Lieut., subsequently transferred to Royal Air Force as a Lieut. April 1918. Served at Home and in France.

JAMES FREDERICK HAYNES ATKEY.

Admitted Nov. 1901. Member of Atkey & Son, of 9 Sackville Street, Piccadilly, W. Joined Aug. 1915 as Private, Inns of Court O.T.C. Gazetted 2nd Lieut. 3/2nd North Midland Royal Field Artillery (T.) Dec. 1915, promoted Lieut. about August 1917, Capt. about Aug. 1918. Served in France Feb. 1917 to Sept. 1918. Wounded Sept. 3, 1918.

ALFRED JOHN ATKINS.

Admitted May 1917. Managing Clerk to Hodding & Jackson, of Salisbury. Enlisted Nov. 20, 1914, in 6th (Cyclist) Batt. Royal Sussex Regt. as a Motor-Cyclist Dispatch Rider with rank of Lance-Corporal. Discharged on March 10, 1915, as Medically Unfit for Further Service owing to defective vision.

CECIL CHARLES ATKINS.

Admitted Oct. 1904. Practised at Lowestoft. Served as Lieut. 6th (Cyclist) Batt. Suffolk Regt.

GEORGE JAMES MURRAY ATKINS.

Admitted Jan. 1897. With Gibson & Weldon, 27 Chancery Lane, London. Joined July 1917 as Cadet in the Garrison Officers Cadet Batt., Cambridge. Gazetted 2nd Lieut. 1st Garrison Batt. Worcester Regt. Sept. 17, 1917, Staff Lieut. R.T.O. France, June 8, 1918. Served in France.

JOHN LLOYD ATKINS.

Articled to Percy William Leighton Earle, of Merthyr Tydfil. Enlisted Jan. 1916 as Private, 28th Batt. Royal Fusiliers. Gazetted Sub-Lieut. in the Royal Naval Volunteer Reserve and attached to Royal Naval Division March 1, 1917. Served at Home and in France.

ARTHUR ATKINSON.

Admitted Nov. 1886. Member of Atkinson & Stainer, of Folkestone. Mobilised Aug. 1914 as Major 4th Batt. The Buffs (East Kent Regt.) (T.).

BERNARD STEWART ATKINSON.

Articled to W. Walford, of Walsall. Joined 1914 as Private, Inns of Court O.T.C., subsequently receiving his Commission and promoted to A/Capt. South Staffordshire Regt. Killed in action at Bourlon Wood, Nov. 30, 1917.

GEORGE JAMES ATKINSON.

Admitted Nov. 1902. Managing Clerk with Messrs. Burd, Pearse, Prickman & Brown, of Okehampton, Devon. Joined Sept. 26, 1916 as Ordinary Seaman, Royal Naval Volunteer Reserve. Commissioned Sub-Lieut. R.N.V.R. Dec. 10, 1917, promoted Lieut. Dec. 10, 1918. Served with the Grand Fleet (Destroyer Flotillas) and in the Mediterranean (Motor Launch Patrol.)

JOSEPH ALBERT ATKINSON.

Admitted June 1916. Of Leeds. Served as Lance-Bombadier 16th Heavy Battery, Royal Garrison Artillery.

NORMAN EVANS ATKINSON.

Articled to C. E. Atkinson, of Harrogate. Served as Lieut. 3rd Batt. West Yorkshire Regt Once mentioned in Dispatches.

REGINALD DOUGLAS ATKINSON.

Admitted July 1904. Of Bangkok, Siam. Served as Capt. 6th Reserve of Cavalry.

JAMES ATTENBOROUGH.

Admitted Oct. 1907. Member of Stanley Attenborough & Co., 18 Piccadilly, London. Mobilised Aug. 1914 as Major, 2nd Batt. London Regt., promoted Lieut.-Col. Dec. 1914. Four times mentioned in Dispatches. Awarded the C.M.G. and T.D. Served at Malta, France, and Home.

RALPH ERNEST ATTENBOROUGH.

Admitted Oct. 1904. Member of Attenboroughs, of 15 & 16 Thavies Inn, Holborn, E.C. Served as Sergeant Inns of Court O.T.C. Subsequently gazetted 2nd Lieut. Inns of Court O.T.C. and promoted Lieut. Lieut. Machine Gun Corps.

HAROLD FREDERIC ATTER.

Admitted Aug. 1901, practising at Wakefield. Joined Oct. 31, 1914, as 2nd Lieut., King's Own Yorkshire Light Infantry, promoted Temp. Lieut. Jan. 1915, Temp. Capt. March 1915, reverted to 2nd Lieut. on alteration of posting Aug. 1916, appointed Staff Capt. 138th Inf. Brigade Sept. 1917, appointed Staff Capt., H.Q. First Army April 14, 1918. Once mentioned in Dispatches. Awarded the O.B.E. (Military Division). Served at Home 1914 to 1916, and in France 1916 to 1919.

RAYMOND GEORGE ATTRIDE.

Admitted June 1913, practised at Wellington College, Berks. Mobilised Aug. 1914 as Lieut. 4th Batt. Royal Berkshire Regt, promoted Capt. Sept. 1914. Once mentioned in Dispatches. Killed in action, Aug. 14, 1916, near Pozières, France.

LESLIE FRANK ATTWATER.

Articled to L. W. Liell, of 110 Bishopsgate, E.C. Joined Jan. 20, 1915, as Private, Hon. Artillery Company. Gazetted 2nd Lieut. Royal Garrison Artillery Sept. 23, 1915, promoted Lieut. July 1917, A/Capt. Sept. 1917. Once mentioned in Dispatches. Served at Home Jan. 1915 to April 1916 and in France May 1916 to May 1919. Slightly wounded July 30, 1917.

JOHN LORIMER AUDEN.

Articled to T. E. Auden, of Burton-on-Trent. Mobilised Aug. 1914 as 1st Lieut. North Staffordshire Regt., promoted Capt. July 1915. Awarded the M.C. Served in France. Blown up by shell at Monchy Sept. 1916.

DUDLEY AUKLAND.

Admitted Aug. 1909, practising at Liverpool. Served as Lieut. 5th Batt. South Lancashire Regt. (T.).

CECIL WALTER AUSTIN

Admitted July 1912. Managing Clerk with Nicholson, Patterson & Freeland, 46 Queen Anne's Gate, London, S.W. Joined Nov. 3, 1914, as 2nd Lieut., Royal Army Service Corps, promoted Lieut. March 1915, Capt. March, 1916. Served in France Jan. 1915 to March 1919.

ROGER LORIMER AUSTIN.

Admitted May 1902, practised at Bristol. Served as Major 1st South Midland (Gloucestershire) Brigade, Royal Field Artillery (T.).

HENRY AUTY.

Admitted May 1879. Member of Auty & Sons, of Sheffield. Served as Lieut. 4th Batt. York and Lancaster Regt.

DOUGLAS HENRY AVORY.

Admitted April 1912, practised at 18 Austin Friars, E.C. Joined Oct. 1914 as 2nd Lieut. 5th Batt. Royal Berkshire Regt., and subsequently promoted Lieut. Once mentioned in Dispatches. Served in France.

EDMUND PORTMAN AWDRY.

Articled to E. M. Awdry, of Chippenham, Wilts. Mobilised Aug. 1914 as 2nd Lieut. Royal Wiltshire Yeomanry. Appointed Adjutant Dec. 1915, and promoted Capt. Feb. 1916. Awarded the M.C. Served in France.

NEVILLE JOHN AWDRY.

Articled to R. B. Wood, of Chippenham. Mobilised Aug. 1914 as Lieut. 4th Batt. Wiltshire Regt., promoted Capt. June 1916, Staff Capt. Poona Brigade, India, Aug. 1916 to December 1917. Served in India December 1914 to Oct. 1919.

HERBERT EDWARD AYRES.

Admitted Dec. 1913. Managing Clerk with Reed & Reed, 1 Guildhall Chambers, Basinghall Street, E.C. Enlisted July 8, 1918, as Private, 28th Batt. County of London Regt. (Artists Rifles), promoted Lance-Corporal Oct. 1918. Served at Home.

PERCY DANFORD ALWARD

Admitted May 1911. Member of Henry J. King & Aylward, of Salisbury. Served as 2nd Lieut. 15th Batt. Hampshire Regt.

FRANCIS ERIC LEONARD BACHE.

Admitted April 1906. Member of Wm. Bache & Sons, of West Bromwich. Enlisted Sept. 1914 as Private, 10th Batt. South Staffordshire Regt. Gazetted 1st Lieut. 10th Batt. South Staffordshire Regt. Nov. 1, 1915, promoted Capt. Feb. 1916. Awarded the M.C. Served at Gallipoli and France. Wounded April 1918.

CHARLES WALTER BACK.

Admitted Nov. 1910. Member of Francis & Back, of Norwich. Enlisted Sept. 2, 1914, as Private, 19th (Service) Batt. Royal Fusiliers. Commissioned 3rd Batt. Norfolk Regt., May 23, 1915, promoted Lieut. July 1917, Capt. Sept. 1917. Awarded the M.C. Served Home, and in Egypt, Palestine, and Syria.

HENRY WILLIAM BACK.

Admitted June 1910. Member of Francis & Back, of Norwich. Mobilised as Lieut., Norfolk Regt. Aug. 4, 1914, promoted Capt. Dec. 1914, Major Sept. 1917. Served at Home, in France, Italy, and Belgium.

HORACE AUBREY BACK.

Admitted Oct. 1906. Member of Surtees, Phillpotts & Co., 6 St. Helen's Place, London, E.C. Joined Feb. 1915, as 2nd Lieut., 3rd Batt. Gloucestershire Regt., subsequently attached in France to 1st Batt. Killed in France Sept. 22, 1916.

HENRY BACKHOUSE.

Articled to Henry Backhouse, of Blackburn. Joined Dec. 13, 1917, Inns of Court O.T.C. Transferred to 2nd Cavalry Officers Cadet School, April 1918, gazetted 2nd Lieut. in 6th Reserve Regt. of Dragoons Oct. 18, 1918. Served at Home.

STANLEY EDGAR BADCOCK.

Admitted May 1904. Member of F. & S. E. Badcock, of Bishop Auckland. Mobilised Aug. 1914 as Capt., Durham Light Infantry. Promoted Major March 1915. Killed in action April 26, 1915, at the 2nd Battle of Ypres.

CYRIL LAUD BADDELEY.

Admitted Dec. 1913. Member of Baddeleys & Co., of 77 Leadenhall Street, E.C. Served as Lieut. Royal Naval Volunteer Reserve.

EDWARD LAWRENCE BADDELEY.

Admitted June 1893. Practised at Manchester. Mobilised Aug. 1914 as Major, 8th Batt. Lancashire Fusiliers. Served in Egypt and Gallipoli. Killed in action at Gallipoli, June 6, 1915.

JAMES ALEXANDER BADDILEY.

Admitted Feb. 1906. Member of Baddiley & Co., of Doncaster. Enlisted June 7, 1915, as Private, Royal Army Service Corps, promoted Corporal Nov. 1915. Served in France Aug. 1915 to Feb 1919.

PERCY BADHAM.

Admitted July 1913. Of Tewkesbury. Served as 2nd Lieut. 5th Batt. Gloucestershire Regt.

GEOFFREY THOMAS BAGGALLAY.

Articled to A. Bathurst, 48 Lincoln's Inn Fields. Mobilised Aug. 1914 as Private, 28th Batt. County of London Regt. (The Artists). Promoted Sergeant Dec. 1914, gazetted Temp. 2nd Lieut. Welch Regt. May 9, 1915, promoted Lieut. South Wales Borderers Aug. 1917, Capt. Aug. 1919. Served in France. Wounded May 24, 1915, and Nov. 20, 1917.

GEORGE BARRY BAGNALL.

Admitted April 1912, practised at 147 Oxford Street, W. Joined Aug. 1914 as Private, 10th Batt. Royal Fusiliers, subsequently gazetted 2nd Lieut. 13th Batt. Rifle Brigade. Served in France. Killed in action April 20, 1917.

BRIAN GRIERSON BAILEY.

Articled to N. C. Bailey, of 5 Berners Street, W. Joined 1914 as Private, Inns of Court O.T.C, subsequently gazetted 2nd Lieut. 9th Batt. County of London Regt. (Queen Victoria's Rifles). Promoted Lieut.

CHARLES FREDERIC BAILEY.

Admitted Aug. 1895. Practising at Leicester. Served as Capt. 4th (Reserve) Batt. Leicestershire Regt. (T.).

EDWARD ALEC HORSMAN BAILEY.

Admitted April 1911. Managing Clerk with Baileys, Shaw & Gillett, of 5 Berners Street, W. 1. Mobilised Aug. 1914 as Major, Royal Field Artillery (T.) Promoted A/Lieut.-Col. July 1917, Lieut.-Col. May 1918, Staff Capt. Royal Artillery Aug. 1914 to April 1916, Brigade-Major Royal Artillery April 1916 to Jan. 1917. Four times mentioned in Dispatches. Awarded D.S.O. Served at Home 1914 to 1915, in France 1915 to 1916, and Egypt and Palestine 1916 to 1918. Invalided Home with dysentery and typhoid Aug. 1918.

GILBERT HOWARD BAILEY.

Admitted April 1907. Member of Cooper, Sons, Marsh & Bailey, of Manchester. Enlisted Nov. 1914 as Ord. Seaman in R.N.V.R. and later promoted to Chief Petty Officer. Transferred to the Army in May 1916 and granted commission as 2nd Lieut. Royal Army Service Corps. Served with the Egyptian Camel Transport Corps from May 1916 to Nov. 1916 in Egypt and Sinai and then transferred to Remount Services and appointed Adjutant of a Camel Remount Depôt at Suez, Egypt, promoted to Capt. and later made Commandant of No. 2 Camel Remount Depôt, Egypt. Once mentioned in Dispatches. Served in Gallipoli, Egypt, and Sinai. Military visits to Arabia, Soudan, and British Somaliland.

WILLIAM HENRY BAILEY.

Admitted May 1900. Town Clerk of Taunton. Mobilised Aug. 1914 as Lieut., Somerset Royal Horse Artillery. Promoted Capt. Nov. 1914, Major March 1918. Served at Home Aug. 1914 to Nov. 1917, Egypt and Palestine Nov. 1917 to May 1918, and France June 1918 to Nov. 1918.

WILLIAM JOHN BAILEY.

Articled to W. J. Bailey, of Newport, Isle of Wight. Enlisted Nov. 1916 as Signaller, Royal Garrison Artillery, subsequently employed as Dispatch Rider, attached R.E. (Signals). Served in France and with British Army of the Rhine.

EDWARD MILLEAR BAILY.

Admitted May 1903. Practising at Glastonbury. Mobilised Aug. 1914 with the Somerset Light Infantry and attained the rank of Major. Served in India and Mesopotamia.

GERARD GIBSON BAILY.

Admitted Feb. 1899. Assistant to N. J. Hughes-Hallett, Clerk of the Peace and of the County Council, Derbyshire. Rejoined the 5th Batt. Sherwood Foresters (Notts and Derby Regt.) as Capt. Oct. 1914. Served in France.

THOMAS BENJAMIN BAINBRIDGE.

Admitted Dec. 1907. Managing Clerk with Balderston, Warren & Pothecary, of Letchworth, Herts, and 32 Bedford Row, W.C. 1. Joined July 5, 1915, as Temp. 2nd Lieut., Royal Army Service Corps (H.T.). Promoted 1st Lieut. Jan. 1916, A/Capt. (attached Salonica Base Headquarters for legal duties) Dec. 1918, subsequently confirmed Temp. Capt. and Courts-Martial Officer, Salonica Base Headquarters as from same date. Once mentioned in Dispatches. Served in Macedonia and Bulgaria Aug. 1916 to Nov. 1918, subsequently throughout the " Army of the Black Sea," generally—Saloncia,

Turkey, Bulgaria, and South Russia, to July 1919, on special legal duties for G.H.Q., H.Q. Lines of Communication, and H.Q. Salonica Base.

ELLIS EYTON BAINES.

Admitted May 1897. Member of Vandercom & Co., 23 Bush Lane, E.C. 4. Mobilised Aug. 1914 as Private, 28th Batt. County of London Regt. (Artists Rifles). Promoted A/Sergt. Nov. 1914, and Company Q.M.S. in Jan. 1915, gazetted Lieut. Army Ordnance Department on June 17, 1915, promoted Capt. March 1917. Served at Home and in France. Died at No. 2 British Red Cross Hospital, Rouen, on Aug. 7, 1918, from illness following service.

STEPHEN HUMPHREY BAINES.

Admitted Nov. 1900. Member of Hazel & Baines, of Oxford. Joined 2/4 Oxford and Bucks Light Infantry (T.) Sept. 15, 1914, as a Private. Commission in Sherwood Foresters 1915, transferred to Labour Corps Sept. 1917, attached 13th Batt. East Lancashire Regt. June 1918, joined 119th Light Trench Mortar Battery July 1918. Served at Home and in France and Belgium. Wounded on the Somme March 1917, and near Armentières Oct. 5, 1918.

ERIC JOHN BAIRSTOW.

Articled to T. S. Steel, of Warrington. Mobilised Aug. 1914 as 2nd Lieut., 1/5th Batt. Cheshire Regt. (T.F.). Promoted Lieut. May 1915, Capt. Sept. 1915. Served 6 months in England and 4 years in France and Belgium.

AUBREY HALLIWELL BAKER.

Articled to E. E. Baker, of Weston-super-Mare. Mobilised Aug. 1914 as Lieut., 4th Batt. Somerset Light Infantry (T.). Promoted Capt. Oct. 1914. Served in India, chiefly on frontier, Oct. 1914 to Feb. 1916, and in Mesopotamia Feb. and March 1916. Killed in action in the advance to Kut March 8, 1916.

CHARLES WILLIAM EVELYN BAKER.

Admitted Feb. 1911. Member of Baker & Sons, of 35 Parliament Street, S.W. Served as Lieut., 8th Batt. Royal West Kent Regt. and Motor Machine Gun Corps, and subsequently promoted Capt.

FRANK JAMES BAKER.

Admitted June 1912, practising at Guildford. Enlisted Aug. 6, 1914, as Private, 13th Batt. County of London Regt. Gazetted Lieut. Royal Flying Corps Feb. 1915, promoted Capt. Aug. 1917, Major (Staff Officer 2nd Class) July 1918. Once mentioned in Dispatches. Served at Home.

GEORGE BRINGLEY AUFRÈRE BAKER.

Articled to B. A. Collins, of Reading. Served as 2nd Lieut., Royal Berkshire Regt. and subsequently promoted Lieut. Awarded the M.C.

GEORGE FREDERICK BAKER.

Admitted Oct. 1910. Member of Baker & Meek, of Willenhall. Enlisted Dec. 10, 1915, as Private, Royal Army Service Corps (M.T.). Sergeant from Feb. 1917, A/Mechanist Staff Sergeant July 1917 to Aug. 1918. Served at Home and in Mesopotamia.

HUGH HASSARD BAKER.

Admitted Aug. 1912. Member of Baker & Sons, of 35 Parliament Street, S.W. Served with the 14th Batt. County of London Regt. (London Scottish).

JOSEPH BAWRON BAKER.

Articled to Charles R. Steele, of 6 Finsbury Square, E.C. 2. Joined May 17, 1915, as Private, Inns of Court O.T.C. Gazetted 2nd Lieut. Royal Warwickshire Regt. Aug. 21, 1915, promoted Lieut. Feb. 1917. Served in Mesopotamia March 1916 to Aug. 1918, and with North Persian Force Aug. 1918 to Feb. 1919. Wounded April 5, 1916, at Felahiged, Mesopotamia.

JOSIAH FERDINAND BAKER.

Admitted April 1913, practised at Burnley. Served as 2nd Lieut. 5th Batt. East Lancashire Regt.

NEVILLE ERNEST BAKER.

Articled to E. E. Baker, of Weston-super-Mare. Joined Aug. 1914 as Motor Cyclist Despatch Rider-Corporal, Royal Engineers (Signals). Sailed for France with First Division Aug. 1914, gazetted 2nd Lieut. Royal Engineers Jan. 1915, Brigade Signal Officer 1915, promoted Lieut., attached to Headquarters 2nd Brigade Tank Corps, 1917. Served in France and Belgium 1914 to 1917. Died of wounds at Voormezeele near Yypres, Belgium, July 31, 1917.

REGINALD LAWRENCE BAKER.

Admitted Dec. 1901, practised at Abergavenny. Mobilised Aug. 1914 as Capt. 3rd Batt. Monmouthshire Regt. Killed in action at Ypres May 8, 1915.

THOMAS MACDONALD BAKER.

Articled to E. T. Hall, of Reading. Mobilised Aug. 4, 1914, as a Lieut., 1/6th Batt. East Surrey Regt. (T.). Promoted Temp. Capt. Oct. 1914, confirmed in rank of Capt. June 1916. Served at Home, Aden, and India. Wounded Jan. 5, 1918.

FRANCIS SHORLAND BALL.

Admitted July 1901, practised at Manchester. Served as Lieut., 1st Batt. The Queen's Royal West Surrey Regt.

FRANK LESLIE BALL.

Admitted Jan. 1905. Member of Godfrey, Warr & Co., of Palmerston House, 34 Old Broad Street, London, E.C. Enlisted Sept. 2, 1914, as Private, in 28th Batt. County of London Regt. (Artists Rifles). Gazetted 2nd Lieut. East Yorkshire Regt. Oct. 3, 1915, promoted Capt. and Adjutant July 1916, A/Major Oct. 1916. Temporarily commanding Battalion Nov. and Dec. 1916. Awarded the M.C. Served in France from Jan. 1915 until taken prisoner at Wytscheate Ridge, April 28, 1918.

JOHN RAYMOND MORTON BALL.

Admitted April 1906. Member of Ball, Smith & Playne, of Stroud, Glos. Called up on Embodiment of Territorial Force Aug. 5, 1914, as Capt., Royal Army Service Corps. Promoted to Major Oct. 1914, and to Lieut.-Col. June 1916. Awarded the T.D. Served in France March 1915, to Nov. 1915, and May 1916, to Sept. 1916.

CECIL BALLS.

Admitted July 1896. Clerk with Richardson, Foxwell & Hart, of Much Hadham, Herts. Served as Corporal, 4th (Reserve) Batt. Essex Regt.

ARTHUR BALMER.

Admitted May 1899. Member of Church, Adams, Prior & Balmer, of 11 Bedford Row, W.C. Joined Dec. 1915 as Sub-Lieut., Royal Naval Volunteer Reserve, promoted Lieut. Dec. 1916. Served in Auxiliary Patrol, North Sea and English Channel, minesweeping and patrol. In command of H.M.M.L. 191 from Aug. 1916 to Feb. 1919. Received share of Admiralty award for destruction of enemy submarine in Aug. 1918.

ARTHUR EDWARD BANES.

Admitted June 1909, practising at 37 & 38 Mark Lane, E.C. Served as Private, 2nd Batt. Hon. Artillery Company.

EDGAR HASLAM BANKS.

Articled to Frederick Jackson, of Nottingham. Joined Aug. 7, 1915, as 2nd Lieut., 11th King's Own Yorkshire Light Infantry, Lieut. Machine Gun Corps Jan. 1918, A/Capt. 58th Machine Gun Batt. Aug. 1918, Lieut. Machine Gun Corps Nov. 1918 to Jan. 1919. Served at Home, France, 1915, Egypt 1916 to 1917, France and Flanders 1917 to 1919.

ERNEST HENRY BANKS.

Admitted Aug. 1909. Member of Banks, Kendall & Taylor, of Liverpool. Served as Capt., 15th Batt. Cheshire Regt.

RUSSELL EVARARD BANKS.

Admitted Aug. 1914. Of Twickenham. Served as 2nd Lieut., East Surrey Regt.

SYDNEY NEAL BANKS.

Articled to J. I. Dodd, of 11 New Square, Lincoln's Inn, W.C. Served as Private, 12th (Service) Batt. Royal Sussex Regt.

HAROLD JAMES THOMAS BANNEHR.

Admitted July 1908. Managing Clerk with Mackrell, Maton & Co., of Cannon Street, E.C. Joined June 3, 1915, the Inns of Court O.T.C. Gazetted 2nd Lieut. 7th Batt. Durham Light Infantry Sept. 29, 1915. Reported missing on Nov. 5, 1916, after an attack near to the Butte de Warlencourt, and on March 20, 1919, the War Authorities presumed his death as, on, or since Nov. 5, 1916.

ERNEST BANNISTER.

Articled to J. H. S. Aitken, of Nelson. Served as Private, 10th T.R. Batt.

WILLIAM WILSON BANNISTER.

Admitted April 1907, practising at Stourbridge. Enlisted Sept. 1914 as Private, Public Schools Batt. Promoted Sergeant Dec. 1914, gazetted 2nd Lieut. 12th Batt. Scottish Rifles May 1915, and subsequently promoted Lieut. 6th Batt. Royal Irish Rifles, and afterwards attached 1st Batt. The Royal Irish. Served in Serbia 1915, Salonica 1916 to 1918, Palestine 1918 till Armistice. Wounded March 18, 1918 (Palestine).

EDWARD SPENCER BANTOFT.

Admitted Feb. 1909. Managing Clerk with Lonsdale & Everidge, of 1 Adam Street, Adelphi, W.C. Joined Oct. 1914 as Private, Inns of Court O.T.C., and promoted Corporal Nov. 1914 and Sergeant Jan. 1915, gazetted 2nd Lieut. 5th City of London Batt. London Regt. (London Rifle Brigade)

April 2, 1915, promoted Lieut. July 1916. Served in France July 1916 to Sept. 1916. Died Sept. 11, 1916 at a Casualty Clearing Station of wounds received in action at Combles the previous day.

HUGH LAWRENCE BANTOFT.

Articled to E. P. Ridley, of Ipswich. Served as Private, 1st East Anglian Field Ambulance, Royal Army Medical Corps.

JAMES HIRST BANYARD.

Admitted March 1913, practised at Leyburn. Given commission as 2nd Lieut., Bedfordshire Regt. in May 1915, and sent to the front in Aug. 1916. Killed in action Sept. 3, 1916.

BRADLEY KING BELL BARBER.

Articled to J. Carter Harrison, of 39 Great James Street, W.C. Served as Private, 28th Batt. County of London Regt. (Artists Rifles).

CYRIL ARTHUR BARBER.

Admitted July 1915. Member of Barbers, of Harrogate. Enlisted Jan. 1916 as Gunner, Royal Field Artillery. Served in France March 1917 to April 1919.

GEOFFREY CAREW BARBER.

Articled to H. E. Donnes, of Scarborough. Mobilised Aug. 1914 as Capt., 5th Batt. Yorkshire Regt. (T.). Served in France April 13 to 25, 1915. Killed in action near St. Julien, Ypres, Belgium, April 25, 1915.

LAURENCE HENRY BARBER.

Admitted Oct. 1908. Member of Watson, Esam & Barber, of Sheffield. Joined Sept. 23, 1914, as Temp. 2nd Lieut., York and Lancaster Regt. (T.F.), promoted Temp. Lieut. Nov. 1914, Temp. Capt. March 1915, Substantive Capt. June 1916, Adjutant 4th (Reserve) Batt. June 1915 to Feb. 1919. Served at Home.

SYDNEY BARBER.

Articled to Francis Barber, of Harrogate. Enlisted Sept. 15, 1914, as Private, 5th Batt. West Yorkshire Regt. Gazetted 2nd Lieut. Royal Field Artillery Oct. 1, 1914, promoted Lieut. July 1917, Capt. Dec. 1917. Served at Home to Nov. 1915, Egypt Dec. 1915 to March 1916, France March 1916 to Dec. 1918, Germany Dec. 1918 to Feb. 1919.

HENRY GLADSTONE BARCLAY.

Admitted May 1904. Of Macclesfield. Joined Nov. 25, 1916, as Lieut., Territorial Force Reserve, promoted Capt. Sept. 1917. Served at Home.

ARTHUR HAMILTON BARDSWELL.

Admitted Nov. 1896. Member of Longueville & Co., of Oswestry. Enlisted Sept. 11, 1918, as Private, 28th Batt. County of London Regt. (Artists Rifles).

JOHN CLAUDE HORSEY BARFIELD.

Admitted Feb. 1913. Managing Clerk with Barfield & Barfield, 1 West Street, Finsbury Circus, London, E.C. Joined Dec. 1914 as 2nd Lieut., Royal Flying Corps. Served in Flanders. Killed whilst flying near Ypres on June 29, 1915.

JOHN FOSTER BARHAM.

Articled to R. A. Pinsent, of Birmingham. Enlisted Aug. 14, 1914, as Private, 16th Batt. Middlesex Regt. Gazetted 2nd Lieut. Royal Army Service Corps, Feb. 8, 1915, promoted 1st Lieut. July 1915, Capt. July 1918. Awarded the M.C. Served at Home, in Ireland, France, and Belgium.

GEOFFREY MENTOR BARK.

Admitted Feb. 1908. Assistant Solicitor to Birmingham Corporation. Joined Nov. 5, 1915, as 2nd Lieut., 4th Batt. Royal Warwickshire Regt., promoted Lieut. July 1917. Served in France Sept. 1916 to April 1917. Wounded April 14, 1917, near la Coulotte.

ARTHUR PRESCOTT BARKER.

Admitted Dec. 1909, practising at 32 Queen Victoria Street, E.C. Joined June 6, 1916, as 2nd Lieut., Royal Army Service Corps (M.T.), promoted Lieut. Dec. 1917. Once mentioned in Dispatches. Served in Serbia Aug. 1916 to April 1919.

CHARLES WILLIAM TONE BARKER.

Admitted Oct. 1910. Member of Dixon & Barker, of Sunderland. Joined Aug. 1914 as Trooper, 15th Hussars. Gazetted Lieut. 15th Batt. Durham Light Infantry 1915, promoted Capt. Sept. 1915. Awarded the M.C. Served in France. Wounded at Fricourt July 1, 1916. Killed at Clery-sur-Somme March 24, 1918.

CLAUDE BARKER.

Admitted July 1884, practising at Sheffield. Mobilised as Capt., West Riding Divisional Royal Engineers, commanded the 49th, 62nd, and 72nd Signal Coys., also had charge of the 3rd Line Grouped Signal Coys., Northern Command, and was 2nd in Command at Biggleswade Signal Depôt from Aug. 1918 to March 1919, promoted Temp. Major Nov. 1914. Substantive Rank June 1916. Mentioned in Dispatches once. Awarded the T.D. Served at Home.

GEOFFREY BARKER.

Articled to F. T. Hunter, of Bradford. Joined Aug. 1914 2/6 Batt. West Yorkshire Regt. Commissioned Sept. 10, 1914, promoted A/Lieut. June 1915, Lieut. June 1916, A/Capt. May 1917. Served at Home until Jan. 1917, after that date in France. Killed in action 1st Battle of Cambrai, Nov. 22, 1917.

GEOFFREY BARKER.

Articled to the late C. M. Barker, of 15 Bedford Row, W.C. Enlisted Oct. 6, 1914, as Private, 1st Sportsman's Batt. Royal Fusiliers. Gazetted 2nd Lieut. Cambridgeshire Regt. June 25, 1915, promoted Lieut. June 1916, Capt. Oct. 1916. Awarded the M.C. Served in France and Belgium.

GEORGE ERNEST BARKER.

Admitted Aug. 1913, practising at Llanelly. Served as Corporal, Royal Army Service Corps.

HAROLD FREDERIC BARKER.

Admitted June 1914. Managing Clerk with Dixon & Barker, of Sunderland. Mobilised Aug. 1914 as Capt., Durham Royal Garrison Artillery (T.),

Capt. 160th Royal Field Artillery (Wearside Brigade) March 1915, promoted Major 1918. Once mentioned in Dispatches. Served in France. Killed on March 29, 1918, at Farpoux in Forward Observation Post.

HOLROYD BIRKETT BARKER.

Admitted May 1910. Member of Hooper & Barker, of Birmingham. Joined 1915 as 2nd Lieut., 134th Siege Battery Royal Garrison Artillery, promoted Lieut. after his death. Served at Home and at Salonica. Died at Salonica Aug. 15, 1917, buried in Mikra Cemetery.

JAMES BARKER.

Articled to Wm. F. B. Warman, of Stroud. Joined May 1916 as Private, Gloucestershire Hussars, afterwards transferred to 6th Batt. Gloucestershire Regt., subsequently promoted to Lance-Corporal. Killed in action near Merville and Calonne April 14, 1918.

JAMES PERCIVAL BARKER.

Admitted Dec. 1913, practised at Harrogate. Served as Lieut., 49th West Riding Divisional Army Service Corps.

JOHN BARKER (Jun.).

Articled to John Barker, of Great Grimsby. Enlisted Sept. 17, 1914, as Private, 10th Batt. Lincolnshire Regt. Commissioned Temp. 2nd Lieut. 10th South Staffordshire Regt. May 12, 1915, transferred to Royal Flying Corps as Pilot May 1917, promoted Lieut. July 1917. Served in France. Wounded Oct. 31, 1917, whilst flying over Menin.

ARTHUR ERNEST LESLIE BARLOW.

Admitted July 1912. Member of Arthur Barlow & Son, of Nottingham. Joined Dec. 10, 1914, as 2nd Lieut., 1/1 Notts. (Sherwood Rangers) Yeomanry, promoted Lieut. June 1916, A/Capt. Aug. 1918. Served in Egypt, Macedonia, and Palestine.

RICHARD MAXWELL BARLOW.

Articled to J. W. Barlow, of Bury. Enlisted May 25, 1916, as Private, 5th Batt. Lancashire Fusiliers. Gazetted 2nd Lieut. May 29, 1917. Awarded the M.C. Served in France. Wounded Sept. 20, 1917, at Schüler Galleries, St. Julien, on the Passchaendale Ridge.

GEORGE WILLIAM BARNARD.

Admitted Jan. 1911. Member of Barnard & Son, of Norwich. Enlisted May 31, 1916, as Private, Argyll and Sutherland Highlanders. Gazetted 2nd Lieut. 1/2 Argyll and Sutherland Highlanders June 26, 1918. Served in France.

BENJAMIN BARNES.

Admitted April 1910. Member of Walmsley & Barnes, of Broadstairs. Joined Oct. 10, 1914, as Private, Inns of Court O.T.C. Gazetted 2nd Lieut. 2/4 King's Own Yorkshire Light Infantry Nov. 24, 1914, promoted Lieut. July 1916, Capt. Oct. 1917. Once mentioned in Dispatches. Served in France and Belgium Aug. 1915 to Aug. 1917. Gassed July 23, 1917, at Nieuport.

CHARLES ERIC BARNES.

Admitted Dec. 1899, practising at Brackley. Joined Oct. 1914 as A.B., Hawke Batt. Royal Naval Division. Gazetted 2nd Lieut. 2nd Batt. Oxford and Bucks Light Infantry, promoted Lieut., April 1918. Served in Gallipoli 1915, Egypt 1916, and France 1917 and 1918. Wounded June 1915 at Gallipoli.

GEORGE HERBERT LEONARD BARNES.

Admitted July 1914. With Tyrrell & Barnes, of Weston-super-Mare and Bristol. Joined Aug. 4, 1916, and served as Lance-Corporal, 6th Batt. Machine Gun Corps in France and Belgium. Wounded Oct. 4, 1917, at Poelcappelle Ridge.

GEORGE MILLARD BARNES.

Articled to William Arnold, of 5 Salters' Hall Court, E.C. Served as Corporal Motor Machine Gun Service, Royal Field Artillery.

HAROLD DOUGLAS BARNES.

Admitted April 1901. Member of Barnes & Butler, 17 John Street, Bedford Row, London, W.C. 1. Mobilised Aug. 5, 1914, as Capt., 7th Batt. London Regt., promoted Major Nov. 1914, joined B.E.F. March 1915, attached Judge-Advocate-General's Office Nov. 1916, Staff (War Office) Feb. 1917, Deputy-Asst.-Adjutant-General (War Office—J.A.G.'s Office), Jan. 1919. Once mentioned in Dispatches. Awarded O.B.E. (Military Division). Served in France 1915. Very severely wounded Battle of Festubert May 16, 1915.

JAMES BARNES.

Admitted Dec. 1896, practising at Portsmouth. Served as Capt., 11th Batt. Royal Warwickshire Regt.

NICOLAS EDMUND BARNES.

Admitted Nov. 1891, practising at Ulverston, Lancashire. Embodied Aug. 4, 1914, as Capt., 4th Batt. The King's Own Royal Lancaster Regt., promoted Major May 1915. Served in Flanders 1915 and 1916 until invalided home, subsequently in England and in Ireland.

THOMAS BARNES.

Admitted May 1902, practising at Carlisle. Joined Sept. 13, 1914, as Private, No. 1 Supernumerary Co. 3/4 Border Regt. Gazetted 2nd Lieut. Sept. 15, 1914, Lieut. Sept. 1915.

THOMAS JAMES BARNES.

Admitted May 1911. Member of Godfrey Warr & Co., 34 Old Broad Street, E.C. Joined Sept. 1914 as A.B., Royal Naval Volunteer Reserve, subsequently commissioned Sub.-Lieut. Discharged (invalided) June 1917. Awarded the O.B.E. Served at Home and at Sea.

BERTRAM LEEDS THOMAS BARNETT, L.R.C.P., L.R.C.M.

Admitted Nov. 1909. Medical Officer of Health for Isle of Ely. Joined Nov. 1914 as Capt., 2nd County of London Army Service Corps. Served at Home. Accidentally killed near Aldershot April 18, 1915.

HARRY BARNICOT.

Admitted April 1908. Managing Clerk with Watson & Chell, of Bury, Lancs. Enlisted Oct. 1906 as Private, Royal Army Veterinary Corps. Gazetted 2nd Lieut. Labour Corps Dec. 1917, attached 1st Garrison Batt. Royal Warwickshire Regt. July to Sept. 1918, then employed on G.H.Q., E.E.F., promoted Lieut. June 1919. Served at Home till June 1918, then in Egypt and Palestine till Dec. 1919.

STANISLAUS BARON.

Admitted April 1907. Member of Taylor, Sons, Bridge & Baron, of Wigan. Served in the Royal Air Force.

ARTHUR MATTHEWS BARRACK.

Admitted Oct. 1906, of Epsom. Enlisted Sept. 5, 1914, as Private, East Surrey Regt., promoted Sergeant. Gazetted Lieut. General List (Recruiting) March 3, 1917. Home Service only.

WALTER ARTHUR BARRAND.

Admitted Oct. 1912. Of Leicester. Served as Private, 4th Batt. Leicestershire Regt.

ARTHUR LESLIE BARRETT.

Articled to Thomas Oerton, of Barnstaple. Enlisted Oct. 16, 1914, as Private, Royal North Devon Hussars. Cadet Inns of Court O.T.C. Feb. 1916, commissioned 2nd Lieut. Devonshire Royal Garrison Artillery Oct. 12, 1916, promoted Lieut. April 1918, Capt. March 1919, and appointed Courts-Martial Officer to the British Army of the Rhine same date. Served at Home and in France, Belgium, and Germany.

FREDERICK GAMBLE BARRETT.

Admitted Jan. 1913, practising with Ernest Bevir & Son, of Devereux Chambers, Temple, W.C. Joined Jan. 31, 1915, as 2nd Lieut., 21st Batt. London Regt., promoted Lieut. Jan. 1916., seconded to 181st Trench Mortar Battery, July 1916 and to Special Employment May 1918. Served in France June 1916 to Nov. 1916, at Salonica Nov. 1916 to August 1917, and in Palestine August 1917 to July 1919.

HERBERT LESLIE CROSTHWAITE BARRETT.

Admitted Nov. 1901. Member of Barrett & Thomson, of Slough, Bucks. Mobilised Aug. 1914 as Capt., Bucks Batt. Oxford and Bucks Light Infantry promoted Temp. Major Mar. 1916, Major June 1916. Awarded the T.D. Served at Home and in France. Invalided from France in 1916.

REGINALD HENRY BARRETT.

Admitted Aug. 1909. Managing Clerk with W. G. Howell, of Cardiff. Joined Oct. 27, 1915, as 2nd Lieut., 4th Batt. East Yorkshire Regt. (T.F.), promoted Temp. Lieut. Aug. 1916, Lieut. July 1917, Temp. Capt. and Courts-Martial Officer Feb. 1919; 25th Provisional Batt. Nov. 1915 to Dec. 1916, 27th Batt. Durham Light Infantry Jan. 1917 to Nov. 1918, 17th Labour Company Nov. 1918 to Jan. 1919, Prosecutions Office, Cologne, Feb. to March 1919, Headquarters, Military Governor Occupied German Territory, March to Sept. 1919. Served at Home, Belgium, and Germany.

GEORGE OLIVER JAMES BARRICK.

Articled to H. A. Armitage, of Newnham & Newent. Enlisted May 25, 1915, as Trooper, Royal Gloucestershire Hussars. Gazetted 2nd Lieut. 3/4 West Riding Brigade Royal Field Artillery Aug. 12, 1916. Served in France. Killed in action, Nov. 6, 1917.

THE HON. WALTER BERNARD LOUIS BARRINGTON.

Admitted Feb. 1901. Member of Norton, Rose, Barrington & Co., of 57½ Old Broad Street, E.C. Joined Dec. 1917 as 2nd Lieut., Royal Army Service Corps, subsequently promoted Temp. Capt. Employed at War Office.

GILBERT LACY BARRITT.

Articled to H. H. Harvey, of Spalding, Lincs. Joined Aug. 28, 1914, as Private, 4th Batt. Lincolnshire Regt. Gazetted 2nd Lieut. 4th Batt. Lincolnshire Regt. (T.F.) March 18, 1915, seconded Observer Royal Flying Corps March 1917, promoted Lieut. April 1917, Pilot Nov. 1917. Served at Home 27 months and in France 30 months. Wounded and prisoner (shot down in aerial combat), Sept. 1, 1918.

ALFRED JAMES BARROW.

Admitted July 1912. Member of Crawshay & Barrow, of Richmond, Surrey. Joined Inns of Court O.T.C. Feb. 1915, subsequently gazetted 2nd Lieut. Lancashire Fusiliers, promoted to Capt. Awarded the M.C. Wounded on March 23, 1918, in France. Prisoner of War at Cassel, Germany, where he died from his wounds on June 24, 1918.

NOEL COGHLAN BARRS.

Articled to W. S. Sharpe, 12 New Court, Carey Street, W.C. Joined Sept. 1914 as Private, Public Schools Corps, subsequently received commission as 2nd Lieut. Royal West Kent Regt. Killed Sept. 15, 1916, in the advance on Fleurs.

EWART CHARLES BARTLETT.

Admitted Dec. 1908. With Geoffrey Colbourne, of Brighton. Mobilised Aug. 1914 as Lieut., Home Counties Divisional Engineers (T.F.), promoted A/Capt. Sept. 1914, A/Major June 1915 to April 1918, raised and commanded 2nd Home Counties (subsequently 67th) Divisional Signal Company Royal Engineers until it was disbanded April 1918, proceeded overseas and joined 40th Divisional Signal Coy. R.E. June 27, 1918, became Substantive Capt. Aug. 1918. Served at Home Sept. 1914 to June 1918, France June 1918 to March 1919.

HOWARD JOHN BARTLETT.

Admitted Feb. 1900, practising at Chichester. Received commission as Lieut. in Royal Army Service Corps Feb. 1915. Gazetted Capt. Sept. 1915. Once mentioned in Dispatches. Stationed at Leeds from Feb. 1915 to Nov. 1916, then sent to Salonica. Died in Hospital at Taranto, Italy, from pneumonia following influenza on Dec. 1, 1918, when on way home from Salonica on leave.

BASIL KELSEY BARTON.

Admitted Nov. 1903, practising at Hull. Served as 2nd Lieut. Royal Field Artillery and attained the rank of Capt. Once mentioned in Dispatches. Awarded the M.C.

CHARLES THOMAS BARTON.

Admitted Dec. 1903. Member of Barton & Sons, of East Dereham. Joined Aug. 18, 1915. as 2nd Lieut., promoted Lieut. July 1917. Served in Egypt and Palestine. Very severely wounded April 19th, 1917, at Gaza, Palestine.

GLYNN HENRY REGINALD BARTON.

Articled to H. Stewart-Moore of 6 Suffolk Street, S.W. Served as Capt. Tank Corps. Mentioned in Dispatches. Awarded the M.C.

TILNEY WALLACE BARTON.

Admitted May 1887, practising at Bournemouth. Commissioned as Staff Capt. July 24, 1915, Special List, promoted Major March 1919, Lieut.-Col. May 1919. Once mentioned in Dispatches. Officer in charge Lands Branch, Headquarter Staff, Southern Command, July 1916, to Dec. 1917, Officer in charge Prisoner War Labour, Dorchester, Dec. 1917 to Oct. 1918, A.A.G. to Military Governor, Jerusalem, Dec. 1918 to March 1919, Claims Bureau, Palestine, March 1919 to May 1919.

WALTER JOHN BARTON.

Admitted April 1900. Member of Barton & Son, of East Dereham, Norfolk. Mobilised Aug. 5, 1914, as Capt., 1/5 Batt. Norfolk Regt., promoted Major Nov. 1914. Served at Gallipoli, Egypt, Sinai Peninsula.

CECIL BARTRAM.

Admitted March 1903. Managing Clerk with Reynolds & Son, of High Wycombe. Mobilised as Capt., 4th Batt. Royal Berkshire Regt. Aug. 1914, promoted Major 1915. Once mentioned in Dispatches. Served at Home 1914 to 1917, France 1917, Italy 1917 to 1919.

HARRY PARRINGTON BARUGH.

Admitted May 1907. Member of Buchannan, Richardson & Barugh, of Guisborough. Joined Feb. 6, 1915, as 2nd Lieut., Royal Army Service Corps, promoted Lieut. July 1915, Capt. April 1916. Twice mentioned in Dispatches. Served at Home till July 1915, France and Belgium July 1915 to Nov. 1917, Italy Nov. 1917 to March 1919.

WILFRED THOMAS DE BERDEWELLE BARWELL.

Admitted March 1896. Member of Crawford & Barwell, of Seaford, now practising on own account at Seaford. Joined Sept. 13, 1914, as Private, 19th Batt. Royal Fusiliers, promoted Corporal Sept. 1914, Sergeant Dec. 1914. Gazetted Lieut. R.T.O. March 1915, Capt. R.T.O. Oct. 1916, Major D.A.D.R.T. July 1918. Served in England till March 1915, in France March 1915 to April 1916, at Home April 1916 to Oct. 1917, and in Italy Oct. 1917 to April 1919.

JOHN CECIL BASSETT.

Admitted May 1907. Member of Bassett, Stanton & Bassett, of Southampton. Served as Major 5th Batt. Hampshire Regt. (T.), and subsequently promoted Lieut.-Col. Served in India.

SPENCER MARTIN EYCKHOLT BATCHELOR.

Admitted July 1908. Member of Browne & Batchelor, of Nice, France. Joined Aug. 13, 1914, as Gunner, 1st Home Counties Royal Field Artillery (T.).

Gazetted 2nd Lieut. Sept. 28, 1914, and attained the rank of Lieut.-Col. March 1919. Served at Home, France, and Flanders. Gassed July 1917.

ROGER BATE.

Articled to J. C. Bate, of Chester. Joined July 1915 as Voluntary Driver British Red Cross (Motor Transport). Ranked as Hon. Lieut. with the Italian Army. Awarded the Fatiche di Guerra (Italy). Served in France Sept. 1915 to Feb. 1916, in Italy Feb. 1916 to Sept. 1917. Discharged Oct. 1917 to join Aeronautical Inspection Dept. (Ministry of Munitions).

ALFRED BATES.

Articled to Alfred Bates, of Morecambe, Lancs. Joined April 7, 1915, as 2nd Lieut., 4th Batt. East Lancashire Regt. (T.F.), promoted Lieut. June 1916, Capt. March 1917. Awarded the M.C. Served at Home April 1915 to Feb. 1917, France March 1917 to Jan. 1919.

ARNOLD FIELDING BATES.

Articled to H. W. Jackson, of Sheffield. Joined Nov. 1914, as Trooper, 2/1 Yorkshire Dragoons. Gazetted 2nd Lieut. with 2/1 Yorkshire Dragoons (T.F.) Sept. 26, 1915, Lieut. with Cavalry Corps Signal Squadron April 1918. Served in France and Belgium from Oct. 1915 to Jan. 1919.

EDMUND CHADWICK BATES.

Admitted Aug. 1903. Of Marylebone Station, N.W. Served as Capt., 1st Batt. Hertfordshire Regt.

FRANCIS OSBORNE BATES.

Articled to J. H. Powell, of Derby. Joined Inns of Court O.T.C. Nov. 23, 1915. Gazetted 2nd Lieut. 5th (T.F.) Batt. The Sherwood Foresters Nov. 1917. Served at Home and in France.

NORMAN MALCOLM BATES.

Admitted April 1912, practising at Wolverhampton. Joined Sept. 21, 1914, as Private, 5th Batt. South Staffordshire Regt. Obtained commission March 1915 in 5th Batt. South Staffordshire Regt. as 2nd Lieut. Served at Home and France. Wounded Oct. 13, 1915, at attack on Hohenzollern Redoubt. Relinquished commission July 30, 1916, on account of wounds.

CECIL WILLIAM BATESON.

Admitted Nov. 1908. Member of Batesons, Warr & Wimshurst, of Liverpool. Joined Aug. 6, 1914, as Sub-Lieut., Royal Naval Volunteer Reserve, subsequently promoted Lieut. Once mentioned in Dispatches.

ROBERT BATH.

Admitted Dec. 1898. Member of Austin & Bath, Glastonbury. Mobilised Aug. 1914 as Capt., Somerset Royal Horse Artillery, promoted Major 1917. Once mentioned in Dispatches. Awarded the M.C. and T.D. Served at Home and in Egypt.

JAMES RICHARD CORT BATHURST.

Admitted Oct. 1916, practising at 27 Chancery Lane, W.C. Joined April 30, 1917, as Acting Paymaster, Army Pay Department. Served at Home.

RALPH CECIL BATLEY.

Admitted Aug. 1887. Of Silton Lodge, Zeals, Wilts. Served at home as Major Dorset Yeomanry. Died Oct. 23, 1917.

CHARLES DORRINGTON BATT.

Articled to Henry Reed, of Sheffield. Served as Private, 2nd (Public Schools) Batt. Royal Fusiliers.

WILLIAM ELLIOTT BATT.

Admitted May 1905, practised at 58 Theobalds Road, W.C. Served as Major commanding 2nd City of London Battery Royal Field Artillery (T.), subsequently promoted Lieut.-Col. Awarded the C.M.G.

GRENVILLE ARTHUR BATTCOCK.

Admitted Jan. 1910. Managing Clerk with Halliley & Morrison, of Bedford. Mobilised Aug. 4, 1914, as Capt., 1/4 Batt. Royal Berkshire Regt, promoted Major April 1916 (Permanent Rank), with 8th Royal Berkshire Regt. July 1917 to Aug. 1917, Second in command 1st Loyal North Lancashire Regt. Aug. 1917 to July 1918. Three times mentioned in Dispatches. Served in France and Italy.

JOSEPH KEITH BATTEN.

Articled to Joseph Batten, of Peterborough. Mobilised Aug. 4, 1914, as Lieut., Bedfordshire Regt. (T.), promoted Capt. 1915. Served at Home and in France. Killed in action on Sept. 27, 1918, at Mœuvres.

MAXWELL CORNISH BATTEN.

Admitted Jan. 1914. Managing Clerk with Trower, Still & Co., 5 New Square, Lincolns Inn, W.C., now with George M. Doe, Great Torrington, Devon. Enlisted Oct. 20, 1915, as Sapper, 3/2 Mounted Divisional Signal Squadron Royal Engineers (T.). Gazetted 2nd Lieut. Royal Garrison Artillery May 19, 1918. Served in Egypt Jan. 1916 to Aug. 1917, at Home Sept. 1917 to Aug. 1918, at Salonica Aug. 1918 to May 1919, and at Constantinople, Army of Occupation, May 1919 to July 1919.

ROBERT HENRY GUY BATTEN.

Articled to Joseph Batten, of Peterborough. Joined Aug. 1914 as Private, Public Schools Batt. Royal Fusiliers. Passed through Sandhurst. Gazetted 2nd Lieut. Northamptonshire Regt. Served in France. Gassed at Loos in 1915, wounded at Villers 1916.

PHILIP HENRY BATTISHILL.

Admitted Dec. 1913. Of Tiverton. Joined as Private, Public Schools Batt. Royal Fusiliers, subsequently gazetted 2nd Lieut. 4th Batt. West Yorkshire Regt, promoted Lieut. Mentioned in Dispatches and awarded the M.C and Bar.

BERTIE CECIL BATY.

Admitted Oct. 1910, practised at Houghton-le-Spring. Joined Oct. 1914, as Private, Durham Light Infantry. Commissioned 2nd Lieut. Durham Light Infantry March 1915, promoted Lieut. May 1915, Capt. Aug. 1915. Served at Home and in France. Killed in action Sept. 16, 1916.

JOHN ARMSTRONG BATY.

Admitted Sept. 1903. Member of Baty & Fisher, of Hexham. Joined Feb. 3, 1916, as Private, Inns of Court O.T.C., and attained the rank of A/Sergeant. Commissioned 2nd Lieut. Northumberland Fusiliers Dec. 19, 1916, promoted Lieut. June 1918. Served in France. Wounded severely April 6, 1917, at Arras.

REGINALD PRIDHAM BAULKWILL.

Articled to A. E. Hopper, of Barnstaple, N. Devon. Enlisted Oct. 1915, as Rifleman, 5th (City of London) Batt. London Regt., London Rifle Brigade. Served in France. Wounded on the Somme.

JOHN FRANCIS BAWTREE.

Admitted Nov. 1902. Member of Bawtree & Sons, of Witham, Kelvedon, and Tiptree, Essex. Joined Oct. 1914, as Lieut., 2/5 Batt. Essex Regt., subsequently promoted Capt. Served at Home.

PERCY ALWYNE BAX.

Articled to A. M. Cohn, of 52 New Broad Street, E.C. Enlisted Oct. 1, 1917, as Gunner, Royal Garrison Artillery, promoted to Lance-Bombardier Nov. 16, 1917. Served at Home.

GEORGE VERNON BAXTER.

Articled to W. K. Baxter, of Huddersfield. Joined Nov. 10, 1914, as Private, 2/7 Batt. West Riding Regt., later Lance-Corporal. Gazetted 2nd Lieut. 10th Batt. Manchester Regt. Feb. 13, 1915, promoted Lieut. June 1916, and A/Capt. May 1918. Served at Home Nov. 1914 to July 1915, Gallipoli July 1915 to Jan. 1916, Egypt—Palestine (Sinai Campaign) Jan. 1916 to Feb. 1917, France Feb. 1917 to May 1917, Home May 1917 to April 1918, France April 1918 to Sept. 1918, Home Sept. 1918 to Aug. 1919. Wounded May 8, 1917, accidentally wounded Sept. 17, 1918.

ROWLAND PERCIVAL BAXTER.

Articled to Chapman & Baxter, of Whitehaven. Enlisted Sept. 9, 1915, as Private, 28th Batt. County of London Regt. (Artists Rifles). Commissioned 2nd Lieut. 5th Batt. Border Regiment Oct. 27, 1915. Served on the Western Front. Wounded at Wytschaete July 27, 1916. Killed in action in the neighbourhood of Martinpuich Sept. 16, 1916.

SYDNEY JAMES BAYLISS.

Admitted Aug. 1909, practising at Bristol. Served as Lieut., 8th Batt. Gloucestershire Regt.

EDWARD REGINALD BAYNES.

Articled to C. G. Kekewich, of 2 Suffolk Lane, E.C. Served as 2nd Lieut., Royal Army Service Corps., promoted Lieut.

NORMAN THOMAS BAYNES.

Articled to Thomas Godfrey Baynes, of Dartford, Kent. Joined Aug. 5, 1915, as Private, Inns of Court O.T.C., transferred to 5th (City of London) Batt. London Regt. (London Rifle Brigade) Jan. 1916, and to the Machine Gun Corps (Infantry) Aug. 1916, promoted Sergeant Jan. 1917, transferred to Royal

Flying Corps Nov. 1917, and subsequently Royal Air Force. Served in France and at Home. Wounded at Festubert June 6, 1917, whilst serving with the 202nd Machine Gun Coy., 197th Brigade, 66th Division.

WILLIAM NELSON BAZELEY.

Admitted July 1910. Member, of Bazeley Barnes, & Bazeleys, of Bideford, Devon. Mobilised Aug. 1914 as Capt., 6th Batt. Devonshire Regt. (T.)., promoted Major May 1915, Lieut.-Col. Jan. 1918. Mentioned in Dispatches. Served in Mesopotamia and India 1919 as Commandant, Murree Hills. Wounded on March 8, 1916, at, or near, Dujailah in Mesopotamia, with Expeditionary Force for relief of Kut.

FRANK DOVETON BAZETT.

Admitted April 1906. Member of Pitman & Bazett, of Newbury and Reading, Berks. Joined Nov. 1915 as 2nd Lieut., 3rd (S.R.) Batt. Royal Berkshire Regt., promoted Lieut. July 1917, A/Capt. Nov. 1917 to May 1918, Temp. Capt. Dec. 1918 to April 1919, 1st Batt. Royal Berkshire Regt. Jan. 1917 to May 1918, Intelligence Officer 99th Infantry Brigade May to Nov. 1918, attached 3rd Army Headquarters as Courts-Martial Officer Nov. 1918 to April 1919. Once mentioned in Dispatches. Awarded the M.C. Served in England Nov. 1915 to Jan. 1917, and in France Jan. 1917 to April 1919. Accidentally injured by bomb when instructing in England May 1916.

CYRIL SHAKESPEAR BEACHCROFT.

Admitted Aug. 1908. Member of Beachcroft, Thompson & Co. of 9 Theobalds Road, W.C. Joined Inns of Court O.T.C. in Aug. 1914 and obtained commission in The Queen's Own Dorset Yeomanry, attaining the rank of Capt. and Adjutant. In order to get to the front, transferred to the Household Batt. of the Guards with the rank of Lieut. Went to France Aug. 29, 1917. Killed in action Oct. 12, 1917.

ALAN BEAL.

Admitted Nov. 1913. Managing Clerk with McColm & Brooke, of Lewisham, S.E. Joined Aug. 5, 1914, as Gunner, " B " Battery Hon. Artillery Company. Gazetted 2nd Lieut. Royal Field Artillery Oct. 21, 1914, promoted Lieut. Aug. 1915, Capt. Sept. 1917. Once mentioned in Dispatches. Awarded the M.C. and French Croix de Guerre avec Palme. Served in England to April 1915 and May to June 1915, France April 1915 and July 1915 to May 1919.

LEONARD FRANK BEAL.

Admitted Oct. 1912. Member of F. Beal & Son, of St. Albans. Enlisted Aug. 1914 as Private, 28th Batt. County of London Regt. (Artists Rifles). Gazetted 2nd Lieut. Bedfordshire Regt. March 1915, promoted Lieut. Aug. 1915, Capt. Oct. 1915, Major Oct. 1917. Awarded the M.C. Served in France. Wounded June 1915.

RICHARD EDWARD BRUCE BEAL.

Admitted July 1901. Member of E. W. & Bruce Beal, 41 Finsbury Pavement, E.C. Joined Nov. 13, 1915, as Lieut, Royal Army Service Corps, promoted Capt. Sept. 1917, Temp. Major D.A.Q.M.G. March 1919. Twice mentioned in Dispatches. Awarded the O.B.E., M.C., White Eagle (Serbian),

St. Stanislas (Russian). Served in Egypt, Salonica, Serbia, Sofia, Bulgaria, Constantinople, South Russia.

EDMUND LANSDOWNE BEALE.
Articled to J. F. Beale, of 16 Great George Street, S.W. Joined 1914 as Private, 14th Batt. County of London Regt. (London Scottish). Subsequently commissioned and posted to the Cambridgeshire Regt., attaining the rank of Capt. Killed in action March 2, 1918.

CHARLES HENRY BEARBLOCK.
Articled to E. G. Thorne, of 22 Aldermanbury, London, E.C. Joined University of London O.T.C. in Aug. 1914. Received commission as Temp. 2nd Lieut. Sept. 1, 1914, and gazetted to 9th Batt. Essex Regt., promoted Lieut. April 1915, and served from that date as Machine Gun Officer of the Batt. Served in France. Wounded Oct. 20, 1915, and died the same day.

BALFOUR WEST BEARD.
Articled to W. J. W. Beard, of 3, 4, and 5 Queen Street, E.C. Served as Lance-Corporal Royal Army Service Corps.

EDWIN CYRIL BEARD.
Articled to H. C. Wanklyn, of Colchester. Enlisted Sept. 16, 1914, as Motor Dispatch Rider, Essex Regt, afterwards joined the University and Public Schools Corps. On March 5, 1915, granted commission as 2nd Lieut. 5th Batt. Essex Regt., and afterwards, while abroad, promoted Lieut. On Sept. 25, 1915, sailed for the Dardanelles, afterwards served in Egypt. On March 29, 1917, reported wounded and missing after the 1st Battle of Gaza, subsequently presumed killed.

HAROLD INGHAM BEARDER.
Admitted Dec. 1908, practising at Halifax. Joined April 16, 1917, as Private, Inns of Court O.T.C. Gazetted 2nd Lieut. Royal Garrison Artillery (S.R.) March 3, 1918, and posted to 375th Siege Battery, France, June 20, 1918.

AMOS BEARDSLEY.
Articled to L. N. Holden, of Lancaster. Mobilised Aug. 1914 as 2nd Lieut., 4th Batt. The King's Own Royal Lancaster Regt. (T.F.). Resigned July 1916, rank Lieut. Joined Royal Field Artillery Aug. 1916 as Gunner, transferred to Machine Gun Corps (H.B.) (Tanks) Feb. 1917, subsequently promoted to Corporal. Awarded the M.M. Served in France May 1915 to June 1916 and July 1917 to Jan. 1919.

ARTHUR LIONEL BEARDSLEY.
Admitted Oct. 1906. Member of Woolley, Beardsley & Bosworth, of Loughborough. Served as Sergeant 11th Batt. South Lancashire Regt.

GERALD BEAUMONT.
Admitted Sept. 1903. Member of Harrison Beaumont & Smith of Wakefield. Enlisted Sept. 3, 1914, as Private, Essex Yeomanry. Gazetted 2nd Lieut. King's Own Yorkshire Light Infantry, Oct. 26, 1914, promoted Lieut.

Jan. 1915, Capt. June 1915, Major April 1917. Awarded the M.C. and Bar. Served in France.

JOHN BEECROFT BEAUMONT.

Admitted Jan. 1910. Member of Beaumont & Son, of Leeds. Mobilised Aug. 1914 as 2nd Lieut., Northern Signal Companies, Royal Engineers, promoted Lieut. June 1916. Served in Egypt, Palestine and Syria.

KENNETH MACDONALD BEAUMONT.

Admitted Oct. 1910. Member of Beaumont & Son, of 66 Gresham House, Old Broad Street, E.C. Joined Sept. 18, 1914, as Lieut., Royal Army Service Corps, promoted Capt. Dec. 1914, Major Dec. 1915, D.A.D.S. July 1917 to May 1919. Mentioned three times in Dispatches. Awarded the D.S.O. Served at Home Sept. 1914 to March 1915, and at Gallipoli, Mudros, Egypt, Palestine and Syria March 1915 to May 1919.

THOMAS NICHOLLS BEAVAN.

Admitted Aug. 1899. Member of Weld & Beavan, of 9 Bedford Row, W.C. Enlisted June 1916 as Private, Bedfordshire Regt. Gazetted 2nd Lieut. Leinster Regt. Aug. 1917. Served in France Oct. to Dec. 1917, when invalided home, and in France and Belgium July 1918 to Dec. 1918.

JOHN PICKARD BECHER.

Admitted Nov. 1902. Member of Toynbee & Co., of Lincoln, and Larken & Co., of Newark. Mobilised Aug. 1914 as Major, 8th Batt. Notts and Derby Regt. (Sherwood Foresters) (T.). Once mentioned in Dispatches. Awarded the D.S.O. Served in France. Wounded in the attack on the Hohenzollern Redoubt, died from the wound in Hospital Jan. 1, 1916.

JAMES FRANCIS ADAMS BECK.

Admitted Sept. 1907. Member of Parson, Lee & Co., of 24 Lime Street, London, E.C. Enlisted March 29, 1917, as a Gunner in the Essex and Suffolk Royal Garrison Artillery. Gazetted 2nd Lieut. Royal Army Service Corps March 28, 1918. Served at Home March 1917 to April 1918, and in France April 1918 to Feb. 1919.

REGINALD ARTHUR BECK.

Articled to A. E. Crane, of 44 Bedford Row, W.C. Mobilised Aug. 1914 as Driver, Hon. Artillery Company, subsequently gazetted 2nd Lieut. Royal Horse Artillery and attained the rank of Capt. and Adjutant. Mentioned in Dispatches. Severely wounded in France, March 24, 1918.

WILLIAM CRABBE BECK.

Admitted Jan. 1913. Member of Neve, Beck & Kirby, 21 Lime Street, E.C. Mobilised Aug. 4, 1914, as Capt. in 4th London Howitzer Brigade, subsequently Capt. in Royal Field Artillery, promoted full Major Nov. 1917. Twice mentioned in Dispatches. Served at Home, in France, Salonica, Egypt, and Palestine. Killed in Palestine March 28, 1918.

CECIL BEDFORD.

Admitted Aug. 1910, practising at Ilford, Essex. Enlisted Sept. 1916 as Telegraphist, Royal Naval Volunteer Reserve. Served at Home Sept. 1916 to Jan. 1919.

SEATON HALL BEDFORD.

Admitted Feb. 1914. Of Sheffield. Joined Aug. 6, 1914, as Private, 1st Hon. Artillery Company. Gazetted 2nd Lieut. 2nd Batt. Royal Berkshire Regt. May 7, 1916. Served in France. Killed in action, July 1, 1916.

LEONARD JAMES BEDWELL.

Articled to H. B. Ashton, of Bury St. Edmunds. Enlisted Sept. 19, 1914, as Private, 19th (S.) Batt. Royal Fusiliers. Gazetted 2nd Lieut. 3rd Batt. East Surrey Regt. May 18, 1915, seconded 2nd Lieut. Machine Gun Corps July 1916, promoted Temp. Lieut. Machine Gun Corps Dec. 1916, Substantive Lieut. East Surrey Regt. July 17, 1917. Once mentioned in Dispatches. Served in Macedonia Nov. 1916 to Dec. 1918, and at Home Dec. 1918 to July 1919.

FRANCIS BERNARD WYNTER BEE.

Admitted June 1914. Managing Clerk with Martineau & Reid, 2 Raymond Buildings, Gray's Inn, W.C. Mobilised July 29, 1914, as Lieut., Dorset Royal Garrison Artillery (T.F.), promoted Temp. Capt. June 1915, Capt. June 1916, A/Major May 1917, Adjutant Dorset Royal Garrison Artillery (T.F.) during whole of 1915. Once mentioned in Dispatches. Served in France Oct. 1916 to July 1917, and April 1918 to March 1919.

WILLIAM SORBY MARDON BEEBY.

Admitted May 1913, practising at Sheffield. Enlisted Aug. 1914 as Private, York and Lancaster Regt. Gazetted 2nd Lieut. 1914, promoted Lieut. 1915, Capt. 1916. Killed in action at Bullecourt, May 4, 1917.

FRANCIS WILLIAM BEECH.

Admitted Aug. 1911, practised at Pontypridd. Served as A/Paymaster (Worcestershire Regt.), Army Pay Department.

JOHN LESLIE BEECH.

Articled to C. H. Beech, of Manchester. Enlisted Sept. 4, 1914, as Private, 20th Batt. Royal Fusiliers, transferred to the Labour Corps in 1917, promoted Lance-Corporal and retransferred to the Royal Fusiliers Feb. 1918. Served at Home and France. Wounded July 16, 1916.

PHILIP BEILBY BEECROFT.

Admitted Dec. 1908. Assistant Solicitor Walsall Corporation. Joined April 29, 1916 as Private, Royal Army Service Corps (M.T.), and subsequently promoted A/Sergeant. Gazetted 2nd Lieut. Royal Army Service Corps (M.T.) Sept. 10, 1917, promoted Lieut. March 1919. Served in Flanders, France, and with the Rhine Army Nov. 1918 to July 1919.

STANLEY BEECROFT.

Articled to W. G. Beecroft, of Leigh-on-Sea, Essex. Enlisted Sept. 9, 1914, as Private (Dispatch Rider), 17th Batt. Royal Fusiliers, transferred as 2nd Class Air Mechanic Royal Flying Corps (Motor Cyclist) May 1915, promoted to 1st Class Air Mechanic Aug. 1916, and to Corporal Jan. 1918. Awarded the Italian Medal. Served at Home, Belgium, France and Italy from 1915 to 1919.

WILLIAM ROBERT BEER.

Articled to William Beer, of Kingsbridge. Served as 2nd Lieut. 5th Batt. Devonshire Regt. Served in India.

ROBERT HENRY STEWART EDLESTONE BEHREND.

Admitted Oct. 1897. Member of R. H. Behrend & Co., of 17 Surrey Street, W.C. Joined 1915 as Capt., 23rd Batt. London Regt., temporarily attached War Office Staff 1917, Staff Capt. 1918, Brevet-Major 1919. Twice mentioned in Dispatches. Served at Home and in France.

ERIC BELDON.

Articled to Albert Beldon, of Bradford. Served as 2nd Lieut., West Yorkshire Regt.

HOWARD BELDON.

Admitted March 1915, practised at Bradford. Served with the 6th Batt. West Yorkshire Regt.

ERIC HERBERT BELK.

Articled to F. W. Yeates, of 23 Surrey Street, W.C. Enlisted Sept. 1914, as Private, 4th Batt. Queen's Own Cameron Highlanders, recommended for commission. Served in France. Killed at the Battle of Loos Sept. 28, 1915.

ALAN THORPE BELL.

Articled to Thomas Bell, of Stockport. Served as Private Royal Army Service Corps (M.T.).

BERNARD ARTHUR BELL.

Articled to W. J. Stuart, of Hull. Joined Sept. 2, 1914, as 2nd Lieut., Duke of Wellington's West Riding Regt., promoted Lieut. Sept. 1914, Temp. Capt. Dec. 1915, Permanent Capt. July 1916. Served in France 1915. Severely wounded in June 1915. Incapacitated for further Active Service.

CECIL CHARLES BELL.

Admitted May 1913. Member of C. C. Bell & Son, of Bedford. Enlisted Jan. 1916, as Private, 28th Batt. County of London Regt. (Artists Rifles). Gazetted 2nd Lieut. Lancashire Fusiliers Sept. 1917. Killed Nov. 28, 1917.

ERIC WALTER BELL.

Admitted March 1901, practising at 22 Red Lion Square. Joined Dec. 23, 1914, as 2nd Lieut., 10th Batt. Royal Welch Fusiliers. Promoted 1st Lieut. March 1915, Capt. July 1915, appointed Railway Traffic Officer Aug. 1916. Served in France 1915 to 1919. Gassed April 30, 1916, at Kimmel Hill.

GEORGE FRANCIS BELL.

Admitted Feb. 1902. Member of Davies, Balkwill & Bell, of Newcastle-upon-Tyne. Joined Aug. 1914 as 2nd Lieut., 6th Batt. Northumberland Fusiliers, subsequently promoted Capt. Twice mentioned in Dispatches. Served in France 3 years. Wounded Dec. 1915 and Jan. 1916.

HERBERT ALFRED BELL.

Admitted Nov. 1893, practising at Gainsborough. Mobilised Aug. 1914, as Capt., 5th Batt. Lincolnshire Regt, promoted Major Jan. 1917. Served in Ireland Easter 1916, and in France March 1917 to Feb. 1919.

JOHN HERBERT BELL.

Admitted Dec. 1899. Member of Theodore Bell & Co., of 3 Salters' Hall Court, Cannon Street, E.C. Served as Private, 5th (Reserve) Batt. East Surrey Regt., subsequently gazetted 2nd Lieut. Territorial Force Reserve, and attained the rank of Capt, appointed Adjutant and Quartermaster Donnington Hall Prisoners of War Camp.

JOHN SACKVILLE BELL.

Admitted Aug, 1900, practising at Kingston-on-Thames. Joined May 9, 1916, as Assistant Paymaster, Royal Naval Volunteer Reserve. Served at Home.

LIONEL STUART BELL.

Admitted Oct. 1913. Of Plumstead. Served as Private, Royal Army Veterinary Corps.

ROBERT WILLIAM BELL.

Articled to David Main, of Carlisle. Joined March 25, 1915, as Quartermaster, British Red Cross Society. Once mentioned in Dispatches. Served at Home.

SYDNEY JAMES BELL.

Articled to Ernest Hadfield, of Southport. Joined March 1915 Inns of Court O.T.C. Gazetted 2nd Lieut. 7th Batt. King's Liverpool Regt. July 19, 1915. Served in France. Wounded at Guedecourt Sept. 25, 1916, and died in Manchester Hospital Oct. 13, 1916.

TOM GEORGE BELL.

Admitted July 1899, practising at South Shields. Joined March 29, 1915, as Capt., 4th Northumbrian (How.) Brigade Royal Field Artillery (T.). Served at Home March 1915 to Nov. 1918, and in France Nov. 1918 to June 1919.

WILSON BELL.

Admitted July 1904. Assistant Solicitor to the West Riding of Yorks County Council. Joined Nov. 23, 1914, as 2nd Lieut., King's Own Yorkshire Light Infantry, promoted Lieut. March 1915, Capt. May 1915. Served in France. Killed in action March 15, 1917, at Puisieux-au-Mont, near Bapaume, France.

CUTHBERT BELLORD.

Articled to E. J. Bellord, of 8 Waterloo Place, S.W. Served as 2nd Lieut. King's Shropshire Light Infantry.

EDWARD MILLIGEN BELOE.

Admitted March 1895, practising at Lynn, Norfolk. Served as Capt. Royal Defence Corps.

EDWARD JOSEPH BELTON.

Admitted April 1892, practised at 35 Bloomsbury Square, W.C. Served as Private Public Schools Corps.

LESLIE ALAN BENDLE.

Articled to F. W. Halton, of Carlisle. Joined Oct. 5, 1914, as 2nd Lieut., 4th Batt. Border Regt. Promoted Lieut. June 1916, Capt. July 1917, attached to 4th Batt. Dorset Regt. (T.F.) from Aug. 1916. Served in India and Burma Oct. 1914 to Aug. 1916, Mesopotamia Aug. 1916 to Feb 1919.

GERALD CARR BENHAM.

Admitted Oct. 1906. Member of Sparling, Son & Benham, of Colchester. Mobilised Aug. 1914, as Lieut., 8th (Cyclist) Batt. Essex Regt, promoted Capt. Aug. 26, 1914, A/Major Sept. 1916, Substantive Major Nov. 1919, Adjutant 8th Batt. Essex Regt. Sept. 1914 to Sept. 1916. Once mentioned in Dispatches. Awarded the M.C. Served at Home and in France. Wounded Sept. 17, 1918, near St. Quentin.

THOMAS JOSEPH BENJAMIN.

Admitted April 1912, practising at Liverpool. Joined Aug. 28, 1914, as Private, 5th Batt. The King's Liverpool Regt. (T.), promoted Lance-Corporal Feb. 1915, gazetted 2nd Lieut. June 9, 1915 (while in France), and posted to same Batt, promoted Lieut. Aug. 1916, Temp. Capt. May 1918. Served in France continuously Feb. 1915 to Aug. 1916, subsequently (incapacitated) on administrative duties at Home. Wounded Guillemont (Somme) Aug. 9, 1916.

ARTHUR CAMPION BENNETT.

Admitted Feb. 1907, practising at West Hartlepool. Mobilised Aug. 1914 as Capt., Durham Royal Garrison Artillery (T.F.), promoted Major June 1916, seconded for service with Royal Garrison Artillery (Regular Forces) Dec. 1915. Served in France and Belgium.

DONALD BENNETT.

Admitted Jan. 1913, practising at Bristol. Served as Private, South Midland Field Ambulance, Royal Army Medical Corps.

EDWARD BENNETT.

Articled to C. R. E. Pattenden, of 12 Bernard Street, Russell Square, W.C. Joined Jan. 22, 1917, as Ordinary Seaman, Royal Naval Volunteer Reserve. Appointed Decoder H.M.S. *Artois*, 10th Cruiser Squadron, July 6, 1917. Served on Iceland Patrol and with North Atlantic Convoys.

ERNEST WILLIAM BENNETT.

Admitted March 1892, practising at Worthing. Rejoined 4th Batt. Royal Sussex Regt. with rank of Capt., on Sept. 23, 1914, transferred to Territorial Force Reserve on Oct. 4, 1915. Served at Home.

GORDON BENNETT.

Articled to A. H. Dolman, of Abertillery. Served as Lieut., 3rd Batt. Monmouthshire Regt.

GUY WHITTEM BENNETT.

Articled to Stilgoes of 24 Essex Street, W.C. Served as 2nd Lieut., 9th Batt. Shropshire Light Infantry.

HENRY MALCOLM BENNETT.

Articled to Thomas Bennett, of Deddington. Served as Private, Inns of Court O.T.C. and subsequently gazetted 2nd Lieut. 20th Batt. County of London Regt. Promoted Lieut.

IVAN PROVIS WENTWORTH BENNETT.

Articled to H. A. Merriman, of Guildford. Joined Sept. 3, 1914, as 2nd Lieut., 7th Batt. The Queen's Royal West Surrey Regt., promoted Capt. Nov. 1915. Served in France. Killed at Trones Wood, Somme, July 13, 1916.

JULIEN FREDERICK CHARLES BENNETT.

Admitted Aug. 1893, practising as Harston & Bennett, of 35 Lincoln's Inn Fields, London. Mobilised Aug. 4, 1914, whilst serving in London Rifle Brigade as a Sergeant. Received commission in this Regt. Oct. 14, 1914, and posted to 2nd Batt., promoted 1st Lieut. Jan. 1915 and Capt. Jan. 1915, appointed Adjutant of 3rd Batt. same day and served as such until Aug. 1918, granted permanent rank of Capt. July 11, 1917, transferred to Royal Air Force with temporary commission in that Force as Lieut. Administrative on Sept. 1918, promoted Capt. Administrative Nov. 1918, acted as Adjutant at No. 1 Stores Depôt, Kidbrooke, from Sept. 1918 until April 1919. Served at Home.

RONALD CLAUDE BENNETT.

Articled to C. H. Bennett, of 68 Coleman Street, E.C. 4. Joined Aug. 1915 as Voluntary Ambulance Driver, British Red Cross Society. Served in France Sept. 1915 to March 1916 and at Home Jan. 1917 to Feb. 1919.

THOMAS GERALD BENNETT.

Articled to C. H. Waugh, of Haywards Heath. Served as 2nd Lieut., 6th (Cyclist) Batt. Royal Sussex Regt. and the Machine Gun Corps. Attained the Rank of Capt.

WILLIAM PORTER BENNETT.

Articled to Le Brasseur & Oakley, of 40 Carey Street, W.C. Served as Lieut. 2nd Batt. Border Regt.

WILLIAM RICHARD BENNETT.

Admitted Nov. 1899, practising at 10 King's Bench Walk, Temple, E.C. Enlisted in the ranks Sept. 16, 1914, commissioned 2nd Lieut., Royal Army Service Corps Sept. 25, 1914, promoted 1st Lieut. Dec. 1914, Capt. March 1915. Served at Home.

BARZILLAI BECKERLEG BENNETTS.

Admitted May 1905, practising at Penzance, Cornwall. Enlisted Sept. 4, 1914, as Trooper, Royal 1st Devon Yeomanry, gazetted 2nd Lieut. 13th Batt. Argyll and Sutherland Highlanders Dec. 1914, attached 12th Batt. Sept. 1915 (to proceed to France with them), promoted Lieut. and Adjutant 1916, Capt. 1917. Once mentioned in Dispatches. Served in France 1915, Salonica 1915 to Nov. 1918, Ireland Dec. 1918 to Feb. 1919.

ARTHUR CRICHTON STUART BENNING.

Admitted Nov. 1906, practising at Birmingham and Dunstable. Mobilised Aug. 1914 as Capt., Bedfordshire Yeomanry, promoted Major May 1915. Twice mentioned in Dispatches. Served in France June 1915 to April 1919 with 9th Cavalry Brigade, 1st Cavalry Division.

BERNARD JOHN BENSON.

Articled to Reginald Benson, of Sheffield. Enlisted Sept. 10, 1914, as Private, 12th Batt. York and Lancaster Regt., transferred as Sapper 52nd (A.W.) Coy. Royal Engineers. Served in France

HENRY LAURENCE BENSON.

Admitted Dec. 1912. Managing Clerk with Cuthbert Bainbridge, of Newcastle-upon-Tyne. Joined Aug. 5, 1914, as Private, 6th Northumberland Fusiliers and promoted to Sergeant, subsequently gazetted 2nd Lieut. in same Regt. Once mentioned in Dispatches. Served in France and Belgium. Killed in action April 11, 1916, at Kemmel.

ALFRED HARDY BENTLEY.

Admitted May 1903. Member of Druces & Attlee, of 10 Billiter Square, E.C. Served as Private, Hon. Artillery Company, subsequently gazetted Lieut. Royal Army Ordnance Dept.

WILLIAM BENTLEY.

Admitted Feb. 1907. Member of Carter, Bentleys & Gundill, of Pontefract. Served as 2nd Lieut., 5th Batt. King's Own Yorkshire Light Infantry and subsequently promoted Lieut.

WILLIAM HENRY BENTLEY.

Articled to W. H. Tyrer, Town Clerk of Wigan. Enlisted Feb. 14, 1917, as Private, Royal Army Service Corps (M.T.), transferred to 8th Training Reserve Batt. March 1917, gazetted 2nd Lieut. Royal Flying Corps, Jan. 18, 1918. Served at Home Feb. 1917 to April 1918, France April 1918 to Sept. 1918, Home Oct. 1918 to March 1919.

BENYON RUDGARD BENYON-WINSOR.

Admitted March 1913. Of Swansea. Served as Lieut., 1st Welsh (Howitzer) Brigade, Royal Field Artillery (T.) and attained the rank of Major.

ALEXANDER BERESFORD.

Admitted Jan. 1905. Member of Albery, Lucas & Beresford, of Petersfield and Midhurst. Served as Lieut., 35th Divisional Train, Royal Army Service Corps.

OTTO LEOPOLD BERGENDORFF.

Articled to S. G. Hooper, of Dudley. Enlisted Nov. 21, 1914, as Gunner, 6th South Staffs Battery Royal Field Artillery. Awarded the M.M. Served in France. Gassed Nov. 1917.

FRANCIS RATTRAY BERGH.

Admitted Nov. 1897. Member of Oldfields, of 13 Walbrook, E.C. 4. Enlisted Aug. 13, 1916, as Private, Royal Fusiliers. Gazetted 2nd Lieut. Labour Corps Aug. 19, 1917, promoted A/Capt. March 1918, appointed "Labour Superintendent" with rank of A/Capt. Nov. 1918. Served in France.

CHARLES WALTER BERKELEY.

Admitted Dec. 1891. Practising at 25 Bedford Row, London, W.C. Mobilised Aug. 1914 as Major and Hon. Lieut.-Col., 7th Batt. London Regt.,

Lieut.-Col. Commanding 2/7 Batt. London Regt. Nov. 1914 to June 1917 in England and France, Area Group Commandant June 1917 to April 1919. Promoted Colonel Nov. 1918. Once mentioned in Dispatches. Served in France.

GEORGE NORMAN BERNEY.

Articled to J. T. Goddard, of 10 Serjeant's Inn, Temple, E.C. Enlisted Aug. 1914 and shortly afterwards received a commission in the Herefordshire Regt., attaining the rank of Capt. Killed in action in Palestine on Nov. 6, 1917.

NOËL BERRIDGE.

Admitted Feb. 1911. With Burn & Berridge, 11 & 12 Southampton Street, Bloomsbury, W.C. Joined Aug. 9, 1914, as Private, 1st Batt. Hon. Artillery Company. Invalided out Aug. 9, 1916. Served in Flanders 1915.

CHARLES BERRY.

Admitted Sept. 1899, practising at Tunbridge Wells, Kent. Joined June 26, 1917, as Cadet, Garrison Officers Cadet Batt. Gazetted 2nd Lieut. 4th Batt. Royal Sussex Regt. Aug. 18, 1917, promoted Temp. Capt. and Courts-Martial Officer, 4th T.R. Brigade, Sept. 1918. Served at Home.

JOHN ANTHONY BERRY.

Admitted April 1910. Managing Clerk with G. R. Hubbard, of 40 Chancery Lane, W.C. Joined 15th Batt. County of London Regt. (Civil Service Rifles) on Aug. 5, 1914. After serving during the winter in trenches, sent to Officers' Training Camp at Boulogne, and given a Commission as 2nd Lieut. 2nd Batt. Gordon Highlanders. Killed at the Battle of Loos Sept. 18, 1915.

THOMAS ALGERNON SCHOLES BERRY.

Admitted June 1907. Practising at Swinton, nr. Manchester. Enlisted Sept. 1, 1914, as Gunner, Royal Field Artillery, Corporal Feb. 1915, Sergeant April 1915, Battery Quartermaster-Sergeant May 1915, Battery Sergeant-Major Jan. 1916, transferred to Royal Garrison Artillery Aug. 1917, appointed Sergeant (Artillery Clerk), subsequently Staff Sergeant on the Staff of Royal Artillery Headquarters, Italy (Superintending Clerk to Staff Capt. R.A.G.H.Q., Italy). Twice mentioned in Dispatches. Awarded the M.S.M. Served in Ireland Sept. 1914 to March 1915, England March 1915 to July 1915, Belgium and France July 1915 to Nov. 1917, Italy Nov. 1917 to Jan. 1919.

HAROLD RICHARD BETTINSON.

Articled to George Alfred Bettinson, of Birmingham. Enlisted May 1, 1917, as Private, 3rd Batt. Royal Warwickshire Regt. Gazetted 2nd Lieut. Machine Gun Corps Oct. 27, 1917. Awarded the M.C. Served in France. Gassed Oct. 9, 1918, at Armentières.

THEOPHILUS HAMILTON BEVAN.

Admitted Aug. 1918. Practising at 1 Bush Lane. Enlisted April 1916 as Private, East Surrey Regt. Gazetted 2nd Lieut. Royal Garrison Artillery (S.R.) Jan. 1917, promoted Lieut. July 1917. Served at Home.

REGINALD EDGAR MORRIS BEW.

Articled to J. A. M. Bew, of Chichester. Served as Private, Royal Army Service Corps (M.T.).

EDWARD NEVILLE BEWLEY.

Admitted Dec. 1911. Practised at 40 Chancery Lane, W.C. Joined the Inns of Court O.T.C. in June 1915, and was afterwards gazetted 2nd Lieut. Sherwood Foresters, Notts and Derby Regt. Killed in action June 26, 1917.

ERNEST RUDOLPH NEVILLE BEWLEY.

Articled to H. N. Bewley, of Liverpool. Served as 2nd Lieut., XI. Army Corps Cyclist Batt.

HARRY MAX BEYFUS.

Admitted Nov. 1909. Managing Clerk with Beyfus & Beyfus, of 32 Sackville Street, W. Joined Nov. 14, 1916, as Ordinary Seaman. Served in Eastern Mediterranean, H.M.S. *St. George*, from Jan. 1917. to Nov. 1917. Then attached as Interpreter and Telephonist with French Navy till Jan. 1919.

FREDERICK ARNOLD BIDDLE.

Admitted Nov. 1902. Member of Biddle, Thorne, Welsford & Gait, of 22 Aldermanbury, E.C. Enlisted Corps of School of Musketry, Sept. 16, 1914. Received commission as Lieut. Territorial Force Reserve July 11, 1915, promoted Capt. Nov. 1915. Served at Home and in France.

CECIL FRANCIS GILMOUR BILBROUGH.

Articled to A. S. Cardew, of Lennox House, Norfolk Street, W.C. Served as Private, 12th Batt. Lond. Regt., subsequently gazetted 2nd Lieut. Middlesex Regt. and promoted Lieut.

SAMUEL WALTER BILLINGS.

Admitted April 1902. Practised at Cheltenham. Served as a Private in Universities and Public Schools Batt. Royal Fusiliers. Died Jan. 3, 1916, of wounds received in action the previous day.

CLAUDE HERBERT EVELYN BILTON.

Articled to Ernest Bird, of 9 Young Street, Kensington, W. Served as 2nd Lieut. and Dispatch Rider, Cyclist Batt. Black Watch.

HAROLD BERTRAM BINGHAM.

Admitted July 1913. Managing Clerk with Mead & Sons, of 116 Jermyn Street, S.W. 1. Enlisted Sept. 2, 1914, as Private, 18th (P.S.) Batt. Royal Fusiliers. Gazetted 2nd Lieut. Royal Sussex Regt. July 1916, 2nd Lieut. Royal Field Artillery, April 1917 promoted Lieut. Oct. 1919. Served at Home and in France.

LEONARD BINGHAM.

Admitted June 1915. Practising at 65 Coleman Street, E.C. Enlisted Feb. 28, 1916, as Signaller, Royal Horse and Royal Field Artillery. Served in France 1917 to 1918.

BENJAMIN BERNARD BINKS.

Articled to William Harrison, of Leeds. Served as 2nd Lieut., West Riding Army Service Corps (T.) and afterwards promoted Lieut.

HENRY FREDERICK DUDLEY BINGLEY.

Admitted April 1912. Managing Clerk with Shepheards & Walters, of 4 Broad Street Place, Finsbury Circus, E.C. Joined Dec. 1916 as Cadet, Royal

Garrison Artillery School, Handel Street, London. Gazetted 2nd Lieut. Royal Garrison Artillery Jan. 13, 1917, promoted Lieut. July 1918. Served at Home.

CLEMENT STANLEY BINNS.

Admitted March 1908. Member of Newsom & Binns, of Sheffield. Joined May 1915 as 2nd Lieut., Northumberland Fusiliers (1st Tyneside Scottish). Served in France. Missing, believed killed, July 1, 1916.

ARTHUR LYLE BIRCH.

Admitted Feb. 1901. Member of Birch, Cullimore & Co., of Chester. Joined Nov. 27, 1915, as 2nd Lieut., 5th Batt. Cheshire Regt., subsequently promoted Lieut.

FRANK BIRCH.

Admitted Dec. 1905. Managing Clerk with Kirby, Millett & Ayscough, of 2 and 3 The Sanctuary, Westminster, S.W. Enlisted June 9, 1916, as Private, 8th Reserve Cavalry. Gazetted 2nd Lieut. 3rd Batt. West Yorkshire Regt. April 26, 1917, promoted Lieut. Oct. 1918. Served at Home June 1916 to June 1917, and Dec. 1917 to March 1918, and in France and Flanders June to Dec. 1917, and in March 1918. Wounded on Somme March 25, 1918.

GEORGE BIRCH.

Admitted May 1896, practising at Lichfield. Joined Oct. 1914 as Acting Paymaster, Army Pay Department. Once mentioned in Dispatches. Served at Home.

ERNEST ROY BIRD.

Admitted July 1905. Member of Wedlake, Letts & Birds, and Tahourdin & Birds, of 11 Serjeant's Inn, and Ernest Bird & Sons, of 9 Young Street, Kensington. Mobilised Aug. 4, 1914, as Private, 16th Batt. County of London Regt. (Queen's Westminster Rifles), subsequently promoted Company Sergeant-Major. Served at Home.

ERNEST WILLIAM BIRD.

Admitted April 1902. Member of Bartley, Bird & Co., of Liverpool. Served as Private, 10th Batt. King's Liverpool Regt. (Liverpool Scottish), subsequently gazetted 2nd Lieut. in same Batt. and Regt. and attained the rank of Capt. Mentioned in Dispatches.

HENRY SODEN BIRD.

Admitted Nov. 1902. Member of H. Soden Bird & Sons, of Newcastle-upon-Tyne. Served as Gunner and Signaller, 297th Siege Battery Royal Garrison Artillery. Awarded the M.M.

NORMAN DOUGLAS BIRD.

Admitted Dec. 1905. Member of J. Hopley Pierce & Bird, of Wrexham. Enlisted May 1916 as Gunner, Lancashire and Cheshire Garrison Artillery (T.). Obtained commission in Royal Garrison Artillery in April 1918. Served at Home and in France.

STANLEY TREADGOLD BIRD.

Articled to C. A. Pryce, of Abingdon, Berks. Enlisted Sept. 8, 1914, as a Private, 28th Batt. County of London Regt. (Artists Rifles), later sent to the

Artists' Officers Training School at St. Omer. Gazetted Temp. 2nd Lieut. King's Royal Rifles Sept. 19, 1915, and joined the 7th Batt. at the Front that month. Served in France. Wounded near Ypres on Dec. 6, 1915, and invalided home until May 1916. Rejoined Regiment in France, and again severely wounded at Derrancourt Aug. 19, 1916. Died at the Corps Dressing Station Aug. 20, 1916.

WALTER LEONARD BIRD.

Admitted May 1909, practising at Bradford. Served as 2nd Lieut., 10th Batt. King's Liverpool Regt. (Liverpool Scottish). Promoted Lieut.

JOSEPH HORNBY BIRLEY.

Admitted March 1907. Enlisted 1914 as Private, 3rd (Public Schools) Batt. Royal Fusiliers, subsequently commissioned and posted to the Manchester Regt., attaining the rank of Capt. Killed in action Sept. 2, 1918.

HENRY ANTHONY BIRRELL-ANTHONY.

Articled to B. L. Reynolds, of High Wycombe. Served as 2nd Lieut., Monmouthshire Regt.

REGINALD BARTLEMORE GROSVENOR BIRTILL.

Admitted Dec. 1906. Formerly practising at South Molton, N. Devon. Enlisted Dec. 11, 1916, as Private, Depôt Devonshire Regt. Gazetted 2nd Lieut. 6th Batt. Devonshire Regt. Jan. 30, 1918, subsequently promoted A/Capt. 15th Batt. Hampshire Regt. Served in France May to July 1917 and Oct. 1918 to Feb. 1919.

WILLIAM THOMAS WATKINS BIRTS.

Admitted Nov. 1907, practising at 65 Coleman Street, E.C. 2. Joined March 1916 as 2nd Lieut., 16th Batt. County of London Regt. (Queen's Westminster Rifles), subsequently promoted Lieut. Served in France. Invalided home with trench fever Aug. 1917.

THOMAS HUME BISCHOFF.

Admitted Dec. 1910. Member of Bischoff & Co., of 4 Great Winchester Street, London, E.C. Joined Oct. 1915 as 2nd Lieut., Royal Field Artillery. Promoted Lieut. April 1917, Adjutant 187th Brigade R.F.A. Jan. 1917, Staff Capt. (41st Divisional Artillery) T/Capt. April 1917. Once mentioned in Dispatches. Awarded the M.C. Served in France and Belgium May 1916 to Nov. 1917, and March 1918 to Dec. 1918, Italy Nov. 1917 to March 1918.

BERTRAM LEWIS BISGOOD.

Admitted Aug. 1905. Member of Hatchett Jones, Bisgood, Marshall & Thomas, of 48 Mark Lane, E.C. Served as 2nd Lieut., "C" Anti-Aircraft Battery, Royal Garrison Artillery.

GEORGE RENDEL BISHOP.

Admitted Nov. 1917. Assistant Solicitor Hammersmith Borough Council. Joined June 1912 as 2nd Lieut., Northamptonshire Regt., subsequently promoted to Lieut.

GERALD BISHOP.

Articled to A. E. Phipps, of Northampton. Joined Nov. 2, 1914, as Private, Inns of Court O.T.C. Gazetted 2nd Lieut. 4th Res. Batt. Northamptonshire Regt. Feb. 4, 1915. Promoted Lieut. Nov. 1915, Capt. July 1917. Served in France Dec. 1916 to March 1917, and Nov. 1918 to Feb. 1919. Severely wounded March 4, 1917.

GERALD CLEMENT WILLIAM BISHOP.

Articled to his father, F. W. Bishop, of Bridgwater. Joined the Public School Corps of *The Hawke* Batt. Royal Naval Volunteer Reserve in Jan. 1915. Went to Gallipoli in April 1915 where he was wounded, remained there until the evacuation. Subsequently returned home to train for commission. Posted 2nd Lieut. to 6th Batt. Middlesex Regt. Went to France July 1917. Killed in action Aug. 12, 1917.

JOHN WALTON BISHOP.

Admitted March 1902, practising at Llanelly and Ammanford. Mobilised Aug. 1914 as 2nd Lieut., Pembroke Yeomanry, appointed Capt. Nov. 1914, Major Nov. 1916. Awarded the T.D. Served at Home 1914 to 1915, Egypt and Palestine 1916 to 1917, Home 1918 to 1919.

JOSEPH GEORGE BISHOP.

Admitted April 1892, practising at Abergavenny. Served as Major, 3rd Batt. Monmouthshire Regt. (T.) and promoted to Lieut.-Col. Attached to Staff. Awarded the O.B.E.

JOSEPH RICHARD BISHOP.

Admitted Nov. 1908. Assistant Solicitor Great Western Railway Co. Served as Staff Lieut., Royal Engineers (Signal Service).

WILLIAM HENRY BLABER.

Admitted Dec. 1893. Member of Robinson & Blaber, of 23 Philpot Lane, E.C. Served as Lieut., 1st Home Counties Brigade, Royal Field Artillery (T.)

ALEXANDER MACGREGOR BLACK.

Admitted Nov. 1902. Member of Foyer, White, Borrett & Black, of 26 Essex Street, Strand, W.C. Joined Nov. 1914 as Lieut., 14th Batt. Northumberland Fusiliers, promoted Capt. 1915, Major 1917. Twice mentioned in Dispatches. Awarded the D.S.O. Served at Home 1914 to 1915 and in France 1915 to 1919.

LEONARD ARTHUR BLACKBURN.

Articled to W. M. Jenner, of 15 Walbrook, E.C. 4. Joined Aug. 4, 1914, as 2nd Lieut., 6th Batt. Royal Sussex Regt., promoted Lieut. Oct. 1914, Captain March 1915. Transferred to Household Batt. June 1917. Served in France. Wounded in front of Peronne on March 21, 1918, during the retreat.

ALPHONSUS BLACKMORE.

Admitted Aug. 1909, practising at Doncaster. Joined July 1915 as 2nd Lieut., Army Service Corps, promoted Lieut. Dec. 1915, Capt. March 1916. Served at Home.

BASIL BERNARD BLACKWELL.

Admitted May 1909. Member of W. B. Blackwell & Co., of 1 Mitre Court Chambers, Temple, E.C. Joined May 1915 as Private, Inns of Court O.T.C.

Gazetted 2nd Lieut. 8th Batt. Royal West Kent Regt. (The Buffs). Served in France. Killed in action on Sept. 3, 1916, at Selville Wood.

CHARLES BLACKWELL.
Admitted Oct. 1914. Of 3 Gray's Inn Square, W.C. 1. Joined Aug. 1914 as Private, Hon. Artillery Company. Subsequently gazetted 2nd Lieut. Royal Fusiliers. Served in France and Flanders. Killed in action July 20, 1915.

HENRY DAWSON BLADES.
Admitted Sept. 1890, practising at Sedbergh, Yorkshire. Enlisted Oct. 1914 as Private, The King's Own Royal Lancaster Regt. Served in France Feb. 1915 to April 1915, and Feb. 1917 to May 1918. Wounded April 24, 1915, at 2nd Battle of Ypres.

GEORGE CHAMBERS BLAGDEN.
Admitted Jan. 1908. Managing Clerk with Coward, Hawksley, Sons & Chance, of 30 Mincing Lane, London, E.C. Joined June 6 1918, as Private, Inns of Court O.T.C., and subsequently served as Cadet, 22nd (Garrison) Officers Cadet Batt.

CLAUDE EDMUND LANGLEY BLAGG.
Articled to A. J. C. Mackarness, of Petersfield, Hants. Joined Nov. 6, 1914, as Petty Officer, Royal Navy (despatch rider motor cyclist). Appointed Leading Mechanic Royal Naval Air Service (Wireless Operator in Airships) Sept. 1915. Served in Home Naval Air Stations Nov. 1914 to April 1917, and in Southern Adriatic ashore and afloat April 1917 to Jan. 1919.

FRANCIS OSMOND BLAGG.
Articled to F. E. Blagg, of Portsmouth. Mobilised Aug. 1914 as Lieut., 6th Batt. Hampshire Regt. Promoted Temp. Capt. Nov. 1914, Capt. (substantive) Feb. 1915, A/Major Dec. 1918, A/Lieut.-Col. Jan. 1919 to April 1919, when reverted to permanent substantive rank of Capt. Served at Home Aug. 1914 to Oct. 1914, India Oct. 1914 to Sept. 1917, Mesopotamia Sept. 1917 to Dec. 1917, India Dec. 1917 to June 1919.

HAROLD EPHRAIM BLAIBERG.
Admitted June 1905, practising at 18 Ironmonger Lane, E.C. Joined Sept. 18, 1914, as 2nd Lieut., 3rd Reserve Cavalry Regt., transferred to Royal Warwickshire Regt. Special Reserve as Lieut. July 1917. Served in France. Wounded April 14, 1917 and June 1918.

JOHN BLAIR.
Admitted June 1900. Member of Faithfull, Owen, Blair & Wright, of Dacre House, Victoria Street, S.W. 1. Enlisted Sept. 5, 1914, as Trooper, Lothians and Border Horse, granted commission in Royal Scots Dec. 23, 1914. Subsequently promoted Temp. Capt.

FRANK BLAIR-ALLEN.
Admitted Oct. 1911. Member of Nicholson & Blair-Allen, of Sunderland. Joined Sept. 1914 as Private, 7th Batt. Durham Light Infantry and afterwards promoted Lance-Corporal. Served in France and Belgium. Killed in action May 23, 1915, in 2nd Battle of Ypres.

DENIS HENRY BLAKE.

Admitted May 1912. Of Great Yarmouth. Enlisted Sept. 3, 1914, as Private, 6th Batt. Northamptonshire Regt. Commission in 6th Batt. Bedfordshire Regt. Sept. 1914, promoted Capt. April 1915. Once mentioned in Dispatches. Served at Home, France, War Office (Intelligence Department) Sept. 1917, British and Canadian Recruiting Mission in U.S.A. 1918. Wounded Oct. 1915 at Hannescamp, June 1916 at La Douelles, Nov. 1916 at Thiepval, April 1917 at Battle of Arras.

EDWARD WILLIAM RICHMOND BLAKE.

Articled to E. J. Blake, of Crewkerne, Somerset. Joined Aug. 1916, as Private, Somerset Light Infantry. Gazetted 2nd Lieut. 4th Batt. Somerset Light Infantry March 9, 1917. Went to France on May 6, 1917, and attached to the 8th Batt. Somerset Light Infantry. Killed in action at the Battle of Wytescheat July 31, 1917.

GEORGE VICTOR BLAKE.

Admitted Feb. 1910. Managing Clerk with Longueville & Co., of Oswestry. Joined Nov. 1916, as Private, Inns of Court O.T.C., and subsequently promoted Corporal. Gazetted 2nd Lieut. 1st Batt. King's Shropshire Light Infantry Jan. 22 1917. Served in France from Feb. 1917, until killed in action at Marcoing, in the battle of Cambrai, Dec. 2, 1917.

JOHN HUMPHREY BLAKE.

Admitted June 1914. Clerk with Sparks & Blake, of Crewkerne, Somerset. Mobilised Aug. 1914, as 2nd Lieut., 5th Batt. Somerset Light Infantry (T.), promoted 1st Lieut. Aug. 1914, Capt. June 1916. Station Staff Officer at Kasauli (India) April 1915 to April 1916. Assistant Staff Capt. 233rd Inf. Bde. E.E.F. Feb. 1918 to Sept. 1918. A.D.C. to G.O.C. 75th Division E.E.F. Sept. 1918 to May 1919. Served at Home till Oct. 1914, India Oct. 1914 to April 1917, Egypt and Palestine May 1917 to May 1919.

LEONARD NICHOLSON BLAKE.

Admitted Jan. 1903. Member of Blake, Reid & Lapthorn, of Portsmouth. Served as Capt. and Quartermaster, 5th Southern General Hospital, Royal Army Medical Corps (T.).

PHILIP JESSOP BLAKE.

Admitted Dec. 1905. Member of Wake & Sons, of Sheffield. Served as Gunner, Royal Garrison Artillery.

DOUGLAS BLANCHARD.

Admitted May 1911. Managing Clerk with J. H. Hutchings, of Teignmouth, S. Devon. Enlisted Nov. 27, 1914, as Private, 18th Batt. Royal Fusiliers. Gazetted 2nd Lieut. 3rd Dorset Regt. (Special Reserve) May 1915. Attached 3rd Middlesex Regt. Oct. 1915. Appointed Salvage Officer 28th Division Dec. 1916, promoted Lieut. July 1917. Attached 819 Employment Coy. Labour Corps Aug. 1918. Attached 3rd Echelon G.H.Q., B.S.F., Nov. 1918. Appointed Staff Lieut., 1st Class, Jan. 1919. Served at Home Nov. 1914 to Sept. 1915, France Oct. 1 to 25, 1915, Egypt Oct. 1915 to Jan. 1916, Salonica Force Jan. 1916 to June 1919.

VICTOR BLANCHARD.

Articled to W. E. Hart, of Sheffield. Joined March 1918, as Cadet, No. 14 Officers' Cadet Batt. Gazetted 2nd Lieut. 3rd York and Lancaster Regt. Sept. 1918, attached 2/6 Durham Light Infantry March 1919. Served at Home and in France.

WILLIAM EDWARD MOERAN BLANDY.

Admitted June 1913. Member of Blandy & Blandy, of Reading. Mobilised Aug. 1914, as Capt., 4th Batt. Royal Berkshire Regt. (T.F.). Served in France 1915 to 1916. Wounded Aug. 14, 1916, at Ovillers (Somme). Invalided out March 4, 1917.

WILLIAM DESMOND BLATCH.

Admitted Nov. 1913, practised at Southampton. Served as a Trooper, Hampshire Yeomanry (Carabiniers). Subsequently gazetted 2nd Lieut. Derbyshire Dragoons, promoted Lieut.

STEWART LENTON BLAXLEY.

Admitted Jan. 1912. Clerk with Alfred Truman, of Bicester, Oxon. Joined Nov. 22, 1915, as Private, Inns of Court, O.T.C. Gazetted 2nd Lieut. 2nd Batt. Royal Welsh Fusiliers Nov. 23, 1916. Served in France. Killed in action at Héninel, near Arras, April 23, 1917.

HENRY BLECKLY.

Articled to E. L. Sandbach, of Manchester. Served as 2nd Lieut., Cheshire Yeomanry, promoted Lieut.

SIDNEY THOMAS BLEWETT.

Articled to R. A. Jones, of Swansea, Glam. Joined June 1917, as Convoy Signalman, Royal Naval Volunteer Reserve. Served in the Mediterranean and at Ports between Gibraltar and Port Said.

ARTHUR JOSEPH BLISS.

Admitted Oct. 1911. Member of Bliss & Sons, of High Wycombe. Joined Aug. 6, 1914, as Private, Royal Army Medical Corps. Subsequently gazetted 2nd Lieut. (4th Prince of Wales) The Leinster Regt. Served in France. Killed in action at Ginchy Sept. 9, 1916.

HENRY NORMAN BLISS.

Admitted April 1905. Member of Edell & Co., of 4/6 King Street, Cheapside, E.C. Joined Inns of Court O.T.C. Sept. 11, 1915, and attained the rank of Sergeant. Gazetted 2nd Lieut. 56th Divisional Field Artillery, A/280 Brigade, 1918. Served at Home and in France.

WILLIAM THOMAS BARNARD BLOCK.

Admitted July 1902. Member of Block & Cullingham, of Ipswich. Served as Lieut. Royal Garrison Artillery.

FREDERICK HYMAN BLOOM.

Admitted March 1915, practising at Middlesbrough. Served as Lance-Corporal Royal Engineers.

HENRY BLOOM.

Admitted May 1912. Practised at Middlesbrough. Joined the Durham University O.T.C. on the outbreak of war and gazetted 2nd. Lieut. 12th (S.)

Batt. Yorkshire Regt. (Teeside Pioneers). Killed in action in France Feb. 14, 1917, whilst serving as a machine-gun officer.

ALFRED HERBERT BLUNDELL.

Admitted Dec. 1891. Member of Blundell, Baker & Co., of 16 Serjeant's Inn, E.C. Served as 2nd Lieut., 28th Batt. County of London Regt. (Artists Rifles), and subsequently promoted Capt.

CHARLES WINNALL BLUNDELL.

Admitted Oct. 1892. Managing Clerk with Sole, Turner & Knight, of 69 Aldermanbury, E.C. Mobilised Aug. 1914, as Col.-Sergeant, 16th Batt. County of London Regt. (Queen's Westminster Rifles), promoted Company Sergeant-Major Nov. 1914. Served at Home.

JOHN WARDEN BLUNT.

Admitted Oct. 1905, practised at Leicester. Served as Capt., Leicestershire Royal Horse Artillery.

CHARLES FREDERICK TOLMÉ BLYTH.

Admitted May 1892. Member of Blyth, Dutton, Hartley & Blyth, of 112 Gresham House, Old Broad Street, E.C. Served as Lieut.-Col., Royal Army Service Corps (T.) Once mentioned in Dispatches. Awarded the C.M.G.

MAURICE McAUSLANE BLYTH.

Admitted Nov. 1901, practising at 6 New Court, Lincoln's Inn, W.C. 2. Enlisted Sept. 1914, as Private, 19th (Public School) Batt. Royal Fusiliers. Discharged Dec. 1914 owing to serious illness.

THOMAS TOLMÉ BLYTH.

Admitted Dec. 1906. Member of Blyth, Dutton, Hartley & Blyth, of 112 Gresham House, Old Broad Street, E.C. Served as Lieut., Royal Army Service Corps (T.), and subsequently promoted Capt.

ARTHUR ALLISTER BLYTON.

Articled to E. Van Houtte Blyton, of Spalding. Joined Aug. 27, 1914, as Private, 4th Batt. Lincolnshire Regt. (T.). Gazetted 2nd Lieut. 4th North Midland (Howitzer) Brigade (T.) Nov. 25, 1914, transferred to "C" Battery, 34th (Army) Brigade Royal Field Artillery July 1917, to "B," "A," "C," 277th (Army) Brigade, Dec. 1917, and to "A" Battery, 70th Brigade, 15th Division, in June 1918. Served in France and Belgium from Nov. 11, 1915, until killed in action at Pont-à-Trois, Gueules, France, on Sept. 5, 1918. Buried in English Cemetery at Vis-en-Artois, France.

HENRY AUBREY BLYTON.

Admitted June 1913. Managing Clerk with E. Van Houtte Blyton, of Spalding. Joined March 29, 1916, as Private, Royal Army Service Corps, promoted to Sergeant April 1916, Staff Sergeant-Major July 1916. Gazetted 2nd Lieut. Royal Army Service Corps Aug. 31, 1917, promoted Lieut. March 1919. Served at Home.

HAROLD ARTHUR PALMER BOCKETT.

Articled to Arthur Bockett, of Amberley House, Norfolk Street, Strand, W.C. Joined Nov. 24, 1915, as Private, Hon. Artillery Company. Gazetted

2nd Lieut. 2nd Batt. Hon. Artillery Company Dec. 16, 1916. Served in France. Killed in action May 4, 1917.

MYLES BODDINGTON.

Articled to Alfred Whitworth, of Manchester. Enlisted Sept. 1914, as Private, 5th Batt. King's Shropshire Light Infantry. Subsequently gazetted 2nd Lieut. 6th Batt. of same Regt. and attained the rank of Capt. Awarded the M.C. Served in Belgium and France July 1915 to July 1916. Killed in action near Ypres July 1, 1916.

RALPH THOMAS BODDINGTON.

Admitted March 1909. Member of Hooper, Ryland & Boddington, of Birmingham. Joined March 1916, as 2nd Lieut., 10th Batt. London Regt., subsequently promoted Lieut. Killed at Beersheba, Palestine, Nov. 2, 1917.

HAROLD OWEN BODVEL-ROBERTS.

Admitted Aug. 1908. Of Carnarvon. Joined Aug. 1914, as 2nd Lieut., City of London Batt., London Regt. Once mentioned in Dispatches. Awarded the M.C. Served in France. Wounded at Loos Sept. 25, 1915 (where he earned the M.C.) and died from the wounds then received at Le Tréport, France, on Nov. 18, 1915.

GEORGE FRANKLAND BOLAM.

Admitted April 1909, practising at Gateshead. Served as Lieut. 9th Batt. Durham Light Infantry.

ARTHUR BOLDEN.

Admitted Aug. 1906. Member of Strong & Bolden, of 70 Gracechurch Street, E.C. Joined Sept. 1914, as Able Seaman, Royal Naval Volunteer Reserve (Anti-Aircraft Corps). Commissioned Sub-Lieut. Royal Naval Volunteer Reserve (Auxiliary Patrol) 1916, and promoted Lieut. 1917. In command of Minelayers 311 and (later) 313.

CHARLES BENSLY BOLINGBROKE.

Articled to E. M. Calvert, of Norwich. Served as Lieut., 6th (Cyclist) Batt. Norfolk Regt., and attained the rank of Capt.

ARTHUR EDWARD BOLTER.

Articled to P. H. Freeman, of 3 South Square, Gray's Inn, W.C. Served as Private, 28th Batt. County of London Regt. (Artists Rifles). Subsequently obtained commission in Machine Gun Corps and promoted Lieut.

CHARLES ALBERT BOLTER.

Admitted May 1911. On the Solicitor's Staff of Great Western Railway Co. Enlisted Sept. 3, 1914, as Private, 28th Batt. County of London Regt. (Artists Rifles), was drafted to France in Jan. 1915, in Aug. 1915 was appointed a Sergeant-Instructor in Machine Gun School in France, on April 26, 1917, was gazetted 2nd Lieut. Machine Gun Corps. Killed in action near Bailleul, France, on April 12, 1918.

EDWARD TREVOR BOLTON.

Admitted Feb. 1909. Member of Bolton Bros., of 43 Great Tower Street, E.C. Enlisted Oct. 1914 as Private, in 23rd (Sportsman's) Batt. Royal

Fusiliers. Gazetted 2nd Lieut. 11th Batt. Suffolk Regt. Sept. 16, 1916, and promoted Lieut. March 1918. Once mentioned in Dispatches. Served in France from Nov. 1915 to date of his death. Wounded in battle of Arras April 9, 1917. Killed in action on April 10, 1918.

FREDERICK WILLIAM GEORGE BOLTON.

Admitted Nov. 1899. Member of Bolton & Tabor, of Letchworth, Herts. Enlisted Nov. 22, 1914, as Private, 28th Batt. County of London Regt. (Artists Rifles). Gazetted Temp. 2nd Lieut. April 1915, promoted Temp. Lieut. July 1915, Temp. Capt. March 1918 Army Printing and Stationery Services. Once mentioned in Dispatches. Served in France and Italy May 1915 to March 1919.

WILLIAM SPROULE BOLTON.

Admitted June 1911. Member of E. Trevor Bolton & Co., of Great Tower Street, E.C. Enlisted as a Private in 23rd Royal Fusiliers (Sportsman's Batt.) and went to France Nov. 1915. Wounded at the battle of Beaumont Hamel in Nov. 1916, promoted Sergeant 1917. Died Feb. 7, 1919, of pneumonia just after being demobilised.

ALFRED DALTON BOND.

Admitted May 1907. Member of Newman & Bond, of Barnsley. Joined Oct. 1914, as 2nd Lieut., 5th Batt. York and Lancaster Regt. (T.F.). Served at Home. Died of pneumonia at Scarborough May 22, 1916.

EDWIN RAYMOND BOND.

Admitted Oct. 1913. Of Cardiff. Served as Major, Royal Air Force.

HUBERT SAMUEL EMERY BOND.

Articled to S. O. Jenkins, of Cardiff. Joined May 1915 on probation. Obtained commission in the 7th Welsh Cyclists as Sub-Lieut. on Aug. 19, 1915, transferred into Royal Air Force Oct. 1916. Fell at Hounslow through machine going to pieces June 14. Died at Bryanston Square Hospital on June 17, 1917.

ERNEST EDGAR BONE.

Admitted May 1911. Member of Ernest E. Bone & Son, of Llandudno and Colwyn Bay. Served as Private, The Rand Rifles, Transvaal.

GEOFFREY FOSTER BONE.

Articled to F. J. Bone, of Devonport. Mobilised Aug. 1914, as 2nd Lieut., Devon Royal Engineers, promoted Lieut. Jan. 1915, Capt. June 1916, joined Royal Flying Corps Sept. 1915, joined Machine Gun Corps Sept. 1917. Served at Gibraltar April to Sept. 1915, France Feb. to April 1916, Mesopotamia Nov. 1917 to March 1919.

JOHN BONE.

Admitted Nov. 1905. Member of Allan B. Bone & Son, of Devonport. Mobilised Aug. 1914 as 2nd Lieut., Royal Engineers (T.F.), promoted Lieut. June 1916, A/Capt. and Adjutant to C.R.E. 17th Division, July 1918. Served at Home Aug. 1914 to March 1915, Gibraltar March 1915 to Nov. 1916; Home Nov. 1916 to March 1917, France March 1917 to Jan. 1919.

CLAUDE HERBERT DICK BONNETT.

Admitted Feb. 1912; practised at Hounslow. Served as 2nd Lieut., 10th Batt. Royal Fusiliers. Awarded the O.B.E.

JAMES PATTERSON BONNEY.

Admitted Oct. 1909. Member of Wilding, Son & Bonney, of Blackburn, and Wilding, Bonney & Pegge, of Manchester. Joined Nov. 1915, as Private, Inns of Court O.T.C. Gazetted Lieut. 351st Siege Battery Royal Garrison Artillery. Served in France. Killed in action Oct. 6, 1917.

TREVOR IEUAN BONNOR-MAURICE.

Admitted Dec. 1911. Member of Bircham & Co., of 46 Parliament Street, Westminster. Mobilised Aug. 1914, as Lieut., 1/1 Montgomeryshire Yeomanry, subsequently changed into 1/1 Lincolnshire Yeomanry, promoted Capt. in 1915. Served in the Palestine Campaign from March 1916 to July 1919.

CYRIL ARTHUR BONSER.

Admitted Oct. 1913. Member of Hopkin & Bonser, of Sutton-in-Ashfield, and Mansfield, Notts. Enlisted Oct. 11, 1916, as Gunner, Royal Garrison Artillery and attained the rank of Regimental Sergeant-Major. Served at Gibraltar, Egypt, France, Belgium, and Germany.

EDWIN KENNETH BONSEY.

Articled to G. O. Jones, of Liverpool. Joined Dec. 1915, as Private, Inns of Court O.T.C. Gazetted 2nd Lieut. 99th Siege Battery Royal Garrison Artillery Feb. 1917. Gassed on June 25, 1918, and died in hospital on July 2, 1918.

CHARLES WILLIAM BOOTE.

Articled to J. W. Cocks, of Liverpool. Joined Aug. 8, 1914, as 2nd Lieut., 8th Batt. Cheshire Regt., promoted Lieut. Jan. 1915, Capt. Sept. 1915. Served at Gallipoli and Mesopotamia. Killed in action April 4–5, 1916.

CHARLES VICTOR BOOTH.

Admitted Dec. 1910. Managing Clerk with F. A. C. Redden, of 17 Victoria Street, S.W. Serving in the Inns of Court O.T.C. at outbreak of war. Gazetted 2nd Lieut. 8th Batt. Suffolk Regt. Sept. 17, 1914, promoted Lieut. Dec. 1914, Capt. April 1915, transferred Labour Corps Oct. 1917, and to the Royal Air Force, Sept. 1918. Served at Home Aug. 1914 to July 1915, in France July 1915 to Feb. 1916, Home Feb. 1916 to March 1919.

GERALD ASTLEY BOOTH.

Articled to R. H. Langley, of 4 Bedford Row, W.C. Enlisted in Hon. Artillery Company (Infantry) as a Private on Sept. 5, 1914, and attained the rank of Sergeant. Gazetted 2nd Lieut. Hon. Artillery Company Dec. 1916 and promoted Lieut. June 1918. Served in France Feb. 1915 to April 1917, remainder of time at Home. Wounded April 23, 1917, at Gavrelle, France.

HAROLD GORDON BOOTH.

Admitted Jan. 1911. Of Leeds. Enlisted Sept. 6, 1916, as Private, Royal Army Service Corps (M.T.). Commissioned 2nd Lieut. in same Regt. May 13, 1918. Served at Salonica.

HERBERT BOOTH.

Admitted April 1910. Managing Clerk with Robert Innes, of Manchester. Joined Nov. 1915, as Sapper, Royal Engineers, promoted Corporal March 1916, Sergeant Oct. 1916, Engineer Clerk with 15th Divisional R.E. Headquarters, B.E.F., from March 1916 to March 1919. Mentioned in the " Peace " Dispatch. Served in France and Belgium.

HOLLAND BOOTH.

Articled to H. Lang-Coath, of Swansea. Enlisted Aug. 7, 1914, as Private, 7th Batt. Welch Regt. (T.F.), transferred to 4th Batt. Oxford and Bucks Light Infantry (T.F.) May 1916. Commissioned in France, and gazetted to 12th Batt. York and Lancaster Regt. Feb. 21, 1917. Served in England and East Coast until May, 1916, and in France May 1916 to Aug. 1917. Wounded at Fresnoy, near Arras, Aug. 11, 1917.

ARTHUR CARY HAMPTON BORRER.

Admitted April 1905. Managing Clerk with Boodle, Hatfield & Co., of 53 Davies Street, W. Enlisted Jan. 1917, as Private, 28th Batt. County of London Regt. (Artists Rifles). Gazetted 2nd Lieut. Royal Army Ordnance Corps Sept. 1917, promoted Lieut. Dec. 1918. Served at Home and in Macedonia.

GEORGE KENYON FORSTER BORRETT.

Articled to F. C. H. Borrett, of Rochester. Joined Sept. 22, 1914, as 2nd Lieut., 1st Royal Guernsey Militia, promoted Lieut. 1st Royal Guernsey Light Infantry Dec. 16, 1916. Served at Home and in France and Belgium. Taken prisoner Dec. 1, 1917, at Battle of Cambrai.

ERNEST BORRIE.

Admitted March 1910. Member of Albert Borrie & Sons, of Middlesbrough. Served as Lance-Corporal, 4th (Reserve) Batt. King's Own Royal Lancaster Regt.

ROBERT GEOFFREY BORWICK.

Articled to the Hon. Sir Charles Russell, Bart., of 37 Norfolk Street, W.C. Served as Lieut., 1st Batt. Herefordshire Regt.

ERIC LEVER BOSTOCK.

Admitted Nov. 1910, practising at Liverpool. Served as Private, 1st (City) Batt. King's Liverpool Regt. Subsequently gazetted 2nd Lieut. " H " Batt. Tank Corps.

JAMES BAXENDALL BOSWELL.

Articled to J. R. Ford, of Leeds. Mobilised as Capt. and Quartermaster, 2nd West Riding Field Ambulance, Royal Army Medical Corps (T.F.). Promoted Major. Died March 23, 1916, at Beckett's Park Hospital, Leeds.

JOHN DUMVILLE BOTTERELL.

Admitted June 1910. Member of Botterell & Roche, of 24 St. Mary Axe, E.C. Served as Capt., West Kent Yeomanry.

PERCY DUMVILLE BOTTERELL.

Admitted Dec. 1906. Member of Botterell & Roche, of 24 St. Mary Axe, E.C. Served with the Royal Naval Volunteer Reserve. Subsequently Assistant Commercial Attaché at The Hague. Appointed a C.B.E.

GEORGE RHODES BOTTOMLEY.

Articled to Maurice Gaunt, of Bradford. Mobilised Aug. 5, 1914, as Gunner, 4th (West Riding) Howitzer Brigade, Royal Field Artillery (T.F.). Gazetted 2nd Lieut. West Riding Royal Field Artillery, March 25, 1915, promoted to Lieut. 62nd Division, B.E.F., June 1916, A/Capt. Feb. 1918. Served at Home 2 years, in France 2 years, and in Germany 4 months.

ARTHUR ERNEST ESSINGTON BOULTON.

Admitted Nov. 1902. Member of Gales, Boulton & Son, of Sunderland. Joined Oct. 5, 1914, as Lieut., Royal Field Artillery (T.F.), promoted Capt. Oct. 1915. Served in France and Flanders.

ARTHUR WARDLE BOULTON.

Admitted April 1912. Managing Clerk with R. T. Adderly, of Longton, Stoke-on-Trent. Joined Nov. 28, 1914, as 2nd Lieut., 10th (Service) Batt. North Staffordshire Regt., sailed for Dardanelles May 1915, landed Cape Helles, June 6, attached to 5th East Lancs. Regiment (T.F.), in Oct. was Brigade Bombing Officer, left (wounded) on Oct. 29, at Malta in Hospital until Dec. 23, sent to England, three months' Sick Leave, Recruiting Officer April to Aug. 1916 with 3rd Training Reserve Batt. (Lieut. while so employed) until April 1917, then went to France and attached to 5th North Staffordshire Regt. (T.F.), left France (wounded) July 25, 1917, in Hospital until May 30, 1918, promoted Lieut. June 2, 1917.

HUGH DELABERE BOUSFIELD.

Admitted Oct. 1904. Member of Dibb & Co., of Leeds. Embodied with 7th West Yorkshire Regt., Aug. 3, 1914, with rank of Major, commanded 1/5 Batt. West Yorkshire Regt. with rank of Lieut.-Col. from July 1916 to Oct. 1917. Twice mentioned in Dispatches. Awarded the D.S.O., C.M.G., T.D., French Croix de Guerre, Belgian Croix de Guerre. Served in France April 1915 to April 1919. Wounded at Passchendaele. Taken prisoner at Kemmel Hill when Liaison Officer with the French Army.

ERNEST STANLEY BOUSTRED.

Admitted Dec. 1913. Member of H. Boustred & Son, of 74 Coleman Street, E.C. Enlisted Aug. 28, 1914, as Private, 13th Batt. London Regt. (Kensingtons), transferred Nov. 1915 to Royal Field Artillery as Signaller. Served in Mesopotamia.

FREDERICK EDGAR BOWDEN.

Admitted May 1904. Member of Foot & Bowden, of Plymouth. Joined Sept. 4, 1914, as Lance-Corporal, 30th Coy. Royal Engineers, promoted Corporal Sept. 1914, Sergeant Feb. 1915. Gazetted 2nd Lieut. Devonshire Royal Engineers March 4, 1915, promoted Lieut. Aug. 1915, A/Capt. Sept. 1917. Once mentioned in Dispatches. Served at Home 1914 to 1916, and in Egypt, Palestine, and Syria 1917 to 1919.

HUBERT MOXHAY BOWDEN.

Admitted July 1909, practising at 221B Hammersmith Road, London, W. Enlisted Aug. 30, 1916, as Private, London Regt., and subsequently served in Middlesex Regt. and 686th Home Service Employment Company, Labour Corps.

ALFRED JOHN HAMILTON BOWEN.

Admitted July 1909. Member of Bowen & Son, of Pontypool. Mobilised Aug. 1914, as Captain, 2nd Batt. Monmouthshire Regt. (T.), and was promoted to Lieut.-Col. in command of Regt. Aug. 1915. Three times mentioned in Dispatches. Awarded the D.S.O. and Bar. Served in France. Killed in action at Sailisel March 2, 1917.

HUGH STORER BOWEN.

Admitted June 1909, practising at Canterbury. Joined Oct. 1914, as Capt., 12th Batt. Essex Regt, promoted Major Aug. 1917. Served at Gallipoli Sept. 1915 to Jan. 1916, Egypt Jan. to March 1916, and France April 1916 to Aug. 1918.

LESLIE HAROLD BOWEN.

Admitted Oct. 1913, practised at 12 New Court, Carey Street, W.C. Served as 2nd Lieut., 3rd (attached 1st) Batt. Lincolnshire Regt. Killed in France on Dec. 22, 1915, whilst on patrol duty.

WILLIAM THOMAS BOWEN-HAMER.

Articled to E. P. Careless, of Llandrindod Wells. Joined Feb. 8, 1915, as Driver, 2nd "B" Battery, Hon. Artillery Company, subsequently posted Gunner, promoted Lance-Bombardier 1916 and Bombardier 1917. Served at Home, and for last two years of war in France, Belgium, and Germany. Wounded Aug. 1918.

BASIL CEDRIC BOWER.

Admitted April 1914. Of Swinton. Served as Motor Ambulance Driver, British Red Cross Society.

GEOFFREY ARTHUR HOLME BOWER.

Admitted Nov. 1912. Managing Clerk with Bower, Cotton & Bower, 4 Bream's Buildings, Chancery Lane, E.C. Mobilised Aug. 1914, as Capt., 7th Batt. Middlesex Regt. (T.F.), promoted Major June 1916. Three times mentioned in Dispatches. Awarded the M.C. Served at Home Aug. 1914, Gibraltar Sept. 1914 to Feb. 1915, Home Feb. 1915 to March 1915, France March 1915 to July 1919, except Oct and Nov. 1917, when at Staff Course, Cambridge.

JOHN ALBERT BOWER.

Articled to J. C. Waddington, of Burnley. Joined Dec. 1914, as Gunner, Royal Field Artillery, promoted Corporal Feb. 1915. Gazetted 2nd Lieut. Royal Horse and Royal Field Artillery April 5, 1915, promoted Lieut. July 1917, appointed Signalling Instructor 1st Army Signal School 1918. Served at Home and in France. Injured at duty, Somme, August 1916.

SIDNEY WATKIN BOWES.

Articled to Arthur H. Neve, of Tonbridge. Enlisted Dec. 11, 1915, as Private, 3rd Batt. East Surrey Regt., transferred July 1916 to 4th Batt.

Northumberland Fusiliers. Gazetted 2nd Lieut. Lincolnshire Regt. April 1917, transferred to the King's Own Yorkshire Light Infantry 1918, promoted Lieut. Nov. 1918. Served with British Salonica Force.

GEORGE HUTTON BOWES-WILSON.

Admitted April 1902, practised at Middlesbrough. Mobilised as Capt., 4th Batt. Yorkshire Regt. (T.). Served at Home and in France and Belgium 1914 and 1915. Killed in action near Ypres June 17, 1915.

EUSTACE GILBERT BOWHAY.

Admitted July 1912, practised at Great Torrington, North Devon. Mobilised Aug. 1914, as Lieut., 6th Batt. Devonshire Regt., promoted Capt. Oct. 1914. Served in India 1914 and 1915, and in Mesopotamia 1916. Killed in action in Battle of Es Sinn, Mesopotamia, March 8, 1916.

HUMPHREY CHARLES BRADSHAW BOWLES.

Admitted April 1909, practising at Worthing. Mobilised Aug. 1914, as 2nd Lieut., 1st Home Counties Brigade Royal Field Artillery (T.F.), promoted Lieut. Nov. 1914, Captain March 1918. Served in India Oct. 1914 to Dec. 1915, Mesopotamia (Kut Relief Force) Dec. 1915 to June 1916, France 1917.

EDWYN RANDOLPH BOWLING.

Articled to J. W. C. Frere, of 28 Lincolns Inn Fields, W.C. Enlisted 1914, as Private, Sportsman's Batt. Royal Fusiliers. Gazetted 2nd Lieut. 9th Batt. Royal West Kent Regt. Killed in action June 4, 1916.

GILBERT BOWLING.

Articled to William Mossop, of Burnley. Enlisted Dec. 21, 1915, as Private, Denbighshire Yeomanry, promoted Lance-Corporal May 1917, Depôt Hussar Regts., Yorks, Corporal Oct. 1917. Served in England.

ANTHONY HARVEY BOWMAN.

Articled to A. N. Bowman, of Carlisle. Mobilised Aug. 1914, as Capt., 1st Cumberland Howitzer Battery (T.), transferred to Regular Army as 2nd Lieut. Royal Field Artillery 1915. Served at Gallipoli and in France. Died May 20, 1916, of wounds received in action near Arras, May 19.

JOHN BROUGHTON BOWMAN.

Admitted April 1898, practising at South Shields. Mobilised Aug. 1914, as Major, 7th Batt. Durham Light Infantry, promoted Lieut.-Col. Nov. 1914. Awarded the T.D. Served at Home.

CHARLES MEATHERINGHAM BOWSER.

Admitted Nov. 1907. Member of Mossop & Mossop, of Long Sutton, Lincs. Enlisted Nov. 2, 1916, as Gunner, Royal Garrison Artillery. Gazetted 2nd Lieut. Royal Army Service Corps Feb. 18, 1918. Served at Home to Nov. 1916, at Gibraltar Dec. 1916 to July 1917, Home Aug. 1917 to May 1918, Mesopotamia June 1918 to Feb. 1919.

LEONARD ARTHUR BOX.

Admitted June 1910. Member of W. W. Box & Co., of 28 Great James Street, Bedford Row, W.C. Joined Aug. 23, 1917, as Lieut., Royal Defence Corps.

RICHARD EDWARD BOX.

Admitted July 1907, practising at Oxford. Enlisted Oct. 10, 1914, as Private, 4th Batt. Royal Berkshire Regt., promoted Sergeant 1916, Sergeant-Major 1917 10th Royal Fusiliers (attached Intelligence B). Once mentioned in Dispatches. Awarded Médaille Militaire (Croix de Guerre) (French). Served in France and Belgium (4 years in all).

ALLEYNE PERCIVAL BOXALL.

Admitted April 1908. Member of Boxall & Boxall, of 22 Chancery Lane, W.C. Mobilised Aug. 1914, as Major, 1st Home Counties Brigade, Royal Field Artillery. Served with 307th Brigade Royal Field Artillery, 165th Brigade Royal Field Artillery, and 28th (Army) Brigade Royal Field Artillery, promoted Lieut.-Col. 1917, commanded 330th Brigade Royal Field Artillery Sept. 1918 to April 1919. Twice mentioned in Dispatches and in 5th Army Orders (for bravery). Awarded the T.D. Served in India 1914 to 1915, and in France and Flanders 1916 to 1919. Wounded (gas shell) Sept. 11, 1917, at 3rd Battle of Ypres.

FRANK STUART BOXALL.

Admitted Nov. 1910. Managing Clerk with Sir H. Kingsley Wood & Co., 15 Walbrook, E.C. Enlisted Sept. 8, 1914, as Private, 28th Batt. County of London Regt. (Artists Rifles). Gazetted 2nd Lieut. 19th (Service) Batt. Manchester Regt. Jan. 15, 1915, promoted Lieut. Sept. 1915, Capt. June 1917, Court-Martial Officer Feb. 1918, gazetted to Intelligence Staff May 1919. Once mentioned in Dispatches. Served in France and Belgium 1915 to 1917.

REGINALD JOHN BOYCE.

Admitted Nov. 1897, practised at Norwich. Served as Lieut., Royal Defence Corps.

HAROLD CHARLTON BOYCOTT.

Admitted Oct. 1898, Solicitor to the Northampton Brewery Co. and also practising at Northampton. Joined March 29, 1916, as Private, 28th Batt. County of London Regt. (Artists Rifles). Received commission as 2nd Lieut. Coldstream Guards Aug. 4, 1916. Went to France Jan. 1917, appointed Asst. Adjutant to C.R.E. Guards Division, Nov. 1917, promoted Lieut. Feb. 1918. Killed in action March 21, 1918. Buried at Arras.

ERNEST ALEXANDER BOYER.

Articled to Stephen Miall, of Fore Street, E.C. Joined July 1916, as Private, 28th Batt. County of London Regt. (Artists Rifles). Gazetted 2nd Lieut. 7th Batt. London Regt. Jan. 1917, joined the 11th Batt. in France March 1917, attached to 22nd Batt. Jan. 1918. Served at Home and in France. Officially reported killed in action April 5, 1918, at Aveluy Wood, near Martinsart.

WILLIAM ARCHIBALD BOYES.

Admitted July 1898, practising as Boyes & Son, at Barnet, Herts. Enlisted Aug. 9, 1914, as Private, Royal Army Medical Corps. Discharged Dec. 9, 1914, as "special case" to resume official civilian duties. Served at Home.

ALAN ANDERSON BOYLE.

Articled to William Boyle, of Liverpool. Served as Private, 10th Batt. King's Liverpool Regt. (Liverpool Scottish). Subsequently obtained commission in the Royal Marines, and attained the rank of Capt.

ERNEST PATRICK CHARLES BOYLE.

Admitted Jan. 1888. Rejoined Hon. Artillery Company on outbreak of war and gazetted Capt. in Sept. 1914. Went to France Jan. 1915. Shot through the lungs in June 1916, spent some months in hospital undergoing serious operation, subsequently returned to the front. Wounded in the face Oct. 1916, and appointed A/Lieut.-Col. Awarded the D.S.O. Killed in action Feb. 1917.

PERCY BRABY.

Admitted Oct. 1889. Member of Braby & Waller, of Dacre House, Arundel Street, Strand, W.C. Joined June 21, 1915, as A.B., Royal Naval Air Service Anti-Aircraft (whole time). Gazetted 2nd Lieut. Royal Garrison Artillery March 1916, promoted to Lieut. Sept. 1917. Served at Home.

ARTHUR ARMISTEAD BRACEWELL.

Admitted Dec. 1908. Member of J. & A. A. Bracewell, of Colne, Lancs. Enlisted April 3, 1917, as Gunner, Royal Garrison Artillery and subsequently promoted Corporal. Granted commission May 5, 1918. Served at Home.

GEOFFREY JOHN BRACEY.

Admitted June 1909. Member of Chamberlin, Talbot & Bracey, of Gt. Yarmouth and Lowestoft. Joined Aug. 4, 1914, as Private, 5th Batt. Norfolk Regt. Capt. and Adjutant 2/5 Batt. Norfolk Regt. 1915 and 1916, second in command Sept. 1916, promoted Major 1916, went to France Feb. 1917 and became second in command of 11th Batt. King's Own Royal Lancaster Regt, joined 63rd (Royal Naval) Division July 1918 as second in command of 7th Royal Fusiliers, and afterwards as second in command of 1/28 Batt. County of London Regt. (Artists Rifles), invalided home with trench fever June 1918, returned to France in Oct. 1918, and took over a German Prisoner of War Camp.

GUY BRACHER.

Admitted Oct. 1912. Member of Bracher & Son, of Maidstone. Joined Sept. 3, 1914, as Private, Universities and Public Schools Batt. Gazetted 2nd Lieut. 3rd Batt. East Kent Regt. (The Buffs) May 16, 1915. Served in France. Killed in action outside Albert July 3, 1916.

WILLIAM VICTOR ALLEN BRACHER.

Articled to Septimus Brutton, of Portsmouth. Joined Nov. 1915, as Private, 28th Batt. County of London Regt. (Artists Rifles). Served in France Feb. to May 1916. Died of enteric fever May 9, 1916.

JOHN FOWLER BRADBURY.

Admitted Feb. 1910. Member of Saunders, Bradbury & Breakwell, of Birmingham. Served as Capt. and Adjutant, South Midland Divisional Royal Army Service Corps (T.).

PAUL BRADDON.

Articled to William Sharp, of 11 Arundel Street, Strand. Joined Oct. 16, 1915, as 2nd Lieut., 2/5 Batt. East Surrey Regt., promoted Lieut. July 1917, attached as 2nd Lieut. to 21st Batt. King's Royal Rifles Oct. 1916 to March 1917, attached to War Office as Cypher Officer Dec. 1917 to April 1919. Served in France.

FRANCIS GARFIELD BRADFORD.

Admitted Feb. 1908, practising at Yeovil, Somerset. Joined Dec. 1915, as 2nd Lieut., Royal Field Artillery, promoted Lieut. July 1917. Served at Home and in France.

SIR AUGUSTUS MONTAGUE BRADLEY.

Admitted Nov. 1886, practising at Dover. Joined March 17, 1915, as Lieut.-Col., commanding 296th Brigade Royal Field Artillery, Lieut.-Col. commanding group of 2 Howitzer Brigades July 1916 to Oct. 1916, Lieut.-Col. commanding 65th Divisional Amm. Col. Oct. 1916 to Feb. 1918. Served in the Irish Rebellion, April 1916.

JOSEPH ROWLAND BRADLEY.

Admitted Nov. 1903. Clerk with Baker & Co., of Weston-super-Mare. Enlisted March 3, 1917, as Private, 3rd Batt. Devonshire Regt, transferred to 4th Batt. July 1917. Served in Mesopotamia July 1917 to April 1919.

WILLIAM BERTRAM BRADLEY.

Admitted Nov. 1898, practising at Monmouth. Served as Capt. and Hon. Major, Glamorgan Royal Garrison Artillery (T.).

ALFRED EXELBY BRADSHAW.

Articled to Jos. H. Bate, of Wrexham. Enlisted Dec. 11, 1915, as Pioneer, Royal Engineers (Signals), Sapper Army Signal Coy. Sept. 1917, promoted Corporal Oct. 1917, A/Sergeant June 1919, Chief Signal Officer, G.H.Q. Once mentioned in Dispatches. Served in Mesopotamia 1916 to 1919.

STANLEY GOODWIN BRADSHAW.

Admitted Aug. 1913. Member of C. G. Bradshaw & Waterson, of 16 Finsbury Square, E.C. Serving in the Inns of Court O.T.C. at outbreak of war. Gazetted 2nd Lieut. 8th Batt. East Lancashire Regt. Sept. 19, 1914, promoted Lieut. Dec. 1914, Capt. March 1915. Awarded the M.B.E. (Military Division). Served in France Aug. 1915 to May 1916.

HERBERT BRADWELL.

Admitted Nov. 1901, practising at Nottingham. Served as Capt., 7th Batt. Notts and Derby Regt. (Sherwood Foresters) (T.). Subsequently promoted Major.

JOHN ATKINS BRAIN.

Admitted Dec. 1914. Member of Brain & Brain, of Reading. Enlisted Feb. 15, 1916, as Private, Inns of Court O.T.C. (previously served with the Red Cross in France from Sept. 1915 to Jan. 1916). Gazetted 2nd Lieut. 4th Batt. Royal Berkshire Regt. July 22, 1916, promoted Lieut. Jan. 1918. Served in France Aug. 1916 to March 1918. Wounded at Villers Brettoneaux March 30, 1918.

BRIAN BRAMALL.

Articled to Sidney White, of 23 Leadenhall Street, E.C. Served as 2nd Lieut., 10th Batt. Middlesex Regt. and attained rank of Capt.

CLAUD ARTHUR BRAMALL.

Articled to A. M. Bramall, of 3 Verulam Buildings, Gray's Inn, W.C. Joined Aug. 4, 1914, as Private, 1st Batt. Hon. Artillery Company, promoted Corporal March 1915, Sergeant April 1915. Gazetted 2nd Lieut. General List Nov. 1916, 2nd Class Staff Lieut. Dec. 1916, 1st Class Staff Lieut. May 1918. Served in France Sept. 1914 to Dec. 1914 and Dec. 1916 to March 1919.

RALPH CYRIL LOCKHART BRANDON.

Articled to William Elam, of 80 Cheapside, E.C. Served as Private, 19th (Service) Batt. Royal Fusiliers. Subsequently obtained commission in 5th (Reserve) Batt. Middlesex Regt. and promoted Lieut.

HENRY NORMAN HUGH BRANSOM.

Admitted Oct. 1914, practised at 66 Berners Street, W. Served as Sub-Lieut. Royal Naval Volunteer Reserve (minesweeper).

DOUGLAS STEPHENSON BRANSON.

Articled to G. E. Branson, of Sheffield. Mobilised Aug. 1914, as 2nd Lieut., 4th (Hallamshire) Batt. York and Lancaster Regt., promoted Lieut. Oct. 1914, Capt. July 1916, A/Major Aug. 1916, A/Lieut.-Col. April 1917. Five times mentioned in Dispatches. Awarded the D.S.O. and 2 bars and the M.C. Served in France and Belgium and with Army of Occupation. Wounded April 1918 and Nov. 1918.

FREDERICK HENRY EWART BRANSON.

Admitted Nov. 1902. Member of Linklater & Co., of 2 Bond Court, E.C. 4. Joined Sept. 1915 as Temp. Lieut. Royal Army Ordnance Corps. Deputy Assistant Director of Equipment and Ordnance Stores at War Office Oct. 1916 to Jan 1919, Temp. Capt. Oct. 1916, Temp. Major (about) Feb. 1918. Once mentioned in Dispatches. Awarded the O.B.E. (Military Division). Served at Home.

RAYMOND HELTON BRANTHWAITE.

Admitted June 1913. Member of Lynde & Branthwaite, of Manchester. Joined Oct. 22, 1914, as 2nd Lieut., 7th Batt. Manchester Regiment, promoted Lieut. June 1915, Capt. Oct. 1915. Once mentioned in Dispatches. Served in France.

HENRY BENEDICT LINTHWAITE BRAUND.

Articled to F. H. Hayllar, of Brighton. Served as Capt., 6th Batt. Wiltshire Regt.

CECIL FRANCIS BRAY.

Admitted March 1908. Member of Bray & Bray, of Leicester. Enlisted Feb. 1916, as Private, 28th Batt. County of London Regt. (Artists Rifles), transferred July 1916 to Royal Field Artillery Cadet School. Gazetted 2nd Lieut. Royal Field Artillery Oct. 1916. Served in France and in Ireland.

HERBERT GEORGE BREDE.

Admitted Nov. 1919, practised at Ilfracombe. Served as Lieut., 6th (Reserve) Batt. Devonshire Regt (T.).

CHARLES EDWARD BREESE.

Admitted Dec. 1889. Member of Charles E. Breese & Co., of Portmadoc and Criccieth. Served as Capt., Royal Welch Fusiliers.

PERCIVAL JAMES BRETHERTON.

Admitted Dec. 1907. Member of Bretherton & Sons, of Gloucester. Joined May 10, 1915, as 2nd Lieut., Gloucestershire Regt., promoted Temp. Lieut. Dec. 1915 and reverted Aug. 1916, promoted Lieut. (full rank) July 1917, attached 2nd Batt. Devonshire Regt. June 1918 to Feb. 1919, promoted A/Capt. June 1918. Awarded the M.C. Served in France. Wounded Dec. 15, 1916, and Aug. 16, 1917.

WALTER GUY NICHOLAS BRETON.

Admitted April 1909, practised at Hanley, Staffs., in partnership with W. H. Breton. Joined Sept. 14, 1914, as 2nd Lieut., Royal Garrison Artillery, promoted Lieut. Jan. 1915, Adjutant April 1915, Capt. Oct. 1915, Major Nov. 1916. Twice mentioned in Dispatches. Awarded the D.S.O. Served in France and Belgium. Killed at Ypres Sept. 14, 1917.

ALAN BREWER.

Articled to W. L. Oxley, of Sheffield. Served as Private, 5th (Sheffield City) Batt. York and Lancaster Regt.

EDGAR BEWICK BREWER.

Articled to E. T. Gurdon, of 28 Lincoln's Inn Fields, W.C. Enlisted Sept. 26, 1914, as Private, 7th Batt. London Regiment (T.F.), promoted Lance-Sergeant about Jan. 1915. Commissioned as 2nd Lieut. in same Regiment May 5, 1915, promoted Lieut. Oct. 1915, Capt. Nov. 1916, attached to 140th Trench Mortar Battery May 1916 to Nov. 1917, and commanded this Battery Nov. 1916 to Nov. 1917, gazetted as relinquishing commission on account of ill-health contracted on active service July 26, 1918. Once mentioned in Dispatches. Awarded the M.C. Served in France Oct. 1915 to Dec. 1917.

ARTHUR BREWIS.

Admitted Nov. 1897. Member of Brewis & Sons, of St. Helens, Lancs. Served as Capt., 5th Batt. South Lancashire Regt. (T.), and subsequently promoted Major.

HAVARD NOEL BRIDGWATER.

Admitted June 1903, practising at Sheringham and Holt, Norfolk. Mobilised Aug. 1914, as Capt., 3rd Batt. Norfolk Regt., promoted Major, Aug. 1917. Three times mentioned in Dispatches. Awarded the O.B.E. and D.S.O. Served in Gallipoli, Egypt, and Palestine.

LOUIS BERNARD BRIERCLIFFE.

Admitted June 1911. Member of Hulton, Harwood & Briercliffe, of Bolton. Joined Sept. 1915, as 2nd Lieut., 3rd East Lancashire Brigade, Royal Field Artillery. Served at Home and in France. Killed in action at Arras March 31, 1917. Buried at Haute Avesnes, France.

JOHN WILLIAM BRIGDEN.

Admitted Dec. 1909. Of Ipoh, Straits Settlements. Served as 2nd Lieut., 6th Batt. Queen's Royal West Surrey Regt.

BRIAN DUDLEY BRIGG.

Admitted Jan. 1914, practising at Harpenden, Herts. Joined Sept. 1914, as Cadet, University of London O.T.C., and subsequently Lance-Sergeant. Gazetted Temp. 2nd Lieut. 8th Batt. Royal Berkshire Regt. Nov. 27, 1914, promoted Lieut. July 1917, attached 26th Divisional Cyclist Coy. July 1915, attached 12th Corps Cyclist Batt. Dec. 1916. Served at Home Nov. 1914 to Sept. 1915, in France Sept. to Nov. 1915, in Macedonia Nov. 1915 to Dec. 1918, in Caucasus Dec. 1918 to Jan. 1919.

ALBERT BRIGGS.

Admitted March 1, 1915. Managing Clerk with Roland W. Robinson, of Blackpool. Joined Jan. 18, 1916, as Sapper, Royal Engineers, promoted Lance-Corporal July 1916, Sergeant Sept. 1916. Gazetted 2nd Lieut. Inland Water Transport, Royal Engineers, March 10, 1917, promoted Lieut. June 1917, Capt. Feb. 1918. "Brought to knowledge of Secretary of State for War for valuable services rendered." Awarded the O.B.E. Served at Home.

JOHN JAMES BRIGGS.

Admitted Dec. 1912. Member of James Freeman & Briggs, of Bradford. Joined Sept. 10, 1914, as 2nd Lieut., 6th Batt. West Yorkshire Regt., promoted Lieut. June 1916. Served in France and Belgium Aug. 1916 to March 1919.

GEORGE AUGUSTIN BRIGHOUSE.

Admitted Oct. 1911. Of Ormskirk. Served as Private, 4th Batt. King's Liverpool Regt. Afterwards gazetted 2nd Lieut. 20th (Service) Batt. King's Liverpool Regt., and attained the rank of Capt. Mentioned in Dispatches.

ROBERT WALES BRIGHOUSE.

Admitted Dec. 1897. Member of Brighouse, Jones & Co., of Ormskirk. Served as Lieut., Royal Army Service Corps (T).

ALFRED STANLEY BRIGHT.

Admitted Feb. 1910. Member of J. & A. Bright, of Nottingham. Joined Oct. 1914, as 2nd Lieut., 7th Batt. Notts. and Derby Regt. (Sherwood Foresters), promoted Lieut. Oct. 1915, Capt. Sept. 1916. Served on the Western Front. Wounded May 1915, Nov. 1915, and March 1918. Taken prisoner March 21, 1918.

ARCHIBALD VICCARS BRIGHT.

Admitted July 1910. Clerk with J. & A. Bright, of Nottingham. Joined Sept. 1914, as Private, 12th Batt. Notts and Derby Regt. Gazetted 2nd Lieut. 3rd Batt. Notts and Derby Regt. March 1915, promoted Lieut. 1916. Served at Home and in France. Killed in action in Battle of Messines June 7, 1917.

BASIL HERBERT BRIGHT.

Articled to F. H. Bright, of Maldon, Essex. Joined Feb. 9, 1915, as 2nd Lieut., 7th Batt. Worcestershire Regt., promoted Temp. Lieut. Nov. 1915, transferred to command 82nd Trench Mortar Battery Jan. 1916, afterwards changed to 144 T.M.B., promoted A/Capt. June 14, 1916. Twice mentioned in Dispatches. Awarded the M.C. Served at Home Feb. 1915 to July 1915, France July 1915 to Nov. 1917, Italy Nov. 1917 to Jan. 1919, Home Jan. 1919 to Aug. 1919. Wounded slightly Sept. 3, 1916, near Beaumont-Hamel.

FREDERICK GERALD BRIGHT.

Admitted June 1912. Member of F. H. Bright & Son, of Witham and Maldon, Essex. Mobilised Aug. 4, 1914, as Lieut., 5th Batt. Essex Regt., promoted Capt. Dec. 1914, Staff-Capt. 161st Inf. Brigade July 1915, D.A.Q.M.G. Kantara area E.E.F. Aug. 1917, D.A.Q.M.G. 60th Division (with rank of Major) April 1918 to March 1919. Twice mentioned in Dispatches. Awarded the M.C. and the Order of the Nile (4th Class). Served at Home Aug. 1914 to July 1915, Gallipoli Aug. 1915 to Dec. 1915, Egypt Dec. 1915 to Jan. 1917, Palestine Jan. 1917 to March 1919.

WILLIAM ARTHUR BRIGHT.

Admitted Dec. 1904, practising at 15 George Street, Mansion House, E.C. Enlisted Jan. 14, 1916, as Driver, Royal Army Service Corps. Subsequently received commission and promotion to A/Capt. Royal Army Service Corps. Served at Home.

EDGAR WILLIAM BRIGHTEN.

Admitted March 1904. Member of Brown & Brighten, of 4 Mitre Court, E.C. Served as Major, 5th Batt. Bedfordshire Regt. (T.), promoted Brevet Lieut.-Col. Mentioned in Dispatches. Awarded the Order of C.M.G. and the D.S.O.

GEORGE STANLEY BRIGHTEN.

Admitted Nov. 1911. Member of Brighten & Lemon, of 1 Crutched Friars, London, E.C., and Antwerp. Enlisted Aug. 1914, as Private, Public Schools Batt. Royal Fusiliers. Gazetted 2nd Lieut. 8th Batt. The King's Liverpool Regt. Nov. 17, 1914, and attained the rank of A/Major in that Regiment, joined the 5th Batt. Lancashire Fusiliers March 1917 as 2nd in Command and subsequently promoted to Lieut.-Col. Three times mentioned in Dispatches. Awarded the D.S.O. and Bar, Chevalier de l'Ordre de la Couronne (Belgium) and Croix de Guerre (Belgium). Served from May 3, 1915, to March 1919 in France and Belgium.

FRANK PUDEY BRINDLEY.

Admitted Nov. 1903, practising at 37 Norfolk Street, Strand, W.C. Joined Jan. 18, 1918, as Paymaster Sub-Lieut., Royal Naval Volunteer Reserve, appointed Secretary to Chief of Staff, Vice-Admiral North of Ireland, June 1918. Served on North Coast of Ireland.

WALTER DYSON BRISCOMBE.

Admitted Nov. 1904, practising at Southport. Enlisted Feb. 1917, as Private, Army Pay Corps, promoted Corporal Feb. 1918. Served over 2 years in France.

FRANK BRITCLIFFE.

Admitted Dec. 1912. Member of Britcliffe & Son, of Accrington. Mobilised Aug. 1914, as Lieut., 5th Batt. East Lancashire Regt., promoted Capt. June 1916. Awarded the M.C. Served in Egypt 1914, Gallipoli 1915, Sinai 1916, France and Belgium 1917 to 1918. Severely wounded Aug. 24, 1918, at Miraumont, France.

ARNOLD BRITTAIN.

Admitted April 1912, practising at Sheffield. Served as Private, Royal Army Medical Corps (T.).

LEONARD HALL BRITTAIN.

Articled to W. J. Bradford, of Rotherham, Yorkshire. Enlisted Feb. 22, 1917, as Trooper, 19th Hussars, transferred to 1/1 Staffordshire Yeomanry July 1918. Served at Home and in Egypt.

WILLIAM BRITTAIN.

Admitted Jan. 1898. Managing Clerk with Baileys, Shaw & Gillett, 5 Berners Street, W. Enlisted Sept. 3, 1918, as Driver, Royal Army Service Corps. Subsequently gazetted Temp. 2nd Lieut. Royal Army Service Corps. Served at Home.

JOHN ERIC BROAD.

Articled to T. H. Bower, of 4 Bream's Buildings, E.C. Joined Aug. 1914, as Private, 28th Batt. County of London Regt. (Artists Rifles). Gazetted 2nd Lieut. Hertfordshire Regt. Dec. 2, 1915, promoted Lieut. Dec. 1916. Served in France March to Oct. 1915, and Oct. 1917 to March 1918. Killed in action at Mont St. Quentin, near Peronne, France, March 23, 1918.

JOHN MOXON BROAD.

Admitted April 1911. Member of Broad & Son, of 1 Great Winchester Street, E.C. Joined Sept. 16, 1914, as 2nd Lieut., 60th London Divisional Train, Royal Army Service Corps, promoted Lieut. Nov. 1914, Capt. Jan. 1915, transferred to Infantry July 1918 and posted to 2/19 Batt. London Regt., retransferred to Royal Army Service Corps Dec. 1918. Served in France June to Dec. 1916, Salonica Jan. to June 1917, Palestine June 1917 to Jan. 1919.

CROSSLEY ST. JOHN BROADBENT.

Admitted Dec. 1907, practising at Darwen. Served as Capt., 4th Batt. East Lancashire Regt. (T.), and afterwards promoted Major.

ROBERT ALEXANDER LONGMAN BROADLEY.

Admitted Jan. 1909, practising at 4 Elm Court, E.C. Served in France with Red Cross Oct. 1914 to Feb. 1915. Gazetted Lieut. Royal Army Service Corps Sept. 1915, promoted A/Capt. Oct. 1917. Served at Home and in France.

JOSEPH BROATCH.

Admitted March 1884. Member of Broatch & Son, of Keswick. Served as Capt. and Hon. Major, 4th Batt. Border Regt. (T.).

EDWARD HOWARD BROCKLEHURST.

Admitted Feb. 1903. Member of Blunt & Brocklehurst, of Macclesfield. Enlisted March 7, 1916, as Private, 28th Batt. County of London Regt. (Artists Rifles), transferred as Private to Royal Army Service Corps April 1916. Gazetted 2nd Lieut. Royal Army Service Corps, May 1916, promoted Lieut. Nov. 1917, A/Capt. May 1917 to Jan. 1919. Once mentioned in Dispatches. Served in France and Belgium.

THOMAS POWNALL BROCKLEHURST.

Admitted Dec. 1912. Managing Clerk with Bell, Brodrick & Gray, of Queen Victoria Street, E.C. Joined Aug. 16, 1914, as Private, 28th Batt. County of London Regt. (Artists Rifles). Gazetted 2nd Lieut. Queen's Royal West Surrey Regt. May 1915, promoted Capt. Aug. 1915. Served at Home and in France. Killed in action July 1, 1916, at Mametz, Battle of Somme.

RALPH ZOUCH BROCKMAN.

Admitted July 1913, practised at Folkestone. Joined Jan 25, 1916, as Gunner, Royal Horse Artillery. Gazetted 2nd Lieut. Royal Field Artillery June 20, 1916. Awarded the M.C. Served in France 1916 and 1917. Killed at Messines, Belgium, Sept. 29, 1917.

RANDOLPH CHARLES ZOUCH DRAKE BROCKMAN.

Admitted Oct. 1910, practising at Folkestone. Joined the 105th Fusiliers (Saskatoon) as Private. Provisional Lieut. 105th Fusiliers Aug. 1915, Lieut. 107th Batt. Canadian Pioneers Dec. 1915, transferred as Lieut. to Lord Strathcona's Horse (R.C.) May 1918 in France. Served in Canada and France.

ALEXANDER BRODIE.

Admitted Nov. 1900. Member of Budd, Brodie & Hart, of 33 Bedford Row, W.C. Served as 2nd Lieut., 16th Batt. County of London Regt. (Queen's Westminster Rifles) and afterwards promoted Lieut.

EDWARD BRODRICK.

Admitted May 1914, practised at Blackburn. Served as Lieut., 13th Batt. Manchester Regt.

OLIVER BROGDEN.

Admitted July 1904, practising at Leigh, Lancashire. Joined Nov. 3, 1916, as Private, Cheshire Regt. Served 15 months on East Coast, 15 months in Palestine and Salonica.

WILLIAM FREDERICK BROGDEN.

Admitted Nov. 1907. Member of Brogden & Son, of Lincoln. Served as Lieut., 11th Batt. Suffolk Regt.

JOHN NEVILLE BROMET.

Articled to G. A. Bromet, of Tadcaster. Joined Sept. 6, 1914, as Private, Middlesex Battalion Public School and University Corps. Gazetted 2nd Lieut. Royal Field Artillery Oct. 17, 1914, promoted Lieut. July 1915. Served in France. Killed in action at Gouzeaucourt, near Cambrai, Nov. 30, 1917.

ARTHUR STANLEY BROOKES.

Admitted Oct. 1906, practising at Bristol. Joined April 10, 1915, as Lieut. and Quartermaster, 2/3 South Midland Field Ambulance 61st Division. Served in France May 1916 to Jan. 1919.

JOHN CHARLES BROOKHOUSE.

Admitted Aug. 1901, practising at 8 & 9 Queen Street, Cheapside, E.C. Joined Nov. 1915, as 2nd Lieut., Royal Garrison Artillery. Embarked for Salonica on staff of 61st Heavy Artillery Group Aug. 1916, promoted Lieut. Nov. 1916, Staff-Lieut. 1st Class Headquarters Heavy Artillery 21st Corps Dec. 1917, promoted Capt. April 1918, posted to 422nd Siege Battery Aug. 1918, promoted A/Major Dec. 1918. Served at Salonica Aug. 1916 to Sept. 1917, Palestine Sept. 1917 to Dec. 1918, Egypt. Dec. 1918 to Feb. 1919.

FRANK SMITH BROOKS.

Articled to A. P. Brooks, of Southport. Served as 2nd Lieut., 20th Batt. Manchester Regt. Killed in action in France July 1, 1916.

HENRY JAMES BROOKS.

Articled to C. S. Preston, of 35 Lincoln's Inn Fields, W.C. Served as Sergeant, Inns of Court O.T.C. Afterwards gazetted to the Manchester Regt., and attained the rank of Major. Awarded the D.S.O. and the M.C.

RICHARD BASIL DIGBY BROOKS.

Articled to Richard Brooks, of 24 Lawrence Lane, Cheapside, E.C. Joined Sept. 1914 Inns of Court O.T.C. Gazetted 2nd Lieut. 2/7 Batt. Middlesex Regt., appointed Staff-Capt. R.T.O. Headquarters of Administrative Services Department General List Dec. 1917.

JOHN WILLIAM FRANK BROOM.

Admitted June 1910. Member of Steel & Broom, of Cheltenham. Enlisted June 11, 1917, as Private, Worcestershire Regt., transferred to 639th Home Service Employment Coy. Labour Batt., subsequently transferred to Reserve for service as an Official, Ministry National Service. Served at Home.

GEOFFREY BROOME.

Admitted Nov. 1904. Of 36 Bedford Row, W.C. Served as 2nd Lieut., Queen's Royal West Surrey Regt.

MALAM (MAX) BROTHERS.

Admitted Dec. 1907. Member of Malam Brothers & Son, of Blackburn. Joined Aug. 1914, as 2nd Lieut., 2/4 Batt. East Lancashire Regt., and attained the rank of Capt. Served in France. Killed in action at Givenchy May 28, 1917.

ARNOLD LESLIE THACKHALL BROWETT.

Admitted Dec. 1909. Member of Browetts, of Coventry. Rejoined Aug. 1914 the 7th Batt. Royal Warwickshire Regt. with the rank of Capt. Went to France May 1916. Killed in trenches at Neuve Chapelle July 5, 1916.

ALFRED WILLIAMSON BROWN.

Articled to J. F. Read, of Liverpool. Enlisted Jan. 25, 1916, as Private, 28th Batt. County of London Regt. (Artists Rifles). Commissioned 2nd Lieut. 9th Batt. King's Liverpool Regt. July 10, 1916, promoted Lieut. April 1917. Served at Home Jan. to Oct. 1916, in France Oct. 1916 to Feb. 1918, at Home Feb. 1918 to Jan. 1919. Wounded at Ypres June 16, 1917.

ARTHUR CASSELS BROWN.

Articled to H. E. Bury, of 47 Lincoln's Inn Fields, W.C. Enlisted Nov. 5, 1914, as Private, 14th London Regt. (London Scottish), promoted Lance-Corporal April 1915. Gazetted 2nd Lieut. 4th Batt. Cameron Highlanders (T.F.) July 2, 1915, promoted Lieut. Nov. 1915, reverted to 2nd Lieut. on being seconded for duty with Machine Gun Corps Aug. 1916, promoted Lieut. Feb. 1917, appointed Assistant Adjutant Headquarters Training Group B Machine Gun Training Centre Jan. 1918. Served in France Oct. 1916 to April 1917. Wounded at Chérisy April 26, 1917.

CHARLES BROWN.

Admitted July 1902. Managing Clerk with Balderston & Warrens, 32 Bedford Row, W.C., and Baldock, Herts. Enlisted Dec. 1914, as Gunner,

2/A Battery Hon. Artillery Company. Commissioned in Labour Corps Jan. 1918 as 2nd Lieut. and posted to 99th Labour Company. Served in France June 1917 to June 1919.

CHARLES ANTHONY BROWN.

Admitted Feb. 1900, practising at 57 Gracechurch Street, London, E.C. Joined Jan. 1917, as Cadet, Garrison Officers' Cadet Batt. Gazetted 2nd Lieut. 3rd Garrison Batt. Royal Welch Fusiliers March 1917, transferred 2nd Garrison Batt. June 1917, promoted Lieut. Sept. 1918. Served in Egypt.

COLIN EDWIN BROWN.

Admitted April 1901. Member of Colin Brown, Wilkinson & Wharton, of Whitby and Scarborough. Enlisted Dec. 13, 1915, as Gunner, Royal Garrison Artillery, promoted Bombardier about Dec. 1917. Served in France.

EDWARD FREDERICK MONTAGU BROWN.

Admitted Feb. 1909. Member of Henry Vickers, Son & Brown, of Sheffield. Joined Aug. 1914, as Private, Universities and Public Schools Batt. 18th Royal Fusiliers, afterwards Sergeant in same Regt. Subsequently 2nd Lieut. and Lieut. in 1st Batt. Hertfordshire Regt. Died of wounds in France Jan 8, 1918.

ERNEST VICTOR BROWN.

Admitted Jan. 1903. Member of Goodall, Brown & Willatt, of Nottingham. Served as Lieut., Royal Garrison Artillery.

EVERARD KENNETH BROWN.

Admitted Feb. 1903. Member of Kenneth Brown, Baker, Baker & Co., of Lennox House, Norfolk Street, Strand, W.C. Joined Aug. 16, 1917, as Temp. 2nd Lieut., Special List, promoted Temp. Lieut. Nov. 1917, Intelligence Officer Northern Command Sept. 1917 to Feb. 1919, Temp. Capt. July 1918, Staff-Lieut. I (B) Northern Command Nov. 1917 to July 1918, Staff-Capt. for Defence of the Realm Regulations Northern Command July 1918 to Feb. 1919. Awarded the M.B.E. (Military Division). Served at Home.

FRANCIS JOHN BROWN.

Articled to Cecil Crust, of Spalding. Served as a Private in Lewis Machine Gun Section Middlesex Regt. Killed in action in France on Aug. 26, 1916.

FREDERIC HOLIFIELD BROWN.

Admitted Nov. 1907. Member of Penman & Brown, of 19 Holborn Viaduct, E.C. Joined Oct. 1914, as Private, Hon. Artillery Company. Served in France. Wounded severely Feb. 1915. Died of influenza Nov. 26, 1918.

FREDERICK WILLIAM GRAY BROWN.

Admitted Aug. 1910, practised at 22 Chancery Lane, W.C. Served as Lieut., 18th Batt. County of London Regt. (London Irish Rifles).

GEORGE WILLIAM FREDERICK BROWN.

Admitted Feb. 1890, practising at Barnstaple. Served as Major, 6th Batt. Devonshire Regt.

HAROLD GEORGE BROWN.

Admitted Aug. 1900. Member of Linklater & Brown, of 2 Bond Court, E.C. Served as Chief Petty Officer, Royal Naval Volunteer Reserve.

HENRY FORESTER BROWN.

Articled to G. F. S. Brown, of Worcester. Served as 2nd Lieut., Royal Army Service Corps, and afterwards promoted Lieut.

HENRY OSWALD BROWN.

Admitted Oct. 1912, practising at Doncaster. Joined Jan. 18, 1915, as 2nd Lieut., 5th Batt. King's Own Yorkshire Light Infantry (T.F.), promoted Lieut. Aug. 1915, Capt. June 1917. Served at Home Jan. 1915 to Dec. 1916, France Dec. 1916 to Dec. 1917, Home Dec. 1917 to Feb. 1919. Wounded May 1917 Croisilles-Bullecourt, and Nov. 27, 1917, Bourlon (Cambrai).

HENRY PINDER BROWN.

Admitted Jan. 1898, practising at 240 High Holborn, W.C. Mobilised Aug. 1914, as Batt. Quartermaster-Sergeant, 28th Batt. County of London Regt. (Artists Rifles). Commissioned as 2nd Lieut. in Jan. 1915, promoted Lieut. April 1915, and Capt. July 1916, seconded for duty on Staff R.T.E. in Sept. 1916. Awarded the T.D. Served at Home till April 1915, France April to June 1915, Home June 1915 to June 1916, France and Belgium June 1916 to April 1919.

JOHN HOPE BROWN.

Admitted Aug. 1896. Member of Brown, Auld & Brown, of Whitehaven. Joined Sept. 1914, as Major, 5th Batt. Border Regt. Served at Home.

MAURICE BLUMFIELD BROWN.

Admitted June 1910. Managing Clerk with Godwin & Son, 63 Wool Exchange, Coleman Street, E.C. Mobilised Aug. 1914, as Private, Hon. Artillery Company (Infantry). Obtained commission in Hon. Artillery Company June 1915, promoted Capt. Aug. 1917. Awarded the M.C. Served at Home, in France, and in Italy. Wounded Nov. 1914.

PHILIP JOHNSON BROWN.

Articled to H. P. Addleshaw, of Manchester. Served as Corporal, Army Pay Corps.

RONALD STEWART BROWN.

Admitted Dec. 1898. Member of Collins, Robinson, Driffield, Cleyton & Stewart Brown, of Liverpool. Joined April 1915, as 2nd Lieut., 2/1 Duke of Lancaster's Own Yeomanry, promoted Capt. and Adjutant Nov. 1916.

STANLEY GORDON BROWN.

Articled to John Errington, of Carlisle. Joined Feb. 1915, as Seaman, Royal Naval Division. Served at Gallipoli. Killed 1915, shortly after the expedition landed.

WILLIAM BROWN.

Admitted Oct. 1909, practised at Sunderland. Enlisted Sept. 2, 1914, as Private, Durham Light Infantry. Served in France. Reported missing May 26, 1915.

WILLIAM CUTHBERT BROWN.

Admitted Feb. 1909. Of the Port of London Authority. Served in the Hon. Artillery Company. Afterwards obtained commission in the Durham

Light Infantry, and attained the rank of Capt. Mentioned in Dispatches. Awarded the M.C.

WILLIAM HELMSLEY BROWN.

Admitted Nov. 1905. Member of Royds, Rawstorne & Co., of 46 Bedford Row, W.C. Served as Assistant Paymaster, Royal Naval Volunteer Reserve.

WILLIAM LEONARD BROWN.

Admitted Feb. 1915. Of Buxton. Joined Jan. 1915, as 2nd Lieut., 6th Batt. Notts and Derby Regt. (Sherwood Foresters), and subsequently appointed Brigade Intelligence Officer. Killed in action in France Sept. 25, 1915.

WILLIAM LINFORD BROWN.

Admitted April 1910, practising at Exeter. Enlisted March 30, 1916, as Private, Worcestershire Regt. Served in France. Wounded.

WILLIAM STANLEY ALSTON BROWN.

Admitted Nov. 1901. Member of W. H. Brown & Son, of Bristol. Enlisted June 14, 1916, as Private, 5th Batt. North Staffordshire Regt., promoted Corporal Aug. 1916. Commissioned 2nd Lieut. Jan. 5, 1917, 1st Lieut. July 1918, Capt. Dec. 1918, and appointed a Courts-Martial Officer. Served in France.

JOHN EDWARD BROWN-HUMES.

Admitted April 1909. Member of Douglas & Humes, of Bishop Auckland. Served as Lieut., 7th Batt. Durham Light Infantry (Pioneers).

ARTHUR NORMAN BROWNE.

Articled to Arthur Browne, of Warrington. Served as Private, 5th City of London Batt. London Regt. (London Rifle Brigade).

CHARLES HOWE BROWNE.

Articled to A. E. Pratt, of 142 Holborn Bars, London, E.C. 1. Enlisted June 1916, as Gunner, Devonshire Royal Garrison Artillery (T.F.). Gazetted 2nd Lieut. Devonshire Royal Garrison Artillery (T.F.) June 1, 1917, promoted Lieut. Dec. 1918. Served at Home.

HAROLD ST. JOHN BROWNE.

Admitted Dec. 1905. Member of Browne & Wells, of Northampton. Mobilised Aug. 4, 1914, as Capt., 4th Batt. Northamptonshire Regt., promoted A/Major March 1917. Awarded the M.C., T.D., and the Order of the Nile. Served at Gallipoli, Egypt, and Palestine.

CLIFFORD BRUMFITT.

Admitted Nov. 1907, practising at Morley, near Leeds. Enlisted Sept. 6, 1916, as Gunner and Signaller, Royal Field Artillery. Served with Salonica Forces in Macedonia.

GEORGE RICHARD BRUMFITT.

Admitted April 1912, practising at Barnsley. Enlisted Nov. 13, 1916, as Private, West Yorkshire Regt., transferred to Army Pay Corps Jan. 1917, promoted Corporal Nov. 1917. Served at Home.

GEORGE KINGSTON HALL BRUTTON.

Admitted Aug. 1891. Of Hong Kong. Served as Major, Labour Corps.

HENRY LIONEL BRUTTON.

Admitted Oct. 1910. Member of Reid, Sharman, White & Brutton, of 52 Bedford Row, W.C. Joined Sept. 20, 1914, as 2nd Lieut., Queen's Own Worcestershire Hussars, Capt. and Adjutant Feb. 1915 to Sept. 1917, transferred as Capt. to 2/8 Batt. Worcestershire Regt. April 1918. Served in France April 1918 to Feb. 1919.

WILLIAM GLYNES BRUTY.

Admitted Dec. 1896. Member of Duffield, Bruty & Co., 18 Broad Street Avenue, E.C., and Waltham Abbey. Joined Jan. 15, 1915, as 2nd Lieut., Special Supply Coy., 24th Batt. County of London Regt., Lieut. June 1915 Royal Defence Corps, transferred to General List of Regular Army 1917, appointed Assistant Provost Marshal at Headquarters Eastern Command March 1917 to March 1919, rank Capt. Once mentioned in Dispatches. Awarded the M.B.E. (Military Division). Served at Home.

FREDERICK STAWELL BRYAN.

Admitted Dec. 1905. Member of Bryan & Bryan, of Hindley. Served as 2nd Lieut., 9th Batt. Middlesex Regt. Awarded the M.C.

GUY WILLOUGHBY STAWELL BRYAN.

Articled to H. J. W. Holt, of 12 Great Marlborough Street, W. Enlisted Sept. 4, 1914, as Private, 19th (Service) Batt. Royal Fusiliers. Gazetted 2nd Lieut. 13th Batt. Hampshire Regt. March 12, 1915, promoted Lieut. 10th Batt. Hampshire Regt. July 1917. Once mentioned in Dispatches. Awarded the Italian Silver Medal for Valour. Served in Macedonia.

GUY WYNDHAM BRYAN.

Admitted April 1901. Of 14 Old Jewry Chambers, E.C. Served as Bombardier, Royal Garrison Artillery.

HENRY NORMAN BEECHER BRYANT.

Admitted Oct. 1909. Member of Beecher, Bryant & Co., of 17 Gracechurch Street, E.C. Enlisted April 10, 1917, as Gunner, Royal Garrison Artillery, appointed Bombadier June 1919. Served in India Sept. 1917 to Nov. 1919, N.W. Frontier 3rd Afghan War May to Sept. 1919.

SYDNEY BRYANT.

Admitted April 1910. Member of Bryant, of Pontypridd. Joined Nov. 1915, as Sapper, Royal Engineers. Served at Home, in France, and in Italy.

CHARLES JOHN BRYDEN.

Admitted Sept. 1899. Member of Keene, Marsland, Bryden & Besant, of 15 Seething Lane, E.C. Mobilised Aug. 4, 1914, as Sergeant, 14th Batt. County of London Regt. (London Scottish). Commissioned 2nd Lieut. Sept 22, 1915 (London Scottish), promoted Lieut. March 1917. Served in France Sept. 1914 to Feb. 1919.

PATRICK BRYDONE.

Admitted Dec. 1902, practising at Tonbridge. Served as 2nd Lieut., Royal Army Service Corps (M.T.).

EDWARD ALAN BRYNING.

Admitted Oct. 1910, practising at Preston. Served as 2nd Lieut., Royal Field Artillery, afterwards promoted Lieut. and attached to Royal Engineers (Signal Service). Mentioned in Dispatches.

WILLIAM ERNEST MARSHALL BUCHANAN.

Admitted June 1894. Temporary Clerk with Public Trustee, Kingsway. Enlisted Sept. 5, 1915, as Private (Driver), Royal Army Service Corps (M.T.). Served in France Nov. 1915 to May 1918, Ireland Sept. to Dec. 1918. Invalided from France May 1918. Discharged unfit Dublin 1918.

ALEXANDER BUCHANNAN.

Admitted June 1901, practised at Thirsk. Joined May 17, 1915, as 2nd Lieut., 6th Batt. West Yorkshire Regt. (T.), promoted Temp. Capt. April 1916. Attached to 16th Batt. on going to France with the rank of 2nd Lieut. Served in France from Jan. to July 1917. Killed in action near Arras July 21, 1917.

GEORGE HERBERT BUCHANNAN.

Admitted May 1900. Member of Forsdike, Buchannan & Giles, of Cardiff. Joined Dec. 30, 1915, as 2nd Lieut., subsequently promoted to Capt.

WILLIAM DOVER WAY BUCKELL.

Admitted Oct. 1913. Managing Clerk with Buckell & Drew, of Newport and Ventnor, Isle of Wight. Joined Oct. 1914, as Corporal, Royal Engineers, discharged July 1, 1915 (medically unfit on account of injuries received while on Active Service in France). Rejoined Sept. 1916, as Cadet, Machine Gun Corps. Gazetted 2nd Lieut. Machine Gun Corps Jan. 1917, promoted Lieut. July 1918. Once mentioned in Dispatches. Awarded the M.C. Served in France Oct. 1914 to Jan. 1915, and April 1917 to May 1918. Injured in France Jan. 1, 1915, wounded March 22, 1918.

EDMUND CECIL GLADSTONE BUCKLEY.

Admitted April 1912. Managing Clerk with Whitley & Co., of Liverpool. Mobilised Aug. 1914, as 2nd Lieut., 6th (Rifle) Batt. King's Liverpool Regt., promoted Capt. March 1915. Served in Belgium and France. Killed in action near Guillemont, Aug. 5, 1916. Buried at Carnoy.

GILBERT BUCKLEY.

Admitted Feb. 1899, practising at Manchester. Served as Private, Royal Army Service Corps, attached 52nd Brigade Headquarters, Royal Garrison Artillery.

JOSEPH MICHAEL BUCKLEY.

Articled to Hutchison & Cuff, of 6 Stone Buildings, Lincoln's Inn Fields. Joined Aug. 1914, as Private, 28th Batt. County of London Regt. (Artists Rifles). Gazetted 2nd Lieut. 9th Batt. The Rifle Brigade Sept. 1915, and subsequently promoted Capt. and Adjutant. Awarded the M.C. Served in France and Belgium. Wounded on the Somme in Aug. 1916. Killed at Passchendaele Dec. 22, 1917.

JAMES DOUGLAS BUCKTON.

Admitted Feb. 1884. Of Warrington. Joined Nov. 23, 1914, as Major and Hon. Lieut.-Col., No. 2 Supernumerary Coy., 5th Batt. Gloucestershire Regt. Served in England.

CHARLES WILLIAM BUCKWELL.

Admitted June 1906, practising at Brighton and Battle. Mobilised Aug. 1914, as Capt., Royal Engineers (T.), promoted Major Feb. 1915. Mentioned in Dispatches. Served at Home and in France. Suffered from shell-shock April 15, 1918.

THOMAS LAURENCE BUDD.

Admitted Aug. 1913. Managing Clerk with F. A. Sarjeant, of Reading, Berks. Joined Wessex Signal Coy., Royal Engineers (T.F.) Sept. 2, 1914, promoted Corporal Nov. 1914, 27th Div. Signal Coy., Sergeant 1917, 58th Div. Signal Coy. Served in France.

FREDERIC VINCENT BUDDEN.

Admitted April 1908, practising at Dover. Joined Aug. 20, 1914, 3rd Home Counties Brigade Royal Field Artillery (T.), afterwards called 222nd Brigade Royal Field Artillery, promoted A/Capt. April 1917 (Substantive Capt. Nov. 1918), A/Major Oct. 1918, relinquished Acting rank Sept. 1919. Served in India Oct. 1914 to May 1916, Mesopotamia May 1916 to April 1919, India and Afghan Campaign April to Aug. 1919.

LIONEL BUDDEN.

Articled to M. J. Raymond, of Wimborne. Served as Private, Royal Army Medical Corps.

WILLIAM HATTON BUDGE.

Admitted Feb. 1907, practising at Poole, Dorset. Mobilised Aug. 1914, as Capt., Dorset Royal Garrison Artillery, promoted Major 1917. Once mentioned in Dispatches. Served at Home Coast Defence.

JAMES ROSTRON BUGLER.

Articled to R. W. Bugler, of Haslingden, Lancs. Joined as Private, East Lancashire Regt., and promoted to Corporal. Gazetted 2nd Lieut. 3rd Batt. Dorset Regt., attached to 3/3 Gurkha Rifles, E.E.F. Served in Palestine and Egypt.

REGINALD BULGIN.

Admitted Oct. 1913. Of Brixham. Served as Private, 28th Batt. County of London Regt. (Artists Rifles). Afterwards gazetted 2nd Lieut. Royal Fusiliers and attached 23rd Batt. London Regt. Mentioned in Dispatches.

ROLAND JOHN HOWARD BULL.

Admitted Dec. 1913. Member of Bull & Bull, 3 Stone Buildings, Lincoln's Inn, W.C., and Hammersmith, W. Gazetted 2nd Lieut. 16th Batt. County of London Regt. (Queen's Westminsters) Aug. 24, 1914, promoted Lieut. April 1915, Capt. May. 1917, seconded Signal Service with the 8th Heavy Artillery Group. Served at Home and in Flanders and France. Killed accidentally July 13, 1917, at Canada Farm, Elverdinghe, N.W. of Ypres.

REGINALD BULLIN.

Admitted Nov. 1901, practising as Edmonds & Bullin, at Portsmouth. Mobilised Aug. 4, 1914, as Capt., 6th Duke of Connaught's Own Hampshire Regt., promoted Temp. Major July 1915, Major (Substantive rank) June 1916, seconded to 2/6 Hampshire Regt. as Adjutant from Oct. 1914 to Feb. 1915, seconded to 84th Provisional Batt. (Hampshire Regt.) as Adjutant from Feb. to July 1915, Second in Command of 17th Hampshire Regt. from July 1915 to Feb. 1919, President of numerous District Courts-Martial and also Judge-Advocate at various General Courts-Martial during the War, and for a time acted as legal adviser to Brigade Headquarters. "Name brought to the notice of Secretary of State for War for valuable services in connection with the War." Awarded the T.D. Served at Home.

JAMES HOWEL BULLOCH.

Admitted April 1901. Member of Slibbard, Gibson & Co., and Thomas Cooper & Co., of 21 Leadenhall Street, London, E.C. Joined April 1917, as Lieut., Royal Naval Volunteer Reserve. Served in the North Sea. Special service in connection with Scandinavian Convoys.

HENRY ACTON LINTON BULLOCK.

Admitted May 1910. Member of Goate & Bullock, of Coventry. Served as 2nd Lieut., 7th Batt. Royal Warwickshire Regt. Killed in action 1916.

LANCELOT CLAUDE BULLOCK.

Admitted Dec. 1903. Member of Wadeson & Malleson, and Markby, Stewart & Co., of 7 Devonshire Square, E.C. Joined Sept. 15, 1916, as Cadet. Gazetted 2nd Lieut. Royal Garrison Artillery Dec. 11, 1916, Staff-Lieut. June 1918, Staff-Capt. Aug. 1918. Served in France.

ERNEST BULLOUGH.

Admitted Aug. 1910. Member of Wilson & Bullough, of Wigan. Commissioned Feb. 28, 1915, as 2nd Lieut. in 14th Batt. Manchester Regt., promoted Capt. March 1916, subsequently went overseas (France) to 20th Manchesters and invalided with Trench Fever. After discharged from Hospital served on Irish Command Discharge Centre, Dublin, until Jan. 1919. Served at Home and in France.

JAMES BULLPITT.

Admitted Feb. 1905, practising at Upper Norwood. Joined Aug. 5, 1914, as Private, 28th Batt. County of London Regt. (Artists Rifles), transferred to Machine Gun Corps, and commissioned in Oct. 1916, promoted Lieut. March 1918. Once mentioned in Dispatches. Awarded the M.C. Served in France Oct. 1914 to Feb. 1919.

CHARLES GILBERT BUNTING.

Admitted June 1911, practising at West Hartlepool. Enlisted March 29, 1916, as Gunner, Royal Garrison Artillery (T.), promoted Bombardier Sept. 1916. Gazetted 2nd Lieut. Royal Garrison Artillery (T.) April 30, 1917, promoted Lieut. Sept. 1918. Served on Coast Defence.

EDWARD D'ARCY BURBIDGE.

Admitted Dec. 1897. Member of Burbidge & Trestrail, of Bristol. Mobilised Aug. 5, 1914, and served as Capt., Royal Horse and Royal Field Artillery (T.F.). Served in France March 1915, Italy Nov. 1917, returned to England Jan. 1919.

JOHN DENIS BURCH.

Articled to J. R. Lloyd, of Bristol. Served as Trooper, 3rd Batt. North Somerset Yeomanry.

JAMES MELVILL BURCHELL.

Admitted Oct. 1911, practised at 5 The Sanctuary, Westminster. Served as Private, 23rd Batt. County of London Regt. Afterwards gazetted 2nd Lieut. 9th Batt. County of London Regt. (Queen Victoria's Rifles), promoted Lieut. and appointed Staff-Capt. Mentioned in Dispatches. Awarded the O.B.E.

LESLIE CORBET BURCHER.

Articled to F. E. Burcher, of Kidderminster. Joined March 25, 1915, as 2nd Lieut., Worcestershire Regt., 2nd Lieut. Royal Flying Corps. Dec. 1915., Certificated Pilot June 3, 1916, Lieut. Oct. 1916, Capt. March 1918, transferred to Royal Air Force as Capt. April 1, 1918. Served at Home and in France.

GEOFFREY ERIC BURDEKIN.

Articled to B. T. Burdekin, of Sheffield. Received commission as 2nd Lieut. Notts and Derby Regt. (Sherwood Foresters) Aug. 1914, and subsequently attached to 1st Batt. Loyal North Lancashire Regt. Served in France. Killed at Beuvry Jan. 26, 1915.

EDWARD PRIESTLEY BURDETT.

Articled to R. G. Layton, of Liverpool. Served as 2nd Lieut., 3rd Batt. South Lancashire Regt., and afterwards promoted Lieut. Also held commission in Royal Air Force.

THOMAS GEORGE DEANE BURDETT.

Articled to W. Hughes Jones, of Aberystwyth, and afterwards Managing Clerk with Smith Davies & Co., Aberystwyth. Joined Sept. 2, 1914, as Lieut., 7th Batt. Royal Welch Fusiliers., promoted Capt. May 1916. Once mentioned in Dispatches. Awarded the M.C. Served at Gallipoli, Egypt, and Palestine from Sept. 1915 to Nov. 1917. Killed in action in Palestine Nov. 6, 1917.

WILLIAM EDWARD PARRY BURGES.

Admitted April 1884. Member of Burges & Sloan, of Bristol. Served as Colonel commanding Bristol Batt. Gloucestershire Regt.

ROBERT EDWARD BURGESS.

Articled to L. W. Taylor, 1 New Square, Lincoln's Inn, W.C. Mobilised Aug. 1914, as 2nd Lieut., Royal Field Artillery, promoted Lieut. Sept. 1914, Capt. Oct. 1918. Served in France.

EDWARD LESLIE BURGIN.

Admitted Aug. 1909. Member of Denton Hall & Burgin, of 3 Gray's Inn Place, W.C., and Paris. Joined June 28, 1917, as Private, Inns of Court O.T.C. Direct commission as 2nd Lieut. to General List, attached Intelligence Corps, Nov. 30, 1917. Once mentioned in Dispatches. Awarded the Croce di Guerra (Italian). Served at Home and subsequently in Italy.

HAROLD CHARLES BURGIN.

Admitted Feb. 1913. Of 3 Gray's Inn Place, London W.C. Gazetted Lieut. 11th Batt. County of London Regt. Aug. 31, 1914, promoted Capt. and Adjutant May 1915, Staff-Lieut. (1st Class) June 1918 Headquarters, Aldershot Command, Aldershot. Once mentioned in Dispatches. Served at Home and in France. Suffered from shell-shock.

FREDERIC BURGIS.

Admitted July 1906. Member of Walter Burgis & Co., of 31 Bridge Row, London, E.C. Joined July 19, 1917, as Private, Inns of Court O.T.C. Gazetted May 1, 1918, as 2nd Lieut. King's Shropshire Light Infantry. Served at Home.

GEORGE BERNARD BURKE.

Articled to James Ball, of 10 Gray's Inn Place, Gray's Inn, W.C. Enlisted Dec. 4, 1916, as Private, Royal Army Service Corps (M.T.), transferred to Royal Flying Corps, as 2nd Air Mechanic, March 1917. Served at Home, in France, and in Italy.

ROLAND CLIVE WALLACE BURN.

Admitted Dec. 1912. Member of Burn & Berridge, of 11 Old Broad Street, E.C. Served as 2nd Lieut., Sussex Yeomanry, attaining the rank of Capt., and as Major Cavalry Machine Gun Corps.

EDWARD CHRISTIAN BURNELL.

Articled to F. W. Scorah, of Sheffield. Enlisted Aug. 1, 1916, as Private, Royal Army Service Corps (M.T.). Served in Mesopotamia Aug. 17 to Aug. 28, 1917, and in India Aug. 1917 to July 1919.

LEIGH MATHIESON BURNETT.

Articled to P. M. Randall, of Southampton. Joined Sept. 20, 1916, as Private, Labour Corps.

EDWARD ALFRED BURNIE.

Admitted Nov. 1901, practising at 59 & 60 Gracechurch Street, London, E.C. Enlisted May 31, 1917, as Driver, Royal Army Service Corps (H.T.). Gazetted 2nd Lieut. 62nd Divisional Train, Royal Army Service Corps, July 29, 1917, promoted Lieut. Jan. 1919. Served in France Aug. 1917 to December 1918, and in Germany Dec. 1918 to April 1919.

SIDNEY JOHNSTONE BURNIE.

Admitted April 1905, practising at Nottingham. Served as Lance-Corporal, Royal Engineers (Signals).

CLIFFORD JOHN FREDERICK BURR.

Admitted July 1910. Managing Clerk with Light & Fulton, of 1 Laurence Pountney Hill, E.C. Mobilised at outbreak of War, as Lieut., 5th Batt. Royal West Kent Regt., and sent to India. Died at Jhansi, India, on May 6, 1915.

SEPTIMUS HENRY BURRA.

Admitted Jan. 1913. Of 2 Raymond Buildings, Gray's Inn, W.C. Served as Lieut., Royal Field Artillery (T.).

CHARLES HEARN OSCAR DUDLEY BURRELL.

Articled to J. A. Davies, of Liverpool. Joined Aug. 15, 1914, as 2nd Lieut., 3rd Batt. Leicestershire Regt., transferred to 1st Batt. June 1915, promoted

Lieut. Sept. 1916, Adjutant Sept. 1916, A/Capt. Feb. 1917. Once mentioned in Dispatches. Awarded the M.C. Served in France and Belgium. Wounded Dec. 1917; gassed.

JOHN STAMP GARTHORNE BURRELL.

Admitted Oct. 1910. Managing Clerk with Potts, Potts & Gardner, of Chester. Joined Universities and Public Schools Batt. Royal Fusiliers Sept. 1914. Commissioned 2nd Lieut. 4th Batt. The Cheshire Regt. Oct. 10, 1914, attached to the Staff of 55th Infantry Brigade June and July 1915, embarked with his Regt. for Gallipoli July 1915. Killed in action at Suvla Bay, Gallipoli, Aug. 9, 1915.

RAYMOND FRANCIS TOPHAM BURRELL.

Articled to J. A. Burrell, of 66 Lincoln's Inn Fields, W.C. Joined Inns of Court O.T.C. Aug. 4, 1914. Gazetted 2nd Lieut. Queen's Own Royal West Kent Regt. Nov. 4, 1914. Served at Home and in France. Killed in action at Loos Sept. 26, 1915.

WILLIAM TEMPLE BURRIDGE.

Admitted Oct. 1904, practised at Wellington, Somerset. Served as Capt., 5th. (Reserve) Batt. Somerset Light Infantry (T).

HAROLD RUTHVEN BURRILL.

Articled to Charles Scriven, of Leeds. Joined Oct. 19, 1914, as Temp. 2nd Lieut., 12th Batt. King's Own Yorkshire Light Infantry, promoted Temp. Lieut. Dec. 1914, Temp. Capt. March 1915, appointed Brigade Machine Gun Officer 93rd Infantry Brigade April 1915, transferred to General List June 1915, transferred to Machine Gun Corps July 1916, Temp. Major July 1916, appointed Divisional Machine Gun Officer 28th Division Feb. 1918. Once mentioned in Dispatches. Served at Home Oct. 1914 to Nov. 1915, Aug. 1917 to Jan. 1918, in France Nov. and Dec. 1915, April 1916 to July 1917, Egypt Jan. to March 1916, Salonica Feb. to Nov. 1918, Turkey Dec. 1918 to March 1919.

HUMPHREY SANDFORD BURRINGTON.

Admitted June 1911, practised at Bridgwater and Burnham. Served as Private, 6th (Service) Batt. Somerset Light Infantry. Afterwards obtained commission in Somerset Light Infantry and promoted Lieut.

BENJAMIN PALMER BURROUGHS.

Admitted July 1893, practising at Liverpool. Joined March 30, 1915, as Major, Royal Field Artillery, Staff-Capt. June 1916 3rd Army Railheads. Served in France.

ARTHUR CECIL BURROWS.

Articled to H. W. Jelf, of 12 Norfolk Street, Strand, W.C. Served as 2nd Lieut., 9th Batt. Lincolnshire Regt., and attained the rank of Temp. Capt. Awarded the M.C.

JOHN BURROWS.

Admitted April 1915. Member of Davies & Burrows, of Leeds. Joined July 1st, 1915, as 2nd Lieut., 6th Batt. West Yorkshire Regt., promoted Lieut. in 1916 whilst instructing in Machine Gun work; on return from France was Courts-Martial Officer to West Reserve Brigade (T.F.). Served in France 1916. Wounded on Somme on Sept. 3 at Thiepval, and evacuated for gas poisoning.

HOWARD FRANCIS BURT.

Admitted April 1907. Managing Clerk with W. Bishop, Solicitor to L. and S.W. Railway Company, Waterloo Station, S.E. Joined Sept. 23, 1914, as 2nd Lieut., Royal Field Artillery, promoted Lieut. Sept. 1915, Capt. Dec. 1915, A/Major Jan. 1917, Temp. Major April 1918. Twice mentioned in Dispatches. Awarded the M.C. Served continuously in France, Belgium, and Germany from Nov. 1914 to March 1919.

WALTER GEORGE BURT.

Admitted Nov. 1911. Of Barnsley. Served as Private, 28th Batt. County of London Regt. (Artists Rifles), subsequently gazetted 2nd Lieut., 14th Batt. York and Lancaster Regt., promoted Lieut. July 1917.

CECIL BURTON.

Articled to Arthur E. Burton, of 10 Norfolk Street, Strand, W.C. Joined Sept. 22, 1914, as Lance-Corporal, 22nd (Service) Batt. Royal Fusiliers. Gazetted Nov. 15, 1917, 2nd Lieut. 20th Divisional Signal Company, Royal Engineers, i/c 59th Infantry Brigade Signals. Once mentioned in Dispatches. Awarded the M.C. Served at Home, and in France Nov. 1915 to Feb. 1919. Wounded Nov. 13, 1916, at Beaumont Hamel.

CHARLES ERNEST BURTON.

Admitted Feb. 1914. Member of Becke, Green & Stops, of Northampton. Joined June 1915, as Private, Inns of Court O.T.C. Gazetted 2nd Lieut. 2nd Batt. Monmouthshire Regt. (T.F.) Dec. 1915, promoted Lieut. July 1917, A/Capt. and Adjutant attached 24th Denbighshire Yeomanry Batt. Royal Welch Fusiliers Aug. 1918. Served in France May 1916 to March 1917, May to Oct. 1918, at Home March to Oct. 1917, in Palestine Oct. 1917 to May 1918.

EDMUND GERALD BURTON.

Admitted Nov. 1902. Member of Burton & Snell, of Daventry. Served with the Royal Army Service Corps.

GUY PRITCHARD BURTON.

Articled to N. T. Davidson, of 10 & 11 Lime Street, E.C. Joined May 10, 1915, as 2nd Lieut., Royal Army Service Corps, promoted Lieut. Aug. 1916. Served at Gallipoli June to Nov. 1915, at Home Nov. 1915 to Feb. 1917, in France and with the Army of the Rhine Feb. 1917 to Sept. 1919.

RICHARD AMERY BURTON.

Articled to F. J. Poole, of Widnes. Joined Aug. 25, 1914, as Private, 10th (Service) Batt. Royal Fusiliers. Gazetted 2nd Lieut. Rifle Brigade May 1917, promoted Lieut. Dec. 1918. Served in France. Wounded July 15, 1916, Somme (Pozières), and Nov. 1917 at Cambrai, 1st Battle.

EDMOND WILLIAM BURY.

Admitted Dec. 1913. Member of H. E. & W. Bury, of 47 Lincoln's Inn Fields, W.C. Joined 1914, as 2nd Lieut., 11th (Service) Batt. King's Royal

Rifle Corps, promoted Lieut. Feb. 1915, and afterwards to Capt. Served in France. Killed in action at Laventie Dec. 5, 1915.

HAROLD STERNDALE ENTWISLE BURY.

Articled to H. E. Bury, of 47 Lincoln's Inn Fields, W.C. Joined Aug. 1914, as 2nd Lieut., Grenadier Guards. Served in France. Killed in action at Guinchy, Jan. 26, 1915.

HUGH BURY.

Admitted April 1911, practised at Barnsley, Yorks. Joined Aug. 1914, as Private, 2nd King Edward's Horse. Gazetted Lieut. Royal Sussex Regt. Oct. 1914, promoted Capt. March 1915. Served in France. Wounded Sept. 27, and Oct. 1, 1915. Taken prisoner Oct. 3, 1915.

THOMAS OSWELL BURY.

Admitted Nov. 1904. Member of Bury & Bury, of Wrexham. Mobilised Aug. 1914, as Capt., 4th Batt. Royal Welch Fusiliers (T.F.), promoted Major June 1916, Lieut.-Col. March 1918, attached 1/24 Batt. London Regt. April 1917 to March 1918, commanded 1/20 Batt. London Regt. July and Aug. 1918. Once mentioned in Dispatches. Served in France 3 years—remainder of time in England.

GRAHAM SHURMUR BUSH.

Articled to A. W. Taylor, of Bristol. Joined Sept. 29, 1914, as Corporal Dispatch Rider, Royal Engineers. Gazetted 2nd Lieut. Somerset Light Infantry April 7, 1915, transferred to Royal Flying Corps Sept. 1915, promoted Lieut. Royal Air Force Dec. 1916. Served in France. Wounded May 1916.

HERBERT FULFORD BUSH.

Articled to C. S. Tomlinson, of 50 Lincoln's Inn Fields, W.C. Joined Sept. 11, 1914, as Lieut., Royal Army Service Corps, promoted Capt. Feb. 1915, Major June 1916, S.S.O. 25th Division, D.A.D.S. 2nd Army. Once mentioned in Dispatches. Awarded D.S.O. Served in France 1916 to 1918, and at Cologne 1918 and 1919.

HORACE BUSHELL.

Admitted Jan. 1913, practised at York. Joined Sept. 7, 1914, as Private, 21st Batt. Royal Fusiliers. Received commission in Machine Gun Corps Sept. 1916, promoted Lieut. June 1917, and Capt. March 1918. Served in France. Killed in action near Chérisy, Sept. 6, 1918.

FRANK HOWARD BUTCHER.

Admitted Dec. 1910. Managing Clerk with Slaughter & May, of 18 Austin Friars, E.C. Joined Jan. 16, 1917, as Ordinary Seaman, Royal Navy.

OSBORNE ARTHUR BUTCHER.

Admitted April 1904, practising at 30 Coleman Street, E.C. Gazetted Flight Sub-Lieut. Royal Naval Air Service May 17, 1915, promoted Flight Lieut. Oct. 1916, A/Flight Commander Aug. 1917, Flight Commander (confirmed) Dec. 1917, transferred to Royal Air Force as Capt. April 1918, A/Lieut.-Col. May 1918. Awarded the D.S.C. Served at the Dardanelles May 1915 to April 1916, with the Grand Fleet July 1916 to Nov. 1917, and in the Mediterranean Nov. 1917 to March 1919.

ROBERT WHITTAKER BUTCHER.

Admitted June 1909. Member of Butcher & Barlow, of Manchester. Mobilised Aug. 1914, as Lieut., 5th Batt. Lancashire Fusiliers, subsequently promoted Lieut. Once mentioned in Dispatches. Awarded the M.C. Served at Gallipoli. Wounded June 4, 1915.

ALEC WILLIAM BUTLER.

Articled to F. W. Butler, of Horsham. Joined Oct. 1, 1914, as Private, Inns of Court O.T.C. Gazetted Nov. 25, 1914, 2nd Lieut. 4th Batt. Royal Sussex Regt., seconded to Machine Gun Corps May 1916, promoted Lieut. (T.F.) June 1916, Capt. (T.F.) June 1917. Served at Home Oct. 1914 to July 1915, Gallipoli July to Dec. 1915, Egypt and Palestine Dec. 1915 to Jan. 1919.

CLIFFORD HICKS BUTLER.

Admitted June 1908. Assistant Clerk of Peace, Cambridge County. Joined Oct. 1914, as Private, University and Public Schools Batt. Royal Fusiliers. Gazetted 2nd Lieut. 5th Batt. Black Watch Aug. 1915. Served in France. Killed in action at Battle of Arras April 23, 1917.

FRANCIS NOEL BUTLER.

Admitted Dec. 1899. Member of Wilkinson & Butler, of St. Neots, Hunts. Mobilised Aug. 1914, as Lieut.-Col., 5th Batt. Bedfordshire Regt. Served at Home and in France.

ERNEST THOMAS BUTLIN.

Admitted May 1905, practising at Manchester. Joined Aug. 21, 1915, as 2nd Lieut., 7th Batt. Cheshire Regt. (T.F.), afterwards attached to 2nd Batt. Monmouthshire Regt., promoted Lieut. July 1917, A/Capt. Sept. 1918. Served at Home Aug. 1915 to Oct. 1916, in France Oct. 1916 to Oct. 1918.

JOHN ALEC STEUART BUTT.

Articled to A. E. M. Taylor, of 4 Trafalgar Square, W.C. Joined Aug. 28, 1914, as Private, Hon. Artillery Company. Gazetted 2nd Lieut. 7th (Service) Batt. Duke of Cornwall's Light Infantry, and subsequently promoted Capt.

THOMAS GEORGE CECIL BUTT.

Articled to Thomas Brandon, of Manchester. Served as Private, Duke of Lancaster's Imperial Yeomanry.

FRANCIS SAM BUTTER.

Admitted April 1912, practising at Shrewsbury. Joined Aug. 16, 1915, as 2nd Lieut., Royal Army Service Corps, promoted Lieut. Dec. 1915, Capt. Sept. 1916. Awarded the O.B.E. (Military Division). Served in Egypt, Cyprus, and Palestine.

HAROLD BUTTERLEY.

Articled to J. Hewitt, of Barnsley. Served as 2nd Lieut., Barnsley (Service) Batt. York and Lancaster Regt.

JOHN FREDERICK BUTTLE.

Admitted Nov. 1911. Managing Clerk with William Buttle, of 15 Basinghall Street, E.C. Joined Oct. 11, 1916, as Private, Inns of Court O.T.C., promoted Lance-Corporal about Jan. 1917. Served at Home.

THOMAS KERSHAW BUXTON.

Articled to James Chapman, of Manchester. Joined May 21, 1917, as Private, 1st Batt. Herefordshire Regt., appointed Lance-Corporal Dec. 1917, promoted Corporal Feb. 1918 in the 4th (Reserve) Batt. "The King's" (Shropshire Light Infantry). Served at Home.

JOHN BYERS.

Admitted Oct. 1905. Member of Steel, Maitland & Byers, of Sunderland. Served as Private, 2nd (Public Schools) Batt. Royal Fusiliers.

JOHN ROBSON BYERS.

Articled to G. Norman Barker, of Ilkeston, Notts. Joined Jan. 20, 1915, as Cadet. Gazetted 2nd Lieut. 4th Batt. Notts & Derby Regt. (Sherwood Foresters) May 7, 1915, promoted Lieut. Aug. 1917. Served in France. Wounded July 1, 1916.

EDMUND JAMES WIDDRINGTON BYRNE.

Admitted Aug. 1903, practised at 7 Lothbury, E.C. Joined Aug. 4, 1914, as Private, Inns of Court O.T.C. Gazetted Lieut. South Wales Borderers (S.R) Sept. 23, 1914, promoted Capt. May 1915. Served in France Dec. 1914 (wounded), Dardanelles Aug. 1915, Egypt Jan. 1916, France March 1916. Killed in action at Albert, France, April 29, 1916.

FRANCIS BERNARD BYRNE.

Articled to W. B. Thursfield, of Birmingham. Served as Private, 2nd City of Birmingham Batt., and subsequently gazetted 2nd Lieut. 16th (Service) Batt. Royal Warwickshire Regt.

LOUIS FREDERICK BYRNE.

Articled to E. B. Lisle, of Newcastle-on-Tyne. Gazetted 2nd Lieut. Northumberland Fusiliers Nov. 13, 1914. Served at Home and in France. Killed in action in Somme battle July 1, 1916.

CYRIL WEST BYWATERS.

Admitted Dec. 1911. Managing Clerk with Julius H. White, of 40/44 Holborn Viaduct. Enlisted March 1917, as Gunner, Royal Horse Artillery. Gazetted 2nd Lieut. Royal Field Artillery Oct. 1917, promoted Lieut. April 1919. Served in France.

HENRY WILLIAM CADBURY-BROWN.

Admitted July 1906. Of Sarratt, Herts. Served as 2nd Lieut., Royal Army Service Corps, and subsequently attained the rank of Capt.

ALFRED ARMSTRONG CADDICK.

Admitted July 1894. Member of Caddick & Walker, of West Bromwich and Birmingham. Served as Major, 8th Batt. Royal Warwickshire Regt. (T.). Once mentioned in Dispatches. Trained in England from Aug. 1, 1914, went to France in spring of 1915, and remained until killed in action at the Battle of the Somme July 1, 1916.

REGINALD HARRY CADE.
Articled to J. Ogden Hardicker, of Manchester. Joined Aug. 1914, as 2nd Lieut., 7th Batt. Lancashire Fusiliers, and attained the rank of Major. Served in Egypt, Gallipoli, and in France. Twice wounded. Killed in action Oct. 1918.

JOHN ARCHIBALD CAHILL.
Admitted Feb. 1913. Member of Williams & James, of Norfolk House, Strand, W.C. Joined Aug. 1914, as Private, 28th Batt. County of London Regt. (Artists Rifles). Gazetted 2nd Lieut. 2nd Batt. Royal Berkshire Regt. Feb. 14, 1915, promoted Lieut. Oct. 1915, and Capt. Feb. 1916. Once mentioned in Dispatches. Awarded the M.C. Served in France and Flanders. Wounded at Neuve Chapelle in 1915 and on the Somme in July 1916. Killed in action at Zonnebeke, near Ypres, Aug. 16, 1917.

HERBERT PORRITT CAIN.
Admitted Dec. 1903, practised at Ramsbotham. Joined Oct. 10, 1914, as 2nd Lieut., 5th Batt. East Lancashire Regt., promoted Temp. Lieut. Jan. 1915, Permanent Lieut. Aug. 1917, Temp. Capt. May 1915, Permanent Capt. Sept. 1917. Served at Home 1914, 1915, and 1916, and in France 1917, 1918.

HARRY CALDECUTT.
Admitted Dec. 1905. Managing Clerk with Sedgley, Caldecutt & Co., of Knutsford, Cheshire. Mobilised, as Capt., 5th Batt. Cheshire Regt. Aug. 1914. Served in France Feb. to Sept. 1915 and March 1916 to July 1918.

JOHN LINDOW CALDERWOOD.
Admitted Nov. 1912. Member of Townsend, Wood & Calderwood, of Swindon. Served as 2nd Lieut., 15th Batt. King's Liverpool Regt., and attained the rank of Capt. Mentioned in Dispatches.

JOHN CALLAWAY.
Admitted Feb. 1885, practising at Westbury, Wilts. Joined Sept. 1914, as Capt., 2/4 Batt. Wiltshire Regt., went to India Dec. 1914, and in March 1918 appointed A.D.J.A.G. Southern Command, Poona, India. Served in India practically all the time.

LAURENCE FREDERICK CALLINGHAM.
Admitted Feb. 1913, practising at 1 New Square, Lincoln's Inn, W.C. Enlisted Aug. 5, 1914, as Private, 28th Batt. County of London Regt. (Artists Rifles), promoted Lance-Corporal April 1915 (in France). Obtained commission as Sub-Lieut. Royal Naval Division May 1915, attached to Hood Batt. (Gallipoli and France), transferred to Royal Naval Volunteer Reserve, Sea Service, March 1917, promoted Lieut. 1917. Served in France and Belgium Nov. 1914 to May 1915, Gallipoli and Ægean Isles Oct. 1915 to May 1916, France May 1916 to Nov. 1916, Sea Service March 1917 to Jan. 1919. Wounded at capture of Beaucourt by the Royal Naval Division Nov. 13, 1916.

CHARLES WILLIAM CALLIS.
Admitted July 1883. Member of Callis & Woosnam, of Blackpool. Served as Capt., 4th Batt. Loyal North Lancashire Regt. (National Reserve).

JOHN ALBERT FREDERICK CALLIS.

Articled to C. W. Callis, of Blackpool. Served as 2nd Lieut., 4th Batt. Manchester Regt., and attained the rank of Capt.

GEORGE BLAYLOCK CALVERT.

Admitted April 1912. Member of Trevor C. Griffiths & Co., of Blackwood, Mon. Joined Dec. 1916, as Paymaster Sub.-Lieut., Royal Naval Volunteer Reserve, H.M.S. *Pembroke*, served on H.M.S. *Actaeon* Jan. 1917 to May 1919. Served at Home (Harbour Service).

JOSEPH HARRISON CALVERT.

Articled to T. Lamb, of 22 Chancery Lane, W.C. Joined April 1916, as Gunner, Royal Field Artillery (T.F.). Gazetted 2nd Lieut. Royal Field Artillery (S.R.) Jan. 13, 1917, promoted Lieut. July 13, 1918. Once mentioned in Dispatches. Awarded the M.C. Served in France.

REGINALD CULLEN CALVERT.

Admitted Jan. 1911. Member of Calvert & Son, of Leeds. Mobilised Aug. 1914, as Lieut., 7th Batt. West Yorkshire Regt. (Leeds Rifles), and subsequently promoted Capt. Served in France. Wounded in 1915, and invalided home. Rejoined his Unit, and subsequently wounded in July 1916. Died in Casualty Clearing Station July 15, 1916.

ALEXANDER BOSWELL CAMPBELL.

Admitted Jan. 1901, practised at Hastings. Joined Aug. 1914, as Capt., Sussex Yeomanry, attached as Lieut. Royal Sussex Pioneer Batt. Served at Home and in France. Died of wounds received in action in France Sept. 13, 1917.

COLIN CAMPBELL.

Articled to Peregrine Thomas, Town Clerk of Burnley. Joined Sept. 28, 1915, as Sapper, Royal Engineers. Served in German East Africa.

GEORGE LESLIE CAMPBELL.

Admitted Aug. 1906. Member of Caporn & Campbell, of St. Bride's House, Salisbury Square, E.C. Served as Quartermaster-Sergeant, 330th Road Construction Coy., Royal Engineers.

GEORGE RUPERT ALLAWAY CAMPBELL.

Admitted Feb. 1906, practised at 10 Coleman Street, E.C. Served as 2nd Lieut., 22nd Batt. Middlesex Regt., subsequently invalided out of the Army.

WILLIAM EDWARD HARRISON CAMPBELL.

Articled to J. C. Morton, of Sunderland. Joined May 15, 1915, as Cadet, Durham University O.T.C. Gazetted 2nd Lieut. 3/1 West Riding Brigade, Royal Field Artillery (T.), Aug. 17, 1915, promoted Lieut. June 1916. Served at Home, France and Belgium Feb. to May 1917 and Sept. to Nov. 1917, Italy Nov. 1917 to Nov. 1918. Wounded at Zillebeke, Belgium, April 26, 1917.

WILLIAM THOMAS CAMPBELL-JONES.

Admitted Oct. 1906, practising at Haverfordwest. Served as Major, 4th Batt. Welch Regt.

HERBERT WILTON CAMPION.

Articled to H. G. Campion, of 5 Queen Victoria Street, E.C. Joined July 13, 1914, as Midshipman, London Division Royal Naval Volunteer Reserve, promoted Sub.-Lieut. Dec. 1914, Flight Sub.-Lieut. Sept. 1915, Flight Lieut. April 1917, Capt. April 1918. Served in Belgium 1914, France 1915, Coastal Patrol (Pilot flying) 1916 to 1918, France and Belgium 1918 and 1919, Taken prisoner on Oct. 9 and 12, 1914.

WALTER HOWARD CANDLER.

Admitted Dec. 1901, practising at Bognor. Joined Jan. 29, 1915, as Private, 11th Batt. Royal Sussex Regt., promoted Lance-Corporal, Dec. 1915. Served in France March 1916 to Jan. 1917 and Aug. 1917 to April 1918. Wounded March 30, 1918.

FRANK CUTHBERT CANE.

Admitted Feb. 1917. Clerk with Henry Cane, of Brighton. Joined Sept. 25, 1917, as Private, Royal Sussex Regt., transferred to Army Pay Corps Dec. 1917, promoted Corporal Oct. 1918. Served at Home.

WILLIAM JOHN CANTON.

Admitted Dec. 1909, practising at Dowlais. Mobilised Aug. 1914, as Lieut., South Wales Borderers (T.F.), Capt. and Adjutant from Nov. 1914 to end of War. Once mentioned in Dispatches. Served at Home, and in France and Germany.

ERNEST AMPHLETT CAPEL.

Admitted May 1898. Member of Lambe, Carless & Capel, of Hereford. Mobilised Aug. 1914, as Capt., 1st Batt. Herefordshire Regt. (T.F.), promoted Major June 1916. Awarded the M.C. and T.D. Served at Home 1914, Gallipoli 1915, Egypt and Palestine 1916, 1917, 1918. Wounded in Suvla Bay landing Aug. 9, 1915.

GEOFFREY NOEL CAPNER.

Admitted Feb. 1906. Managing Clerk with Slater & Co., of Darlaston. Joined Aug. 6, 1915, as 2nd Lieut., 5th Batt. South Staffordshire Regt., promoted Lieut. May 1917. Served in France 1916, 1917, 1918.

EDWARD ORFORD CAPON.

Admitted Dec. 1897. Member of Capon & Elliott Smith, of 29 Bedford Row, W.C. Served as Lieut., 73rd Protection Coy., Royal Defence Corps.

JOHN VICTOR CARD.

Admitted Aug. 1911. Managing Clerk with Wm. G. Card, of 11 Milk Street Buildings, Cheapside, E.C. Enlisted Sept. 1914, as Private, Grenadier Guards. Subsequently commissioned and attained the rank of Capt. in East Surrey Regt. Awarded the M.C. Served in France, Salonica, East Africa, and Russia. Killed in action near Archangel March 25, 1919.

D'ARCY CARDEN.

Articled to Herbert Carden, of Brighton. Joined Dec. 1914, as Lieut., 2nd Home Counties Brigade Royal Field Artillery, promoted to Capt. Jan. 1916 and Major Nov. 1918. Served at Home 1914 to April 1917, Palestine April 1917 to May 1918, France May to Dec. 1918.

PHILIP SIDNEY CARDEN.

Admitted Nov. 1901. Member of Cardens, of Brighton. Mobilised Aug. 4, 1914, as Sergeant, Sussex Yeomanry. Gazetted 2nd Lieut. Royal Army Service Corps (T.F.) Sept. 1914, promoted Lieut. Dec. 1914, Capt. Aug. 1915. Twice mentioned in Dispatches. Served in France from Dec. 1914 to Feb. 1919.

CECIL DACRE CARDER.

Admitted Feb. 1906. Member of Carder & Carder, of Dover. Mobilised Aug. 1914, as Major, 1st Kent Battery Royal Field Artillery (3rd Home Counties Brigade). Once mentioned in Dispatches. Served in India 1914, Mesopotamia 1916 to 1919.

HENRY CARDWELL.

Admitted Dec. 1914. Solicitor with Tatham, Worthington & Co., of Manchester. Joined Aug. 1915, as Cadet, Manchester University O.T.C. Gazetted 2nd Lieut. Lancashire Fusiliers Oct. 1915, promoted Lieut. July 1917. Wounded at Arras May 3, 1917. Discharged on account of wounds received on active service Feb. 1918.

ARCHIBALD LINDSAY CARELESS.

Admitted July 1896. Member of E. P. & A. L. Careless, of Llandrindod Wells. Served as Major, Brecknockshire Batt. South Wales Borderers (T.).

NIGEL EDWARD CAREY.

Admitted Aug. 1902, practising at 5 Verulam Buildings, Gray's Inn, W.C. Mobilised Aug. 1914, as Corporal, Inns of Court O.T.C. Gazetted 2nd Lieut. The Rifle Brigade Sept. 1914, promoted Lieut. June 1915. Served in France and at Home.

WILFRID TOWNSHEND CARLESS.

Admitted March 1897. Member of Lambe, Carless & Son, of Hereford. Mobilised Aug. 1914, as Major, 1st Batt. Herefordshire Regt. Served at Home and at Gallipoli. Present at Suvla Bay landing Aug. 1915. Missing in Gallipoli as from Aug. 12, 1915, subsequently presumed by War Office to have been killed on that day.

JOHN ARTHUR CARLILE.

Articled to Arthur Atkinson, of Folkestone. Joined Oct. 1914, as Private, Inns of Court O.T.C. Gazetted 2nd Lieut. 18th Batt. Notts & Derby Regt. (Sherwood Foresters), promoted Capt. 7th Batt. Leicestershire Regt., attached to 7th Batt. Essex Regt., appointed A/Staff-Capt. Once mentioned in Dispatches. Served in France. Wounded at Somme (Cambrai Wood). Died from effects Dec. 25, 1919.

WILLIAM HOOTON CARLILE.

Admitted Dec. 1913. Managing Clerk with Frank Allen, of Doncaster. Joined May 21, 1917, as Private, Royal Army Veterinary Corps, promoted Corporal. Served at Home.

HENRY BARRY CARLISLE.

Articled to E. J. Carlisle, of Manchester. Joined Oct. 6, 1914, as 2nd Lieut., 2/6 Batt. Lancashire Fusiliers, promoted Lieut. Jan. 1916, Capt. June 1916, Major Sept. 1918. Seconded to Machine Gun Corps March 1916. Served at

Home Oct. 1914 to Aug. 1915, Gallipoli Aug. to Dec. 1915, Egypt Dec. 1915 to Feb. 1917, France Feb. 1917 to June 1918, Home June 1918 to Jan. 1919.

THOMAS TONKIN CARLYON.

Articled to E. L. Carlyon, of Truro. Joined Sept. 4, 1916, as Private, 1/7 Batt. Devonshire Regt. Gazetted 2nd Lieut. Cornwall Royal Garrison Artillery (T.) Dec. 24, 1917. Served in France. Killed in action June 28, 1918.

PHILIP WILLIAM POOLE CARLYON-BRITTON.

Admitted March 1886. Member of Upton, Britton & Lumb, of 43 Bedford Square, W.C. Gazetted Dec. 9, 1914, as Major, 14th Batt. West Yorkshire Regt., second in command of 12th Batt. West Yorkshire Regt. Granted honorary rank of Major in the Army Sept. 1918. Served at Home (with occasional visits to France) from Dec. 1914 to April 1916, and in Belgium and France from April 1916 to Sept. 1918.

RAYMOND CARLYON CARLYON-BRITTON.

Articled to Mellor Lumb, of 43 Bedford Square, W.C. 1. Director of Motor Department of the British Committee of the French Red Cross 1915 to Aug. 1918, Sub.-Lieut. Royal Naval Volunteer Reserve (Hydrophone Service) Aug. 1918 until Nov. 18, 1918, Mine-sweeping in Black Sea, Nov. 18 to Dec. 12, 1918, attached to Staff of Admiral the Hon. Sir Arthur Somerset Gough-Calthorpe, K.C.B., K.C.M.G., &c., British High Commissioner, Constantinople, and lent to Foreign Office for such service, Dec. 12, 1918, to April 1919. King's Messenger from Constantinople to Paris Conference and Foreign Office, London, April 1919.

WILLIAM EDWIN BLAKE CARN.

Articled to W. G. Carn, of Kingston-on-Thames. Mobilised Aug. 1914, as Trooper, 1st County of London Yeomanry (Middlesex Hussars). Gazetted 2nd Lieut. 10th (Scottish) T.F. (Res.) Batt. King's Liverpool Regt. March 21, 1917, A/Capt. May to Sept. 1918 whilst Assistant Commandant to Western Command Anti-Gas School, Substantive Lieut. Sept. 1918. Served at Home, Egypt, Gallipoli, Dublin, France, and Belgium.

THOMAS MANSEL NICHOL CARNE.

Articled to J. W. Botsford, of Cardiff. Served as 2nd Lieut., 16th (Cardiff City) Batt. The Welch Regt.

WILLIAM BIRCH CARNLEY.

Admitted Dec. 1909. Member of Culross & Co., of 13 Old Cavendish Street, W. Joined Feb. 14, 1916, as Private, Inns of Court O.T.C. Gazetted 2nd Lieut. Royal Army Ordnance Department July 18, 1916, promoted Lieut. Oct. 1916, Lieut. Royal Flying Corps Jan. 1917, Capt. July 1917. Served at Home.

CHARLES ERNEST CARPENTER.

Articled to T. A. Needham, of Manchester. Joined Nov. 15, 1916, as Private, in Royal Army Service Corps, on the Adjutant-General's Branch of the Staff at General Headquarters France and Italy, promoted A/Sergeant July 1918, and Probationer for commission in the Army Pay Department up to date of Armistice. Served at Home Nov. to Dec. 1916, France Dec. 1916 to Nov. 1917, Italy Nov. 1917 to March 1918.

FRED HAROLD CARPENTER.

Admitted May 1916, practising at Brighton. Joined July 17, 1916, as Private, 1/6 Batt. Royal Sussex Regt. Gazetted 2nd Lieut. 4th (Reserve) Batt. Royal Sussex Regt. March 1, 1917, Adjutant Brigade Signal School, Southborough, Aug. 1917, promoted Lieut. Sept. 1, 1918. Served in France. Gassed Oct. 1918, and invalided Home.

JAMES SIDNEY CARPENTER.

Admitted July 1899, practising at Bath. Joined 1916 as 2nd Lieut., Royal Army Ordnance Corps, subsequently promoted Lieut. Served at Home, Southern and Eastern Commands.

GEORGE ARTHUR BUXTON CARR.

Admitted Aug. 1889. Member of C. R. Randall & Son, of 4 Copthall Buildings, E.C. Mobilised Aug. 5, 1914, as Major, 1/24 Batt. London Regt. (The Queen's), promoted to Substantive Lieut.-Col. in same Regt. May 1916. Placed on Territorial Force Reserve Sept. 1918. Once mentioned in Dispatches. Awarded D.S.O. and T.D. Served at Home Aug. 1914 to March 1915, France March 1915 to July 1917, Home July 1917 to Sept. 1918. Slightly wounded Dec. 24, 1916.

HERBERT GEORGE CARR CARR-ELLISON.

Admitted Nov. 1899. Member of Leadbitter & Harvey, of Newcastle-upon-Tyne. Joined Aug. 4, 1914, as Capt., Northumberland Hussars Yeomanry, attached 21st (E. of I.) Lancers March 1917 to Oct. 1919, Staff-Capt. North-West Frontier Force Headquarters May to Sept. 1919. Served at Home Aug. 1914 to Jan. 1917, India Jan. 1917 to Nov. 1919, Afghan Frontier May to Sept. 1919.

HAROLD CARRINGTON.

Admitted Feb. 1912. Member of Carrington & Leonard, of Barnsley. Served as 2nd Lieut., 5th Batt. Durham Light Infantry.

JOHN CARRINGTON.

Admitted Feb. 1883. Member of Carrington & Leonard, of Barnsley. Joined Sept. 5, 1916, as Major, Royal Engineers. Served as Major and O.C. 228th Field Coy. Royal Engineers.

ROBERT CARRUTHERS.

Admitted Jan. 1881, practising at Liverpool. Served as Lieut.-Col., Recruiting Staff 8th Regimental District.

THOMAS WRIGHT CARSON.

Admitted Dec. 1907, practised at Llanelly. Gazetted 2nd Lieut. 6th Batt. Duke of Wellington's Own West Riding Regt. shortly after the outbreak of the War. Reported missing on Dec 27, 1915, and official news of his death was received from Germany.

CHARLES COPLESTONE CARTER.

Articled to Grylls & Cowland, of Launceston. Served as Private, 2nd Public Schools Batt. Royal Fusiliers.

HARRY OSBORNE CARTER.

Admitted Dec. 1908, practising at 16 Victoria Street, Westminster, S.W. Joined Feb. 1915, as 2nd Lieut., 8th Batt. Middlesex Regt., promoted Capt. 1918. Once mentioned in Dispatches. Served in Gibraltar, Egypt, and England.

HUBERT CARTER.

Admitted Feb. 1909, practising at Bath. Served as Lieut., 8th Batt. Somerset Light Infantry.

ISIDORE ONSLOW GOODRICHE CARTER.

Admitted Oct. 1908. Of 28 Cathcart Hill, N. 19. Served as Pay Sub-Lieut., Royal Naval Volunteer Reserve, on H.M.S. *Iron Duke*.

JOHN FREDERICK HEATHCOTE CARTER.

Admitted March 1908. Member of Frank Simmonds & Carters, of Broad Street House, E.C. Joined Dec. 29, 1915, as Private, Inns of Court, O.T.C. Subsequently gazetted Lieut. King's Shropshire Light Infantry.

ROBERT CHARLES HEATHCOTE CARTER.

Admitted March 1908. Member of Frank Simmonds & Carters, of Broad Street House, E.C. Served as Lieut., 4th Batt. King's Shropshire Light Infantry.

RONALD NORMAN CARTER.

Articled to H. W. Carter, of 61 Carey Street, Lincoln's Inn, W.C. Joined April 7, 1915, as Cadet, Inns of Court O.T.C. Gazetted 2nd Lieut. 3rd Batt. Dorset Regt. July 28, 1915, transferred to the Royal Flying Corps June 1916, promoted Lieut. Dec. 1917. Served in France. Shot down and taken prisoner while flying on Sept. 20, 1916, in France. Repatriated from Germany on Dec. 18, 1918.

THOMAS HEALEY HUNTON CARTER.

Admitted Nov. 1903, practising at Newhaven & Seaford. Joined Nov. 16, 1914, 5th Batt. Royal Warwickshire Regt., and attained the rank of A/Major Aug. 1916. Twice mentioned in Dispatches. Awarded the D.S.O. Served at Home and in France. Invalided owing to illness in Oct. 1916.

DAVID JAMES CARTWRIGHT.

Articled to J. W. Piercey, of Huddersfield. Joined April 11, 1916, as Private, 3rd Batt. West Riding Regt., transferred to Home Service Employment Coy. during early part of 1917 on account of Medical Disability, and promoted Corporal. Served at Home.

FREDERICK HAWKSLEY TALBOT CARTWRIGHT.

Admitted March 1903. Assistant Solicitor to the County Council of the West Riding of Yorkshire, County Hall, Wakefield. Mobilised Aug. 1914, as Lieut., 1/4 Batt. King's Own Yorkshire Light Infantry, promoted Capt. 1914, Major 1918. Served in France 1915 and 1917, during which time he was twice invalided home.

HENRY JOSEPH CARTWRIGHT.

Articled to A. H. Bikker, of 3 New Court, W.C. Served as 2nd Lieut., 10th Batt. Bedfordshire Regt.

HUBERT SCOTT CARTWRIGHT.

Admitted June 1901. Member of Roy & Cartwright, of 4 Brick Court, Temple, E.C. Mobilised Aug. 1914, as Capt., 14th Batt. County of London Regt. (London Scottish), promoted Temp. Major Oct. 1915, Major (Substantive) May 1916. Awarded T.D. and Croix de Guerre (French). Served in France and Belgium Sept. to Dec. 1914, France June to Nov. 1916, Salonica Nov. to Dec. 1916. Wounded at Givenchy Dec. 23, 1914.

VINCENT HENRY CARTWRIGHT.

Admitted Oct. 1908. Member of Freeth, Rawson & Cartwright, of Nottingham. Joined Sept. 20, 1914, as 2nd Lieut., Royal Marine Artillery, promoted Lieut. Jan. 1915, Capt. July 1915, Major June 1917. Twice mentioned in Dispatches. Awarded the D.S.O. and French Croix de Guerre. Served in France.

ROBERT JOHNSTON CARUTHERS-LITTLE.

Admitted Aug. 1910. Member of Edward Palling Little, of Stroud, Glos. Mobilised Aug. 4, 1914, as Capt., Gloucestershire Regt., promoted Major June 1916, 4th (Reserve) Batt. Gloucestershire Regt. Nov. 1916 to March 1917, 1st Garrison Batt. Northamptonshire Regt. May to Nov. 1917, 1/4 Northampton Regt. Nov. 1917 to July 1919. Once mentioned in Dispatches. Served at Home Aug. 1914 to Mar. 1915, France Mar. 1915 to July 1916, Home July 1916 to Mar. 1917, Egypt April to Nov. 1917, Palestine and Egypt Nov. 1917 to July 1919. Wounded July 23, 1916. Torpedoed *Arcadian* April 1917.

ALFRED CEDRIC CARVER.

Articled to R. A. Wright, of Manchester. Served as 2nd Lieut., 14th Batt. Cheshire Regt.

FRANK TOM CARVER.

Admitted Dec. 1899. Member of David Allen & Carver, of Hereford. Mobilised Aug. 5, 1914, as 2nd Lieut., 1st Batt. Herefordshire Regt. (T.F.), promoted Capt. and Adjutant Sept. 1914, appointed Major on Headquarters Staff of the Western Command Depôt, Heaton Park, June 1916, appointed to Headquarters Staff of Navy and Army Canteen Board May 1917, appointed D.A.Q.M.G. Headquarters, Western Command, Chester, from May 1918 to Jan. 1920, with rank of Major. Injured through a horse accident while training in Aug. 1915 and found unfit for General Service.

GILBERT SQUAREY CARVER.

Admitted April 1903. Of Singapore. Served as 2nd Lieut., 14th Batt. Cheshire Regt.

WALTER LIONEL CARVER.

Admitted July 1907. Managing Clerk with Baker & Lillington, of Weston-super-Mare. Joined Aug. 28, 1914, as 2nd Lieut., 1st Batt. Herefordshire Regt. (T.), promoted Lieut. Jan. 1915, Capt. Oct. 1915. Served at Suvla Bay Aug. to Nov. 1915, and with Egyptian E.F. 1916 and 1917. Killed in action at Khuweilyeh Nov. 6, 1917.

LAUNCELOT SULYARDE ROBERT CARY.

Articled to W. J. Sloan, of Bristol. Served as 2nd Lieut., Devonshire Regt. Killed in action July 20, 1916.

DONALD ALBERT STEVENSON CASH.

Articled to A. J. Cash, of Derby. Joined April 10, 1916, as Private, 4th Batt. Royal Scottish Fusiliers, promoted Corporal Feb. 1917. Gazetted 2nd Lieut. 5th Batt. Notts and Derby Regt. (Sherwood Foresters) June 26, 1918. Served in France 1917.

CHARLES PARKINSON CASS.

Admitted Nov. 1901, practising at Keighley, Yorks. Mobilised Aug. 1914, as Major, 6th Batt. West Riding Regt. Demobilised Nov. 15, 1918, to be loaned to Ministry of National Service. Awarded the T.D. Served in France and at Home.

DEMETRIUS JOHN CASSAVETTI.

Admitted Nov. 1909. Member of Orr Dignam & Co., of Finsbury House, Blomfield Street, E.C. Joined July 1, 1917, as 2nd Lieut., General List, promoted Lieut. R.T.D. Mediterranean Lines of Communication Staff July 1917. Served in France and Mediterranean Lines of Communication.

CHARLES ERNEST CASTELLAN.

Admitted April 1900. Member of Hennen, Edgelow & Castellan, of Quality Court, Chancery Lane, W.C. Served as Major, 2nd East Anglian Brigade Royal Field Artillery.

LEON BENHAM CASTELLO.

Admitted May 1905. Member of Bull & Bull, of 3 Stone Buildings, Lincoln's Inn, W.C. Joined May 3, 1915, as 2nd Lieut., 5th Batt. Royal Irish Rifles, seconded Machine Gun Corps Nov. 1915, seconded Intelligence Corps June 1916. Once mentioned in Dispatches. Awarded the Legion of Honour and Croix de Guerre. Served in France.

BASIL LANGFORD HARVE CASTLE.

Articled to J. Ballard of Bournemouth. Served with the Royal Flying Corps. Afterwards obtained commission in Royal Army Service Corps and attained the rank of Lieut.

CLAUDE MONTAGU CASTLE.

Admitted Jan. 1903, practising at 4 Bishopsgate, E.C. Joined Dec. 23, 1914, as Capt., Royal Irish Rifles (Ulster Division). Awarded the M.C.

GODFREY ERNEST CASTLE

Admitted Feb. 1910. Member of Whitley & Co., of Liverpool. Served as Lieut., 3rd West Lancashire Brigade, Royal Field Artillery, and attained the rank of Capt. Mentioned in Dispatches and awarded the M.C.

TREVOR CASTLE.

Admitted July 1903, practising at 79 Lombard Street, E.C. Served as Capt., 6th (Reserve) Batt. East Surrey Regt.

WILLIAM HENRY CASTLE.

Admitted May 1903, practising at 44 Pembroke Road, Kensington, W. Joined Sept. 2, 1914, as Private, 19th (Service) Batt. Royal Fusiliers. Gazetted 2nd Lieut. 7th Batt. Royal Fusiliers May 18, 1915, transferred Royal Army Service Corps Sept. 1917, promoted Lieut. March 1919. Served in Greek Macedonia and Serbia Jan. 1916 to Jan. 1919.

THOMAS HILL CASWELL.

Admitted Nov. 1901. Managing Clerk with Hunt & Hunt, of 14 Old Jewry Chambers, Cheapside, E.C. Joined Nov. 11, 1914, as Lieut., in Royal Army Service Corps, promoted Capt. Nov. 1915. Served in France March 1915 to Nov. 1918. Invalided home in Nov. 1918 suffering from rheumatism.

HAROLD ARMAND CATEAUX.

Admitted March 1906, practised at Richmond, Surrey. Served as Private, Royal Army Medical Corps.

WALTER NOEL CATLOW.

Articled to B. W. Edwards, of Leicester. Joined Oct. 10, 1914, as 2nd Lieut., 46th (N.M.) Divisional Train Royal Army Service Corps (T.F.), promoted A/Lieut. Oct. 1915, confirmed in rank June 1916, seconded to London Regt. March 1918, attached 8th (Reserve) London Regt. Jan. to May 1918, attached 1/21 London Regt. (1st Surrey Rifles) May 1918, promoted A/Capt. and Adjutant Sept. 1918 to June 1919. Once mentioned in Dispatches. Served in France Feb. 1915 to Nov. 1917 and May 1918 to May 1919.

CHARLES BURNEY CATNACH.

Articled to A. L. Bird, of Newcastle-upon-Tyne. Joined May 6, 1915, as 2nd Lieut., 4th Batt. Northumberland Fusiliers (T.F.), transferred to Royal Flying Corps July 1916, gazetted a Flying Officer (Observer) Jan. 1917, promoted Lieut. Jan. 1917, gazetted Flying Officer (Pilot) Dec. 1917. Served various periods at Home, in France Sept. 1916 to April 1917, in Salonica Jan. 1918 to March 1919.

GLANVILL RICHARD CATTARNS.

Admitted Dec. 1908. Member of Cattarns & Cattarns, of Leadenhall Street, E.C. Joined Aug. 1914, as 2nd Lieut., South Lancashire Regt., promoted Lieut. and Capt. 1915, A/Major 1916. Twice mentioned in Dispatches. Awarded the M.C. Served at Gallipoli and Mesopotamia. Killed in action Feb. 12, 1917.

EUSTACE SHIPSTONE CATTLE.

Articled to Frederic Cattle, of Ilkeston. Joined Aug. 1914, as 2nd Lieut., 4th Batt. York and Lancaster Regt., promoted Lieut. 1915. Awarded the M.C. Served in France. Reported missing, believed killed, near Thiepval July 7, 1916.

CHARLES STEWART CAUTHERLEY.

Admitted Nov. 1903. Managing Clerk with Druces & Attlee, of 10 Billiter Square, E.C. Mobilised Aug. 1914, as Private, Hon. Artillery Company, and attained the rank of Company Sergeant-Major. Subsequently gazetted Lieut. Hertfordshire Regt. Served in France and Flanders Sept. 1914 to Oct. 1915 and April 1916 to April 1918. Suffered from shell shock Sept. 1916. Killed in action at Voormezeele, near Kemmel, April 26, 1918.

STEPHEN AYLWIN CAVE.

Admitted Feb. 1904, practising at Wellington College, Berks. Joined July 11, 1917, as Private, Royal Berkshire Regt., transferred to Army Pay Corps Sept. 1917. Discharged April 4, 1918. Served at Home.

WILLIAM THOMAS CHARLES CAVE.

Admitted Dec, 1907. Member of E. F. Turner & Sons, of 115 Leadenhall Street, E.C. Served as 2nd Lieut., Inns of Court O.T.C., and attained the rank of Capt.

NORMAN CAYLEY.

Admitted Nov. 1899. Managing Clerk with Waterhouse & Co., of 10/12 Bishopsgate, E.C. Joined Aug. 1915, as 2nd Lieut., Royal Garrison Artillery, promoted Lieut. July 1917, A/Capt. Sept. 1917 to April 1918, with 24th Heavy Battery Royal Garrison Artillery Dec. 1915, with the Field Survey Company (Observation Branch) in command of an Observation Group July 1916 to April 1918, A.D.C. to G.O.C. 29th Division April 1918 to March 1919. Served in Belgium, France, and Germany Dec. 1915 to March 1919.

CHARLES ROBERT CHADWICK.

Admitted Nov. 1912. Member of Arnold Chadwick, Fooks & Co., of 60 Carey Street, Lincoln's Inn, W.C. Joined Aug. 1914, as Private, 18th Batt. Royal Fusiliers (1st Public School Batt.). Gazetted 2nd Lieut. 3rd Batt. The Queen's Own (Royal West Kent) Regt. May 9, 1915, promoted Lieut. July 1917. Served with Mesopotamian Expeditionary Force.

HAROLD CHADWICK.

Articled to William Johnston, of Stockport. Joined Dec. 12, 1914, as Private, 6th (Reserve) Batt. Cheshire Regt., and attained the rank of Regimental Quartermaster-Sergeant. Gazetted 2nd Lieut. Durham Light Infantry Oct. 30, 1917, and posted to 19th Batt. Jan. 1918, appointed Batt. Education Officer Nov. 1918. Awarded the M.C. Served at Home Dec. 1914 to Jan. 1918 and in Belgium and France Jan. 1918 to Feb. 1919. Wounded slightly Nov. 4, 1918.

HERBERT FRANCIS CHADWICK.

Admitted April 1896. Member of Chadwick, Son & Nicholson, of Dewsbury. Served as Capt., 12th (Service) Batt. King's Own Yorkshire Light Infantry (Miners).

JOHN CHADWICK.

Articled to Louis Chadwick, of 60 Carey Street, Lincoln's Inn, W.C. Joined Sept. 2, 1914, as Private, 18th Service (1st P.S.) Batt. Royal Fusiliers. Gazetted 2nd Lieut. 5th Batt. (Special Reserve) Royal Dublin Fusiliers May 23, 1915, promoted Lieut. July 1917. Served at Home Sept. 1914 to May 1916 and July 1916 to June 1918, and in France May to July 1916 and July 1918 to Jan. 1919. Wounded July 1, 1916.

LEONARD ARTHUR CHADWICK.

Articled to J. P. Chadwick, of 67 Tooley Street, S.E. Mobilised Aug. 1914, as Gunner, "B" Battery, Hon. Artillery Company, and attained the rank of Sergeant. Gazetted 2nd Lieut. Royal Field Artillery Dec. 1915, promoted Lieut. Sept. 1917, and Capt. Oct. 1918. Awarded the M.C. Served at Home Aug. 1914 to April 1915, Egypt and Aden April to Dec. 1915, France May 1916 to Nov. 1918, Germany Dec. 1918 to Oct. 1919. Wounded at Ypres Oct. 10, 1917, and Oct. 30, 1917, and at Cambrai Oct. 8, 1918.

HENRY CECIL CHALKER.

Admitted Dec. 1910. Member of Stewart & Chalker, of Wakefield. Mobilised Aug. 1914, as Capt., 4th Batt. King's Own Yorkshire Light Infantry. Invalided May 3, 1918. Once in List of Mentions by Secretary of State for War Feb. 1917. Served at Home.

OSCAR BERNARD CHALLENOR.

Articled to Bromley Challenor, of Abingdon, Berks. Mobilised Aug. 1914, as Lieut., 1/4 Batt. Royal Berkshire Regt. (T.F.), promoted Capt. Aug. 1916. Once mentioned in Dispatches. Awarded the M.C. Served in France March 1915 to Nov. 1917, and in Italy Nov. 1917 to March 1919. Wounded in France Aug. 1915, and in Italy Sept. 1918.

WILLIAM FRANCIS CHALLINOR.

Admitted Oct. 1906. Member of Challinors & Shaw, of Leek, Staffs. Mobilised Aug. 1914, as Major, 2nd North Midland Brigade, Royal Field Artillery, Temp. Lieut.-Colonel to command 46th Divisional Ammunition Column Feb. 1916. Once mentioned in Dispatches. Awarded the D.S.O. Served in France Feb. 1915 to Oct. 1916. Discharged medically unfit Dec. 1917.

ARTHUR BRACEBRIDGE CHALLIS.

Admitted June 1897. Member of Hayward, Smith & Challis, of Rochester. Joined 1914, as 2nd Lieut., Heavy Battery Home Counties (Kent) Royal Garrison Artillery, subsequently promoted Major. Killed in action Sept. 21, 1918.

WILLIAM GUY FAWCETT CHALLIS.

Articled to J. F. Guillaume, of Bournemouth and London. Joined the 1st Sportsman's Batt. as Private in Oct. 1914. Received his commission as 2nd Lieut. 3rd Batt. Hampshire Regt. May 1915, promoted Lieut. July 1916. Served at Home and in Flanders. Killed in action Ploegsteert July 13, 1916.

NORMAN GRANT CHALMERS-HUNT.

Admitted Aug. 1905, practising at Ware. Joined Sept. 1914, as Private, Herts National Reserve. Gazetted 2nd Lieut. Royal Army Service Corps (M.T.) June 28, 1915, promoted Lieut. Feb. 1916, Capt. Oct. 1918. Served in France Aug., Sept., and Oct. 1915, and Aug. 1917 to Sept. 1918.

FRANCIS WALTER CHAMBERLAIN.

Admitted Dec. 1913. Member of Chamberlain & Co., of 1 Stone Buildings, Lincoln's Inn, W.C. Joined Oct. 1, 1914, as Trooper, Public Schools Mounted Corps. Gazetted 2nd Lieut. Royal Field Artillery May 29, 1915, promoted Lieut. July 1916. Served in France. Wounded July 12, 1917, and April 18, 1918.

HENRY SEYMOUR CHAMBERLAIN.

Admitted June 1906, practising at Bognor. Joined Nov. 9, 1914, as Lieut., Royal Army Service Corps, promoted Capt. Aug. 1915, Major Feb. 1917. Served in Dublin Nov. 1914 to Feb. 1915, France Feb. 1915 to Sept. 1917, Egypt Nov. 1917 to Jan. 1919.

NEVILLE GRAHAME CHAMBERLAIN.

Articled to T. M. Pritchard, of Painters' Hall, E.C. Mobilised Aug. 1914, as Trooper, Inns of Court O.T.C. Commissioned Oct. 10, 1914, in London Brigade Royal Garrison Artillery (T.F.), promoted Lieut. Nov. 1915, A/Capt. Nov. 1917. Once mentioned in Dispatches. Served in France and Belgium March 1915 to Oct. 1918.

EDWARD PERCY CHAMBERS.

Admitted Feb. 1893. Member of Chambers & Chambers, of Brighouse, Yorks. Mobilised Aug. 1914, as Major, 1/4 Batt. Duke of Wellington's (West Riding) Regt., promoted Lieut.-Col. May 1915, transferred to Reserve June 11, 1918, with rank of Major. Awarded Chevalier du Mérite Agricole. Served in France and Belgium April 1915 to March 1918.

KENNETH WILLIAM GLENDOWER MATHER CHAMBERS.

Admitted Nov. 1911. Member of Chambers & Chambers, of Denton, Gorton, and Ashton-under-Lyne. Joined Sept. 27, 1917, as Private, Inns of Court O.T.C. Commissioned May 13, 1918, as 2nd Lieut. Royal Army Service Corps (M.T.). Served in France, Italy, Greece, Macedonia, Serbia, Bulgaria, and Hungary, with British, French, and Serbian Armies.

LESLIE BERT CHAMBERS.

Articled to Edmund Huntsman, of Nottingham. Gazetted July 10, 1915, 2nd Lieut. 3rd Batt. York and Lancaster Regt., promoted Lieut. Feb. 1917, A/Capt. June 1917, transferred as Observer to Royal Flying Corps, Aug. 1917. Once mentioned in Dispatches. Awarded the M.C. and Bar. Served at Home until June 1916, and in France and Belgium until April 1918. Wounded Feb. 1917 at Hooge, air crash in France April 1918.

PHILIP HENRY CHAMPERNOWNE.

Admitted Oct. 1886. Member of Wigan, Champernowne & Prescott, of Norfolk House, Victoria Embankment, W.C. Served as Major, 4th Batt. Royal Berkshire Regt.

ALBERT EDWARD GURNEY CHAMPION.

Admitted May 1896. Member of Lefroy & Champion, of Bournemouth. Joined Sept. 2, 1914, as Lieut., Royal Field Artillery, promoted A/Capt. March 1917, Substantive Capt. Nov. 1917. Served nearly 3 years in France, remainder of service in England. Accidentally wounded March 1917.

BERNARD CHAMPNESS.

Admitted May 1913. Member of W. H. Champness & Co., of 14 Serjeant's Inn, E.C. Joined Nov. 10, 1914, as Private, 28th Batt. County of London Regt. (Artists Rifles). Nominated for commission Sept. 6, 1915, but subsequently transferred to 15th Batt. London Regt. (Kensingtons) for immediate service 1916. Went to France June 1916 as Private, and killed before admission to Officer Cadet unit. Killed in action near Neuville St. Vaast July 27, 1916. Buried at Ecoivres Cemetery, near Mont St. Eloi.

JOHN DALRYMPLE CHAMPNEYS.

Articled to R. M. Welsford, of 22 Aldermanbury, E.C. Joined 1914, as Lieut., 6th Batt. Leicestershire Regt. Mortally wounded at Berles-aux-Bois,

France, and captured by Germans Nov. 22, 1915. Died of wounds Nov. 23, 1915. Buried at Monchy.

FRANK MERYON CHANCE.

Articled to Robert Coward, of 30 Mincing Lane, E.C. Joined Aug. 6, 1914, as Private, 21st Batt. County of London Regt. Gazetted 2nd Lieut. 24th Batt. of London Regiment (The Queen's) Dec. 15, 1914. Served in France March to May 1915. Killed in action at Givenchy May 25, 1915.

EDGAR CHARLES CHANCELLOR.

Articled to Sir George H. Radford, of 27 Chancery Lane, W.C. Joined Dec. 20, 1915, as Private, 5th Batt. Royal Fusiliers. Gazetted 2nd Lieut. (Special Reserve) 6th Batt. Rifle Brigade Dec. 19, 1916, promoted Lieut. June 1918. Served in France. Wounded Nov. 30, 1917, near Bellenglise (Somme).

OSBORN ROBERT MOSELEY CHANNER.

Admitted Nov. 1903. Member of Channer & Channer, of Taunton. Served as Major, West Somerset Yeomanry.

ALBERT LACY CHAPMAN.

Admitted June 1913. At time of joining Managing Clerk with Messrs. Winterbotham, Gurney & Co., Solicitors, Cheltenham, now Managing Clerk with Messrs. R. & C. B. Masefield, Ledbury. Joined June 18, 1917, as Private, 3rd Batt. Gloucestershire Regt., transferred to the Labour Corps March 1918 and shortly after promoted A/Sergeant. Served at Salonica.

ALFRED JOHN CHAPMAN

Articled to B. C. Newbold, of Burton-on-Trent. Joined Sept. 1914, as Private, 21st Batt. Royal Fusiliers (Universities and Public Schools). Gazetted 2nd Lieut. Royal Flying Corps 41st Squadron Sept. 5, 1916. Served in France as a Private Nov. 1915 to May 1916 and as Royal Flying Corps Scout Pilot June to Sept. 1917. Killed in aerial fight over the enemy's lines near Cambrai Sept. 18, 1917.

CYRIL EDWARD WORSLEY CHAPMAN..

Articled to Henry Fielding, of Canterbury. Served as 2nd Lieut., Royal Field Artillery, and afterwards promoted Lieut.

HENRY ROBINSON CHAPMAN.

Admitted May 1909. Member of Chapman & Wilkinson, of Leyburn, Yorks. Joined Sept. 1, 1914, as Private, Universities and Public Schools Batt. Commissioned Lieut. 5th Batt. Yorkshire Regt. Sept. 29, 1914, promoted Capt. May 1915. Once mentioned in Dispatches. Served in Belgium, France, and Home.

HORACE CHAPMAN.

Admitted Oct. 1912, practised under style of Dawson & Chapman, at Leeds. Joined Aug, 17, 1916, as 2nd Air Mechanic, 40th Squadron Royal Flying Corps. Went to France Dec. 31, 1916. Died in Souvenir Hospital, St. Omer, France, April 22, 1917.

JAMES TAYLOR CHAPMAN.

Articled to James Chapman, of Manchester. Served as Private, 28th Batt. County of London Regt. (Artists Rifles).

LAWRENCE VAUGHAN CHAPMAN.

Articled to H. F. Cracknell, of 3 Lancaster Place, Strand, W.C. Joined Reserve of Officers after serving in London University O.T.C. Gazetted 2nd Lieut. 6th Batt. The Rifle Brigade Aug. 5, 1914, transferred to 2nd Batt. and left for the front May 1915, promoted Lieut. June 1915. Served in France and Belgium. Killed at Battle of Loos Sept. 25, 1915.

JAMES CHAPMAN-WALKER.

Admitted Dec. 1900. Member of Chapman-Walker & Shephard, of 25 Dover Street, W. Served as Capt., A/Major, Royal Army Service Corps.

AUBREY TORRINGTON CHAPPLE.

Admitted Jan. 1908. Member of Chapple & Son, of 79 Gresham Street, E.C. Joined Sept. 1916, as Private, Royal Army Service Corps (M.T.). Served at Home. Died of spotted fever in Fulham Military Hospital May 3, 1917.

HENRY TORRINGTON CHAPPLE.

Admitted Nov. 1906, practising at 2A Guildhall Chambers, Basinghall Street, E.C. Joined April 16, 1917, as Driver, Royal Army Service Corps (H.T.). Served in England 6 months, France remainder of time.

REGINALD PENDRILL ST. JOHN CHARLES.

Admitted Dec. 1901. Member of H. P. Charles & Son, of Neath, Glam. Joined Jan. 22, 1917, as Private, Inns of Court O.T.C. Gazetted 2nd Lieut. Royal Garrison Artillery (31st Siege Battery) Jan. 6, 1918. Served in France.

CHARLES PERCY CHARLESWORTH.

Admitted Dec. 1889. Member of Charlesworth & Wood, of Skipton. Served as Capt., 6th Batt. Duke of Wellington's West Riding Regt.

JOHN CHARLESWORTH.

Articled to W. W. Gibson, of Newcastle-upon-Tyne. Joined Oct. 5, 1914, as Private, 53rd Field Ambulance Royal Army Medical Corps. Gazetted 2nd Lieut. 5th Batt. Manchester Regt. April 24, 1915, promoted Lieut. June 1916. Once mentioned in Dispatches. Served in Gallipoli Aug. to Dec. 1915, France July 1916 to Oct. 1917, Italy Oct. 1917 to Sept. 1918, France Sept. to Oct. 1818. Wounded near Beaurevoir Oct. 8, 1918.

WILLIAM CHARLESWORTH.

Articled to P. B. Mather, of Chesterfield. Joined Nov. 13, 1915, as Private, Notts and Derby Regt. (Sherwood Foresters). Gazetted 2nd Lieut. in same Regt. Jan. 29, 1916, promoted Lieut. July 1917, Staff-Lieut. General List 1919. Served at Home, France, Belgium, Germany. Wounded at Somme Sept. 29, 1916, and at Passchendaele Sept. 26, 1917.

CHRISTOPHER COLIN CHARLTON.

Admitted April 1910. Managing Clerk with William Bell & Sons, of Sunderland. Joined March 1, 1915, as 2nd Lieut., Royal Field Artillery, subsequently promoted Capt. Awarded the French Croix de Guerre. Served in France Jan. 1916 to Dec. 1918.

ARTHUR EDMUND WEBSTER CHARSLEY.

Admitted Dec. 1887, practising at Beaconsfield, Bucks. Mobilised Aug. 1914, as Capt., 1st Batt. Bucks Rifle Volunteers. Re-gazetted Bucks Batt.

Oxford and Bucks Light Infantry (No. 1 Supply Coy.), Dec. 1, 1914, transferred No. 11 Coy. Royal Defence Corps June 1916. Discharged April 30, 1917. Served at Home.

ERIC HAROLD CHATER.

Articled to Trevor Pollard, of Brighton. Served as 2nd Lieut., Oxford and Bucks Light Infantry.

FRANK KENTISH CHATER.

Admitted Jan. 1886, practising at Lincoln's Inn Chambers, 40 Chancery Lane, W.C. Rejoined from Militia July 22, 1915, as Capt., The Welch Regt., served on Staff of Western Command School of Instruction for Infantry Officers, Kinmel Park, N. Wales, and Knowsley, Dec. 1915 to Jan. 1917, served on Staff of No. 1 School of Instruction for Infantry Officers, Brocton, Stafford, June 1917 to June 1918, 3rd Batt. The Welch Regt., Redcar, Yorks., July 1918 to Jan. 1919.

EDWARD ALFRED CHATHAM.

Articled to Edward Chatham, of Manchester. Joined O.T.C. at outbreak of war. Gazetted 2nd Lieut. Shropshire Light Infantry July 13, 1915, transferred to 13th Batt. West Yorkshire Regt. Dec. 1915. Served at Home.

FREDERICK CHARLES CHATT.

Admitted Jan. 1906, practising at Newcastle-on-Tyne. Joined Aug. 1914, as Private, Infantry. Subsequently commissioned and attained the rank of Capt.

JAMES CHATTERTON.

Articled to Henry Tweed, of Horncastle, Lincs. Joined Sept. 10, 1914, as Private, 7th Batt. London Regt. (T.F.). Gazetted 2nd Lieut. 7th Batt. London Regt. May 5, 1915, promoted Lieut. June 1916 and Temp. Capt. Oct. 1916, relinquished Temp. rank of Capt. March 1917 and gazetted A/Capt. Oct. 1917, transferred to the Royal Flying Corps. Nov. 1917, being gazetted Flying Officer April 1918. Awarded the M.C. Served at Home and France. Total service in France 32 months. Wounded Dec. 21, 1915.

RICHARD CHATTERTON.

Articled to Henry Tweed, of Horncastle, Lincs. Joined Nov. 22, 1915, as Private, 28th County of London Regt. (T.F.) (Artists Rifles). Gazetted 2nd Lieut. Royal Garrison Artillery Aug. 28, 1916, and posted to 192nd Heavy Battery Sept. 1916, promoted Lieut. Feb. 1918. Twice mentioned in Dispatches. Awarded the M.C. and French Croix de Guerre (en Vermeuil). Served 2 years with the British Salonica Forces in Greece, Serbia, and Bulgaria.

PHILIP ROBERT CHAUNDLER.

Articled to Henry Chaundler, of Biggleswade. Served as 2nd Lieut., 5th (Service) Batt. Bedfordshire Regt. (T.) and Machine Gun Corps., attained the rank of Lieut. Mentioned in Dispatches. Awarded the M.C.

ALEXANDER ROBERT CHEALE.

Admitted Nov. 1908. Member of Cheale & Son, of Tunbridge Wells. Mobilised Aug. 1914, as Capt., 1/4 Batt. The Queen's Own Royal West Kent

Regt., Adjutant Oct. 1914 to March 1916, promoted Major June 1916. Served at Home Aug. to Oct. 1914, India Oct. 1914 to Feb. 1919.

THOMAS JOHN CHELLEW.

Admitted May 1892, practising at St. Ives, Cornwall. Mobilised Aug. 3, 1914, as Major, Cornwall Royal Garrison Artillery (T.), promoted Lieut.-Col. Aug. 1914 on appointment to command of Brigade. Twice mentioned in Dispatches. Awarded O.B.E. (Military). Served at Home.

GEORGE JOSEPH CHESHIRE.

Admitted Aug. 1913. Managing Clerk with Wm. Sutton, of Newcastle-upon-Tyne. Joined Nov. 12, 1915, as Private, 3rd Batt. Northumberland Fusiliers, subsequently promoted Lance-Corporal. Served at Home.

PHILIP GEORGE CHESTERMAN.

Admitted June 1907. Member of W. T. Chesterman & Sons, of Bath. Joined July 20, 1915, as Orderly, Friends' Ambulance Unit, connected with British Red Cross Society. Served in France.

WILLIAM PAUL CHESTERMAN.

Admitted Dec. 1902. Member of W. T. Chesterman & Sons, of Bath. Joined April 1917, as Private, Hon. Artillery Company. Discharged Aug. 1918. Served in France and Italy. Wounded near Ypres Oct. 1917.

HENRY ARTHUR CHETHAM.

Admitted Aug. 1905. Member of Harris, Chetham & Cohen, of 25 Finsbury Square, E.C. Joined May 1916, as 2nd Lieut., Royal Garrison Artillery, promoted Lieut. Once mentioned in Dispatches. Served in France 2½ years.

ARTHUR EDWARD CHEVALIER.

Admitted Sept. 1887. Member of Duncan Oakshott, Baxter & Chevalier, of Liverpool. Joined July 1, 1915, appointed to command of 26th Supernumerary Company, King's Liverpool Regt., Substantive Capt. throughout, transferred in Aug. 1916 to the Territorial Force Reserve (General List) and appointed a Staff Adjutant at Knockaloe Alien Prisoners of War Camp, Isle of Man. Home service.

GILBERT HELE CHILCOTT.

Admitted Dec. 1878, practising at Truro. Joined Sept. 1914, as Major, 4th (Reserve) Batt. Duke of Cornwall's Light Infantry. Discharged July 1916. Once mentioned in Dispatches. Awarded C.M.G. No fighting service. Served in India and at Home.

DAVID LESLIE CHILD.

Admitted Feb. 1913. Of 17 Paternoster Row, E.C. Joined Feb. 5, 1915, as 2nd Lieut., 2nd City of London Batt. Royal Fusiliers, promoted Lieut. early in 1916. Served at Malta, Egypt, Dardanelles, and France. Killed in action at Ginchy, France, Sept. 11, 1916, in command of Machine Guns.

CLAUDE ALAN CHILTON.

Admitted Nov. 1899. Member of Chilton & Sons, of Bristol. Joined March 11, 1915, as 2nd Lieut., Royal Engineers, promoted Temp. Lieut. March 1916, Substantive June 1916, Temp. Capt. July 1916, Temp. Major Sept. 1919,

Deputy Assistant Director Engineers Stores Nov. 1919. Served at Home (East Coast Defences) 1916, and in France Jan. 1917 to Feb. 1918.

WILLIAM ARTHUR CHISLETT.

Articled to W. J. Board, Town Clerk, Nottingham. Joined March 5, 1915, as 2nd Lieut., Royal Horse and Royal Field Artillery, promoted Lieut. Oct. 1916. Served Home, France, and Flanders. Invalided home with broken shoulder in August 1916 and again invalided home with pneumonia in March 1917.

ERNEST EDWARD CHITTY.

Admitted Dec. 1901. Member of Chitty & Scorer, of Dover. Joined Nov. 1916, as Private, East Kent Regt. (The Buffs). Gazetted 2nd Lieut. 5th Batt. Royal Fusiliers March 28, 1917, transferred to 7th Batt. May 1917, promoted Lieut. Sept. 1918. Served in France and Belgium.

HUGH VALENTINE CHOLMELEY.

Articled to J. W. C. Frere, of 28 Lincoln's Inn Fields, and afterwards Managing Clerk with Frere, Cholmeley & Co. Joined July 1915, as Private, Inns of Court O.T.C. Gazetted 2nd Lieut. Grenadier Guards (Special Reserve) Sept. 15, 1915. Served in France 1915 to 1916. Killed in action in the Ypres Salient April 1916 while attached to Machine Gun Corps.

ARTHUR REGINALD CHORLEY.

Admitted April 1894. Member of Barr, Nelson & Co., of Leeds. Enlisted Sept. 3, 1914, as Private, 4th Batt. King's Own Yorkshire Light Infantry, and attained the rank of Sergeant. Gazetted 2nd Lieut. in same Battalion Oct. 1915, promoted Lieut. 1916, A/Capt. in July 1917, Assistant Staff-Capt. to 148th Infantry Brigade from Dec. 1916 to March 1918, appointed Staff-Capt. March 1918. Twice mentioned in Dispatches. Served in France and Belgium. Died of wounds at Boulogne-sur-Mer, France, April 29, 1918.

FRANCIS EDWARD CHORLEY.

Articled to R. F. Chorley, of Kendal. Joined June 6, 1918, as Private, 53rd Batt. Cheshire Regt. Served at Home, France, and Germany.

HERBERT CHORLEY.

Admitted Dec. 1904, practising at St. Helens, Lancashire. Joined Aug. 4, 1914, as Sapper, Royal Engineers, promoted Corporal Sept. 1914. Gazetted Temp. 2nd Lieut. Royal Army Service Corps (M.T.) March 23, 1917, Temp. Lieut. Sept. 1918. Served in England 1914 to 1915, France and Belgium 1916 to 1918, Germany 1919.

RICHARD CLEASBY CHORLEY.

Articled to R. F. Chorley, of Kendal. Served as Trooper, Cumberland and Westmorland Yeomanry.

JOHN STANLEY CHOWN.

Admitted April 1909. Member of Hewitt, Woollacott & Chown, of 158 Leadenhall Street, E.C. Joined May 15, 1916, as Rifleman, 5th City of London Batt. London Regt. (London Rifle Brigade), promoted Lance-Corporal July 1916. Gazetted 2nd Lieut. March 1, 1917, promoted Lieut. Sept. 1918. Awarded the M.C. Served at Home and in France April 1917 to March 1918. Taken prisoner near St. Quentin, March 21, 1918.

CECIL TILSON CHOWNE.

Admitted Jan. 1900, practising at Bath. Served as Lieut., West Somerset Yeomanry.

ALBERT CHRISTIAN.

Articled to Botterell & Roche, of 24 St. Mary Axe, E.C. Served as Private, Oxford and Bucks Light Infantry.

HERBERT JAMES CHRISTIE.

Admitted June 1905, practising at 109 Cheapside, E.C., and Osterley Park. Served as Private, 28th Batt. County of London Regt. (Artists Rifles), and afterwards gazetted 2nd Lieut. Middlesex Regt.

EDWARD GEOFFREY CHUBB.

Admitted April 1895, practised at 41 Moorgate Street, E.C. Joined Dec. 1914 as Capt., Middlesex Regt., transferred to West Surrey Regt. April 1915. Served in France. Killed in action July 12, 1915.

ERNEST FRANK CHURCHILL.

Admitted Feb. 1909. Managing Clerk with Hewett & Churchill, of Reading. Joined Dec. 14, 1914, as Private, Inns of Court O.T.C. Gazetted 2nd Lieut. Royal Engineers March 1, 1915, promoted Lieut. Aug. 1915, Capt. May 1918, A/Major, Nov. 1918. Twice mentioned in Dispatches Awarded the M.C. Served in France and Germany 1915 to 1919.

JOHN ABELL VYVYAN CHURCHILL.

Admitted March 1906. Practising as Noon, Clarke & Churchill, of 31 Great St. Helens, E.C. Served as Petty Officer, Royal Naval Air Service. Afterwards obtained commission in the Tank Corps and promoted Lieut. Mentioned in Dispatches. Awarded the M.C.

ALLAN ROBERT CHURCHMAN.

Articled to E. C. Rawlings, of 2 Walbrook, E.C. Served as Petty Officer, Motor Cyclist Scouts, Royal Naval Air Service, and afterwards as Capt. Royal Air Force. Awarded the D.F.C.

WILLIAM ARTHUR VERE CHURTON.

Admitted Nov. 1901. Member of W. H. Churton & Son, of Chester. Mobilised Aug. 1914 as Capt., 1/5 Batt. Cheshire Regt., promoted Major, June 1916, Temp. Lieut-Col., Feb. 1918. Three times mentioned in Dispatches. Awarded the D.S.O. and T.D. Served in France and Belgium Feb. 1915 to Armistice.

WILLIAM LOUIS CLABBURN.

Admitted Nov. 1902. Member of Clabburns, of Norwich. Joined Oct. 21, 1914, as Lieut., 4th Batt. Norfolk Regt. (T.F.), promoted Capt. Nov. 1914. Served at Home.

BARNARD AUBREY CLAPHAM.

Admitted Oct. 1904. Member of Rooker, Matthews & Co., of Plymouth. Joined Oct. 1914 Public School Corps. Subsequently commissioned and promoted to Lieut., 4th Batt. Essex Regt. Served in Egypt and Palestine. Died of wounds at Gaza, Palestine, March 27, 1917.

HENRY SHEFFIELD CLAPHAM.

Admitted May 1897, practising at 2 Broad Street Place, E.C. Joined Sept. 2, 1914, as Private, Hon. Artillery Company, promoted Sergeant Sept. 1915, Company Quartermaster-Sergeant Jan. 1916. Gazetted 2nd Lieut. Royal Army Ordnance Corps. Oct. 30, 1916, promoted Lieut. Jan. 1917, Served at Home Sept. to Dec. 1914, and in France and Flanders Dec. 1914 to April 1919. Slightly wounded Sept. 30, 1915.

PERCIVAL ALFRED CLAPHAM.

Admitted July 1896, practising at 11 New Square, Lincoln's Inn, W.C. Joined Nov. 1916, as Private, 28th Batt. County of London Regt. (Artists Rifles). Served at Home.

ALBERT DOUGLAS McKILLOP CLARK.

Articled to W. T. Wilkinson, of Weymouth. Joined Aug. 4, 1914, as 2nd Lieut., Royal Garrison Artillery (T.), promoted Lieut. Nov. 1914, Capt. Aug. 1916, Major July 1917. Once mentioned in Dispatches. Served in France Dec. 1915 to Dec. 1918.

ALBERT NETTLETON CLARK.

Admitted March 1911. Member of Hodding & Clark, of St. Albans. Mobilised Aug. 1914, as Lieut., Inns of Court O.T.C., transferred to 2/24 Batt. London Regt. (The Queen's) April 1916, promoted A/Major Nov. 1917. Once mentioned in Dispatches. Awarded the M.C. Served in France 1916, Salonica 1916 to 1917, Egypt and Palestine 1917 to 1918, and France 1918. Wounded Sept. 18, 1918.

CHARLES ERIC CLARK.

Articled to A. E. Morton, of Nottingham. Served as Private, Royal Army Ordnance Corps.

GEORGE FREDERICK CLARK.

Admitted Aug. 1895, practising at 35 Bucklersbury, E.C., and 718 Fulham Road, Fulham, S.W. Joined Dec. 1916, as Lieut., Worcestershire Regt., promoted Capt. April 1917, transferred to Royal Flying Corps March 1918, Capt. Royal Air Force S.O. III. Oct. 1918, Major Nov. 1918. Served at Home.

JOHN EVELYN CLARK.

Articled to Jonathan Clark, of 1 Devonshire Terrace, W. Mobilised Aug. 1914, as Lieut., Royal Army Service Corps, promoted Capt. and Adjutant 48th Div. Train. Twice mentioned in Dispatches. Served in Belgium, France and Italy.

LIONEL MELVILLE CLARK.

Admitted March 1903. Member of Blunt, Clark & Co., 95 Gresham Street, E.C. Joined May 31, 1915, as Lieut., Royal Army Service Corps, promoted Capt. Dec. 1915, Major April 1917, appointed D.A.D.S., Feb. 1919. Twice mentioned in Dispatches. Awarded the O.B.E. Served at Home May to Sept. 1915, Mudros and Gallipoli Sept. 1915 to Jan. 1916, Egypt and Palestine Jan. 1916 to June 1919.

MALCOLM CLARK.

Articled to W. A. Thomson, of 3 King's Bench Walk, Temple, E.C. Joined Aug. 1914, as Trooper, Inns of Court (Cavalry), afterwards promoted Lance-Corporal. Gazetted 2nd Lieut. Royal Army Service Corps (H.T.) Nov. 11, 1914, promoted Lieut. Nov. 1915, Capt. and Adjutant Aug. 1917 to Feb. 1919. Served at Home and Salonica Jan to July 1916. Suffered from malaria and dysentery.

WALTER DOUGLAS CLARK.

Admitted May 1915. Member of J. H. Clark, of West Bromwich and Smethwick. Joined Nov. 11, 1915, as 2nd Class Air Mechanic, Royal Flying Corps, promoted 1st Class Air Mechanic 1916, and Corporal Mechanic 1918. Served at Home and in France.

WALTER TREVELYAN CLARK.

Admitted July 1916. Member of Clark & Smith, of Malmesbury, Wilts. Joined June 21, 1917, as Gunner, Royal Garrison Artillery, promoted Corporal Nov. 1917, joined 512th Siege Battery Dec. 1917, 32nd Siege Battery June 1918. Gazetted 2nd Lieut. Royal Garrison Artillery April 12, 1919. Served in France. Wounded at Caestre, Aug. 3, 1918.

WILFRED JOHN CLARK.

Admitted Feb. 1908, practising at Rotherham. Joined June 30, 1917, as Private, Royal Army Service Corps (M.T.). Served at Home and with Egyptian Expeditionary Force.

WILLIAM SCOTT CLARK.

Admitted Dec. 1907, practising at Carlisle. Joined Sept. 3, 1914, as Private, 1/4 Batt. The Border Regt. (T.F.). Gazetted 2nd Lieut. in same Regt. March 1916, promoted Lieut. Sept. 1917. Served in India 1914 to 1919.

ARTHUR CLARK.

Admitted Feb. 1892. Of 189 Holloway Road, N. Served as 2nd Lieut., Royal Army Service Corps.

CECIL SOMERS CLARKE.

Admitted Oct. 1884, practising at Brighton. Mobilised and served as Colonel, 6th (Cyclist) Batt. Royal Sussex Regt. Awarded V.D. Served at Home and in France.

CHARLES FREDERICK LORISTON CLARKE.

Admitted Nov. 1893. Member of Tanner & Clarke, of Bristol and Wotton-under-Edge, Glos. Joined May 27, 1918, as Lieut., Royal Naval Volunteer Reserve. Served at Home at Devonport on the Admiral's Staff (Intelligence Department).

DERRICK ANSELL CLARKE.

Articled to Joseph Ansell, of Birmingham. Joined Sept. 19, 1914, as 2nd Lieut., 5th Batt. South Staffordshire Regt., promoted Capt. June 1916, Adjutant 1915 to 1919. Once mentioned in Dispatches. Awarded the M.B.E. (Military). Served at Home and in France (draft conducting).

DONALD CLARKE.

Articled to A. J. Clarke, of High Wycombe. Joined Aug. 1914, as Private, Hon. Artillery Company. Gazetted 2nd Lieut. Royal Flying Corps June 1916. Served in France 1914 to 1916. Killed in action Aug. 26, 1916.

EDGAR CHARLES GILBERT CLARKE.

Admitted June 1913, practising at Birmingham. Served as 2nd Lieut., 6th Batt. Royal Worcestershire Regt., promoted Lieut.

ERIC CLARKE.

Admitted Feb. 1901. Member of Murton & Clarke, of Cranbrook and Hawkhurst, Kent. Mobilised Aug. 1914, as Capt., Royal West Kent Regt., (The Buffs), promoted Temp. Major Oct. 1914, Major June 1916. Served in India 1914 and 1915, and in Mesopotamia 1915 and 1916. Wounded (severely) at Battle of Sheikh Saad, Mesopotamia, on Jan. 7, 1916. Relinquished commission, on account of ill-health caused by wounds received in action, on Dec. 18, 1918.

ESKRICKE JOSEPH CLARKE.

Articled to W. H. Clarke, of Leeds. Mobilised Aug. 4, 1914, as Lieut., 7th Batt. West Yorkshire Regt., promoted Capt. Aug. 1914, Major Nov. 1916, seconded to command 62nd Divisional Cyclist Company March 1915, attached 18th Corps Staff (in France) Jan. to April 1918, and A/D.A.Q.M.G. on several occasions during this period and also throughout the German offensive (March and April 1918), appointed to command of 19th Corps Cyclist Batt. in France April 1918. Twice mentioned in Dispatches. Awarded French Croix de Guerre (with Silver Star). Served at Home 1914 to Jan. 1917, France Jan. 1917 to June 1919.

FRANCIS EAGLE CLARKE.

Admitted April 1910. Member of Clarke & Son, of Leeds and Filey. Joined July 1917, as Gunner, Royal Garrison Artillery (2/1 North Riding Heavy Battery), and attained the rank of Sergeant. Served at Home.

GEOFFREY PEARD CLARKE.

Articled to C. P. Clarke, of Taunton. Joined Dec. 4, 1914, as 2nd Lieut., 5th Batt. Somerset Light Infantry (T.F.), promoted Temp. Lieut. Sept. 1915, relinquished Temp. Lieut. April 1917, promoted Lieut. July 1917, A/Capt. Oct. 28, 1917. Awarded the M.C. Served in India March 1916 to April 1917, Egypt and Palestine April 1917 to Dec. 1918. Wounded at El-Jib Nov. 23, 1917.

HARRY COLIN CLARKE.

Admitted May 1903, practised at Shrewsbury until 1910, when he went to British Columbia. Joined the Army soon after the outbreak of War and reached the rank of Capt. in the Royal Army Service Corps. Killed in action 1916.

HENRY HAROLD CLARKE.

Admitted June 1909, practised at Shrewsbury. Served as Capt., 3rd Batt. Royal Welch Fusiliers.

HENRY PALLISTER CLARKE.
Admitted Dec. 1911. Of 23 College Hill, E.C. Served as Private, 3rd City of London Field Ambulance, Royal Army Medical Corps, afterwards gazetted 2nd Lieut. The Queen's Royal West Surrey Regt., and promoted Lieut. Mentioned in Dispatches. Awarded the M.C.

JAMES FRANCIS CLARKE.
Admitted April 1900. Of 29 Trevor Square, Knightsbridge. Served as Private, 15th Batt. County of London Regt. (Civil Service Rifles).

JOHN LAURENCE CLARKE.
Admitted July 1910, practised at 31 Great St. Helen's, E.C. Served as Private, Hon. Artillery Company.

JOHN TURNER PARKER CLARKE.
Admitted June 1907, practising at Whitchurch, Hants. Served as Capt., Wessex Divisional Train, Royal Army Service Corps (T.).

JOSEPH SPOTTISWOODE CLARKE.
Admitted Feb. 1, 1916, practising at Doncaster. Joined Jan. 29, 1917, as Private, West Yorkshire Regt., promoted Lance-Corporal Oct. 1917, Corporal March 1918. Served at Home (No. 2 Infantry Records, York).

NOEL OLIVER CLARKE.
Admitted Feb. 1911. Member of J. B. Clarke & Co., of Birmingham. Joined Aug. 15, 1914, as 2nd Lieut., 3rd Batt. North Staffordshire Regt., promoted Lieut. March 1915, Capt. Dec. 1915. Served at Home Sept. 1914 to March 1915, March 1916 to Jan. 1919, France March 1915 to March 1916. Wounded at St. Jean, Ypres, June 22, 1915, and at Hooge, Ypres, Feb. 27, 1916.

REGINALD JAEGER CLARKE.
Admitted May 1892, practising at Liverpool. Mobilised Aug. 4, 1914, as Major, 9th Batt. King's Liverpool Regt., given the command of a company in the 21st (Labour) Batt. Cheshire Regt. Aug. 1916, promoted A/Lieut.-Col. in command of 21st Batt. Cheshire Regt. Dec. 1916, and subsequently employed as Assistant Labour Commandant in the organisation and command of Labour Bureaux and as Courts-Martial Officer of No. 1 Area, transferred as Courts-Martial Officer to No. 1 District Oct. 1919. Awarded Volunteer Long Service Medal and T.D.

WILLIAM SEFTON CLARKE.
Admitted Nov. 1894, practising at Bristol. Mobilised Aug. 1914, as Capt., 4th Batt., Gloucestershire Regt., and subsequently promoted to Major. Served in France March 1915 to Feb. 1916.

ALFRED BAIRSTOW CLARKSON.
Admitted Dec. 1907. Member of Spencer, Clarkson & Co., of Keighley. Mobilised Aug. 1914, as Capt., 6th Duke of Wellington's Regt., promoted Major June 1916, A/Lieut.-Col. Nov. 1918, reverted to Major Dec. 1918. Twice mentioned in Dispatches. Awarded the M.C. and D.S.O. Served in France April 1915 to Feb. 1919. Wounded (very slightly) July 1915.

CHARLES CLARKSON.

Admitted Nov. 1904. Member of James Clarkson & Son, of Halifax. Served in France as Capt., 2/4 Duke of Wellington's West Riding Regt. Died Feb. 11, 1917, of wounds received in action.

WILFRID BAIRSTOW CLARKSON.

Articled to J. N. Clarkson, of Keighley. Enlisted Sept. 15, 1914, in 21st Batt. Royal Fusiliers. Gazetted 2nd Lieut. Royal Garrison Artillery Oct. 5, 1914, promoted Lieut. Jan. 1916, A/Capt. Jan. 1917, A/Major Nov. 1917. Once mentioned in Dispatches. Awarded the D.S.O. Served in France.

FREDERIC HARDEN CLAY.

Admitted April 1908, practised at Bristol. Served as 2nd Lieut., Somerset Yeomanry.

EDWIN CLAYTON.

Admitted May 1910. Member of H. B. Clayton & Son, of Nottingham. Served as Gunner, Royal Garrison Artillery, afterwards gazetted 2nd Lieut. 3rd Batt. Suffolk Regt.

FRANK CLAYTON.

Admitted June 1907. Member of H. B. Clayton & Son, of Nottingham. Enlisted 1915 and served in Officers' Cadet Batt. at Cambridge until Oct. 1916. Gazetted 2nd Lieut. Notts and Derby Regt. (Sherwood Foresters) Oct. 1916, promoted Lieut. April 1917. Twice mentioned in Dispatches. Served at Home and France.

GEOFFREY SHAW CLAYTON.

Admitted Nov. 1903. Member of Bramwell, Clayton & Clayton, of Newcastle-on-Tyne. Enlisted Oct. 31, 1914, as Private, 18th (Service) Batt. King's Liverpool Regt. Commissioned as 2nd Lieut. Nov. 23, 1914, promoted Capt. Feb. 1915, Major March 1915, Lieut.-Colonel Feb. 1918. Once mentioned in Dispatches. Awarded the D.S.O. Served in France. Nov. 1915 to Dec. 1918.

HAROLD VERNEY CLAYTON.

Articled to H. J. Berry, of Manchester. Joined Dec. 6, 1914. Gazetted Lieut. Manchester Regt. Dec. 1916, promoted Capt. Oct. 1917. Awarded the M.C. Served in Gallipoli and France. Wounded Aug. 26, 1916.

LANCELOT JAMES CLAYTON.

Admitted Jan. 1905. Managing Clerk with Clayton, Sons & Fargus, 10 Lancaster Place, Strand, W.C. Joined Aug. 29, 1914, as Private, 15th Batt. London Regt. (Civil Service Rifles). Gazetted 2nd Lieut. 1/5 Gloucestershire Regt. March 17, 1915, promoted Lieut. June 1916. Served in France July 1915 to March 1916 and June and July 1916. Wounded near Ovillers, France, July 23, 1916.

GUY VERNON HEUKENSFELDT CLAYTON-SMITH.

Articled to W. E. Clayton-Smith, of Pontefract. Joined Feb. 1, 1917, as Private, Inns of Court O.T.C. Gazetted 2nd Lieut. 3rd Batt. King's Own Yorkshire Light Infantry Nov. 28, 1917. Served at Home.

STANLEY WILLIAM CLEAVE.

Articled to C. T. K. Roberts, of Exeter. Joined Feb. 22, 1915, as Rifleman, 28th Batt. County of London Regt. (Artists Rifles). Gazetted 2nd Lieut. 2/17 Batt. London Regt. Jan. 26, 1916, promoted Lieut. July 1917. Served in France May to Sept. 1915 and June to Oct. 1916, Salonica Dec. 1916 to May 1917, Egypt and Palestine May 1917 to Feb. 1919. Wounded May 1, 1918.

CHARLES MITCHELL CLEGG.

Admitted Aug. 1913. Member of Dibb & Clegg, of Barnsley. Joined Oct. 19, 1914, as 2nd Lieut., 5th Batt. York and Lancaster Regt. (T.F.), transferred to Royal Army Service Corps June 1916, promoted Temp. Lieut. Dec. 1917, appointed A/Capt. May 1917. Once mentioned in Dispatches. Served at Home Oct. 1914 to Aug. 1916, France Aug. 1916 to Feb. 1919.

FRANK CECIL CLEGG.

Articled to R. H. Greenwood, of Kendal. Joined the Army on the outbreak of war, being given a commission in the 6th Batt. Border Regt., promoted Capt. July 1915 and left for the Dardanelles directly after. Killed in action Aug. 22, 1915.

JOHN CLEGG.

Admitted Dec. 1905. Managing Clerk with Jackson & Co., of Rochdale. Mobilised Aug. 4, 1914, as Sergeant, 6th Batt. Manchester Regt. Served in Egypt and Gallipoli Peninsula. Killed in action at Gallipoli June 4, 1915.

JOSEPH CLEGG.

Admitted May 1905. Member of Clegg & Baines, of Leeds. Joined Dec. 1914 as Lieut., 6th Batt. King's Own Yorkshire Light Infantry, promoted Capt. Aug. 10, 1916, appointed Brigade Intelligence Officer Aug. 23, 1916. Served in France. Killed in action Sept. 16, 1916.

WILLIAM JOHN CLEGG.

Articled to L. J. Clegg, of Sheffield. Joined Nov. 12, 1915, as 2nd Lieut., 1/1 Queen's Own Yorkshire Dragoons, and subsequently promoted Lieut. Awarded the M.C. Served in France, Belgium, Germany Sept. 1916 to May 1919.

OSWALD CLEMENT.

Admitted Oct. 1904. Managing Clerk with Parker Garrett & Co., St. Michael's Rectory, Cornhill, E.C. Joined Feb. 18, 1918, as A.C. II. Royal Naval Air Service, afterwards Royal Air Force. Served at Home.

AYLMER GUSTAVUS CLERK.

Admitted July 1911. Managing Clerk with Murray, Hutchins & Co., 11 Birchin Lane, E.C. Mobilised, as Capt., 1st Batt. Hertfordshire Regt. (T.F.), promoted Major June 1916. Three times mentioned in Dispatches. Awarded D.S.O. and M.C. Served in France and Belgium. Four times wounded.

JOHN PENRHYN CLEWS.

Admitted Nov. 1911. Member of Isle & Clews, of York. Joined May 29, 1916, as Private, Royal Army Ordnance Corps, transferred to Royal Flying Corps June 1916, promoted Sergeant Jan. 1917. Granted commission in Royal Air Force Nov. 1918. Served in England and France.

FRANCIS ERNEST CLIFFORD.

Admitted April 1904, practising at 36 Great James Street, Bedford Row. Mobilised Aug. 4, 1914, as 2nd Corporal, London Mounted Brigade Royal Army Service Corps (T.F.), transferred to 2nd London Mounted Brigade Royal Army Service Corps with rank of Corporal April 1915, promoted Sergeant Sept. 1915, Staff-Sergeant March 1916. Commissioned 2nd Lieut. Aug. 26, 1917, posted to 49th Divisional Train, Royal Army Service Corps, Sept. 1917. Served on East Coast Sept. 1914 to June 1917, Belgium and France Sept. 1917 to Jan. 1919. Wounded April 12, 1918.

HORACE MONTAGUE CLIFFORD.

Admitted May 1904. Member of Cliffords, of Derby and Loughborough. Joined Oct. 1, 1914, as Capt., 5th Batt. Notts and Derby Regt. (Sherwood Foresters) (T.F.), Adjutant 5th (Reserve) Sherwood Foresters March 1915 to May 1917, A/Major March to April 1918. Served in France Sept. 1917 to April 1918. Wounded at Kemmel, April 14, 1918.

SIDNEY WILLIAM CLIFT.

Admitted April 1912. Member of Rollason, Clift & Co., of Birmingham. Served as Capt., Royal Garrison Artillery.

PERCY JAMES CLIFTON.

Admitted Dec. 1910. Member of William A. Crump & Son, of 17 Leadenhall Street, E.C. Mobilised Aug. 1914, as Capt., Royal Field Artillery (T.), promoted Major Dec. 1914. Twice mentioned in Dispatches. Awarded the D.S.O. Served in France. Killed in action Aug. 26, 1918.

WILFRID CLOTHIER.

Admitted Nov. 1909, practised at Liverpool. Served as Private, Hon. Artillery Company.

MAURICE ISACKÉ CLUTTERBUCK.

Admitted Nov. 1912. Member of Lane, Clutterbuck & Co., of Birmingham. Joined Aug. 11, 1914, as 2nd Lieut., 3rd South Midland Brigade Royal Field Artillery, promoted Lieut. Nov. 1914, and afterwards Capt., Staff-Capt. Dec. 1916, Major July 1918. Once mentioned in Dispatches. Served in France March 1915 to Nov. 1918.

STEPHEN JAMES COALES.

Admitted Feb. 1903, practised at Wellingborough. Joined Sept. 29, 1915, as 2nd Lieut., Royal Sussex Regt., subsequently transferred to Royal West Kent Regt. Served in France. Died of wounds Sept. 18, 1916, Battle of the Somme.

GEORGE THOMAS COATES.

Admitted April 1907. Member of Maynard & Coates, of Preston. Served as 2nd Lieut., 16th Battery Royal Field Artillery.

WILLIAM HUTCHINSON COATES.

Admitted Jan. 1912, practising at Grimsby, Lincolnshire. Joined Aug. 1918, as Paymaster Sub-Lieut., Royal Naval Volunteer Reserve. Served on Staff of Commander-in-Chief, Queenstown, Ireland.

KENNETH RHODES COBB.

Admitted Jan. 1901. Member of J. H. & K. R. Cobb, of 7 New Court, Lincoln's Inn, W.C. At outbreak of war joined the O.T.C. and later received a commission in the 15th Batt. King's Royal Rifle Corps, promoted Capt. early in 1915 and attached to the 1st Batt. Royal Inniskilling Fusiliers. Killed in action at the Dardanelles July 1, 1915.

RICHARD COBBETT.

Admitted Nov. 1902. Member of Cobbett, Wheeler & Cobbett, of Manchester. Joined Nov. 1915, as 2nd Lieut., Cheshire Yeomanry, Capt. A.P.M. No. 6 Cheshire Area, Western Command, March 1917 to Aug. 1918. Served at Home.

FRANCIS ALFRED WORSHIP COBBOLD..

Admitted Feb. 1908. Member of Cobbold, Sons & Menneer, of Ipswich. Mobilised Aug. 1914, as Capt., Essex and Suffolk Royal Garrison Artillery, promoted Major in 1916. Once mentioned in Dispatches. Awarded the D.S.O. Served on Coast Defences, Harwich and Felixstowe, 1914 and 1915, France and Belgium 1916 and 1917. Wounded at Ypres July 4, 1917.

CHARLES COBURN.

Admitted Oct. 1909. Employed with Royal Pension Fund for Nurses, Buckingham Street, Strand, W.C. Gazetted 2nd Lieut., King's Royal Rifle Corps Oct. 30, 1916. Reported missing July 31, 1917, at Hollebecke, subsequently officially presumed to have been killed in action on that date.

FRANCIS COBURN.

Admitted April 1900. Formerly member of Coburn & Co., 11 St. Helen's Place, E.C., now retired from the firm. Enlisted Dec. 1914, as Private, Inns of Court O.T.C. Gazetted 2nd Lieut. King's Royal Rifle Corps May 15, 1915, promoted Lieut. Feb. 1916, Capt. General List Oct. 1918, Major (as D.A.Q.M.G.) May 1919. Served at Home, in India, and on North-West Frontier.

DONALD HENRY COCHRANE.

Articled to David Cochrane, of Birmingham. Joined Nov. 17, 1914, as Private, Royal Army Medical Corps (T.F.). Served in France.

JOHN GEDDES HUNTER COCKBURN.

Admitted Aug. 1903. Member of Cockburn, Gostling & Cockburn, of Brighton. Mobilised Aug. 4, 1914, as Capt., 6th (Cyclist) Batt. Royal Sussex Regt. (T.). Served in India and Waziristan and North-West Fronteir.

REGINALD STAPYLTON COCKBURN.

Articled to R. C. Nesbitt, of 7 Devonshire Square, Bishopsgate, E.C. Joined Aug. 5, 1914, as Private, Inns of Court O.T.C. Gazetted 2nd Lieut. King's Royal Rifle Corps Sept. 12, 1914, promoted Lieut. Nov. 1914, Capt. Dec. 1915, Major Jan. 1917, Major A.D.C. to S.O.C. 63rd (R.N.) Division Aug. 1918. Awarded the M.C. Served at Home Aug. 1914 to July 1915, and in France July 1915 to Jan. 1919.

CHARLES WHALLEY COCKRILL.

Admitted July 1910. Assistant Prosecuting Solicitor to the Corporation of Bradford. Joined July 1916 as 2nd Lieut., West Riding Brigade Royal

Field Artillery, promoted Lieut. Aug. 1917. Served in France. Killed in action at Ronssoy, Feb. 2, 1918, and buried at Villas Faucan.

WALTER RACKWOOD COCKS.

Admitted May 1903. Member of Cocks & Tucker, of Exeter. Mobilised Aug. 1914, as 2nd Lieut., Devon (Fortress) Royal Engineers, promoted Temp. Lieut. Jan. 1915, Substantive June 1916, A/Capt. March 1915. Served at Home Aug. 1914 to March 1915, Gibraltar March 1915 to Nov. 1916, France and Belgium March 1917 to June 1919.

FRANCIS GEOFFREY COCKSHOTT.

Admitted Dec. 1905. Of Southport and Canada. Served as Private, 16th (Saskatchewan) Light Horse.

THOMAS ARTHUR CODNER.

Admitted Feb. 1913. Managing Clerk with Hooper & Wollen, of Torquay, Devon. Enlisted Aug. 1914 in Public Schools Corps. Commissioned in Royal Field Artillery Oct. 9, 1914, promoted Lieut. Nov. 1915, and Substantive Rank of Capt. Jan. 1916. Twice mentioned in Dispatches. Served in France July 1915 to July 1919.

EDWIN HENRY COE.

Admitted Nov. 1913, practising at 6 Princes Street, Hanover Square, W. Mobilised Aug. 4, 1914, with West Kent (Queen's Own) Yeomanry. Gazetted Temp. 2nd Lieut. Royal Field Artillery Jan. 7, 1915, subsequently promoted Lieut., then Capt., and later A/Major. Awarded the M.C. Served at Home until Sept. 1915, France Sept. and Nov. 1915, Home until June 1916, France June 1916 to Oct. 1917, Italy Oct. 1917 to March 1918, France March to Oct. 1918. Wounded three times.

JOHN THEODORE COGGINS.

Admitted July 1911. Member of Foster & Wells, of Aldershot and Farnborough. Joined May 1918, as Private, Inns of Court O.T.C. Served at Home.

EDWARD MOLYNEUX COHAN.

Articled to G. M. Magee, of Liverpool. Mobilised Aug. 1914, as 2nd Lieut., 1st West Lancs. Brigade Royal Field Artillery (T.). Killed Aug. 5, 1914, as the result of an accident, during mobilisation, when on duty on Salisbury Plain.

ARTHUR SAVILLE COHEN.

Admitted May 1901, practising at 23 College Hill, E.C. Joined June 30, 1916, Barrack Warden, acting rank of Sergeant-Major, Royal Army Service Corps. Gazetted Jan. 4, 1917, as 2nd Lieut. Royal Army Service Corps, promoted Lieut. July 1918. Served at Home and in Italy.

SYDNEY COHEN.

Admitted Oct. 1913. Member of Osborne & Osborne, of 119 London Wall, E.C. Served as Rifleman, 21st Batt. London Regt.

LEIGH RIGBY COKE.

Admitted Feb. 1903. Member of Kingsford, Drake & Coke, of Ashford, and Hythe, Kent. Enlisted Sept. 4, 1914, as Private, 5th Batt. East Kent Regt. (The Buffs). Gazetted 2nd Lieut. 8th Batt. Hampshire Regt. May

1915 and attained the rank of Capt. Served in Palestine. Killed in action at Gaza Nov. 2, 1917.

ROBERT WILLIAM GREEN COLBECK.

Articled to J. R. Green, of Wakefield. Joined Dec. 9, 1915, as Private, King's Own Yorkshire Light Infantry. Served in France and at Home.

WILLIAM HENRY COLBECK.

Admitted Nov. 1914, practising at Leeds. Served as 2nd Lieut., 17th (Service) Batt. West Yorkshire Regt., promoted Lieut.

GEOFFREY COLBOURNE.

Admitted Nov. 1912, practising at Brighton. Joined May 17, 1916, as Private, 3/1 Sussex Yeomanry. Gazetted 2nd Lieut. Royal Fusiliers March 28, 1917, A/Capt. and A/Adjutant Nov. 1917 to Feb. 1918, promoted Capt. Feb. 1918. Served at Home May 1916 to May 1917, France May 1917 to Feb. 1919. Wounded at Fontaine-les-Croissilles June 24, 1917, and at Ablainzeville (gas) June 30, 1918.

HENRY STARKEY COLDICOTT.

Admitted Nov. 1875, practising at 22 Basinghall Street, E.C. Appointed Colonel commanding 2/21 Batt. London Regt. Sept. 9, 1914, and to the 3/21 Batt. Dec. 1915, became Chief Military Representative in Birmingham Recruiting Area Sept. 1916. Went to France June 1917 and was attached to 4th, 5th, and 13th Corps successively, being employed in various capacities. Once mentioned in Dispatches. Served at Home until June 1917, France June 1917 to May 1919.

ERIC COLEBY.

Admitted Oct. 1911. Of Marylebone Station, N.W. Served as Bombardier, Motor Machine Gun Section, Royal Field Artillery.

CLARENCE WATKINS COLEMAN.

Admitted Nov. 1912, practising at 13 Devonshire Square, E.C. Joined Sept. 14, 1914, as Private, Royal Fusiliers, and subsequently promoted to Sergeant. Served at the Dardanelles, in Egypt, and in France. Wounded in France Sept. 9, 1916.

ROBERT EDWIN COLEMAN.

Articled to George Coleman, of Hove. Joined Nov. 21, 1914, as 2nd Lieut., Sussex Royal Garrison Artillery, promoted Lieut. Sept. 1917. Served at Home and in France.

STANLEY ALLFORTH COLEMAN.

Articled to Noel O. Clarke, of Birmingham. Joined April 10, 1916, as Cyclist, the 25th (County of London) Cyclist Batt., transferred, as Rifleman, to 12th Batt. Royal Irish Rifles (Ulster Division) Feb. 1917. Served in France. Prisoner of War March 21, 1918, to Jan. 15, 1919, taken before St. Quentin,

WALTER ROBERT GRANVILLE COLEMAN.

Articled to E. A. Burnie, of 59 & 60 Gracechurch Street, E.C. Joined July 8, 1918, as Private, Royal Sussex Regt., promoted Lance-Corporal Aug. 1918. Served at Home.

JOHN MONCK CAMPION COLES.

Articled to J. B. C. Coles, of Eastbourne. Served as Corporal, 10th Batt. Royal Sussex Regt. Afterwards 2nd Lieut. 11th Batt., North Staffordshire Regt., gazetted Temp. Capt. while holding appointment of Divisional Courts-Martial Officer on Headquarter Staff Northern Command. Awarded the M.B.E.

HENRY WILLIAM HOWELL COLLETT.

Admitted July 1914. Of Liverpool. Served as Private, 17th (Service) Batt. King's Liverpool Regt. Killed in action.

JAMES HENRY COLLIER.

Admitted Feb. 1908. Member of Oswald Hickson, Collier & Co., of 6 Moorgate Street, E.C. Joined Oct. 1914, as 2nd Lieut., 4th Batt. Northamptonshire Regt., and subsequently promoted to Major.

OSWALD COLLIER.

Admitted Dec. 1901, practised at 63 Queen Victoria Street, E.C. Served as Lieut., 9th Batt. Border Regt.

HARRY COLLINGS.

Admitted Aug. 1913. Member of Field, Cunningham & Collings, of Sale, Cheshire, and also at Manchester. Joined Sept. 27, 1915, as Private, 29th (Reserve) Batt. Royal Fusiliers, promoted Corporal March 1916, A/Sergeant May 1919. Served on North-West Frontier in India May to Sept. 1919

GEOFFREY ABDY COLLINS.

Admitted Dec. 1913. Member of Peake, Bird, Collins & Co., of 6 Bedford Row, W.C. Served as 2nd Lieut., 11th Batt. The Rifle Brigade.

HENRY AIKEROYDE COLLINS.

Admitted July 1909. Managing Clerk with J. A. Collins, of 1 New Square, Lincoln's Inn. Mobilised Aug. 5, 1914, as Corporal, National Reserve. Enlisted Inns of Court Sept. 1914. Gazetted 2nd Lieut. 9th Batt. Middlesex Regt. (T.F.) Oct. 3, 1914, promoted Temp. Capt. Nov. 1914, transferred to Ministry of Munitions May 1917, relinquished Temp. rank of Capt. and promoted to 1st Lieut. Posted Royal Engineers Experimental Station, Porton, seconded for service with Royal Engineers. Gazetted A/Capt. Feb. 1919. Served at Home.

HENRY AKERMAN DESMOND COLLINS.

Admitted Dec. 1904. Assistant Solicitor Metropolitan Water Board, Savoy Street, W.C. Mobilised Aug. 1914, as Capt., 11th Batt. County of London Regt., Temp. Major Sept. 1916 to March 1917. Served with Mediterranean Expeditionary Force, Gallipoli, July to Oct. 1915, and with Egyptian Expeditionary Force June 1916 to May 1917.

HORACE ALEXANDER COLLINS.

Articled to E. A. Collins, of 238 Edgware Road, W. Joined Sept. 8, 1914, as Private, 28th Batt. County of London Regt. (Artists Rifles). Gazetted 2nd Lieut. South Staffordshire Regt. Nov. 9, 1914, afterwards appointed Divisional Signalling Officer, promoted Lieut. March 1917. Served in France. Killed in action at Kemmel Hill Sept. 18, 1917.

JAMES ADOLPHUS COLLINS.

Admitted May 1887, practising at 1 New Square, Lincoln's Inn, W.C. Joined March 10, 1915, as Lieut., 14th Supernumerary Coy., 2/6 Batt. Essex Regt., Lieut. 24th Batt. The Rifle Brigade Nov. 1915, promoted Capt. Nov. 1917. Served at Home and in India.

PHILIP COLLINS.

Admitted Oct. 1905. Member of Peake, Reed, Collins & Co., of 6 Bedford Row, W.C. Joined August 1914, as 2nd Lieut., The Rifle Brigade, and attained the rank of Capt. Killed in action at Hooge July 30, 1915.

ARTHUR AMERY COLLINSON.

Admitted Nov. 1907. Managing Clerk with Waltons & Co., of 101 Leadenhall Street, E.C. Joined Aug. 5, 1914, as Private, Hon. Artillery Company. Gazetted 2nd Lieut. 9th Batt. East Surrey Regt. Sept. 22, 1914, promoted Lieut. Dec. 1914, Capt. May 1915. Served in France. Reported missing at the Battle of Loos Sept. 25–26, 1915, and officially believed to have been killed in action on that date.

CHARLES HERBERT COLLIS.

Admitted July 1880, practising at Stourbridge. Served as Col., South Midland Division Royal Army Service Corps (T.).

FRANK REGINALD COLLIS.

Articled to Frank Collis, of Stoke-upon-Trent. Mobilised Aug. 1914, as Lieut., Royal Field Artillery, promoted Capt. June 1915, Major Commanding D/77th Brigade 16th Irish Division 1916. Served in France Jan. 1915 to Sept. 1916. Killed in action at Combles Sept. 27, 1916.

GEORGE DOUGLAS COLLIS.

Articled to F. L. Dickson, of Hanley. Served as 2nd Lieut., 6th Batt. North Staffordshire Regt.

HERBERT CHARLES CLIVE COLLIS.

Articled to Frank Collis, of Stoke-upon-Trent. Joined April 1917, as Cadet, Royal Field Artillery. Gazetted 2nd Lieut. A/277th Brigade Royal Field Artillery Oct. 1, 1917, promoted Lieut. Jan. 1919. Awarded the M.C. Served in France 1917 to 1919. Wounded Feb. 27, 1918.

MAURICE JAMES COLLIS-SANDES.

Admitted Jan. 1913, and at the outbreak of War was about to be admitted a partner in the firm of Young, Jones & Co., of 2 Suffolk Lane, E.C. Gazetted 2nd Lieut. 11th (Service) Batt. Royal Fusiliers, and subsequently promoted to Capt. Once mentioned in Dispatches. Killed in action Feb. 17, 1917.

EDGAR HENRY COLLISON.

Articled to E. M. Calvert, of Norwich. Joined Sept. 1914 as 2nd Lieut., 1/4 Batt. Norfolk Regt., and served with that regiment at Gallipoli. Invalided home with enteric fever and subsequently joined the Royal Flying Corps. Died from the effects of a flying accident in Norfolk, June 26, 1916.

EDWIN READ COLLISSON.

Admitted Feb. 1910. Member of G. R. Thorne, Sons & Co., of Wolverhampton. Mobilised Aug. 1914, and served for some months as Transport

Officer. Went to France Feb. 1915 and promoted Capt. and Adjutant 1/6 South Staffordshire Regt. Killed in action Oct. 13, 1915.

ARTHUR THOMAS COLMAN.

Admitted Feb. 1904, practised at 21 Essex Street, Strand, W.C. Joined Sept. 1914, as Private, Australian Voluntary Hospital, and in May 1915 joined Inns of Court O.T.C., transferred subsequently as Private to 7th Batt. Middlesex Regt. Served in France, Wounded Aug. 27, 1916, and died Aug. 28, 1918. Buried at Ligny-sur-Canehe.

CLEMENT GEORGE COLMAN.

Admitted May 1911, practised at 25 Bedford Row, W.C. Joined July 26, 1915, as Lieut., Army Pay Department, promoted Capt. July 1918. Served in France.

FREDERICK JOHN COLSON.

Admitted July 1899, practising at 22 Walbrook, E.C. Joined Aug. 6, 1914, as Private, 15th Batt. County of London Regt. (Civil Service Rifles), and afterwards promoted Lance-Corporal. Gazetted 2nd Lieut. Somerset Light Infantry Dec. 15, 1916, promoted Lieut. June 1918. Recruiting Officer and Military Representative (Finsbury) March 1917, Chief National Service Representative, County of Kent, Oct. 1918. Served at Home.

AUGUSTUS GILBERT COLVILE.

Admitted Jan. 1899. Member of Adams & Colvile, of 5 Frederick's Place, Old Jewry, E.C. Joined Sept. 28, 1914, as Capt., 22nd (Service) Batt. Royal Fusiliers, Staff-Capt. 24th Training Reserve Brigade Feb. 1917 to Jan. 1918. Served at Home.

ROBERT GEORGE COMMIN.

Admitted Feb. 1911. Member of Stanley Robinson & Commin, of 170 Strand, W.C., and St. Albans. Joined Dec. 9, 1915, as Private, 28th Batt. County of London Regt. (Artists Rifles). Obtained commission May 28, 1917, and posted to 3rd Batt. West Yorkshire Regt., posted to 21st (Service) Batt. July 1917, rank Lieut. Served at Home till July 26, 1917, and in France July 1917 to Jan. 1919.

GERALD EDMONDS COMPSTON.

Admitted Oct. 1910. Member of Rollit, Sons & Compston, of 3 Mincing Lane, E.C. Joined July 17, 1918, as Private, Inns of Court O.T.C., promoted Lance-Corporal Aug. 1918. Served at Home.

JOHN HEXT COMYNS.

Admitted Dec. 1901, practised at Torquay. Served as 2nd Lieut., 1st Batt. Hertfordshire Regt., and afterwards promoted Lieut. Given the rank of Capt. whilst Courts-Martial Officer.

JOHN CONCHAR.

Admitted June 1911. Member of Sugden, Dewhirst & Conchar, of Bradford. Joined Aug. 12, 1914, as Lance-Corporal (Dispatch Rider), Royal Engineers, promoted Sergeant Dec. 1916. Gazetted 2nd Lieut. West Yorkshire Regt. May 6, 1915, appointed Courts-Martial Officer, Tees Garrison, Nov. 1916,

Temp. Capt. General List May 1917. Served in France Nov. 1915 to Feb. 1916. Wounded at St. Eloi Jan. 24, 1916.

ALLAN GEORGE CONDI.

Articled to C. W. Allan Hodgson, of Carlisle. Joined July 1915, as 2nd Lieut., 5th Batt. Border Regt. Served in France. Killed in action Oct. 1, 1916.

GEORGE AUGUSTUS VICTOR CONNOLLY.

Admitted Dec. 1909, practising in Solicitor's Department, South-Eastern & Chatham Railways. Gazetted 2nd Lieut. Royal Sussex Regt. Sept. 1914. Invalided from the Service Sept. 1915.

CLIFFORD GLOVER CONOLLY.

Admitted Oct. 1904. Member of White & Leonard, of Bank Buildings, Ludgate Circus, E.C. Served as Lieut., Royal Army Service Corps.

ALAN PENROSE COODE.

Admitted Nov. 1896. Member of Coodes, of St. Austell. Mobilised Aug. 1914, as Capt., Duke of Cornwall's Light Infantry, promoted Major June 1916. Once mentioned in Dispatches. Served in India 1914 and 1915, Aden 1916, Palestine and Egypt 1917 and 1918.

FREDERICK JOHN MERVYN COOK.

Articled to W. F. Cook, of Bristol. Mobilised Aug. 4, 1914, as Trooper, Royal Gloucestershire Hussars, transferred to 16th Machine Gun Squadron, E.E.F. 1916. Granted commission in 8th Batt. Somerset Light Infantry Nov. 28, 1917, promoted Lieut. Jan. 1919. Served at Home 1914 to March 1915, Egypt April to Aug. 1915, Gallipoli (Suvla Bay) Aug. to Dec. 1915, Sinai and Palestine Dec. 1915 to Aug. 1917, France and Belgium April 1918 to March 1919.

GEORGE ROPE COOK.

Admitted Aug. 1900. Member of Hannay, Horton & Cook, of Liverpool. Served as Private, 28th Batt. County of London Regt. (Artists Rifles).

JAMES WATSON COOK.

Articled to W. A. Cook, of Southport, Lancs. Joined Aug. 31, 1914, as Private, 7th Batt. King's Liverpool Regt. (T.F.). Promoted Sergeant July 1916. Commissioned Dec. 1916, and posted to 7th Batt. King's Liverpool Regt. Jan. 1917, promoted Lieut. June 1918, A/Capt. Jan. 1918. Awarded M.C. and Bar. Served in France from March 1915 to July 1916 and Feb. 1917 to Sept. 1918, and in Germany, Army of Rhine, Feb. to Nov. 1919.

PERCY MELLOWS COOK.

Admitted Oct. 1908. Assistant Solicitor to the Bournemouth Corporation. Joined Aug. 1915, as Private, 28th Batt. County of London Regt. (Artists Rifles). Gazetted 2nd Lieut. King's Royal Rifle Corps Dec. 6, 1915, promoted Lieut. Sept. 1916, A/Capt. Sept. 1916. Served in France. Killed in action near Flers Oct. 4, 1919.

VICTOR CHANDLER COOK.

Admitted June 1911, practising at 11 Mansion House Chambers, Queen Victoria Street, E.C. Joined Sept. 6, 1914, as Private, Hon. Artillery Company, promoted Lance-Corporal June 1915, Corporal July 1915. Gazetted 2nd Lieut. Royal Army Service Corps Sept. 21, 1915, promoted Lieut. May 1916, Capt. Dec. 1917. Once mentioned in Dispatches. Awarded O.B.E. Served in France Dec. 1914 to June 1919.

CHARLES TAYLOR COOKE.

Admitted June 1906. Member of John H. Cooke & Sons, of Winsford. Mobilised Aug. 1914, as Lieut., 7th Batt. Cheshire Regt., promoted Capt. 1915. Served at Home and at Gallipoli. Missing at Suvla Bay on Aug. 10, 1915, and afterwards presumed killed.

FREDERICK HORACE COOKE.

Admitted July 1895, practising at Crewe. Joined French Red Cross as Motor Driver July 1916. Awarded Croix de Guerre (French). Served in France.

GUY PROUDFOOT COOKE.

Articled to D. F. Cooke, of 17 Coleman Street, E.C. Mobilised Aug. 1914, as Ordinary Seaman, Royal Naval Volunteer Reserve, appointed Leading Seaman Aug. 1914. Gazetted Sub-Lieut. Dec. 29, 1914. Served in Antwerp expedition Oct. 1914, and at Gallipoli Feb. 1915. Killed in action at Gaba Tepe, Gallipoli, May 3, 1915.

HERBERT EDGAR COOKE.

Admitted June 1906. Member of Meade, King, Cooke & Co., of Bristol. Joined Sept. 3, 1914, as Private, Royal Fusiliers. Gazetted Dec. 1914 2nd Lieut. 2/1 Pembroke Yeomanry, promoted Lieut. 1916, Capt. 1918, attached Deputy A.P.M., Manchester. Served at Home and in France.

JOHN KEMP COOKE.

Admitted June 1903. Member of John H. Cooke & Sons, of Winsford, Cheshire. Mobilised Aug. 1914, as Major, 7th Batt. Cheshire Regt. Served at Home. Died July 29, 1915.

NORMAN FREDERIC COOKE.

Articled to J. B. Cooke, of Wakefield. Joined Sept. 20, 1914, as Private, 15th Batt. West Yorks. Regt. Gazetted 2nd Lieut. 10th Batt. North Staffordshire Regt. Sept. 27, 1915, promoted Lieut. July 1917. Served at Home Sept. 1914 to July 1916 and Nov. 1916 to March 1918, France July to Nov. 1916 and March 1918 to Jan. 1919. Wounded at Grandcourt Nov. 18, 1916, and at Lens May 11, 1918.

REGINALD BERTRAM COOKE.

Admitted Jan. 1906. Member of Colman & Knight, of 3 Verulam Buildings, Gray's Inn, W.C. Joined April 1916, as Private, Royal Army Service Corps. Gazetted 2nd Lieut. Royal Army Service Corps July 4, 1916, promoted Lieut. Jan. 1918. Served in France July 1916 to Dec. 1918.

REGINALD CHARLES COOKE.

Admitted March 1911, practised at Weston-super-Mare and Cardiff. Enlisted Aug. 1914, as Private, 11th Batt. Welch Regt. Gazetted 2nd Lieut. 9th Batt. Welch Regt. 1915. Twice mentioned in Dispatches. Awarded the M.C. Served in France. Killed in action at Contalmaison on July 7, 1916.

THOMAS COOKSEY.

Admitted Feb. 1904. Member of Thomas Cooksey & Co., of Old Hill, Staffs. Joined Oct. 1914, as 2nd Lieut., 6th Batt. Worcestershire Regt., promoted Capt. May 1916. Served at Home, France, and Serbia.

THOMAS OWEN COOKSEY.

Admitted Oct. 1908. Managing Clerk with W. J. Pitt, of Bridgenorth, Shropshire. Joined Feb. 4, 1915, as Lieut., Royal Army Ordnance Department, promoted Capt. Nov. 1918. Served at Home.

JOHN POWER HICKS COOKSON.

Admitted Oct. 1913. Managing Clerk with Brydges, Mellersh & Mellersh, of Cheltenham. Joined Sept. 1914, as Private, 2nd Public Schools Batt. Royal Fusiliers. Gazetted 2nd Lieut. March 1915, promoted Lieut. Dec. 1915, Capt. March 1916. Served at Home and France and Belgium.

CHARLES STANLEY COOMBE.

Admitted July 1903. Member of Gould & Coombe, of Sheffield. Joined Oct. 12, 1914, as 2nd Lieut., 4th Batt. York and Lancaster Regt., promoted Lieut. and Quartermaster Jan. 1915, Capt. and Quartermaster June 1918. Once mentioned in Dispatches. Served in France, Belgium, and Germany.

PHILIP GURNEY COOMBS.

Articled to Thomas Green, of Oundle, Northamptonshire. Joined Aug. 1914, as 2nd Lieut., Northamptonshire Regt., promoted Capt. Nov. 1915, transferred to Royal Garrison Artillery Sept. 1916 as Lieut. Served in France.

ALBERT GORDON COOPER.

Admitted April 1915, practised at Barnsley. Served as Private, Royal Fusiliers. Killed in action.

EDWARD VICTOR BRODIE COOPER.

Articled to J. L. Norris, of Stroud. Served as Private, 5th (Reserve) Batt. Gloucestershire Regt.

ERNEST READ COOPER.

Admitted July 1888, practising at Southwold, Suffolk. Gazetted Major commanding 3rd Vol. Batt. Suffolk Regt. Sept. 1, 1916. Served 2 months whole-time service in command of Special Service Company on East Coast during July and Aug. 1918. Once mentioned in dispatches.

FRANK COOPER.

Admitted April 1901. Member of James F. Addison & Cooper, of Walsall. Served as Corporal, 13th Company Royal Army Service Corps (M.T.).

FRANK COOPER.

Articled to William Irons, of Sheffield. Enlisted Oct. 1, 1915, as Rifleman, 5th City of London Batt. London Regt. (London Rifle Brigade), transferred to King's Royal Rifle Corps, Oct. 1916, promoted Lance-Corporal Nov. 1916. Killed Feb. 7, 1917, by rifle grenade when on duty in the trenches near Ypres.

GEOFFREY HERBERT COOPER.

Admitted Nov. 1912, practised at Manchester. Served as 2nd Lieut., 2nd East Lancashire Brigade, Royal Field Artillery (T.), and afterwards promoted Lieut.

JOHN GRAHAM COOPER.

Admitted Dec. 1904, practising at Birmingham. Joined Sept. 2, 1914, as Private, 1/6 Batt. Royal Warwickshire Regt. Gazetted 2nd Lieut. Sept. 19, 1915, Royal Warwickshire Regt., promoted Lieut. July 1917, A/Capt. June 1918. Once mentioned in Dispatches. Served in France March 1915 to Nov. 1917, Italy Nov. 1917 to Oct. 1918.

JOHN STUART COOPER.

Admitted April 1909, practising at Newcastle-on-Tyne. Served as Lieut., Royal Army Service Corps, and attained the rank of Major.

LANCELOT HEAD COOPER.

Articled to W. May, of 18 Austin Friars, E.C. Served as 2nd Lieut., 3rd Batt. Royal West Kent Regt.

REGINALD BRODIE COOPER.

Admitted Dec. 1899. Managing Clerk with Baileys, Shaw & Gillett, of 5 Berners Street, W. Joined June 1916, as Cadet, 28th Batt. County of London Regt. (Artists Rifles). Gazetted 2nd Lieut. Royal Garrison Artillery (S.R.) Nov. 30, 1916, promoted Lieut. May 1918. Served at Home till Aug. 1917, Gibraltar Aug. 1917 to Feb. 1919.

THOMAS COOPER.

Admitted Dec. 1906. Member of Hindle, Son & Cooper, of Darwen, Lancs. Joined Dec. 1915, as 2nd Lieut., 4th Batt. East Lancashire Regt. and subsequently promoted to Lieut. Severely wounded on the Somme May 24, 1918.

WILLIAM GORDON COOPER.

Articled to T. A. Higson, of Manchester. Served as Private, Royal Army Service Corps (M.T.).

WILLIAM HEINEKEN COOPER-HORSFALE.

Admitted Aug. 1891, practised at Northallerton. Joined Jan. 1915, as Capt., 4th Batt. Yorkshire Regt., transferred to Ministry of National Service May 1918. Served at Home.

WALLACE GRAHAM HOZIER COOPER-KING.

Admitted Dec. 1900, practising at 6 New Court, Carey Street, W.C. Joined July 22, 1915, as 2nd Lieut., 11th Batt. North Staffordshire Regt., promoted Lieut. May 1917. Served in France and Belgium July to Nov. 1916 and July to Dec. 1918.

ALEC COOPMAN.

Articled to E. H. Coopman, 5 Giltspur Street, Holborn, E.C. Joined Sept. 2, 1914, as Private, 20th Batt. Royal Fusiliers. Served in France only.

GEOFFREY SILVERWOOD COPE.

Articled to W. Silverwood Cope, of 5 New Court, Lincoln's Inn, W.C. Was in Inns of Court O.T.C. at outbreak of War. Medically examined and rejected as unfit for military service. Joined Headquarters Staff of Royal Red Cross Society Nov. 1914, equipped and was Transport Officer and subsequently secretary of King George Military Hospital, Stamford Street, S.E., from its foundation to its close. Awarded M.B.E. Served at Home.

CHARLES EDWARD FRASER COPEMAN.

Admitted Dec. 1895, practising at Wisbech, Cambs. Mobilised Aug. 1914 as Lieut.-Col. commanding 1st (Service) Batt. Cambridgeshire Regt., promoted Col. 1918, transferred to 9th Batt. Northamptonshire Regt. Name brought to the notice of Secretary of State for War on three occasions. Awarded C.M.G. and T.D. Served in France Feb. to May 1915 and at Home on East Coast.

JOHN YOUNG COPEMAN.

Admitted Oct. 1910, practising at Victoria, British Columbia. Joined Sept. 5, 1914, as Private, Royal Army Service Corps (M.T.), promoted Corporal Sept. 1914, Sergeant Nov. 1914. Gazetted 2nd Lieut. 3rd Batt. Leicestershire Regt. Sept. 1915, promoted Lieut. July 1917, Temp. Capt. attached 181st Infantry Brigade June 1918. Twice mentioned in Dispatches. Served in France Sept. 1914 to Sept. 1915, Mesopotamia June 1916 to Dec. 1917, Egyptian Expeditionary Force and Palestine Jan. 1918 to Feb. 1919.

HAROLD WALLACE COPLAND.

Articled to Charles Owen, of Stafford. Joined Sept. 1914, as Trooper, Staffordshire Yeomanry. Commissioned 2nd Lieut. Royal Field Artillery Nov. 5, 1914, promoted Lieut. July 1917, Capt. Aug. 1917. Served at Home and in France.

HENRY TOWNSEND COPLAND.

Admitted Nov. 1902, practising at Sheerness. Joined May 1918, as Private, Inns of Court O.T.C. Gazetted 2nd Lieut. The Queen's Own Royal West Kent Regt. Served at Home.

MAURICE COPLAND.

Admitted May 1902. Member of Copland & Sons, of 7 Union Court, Old Broad Street, E.C., and Chelmsford. Served as Private, 5th (Cinque Ports) Batt. Royal Sussex Regt. (T.). Died at the Stationary Hospital, Boulogne, on March 21, 1915.

REGINALD WALLACE COPLAND.

Articled to Charles Owen, of Stafford. Mobilised Aug. 4, 1914, as 2nd Lieut., 5th Batt. North Staffordshire Regt., promoted Lieut. Sept. 1914., transferred to Indian Army in Aug. 1917 to 3/1 K.G.O. Gurkha Rifles as Lieut., promoted Capt. April 1919. Served at Home 1914 to 1915, France 1915 to 1916, Home in 1916, France 1916 to 1917, India 1917 to 1919. Killed outside Fort Sandeman, Baluchistan, during the Afghanistan War, on July 26, 1919.

ALFRED BERESFORD COPLEY.

Admitted Jan. 1914, practised at Rotherham. Served as 2nd Lieut., Machine Gun Corps. Killed in action Aug. 26, 1917.

ADRIAN GRAY CORBETT.

Admitted Oct. 1911. Member of Slaughter & May, of 18 Austin Friars, E.C. Served as 2nd Lieut., Sussex Yeomanry. Awarded the Order of the Crown of Italy (Officer).

ROWLAND GEORGE CORBETT.

Admitted Oct. 1912. Managing Clerk with Fowler, Langley & Wright, of Wolverhampton. Joined Oct. 20, 1915, as Private, Royal Army Service

Corps (M.T.), promoted Corporal June 1916. Served at Home Oct. 1915 to Feb. 1916, France Feb. 1916 to Nov. 1917, Italy Nov. 1917 to Feb. 1919.

CLIVE SHEWELL CORDER.

Articled to W. S. Burton, of Newcastle-upon-Tyne. Joined April 1918, as Cadet, Durham University O.T.C. Served at Home.

BENJAMIN SPRINGBETT CORKE.

Admitted May 1896, practised at Gloucester. Joined April 30, 1917, 1st Regt. of the French Foreign Legion. Awarded Croix de Guerre (Silver Star). Served in France and Belgium.

NIGEL ARTHUR CORKE.

Articled to J. F. Duncan, 6 Old Jewry, E.C. Joined Oct. 13, 1914, as Private, Hon. Artillery Company. Served at Home Oct. 1914 to Jan. 1915 and Feb. 1915 to Aug. 1916, B.E.F. France, Jan. to Feb. 1915. Discharged Aug. 26, 1916.

ALFRED LINGHAM CORLETT.

Articled to Arthur Draycott, of Liverpool. Served as 2nd Lieut., 5th Batt. South Lancashire Regt., and attained the rank of Capt.

EDWARD JAMES CORNISH.

Articled to W. J. Sloan, of Bristol. Joined March 2, 1915, as 2nd Lieut., 1/4 Batt. Gloucestershire Regt., promoted Lieut., seconded to 51st (H.D.) Machine Gun Batt. June 6, 1918. Served in France and Germany. Wounded at Ypres, Aug. 16, 1917.

THOMAS HENRY CORNISH.

Admitted Jan. 1886. Member of T. H. & J. B. Cornish, of Penzance. Mobilised through National Reserve Aug. 4, 1914, as Col., 4th Batt. Duke of Cornwall's Light Infantry (T.), served as R.O. until Sept. 1915, then appointed Sub-Area Commander, No. 1 Cornwall. Served at Home.

PETER CHURCHILL CORNISH-BOWDEN.

Admitted Feb. 1900, practising at Newton Abbot, Devon. Joined June 12, 1916, as Private, 4th Batt. Devonshire Regt. (36th Provisional Batt.). Gazetted 2nd Lieut. 3rd (Foreign Service) Garrison Batt. Bedfordshire Regt. Feb. 11, 1917, transferred from 3rd (Foreign Service) Garrison Batt. Bedfordshire Regt. (at Rangoon) and to 25th Batt. Middlesex Regt. (at Singapore), promoted Lieut, Aug. 1918. Served at Home until March 1917, Burma to Nov. 1917, Singapore to July 1918, Siberia Aug. 1918 to Feb. 1919, Hong Kong March 1919, Home May to June 1919.

GUY TEMPLE CORRIE.

Articled to C. S. Hind, Ormond House, E.C. Joined Nov. 19, 1914, as A.B., Hawke Battalion Royal Naval Division. Gazetted 2nd Lieut. Royal Warwickshire Regt. Nov. 23, 1915, promoted Lieut. July 1917, Inspector of Propellants 1917 to 1919. Served in Gallipoli 1915, France 1916. Wounded at Delville Wood, France, July 28, 1916.

OWEN CECIL KIRKPATRICK CORRIE.

Admitted Dec. 1909. Managing Clerk with R. S. Taylor, Son & Humbert, 4 Field Court, Gray's Inn, W.C. Joined Aug. 5, 1914, as Private, Inns of Court

O.T.C. (Squadron). Gazetted 2nd Lieut. North Somerset Yeomanry Jan. 6, 1915, O.C. No. 9 (afterwards X/33) Trench Mortar Battery July 1915 to April 1916, A/Lieut. Dec. 1915, A/Capt., Trench Mortar Officer, 39th Division, B.E.F., April 1916 to May 1917, promoted Lieut. July 1917, A/Capt. Trench Mortar Officer, 54th Division, E.E.F., Sept. 1917 to Feb. 1918, transferred to Royal Field Artillery (T.F.), attached 272nd Brigade Aug. 1918, Temp. Capt., Military Magistrate, Nablus, and Judicial Officer, Haifa, March 1919, Temp. Major, Vice-President, Court of Appeal, Jerusalem, April 1919. Once mentioned in Dispatches. Awarded the M.C. Served in France June 1915 to July 1917, and in Palestine from July 1917.

JOHN SIDNEY CORSER.

Admitted June 1904, practised at Wellington, Shropshire. Served as Private, 5th Batt. Shropshire Light Infantry.

JAMES RUSSELL CORT.

Admitted Dec. 1908, practised at Manchester. Served as Lieut., Seaforth Highlanders.

RALPH EDGAR COSTELLO.

Articled to Henry Clarkson, of 9 Ironmonger Lane, E.C. Served as 2nd Lieut., 10th Batt. Duke of Wellington's West Riding Regt.

JOHN NICHOLDS FRANKLIN COTTERELL.

Articled to John N. Cotterell, of Walshall. Joined March 25, 1918, as Cadet at No. 3 Royal Field Artillery Officers' Cadet School, Weedon. Gazetted 2nd Lieut. Sept. 16, 1918, posted to 14th Battery 3A Reserve Brigade. Served at Home (Southern Command).

ROBERT ARTHUR COTTON.

Articled to John Davies, of Llanidloes, North Wales. Joined March 11, 1915, as Private, 2/7 Batt. Royal Welch Fusiliers. Gazetted 2nd Lieut. to 5th Batt. East Lancashire Regt. May 21, 1915, Lieut. and Quartermaster May 1915, seconded to Machine Gun Corps March 1918. Served at Home March 1915 to Oct. 1916 and March 1918 to July 1918, Egypt and Sinai Oct. 1916 to March 1917, France March 1917 to March 1918 and July 1918 to Oct. 1918. Wounded Aug. 31, 1918.

JONATHAN COUCH.

Articled to John Stephens, of St. Austell. Embodied as Corporal in the Royal 1st Devon Yeomanry Aug. 5, 1914, promoted Sergeant Oct. 1915, Squadron-Quartermaster-Sergeant March 1916. Granted commission as 2nd Lieut. 2nd Batt. Wiltshire Regt. March 27, 1918. Served at Home and in France. Wounded Nov. 5, 1918.

CHARLES DOUGLAS COULBY.

Articled to J. A. H. Green, of Nottingham. Joined March 16, 1915, as 2nd Lieut., 7th (Robin Hood) Batt. The Sherwood Foresters, promoted Lieut. Dec. 1916, seconded Tank Corps Jan. 1918, A/Capt. Oct. 1918, Temp. Capt. Dec. 1918. Served in France 1915, 1916, 1917, 1918. Wounded at Hohenzollern Redoubt Oct. 13, 1915.

AUBREY EWAN COULTON.

Admitted April 1913. Member of Coulton & Son, of King's Lynn. Mobilised Aug. 1914, as Capt., 6th Batt. Norfolk Regt. Went to France attached to the Royal Warwickshire Regt., and was killed in action at Laventie July 19, 1916.

WILLIAM HENRY COUPE.

Admitted March 1909. Member of Coupe & Harrison, of Preston, Lancs. Joined Sept. 15, 1916, as Private, Loyal North Lancashire Regt., transferred to Army Pay Corps Nov. 1916, to 3rd King's Own Scottish Border Regt. Aug. 1918, and attained the rank of Corporal both in the Army Pay Corps and in the Border Regt. Served at Home.

CECIL HALES COURT.

Admitted Dec. 1913. Member of W. H. Court & Son, of 181 Piccadilly, W. Mobilised Aug. 1914, as Private, Inns of Court O.T.C. Gazetted 2nd Lieut. 19th Batt. London Regt. Oct. 3, 1914, promoted Lieut. June 1916, A/Capt. Nov. 1916, Captain Aug. 1918, Staff-Lieut. War Office Nov. 1918. Served at Home.

WILLIAM COURT.

Articled to F. J. Argles, of Maidstone. Joined Dec. 11, 1915, as Private, 15th (T.R.) Batt., promoted Lance-Corpl. Manchester Regt., transferred to Royal Garrison Artillery. Commissioned 2nd Lieut. April 15, 1918. Served in France.

ALEXANDER PANTÉLIS COUSTAS.

Articled to J. J. Stavridi, of 40 Old Broad Street, E.C. Served as Staff-Sergeant-Major, Royal Army Service Corps.

DOUGLAS FREEMAN COUTTS.

Articled to W. M. Walter, of 31 Budge Row, E.C. Served as 2nd Lieut., 10th Batt. London Regt.

HERBERT JOHN COVE.

Admitted Nov. 1898, practised at Northampton. Served as 2nd Lieut., Northamptonshire Yeomanry.

CHARLES STUART COW.

Admitted Oct. 1904. Member of Horsley & Weightman, of 1 Guildhall Chambers, Basinghall Street, E.C. Joined June 1917, as Private, Inns of Court O.T.C. Gazetted 2nd Lieut. Royal Army Service Corps Oct. 1917. Served in France and at Home.

HENRY WALTER COWEN.

Articled to George Elder, of Newcastle-upon-Tyne. Joined May 8, 1916, as Dispatch Rider with Signal Section of Royal Engineers. Gazetted 2nd Lieut. Royal Garrison Artillery in 1918. Killed in action in France on or about Sept. 27, 1918.

MYER HENRY COWEN.

Articled to Joseph Cohen, of Birmingham. Joined July 26, 1917, as Private, Royal Warwickshire Regt., promoted Corporal July 1918, transferred to Army Pay Corps immediately after joining the Forces. Served at Home.

CLIFFORD HORACE HENRY COWL.

Admitted April 1908. Member of Arthur E. Cowl & Son, of Great Yarmouth. Joined Jan. 15, 1919, as Private, 28th Batt. County of London Regt. (Artists Rifles), promoted Lance-Corporal 1915, Corporal 1916. Gazetted 2nd Lieut. 5th (Reserve) Batt. Durham Light Infantry March 10, 1917, seconded to 12th Infantry Labour Company Lincolnshire Regt. March 1917, promoted Lieut. Sept. 1918. Served at Home Jan. 1915 to March 1917, and in Belgium and France March 1917 to Feb. 1919.

HENRY LETHBRIDGE COWLARD.

Admitted July 1905. Member of Cowlard, Grylls & Cowlard, of Launceston. Joined Sept. 18, 1914, as Capt., 10th Batt. Welch Regt., Staff-Capt. 76th Infantry Brigade, 25th Division, Jan. 1915. Served at Home and in France and Belgium.

GEORGE HAMILTON IVENS COWLEY.

Admitted Nov. 1908, practising at Coventry. Served as 2nd Lieut., 90th Heavy Battery Royal Garrison Artillery.

JOHN NORMAN COWLEY.

Admitted Jan. 1912. Of Boxmore, Herts. Joined Sept. 7, 1914, as Private, 28th Batt. County of London Regt. (Artists Rifles). Gazetted 2nd Lieut. 4th Batt. East Anglian Field Artillery Brigade Feb. 20, 1915, promoted Lieut. Dec. 1915, Capt. and Adjutant 19th Brigade Royal Horse Artillery July 1917. Once mentioned in Dispatches. Served in France Nov. 1914 to Feb. 1915, Egypt and Palestine Feb. 1915 to Oct. 1918.

RONALD FOSTER COWLISHAW.

Admitted Feb 1911. Member of Cowlishaw & Son, of Uttoxeter. Served as Private, 10th Batt. Royal Fusiliers. Subsequently gazetted 2nd Lieut. 5th Batt. North Staffordshire Regt.

BERNARD KILMISTER COX.

Admitted March 1912, practising at Leeds. Served as Sergeant, 30th Motor Ambulance Convoy.

CECIL HAMMOND COX.

Articled to E. A. B. Cox, of Birmingham. Joined Aug. 21, 1915, as Private, Royal Army Medical Corps, promoted Sergeant April 1916. Served in France.

DUDLEY ALFRED COX.

Articled to J. F. Fowler, of 1 York Buildings, Adelphi, W.C. Joined Sept. 15, 1914, as 2nd Lieut., The East Yorkshire Regt., promoted Lieut. Oct. 1914, Capt. Sept. 1915. Once mentioned in Dispatches. Awarded the M.C. Served in France 1914 to 1915 (6 months), Alexandria Nov. 1915 (1 month), Macedonia Dec. 1915 to Aug. 1918, Constantinople March 1919 (1 month). Slightly wounded at Loos Oct. 1915.

EDWARD GEOFFREY HIPPISLEY COX.

Admitted Feb. 1907. Member of Dyson, Bell & Co., of 3A Dean's Yard, Westminster, S.W. Mobilised Aug. 1914, as Lieut., 16th Batt. County of London Regt. (Queen's Westminster Rifles), promoted Capt. Sept. 1914, Brevet Major in Army June 1917, Major (Substantive) Sept. 1917, Temp. Lieut.-Col.

in Army May 1918, On Staff, Staff-Capt. July 1915, D.A.Q.M.G. March 1916, D.A.A.G. Aug. 1917, A.A.G. May 1918 (London District). Twice mentioned in Dispatches. Awarded Brevet Major in Army, C.B.E. (Military). Served in France and at Home.

HARLEIGH COX.

Articled to W. F. Long, of Bath. Mobilised Aug. 1914, as Lieut., 1st Batt. Gloucestershire Regt., and promoted Capt. 8th Batt. Gloucestershire Regt. Dec. 27, 1914. Killed in action near the village of La Boiselle July 3, 1916.

LEONARD CHARLES COX.

Admitted Oct. 1909. Member of Byrch, Cox & Sons, of Evesham. Joined Nov. 1915, as Private, Inns of Court O.T.C. Commissioned Lieut. Worcestershire Regt. 1916. Served in France. Wounded March 1918.

SYDNEY GEORGE COX.

Admitted March 1908. Member of Coad & Cox, of 27 Old Jewry, E.C. Joined July 5, 1916, as Private, 10th Batt. Middlesex Regt. Gazetted 2nd Lieut. 1/8 Batt. Middlesex Regt. March 28, 1917, promoted Lieut. Sept. 1918. Served in France.

TARRANT DORAN COX.

Admitted May 1910. Managing Clerk with Francis & Crookenden, of 23 Lincoln's Inn Fields W.C. Joined Aug. 26, 1914, as Rifleman, 9th Batt. King's Royal Rifle Corps, promoted Lance-Corporal 8th Batt. Sept. 1915. Served in Belgium and France May 1915 to July 1916. Wounded at Ypres July 11, 1915, and at Arras July 1, 1916. Discharged through wounds received in action Oct. 20, 1916.

BASIL COZENS-HARDY.

Admitted July 1911. Member of Cozens-Hardy & Jewson, of Norwich. Joined Oct. 21, 1914, as 2nd Lieut., 4th (Reserve) Batt. Norfolk Regt., promoted Lieut. 1916, Capt. Aug. 1917. Served at Home to Aug. 1918, and in France Aug. to Sept. 1918. Wounded—leg amputated—near St. Quentin Sept. 18, 1918.

NEWMAN CRABTREE.

Admitted Jan. 1897. Member of Clough & Crabtree, of Cleckheaton. Joined Aug. 15, 1914, as Private, 4th Batt. West Riding Regt. Gazetted Lieut. West Yorkshire Regt. Sept. 23, 1914, promoted Capt. Dec. 1914, A/Major Nov. 1916 to Jan. 1917. Awarded the M.C. Served at Home and France.

RONALD ARTHUR CHARLES CRADOCK-HARTOPP.

Admitted Feb. 1905. Formerly member of Marcy & Hartopp, of 7 New Square, Lincoln's Inn, W.C. Joined Sept. 15, 1914, as Private, University and Public Schools Batt. 20th Royal Fusiliers, Company Quartermaster-Sergeant Sept. 1914. Gazetted Lieut. Royal Flying Corps Oct. 23, 1917. Served at Home and France. Invalided from France 1916 with trench fever and neuritis contracted on active service.

GEOFFREY ETHELBERT CRAGG.

Admitted July 1910, practised at Reigate. Mobilised Aug. 1914, as Sergeant, 5th Batt. Queen's Royal West Surrey Regt., volunteered in Aug.

1915 to go from India to Persian Gulf, and reverted to Corporal. Served at Home, in India, and in Mesopotamia. Died of dysentry at Kut-el-Amara on Oct. 17, 1915.

ALLEN HOYTE CRAIG.

Admitted April 1909. Managing Clerk with James Mellor & Coleman, of 12 Coleman Street, E.C. Joined Nov. 10, 1914, as Private, Royal Army Service Corps (M.T.). Gazetted 2nd Lieut. Royal Army Service Corps Sept. 14, 1915, and attained the rank of A/Capt. Served in British Expeditionary Force Nov. 1914 to Nov. 1918, and afterwards with British Army of the Rhine.

THOMAS EDGAR CRAIK.

Articled to J. H. Craik, of Batley. Mobilised Aug. 1914, as 2nd Lieut., 4th King's Own Yorkshire Light Infantry (T.F.), promoted Lieut. June 1914, Capt. Nov. 1915, Major (temporary rank in Machine Gun Corps) Feb. 1918. Awarded the M.C. Served in England till Sept. 1915 and from Dec. 1917 to Dec. 1918, and in France and Belgium Sept. 1915 to Dec. 1917.

PERCY CRAMPTON.

Admitted June 1913. Member of T. R. Dootson, of Leigh. Joined May 1915, as Private, Inns of Court O.T.C. Gazetted Lieut. 2/5 Batt. Loyal North Lancashire Regt. Aug. 1915. Once mentioned in Dispatches. Awarded the M.C. Served in France. Wounded May 24, 1917.

ALBERT CHARLES CRANE.

Articled to F. W. Beck, of 21 Lime Street, E.C. Served as Corporal, Machine Gun Corps. Killed in action in France July 23, 1916.

LUCIUS FRANCIS CRANE.

Admitted Dec. 1907. Member of Francis Miller & Steele, of 6 Finsbury Square, E.C. Joined Sept. 1915, as Cadet, 28th Batt. County of London Regt. (Artists Rifles). Gazetted 2nd Lieut. 14th Batt. Worcestershire Regt. Aug. 4, 1917. Served in France. Gassed March 1918. Killed in action near Cambrai Oct. 8, 1918.

PERCIVAL JETHRO CRANG.

Articled to J. T. Bond, of Plymouth. Joined Aug. 1, 1915, as Private, Argyll and Sutherland Highlanders. Gazetted 2nd Lieut. Devonshire Regt. Oct. 25, 1916, went to France Nov. 1916. Served at Home and in France. Placed on retired list through ill-health contracted on active service July 8, 1918. Totally incapacitated from "retirement." Died from effects on March 18, 1920.

LEONARD GEORGE CRAUFORD.

Admitted Dec. 1910, practising at 69 Chancery Lane, W.C. Joined Oct. 1916, as Sapper, London Electrical Engineers, promoted Corporal June 1918. Served at Home (Anti-Aircraft).

ALEXANDER BASIL CRAWFORD.

Admitted June 1914, practised at Boston, Lincs. Enlisted Aug. 1914, as Private, 4th Batt. Lincolnshire Regt. (T.). Gazetted 2nd Lieut. 14th Batt. Notts and Derby Regt. Feb. 1915, promoted Capt. 17th Batt. West Yorkshire Regt. Sept. 1915. Killed in action near Richboorg St. Vaust May 16, 1916.

FRANK SPENCER CRAWFORD.

Articled to R. H. Spencer, of Tredegar, Mon. Joined Sept. 21, 1914, as 2nd Lieut., 3rd Batt. Monmouthshire Regt., promoted Lieut. Feb. 1915, Capt. Dec. 1916, attached 18th Batt. Middlesex Regt. Aug. 1916 to Oct. 1917, and to 9th Batt. Cheshire Regt. Feb. to Sept. 1919. Served at Home 1½ years, and in France and with Army at the Rhine 3½ years. Seriously wounded, Ypres Salient, May 3, 1915.

HAMILTON WALKER CRAWFORD.

Admitted May 1905. Member of Ingledews, Sons & Crawford, of Swansea. Joined Feb. 9, 1915, as 2nd Lieut., 2/1 Pembroke Yeomanry, promoted Lieut. 1916, seconded Machine Gun Corps (Cavalry) 1918. Served at Home.

HUGH CRAWFORD.

Articled to R. W. Brighouse, of Ormskirk. Served as Private, 17th (Service) Batt. King's Liverpool Regt. Killed in action.

WILLIAM LINDSAY CRAWFORD.

Admitted March 1909, practising at Doncaster. Gazetted 2nd Lieut., 5th Batt. King's Own Yorkshire Light Infantry Aug. 28, 1914, promoted Lieut. 1915, Capt. June 1916. Awarded the M.C. and Croix de Guerre (gold star). Served in France, Belgium, and Germany.

FRANCIS SEYMOUR CRAWSHAW.

Articled to G. H. Simpson, of Sheffield. Joined the Machine Gun Corps in January 1916 as a Private. Served at Salonica. Died of disease in Hospital at Salonica Sept. 19, 1918.

FRANCIS CRAZE.

Admitted Jan. 1911. Of Canada. Served as 2nd Lieut., 5th Batt. Duke of Cornwall's Light Infantry, attached 6th Batt. Devonshire Regt., promoted Lieut., held the rank of Capt. whilst Courts-Martial Officer.

ROBERT HENRY HERBERT CREAK.

Admitted Nov. 1886, practising at Birmingham. Was Major, 8th Batt. Worcestershire Regt., at outbreak of War. Retained same rank except for short period as A/Lieut.-Col. in France. Served in 7th (Reserve) Batt. Worcesteshire Regt. after return to England. Served in France and Belgium March 1915 to April 1916, and remainder at Home.

HARRY WILLIAM HAY CREASY.

Articled to R. J. Cooke, of 22 Surrey Street, Victoria Embankment, W.C. Joined Aug. 5, 1914, as Private, Inns of Court O.T.C. Gazetted 2nd Lieut. 10th Batt. Devonshire Regt. Sept. 19, 1914, promoted Temp. Lieut. 11th Batt. Essex Regt. Oct. 1915, Temp. Capt. March 1916. Awarded the M.C. Served in France Oct. 1915 to June 1916. Killed in action June 13, 1916.

CHARLES EDWARD VICTOR CREE.

Articled to his father, A. W. Cree, of 13 Gray's Inn Square, W.C. Joined Sept. 1914, as Private, Inns of Court O.T.C. Subsequently gazetted 2nd Lieut. 6th Batt. Notts and Derby Regt. (Sherwood Foresters), proceeded to France July 1915, and promoted Lieut. Oct 1915. Killed in action July 20, 1916.

HERBERT EDWARD CREE.

Admitted Feb. 1895. Member of Cree & Turner, of 109 Jermyn Street, St. James's, S.W. Joined Oct. 1914, as A.B., Royal Naval Volunteer Reserve, subsequently promoted Chief Petty Officer.

JOHN FRANCIS GEORGE CREE.

Admitted Aug. 1907. Member of Cree & Son, of 13 Gray's Inn Square, W.C. Served as 2nd Lieut., 9th Batt. Bedfordshire Regt., afterwards transferred to the Welch Regt. and promoted Lieut.

CHARLES NUGENT CREECH.

Articled to W. H. Creech, of Blandford and Sturminster Newton. Joined Sept. 7, 1914, as Gunner, 1st Dorset Battery Royal Field Artillery (T.), transferred to Headquarters 217th Brigade Royal Field Artlllery in 1916 with rank of Bombardier. Served at Home Sept. to Oct. 1914, and in India Nov. 1914 to March 1919.

LESLIE CREERY.

Articled to N. H. Wightwick, of Canterbury. Served as Private, Public Schools Batt. Royal Fusiliers, afterwards gazetted 2nd Lieut. 4th Batt. Royal West Kent Regt., promoted Lieut. July 1917.

ALFRED CRERAR.

Admitted April 1898, practising at Maryport, Cumberland. Gazetted Dec. 1, 1915, 2nd Lieut. 3/4 East Lancashire (Howitzer) Brigade Royal Field Artillery, promoted Temp. Lieut. Jan. 1916, Lieut. July 1917, A/Capt. No. 3 Siege Artillery Reserve Brigade Royal Garrison Artillery Oct. 1917. Served at Home only.

EDWARD ARTHUR CRESSWELL.

Admitted April 1905. Managing Clerk with Neve Thorneycroft & Co., of Wolverhampton. Rejoined Aug. 4, 1914, as Lieut., 6th Batt. South Staffordshire Regt. (T.), promoted Capt. May 1915. Served in France Feb. to Oct. 1915. Killed in action Oct. 13, 1915.

FRANCIS NATHANIEL CRESWICK.

Admitted Nov. 1899, practising at Sheffield. Joined Sept. 7, 1914, as Lieut. (T.F. General List), Supernumerary Company attached West Yorkshire Regt. (T.F.), promoted Capt. April 1915, transferred to Royal Defence Corps May 1916, 1st Garrison Batt. King's Own Yorkshire Light Infantry May 1917, attached 1st Garrison Batt. Northumberland Fusiliers Nov. 1917. Served at Home Sept. 1914 to Nov. 1917, and at Malta Nov. 1917 to March 1919.

GEORGE WALTON CRICKETT.

Admitted June 1908. Member of Charles Howard & Co., of Manchester. Joined Aug. 1914 as Private. Gazetted 2nd Lieut. North Staffordshire Regt., and subsequently promoted Lieut. Served in France and India.

LAWRENCE LAYTON CRISP.

Articled to J. B. Allan, of 7 King's Bench Walk, Temple, E.C. Joined Sept. 3, 1914, as Private, 18th Batt. Royal Fusiliers. Gazetted 2nd Lieut. 13th Batt. The Cheshire Regt. Feb. 27, 1915, promoted Lieut. July 1917,

Capt. Labour Corps April 1918. Served in France Sept. 1915 to Feb. 1916 and Aug. 1916 to April 1919. Wounded in Battle of the Somme Oct. 1916.

ARCHIBALD THOMAS CROCKER.

Admitted Dec. 1912, practising at 21 Buckingham Street, W.C. Served as Corporal, Royal Army Service Corps.

WALTER ANGUS CROCKER.

Articled to W. C. Crocker, 93 Gresham Street, E.C. Joined Sept. 7, 1914, as Private, 17th (Service) Batt. Royal Fusiliers, attached 5th Machine Gun Company Nov. 1915 to March 1916, transferred to 85th Company Machine Gun Corps Nov. 1916 to Feb. 1919. Served at Home Sept. 1914 to Nov. 1915 and March to Oct. 1916, France Nov. 1915 to March 1916, Salonica Oct. 1916 to Dec. 1918, Constantinople Dec. 1918 to Jan. 1919. Wounded at Souchey (France) March 30, 1916.

WILLIAM CHARLES CROCKER.

Admitted July 1912, practising at 93 Gresham Street, E.C. Joined June 9, 1917, as Private, 28th Batt. County of London Regt. (Artists Rifles). Gazetted 2nd Lieut. 4th Batt. Dorsetshire Regt. June 1918, attached 1st Batt. Oct. 1918. Awarded the M.C. Served in France.

ERIC BERTRAM CROCKFORD.

Articled to A. L. Crockford, of Birmingham. Joined Sept. 1914, as Private, 14th Batt. Royal Warwickshire Regt. Gazetted 2nd Lieut. 6th Batt. Royal Warwickshire Regt. Aug. 1915, subsequently promoted Lieut. Served in France in 1916 and 1918.

LESLIE CHARLES CROCKFORD.

Admitted May 1913. Managing Clerk with Arthur L. Crockford, of Birmingham. Mobilised Aug. 1914, as Lieut., 6th Batt. Royal Warwickshire Regt. (T.F.), promoted Capt. March 1916, Staff-Capt. 143rd Infantry Brigade 1917, Brevet Major June 1918, D.A.Q.M.G., G.H.Q. (Italy), Oct. 1918. Twice mentioned in Dispatches. Awarded the M.C. and Italian Croce di Guerra. Served in England Aug. 1914 to March 1915, France March 1915 to Nov. 1917, Italy Nov. 1917 to March 1919.

DESMOND WARRICK CROFT.

Articled to E. H. Freshfield, of 31 Old Jewry, E.C. Mobilised Aug 1914, as Private, Inns of Court O.T.C. Commission in 5th Batt. South Wales Borderers Sept. 1914, promoted Lieut. Jan. 1915, Capt. Aug. 1915, Major March 1917. Twice mentioned in Dispatches. Awarded the D.S.O. and M.C. Served in France July 1915 to June 1917 and Nov. 1917 to April 1918. Twice wounded.

LEONARD WILBERFORCE CROFT.

Admitted Oct. 1905, practised at 68 Aldersgate Street, E.C. Served as Lieut., 9th Batt. East Lancashire Regt., and subsequently promoted Capt. Mentioned in Dispatches. Awarded the M.C.

EDWARD SPENCER CROFT-SMITH.

Articled to Wm. J. Robbins, of 218 Strand, W.C. Mobilised Aug. 1914 as Private, 28th Batt. County of London Regt. (Artists Rifles). Gazetted

2nd Lieut. King's Royal Rifle Corps March 1915. Served in France. Reported missing May 10, 1915, subsequently presumed to have been killed on that date.

HENRY CROFTON.

Admitted March 1903, practising at South Shields and Haltwhistle. Joined June 30, 1917, as Private, West Yorkshire Regt., subsequently promoted Corporal Army Pay Corps. Served in Egypt.

JOHN CECIL CROFTS.

Admitted March 1915. Of 92 Great Tower Street, E.C. Joined 1915, as Private, East Kent. Regt. (The Buffs). Gazetted 2nd Lieut. The Suffolk Regt. 1916, promoted Lieut. Labour Corps 1917. Served in France.

ALFRED CROMPTON.

Admitted Dec. 1911. Member of W. W. Crompton & Son, of Bury. Joined July 12, 1915, as 2nd Lieut., 11th Batt. North Staffordshire Regt., promoted Lieut. Jan. 1917. Served in France and Belgium. Severely wounded at Wytcheate Ridge, July 21, 1917, and at Havrincourt Wood (Cambrai), Sept. 15, 1918.

NEVILLE CROMPTON.

Articled to T. R. Bertwhistle, of Bury. Joined Dec. 18, 1914, as 2nd Lieut., attached to Royal Flying Corps Nov. 1916, promoted Lieut. Nov. 1917, transferred to Royal Air Force April 1918, promoted Capt. and Flight-Commander April 1918. Once mentioned in Dispatches. Served at Home Dec. 1914 to Feb. 1916, Egypt Feb. 1916 to April 1917, France May 1917 to Feb. 1919.

WILLIAM EARLE CROMPTON.

Admitted April 1908. Member of Crompton & Crompton, of Bolton, Lancs. Served as Private, Royal Army Service Corps (M.T.).

LESLIE ARTHUR CROOK.

Articled to Merton A. Jones, of 11 Old Jewry Chambers, E.C. Mobilised Aug. 1914 with 28th Batt. County of London Regt. (Artists Rifles), went to France in Oct. 1914, and given a commission in The Queen's Royal West Surrey Regt. in Jan. 1915, promoted Capt. in July 1917. Twice mentioned in Dispatches. Awarded the M.C. Served in France and Belgium. Wounded three times. Killed in action Sept. 25, 1917.

CECIL WOODROW CROSS.

Admitted Nov. 1899. Member of Beckingsale, Greenwood, Tucker & Cross, 34 Copthall Avenue, E.C. Joined Nov. 16, 1914, as A.B., Royal Naval Volunteer Reserve. Subsequently gazetted Temp. Lieut.-Commander. Awarded O.B.E. (Military Branch).

EDWARD PEEL CROSS.

Admitted Aug. 1895, practising at Harrogate. Mobilised Aug. 1914, as Capt., 5th Batt. West Yorkshire Regt., promoted Major Jan. 1915. Gazetted to T.F. Reserve June 1918. Served at Home.

GEORGE HENRY CROSS.

Admitted May 1910, practised at Prescot. Served as Private, 10th Batt. King's Liverpool Regt. (Liverpool Scottish). Afterwards obtained commission in King's Liverpool Regt. and promoted Lieut.

JAMES HUNSDON CROSS.

Admitted July 1902, practising at Cardiff. Joined Sept. 4, 1914, as Private, Royal Fusiliers. Gazetted 2nd Lieut. The Welch Regt. May 4, 1915, promoted Lieut. Feb. 1916, transferred to 1st Batt. Tank Corps Dec. 1916, promoted Capt. Sept. 1918. Served in France and Belgium. Wounded and gassed at Villiers Bretonneux April 17, 1918.

PHILIP ANDREW CROSS.

Articled to E. W. Pierce, of Liverpool. Joined March 29, 1915, as Sub-Lieut., Royal Naval Volunteer Reserve, promoted Lieut. March 1916. Served in Home waters 1915 to 1916, and at Gibraltar 1917, 1918, 1919.

MARLBOROUGH EVELYN BEDFORD CROSSE.

Articled to H. B. E. Barwell-Ewins, of Birmingham. Enlisted Sept. 1914, as Private, 28th Batt. County of London Regt. (Artists Rifles). Went to France Oct. 26, 1914, and was there transferred to 2nd Batt. Yorkshire Regt. (The Green Howards) on Nov. 13, 1914, having received a commission as 2nd Lieut. and appointed Machine Gun Officer. Killed in action March 14, 1915.

CECIL CROSSKEY.

Admitted Feb. 1882. Member of Mathews, James & Crosskey, of Birmingham. Mobilised, as Major, Royal Army Service Corps, promoted Lieut.-Col. June 1916. Twice mentioned in Dispatches. Awarded O.B.E. (Military Division). Served at Home and in France and Belgium.

GUY ROBERT CROUCH.

Admitted Dec. 1912. Managing Clerk with Parrott & Coales, of Aylesbury. Mobilised Aug. 4, 1914, as Lieut., Oxford and Bucks Light Infantry (T.F.), promoted Temp. Capt. Sept. 1914, Capt. July 1916, A/Major Aug. 1918, attached to 1/5 Batt. Gloucester Regt. July 1918. Once mentioned in Dispatches. Awarded the M.C. Served at Home Aug. 1914 to March 1915, France March 1915 to Nov. 1917, Italy Nov. 1917 to Sept. 1918, and again in France Sept. 1918 to Jan. 1919. Wounded in front of Peronne Feb. 28, 1917.

LIONEL WILLIAM CROUCH.

Admitted Dec. 1909, practised at Aylesbury. Mobilised Aug. 4, 1914, as Capt., 1st Bucks. Batt. Oxford and Bucks Light Infantry. Served at Home Aug. 1914 to March 1915, and then in France. Killed in action in the 1st Battle of the Somme July 21, 1916.

ARTHUR ARNOLD CROW.

Articled to F. W. Mander, of 7 New Square, Lincoln's Inn, W.C. Joined Aug. 1914, as Private, 28th Batt. County of London Regt. (Artists Rifles). Gazetted 2nd Lieut. 5th Batt. Loyal North Lancashire Regt. Nov. 26, 1914, promoted 1st Lieut. Dec. 1914, Capt. July 1915, appointed Adjutant of Officers' Instruction School, Tunbridge Wells, in the spring of 1915. In July 1916 resigned commission on account of ill-health. Subsequently went to Messines to assist Church Army in canteen work. On passing of the Review of Exemption Act in 1917 at once presented himself for examination, and was marked fit for active service. As, however, previous medical boards had refused to allow him to proceed to France as a commissioned officer, he enlisted in the Essex Regt. as a Private, proceeding to France on Sept. 7, 1917. He was killed Oct. 10, 1917, in the attack on the Passchendaele Ridge, 3rd Battle of Ypres.

GEORGE BERTRAM CROWDER.

Admitted Feb. 1902. Member of Vizard, Oldham, Crowder & Cash, of 51 Lincoln's Inn Fields, W.C. Joined Nov. 1, 1915, as 2nd Lieut., Royal Garrison Artillery (S.R.), promoted Lieut. July 1917, A/Capt. and Adjutant Aug. 1918. Once mentioned in Dispatches. Served in Serbia Aug. 1916 to Nov. 1918.

GODFREY DEVERIL CROWTHER.

Admitted Aug. 1902, practising at Plymouth. Served as Lieut., Devonshire Royal Garrison Artillery and subsequently promoted Capt.

JOHN EDWARD MARMADUKE CROWTHER.

Admitted July 1905. Member of Hargreaves & Crowthers, of 23 Abingdon Street, Westminster, S.W. Joined Dec. 28, 1914, as Private, 28th Batt. London Regt. (Artists Rifles). Gazetted 2nd Lieut. 11th Batt. East Surrey Regt. March 10, 1915, promoted Lieut. 13th Batt. July 1917. Awarded the M.C. Served at Home Dec. 1914 to May 1916, Sept. 1916 to May 1917, and March 1918 to Feb. 1919, and in France May to Sept. 1916, and May 1917 to March 1918. Wounded in attack on Flers Sept. 15, 1916, and in attack on Mory March 23, 1918.

PHILIP MAIN CROWTHER.

Admitted July 1914, practised at Bradford. Joined Sept. 1914, as Private, 6th Batt. West Yorkshire Regt. Commissioned May 1917 to 5th Batt. West Yorkshire Regt., gazetted Lieut. Nov. 1918. Served in France. Wounded at Thiepval July 14, 1916.

THOMAS PERCY CROYSDALE.

Articled to F. W. R. Hore, of 52 Lincoln's Inn Fields, W.C. Served as Lieut., 8th City of London Batt. London Regt. (Post Office Rifles) and subsequently promoted Capt.

ROBERT BARNARD CRUICKSHANK.

Admitted Dec. 1901, practising at Gosport, Hants. Joined June 1916, as Cadet Gunner, Royal Garrison Artillery. Gazetted 2nd Lieut. Royal Garrison Artillery (S.R.) Aug. 11, 1916, promoted Lieut. Feb. 1918. Served with 2nd Mobile Brigade, Royal Garrison Artillery Anti-Aircraft, Home, East Coast, and London Defences.

ROBERT SCOTT CRUICKSHANK.

Admitted April 1906, practised at 10 Billiter Square, E.C. Served as Lieut., Royal Army Service Corps and attained the rank of Temp. Major. Mentioned in Dispatches and awarded the O.B.E.

BERTRAM EVERSLEY CRUMP.

Admitted May 1905. Member of Crump, Duignan & Crump, of Walsall. Joined Aug. 31, 1917, as Private, Inns of Court O.T.C. Gazetted 2nd Lieut. Royal Army Service Corps Jan. 1, 1918. Served in France.

DUDLEY JAMES CRUMP.

Admitted May 1901. Member of William A. Crump & Son, of 17 Leadenhall Street, E.C. Joined March 22, 1915, as 2nd Lieut., 3/9 Batt. Middlesex Regt., promoted Lieut. Sept. 1915, Capt. March 1918, attached 24th Batt. The Rifle Brigade March 1917. Served at Home and India. Appointed on Staff, India, 1917.

ELDON ANNESLEY CRUMP.

Admitted April 1899. Member of Crump, Duignan & Crump, of Walsall. Mobilised Aug. 1914, as 2nd Lieut., South Staffordshire Regt., promoted Major Oct. 1914, Lieut.-Col. Commanding 5th (Reserve) Batt. South Staffordshire Regt. Nov. 1915. Once mentioned in Dispatches. Awarded the O.B.E. Served at Home.

WILLIAM GEOFFREY CRUMP.

Articled to William Clifton, of 17 Leadenhall Street, E.C. Joined June 27, 1915, as 2nd Lieut., 3rd Batt. The London Regt., promoted Lieut. Machine Gun Corps (Cavalry) Jan. 1, 1917, Lieut. Tank Corps Sept. 1917, Temp. Capt. Oct. 1918, Adjutant Dec. 1918. Twice mentioned in Dispatches. Served in France 2 years.

ERNEST FREDERIC CRUNDWELL.

Admitted Oct. 1912. Member of Cotter & Crundwell, of Farnham. Joined Aug. 11, 1914, as Private, 1/5 Batt. The Queen's Royal West Surrey Regt. (T.F.). Gazetted 2nd Lieut. 4th Batt. The Queen's Royal West Surrey Regt. March 27, 1917, promoted Lieut. Sept. 1918. Served in India Oct. 1914 to Dec. 1915, Mesopotamia Dec. 1915 to July 1916, Palestine June to Aug. 1917, Egypt Aug. 1917 to Sept. 1918, India Sept. 1918 to June 1919.

CYRIL KEITH CULLEN.

Articled to J. K. Allerton, of Worthing. Joined Dec. 27, 1915, as Private, 14th Batt. County of London Regt. (London Scottish), transferred March 1918 to Royal Flying Corps as Cadet Pilot. Subsequently gazetted 2nd Lieut. Served at Home 1916 and 1918, France 1917. Slight shrapnel wound May 1917.

GEORGE CHARLES HENRY CULLEY.

Articled to H. H. Cole, of Norwich. Joined Aug. 24, 1914, as 2nd Lieut., Norfolk Regt. Gazetted Lieut. April 1915, joined Machine Gun Corps in 1916, gazetted Capt. June 1916, joined Royal Flying Corps Sept. 1916. Served at Home 1914, Gallipoli 1915, Egypt 1916 and 1917, France 1918. Crashed at Aboukir, Egypt, in aeroplane Feb. 19, 1917.

CHARLES CULLIMORE.

Articled to John Cullimore, of Chester. Mobilised Aug. 1914, as 2nd Lieut., Cheshire Brigade Royal Field Artillery (T.F.), and attained the rank of Capt. (A/Major). Wounded at the Battle of Gaza, Palestine.

WILLIAM CULLIMORE.

Admitted April 1913. Managing Clerk to Birch, Cullimore & Co., of Chester. Mobilised Aug. 1914, as Private, Territorial Force. Subsequently gazetted Lieut. 5th Batt. Cheshire Regt.

GEORGE CHARLES HENRY CULLEY.
Articled to H. H. Cole, of Norwich. Served as Lieut., 4th Batt. Norfolk Regt., and as Flying Officer, Royal Flying Corps.

CHARLES HILL CULROSS.
Admitted Sept. 1905. Member of Culross & Co., of 13 Old Cavendish Street, W. Joined March 1915, as Lieut., R.T.O. Invalided from Service March 1916. Served in France and Central Force, Horse Guards.

JAMES CUMBERBIRCH.
Admitted May 1912, practising at Macclesfield. Served as Corporal, Royal Army Service Corps (M.T.).

JOHN LEONARD CUNLIFFE.
Articled to T. H. Davies-Colley, of Manchester. Joined Nov. 1914, as Lieut., 21st Batt. Manchester Regt., promoted Capt. June 1916. Served at Home Nov. 1914 to Sept. 1915, France Sept. 1915 to Sept. 1916. Killed in action at Delville Wood Sept. 4, 1916.

GRAHAM CUNNINGHAM.
Admitted Feb. 1915, practising at Chingford. Joined Aug. 14, 1915, as 2nd Lieut. 5th Batt. Royal Fusiliers, promoted Lieut. July 1917, A/Adjutant 4th Royal Fusiliers (France) 1916, Capt. and Adjutant 5th Royal Fusiliers 1917 to 1918, Capt. and Adjutant Headquarters Repatriated Prisoners of War Reception Camps, Canterbury. Served at Home and in France.

ERNEST CHARLES CURRAN.
Admitted April 1904. Member of Jackson, Elwell & Curran, of 65 Coleman Street, E.C. Joined July 1915, as Private, 28th Batt. County of London Regt. (Artists Rifles). Gazetted 2nd Lieut. Royal Army Service Corps Oct. 1915, promoted Capt. Nov. 1918. Served at Home July 1915 to Oct. 1917, France Oct. 1917 to March 1919.

GEORGE PATRICK CURRAN.
Admitted Aug. 1911, practised at 11 Talbot Road, Bayswater. Joined March 3, 1916, as Rifleman, 2nd Batt. County of London Regiment (London Irish Rifles). Served at Home, at Salonica, and with the Egyptian Expeditionary Force. Died at 26th Casualty Clearing Station, Ludd, Syria, May 21, 1918, from malignant malaria.

CURZON CURSHAM.
Admitted Oct. 1911. Member of Bernard Wright & Cursham, of Nottingham. Commissioned 2nd Lieut. 2/8 Batt. Notts and Derby Regt. (Sherwood Foresters) (T.F.) Nov. 12, 1914, promoted Lieut. (Permanent) July 1916, seconded to Machine Gun Corps Jan. 1918. Served in England 1914 to April 1916, Irish Rebellion April 1916, France Feb. 1917 to Feb. 1919.

LIONEL CHARLES ALFRED CURTIES.
Articled to F. G. Stenning, of Maidstone. Joined Sept. 18, 1914, as Private, University and Public Schools Corps. Gazetted 2nd Lieut. 8th (Service) Batt. East Kent Regt. (The Buffs), promoted Capt. June 1915 and attached to Staff of 72nd Infantry Brigade, appointed Brigade Machine

Gun Officer. Served in France. Reported missing, believed killed, at the Battle of Loos Sept. 26, 1915, since presumed by the War Office killed in action on that date.

ALEC CHARLES CURTIS.

Articled to Henry Pomeroy, of Bristol. Joined Aug. 14, 1914, as Trooper, 1/1 North Somerset Yeomanry, and discharged medically unfit for further service after injuries received in Flanders on Jan. 23, 1915. Re-enlisted as Private, Royal Army Medical Corps, on recovery on Aug. 15, 1915, joined the 100th Field Ambulance as a Corporal in France Nov. 1915, appointed A/Sergeant July 1917. Served in Flanders Nov. to Dec. 1914, and in France Nov. 1915 to Nov. 1916. Wounded at Ypres Dec. 1914.

ALFRED EDWIN IFOR CURTIS.

Admitted Feb. 1913. Member of Alfred Curtis & Son, of Neath, Glamorganshire. Joined April 1915, as Private, 23rd (Service) Batt. Royal Fusiliers. Commissioned 2nd Lieut. 6th Batt. The Welch Regt. Sept. 1915, Temp. Lieut. Sept. 1916, Permanent Lieut. Sept. 1917, A/Capt. and A/Adjutant Oct. 1917. Served at Home and France.

HENRY CURTIS.

Admitted Aug. 1905. Member of Barret & Curtis, of Leeds & Otley. Joined March 1916, as Private, 3/4 Batt. Cameron Highlanders, subsequently promoted Sergeant 653rd Employment Coy. General Headquarters, Ireland. Served in England and Ireland.

HENRY GEORGE CURTIS.

Admitted April 1907, practising at Southend-on-Sea. Served as Lance-Corporal, 22nd Batt. Royal Fusiliers.

OSWALD TREVOR CURTIS.

Articled to Harold W. Mooring Aldridge, of Bournemouth. Joined May 4, 1916, as Private, Hon. Artillery Company (Infantry), transferred to Royal Air Force to train for commission July 1918. Appointed Flight Cadet Nov. 1918. Discharged on appointment to Honorary Commission in Reserve of Officers. Served in France.

WALTER LAWRENCE CURTLER.

Articled to W. T. Curtler, of Worcester. Mobolised Aug. 1914, as Lieut., 8th Batt. Worcestershire Regt. (T.F.), promoted Capt. June 1915. Entered Indian Army (Gurkha Rifles) as Lieut. July 1917, promoted Capt. May 1919. Served in France March 1915 to Nov. 1916. Wounded June 1915.

ARTHUR ROBERT CUSHING.

Admitted Nov. 1905, practising at 28 Bedford Row, W.C. Joined the Ambulance Column attached to London District of the British Red Cross Society on March 15, 1915, as a Driver, and ultimately became a Quartermaster and head of the Car Department. Served at Home.

CLEMENT ARCHIBALD CUSSE.

Admitted Feb. 1912. Managing Clerk to Houseman & Co., of 6 New Court, Carey Street, W.C. Joined Oct. 20, 1914, as Private, Inns of Court

O.T.C. Obtained a commission and attained the rank of Major 1/4th Batt. Devonshire Regt., D.A.Q.M.G. Mesopotamia. Once mentioned in Dispatches.

JOHN CUTHBERT.

Admitted July 1899. Member of Percy Short & Cuthbert, of Donington House, Norfolk Street, Strand, W.C. Joined May 30, 1916, as Gunner, Royal Field Artillery. Discharged (unfit for service owing to ill-health in consequence of service) April 9, 1918. Served in France and Belgium Oct. 1916 to Oct. 1917.

ROBERT FREDERICK CUTHBERT.

Admitted May 1901. Member of Ravenor & Cuthbert, of Witney, Oxon. Joined Sept. 14, 1914, as 2nd Lieut., 4th Batt. Oxford and Bucks Light Infantry, promoted Capt. June 1916, Adjutant June 1916 to July 1918. Awarded the M.C. Served in France. Wounded near Arras Nov. 13, 1917.

JOHN WILLIAM CUTHBERTSON.

Admitted Oct. 1915, practising at Blyth, Northumberland. Joined Feb. 20, 1917, as Private, Royal Army Service Corps, and subsequently promoted Corporal. Served at Home.

GERALD WARING CUTLER.

Admitted March 1901. Member of Cutler & Allingham, of 15 Duke Street, St. James's, S.W. Served as Capt., Royal Army Ordnance Corps.

HOWARD FRANCIS DADDS.

Articled to W. A. G. Davidson, of Bank Buildings, Acton, W. Joined May 12, 1915, as Private, 2nd Batt. Hon. Artillery Company, promoted Sergeant 1919, transferred to 1st Batt. in France. Served at Home May 1915 to July 1916, in France July 1916 to Jan. 1919, and with Army of the Rhine Jan. to April 1919.

WALTER LEWIS DAGG.

Admitted Aug. 1881, practising at 65 Long Acre, W.C. Served as Farrier Sergeant-Major, Transport and Remount Department, attached Royal Army Service Corps.

CEDRIC HUNTON DAGGETT.

Articled to W. W. Gibson, of Newcastle-upon-Tyne. Joined Sept. 1914, as Private, 9th Batt. Northumberland Fusiliers. Gazetted 2nd Lieut. 21st Batt. Northumberland Fusiliers (2nd Tyneside Scottish), promoted Capt. and transferred to the 23rd Batt. Awarded the M.C. Served in France. Killed in a night raid at Armentières Feb. 11, 1917.

CHARLES LOUIS D'ALBANI.

Articled to A. J. D'Albani, of Newmarket. Served as Lieut., 3rd Batt. Suffolk Regt., subsequently promoted Capt. and transferred to the Indian Army.

ALWYNE PERCY DALE.

Admitted Oct. 1906, practised at Knaresborough and York. Mobilised Aug. 1914, as Capt., 5th Batt. West Yorkshire Regt. (T.), and subsequently promoted Major. Awarded the O.B.E. Served in France. Killed in action March 1, 1917.

CECIL HALSTED DALE.

Admitted April 1909. Member of Halsted Dale & Son, of 17 Finsbury Square, E.C. Joined as Private, Hon. Artillery Company, and subsequently gazetted Lieut. in same Regt. Served in Italy.

DONALD HALE DALE.

Admitted May 1912, practising at 6 South Square, Gray's Inn, W.C. Joined Nov. 11, 1914, as 2nd Lieut., Royal Army Service Corps, promoted Lieut. July 1915, and Capt. March 1916, transferred to 1/88 Carnatic Infantry Sept. 1918. Served in Macedonia Dec. 1916 to Sept. 1918, and in India Sept. 1918 to Sept. 1919.

ROBERT JACOMB NORRIS DALE.

Admitted Dec. 1909. Managing Clerk with Dale & Co., of 75 Cornhill, E.C. Joined Aug. 4, 1914, as Private, 28th Batt. County of London Regt. (Artists Rifles). Gazetted 2nd Lieut. 9th Batt. Manchester Regt. June 18, 1915, subsequently promoted Lieut. and attached to Royal Flying Corps. Served in Gallipoli, Egypt, and Italy. Killed in Italy while observing in captive balloon Jan. 31, 1917.

HUGH WALDRON DALLAS.

Articled to J. H. Dallas, 12 Old Jewry Chambers, E.C. Joined, as 2nd Lieut., 8th Batt. Norfolk Regt., promoted to Capt. Joined the Indian Army in 1919.

WILLIAM FREDERICK DALLAS.

Articled to R. R. Linthorne, Town Clerk of Southampton. Gazetted 2nd Lieut. Hampshire Regt. Oct. 8, 1914, attached to 6th Batt. East Lancashire Regt. in Sept. 1915, Temp. Capt. from Sept. 18 to Oct. 3, 1915, inclusive. Gazetted as granted a commission as 2nd Lieut. in The Welch Regiment (Permanent Army) Feb. 10, 1916, but pending joining that Regt. remained with the 6th Batt. East Lancashire Regt. as Lieut., and subsequently as A/Capt. Served at Gallipoli from Sept. 1915 to the time of the Evacuation, and afterwards in Mesopotamia. Killed in action at Sanna-i-Yat April 9, 1916, whilst serving with the Kut Relief Force.

ARTHUR DOUGLAS DALLOW.

Admitted Nov. 1907. Member of Dallow & Dallow, of Wolverhampton. Mobilised Aug. 5, 1914, as Sergeant, Queen's Own Royal Staffordshire Yeomanry. Gazetted Lieut. Royal Field Artillery Feb. 1915, promoted Capt. Oct. 1915. Once mentioned in Dispatches. Served in France 1916, Irish Rebellion 1916, France 1917, 1918, 1919.

CHAMPNEYS JOHN DALRYMPLE.

Articled to R. M. Welsford, of 22 Aldermanbury, E.C. Served as Lieut., 6th Batt. Leicestershire Regt.

ROBERT CECIL DALTON.

Admitted Jan. 1914. Member of Phillips, Evans & Dalton, of Stamford. Joined Sept. 4, 1914, as Private, 24th Batt. London Regt. Gazetted Lieut. 16th Batt. County of London Regt. (Queen's Westminster Rifles) in Feb. 1915, promoted Capt. in Indian Reserve Officers. Awarded the M.C. Served in France, Salonica, Palestine, and India. Wounded in Salonica.

WILLIAM EDWARD D'ANGIBAU.

Admitted Nov. 1913, practising with D'Angibau & Malim, of Boscombe, Hants. Joined Oct. 1, 1914, as 2nd Lieut., 7th Batt. Hampshire Regt., promoted Lieut. June 1916, attached Machine Gun Corps Sept. 1917. Served on North-Western Frontier twice, including Afghan Campaign, and India.

ALFRED MARTIN GEORGE DANIEL.

Admitted Dec. 1906. Member of Cruttwells, Daniel & Cruttwell, of Frome. Joined Nov. 1, 1914, as Lieut., 4th Batt. Somerset Light Infantry (T.F.), transferred to The Rifle Brigade (T.F.), Sept. 1915, A/Brigade General Officer 228th Infantry Brigade (28th Division), Salonica Forces, Aug. to Dec. 1918, A/Field Cashier Gen. Ross' Force, Bulgaria, Nov. 1918 to Jan. 1919, promoted Capt. Nov. 1918, to date from Dec. 23, 1917. Once mentioned in Dispatches. Served at Home Nov. 1914 to Jan. 1916, Egypt Jan. to April 1916, Cyprus April to May 1916, British Salonica Forces May 1916 to April 1919.

HENRY EDWIN DANIEL.

Admitted Jan. 1897, practising at Manchester. Commissioned April 25, 1915, as Lieut., No. 1 Supernumerary Coy. 4th Batt. The Welch Regt. Gazetted Lieut. 22nd Batt. The Rifle Brigade (T.F.) Nov. 1915. Served at Home and in Egypt, Cyprus, Lemnos, and Thasos, afterwards at Home. Contracted malaria in the Island of Thasos, and lost sight of left eye.

HENRY KENYON DANIEL.

Admitted Aug. 1897. Member of K. & W. Daniel, of Ramsgate and Margate. Commissioned Oct. 14, 1914, as Capt. Royal Field Artillery (T.), promoted Temp. Major Jan. 1915, Permanent Major Aug. 1917. When in France commanded "B" Battery, 180th Brigade. Once mentioned in Dispatches. Served at Home Oct. 1914 to Aug. 1917 and from Oct. 1918 to March 1919, and in France Aug. 1917 to Oct. 1918.

JOHN ARTHUR DANIEL.

Admitted Jan. 1908. Member of Simons, Smyth & Daniel, of Merthyr Tydfil. Joined May 1917, as Gunner, Royal Garrison Artillery, promoted Corporal (B.C.A.) Nov. 1917. Served in France.

NOEL THOMAS DANIEL.

Articled to W. L. Moore, of Newport, Mon. Joined Oct. 21, 1915, as Gunner, 4th Welsh Brigade Royal Field Artillery, transferred to B/87th Brigade upon proceeding to France Sept. 16, 1916. Served in France and Belgium. Killed in action April 25, 1918.

STANLEY MAYOU DANIEL.

Admitted March 1902, practising at Witham, Essex. Joined Jan. 29, 1918, as Gunner, Royal Garrison Artillery. Served in France.

JOHN ARTHUR HELTON DANIELL.

Admitted Feb. 1901. Member of J. L. & E. T. Daniell, of Bristol. Served as a Sergeant in 345th Siege Battery Royal Garrison Artillery. Killed in action July 1, 1917.

THOMAS EDWARD ST. CLARE DANIELL.
Admitted Feb. 1912. Managing Clerk with Mackrell & Ward, of 33 Walbrook, E.C. Joined Aug. 30, 1914, as Private, 28th Batt. County of London Regt. (Artists Rifles) and attained the rank of Sergeant. Gazetted 2nd Lieut. Royal Fly ng Corps Sept. 1915, promoted Capt. Jan. 1916, Major June 1916. Deputy Assistant Director of Aircraft Equipment (rank Major) Feb. 1917, Assistant (rank Lieut.-Col.) March 1917, Deputy Director (rank Col.) April 1918. Three times mentioned in Dispatches and awarded O.B.E. and M.C. Served in France and at Home.

DOUGLAS ARCHIBALD DANIELS.
Admitted Feb. 1916, practising at Chatham. Served as Private, Royal Army Service Corps (M.T.).

WILLIAM LEIGHTON DANN.
Admitted Oct. 1912, practised at Derby. Served as Private, 1st Batt. North Staffordshire Regt.

MAURICE DAPHNE.
Admitted Dec. 1908, practising at 71 Lincoln's Inn Fields, W.C. Joined April 17, 1917, as Private, Royal Army Service Corps (M.T.). Gazetted 2nd Lieut. Royal Army Service Corps (M.T.) April 20, 1918. Served in ranks at Home, commissioned service in France.

HAROLD DUKINFIELD DARBISHIRE.
Admitted Jan. 1908. Member of Gibbons, Arkle & Darbishire, of Liverpool. Mobilised Aug. 1914, as Lieut., West Lancs (Howitzer) Brigade Royal Field Artillery (T.F.), promoted Capt. July 1916, Major July 1918. Served in Gallipoli, Egypt, and Palestine.

WILFRED DARBYSHIRE.
Articled to T. R. Dootson, of Leigh, Lancs. Joined Jan. 13, 1916, as Private, Royal Fusiliers. Served in England Jan. to July 1916, and in France July 1916 to April 1917. Killed in action April 16, 1917.

HUGH CUFF DARKE.
Admitted Jan. 1905. Deputy Clerk for the County and Clerk of the Peace for East Sussex. Mobilised Aug. 1914, as Major, 1st Home Counties Brigade Royal Field Artillery. Served at Home, India, and Mesopotamia. Died at Lahore July 12, 1916.

FRANK GEORGE DARLING.
Articled to F. B. Darling, of Birmingham. Served as Private, Hon. Artillery Company (Infantry).

HENRY CLAYTON DARLINGTON.
Admitted March 1904. Member of Peace & Darlington, of Liverpool and Wigan. Commanding 1/5 Batt. Manchester Regt. Sept. 12, 1914. Three times mentioned in Dispatches and awarded the C.M.G. and Order of Crown of Italy (Officer). Served in Egypt Sept. 1914 to April 1915, Dardanelles April to Oct. 1915, Sinai Feb. 1916 to Feb. 1917, France Feb. 1917 to 1919.

CHARLES JOSEPH CROUGHTON DAVENPORT.

Admitted May 1908, practising at 133 Aldersgate Street, E.C. Joined Reserve Dec. 1915. Gazetted 2nd Lieut. Royal Army Service Corps Nov. 13, 1916, promoted Lieut. May 1918. Served in France 1916 to 1918.

HAROLD DAVENPORT.

Articled to Gordon Cox, of Tower Royal, Cannon Street, E.C. Served as 2nd Lieut., 9th (Service) Batt. West Yorkshire Regt., promoted Lieut. Aug. 1915.

HUGH NARES DAVENPORT.

Admitted July 1911. Member of Davenport & Rose, of Oxford. Joined Sept. 1914, as Lieut., 4th Batt. Oxford & Bucks Light Infantry, subsequently promoted Capt. and Major, attached to 2/6 Batt. Royal Warwickshire Regt. Awarded the M.C. and recommended for Bar. Served in France. Reported missing March 26, 1918, since presumed killed on that date near Verlaines.

DONALD WOODWARD DAVEY.

Articled to W. L. Yorath, of Cardiff. Joined Aug. 4, 1914, as Gunner, Royal Field Artillery (T.F.). Gazetted Lieut. 5th Batt. The Welch Regt. Oct. 1914, Lieut. Royal Field Artillery (T.F.) March 1915, A/Capt. May 1919. Served at Home and in France.

ALEXANDER CHARLES ROBERT DAVID.

Articled to G. N. David, of Cardiff. Joined Nov. 30, 1914, as Temp. 2nd Lieut. Royal Field Artillery, promoted Temp. Lieut. March 1916, A/Capt. Oct. to Dec. 1916, March to May 1918, and in July 1918, A/Major Jan. 1919. Served with 25th Division throughout while in France. Awarded the M.C. Served at Home Nov. 1914 to Sept. 1915, and Aug. 1917 to March 1918, and in France Sept. 1915 to Aug. 1917 and March 1918 to Feb. 1919.

GEORGE NEVILE DAVID.

Admitted Oct. 1911. Member of George David & Co., of Cardiff. Joined July 22, 1916, as Private, 19th (Reserve) Batt. King's Royal Rifle Corps. Gazetted to 1st (Reserve) Garrison Batt. The Suffolk Regt. Feb. 11, 1917 transferred to Labour Corps March 1917. Served at Home, and in France March to Aug. 1917.

THOMAS JENKINS DAVID.

Admitted Nov. 1904, practising at 15 Waterloo Place, Pall Mall, S.W. Mobilised Aug. 1914, as Capt., Glamorgan Royal Horse Artillery, promoted Temp. Major Nov. 1914, Major June 1916. Once mentioned in Dispatches. Awarded the D.S.O. and T.D. Served in France. Wounded Oct. 1917.

ERNEST ALEXANDER DAVIDSON.

Admitted Feb. 1907. Member of Gard, Lyell, Betenson & Davidson, of 2 Gresham Buildings, Basinghall Street, E.C. Joined April 9, 1917, as Gunner, Royal Garrison Artillery, promoted Bombardier June 1917. Served at Home April 1917 to Jan. 1918, and in France Jan. to Dec. 1918.

ALUN EDWARDS DAVIES.

Admitted March 1909, practised at Grimsby. Served as Private, 10th (Service) Batt. Lincolnshire Regt., and subsequently promoted to Sergeant.

ARNOLD WALTERS DAVIES.

Admitted Feb. 1910, practising at Lampeter. Joined May 5, 1915, as 2nd Lieut., Royal Engineers (Welsh Field Coy.), promoted Lieut. Dec. 1915, and transferred to 438th (Cheshire) Field Coy. Royal Engineers Nov. 1916. Served in France and Belgium.

ARROL EWART DAVIES.

Admitted Aug. 1913, practising at Tenby, and Milford Haven. Joined Jan. 29, 1915, Royal Flying Corps. Discharged unfit April 1915, re-enlisted June 1915 Pembroke Yeomanry (T.F.), transferred The Welch Regt. Aug. 1916, transferred Hampshire Regt. Nov. 1916, attached Royal Engineers, transferred Labour Corps for special duty Feb. 1918. Rank on demobilisation O.R. Q.M.-Sergeant. Served at Home, Egypt, and Salonica. Invalided with malaria.

ARTHUR RUSSELL DAVIES.

Articled to W. P. Davies, of 60 Uxbridge Road, Shepherd's Bush. Joined Feb. 17, 1917, as Driver, Royal Horse Artillery. Gazetted 2nd Lieut. Royal Garrison Artillery Sept. 1, 1917. Served in France and Belgium Oct. 1917 to Nov. 1918. Invalided Home in Nov. 1918.

DAVID OSWALD DAVIES.

Admitted April 1896, practised at Dolgelly and Barmouth. Mobilised Aug. 1914, as Lieut., 7th Batt. Royal Welch Fusiliers (T.), promoted Capt. Aug. 1914. Relinquished commission on account of ill-health May 10, 1916, and granted hon. rank of Capt. Served at Home. Died May 21, 1917, as result of illness contracted while serving with the Army.

EDWARD DAVIES.

Articled to T. B. R. Wilson, of Newport, Mon. Joined Oct. 13, 1914, as 2nd Lieut., 1st Batt. Monmouthshire Regt. (T.F.), promoted Lieut. 1916, transferred to T.F. Reserve Sept. 15, 1916. Served in France. Wounded at Hohenzollern Redoubt Oct. 13, 1915.

EDWARD SMITH THOMAS DAVIES.

Admitted Feb. 1914, practising at Bridgend, Glam. Joined Aug. 4, 1914, 1/5 Batt. The Welch Regt., seconded Machine Gun Corps, rank Capt. Served at Gallipoli 1915, Tripoli 1917, Egypt 1917. Wounded Gallipoli Aug. 1915. Discharged Nov. 1917.

ERIC DAVIES.

Admitted Aug. 1914. Managing Clerk with Bristows, Cooke & Carpmael, of 1 Copthall Buildings, E.C. Mobilised Aug. 4, 1914, as 2nd Lieut., Notts (Sherwood Rangers) Yeomanry, promoted Lieut. Sept. 1914, Capt. Nov. 1915. Served in Egypt April to Aug. 1915, Gallipoli Aug. to Dec. 1915, Egypt Dec. 1915 to Feb. 1916, Salonica Feb. to Dec. 1916, Palestine and Egypt July 1917 to May 1919. Wounded Sept. 1915 and Nov. 1917.

ERNEST HENRY DAVIES.

Admitted May 1886, practising at 13 Great James Street, Bedford Row, W.C. Went to France in Jan. 1915 as Volunteer Ambulance Driver for British Ambulance Committee, attached 8th Corps French Army, was Commandant of Section from March to June 1916, when returned to England. Joined Royal Naval Volunteer Reserve (Anti-Aircraft Corps) in Jan. 1917, obtained discharge in Sept. 1918, and returned to Ambulance Section in France, as Sous-Chef (2nd in Command) attached to 72nd Div. French Army, and remained till discharged on Feb. 13, 1919. Awarded Croix de Guerre (French). Served in France with French Army, and at Home.

EUSTACE ARTHUR DAVIES.

Admitted March 1904, practising at Cardiff. Joined Sept. 3, 1917, as Private, Royal Army Service Corps (M.T.). Served in Italy.

FAIRFAX LLEWELLYN DAVIES.

Articled to Fairfax Davies, of North Walsham, Norfolk. Joined Sept. 14, 1914, as Private, 1/6 Cyclist Batt. 6th Norfolk Regt. Gazetted 2nd Lieut. in same Regt. Oct. 1914, and in July 1916 attached to 2/8 Batt. West Yorkshire Regt. as Lieut. Served at Home until Jan. 1917, then until date of death in France. Killed on night patrol duty July 8, 1917.

GEORGE HERBERT OAKLEY DAVIES.

Admitted Oct. 1909, practised at 62 Old Broad Street, E.C. Served as Private, 32nd Batt. London Regt.

GWYN HOWARD DAVIES.

Admitted March 1910. Member of Kimber Bull, Howland, Clappé & Co., of 6 Old Jewry, E.C. Served as Private, 1st Batt. Hon. Artillery Company.

HENRY HOWELLS DAVIES.

Articled to D. J. Davies, of Cardiff. Joined May 1915, as Private, 3/5 Batt. The Welch Regt., and attained the rank of Sergeant. Gazetted 2nd Lieut. Royal Defence Corps Sept. 7, 1916, promoted Lieut. March 1918, transferred to South Wales Borderers April 1919. Served at Home May 1915 to April 1919, France and Belgium April to Oct. 1919.

HUGH VERNON MORRIS DAVIES.

Admitted April 1910, practising at Guildford. Served as Private, 5th (Reserve) Batt. The Queen's Royal West Surrey Regt.

JENKIN MORGAN DAVIES.

Admitted Feb. 1913, practising at Neath, Glam. Joined May 11, 1916, as Driver, Royal Field Artillery, subsequently promoted Bombardier. Served in Egypt and Palestine.

JOHN BERTIE DAVIES.

Admitted Oct. 1907, practising at Merthyr Tydfil. Joined Nov. 4, 1915, as Private, Royal Army Medical Corps. Served in France.

JOHN NORMAN DAVIES.

Articled to Joseph Davies, of Aberystwyth. Joined March 3, 1915, as 2nd Lieut., 7th Batt. Royal Welch Fusiliers, promoted Lieut. June 1916. Served in Egypt.

JOSEPH DAVIES.

Admitted June 1908, practising at St. Helens, Lancs. Served as Private, 710th Coy. Royal Army Service Corps (M.T.).

JOSEPH GORDON DAVIES.

Admitted Oct. 1911. Member of Joseph Davies & Son, of Aberystwyth. Joined Jan. 6, 1916, as Gunner in the Royal Field Artillery. Gazetted 2nd

Lieut. Royal Garrison Artillery Dec. 18, 1916, promoted Lieut. June 1918. Served in France Feb. 1917 to Dec. 1918.

NOEL HIER DAVIES.

Articled to H. G. P. Venables, of Cardiff. Served as 2nd Lieut., 4th Welsh Brigade Royal Field Artillery. Promoted Lieut.

OWEN GILBERT DAVIES.

Articled to C. P. Yearsley, of Welshpool. Joined Oct. 5, 1914, as Corporal, North Wales (University and Public Schools) Batt. 16th Royal Welch Fusiliers. Commissioned 2nd Lieut. Royal Garrison Artillery Nov. 18, 1914, transferred to Indian Mountain Battery, commission made permanent May 1915, promoted Lieut. July 1916, and subsequently A/Capt. Awarded the M.C. Served on North-West Frontier of India 1915 and 1916, also in 1919, East Africa 1917 and 1918, Mesopotamia 1919.

PHILIP EDGAR DAVIES.

Articled to W. F. O. Edmonds, of 13 Clifford's Inn, E.C., and Mortlake. Joined 1915, as Private, 3rd Batt. East Surrey Regt. and attained the rank of Corporal. Served at Home. Died of blood poisoning at Dover Jan. 1917.

WALTER CRADOC DAVIES.

Admitted Nov. 1904. Member of Evan R. Davies & Davies, of Pwllheli. Commissioned Lieut. T.F. Reserve Oct. 1915, promoted Temp. Capt. Sept. 1917. Served at Home. Appointed Appeal Military Representative March 1916.

WILLOUGHBY ARLINGHAM DAVIES.

Articled to R. H. A. Davies, of Crickhowell. Joined Aug. 9, 1914, as Private, Hon. Artillery Company (Infantry). Commissioned Flight Sub-Lieut. Royal Naval Air Service July 11, 1915, promoted Flight Lieut. Dec. 1916, Flight Commander June 1917, subsequently Capt. Royal Air Force. Served in France 1914 to 1915, East Coast Sea Patrols (Seaplanes) 1916 to 1917, Instruction Patrols 1918 to 1919.

ARCHIBALD EDWARD KENNETT DAVIES-BUNTON.

Admitted June 1910, practising at Wareham, Dorset. Joined Sept. 12, 1914, as 2nd Lieut., 4th Batt. Dorset Regt. (T.F.), promoted 1st Lieut. June 1916, Capt. Feb. 1918, transferred to Royal Air Force April 1918 as Flight Lieut. Once mentioned in Dispatches. Served at Home Sept. 1914 to Feb. 1916, India Feb. 1916 to July 1917, Palestine Aug. 1917 to Oct. 1918. Wounded Nov. 21, 1917.

THOMAS HENRY DAVIES-COLLEY.

Admitted Nov. 1891. Member of Slater, Heelis & Co., of Manchester. Mobilised 1914, as Lieut.-Col., 2/6 Batt. Manchester Regt. Served at Home.

ARTHUR HARVARD DAVIS.

Admitted Oct. 1913. Of Whitchurch. Served as 2nd Lieut., 11th Batt. Worcestershire Regt.

BARNARD BURRELL DAVIS.

Admitted April 1914, practising at Cannock, Staffs. Joined Sept. 4, 1914, as Private, 5th Batt. South Staffordshire Regt. (T.F.), promoted Lance-Corporal in Oct., Corporal in Nov. Gazetted 2nd Lieut. Sept. 5, 1916, promoted

Lieut. March 1918. Served at Home Sept. 1914 to Feb. 1915, Flanders and France Feb. 1915 to March 1916, Home May to Oct. 1916, France Oct. 1916 to Feb, 1917.

CHARLES HERBERT DAVIS.

Articled to C. F. Davis, of 15 & 16 Railway Approach, London Bridge, S.E. Joined April 1917, as Private, 28th Batt. County of London Regt. (Artists Rifles). Gazetted 2nd Lieut. 8th Batt. East Surrey Regt. Dec. 17, 1917, attached to 7th Batt. The Queen's Royal West Surrey Regt. in France. Served at Home and in France. Wounded Aug. 23, 1918, at Albert, France.

EDWARD WILLIAM DAVIS.

Admitted Oct. 1910. Of British Columbia. Served as 2nd Lieut., 10th Batt. King's Own Royal Lancaster Regt.

GUY CLIFTON DAVIS.

Articled to H. J. Shepard, of 40 Chancery Lane, W.C. Joined Sept. 1914 as Private, Inns of Court O.T.C. Gazetted 2nd Lieut. 7th Batt. Northumberland Fusiliers Feb. 1915, and went to the Front following April, promoted Lieut. June 1916. Wounded April 19, 1918. Died in Casualty Station in France May 11, 1918.

JOHN ALBERT DAVIS.

Admitted Aug. 1913, practising at 227–8 Strand, W.C. Served as 2nd Lieut., 1st City of London Brigade Royal Field Artillery.

JOHN HARVARD DAVIS.

Admitted Aug. 1909, practising at Cardiff. Enlisted Jan. 19, 1917, as Private, Inns of Court O.T.C. Subsequently gazetted 2nd Lieut. Royal Garrison Artillery (T.F.) Served in France.

KENNETH JAMES DAVIS.

Articled to G. J. Davis, of 1 Gresham Buildings, Basinghall Street, E.C. Mobilised Aug. 5, 1914, as Private, 5th Batt. City of London Regt. (London Rifle Brigade), promoted Sergt. and attached Headquarters 174th Infantry Brigade Sept. 5, 1915. Gazetted 2nd Lieut. Labour Corps Dec. 5, 1917. Served at Home Aug. 1914 to Jan. 1917, and in France Jan. 1917 to May 1919.

LAWRENCE MICHAEL DAVIS.

Admitted Jan. 1915. Assistant Solicitor to Port of London Authority, Victoria Embankment, E.C. Joined June 26, 1917, as Private, 2/3 County of London Yeomanry. Gazetted 2nd Lieut. 2/3 County of London Yeomanry May 17, 1919. Served at Home.

LEO EDWIN DAVIS.

Articled to H. J. Davis, of Liverpool. Joined Sept. 1914, as Lieut., King's Liverpool Cadet Batt. Gazetted 2nd Lieut. 5th Batt. Manchester Regt. Jan. 1915. Served at Gallipoli. Killed in action at Krithia during Suvla Bay operations Aug. 6, 1915.

REGINALD GEORGE DAVIS.

Admitted Dec. 4, 1888, practising at 58 Finsbury Pavement, E.C. Mobilised Aug. 5, 1914, as Orderly Room Sergeant, 5th City of London Batt. London Regt. (London Rifle Brigade), promoted Colour-Sergeant Dec. 1914 and Regimental Quartermaster-Sergeant June 1918. Served at Home during the War with 1st and 2nd Batts. London Rifle Brigade, 101st Provisional Batt., 30th and 25th Batts. London Regt., 1st City of London Batt. (London Regt.) Royal Fusiliers, and 38th, 39th, and 42nd Batts. Royal Fusiliers.

RICHARD JOHN DAVIS.

Admitted Jan. 1900, practising at 35 North End Road, West Kensington, W. Joined Jan. 1915, as an A.B., Royal Naval Volunteer Reserve. Granted commission as Assistant Paymaster Royal Naval Volunteer Reserve April 6, 1916, and promoted Paymaster-Lieut. Sept. 1918. Served on Admiralty War Staff and Shipping Intelligence Officer, Liverpool.

SIDNEY GEORGE DAVIS.

Admitted Nov. 1915. Member of Bulcraig & Davis, of Donnington House, Norfolk Street, Strand, W.C. Joined Jan. 1917, as Lieut., Special List Jan. 15, 1917, transferred Nov. 1917, after being attached to D.R.1/B., War Office, to Ministry of National Service, Headquarters, Registration Department, whilst unfit for General Service. Awarded O.B.E. Served at Home.

GEOFFREY CUTHBERT DAVISON.

Articled to H. C. Davies, of Norwich. Served as Private, Public Schools Batt. Royal Fusiliers.

RICHARD ELMER DAVISON.

Articled to H. H. Bowyer, of 2 Walbrook, E.C. Joined Nov. 3, 1915, as Rifleman, 16th Batt. County of London Regt. (Queen's Westminster Rifles). Served at Home, and went to France in June 1916. Killed in a bombing raid in Leuze Wood, near Combles, Sept. 10, 1916.

ROBERT PICKERING DAVISON.

Admitted May 1913, practising at 26 Bush Lane, E.C. Enlisted Dec. 14, 1914, as Private, 24th Batt. Royal Fusiliers, discharged permanently unfit June 19, 1917. Rejoined voluntarily May 10, 1918, as Cadet, No. 4 Officers Cadet Batt. Gazetted 2nd Lieut. Northumberland Fusiliers Jan. 1919. Served at Home Dec. 1914 to Nov. 1915, Jan. to April 1916, and Dec. 1916 to Feb. 1919, and in France Nov. 1915 to Jan. 1916, and April to Dec. 1916. Wounded at Givenchy Dec. 28, 1915, and at Beaumont Hamel Nov. 13, 1916.

EDWARD WILLIAM DAVY.

Admitted July 1905. Managing Clerk with W. H. Davy, of Temple Cloud, Somerset. Joined June 1915, as Private, Hon. Artillery Company. Gazetted 2nd Lieut. in Royal Field Artillery Feb. 1917, afterwards promoted Lieut. Served in France.

HENRY RAWLE DAVY.

Admitted Sept. 1897. Managing Clerk to Stone, Thomas & King, of Bath. Joined 1915, as Private, 5th Batt. Royal Fusiliers. Served in France and Belgium. Died Oct. 20, 1917, of wounds received in action near Poperinghe the day before.

SAMUEL CHARLES DAVY.

Articled to W. H. Davy, of Temple Cloud, Bristol. Served as 2nd Lieut., Royal Scots Fusiliers, promoted Lieut. July 1917.

GEORGE COODE DAW.

Admitted Oct. 1905. Member of Ellis, Peirs & Co., of 17 Albemarle Street, W. Joined Aug. 11, 1915, as Sub-Lieut., Royal Naval Volunteer Reserve, Temp. Lieut. Royal Garrison Artillery Aug. 11, 1916, Temp. Capt. April 26, 1918. Once mentioned in Dispatches. Served at Home.

REGINALD SAMUEL DAW.

Admitted Jan. 1904. Member of Nisbet, Daw & Nisbet, of 35 Lincoln's Inn Fields, W.C. Joined Oct. 1914 Inns of Court O.T.C. Gazetted Lieut. 9th Batt. King's Royal Rifle Corps Nov. 1914, promoted Capt. March 1915. Twice mentioned in Dispatches. Served in France. Killed in action at Delville Wood Aug. 25, 1916.

WILLIAM FABYAN BENNETT DAW.

Articled to Montague Ellis, of 17 Albermarle Street, W. Served as Private, 14th Batt. County of London Regt. (London Scottish).

EDWIN POMLEY DAWES.

Admitted April 1903. Member of Dawes & Son, of Rye, Sussex. Mobilised Aug. 1914, as Capt., 5th (Cinque Ports) Batt. Royal Sussex Regt. Served in France Feb. 1915 to June 1915, when returned to England after having been buried, suffering from loss of memory, a Provost-Marshal Purfleet Nov. to Dec. 1915, Appeal Military Representative in West Sussex March 1915 to July 1916. Called upon to resign commission owing to ill-health contracted on Active Service Jan. 3, 1918, and retain rank of Capt.

MICHAEL STILEMAN DAWES.

Admitted Nov. 1914. Member of Dawes & Sons, of 2 Birchin Lane, E.C. Joined March 28, 1916, as Sergeant Instructor, C.U.O.T.C., attached Royal Engineers (Signals). Served at Home.

CHARLES JOHN RANDLE DAWKINS.

Articled to C. W. M. Price, of 10 Lincoln's Inn Fields, W.C. Served as 2nd Lieut., 9th Batt. The Welch Regt. Killed in France Sept. 25, 1915.

FREDERICK SAMUEL SHELLEY DAWKINS.

Articled to Robt. Carter, of 4 Gray's Inn Square, W.C. Joined Feb. 1916, as Private, Royal Fusiliers, promoted Lance-Corporal Aug. 1916. Gazetted 2nd Lieut. Machine Gun Corps July 28, 1917, promoted Lieut. Jan. 1919. Served in France. Taken prisoner and wounded at Kemmel Hill April 25, 1918.

COLIN AUFRÉRE DAWSON.

Articled to William Dawson, of 2 New Square, Lincoln's Inn, W.C. Joined Aug. 14, 1916, as Private, Royal Army Service Corps. Gazetted 2nd Lieut. Royal Army Service Corps Oct. 7, 1917. Served at Home, Italy March 1917, Salonica May 1917, attached 1st Serbian Army Oct. 1917 to Jan. 1919.

FRANCIS THOMAS PRESSLAND DAY.

Articled to A. J. Darnell, of Northampton. Served as 2nd Lieut., 11th Batt. West Yorkshire Regt.

GEORGE LEWIS DAY.

Articled to G. D. Day, of St. Ives and Huntingdon. Mobilised Aug. 1914, as Lieut., Huntingdonshire Cyclist Batt., served with this Regt. in earlier part of War, then in France for 18 months with Gloucestershire Regt., later with 3rd Batt. Bedfordshire Regt., attained the rank of Major. Once mentioned in Dispatches. Wounded near Villers Bretoneaux March 30, 1918.

HORACE ALFRED DAY.

Articled to H. D. M. Barnett, of Leicester. Joined Oct. 13, 1914, as Chief Petty Officer, Royal Naval Volunteer Reserve. Gazetted Sub-Lieut. Dec. 19, 1915, Lieut. Royal Marines Aug. 1916, Capt. Dec. 1918. Twice mentioned in Dispatches and awarded M.C. Served in Gallipoli May 1915 to Feb. 1916, and in France and Belgium April 1916 to May 1919. Wounded Gallipoli June 1916, and gassed in France March 1918.

RICHARD DAY.

Articled to Ben. Day, of Leeds. Mobilised Aug. 1914, as Lieut., Royal Field Artillery (T.) and subsequently attained the rank of Major. Awarded the M.C. and Bar. Served in France throughout from the spring of 1915, and was in command of his Battery at the Passchendaele Ridge. Killed in action Feb. 23, 1918.

THOMAS FAIRCHILD DAY.

Admitted March 1907, in practice at Ilfracombe. Joined Aug. 4, 1914, as Lieut., Royal Garrison Artillery (T.F.), subsequently promoted to Capt.

GILBERT WILLIAM DAYNES.

Admitted July 1906. Member of J. W. C. Daynes, Son & Keefe, of Norwich. Mobilised Aug. 5, 1914, as Major, 1st East Anglian Brigade Royal Field Artillery (T.). Remained in 1st East Anglian Brigade to Aug. 1916, 533rd Howitzer Battery Sept. to Oct. 1916, 95th Brigade Oct. 1916 to July 1918, promoted Lieut.-Col. July 1918, with 64th Divisional Artillery Aug. 1918 to Jan. 1919. Once mentioned in Dispatches. Served at Home Aug. 1914 to Oct. 1916, France Oct. 1916. to July 1918, Home July 1918 to Jun. 1919. Wounded at Battle of Arras April 22, 1917.

GERALD MARMADUKE DE LANGPORT DAYRELL.

Admitted March 1898. Member of Charles & Dayrell, of 67 Moorgate Street, E.C. Served as Major, 5th (Reserve) Batt. Bedfordshire Regt.

ALFRED STANLEY DEACON.

Articled to Walter Watts, of Bristol. Joined Aug, 17, 1914, as Private, 6th Batt. Gloucestershire Regt. Gazetted 2nd Lieut. Feb. 1915 and attached to 11th Batt. Gloucestershire Regt., promoted Lieut. July 1915, attached to West African Frontier Force, sent to West Coast of Africa in July 1915, served through the Cameroon Expedition, returned to England July 1916, attached to 3rd Gloucestershire Regt. in Nov. 1916 and sent to France. Killed at Assevillers, near Dompierre, Feb. 28, 1917.

ARTHUR EDWARD COLE DEACON.

Admitted May 1902. Managing Clerk with Dod, Longstaffe & Fenwick, of 16 Berners Street, W. Joined Nov. 1915, as Private, Army Cyclist Corps. Gazetted 2nd Lieut. 5th (Cinque Ports) Batt. Royal Sussex Regt. Jan. 1916, appointed Recruiting Officer Feb. 1917, gazetted A/Capt. whilst employed as Chief Registration Officer of an Area Oct. 1917, appointed Assistant

Legal Adviser, London Region of Ministry of National Service Nov. 1917. Served at Home.

HORACE AUGUSTUS DEACON.

Articled to Frank Naylor, of Jaspar House, Copthall Avenue, E.C. Joined Oct. 1914, as Private, 13th Batt. County of London (Princess Louise's Kensington) Regt. Gazetted 2nd Lieut. Feb. 13, 1915, promoted Lieut. Aug. 15, 1915, A/Capt. Jan. 1917. Served in France. Wounded at Vimy Ridge, outside Lens, April 23, 1917.

REGINALD WILLIAM JOHN DURAND DEACON.

Admitted July 1899. Member of Stephens & Wright, of St. Austell, Cornwall. Joined Dec. 1914, as Lieut., Gloucestershire Regt., promoted Capt. May 1916, Major (Brevet) June 1919. Awarded M.C. Served in Gallipoli 1915, Mesopotamia 1916 (First Kut Relief Expedition), and 1916 to 1917 (to Baghdad), India, General Staff, Army Headquarters, 1918, Home, General Staff, War Office, 1918 to 1920.

WALTER JOHN DEACON.

Admitted April 1910, practising at Peterborough. Joined Nov. 1915, as Lieut., East African Veterinary Corps, Lieut. King's African Rifles April 1917 to Dec. 1918. Served in British East Africa.

CHARLES JOSEPH JOHN KING DEAKIN.

Admitted June 1914. Managing Clerk with Messrs. Onions & Davies, of Market Drayton. Joined Sept. 1914, as Private, in Public School Batt., promoted Sergeant Jan. 1915. Gazetted 2nd Lieut. 16th Batt. Middlesex Regt. May 1915. Served at Home Sept. 1914 to Nov. 1915, then went to France. Died July 2, 1916, from wounds received on July 1, 1916, at Beaumont Hamel in Battle of Somme.

CHARLES FREDERICK ELLIS DEAN.

Admitted Nov. 1902. Member of Pulman & Dean, of Lutterworth and Rugby. Joined Dec. 31, 1914, as Private, 19th Batt. Royal Fusiliers. Gazetted 2nd Lieut. 4th Batt. Lincolnshire Regt. March 28, 1917, promoted Lieut. Sept. 1918. Served in France. Wounded Dec. 31, 1915.

LEONARD LAWSON DEAN.

Articled to his father, A. H. Dean, of Manchester. Passed into Sandhurst and was gazetted 2nd Lieut. Loyal North Lancashire Regt. April 1917. Killed in action Oct. 3, 1918.

FREDERICK LLEWELYN DEANE.

Admitted Aug. 1908. Member of Wilson & Deane, Bracknell, Berks. Joined 1915, as Private, 15th Batt. County of London Regt. (Civil Service Rifles). Served at Home and in France. Killed in action on the Somme Sept. 15, 1916. Buried at Bazentin-le-Grand.

HENRY JOHN DEANE.

Admitted May 1897, practising at Loughborough. Joined Aug. 5, 1914, as Private, 5th Batt. Leicestershire Regt., promoted Sergeant Sept. 1914. Gazetted Lieut. and Quartermaster Leicestershire Regt. Sept. 15, 1914, promoted Capt. and Quartermaster Sept. 1917, transferred to T.F. Reserve Nov. 1917. Served at Home.

REGINALD SLEIGHT DEARDEN.
Articled to H. S. Thompson, of Harrogate. Joined Sept. 1914, as Private (University and Public Schools Batt.), 21st Royal Fusiliers, went to France in Nov. 1915 as Divisional Cyclist with 33rd Division, and in May 1916 joined as a bomber 1st Batt. Cameronians (Scottish Rifles). Killed in action in the Battle of the Somme July 16, 1916.

CHARLES DEARDS.
Admitted Jan. 1907. Member of Leoni & Deards, of 31 Bedford Row, W.C. Joined Sept. 1916, as 2nd Lieut., No. 19 Kite Balloon Section Royal Flying Corps, subsequently promoted to Lieut. Royal Air Force. Served in France. Died at No. 8 General Hospital, Rouen, Oct. 5, 1918, of blood poisoning sustained after a descent in a parachute.

ERNEST ARTHUR DE BURIATTE.
Admitted March 1910. Member of de Buriatte & Bowen, of 7 Ely Place, E.C. Served as 2nd Lieut., Royal Field Artillery, promoted Lieut. Feb. 1916, Temp. Capt. on Staff at Malta Jan. 1919.

WILLIAM DE CAUX.
Admitted April 1905, practised at 10 Staple Inn, W.C. Joined Sept. 1914 Inns of Court O.T.C. Gazetted 2nd Lieut. Norfolk Regt. Dec. 9, 1914, promoted Lieut. Feb. 1915, Capt. Oct. 1915. Served at Home and in France. Killed in action at the Battle of the Somme Sept. 15, 1916.

VIVIAN DEER.
Admitted July 1910. Member of Deer & Deer, of Port Talbot. Joined Aug. 29, 1914, as 2nd Lieut., 7th Batt. The Welch Regt., promoted Lieut. April 29, 1915, attached 6th Batt. The Welch Regt. May 1917, promoted Capt. June 1917. Served on East Coast Aug. 1914 to May 1917, France May 1917 to Sept. 1918, Home Sept. 1918 to March 1919.

ESMÉ MORTON DE FLEURY.
Articled to Oswald Hanson, of 44 Hammersmith Road, W. Joined March 1916, as Cadet, Bristol University O.T.C. Gazetted 2nd Lieut. Royal Flying Corps May 1917, Sub-Lieut. Royal Naval Volunteer Reserve July 1918. Served at Home and at Sea.

JOHN BERKELEY DE FONBLANQUE.
Articled to R. S. Taylor, of 5 Gray's Inn Square, W.C. Served as 2nd Lieut., Worcestershire Regt., and subsequently promoted Lieut.

CURT GUSTAV DEHN.
Admitted March 1906. Member of Dunderdale and Dehn, of 85 London Wall, E.C., and Manchester. Joined July 1916, as Private, Inns of Court O.T.C. Gazetted 2nd Lieut. 3rd Wiltshire Regt. March 1, 1917, Station Staff Officer Allahabad, India, May 1918, promoted Lieut. Sept. 1918. Served in England July 1916 to July 1917, India Sept. 1917 to Dec. 1918.

REGINALD DE KUSEL.

Admitted Feb. 1911, practised at 24 Austin Friars, E.C. Served as 2nd Lieut., 48th Brigade Royal Field Artillery.

JAMES LOMBARD DE LA COUR.

Admitted Nov. 1913. Of 45 Redcliffe Gardens, South Kensington. Served as Lieut., 16 Batt. London Regt.

WILFRED LAWSON DELL.

Admitted March 1911, practising at 17–18 Basinghall Street, E.C. Joined Nov. 1914, as Private, Hon. Artillery Company (Infantry), promoted Corporal Dec. 1915, Signal Sergeant June 1916. Commissioned in King's Own Yorkshire Light Infantry June 1917, appointed Assistant Adjutant May 1918, promoted Lieut. Dec. 1918. Served on Western Front April 1915 to Jan. 1917, and Aug. 1917 to Jan. 1918.

ROBERT COVENTRY DENBY.

Admitted April 1907, practising at Coventry. Served as 2nd Lieut., Royal Army Service Corps, promoted Lieut. Nov. 1917.

REGINALD IVESON DENHAM.

Admitted Feb. 1913, practising at 170 Piccadilly, W. Mobilised Aug. 1914, as Capt., Royal Engineers, promoted Major June 1916. Once mentioned in Dispatches. Awarded the M.C. Served with Mediterranean Expeditionary Force Feb. to Oct. 1915, British Expeditionary Force June 1916 to Nov. 1917, and Italian Expeditionary Force Nov. 1917 to Nov. 1918.

GEORGE WILLIAM DENMAN.

Admitted Nov. 1912. Member of Edwin Boxall & Kempe, of Brighton. Served as 2nd Lieut., Royal Garrison Artillery.

THOMAS HIERCY DENMAN.

Admitted Dec. 1888. Of East Retford. Served as Major, Territorial Reserve, attached 8th Batt. Notts and Derby Regt. (Sherwood Foresters) (T).

WILFRID DENNES.

Articled to his father, E. T. M. Dennes, of 22 Chancery Lane, W.C. Served as 2nd Lieut., Royal Field Artillery, and subsequently promoted Capt. Awarded the M.C. and Bar. Killed in action March 21, 1918.

HENRY LARDNER DENNYS.

Admitted Dec. 1907. Of Hong Kong. Served as Lieut. (A/Capt.), 3rd Chinese Coy. Labour Corps.

CYRIL ASTON DENYER.

Admitted May 1901. Member of Cox & Co., 17 Tower Royal, Cannon Street, E.C. Joined Aug. 21, 1916, as 2nd Lieut., Royal Army Service Corps (M.T.), promoted Lieut. Feb. 1918. Served in France Aug. 1916 to Feb. 1918, Belgium Feb. to Dec. 1918, Germany Dec. 1918 to Feb. 1919.

HORACE FREDERICK DENYER.

Admitted June 1902. Managing Clerk with Messrs. Reeves, of 42 Old Broad Street, E.C. Mobilised Aug. 1914, as Sergeant, Middlesex Hussars

(1st County of London Yeomanry), promoted Sergeant-Major 1915. Gazetted 2nd Lieut. 12th Batt. Cheshire Regt. Feb. 1915, promoted Lieut. July 1917. Once mentioned in Dispatches. Served at Home Aug. 1914 to April 1915, in Egypt, Gallipoli, and Salonica Feb. 1916 to July 1917. Wounded at Battle of Chocolate Hill, Gallipoli. Killed July 13, 1917, at Horse Shoe Hill, Salonica.

ALAN DE PENNINGTON.

Admitted March 1911, practised at Blackburn. Served as 2nd Lieut., 4th Batt. East Lancashire Regt.

GERALD LISLE ALEXANDER DE ROUGEMONT.

Articled to, and Managing Clerk with, E. F. Turner & Sons, 115 Leadenhall Street, E.C. Joined March 1916, as Private, Royal Army Service Corps (M.T.), and subsequently promoted Corporal. Served with the Salonica Expeditionary Force. Died Aug. 10, 1919, of malaria contracted while on active service.

ARTHUR DANIEL DERVICHE-JONES.

Admitted Dec. 1897, practised at Liverpool. Served as Private, 10th Batt. King's Liverpool Regt. (Liverpool Scottish), and subsequently obtained a commission in the 1st Batt. Liverpool Regt., transferred to the King's Own Royal Lancaster Regt., and attained the rank of Capt. Mentioned in Dispatches. Awarded the D.S.O. and Bar, and the M.C.

JOHN LINDSAY DEUCHAR.

Admitted Feb. 1912, practised at Knutsford. Served as 2nd Lieut., Machine Gun Corps, promoted Lieut. June 1918.

ROLAND ELLIS DE VESIAN.

Admitted Dec. 1884, practised at 8 Old Jewry, E.C. Served as Major, Musketry Instructor 36th Infantry Brigade, and subsequently as Lieut.-Col. 8th (City of London) Batt. London Regt. (Post Office Rifles).

THOMAS VALENTINE DEVEY.

Admitted March 1910, practised at Newcastle-on-Tyne. Served as Gunner, Royal Garrison Artillery. Gazetted 2nd Lieut. Royal Garrison Artillery April 8, 1918.

HATTON BERTRAM ST. JOHN DE VINE.

Admitted Jan. 1909, practised at Tipton, Staffs, until 1911. Ordained and appointed Curate at Birmingham Cathedral. Appointed Chaplain to the Forces and attached to the West Riding Regt., and subsequently to a Scottish Regt. Killed April 27, 1916.

FERAY VULLIAMY DEVONSHIRE.

Articled to Sir John J. Stavridi, of 40 Old Broad Street, E.C. Mobilised Aug. 5, 1914, as 2nd Lieut., Middlesex Hussars (1st County of London Yeomanry), 2nd Lieut. 7th (Queen's Own) Hussars March 1916, attached Royal Air Force July 1917, Flight-Commander Nov. 1917. Once mentioned in Dispatches. Served at Home until April 1915, at Gallipoli 1915, Egypt 1916, India 1916 to 1917, Mesopotamia Nov. 1917, Afghan War 1919. Killed in action Afghan Border July 20, 1919.

GILBERT DEWAR.

Admitted May 1909, practising at 353 Strand, W.C. Joined Sept. 5, 1914, as Private, Hon. Artillery Company. Commissioned 2nd Lieut. Royal Army Ordnance Corps March 1917, promoted Lieut. June 1917, A/Capt. Jan. 1919. Served in France Dec. 1914 to March 1917, and in Italy March 1917 to 1920.

ARTHUR AUGUSTUS BLATHWAYT DEWING.

Admitted Nov. 1906. Member of Welchman & Dewing, of Wisbech. Joined Jan. 1915, as 2nd Lieut., 5th Batt. Royal Sussex Regt. (T.). Served in France. Injured in accident—run down by W.O. lorry, result of which left leg amputated. Discharged Nov. 1916.

CHARLES ESMOND DE WOLFF.

Articled to A. B. Watson, of 12 Bouverie Street, Fleet Street, E.C. Gazetted 2nd Lieut. 5th (C.P.) Royal Sussex Regt. Nov. 7, 1914, attached Royal Army Ordnance Department June 1915 as Lieut., promoted Capt. Oct. 1916, Major May 1918, Lieut.-Col. Feb. 1919. Three times mentioned in Dispatches. Awarded C.B.E. and O.B.E. (Military Division). Served at Home, Salonica (whole time to end of War with Bulgaria and Turkey), and South Russia (British Military Mission).

CHARLES DIBDIN.

Articled to R. W. Dibdin, of 23 Red Lion Square, W.C. Joined Nov. 23. 1914, as 2nd Lieut., Royal Army Service Corps, promoted Lieut. Jan. 6, 1915. Served in France July 1915 to Nov. 1917.

CEDRIC CHARLES DICKENS.

Admitted Nov. 1913. Managing Clerk with Coward & Hawkesley, Sons & Chance, of 30 Mincing Lane, E.C. Mobilised Aug. 1914, as Capt., 13th Batt. County of London Regt. (Kensington), promoted Major Dec. 1915. Once mentioned in Dispatches. Served at Home, in Belgium, and in France, Wounded at Laventie Feb. 22, 1915. Killed in action at Linge Wood (Battle of the Somme) Sept. 9, 1916.

ARTHUR GEORGE DICKINS.

Admitted Feb. 1906. Member of Hunt & Dickins, of Nottingham. Joined Jan. 10, 1918, as Air Mechanic, Royal Flying Corps. Served at Home.

ARNOLD VICTOR DICKINSON.

Articled to F. E. Forster, of Newcastle-upon-Tyne. Joined Oct. 1914, as Cadet, Durham University O.T.C. Commissioned 2nd Lieut. 7th Batt. Durham Light Infantry Aug. 23, 1915, promoted Lieut. Aug. 1917. Served at Home Oct. 1914 to June 1916, and in France June 1916 to Feb. 1918. Wounded at Ypres Feb. 12, 1918. Discharged Sept. 21, 1918, on account of wounds.

CHARLES LEMPRIERE HERBERT DICKINSON.

Articled to C. D. Heaton, of Burslem. Served as Lieut., 3rd Batt. Leicestershire Regt.

FRANK DICKINSON.

Admitted Jan. 1911, practised at Leicester. Served as Private, 4th Batt. Leicestershire Regt.

HAROLD CROWTHER DICKINSON.

Admitted Jan. 1909. Member of John Dickinson & Son, of Wakefield. Served as Chief Petty Officer, Royal Naval Volunteer Reserve.

JAMES DICKINSON.

Admitted April 1912. Member of Thomas Cooper & Co., and Stibbard Gibson & Co., of 21 Leadenhall Street, E.C. Served as Capt., Royal Field Artillery.

JOHN DANIEL DUNCAN DICKINSON.

Admitted July 1901. Of Petrograd, Russia. Served as Private, Royal Army Medical Corps.

JOHN HERBERT DICKINSON.

Admitted Dec. 1892, practising at St. Helens, Lancs. Served as Capt., 5th Batt. South Lancashire Regt., and subsequently promoted Major. Mentioned in Dispatches. Awarded the M.C.

JOHN ROBERT DICKINSON.

Articled to John Gardner, of Liverpool. Served as Trooper, Duke of Lancaster's Own Yeomanry, subsequently obtained a commission in the 8th Batt. King's Own Royal Lancaster Regt. and attained the rank of Capt. Mentioned in Dispatches. Awarded the M.C. and Bar.

LEONARD TAYLOR DICKINSON.

Admitted April 1911. Member of J. L. Dickinson & Sons, of Weston-super-Mare. Joined Aug. 1914, as Private, North Somerset Yeomanry. Served in France and Belgium. Killed in action at Vlamertinghe, Belgium, Nov. 17, 1914.

RICHARD DICKINSON.

Admitted Nov. 1905. Of Manchester. Served as Lance-Corporal, Royal Welch Fusiliers.

RONALD FRANCIS BICKERSTETH DICKINSON.

Admitted July 1910. With Hill, Dickinson & Co., of Liverpool. Mobilised Aug. 1914, as Capt., 10th Batt. King's Liverpool Regt. (Liverpool Scottish). Once mentioned in Dispatches. Served in France and Belgium. Killed in capture of German trenches at Hooge on June 16, 1915.

THOMAS ARTHUR DICKINSON.

Articled to Henry A. May, of Wolverhampton. Joined Inns of Court O.T.C. May 1915, subsequently gazetted 2nd Lieut. 6th Batt. South Staffordshire Regt. Served in France. Killed in action at Battle of Somme July 1, 1916.

ARTHUR HUBERT DICKSON.

Admitted April 1910. Member of W. J. Dickson & Sons, of Kirkham. Granted commission 2nd Lieut. Loyal North Lancashire Regt. Sept. 1914 and attached to the 47th Regimental District as Recruiting Officer, subsequently transferred from Kirkham to Preston. Died Oct. 7, 1915.

FREDERIC LIVINGSTONE DICKSON.

Admitted June 1905. Member of Challinors & Dickson, of Hanley. Mobilised Aug. 4, 1914, as 2nd Lieut., Cheshire Brigade Royal Field Artillery

(T.), promoted Lieut. Sept. 1914, Capt. Feb. 1915. Once mentioned in Dispatches. Served at Home till 1917, Egypt July to Sept. 1917, Palestine Sept. 1917 to Armistice.

GERALD HECTOR DICKSON.

Admitted Aug. 1904. Member of Buck & Dicksons, of Preston. Served as 2nd Lieut., 4th Batt. Loyal North Lancashire Regt., and subsequently attained the rank of Capt.

JOSEPH WILLIAM EDMUND DICKSON.

Articled to Edmund Dickson, of Garstang, Lancs. Joined Oct. 10, 1914, as Private, Inns of Court O.T.C. Gazetted 2nd Lieut. 3rd Batt. Seaforth Highlanders Jan. 13, 1915, promoted Lieut. Feb. 1916, Capt. June 1918. Once mentioned in Dispatches. Awarded the M.C. Served in France, Mesopotamia, Palestine, India, and Egypt. Wounded June 21, 1915, July 6, 1916, and May 21, 1917.

VINCENT HAMILTON DICKSON.

Admitted June 1899. Member of Dickson, Barnes & Dickson, of Chester. Mobilised Aug. 1914, as Major, Cheshire Brigade Royal Field Artillery (T.F.), served with Cheshire Brigade until July 1917 and with 330th Brigade Nov. 21, 1917, to May 1919, A/Lieut.-Col. Jan. to Feb. 1919. Once mentioned in Dispatches. Awarded the D.S.O. and T.D. Served in France Nov. 1915 to Feb. 1916 and Nov. 1917 to May 1919, Egypt and Palestine Feb. 1916 to July 1917.

WILLIAM HERBERT DICKSON.

Admitted Feb. 1901, practising at Chippenham. Joined 14th Batt. County of London Regt. (London Scottish) in 1916 and was later attached to an O.T.C. at Gales. Gazetted 2nd Lieut. Loyal North Lancashire Regt. Killed in action in France, June 7, 1917.

ESSEX LOFTUS DIGBY.

Admitted Feb. 1904, practised at Cardiff. Served as 2nd Lieut., 296th Brigade Royal Field Artillery, promoted Lieut. July 1917.

MALCOLM ALEXANDER MELDON DILLON.

Admitted April 1914, practising at Liverpool. Served as 2nd Lieut., Royal Naval Volunteer Reserve.

PERCY ETTY DIMES.

Admitted Nov. 1901, practising in Solicitor's Department, London County Council. Joined Nov. 1915, as Private, 28th Batt. County of London Regt. (Artists Rifles), promoted Lance-Corporal June 1916, Corporal Nov. 1916, transferred to Royal Flying Corps Aug. 1917, Sergeant Instructor in Aerial Gunnery Dec. 1917. Served at Home Training Stations.

JOHN FRANCIS DOUGLAS DIMOCK.

Admitted Feb. 1912. Member of Mee & Co., of Retford. Joined Sept. 1914, as 2nd Lieut., 8th Batt. Notts and Derby Regt. (Sherwood Foresters), promoted Lieut. Nov. 1915, Capt. June 1916, A/D.A.Q.M.G. 59th D.H.Q. Oct. 1918 to May 1919. Once mentioned in Dispatches. Awarded O.B.E. (Military Division). Served at Home, Ireland, and in France.

HUGH KENNETT DINN.

Admitted Aug. 1909. Member of Dinn & Son, of 2 Gresham Buildings, Basinghall Street, E.C. Joined Sept. 1914, as Private, 5th City of London Batt. London Regt. (London Rifle Brigade). Gazetted 2nd Lieut. King's Royal Rifle Corps April 1, 1915, promoted Lieut. Oct. 1916. Served at Home Sept. 1914 to May 1915, and Oct. 1915 to Oct. 1919, France June to Oct. 1915. Wounded at Loos Sept. 25, 1915.

ROBERT MALAM DIX.

Admitted Feb. 1904, practising at Cranbourn Street, W.C. Joined April 1916, as Lieut., General List, promoted Capt. Jan. 1917, Major Aug. 1918, transferred to Royal Army Service Corps July 1918. Twice mentioned in Dispatches. Awarded the O.B.E. (Military). Served at Home, with E.E.F. Sept. 1917 to May 1918, Army of the Rhine May 1918 to Oct. 1919.

ARTHUR CARLYNE NIVEN DIXEY.

Admitted July 1913, practising at Barrow-in-Furness. Served as Lieut., 4th Batt. East Lancashire Regt.

BURLEIGH HARRY JOHN DIXON.

Admitted Aug. 1896. Of Redland, Bristol. Enlisted June 3, 1915, as Private, 4th Batt. Gloucestershire Regt. Served in France.

CLIVE DIXON.

Articled to J. A. Dixon, of Gateshead. Joined Aug. 15, 1918, as Cadet, Royal Field Artillery.

CYRIL MAXFIELD DIXON.

Articled to P. K. Wake, of Sheffield. Mobilised Aug. 1914 and served as Lieut., 4th Batt. York and Lancaster Regt. (Hallamshire Rifles). Killed in action in France Aug. 30, 1915.

FRANCIS DIXON.

Admitted July 1902. Member of Peckover, Scriven & Co., of Leeds. Joined Oct. 19, 1914, as 2nd Lieut., 1st Batt. Herefordshire Regt., promoted Temp. Capt. Jan. 1915, A/Capt. July 1917, attached 234th Infantry Batt. as Lieut. Aug. 1917, and to King's Shropshire Light Infantry Oct. 1917. Served at Home and in France. Severely wounded at Nesle March 25, 1918.

JAMES MAURICE DIXON.

Admitted April 1913. Member of Jacobs, Dixon & Sons, of Hull. Joined, as Gunner, Royal Garrison Artillery, and promoted Bombardier, subsequently transferred as Cadet to the Royal Garrison Artillery Cadet School, Maresfield Park, Sussex, and gazetted 2nd Lieut. April 1919.

JOHN HARRISON DIXON.

Admitted Jan. 1912. Member of Dixon, Ward & Dixon, of 1 Lancaster Place, Strand, W.C. Joined Nov. 1916, as Gunner, Royal Horse Artillery. Gazetted 2nd Lieut. Royal Field Artillery May 1917, promoted Lieut. Nov. 1918. Served with Salonica Expeditionary Force.

PETER SYDENHAM DIXON.

Admitted June 1905. Formerly Assistant Solicitor to C. B. Hodgson, of Carlisle, Clerk of the Peace for Cumberland, and afterwards of Hong Kong.

Joined the Hong Kong Volunteers in 1914. Gazetted 2nd Lieut. 7th Batt. Royal Sussex Regt. May 1916, promoted Lieut. 1917. Served at Home, in Belgium, and in France. Killed near Albert, France, 1918.

EDGAR STANBURY DOBELL.
Articled to J. P. Dobell, of Plymouth. Joined Nov. 9, 1915, as Private, Coldstream Guards, promoted Corporal Sept. 1918, Sergeant Feb. 1919. Once mentioned in Dispatches. Served at Home 1915, France and Belgium 1916, 1917 and 1918, Germany 1919.

REGINALD CRAWSHAW DOBSON.
Admitted June 1906. Member of Hewson, Goodall & Dobson, of Leeds. Joined Jan 3, 1916, as Private, Inns of Court O.T.C. Gazetted 2nd Lieut. Royal Garrison Artillery (S.R.) Sept. 28, 1916, promoted A/Capt. Oct. 1917, Substantive Lieut. March 1918, A/Major Oct. 1918. Awarded the M.C. Served in France and Belgium with 23rd Siege Battery.

THOMAS KING DOBSON.
Admitted Nov. 1909, practising at Thornaby-on-Tees. Joined Nov. 1914, as Private, Hon. Artillery Company (Infantry). Gazetted 2nd Lieut. (S.R.) Royal Garrison Artillery July 1, 1915, promoted Lieut. 1917, A/Capt. 1918. Served at Home, France March to May 1915, Dardanelles Sept. 1915 to Evacuation, Egypt Jan. to April 1916, Salonica April to Aug. 1916. Wounded near Ypres May 22, 1915.

ARTHUR LEIGH DODD.
Articled to T. H. & T. Dodd, of Preston. Served as Private, King's Liverpool Regt.

CHARLES LEONARD DODD.
Admitted Sept. 1912, practising at Liverpool. Served as Lance-Corporal, 7th Batt. King's Liverpool Regt.

WILFRID THOMAS DODD.
Admitted Oct. 1909. Member of Miller, Taylor & Holmes, of Liverpool. Served as Capt., Western Army Troop Signal Coy. Royal Engineers (T.), and subsequently promoted Major. Twice mentioned in Dispatches. Awarded the D.S.O.

GEORGE HEPPLE DODDS.
Admitted Dec. 1910, practised at Newcastle-upon-Tyne. Served as Lieut., Northumbrian Divisional Royal Engineers (T.), promoted Capt. June 1916.

FRED STANLEY DODSON.
Admitted March 1907, practising at Taunton. Joined Sept. 21, 1914, as Lieut., Somerset Light Infantry, promoted Capt. Dec. 1914, Major June 1917. Once mentioned in Dispatches. Served in France and England.

BENJAMIN DODSWORTH.
Admitted Nov. 1906. Member of Gray & Dodsworth, of 1 Bank Buildings, Princes Street, E.C., and York. Served as Capt., Territorial Force Reserve, attached to the American Mission at Tours.

LEONARD LUMLEY SAVAGE DODSWORTH.

Articled to W. S. Hannam, of Leeds. Served as 2nd Lieut., 12th Batt. West Yorkshire Regt.

GEORGE NEWBOULD DODWORTH.

Admitted Nov. 1901, practising at Sheffield. Mobilised Aug. 4, 1914, as Capt., Royal Engineers (T.F.), promoted to Major Nov. 1914. Once mentioned in Dispatches. Served in France 1914, 1916, and June 1918 to Feb. 1919, Gallipoli March to Sept. 1915.

LEO DOHERTY.

Admitted Feb. 1911. Member of Shippey, Earley & Doherty, of Manchester. Joined May 29, 1916, as Gunner, Royal Garrison Artillery, subsequently promoted Corporal. Served at Home.

REGINALD CHAMBERLAIN DOIDGE.

Admitted Feb. 1913, practised at Ashton-under-Lyne. Joined 1914, as Private, South Notts Hussars (T.). Gazetted 2nd Lieut. Lancashire Fusiliers, and subsequently promoted to Capt. Accidentally killed at Calonne, France, on March 2, 1916, consequent on the explosion of a defective bomb as he was instructing his Company.

KENNETH VERE DOLLEYMORE.

Admitted April 1905. Member of Richardson, Sadlers & Callard, 3 St. James's Street, S.W. Joined Dec. 13, 1914, as A.B., Royal Naval Volunteer Reserve. Gazetted Sub-Lieut. Royal Naval Volunteer Reserve Nov. 27, 1915, promoted Lieut. Nov. 1917, and Adjutant Dec. 1918 to March 1919. Served at Home for Anti-Aircraft Work.

JOHN COLIN DOMINY.

Admitted Dec. 1902. Member of Robins, Westlake & Dominy, of Southampton. Mobilised Aug. 4, 1914, with 5th Batt. Hampshire Regt. Sailed for India Oct. 9, 1914, in rank of Capt., became Major June 1916. Served in India, Afghan War 1919.

FRANK DOMVILLE.

Articled to Arthur Browne, of Warrington. Served as Private, 11th Batt. King's Royal Rifle Corps.

MALCOLMSON GARDINER DONAHOO.

Admitted Feb. 1901, practised at 28 St. Swithin's Lane, E.C. Joined Oct. 8, 1914, as Private, Sportsman's Batt. Royal Fusiliers. Obtained commission as 2nd Lieut. 8th Batt. King's Own Yorkshire Light Infantry Feb. 21, 1915, promoted Lieut. July 1916, A/Capt. Aug. 1916. Awarded the M.C. Served in France Aug. 1915 to Jan. 1917. Died of wounds Jan. 31, 1917.

STUART BURTON DONALD.

Admitted July 1902, practising at Union Bank Buildings, Ely Place, E.C. Mobilised Aug. 1914, as Lieut., Kent Cyclist Batt. (T.F.), promoted Capt. Dec. 1914, attached 5th Batt. East Kent Regt. (The Buffs) (T.F.) June 1916. Served at Home Aug. 1914 to Aug. 1916, and Sept. 1916 to Jan.

1917, France Aug. to Sept. 1916, Greece, Turkey, Bulgaria, Rumania (Salonica Army) Jan. 1917 to April 1919. Wounded Sept. 1916.

ARTHUR LESLIE DONALDSON.

Articled to B. D. Webster, of Newton Abbot. Served as Lieut., 13th Batt. Rifle Brigade.

NEVILE SAVAGE DONE.

Admitted Dec. 1904. Managing Clerk with Speechly & Co., of 10 New Square, Lincoln's Inn, W.C. Joined June 1916, as Private, London University O.T.C., and in Sept. 1916 transferred as Private to 16th Batt. County of London Regt. (Queen's Westminster Rifles). Gazetted 2nd Lieut. 6th Batt. Royal Fusiliers March 1917, attached 22nd Batt. Served at Home June 1916 to Feb. 1917, and in France Feb. to March 1917. Killed in action at Irles, Somme, March 10, 1917.

EDMUND RUSSELL DONISTHORPE.

Admitted Dec. 1891. Member of Donisthorpe & Co., of Swan House, Gt. Swan Alley, E.C. Joined Sept. 1914, as Lieut., 2/1 Bucks Batt. Ox. and Bucks Light Infantry, Capt. Dec. 1914, O.C. Company R.D.C., O.C. Troops Coventry, Law Officer Winchester. Once mentioned in Dispatches. Served at Home.

WILLIAM RALPH DONNE.

Articled to T. F. Ivens, of Kidderminster. Served as Trooper, Queen's Own Worcestershire Yeomanry, and afterwards as Lieut. Warwickshire Regt., attached 2nd Batt. Shropshire Light Infantry.

ROY HOLDSWORTH DORÉ.

Admitted Nov. 1913. Managing Clerk with Paterson, Candler & Sykes, of 8 Bream's Buildings, E.C. Joined Aug. 1914, as Private, Inns of Court O.T.C. Gazetted 2nd Lieut. 9th (Service) Batt. The Welch Regt. Sept. 1914. Served at Home. Discharged Jan. 1915.

GEOFFREY CHARLES HERBERT DORMAN.

Articled to C. H. Dorman, of 23 Essex Street, W.C. Served as 2nd Lieut., Royal Engineers, promoted Lieut. July 1917.

HERBERT DALE DOUBLE.

Admitted Nov. 1903. Member of Alfred Double & Sons, 91 Fore Street, E.C. Joined June 29, 1917, as Private, Royal Army Service Corps. Gazetted 2nd Lieut. Royal Army Service Corps Aug. 26, 1917. Served at Home.

HENRY KENNETH DOUGLAS.

Admitted Oct. 1911. Member of Cooper & Co., of Newcastle, Staffs. Joined Jan 14, 1915, as Sub-Lieut., Royal Naval Volunteer Reserve, promoted Lieut. 1916, Lieut.-Commander 1918. Served at Gallipoli, Salonica, and in France. Wounded in Gallipoli Dec. 11, 1915. Invalided out of the Army Oct. 1918. Died from tuberculous disease contracted whilst on Active Service on May 22, 1919.

JOHN MALCOLM DOUGLAS.

Admitted July 1905. Member of Adam Douglas & Son, of Alnwick and Amble. Joined Nov. 23, 1915, as Private, Royal Army Medical Corps, appointed A/Corporal Feb. 1918. Served at Home.

MALCOLM GORDON DOUGLAS.

Admitted June 1906, practised at 6 Old Jewry, E.C. Served as Capt. and Adjutant, Hon. Artillery Company, and promoted Major Nov. 1916. Three times mentioned in Dispatches. Awarded the D.S.O. and M.C.

JACK MILDRED DOULTON.

Articled to R. W. B. Buckland, of 23 Bush Lane, E.C. Served as Private, Public Schools Batt. Middlesex Regt.

JOHN BULLOUGH DOUTHWAITE.

Admitted Feb. 1906, practised at Lancaster. Enlisted Oct. 1914 in the Royal Army Service Corps. Died of malaria at Nairobi, East Africa, whilst serving.

KENNETH TOWNLEY DOWDING.

Articled to H. M. Crookenden, of 3 New Square, Lincoln's Inn Fields, W.C. Joined Aug. 7, 1914, as Private, 5th City of London Batt. London Regt. (London Rifle Brigade). Gazetted 2nd Lieut. The Queen's Royal West Surrey Regt. Jan. 12, 1915, promoted Lieut. June 1915, joined Royal Flying Corps Sept. 1915, promoted Capt. May 1916, Major Jan. 1917, Capt. Royal Air Force Feb. 1918, Squadron Leader Aug. 1918. Awarded the D.F.C. Served in France March to Dec. 1916 and May to Aug. 1918, and in Italy Nov. 1917 to Jan. 1918.

FREDERICK HENRY DOWKER.

Admitted April 1902. Managing Clerk with Wainwright & Co., 9 Staple Inn, W.C., and afterwards of Southern Rhodesia. Joined Oct. 3, 1914, as Private, 23rd (1st Sportman's) Batt. Royal Fusiliers, promoted Lance-Corporal 1915. Served in France. Killed in capture of Delville Wood July 29, 1916.

ARTHUR EDWARD DOWLEY.

Admitted April 1902. Member of Geo. Brown, Son & Vardy, 56 Finsbury Pavement, E.C. Joined May 1916, as Rifleman, 3/5 City of London Batt. London Regt. (London Rifle Brigade), promoted Lance-Corporal Oct. 1916. Gazetted 2nd Lieut. 5th (Reserve) Batt. East Surrey Regt. (T.F.) April 1917, attached 8th Batt. July 1917, promoted Lieut. Oct. 1918. Awarded the M.C. Served at Home, in Belgium, and in France.

RALPH PATRICK O'BRIAN DOWLING.

Admitted July 1909, practised at Ilkley. Served as Lance-Corporal, Duke of Wellington's West Riding Regt.

THOMAS DOWLING.

Admitted April 1895, practising at Bishop Auckland. Mobilised Aug. 6, 1914, with rank of Major, Royal Army Service Corps, promoted A/Lieut.-Col. Jan. 1916, reverted to rank of Major Dec. 1916, promoted Lieut.-Col. Aug. 1917, to date from June 2, 1916. Three times mentioned in Dispatches. Awarded O.B.E. (Military Division) and Belgian Croix de Guerre. Served at Home Aug. 1914 to April 1915 and Dec. 1915 to Dec. 1916, Belgium and France April to Dec. 1915, Dec. 1916 to Nov. 1917, and March to Dec. 1918, Italy Nov. 1917 to March 1918. Germany Jan. to July 1919.

FRANCIS PATTON DOWN.

Admitted March 1899. Member of Down, Scott & Down, of Dorking. Joined Nov. 1914, as 2nd Lieut., The Queen's Royal West Surrey Regt., transferred to Royal Garrison Artillery Nov. 1915, promoted Lieut. July 1917, Capt. Feb. 1918. Once mentioned in Dispatches. Served at Home Nov. 1914 to Oct. 1916, and at Salonica Oct. 1916 to June 1919.

ERIC LIDIARD DOWNEY.

Admitted Jan. 1913, practising at Croydon. Served as 2nd Lieut., 10th Batt. Suffolk Regt., and subsequently promoted to Capt.

HAROLD CORBETT DOWNING.

Admitted Dec. 1906. Member of Downing & Handcock, of Cardiff. Joined Oct. 1914, as 2nd Lieut., 5th Batt. The Welch Regt. (T.F.), promoted Lieut. Nov. 1915, Capt. June 1916. Once mentioned in Dispatches. Served at Home Oct. 1914 to Sept. 1915 and Sept. 1917 to March 1919, Gallipoli Sept. to Dec. 1915, Egypt and Palestine Dec. 1915 to Aug. 1917. Wounded Gaza March 26, 1917.

HUMPHREY DOWSON.

Articled to Walter Dowson, of 19 Surrey Street, W.C. Enlisted Aug. 1914 in the Hon. Artillery Company. Received a commission as 2nd Lieut. King's Royal Rifle Corps Nov. 11, 1914, promoted Lieut. in 15th Batt. March 1915, Capt. 9th Batt. Aug. 1916. Once mentioned in Dispatches. Awarded the M.C. Served in France. Reported wounded and missing, and eventually considered killed in the Battle of the Somme Sept. 15, 1916.

NOEL CECIL DOWSON.

Admitted June 1908. Member of Dowsons, of 18 Adam Street, Adelphi, W.C. Joined Aug. 16, 1915, as 2nd Lieut., Royal Army Service Corps, promoted Lieut. Dec. 1915, A/Capt. and Adjutant Nov. 1917. Once mentioned in Dispatches. Served in Gallipoli 1915, Egypt 1916 and 1917, France 1918.

SYDNEY HOUGHTON DOWSON.

Admitted Dec. 1909. Of West Meon, Hants. Joined Sept. 1914, as Private, 28th Batt. County of London Regt. (Artists' Rifles). Gazetted 2nd Lieut. 1st Batt. Royal Warwickshire Regt. July 1915, subsequently A/Capt. General List. Awarded the M.C. Served in France Jan. 1915 to April 1918. Wounded June 1916.

ARCHIBALD STANLEY DRABBLE.

Admitted Nov. 1913, practising at Wirksworth. Served as Private, Public School Corps, and subsequently gazetted 2nd Lieut. Machine Gun Corps.

HERBERT HARDY DRABBLE.

Admitted Feb. 1911, practising at Sheffield. Joined Dec. 17, 1914, as 2nd Lieut., 4th Batt. York and Lancaster Regt (T.F.), promoted Lieut. Aug. 1915, A/Capt. Nov. 1915, Substantive Capt. Aug. 1916. Served in France and Belgium. Wounded Nov. 11, 1917.

FRANCIS HUBERT DRAKE.

Admitted Feb. 1913, practising at Haslemere, Surrey. Joined April 13, 1915, as 2nd Lieut., 4th Batt. Duke of Cornwall's Light Infantry, promoted

Lieut. July 1, 1917, Capt. (local rank) from Jan. 1918. Served in Mesopotamia and India.

FREDERIC AUGUSTUS DRAKE.

Admitted June 1907. Member of Williams & James, Norfolk House, Thames Embankment, W.C. Joined June 1915, as 2nd Lieut., Warwickshire Yeomanry, promoted Capt. and Adjutant 1917. Served at Home and Egypt and Palestine. Wounded in Battle of Gaza April 1917. Drowned in the sinking of H.M.T. *Leasowe Castle*, torpedoed off Alexandria, May 27, 1918, on the Regt. returning to England *en route* for France.

CONRAD HAMPDEN DRAYTON.

Admitted Dec. 1908, practising at 6 Bond Court, Walbrook, E.C. Served as Major, Home Counties Royal Army Service Corps.

ROBERT HARRY DRAYTON.

Articled to Roberts & Andrew, of Exeter. Served as Sergt., 2nd Batt. Public School Corps.

JOHN HENRY DRESSER.

Admitted E. 1875. Member of Dresser & Earl, of 89 Chancery Lane, W.C. Served as Major, Home Counties Royal Army Service Corps (T.).

ALFRED LIONEL DREW.

Admitted Oct. 1911. Member of Nisbet, Drew & Loughborough, of 23 Austin Friars, E.C. Joined Aug. 8, 1914, as Private, Hon. Artillery Company (Infantry). Gazetted 2nd Lieut. Royal Army Service Corps June 23, 1915, promoted Lieut. Aug. 1915, Capt. Sept. 1917. Once mentioned in Dispatches. Served at Home.

JOHN HAWORTH DRIVER.

Admitted Nov. 1910, practising at Guiseley, near Leeds. Joined Dec. 5, 1915, as Private, Inns of Court O.T.C. Gazetted 2nd Lieut. 4th Batt. Loyal North Lancashire Regt. March. 1, 1917, promoted Lieut. Sept. 1918. Served in France April 1917 to Oct. 1917. Wounded July 28, 1917, and Oct. 26, 1917.

GEOFFRY TREMENHEERE DRUITT.

Articled to James Druitt, of Bournemouth. Mobilised Aug. 1914 with 7th Batt. Hampshire Regt., promoted Capt. (Temp.) Sept. 1914, Capt. (Substantive) June 1916, detached from Regiment on Staff duties 1916 and 1917, D.A.A. and Q.M.G. Presidency Brigade, Calcutta, Oct. 1916 to Jan. 1918. Served in India 1914 to 1918, Aden Field Force 1918 to 1919.

JAMES VICTOR DRUITT.

Admitted Oct. 1910. Managing Clerk with J. & W. H. Druitt, of Bournemouth. Mobilised Aug. 5, 1914, as Capt., 7th Batt. Hampshire Regt. Served at Home.

ROBERT EVERARD DRUITT.

Admitted April 1908, practising at Christchurch, Hants, and Bournemouth. Joined Sept. 14, 1914, as Capt., 8th Batt. Middlesex Regt. (T.F.), with 11th Batt. July 1916 to Jan. 1917, 7th (Reserve) Batt. March to Oct. 1917, 23rd Cheshire Regt. Oct. 1917 to Feb. 1919, A/Major July 1918 to Feb.

1919. Once mentioned in Dispatches. Served in Gibraltar Feb. to Aug. 1915, Egypt Sept. 1915 to May 1916 (Senassi Campaign Nov. 1915 to May 1916), France May 1916 to Jan. 1917 and May 1918 to Feb. 1919.

THOMAS HENRY DUCKHAM.

Admitted May 1911, practising at 5 Verulam Buildings, Gray's Inn, W.C. Served as Lieut., 4th Welsh Brigade Royal Field Artillery, and subsequently promoted Capt.

ORLANDO HARRY DUCKSBURY.

Articled to A. C. Dickson, of Preston. Joined Aug. 1914, as Private, 5th Batt. King's Own Royal Lancaster Regt. Gazetted 2nd Lieut. Loyal North Lancashire Regt. Sept. 1915. Served in France. Wounded in May 1915 and again in 1916, when taken prisoner.

GEORGE REGINALD JOSEPH DUCKWORTH.

Articled to T. H. Clarke, of Preston. Joined Oct. 2, 1914, as Private, 21st Batt. Royal Fusiliers. Commissioned to 7th (Special Reserve) Batt. Royal Fusiliers July 7, 1916, promoted Lieut. Jan. 1918. Served at Home and France. Wounded at Beaumont Hamel, Nov. 13, 1916. Taken prisoner in the withdrawal on March 23, 1918, near Leschelles and Rocquegney.

WILLIAM DUCKWORTH.

Admitted Dec. 1909, practised at Liverpool. Enlisted, as Private, 10th (Scottish) Batt. King's Liverpool Regt. Served in France. Died Sept. 17, 1918, of illness contracted on service.

HARVEY STEEVENS DUDER.

Admitted Dec. 1898. Assistant Prosecuting Solicitor for the City of Liverpool. Joined Nov. 30, 1914, as 2nd Lieut., 8th (Irish) Batt. King's (Liverpool) Regt., subsequently attained the rank of Major. Served in France. Killed in action July 31, 1917.

ERIC WHITTINGTON DUDLEY.

Admitted Aug. 1908. Managing Clerk with Parker, Garratt & Co., St. Michael's Rectory, Cornhill, E.C. Joined Aug. 1914, as Private, Hon. Artillery Company. Gazetted 2nd Lieut. 13th Batt. Royal Sussex Regt. Dec. 1915. Missing from June 30, 1916, at Richbourg, Belgium.

SAMUEL HUGH DUFF.

Admitted Jan. 1907, practised at Plymouth. Served as Private, Devonshire Regt., and subsequently gazetted 2nd Lieut. 8th Batt. Devonshire Regt. Awarded the M.C.

CLEMENT BERNARD DUKE.

Articled to Horace Duke, of 18 & 19 Ironmonger Lane, E.C. Joined Nov. 1916, as Private, Royal Army Ordnance Corps. Served in France with Nos. 8 (Medium) and 32 (Light) Ordnance Mobile Workshops.

DOUGLAS ST. JOHN DUKE.

Admitted April 1901. Member of Holloway, Blount & Duke, of 24 Lincoln's Inn Fields, W.C. Served as Lieut., Royal Naval Volunteer Reserve (Motor Boat Patrol).

HORACE DUKE.

Admitted June 1906. Member of F. Duke & Son, of 18 & 19 Ironmonger Lane, E.C. Joined April 10, 1917, as Air-Craftsman, 2nd Grade, Royal Naval Air Service, transferred to Royal Air Force April 1918, promoted Corporal July 1918. Served at Home.

JOSEPH DUKE.

Admitted May 1900, practising at Ilminster. Mobilised Aug. 1914, as Lieut., 1/5 Batt. Somerset Light Infantry, promoted Temp. Capt. Oct. 1914, Substantive Capt. June 1916, Staff Capt. (Alexandria District) Feb. 1918 to Sept. 17, 1919. Created officer of "The Order of the Nile" and Knight of "The Order of the Crown of Italy." Served at Home Aug. to Oct. 1914, in India Nov. 1914 to April 1917, and in Palestine and Egypt May 1917 to Sept. 1919.

FINLAY DUN.

Admitted May 1888. Member of Gill, Archer, Maples & Dun, of Liverpool. Joined Oct. 2, 1914, as Capt., 10th Batt. King's Liverpool Regt. (Liverpool Scottish). Served at Home. Discharged Nov. 1, 1916.

ERNEST BOLTON DUNCAN.

Admitted June 1907. Managing Clerk with F. A. C. Redden, of 17 Victoria Street, Westminster, S.W. Joined Jan. 5, 1916, as Private, Inns of Court O.T.C. Gazetted 2nd Lieut. 4th Batt. London Regt. Dec. 19, 1916, promoted Lieut. June 1918, A/Capt. Oct. 1917. Served at Home.

JAMES FERGUS DUNCAN.

Admitted Dec. 1894, practising at 3 Coleman Street, E.C. Joined Aug. 4, 1914, as Lieut., Royal Horse Artillery, promoted Major Feb. 1915, Lieut.-Col. April 1915. Three times mentioned in Dispatches. Awarded the D.S.O. Served in France.

WALTER DUNCAN.

Admitted June 1912. Managing Clerk with Alsop, Stevens, Crooks & Co., of Liverpool. Mobilised, as Private, 6th Batt. King's Liverpool Regt. at outbreak of War. Gazetted 2nd Lieut. 8th Batt. King's Liverpool Regt. Nov. 1914, promoted Lieut. Jan. 1916, Lieut. Home Intelligence Staff Aug. 1918. Once mentioned in Dispatches. Served in France. Taken prisoner at Guillemont, Aug. 8, 1916. Escaped from Lüdingshafen on Rhine and crossed Dutch Frontier Feb. 5, 1918. Died of pneumonia Dec. 19, 1918.

ROBERT WILLIAM LAYARD DUNLOP, C.I.E.

Admitted April 1893. Of Bombay. Served as Lieut.-Col. commanding 3rd (Reserve) Batt., 14th Batt. County of London Regt. (London Scottish), and subsequently of the Royal Horse and Royal Field Artillery. Mentioned in Dispatches. Awarded the D.S.O.

CECIL WILLIAM DUNN.

Admitted April 1888. Member of S. B. Cohen, Dunn & Co., of Audrey House, Ely Place, E.C. Joined Aug. 1914, as Petty Officer, Royal Naval Volunteer Reserve, London Division. Commission as Assistant Paymaster Jan. 1915, Staff Paymaster Aug. 1915, Paymaster Lieut.-Commander Oct.

1917. Served at Royal Naval Depôt, Crystal Palace, and Royal Naval Barracks, Portsmouth, Staff Officer on the Permanent Staff.

JOHN ROBERT COLLARD DUNN.

Admitted Aug. 1911, practised at Porth, Glamorgan. Joined Sept. 6, 1914, as Private, 1/5 Batt. The Welch Regt. (T.). Gazetted 2nd Lieut. 1/5 Batt. The Welch Regt. (T.) April 15, 1915. Served at Home and at Gallipoli. Killed in action at Suvla Bay Aug. 10, 1915.

BERTRAM RICHARD DUNNING.

Articled to W. T. M. Snow, of Exeter. Joined Sept. 18, 1914, as Private, Royal Fusiliers. Gazetted 2nd Lieut. 10th Batt. Devonshire Regt. Sept. 22, 1914, promoted Lieut. March 1914, Capt. April 1917. Once mentioned in Dispatches. Served in France Sept. to Dec. 1915, and in Macedonia Dec. 1915 to June 1919.

STUART CHARLES STEPHEN DUNPHY.

Admitted Jan. 1909, practising at Llandudno. Joined Jan. 26, 1915, as Staff-Sergeant-Major, Royal Army Service Corps. Served at Home, in France, and in North Russia.

REGINALD MARTIN DUNSFORD.

Admitted Oct. 1908, practised at Southampton. Joined Oct. 1914, as Private, 16th Batt. County of London Regt. (Queen's Westminsters). Gazetted 2nd Lieut. Royal Garrison Artillery March 2, 1915, promoted Lieut. June 1916, Capt. Aug. 1918, posted to 16th Siege Battery. Served in France. Died on leave, septic pneumonia, Oct. 1918.

CHARLES HINTON DU PRE.

Admitted Dec. 1905. Member of Foyer & Co., of 26 Essex Street, W.C. Served as Lieut., Royal Army Service Corps. Mentioned in Dispatches. Awarded the M.C.

WILLIAM MAITLAND DURANT.

Articled to C. F. L. Clarke, of Bristol. Gazetted 2nd Lieut. 1/6 Batt. Gloucestershire Regt. Oct. 15, 1914, promoted Lieut. June 1916, A/Capt. Machine Gun Corps June 1917, Capt. Gloucestershire Regt. March 1918. Served in France May 1915 to Sept. 1917 and May to June 1918. Gassed May 29, 1918.

ERIC ALEXANDER OGILVIE DURLACHER.

Articled to E. J. Bellord, of Waterloo Place, S.W. Enlisted Aug. 1914 in Universities and Public Schools Batt. Royal Fusiliers. Gazetted 2nd Lieut. (Reserve of Officers) May 1915, attached 4th Batt. Worcestershire Regt., promoted Capt. April 1917. Awarded the M.C. Served in France. Killed at Croiselles, France, May 20, 1917.

GUY DURNFORD.

Admitted June 1907. Member of Durnford & Son, of 9 King's Bench Walk, Temple, E.C. Served as 2nd Lieut., 4th Batt. London Regt. Royal Fusiliers.

BERNARD HARRY DURRANT.

Articled to L. C. Miller, of Norwich. Joined Oct. 1, 1914, as Private, 2/4 Batt. Norfolk Regt. Gazetted 2nd Lieut. 10th Batt. Norfolk Regt. Oct. 21,

1915, 2nd Lieut. Machine Gun Corps April 10, 1916, Lieut. Machine Gun Corps May 1917, Lieut. 37th Div. Signal Company Royal Engineers July 1918. Once mentioned in Dispatches. Awarded the M.C. Served at Home Oct. 1914 to Oct. 1916, and in France Oct. 1916 to Jan. 1919.

FRANK WILLIAM DUST.

Admitted Oct. 1912. Member of Alderson, Son & Dust, of Sheffield. Mobilised Aug. 1914, as Lieut., 3rd West Riding Brigade Royal Field Artillery (T.), promoted Capt. March 1915, Major Dec. 1916. Awarded the M.C. Served in England Aug. 1914 to March 1915, and in France and Belgium March 1915 to April 1917. Killed in action at Lens April 23, 1917.

CHARLES DUTTON.

Articled to James Dutton, of Bolton. Joined Sept. 3, 1914, as Private, Public Schools Batt. Gazetted 2nd Lieut. 10th Batt. Lancashire Fusiliers Sept. 26, 1914. Killed in action in France July 7, 1916.

HARRY ST. JOHN DUTTON.

Admitted March 1899. Member of James Dutton & Son, of Bolton. Joined Jan. 17, 1917, as 2nd Lieut., 12th Batt. Loyal North Lancashire Regt., promoted Lieut. July 1918. Served in Palestine July 1917 to May 1918, France June to Nov. 1918.

HUGH THOMPSON DUTTON.

Admitted May 1910, practising at Chester. Joined May 26, 1916, as Gunner, Antrim Royal Garrison Artillery, promoted to Bombardier Nov. 1916, transferred to Intelligence Police, Sept. 1917, Sergeant Intelligence Police Dec. 1917, Sergeant Royal Fusiliers Jan. 1919. Served in Ireland May 1916 to Sept. 1917, France Sept. 1917 to Jan. 1919, England Jan. to March 1919.

RICHARD DUTTON.

Articled to H. P. May, of Blackpool. Joined Jan. 1915, as Private, Public Schools Batt. Royal Fusiliers, appointed 2nd Lieut. Royal Flying Corps Sept. 6, 1916. Served in France. Killed while flying in Belgium, Aug. 19, 1917. Interred at Oudenberg lès Ostende, Belgium.

TOM DUERDIN DUTTON.

Admitted Sept. 1916. Of 80 Rochester Row, S.W. Mobilised Aug. 5, 1914, as Rifleman, 16th Batt. County of London Regt. (Queen's Westminster Rifles). Served in France and Belgium.

CHARLES NETTELTON DYER.

Admitted June 1905. Of Croydon. Mobilised Aug. 1914, as Capt., "A" Battery, Hon. Artillery Company. Served in Egypt, on Suez Canal, May 1915 to Jan. 1916 and March to July 1916, and on North-West Frontier Jan. to March 1916. Died of enteric fever in Stationary Hospital, Suez, July 14, 1916.

EDWARD ARNOLD DYER.

Admitted Jan. 1896, practised in Canada. Joined Oct. 1914, as A/Capt., Remount Department, 1st Canadian Contingent, transferred as Lieut. to 9th Batt. Shropshire Light Infantry Feb. 1915, attached 1st Batt. Border Regt. for Gallipoli May 1915. Served at Gallipoli May and June 1915. Killed in action at Gallipoli June 28, 1915.

HENRY LIONEL DYMOKE.

Articled to K. Hunnybun, of Huntingdon. Served as 2nd Lieut., Huntingdonshire Cyclist Batt., and subsequently attained the rank of Capt.

HUGH EDWARD LUBBOCK DYNE.

Admitted April 1911. Managing Clerk with St. Barbe Sladen & Wing, of 7 Queen Anne's Gate, Westminster. Joined Sept. 2, 1914, as Private, 28th Batt. County of London Regt. (Artists Rifles). Gazetted 2nd Lieut. 5th Batt. The Queen's (T.F.) Oct. 29, 1915, promoted Lieut. July 1917, attached 1st Batt. The Queen's Nov. 1917. Served at Home Sept. 1914 to Nov. 1917, and in France Nov. 1917 to Jan. 1919.

ERIC DYSON.

Articled to T. A. Dyson, of Gainsborough, Lincolnshire. Mobilised Aug. 1914, as 2nd Lieut., 5th Batt. Lincolnshire Regt. (T.F.), promoted Lieut. Dec. 1914. Served in France and Belgium Feb. to May 1915. Wounded May 20, 1915. Gazetted out on account of ill-health Nov. 5, 1917.

WILLIAM ELLIS DYSON.

Admitted March 1898. Member of Bingley & Dyson, of Sheffield. Joined March 24, 1916, as Private, 3/5 Batt. York and Lancaster Regt., appointed Sergeant Sept. 1916. Served at Home.

JOHN IRELAND EAGER.

Articled to P. G. Eager, of Horsham, Sussex. Joined May 8, 1918, as Sapper, Royal Engineers. Served at Home.

GUY TRYON EAGLETON.

Articled to John Eagleton, of 40 Chancery Lane, W.C. Served as Private, Hon. Artillery Company. Subsequently obtained commission in Royal Horse and Royal Field Artillery and promoted Lieut.

ARTHUR NOEL EALAND.

Admitted July 1908. Member of Houchen, Greenland & Co., of Thetford, Norfolk. Joined April 1915, as Ambulance Driver, Red Cross Society, and served in France. Gazetted 2nd Lieut. 4th Dragoons June 1917, and in Feb. 1918 transferred to Royal Air Force as 2nd Lieut. in Wireless Section. Accidentally killed July 15, 1918, during a testing flight of wireless telephony.

FRANCIS DAW SHERBROOKE EALES.

Admitted Oct. 1914, practised at 61 Carey Street, W.C. Served as 2nd Lieut., 9th Batt. Leicestershire Regt. Reported missing, believed killed.

LLEWELLYN EARDLEY EARDLEY-SIMPSON.

Admitted Nov. 1914. Of Derby. Mobilised with Territorial Force Reserve, promoted Capt. 4th North Midland (Howitzer) Brigade Royal Field Artillery (T.F.) July 1915, Major April 1918. Served at Home Feb. 1915 to March 1918, France March 1918 to May 1919.

JOHN WILLIAM ARTHUR EARLE.

Admitted Aug. 1914. Member of Earle, Sons & Co., of Manchester. Joined Dec. 1, 1915, as 2nd Lieut., Irish Guards, promoted to Lieut. (A/Capt.).

FREDERICK ARCHIBALD EAST.

Articled to F. J. East, of 127 Moorgate Station Chambers, E.C. Joined May 8, 1916, as Private, 2nd Batt. Hon. Artillery Company. Served in France and Italy. Died at 22nd Field Ambulance, Asiago, Italy, from wounds received in action.

REGINALD CHARLES EASTERBROOK.

Admitted Nov. 1914. Managing Clerk with Hodding & Jackson, of Salisbury. Joined April 1917, as 2nd Lieut., Royal Army Service Corps (H.T.), transferred to Camel Transport Corps as Lieut. Nov. 1918. Served in Egypt and Palestine.

CHARLES MORTIMER EASTLEY.

Articled to C. H. Eastley, of Paignton. Joined Sept. 1914, as 2nd Lieut., 4th Wessex Brigade, Royal Field Artillery (T.F.), promoted Lieut. June 1916, transferred to Royal Flying Corps Oct. 1916. Served in India 1914 to 1917, Egypt 1917, India 1917 to 1918, Baluchistan 1918, Aden 1918, Egypt 1919, India and Afghan operations 1919.

JOHN EDWARD EASTLEY.

Articled to J. B. Eastley, of Paignton, Devon. Joined Aug. 11, 1914, as 2nd Lieut., promoted Temp. Lieut. Sept. 1914, Temp. Capt. Aug. 1915. Joined 6th Batt. Somerset Light Infantry, and went overseas with this Battalion. After being wounded, served in various Reserve Batts. of the Somerset Light Infantry and eventually served as Staff-Capt. of the 193rd Infantry Brigade. Served in France from May to Sept. 1915. Wounded Sept. 19, 1915.

HAROLD EASTON.

Admitted Jan. 1900. Member of Gale & Easton, of Hull. Joined Oct. 1914, as Lieut., East Riding Royal Garrison Artillery, promoted Capt. Oct. 1915. Served in England and Ireland to Nov. 1918, and in France Nov. 1918 to Feb. 1919.

CHRISTOPHER WILLIAM EASTWOOD.

Admitted Nov. 1905, practising at Blackburn. Served as Private, 677th Employment Company.

FREDERICK EAVES.

Admitted Oct. 1908, practising at Lancaster. Served as Capt., 5th Batt. King's Own Royal Lancaster Regt., and attained the rank of Lieut.-Col. Twice mentioned in Dispatches. Awarded the D.S.O.

HAROLD CHARLES EAVES.

Admitted July 1902, practising at Birmingham. Served as Private, 639th (H.S.) Employment Coy.

GEORGE STRACHAN JOHN FULLER EBERLE.

Admitted Oct. 1906. Member of Bevan, Hancock, Boucher & Eberle, of Bristol. Served as Major, South Midland Divisional Royal Engineers (T.). Mentioned in Dispatches. Awarded the D.S.O.

ALEXANDER EDDY.

Admitted Feb. 1904. On Staff of Solicitor to L. & N.W. Ry. Co., Euston Station. Joined Oct. 1914, as A.B., Royal Naval Volunteer Reserve Anti-

Aircraft Corps (London), promoted Chief Petty Officer Feb. 1915. Gazetted Sub-Lieut. Oct. 6, 1918. Served in London and Home Waters.

EDWARD MURRAY CHARLES EDE.

Admitted June 1912. Member of Ede & Jeans, of 50 Bedford Row, W.C. Served as 2nd Lieut., 7th (Service) Batt. South Wales Borderers. Subsequently transferred to South Staffordshire Regt. and attained the rank of Capt.

IVAN JAMES EDELL.

Articled to J. F. Edell, of King Street, Cheapside, E.C. Joined Nov. 9, 1914, as Private, Hon. Artillery Company. Gazetted 2nd Lieut. Royal Field Artillery (T.F.) Sept. 25, 1915, promoted Lieut. June 1916. Awarded the M.C. Served in France May 1916 to July 1917, Salonica Aug. 1918 to Feb. 1919. Wounded July 22, 1917.

ROBERT GERALD EDGAR

Admitted Feb. 1911. Member of Boote, Edgar, Grace & Rylands, of Manchester. Joined March 9, 1909, as 2nd Lieut., 1/6 Batt. Manchester Regt. (T.F.), promoted Lieut. Aug. 1914, Capt. Aug. 1914. Served in Egypt and at Gallipoli. Killed in the attack on Achi Baba, Gallipoli, June 4, 1915.

ALBERT HENRY EDGINGTON.

Admitted Sept. 1905, practised at Worcester, and afterwards went to Australia. Joined Aug. 10, 1914, as Private, First Australian Naval and Military Expedition. After six months service at German New Guinea returned to Sydney and rejoined for service April 1915, went to Egypt, then to the Dardanelles as Private 4th Batt. Australian Imperial Force. Died of dysentery and gastritis at Mudros Aug. 20, 1915.

EDWARD FRANCIS COPPENHALL EDLESTON.

Admitted Nov. 1901, practised at Stafford. Attested Dec. 4, 1915. Proceeded to France Sept. 1916 as Signaller 166th Siege Battery, Royal Garrison Artillery. Wounded Sept. 19, 1918.

ROBERT RAINFORD EDLESTON.

Admitted July 1898, practising at Crewe, Cheshire. Served as Gunner, Royal Garrison Artillery.

JOE EDMANSON.

Articled to C. J. F. Atkinson, of Otley. Joined July 1, 1915, as 2nd Lieut., King's Own Yorkshire Light Infantry. Served in France. Killed on Somme July 3, 1916.

ROBERT EDMOND.

Admitted Feb. 1909. Managing Clerk with Birdsall, Cross & Black, of Scarborough. Joined Aug. 1917, as Sub-Lieut., Royal Naval Volunteer Reserve, serving in Auxiliary Patrol, transferred to Salvage Section Jan. 1918, promoted Lieut. and Assistant Salvage Officer June 1918. Awarded O.B.E. (Military Division). Served in England (part time afloat).

EDWIN ARTHUR EDMONDS.

Admitted April 1900, practising at Broadway House, Walham Green, S.W. Joined Aug. 21, 1916, as Private, Royal Army Service Corps (M.T.) Gazetted

2nd Lieut. Nov. 20, 1916, promoted Lieut. May 1918. Once mentioned in Dispatches. Served in France.

CYRIL ARTHUR EDMONDSON.

Articled to F. J. Mote, of 1 South Square, Gray's Inn, W.C. Joined Sept. 1914 Royal Naval Division. Commissioned Feb. 1915 as Sub-Lieut., promoted Full Lieut. 1916. Once mentioned in Dispatches. Served at Gallipoli and in France. Killed in action Nov. 13, 1916.

FRANCIS TRIVETT EDMUNDS.

Admitted Oct. 1913, practised at Bournemouth. Served as Corporal, 9th Batt. Hampshire Regt.

CHARLES ROBERT EWBANK EDMUNDSON.

Admitted Feb. 1914. Of Masham and Ripon, Yorkshire. Enlisted Sept. 1914, as Private, Middlesex Regt. and ten days later was given a commission and attached to the 8th Batt. Yorks. and Lancashire Regt., promoted Lieut. Jan. 1915, Capt. Feb. 1915. Awarded a posthumous M.C. Killed on the Somme July 1, 1916.

ERIC JAMES EDWARD.

Admitted July 1905. Member of Edward & Childs, 11 Great St. Helen's, E.C. Joined Nov. 9, 1914, as Chief Petty Officer, Royal Naval Volunteer Reserve (London A.A.C.). Sub-Lieut. June 1915, Lieut. Nov. 1915, transferred at own request to Lieut. Royal Garrison Artillery April 1917. Served in France 1915, at Sea, H.M.S. *City of Oxford*, Dover Patrol, Grand Fleet, Battle Cruiser Force 1916 to 1917, France 1917. Taken prisoner at Cambrai Nov. 30, 1917.

ARTHUR EDWARDS.

Admitted Dec. 1903, practised at 57 Moorgate Street, E.C. Joined Oct. 1914, as Private, 5th City of London Batt. London Regt. (London Rifle Brigade). Subsequently gazetted 2nd Lieut. East Kent Regt. (The Buffs). Served in France. Wounded at Ypres May 1915. Killed at Ypres June 15, 1917.

ARTHUR TREVELLYN EDWARDS.

Articled to L. Morgan, of Cardiff. Joined Jan. 15, 1915, as Private, 21st (Service) Batt. Royal Fusiliers. Gazetted 2nd Lieut. Machine Gun Corps Sept. 5, 1916. Served in France and Belgium. Wounded at 3rd Battle of Ypres July 31, 1917. Discharged June 30, 1918.

CYRIL ERNEST EDWARDS.

Admitted April 1915. Member of E. Edwards & Son, of East Ham, E., and 21 College Hill, E.C. Joined Dec. 4, 1915, as 2nd Lieut., Royal Fusiliers, promoted Capt. Sept. 1916, Major July 1917, A/Brigade-Major 124th Infantry Brigade April to June 1918. Three times mentioned in Dispatches. Awarded the D.S.O., M.C., and Croix de Guerre avec Palmes (French). Served at Home Dec. 1915 to May 1916, France May 1916 to Nov. 1917, and Feb. to Dec. 1918, and in Italy Nov. 1917 to Feb. 1918.

EDGAR MAURICE EDWARDS.

Articled to F. S. Pearson, of Birmingham. Served as 2nd Lieut., South Midland Division Royal Army Service Corps, and attained the rank of Capt. Mentioned in Dispatches. Awarded the M.C.

ERIC WILSON EDWARDS.

Admitted Feb. 1915. Member of Braikenridge & Edwards, 16 Bartlett's Buildings, E.C. Joined Jan. 8, 1916, as Temp. 2nd Lieut., The Queen's Royal West Surrey Regt., promoted Lieut. April 1917, A/Capt. Sept. 1917. Served in France, on the Somme during autumn and winter of 1916; took part in Battle of Arras Easter 1917. Killed at Chapel Hill, near Gouzeaucourt, Nov. 30, 1917.

FREDERICK HENRY EDWARDS.

Admitted July 1902, practising at Swansea. Served as Capt., 1st Welsh (Howitzer) Brigade Royal Field Artillery, and subsequently promoted Major.

GERALD BRACTON EDWARDS.

Articled to G. W. Edwards, of Liverpool. Mobilised Aug. 4, 1914, as 2nd Lieut., 5th Batt. The King's Liverpool Regt., promoted Lieut. Aug. 8, 1914, Capt. June 1916, seconded to Signal Service from Nov. 1913 to April 1917, restored to 5th Batt. The King's Liverpool Regt. April 1917. Once mentioned in Dispatches. Awarded the M.C. Served in France. Taken prisoner near Festubert April 9, 1918.

HAROLD MOLYNEUX EDWARDS.

Admitted Oct. 1904. Member of Weldon & Edwards, of 10 New Broad Street, E.C. Joined Sept. 3, 1914, as Private, Royal Army Service Corps, promoted Sergeant Sept. 1914. Gazetted Lieut. Royal Naval Air Service 1917, promoted Capt. Royal Air Force 1918. Served in France and Flanders Sept. 1914 to Jan. 1915.

JOHN VERNEY EDWARDS.

Articled to Ernest Kammerer, of Llanelly. Joined Nov. 1914, as Trooper, 2nd Pembroke Yeomanry, transferred July 1915 to Inns of Court O.T.C. Gazetted 2nd Lieut. 5th Batt. Royal Welch Fusiliers Aug. 4, 1916, promoted Lieut. Feb. 1917. Served at Home, in France, and in North Russia—Murman Coast and Archangel. Gassed Sept. 1917.

OWEN BYDDER EDWARDS.

Admitted Oct. 1907, practising at Holyhead. Joined Sept. 29, 1914, as Capt., 22nd Batt. The Rifle Brigade. Served in Egypt and Salonica.

PATRICK HARRINGTON EDWARDS.

Admitted Jan. 1898. Member of Harrington, Edwards & Cobban, of 33 Southampton Street, Strand, W.C. Joined Oct. 6, 1914, as Sub-Lieut., Royal Naval Volunteer Reserve, promoted Lieut. June 1915, Lieut.-Commander Dec. 1915, Commander Dec. 1917. Three times mentioned in Dispatches. Awarded the D.S.O. and Bar, the Croix de Guerre, and the Order of St. Vladimir and the Order of St. Anne. Served in Egypt (Defence of Suez Canal), Gallipoli landing and evacuation, Stavros (Salonica), France, Raid on Zeebrugge in H.M.S. *Vindictive*; at sea, Archangel, Onega, and Pinega Fronts. Wounded twice in Gallipoli, once in France, and once at Zeebrugge.

PERCY JOHN EDWARDS.

Admitted May 1900, practised at Woking. Served as 2nd Lieut., Royal Dublin Fusiliers, and subsequently promoted Lieut.

TREVOR LOUIS EDWARDS.

Admitted Nov. 1910. Member of Harrington, Edwards & Cobban, 33 Southampton Street, Strand, W.C. Joined Sept. 1914, as 2nd Lieut., Royal Marine Light Infantry (Plymouth Batt.), promoted Lieut. 1915, Capt. 1916. Served in Egypt (Defence of Suez Canal), Gallipoli, and in France. Killed in action at Passchendaele Oct. 26, 1917.

WILLIAM GERALD HOWELL POWELL EDWARDS.

Articled to F. Kinder, of 25 Lincoln's Inn Fields, W.C. Served as 2nd Lieut., Sussex Yeomanry.

WILLIAM RICHARD EDWARDS.

Admitted Dec. 1899, practised at Aberdare. Served as Sergeant, Royal Fusiliers.

ZACHARIAH BENJAMIN EDWARDS.

Admitted June 1912. Member of Ernest Simmons & Co., of 199 Piccadilly, W. Served as 2nd Lieut., 24th Batt. County of London Regt.

MONTAGUE FLAMANK EDYVEAN.

Admitted May 1905, practising at Bodmin, Cornwall. Mobilised Aug. 5, 1914, as Capt., 5th Batt. Duke of Cornwall's Light Infantry (T.F.). Served at Home.

NORMAN EDYVEAN-WALKER.

Articled to C. H. Fuller, of Rugby. Joined Sept. 15, 1914, as Private, 19th Batt. Royal Fusiliers, promoted Corporal 1915. Received commission in same Regiment July 1, 1915. Served at Home and in France. Wounded Aug. 9, 1916, Somme Battle.

THOMAS MACDONALD EGGAR.

Admitted Nov. 1907, practising at Winchester House, E.C., and Brighton. Joined Aug. 25, 1914, as Private, 14th Batt. London Regt. (London Scottish). Gazetted 2nd Lieut. in same Batt. April 7, 1915, promoted Lieut. July 1916, Capt. Dec. 1917, seconded to Royal Flying Corps as Staff Officer and Temp. Capt. July 1916, promoted Major April 1918, and Lieut.-Col. Sept. 1918. Once mentioned in Dispatches. Awarded O.B.E. Served in England and France. Wounded Nov. 9, 1914, and Oct. 13, 1915.

JOHN FOLEY EGGINTON.

Articled to W. H. Egginton, of Birmingham. Joined Dec. 2, 1915, as Gunner, Royal Field Artillery, posted to 89th Battery, 16th Brigade, promoted A/Bombardier June 1917. Granted commission in Indian Army June 7, 1918, and posted to 2/11 Rajputs, posted to 12th Special Reserve Batt. April 1919, and appointed Adjutant, A/Capt. May 1919, promoted Temp. Lieut. (A/Capt.) June 1919. Served in India, North-West Frontier.

CLIFFORD CAUNT ELBORNE.

Admitted March 1914. Member of Elborne & Son, of Nottingham. Joined Sept. 6, 1914, as Private, 9th Batt. King's Royal Rifle Corps, and attained the rank of Sergeant. Gazetted 2nd Lieut. 18th Batt. Notts and Derby Regt. (Sherwood Foresters) Oct. 20, 1915, transferred to 13th Batt. Yorkshire Regt. May 1916, attained the rank of Capt. Served in France.

JAMES MATTHEWS ELDRIDGE.

Admitted Feb. 1906, practising at Oxford. Joined Sept. 1914, as Private, 7th Batt. Oxford and Bucks Light Infantry. Gazetted Lieut. 7th Batt. Royal Berkshire Regt. Oct. 10, 1914, promoted Capt. Dec. 1914, appointed Adjutant Dec. 1914, Major Oct. 1917, 2nd in command 14th Batt. King's Liverpool Regt. May 1918. Served in France 1915 and 1918, Macedonia 1915 to 1918.

ROBEY JAMES ELDRIDGE.

Admitted April 1904. Member of James Eldridge & Sons, of Ryde, Cowes, and Newport, Isle of Wight. Joined Oct. 24, 1916, Hants Yeomanry (Cyclists), promoted Corporal. Appointed A/Paymaster Army Pay Department Nov. 1918. Served at Home.

CHRISTOPHER JOHN ELGIE.

Admitted July 1897, practised at West Hartlepool. Served as Capt., Royal Garrison Artillery.

VIVIAN ARTHUR ALSAGER ELGOOD.

Articled to C. A. Elgood, 218 Strand, W.C. Mobilised Aug. 1914, as Private, Inns of Court O.T.C. Gazetted 2nd Lieut. 19th Batt. London Regt. Oct. 3, 1914, promoted Lieut. May 1915, Capt. Aug. 1918. Awarded the M.C. Served in France June to Nov. 1916, Salonica Dec. 1916 to June 1917, E.E.F. June 1917 to Sept. 1918. Wounded Dec. 8, 1917.

EDWARD GRANVILLE ELIOT.

Admitted Feb. 1904. Member of Kennedy, Ponsonby, Ryde & Co., of 45 Russell Square, W.C. Joined Oct. 1914, as Chief Petty Officer, Royal Naval Volunteer Reserve, transferred to Army. Commissioned as Capt. Royal Garrison Artillery March 1915, appointed Staff Lieut. Heavy Artillery Oct. 1918. Served in France.

ERNEST ELLEN.

Admitted Dec. 1904, practising at 44 Chancery Lane, W.C. Joined Sept. 11, 1916, as Sapper, Royal Engineers. Served in France.

GILBERT STRANGE ELLIOT.

Admitted April 1894. Formerly member of Robinson, May & Elliot, of 22 Charterhouse Square, E.C. Served as Private, 19th (Service) Batt. Royal Fusiliers.

CHARLES ALBERT ELLIOTT.

Articled to Edward Bramley, of Sheffield. Joined Aug. 1914, as Private, Hon. Artillery Company. Gazetted 2nd Lieut. West Yorkshire Regt. Aug. 1914, promoted Lieut. March 1915. Served in Gallipoli. Wounded Aug. 9, 1915. Discharged July 1, 1916.

CLARENCE WILLIAM ELLIOTT.

Articled to E. W. Candler, of 8 Breams Buildings, E.C. Joined Dec. 18, 1916, as Private, Inns of Court O.T.C. Subsequently gazetted 2nd Lieut. 1st Batt. The Queen's Royal West Surrey Regt. Killed in action April 14, 1918.

HERBERT GEORGE UNDERWOOD ELLIOTT.

Admitted June 1880, practising at Newport, Shropshire. Served as Capt., 4th Batt. King's Shropshire Light Infantry and subsequently Royal Defence Corps.

KENNETH ELLIOTT.

Articled to Thomas Lumsden, of Gateshead. Served as 2nd Lieut., 4th Northumbrian Howitzer Brigade, Royal Field Artillery (T.).

ARTHUR THOMAS ELLIS.

Admitted Aug. 1904. Member of Swepstone, Stone, Barber & Ellis, of 9 St. Helen's Place, E.C. Served as Sergeant, 29th Batt. Middlesex Regt.

BERNARD HENRY ELLIS.

Admitted Feb. 1908. Member of Peters & Ellis, of 2A Guildhall Chambers, Basinghall Street, E.C. Mobilised Aug. 1914, as Chief Petty Officer, Royal Naval Volunteer Reserve, served with Royal Naval Division, Benbow Batt., at Antwerp. Mentioned in Dispatches. Awarded the D.C.M. Landed at Gallipoli May 1915 and remained there until the evacuation. Commissioned Temp. Sub-Lieut. Royal Naval Volunteer Reserve Oct. 1915, promoted Temp. Lieut. and Adjutant Nov. 1915, Temp. Lieut.-Commander Oct. 1916. Served at Stavros Feb. to April 1916, in France May 1916 to April 1918—with Anson Batt. June 1915 to April 1917 (4 months in command), Hood Batt. April 21 to April 30, 1917, and since April 1917 in command of Hawke Batt. Awarded the D.S.O. Died of wounds in France April 21, 1918.

CECIL MONTAGUE JACOMB ELLIS.

Articled to Montague Ellis, of 17 Albemarle Street, W. Joined Oct. 21, 1914, as 2nd Lieut., 5th Batt. Hampshire Regt., promoted Lieut. Dec. 1, 1915, A/Capt. June 1, 1917, seconded to Intelligence Corps Sept. to Dec. 1918. Once mentioned in Dispatches. Served in England Oct. to Dec. 1914, India—Secunderabad Jan. 1915 to March 1917, E.E.F.—Egypt and Palestine April 1917 to Nov. 1918, and Syria Dec. 1918 to March 1919.

CHARLES HAROLD ELLIS.

Admitted June 1908. Member of Ellis & Ellis, of Maidstone. Joined April 23, 1917, as Stoker II., Royal Navy, H.M.S. *Pembroke*. Appointed Paymaster Sub-Lieut. Royal Naval Volunteer Reserve, H.M.S. *Pactolus*, Sept. 1917. Served in Home waters.

EDWARD WHITE ELLIS.

Articled to F. B. Aglionby, of Portland House, Basinghall Street, E.C. Joined Sept. 1914, as Private, Public Schools Battalion, Royal Fusiliers. Gazetted Sub-Lieut. Royal Naval Division, Hawke Batt., April 1915, promoted Lieut. Dec. 1916. Served at the Dardanelles Aug. 1915 to May 1916, and in France May 1916 to Feb. 1917. Killed in action near Beaumont Hamel Feb. 3, 1917.

FREDERIC ROBBINS ELLIS.

Articled to J. V. Thomas, of Penzance, Cornwall. Mobilised Aug. 1914, as Lieut., 1/4 Batt. Duke of Cornwall's Light Infantry, attached 2nd Batt. Dorset Regt. May 1918, promoted Capt. June 1916. Served at Home till Oct. 1914, India till May 1915, Mesopotamia till April 1916, and with British Military Mission to East Russia at Vladivostok July to Dec. 1919. Taken prisoner on fall of Kut-el-Amara April 29, 1916, remained prisoner till Aug. 1918 when effected escape.

GEORGE JEWEL LISTER ELLIS.

Admitted March 1885. Member of Dangerfield & Blythe, 26 Craven Street, W.C. Recommissioned in Army May 15, 1915, as Capt. R.O., transferred Ministry of National Service Feb. to Nov. 1918.

HENRY CARTHEW ELLIS.

Articled to Arthur Ellis, of Burslem. Joined Inns of Court O.T.C. in Oct. 1914. Gazetted 2nd Lieut. Cheshire Regt., promoted Capt. Indian Army. Served in Gallipoli, Mesopotamia, Palestine, and Afghanistan.

HENRY LEE ELLIS.

Articled to J. R. B. Gregory, of 1 Bedford Row, W.C. Joined Sept. 8, 1914, Inns of Court O.T.C. Gazetted 2nd Lieut. Notts and Derby Regt. (Sherwood Foresters) Dec. 18, 1914, promoted Lieut. July 1917. Served in France Aug. and Sept. 1915, and Dec. 1915 to April 1918. Wounded Sept. 30, 1915.

PHILIP FREDERICK ELLIS.

Admitted Sept. 1907. Managing Clerk with Arthur Ellis, of Burslem. Joined Sept. 1914, as Capt., 5th Batt. North Staffordshire Regt. Served at Home only as Adjutant and Second in Command of a Batt. Discharged on account of ill-health.

WILLIAM TWIGGE ELLIS.

Admitted Oct. 1889, practising at Llanwrst. Served as Lieut., 5th Batt. Royal Welch Fusiliers.

GERALD ROCHFORT ELLIS-DANVERS.

Admitted Dec 1914. Member of Ellis & Ellis, of 10 Little College Street, Westminster, S.W. Joined Nov. 1916, as Private, Inns of Court O.T.C. Gazetted 2nd Lieut. The Queen's Royal West Surrey Labour March 1917, 2nd Lieut. 94th Labour Coy. July 1917, Capt. and Adjutant 18th Labour Group March 1918. Served at Home and in France.

ALBAN CEDRIC ELLISON.

Admitted Jan. 1913. Member of Ellison & Fyffe, of Sheffield. Served as Chief Petty Officer, H.M. Navy.

BEDE DALTON ELLISON.

Articled to T. W. Ellison, of Glossop, Derbyshire. Joined Feb. 29, 1916, as Private, 3rd Batt. South Lancashire Regt., promoted Corporal (acting) July 1916, reverted to Private on proceeding overseas to 9th Batt., attached to Royal Army Ordnance Corps April 1919, promoted Corporal Oct. 1919, Served at Home Feb. to Aug. 1916 and March to Sept. 1918, Salonica Aug. 1916 to March 1918, France Sept. 1918 to Dec. 1919.

SIDNEY FREDERICK ELLISON.

Admitted Jan. 1901. Member of Ellison & Co., of Cambridge. Served as Lieut., Royal Army Service Corps.

STANLEY JOHN ELLISON.

Articled to John Ellison, of Birmingham. Joined Oct. 1915, as 2nd Lieut., 5th Batt. South Staffordshire Regt. (T.). Served in France. Reported missing, afterwards presumed killed, at Gommecourt July 1, 1916.

THOMAS FREDERICK ELLISON.

Admitted Jan. 1912. Member of Watkins, Pulleyn & Ellison, of 6 South Square, Gray's Inn, W.C. Joined Sept. 29, 1914, as Private, Inns of Court O.T.C. Gazetted 2nd Lieut. Royal Garrison Artillery (T.) Nov. 4, 1914, promoted Lieut. June 1916, A/Capt. Aug. 1917. Once mentioned in Dispatches. Served at Home and France.

WILLIAM RONALD ELLISON.

Articled to J. W. Alsop, of Liverpool. Served as 2nd Lieut., Royal Field Artillery. Died of wounds June 20, 1915.

WILLIAM ELMHIRST.

Articled to C. E. Elmhirst, of York. Joined Oct. 1914, as 2nd Lieut., 9th Batt. East Yorkshire Regt., promoted Lieut., then Capt., transferred to 8th Batt. Oct. 1916. Served at Home and in France. Killed in action at Serres Nov. 13, 1916.

FREDERICK LESLIE ELSWORTH.

Articled to Frederick Lindsay, of Liverpool. Joined Nov. 4, 1914, as Rifleman, 2/6 Batt. King's Liverpool Regt., transferred to 2/5 Batt. Gloucestershire Regt. as Corporal Feb. 1916. Granted commission as 2nd Lieut. 18th (City) Batt. King's Liverpool Regt. May 30, 1917., attached to 8th (Irish) Batt. June 1918, promoted to Lieut. Nov. 1918. Once mentioned in Dispatches. Served in England 2 years, France 2 years 3 months. Wounded Aug. 18, 1916.

CHARLES ADRIAN ASHFORD ELTON.

Admitted Nov. 1904, practising at Birmingham. Joined Aug. 9, 1914, as Private, 1/6 Batt. Royal Warwickshire Regt. Gazetted 2nd Lieut. in same Regt. Sept. 1915, Lieut. March 1916, Capt. Nov. 1916, Major and D.A.D.R.T. Feb. 1918. Twice mentioned in Dispatches. Awarded the D.S.O. Served in France.

CLAUDE SIMEON ELWELL.

Admitted Nov. 1902. Member of Fox, Whittuck, Pitt & Elwell, of Bath. Joined Aug. 1916, as Lieut., Territorial Force Reserve General List, promoted Capt. Sept. 1917. Served at Home.

WALTER DOUGLAS ELWIN.

Admitted Oct. 1913. Of Dover. Joined Sept. 18, 1914, as 2nd Lieut., Royal Engineers, promoted Capt. March 1915. Served at Home.

THOMAS WILLIAM EMERSON.

Admitted Oct. 1906, practising at Plymouth. Joined Jan. 9, 1917, as Lieut., Territorial Force Reserve. Awarded M.B.E. (Military Division). Served at Home (War Office and Ministry of National Service).

HUBERT JOSEPH EMERY.

Admitted April 1907, practising at Stratton-on-the-Fosse, near Bath. Joined May 1916, as Private, Royal Army Ordnance Corps, promoted Lance-Corporal Nov. 1916, transferred to 3rd East Lancashire Regt. July 1917. Commissioned in Royal Army Ordnance Dept. Aug. 1917. Served at Home May 1916 to June 1918, and in France and Belgium June 1918 to April 1919.

JAMES EMERY.

Admitted Feb. 1883. Member of Emery & Emery, of Ramsgate and Broadstairs. Served as Capt., No. 5 Coy. (Supernumerary) 4th Batt. East Kent Regt. (The Buffs), later as Capt. 108th Coy. Royal Defence Corps. At Home Oct. 1914 till Jan. 1917.

THOMAS SMYTHE EMERY.

Admitted Jan. 1911. Member of Emery & Emery, of Ramsgate and Broadstairs. Joined July 1914, as Lieut., Home Counties Division Staff (Signal Corps), Lieut. Royal Engineers, 84th Brigade Staff, Ypres, Jan. 1915, Capt. 1915, Major 1916, Major 2nd in Command 7th Batt. Middlesex Regt. autumn 1916, Temp. Command early 1917, transferred 76th Punjabis Aug. 1917, Indian Native Army Staff 1918 and 1919. Awarded the M.C. Served at Home 1914, Belgium, Flanders 1915, Home 1915, France 1916 to 1917, South Africa 1917, N.W. Frontier 1917, Punjab 1918 to 1919, Afghanistan and Waziristan 1919. Wounded seriously Ypres May 1915.

EDWIN EMLEY.

Admitted April 1892. Member of Fred & Edwin Emley, of Newcastle-on-Tyne. Joined April 2, 1916, as Lieut., Territorial Force Reserve (Observer Corps), transferred to Royal Flying Corps as Lieut. Oct. 6, 1917, promoted A/Capt. Sept. 1918. Once mentioned in Dispatches. Served at Home from Oct. 1917 under London Aerial District Area.

MAURICE WOODMAN EMLEY.

Admitted Nov. 1908. Member of E. F. & H. Landon, of 53 New Broad Street, E.C. Mobilised Aug. 1914, as Capt., Royal Engineers (T.F.), promoted Major Oct. 1918. Twice mentioned in Dispatches. Awarded the O.B.E. Served in France and at Home. Wounded Ypres April 20, 1915.

ERNEST ARNOLD EMMET.

Admitted Nov. 1901. Member of Emmet & Co., of 14 Bloomsbury Square, W.C. Enlisted Sept. 1914, as Private, Hon. Artillery Company. Gazetted Capt. Gloucestershire Regt. Dec. 1914, Adjutant 11th Batt. April 1915, General List (Staff Capt. War Office) Sept. 1918, promoted Major Nov. 1918. Awarded O.B.E. (Military Division). Served at Home and in France. Wounded at Ypres Sept. 1917, and on Cambrai Front Jan. 1918.

HERBERT WILLIAM THACKRAY EMPSON.

Admitted May 1918, practising at North Walsham. Served as Capt., Royal Defence Corps.

CECIL HOWARD EMSLEY.

Articled to R. G. Emsley, of Leeds. Mobilised Aug. 1914, as Lieut., 1st West Riding Brigade Royal Field Artillery, promoted Capt. June 1916, Major

July 1917. Once mentioned in Dispatches. Served in Belgium and France April 1915 to Feb. 1919. Wounded Oct. 1917.

ERNEST ARTHUR ENFIELD.
Admitted Oct. 1906, practising at 10 Billiter Square, E.C. Served as 2nd Lieut., Royal Army Service Corps.

FRANK ENGLAND.
Admitted June 1909. Member of Broadley, England & Co., of 265 Strand, W.C. Joined Oct. 5, 1914, as Lieut., 10th (Service) Batt. King's Royal Rifle Corps., promoted Capt. April 1915, subsequently appointed A.P.M. rank of Staff Capt. Once mentioned in Dispatches. Served in France July 1915 to April 1916, Home April 1916 to Nov. 1917, Italy Nov. 1917 to March 1919. Wounded March 20, 1916.

RICHARD CORNFORTH ENGLISH.
Admitted Nov. 1909. Member of English & Son, of Stamford. Joined at commencement of War, as Private, Royal Army Service Corps. Subsequently gazetted 2nd Lieut. in same Regt. and afterwards promoted Lieut. Served in Flanders. Died on Service July 25, 1916.

SIDNEY JOHN ENNION.
Admitted May 1895, practising at Newmarket, Suffolk. Mobilised Aug. 1914, as Capt., 5th Batt. Suffolk Regt. (T.F.), Major (Temp.) Dec. 1914 to June 1916, retiring as Major. Served at Home Aug. 1914 to June 1916.

HENRY AINSLEY ENOCH.
Admitted April 1915, practising at Swansea. Served as Lieut., Tank Corps.

CYRIL FULLAND ENTWISTLE.
Admitted Feb. 1910, practising at Manchester, and Bolton, Lancs. Joined April 22, 1915, as 2nd Lieut., Essex and Suffolk Royal Garrison Artillery (T.), promoted Lieut. Nov. 1915, A/Capt. Dec. 1916, A/Major April 1917. Once mentioned in Dispatches. Awarded the M.C. Served on Coast Defence and Anti-Aircraft, Harwich Defences, and in France Dec. 1916 to Armistice.

FREDERICK ENTWISTLE.
Admitted Oct. 1911, practising at Middleton. Joined April 2, 1917, 15th Batt. County of London Regt. (Civil Service Rifles). Served in France. Wounded Aug. 8, 1918—left arm amputated.

JOHN PERRIN ERRINGTON.
Admitted Feb. 1905. Member of J. Errington & Son, of Carlisle. Mobilised Aug. 1914, as 2nd Lieut., 1/4 Batt. Border Regt., promoted Capt. Oct. 1914, went with Regt. to Burma, on Staff, Indian Army, as Temp. Major, Capt. Commandant of English Cadets at Subáthu Training College June 1917, with Indian Army Colonel established large training school at Násik, near Bombay, and appointed Assistant Commandant March 1918, Deputy Assistant Adjutant General at Central Headquarters, Lahore, June 1919. Awarded O.B.E. and T.D. Served in Burma and India.

BERNARD EVANS.

Admitted Oct. 1912, practised at 235 Westminster Bridge Road, S.E. Enlisted soon after the outbreak of War, and later became a Lieut. in the Middlesex Regt., subsequently transferred to the Royal Flying Corps. Reported missing on April 8, 1917, subsequently officially reported killed in aerial combat on that day.

CORRIS WILLIAM EVANS.

Admitted June 1912, practised at 1 Lloyds Avenue, E.C. Served as Private, Public Schools Batt. Middlesex Regt.

CYRIL HENRY SHENTON EVANS.

Admitted Oct. 1908, practising at Chard, Somerset. Joined Nov. 1916 Royal Naval Air Service (Motor Boat Section) A.C. Discharged Feb. 1918, and joined 14th Batt. County of London Regt. (London Scottish) as Private July 1918. Served at Home.

DANIEL DOUGLAS POLE EVANS.

Articled to George David, of Cardiff. Joined Nov. 30, 1914, as Temp. 2nd Lieut., Royal Field Artillery, promoted Temp. Lieut. March 1916, A/Capt. April to June 1917, Temp. Capt. Aug. 1917, A/Major Aug. 1918 to Sept. 1919, reverted to Temp. Capt. Sept. 1919. Awarded the M.C. and two Bars. Served at Home Nov. 1914 to Sept. 1915 and June to Sept. 1919, France Sept. 1915 to June 1919, and in South Russia from Sept. 1919.

DAVID CAROLAN EVANS.

Articled to H. R. W. Woods, of 54 Chancery Lane, W.C. Served as Sub-Lieut., Royal Naval Volunteer Reserve.

DUDLEY EVANS.

Admitted March 1911. Member of Boyce & Evans, of 14 Stratford Place, W. Joined April 3, 1917, as Private, Inns of Court O.T.C. Gazetted 2nd Lieut. 9th Batt. King's Own Yorkshire Light Infantry Dec. 18, 1917. Served in France. Wounded and taken prisoner at Kemmel Hill April 26, 1918.

EDMUND RHYDDERCH EVANS.

Admitted June 1910, practising at Aberdare. Served as Private, Royal Air Force.

EDWARD BROCKLEBANK EVANS.

Admitted Oct. 1910. Member of George, Davies & Evans, of Cardigan. Joined May 15, 1916, as Driver, Royal Field Artillery, promoted Bombadier June 1918, Corporal Oct. 1918. Served in France 1916 to 1918.

EMRYS HUNTER EVANS.

Admitted Nov. 1909. Member of Arthen, Owen & Evans, of Pwllheli. Mobilised Aug. 1914, as Lieut., 6th Batt. Royal Welch Fusiliers, promoted A/Capt. Nov. 1914, Capt. Aug. 1915, A/Major Dec. 1915 to Jan. 1916, and Sept. to Dec. 1917, A/Lieut.-Col. Dec. 1917 to Jan. 1918, A/Major Jan. to March 1918, A/Lieut.-Col. April to Aug. 1918, Temp. Lieut.-Col. 1st Batt. Herefordshire Regt. Nov. 1918 to June 1919. Once mentioned in Dispatches. Awarded the

M.C. and Bar. Served at Home Aug. 1914 to July 1915, Suvla Bay July to Dec. 1915, Egypt Dec. 1915 to March 1916, Palestine March 1916 to Aug. 1918, and in France and Belgium Sept. 1918 to Jan. 1919, Army of Occupation (Germany) Jan. to March 1919, Belgium March to May 1919. Wounded at Gaza March 26, 1915.

ERNEST ROBERT EVANS.

Admitted June 1899. Member of Evans & Son, of Ely, Cambs. Mobilised Aug. 1914, as Trooper, King's Own Royal Regt. (1/1 Norfolk Yeomanry), promoted to Troop Sergeant and Musketry Instructor Oct. 1914. Served at Home. Discharged Nov. 19, 1915.

FRANCIS ALFRED EVANS.

Articled to Dixon & Mason, of Pewsey, Wilts. Joined April 3, 1918, as Private, Inns of Court O.T.C., transferred to No. 8 Officers Cadet Batt. as an Officer-Cadet Oct. 1918. Served at Home.

FRANCIS VAUGHAN EVANS.

Admitted March 1915, practised as J. Tickle & Co., at 63 Cheapside, E.C. Served as a Private in Royal West Kent Regt. Killed in action Oct. 24, 1917.

FRANK TAYNTON EVANS.

Admitted Nov. 1902, practising at Newport, Mon. Served as Capt., 1st (Reserve) Batt. Monmouthshire Regt. (T.).

GUY EDWARD EVANS.

Admitted April 1911, practising at Highgate, N. Joined 1916, as Private, 14th Batt. County of London Regt. (London Scottish). Served in France. Wounded at Arras May 1917. Discharged Jan. 9, 1918.

HOWELL ARNOLD EVANS.

Articled to William Thomas, of Aberdare. Joined Nov. 24, 1914, as 2nd Lieut., 5th Batt. The Welch Regt., promoted Lieut. Jan. 1917, Capt. Feb. 1918. Once mentioned in Dispatches. Awarded the M.C. Served at Home Nov. 1914 to Aug. 1915, Suvla, Egypt, and Palestine Aug. 1915 to Aug. 1919.

HUGH JOHN HOWELL EVANS.

Admitted April 1896. Member of Gold, Edwards & Co., of Denbigh. Served as Major, Denbighshire Hussars.

ILLTYD MOY EVANS.

Articled to J. M. Evans, of Swansea. Joined Aug. 4, 1914, as Private, 7th Batt. The Welch Regt., transferred to 13th Batt. and promoted Corporal. Gazetted 2nd Lieut. in same Batt. and subsequently promoted Lieut. Served at Home and in France.

IVAN AMPHLETT EDWARDES EVANS.

Articled to Porter, Amphlett & Co., of Colwyn Bay. Joined Sept. 3, 1914, as Private, 19th Batt. Royal Fusiliers. Commissioned 2nd Lieut. 17th Batt. The Welch Regt. June. 21, 1915, promoted Temp. Lieut. June 1915, Temp. Capt. April 1916, transferred General List New Armies April 1917, promoted Temp. Major Jan. 1919. Awarded the M.C. Served in France June 1916 to March 1919.

IVOR EVANS.

Admitted Jan. 1908. Member of Roberts & Evans, of Aberystwyth. Joined Aug. 6, 1916, as 2nd Lieut., Royal Field Artillery, seconded to Royal Garrison Artillery, 288th Siege Battery, Nov. 1916, A/Capt. and Adjutant Siege Artillery, Reserve Brigade, June to Nov. 1917, Lieut. 3rd Siege Artillery Reserve Brigade Nov. 1917 to Jan. 1919. Served at Home.

JOHN DAWE EVANS.

Admitted Oct. 1913. Member of Enoch, Evans & Son, of Walsall. Joined Oct. 23, 1916, as Private, Royal Army Service Corps (M.T.). Served in France and Belgium Nov. 1916 to March 1919.

JOHN HUGHES EVANS.

Articled to C. A. Jones, of Carnarvon. Served as Lieut., 6th Batt. Royal Welch Fusiliers.

JOHN THOMAS EVANS.

Articled to E. W. Davies, of Carnarvon and London. Joined Sept. 9, 1914, as Trooper, Denbighshire Hussars Imperial Yeomanry, promoted Sergeant and transferred to Welsh Border Brigade Coy. Royal Army Service Corps March 1915. Gazetted 2nd Lieut. 6th Batt. Royal Welch Fusiliers Nov. 30, 1915, promoted Lieut. 4th Batt. Oct. 1917. Served in France. Gassed at Messines June 10, 1917. Wounded at Avelny Wood April 10, 1918.

LESLIE WYNN EVANS.

Articled to O. W. Owen, of Liverpool. Served as 2nd Lieut., 1/17th Batt. London Regt.

REES TUDOR EVANS.

Admitted March 1913. Of Merthyr Tydfil. Mobilised Aug. 1914 as Capt., 1/5 Batt. The Welch Regt. Served at Home and at Suvla Bay. Killed in action Aug. 10, 1915.

RICHARD WILLIAM PICTON EVANS.

Admitted Dec. 1898. Member of Jenkins & Evans, of Cardigan. Served as a Major, The Welch Regt. Died at Gaza, Syria, on Sept. 13, 1918.

ROBERT CHARLES EVANS.

Admitted June 1911. Member of W. R. Evans, Lloyd & Evans, of Wrexham. Joined Nov. 1914, as Private, 19th Batt. Royal Welch Fusiliers. Afterwards gazetted 2nd Lieut. 15th Batt. The Welch Regt. Served in France. Wounded in July 1917. Killed near Thiepval Aug. 24, 1918.

STUART EVANS.

Articled to Henry Dixon, of Bristol. Joined Nov. 16, 1914, as 2nd Lieut., 6th (Service) Batt. South Wales Borderers (Pioneers), promoted Lieut. Dec. 1916, Capt. May 1918, transferred to Indian Army Reserve of Officers Oct. 1917 and attached to 130th K.G.O. Baluchis. Once mentioned in Dispatches. Awarded the M.C. Served in France Sept. 1915 to May 1916, India Dec. 1917 to May 1918, Palestine June to Nov. 1918, Egypt Nov. 1918 to March 1919. Accidentally wounded in France Feb. 20, 1916. Wounded on Vimy Ridge May 16, 1916.

THOMAS EVANDER EVANS.

Admitted Dec. 1907, practising at Hoddesdon, Herts, and, 1 Gray's Inn Square, W.C. Joined Sept. 3, 1914, as Private, 28th Batt. County of London Regt. (Artists Rifles). Commissioned as 2nd Lieut. Royal Welch Fusiliers Jan. 28, 1915, promoted Temp. Lieut. Oct. 1916. Once mentioned in Dispatches. Awarded the M.C. and Bar. Went to France with 11th Batt. Royal Welch Fusiliers Sept. 1915, transferred to Balkans Nov. 1915, evacuated wounded to England Aug. 1917, Military Intelligence Directorate, War Office, Dec. 1917 to July 1918, Limerick Aug. to Sept. 1918, to France Sept. 16, 1918, wounded for third time and evacuated to England Oct. 8, 1918, Military Secretary's Department, War Office, Dec. 1918 to April 1919. Wounded near Smol, Macedonia, Oct. 1916; near Krastali, Serbia, May 1917; near Villers Bretoneux, Cambrai, Oct. 8, 1918.

THOMAS FORCER EVANS.

Admitted Jan. 1914, practising at Holyhead. Served as Lieut., 6th Batt. Royal Welch Fusiliers.

WALTER HENRY FREKE EVANS.

Articled to A. A. Bains, of Brighton. Served as 2nd Lieut., 1st Home Counties (Sussex) Brigade Royal Field Artillery (T.), promoted Lieut. June 1916.

WALTER VAUGHAN EVANS.

Admitted June 1914, practising at Fishguard. Joined Aug. 4, 1914, as Corporal, Pembroke Royal Garrison Artillery (T.F.), promoted Sergeant 1915. Gazetted 2nd Lieut. Pembroke Royal Garrison Artillery (T.F.) Aug. 6, 1916, with Hon. Rank of a Lieut. Served at Home. Had to relinquish commission on account of sickness contracted whilst serving June 1918.

WILLIAM DAVID RUSSELL EVANS.

Articled to T. A. Rees, of Merthyr Tydfil. Mobilised Aug. 1914, as 2nd Lieut., 5th Batt. The Welch Regt. (T.F.), promoted Lieut. Nov. 1914. Served at Home Aug. 1914 to June 1915, and at Gallipoli, Suvla Bay Landing, Aug. 8 and 9, 1915. Wounded and missing Aug. 10, 1915.

REGINALD WYNNE EVANS-VAUGHAN.

Articled to R. H. Gaby, of Hastings. Joined Sept. 9, 1914, as Private, 5th Batt. Royal Sussex Regt., transferred to 4th Batt. in 1916, and to 4th Batt. Norfolk Regt. Aug. 1918. Served in France Feb. 1915, Egypt Nov. 1916, and subsequently the whole of the Palestine Campaign. Wounded at "The Keep," la Boiselle, July 24, 1916.

JAMES EVERIDGE.

Admitted Aug. 1905. Member of Lonsdale & Everidge, of 1 Adam Street, Adelphi, W.C. Mobilised Aug. 1914, as Lieut., Surrey Yeomanry, promoted Capt. 1914, and subsequently Major Royal Air Force. Awarded the M.C. Served at Home, France, and Mesopotamia.

HAROLD EVES.

Admitted July 1908, practised at 12 Bouverie Street, E.C. Served as Sub-Lieut., Royal Naval Volunteer Reserve.

CHARLES ARIEL EVILL.

Admitted Feb. 1898. Member of Evans & Evill, of Chepstow. Mobilised Aug. 1914, as Capt., 1st Batt. Monmouthshire Regt. (T.F.), promoted Majo May 1915, Lieut.-Col. Aug. 1915, in command of 1st Batt. Aug. 1915 to May 1918. Once mentioned in Dispatches. Awarded the D.S.O. Served in France Feb. 1915 to May 1918. Wounded May 1915. Gassed Oct. 1915.

JOSEPH EWART.

Admitted Nov. 1901. Served as A/Sergeant, Aldershot Siege School, Royal Garrison Artillery.

HENRY GREY FABER.

Admitted Oct. 1911. Member of Faber, Fawcett & Faber, of Stockton-on-Tees. Mobilised Aug. 1914 as Capt., 5th Batt. Durham Light Infantry, promoted Major June 1916. Once mentioned in Dispatches. Served at Home and in Flanders and France. Wounded May 24, 1915.

GORDON LANCASTER MOUNTFORD FÂCHE.

Admitted Nov. 1912, practising at 13 John Street, Bedford Row, W.C. Joined Aug. 4, 1914, as Private, Inns of Court O.T.C. Gazetted 2nd Lieut. 8th Batt. The Suffolk Regt. Sept. 19, 1914, promoted Major Aug. 1917. Awarded M.C. and Bar. Served in France July 1915 to Jan. 1919. Wounded April 1916.

COLLINGWOOD CHRISTOPHER FAILES.

Articled to J. A. Parsons, of King's Lynn. Joined Nov. 4, 1915, as Trooper, Inns of Court O.T.C. Gazetted 2nd Lieut. Royal Field Artillery (S.R.) Nov. 11, 1916, promoted Lieut. May 1918. Once mentioned in Dispatches. Served at Home and in France.

ERNEST HULFORD FAIRBAIRN.

Articled to M. T. Fairbairn, of 18 Finsbury Square, E.C. Joined Aug. 31, 1915, as Air-Mechanic, Royal Naval Air Service, Petty Officer April 1917, Sergeant Royal Air Force April 1918, Flight Sergeant July 1918. Served at Home Aug. 1915 to Nov. 1916, and in France Nov. 1916 to Aug. 1918.

GORDON GRANGE FAIRBAIRN.

Articled to Alfred Ellis, of 30 John Street, Bedford Row, W.C. Joined Nov. 12, 1914, as Private, 14th Batt. County of London Regt. (London Scottish). Gazetted 2nd Lieut. 2/1 Royal Gloucestershire Hussars Jan. 28, 1916, transferred to Royal Flying Corps Oct. 1916, promoted A/Capt. April 1918, A/Major Nov. 1918. Served at Home and in France. Wounded at Loos Oct. 13, 1915, and while flying at Arras April 22, 1917.

HENRY FREDERIC NOEL FALKNER.

Admitted Nov. 1906. Member of Falkner, Son & Roberts, of Louth, Lincolnshire. Mobilised Aug. 1914, as Capt., 5th Batt. Lincolnshire Regt. Served through the Dublin rebellion in April and May 1916, and in France from Aug. 1916. Killed in action Oct. 11, 1916, and buried in Vermelles British Cemetery, France.

ROY FARADAY.

Articled to C. R. Callard, of 3 St. James's Street, S.W. Joined Sept. 5, 1914, as Private, 28th Batt. County of London Regt. (Artists Rifles). Gazetted 2nd Lieut. 2/6 Batt. City of London R gt. Feb. 26, 1915, promoted Temp. Lieut. Oct. 1915, and confirmed in rank June 1916. Served at Home and in France. Killed in action on the Messines Ridge June 7, 1917.

JOHN GERALD FARDELL.

Articled to John Fardell, of Ryde, I. of W. Mobilised Aug. 4, 1914, as Lieut., 8th (Princess Beatrice's Isle of Wight Rifles) Batt. The Hampshire Regt., promoted to Capt. Once mentioned in Dispatches. Served in Gallipoli 1915, Mesopotamia, Persia, Transcaspia, and Russian Turkestan 1916 to 1919.

FREDERICK BRIAN ARTHUR FARGUS.

Admitted Feb. 1911. Member of Clayton, Sons & Fargus, of 10 Lancaster Place, Strand, W.C. Mobilised Aug. 1914 as Lieut. in command of Machine Gun Secton, 9th City of London Batt. London Regt. (Queen Victoria's Rifles). Served in Flanders. Killed in action near Wulverghem, Flanders, Jan. 1, 1915.

FRANK MORLEY FARMER.

Admitted Dec. 1900. Assistant Solicitor, West Riding County Council. Joined June 20, 1916, as Private, Royal Army Service Corps (M.T.), promoted Lance-Corporal Nov. 1916, Corporal Dec. 1916. Commissioned in Royal Army Service Corps July 29, 1917, promoted Lieut. Jan. 1919. Awarded M.B.E. (Military Division). Served 6 months in War Office (Q.M.G. 3), and in France and Belgium Aug. 1917 to Feb. 1919.

JAMES CLEVELAND FARMER.

Articled to J. S. Farmer, of Stockton-on-Tees. Served as Bombardier, Somerset Royal Horse Artillery (T.).

SYDNEY MORLEY FARMER.

Admitted Jan. 1911. Member of R. J. Jones, Sephton, Rollo & Farmer, of Liverpool. Served as Private, Inns of Court O.T.C.

DUDLEY HERBERT FARNFIELD.

Admitted Oct. 1913. Member of J. A. & H. E. Farnfield, of 90 Lower Thames Street, E.C. Joined May 24, 1916, as Sub-Lieut., Royal Naval Volunteer Reserve, promoted Lieut. May 1917. Served in Belgium, France, and English Channel and West Coast of England.

LESLIE FARNFIELD.

Admitted April 1908. Member of J. A. & H. E. Farnfield, of 90 Lower Thames Street, E.C. Commissioned as Sub-Lieut. Royal Naval Volunteer Reserve May 12, 1916, promoted Lieut. June 1917. Served with Auxiliary Patrol afloat and subsequently on Staff of Admiral Charles H. Dare, Milford Haven, for duty ashore.

JOHN PHILIP FARR.

Admitted April 1912. Managing Clerk with Harold Easton, of Leominster. Joined Oct. 1914, as Private, 23rd Batt. Royal Fusiliers (Sportsman's Batt.), promoted Lance-Corporal Signal Section March 1916. Served in France. Leg shattered with shrapnel Delville Wood July 27, 1916. Died after amputation Aug. 3, 1916, at Abbeville, buried in Cemetery at Abbeville, Aug. 4, 1916.

HUBERT LISTER FARRAR.

Admitted Nov. 1904. Member of Farrar & Co., of Manchester. Joined March 16, 1915, as 2nd Lieut., Royal Field Artillery, promoted Lieut. Aug. 1915, appointed Adjutant of 30th Divisional Ammunition Column same date, appointed A.D.C. to C.R.A. 30th Division May 1916, Reconnaissance Officer to C.R.A. 30th Division Jan. 1917 Staff Capt. R.A., 11th Division, July 1917, Temp. Capt. July 1917, Staff Capt. R.A., VII Corps, March 1918. Twice mentioned in Dispatches. Served at Home March to Nov. 1915, France Nov. 1915 to Feb. 1919.

BEDE FARRELL.

Admitted Jan. 1905, practised at Hull. Mobilised Aug. 1914 as Capt., 4th Batt. East Yorkshire Regt. Served in France. Killed in action near Ypres April 24, 1915.

HAROLD MARSON FARRER.

Admitted Feb. 1914. Member of Farrer & Co., of 66 Lincoln's Inn Fields, W.C. Joined Oct. 1, 1914, as Temp. Sub-Lieut., Royal Naval Division, promoted Temp. Lieut. July 1915, Temp. Capt. General List (Army) April 1917, Temp. Major March 1918. Once mentioned in Dispatches. Served in Gallipoli March to Aug. 1915, France April 1917 to Jan. 1919.

SIDNEY VANNER FARRINGTON.

Admitted Nov. 1911. Member of Farrington & Winterton, of Brighton. Gazetted 2nd Lieut. Sussex Royal Garrison Artillery (T.) Oct. 18, 1915, promoted Lieut. June 1916, A/Capt. Jan. 1918. Served at Home and France. Wounded near Messines May 26, 1917.

WILLIAM BOWKER FARRINGTON.

Admitted Feb. 1902, practised at Manchester. Joined Feb. 1916, as Private, Inns of Court O.T.C. Gazetted 2nd Lieut. 1/6 Batt. Manchester Regt. Feb. 1917. Killed in France March 25, 1918.

CYRIL FAWCETT.

Articled to the late Wm. Fawcett, of Leeds. Joined Oct. 1914, as 2nd Lieut., Royal Army Service Corps (T.F.), promoted Lieut. June 1915, transferred to Gloucestershire Regt. 1917. Served in France 1916 to 1918.

GEOFFREY FAWCETT.

Articled to the late Wm. Fawcett, of Leeds. Joined Sept. 1914, as 2nd Lieut., Royal Army Service Corps (T.F.), promoted Lieut. Feb. 1915, transferred to London Regt. 1917. Served in France 1915 to 1918. Killed June 14, 1918.

HERBERT WILKINSON FAWCETT.

Admitted Dec. 1904. Member of Richardson, Son & Fawcett, of Bridlington. Served as Corporal, Royal Army Service Corps (M.T.).

WILLIAM GEORGE STEWART FAWKES.

Admitted Oct. 1910. Member of Scriven, Terry & Fawkes, of Northampton. Served as Lieut., 5th Batt. Norfolk Regt. Wounded at Gallipoli Aug. 1915 and taken prisoner by the Turks.

GEORGE OSWALD FEA.

Admitted Dec. 1901, practised at Hull and Bridlington. Joined Oct. 10, 1914, as Trooper, Queen's Own Yorkshire Dragoons (Yeomanry), transferred as Private to 13th Batt. Yorkshire Regt. Sept. 1917. Served in Flanders and France July 15, 1915, to Nov. 1917. Wounded in action Nov. 23, 1917, and afterwards killed on the same date at Bourlon, France.

GEORGE ALAN FEARNSIDE.

Admitted Oct. 1909, practising at Leeds. Joined Nov. 1915, as Private, Inns of Court O.T.C. Commissioned in Royal Field Artillery Dec. 4, 1916, promoted Lieut. June 1918. Served in France. Wounded April 23, 1917.

WILLIAM DAVIES FEATHERSTONE.

Articled to H. J. Goodwin, of Birmingham. Joined Dec. 1915, as 2nd Lieut., 3rd South Midland Battery, Royal Field Artillery, promoted Lieut. June 1917. Awarded the M.C. Served in France. Wounded July 25, 1917. Killed at Villers au Flos, near Bapaume, March 23, 1918.

LEO BURTON FEENY.

Admitted Nov. 1901. Of Boston, Massachusetts, U.S.A. Served with the McGill University Overseas Corps and 38th Batt. Infantry Canadian Expeditionary Force.

CHARLES ARTHUR FELL.

Articled to E. P. Williams, of 79 Lombard Street, E.C. Joined July 15, 1915, as Private, Inns of Court O.T.C. Gazetted 2nd Lieut. Royal Field Artillery July 14, 1916, promoted A/Lieut. July 1917, Lieut. Jan. 1918. Served in Ireland July 1916 to Jan. 1917, France March 1917 to March 1918. Taken prisoner March 21, 1918, repatriated Dec. 2, 1918.

THOMAS BRUCE FELTHAM.

Articled to H. S. K. Feltham, of Crewe. Enlisted Sept. 5, 1914, as Private, 20th (Public Schools) Batt. Royal Fusiliers, subsequently promoted to Lance-Corporal. Served in France 1915 to 1916. Wounded June 1916. Discharged owing to wounds in 1917.

JOHN HERBERT FELTON.

Articled to R. E. Steel, of Cheltenham. Joined Sept. 11, 1914, as Private, 2/5 Batt. Gloucestershire Regt., transferred as Sapper Royal Engineers Signal Service (Motor Cyclist) Dec. 1915, and later Dispatch Rider Corporal. Served at Home 1914 to 1916, France 1916 to end of 1917, and in Italy May 1918 to Armistice.

DOUGLAS WILLIAM FENTON FENTON-JONES.
Admitted March 1912. Member of Bishop & Fenton-Jones, of 76 Kingsland High Street, E. Served as Capt., Royal Army Ordnance Corps.

MELVILL COLLINGWOOD FENWICK.
Articled to T. C. Fenwick, of 16 Berners Street, W. Joined Sept. 1914 as 2nd Lieut., 6th Batt. Suffolk Regt., subsequently promoted Lieut. and Capt. Served at Home and in France.

JOHN JOHNSON TILL FERENS.
Admitted June 1898. Member of Ferens & Sanderson, of Hull. Joined June 1915 as 2nd Lieut., 2/4 Batt. East Yorkshire Regt., promoted Lieut. June 1916, A/Capt. Sept. 1918, attached to 10th Batt. Served at Home, Bermuda, and France.

JOHN EDWARD FEW.
Admitted Nov. 1902, practising at Cambridge. Temporarily employed as Company Commander in 11th (Cambs.) Batt. Suffolk Regt. Sept. 1914. Commissioned Capt. in 2/1 Batt. Cambs. Regt. (T.F.) Nov. 3, 1914. Posted to 62nd Prov. Batt. as Capt. June 1915, transferred to 13th (Cambs. Reserve) Batt. Suffolk Regt. May 1916, attached Aldershot Command Anti-Gas School Oct. 1917. British Military Mission to U.S.A., Assistant Instructor Nov. 1917, posted to 3rd Batt. Suffolk Regt. Aug. 1918. Served at Home, and at Camp Funston, Kansas, U.S.A., Nov. 1917 to Aug. 1918.

WILLIAM ARCHDALL FFOOKS.
Articled to E. A. Ffooks, of Dorchester. Served as 2nd Lieut., 8th Batt. Duke of Cornwall's Light Infantry.

ARTHUR DILLWYN FFOULKES-JONES.
Articled to E. Ffoulkes-Jones, of Llangollen, N. Wales. Joined Sept. 30, 1915, as 2nd Lieut., 4th Batt. Royal Welch Fusiliers, promoted Lieut. June 1916, A/A.D.C. to G.O.C. 47th Div. during Aug. and Sept. 1917, Temp. A.D.C. to G.O.C. 41st Div. Oct. 1918, transferred to the Camouflage Park Royal Engineers until April 1919. Served in France and Belgium. Wounded at Battle of Cambrai, at Boulon Wood, Nov. 2, 1917.

EDMUND VENTRIS FIELD.
Articled to Cecil Brodrick, of Ormond House, 63 Queen Victoria Street, E.C. Mobilised Aug. 4, 1914, as 2nd Lieut., 13th (Princess Louise's Kensington) Batt. The London Regt., promoted Lieut. Aug. 1914, Capt. Jan. 1916. Served at Home and in France. Wounded Dec. 7, 1914, and Sept. 25, 1916.

HERRICK REVELEY FIELD.
Articled to John Field, of Manchester. Joined Nov. 1915, as Private, Manchester Regt. Gazetted 2nd Lieut. Tank Corps Feb. 28, 1919. Served in France. Invalided Home Dec. 2, 1916.

MARK GWENDWR FIELD.
Admitted Jan. 1910. Member of Field & Sons, of Leamington. Mobilised Aug. 1914, as Lieut., 4th South Midland Howitzer Brigade Royal Field Artillery

(T.F.), promoted Capt. June 1916. Served in Flanders and France, went to France March 1915. Invalided home sick Oct. 16, 1916. Severely wounded at Ypres Oct. 7, 1917.

SIDNEY FIELD.
Admitted Jan. 1900. Member of Field & Sons, of Liverpool. Served with the 6th Batt. King's Liverpool Regt. (T.).

SYDNEY RIACH FIELD.
Admitted Dec. 1908. Member of Field & Sons, of Leamington. Mobilised Aug. 1914, as Lieut., 4th South Midland (Howitzer) Brigade Royal Field Artillery (T.), promoted Capt. Aug. 1914, Major June 1915. Served at Home and in France. Wounded at Fauquiesart, France, July 18, 1916.

CARYL HILLYARD FIELD-FISHER.
Admitted Aug. 1909. Member of Carter & Fisher, of Torquay. Joined March 22, 1916, as Private, Hon. Artillery Company, subsequently promoted Corporal. Served as sniper in the 2nd Batt. at Ploegsteert in Belgium Oct. 1916, and subsequently on the Somme, at Beaumont Hamel, Nov. and Dec. 1916.

EDWIN EWART FIELDHOUSE.
Articled to J. W. Piercy, of Huddersfield. Joined Nov. 20, 1914, as A.B., Hawke Batt. Royal Naval Division, Third Writer R.N. July 1916 to Dec. 1917, Paymaster Sub-Lieut. Royal Naval Reserve Dec. 1917 to Aug. 1919, Secretary to British Naval Attaché, Embassy, Rome. Awarded Cavalier of the Order of the Crown of Italy. Served at Home, and at Gallipoli with Royal Naval Division May to Dec. 1915, at British Embassy, Rome, Feb. 1918 to Aug. 1919.

EDWARD FLEMING FIELDING.
Admitted Jan. 1905. Member of Fuller, Whittington & Fielding, of Bath. Joined Feb. 1915, as 2nd Lieut., 9th Batt. Somerset Light Infantry, and subsequently promoted Lieut. and attached to West African Regt. Served at Home and in the Cameroons, West Africa. Killed in Action Oct. 24, 1915.

HERBERT HILTON FIELDING.
Admitted Feb. 1913, practised at Manchester. Joined Feb. 15, 1916, as Private, 6th Batt. Manchester Regt., promoted Lance-Corporal April 1916. Gazetted 2nd Lieut. Manchester Regt. Nov. 28, 1916. Went to France Jan. 1917, attached to 22nd Batt. Killed in action at Croisilles March 28, 1917, and buried in the St. Leger British Cemetery.

ERNEST GERARD FINCH.
Admitted Nov. 1893, practising at Liverpool. Mobilised Aug. 1914, as Capt., 9th Batt. King's Liverpool Regt., promoted Major Feb. 1916. Served in Egypt 1914 to 1915, and at Home.

FRED JAMES FINCH.
Admitted April 1914, practising at Gravesend. Joined May 1917, as Private, Inns of Court O.T.C., and subsequently became Sergeant. Served at Home.

GEORGE FLADGATE FINCH.

Articled to C. S. Raymond-Barker, 9 New Square, W.C. Mobilised Aug. 1914, as Private, Inns of Court O.T.C. Gazetted 2nd Lieut. 12th Batt. The Rifle Brigade Sept. 22, 1914, promoted Lieut. Jan. 1915, Capt. Feb. 1915, appointed General Staff Officer (3rd Grade) 64th Division, Norwich, Dec. 1916, and to Headquarters, First Army, France, May 1918. Twice mentioned in Dispatches. Served at Home Aug. 1914, to July 1915 and Aug. 1916 to Sept. 1917, France July 1915 to Aug. 1916 and Sept. 1917 to Jan. 1919. Wounded Ypres Feb. 12, 1916.

HARRY FINCH.

Admitted Dec. 1907. Member of Courtenay, Croome & Finch, of 3 Lombard Court, Gracechurch Street, E.C. Joined Feb. 10, 1915, as Private, Royal Army Service Corps and immediately promoted Staff Sergeant. Gazetted 2nd Lieut. in same Regt. Dec. 1, 1917. Served in France practically whole time.

JAMES BASS FINCH.

Articled to J. H. Hutchings, of Teignmouth. Joined Nov. 20, 1915, as Private, Inns of Court O.T.C. Obtained commission in Royal Flying Corps Jan. 24, 1917, as Flying Officer, transferred to Royal Air Force and promoted Lieut. April 1918. Served in France. Wounded in aerial combat in France Aug. 26, 1917.

WILLIAM GERARD FINCH.

Admitted Feb. 1900. Member of Finch, Johnson & Co., of Preston. Served as Major, 9th Batt. King's Liverpool Regt. (T.F.R.).

DONALD GEORGE FINCHAM.

Articled to H. C. Wanklyn, of Colchester. Joined Nov. 27, 1916, as Private, Notts and Derby Regt. (Sherwood Foresters), appointed Lance-Corporal May 1918. Served at Home.

ALFRED GUSTAVE FINDEISEN.

Admitted Sept. 1899. Member of Dymond, Findeisen & Tosswill, of Torquay. Served as Lance-Corporal, 30th Batt. Middlesex Regt.

ALEXANDER WYNAND FINDLAY.

Admitted June 1902, practising at 142 Holborn Bars, E.C. Joined Nov. 13, 1914, as Private, 14th Batt. County of London Regt. (London Scottish). Served in France March 1915 to Nov. 1916. Invalided home with trench fever. Discharged April 29, 1918.

ANDREW FINDLAY

Articled to Sir W. W. Rutherford, M.P., of 48 Cannon Street, E.C. Joined April 23, 1917, as Gunner, Royal Garrison Artillery, promoted Corporal March 1918. Served at Home.

ROBERT LESLIE FINNIS.

Admitted Nov. 1901. Member of Finnis, Downey, Linnell & Chessher, of 5 Clifford Street, Bond Street, W. Served as 2nd Lieut., Royal Air Force.

DENIS GORDON FIRTH.

Articled to J. H. T. Wharton, of Southampton. Mobilised Aug. 1914, as Lieut., 1/5 Batt. Hampshire Regt., promoted Capt. June 1916. Served in India Nov. 1914 to Dec. 1915, Mesopotamia Dec. 1915 to April 1916, India April 1916 to March 1919. Wounded at Sunnaiyat, Mesopotamia, April 6, 1916.

HAROLD WHITELEY FIRTH.

Articled to Sir Robert Fox, of Leeds. Joined Jan. 15, 1916, as 2nd Lieut., Northumberland Fusiliers, promoted Lieut. July 1917, Capt. July 1918. Awarded the M.C. Served in France. Wounded April 9, 1917, and Aug. 17, 1918. Taken prisoner at Beaumont Hamel Aug. 17, 1918.

HENRY FIRTH.

Admitted Oct. 1911. Member of Wilson & Firth, of Ashton-under-Lyne. Joined Oct. 1, 1917, as Private, Army Pay Corps, promoted Corporal Oct. 1918. Served at Home.

WILLIAM HENRY FIRTH.

Admitted Feb. 1915. Member of Firth & Firth, of Bradford. Joined Dec. 20, 1916, as Sapper, Railway Operating Division, Royal Engineers, promoted Corporal Sept. 1918. Served in France and Belgium.

ARTHUR REGINALD COLBORNE FISHER.

Articled to R. H. Carpenter, of Bristol. Joined Oct. 28, 1914, as Trooper, North Somerset Yeomanry. Gazetted 2nd Lieut. Royal Garrison Artillery Nov. 12, 1914, promoted Lieut. July 1917. Served at Home, Jamaica, and France.

EDWARD LINDESAY FISHER.

Admitted Nov. 1902, practising at Huddersfield. Joined Sept. 1914, as 2nd Lieut., 2/5 Batt. Manchester Regt., promoted Temp. Lieut. Nov. 1914, Temp. Capt. Jan. 1915, Substantive Capt. June 1916, Temp. Major Oct. 1916, A/Major Aug. 1917. Once mentioned in Dispatches. Served in France. Wounded at Hervilly Wood March 22, 1918, and subsequently taken prisoner same day.

GEORGE WILLIAM FISHER.

Admitted Oct. 1913. Member of Morris & Bristow, of 41 Bedford Row, W.C. Served as 2nd Lieut., 1st County of London Brigade, Royal Field Artillery (T.), promoted Lieut. June 1916. Mentioned in Dispatches.

GERALD LEAROYD HAMMOND FISHER.

Articled to H. J. Sharman, of Liverpool. Joined Sept. 1914, as Private, 6th Batt. King's Liverpool Regt. Obtained commission about Feb. 1915 with 1/8 (Irish) Batt. King's Liverpool Regt. as 2nd Lieut., promoted Lieut. Oct. 1915, attached to 164th Machine Gun Company Feb. 1916. Served in France. Believed to have been killed on Aug. 8, 1916, by gas shell. War Office's Report, missing, believed killed.

HENRY JOHN FISHER.

Admitted Oct. 1905. Member of Deacon & Co., of 9 Great St. Helen's, E.C. Joined Oct. 1914, as Private, Inns of Court O.T.C. Commissioned

2nd Lieut. Inns of Court O.T.C. Oct. 1915, promoted Lieut., subsequently seconded for special service at Headquarters. Served at Home.

OAKDEN FISHER.

Admitted Nov. 1910, practising at Heathfield, Sussex. Mobilised Aug. 1914, as 2nd Lieut., Glamorganshire Yeomanry (T.F.), promoted Capt. July 1916, attached 24th Batt. (Pembroke and Glamorgan Yeomanry Batt.) The Welch Regt. Jan. 1917. Once mentioned in Dispatches. Awarded the Croix de Guerre. Served at Home 1914 to 1916, Egypt 1916 to Jan. 1917, Palestine 1917 to March 1918, France 1918 to 1919. Wounded Dec. 27, 1917.

STANLEY JOSEPH FISHER.

Articled to John Tyson, of Dalton-in-Furness. Joined June 26, 1916, as Pioneer, Special Brigade, Royal Engineers, promoted Lance-Corporal. Subsequently gazetted 2nd Lieut. Loyal North Lancashire Regt. Served 2 years in France.

EDWARD JOHN FITZGERALD.

Admitted July 1912, practising at Newcastle-on-Tyne. Served as Private, 1/7 Batt. Northumberland Fusiliers.

JOHN WILLIAM FITZHERBERT-BROCKHOLES.

Articled to F. J. Weld, of Liverpool. Mobilised Aug. 4, 1914, as Lieut., Duke of Lancaster's Own Yeomanry, promoted Capt. June 1916. Awarded the M.C. Served in France May 1915 to April 1919.

THOMAS FLAVELL.

Admitted Nov. 1905. Member of Preston, Son & Flavell, of Hinckley. Served as a Cadet, and gazetted 2nd Lieut. Royal Garrison Artillery April 3, 1919.

NEVILLE GEORGE FLAWN.

Admitted April 1906. Assistant Solicitor Great Central Railway Co., Marylebone Station, N.W. Joined May 1916, as Private, 28th Batt. County of London Regt. (Artists Rifles). Commissioned Nov. 1916 as 2nd Lieut. Royal Garrison Artillery, subsequently promoted Lieut. Served in France. Invalided home from France and discharged Feb. 1918.

ERNEST FLETCHER.

Admitted July 1894. Member of Watkins, Son & Fletcher, of Atherton. Served as Major, 5th Batt. Manchester Regt. (T.).

FRANK CASTLE FLETCHER.

Articled to N. D. Walker, of Newcastle-on-Tyne. Joined Aug. 12, 1914, as Lieut. and Quartermaster, Northumbrian Divisional Clearing Hospital, Royal Army Medical Corps (T.F.), promoted Capt. and Quartermaster Oct. 1917. Served at Home Aug. 1914 to Jan. 1917, and in France Jan. 1917 to Aug. 1919.

VICTOR ROBERT FLETCHER.

Admitted Oct. 1910. On staff of the Solicitor to the Board of Trade, Great George Street, S.W. Mobilised Aug. 1914, as Private, Inns of Court O.T.C., promoted Lance-Corporal Aug. 1914. Gazetted 2nd Lieut. 21st

Batt. The London Regt. (First Surrey Rifles) Sept. 23, 1914, promoted Lieut. June 1916, Capt. May 1917. Served in France Dec. 1917 to June 1918. Remainder of time at Home.

FRANK STUART FLEURET.

Admitted Feb. 1912. Member of Coldham, Birkett & Fleuret, of 27 Chancery Lane, W.C. Served as 2nd Lieut., 5th Batt. East Kent Regt. (The Buffs), promoted Lieut. June 1916.

HERBERT FLOWERS.

Admitted March 1908. Member of G. A. Flowers & Son, of Steyning, Sussex. Joined Sept. 1914, as Private, Public School Corps. Gazetted 2nd Lieut. 5th Batt. Royal West Kent Regt. June 30, 1915. Served in France. Killed at Battle of Delville Wood Aug. 31, 1916.

ALFRED EDWARD FLOYD.

Admitted Aug. 1901, practising at Dunmow, Essex. Served as Capt., 7th (Vol.) Batt. Essex Regt.

ERIC GASKELL FLOYD.

Admitted April 1910, practising at 76–78 Swinton Street, Gray's Inn Road, W.C. Served as Lieut. and Quartermaster, 3rd Welsh Field Ambulance, Royal Army Medical Corps (T.), promoted Capt. Nov. 1917. Mentioned in Dispatches.

REGINALD LAKE FLUX.

Admitted July 1912, practising at Ryde. Mobilised Aug. 1914, as 2nd Lieut., 1/5 Hants. Battery Royal Field Artillery (T.F.), and subsequently promoted Capt. Awarded the M.C. Served in Mesopotamia, Kut-el-Amara.

HARDWICKE KENYON FOERS.

Admitted Jan. 1916. Assistant Solicitor with Town Clerk of Rotherham. Joined Dec. 17, 1915, as Private, Inns of Court O.T.C. Gazetted 2nd Lieut. 3/3 London Brigade, Royal Field Artillery, promoted Lieut. Aug. 1918. Served in France. Wounded at Paschendaele Ridge Oct. 8, 1917.

FRANK WILSON FOLEY.

Admitted Feb. 1904, practising at Bolton. Served as Major, 4th Batt. Loyal North Lancashire Regt.

HENRY ARTHUR FOLEY.

Articled to E. E. Baker, of Weston-super-Mare. Joined Aug. 31, 1914, as Private, 6th Batt. Somerset Light Infantry. Gazetted Temp. 2nd Lieut. 7th Batt. Somerset Light Infantry Dec. 12, 1915, promoted Lieut. April 1917, A/Capt. Dec. 1916. Awarded the M.C. Served in France May 1915 to March 1918. Wounded at Lesbœufs Sept. 16, 1916, and at Langemarck Aug. 16, 1917. Taken prisoner near Ham March 24, 1918. (Camps, Rastatt and Grandeuz).

GEORGE HOWARD FOORD.

Admitted Nov. 1909. Member of Foord & Son, of 16 Philpot Lane, E.C. Joined March 1915 as 2nd Lieut., Royal Army Service Corps, promoted Lieut.

Sept. 1915. Served at Home and at Gallipoli. Died Oct. 13, 1915, of wounds received in action at Cape Helles.

HERBERT QUALLETT FOORD.

Admitted Oct. 1914. Member of Foord & Son, of 16 Philpot Lane, E.C. Joined Sept. 1914, as Private, Inns of Court O.T.C. Gazetted 2nd Lieut. 8th Batt. Royal West Kent Regt. Feb. 10, 1915, 2nd Lieut. 8th Batt. The Queen's Regt. Oct. 15, 1915, Capt. General List, appointed Courts-Martial Officer Thames and Medway Garrison, Chatham, Oct. 26, 1916 (B.E.F. France, Oct. 1915 to June 1916), Capt. Royal West Kent Regt., Courts-Martial Officer Hounslow Area, Hounslow, from Sept. 1919. Once mentioned in Dispatches (Home). Served at Home and in Flanders.

FOSTER LAKE FOOTNER.

Admitted Feb. 1905. Member of G. B. Footner & Son, of Romsey, Hants. Mobilised Aug. 1914, as Major, 4th Batt. Hampshire Regt. (T.). Once mentioned in Dispatches. Awarded the D.S.O. Served in India and Mesopotamia. Wounded during siege of Kut Dec. 9, 1915, and Jan. 11, 1916. Taken prisoner at Kut-el-Amara April 29, 1916.

ALBERT EDWARD FORBES.

Admitted April 1905. Member of Forbes & Nixon, of Middlesbrough. Joined Feb. 8, 1917, Royal Field Artillery and subsequently transferred to Royal Garrison Artillery. Served in France.

RONALD MYLNE FORD.

Admitted Oct. 1910. Member of Cooper & Co., Newcastle, Staffs. Joined Aug. 1914 as Private, Inns of Court O.T.C. Gazetted 2nd Lieut. 3rd Batt. South Wales Borderers (Special Reserve) Oct. 7, 1914, promoted to Lieut. May 1915. Awarded Croix de Guerre with Palms (French). Went to France March 1915, rejoined Special Reserve June 1916, since when served in England. Wounded on Hill 70 at Loos Nov. 28, 1915.

WILLIAM FORD.

Articled to A. R. Ford, of 4 South Square, Gray's Inn, W.C. Joined March 25, 1915, as 2nd Lieut., 7th Batt. Royal Fusiliers, promoted Lieut. March 1918. Served in France. Wounded on the Ancre Nov. 13, 1916. Discharged March 21, 1918, on account of wounds.

WILLIAM ALLIN FORD.

Articled to W. H. Hortin, of St. Lawrence House, Trump Street, King Street, E.C. Joined Sept. 7, 1914, as Private, 20th Batt. County of London Regt. (T.F.). Commissioned in France Jan. 31, 1916, to 5th Batt. Oxfordshire and Buckinghamshire Light Infantry, promoted Lieut. March 1917, and Capt. Aug. 1917. Served in France March 1915 to Oct. 1917. Wounded at Gheluvett, Menin Road, Flanders, Oct. 17, 1917.

ARCHIBALD CLAUDE FORMAN.

Admitted Nov. 1902, practising at 58 Lombard Street, E.C. Mobilised Aug. 2, 1914. Commissioned Royal Naval Volunteer Reserve Oct. 7, 1914, from Chief Petty Officer, with Royal Naval Division till April 1915, thence

H.M. Naval Base, Larne, Ireland, promoted Lieut. Royal Naval Volunteer Reserve Aug. 1915. Received thanks of Admiralty April 12, 1918. Served at the Admiralty and in Ireland.

ARTHUR TEMPLE FORMAN.

Admitted Dec. 1906. Member of Gray & Dodsworth, of 1 Bank Buildings, Prince's Street, E.C., and York. Joined Nov. 1915, as Lieut., Royal Army Ordnance Corps, promoted Capt. Jan. 1918. Once mentioned in Dispatches. Served at Home till Oct. 1916, Mesopotamia Oct. 1916 to Dec. 1918.

ARTHUR LIVESEY FORRESTER.

Admitted Nov. 1902. Member of Forrester, Moir & Co., of Malmesbury, Wilts. Served as Capt., 3rd Wessex Brigade, Royal Field Artillery.

ALFRED WILLIAM FORSDIKE.

Articled to W. E. Hart, of Sheffield. Joined Sept. 1914, as 2nd Lieut., Royal Field Artillery, promoted A/Capt. April 1917, Capt. Jan. 1918. Three times mentioned in Dispatches. Served at Home, Egypt, Greece, Bulgaria, Serbia (Serbian Retreat 1915), Salonica (Struma Valley), and Palestine.

HENRY PHILIP FORSHAW.

Admitted April 1903. Member of Forshaw, Parker & Co., of Preston. Served as Capt., 5th (Reserve) Batt. King's Own Royal Lancaster Regt. Mentioned in Dispatches. Awarded the M.C. and Bar.

JOHN FORSHAW.

Admitted April 1915. Of Liverpool. Joined May 1915, as 2nd Lieut., 8th Batt. King's Liverpool Regt., subsequently resigned commission, and in 1917 became Private in 2nd Batt. Hon. Artillery Company (Infantry). Served in France and Italy.

PERCIVAL ARMORER FORSTER.

Admitted Nov. 1911. Member of Partridge & Co., of King's Lynn. Joined Oct. 10, 1914, as 2nd Lieut., 3rd Batt. Yorkshire Regt. (S.R.), promoted Lieut. Feb. 1915, Temp. Capt. Oct. 1915, seconded to Machine Gun Corps. Feb. 1916. Reverted to Permanent Rank, promoted Temp. Capt. Machine Gun Corps April 1916. Once mentioned in Dispatches. Awarded the M.C. Served at Home Oct. 1914 to May 1915, France May 1915 to Nov. 1916, Home Nov. 1916 to termination of War.

WILLIAM FORSTER.

Articled to F. H. Chance, of 30 Mincing Lane, E.C. Joined Feb. 6, 1916, as Private, 29th Batt. Royal Fusiliers, and afterwards transferred to 8th Batt. Served at Home Feb. to Aug. 1916, and in France Aug. to Oct. 1916. Killed in action near Gueudecourt Oct. 7, 1916.

WILLIAM OXLEY FORSTER.

Articled to J. E. Gibson, of Newcastle-on-Tyne. Joined March 26, 1915, as Lieut., 8th Batt. Durham Light Infantry. Served in France. Killed Sept. 22, 1916.

SAMUEL SANFORD FORSYTH.

Admitted Aug. 1909. Managing Clerk with R. A. Rotherham, of Coventry, Joined Aug. 6, 1914, as Gunner, Royal Field Artillery, promoted Bombardier.

Given commission Sept. 23, 1914, A.D.C. to General F. Wing, A.D.C. to General Sandilands, given Command of Trench Mortar Battery Sept. 1915. Once mentioned in Dispatches. Served in France. Killed at Hooge, near Ypres, Sept. 25, 1915.

ALBERT EDWARD MUSPRATT FORTESCUE.

Admitted Apil 1906, practising at Donington House, Norfolk Street, W.C. Joined June 10, 1918, as 2nd Lieut. (A/Capt.), Royal Air Force, promoted Flying Officer (A/Flight-Lieut.) Dec. 1919. Awarded O.B.E. Served at Home.

CHARLES LAWRENCE FORTESCUE.

Articled to Charles Fortescue, of Banbury, Oxon. Joined Oct. 8, 1914, as Capt., Commanding 3rd (Service) Coy. 4th Batt. Oxford and Bucks Light Infantry, appointed Adjutant Lines of Communication, Southern Command, Aug. 1915, Adjutant No. 3 Area, Royal Defence Corps, Southern Command, Feb. 1917, Officer Commanding 252 P. Coy. Oct. 1918, Adjutant, P.W. Staff, Western Command, July 1919, Commandant of same Nov. 1919. Served at Home.

EDWARD CLAUDE FORTESCUE.

Admitted Jan. 1901. Member of Stockton, Sons & Fortescue, of Banbury. Mobilised Aug. 5, 1914, as Capt., 4th Batt. Oxford and Bucks Light Infantry, promoted Substantive Major June 1916, appointed Courts-Martial Officer Dec. 18, 1918, in France. Awarded the T.D. Served in France.

HAROLD WILSON FORTUNE.

Admitted Feb. 1906, practising at Harrogate. Joined May 1917, as Aircraftsman II., Royal Naval Air Service, promoted Aircraftsman I., Leading Hand, transferred to Royal Air Force as Corporal Clerk. Served in France and England.

WILLIAM GRAHAM FORWARD.

Admitted Feb. 1900. Member of William Forward & Sons, of Axminster. Mobilised Aug. 1914, as Capt., 1/4 Batt. Devonshire Regt. (T.F.), promoted Major May 1917. Awarded the T.D. Served in India Oct. 1914 and Mesopotamia Jan. 1916 to April 1919.

BARTHOLOMEW FOSKETT.

Admitted Dec. 1908, practising at Newcastle-on-Tyne. Joined Oct. 13, 1915, as 2nd Lieut., Royal Field Artillery, promoted Lieut. June 1916, Capt. Aug. 1917, Adjutant 78th Brigade July 1917 to March 1918, Military Operations Department, War Office, London, July 1918 to March 1919. Awarded the M.C. Served at Home Oct. 1915 to Nov. 1916 and July 1918 to March 1919, and in France and Flanders Nov. 1916 to March 1918. Wounded on Arras Front April 20, and 24, 1917. Gassed Cambrai Front March 21 to 26, 1918.

NOËL FOSKETT.

Admitted Dec. 1914, practising at 9 Bush Lane, Cannon Street, E.C. Joined Dec. 16, 1916, as Private, 28th Batt. County of London Regt. (Artists Rifles). Gazetted 2nd Lieut. Machine Gun Corps Sept. 26, 1917. Served in Belgium Oct. 1917 to Dec. 1917, Italy Dec. 1917 to April 1918, France and Belgium April 1918 to March 1919. Wounded June 28, and Oct. 6, 1918.

ARTHUR WILLIAM FOSTER.

Articled to E. P. Foster, of Wells, Somerset. Joined Nov. 9, 1914, as O.S., Royal Naval Volunteer Reserve, promoted A.B. March 1915. Gazetted 2nd Lieut. Special Reserve Royal Field Artillery, March 27, 1917. Served at Gallipoli and Dardanelles May 1915 to Aug. 1916, and in France Aug. 1917 to May 1918. Wounded May 16, 1918.

EDWARD WADE FOSTER.

Articled to E. P. Foster, of Wells, Somerset. Joined July 3, 1917, as Private, Army Pay Corps, promoted Corporal July 1918. Served at Home.

ERNEST HENRY FOSTER.

Admitted April 1894. Member of Walter & E. H. Foster, of Leeds. Employed on War Work at Lands Branch, War Office.

FERMIAN LE NEVE FOSTER.

Admitted Dec. 1910. Member of Warren, Murton, Miller & Foster, of 45 Bloomsbury Square, W.C. Served as 2nd Lieut., Inns of Court O.T.C., promoted Capt. June 1916, and subsequently employed at Ministry of Labour.

GEORGE EDWARD FOSTER.

Articled to A. W. Price, of Northampton. Joined Sept. 14, 1914, as Private, 7th Batt. Northamptonshire Regt., later Lance-Corporal. Commissioned as 2nd Lieut. 2nd Batt. Monmouthshire Regt. Jan. 22, 1915, appointed Lieut. July 1915, and A/Capt. Oct. 1917. Served in France July 1915 to Aug. 1916 and Oct. 1917 to April 1918. Wounded Aug. 1916. Captured April 12, 1918, and interned in Grandenz, Poland. Repatriated Dec. 21, 1918.

HORACE HARFORD FOSTER.

Admitted Feb. 1907, practising at Malvern. Served as 2nd Lieut., Herefordshire Regt., promoted Lieut. July 1917.

HUGH MATHESON FOSTER.

Admitted Nov. 1907. Member of Foster & Wells, of Aldershot. Mobilised Aug. 1914, as Capt., 1/4 Batt. Hampshire Regt. (T.F.), promoted Major Sept. 5, 1919. D.A.A.G. 4th (India) Division. Awarded the T.D. Served in Mesopotamia and Persia 1915 to 1916, and in India 1916 to 1919.

RENNIE JAMES FOSTER.

Admitted Sept. 1907. Managing Clerk with Gaunt, Foster & Co., of Bradford. Joined Aug. 5, 1914, as Private, 1/6 Batt. West Yorkshire Regt., subsequently promoted Corporal. Awarded the M.M. Served in France and Belgium April 1915 to June 1918. Wounded at Battle of Somme July 20, 1916.

ROBERT TONGE FOSTER.

Articled to W. A. Foster, of Hull. Joined Oct. 1914, as Private, Inns of Court O.T.C. Gazetted 2nd Lieut. East Riding Yorkshire Yeomanry Feb. 26, 1915, promoted Lieut. 2nd Reserve Cavalry Regt. Aug. 1917. Served in France.

WILLIAM FOSTER.

Articled to J. A. H. Green, of Nottingham. Joined March 13, 1915, as 2nd Lieut., 2/7 Batt. Notts and Derby Regt. (Sherwood Foresters), promoted Lieut. Oct. 1915, Capt. and Adjutant March 1918. Once mentioned in

Dispatches. Awarded the M.C. Served at Home and in France and Belgium. Wounded April 23, 1917.

PETER ROBERTS FOULKES-ROBERTS.

Articled to A. Foulkes-Roberts, of Denbigh, N. Wales. Mobilised Aug. 1914, as Lieut.,4th Batt. Royal Welch Fusiliers, promoted Temp. Capt. July 1915, Substantive Capt. Oct. 1915. Once mentioned in Dispatches. Awarded the M.C. Served in France June 1915 to March 1918. Wounded and taken prisoner March 23, 1918. Repatriated Nov. 28, 1919.

JOHN ALFRED ARNOTT FOUNTAIN.

Articled to C. F. Booth, of 4 Bedford Row, W.C. Joined Nov. 23, 1914, as Private, 12th Batt. Royal Sussex Regt. Gazetted 2nd Lieut. 10th Batt. King's Own Yorkshire Light Infantry Feb. 24, 1915. Served in France. Killed between Fricourt Wood and La Boiselle July 1, 1916.

ARTHUR CLIFFORD FOUNTAINE.

Admitted Dec. 1900, practised at 27 Chancery Lane, W.C. Served as Lieut., 60th Garrison Batt. Royal Welch Fusiliers.

REGINALD WEST FOVARGUE.

Articled to H. W. Fovargue, of Eastbourne. Joined Sept. 4, 1914, as Private, 18th Batt. Royal Fusiliers, Public Schools Brigade. Gazetted 2nd Lieut. 2/2 Home Counties Brigade Royal Field Artillery Feb. 26, 1915, promoted Lieut. June 1916, and A/Capt. Oct. 1918. Served at Home Sept. 1914 to March 1916 and April 1916 to Oct. 1917, France April 1 to April 17, 1916, Mesopotamia Oct. 1917 to May 1919, and in India May to Sept. 1919.

SYDNEY JOHN FOWLER.

Admitted Nov. 1897. Member of Fowler & Co., of Oakham, Rutland. Mobilised Aug. 1914, as Capt., 5th Batt. Leicestershire Regt. Served in France Oct. to Dec. 1915, remainder of time in England.

ROBERT JOHN FOWLES.

Articled to A. E. Ellis, of 6 King's Bench Walk, Temple, E.C. Served as Private, Hon. Artillery Company. Obtained commission in Hon. Artillery Company and promoted Lieut. June 1918. Held rank of Capt. whilst Courts-Martial Officer. Mentioned in Dispatches. Awarded the M.C.

ARTHUR CECIL FOX.

Articled to Peregrine Thomas, of Burnley. Served as Private, 70th Training Reserve Batt., Ripon.

JEREMIAH HASLAM FOX.

Admitted Dec. 1895, practising at St. Helens, Lancs. Served as Major, West Lancashire Division Royal Engineers.

JOHN FOX

Admitted June 1905. Assistant Registrar of Friendly Societies, British Museum, Montague Place, W.C. Joined May 8, 1915, as Temp. 2nd Lieut., Royal Army Service Corps, promoted Temp. Lieut. Sept. 1915, Temp. Capt. Dec. 1915, A/Major Aug. 1917, D.A.D.S., G.H.Q., 1st Echelon, E.E.F., Dec. 1917, Temp. Major, Staff, Feb. 1918. Twice mentioned in Dispatches. Awarded the O.B.E. (Military Division). Served in Dardanelles July 1915 to Feb. 1916,

Senussi Campaign Feb. to May 1916, Egypt May 1916 to Oct. 1917, Palestine Oct. 1917 to Feb. 1919.

PHILIP HENRY FOX.

Admitted Aug. 1901. Of 119B St. James's Court, Buckingham Gate, S.W. Joined March 1, 1915, as A.B. (Mobile Section, Anti-Aircraft Corps), Royal Naval Volunteer Reserve. Assistant Paymaster Royal Naval Reserve July 1915, Paymaster-Lieut. July 1917. Served with H.M.Y. *Sagonara*, H.M.Y. *Sapitta*, H.M.S. *President*, English Channel, Hebrides, Murman Coast, and Shore Service.

WILLIAM STEPHEN FRANCE.

Admitted July 1886, practising at Wigan. Mobilised Aug. 5, 1914, as Lieut.-Col. (Hon. Col.) Commanding 5th Batt. Manchester Regt. (T.F.), to Command of Details East Lancashire Reserves Depôt Sept. 1914, A.A. and Q.M.G. 66th (East Lancashire) Division Nov. 1914, D.A.Q.M.G. Mersey Garrison Feb. 1917. Once mentioned in Dispatches. Served at Home.

FRANCIS EDWARD FRANCILLON.

Admitted Oct. 1914. Member of H. J. Francillon & Son, of Dursley, Glos. Mobilised Aug. 5, 1914, as Lieut., 1/5 Batt. Gloucestershire Regt., promoted Temp. Capt. May 1915, Substantive Capt. June 1916. Once mentioned in Dispatches. Served in France March 1915 to Nov. 1917, Italy Nov. 1917 to Sept. 1918, France Sept. 1918 to July 1919.

FRANCIS ARCHIBALD FRANCIS.

Admitted April 1910. Member of Marcus & Francis, of 47 Broad Street Avenue, E.C. Joined July 4, 1915, as A.B., Royal Navy Branch, Royal Naval Volunteer Reserve.

GUY LANCELOT BRERETON FRANCIS.

Admitted March 1911. Member of Morgan & Co., of Chepstow. Served as Capt., 1st Batt. Monmouthshire Regt., and afterwards transferred to Royal Army Service Corps (M.T.).

HUGH DOUGLAS PEREGRINE FRANCIS.

Admitted Oct. 1908. Member of Francis & Johnson, of 19 Great Winchester Street, E.C. Joined Aug. 3, 1914, as Private, Inns of Court O.T.C. Gazetted 2nd Lieut. 1/1 East Riding Yeomanry Sept. 25, 1914, promoted Lieut. June 1916, Capt. July 1917, Adjutant Aug. 1915 to April 1918, Capt. and Adjutant 102nd (Lincoln and East Riding Yeomanry) Batt. Machine Gun Corps April 1918 to March 1919. Once mentioned in Dispatches. Awarded the M.C. Served at Home Aug. 1914 to Oct. 1915, Egypt Oct. 1915 to Nov. 1916, Palestine Nov. 1916 to May 1918, France June 1918 to March 1919.

WALTER HAMOND FRANCIS.

Admitted Nov. 1882. Member of Francis & Co., of Cambridge. Joined Jan. 23, 1915, as Capt. and Hon. Major, Royal Defence Corps (formerly 4th Batt. Suffolk Regt.). Served at Home.

CHARLES CLARK FRANK.

Admitted Feb. 1895, practising at Leeds. Joined Nov. 5, 1915, as 2nd Lieut., 7th Batt. Prince of Wales's Own West Yorkshire Regt. (Leeds Rifles), promoted Lieut. July 1917, resigned Commission on the grounds of ill-health caused by wounds and retained the rank of Lieutenant Feb. 25, 1918. Served at Home Nov. 1915 to May 1916, France May to July 1916. Wounded in the attack on the Selmahen Redoubt opposite Thiepval Wood July 1, 1916, and captured the same night. A prisoner in Germany until interned in Holland on May 16, 1918. Repatriated sick Sept. 23, 1918.

ERNEST FRANKLAND.

Admitted Oct. 1908, practising at Middlesbrough. Joined May 1916, as Gunner, Royal Garrison Artillery, promoted Lance-Bombardier Dec. 1918. Served in France.

WALTER BELL FRANKLIN.

Articled to William Graham, of 24 Coleman Street, E.C. Served as 2nd Lieut., King's Royal Rifle Corps.

REGINALD DAVID FRAPE.

Admitted May 1905. Member of Frape & Gauntlett, of Brighton. Joined Nov. 16, 1914, as Private, 13th Batt. Royal Sussex Regt., and subsequently promoted Lance-Corporal. Served in France. Killed in action June 30, 1916.

ARNOLD FREDERICK FRASER.

Admitted Feb. 1913. Member of Fraser & Fraser, of Nottingham. Served as 2nd Lieut., 7th (Service) Batt. South Staffordshire Regt.

CECIL EDWARD REGINALD FRASER.

Admitted Oct. 1905. Member of Fraser & Son, of Nottingham. Joined Sept. 24, 1914, as Private, Notts and Derby Regt. (Sherwood Foresters). Gazetted 2nd Lieut. Aug. 4, 1915, promoted Lieut. Dec. 1915, Capt. May 1918. Twice mentioned in Dispatches. Served at Home, and in France and Belgium.

CECIL EUSTACE WILLIAM FRASER.

Admitted Aug. 1901, practising at Bickley, Kent. Served as Capt. 5th, London Brigade Royal Field Artillery, and promoted Major June 1917.

EDWARD FRASER.

Admitted March 1906. Member of North, Kirk & Co., of Liverpool. Served as 2nd Lieut., Machine Gun Corps.

GORDON FRASER.

Admitted Jan. 1910, practising at Ipswich. Joined Oct. 7, 1914, as 2nd Lieut., 3rd Batt. Suffolk Regt., attached Royal Army Ordnance Corps Dec. 1914, promoted Lieut. Jan. 1915, Capt. Sept. 1916, Major July 1917, appointed to Administrative Staff. Once mentioned in Dispatches. Awarded the M.C. Served in France and Belgium March 1915 to Jan. 1919.

JAMES SCHOLFIELD FRASER.

Admitted Nov. 1900, practised at Ashford, Kent. Mobilised Aug. 1914, as Capt., 5th Batt. East Kent Regt. (The Buffs), and subsequently promoted Major. Served in India and Mesopotamia. Killed at Shaikh Saad, in Mesopotamia, Jan. 13–14, 1916.

WALLACE FRASER.

Admitted April 1899, practised at Liverpool. Joined Aug. 1914, as Private, 19th Batt. King's Liverpool Regt. Gazetted Lieut. in same Regt. Sept. 1, 1914, promoted Capt. Dec. 1914. Served in France. Killed in action at Guillemont July 30, 1916.

ROWLAND WYNNE FRAZIER.

Admitted June 1912. Managing Clerk with Redfern, Hunt & Co., of Frederick's Place, E.C. Joined Sept. 3, 1914, as Ordinary Seaman, Royal Naval Volunteer Reserve, Signalman May 1915. Gazetted Sub-Lieut. Royal Naval Volunteer Reserve Feb. 1, 1916, Observer Lieut. Royal Navy Oct. 1917, Capt. Royal Air Force April 1918. Minesweeping in North Sea May 1915 to Jan. 1916, Flying in Eastern Mediterranean Oct. to Dec 1916. Shot down in Henri Farman Biplane at Gereviz, near Port Lagos, coast of Bulgaria, Dec. 1, 1916. Escaped from Philippopolis Prison Camp Aug. 28, 1918. Recaptured at Chepelari Sept. 8, 1918.

WILLIAM FREAM.

Articled to Ralph Fream, of Gloucester. Served as Lieut., 5th Batt. Gloucestershire Regt.

HERBERT FREEDMAN.

Articled to J. C. Morton, of Sunderland. Joined March 7, 1917, as Gunner in Durham Royal Garrison Artillery, transferred to No. 3 Siege Artillery Reserve Brigade Nov. 1917, and to 176th Siege Battery Feb. 1918. Served with the Italian Expeditionary Force.

ADOLPHUS HYMAN FREEMAN.

Admitted Oct. 1915, practising at 17 Cork Street, W. Joined March 1, 1916, as Rifleman, 3/16 Batt. County of London Regt. (Queen's Westminster Rifles), promoted Lance-Corporal July 1916. Gazetted 2nd Lieut. Royal Army Service Corps (M.T.) Oct. 23, 1916, promoted Lieut. April 1918. Served at Home and in France and Belgium.

GEORGE HERBERT FREEMAN.

Admitted April 1906, practising at 23 Bedford Row, W.C. Joined Dec. 1915, as Private, 28th Batt. County of London Regt. (Artists Rifles). Gazetted 2nd Lieut. Royal Garrison Artillery Aug. 28, 1916, promoted Lieut. Feb. 1918, Capt. and Adjutant March 1918. Twice mentioned in Dispatches. Awarded the M.B.E. Served in Salonica.

GODFREY JOHN TILLEARD FREEMAN.

Admitted Feb. 1905, practising at 30 & 31 Clement's Lane, E.C. Joined Dec. 20, 1915, as Private, Royal Army Medical Corps, became Cadet Royal Army Service Corps Nov. 1918. Served in France May 1916 to Nov. 1918.

JOHN ARTHUR FREEMAN.

Admitted Dec. 1899. Member of Brook, Freeman & Batley, of Huddersfield. Joined Sept. 2, 1914, as Lieut., Duke of Wellington's Regt., afterwards transferred to 2nd Garrison Batt. King's Own Yorkshire Light Infantry. Served in France Jan. to May. 1917. Discharged Oct. 25, 1917, as a result of illness contracted on Active Service.

JOHN GUY FREEMAN.

Admitted Oct. 1914. Member of A. G. Freeman & Son, of 20 Copthall Avenue, E.C. Joined March 1917, as Private, Royal Army Ordnance Corps. Served in France. Discharged Dec. 1917.

ROBERT CLIFFORD FREEMAN.

Articled to C. R. Freeman, of 30A George Street, Hanover Square, W. Mobilised Aug. 4, 1914, as Capt., 12th Batt. London Regt. (T.F.), in command 1st London Divisional Signal Coy. Royal Engineers (T.F.) Aug. 1914, transferred with unit to 29th Division Jan. 1915, acted as O.C. 29th Divisional Signal Coy. at Gallipoli April to Aug. 1915, invalided (dysentery) Aug. 1915, Instructor in Signal Service Training Centre Jan. to April 1916, Inspector of Signalling, Scottish Command, May to Nov. 1916, Staff Course, Cambridge, Nov. to Dec. 1916, G.S.O.III. Fourth Garrison, Edinburgh, Jan. to Nov. 1917, Staff attachments and employed with 2nd Army Signal Coy., France, Nov. 1917 to June 1918, G.S.O.III. 31st Division June 1918 to April 1919. Awarded M.C. and Belgian Croix de Guerre. Served at Home Aug. 1914 to March 1915, and Aug. 1915 to Nov. 1917, Gallipoli April to Aug. 1915, France Nov. 1917 to April 1919.

RUSSELL JOURDAN FREEMAN.

Admitted Nov. 1903. Member of John Newton & Sons, of 27 Clement's Lane, E.C. Served as Bombardier, Royal Field Artillery.

SAMUEL FREEMAN.

Admitted Nov. 1902, practising at Halifax. Joined Sept. 17, 1918, as Victualling Assistant, Royal Navy. Served at Home (at Portsmouth Royal Naval Barracks).

WALTER HANSON FREEMAN.

Articled to W. H. Coles, of Wakefield. Mobilised Aug. 1914, as 2nd Lieut., 5th Batt. West Yorkshire Regt. (T.F.), promoted Lieut. Oct. 1914, Temp. Capt. Sept. 1915, Substantive Capt. June 1916, A/Major Oct. 1918. Awarded the M.C. and Bar. Served at Home Aug. 1914 to April 1915, in France and Flanders April 1915 to March 1919, and in Germany March to Dec. 1919.

WALTER KINGSON FREETH.

Articled to Arthur Gilbert, of 4 Walbrook, E.C. Served as Capt., 12th Batt. Royal Fusiliers.

ALFRED CYRIL FRENCH.

Articled to F. H. Pepper, of Birmingham. Joined Sept. 27, 1917, as Private, Inns of Court, O.T.C., subsequently became Cadet, Royal Artillery, and after demobilisation gazetted as 2nd Lieut. Royal Garrison Artillery. Served at Home.

ROBERT MASON JACKSON FRENCH.

Articled to J. M. French, of Boscombe. Mobilised Aug. 1914, as Lieut., 3rd Batt. Royal Welch Fusiliers, promoted Capt. Feb. 1915, attached to 2nd Batt. Aug. 1914 to Sept. 1915, and to 1st Batt. Sept. 1915. Served in France. Wounded at Loos. Died from wounds Feb. 19, 1916.

WILLIAM GORDON FRENCH.

Admitted June 1909, practising at Bolton, Lancs. Joined Dec. 3, 1915, as 2nd Class Air-Mechanic, Royal Flying Corps, subsequently promoted 1st Class Air-Mechanic Royal Air Force. Served at Home.

GILBERT RAPER FRERE.

Articled to A. F. Foster, of 28 Lincoln's Inn Fields, W.C. Joined Aug. 1914, as Private, Public Schools Batt. Gazetted 2nd Lieut. 10th Batt. The Rifle Brigade Sept. 1915, appointed Adjutant Oct. 1915, promoted Capt. shortly before his death. Served at Home and in France. Wounded Oct. 26, 1915, at Laventie, and died the evening of the same day at the Casualty Clearing Station at Merville, where he was buried.

PHILIP BEAUMONT FRERE.

Articled to L. C. Cholmeley, of 28 Lincoln's Inn Fields, W.C. Joined Aug. 3, 1914, as Rifleman, Inns of Court, O.T.C. Gazetted Temp. 2nd Lieut. 8th Batt. East Surrey Regt. Sept. 12, 1914, promoted Temp. Lieut. Dec. 1914, 2nd Lieut. (Regulars) 1st King's Royal Rifle Corps Aug. 4, 1916, Lieut. and Adjutant Dec. 1916, Temp. Capt. Aug. 1917. Twice mentioned in Dispatches. Awarded the M.C. Served in France and Belgium June 1915 to June 1918. Wounded June 20, 1918.

LEONARD MICHAEL FRIEND.

Admitted Nov. 1907, practising at 167 Seymour Place, W. Served as Lieut., 3rd Batt. Northumberland Fusiliers.

CHARLES PERCIVAL FRIPP.

Articled to G. P. Fripp, of Oldham. Served as Private, 7th Batt. King's Liverpool Regt. (T.).

GEORGE CHRISTIE FRIPP.

Admitted Oct. 1912. Member of Fripp & Son, of Oldham. Served as 2nd Lieut., 10th Batt. Manchester Regt., and promoted Lieut. July 1917. Mentioned in Dispatches. Awarded the M.C.

WILLIAM THOMAS FRODSHAM.

Articled to J. Frodsham, of St. Helens. Joined Oct. 1914, as 2nd Lieut., 2/5 Batt. South Lancashire Regt., promoted Lieut. April 1918. Served in France. Killed in action at Delville Wood Sept. 9, 1916.

ALFRED FROST.

Articled to J. H. Frost, of Birmingham. Served as 2nd Lieut., Guards Machine Gun Regt.

GEORGE CHARLES LOVELL FRY.

Admitted Feb. 1887, practising at 74 Coleman Street, E.C. Joined Aug. 4, 1914, as Transport Sergeant, 28th Batt. County of London Regt. (Artists Rifles). Gazetted Staff Lieut. Special List as Railway Transport Officer April 6, 1916, promoted 1st Class May 1917. Served in France throughout.

THEODORE PENROSE FRY.

Articled to Percy Corder, of Newcastle-on-Tyne. Joined Nov. 6, 1914, as 2nd Lieut., 5th Batt. Durham Light Infantry (T.F.), promoted Lieut. June

1916, Capt. Jan. 1919., Instructor VI. Corps School, B.E.F., Oct. 1917 to Feb. 1919. Served at Home and in France. Wounded at Ypres Dec. 25, 1915.

WILLIAM HENRY FRY.

Articled to A. J. Larcome, of Portsmouth. Enlisted as Private in the Public Schools Batt. Royal Fusiliers at the outbreak of War, and shortly afterwards gazetted 2nd Lieut. 13th Batt. Hampshire Regt. Went to Gallipoli 1915 and remained there until the evacuation, then went to Egypt and finally to France. Seconded to Machine Gun Corps, promoted Lieut. Once mentioned in Dispatches. Killed in action May 26, 1917.

ROBERT LEO FULFORD.

Admitted Feb. 1910, in practice at 33 Bedford Street, W.C. Joined Aug. 28, 1914, as Private, in Infantry. Later gazetted Capt. Royal Army Service Corps. Discharged Aug. 1918.

ALAN LINDSEY FULLALOVE.

Articled to G. S. Ritchie, of Burnley. Joined Feb. 1916, as Sub-Lieut., Royal Naval Volunteer Reserve. Served in H.M.S. *Columnbella*, in 10th Cruiser Squadron, and in H.M.S. *Courageous*, Flag-ship of Vice-Admiral, Light Cruiser Force.

ALFRED WALTER FRANCIS FULLER.

Admitted April 1906. Managing Clerk with Steadman, Van Praagh & Gaylor, of 4 Suffolk Street, Pall Mall East, S.W. Joined Sept. 1914, as Private, Inns of Court O.T.C. Gazetted 2nd Lieut. 9th Batt. Oxford and Bucks Light Infantry March 17, 1915, promoted Lieut. Oct. 1915, Capt. Jan. 1916, attached Tank Corps Jan. 1917, rejoined Regt. April 1917, XII. Corps Trench Mortar Officer and Commandant of T.M. School Jan. to Sept. 1918. Rejoined Regt. Served at Home Sept. 1914 to June 1917, Macedonia (Serbia and Bulgaria) June 1917 to Jan. 1919 with 7th Oxford and Bucks Light Infantry.

GORDON HOWARD FULLER.

Articled to Ernest A. Fuller, of 37 Essex Street, W.C. Joined Oct. 1914, as Private, 5th Batt. East Surrey Regt. Gazetted 2nd Lieut. Oxford and Bucks Light Infantry Jan. 1917, and promoted Temp. Capt. March 1918. Served in India and France. Killed south of Arras July 7, 1918.

EDWARD ARTHUR CRAIG FULTON.

Articled to C. S. Fisher, of 3 Field Court, Gray's Inn. Joined Aug. 6, 1914, as Private, 2nd Batt. Royal Fusiliers, subsequently gazetted Capt. 3rd Batt. Highland Light Infantry. Served at Malta 1914, in France 1915 to 1917, and in India 1918 to 1919. Accidentally wounded at La Gorgue Oct. 25, 1915.

GEORGE KOBERWEIN FULTON.

Admitted July 1910. Member of Hamilton Fulton & Son, of Salisbury. Joined Feb. 1915, as Lieut., Wiltshire Regt., and subsequently attained the rank of Lieut.-Col. 9th Batt. Cheshire Regt. Three times mentioned in Dispatches. Awarded the D.S.O. Served in France. Killed in action April 14, 1918.

CLEMENT BARRINGTON FURMSTON.

Articled to W. M. Wilson, of Alfreton, Derbyshire. Enlisted Nov. 1914, as Private, 21st Batt. Royal Fusiliers, and on Sept. 5, 1916, obtained commission as 2nd Lieut. Machine Gun Corps. Killed in action at Arras April 9, 1917.

ARTHUR SANDERSON FURNISS.

Admitted Nov. 1913. Member of Girbord & Co., of Rotherham. Joined Aug. 6, 1914, as 2nd Lieut., 5th Batt. York and Lancaster Regt., promoted Lieut. Jan. 1915, Capt. May 1915. Served in France. Wounded and taken prisoner at Beaumont Hamel Feb. 22, 1917.

JOHN JAMES FYFFE.

Admitted Nov. 1912. Member of Ellison & Fyffe, of Sheffield. Joined Aug. 1914, as Private, Royal Army Service Corps, and subsequenetly gazetted 2nd Lieut. 9th Batt. West Yorkshire Regt. Served at Gallipoli, Egypt, and France. Killed in action in France in 1916.

LEONARD WILLIAM FYSON.

Articled to B. E. White, of 52 Bedford Row, W.C. Joined Nov. 17, 1915, as Private, 2nd Batt. Hon. Artillery Company (Infantry). Commissioned as 2nd Lieut. 5th Batt. East Surrey Regt. Dec. 19, 1916, promoted Lieut. June 1918. Served at Home and in France. Wounded July 18, 1917.

CYRIL LEICESTER GABELL.

Admitted March 1913, practising at Hereford. Served as 2nd Lieut., 2nd Batt. Monmouthshire Regt., subsequently promoted Capt.

VICTOR JOHN GADBAN.

Admitted Dec. 1904. Member of Downie & Gadban, of Alton, Hants. Served as Temp. Capt., Labour Corps.

JOSEPH HENRY GAIN.

Admitted Oct. 1905, practising at Painters Hall, Little Trinity Lane, E.C. Served as Private, Royal Army Ordnance Corps.

THOMAS ALAN GAINSFORD.

Admitted Feb. 1904. Member of Webster & Co., of Sheffield. Served as 2nd Lieut., Royal Garrison Artillery.

THOMAS GAIR.

Articled to Sir Harcourt E. Clare, of Preston. Joined Aug. 1914, as 2nd Lieut., Royal Field Artillery, promoted Lieut. 1916. Served in France Feb. to Sept. 1917. Killed at Ypres Sept. 9, 1917.

ANTHONY RICHARD GALE.

Admitted April 1910, practising at 11 Queen Victoria Street, E.C. Joined Nov. 12, 1914, as Private, Inns of Court O.T.C. Gazetted Lieut. Royal Army Ordnance Corps Jan. 22, 1915, promoted A/Capt. Feb. 1916, Temp. Capt. Oct. 1917, A/Major Jan. 1918. Once mentioned in Dispatches. Served at Home Nov. 1914 to Jan. 1915, and in France Jan. 1915 to Oct. 1919.

LIONEL ERNEST BRADLEY GALE.

Admitted June 1905, practising at Poole, Dorset. Served as 2nd Lieut., 4th Batt. Hampshire Regt. (T.), attached 68th Labour Company.

REGINALD ALBERT BRADLEY GALE.

Admitted May 1914, practised at Basingstoke. Served as Cadet. Gazetted 2nd Lieut. Royal Garrison Artillery, and subsequently promoted Lieut.

JOHN RUSSELL GALES.

Admitted July 1913. Managing Clerk with Landor & Barrows, of Wolverhampton. Joined Aug. 4, 1914, as 2nd Lieut., 3rd (S.R.) Batt. Durham Light Infantry, promoted Lieut. Sept. 1919, Staff July 1915 to Feb. 1917. Awarded the M.B.E. Served in France and Flanders and with Army of Occupation. Wounded Sept. 20, 1914.

HAROLD EDWIN GALLAHER.

Admitted Nov. 1906, of Sutton, Surrey. Joined May 21, 1915, as 2nd Lieut., 15th Batt. County of London Regt. (Civil Service Rifles) (T.F.), promoted Lieut. Sept. 1916, Staff Lieut. A.C.M.A. No. 29 Area July 1918, Staff Capt. March 1919. Served in France May to Nov. 1916.

JOHN ARTHUR GALLOP.

Admitted Sept. 1905, practising at 4 Great Winchester Street, E.C. Served at Home as Capt., Hertfordshire Regt.

LIONEL RICHMOND GALSWORTHY.

Articled to C. W. Cross, of 34 Copthall Avenue, E.C. Joined Oct. 5, 1914, as Private, 3rd (City of London) Batt. Royal Fusiliers. Commissioned as 2nd Lieut. 15th Batt. Royal Fusiliers Dec. 9, 1914, transferred to Royal Field Artillery Sept. 1917, promoted Lieut. Jan. 1917. Served in France Nov. 1915 to Oct. 1918.

CHARLES LANCELOT GAMBLE.

Admitted April 1909. Of East Moulsey. Joined Aug. 12, 1914, as Lieut., Royal Naval Volunteer Reserve, promoted to Lieut.-Commander. Awarded Croix de Guerre with Palms (French).

JOHN HUNTER GAMBLE.

Admitted April 1909. Managing Clerk with John Gamble, of 95 and 97 Finsbury Pavement, E.C. Joined Sept. 5, 1916, as Private, 3rd Batt. Essex Regt., and subsequently promoted Lance-Corporal, transferred Army Pay Corps as Private Dec. 1917, promoted Corporal Dec. 1918. Served at Home.

JOHN CHARLES BLAGDON GAMLEN.

Admitted Aug. 1910. Member of Morrell, Peel & Gamlen, of Oxford. Joined Oct. 1914 Oxford University O.T.C. Gazetted 2nd Lieut. 3/4 Batt. Oxford and Bucks Light Infantry May 1915, promoted Lieut. and Adjutant Jan. 1916, Lieut. 1/4 Batt. Aug. 1916 to Feb. 1919, Staff Capt. General Headquarters, Italy, Feb. to April 1919. Awarded the M.C. Served in France 1916 to 1917, Belgium 1917, Italy 1917 to 1919.

BEAUMONT EDWARD ZACHARIE GAMMELL.

Articled to P. C. Conway, of 81 Rochester Row, Westminster, S.W. Joined March 2, 1916, as 3rd Air-Mechanic, Royal Flying Corps. Gazetted

2nd Lieut. Royal Flying Corps Aug. 16, 1917, promoted Lieut. April 1918. Served in France. Killed Sept. 4, 1918, by anti-aircraft guns over Germany. Died in German hands.

HUMPHREY PERCIVAL GAMON.

Admitted Nov. 1903. Member of Gamon, Farmer & Co, of Chester. Mobilised Aug. 1914 as Capt., 5th Batt. North Staffordshire Regt., promoted Major July 1917, Staff Capt. 3rd Echelon G.H.Q., France, Aug. 1916, D.A.A.G. Nov. 1918. Twice mentioned in Dispatches. Awarded the O.B.E. (Military Division). Served in France March 1915 to March 1919, except for about a month in Egypt.

HENRY GANDY.

Admitted Oct. 1910. Of Newcastle-upon-Tyne. Served as 2nd Lieut., Northumbrian (North Riding) Royal Garrison Artillery, promoted Temp. Lieut. Nov. 1918.

IRVING BLANCHARD GANE.

Admitted Feb. 1914. Member of Gane & Tattersall, of 106 Leadenhall Street, E.C. Joined Aug. 10, 1914, as Private, 1st Batt. Hon. Artillery Company (Infantry). Subsequently Capt., General Staff Officer 3rd Grade, G.H.Q., E.E.F. Served in France Sept. 1914 to May 1915 and June to Dec. 1916, Salonica Dec. 1916 to June 1917, and Palestine June 1917 to March 1919.

JOSEPH HERBERT GARBUTT.

Articled to H. E. Harrowell, of York. Joined Nov. 1916, as Private, 28th Batt. County of London Regt. (Artists Rifles), promoted Sergeant Oct. 1918. Served in France and Belgium. Killed in action at Harvengt, Belgium, Nov. 10, 1918.

FREDERICK GARD.

Admitted Dec. 1905. Member of Albert Gard & Co., of Devonport. Joined May 17, 1915, Inns of Court O.T.C. Gazetted 2nd Lieut. 9th Batt. Duke of Cornwall's Light Infantry Aug. 21, 1915, and subsequently transferred to 1st Batt., promoted Lieut., for some time held acting rank of Capt. Served at Home, in Flanders, and on the Italian Front. Killed in action June 28, 1918.

STEPHEN ALFRED GARD.

Admitted Aug. 1908. Member of Gard, Rook & Co., of 2 Gresham Buildings, E.C. Joined Aug. 24, 1914, as Private, Hon. Artillery Company, promoted Lance-Sergeant Sept. 1915. Served in France and Flanders. Killed in action Sept. 30, 1915. Buried at Brandhoek, near Poperinghe.

ERIC GORDON GARDINER.

Articled to E. J. Stokes, of 10 Serjeant's Inn, E.C. Joined Sept. 1914 Inns of Court O.T.C. Commissioned to the Lancashire Fusiliers March 1915, promoted Lieut. June 1915, Adjutant April 1916, Capt. Sept. 1916, Second in Command and Major 1918. Once mentioned in Dispatches. Awarded the M.C. Served in France.

EDGAR FREDERIC GARDNER.

Admitted May 1882, practising at Newport, Mon. Joined Feb. 2, 1915, as Lieut., 4th Supernumerary Coy. 1st Batt. Monmouthshire Regt., promoted

Capt. on Supernumerary Staff, Chester, and Adjutant and Supervising Officer (Acting) June 1915. Served at Home. Discharged invalided June 17, 1917.

GEORGE DUDLEY GARDNER.

Articled to G. J. E. Gardner, of Northallerton. Joined Sept. 12, 1914, as 2nd Lieut., 4th Batt. Yorkshire Regt., promoted Lieut. May 1915, transferred Royal Flying Corps July 1915, Capt. Jan. 1917, Major March 1918. Three times mentioned in Dispatches. Awarded the M.C. and Italian Silver Medal for Military Valour. Served at Home Sept. 1914 to Nov. 1915, and Dec. 1918 to April 1919, Egypt Dec. 1915 to July 1916, Macedonia July 1916 to July 1918.

GEORGE HERBERT GARDNER.

Admitted Sept. 1907. Member of Chalmers-Hunt & Gardner, of Ware. Joined Sept. 7, 1914, as Private, 2/28 Batt. County of London Regt. (Artists Rifles). Subsequently became Major.

PHILIP MURRAY GARDNER.

Admitted July 1912. Member of Loxley, Gardner & Sewell, of 1 & 2 Bucklersbury, E.C. Joined March 4, 1915, as Sub-Lieut., Royal Naval Volunteer Reserve, Paymaster Sub-Lieut. April 1916. Served in H.M.Y. *Boadicea II* in Italy.

ROBERT GARDNER.

Admitted Aug. 1904. Member of E. G. Clark & Gardner, of Lancaster. Served as 2nd Lieut., 5th Batt. Royal Lancaster Regt. Killed in action May 5, 1915.

RONALD ARTHUR GARDNER.

Articled to E. H. Clutterbuck, of Birmingham. Joined Oct. 26, 1915, as Private, Royal Army Service Corps, appointed A/Corporal Nov. 1915, but appointment cancelled May 1916 on volunteering for overseas service. Served at Home Oct. 1915 to June 1916 and July 1917 to March 1919, Salonica June 1916 to July 1917.

WILLIAM GARNER.

Admitted Oct. 1892, practising at Hounslow. Served as Lieut.-Col. commanding 8th Batt. Middlesex Regt. Twice mentioned in Dispatches. Awarded the C.M.G. Served in Gibraltar, France, and Home. Wounded 2nd Battle of Ypres May 1915. Discharged June 15, 1917.

ABRAHAM LANGHORN GARNETT.

Admitted May 1878, practising at Burnley. Joined Aug. 13, 1914, as Lieut. and Quartermaster, Royal Army Medical Corps, Capt. and Quartermaster Aug. 1917. Served at Home. Discharged owing to disability June 4, 1918.

NORTON ROCHFORT GARRARD.

Articled to T. E. Baker, of 16 Serjeant's Inn, E.C. Joined Sept. 1, 1914, as Private, Inns of Court O.T.C. Gazetted 2nd Lieut. 6th Batt. North Staffordshire Regt. Nov. 6, 1914, promoted Lieut. (Temp.) Jan. 1915, Capt. (Temp.) May 1916, Lieut. June 1916, A/Capt. June to Oct. 1917 and July to Sept. 1918. Served at Home and in France.

JOHN WHITMORE GARRATT.

Admitted Dec. 1891, practising at Cradley Heath, Staffs. Served as Lieut.-Col., 7th Batt. Worcestershire Regt. till Nov. 1914, after on T.F.R. for 18 months, and then G.S.O. for 15 months in France and Belgium. Served at Home and in France and Belgium. Wounded at Nieppe April 10, 1918.

DOUGLAS THORNBURY GARRETT.

Admitted Jan. 1909. Member of Parker, Garrett & Co., of St. Michael's Rectory, Cornhill, E.C. Joined Feb. 1917, as Lieut., Royal Naval Volunteer Reserve. Served at Home, Gibraltar, and Sierra Leone, West Africa.

NEWSON LITTLEWOOD GARRETT.

Admitted Aug. 1893. Member of Minchin, Garrett & Co. of 4 Stone Buildings, Lincoln's Inn, W.C. Joined April 1915, as Capt., King's Royal Rifle Corps, promoted Major Oct. 1915. Served at Home and in France.

DAVID LYNDSAY STRANACK GASKELL.

Articled to Thomas Mears, of Great George Street, Westminster, S.W. Joined Aug. 10, 1914, as Private, Hon. Artillery Company, and subsequently promoted Corporal. Gazetted Lieut. in Cardiff City Batt. The Welch Regt. May 20, 1915. Served in France. Fatally wounded at bomb practice Jan. 11, 1916. Died Jan. 12, 1916.

JOHN CLARE GASKELL.

Admitted Nov. 1910. Member of Gaskell & Co., of Cardiff. Mobilised Aug. 8, 1914, as Major, 2nd Welsh Brigade, Royal Field Artillery, promoted Brigade-Major 53rd Division Sept. 1915, Lieut-Colonel commanding 261st Brigade April 1917 and 262nd Brigade July 1917 to end of War. Once mentioned in Dispatches. Served at Home 1914 to 1915, France 1915 to 1916, Egypt, Palestine, and Syria 1916 to 1919.

WALLISS WILLIAM PENN GASKELL.

Admitted Nov. 1902, practised at 214 Bishopsgate, E.C. Mobilised Aug. 4, 1914, with Inns of Court O.T.C. Gazetted 2nd Lieut. 24th Batt. County of London Regt. (The Queen's) Feb. 1915. Served in France. Killed in action at La Bassée May 25–26, 1915.

ARTHUR JOHN GATELEY.

Admitted Nov. 1907. Member of Stephen Gateley & Sons, of Birmingham. Joined Dec. 4, 1914, as Lieut., King's Liverpool Regt., promoted Capt. Oct. 1915, transferred to Cheshire Regt. Jan. 1916. Served at Home Dec. 1914 to Jan. 1916 and Nov. 1916 to April 1918, Salonica Jan. to Nov. 1916, France April 1918 to March 1919.

ERIC CHASEMORE GATES.

Admitted Jan. 1914. Managing Clerk with Pontifex, Pitt & Johnson, 16 St. Andrew Street, Holborn Circus, E.C. Joined Sept. 1914, as Lieut., 13th Batt. County of London Regt. (Kensington), promoted Capt. Feb. 1915. Killed at Neuve Chapelle March 12, 1915.

KENNETH FRANCIS DRAKE GATTIE.

Articled to J. B. Watford, of Abergavenny. Served as Capt., 3rd Batt. Monmouthshire Regt., subsequently transferred to South Wales Borderers, appointed Brigade-Major April 1919. Twice mentioned in Dispatches. Awarded the D.S.O. and M.C.

ALFRED GAUKROGER.

Admitted Oct. 1906, practising at Bradford, Yorks. Joined Dec. 28, 1917, as Paymaster Sub-Lieut., Royal Naval Volunteer Reserve. Served in Bermuda, West Indies, Dec. 1917 to Dec. 1918, as Assistant to Naval Intelligence Officer. Secretary to Senior Naval Officer, Leith, Jan. to July 31, 1919.

CUTHBERT VIVIAN GAULTER.

Articled to J. R. Gaulter, of Fleetwood. Joined Sept. 1914, as 2nd Lieut., 1/5 Batt. King's Own Royal Lancaster Regt., promoted Lieut. June 1915, attached Royal Flying Corps Dec. 1916. Served in France. Killed May 17, 1917.

ARTHUR GAUNT.

Admitted May 1910. Assistant to the Solicitor, North Eastern Railway Company, York. Mobilised Aug. 1914, as 2nd Lieut., 5th Batt. (P.W.O.) West Yorkshire Regt., promoted Lieut. Sept. 1914, Capt. June 1916. Once mentioned in Dispatches. Awarded the O.B.E. (Military Division). Served in France. Wounded at Thiepval Sept. 28, 1916.

MAURICE GAUNT.

Admitted April 1902. Member of Gaunt, Foster & Co., of Bradford. Joined June 1916, as Private, Royal Army Service Corps (M.T.). Gazetted 2nd Lieut. in same Regt. July 1917. Served in Salonica and at Malta.

ROBERT ROBINS GEACH.

Admitted March 1912. Member of Burley & Geach, of Petersfield, Hants. Served as Sergeant, 2nd London Sanitary Company.

HENRY LESLIE GEARE.

Admitted May 1909. Member of Geare & Son, of 27 Chancery Lane, W.C. Mobilised Aug. 4, 1914, as Colour-Sergeant, Inns of Court O.T.C. Gazetted 2nd Lieut. Inns of Court O.T.C. Aug. 18, 1914, promoted Lieut. May 1915, Temp. Capt. July 1915, Capt. June 1916, attached to 56th Division, B.E.F., July 1916, and to The Rifle Brigade Aug. 1918, posted to 1st Batt. King's Own Yorkshire Light Infantry Nov. 1918 and to 6th Batt. Royal Inniskilling Fusiliers Dec. 1918, appointed D.A.P.M. of Sub-Area of No. 4 Area April 1919. Served at Home and in France and Belgium.

THOMAS GEE.

Articled to Gee & Edwards, of Swansea. Joined Sept. 1914, as Private, Glamorganshire Yeomanry. Gazetted 2nd Lieut. 120th Brigade Royal Field Artillery March 1915, promoted Lieut. (Temp. Capt.) 1916. Resigned owing to ill-health with rank of Temp. Lieut. 1917. Once mentioned in Dispatches. Served at Home and in France. Contracted diseased hip whilst in France. Died Nov. 13, 1917.

WILLIAM CHARLES COLEMAN GELL.

Admitted Feb. 1914. Managing Clerk with Parker, Garrett & Co., of St. Michael's Rectory, Cornhill, E.C. Embodied Aug. 4, 1914, as 2nd Lieut., Warwickshire Regt., promoted Temp. Lieut. Aug. 1914, Temp. Capt. June 1915, Substantive Capt. June 1916, Temp. Major Oct. 1916, A/Lieut.-Col.

May 1917, Temp. Lieut.-Col. Jan. 1919. Three times mentioned in Dispatches. Awarded D.S.O. and Bar, M.C., Italian Silver Medal for Valour and Brevet Majority. Served in France March 1915 to Nov. 1917, and in Italy Nov. 1917 to Feb. 1919. Wounded July 1, 1916.

CHARLES WEBSTER REDE GELL-WOOLLEY.

Admitted July 1887. Member of FitzHugh, Woolley, Baines & Woolley, of Brighton. Recommissioned as Major, Territorial Force General Reserve, Nov. 19, 1914, served with National Reserve from Nov. 1914 to Oct. 1915 when transferred to Territorial Royal Field Artillery (Home Counties Brigade). Served at Home.

FRANCIS STEWART GENTLE.

Articled to J. K. Nye & Donne, of Brighton. Served as 2nd Lieut., Sussex Yeomanry (T.), promoted Lieut. June 1916.

ARTHUR LLEWELYN GEORGE.

Articled to William George, of Llanidloes. Joined April 10, 1917, as Private, Royal Army Ordnance Corps. Died at Port Tewfik, Suez, Egypt, on June 28, 1919.

EDWARD HERBERT GEORGE.

Admitted Oct. 1904, practising at Mountain Ash. Served with the Royal Air Force at Malta.

THOMAS HENRY MARSHALL GEORGE.

Admitted July 1907, of Trowbridge, Wilts. Joined Nov. 18, 1914, as Capt., 4th Batt. The Welch Regt. Served at Home.

HENRY HAMILTON GEPP.

Admitted Jan. 1902, practising at Chelmsford. Mobilised Aug. 4, 1914, as Capt., Essex Yeomanry. Served at Home Aug. 1914 to Nov. 1916, and in France Nov. 1916 to March 1919.

DOUGLAS STUART GIBBON.

Admitted Feb. 1908. Member of Ward, Perks & Terry, of 85 Gracechurch Street, E.C. Joined O.T.C. in Jan. 1915. Subsequently became a Capt., Royal Welch Fusiliers. Awarded the M.C. Wounded outside Hohenzollern Redoubt Dec. 1915, and in Salonica March 1917.

EVAN REES GIBBON.

Articled to F. L. Cooper, of Newport, Mon. Joined Dec. 1915, as Private, South Wales Borderers. Gazetted 2nd Lieut. in same Regt. 1916, promoted Capt. 1917. Served in France.

JOHN ERRINGTON GIBBS.

Admitted April 1906. Member of John E. Gibbs & Co. of 32 King Street Cheapside, E.C. Joined Dec. 2, 1914, as Private, Hon. Artillery Company, promoted Lance-Corporal March 1915, Sergeant July 1916, Company Sergeant-Major Instructor Nov. 1917. Served in France at G.H.Q., Lewis Gun School.

ALAN GRAEME GIBSON.

Admitted April 1900. Member of Stibbard, Gibson & Co. and Thomas Cooper & Co., of 21 Leadenhall Street, E.C. Joined Jan. 2, 1915, as Lieut.,

Royal Army Service Corps (H.T.), promoted Capt. Feb. 1915, Major May 1918. Served in Salonica Oct. 1915 to Nov. 1917, and in Palestine Dec. 1917 to Nov. 1918.

BERTRAND DEES GIBSON.

Admitted Oct. 1899. Member of W. & B. D. Gibson, of Hexham. Mobilised Aug. 1914, as Major, Northumberland Fusiliers, promoted Lieut.-Col. Aug. 1915, with command of the 4th Batt. Northumberland Fusiliers (T.F.), and Substantive Lieut.-Col. March 1918. Four times mentioned in Dispatches. Awarded the D.S.O. and the Croix de Guerre with Palms (French). Served in France from April 1915 to May 1918. Killed May 27, 1918, near Craonne.

CHARLES OSBORNE PROVIS GIBSON.

Admitted Oct 1904. Member of Clayton & Gibson, of Newcastle-upon-Tyne. Joined Sept. 16, 1914, as 2nd Lieut. 1/4 Batt. Northumberland Fusiliers (T.F.), and attained rank of Capt., Staff Capt. 62nd Infantry Brigade Nov. 1915, Staff Capt. Cromarty Garrison Jan. 1919. Twice mentioned in Dispatches. Awarded M.C. Wounded in France May 27, 1918.

FRANK ARCHIBALD STANLEY GIBSON.

Articled to F. G. Allen, of Portsmouth. Joined Sept. 5, 1914, as Gunner, Hampshire Royal Garrison Artillery (T.). Subsequently became Lieut. 6th Batt. Hampshire Regt. (T.). Served in India and Mesopotamia June 1916 to March 1919.

GEOFFREY CURREY GIBSON.

Admitted Feb. 1913. Managing Clerk with Andrew, Wood, Purves & Sutton, of 8 & 9 Great James Street, Bedford Row, W.C. Commissioned Aug. 15, 1914, as 2nd Lieut., 3rd Batt. Essex Regt. (S.R.), transferred to 1st Batt. May 1915, promoted Temp. Lieut. Aug. 1915, Lieut. Sept. 1915, Capt. Sept. 1916, invalided to England Dec. 1915, employed Secretariat, Ministry of Munitions, April to June 1916, rejoined 3rd Batt. Essex Regt. June 1916, Assistant Adjutant June 1916 to Feb. 1917, rejoined 1st Batt. in France April 1917, attached Headquarters 29th Division June to Sept. 1917, invalided to England Sept. 1917, attached Headquarters Harwich Garrison Oct. to Dec. 1917, Staff Capt. 12th Cyclist Brigade, Canterbury, Oct. 1918 to March 1919. Served in Gallipoli and France. Wounded in Gallipoli June 6, 1915.

JAMES BAILY GIBSON.

Admitted Aug. 1901, practising at Beaconsfield, Bucks. Joined British Red Cross Society Oct. 1914. Gazetted 2nd Lieut. Royal Army Service Corps June 1916, and subsequently promoted Lieut. Awarded the M.B.E. Served in France and Belgium Oct. 1914 to May 1915, Salonica Aug. to Nov. 1916, Home Nov. 1916 to Feb. 1919.

NORMAN GIBSON.

Admitted Oct. 1905. Member of Goy, Cross & Co., of Barton-on-Humber, Scunthorpe, and Winterton. Joined July 10, 1915, as 2nd Lieut., 4th Batt. East Yorkshire Regt, and subsequently promoted Lieut., posted to 7th Batt. when serving in France. Served at Home July 1915 to Nov 1916, Bermuda

Nov. 1916 to May 1917, France July 1917 to March 1918. Taken prisoner near Le Sars, March 25, 1918. Repatriated Dec. 18, 1919.

REGINALD GIBSON.

Admitted Dec. 1912. Member of W. R. & R. Gibson, of Newcastle-upon Tyne. Served as 2nd Lieut., Northumbrian Divisional Royal Engineers, promoted Lieut. in June 1916. Mentioned in Dispatches.

THOMAS GEORGE GIBSON.

Admitted Jan. 1912. Of the Solicitor's Department, H.M. Customs & Excise, London, E.C. Joined Sept. 25, 1914, as 2nd Lieut., 15th Batt. West Yorkshire Regt., attained the rank of Major in Oct. 1916. Once mentioned in Dispatches. Served in Egypt Dec. 1915 to March 1916, France March 1916 to April 1919. Wounded Aug. 20, 1916.

WILLIAM REGINALD GIBSON.

Articled to J. F. Burnicle, of Sunderland. Gazetted as Sub.-Lieut., Royal Naval Volunteer Reserve Jan. 11, 1916, and appointed to H.M.S. *Victory* for Royal Naval Division, promoted Lieut. Dec. 1917 (when on Active Service appointed to the Hood Batt. of the Royal Naval Division). Awarded the M.C. and Bar. Served in France and Flanders Dec. 1916 to Jan. 1919. Gassed slightly.

RONALD GEORGE GIBSON-ROBINSON.

Articled to G. A. Baker, of Norfolk House, Laurence Pountney Hill, E.C. Joined Sept. 1916, as Private, 5th Batt. Northumberland Fusiliers, Lance-Corporal Dec. 1916. Gazetted 2nd Lieut. 8th Batt. Royal Sussex Regt. Oct. 1917, promoted Lieut. May 1919. Served in France. Wounded on the Somme Aug. 8, 1918.

CHARLES SYDNEY GIDDINS.

Admitted Dec. 1891. Member of Holder & Wood, of 6 Martin's Lane, Cannon Street, E.C. Served as Able Seaman, Royal Naval Air Service (Anti-Aircraft Corps).

JOHN GIDLEY.

Admitted Feb. 1892, practising at Chagford, Devon. Served as Capt., 11th Batt. Devonshire Regt.

LIONEL EDWIN GIFFEN.

Articled to H. C. Turner, of 80 Finsbury Pavement, E.C. Joined Sept. 20, 1914, as Private, 28th Batt. County of London Regt. (Artists Rifles). Gazetted 2nd Lieut. 25th Batt. London Regt. Aug. 8, 1915, promoted Lieut. Jan. 1916, Temp. Capt. May 1916, Lieut. March 1917, Lieut. Indian Army Reserve 1/50 Kurman Rifles Feb. 1918, Permanent Capt. Aug. 1919. Served at Home, in France 1917, India Dec. 1917 to Nov. 1919. Wounded at Arras on May 3, 1917.

BERTIE JOHN GILBERT.

Admitted June 1909, practising at Southsea. Joined Feb. 1915 as Capt., 13th Batt. Warwickshire Regt., transferred to 1st Garrison Batt. Oxford and Bucks Light Infantry and went to India in autumn 1915. Served in Mesopotamia R.A.O.C. 1918.

JOHN CLIFFORD WILSON GILBERT.

Admitted March 1903. Member of J. Wilson-Gilbert & Co., of Norwich. Served as Lieut., Home Defence Corps.

LIONEL ALFRED GILBERT.

Admitted July 1905, practising at Bognor. Served as Lieut., 4th Batt. Hampshire Regt., subsequently promoted Capt.

THOMAS NORMAN GILBERT.

Admitted Aug. 1906. Managing Clerk with Barlow, Barlow & Lyde, of 165 Fenchurch Street, E.C. Joined Nov. 4, 1915, as 2nd Air Mechanic, Royal Flying Corps. Gazetted 2nd Lieut. Royal Flying Corps Oct. 1, 1916, promoted Lieut. April 1917, Capt. Jan. 1918. Served at Home, Canada, and after Armistice in France and Germany.

OSWALD BISSILL GILES.

Admitted March 1911. Member of Millington, Simpsons & Giles, of Boston, Lincs. Mobilised Aug. 4, 1914, as Lieut., North Midland Brigade Royal Field Artillery, promoted Capt. Jan. 1915, Major 1918, commanding a 4·5 Howitzer Battery in 95th Brigade, 21st Division, from June 1918 to the Armistice. Served in France and Belgium Feb. 1915 to March 1917, invalided home March 1917 to May 1918, in France May 1918 until after the Armistice.

RUSSELL ROSS GILES.

Articled to H. R. Giles, of 3 & 4 Clement's Inn, W.C. Joined Oct. 10, 1914, as Private, 8th Batt. Essex Regt. Gazetted 2nd Lieut. 2/12 Batt. London Regt. March 15, 1915, with the 2nd London Divisional Cyclists May 1915, and with 60th Divisional Cyclist Company June 1915, promoted A/Lieut. Dec. 1915, Lieut. June 1916, with the 18th Cyclist Batt. Jan. 1917, promoted Capt. June 1917, with the Household Machine Gun Brigade Aug. 1918, and the III. Corps Cyclist Batt. as A/Major Feb. 1919. Served at Home to June 1916, thereafter France and Belgium. Slightly gassed, subsequently pneumonia.

HUMPHREY LIVINGSTON GILKS.

Admitted April 1910. Member of Moon, Gilks & Moon, of 24 Bloomsbury Square, W.C. Mobilised Aug. 1914, as 2nd Lieut., 28th Batt. County of London Regt. (Artists Rifles), promoted Lieut. Sept. 1914, Capt. June 1915, seconded as Adjutant to 1/6 Batt. City of London Regt. Feb. 1916 to Feb. 1918. Served in England with the 2nd Artists Rifles until Nov. 1918, then went to France again and served with the 1st Artists Rifles until Feb. 1919. Once mentioned in Dispatches. Awarded the M.C. Served in England Aug. to Oct. 1914 and Feb. to Nov. 1918, France Oct. 1914 to Feb. 1918 and Nov. 1918 to Feb. 1919. Wounded July 27, 1917.

BASIL EVERY GILL.

Articled to T. H. Gill, of Devonport. Joined Sept. 1914, as 2nd Lieut., 6th Batt. Duke of Cornwall's Light Infantry. Entered Sandhurst Dec. 1914, gazetted Lieut. 2nd Batt. Yorkshire Regt. May 12, 1915. Served in France. Killed in action Oct. 18, 1916.

CHARLES TREVERBYN GILL.

Articled to F. C. Maples, of 6 Frederick's Place, Old Jewry, E.C. Joined Sept. 1914 as Private, 16th (Public Schools) Batt. Middlesex Regt. Received commission in April 1915 as 2nd Lieut. Manchester Regt. Served in France. Killed July 1, 1915.

CLAUDE ARUNDEL GILL.

Articled to Alfred Appleby, of Newcastle-upon-Tyne. Served as Corporal, 24th Batt. County of London Regt.

EDWIN HENRY GILL.

Articled to H. E. Tudor, of 27 Chancery Lane, W.C. Joined Nov. 25, 1915, as Rifleman, 16th Batt. County of London Regt. (Queen's Westminster Rifles). Served at Home. Discharged June 16, 1916.

JOHN HENRY GILL.

Admitted Jan. 1896. Member of Hallett, Creery & Co., of Ashford, Kent. Joined Sept. 1, 1914, as Private, 5th Batt. East Kent Regt. (The Buffs). Commissioned Temp. Lieut. East Yorkshire Regt. Feb. 3, 1915, promoted Temp. Capt. West Yorkshire Regt. June 1915, Temp. Major Dec. 1915, A/Lieut.-Col. Labour Corps Dec. 1917, relinquished commission Sept. 13, 1918, on account of ill-health contracted on Active Service and granted Hon. rank of Major. Twice mentioned in Dispatches. Awarded D.S.O. Served in France. Wounded March 31, 1916, and Aug. 31, 1917.

ROBERT HARWAR GILL.

Admitted Feb. 1899. Sole Member of Wallace, Gill & Son, of Knaresborough, Yorks. Mobilised Aug. 1914, as Capt., 10th Batt. Duke of Wellington's Regt., promoted Major 1916. Three times mentioned in Dispatches. Awarded the D.S.O. Served in France and Belgium 1915 to 1917 and in Italy 1917 and 1918. Twice wounded Piave Oct. 27, 1918.

RICHARD FRANCIS GILLETT.

Admitted Feb. 1913. Managing Clerk with Adams & Colvile, of 5 Frederick's Place, Old Jewry, E.C. Joined May 1915, as Private (Motor Driver), Royal Army Service Corps (M.T.). Served in France. Killed in action Aug. 7, 1916.

WILLIAM ALAN GILLETT.

Admitted Nov. 1902. Member of Baileys, Shaw & Gillett, of 5 Berners Street, W. Served as Lieut.-Col., 5th Batt. East Surrey Regt. Awarded the T.D. Served in France 1916, 1918, commanded 11th Batt. Somerset Light Infantry Sept. 1918 to March 1919 in France.

HENRY THOMAS GILLING.

Admitted March 1889. Member of Gilling & Goodfellow, of Cardiff. Mobilised Aug. 5, 1914, as Lieut.-Col., in command of 2nd Welsh Brigade Royal Field Artillery, subsequently 266th Brigade, then 267th Brigade, then commanded 343rd Brigade and 68th Divisional Ammunition Column. Awarded the O.B.E. (Military). Served at Home, France (B.E.F.), Egypt (E.E.F. Western Desert and Sinai).

FRANK GILLSON.

Admitted March 1892, practising at Fareham, Hants. Mobilised Aug. 1914, as Capt., Hampshire Royal Horse Artillery, promoted Major June 1916. Once mentioned in Dispatches. Served at Home and Ireland till March 1917, and July 1917 to Feb. 1918, France and Flanders March to July 1917, and Feb. to Dec. 1918. Wounded July 8, 1917.

CHARLES WILLIAM GILMOUR.

Admitted Feb. 1913, practising at 68 Aldermanbury, E.C. Joined Sept. 2, 1914, as Private, 28th Batt. County of London Regt. (Artists Rifles), subsequently became Lieut. Machine Gun Corps. Wounded at Bullecourt (France) May 15, 1917.

DENNIS BARTON GINN.

Admitted Dec. 1905. Member of Ginn & Co., of Cambridge. Joined Sept. 8, 1914, as Trooper, Lovat Scouts. Commissioned in Suffolk Yeomanry March 3, 1915, promoted Capt. July 1916. Served in Dardanelles, Egypt, Palestine, and France.

HAROLD ERNEST GIRLING.

Admitted Jan. 1913, practising at 36 Furnival Street, Holborn, E.C. Joined Sept. 14, 1914, as Rifleman, 12th Batt. London Regt. Served in France March to May 1915. Wounded May 8, 1915. Taken prisoner at 2nd Battle of Ypres on May 8, 1915. Sent to Switzerland for internment in Aug. 1916, and repatriated in Sept. 1917. Discharged Dec. 14, 1917.

ISAAC JOSEPH GIRLING.

Admitted April 1914, practising at Newcastle-on-Tyne. Joined Sept. 7, 1914, as Private, Hon. Artillery Company. Gazetted 2nd Lieut. 2nd (Reserve) Batt. Prince of Wales's North Staffordshire Regt. Sept. 27, 1915, promoted Lieut. 9th (Service) Batt. July 1, 1917. Served in Flanders and France.

HENRY PATERSON GISBORNE.

Admitted Dec. 1912. Member of Munton, Morris & Co., of Temple Chambers, Temple Avenue, E.C. Served as Lieut., Duke of Wellington's (West Riding) Regt.

HUGH MARSHALL GISBY.

Admitted Aug. 1904. Member of Gisby & Son, of Ware, Herts. Joined April 4, 1916, as Private, Royal Army Service Corps, promoted A/Sergeant Aug. 1916, Sergeant Dec. 1917. Served in France Sept. 1916 to Jan. 1919.

HARRY NEVILLE GITTINS.

Admitted May 1913. Member of F. & H. N. Gittins, of Liverpool. Mobilised Aug. 1914, as 2nd Lieut., Lancashire and Cheshire Royal Garrison Artillery, promoted Lieut. Jan. 1915, Capt. Jan. 1917. Served at Home till Sept. 1916, and in France Sept. 1916 to March 1917. Died of pneumonia at Gezaincourt, France, March 20, 1917.

ROBERT PHILLOTT GLADSTONE.

Admitted Aug. 1901, practised at Dartford, Kent. Served as Lieut., 13th Princess Louise's Kensington Batt. London Regt., promoted Capt. June

1916, appointed Deputy Military Governor Sept. 1918. Mentioned in Dispatches.

FRANK GLANVIL GLANFIELD.

Admitted Jan. 1903. Member of Williams & Glanfield, of Lincoln. Served as Lieut., Territorial Force Reserve.

PERCY GLANFIELD.

Admitted Jan. 1907, practising at Torquay. Gazetted Lieut. Dorset National Reserve (T.F.) Jan. 1, 1915, appointed Appeal Military Representative of Worcestershire with rank of Capt. in March 1916 and held that appointment until end of War.

ARTHUR GORDON GLANVILLE.

Admitted June 1913. Member of Glanville & Glanville, of Portsmouth. Joined Oct. 21, 1914, as 2nd. Lieut., 6th Batt. Hampshire Regt. (T.F.), promoted A/Lieut. July 1915, Substantive Lieut. June 1916, A/Capt. July 1917. Served at Home.

WILLIAM BRUCE GLASSON.

Admitted June 1912. Managing Clerk with Philip Baker & Co., of Birmingham. Joined Sept. 17, 1914, as Private, 15th (Service) Batt. Royal Warwickshire Regt. Served in France Nov. 1915 to Dec. 1916. Wounded slightly July 1916; dangerously Sept. 1916, Battle of the Somme. Died as result of his wounds Feb. 24, 1919.

ARTHUR RIMINGTON GLAZEBROOK.

Articled to J. C. Atkinson, of Leeds. Mobilised Aug. 1914, as 2nd Lieut., 7th Batt. West Yorkshire Regt. (Leeds Rifles) (T.F.), promoted Lieut. Oct. 1915, Capt. June 1916. Once mentioned in Dispatches. Awarded the M.C. Served at Home and in France. Wounded Dec. 8, 1915.

JOHN JOSEPH GLEDHILL.

Admitted April 1900. Member of Eastwoods, Sutcliffes, Sager & Gledhill, of Todmorden. Mobilised Aug. 1914, as Capt., 6th Batt. Lancashire Fusiliers (T.F.), promoted Major 1915, Lieut.-Col. 1916. Once mentioned in Dispatches. Served in Egypt Sept. 1914 to April 1915, Gallipoli April to July 1915, Home 1916, Sinai and Palestine Aug. 1916 to Dec. 1916, America April to Dec. 1918. Wounded Gallipoli May 6, 1915.

GEORGE CROSFIELD GLENNY.

Admitted Nov. 1903. Of Carlisle. Served as Private, Royal Army Service Corps (M.T.).

FRANCIS GLOVER.

Admitted Nov. 1909. Member of Francis Glover & Son, of Bath. Joined July 3, 1917, as Private, Royal Army Service Corps (M.T.), promoted Lance-Corporal Dec. 1917, attached 481st Siege Battery, Royal Garrison Artillery. Served in France.

JOHN GRENSIDE GLOVER.

Articled to T. E. Catterall, of Wakefield. Joined the Yorkshire Yeomanry as a Trooper, and subsequently gazetted 2nd Lieut. King's Own Yorkshire Light Infantry. Killed in action.

WILLIAM GREY GLOVER.

Admitted Nov. 1896, practising at St. Mary's Chambers, 14 St. Mary Axe, E.C. Joined March 16, 1916, as an Ordinary Seaman in Royal Navy. Received commission as Lieut. Royal Naval Volunteer Reserve, Naval Transport Officer, 3rd Grade, June 6, 1918. Served in H.M.S. *Pembroke* March to April 1916, H.M.S. *Vanguard* April to Nov. 1916 (present at the Battle of Jutland), H.M.S. *Campania* Nov. to Dec. 1916, Admiralty (Trade Division) Jan. 1917 to Feb. 1918, Naval Transport Office Leith July 1918 to Jan. 1919.

IOAN YNYR GLYNNE.

Articled to J. Glynne Jones, of Bangor, N. Wales. Joined Nov. 1915, as Bombardier, University College of North Wales O.T.C. Gazetted Temp. 2nd Lieut. West Yorkshire Regt. Jan. 22, 1916, promoted Lieut. July 1917, Capt. April 1918. Awarded the M.C. Served at Home and in France and Italy. Wounded at Hébuterne March 1917.

ERNEST GODDARD.

Admitted Nov. 1911. Member of Peacock & Goddard, of 3 South Square, Gray's Inn, W.C. Joined Oct. 1916 as Officer Cadet. Gazetted 2nd Lieut. 1st (H.S.) Garrison Batt. East Yorkshire Regt. 1917, Staff Lieut. (Intelligence Officer) Headquarters, Eastern Command, (1917 to 1919). Awarded the M.B.E. Served at Home.

LESLIE ALLISON GODFREE.

Admitted April 1907, formerly practising at Brighton. Joined, as 2nd Lieut., Royal Field Artillery (T.F.), promoted Lieut. June 1916, A/Capt. Aug. 1917, appointed Staff Capt. R.A. Jan. 1919 (with temp. rank of Capt. in the Army). Once mentioned in Dispatches. Awarded the M.C. Served at Home Oct. 1915 to March 1917, and in France March 1917 to end of War.

CECIL ARNOLD GODFREY.

Admitted March 1906. Member of Hind & Godfrey, of Nottingham. Joined March 1916, as Private, Oxford and Bucks Light Infantry. Commissioned 2nd Lieut. Loyal North Lancashire Regt. June 1916, promoted Lieut. Feb. 1917, Capt. April 1917, appointed Staff Capt. May 1918, and promoted Major June 1919. Three times mentioned in Dispatches. Awarded the M.C., and the Belgian Chevalier de l'ordre de la Couronne and Croix de Guerre. Served in France and Belgium Aug. 1916 to Nov. 1918.

WILFRID HENRY GODFREY.

Admitted May 1904, practising at 4 & 5 West Smithfield, E.C. Joined June 21, 1916, as Sub-Lieut., Royal Naval Volunteer Reserve (Yacht Patrol), promoted Lieut. June 1917 (Auxiliary Patrol), Lieut. (in command) M.L. 227 June 1918. Served in North Sea.

STEPHEN GODLEE.

Admitted June 1911. Member of Wragge & Co., of Birmingham. Joined Oct. 28, 1914, as 2nd Lieut., Royal Garrison Artillery (T.), promoted Temp. Lieut. July 1915, Lieut. June 1916, A/Capt. Feb. to June 1917, Nov. 1917 to April 1918, Capt. Jan. 1919. Served in France. Wounded June 27, 1917, and May 3, 1918

JAMES STANLEY POOL GODSELL.

Admitted Dec. 1903. Managing Clerk with Sir Charles E. Longmore, K.C.B., of Hertford. Joined Oct. 1914 as Private, Inns of Court O.T.C. Gazetted 2nd Lieut. Gloucestershire Regt. Dec. 6, 1914, transferred to General List, Temp. Capt. whilst specially employed on Legal Duties at General Headquarters, Salonica, B.S.F., March 1917 to Nov. 1919, Staff Capt. Headquarters, Lines of Communication, British Salonica Force and British Army of the Black Sea Nov. 1918 to July 1919. Twice mentioned in Dispatches. Awarded the M.B.E. (Military Division). Served at Home till Jan. 7, 1916, Egypt Jan. to March 1916, Salonica April 1916 to June 1919.

HUGH GOFF.

Admitted April 1911. Clerk with Attwater & Liell, of 110 Bishopsgate, E.C. Joined Oct. 1, 1914, as Private, 2/1 West Kent (Queen's Own) Yeomanry, promoted Sergeant 1915, transferred to 7th Batt. Royal West Kent Regt. April 1918 with rank of Sergeant. Awarded the M.M. Served at Home and in France.

WILLIAM GOFFEY.

Admitted Oct. 1906. Managing Clerk with Hill, Dickinson & Co., of Liverpool. Gazetted March 25, 1915, 2nd Lieut. 6th (Rifle) Batt. The King's Liverpool Regt. (T.F.), subsequently promoted Lieut. (Substantive). Served in France. Wounded 3rd Battle of Ypres July 31, 1917.

CECIL ARGO GOLD.

Admitted Jan. 1913. With Chester, Broome & Griffithes, of 36 Bedford Row, W.C. Joined Nov. 24, 1914, as 2nd Lieut., Royal Berkshire Regt., promoted Lieut. and Adjutant Oct. 1915. Once mentioned in Dispatches. Served in France. Killed at Ovillers July 3, 1916.

PHILIP GOLDBERG.

Articled to H. H. Brown, of Gravesend. Joined Dec. 9, 1915, as Private, 28th Batt. County of London Regt. (Artists Rifles). Gazetted 2nd Lieut. Middlesex Regt. July 7, 1916, promoted Lieut. Jan. 1918. Served at Home and in France.

CHARLES SPENCER GOLDING.

Admitted Feb. 1905. Member of Golding, Hargrove & Golding, of 99 Cannon Street, E.C. Joined Oct. 1914, as Chief Petty Officer, Royal Naval Volunteer Reserve. Gazetted Sub-Lieut. Nov. 1914, Lieut. May 1915, transferred to Royal Garrison Artillery as Capt. June 1916, promoted Major Nov. 1917. Served at Home and in France.

GEOFFREY RAMSEY GOLDINGHAM.

Articled to F. W. Atkey, of 9A Sackville Street, W. Served as Private, 14th Batt. County of London Regt. (London Scottish). Subsequently obtained commission in the Royal Marines and attained the rank of Capt. Mentioned in Dispatches. Awarded the M.C. and Bar.

HENRY CLAUDE GOLDSMITH.

Admitted May 1911. Managing Clerk with Aldous & Gotelee, of Ipswich. Joined Sept. 3, 1914, as Private, 19th (Service) Batt. Royal Fusiliers. Gazetted

2nd Lieut. 10th Batt. Suffolk Regt. March 26, 1915, promoted A/Capt. Jan. 1918. Awarded the M.C. Served in Egypt and Palestine. Wounded at 3rd Battle of Gaza Nov. 2, 1917.

HENRY MILLS GOLDSMITH.

Admitted Jan. 1914, practised at Devonport. Served as Lieut., Devonshire Regt., attached 2nd Lincoln Brigade, Machine Gun Officer 25th Brigade. Killed in action near Fromelles May 9, 1915.

WILLIAM GOMM.

Admitted Dec. 1912. Managing Clerk with Hutchinson, Sons & Gomm, 1 Lincoln's Inn Fields, W.C. Joined July 2, 1917, as Private, 103rd Training Reserve Batt., transferred to Labour Corps on medical grounds Oct. 1917. Served in England, France, and Germany.

GEORGE PERCY GOODALL.

Admitted Feb. 1901. Member of Beaumont & Goodall, of Nottingham. Enlisted Oct. 1914 as Private in the Notts and Derby Regt. (Sherwood Foresters), and shortly afterwards gazetted Lieut. in the 10th Batt. of that Regt., promoted Capt. Dec. 1914, and went to France July 1915. Killed in action in Flanders Feb. 16, 1916.

MARCUS HERBERT GOODALL.

Articled to J. H. Cockburn, of Rotherham. Obtained his commission in the York and Lancaster Regt. Aug. 16, 1914, and went to the Front in April 1915, promoted Temp. Capt. Feb. 8, 1916. Wounded Sept. 1915. Died July 14, 1916, of wounds received in action on July 5.

TOM GOODALL.

Admitted Dec. 1909. Managing Clerk with E. B. Wilson & Topham, of Mirfield. Joined Dec. 10, 1914, as 2nd Lieut., 2/5 Batt. Duke of Wellington's West Riding Regt., promoted A/Lieut. March 1915, A/Capt. Oct. 1915, Lieut. June 1916, Capt. May 1917, A/Major Dec. 1917 to Feb. 1918. Served with 2/5 Batt. Duke of Wellington's Regt. Dec. 1914 to Feb. 1918, and with 5th Batt. Feb. to March 1918. Once mentioned in Dispatches. Awarded D.S.O. and M.C. Served in France. Wounded March 31, 1917, and March 29, 1918.

EDWARD LIONEL GOODCHILD.

Articled to his father, Herbert Goodchild, of Norwich. Joined Sept. 1914, as Private, 8th Batt. Norfolk Regt. Served in France. Badly wounded April 26, 1916, and died in Corbie Hospital April 28, 1916.

HUGH NAPIER GOODCHILD.

Admitted Oct. 1914, practising at Norwich. Served as 2nd Lieut., Royal Field Artillery.

WILLIAM WINTER GOODE.

Admitted Nov. 1893. Member of Louch, Son & Goode, of Langport and North Curry, Somerset. Joined Oct. 3, 1914, as Capt., 5th Batt. Somerset Light Infantry. Temporary Major for a short time while 2nd in Command in 1917. Served in India.

THOMAS WILLIAM WADE GOODERIDGE.

Admitted Dec. 1910. Conveyancing Solicitor to the Essex County Council, Chelmsford. Joined Sept. 1, 1914, as Private, Royal Army Medical Corps, promoted Lance-Corporal Sept. 1916. Gazetted 2nd Lieut. Royal Field Artillery Oct. 1917, promoted Lieut. April 1919. Served in France March 1915 to March 1918. Captured at Urvillers near St. Quentin March 21, 1918.

FREDERICK OWEN GOODMAN.

Admitted Dec. 1903, practising at Portsmouth. Joined Dec. 1915, as 2nd Lieut., 2/6 Batt. Hampshire Regt., and subsequently promoted Lieut. Transferred to Dorset Regt. and later to Machine Gun Corps. Served in France Dec. 1917 to July 1918.

GODFREY DAVENPORT GOODMAN.

Admitted March 1890. Member of Bennett & Co., of Buxton & Chapel-en-le-Frith. Mobilised Aug. 5, 1914, as Major, 6th Batt. Notts and Derby Regt. (Sherwood Foresters), promoted Lieut.-Col. Oct. 1914, Col. Oct. 1918, Brigadier-General, Commanding 52nd Infantry Brigade Nov. 1916 to March 1917, and the 21st Infantry Brigade March 1917 to June 1919. Five times mentioned in Dispatches. Awarded C.M.G., D.S.O., and Croix de Guerre (Belgique). Served in France and Belgium Feb. 1915 to June 1919. Wounded Sept. 2, 1918.

MONTAGUE GOODMAN.

Admitted July 1898. Member of Goodman, Saunders, Squires & Co., of 21 St. Helen's Place, E.C. Served as Lieut., Royal Army Service Corps (M.T.).

ERNEST GOODRIDGE.

Articled to E. E. Burgess, of Doncaster. Joined Nov. 1915, as Private, King's Royal Rifle Corps, and subsequently promoted Corporal. Killed in action on the Somme Oct. 4, 1916.

FREDERICK CLAUDE GOODWIN.

Admitted Dec. 1911. Practising at 32 Bedford Row, W.C. Joined May 1917, as Private, Inns of Court O.T.C. Commissioned in Territorial Force (Yeomanry) and gazetted to Scottish Horse as 2nd Lieut. March 1918, Assistant Staff Capt. Brigade Headquarters Aug. 1918. Served at Home.

HAROLD JAMES GOODWIN.

Admitted Oct 1912. Member of Ryland, Martineau & Co., of Birmingham. Enlisted as Gunner, Royal Garrison Artillery. Subsequently obtained commission as 2nd Lieut. 135th Battery Royal Garrison Artillery. Served in France. Killed in action at Arras April 24, 1917.

ALEXANDER WOOD GOOLDEN.

Articled to C. S. Raymond-Barker, of 9 New Square, Lincoln's Inn, W.C. Enlisted Aug. 1914, as Private, 28th Batt. County of London Regt. (Artists Rifles). Gazetted Temp. 2nd Lieut. 1st Batt. East Surrey Regt. May 1915, joined the Indian Army and went to Karachi July 1917, and attained rank of Temp. Capt. Served in France Oct. 1914 to Aug. 1915, South Persia March 1918 to March 1919, North-West Frontier April to July 1919.

Severely wounded in France Aug. 1915. Killed in action at Barber, near Fort Sandeman, July 15, 1919.

COLIN GRAHAM GORDON.

Articled to Graham Gordon, of 37 Golden Square, W. Served as Lance-Corporal, 14th Batt. County of London Regt. (London Scottish).

GEORGE GORDON.

Articled to J. H. Milner, of Leeds. Joined Aug. 4, 1914, as Private, Leeds University O.T.C., promoted Sergeant Feb. 1915. Commissioned 2nd Lieut. Dec. 1915. Before transfer to Reserve held Staff Appointment as Officer in charge of Courts-Martial to Headquarters West Riding Brigade. Served at Home and in France.

JAMES MILLER GORDON.

Articled to George Slade, of 90 Cannon Street, E.C. Served as 2nd Lieut., 9th Batt. Royal Scots Fusiliers.

STEPHEN JEFFERSON GORDON.

Admitted Nov. 1907. Member of Gordon, Hunter & Duncan, of Bradford. Mobilised Aug. 1914, as Lieut., 6th Batt. West Yorkshire Regt., promoted Capt. 1916. Served at Home till April 1915, then to France. Invalided June 1915, served Ministry of Munitions till May 1917, went to France June 1917, invalided Aug. 1917. Deputy Controller Ministry of Munitions Sept. 1917 to Jan. 1919.

ARTHUR HOLMES GORE.

Admitted July 1893. Member of Gore & Munro, of Bristol. Adjutant of United Arts Batt. Aug. 1914, joined 8th Batt. Hampshire Regt. as Capt., gazetted Jan. 1915. Landed at Suvla Bay Aug. 10, 1915. Killed at Anafata Aug. 12, or 13, 1915.

ARNOLD KENNETH GORNALL.

Admitted July 1911. Member of A. H. & A. K. Gornall, of Blackburn. Served as Private, Army Pay Corps.

HENRY CONRAD GORTON.

Admitted Dec. 1906, practised at St. Anne's-on-the-Sea. Served as Lieut., 14th Batt. Royal Welch Fusiliers, promoted Capt.

OSCAR GEORGE GOSDEN.

Admitted Dec. 1900, practising at 17 Clairview Road, Streatham, S.W. Joined March 31, 1916, as Private, Royal Army Ordnance Corps, transferred to Middlesex Regt. June 1916, and subsequently promoted to Sergeant 10th Batt. Served at Home to Aug. 1917, afterwards in India.

REGINALD RIDLEY LITCHFIELD GOSLING.

Articled to John Hodge, of Weston-super-Mare. Joined Nov. 14, 1916, as Aircraftsman, Royal Naval Air Service, promoted Leading Aircraftsman Aug. 1917, Petty Officer Nov. 1917, Flight-Sergeant Royal Air Force May 1918. Served at War Stations Royal Naval Air Service at Newlyn and Plymouth (seaplanes) Dec. 1916 to Sept. 1918, and at Wing Headquarters, Ireland, Sept. 1918 to Jan. 1919.

LESLIE LAWRENCE GOSNEY.

Admitted Dec. 1915. Of Croydon. Joined March 6, 1915, as 2nd Lieut., 4th Batt. The Queen's Royal West Surrey Regt., promoted Lieut. Dec. 1915, Capt. June to Aug. 1918, Staff Capt. June to Nov. 1919. Served at Home March 1915 to June 1916, India July 1916 to Nov. 1917 and Aug. 1918 to Oct. 1919, Mesopotamia Nov. 1917 to Aug. 1918, Afghan War May to Oct. 1919.

HUBERT JOHN GOSS.

Articled to H. S. K. Feltham, of Crewe. Enlisted Aug. 1914, as Private, 10th Batt. Royal Fusiliers. Gazetted Temp. 2nd Lieut. 10th Batt. Cheshire Regt. June 1916. Awarded the M.C. Served in France. Severely wounded in Battle of the Somme July 14, 1916. Presumed killed in action on or since July 15, 1916.

ROBY MYDDLETON GOTCH.

Articled to J. T. Perry, of Nottingham. Mobilised Aug. 1914, as Lieut., 7th Batt. Notts and Derby Regt. (Sherwood Foresters) (T.), promoted Temp. Capt. and Adjutant July 1915, Capt. July 1916. Once mentioned in Dispatches. Served at Home Aug. 1914 to Feb. 1915, thereafter in France and Belgium. Reported wounded and missing July 1, 1916, subsequently presumed killed.

GORDON LESLIE GOTELEE.

Articled to J. B. Hartley, of 112 Gresham House, E.C. Served with the Cyclist Corps.

ALBERT ERNEST GOTT.

Admitted April 1910. Managing Clerk with E. H. Davies & Co., of 13 Great James Street, Bedford Row, W.C. Joined July 1915, as Private, Inns of Court O.T.C. Gazetted 2nd Lieut. Royal Warwickshire Regt. Oct. 1915, proceeded to France May 1916 and attached to 10th Batt. Killed near Beaumont Hamel Nov. 18, 1916.

GUY WOLFE GOTTO.

Admitted July 1913. Member of Aylett & Gotto, of 105 Cheapside E.C. Joined Aug. 16, 1915, as 2nd Lieut., Royal Army Service Corps, promoted Lieut. June 1917, Capt. June 1918. Served in France Sept. 1915 to Feb. 1916, Palestine Feb. 1918 to Jan. 1919.

JOHN BOLLE TYNDALE GOUGH.

Admitted Nov. 1902. Member of Jessopp & Gough, of Waltham Abbey. Mobilised Aug. 1914, as Capt., 1st Batt. Hertfordshire Regt., and promoted Major June 1916. Served at Home Aug. 1914 to Feb. 1916, Mesopotamia Feb. to July 1916, Home July 1916 to Nov. 1917, France Nov. 1917 to March 1918. Killed in action between Epéhy and Villers Fancon March 22, 1918.

ALFRED KENNETH GOULD.

Articled to C. J. Haydon, of Bournemouth. Served as 2nd Lieut., Royal Sussex Regt.

HENRY CONINGSBY GOULD.

Admitted April 1906, practised at Exeter. Served as Lieut., Devon and Cornwall Brigade, Royal Army Service Corps, subsequently promoted Major.

HUGH PEARCE GOULD.

Admitted Jan. 1907. Member of Dennes, Lamb & Pearce Gould, of 22 Chancery Lane, W.C. Joined May 1916, as 2nd Lieut., Welch Guards, promoted Lieut. April 1917, attached Guards Machine Gun Regt. Served in France.

EDWARD LEO GOULDEN.

Admitted June 1914. Managing Clerk with Edward Henry Coopman, of 5 Giltspur Street, E.C. Joined Aug. 20, 1914, as Trooper, Royal East Kent Mounted Rifles. Gazetted 2nd Lieut. Royal Field Artillery (T.F.) Jan. 27, 1915, promoted Lieut. June 1915. Served in France. Wounded at Arras April 10, 1918.

ERNEST OSMUND GOULDEN.

Articled to F. W. Hardman, of Deal. Served as 2nd Lieut., Royal West Kent Regt., promoted Lieut. July 1917. Mentioned in Dispatches and awarded the M.C.

HENRY GOVER.

Admitted May 1911. Member of Henry Gover & Son, of 5 Monument Street, E.C. Joined Sept. 1915, as Private, Inns of Court O.T.C. Gazetted 2nd Lieut. Royal West Kent Regt. June 1916, promoted Lieut. Feb. 1918 (attached 1/2 Batt. London Regt.), Capt. March 1918. Once mentioned in Dispatches. Served at Home and in Belgium and France.

WILLIAM CYRIL GOVER.

Admitted Nov. 1903. Of Newcastle-on-Tyne. Joined Aug. 1914, as Private, 21st Batt. Royal Fusiliers. Gazetted 2nd Lieut. Royal Garrison Artillery (Special Reserve) Aug. 19, 1916, promoted Capt. Nov. 1916. Awarded O.B.E. (Military). Served at Home and in France.

CECIL NEWTON GRAHAM.

Admitted Jan. 1909. Member of Hodding & Co., of Worksop, Notts. Joined Nov. 4, 1914, as Petty Officer, Royal Naval Air Service, afterwards Royal Naval Armoured Car Division. Joined Royal Army Service Corps in May 1916 as Lieut. Twice mentioned in Dispatches. Awarded the M.C. Served in Gallipoli March to Oct. 1915, Egypt Oct. 1915 to Jan. 1916, France Aug. 1916 to Jan. 1919.

CHARLES RONALD GRAHAM.

Admitted Feb. 1914. Member of Lawrence, Graham & Co., of 6 New Square, Lincoln's Inn, W.C. Joined Oct. 10, 1914, as 2nd Lieut., Intelligence Corps, promoted Lieut. Oct. 1915, Capt. (General List) attached General Service Headquarters Lines of Communication Aug. 1916. Twice mentioned in Dispatches. Awarded O.B.E. (Military). Served in France.

ERNEST FREDERIC GRAHAM.

Articled to S. H. Graham, of Longton, Stoke-on-Trent. Joined Nov. 17, 1914, as Gunner, North Midland (Staffs.) Royal Garrison Artillery (T.F.). Gazetted 2nd Lieut. North Midland Brigade, Royal Field Artillery (T.F.) Sept. 15, 1915, promoted Lieut. June 1916. Awarded the M.C. Served in France March 1916 to Nov. 1917, Italy Nov. 1917 to Jan. 1919.

EVELYN RONALD BRODRICK GRAHAM.

Admitted Feb. 1909, practising at 222 Strand, W.C. Joined April 1917, as Private, Inns of Court O.T.C., promoted Lance-Corporal Sept. 1917. Commissioned 2nd Lieut. 22nd Batt. London Regt. May 1918. Served in Egypt and Palestine.

HARRIMAN GRAHAM.

Articled to Geo. Elder, of Newcastle-upon-Tyne. Joined Dec. 2, 1915, as 2nd Lieut., 3rd Batt. The Black Watch, promoted Lieut. July 1917. Served in Macedonia Feb. 1917 to July 1918, France July 1918 to April 1919. Wounded Nov. 3, 1917.

HARTLEY GRAHAM.

Admitted Dec. 1900, practising at Penrith. Joined July 23, 1917, as Private, 1st Batt. Border Regt. Gazetted 2nd Lieut. 3rd (Reserve) Garrison Batt. Royal Welch Fusiliers Oct. 16, 1917, attached 88th Labour Coy. March 1918, and to 12th Batt. North Staffordshire Regt. June 1918, A/Capt. Prisoners of War Coy. Sept. 1918. Served at Home to March 1918, and in France March 1918 to Feb. 1919.

HENRY FERGUS GRAHAM.

Articled to A. S. Legg, of 13 Bedford Row, W.C. Joined Sept. 1, 1914, as 2nd Lieut., Royal Field Artillery, promoted Lieut. Aug. 1917, A/Capt. Aug. 1918, A/Major Sept. 1918. Once mentioned in Dispatches. Served in Egypt June 1915, Serbia Sept. 1915, France May 1916 to April 1920. Twice wounded.

HENRY SALKELD GRAHAM.

Admitted Dec. 1911. Managing Clerk with Graham & Graham, of Fowey, Cornwall. Mobilised Aug. 1914, as Lieut., Cornwall (Fortress) Royal Engineers, promoted Capt. Oct. 1914. Twice mentioned in Dispatches. Served at Home Aug. 1914 to Jan. 1915, France Jan. 1915 to March 1919.

NORMAN GRAHAM.

Articled to R. J. Steele, of Carlisle. Joined Nov. 1915, as Private, Inns of Court O.T.C. Gazetted 2nd Lieut. 4th Batt. Border Regt. Sept. 1916, promoted Lieut. Feb. 1918. Served in France Oct. 1916 to Dec. 1918. Wounded at Monchy-le-Preux in the Battle of Arras May 19, 1917. Taken prisoner in the German Offensive March 21, 1918.

HUGH GRAMSHAW.

Admitted July 1909. Member of Lamport, Bassett & Hiscock, of Newport, Isle of Wight. Joined Sept. 1914 Public School Batt. Royal Fusiliers. Appointed 2nd Lieut. 3rd Batt. Staffordshire Regt. May 20, 1915. Served at Home. Died of pneumonia at Scaffold Hill Hospital Feb. 28, 1916.

HERBERT CECIL GRANT.

Admitted Nov. 1898, practising at 27 King Street, Cheapside, E.C. Served as A/Paymaster, Army Pay Department.

NORMAN STANLEY GRANT.

Articled to B. E. Poppleton, of Castleford. Mobilised Aug. 4, 1914, as Lance-Corporal, 1/5 Batt. King's Own Yorkshire Light Infantry, promoted Corporal Oct. 1914, Sergeant March 1915, Staff-Sergeant April 1915, Company

Quartermaster-Sergeant July 1917. Served in England Aug. 1914 to April 1915, France, Belgium, and with Army of Occupation Germany April 1915 to March 1919. Gassed at Nieuport July 1917.

ARTHUR GLENDOWER GRAVES.

Articled to H. G. Pritchard, of 12 New Court, W.C. Joined Sept. 1914, as Private, 28th Batt. County of London Regt. (Artists Rifles). Gazetted 2nd Lieut. Somerset Light Infantry Dec. 17, 1914, transferred to Royal Flying Corps Aug. 1916, promoted Lieut. Aug. 1917, embodied with Royal Air Force April 1918. Served in France Aug. 1917 to Feb. 1918.

ELIOTT CECIL GEORGE GRAY.

Admitted Dec. 1901. Of the Treasury Solicitor's Department, Storey's Gate, S.W. Joined Sept. 14, 1914, as Private, 16th Batt. Middlesex Regt. Gazetted Temp. Lieut. Royal Army Service Corps Feb. 5, 1915, promoted Temp. A/Capt. July 1917, Temp. Capt. and Adjutant May 1918. Once mentioned in Dispatches. Awarded the M.B.E. (Military Division). Served in France.

FRANCIS JAMES GRAY.

Admitted April 1903. Member of Frank Gray & Darby, of Oxford, served as Private, Intelligence III. Corps Headquarters, France.

GEORGE DONALD GRAY.

Admitted April 1912. Member of James Gray & Son, of Barnsley, Yorks. Joined Nov. 1914, as 2nd Lieut., King's Own Yorkshire Light Infantry, promoted Lieut. Jan. 1915, Capt. May 1917. Served in France. Died of wounds received in France May 5, 1917.

JOHN MILNER GRAY.

Articled to C. Brodrick, of 63 Queen Victoria Street, E.C. Served as 2nd Lieut., 8th Batt. Notts and Derby Regt. (Sherwood Foresters), and subsequently attained the rank of Capt.

LEONARD GRAY.

Admitted Feb. 1903, practised at Chelmsford and Ongar. Joined, as 2nd Lieut., Essex Regt. and subsequently promoted Lieut. Served in the Dardanelles. Died abroad of enteric July 31, 1917.

VIVIAN SEATON GRAY.

Articled to W. S. Gray, of Whitby. Served as 2nd Lieut., Mechanical Transport Royal Army Service Corps, and subsequently attained the rank of Major.

WILFRED RONALD GRAY.

Articled to Nelson Crowther, of 10 Lincoln's Inn Fields, W.C. Served as 2nd Lieut., East Kent Regt., promoted Lieut. Nov. 1918. Mentioned in Dispatches and awarded the M.C.

ROBERT BENJAMIN GRAYSON.

Articled to Arnold Slater, of Sheffield. Joined Dec. 18, 1914, as A.B., Royal Naval Volunteer Reserve, promoted Chief Petty Officer 1915, gazetted 2nd Lieut. Royal Garrison Artillery Sept. 1916, promoted Lieut. March 1918. Served in France and Belgium.

ALFRED ERNEST GREAVES.

Admitted April 1897, practising at Wakefield. Rejoined 1/4 Batt. King's Own Yorkshire Light Infantry Aug. 4, 1914, as 2nd Lieut., promoted Lieut. Aug. 1915. Once mentioned in Dispatches. Served in France and Belgium April 1915 to Jan. 1919.

FREDERIC GREAVES.

Articled to J. W. Greaves, of Manchester. Joined Nov. 14, 1914, as Private, 9th Batt. (Highlanders) Royal Scots, transferred to Cameronians (Scottish Rifles) Aug. 1916. Gazetted 2nd Lieut. King's Own Royal Lancaster Regt. June 6, 1917, transferred to Loyal North Lancashire Regt. Dec. 1917. Served at Home and in France. Slightly wounded south of Menin Road July 31, 1917, gassed at Givenchy April 21, 1918. Killed in action at Givenchy June 1, 1918.

THOMAS GREAVES.

Admitted Jan. 1909. With Davies, Sanders & Swanwich, of Chesterfield. Joined March 5, 1915, as 2nd Lieut., 6th Batt. Notts and Derby Regt. (Sherwood Foresters) (T.F.), promoted Lieut. Aug. 1915, gazetted Adjutant Jan. 1916, Capt. Nov. 1917. Served in France. Wounded at Gore July 1, 1918, and died of wounds the same day. Buried at Pernes British Cemetery.

GEORGE LEWIS FITZCLAIR GRECE.

Admitted Aug. 1913. Of Gresham House, Old Broad Street, E.C. Served as Corporal 1st Class A.M., Royal Air Force.

ARTHUR GREEN.

Admitted July 1909, practised at Manchester. Served as Lieut., Manchester Regt. Killed in action April 1918.

CECIL JOHN TINDELL GREEN.

Admitted Dec. 1912, practising at Sunderland. Served as Gunner, Hon. Artillery Company, and subsequently gazetted Lieut. Royal Army Service Corps.

DIGBY GREEN.

Admitted Dec. 1911. Managing Clerk with Geo. D. Day, of St. Ives, Huntingdonshire. Mobilised Aug. 4, 1914, as Private, 1/1 Hunts Cyclist Regt. (T.), transferred to Inns of Court O.T.C. Jan. 1916. Commissioned 2nd Lieut. Royal Garrison Artillery (S.R.) Nov. 2, 1916, promoted Lieut. May 1918, posted to 47th Siege Battery Dec. 1916. Awarded the M.C. Served in England Aug. 1914 to Dec. 1916, in France Dec. 1916 to Dec. 1918.

DOUGLAS GREEN.

Admitted Nov. 1901, practising at Boroughbridge, Yorks. Mobilised Aug. 1914, as 2nd Lieut., 5th Batt. West Yorkshire Regt., subsequently promoted Lieut. and Capt., appointed Staff Capt. 146th Infantry Brigade April 1917. Once mentioned in Dispatches. Awarded M.C. Served in France and Belgium April 1915 to Armistice. Wounded and gassed April 1918.

ERNEST EDWARD GREEN.

Admitted Feb. 1906. Member of Waldron, Sons & Green, of Cardiff. Mobilised Aug. 4, 1914, as Capt., 7th Batt. The Welch Regt., promoted Staff Capt. July 1915, Temp. Major Sept. 1915, Substantive Major June 1916. Twice mentioned in Dispatches. Served in France.

GEORGE MORGAN GREEN.

Articled to W. J. Lake, of 61 Carey Street, Lincoln's Inn, W.C. Joined Oct. 3, 1914, as Private, 19th Batt. Royal Fusiliers (P.S. Brigade), transferred to 23rd Batt. Royal Fusiliers (Sportsman's) 1916. Invalided Home April 1917, transferred to Labour Corps Oct. 1917. Served in France 1915, 1916, 1917. Wounded Jan. 1916.

HAROLD FRANCIS GREEN.

Admitted Dec. 1904, practising at 5 Bloomsbury Square, W.C. Joined June 1916, as Private, Grenadier Guards. Gazetted 2nd Lieut. 26th Batt. Royal Fusiliers, subsequently transferred (Sept. 1918) to Royal Air Force with rank of Capt. Served in France. Wounded and blown up on the Piavé (Montello Sector) Dec. 1917.

JOHN ALFRED HENDERSON GREEN.

Admitted April 1883, practising at Nottingham. Joined Nov. 21, 1914, as Capt., 7th (Robin Hood) Batt. Notts and Derby Regt. (Sherwood Foresters). Awarded C.B.E. Served at Home.

RALPH BARCHAM GREEN.

Articled to W. Godden, of 34 Old Jewry, E.C. Joined Sept. 15, 1914, as Private, 19th Batt. Royal Fusiliers (2nd Batt. U.P.S. Brigade). Gazetted 2nd Lieut. 9th Batt. Royal West Kent Regt. Oct. 8, 1914, transferred to Army Cyclist Corps Aug. 1915, promoted Lieut. Dec. 1915, Capt. June 1916, with No. 2 Traffic Control Coy. April 1917, Provost Reinforcement Officer April 1918, Deputy Assistant Provost-Marshal Nov. 1918. Awarded M.C. Served in France and Belgium. Wounded in Ypres Sept. 5, 1917.

RICHMOND EDWARD ORMOND LYTTLETON GREEN.

Articled to F. L. Green, of Presteign. Joined Oct. 1914 as 2nd Lieut., 6th Batt. King's Shropshire Light Infantry. Served at Home, and in Belgium and France. Killed at Ypres on Feb. 19, 1916.

STUART ANSWORTH GREEN.

Admitted April 1904. Member of Robin Hamp & Green, of 22 Southampton Street, W.C. Joined July 1916, as Private, Royal Army Service Corps. Gazetted 2nd Lieut. 1st Brigade Tank Corps, promoted Lieut. Royal Army Service Corps (Guards Div. M.T. Company). Served at Home and in France.

WALTER GREEN.

Admitted May 1903. Member of Green & Son, of Howden, Selby, and Market Weighton. Mobilised Aug. 4, 1914, as Capt., 5th Batt. East Yorks Regt., promoted Major 1916. Served at Home and in France.

WALTER HOWARD GREEN.

Admitted April 1900, practising at Birmingham. Joined Oct. 16, 1917, as Private, Royal Army Service Corps. Served at Home.

WILLIAM EDWARD GREEN.

Articled to William Simpson, of Leicester. Joined March 1916, as Rifleman, 5th City of London Batt. London Regt. (London Rifle Brigade), promoted Lance-Corporal July 1916. Gazetted 2nd Lieut. in same Batt. Jan. 25, 1917, and promoted Lieut. July 1918. Served at Home and in France and

Belgium. Wounded in Battle of Menin Road near Ypres and St. Julien Sept. 20, 1917.

EDWARD WHITAKER GREENE.

Admitted March 1904. Managing Clerk with Torr & Co., of 38 Bedford Row, W.C. Joined Sept. 29, 1914, as Private, Inns of Court O.T.C., and attained the rank of Company-Quartermaster-Sergeant. Gazetted 2nd Lieut. in same Regt. Sept. 12, 1915, promoted Lieut. June 1916, Capt. Aug. 1918, attached Hertfordshire Regt. July 1918. Served at Home, and in France Feb. to March 1918.

FRANCIS PEMBERTON GREENER.

Admitted May 1908. Managing Clerk with Corbin, Greener & Cook, of 52 Bedford Row, W.C. Joined Aug. 1914, as Lieut., 2nd Batt. East Surrey Regt. Served in France. Killed Feb. 15, 1915.

FREDERICK WILLIAM RIDGE GREENHILL.

Articled to William Sweetland, of 4 Cullum Street, Fenchurch Street, E.C. Joined 28th Batt. County of London Regt. (Artists Rifles) Nov. 1915. Gazetted 2nd Lieut. 3rd Batt. Grenadier Guards, and subsequently promoted Lieut. Killed in action in France Oct. 10, 1917.

GARNET ARTHUR CLAUDE GREENOP.

Articled to A. J. Greenop, of Bush Lane House, E.C. Enlisted Sept. 1914, as Private, 5th Batt. County of London Regt. (London Rifle Brigade). Went to France Nov. 1914. Gazetted 2nd Lieut. Royal Field Artillery Dec. 1, 1915. Killed in action July 8, 1916.

HENRY GREENWAY.

Admitted April 1882. Member of Greenway & Sons, of Newquay, Cornwall. Served as Lieut., 4th Batt. Duke of Cornwall's Light Infantry.

ARTHUR FORTESCUE GREENWOOD.

Admitted April 1902, practising at 10 New Broad Street, E.C. Served from March to Aug. 1915 as A.B., Royal Naval Volunteer Reserve Anti-aircraft Division, promoted Chief Petty Officer April 1, 1915. Served at Home: East Coast Mobile-gun Section. Discharged Aug. 12, 1915.

CHARLES GREENWOOD.

Admitted Dec. 1878. Member of Greenwood & Greenwood, of 1 Mitre Court Buildings, Temple, E.C. Mobilised Aug. 2, 1914, as Paymaster, London Division Royal Naval Volunteer Reserve, appointed Paymaster of Drake Batt. Royal Naval Division until Nov. 1914, when appointed by the Admiralty Secretary to Commodore Sir Richard Williams Bulkeley, Bart., C.B., Royal Naval Reserve, promoted Staff Paymaster Feb. 1915, and to Fleet Paymaster (Paymaster Commander) July 1918. Awarded the O.B.E. Accompanied the Troops, Royal Naval Division, on expedition towards Antwerp 1914, recalled to take up above appointment as Secretary to Commodore. Served in H.M.S. *Victory VI.*

GEORGE GREENWOOD.

Articled to B. Greenwood, of Dewsbury. Served as Capt., 4th Batt. King's Own Yorkshire Light Infantry.

HARRY RICHARD GREENWOOD.

Articled to E. E. Winterbotham, of 1 Frederick's Place, Old Jewry, E.C. Joined Sept. 8, 1917, as Air-craftsman, 2nd Class, Royal Naval Air Service, promoted Air-craftsman, 1st Class, March 8, 1918, transferred to Royal Air Force as Private, 1st Class, April 1918, promoted Corporal and remustered as Corporal Clerk June 1918, appointed A/Sergeant Clerk Sept. 1918. Served at Home.

JAMES GREENWOOD.

Articled to Stanley Gummer, of Rotherham. Joined Oct. 25, 1915, as Driver, 2/1 West Riding Royal Horse Artillery (T.). Discharged and re-enlisted in the Royal Engineers Feb. 1916. Served at Home Oct. 1915 to March 1916, and in France March 1916 to Feb. 1919. Severely gassed March 21, 1919.

JOSEPH JAMES GLEDHILL GREENWOOD.

Admitted Nov. 1913. Managing Clerk with H. Syd Powell, of Pocklington. Joined Sept. 1, 1914, as Trooper, Yorkshire Hussars (T.F.), promoted Lance-Corporal Oct. 1914. Gazetted 2nd Lieut. West Yorkshire Regt. Nov. 30, 1914, promoted Capt. Feb 1917, Adjutant May 1917 to Feb. 1918, attached 16th O.C. Batt. Sept. 1918 to Jan. 1919. Once mentioned in Dispatches. Served in France Sept. and Oct. 1915, March to July 1916, and Oct 1916 to May 1918. Wounded Sept. 26, 1915, July 14, 1916, and May 30, 1918.

RANOLF NELSON GREENWOOD.

Admitted April 1913. Member of Travers, Smith, Braithwaite & Co., of 4 Throgmorton Avenue, E.C. Commissioned as 2nd Lieut., Cheshire Regt. Special Reserve Sept. 22, 1914, joined 1st Batt. April 1915, appointed Officer Commanding Company May 1915 and Adjutant Sept. 1915, attached to Brigade Headquarters March to July 1916, rejoined Regt. acting Second in Command Oct. and Nov. 1916, appointed Staff Capt. 1st Army Headquarters Feb. 1917, appointed D.A.A.G. 16th Division April 1918, promoted Temp. Lieut. June 1915, Temp. Capt. Nov. 1915, Substantive Capt. Aug. 1916, Temp. Major April 1918. Twice mentioned in Dispatches. Awarded the M.C. Served in France April 1915 to Feb. 1919.

CHARLES LEWIS GREGORY.

Admitted April 1900. Member of Bartlett & Gregory, of 6 New Square, Lincoln's Inn, W.C. Enlisted Dec. 9, 1915, as Private, 2nd Batt. Hon. Artillery Company. Served in France, and in Italy Nov. 1917 to Dec. 1918.

FREDERIC GEORGE GREGORY.

Articled to F. W. A. Cushman, of Brighton. Joined Oct. 23, 1915, as Private, Royal Army Ordnance Corps, transferred to Lancashire Fusiliers Sept. 1917. Granted commission as 2nd Lieut. Duke of Cornwall's Light Infantry Aug. 28, 1918. Served at Home Oct. to Dec. 1915 and Dec. 1917 to Oct. 1918, and in France Jan. 1916 to Dec. 1917, and Salonica Force Oct. 1918 to April 1919.

FREDERICK CHARLES GREGORY.

Admitted May 1905. Member of Peacock, Gregory & Son, of Liverpool. Mobilised Aug. 1914, as Capt., Cheshire Regt., promoted Major Aug. 1915.

Once mentioned in Dispatches. Awarded the D.S.O. and T.D. Served in Gallipoli and France. Wounded at Suvla Bay Aug. 1915.

JAMES LANGDALE GREGORY.

Admitted Feb. 1900. Member of Howe & Gregory, of Bradford. Joined Feb. 1915, as Private, Public School Batt. Royal Fusiliers. Gazetted 2nd Lieut. Yorkshire Regt. Nov. 1916, and afterwards attached to the Royal Engineers. Served on the Western Front. Killed near Ypres May 13, 1917. Buried at Zillebeke.

JAMES WILLIAM RYE GREGORY.

Admitted June 1910. Of Liverpool. Served as Private, 829th Area Employment (Artisan) Company.

REGINALD GREGORY.

Admitted June 1912. Managing Clerk with Ralph Fream, of Gloucester. Joined Feb. 1918, as Gunner, 170th Siege Battery, Royal Garrison Artillery Subsequently 2nd Lieut. Gloucester Volunteer Regt. Served in France on Cambrai front.

IAN BORTHWICK GREIG.

Articled to T. S. Hillas-Drake, of 50 Old Broad Street, E.C. Served as 2nd Lieut., 8th Batt. Duke of Cornwall's Light Infantry, subsequently promoted Capt. Mentioned in Dispatches. Awarded the M.C.

HAROLD CUTCLIFFE GRENSIDE.

Admitted Nov. 1905. Member of Grenside & Son, of 3A Dean's Yard, Westminster. Joined May 1916, as Private, 28th Batt. County of London Regt. (Artists Rifles). Gazetted 2nd Lieut. Royal Garrison Artillery (S.R.) May 1, 1917, promoted Lieut. Nov. 1918. Served at Home and in France.

JOHN GRETTON.

Admitted March 1909, practising at Derby. Joined March 1, 1916, as Lieut., Territorial Force Reserve, promoted A/Capt. Dec. 1916, transferred to 25th Batt. The Rifle Brigade Aug. 1918, relinquished Acting Rank of Capt. Served in France.

CYRIL HOWARD GREVILLE-SMITH.

Articled to F. C. Greville-Smith, of 2 Clement's Inn, W.C. Served as Capt., 8th Batt. Middlesex Regt.

HENRY BENNETT GRIBBLE.

Admitted July 1905. Formerly Member of Gribble & Co., of 38 Bedford Row, London, W.C., afterwards practised at Victoria, and Kelowna, B.C. Enlisted as Trooper, 11th Canadian Mounted Rifles, at Vermont, B.C., April 1915. Regiment came to England March 1916. After attack of laryngitis with the Pay Office in London. Joined 1st Canadian Reserve Batt. at Seaford Aug. 1917. While there suffered from tuberculosis. Sent to a Sanatorium at Hastings for 6 months' treatment, and discharged June 1918 with both lungs seriously affected. Died Dec. 19, 1919.

HENRY JOHN CAREW GRIBBLE.

Admitted Dec. 1908, of Bristol. Served as 2nd Lieut., 6th Batt. Devonshire Regt., promoted Lieut. July 1917.

ALFRED EDWIN BARLOW GRIFFIN.

Admitted Dec. 1914, of St. Helens, Lancs. Joined Feb. 23, 1916, as Sapper, Royal Engineers, Searchlight Company. Served in Mesopotamia and India.

HENRY HALL GRIFFITH.

Articled to A. F. Griffith, of Brighton, and 37 Queen Victoria Street, E.C. Joined June 2, 1916, as Sub.-Lieut., Royal Flying Corps, and subsequently promoted Capt. Served in France. Killed in an aeroplane accident at Dartford Nov. 2, 1917.

JOSEPH GRIFFITH.

Admitted Sept. 1905, practising at Newcastle-under-Lyme. Mobilised Aug. 4, 1914, as Capt., 5th Batt. North Staffordshire Regt., promoted Major Nov. 1915. Served in France, Belgium, and Egypt. Discharged March 1918.

TREVOR LLEWELYN GRIFFITH.

Articled to James Amphlett, of Colwyn Bay. Joined July 6, 1915, as Gunner, Royal Field Artillery. Gazetted 2nd Lieut. Royal Field Artillery Jan. 30, 1917, promoted Lieut. Aug. 1917. Served in France. Killed in Ypres Oct. 30, 1917.

WALTER STANLEY CURRIE GRIFFITH.

Admitted May 1905, practised at 31 Walbrook, E.C. Joined Aug. 22, 1914, as Private, 6th Batt. Leinster Regt., promoted Sergeant Dec. 1914. Gazetted 2nd Lieut. in same Regt. April 1915. Killed Aug. 7, 1915, at Gallipoli.

FREDERICK GRIFFITHS.

Admitted June 1909, practising at Kidsgrove. Joined May 14, 1918, as 3rd Clerk, 38th Squadron, Royal Air Force, subsequently Private Royal Naval Air Service. Served at Home May to Oct. 1918, and in France and Belgium Oct. 1918 to Feb. 1919.

HENRY JOHN MARTIN SAUNDERS GRIFFITHS.

Admitted April 1909, practising at Llansamlet. Served as Lieut., 53rd Batt. Royal Fusiliers.

JOHN ERNEST GRIFFITHS.

Admitted Oct. 1911, practising at Stockport. Joined Sept. 3, 1917, as Gunner, Royal Garrison Artillery. Served in France.

JOHN HENRY GRIFFITHS.

Admitted Dec. 1905, practising at Swansea. Joined Sept. 19, 1914, as Private, Royal Army Service Corps (M.T.), promoted A/Sergeant July 1915, Sergeant Nov. 1917, A/Mechanist-Staff-Sergeant Dec. 1917. Served in Salonica.

ROBERT TREVOR GRIFFITHS.

Articled to R. T. Griffiths, of Hay, Breconshire. Joined March 14, 1915, as 2nd Lieut., 2/1 Brecknockshire Batt. South Wales Borderers (T.F.), promoted Lieut. Sept. 1915, attached to 2/7 Batt. Royal Welch Fusiliers Sept. 1915, to 23rd Batt. June 1918, and to 6th Batt. South Wales Borderers Sept. 1918. Served at Home March 1915 to Sept. 1918, and in France Sept. 1918 to April 1919.

THOMAS GRIFFITHS.

Admitted Jan. 1909, practising at 44 Bedford Row, W.C. Joined Sept. 1914, as Lieut., Royal Naval Volunteer Reserve. Served in Home Waters: North Sea and English Channel.

PERCY GRIFFITHS-AVERILL.

Admitted Jan. 1915. Member of Greville & Averill, of 135 Edgware Road W. Served with the 1st British Ambulance Unit. Awarded Croce al Merito di Guerra (Italian).

EDWARD NORMAN GRIMWADE.

Admitted Feb. 1910. Member of Farmans, of 329 High Holborn, W.C. Joined April 10, 1917, as Private, Inns of Court O.T.C., and promoted to Lance-Sergeant.

HUGH NOEL GRIMWADE.

Admitted July 1910. Managing Clerk with Foster, Calvert & Marriott, of Norwich. Joined Aug. 4, 1914, as Private, 6th Batt. Norfolk Regt. Commissioned to 12th Batt. Durham Light Infantry Feb. 23, 1915, promoted A/Capt. General List Nov. 1916, Substantive Lieut. July 1917, Substantive Capt. May 1918, Brevet Major Jan. 1919. Four times mentioned in Dispatches. Awarded D.S.O., M.C., and Croce di Guerra (Italian) and Brevet Majority. Served at Home Aug. 1914 to Aug. 1915, France Aug. 1915 to Nov. 1917, Italy Nov. 1917 to April 1919, Egypt April to Sept. 1919.

DAVID GROOM.

Admitted April 1909, practising at Newcastle-upon-Tyne. Served as Private, 2/23 Batt. London Regt.

THOMAS ALEXANDER GROSE.

Admitted April 1909, practising at 12 Bedford Row, W.C. Joined May 1916, as Gunner, Royal Garrison Artillery. Commissioned in Royal Garrison Artillery Dec. 1916, promoted Lieut. June 1918. Served at Home to Jan. 1917, France to April 1917, Salonica Aug. 1918 to March 1919. Wounded on Somme April 1917.

EDWARD GEORGE GROUND.

Admitted June 1911. Of 210 Finchley Road, N.W. Mobilised Aug. 1914, as 2nd Lieut., 11th Batt. London Regt.(Finsbury Rifles), and subsequently promoted Lieut. Served at Home and at Gallipoli. Wounded, reported missing by War Office, Aug. 15, 1915, since presumed killed in action on that day.

ALEXANDER OLIVER GEORGE MANTEL GROVE.

Admitted Nov. 1902, practising at Dudley. Served as Lieut., 7th Batt. Worcestershire Regt.

ERNEST RICHARD GROVE.

Articled to E. H. Grove, of Halesowen. Joined Jan. 20, 1917, Inns of Court O.T.C. Gazetted 2nd Lieut., 7th Batt. King's Liverpool Regt. July 1917, afterwards transferred to 12th Batt. Served in France Dec. 1917 to Feb. 1918. Killed in action near Geluvelt Feb. 10, 1918.

JOSEPH GROVES.

Admitted Feb. 1905, practised at Scarborough. Served as Capt., 6th Batt. Duke of Wellington's West Riding Regt.

LYNDHURST GEORGE GROVES.

Admitted July 1915, practising at Portsmouth. Joined June 9, 1917, as Paymaster Sub-Lieut., Royal Naval Volunteer Reserve. Served at Home and Ireland.

CHARLES GRUNDY.

Admitted Nov. 1903. Son of Albert Walker Grundy, of Manchester. Joined Sept. 1914, as Private, Princess Patricia's Canadian Light Infantry. Served in France and Belgium. Killed at Zonnebeke, near Ypres, Belgium, April 16, 1915.

GEOFFREY STEWART GRUNDY.

Admitted March 1911. Managing Clerk with Spyer & Co., of Austin Friars House, E.C. Joined Aug. 1914, as Private, Hon. Artillery Company. Served in France and Belgium. Killed in action near St. Eloi April 14, 1915.

VICTOR GRUNHUT.

Admitted Feb. 1893, practising at South Shields. Mobilised Aug. 1914, as Capt., 4th Northumbrian (Howitzer) Brigade Royal Field Artillery, promoted Major Sept. 1916 and commanded the 2nd and 3rd Line 4th Northumbrian (Howitzer) Brigade Royal Field Artillery. Placed on Territorial Reserve on Nov. 22, 1917. Served at Home.

CHARLES HENRY TRAVERS GUEST.

Articled to T. R. Dootson, of Leigh, Lancs. Joined Jan. 13, 1916, as Private, Royal Fusiliers. Served in England Jan. to July 1916 and then in France. Killed in action July 31, 1916.

LESLIE BATE GUEST.

Articled to Heywood & Ram, of 222 Strand, W.C. Joined Oct. 2, 1914, as Private, Inns of Court O.T.C. Gazetted 2nd Lieut. 1/7 Batt. Royal Warwickshire Regt. Feb. 21, 1915, promoted Lieut. July 1917, Batt. Signalling Officer, and for some time in Italy Signalling Officer to 143rd Infantry Brigade, A/Capt. several times. Once mentioned in Dispatches. Awarded Italian Bronze Medal for Valour. Served in France and Belgium Aug. 1915 to Nov. 1917, Italy Dec. 1917 to Dec. 1918.

REGINALD GUILLAUME.

Admitted Feb. 1913. Member of Guillaume & Sons, of 9 Salisbury Square, E.C. Joined May 28, 1918, as Private, Royal Army Service Corps (M.T.). Served at Home.

FRANCIS WILLIAM GULLICK.

Admitted Dec. 1903, practising at 171 Queen Victoria Street, E.C. Served as A/Paymaster, Army Pay Department.

STANLEY GUMMER.

Admitted March 1912. Member of Gichard, Gummer, & Furniss, of Rotherham. Joined Aug. 1914, as Private, 12th Batt. York and Lancaster

Regt. Gazetted 2nd Lieut. 5th Batt. York and Lancaster Regt. Dec. 1914, promoted Capt. Dec. 1915. Served in France and Belgium. Killed at Passchendaele Oct. 9, 1917.

LIONEL LESLIE GUNN.

Admitted Oct. 1913. Member of Lord & Gunn, of 64 Basinghall Street, E.C. Served as Lieut., Royal Army Service Corps.

JOHN HUGH GUNNER.

Admitted Jan. 1909. Member of Gunner & Sons, of Bishop's Waltham. Mobilised Aug. 1914, as 2nd Lieut., Hants Carabiniers (Yeomanry), promoted Capt. and Adjutant May 1915, Temp. Major Feb. 1916, reverted to Capt. 1917, attached to 15th Batt. Hampshire Regt. April 1918. Served in Flanders and France. Killed in action at Mount Kemmel Aug. 9, 1918.

HENRY SEATLE GUNSON.

Admitted April 1908, practising at Haywards Heath. Served as 2nd Lieut., 4th Batt. Royal Sussex Regt., promoted Lieut. July 1917.

CLEMENT HENDERSON GURNEY.

Admitted May 1905. Member of Devonshire, Monkland & Co., of 1 Frederick's Place, Old Jewry, E.C. Served as Lieut., 10th Batt. Norfolk Regt. Mentioned in Dispatches and awarded the D.S.O. and Bar.

FRANCIS JAMES WARD GURNEY.

Articled to Henry Chaundler, of Biggleswade, Beds. Mobilised Aug. 4, 1914, as Lance-Corporal, Bedfordshire Yeomanry, attached to Headquarters Warwickshire Infantry Brigade Aug. to Oct. 1914, with Bedfordshire Yeomanry Oct. 1914 to Jan. 1915, attached to Headquarters South Midland Infantry Brigade Jan. to May 1915. Gazetted 2nd Lieut. 5th Bedfordshire Regt. July 24, 1915, promoted Lieut. July 1917, appointed to command 162nd Light Trench Mortar Battery, with acting rank of Capt. Aug. 1918. Served in France March to May 1915, Egypt and Palestine Nov. 1915 to Feb. 1919.

KENNETH GERARD GURNEY.

Admitted Jan. 1913. Managing Clerk with Janson, Cobb & Co., of 22 College Hill, E.C. Joined May 23, 1916, as Private, 28th Batt. County of London Regt. (Artists Rifles). Received commission as 2nd Lieut. 5th Batt. Gloucestershire Regt. Dec. 19, 1916, transferred to 2/6 Batt. Feb. 1917. Served in France Feb. 1917 to Dec. 1917. Wounded near la Vacquérie Dec. 2, 1917. Found by German search party on Dec. 4 after lying out forty-eight hours, and taken to Walincourt Military Hospital. Died from effects of wound Dec. 17, 1917.

WILLIAM GUTHRIE.

Admitted Nov. 1906, practised at Newcastle-upon-Tyne. Served as 2nd Lieut., Labour Coy.

ALBERT NORMAN GUTTERIDGE.

Admitted Nov. 1909. Member of Middleton & Gutteridge, of Dunstable. Joined April 22, 1915, as 2nd Lieut., 17th Batt. County of London Regt. (T.F.), promoted Lieut. June 1917. Served in France. Wounded on Somme Oct. 1, 1916.

HENWOOD GUY.

Admitted Nov. 1912, practising at Bodmin. Joined as Private, Inns of Court O.T.C. Gazetted 2nd Lieut. No. 2 Heavy Battery Cornwall Royal Garrison Artillery (T.), promoted Lieut. June 1916.

RICHARD BERTRAM GUY.

Admitted Dec. 1908. Member of Guy & Gribble, of Cardiff and Penarth. Joined May 1917, as Assistant Paymaster, Royal Naval Volunteer Reserve. Gazetted Lieut. Royal Air Force April 1, 1918. Served in Italy and at Home.

CLAUD JAMES MATTHEW GWATKIN.

Admitted April 1913. Of Abergavenny. Served as 2nd Lieut., 3rd Batt. Monmouthshire Regt.

GERALD CROWTHER GWYNN.

Admitted Jan. 1905. Member of Gwynn, Onslow & Co., of Bristol. Joined Oct. 21, 1914, as Capt., 4th Batt. Gloucestershire Regt. Temp. Major 1915 to 1917. Later Staff Capt. XVII. Corps, B.E.F., France. Once mentioned in Dispatches. Served in France 1916 to 1919.

HUBERT LLEWELYN GWYNNE.

Articled to A. H. Shaw, of Leek. Gazetted 2nd Lieut., 11th Batt. North Staffordshire Regt, July 22, 1915. Served at Home Aug. 1915 to July 1916, and in France July to Nov. 1916. "Missing, believed killed," on the Somme Nov. 19, 1916.

NORMAN HACKER.

Admitted Nov. 1912. Member of Hacker & Michelmore, of Newton Abbot. Mobilised Aug. 1914, as Lieut., 5th Batt. Devonshire Regt. (T.) and sent to India. Volunteered for service in Mesopotamia and attached to 2nd Batt. Dorset Regt. Gazetted Capt. (Regular Army) July 1916. Served in India Oct. 1914 to Dec. 1915, Mesopotamia Dec. 1915 to Oct. 1917. Wounded in Battle of Jebel Hamriu March 25, 1917. Killed Oct. 26, 1917.

ALFRED HACKING.

Admitted Jan. 1908. Member of Chamberlayne, Hacking & Co., of 45 Parliament Street, S.W. Joined Aug. 1914, as Private, Royal Fusiliers. Gazetted Lieut. Notts and Derby Regt. (Sherwood Foresters) Sept. 1914, promoted Capt. Dec. 1915, Lieut.-Col. Aug. 1918. Three times mentioned in Dispatches. Awarded the D.S.O. and Bar and M.C. Served in France Feb. 1915 to Oct. 1918. Wounded at Ramicoort Oct. 3, 1918.

HORACE BOOTH HACKNEY.

Articled to G. L. Pedley, of Tunstall, Staffordshire. Joined Sept. 7, 1914, as Private, 5th Batt North Staffordshire Regt., promoted Corporal June 1915. Gazetted 2nd Lieut. Middlesex Regt. Sept. 15, 1915, promoted Lieut. Jan. 1917. Awarded French Croix de Guerre with Silver Star. Served at Home Sept. 1914 to April 1916, France April 1916 to Nov. 1917, Italy Nov.

1917 to Feb. 1918, France and Germany Feb. 1918 to Feb. 1919. Gassed Sept. 1918.

ALAN HACKWORTH.

Articled to F. S. Gaylor, of 4 Old Burlington Street, W. Joined Aug. 1914, as Private, Inns of Court, O.T.C. Transferred Sept. 1914 as Gunner B. Battery, Hon. Artillery Company. Gazetted 2nd Lieut. Royal Field Artillery Oct. 14, 1916, promoted Lieut. April 1918. Once mentioned in Dispatches. Served in Egypt and Aden April 1915 to May 1916, and in France Dec. 1916 to April 1919. Gassed Aug. 1918.

ALBERT VICTOR LEOPOLD HADAWAY.

Admitted Nov. 1911. Practised at North Shields. Served as Private, 2nd Sportsman's Batt. Royal Fusiliers. Subsequently gazetted 2nd Lieut. 4th Batt. Durham Light Infantry, promoted Lieut. July 1917. Also in Machine Gun Corps.

ALBERT VICTOR HADEN.

Articled to H. L. Lester, of Walsall. Joined Sept. 17, 1915, as Rifleman, in the 2/9 Batt. County of London Regiment (Queen Victoria's Rifles). Gazetted 2nd Lieut. Machine Gun Corps Dec. 29, 1916, promoted Lieut. July 1918. Served in France and Belgium. Wounded at or near Wytschaete, Belgium, July 24, 1917.

WILLIAM HELM HADFIELD.

Admitted June 1907. Member of Lake, New, & Hadfield, of Stockport. Joined March 1, 1917, as Private, Inns of Court, O.T.C. Subsequently gazetted 2nd Lieut. Gloucestershire Regt.

WILLIAM HADGKISS.

Articled to George Thomas, of Redditch. Served as 2nd Lieut., 11th (Service) Batt. Loyal North Lancashire Regt.

ARTHUR WILLIAM HADRILL.

Admitted May 1900. Member of Mackrell, Maton, Godlee & Quincey, of 21 Cannon Street, E.C. Joined Hon. Artillery Company, as Private, on outbreak of War. After a few months gazetted 2nd Lieut. Lincolnshire Regt., promoted Lieut. March 1915. Went to the Dardanelles, attached 1st Batt. Royal Munster Fusiliers July 1915. Killed in action at Suvla Bay Aug. 12, 1915.

AMYAND JAMES RIDER HAGGARD.

Articled to A. F. Francis, of 23 Lincoln's Inn Fields, W.C. Joined Aug. 7, 1914, as Private, 5th City of London Batt. London Regt. (London Rifle Brigade). Gazetted 2nd Lieut. in same Batt. Oct. 11, 1914, promoted Lieut. The Queen's Regt. Nov. 1915, G.S.O. III. Northern Command June 1917 to Feb. 1918. Served in France 1916 to 1918. Wounded July 1, 1916, and gassed Sept. 29, 1918.

BERNARD HAGGIS.

Articled to J. W. Stocker, of 150 Fenchurch Street, E.C. Joined Sept. 9, 1914, as Private, 28th Batt. County of London Regiment (Artists Rifles). Transferred to Meteorological Section, Royal Engineers, Aug. 1915, promoted

Corporal Aug. 1915 and Sergt. March 1918. Once mentioned in Dispatches. Served at Home Sept 1914 to Jan. 1915, in France Jan. 1915 to Jan. 1918, and in Italy Jan. 1918 to Jan. 1919.

CHARLES DOUGLAS HAGON.

Admitted March 1910. Managing Clerk with Hagon & Teek, of Bridgwater. Joined March 25, 1916, as Private, Somerset Light Infantry. Gazetted 2nd Lieut. in same Regt. March 1917. Served at Home and in France. Wounded in France July 1917. Died of wounds Aug. 3, 1917.

WILFRED HAGUE.

Admitted May 1913, practising at Sedbergh, Yorks. Served as Trooper, Westmorland and Cumberland Yeomanry.

JAMES JOHNSON HAIGH.

Admitted June 1912, practising at Selby. Served as Private, 1st Sportsman's Batt. Royal Fusiliers. Subsequently obtained commission in 5th Batt. York and Lancaster Regt., promoted Lieut. July 1917. Mentioned in Dispatches. Awarded the M.C. Taken prisoner Aug. 1916.

WALTER HAINSWORTH.

Admitted July 1915. Of Doncaster. Served as Lance-Corporal, 53rd (Y.S.) Batt. Yorkshire Light Infantry.

HENRY CHICHELEY HALDANE.

Admitted Dec. 1897. Member of Neish, Howell & Haldane, of 47 Watling Street, E.C. Joined Sept. 5, 1914, as Private, West Kent Yeomanry. Gazetted 2nd Lieut. Lothians and Border Horse Nov. 1914, promoted Lieut. June 1917, Capt. May 1918. Four times mentioned in Dispatches. Awarded O.B.E. (Military Division). Served in France Sept. 1915 to Feb. 1919.

GEOFFREY THOMAS HALE.

Articled to A. H. L. Knapp, of 1 King's Bench Walk, Temple, E.C. Enlisted Sept. 28, 1914, in 28th Batt. County of London Regt. (Artists Rifles). Commissioned in 7th Batt. Royal Berkshire Regt. Nov. 24, 1914, transferred to 9th Batt. July 1915, transferred to Machine Gun Corps Dec. 1915, promoted Temp. Lieut. July 1916, Capt. Dec. 1917, Major July 1918. Served with Machine Gun Corps in 38th, 16th, 19th, 61st, and 35th Divisions. Once mentioned in Dispatches. Served in France May 1916 to April 1919.

JOHN BASELEY HALES.

Admitted July 1914. Of Norwich. Served as Sergeant, Inns of Court O.T.C. Subsequently obtained commission in Oxford and Bucks Light Infantry and promoted Lieut. June 1916. Mentioned in Dispatches. Awarded the M.C.

WILLIAM CLIFFORD HALES.

Articled to A. W. Stirling, of 6 Old Jewry, E.C. Joined Aug. 31, 1914, as Private, Norfolk Regt. Gazetted 2nd Lieut. Royal Berkshire Regt. Mar. 6, 1915. Served in France. Killed in night attack Oct. 23–24, 1916, and buried on battlefield.

ALFRED HALKYARD.

Admitted Feb. 1916. Of Leicester. Joined Nov. 1915, as Private, Inns of Court O.T.C. Gazetted 2nd Lieut. Leicestershire Regt., and promoted

Lieut. March 1918. Mentioned in Dispatches. Awarded the M.C. Captured May 27, 1918. Repatriated Christmas 1918.

ALFRED EDWARD HALL.

Articled to R. A. Burrows, of 27 Chancery Lane, W.C. Served as Gunner, Hon. Artillery Company.

ARTHUR WILLIAM GANE HALL.

Articled to C. Cheesman, of Nottingham. Joined Nov. 1, 1914, as Private, Nottingham University, O.T.C., attached Notts and Derby Regt. Gazetted 2nd Lieut. North Midland Divisional Cyclist Company (T.F.) Feb. 19, 1915, promoted Temp. Lieut. Nov. 1915, transferred to VII Corps Cyclist Batt. (Army Cyclist Corps) April 1917, promoted Substantive Lieut. July 1917. Once mentioned in Dispatches. Served at Home Feb. 1915 to April 1917, France April 1917 to Jan. 1919.

CECIL WILLIAM HALL.

Articled to T. W. Hall, of 61 West Smithfield, E.C. Mobilised Aug. 4, 1914, as Lance-Corporal, 14th Batt. County of London Regt. (London Scottish). Commissioned as Temp. 2nd Lieut. Royal Army Service Corps Aug. 1915, promoted Temp. Capt. July 1916, afterwards Temp. Capt. 1st Batt. Somerset Light Infantry. Once mentioned in Dispatches. Awarded the M.C. Served at Home Aug. to Sept. 1914 and Dec. 1917 to May 1918, and in France Sept. 1914 to Dec. 1917. Wounded at the taking of the Drocourt-Queant Line, Sept. 1918.

CHARLES JOHN ERNEST HALL.

Admitted July 1898. Member of Hall & Co., of Manchester. Served with British Red Cross Society (Cheshire Branch) as Assistant County Director (Transport). Awarded O.B.E.

HARRY HALL.

Admitted April 1893, practised at Hull. Served as Major, East Riding Royal Garrison Artillery.

HENRY SIDNEY HOFMAN HALL.

Admitted May 1909, practising at Birmingham. Served as Temp. Capt., Royal Fusiliers. Mentioned in Dispatches. Awarded the D.S.O.

JAMES MALCOLM HALL.

Articled to J. N. Bailey, of 27 Chancery Lane, W.C. Served as Private, 13th Batt. County of London Regt. (T.)

JOHN HALL.

Admitted May 1882. Member of Hall & Smith, of Bury. Served from Sept. 1914 as Lieut.-Col., 5th Batt. Lancashire Fusiliers.

JOHN HALL.

Admitted Aug. 1903. Of Torquay. Served as Gunner, Royal Garrison Artillery. Died in Hospital Feb. 25, 1917.

JOHN PHILIP HALL.

Articled to J. H. Hall, of Bolton. Joined May 24, 1915, as 2nd Lieut., 2/3 Batt. East Lancashire Royal Field Artillery, promoted Lieut. June 1916. Served in France. Wounded June 1917.

LANCELOT EDEY HALL.

Admitted July 1910. Member of Thomas William Hall & Son, of 61 West Smithfield, E.C. Mobilised Aug. 4, 1914, as Sergeant in 14th Batt. County of London Regt. (London Scottish). Commissioned as Temp. Lieut. Royal Army Ordnance Department May 27, 1915, appointed A/Capt. Feb. 1918, Temp. Capt. Nov. 1918. Served at Home Aug. to Sept. 1914 and April 1915 to March 1919, and in France Sept. 1914 to April 1915.

JOHN WILLIAM HALLAM.

Admitted Feb. 1901, practising at Birmingham. Served as Private, No. 2 School of Observers, Royal Air Force.

LEONARD JAMES HALLETT.

Admitted July 1919. Managing Clerk with Trower, Still, Parkin & Keeling, of 5 New Square, Lincoln's Inn, W.C. Enlisted March 26, 1916, as Private, Royal Army Ordnance Corps, and subsequently promoted Corporal. Served at Home.

GERARD RIVERS HALLIDAY.

Articled to J. C. Warner, of Winchester. Served as 2nd Lieut., 1st Wessex Brigade Royal Field Artillery (T.).

CHARLES STUART HALLINAN.

Articled to Harry Cousins, of Cardiff. Joined Oct. 1915 Inns of Court O.T.C. (Cavalry). Gazetted 2nd Lieut. 3/2 Welsh Brigade Royal Field Artillery June 1916, transferred to the Royal Flying Corps Oct. 1916. Served at Home. Discharged July 18, 1917, after three months in hospital.

CYRIL ERNEST HALLIWELL.

Articled to John Haslam, of Bury. Joined Sept. 1915, as 2nd Lieut., 8th Batt. Bedfordshire Regt., and subsequently promoted Capt.

ROBERT HALSALL.

Admitted Nov. 1912. Member of W. and R. Hodge & Halsall, of Southport. Served as Cadet, Inns of Court O.T.C.

WALTER JOHNSTONE HALSEY.

Admitted Aug. 1899. Member of Halsey, Lightly & Hemsley, of 32 St. James's Place, S.W. Served as Capt., 4th Batt. Bedfordshire Regt.

FREDERIC WILLIAM HALTON.

Admitted Dec. 1895. Member of Halton & Hodgson, of Carlisle. Served as Capt. and Adjutant, 4th Batt. Border Regt., and attained the rank of Lieut.-Colonel.

REGINALD BARNES HAMER.

Articled to Arthur Hamer, of Bolton. Joined Sept. 7, 1914, as Private, 20th (Public Schools) Batt. Royal Fusiliers. Gazetted 2nd Lieut. Manchester Regt. Dec. 21, 1914, promoted Lieut. July 1916. Served in France, Germany, and at Home. Wounded near Trones Wood July 20, 1916, and taken prisoner at Rocquigny, near Bapaume, March 24, 1918, interned at Rostatt (Baden) and then at Graudenz, near Danzig. Returned to England Dec. 21, 1918.

SAMUEL HAMER.

Admitted Jan. 1908. Of Ashton-under-Lyne. Joined Sept. 20, 1915, as Private, Inns of Court O.T.C. Gazetted 2nd Lieut. 32nd Batt. Northumberland Fusiliers April 26, 1916. Went to France June 1916 attached to the 26th Batt. Killed at Arras April 14, 1917.

ALFRED GEORGE HAMILTON.

Articled to H. J. Hobbs, of Bristol. Served as Trooper, Royal Gloucestershire Hussars and afterwards promoted Capt., subsequently transferred to the Royal Army Service Corps as Sergeant.

GEORGE HAMILTON.

Admitted Jan. 1898. Member of Adler & Perowne, of 46 and 47 London Wall, E.C. Mobilised Aug. 6, 1914, from Reserve of Officers (Special Reserve) King Edward's Horse. Major 4th Reserve Cavalry, Tidworth, Aug. 1914 to Jan. 1915, Adjutant and Quartermaster Coast Defence No. 1 Area North March 1915 to May 1916, and to Secret Area, Suffolk, May 1916 to June 1917, Assistant Commandant Prisoners of War Camp, Handforth, July 1917 to June 1919, Commandant and promoted Lieut.-Col. June 1919 to Jan. 1920.

JOHN HAMMILL.

Admitted Aug. 1913, practising at St. Helens. Joined Sept. 18, 1914, as Lieut., 7th (Service) Batt. South Lancashire Regt., promoted Capt. Feb. 1915. Served at Home Sept. 1914 to July 1915, in France July 1915 to June 1916, in India July to Sept. 1917, and in Mesopotamia Sept. 1917 to Feb. 1919.

EDWARD WATKIN HAMMOND.

Admitted July 1913, practising at Pontypridd. Served as Trooper, Glamorganshire Yeomanry.

FREDERICK BASIL HANCOCK.

Admitted Nov. 1913, practising at Shipston-on-Stour. Joined Oct. 21, 1914, as Private, 2/9 Batt. Royal Scots. Commissioned to Kent Cyclist Batt. May 1, 1915, Station Staff-Officer, Ferozepore, India, March 1918 to Oct.1919. Served at Home, in India, Waziristan, and Afghanistan.

JOHN ARNOLD HANCOCK.

Admitted April 1910, practising at Manchester. Served as 2nd Lieut., 7th (Reserve) Batt. Cheshire Regt. (T.).

JOHN JUST HANDCOCK.

Admitted Feb. 1878. Member of Downing & Handcock, of Cardiff. Served as Col., Glamorgan Royal Garrison Artillery (T.).

HAROLD HANDLEY.

Admitted April 1914. Managing Clerk with C. G. Thomson & Wilson, of Kendal. Joined Aug. 29, 1914, as Private, 1/4 Batt. Border Regt. Gazetted 2nd Lieut. 1/5 Batt. East Surrey Regt. April 16, 1918, promoted Lieut. Sept. 1919. Served in Burma and India.

SAMUEL HANDS.

Admitted March 1908, practising at 97 Gresham Street, E.C. Served as Private, City of London Royal Army Medical Corps.

ARTHUR ANDERSON HANHART.

Admitted July 1904. Member of Hanhart & Co., of 20 Southampton Street, High Holborn, W.C. Joined Sept. 1914, as Private, Hon. Artillery Company and attained the rank of Lance-Sergeant. Commission to Royal Garrison Artillery (Special Reserve) July 7, 1916, promoted Capt. June 1918. Served in France Sept. 1916 to March 1919.

WILLIAM HANNA.

Admitted April 1905. Member of Bain & Hanna, of Sunderland. Served as Gunner, Hon. Artillery Company.

CECIL DENBIGH HANNAM.

Admitted Nov. 1910. Member of North & Sons, of Leeds. Joined Sept. 1914, as 2nd Lieut., 2/7 West Yorkshire Regt., promoted Lieut. Nov. 1914, Capt. Feb. 1915. Awarded the M.C. Served at Home and in France. Wounded May 4, 1917, at Bullecourt.

ALEXANDER ARNOLD HANNAY.

Admitted Nov. 1881, practising at 5 Albemarle Street, W. Served with French Red Cross, Chef Adjoint, Convois d'Automobiles. Given the Honorary rank of Lieut. in H.M. Forces. Awarded Croix de Guerre.

HUGH JAMES HANSCOMBE.

Admitted Sept. 1903, practising at Hitchin. Joined Sept. 29, 1914, as Private, City of London Fusiliers. Gazetted Lieut. 10th Batt. South Lancashire Regt. Nov. 30, 1914, promoted Temp. Capt. General List Oct. 1918. Served at Dardanelles and Home. Wounded at Dardanelles June 4, 1915.

HENRY HANSON.

Admitted July 1895. Member of Walker & Hanson, of Nottingham. Joined Oct. 1914, as Capt., 7th (Robin Hood) Batt. Notts and Derby Regt. (Sherwood Foresters). Served in France.

OSWALD HESKETH HANSON.

Admitted May 1898. Member of Beamish, Hanson, Airy & Co., of 60 Lincoln's Inn Fields, W.C. Mobilised Aug. 1914, as Lieut.-Commander, Royal Naval Volunteer Reserve. Served with Naval Division in Flanders 1914. Taken prisoner and shot by the Germans Oct. 11, 1914.

THOMAS REGINALD HANSON.

Articled to A. Wright, of Birmingham. Served with 1st Birmingham Batt. Royal Warwickshire Regt.

THOMAS MILNES HARBOTTLE.

Articled to R. S. Middleton, of Sunderland. Joined Aug. 28, 1914, as Private, 14th Batt. County of London Regt. (London Scottish), promoted Lance-Sergeant Dec. 1914. Gazetted 2nd Lieut. 18th Batt. Durham Light Infantry Jan. 14, 1915, promoted Lieut. July 1916, transferred Royal Engineers Oct. 1916, promoted A/Capt. Nov. 1917, Temp. Capt. Oct. 1918. Awarded the M.C. Served in Egypt, France, Belgium, and Army of Occupation. Wounded Somme July 1, 1916.

TRAVERS BIDDER HARBY.

Admitted June 1889. Member of Stilwell & Harby, of Dover. Served as Sub-Lieut., Royal Naval Volunteer Reserve.

WILLIAM WALLACE HARDEN.

Admitted Jan. 1915, practising at 49 Queen Victoria Street, E.C. Served as 2nd Lieut., 14th Reserve Battery Royal Field Artillery.

JAMES OGDEN HARDICKER.

Admitted July 1893. Member of J. Ogden Hardicker & Hanson, of Manchester. Joined Sept. 1914, as Capt., 7th Batt. Manchester Regt., and subsequently promoted to Lieut.-Col. Discharged in 1917. Died April 7, 1919, of consumption contracted in Gallipoli.

CECIL SUTTON MONTIS HARDING.

Admitted Aug. 1909. Member of Burchell, Wilde & Co., of 36 Victoria Street, S.W. Joined April 1917, as Capt. and Adjutant, General List. Served at Home.

CHARLES FRANCIS HARDING.

Admitted April 1907. Member of Elliott & Harding, of Hastings. Joined Sept. 1914, as Rifleman, 5th Batt. The Rifle Brigade. Discharged owing to ill-health, and subsequently rejoined Jan. 1, 1917, Royal Garrison Artillery and afterwards Labour Corps, attained the rank of Sergeant. Served at Home.

CLIVE SCOTLAND HARDING.

Admitted Oct. 1912, practised at Dorking, Surrey. Served as 2nd Lieut., 4th Batt. East Surrey Regt.

EDWARD SAMUEL HARDING.

Admitted Sept. 1915. Managing Clerk with Harding & Barnett, of Leicester. Joined June 12, 1916, as Ordinary Seaman, Royal Naval Volunteer Reserve. Rated Able Seaman Sept. 1916, Ordinary Telegraphist Jan. 1917, Telegraphist Sept. 1917, Leading Telegraphist Sept. 1918. Served at Home.

LAURANCE HARDING.

Admitted March 1903. Member of Harding & Harding, of 50 Lincoln's Inn Fields, W.C. Joined Aug. 14, 1916, as Private, Royal Army Service Corps (M.T.), promoted Sergeant Dec. 1916. Gazetted 2nd Lieut. Royal Army Service Corps (M.T.) June 24, 1917, promoted Lieut. Dec. 1918. Served in France.

BASIL BROCAS HARDMAN.

Articled to F. W. Hardman, of Deal. Joined Aug. 12, 1914, as Private, 4th Batt. East Kent Regt. (The Buffs). Gazetted 2nd Lieut. Indian Army Reserve of Officers July 29, 1915, and posted to Gurkha Rifles, promoted Lieut. Oct. 1916. Served at Home Aug. to Oct. 1914, India and Burma Dec. 1914 to Aug. 1916, Mesopotamia Aug. 1916 to Oct. 1918. Killed in action near Huwaish, Mesopotamia, Oct. 29, 1918.

PHILIP LEYCESTER HARDMAN.

Articled to F. W. Hardman, of Deal. Joined Aug. 13, 1914, as Private, 4th Batt. East Kent Regt. (The Buffs). Gazetted 2nd Lieut. 6th Gurkha Rifles July 29, 1915, promoted Lieut. July 1916. Served at Home Aug. to Oct.

1914, India Dec. 1914 to Aug. 1916, Mesopotamia Aug. 1916 to Sept. 1918, Salonica Oct. to Nov. 1918, and Russia Dec. 1918 to Jan. 1919.

WILLIAM HOWARD HARDMAN.

Admitted June 1914. Managing Clerk with J. H. Chadwick, of Rochdale. Joined June 28, 1915, as Private, Royal Army Service Corps. Transferred to Royal Garrison Artillery and subsequently gazetted 2nd Lieut. Served in France 1915 to 1918.

HERBERT JUNIUS ALLEN HARDWICKE.

Admitted Dec. 1903. Member of Gaby & Hardwicke, of Bexhill. Served at the School of Military Aeronautics, Royal Air Force.

ALFRED GEORGE HARDY.

Admitted April 1910, practising at 27 Chancery Lane, W.C. Joined April 28, 1917, Royal Flying Corps. Served with the Scottish Command.

HAROLD JOHN HARDY.

Admitted June 1910. Member of W. T. Hindmarsh & Hardy, of Alnwick. Served as Lieut., Royal Army Service Corps.

BERNARD URMSTON HARE.

Articled to H. D. Haslewood, of 139 Temple Chambers, E.C. Served as 2nd Lieut., 14th Batt. Middlesex Regt. Once mentioned in Dispatches. Killed in action at La Bassée Sept. 25, 1915.

EVAN AMYAS ALFRED HARE.

Admitted April 1912, practised at 139 Temple Chambers, E.C. Joined Sept. 1914 28th Batt. County of London Regt. (Artists Rifles). Subsequently gazetted 2nd Lieut. 2nd Batt. Middlesex Regt. Killed in action at Neuve Chapelle March 10, 1915.

DOUGLAS HARRY BERNARD HARFIELD.

Admtted Aug. 1914. Member of Swayne, Havers & Harfield, of Southampton. Joined April 1915, as 2nd Lieut., Hampshire Regt., transferred from 10th (Service) Batt. Hampshire Regt. from original rank to Staff Capt. Lines of Communications, Salonica, Nov. 1917, promoted to D.A.Q.M.G. (Major on General Staff) Salonica Base Jan. 1919, and to 27th Division in Transcaucasia May 1919. Twice mentioned in Dispatches. Awarded the Greek Order of Military Merit. Served at Home April to Oct. 1915, Serbia Nov. to Dec. 1915, Salonica Jan. 1916 to May 1919, Transcaucasia May to Oct. 1919.

PERCY HARFORD.

Admitted April 1910. Member of Elkin, Henriques & Harford, of 3 Salters' Hall Court, Cannon Street, E.C. Joined Oct. 1914, as Private, University of London O.T.C. Gazetted 2nd Lieut. 4th London Royal Field Artillery June 1915, promoted Lieut. June 1916, Capt. Oct. 1918. Once mentioned in Dispatches. Served in France 3 years.

WILLIAM HENRY ROBERT HARGRAUE.

Admitted Jan. 1903, practising at 24 John Street, Bedford Row, W.C. Joined Nov. 12, 1915, as 2nd Lieut., Royal Garrison Artillery, promoted Lieut. and seconded to Army Signal Service Royal Engineers. Served at Home 1915 to March 1917 and in Flanders March 1917 to Jan. 1919.

JAMES BARNARD HARGREAVE.

Admitted Jan. 1914. Member of Brooks, Monk & Hargreave, of Birmingham. Joined Aug. 24, 1914, as 2nd Lieut., 1/6 Batt. Royal Warwickshire Regt., promoted Lieut. July 1916, Capt. June 1917. Served in France. Wounded Aug. 18, 1916.

HARRY HARGREAVES.

Admitted Nov. 1912, practising at Barking. Joined Oct. 8, 1914, as Lieut., 11th (Service) Batt. Cheshire Regt., promoted Capt. Dec. 1914, Major Aug. 1915. Served in France 3 years.

ROBERT HARGREAVES.

Admitted April 1906. Member of Parker, Brailsford & Hargreaves, of Sheffield. Served as Quartermaster-Sergeant Hon. Artillery Company.

RICHARD HARLAND.

Admitted Oct. 1909, practised at Scarborough. Joined June 1917, as Private, 28th Batt. County of London Regt. (Artists Rifles). Gazetted 2nd Lieut. Royal Garrison Artillery March 1918, and posted to 254th Siege Battery. Served in France. Killed in action June 16, 1918.

PERCY HARPER.

Admitted Jan. 1902. Member of Butcher & Harper, of 32 Gresham Street, E.C. Joined June 26, 1916, as Cadet, Royal Garrison Artillery, commissioned Aug. 11, 1916, promoted Lieut. Feb. 1918. Served at Home.

ROBERT HARRADINE.

Admitted Feb. 1900, practising at Broad Street House, E.C. Served as 2nd Lieut., Royal Garrison Artillery.

HUGH VINCENT HARRAWAY.

Admitted Oct. 1906, practising at 12 South Square, Gray's Inn, W.C. Joined May 21, 1917, as Cadet, Royal Army Service Corps. Gazetted 2nd Lieut. No. 2 Water Tank Coy. July 1917, promoted Lieut. Jan. 1919. Served at Home and in France, Belgium, and Germany.

EDWARD AUGUSTINE HEWITT HARRIES.

Admitted Jan. 1904. Member of Riccard & Son, of South Molton, Devon. Joined June 1916, as 2nd Lieut., 4th Batt. The Welch Regt, promoted Lieut.

FRANK SHEARME HARRIES.

Admitted May 1911, practising at Cardiff. Served as Private, 4th Public Schools Batt. Royal Fusiliers.

IVOR HARRIES.

Admitted Feb. 1886, practising at Llanidloes, Montgomeryshire. Joined Jan. 8, 1915, as Private, 24th Batt. Royal Fusiliers, promoted Corporal Oct. 1916, transferred to 105th Training Reserve Batt. March 1917, to 5th Batt. Royal Fusiliers Dec. 1917, and to Army Pay Corps March 1918. Served at Home.

THOMAS MARCHANT HARRIES.

Admitted July 1913. Member of Marchant, Harries & Jones, of Aberdare. Joined Oct. 31, 1916, as Private, Royal Naval Air Service. Served at Home.

HANRY NAZEBY HARRINGTON.

Articled to G. A. Solly, of Birkenhead. Joined Aug. 4, 1914, as Lieut., 3rd Batt. Cheshire Regt, promoted Capt. Feb. 1915. Once mentioned in Dispatches. Served in France. Wounded and taken prisoner Oct. 13, 1914. Interned in Switzerland Nov. 1917, repatriated June 1918.

ARNOLD FRANK STAPLETON HARRIS.

Admitted Jan. 1915. Clerk with Stow, Preston & Lyttelton, of 12 Lincoln's Inn Fields, W.C. Joined Nov. 16, 1914, as Private, Inns of Court O.T.C. Commissioned in Devonshire Royal Garrison Artillery March 3, 1915, promoted Lieut. June 1916, A/Capt. Aug. 1917, A/Major Sept. 1918. Served in France.

ARTHUR ERNEST HARRIS.

Admitted June 1901. Member of Edward Gerrish, Harris & Co., of Bristol. Joined Nov. 1916, as Gunner, Royal Garrison Artillery. Served with British Salonica Force in the Balkans.

ARTHUR LEA HARRIS.

Admitted Dec. 1909. Member of Houghton, Myres & Reveley, of Preston. Joined Aug. 5, 1914, as 2nd Lieut., 4th Batt. Loyal North Lancashire Regt., promoted Capt. 1916. Served in Belgium and France 1915 and 1917. Killed in action at Ypres July 31, 1917.

DONALD FRANK HARRIS.

Articled to F. J. Harris, of Bristol. Joined Sept. 30, 1914, as 2nd Lieut., 6th Batt. Gloucestershire Regt. (T.), promoted Lieut. June 1916, Capt. Dec. 1917, attached Trench Mortar Brigade, 48th Division, B.E.F., May 1917, attached 48th Divisional Artillery Headquarters as Divisional Trench Mortar Officer Sept. 1917. Once mentioned in Dispatches. Served at Home and in France, Belgium, and Italy.

EVAN ARTHUR HARRIS.

Admitted Oct. 1912, practising at Chester. Commissioned Jan. 7, 1916, as 2nd Lieut., 2/5 Batt. Royal Welch Fusiliers, promoted Lieut. July 1917. Served at Home Jan. 1916 to Oct. 1918, and in Palestine and Egypt Oct. 1918 to March 1919.

FREDERIC VIVIAN HARRIS.

Admitted Aug. 1914. In Solicitor's Department of London County Council, 59 Strand, W.C. Joined Dec. 10, 1914, as 2nd Lieut., Royal Fusiliers, employed with 10th Batt. County of London Regt., promoted Lieut. Nov. 1916, Capt. Nov. 1917. Awarded the M.C. Served in Egypt, Palestine, and Syria. Wounded at Gaza Nov. 2, 1917.

HAROLD HENRY HARRIS.

Admitted Jan. 1899. Member of H. S. Harris & Co., of 63 Coleman Street, E.C. Served as Lieut., 3rd County of London Yeomanry (Sharpshooters).

HENRY BLACKWALL HARRIS.

Admitted Aug. 1896. Member of W. Cecil Harris, of Leicester and London. Joined Aug. 1914, as Private, Royal Fusiliers. Obtained commission as Lieut. in 11th Batt. Essex Regt. Sept. 1914, promoted Capt. Dec. 1914, Major Oct.

1915. Served in France and Flanders Aug. 1915 to June 1916. Disabled through accident. Discharged Sept. 1916.

JAMES HERBERT HARRIS.

Articled to R. J. Harris, of Winchester. Mobilised Aug. 1914, as 2nd Lieut., 4th Batt. Hampshire Regt., promoted Lieut. Sept. 1914, Capt. June 1916. Awarded the M.C. Served in India Oct. 1914 to March 1915, and in Mesopotamia March 1915 to April 1916. Taken prisoner by Turks at Fall of Kut-el-Amara April 29, 1916, escaped from Prisoners' Camp in Asia Minor Aug. 7, 1918. Trekked 350 miles to coast of Asia Minor, captured Turkish tug (motor) and crossed to Cyprus 100 miles, arrived there Sept. 13, 1918.

LAWRENCE MONTAGUE HARRIS.

Articled to J. W. Trenfield, of Chipping Sodbury, Glos. Joined Oct. 3, 1917, Royal Naval Air Service (A.C. 2), promoted Royal Navy (Writer) April 1918. Served in Eastern Mediterranean, Malta, and Italy.

MONTGOMERY READER HARRIS.

Admitted Nov. 1908. Of Hong Kong. Served as Capt., 13th Batt. County of London Regt., and promoted Major June 1916. Mentioned in Dispatches. Awarded the M.C.

NATHAN LEONARD HARRIS.

Articled to F. L. Cooper, of Newport, Mon. Joined Sept. 1914, as Private, 1st Batt. Monmouthshire Regt. Gazetted 2nd Lieut. Royal Welch Fusiliers 1915, promoted Capt. 1917. Awarded the M.C. Served in France. Wounded Somme 1916. Killed in action Aug. 1918.

PERCY GRAHAM HARRIS.

Articled to Edgar Hosking, of Liverpool. Joined at outbreak of War as Private, 6th Batt. King's Liverpool Regt. Commission 2nd Lieut. 13th Batt. King's Liverpool Regt. Jan. 1915, attached as Lieut. 2nd Nigerian Regt. W.A.F.F. Dec. 1916. Served Home from outbreak of War to Autumn 1915, and in France to Spring 1916. Wounded May 1916.

THOMAS RICHARD HARRIS.

Admitted Aug. 1905, practising at Swansea. Embodied Aug. 4, 1914, as Capt., 1st Welsh Howitzer Brigade (T.), gazetted Major April 1915. Served in France.

CHARLES EDWARD HARRISON.

Admitted July 1913. Of Liverpool. Served as Private, 3rd West Lancashire Field Ambulance, Royal Army Medical Corps (T.).

CLIFFORD HARRISON.

Admitted Feb. 1912. Member of Harrison & Sons, of Leeds. Served as A/Bombadier, 255th A.A. Section, Royal Garrison Artillery.

EDGAR YATES HARRISON.

Articled to William Harrison, of Manchester. Enlisted Sept. 26, 1914, as Private, 2/7 Batt. Manchester Regt., promoted Lance-Corporal April 1915. Gazetted 2nd Lieut. 8th Batt. Lancashire Fusiliers (T.) July 1915, promoted Lieut. July 1917. Served in France. Wounded at Havrincourt Wood June 7, 1917.

EDWARD CAYLEY HARRISON.

Admitted Oct. 1913. Member of Waterhouse & Co., of 1 New Court, Lincoln's Inn, W.C. Joined Nov. 1911, as 2nd Lieut., Royal Garrison Artillery (T.) and attained the rank of Major. Twice mentioned in Dispatches. Awarded the M.C.

ERIC VERNON HARRISON.

Articled to L. N. Holden, of Lancaster. Joined Jan. 3, 1916, as Driver, " A " Battery. Hon. Artillery Company, subsequently became Corporal Cadet.

EUSTACE JAMES HARRISON.

Admitted Jan. 1905. Member of Field, Sons & Harrison, of Liverpool. Served as Major, 6th Batt. King's Liverpool Regt. (T.), and subsequently promoted Lieut.-Col. Mentioned in Dispatches.

GEOFFREY KESTEVEN HARRISON.

Articled to T. L. Kesteven, of 6 New Square, Lincoln's Inn, W.C Joined July 26, 1912, as 2nd Lieut., 1/5 Batt. East Surrey Regt., promoted Lieut. Aug. 1914, Capt. June 1916, A/Major Oct. 1918 and attached 5th Batt. East Kent Regt. (The Buffs). Once mentioned in Dispatches. Awarded Chevalier de Legion D'Honneur (French). Served in India 1914 to 1915, Mesopotamia 1915 to 1919. Wounded slightly Dec. 19, 1916.

GEORGE ROWLAND DEVEREUX HARRISON.

Admitted Nov. 1902. Member of Harrison & Sons, of Welshpool. Mobilised Aug. 1914, as Major, Montgomeryshire Yeomanry. Served at Home and in Egypt and Palestine.

JOHN STUBBS HARRISON.

Admitted April 1908. Member of Meade, King & Co., of Bristol. Joined Oct. 20, 1914, as 2nd Lieut., 1/1 (South Midland) Royal Field Artillery, promoted Lieut. Jan. 1915, Capt. March 1915, Staff Capt. Royal Artillery Jan. 1916, Staff Capt. General Headquarters, Great Britain, Jan. 1918. Once mentioned in Dispatches. Awarded O.B.E. (Military Division). Served at Home.

LIONEL JOSEPH BRIGGS HARRISON.

Articled to W. H. Briggs, of Derby. Served as 2nd Lieut., 5th Batt. Notts. and Derby Regt. (Sherwood Foresters).

WILLIAM STANFORD-BENNETT HARRISON.

Admitted June 1913. Of Wandsworth, S.W. Mobilised Aug. 1914, as Private, 28th Batt. County of London Regt. (Artists Rifles). Gazetted 2nd Lieut. 9th Batt. Loyal North Lancashire Regt. Jan. 16, 1915. Served in France Nov. 1915 to July 1916. Killed in action at La Boisselle on the Somme July 7, 1916.

WILLIAM STANLEY HARRISON.

Articled to Henry Hughes, of 7 Arthur Street, London Bridge, E.C. Joined May 1, 1918, as Private, Inns of Court O.T.C., transferred as Gunner Royal Field Artillery July 1918. Gazetted 2nd Lieut. Royal Field Artillery (T.) April 5, 1919. Served at Home.

LENNY SEPTIMUS HARRISON.

Admitted Nov. 1908, practising at Southwold, Suffolk, as Cooper & Harrison. Joined March 1, 1915, as 2nd Lieut., 4th Batt. Lincolnshire Regt. (T.), promoted Lieut. June 1916, seconded to 17th Batt. Hampshire Regt. (T.) July 1916, A/Capt. July 1918 till April 1919. Engaged for foreign service but in consequence of injuries received on manœuvres was forced to serve at Home for whole period.

FREDERICK HARDY HARROP.

Admitted Oct. 1912, practising at Manchester. Served as Lieut., 4th Batt. Tank Corps.

CECIL EDGAR HART.

Admitted Dec. 1903, practising at Guildford and Godalming. Joined Aug. 16, 1916, as Private, Royal Army Service Corps (M.T.). Gazetted 2nd Lieut. in same regiment Feb. 1917, promoted Lieut. Aug. 1918. Served in France March 1917 to April 1919. Gassed July 31, 1917.

CECIL HENRY HART.

Articled to L. A. L. North, of 4 Stone Buildings, Lincoln's Inn, W.C. Mobilised Aug. 1914, as Private, 14th Batt. County of London Regt. (London Scottish). Served in France and Belgium. Wounded at Messines Oct. 31, 1914. Taken prisoner at Messines Nov. 11.

HENRY ROBERT HART.

Admitted Dec. 1908. Member of Burton, Yeates & Hart, of 23 Surrey Street, W.C. Joined Aug. 31, 1914, as Private, 15th Batt. London Regt. (Civil Service Rifles). Gazetted 2nd Lieut. East Kent Regt. (The Buffs) (T.) Dec. 19, 1916, promoted Lieut. June 1918. Served in France. Wounded March 1916 and March 1917.

GEOFFREY HAMILTON WILLIAM HARTCUP.

Admitted Oct. 1910. Member of Collisson, Prichard & Barnes, of 27 Bedford Row, W.C. Enlisted Inns of Court O.T.C. June 3, 1915. Gazetted 2nd Lieut. Dorset Royal Garrison Artillery Oct. 8, 1915, promoted Lieut. June 1916, A/Capt. Sept. 1916 (second in command 175th Siege Battery), A/Major Feb. 1917 (Officer Commanding 213th Siege Battery). Once mentioned in Dispatches. Awarded the M.C. Served in France Sept. 1916 to Jan. 1919.

ARTHUR GRAYSON HARTLEY.

Admitted Nov. 1907. Member of Longbourne, Stevens & Powell, of 7 Lincoln's Inn Fields, W.C. Joined Oct. 1914, as Private, 19th (Service) Batt. Royal Fusiliers (Public Schools and University Corps). Gazetted 2nd Lieut. 5th Batt. Bedfordshire Regt. March 1915, and subsequently promoted Lieut. Served in Gallipoli. Relinquished commission, on account of ill-health contracted on active service overseas, Aug. 1917.

CECIL RICHARD HARTLEY.

Admitted Feb. 1914, practised at Rochdale. Served as 2nd Lieut. Duke of Lancaster's Own Yeomanry and attained the rank of Capt. Mentioned in Dispatches.

CHRISTOPHER HARTLEY.

Admitted Oct. 1912. Member of Hartley & Pilgrim, of Colne, Lancs. Gazetted 2nd Lieut. East Lancashire Brigade Royal Field Artillery Aug. 26, 1914, promoted Lieut. Feb. 1915. Served at Home, Egypt, and France. Killed in action near Ypres Sept. 1, 1917.

WILLIAM EDWIN HARTLEY.

Admitted Jan. 1911. Clerk with Michael Abrahams & Co., of 5 Tokenhouse Yard, E.C. Mobilised Aug. 1914 with 28th Batt. County of London Regt. (Artists Rifles). Gazetted 2nd Lieut. 2nd Batt. Cheshire Regt. Aug. 1915. Served in France Oct. 1914 to Oct. 1915. Killed in action at the Hohenzollern Redoubt Oct. 1, 1915.

EDWARD LIDDELL HARTOPP.

Admitted Jan. 1904, practised at 30 Essex Street, Strand, W.C. Served as 2nd Lieut., 5th Batt. Worcestershire Regt. (Special Reserve of Officers).

GORDON GILLOTT HARTWRIGHT.

Admitted Jan. 1908. Managing Clerk with Day & Son, of 2 Millbank House, Westminster, S.W. Rejoined Aug. 11, 1914, in Royal Army Service Corps (T.) with rank 2nd Lieut., promoted Lieut. and subsequently Capt. Served in France.

CHARLES LEWIS HARVEY.

Admitted Jan. 1904. Member of H. H. Harvey & Son, of Spalding, Lincs. Joined Dec. 1914, as 2nd Lieut., 4th Batt. Lincolnshire Regt., promoted Lieut. March 1915, Capt. Aug. 1916. Served in Ireland 1916 and in France 1917. Wounded April 8, 1917. Died from wounds at 2nd London Military Hospital, Chelsea, May 10, 1917.

EDWARD WILLIAM MARSHALL HARVEY.

Articled to F. W. Thompson, of Grantham. Joined June 1917, as Private, West Yorkshire Regt. Served in France.

FREDERICK WILLIAM HARVEY.

Admitted Dec. 1912, practised at Chesterfield. Served as Lance-Corporal, 5th Batt. Gloucestershire Regt. and awarded the D.C.M. Subsequently gazetted 2nd Lieut. in same Regt.

GEORGE JORDENS HARVEY.

Articled to Robert Harvey, of Leicester. Mobilised Aug. 1914, as Lieut., Leicestershire Regt., promoted Capt. May 1915. Served at Home 1914 and in France 1915. Wounded April 13, 1915.

LESLIE HARVEY.

Admitted Jan. 1907. Managing Clerk with Soames, Edwards & Jones, of Lennox House, Norfolk Street, Strand, W.C. Joined 1914, as 2nd Lieut., 8th Batt. Middlesex Regt. Served at Gibraltar 1914 and in France 1915. Killed in action at Ypres April 27, 1915.

REGINALD FREDERICK MELVILLE HARVEY.

Admitted Oct. 1906, practised at Gloucester. Served as Private, Royal Gloucestershire Hussars. Subsequently obtained commission in Queen's

Own Worcestershire Hussars and promoted Lieut. Feb. 1918. Mentioned in Dispatches. Awarded the M.C.

SIDNEY LANCELOT HARVEY.

Admitted Oct. 1904. Member of W. E. Lawrence & Harvey, of Bristol. Served as Capt., 1st Wessex Field Coy. Royal Engineers (T.), and subsequently promoted Major. Twice mentioned in Dispatches. Awarded the M.C.

FREDERICK KEITH HARVEY-SAMUEL.

Articled to F. H. Harvey-Samuel, of 31–34 Basinghall Street, E.C. Joined Nov. 1914, as Private, Inns of Court O.T.C. Gazetted 2nd Lieut. Hertfordshire Regt. March 1915. Served at Home. Resigned Commission owing to ill-health Oct. 1915.

GERALD HARWOOD.

Articled to H. G. Harwood, of 31 Lombard Street, E.C. Enlisted Aug. 31, 1914, as Private, 1st Batt. Hon. Artillery Company. Gazetted 2nd Lieut. 3rd Batt. Suffolk Regt. Jan. 1915, promoted Lieut. Oct. 1916, ultimately joining the Royal Flying Corps in Oct. 1917. Awarded the A.F.C. Served at Home, and in Belgium, France, Mesopotamia, Egypt, and India. Killed as the result of an aeroplane accident May 1, 1919.

MAURICE WELLS HARWOOD.

Articled to J. T. Plowman, of 26 Basinghall Street, E.C. Joined Oct. 17, 1915, as Private, Inns of Court O.T.C. Gazetted 2nd Lieut. Royal Warwickshire Regt. Nov. 22, 1916, promoted Lieut. and Assistant Adjutant and Lewis Gun Officer May 1918. Once mentioned in Dispatches. Served at Home and in France, Belgium, and Italy.

ROBERT HASELDEN.

Articled to Arthur Cotterell, of Walsall. Joined Nov. 11, 1914, as Private, 5th Batt. South Staffordshire Regt. (T.). Served in France. Killed by a German sniper Sept. 1, 1915.

SIDNEY HASLETT.

Admitted March 1902. Member of Martin & Haslett, of 7 Philpot Lane, E.C. Joined Dec. 10, 1915, as Private, Inns of Court O.T.C. Gazetted 2nd Lieut. 11th Batt. London Regt. Nov. 23, 1916, promoted Lieut. May 1918. Served in France.

ROGER JOHN RODWELL HASLEWOOD.

Admitted April 1909, practising at Bridgnorth. Mobilised with Territorial Force at outbreak of War as Capt., 1/4 Batt. The King's Shropshire Light Infantry. Once mentioned in Dispatches. Awarded the M.C. Served in Burma, Straits Settlements, China, and France. Wounded at Neuve Eglise April 15, 1918.

SHEARMAN MONTAGUE HASLIP.

Articled to J. M. Haslip, of 6 Martin Lane, Cannon Street, E.C. Joined Nov. 2, 1915, as 2nd Lieut., Royal Garrison Artillery, promoted Lieut. July 1917. Served in France. Wounded during Battle of the Somme Aug. 31, 1916. Invalided Dec. 15, 1917.

RAYMOND WILLIAM HASTINGS.

Articled to L. C. Harvey, of Spalding and Holbeach. Joined Dec. 7, 1915, as Gunner, Royal Garrison Artillery, subsequently became Bombardier, A/Corporal, and Corporal, B.C.A. Appointed to a Commission Sept. 12, 1918, and posted to 183rd Siege Battery Royal Garrison Artillery. Served in Egypt and Palestine.

FRANK HATCH.

Admitted Dec. 1901. Member of James, James & Hatch, of Wrexham. Joined Dec. 1915, as Private, 21st Batt. Royal Welch Fusiliers. Gazetted 2nd Lieut. 15th Batt. Royal Welch Fusiliers Oct. 1916, promoted Lieut. April 1918. Served in France 1916 to 1918.

NORMAN CLAUD HATCH.

Admitted July 1911. Assistant Clerk to the Lancashire Insurance Committee, Preston. Joined on outbreak of the War, as Private, Yorkshire Hussars, and afterwards transferred to 10th Batt. Royal Fusiliers, subsequently gazetted 2nd Lieut. 3rd Batt. South Lancashire Regt., attached 2nd Batt. Served in France. Killed on the Somme Oct. 21, 1916.

LAWRENCE VICTOR HATFIELD.

Admitted Jan. 1909, practising at Shipley, Yorks. Joined Nov. 2, 1916, as Private, West Yorkshire Regt., transferred to Army Pay Corps Jan. 1917, promoted Corporal May 1918, subsequently transferred to Special Audit Staff. Served at Home.

ROY BERRIMAN HATFIELD.

Admitted Jan. 1912. On outbreak of War was holding the appointment of A.D.C. and Private Secretary to Sir John May, then Governor of Hong Kong, with the local rank of Capt., and at once rejoined the 8th (City of London) Batt. London Regt. (Post Office Rifles) in which he obtained a commission in 1912. Served in France. Mortally wounded at Festubert May 24, 1915. Died the same day at Bethune Hospital and buried in Bethune Cemetery.

GEORGE HATT-COOK.

Admitted April 1909, practised at Northwich. Served as Capt., 5th (Reserve) Batt. Cheshire Regt. (T.), and promoted Major June 1916.

GEOFFREY HATTEN.

Admitted Oct. 1908. Member of Hatten, Winnett & Hatten, of Gravesend. Joined Oct. 1916, as Private, 16th Batt. Essex Regt., transferred to 681st Agricultural Company Dec. 1917, and to 524th H.S. Employment Company Aug. 1918. Served at Home.

ALAN HERBERT HATTON.

Articled to Herbert Hatton, of Warrington. Joined Aug. 26, 1914, as 2nd Lieut., 4th Batt. (P.W.V.) South Lancashire Regt., subsequently promoted Lieut. Served in France and Belgium Feb. to April 1915. Wounded at St. Eloi, near Ypres, April 22, 1915. Discharged for wounds Nov. 5, 1916.

GEORGE ARTHUR LYON HATTON.

Articled to John Venning, of 5 Gray's Inn Square. Joined Sept. 30, 1914, as Temp. Lieut., 6th (Service) Batt. The Queen's Own Royal West Kent

Regt., promoted Temp. Lieut. Dec. 1914, Temp. Capt. Nov. 1915. Served in France and Belgium June 1915 to July 1916. Wounded and taken prisoner at Ovillers July 3, 1916. Repatriated Nov. 18, 1918.

JOHN ALEXANDER HATTRELL.

Articled to C. J. Band, of Coventry. Joined Aug. 1914, as Private, 1/7 Batt. Royal Warwickshire Regt. Gazetted 2nd Lieut. in same Regt. Aug. 1915, promoted Lieut. June 1917, Capt. July 1917 (General List). Served in France.

JOHN ARNOLD HAUGHTON.

Admitted Jan. 1910. Member of Haughton & Haughton, of Bolton. Served as Gunner, No. 7 (Hants) Fire Command, Royal Garrison Artillery.

ARTHUR CLAUDE HAVERS.

Admitted Jan. 1897. Of Mayfield, Sussex. Served as Lance-Corporal, 32nd Batt. Middlesex Regt.

CECIL ROBERT HAVERS.

Admitted Oct. 1914, practising at Norwich. Joined Aug. 1914, as Private, Public Schools Brigade. Gazetted 2nd Lieut. 5th Hampshire Regt. (T.) Dec. 27, 1914, promoted Temp. Lieut. June 1915, Temp. Capt. July 1916, Temp. Lieut. Machine Gun Corps Aug. 1916, A/Capt. Tank Corps May 1917, Temp. Capt. Tank Corps Oct. 1918. Once mentioned in Dispatches Served at Home Aug. 1914 to April 1917 and May to June 1917, and in France April to May 1917 and June 1917 to Jan. 1919. Wounded at Ypres Oct. 1, 1917.

CECIL HAWARD.

Articled to T. H. Wrensted, of 63 Queen Victoria Street, E.C. Joined Inns of Court O.T.C. in Aug. 1914, obtained commission in Middlesex Regt. Oct. 1914 and rose to rank of Capt. in same Regt. Demobilised March 1919. Served in France and Salonica. Wounded and taken prisoner Aug. 1918.

HENRY FRANCIS HAWES.

Articled to J. A. Hammett, of 36 Theobald's Road, W.C. Served as 2nd Lieut., 5th Batt. West Kent Regt., promoted Lieut. June 1916.

HERBERT JOHN HAMBLY HAWKEN.

Admitted July 1910, practising at Plymouth. Joined July 8, 1916, as Gunner, Royal Garrison Artillery, appointed A/Bombardier Oct. 1916, promoted Bombardier Feb. 1918. Served at Home.

REGINALD HAWKEN.

Admitted Sept. 1907, practising at Plymouth. Joined May 16, 1916, as Private, 2/5 Batt. The Queen's Own Royal West Kent Regt., promoted Lance-Corporal Jan. 1917, transferred to 6th Batt. Sept. 1917. Served at Home May 1916 to Sept. 1917 and from latter date in France.

FRANCIS SAMUEL HAWKES.

Admitted April 1893, practised at Bristol. Served as Lieut., 11th Batt. Devonshire Regt., promoted Capt. Aug. 1916.

ALAN GEORGE HAWKINS.

Admitted Jan. 1905, practising at Colchester. Joined June 1915, as 2nd Lieut. 2/7 Batt. Worcestershire Regt. Served at Home. Discharged on account of ill-health Oct. 1916.

CHARLES NEWCOMBE HAWKINS.

Admitted Oct. 1910. Managing Clerk with Freshfields, of 31 Old Jewry, E.C. Joined Oct. 16, 1916, as Private, 28th Batt. County of London Regt. (Artists Rifles). Granted commission as 2nd Lieut. June 17, 1917, and posted to Labour Corps, posted to 431st Agricultural Company Labour Corps Dec. 1917, promoted Lieut. Dec. 1918, A/Capt. and O.C. 431st Agricultural Company Feb. 1919, and became A/Commandant Agricultural Distribution Centre, Bury St. Edmunds, March 1919. Served at Home.

HORATIO HAWKINS.

Admitted Feb. 1884, practising at 37 Essex Street, W.C., and Manchester. Rejoined Nov. 20, 1914, as Major and Hon. Lieut.-Col., subsequently Lieut.-Col. and Honorary Col., commanded 3/7 Batt. Manchester Regt. and 6th (Reserve) Batt. Lancashire Fusiliers July 1915 to March 1918. Served at Home.

GORDON HAWLEY.

Admitted Nov. 1907. Member of S. Pearman Smith & Sons, of Walsall. Joined July 17, 1916, as Private, Royal Army Service Corps. Gazetted 2nd Lieut. in same Regt. Oct. 1916 and attached 175th Siege Battery Royal Garrison Artillery, promoted Lieut. April 1918. Served in France Oct. 1916 to March 1919.

HAROLD STONES HAWORTH.

Admitted Aug. 1902. Member of E. & B. Haworth, of Blackburn. Joined Dec. 5, 1915, as Private, 2/15 Batt. London Regt. (Civil Service Rifles), transferred to Royal Air Force as an Air Mechanic May 1918. Served in France June to Nov. 1916, Salonica Dec. 1916 to July 1917, Palestine July 1917 to Feb. 1918.

LEONARD HAWORTH.

Articled to Harold Fairbrother, of Bolton, Lancashire. Joined Sept. 1915, as Private, 28th Batt. County of London Regt. (Artists Rifles). Commissioned as 2nd Lieut. 1/5 Batt. Loyal North Lancashire Regt. May 1916, promoted Lieut. and held Acting rank of Capt. Served in France and Belgium. Wounded Aug. 1, 1917, and gassed on Somme.

PERCY GEOFFREY DU VAL HAWORTH.

Articled to G. P. Haworth, of Manchester. Joined Sept. 7, 1914, as Private, Public School Batt. Royal Fusiliers. Gazetted 2nd Lieut. 18th Batt. Manchester Regt. Jan. 1915, promoted Lieut. Aug. 1915. Served at Home until Nov. 1915, and in France Nov. 1915 to July 1916. Killed on the Somme July 30, 1916.

HERBERT KEEBLE HAWSON.

Articled to H. W. Jackson, of Sheffield. Joined Aug. 15, 1915, as 2nd Lieut., 3/4 Batt. East Lancashire (Howitzer) Brigade Royal Field Artillery, promoted Lieut. July 1917. Served in France and Belgium May 1916 to Dec. 1918.

FRANK FREDERICK FLINT HAWTHORN.

Admitted April 1913. Member of F. S. Hawthorn & Son, of Uttoxeter. Served as Private, Inns of Court O.T.C. Gazetted 2nd Lieut. Reserve Regt. of Cavalry March 13, 1919.

JACK VALENTINE HAY.

Articled to R. W. Emmet, of 14 Bloomsbury Square, W.C. Joined Aug. 5, 1914, as 2nd Lieut., Intelligence Corps, transferred to Royal Flying Corps Feb. 1917, and to Royal Air Force April 1918. Employed Contre-Espionnage, Intelligence Corps, attached Royal Engineers Nov. 1914 to May 1915 and to Inniskilling Dragoons, Sept. to Nov. 1916. Promoted Lieut. April 1915, Capt. Sept. 1918. Awarded Légion d'Honneur. Served in France and Belgium.

JAMES FREDERICK HAY.

Admitted Dec. 1907. Member of Metcalfe, Sharpe & Hay, of 40 Chancery Lane, W.C. Mobilised Aug. 1914 with the 14th Batt. County of London Regt. (London Scottish) and attained the rank of Capt. Served in France and at Home.

ROBERT ALEXANDER HAYDON.

Admitted Oct. 1908. Member of Rollit, Sons & Compston, of 3 Mincing Lane, E.C. Joined Nov. 1916, as Private, 28th Batt. County of London Regt. (Artists Rifles). Gazetted 2nd Lieut. Royal Garrison Artillery July 1917, promoted Lieut. Jan. 1919, attached to 5th Army Headquarters Feb. to March 1918, and to 4th Army Headquarters April to Dec. 1918. Served in France.

DAVID RITCHIE HAYES.

Admitted July 1908, practising at Leeds. Joined March 3, 1916, as Gunner, Royal Garrison Artillery. Appointed Signaller (1st Class) Oct. 1917, and Signaller Lance-Bombardier March 1918. Served in France with 111th Heavy Battery.

JOHN THOMAS HAYTON.

Admitted Nov. 1917. Member of Todd & Hayton, of Lancaster. Served as A/Lance-Corporal, Army Pay Corps.

JOSEPH HAYTON.

Admitted Jan. 1905. Member of Hayton, Simpson & Fisher, of Cockermouth. Served as Private, 21st Batt. Royal Fusiliers, and afterwards obtained commission in the Border Regt., promoted Lieut. Feb. 1918. Mentioned in Dispatches. Awarded the M.C.

HERBERT CECIL HAYWARD.

Articled to A. H. Hayward, of Leigh, Lancs. Joined April 1918, as Private, 28th Batt. County of London Regt. (Artists Rifles). Served at Home.

DOUGLAS GEORGE HAZARD.

Articled to C. J. Haydon, of Bournemouth. Joined Aug. 4, 1914, as 2nd Lieut., 3rd Batt. King's Shropshire Light Infantry, promoted Lieut. April

1915. Served at Home Aug. 1914 to May 1915 and in Flanders May 8 to 15, 1915. Reported missing, believed killed, at Hooge, near Ypres May 24–25, 1915, and subsequently reported killed in action on that date.

WILLIAM NOEL HAZARD.

Articled to W. H. Hazard, of Harleston, Norfolk. Mobilised Aug. 1914 with 4th Batt. Norfolk Regt. Resigned commission and enlisted in 6th Dragoon Guards 1916. Gazetted 2nd Lieut. 14th Batt. The Welch Regt. 1917. Killed Aug. 26, 1918, in Northern France.

ROLAND HENRY HAZEL.

Admitted March 1909, practising at East Grinstead and South Merstham. Joined Aug. 5, 1914, as Corporal, Royal Engineers. Gazetted 2nd Lieut. in same Regt. Jan. 9, 1916, promoted Lieut. July 1917, Capt. Dec. 1918, Major, Jan. 1920. Once mentioned in Dispatches. Awarded the M.C. Served in France Aug. 1914 to Aug. 1915, and in Egypt, Palestine, and Syria Feb. 1916 to 1920.

THOMAS MAYNARD HAZELRIGG.

Admitted Feb. 1906, practised at Leicester. Served as 2nd Lieut., Lincoln and Leicester Royal Army Service Corps (T.), promoted to Capt. June 1916. Mentioned in Dispatches. Awarded the M.C.

JOHN GUY HEAL.

Admitted Oct. 1912, practising at Bristol. Served as Private, Royal Army Service Corps.

THOMAS LANE CLAYPOLE HEALD.

Admitted Oct. 1913. Of Wigan and Southport. Served as 2nd Lieut., 5th Batt. Cheshire Regt. and attained the rank of Capt. Twice mentioned in Dispatches. Awarded the M.C.

ARTHUR FRANCIS HEANE.

Admitted Feb. 1914, practising at Nottingham. Joined April 1916, and gazetted 2nd Lieut. Royal Garrison Artillery April 1917, promoted Lieut. Oct. 1918. Served in Palestine Aug. 1917 to April 1918, and in France April 1918 to Dec. 1919.

HAROLD SCHOFIELD HEAP.

Admitted Dec. 1908, practising at Ashton-under-Lyne. Joined Dec. 2, 1915, as Private, 28th Batt. County of London Regt. (Artists Rifles). Gazetted 2nd Lieut. York and Lancaster Regt. Dec. 19, 1916, promoted Lieut. June 1918. Served in Salonica.

NORMAN HEAP.

Admitted Dec. 1907. Member of Heap, Marshall & Heeley, of Holmfirth and Huddersfield. Joined Jan. 12, 1907, as Gunner, Royal Field Artillery. Served at Home.

STUART LEIGHTON HEARD.

Admitted Oct. 1913, practising as Assistant Solicitor to Plymouth Corporation. Joined June 21, 1915, as 2nd Lieut., 12th Batt. Worcestershire Regt., transferred to Machine Gun Corps July 1916, promoted Lieut. Jan. 1917. Awarded the M.C. Served at Home June 1915 to Jan. 1916 and Feb.

to June 1919, and Egypt and Palestine Jan. 1916 to Feb. 1919. Wounded at first Battle of Gaza March 26, 1917.

NATHANIEL SALMON HEARLE.

Admitted July 1904, practised at 238 Edgware Road, W. Served as 2nd Lieut., Machine Gun Corps.

GEORGE ROBERT HEATHCOTE.

Admitted Oct. 1898. Member of Heathcote & Webb, of Manchester and Dukinfield. Mobilised Aug. 1914, as Lieut., 6th Batt. Cheshire Regt., promoted Capt. 18th Batt. Manchester Regt. Oct. 1914. Appointed a Military Base Censor with the Egyptian Expeditionary Force Aug. 1916. Served at Home two years, and in Egypt three years.

JOHN GYDE HEAVEN.

Admitted Jan. 1911, practised at Bristol. Served as Capt., South Midland Divisional Royal Engineers.

GUY HEDDERWICK.

Articled to A. S. Jecks, of 24 Austin Friars, E.C. On outbreak of War joined the 2nd County of London Yeomanry (Westminster Dragoons) as a Trooper. Gazetted 2nd Lieut. in the First Reserve Cavalry Aug. 1915 and transferred to the Royal Flying Corps May 1916. Attacked by several enemy aircraft and forced to the ground in the German lines. Reported missing Sept. 22, 1916, and subsequently officially reported as having died.

CHRISTOPHER HENRY HEDDON.

Admitted July 1903, practising at Harrogate and Ripon. Served as Private, Royal Army Service Corps (M.T.).

FRANCIS READE HEDGES.

Admitted Feb. 1902. Member of Hedges & Son, of Wallingford. Mobilised Aug. 1914, as Major, 4th Batt. Royal Berkshire Regt. Served in Belgium, France, and at Home.

HARRY HEELEY.

Articled to William Heeley, of Holmfirth. Joined Sept. 25, 1914, as Private, 1/7 Batt. Duke of Wellington's West Riding Regt., transferred to the 147th Machine Gun Company Oct. 1916. Served in France and Belgium April 1915 to February 1919. Wounded May 25, 1915. Gassed Dec. 19, 1915.

GEORGE HERBERT HEELIS.

Admitted Feb. 1893. Member of E. & E. A. Heelis, of Appleby, Westmorland. Mobilised Aug. 4, 1914, as Capt., 4th Batt. Border Regt., promoted Temp. Major June 1915, Substantive Major June 1916, A/Lieut.-Col. July to Aug. 1917. Served at Home Aug. to Oct. 1914, and in India Oct. 1914 to Dec. 1920.

GUY HOPES HEELIS.

Articled to G. H. Heelis, of Appleby, Westmorland. Joined Sept. 5, 1914, as Private, 1/4 Batt. Border Regt. Gazetted 2nd Lieut. Aug. 26, 1915, promoted Lieut. July 1917. Served in Burma and Mesopotamia. Wounded Sept. 28, 1917.

JOHN ALEXANDER HELLARD.

Admitted June 1906, practised at Colombo. Served with Town Guard Artillery, Colombo, 1914 to 1915. Gazetted 2nd Lieut. 3rd (Reserve) Batt. Somerset Light Infantry June 1915, attached 1st Batt. May 1916. Served in France. Killed in action at the first Battle of the Somme July 1, 1916.

FRANK ARTHUR HELLAWELL.

Admitted Feb. 1905. Managing Clerk with Thomas Dodds, of Newcastle-upon-Tyne. Joined April 2, 1917, as Gunner, Royal Field Artillery. Served in Mesopotamia.

GEOFFREY DAVENPORT HELLIWELL.

Articled to J. H. Rothwell, of Brighouse. Joined Dec. 9, 1915, as 2nd Lieut., 6th Batt. South Staffordshire Regt., subsequently promoted Lieut. Served in France and Italy.

HENRY DAVENPORT HELLIWELL.

Admitted Oct. 1912, practising at Halifax. Mobilised Aug. 4, 1914, as Lieut., 4th Batt. West Riding Regt., promoted Capt. Aug. 1915, attached 20th Batt. Notts and Derby Regt. May to July 1916, transferred to Royal Army Service Corps (M.T.) July 1916. Once mentioned in Dispatches. Served at Home Aug. 1914 to May 1916 and Aug. 1917 to Sept. 1918, France May 1916 to Aug. 1917, Italy Sept. 1918 to Feb. 1919.

RICHMOND PERCIVAL HELLYAR.

Admitted Nov. 1905, practised at Bristol. Served as Company Quarter-master-Sergeant, 1st Public Schools Batt. Royal Fusiliers. Subsequently gazetted Lieut. 27th Divisional Train Royal Army Service Corps (H.T.), promoted Temp. Capt. Sept. 1916. Mentioned in Dispatches.

WILLIAM FRANK HELLYAR.

Articled to W. J. Hellyar, of 35 New Broad Street, E.C. Mobilised Aug. 1914, as Rifleman, 5th City of London Batt. London Regt. (London Rifle Brigade), promoted Lance-Corporal Feb. 1915. Gazetted 2nd Lieut. Royal Army Service Corps (H.T.) July 22, 1915, promoted Lieut. May 1916, Lieut. and Flying Officer (Observer) Royal Flying Corps Oct. 1916, Pilot Oct. 1917, Capt. and Flight Commander Royal Air Force Oct. 1918. Three times mentioned in Dispatches. Served in France and Belgium Nov. 1914 to May 1917. Crashed after collision in mid-air Easter Sunday 1917.

FRANCIS EDGCOMBE HELLYER.

Articled to R. E. Hellyer, of Southsea. Served as Lieut., 9th Cyclist Batt. Hampshire Regt., promoted Capt. June 1916. Mentioned in Dispatches. Awarded the O.B.E.

ROY HELMEROW HELMER.

Admitted Oct. 1908, practising at Barnard Castle. Joined Sept. 1914, as Private, 4th Batt. Yorkshire Regt. (T.), promoted Lance-Corporal Nov. 1914. Commissioned 2nd Lieut. 8th Batt. Yorkshire Regt. Dec. 18, 1914, transferred by order of War Office to Signals Royal Engineers Aug. 1915, promoted Lieut. April 1916, placed in charge of 15th Divisional Artillery Signals March 1917 as A/Capt. Once mentioned in Dispatches. Awarded the M.C. Served in France and Flanders Oct. 1915 to June 1918.

EDWARD CECIL HEMINGWAY.

Admitted Dec. 1909. Member of Marcy, Hemingway & Sons, of Bewdley. Gazetted 2nd Lieut. 2/7 Worcestershire Regt. Sept. 21, 1914, promoted Lieut. June 1915. Served in France. Discharged Nov. 17, 1916, on account of ill-health.

FRANCIS WILLIAM HEMMING.

Admitted Feb. 1913, practised at Worcester. Mobilised Aug. 1914, as Lieut., 8th Batt. Worcestershire Regt. (T.), promoted Capt. June 1915. Served at Home, and in Flanders and France (2 years and 2 months abroad). Wounded April 11, 1917, wounded twice and afterwards killed in action at Guillemont Farm, France, April 24, 1917.

OSWALD ARTHUR HEMPSON.

Admitted Dec. 1909. Member of Hempsons, of 33 Henrietta Street, Strand, W.C. Joined June 6, 1916, as Private, 28th Batt. County of London Regt. (Artists Rifles). Gazetted 2nd Lieut. Royal Field Artillery (S.R.) Jan. 13, 1917, promoted Lieut. July 1918. Served in France. Gassed Sept. 26, 1917.

ARCHIE DOUGLAS HENDERSON.

Admitted Feb. 1910. Member of Shaen, Roscoe, Massey & Co., of 8 Bedford Row, W.C. Joined Sept. 5, 1914, as Private, Norfolk Regt., promoted Lance-Corporal Oct. 1914, Lance-Sergeant Dec. 1914, and Sergeant Feb. 1915. Gazetted 2nd Lieut. March 1915, Capt. July 1915, Major Jan. 1919. Awarded D.S.O. and Order of St. Vladimar (Russian) 4th Class. Served at Home, Egypt, North Russia, France, Italy. Wounded Somme July 1, 1916.

ARTHUR HENDERSON.

Articled to J. H. Waterman, of Regent House, Regent Street, W. Served as Private, 1st Batt. Hon. Artillery Company.

HENRY WALLACE HENDERSON.

Admitted Feb. 1909, practising at Port Talbot. Served as Lieut., Royal Army Service Corps.

MAGNUS CHARLES HENDERSON.

Articled to E. B. Wannop, of Chichester. Joined Dec. 3, 1914, Royal Naval Volunteer Reserve (London) as Ordinary Seaman in the Royal Naval Division. Subsequently gazetted Sub-Lieut. Royal Naval Volunteer Reserve additional for the Royal Naval Division. Served in Gallipoli May 1915 to evacuation, and in France May to Nov. 1916 and Feb. to March 1918. Wounded at Beaucourt, France, Nov. 13, 1916, and gassed at Ribecourt, France, March 17, 1918.

MALCOLM JOHN HENDERSON.

Admitted June 1901. Member of Shaen, Roscoe, Massey & Co., of 8 Bedford Row, W.C. Joined June 1916, as Private, Essex Regt., and attained the rank of Sergeant. Subsequently gazetted 2nd Lieut. Labour Corps attached

Lancashire Fusiliers. Served at home and in France. Taken prisoner whilst on patrol Aug, 8. 1919.

WALTER HENDERSON-CLELAND.

Admitted July 1902, practising at Coventry. Joined June 1915, as 2nd Lieut., 3rd Batt. Cameronians (Scottish Rifles), attached to 2nd Batt. Scottish Rifles in France May 1916, appointed Temp. Capt. and A.P.M. 42nd Division June 1917. Twice mentioned in Dispatches. Awarded the M.C. Served in France and Flanders May 1916 to March 1919.

HERBERT GEORGE HENLEY.

Admitted Feb. 1908. Managing Clerk with Roney & Co., of 42–45 New Broad Street, E.C. Joined Sept. 8, 1914, as Private, 12th Batt. London Regt., promoted Colour-Sergeant Oct. 1914, Company Quartermaster-Sergeant Feb. 1915. Commissioned 2nd Lieut. in Royal Army Service Corps Feb. 27, 1917, transferred to Camel Transport Corps May 1918, promoted Lieut. Aug. 1918. Served in Egypt and Palestine.

FRANK HERBERT HENRI.

Articled to John Watson, of Liverpool. Joined Sept. 11, 1914, as Private, 17th Batt. King's Liverpool Regt. Gazetted 2nd Lieut. Cheshire Regt. Nov. 30, 1914, promoted Lieut. Sept. 1915, Capt. Sept. 1917. Served at Home and in France.

WILLIAM AINSWORTH HENRI.

Articled to Japheth Tickle, of 63 Cheapside, E.C. Joined Nov. 1914, as Private, Inns of Court O.T.C. Gazetted 2nd Lieut. 11th Batt. Northumberland Fusiliers Jan. 1915, promoted Lieut. 1916, Capt. 1918. Awarded the M.C. Served in France and Belgium Aug. 1915 to Oct. 1917, and in Italy Oct. 1917 to Jan. 1919.

RALPH QUIXANO HENRIQUES.

Admitted April 1898. Member of Elkin, Henriques & Harford, of 3 Salters' Hall Court, Cannon Street, E.C. Mobilised at outbreak of War, as Major, 2nd London Divisional Engineers (T.), subsequently Lieut.-Col. Once mentioned in Dispatches. Awarded the T.D. Served in France June to Nov. 1916, Macedonia Nov. 1916 to June 1917, Egypt and Palestine June to Nov. 1917.

CHARLES HENSHALL.

Admitted May 1911, practised at Timperley, Cheshire. Joined 1914, as 2nd Lieut., Manchester Regt., and subsequently promoted Capt. Killed in action July 11, 1916.

ROBERT ALLATT HEPTONSTALL.

Articled to W. V. Dixon, of Wakefield. Served as 2nd Lieut., Barnsley Batt. York and Lancaster Regt., transferred to the Tank Corps and attained the rank of Capt.

JOSEPH HEPWORTH.

Admitted Jan. 1906. Member of Hepworth & Chadwick, of Leeds. Joined June 26, 1916, as Private, Royal Army Service Corps. Gazetted 2nd Lieut. in same Regt. Dec. 19, 1917. Served in France.

ARTHUR GRENVILLE HERBERT.
Admitted July 1904. Member of W. H. & A. G. Herbert, of 10 Cork Street, W. Served as Capt., London University O.T.C., and afterwards gazetted 2nd Lieut. 3rd Batt. East Kent Regt. (The Buffs).

EDWIN SAVORY HERBERT.
Articled to G. A. Macdonald, of 2 and 3 Norfolk Street, Strand, W.C. Joined Nov. 12, 1917, as Ordinary Seaman, Royal Naval Volunteer Reserve, promoted Signalman Aug. 1918. Served on Convoy Service (North America).

RONALD YOUNG HERBERT.
Admitted May 1905. Managing Clerk with Morley, Shirreff & Co., of Gresham House, Old Broad Street, E.C. Joined July 1915, as 2nd Lieut., 13th London Battery Royal Field Artillery, afterwards "A" Battery, 235th Brigade, subsequently promoted Lieut. Once mentioned in Dispatches. Served in France and Flanders Nov. 1915 to Sept. 1917. Wounded on Somme in 1916 and again in 1917. Killed near Wytescheate Wood, Flanders, Sept. 23, 1917.

HORACE FALKLAND HERD.
Admitted May 1910. Managing Clerk with J. B. Cooke, of Wakefield. Mobilised Aug. 1914, as Capt., 3rd Batt. The Welch Regt. Served in France Nov. to Dec. 1914. Killed in action at Festubert Dec. 27, 1914.

RALPH LENOX HERRING.
Articled to W. H. Court, of 181 Piccadilly, W. Joined May 1914, as 2nd Lieut., 4th Batt. London Regt., subsequently Capt. and Adjutant 1st Gurkhas.

WARREN ECCLES HERTSLET.
Admitted Feb. 1901. Member of Eccles Hertslet & Co., of 10 Gray's Inn Place, W.C. Joined 1914, as 2nd Lieut., 10th Batt. County of London Regt. (Hackney) and subsequently promoted Lieut. Killed in action at the Dardanelles Aug. 15, 1915.

THOMAS BERNARD HESLOP.
Admitted Nov. 1913. Member of Heslop & York, of Barnard Castle. Joined June 1913, as 2nd Lieut., 6th Batt. Durham Light Infantry, promoted Lieut. Aug. 1915, Capt. June 1916, A/Major Oct. 1917, A/Lieut.-Col. April 1918. Twice mentioned in Dispatches. Awarded the D.S.O. Served in France and Belgium. Wounded May 30, 1918.

WALTER CRANMER HETHERINGTON.
Admitted Jan. 1914, practising at Ealing; and Gerrard's Cross, Bucks. Joined June 5, 1916, as Private, 1st Garrison Batt. Worcestershire Regt. Granted commission as 2nd Lieut. in Second Line Westmorland and Cumberland Yeomanry, promoted Lieut. May 1919. Served at Home on East Coast Defence, afterwards in Ireland.

WILLIAM HETHERINGTON.
Articled to Joseph Hetherington, of Wigton. Served as Private, Royal Army Service Corps (M.T.).

EDMUND JOHN ROSLIN HETT.

Admitted March 1908. Managing Clerk with Hett, Hett & Davy, of Brigg, Lincolnshire. Joined Oct. 20, 1914, as 2nd Lieut., 5th Batt. Lincolnshire Regt. (T.), promoted Temp. Lieut. Oct. 1915, Capt. June 1916. Once mentioned in Dispatches. Served at Home Oct. 1914 to Oct. 1915 and Feb. to Sept. 1917, in France Oct. 1915 to Feb. 1917 and Sept. 1917 to March 1918. Wounded Aug. 1916. Taken prisoner at Bullecourt March 21, 1918.

FRANCIS PAGET HETT.

Admitted Feb. 1901. Member of Clifford & Hett, Dock House, Billiter Street, E.C. Joined Royal Naval Volunteer Reserve (Auxiliary Patrol), as Sub-Lieut., April 4, 1916, promoted Lieut. May 1917. Served in North Sea, Portsmouth, and Southampton.

WALTER PEARSE HEWETT.

Admitted Dec. 1901. Member of Wreford Brown, Hewett & Co., of 38 Old Jewry, E.C. Mobilised Aug. 4, 1914, as Major, 9th Batt. Middlesex Regt., subsequently Lieut.-Col. commanding same Batt. Once mentioned in Dispatches. Awarded the T.D. Served at Home Aug. to Oct 1914, India Dec. 1914 to Oct. 1917, and Mesopotamia Oct. 1917 to Oct. 1918.

EVELYN LOVELL HEWITT.

Articled to F. A. P. Sylvester, of Trowbridge. Joined Aug. 8, 1914, as 2nd Lieut., Wiltshire Regt., promoted Lieut. Feb. 1915, seconded to West African Regt. June 1915, Temp. Capt. Aug. 1916, Substantive Capt. Jan. 1917. Served in France 1914 and Africa 1915 to 1918.

GEORGE ALFRED GUEST HEWITT.

Articled to Sir Joseph Hewitt, of Barnsley. Mobilised Aug. 1914, as Lieut., York and Lancaster Regt. (T.), promoted Temp. Capt. 1915, permanent rank Capt. and Company Commander July 1917. Served in France. Wounded Ypres Aug. 1, 1915, Somme July 2, 1916. Killed in Bourlon Village Nov. 2, 1917.

SIR JOSEPH HEWITT.

Admitted Dec. 1893, practising at Barnsley. Served as Lieut.-Col., 13th Batt. York and Lancaster Regt. Served at Home.

NEVILLE DEIGHTON MORSE HEWITT.

Articled to W. M. Walter, of 31 Budge Row, E.C. Served as Private, Public Schools Batt. Middlesex Regt.

THOMAS ARMITAGE HEWITT.

Admitted March 1910. Member of Hewitt, Urquhart & Woollacott, of 158 Leadenhall Street, E.C. Joined Sept. 1914, as Rifleman, 5th (City of London) Batt. London Regt. (London Rifle Brigade). Served at Home and in France. Killed in action at Ypres May 3, 1915.

LIONEL MOWBRAY HEWLETT.

Admitted May 1901. Member of Hewlett & Co., of 2 Raymond Buildings, Gray's Inn, W.C. Mobilised Aug. 4, 1914, as Capt., 9th Batt. Middlesex Regt.

Awarded the T.D. Served in India Oct. 1914 to Nov. 1917 and June to Dec. 1918, and Mesopotamia Nov. 1917 to June 1918.

DUDLEY HUGO HEYNES.

Admitted Nov. 1908. Managing Clerk with Pink & Marston, of Portsmouth. Joined June 15, 1916, as Private, 28th Batt. County of London Regt. (Artists Rifles). Commissioned 2nd Lieut. Royal Field Artillery Dec. 1916. Served in France and Flanders. Killed in action at Villers-Bretonneux May 16, 1918.

FREDERICK ARNOLD HEYS.

Admitted Nov. 1910. Member of Reddish & Heys, of Blackburn. Joined Sept. 1914, as 2nd Lieut., 11th Batt. East Lancashire Regt., promoted Lieut. June 1915, Capt. Aug. 1916. Once mentioned in Dispatches. Served at Home and in Egypt and France.

JOHN HARDMAN HEYS.

Articled to C. H. Pickstone, of Radcliffe, Lancs. Joined Aug 1, 1915, as 2nd Lieut., 5th Batt. East Lancashire Regt., promoted Lieut. Oct. 1916, attached from Aug. 1916 to April 1917 to the 5th Batt. Royal Warwickshire Regt. Served in France Aug. 1916 to May 1917. Wounded April 16, 1917, as result of which left leg was amputated. Discharged April 16, 1918.

CHARLES CLEMENT HEYWOOD.

Admitted Oct. 1904. Member of Gardners & Heywood, of Abergavenny. Joined 1915 and gazetted 2nd Lieut., 3rd West Riding Royal Field Artillery (T.), subsequently promoted Lieut. Served in France. Reported missing on April 25, 1918, and subsequently officially reported killed in action on that date.

LEONARD JOHN HEYWOOD.

Articled to M. J. Greener, of 52 Bedford Row, W.C. Joined Sept. 1914, as Private, University and Public Schools Corps, afterwards the 20th Batt. Royal Fusiliers. Served in France. Killed on the Somme in High Wood July 20, 1916.

EDWARD HIBBERT.

Admitted Feb. 1898. Member of Pennington, Hibbert & Westbrook, of Hyde. Joined June 24, 1918, as Driver, Royal Army Service Corps (H.T.).

MARK DAY HICK.

Admitted Feb. 1904. Member of Hick & Hands, of Scarborough. Joined June 1916, as Private, Royal Army Service Corps. Gazetted 2nd Lieut. in same Regt. July 1916, promoted Lieut. Dec. 1917. Served in France Aug. 1916 to March 1919.

DENIS HICKEY.

Admitted Dec. 1917. Clerk with Robert Innes, of Manchester. Joined Nov. 30, 1915, as Private. Gazetted 2nd Lieut. Royal Munster Fusiliers Feb. 20, 1916, promoted Lieut. Oct. 1917. Served at Home and in France. Wounded July 10, 1917.

HUBERT GEORGE HICKMAN.

Admitted June 1903, practising at 34 Clement's Lane, E.C. Served as Able Seaman, Royal Naval Volunteer Reserve (Anti-Aircraft Corps).

TERENCE HICKMAN.

Admitted Aug. 1913. Managing Clerk with Deacon, Gibson & Co., of 9 Great St. Helen's, E.C. Joined Aug. 1914, as Private, Hon. Artillery Company (Infantry). Gazetted 2nd Lieut. 2nd Batt. Leinster Regt. April 1915, promoted Lieut. June 1916. Served in France Sept. 1914 to July 1915 and March to June 1916. Wounded July 1915 and June 1916. Killed in action at Loos June 27, 1916.

CHARLES HUBERT HICKS.

Admitted Jan. 1902, practised at 9 Gray's Inn Square. Gazetted 2nd Lieut., 8th Batt. Notts and Derby Regt. (Sherwood Foresters) Jan. 1916, promoted Lieut. July 1917. Killed in action near Hazebrouck July 21, 1918.

HAROLD COLDSTREAM HICKS.

Admitted May 1905, formerly of Bristol. Served as Capt., 1st (Public Schools) Batt. Royal Fusiliers.

PHILIP HUGH WHITBY HICKS.

Articled to R. A. Pinsent, of Birmingham. Served as 2nd Lieut., 7th Batt. Royal Warwickshire Regt., promoted Lieut. June 1916, A/Capt. Aug. 1918. Awarded M.C.

CUTHBERT GOLLAN HICKSON.

Articled to W. H. Hickson, of Rochdale. Joined Aug. 14, 1914, as Private, Royal Fusiliers. Gazetted Lieut. 1st Batt. East Lancashire Regt. Nov. 27, 1914. Served in France. Wounded March 7, 1916, and March 11, 1918.

RICHARD DOUGLAS HIGG.

Articled to Timbrell & Deighton, of 90 Cannon Street, E.C. Served as Private, Royal West Kent Regt.

HERBERT EDWARD POWELL HIGGINS.

Admitted July 1910, practised at 6 Great James Street, Bedford Row, W.C. Joined Aug. 1914 the 28th Batt. County of London Regt. (Artists Rifles). Subsequently granted a commission in the King's Own Lancaster Regt. and attained the rank of Capt. Served in the Gallipoli Campaign. Killed Gallipoli Peninsula about Aug. 10, 1915.

ALBERT WILFRID HIGGS.

Admitted March 1910. Member of Higgs & Sons, of Brierley Hill, and Lye. Joined Aug. 19, 1916, as Gunner, Royal Garrison Artillery. Gazetted 2nd Lieut. Hampshire Regt. March 1, 1917, transferred to General List with rank of Capt. July 1918. Served in France March 1917 to Jan. 1918, and the remainder of time in England.

RICHARD DOUGLAS HIGGS.

Articled to T. H. Deighton, of 90 Cannon Street, E.C. Joined Sept. 12, 1914, as Private, 1/5 Batt. Royal West Kent Regt. Gazetted 2nd Lieut. 11th Batt. South Staffordshire Regt. Nov. 18, 1915, promoted Lieut. 7th Batt. July 1917. Awarded the M.C. Served at Home, India, and France.

SAMUEL STAGOLL HIGHAM.

Admitted Feb. 1883. Member of Greenwell, Higham & Co., of 4 Berners Street, W. Mobilised Aug. 1914, as Major, 28th Batt. County of London Regt.

(Artists Rifles). Served as A.P.M. 2nd London Division (T.) Aug. 1914, Second in Command No. 15 (Artists Rifles) O.C.B. 1915 to 1916.

WILLIAM THOMPSON HIGHET.

Admitted Oct. 1906. Member of Paisley, Falcon, Skerry & Highet, of Workington, Cumberland. Mobilised Aug. 1914, as Capt., Royal Field Artillery, promoted Major June 1916, A/Lieut.-Col. Nov. 1915 to Feb. 1919. Three times mentioned in Dispatches. Awarded the M.C. Served in Egypt Sept. 1914 to May 1915, Gallipoli May 1915 to evacuation, Palestine Jan. 1916 to Feb. 1917, and France Feb. 1917 to April 1919. Wounded twice, Sept. 29, 1917, and Aug. 15, 1918.

CHARLES BOWYER HIGHMORE.

Admitted Dec. 1910, practised at Dorchester; and 2 Pump Court, Temple, E.C. Rejoined the 28th Batt. County of London Regt. (Artists Rifles) after the outbreak of War and gazetted 2nd Lieut. Machine Gun Corps Jan. 26, 1917. Served at Home and in France. Wounded severely at Monchy June 28, 1917. Invalided out of Army April 23, 1918. Died of pneumonia Feb. 26, 1919.

BERNARD DRAKE HIGMAN.

Articled to H. W. Higman, of St. Austell. Joined April 19, 1915, as Private, Inns of Court O.T.C. Gazetted 2nd Lieut. 25th Batt. London Regt. Dec. 18, 1915, promoted Lieut. July 1916, seconded Royal Flying Corps as Flying Officer Nov. 1916. Served in France Dec. 1916 to March 1918. London Air Defences March 1918 to Armistice.

HENRY OXTOBY HILARY.

Admitted June 1907. Managing Clerk with Messrs. A. & M. W. Platts, of Bingley. Joined Sept. 23, 1916, as Pioneer, Royal Engineers Signal Service, promoted Corporal Oct. 1918. Served in France Jan. to March 1917, Mesopotamia Aug. 1917 to April 1919, India April to Sept. 1919.

FRANCIS CLIFTON HILBERY.

Admitted Feb. 1905. Member of Henry Hilbery & Son, of 4 South Square, Gray's Inn, W.C. Gazetted Sub-Lieut., with seniority May 8, 1916, H.M. Navy, promoted Lieut. May 1917. Employed in Minesweeping, Minelaying, and Patrol and Escort Duty.

MAURICE LAKE HILDER.

Articled to Edward Hilder (his father), of 36 Jermyn Street, St. James's, S.W. Joined Sept. 1914, as Private, Public Schools and Universities Brigade. Gazetted Lieut. Royal Army Service Corps Dec. 1914. Invalided home Sept. 1915, transferred to 5th (attached 23rd) Batt Royal Fusiliers Aug. 1916, promoted Capt. April 1917. Awarded the M.C. Served in Gallipoli June to Sept. 1915, and in France Sept. 1916 to May 1917. Killed near Oppy, in France, May 3, 1917.

PAUL HILDERSHEIM.

Admitted June 1893, practised at 91 Bishopsgate, E.C. Served as Capt., Royal Garrison Artillery.

ARTHUR HILL.

Admitted Jan. 1904, practising at Hitchin, Herts. Joined June 23, 1915, as 2nd Lieut., Sussex Royal Garrison Artillery (T.), promoted Lieut. Dec. 1916, Capt. Jan. 1918. Twice mentioned in Dispatches. Served at Home and in France.

CHARLES GUY ROPER HILL.

Articled to F. C. Hill, of Ormskirk. Mobilised Aug. 1914, as 2nd Lieut., 9th Batt. King's Liverpool Regt., promoted Lieut. Aug. 1915, Capt. Aug. 1918. Awarded M.C. with Bar. Served in England and 26 months in France.

EDWARD HAROLD HILL.

Admitted Oct. 1906. Member of Hill & Douglass, of York. Joined July 6, 1916, as Gunner, Royal Garrison Artillery, promoted to A/Bombardier May 1917. Commissioned 2nd Lieut. Royal Garrison Artillery (T.) Dec. 17, 1917, and posted to 233rd Siege Battery. Served in France.

JAMES CROASDALE HILL.

Articled to N. E. Barnes, of Ulverston, Lancs. Joined June 30, 1915, as Private, Hon. Artillery Company, promoted Corporal Sept. 1916. Served at Home.

JOHN HENRY HILL.

Admitted May 1914. Of Bradford. Joined Oct. 14, 1914, as 2nd Lieut., 4th Batt. West Riding Regt. (T.), promoted Lieut. June 1916. Served at Home.

MALCOLM WALTER HILL.

Admitted March 1914. Of Bradford. Joined Sept. 10, 1914, as 2nd Lieut., 6th Batt. West Yorkshire Regt., seconded to Machine Gun Corps Jan. 1916, promoted Lieut. June 1916, Capt. Jan. 1918. Twice mentioned in Dispatches. Served with British Expeditionary Force July 1915 to March 1918 and June 1918 to April 1919. Wounded Sept. 5, 1916.

MARTIN SPENCER HILL.

Articled to G. L. F. McNair, of 21 Leadenhall Street, E.C. Joined Oct. 14, 1914, as Private, 2/6 Field Ambulance (London) Royal Army Medical Corps (T.), promoted Corporal Sept. 1917, Sergeant Dec. 1917. Served in England 1914 to 1916 and in France 1916 to 1919.

MAURICE CRIDLAND HILL.

Admitted Nov. 1904, practised at Newcastle-upon-Tyne. Joined Sept. 1914 as 2nd Lieut., Northumberland Fusiliers, subsequently promoted Lieut. Served in France. Killed in action at Ypres May 24, 1915.

MURRAY VICTOR BURROW HILL.

Admitted July 1913. Managing Clerk with William Sturges & Co., of 5 Little College Street, Westminster, S.W. Joined Aug. 12, 1914, as 2nd Lieut., 1st Batt. Royal Fusiliers, promoted Lieut. Feb. 1915, Capt. July 1915, Major June 1916, A/Lieut.-Col. Oct. 1916, Major 9th Batt. Royal Sussex Regt. Nov. 1916, Temp. Lieut.-Col. Dec. 1916. Four times mentioned in Dispatches.

Awarded M.C. and D.S.O. and Bar. Served in France Sept. 1914 to March 1918 and July 1918 to May 1919. Wounded March 27, 1918.

ROBERT FARRA HILL.
Articled to J. H. Turner, of York. Joined Sept. 1914, as Private, Royal Army Service Corps, promoted Lance-Corporal Oct. 1914. Gazetted 2nd Lieut. Feb. 1915, promoted Lieut. June 1916, Capt. March 1919. Served at Home Sept. 1914 to July 1915, Gallipoli Aug. to Oct. 1915, Salonica Nov. 1915 to Sept. 1917, Egypt Sept. to Oct. 1917, Palestine Oct. 1917 to Sept. 1918, Syria Sept. 1918 to June 1919.

SYDNEY JAMES HILL.
Admitted Jan. 1906, practising at Liverpool. Joined Dec. 1915, as Trooper, Lancashire Hussars. Gazetted 2nd Reserve Regt. of Hussars Dec. 21, 1916, transferred to Machine Gun Corps Feb. 1918. Served in France. Wounded Sept. 29, 1918, left leg amputated.

WALTER FITZGERALD HILL.
Admitted June 1906, practising at Devereaux Chambers, Temple E.C. Served as Capt., 10th Batt. Highland Light Infantry.

EDWARD LANGDALE HILLEARY.
Admitted Feb. 1897. Of 3 Serjeant's Inn, E.C. Served as Capt., subsequently Major 1st Batt. Lovat Scouts. Three times mentioned in Dispatches. Awarded O.B.E., Greek Order of Military Merit, White Eagle of Serbia. Served in Salonica.

ALFRED CHARLES HILLIER.
Articled to J. S. Carpenter, of Bath. Joined Feb. 15, 1915, as 2nd Lieut., Royal Army Service Corps (M.T.), promoted Lieut. June 1916, A/Capt. for a time in France. Served in France. Invalided from Service, owing to injuries and ill-health contracted on active service, July 1918.

ARTHUR ERNEST HILLS.
Admitted May 1904, practising at 6 King's Bench Walk, Temple, E.C. Served as Major, 5th Batt. Royal West Kent Regt.

JOHN WALLER HILLS.
Admitted Oct. 1897. Member of Rooper & Whateley, of 17 Lincoln's Inn Fields, W.C. Joined Oct. 5, 1914, as Capt., 4th Batt. Durham Light Infantry, promoted Major Nov. 1915, A/Lieut.-Col. July 1916. Once mentioned in Dispatches. Served in France May to Sept. 1916. Wounded on Somme Sept. 30, 1916.

SAMUEL HILTON.
Articled to A. E. Withy, of Swindon, Wilts. Joined Nov. 16, 1914, as Private, 19th (Public Schools) Batt. Royal Fusiliers, subsequently attained the rank of Sergeant and gazetted 2nd Lieut. Royal Fusiliers July 7, 1916, and posted to the 9th (Service) Batt., promoted Lieut. Oct. 1916, appointed A/Adjutant Nov. 1916, Adjutant and A/Capt. Aug. 1917, promoted Capt. Nov. 1917. Once mentioned in Dispatches. Awarded the M.C. Served at Home and France.

WILLIAM ARTHUR HINCHCLIFFE.

Articled to A. E. T. Hinchcliffe, of Huddersfield. Joined Oct. 14, 1914, as 2nd Lieut., 7th Batt. Duke of Wellington's Regt. (T.), promoted Lieut. June 1916, attached 4th Batt. Monmouthshire Regt. 1916 to 1917. Served at Home Nov. 1914 to April 1917 and in France and Belgium April 1917 to May 1919. Trench fever May to July 1918.

ERNEST WILLIAM HINCHLIFFE.

Admitted June 1901, practising at Halifax, Yorks. Joined March 2, 1916, as Private, 14th Batt. County of London Regt. (London Scottish), attached to Intelligence Office, Le Havre, April 1917, and later promoted Corporal and A/Sergeant, appointed to Intelligence Office, Lille, Oct. 1918. Served in France and Belgium.

MAURICE THORP HINCKS.

Admitted Jan. 1908, practising at Leicester. Joined Dec. 8, 1915, as Private, Royal Army Service Corps (M.T.) and attained the rank of Company Quarter-master-Sergeant. Gazetted 2nd Lieut. in same Regt. Dec. 4, 1916, promoted Lieut. June 1915. Once mentioned in Dispatches. Served at Home to Dec. 1916 and Aug. 1919 to Jan. 1920, France and Flanders Dec. 1916 to Feb. 1919, and Germany Feb. to Aug. 1919.

EVERATT HIND.

Admitted Nov. 1887, practising at Goole. Formed and commanded 8th Batt. King's Own Yorkshire Light Infantry in Aug. and Sept. 1914, formed and commanded 2/4 Batt. same Regt. in England and France Oct. 1914 to April 1917, commanded Hind's Batt. Royal Welch Fusiliers May to Sept. 1917, on Staff duties in France Sept. 1917 to Sept. 1918, commanded 80th Labour Group in France Sept. 1918 to May 1919.

LAWRENCE ARTHUR HIND.

Admitted Dec. 1902. Member of Wells & Hind, of Nottingham; and Hinds & Roberts, of 33 Chancery Lane, W.C. Mobilised Aug. 1914, as Capt., 7th (Robin Hood) Batt. Notts and Derby Regt. (Sherwood Foresters), promoted Major 1915, Lieut.-Col. May 1916. Twice mentioned in Dispatches. Awarded the M.C. Served in France. Wounded at Hooge July 1915. Killed Battle of Somme July 1, 1916.

WILLIAM HENRY ROUSSEAU HINDE.

Articled to H. H. Bothamley, of 16 Bedford Row, W.C. Joined Sept. 26, 1914, as 2nd Lieut., Royal Army Service Corps, promoted Lieut. June 1915, Capt. Jan. 1916. Once mentioned in Dispatches. Served at Home. Died of influenza and pneumonia Oct 22, 1918.

FRANK HINDLE.

Admitted July 1911, practising at Haslingden, Lancs. Joined Oct. 10, 1917, as Gunner, Royal Garrison Artillery. Served in France.

FREDERICK HINDLE.

Admitted June 1899. Member of Hindle, Son & Cooper, of Darwen. Joined Sept. 1914, as Private, No. 2 Motor Ambulance Corps. Gazetted

Lieut. Nov. 1917. Awarded Chevalier Legion d'Honneur (French) and Croix de Guerre (two palms and three stars) French. Served in France Sept. 1914 to Jan. 1919.

GEORGE EDWIN SCOTT HINDMARSH.

Admitted Nov. 1904, practised at Bury St. Edmund's. Joined Nov. 1914, as Trooper, 2nd Life Guards. Received commission as 2nd Lieut. 3/1 Batt. Royal Fusiliers (City of London Regt.) Sept. 19, 1915, transferred to 3rd Batt. The Rifle Brigade Nov. 1915. In France May to Sept. 1915, and in India March 1916 to June 1917. Died from heart failure June 16, 1917, in Multan, India.

EVAN JOHN HINDS.

Admitted April 1910, practising at Swansea. Joined March 28, 1916, as Private, Royal Army Service Corps (M.T.), subsequently Lance-Corporal in 336th Siege Battery Ammunition Column. Served in France and Belgium.

GEORGE VERNON HINDS.

Articled to G. P. Hinds, of Goudhurst, Kent. Joined June 2, 1915, as Temp. 2nd Lieut., 10th Batt. Royal West Kent Regt., promoted Lieut. Oct. 1915, transferred to 1st Signal Company Royal Engineers Oct. 1917. Once mentioned in Dispatches. Awarded the M.C. Served in France, Belgium, and with the Army of the Rhine.

CHARLES WILLIAM HINES.

Admitted March 1897. Member of Hines & Son, of Sunderland. Mobilised Aug. 1914, as Major, 7th Batt. Durham Light Infantry (T.). Served in France and Belgium April to May 1915. Killed at or near Wittebroke Farm, near Ypres, May 24, 1915.

HAROLD CUDDEFORD HINGSTON.

Admitted Feb. 1912. Managing Clerk with Ernest Bevir & Son, of Devereux Chambers, Temple, W.C. Joined Dec. 14, 1914, as Private, Inns of Court O.T.C. Commissioned 2nd Lieut. 1st Batt. London Regt. (Royal Fusiliers) April 3, 1915, subsequently promoted Temp. Lieut., Temp. Capt., Assistant Staff Capt. 173rd Brigade while serving in France, and also Assistant to D.A.Q.M.G. 1st Army (Central Force) England for five months prior to going to France. Served at Home and France. Discharged Feb. 1917 on being appointed Assistant Legal Adviser to West Midland Regional Headquarters of Ministry of National Service.

GEORGE ERNEST HINMAN.

Admitted May 1903, practising at 59 Strand, W.C. Joined Sept. 29, 1916, as Private, Inns of Court O.T.C. Commissioned in Royal Garrison Artillery (S.R.) June 1917. Served in Ireland.

JOHN ARTHUR HISLOP.

Admitted June 1914. Member of J. Hislop & Son, of Manchester. Joined 1914, as 2nd Lieut., 19th Batt. Manchester Regt., and attained the rank of Capt. Served at Home and in France. Died at Oxford from operation July 8, 1916.

FREDERICK CECIL HOARE.

Admitted April 1905. Member of Lewis & Sons, of 7 Wilmington Square, W.C. Served as Private, Middlesex Regt.

WILLIAM GEORGE HOBBS.

Admitted Dec. 1913, practised at Kew. Served as Lieut., 8th Batt. Royal Berkshire Regt. Killed in action in France Sept. 25, 1915.

ARTHUR LAWRENCE HOBHOUSE.

Admitted Feb. 1911, practising at 4 Lincoln's Inn Fields, W.C. Joined May 25, 1915, as 2nd Lieut., Royal Army Service Corps., promoted Lieut. March 1916, transferred to General List, Staff-Lieut. Dec. 1916, promoted Staff Capt. March 1919. Served in France Sept. 1915 to May 1919.

ERIC JOHN BENTLEY HOBROW.

Admitted Aug. 1915. Member of Rundle & Hobrow, of 73 Basinghall Street, E.C. Served as Lance-Corporal, 1st Batt. Hon. Artillery Company.

ALFRED CYRIL WHITWORTH HOBSON.

Articled to G. W. Hobson, of Droitwich. Mobilised Aug. 1914, as 2nd Lieut., 2nd South Midland Brigade Royal Field Artillery (T.), promoted Lieut. Jan. 1915, A/Capt. Oct. 1915, Capt. July 1916, A/Major Aug. 1917, Brigade Major R.A., General Headquarters, Italy, April 1918 to Jan. 1919. Twice mentioned in Dispatches. Awarded M.C. and Bar. Served at Home Aug. 1914 to March 1915, France March 1915 to Nov. 1917, and Italy Nov. 1917 to Jan. 1919. Wounded at Ypres Sept. and Nov. 1917.

FRANCIS WILLIAM ELAND HOBSON.

Admitted Nov. 1908, practised at 3–4 Clement's Inn, W.C. Served as 2nd Lieut., 70th Labour Company.

JAMES FALSHAW HOBSON.

Admitted July 1908. Managing Clerk with Maughan & Hall, of Newcastle-upon-Tyne. Joined Sept. 4, 1914, as Private, 21st Batt. Royal Fusiliers. Gazetted 2nd Lieut. 2/8 Batt. Durham Light Infantry June 20, 1915, promoted Temp. Lieut. Nov. 1915, Temp. Capt. Oct. 1916., 2nd Lieut. 1/8 Batt. May 1917, Lieut. June 1917, A/Capt. June 1918, attached 18th Batt. Nov. 1918 to Feb. 1919. Awarded the M.C. Served at Home and France.

NEVILLE HOBSON.

Admitted Feb. 1908, practising at Beverley. Joined Aug. 20, 1914, as Private, 5th Batt. Yorkshire Regt., subsequently attained the rank of Company Sergeant-Major in 16th Batt. King's Royal Rifle Corps. Gazetted 2nd Lieut. 11th Batt. West Riding Regt. June 1915, promoted Lieut. and Adjutant No. 3 Officer Cadet Batt. Feb. 1916, Capt. and Adjutant 2/19 Batt. London Regt. June 1916, Headquarters Staff 60th (London) Division, Dec. 1917 to Dec. 1918. Three times mentioned in Dispatches. Awarded the M.C. Served in France June to Dec. 1916, The Balkans Dec. 1916 to May 1917, and Palestine May 1917 to Dec. 1918.

WILLIAM ANTHONY HOBSON.

Admitted May 1912, practising at Maryport. Served as 2nd Lieut., Lonsdale Batt. Border Regt., subsequently promoted Lieut.

STEPHEN LOTAN HOCKEN.

Admitted Nov. 1914. Assistant to Messrs. Orr, Dignam & Co., of Calcutta. Returned to England June 1915, and in July 1915 joined Inns of Court O.T.C.

Gazetted 2nd Lieut. King's Royal Rifle Corps Nov. 1915. Served in France. Killed in action at Guillemont Sept. 3, 1916.

WILLIAM GEOFFREY HOCKIN.

Admitted Feb. 1904. Member of Hockin, Beckton & Hockin, of Manchester. Joined Nov. 29, 1914, as Lieut., 7th Batt. Lancashire Fusiliers, promoted Temp. Capt. Feb. 1915, Staff-Capt. Aug. 1915, Brigade Major Feb. 1916, Adjutant 1st Volunteer Batt. Manchester Regt. May 1917. Served at Home.

CUTHBERT FRANCIS HODDING.

Admitted Nov. 1909, practised at Salisbury. Mobilised Aug. 1914, as 2nd Lieut., 4th Batt. Wiltshire Regt. and proceeded to India with the Regt., subsequently transferred to the 2nd Gurkha Rifles on the North-Western Frontier until invalided home suffering from "sprue," after a time rejoined Wiltshire Regt. in Ireland. Died Dec. 8, 1918.

HENRY ELLIS HODDING.

Articled to John Hodding, of Worksop. Joined Nov. 1914, as Private, Inns of Court O.T.C. Obtained commission in 10th Batt. Notts and Derby Regt. (Sherwood Foresters), and attained the rank of Lieut. Awarded the M.C. Served in France. Died Nov. 8, 1918, from wounds received near Cambrai Nov. 4.

HENRY CECIL HODGES.

Admitted Oct. 1914. Member of Hart, Scales & Hodges, of Dorking, Surrey. Joined Jan. 3, 1915, as Sub-Lieut., Royal Naval Volunteer Reserve, promoted Lieut. Aug. 1917. Served as Intelligence Officer in H.M.S. *Actaeon.*

REGINALD ARTHUR HODGES.

Admitted Jan. 1909. An Assistant Solicitor to Surrey County Council, Kingston-on-Thames. Mobilised Aug. 1914, as Lieut., 5th Batt. East Surrey Regt., promoted Capt. Nov. 1914. Invalided out Feb. 17, 1915. Served at Home.

WILLIAM LANGHAM HODGES.

Admitted Nov. 1907. Member of Hart, Scales & Hodges, of Dorking. Served as Capt., 5th Batt. The Queen's Royal West Surrey Regt., subsequently promoted Major. Mentioned in Dispatches.

JAMES PERCY HODGKINS.

Articled to William Harding, of Leicester. Served as Private, 4th Batt. Leicestershire Regt.

CHARLES HODGKINSON.

Admitted March 1880. Member of Dransfield & Hodgkinson, of Sheffield. Joined Oct. 1, 1914, as Major, 10th Batt. Manchester Regt., promoted Lieut.-Col. 2/7 Batt. Lancashire Fusiliers June 1915, attached Headquarters Southern Army Nov. 1916. Given the rank of Hon. Col. as a reward for services rendered. Served at Home.

ROBERT FRANK BYRON HODGKINSON.

Admitted July 1900. Member of Hodgkinson & Beevor, of Newark-on-Trent. Mobilised Aug. 1914, as Capt., 8th Batt. Notts and Derby Regt.

(Sherwood Foresters) (T.) and held the Temp. ranks of Major and Lieut.-Col. during the War. Awarded O.B.E. (Military Division). Served in France and at Home. Wounded April 23, 1915.

GEORGE HODGSON.

Articled to Allan Sewart, of Lancaster. Joined Sept. 18, 1914, as Private, 1/4 Batt. Border Regt. Served in India and Burma.

ISAAC HARVEY HODGSON.

Articled to Jos. Broatch, of Keswick. Joined Sept. 12, 1914, as Private, 8th Batt. Border Regt., promoted Sergeant 1914. Granted commission as 2nd Lieut. 10th Batt. Border Regt. Dec. 1914, promoted Lieut. Feb. 1915. Went to Gallipoli in May 1915 to join 1st Batt. Border Regt., was severely wounded at Suvla Bay Aug. 21, 1915, sent home to Netley Hospital, subsequently joined the 3rd Batt. Border Regt, went to France Feb. 12, 1916. Killed in action April 20, 1916, buried at La Neauville-sur-Corbie, France.

JAMES WILLIAM BIRKETT HODGSON.

Admitted Aug. 1902. Member of Allen, Whitfield & Hodgson, of Manchester. Joined Nov. 1916, as 2nd Lieut., Royal Army Service Corps, attached Royal Garrison Artillery Sept. 1917 to Nov. 1918, subsequently promoted Lieut.

JOSEPH PARKIN HODGSON.

Articled to E. R. Pickmere, of Liverpool. Joined Aug. 4, 1914, as Trooper, King Edward's Horse. Commissioned April 1915 1/2 Batt. East Lancashire Brigade Royal Field Artillery, gazetted Lieut. June 1917. Served in Egypt and Palestine May 1915 to Feb. 1919.

RICHARD EVELEIGH HODGSON.

Articled to D. C. Lee, of 46 Queen Victoria Street, E.C. Joined Aug. 1914, as 2nd Lieut., 4th Batt. King's Liverpool Regt. (Special Reserve), promoted Lieut. 1915, transferred to Royal Flying Corps with same rank Nov. 1917. Served in France April 1915 to April 1917, Home April to Nov. 1917. Killed almost in first flight (after gaining wings and posted to 204th Squadron). Shot down by machine gun on returning from a patrol near Dunkirk Sept. 15, 1918.

WILLIAM HARRY HODGSON.

Admitted May 1911, practising at Blackpool. Served as 2nd Lieut., 2/5 Batt. King's Own Royal Lancaster Regt.

WILLIAM WETHERELL HODGSON.

Admitted May 1906, practising at Richmond, Yorks. Joined June 23, 1917, as Private, King's Own Yorkshire Light Infantry. Served in Ireland.

SHIRLEY SAMUEL HODSON.

Admitted May 1905. Of Calcutta. Served as 2nd Lieut., 93rd Burma Infantry, Indian Army.

JOHN STOKER HOGG.

Member of Templer Down & Hogg, of 31 Lombard Street, E.C. Joined Aug. 29, 1914, as Private, 10th Batt. Royal Fusiliers. Gazetted Sept. 4, 1917, 2nd Lieut. Royal Flying Corps, promoted Lieut. Royal Air Force April 1918.

Served in France July 1915 to July 1916 and March 1918 to Feb. 1919, Italy July to March 1918. Wounded July 15, 1916.

CYRIL WALTER HOLCROFT.

Admitted Dec. 1913. Member of Springthorpe & Holcroft, of Birmingham. Joined Sept. 5, 1914, as 2nd Lieut., 8th Batt. Worcestershire Regt., promoted Capt. 1916, Major May 1918. Once mentioned in Dispatches. Awarded the D.S.O. Served in France. Wounded at Ypres Aug. 1917 and at Cambrai Dec. 1917.

EDWARD STANLEY HOLCROFT.

Admitted Jan. 1907, practised at Reading. Served as Capt., 4th Batt. Royal Berkshire Regt. (T.).

GUY PATIENT HOLDEN.

Articled to L. S. Cleaver, of Liverpool. Joined Sept. 12, 1914, as Ordinary Seaman, Royal Naval Division. Gazetted Sub-Lieut. Royal Naval Volunteer Reserve Feb. 6, 1915, promoted Lieut. Jan. 1916. Served at Cape Helles, Gallipoli, Aug. 1915. Invalided Aug. 30, 1916, on account of dysentery contracted on service.

HERBERT CHARLES HOLDEN.

Admitted July 1898. Member of Winder & Holden, of Bolton. Mobilised Aug. 4, 1914, as Capt., Lancashire Fusiliers. Served at Home.

RALPH AINSWORTH HOLDEN.

Admitted April 1905. Member of Richardson, Sowerby, Holden & Co., of 5 John Street, Bedford Row, W.C. Joined Sept. 1917, as Private, Inns of Court O.T.C. Commissioned 2nd Lieut. Royal Garrison Artillery Sept. 1918. Served at Home.

THOMAS WHITE HOLDICH.

Admitted Nov. 1884. Member of Locking, Holdich & Locking, of Hull. Mobilised Aug. 5, 1914, as Major and Second in Command 14th Batt. East Yorkshire Regt. (T.), promoted Lieut.-Col. Sept. 1914, Officer Commanding 2/4 Batt. East Yorkshire Regt. (T.), subsequently Officer Commanding 27th Batt. Durham Light Infantry (T.). Once mentioned in Dispatches. Awarded O.B.E. Served at Home, Coast Defence, and Training. Transferred to Territorial Force Reserve Jan. 30, 1917, on account of ill-health.

HAROLD EVELYN HOLDING.

Admitted Dec. 1912, practising at 13 Golden Square, W. Served as Private, Public Schools Batt. Middlesex Regt.

HAROLD ABERCROMBIE HOLDSWORTH.

Admitted July 1896, practising at 47 Charing Cross Road, W.C. Joined Dec. 16, 1914, as Lieut., Royal Naval Volunteer Reserve. Served in North Sea, North of Scotland, British Channel, West Indies, in command of a number of submarine chasers, mine sweepers, etc. Senior Officer Patrols at Lossiemouth, N.B., Ullapool, N.B., Humber, Littlehampton, and Newhaven. Senior Naval Officer at St. Lucia, British West Indies. Senior Naval Officer Barbados, British West Indies.

VAVASOUR MERVYN HOLDSWORTH.
Admitted Oct. 1914. Managing Clerk with J. D. Arthur, of 171 Queen Victoria Street, E.C. Enlisted Sept. 2, 1914, as Trooper, Royal North Devon Hussars (Yeomanry), promoted Lance-Corporal Oct. 1914, obtained commission as 2nd Lieut. 22nd Batt. London Regt. April 1915. Served in England till July 1915, in France July to Dec. 1915. Killed Dec. 20, 1915, by sniper. Buried in Vermelles Cemetery.

FREDERICK HERBERT HOLE.
Admitted May 1905, practising at Gloucester. Joined Dec. 8, 1915, as 2nd Lieut., Royal Field Artillery (T.), promoted Lieut. July 1917, in Royal Garrison Artillery June 1917 to Feb. 1918, otherwise Royal Field Artillery (T.). Served in France June to Dec. 1916 and May 1918 to March 1919, otherwise at Home.

BASIL THOMAS HOLLAND.
Admitted March 1913. Managing Clerk with C. E. Pettit, of 491 Oxford Street, W. Mobilised Aug. 3, 1914, as Private, 28th Batt. County of London Regt. (Artists Rifles). Gazetted 2nd Lieut. 2nd Black Watch Jan. 1915. Served in France Oct. to March 1914. Killed in action at Neuve Chapelle, March 10, 1915.

JAMES WILLIAM THURSTAN HOLLAND.
Articled to P. N. Stone, of Liverpool. Joined Oct. 4, 1914, as 2nd Lieut., 7th Batt. The King's Liverpool Regt. (T.), promoted Substantive Capt. June 1917. Served in France.

RALPH BERTRAM HOLLAND.
Admitted April 1914, practised at 158 Aldersgate Street, E.C. Joined Aug. 3, 1914, as Private, Inns of Court O.T.C. Gazetted 2nd Lieut. Royal West Kent Regt. Sept. 9, 1914, promoted Lieut. Nov. 1914, Capt. March 1915. Once mentioned in Dispatches. Served in France. Killed at Thiepval (Schwerben Redoubt) Oct. 2, 1916.

RICHARD HOLLAND.
Admitted July 1906. Member of Holland, Rigby, & Williams, of Ashbourne, Derbyshire. Joined July 19, 1918, as Private, Inns of Court O.T.C. Gazetted 2nd Lieut. Royal Marines Sept. 19, 1918. Served at Home.

THOMAS WELSBY HOLLAND.
Admitted Oct. 1910. Member of Holland, Holland & Turner, of Chester, Winsford, and Middlewich. Joined March 1917, as Private, 15th Batt. County of London Regt. (Civil Service Rifles). Gazetted 2nd Lieut. Royal Welch Fusiliers Feb. 1918. Served at Home and in France. Killed in action near Gouzeaucourt Sept. 18, 1918.

PERCY HOOD HOLLICK.
Admitted Oct. 1912. Managing Clerk with W. Henderson Cleland, of Coventry. Joined Aug. 10, 1914, as Private, Hon. Artillery Company. Gazetted 2nd Lieut. 13th Batt. Royal Warwickshire Regt. May 1915, attached to 3rd Batt. March 1916 and to 15th Batt. Jan. 1917, promoted A/Capt. Once

mentioned in Dispatches. Served in France 1914 to 1917. Three times wounded. Killed in action May 9, 1917.

ROLAND HOLLICK.

Admitted Aug. 1906. Member of Roland Hollick & Co., of Coventry. Joined Dec. 20, 1915, as Gunner, Royal Horse Artillery. Gazetted 2nd Lieut. May 1916, promoted Lieut. Nov. 1916. Served in France and England.

HAROLD FOSTER HOLLINRAKE.

Articled to Sir William Cobbett, of Manchester. Joined June 19, 1915, as 2nd Lieut., 6th Batt. Lancashire Fusiliers. Resigned commission March 1917, and immediately enlisted as Private, 5th Batt. Lincolnshire Regt., transferred to 12th Batt. North Staffordshire Regt. and promoted to Sergeant. Served at Home, Gallipoli, Egypt, Sinai Peninsula 1915 to 1916 and in France 1917 to 1918. Killed in action at Hérinnes-lez-Pecq, Belgium, Nov. 8, 1918.

ESMOND MAUDSLEY HOLLINS.

Admitted Jan. 1908, practised at 3 Arundel Street, Strand, W.C. Served as 2nd Lieut., Royal Army Service Corps, promoted Lieut. July 1917.

DENZIL HOLLIS.

Admitted Oct. 1906. Managing Clerk with P. Ashcroft, of The Stag Brewery, Pimlico, S.W. Joined Nov. 8, 1916, as Private, Somerset Light Infantry. Gazetted 2nd Lieut. Royal Field Artillery March 3, 1917, promoted Lieut. Sept. 1918. Served in France and Belgium.

BERNARD HENRY HOLLOWAY.

Articled to J. C. Barnard, of 47 Lincoln's Inn Fields, W.C. Commissioned Sept. 23, 1914, as 2nd Lieut., Royal Sussex Regt., promoted Lieut. Oct. 1914, Capt. Dec. 1914. Served in France. Killed in action near Loos Sept. 27, 1915.

LEONARD CLOUDESLEY HOLLOWAY.

Admitted July 1909. Member of Templeton & Holloway, of 9 King's Bench Walk, Temple. Joined Dec. 12, 1916, as Cadet, Garrison Officer Cadet Batt., Cambridge. Gazetted 2nd Lieut. Worcestershire Regt. Feb. 11, 1917, promoted Lieut. April 1917, A/Capt. Nov. 1917, Capt. April 1918, A/Adjutant Sept. to Nov. 1917, Adjutant Nov. 1917 to July 1918. Served at Home.

JAMES WILLIAM HOLLOWS.

Articled to J. H. Chadwick, of Rochdale. Joined Sept. 1914, as Private, 20th Batt. Royal Fusiliers. Gazetted 2nd Lieut. 4th Batt. Lancashire Fusiliers May 20, 1915, promoted Lieut. July 1917. Served at Home Sept. 1914 to May 1916 and Oct. 1917 to Oct. 1918, and in France and Germany May 1916 to Oct. 1917 and Oct. 1918 to Jan. 1919. Wounded Oct. 1917.

ALEXANDER McARTHUR HOLMAN.

Articled to F. A. Holman, of 1 Lloyd's Avenue, E.C. Joined Aug. 1914, as 2nd Lieut., 6th Dragoon Guards (Special Reserve), promoted Lieut. 1916. Served in France. Wounded Sept. 1916.

ARTHUR LEWIS HOLMES.

Admitted Jan. 1914, practising at Lymington, Hants. Served as 2nd Lieut., Notts and Derby Regt. (Sherwood Foresters).

CHARLES WALKER HOLMES.

Admitted Dec. 1891. Member of Holmes, Son & Pott, of Capel House, New Broad Street, E.C. Joined Oct. 13, 1914, as Capt., Royal Field Artillery. Served at Home.

CYRIL ERNEST JACKSON HOLMES.

Articled to H. J. E. Holmes, of Burnley. Joined Nov. 22, 1915, as 2nd Lieut., 3/5 Batt. East Lancashire Regt., attached to 5th Batt. King's Liverpool Regt. Sept. 1916. Killed in action June 24, 1917, and buried in the British Cemetery at Armentières.

ERIC RICHARD HANBY HOLMES.

Practising at Barnard Castle. Mobilised as Capt., Durham Light Infantry, Served in France and the Balkans.

FREDERICK HOLMES.

Admitted Nov. 1905. Member of Dixon & Holmes, of Worthing. Joined Feb. 11, 1915, as Staff Sergeant-Major, Royal Army Service Corps. Served in France.

LEONARD HOLMES.

Admitted March 1885. Member of Brutton, Holmes & Johnson, of Hove. Mobilised Aug. 1914, as Major, 6th (Cyclist) Batt. Royal Sussex Regt., subsequently promoted Col.

NEWBY HOLMES.

Articled to L. R. Foster, of Sunderland. Served as Private, County Batt. Durham Light Infantry.

THOMAS WILLIAM HOLMES.

Articled to J. E. Wing, of Sheffield. Joined Sept. 10, 1914, as Private, 12th Batt. York and Lancaster Regt., promoted Lance-Corporal Investigation Branch, Provost Branch, Military Foot Police July 1916. Served in Egypt Dec. 1915 to March 1916, and in France and Germany April 1916 to July 1919.

WILLIAM WAINMAN HOLMES.

Admitted Nov. 1904, practising at Bradford, Yorks. Joined Dec. 17, 1916, as Private, Army Pay Corps, subsequently attained the rank of A/Lance-Sergeant. Served at Home.

JOHN CYRIL HOLMS.

Articled to the Hon. Sir Charles Russell, Bart., of 37 Norfolk Street, W.C. Joined Aug. 1914, as 2nd Lieut., 9th Batt. London Regt. Gazetted Capt. July 1915. Served in France Jan. to Sept. 1915. Died of wounds Sept. 10, 1915.

ALAN THOMAS SELBORNE HOLT.

Articled to J. G. Mahaffy, of Manchester. Joined Sept. 28, 1914, as 2nd Lieut., 17th Batt. Manchester Regt., promoted Lieut. Feb. 1917. Awarded M.C. Served in France. Wounded July 30 and Aug. 17, 1916. Wounded and taken prisoner while attacking Chérisy, near Arras, April 23, 1917.

GUY MARRINER WHITTELL HOLT.

Admitted Dec. 1909. Managing Clerk with Broughton, Holt & Middlemist, of 12 Great Marlborough Street, W. Joined Oct. 11, 1915, as 2nd Lieut., Duke of Wellington's West Riding Regt., promoted Lieut. (Staff) Royal Army Service Corps June 1916. Served at Home.

LANCELOT VERE HOLT.

Admitted April 1917, practising at Carmarthen. Served as Lieut., Royal Field Artillery (Jersey Militia).

OLIVER WILLIAM HOLT.

Admitted Dec. 1913. Member of Lupton & Holt, of Manchester. Joined Feb. 13, 1916, as Gunner, 287th Siege Battery, Royal Garrison Artillery. Served in France and Belgium.

CHARLES FIFIELD HOLTOM.

Articled to W. F. Holtom, of Stoke-on-Trent. Joined Aug. 27, 1914, as Private, North Staffordshire Regt., promoted Corporal Oct. 1914. Gazetted 2nd Lieut. in same Regt. Feb. 9, 1915. Served at Home and in France. Wounded Oct. 13, 1915. Died from wounds Aug. 4, 1916.

ARTHUR VALENTINE HOLYOAKE.

Admitted Feb. 1914. Clerk with Scott & Holyoake, of Bromsgrove, Worcestershire. Joined Sept. 1, 1914, as Trooper, Queen's Own Worcestershire Hussars. Gazetted 2nd Lieut. in same Regt. March 1915, promoted Lieut. July 1916, Capt. July 1917. Served in Eastern and Western Egypt. Captured by the Turks at Katia April 23, 1916.

HERBERT JOHN HOOD.

Admitted April 1892, practising at Plymouth. Served as Major, 5th Batt. Duke of Cornwall's Light Infantry.

JOHN SEABORNE HOOK.

Articled to C. A. G. Hayward, of Honiton, Devon. Joined Oct. 6, 1916, as Gunner, No. 7 Reserve Brigade Artillery (T.). Served at Home.

NORMAN EDGAR HOOLEY.

Articled to A. W. Dickins, of Nottingham. Joined 53rd (Young Soldiers) Batt. Leicestershire Regt. Nov. 8, 1918, transferred to 52nd Batt. April 1919. Served at Home and with Rhine Army.

CHARLES VICTOR LISLE HOOMAN.

Articled to W. K. Kitson, of Torquay. Served as Sub-Lieut., Royal Naval Reserve, on staff of Rear-Admiral Simpson.

WILLIAM HENRY HOOPER.

Admitted April 1913, practising at 8 Ely Place, E.C. Joined Aug. 16, 1916, Royal Garrison Artillery. Gazetted 2nd Lieut. 38th (Welsh) Divisional Train Royal Army Service Corps Oct. 1, 1917, promoted Capt. and Adjutant April 1918. Once mentioned in Dispatches. Served at Home Aug. 1916 to Oct. 1917, and in France Oct. 1917 to June 1919.

ROBERT FOWELL HOOPER-WATTS.

Articled to James Morley, of 38 Lincoln's Inn Fields, W.C. Served as Driver, Royal Naval Air Service.

ISAAC DANIEL HOOSON.

Admitted Dec. 1909. Member of Hooson & Hughes, of Wrexham. Joined May 3, 1917, as Aircraftsman, Royal Naval Air Service. Served at Home May 1917 to Feb. 1919.

WALTER HOOTON.

Admitted April 1908, practising at Nottingham. Served as Gunner, Royal Horse Artillery.

JOHN PERCIVAL HOPE.

Admitted Nov. 1899, practised at Cardiff. Served as Capt., King's Liverpool Regt.

ADRIAN EDMUND HOPKINS.

Articled to C. E. Barry, of Bristol. Served as Lieut., 1st Midland Brigade Gloucester Royal Field Artillery. Awarded M.C.

ARTHUR JOHN HOPKINS.

Admitted Jan. 1904, practising at Chesterfield. Served as Capt., 6th Batt. Notts and Derby Regt. (Sherwood Foresters), subsequently promoted Major.

HENRY HOPKINS.

Articled to W. A. Pearson, of York. Served as 2nd Class Air Mechanic, Royal Flying Corps.

CHARLES ALDEN HOPKINSON.

Admitted Jan. 1901, practising at 25 Craven Street, W.C. Served as Leading Seaman, Royal Naval Volunteer Reserve (Anti-Aircraft Corps).

REGINALD HOPWOOD.

Articled to G. H. Hindley, of Liverpool. Joined Sept. 20, 1914, as Private, 4th Batt. Cheshire Regt. and attained the rank of Sergeant. Commissioned Temp. 2nd Lieut. Middlesex Regt. April 1915, promoted Lieut. July 1916, and transferred to The Rifle Brigade Sept. 1916, attached to the Royal Fusiliers Nov. 1918, and subsequently appointed Civil Staff Capt. on the Military Governor's Staff, occupied German Territories. Served at Home, France, Belgium, and Germany. Wounded at Vadencourt, Somme, March 22, 1918.

EDWARD DASHPER HORLEY.

Articled to Edward Horley, of Cardiff. Joined May 14, 1915, as 2nd Lieut., Royal Field Artillery, promoted Lieut. July 1916, and attached to Royal Garrison Artillery Oct. 1916. Served in France. Wounded at Arras April 8, 1917.

ROBERT PHIPPS HORNBY.

Admitted Sept. 1902, practised at 38 Old Jewry, E.C. Served as Lieut., 6th Batt. Lancashire Fusiliers, promoted Capt. June 1916. Mentioned in Dispatches. Awarded the M.C.

BENJAMIN WORTHY HORNE.

Admitted July 1900. Member of Horne & Birkett, of 4 Lincoln's Inn Fields, W.C. Mobilised Aug. 1914, as Private, Hon. Artillery Company, subsequently attained the rank of Sergeant. Served at Home Aug. 1914 to May 1919.

ARTHUR LEONARD HORNER.

Admitted Aug. 1913, practising at 199 Piccadilly, W. Served with Royal Navy Armoured Cars.

FREDERICK JULIAN HORNER.
Articled to George Sutton, of Coventry. Joined Nov. 27, 1914, as 2nd Lieut., Royal Warwickshire Regt., promoted Lieut. 1915, Capt. 1918. Awarded the M.C. Served at Salonica, attached to 2nd Batt. Cheshire Regt. Died of wounds April 15, 1918.

ERNEST JOHN HORNIBLOW.
Articled to H. Jordan, of Reading. Joined Nov. 10, 1914, as Private, 2/14 Batt. County of London Regt. (London Scottish). Served as Piper throughout service. Served in France, Salonica, Egypt, and Palestine.

RONALD FORTESCUE HORNOR.
Admitted June 1912. Member of Blyth & Hornor, of Norwich. Served as Lieut., Royal Army Service Corps.

HAROLD GIBSON HORNSBY.
Admitted June 1910. On the Staff of the Solicitor to H.M. Customs and Excise, Lower Thames Street, E.C. Joined Sept. 20, 1914, as Private, Bristol Batt. Gloucestershire Regt., transferred to 20th Hussars Jan. 1915. Gazetted 2nd Lieut. 11th Batt. Yorkshire Regt. Easter 1915. Served in France from Oct. 1915. Killed in action at Fricourt July 1, 1916.

HAROLD HORSEMAN.
Admitted March 1915. Assistant Solicitor, Public Trustee Office. Joined April 6, 1916, as Private, 4/10 Batt. Middlesex Regt., promoted Sergeant, Officiating Indian Unattached List Nov. 1918. Served on Garrison Duty in India.

EDWARD HORSFALL.
Admitted May 1913, practising at Manchester. Joined Aug. 6, 1914, as 2nd Lieut., 8th (Ardwick) Batt. Manchester Regt. (T.F.), promoted Lieut. May 1915, Capt. June 1916, A/Major March to April 1918, attached to 1/7 Batt. Lancashire Fusiliers as A/Major Oct. 1918. Once mentioned in Dispatches. Awarded the M.C. Served at Home Aug. to Sept. 1914, Cyprus Sept. 1914 to Jan. 1915, Egypt Jan. to April 1915, Gallipoli April 1915 to Jan. 1916, Sinai Jan. 1916 to Feb. 1917, France Feb. 1917 to Feb. 1919. Wounded at Gallipoli May 21, 1915, and Dec. 27, 1915.

WILLIAM EWART HORSLEY.
Articled to J. R. Farrar, of Halifax. Joined Nov. 20, 1915, as Private, Inns of Court O.T.C. Gazetted 2nd Lieut. Duke of Wellington's West Riding Regt. Nov. 23, 1916, promoted A/Capt. Aug. 1917. Served in France Jan. to Oct. 1917 and July 1918 to Jan. 1919.

KENNETH CHARLES HORTON.
Articled to Moody & Woolley, of Derby. Served as Sergeant, Public Schools Batt. Royal Fusiliers.

WALTER HORTON.
Admitted Dec. 1902, practised at Birmingham. Served as 2nd Lieut. 6th Batt. South Staffordshire Regt., promoted Lieut. June 1916.

ARCHIBALD HARDING HOSEGOOD.

Articled to Frank Risdon, of Williton, Somerset. Joined Dec. 1914, as Private, 24th Batt. Royal Fusiliers (2nd Sportsman's), transferred to O.T.C. April 1916. Gazetted 2nd Lieut. 86th Machine Gun Corps Sept. 1916. Served at Home Dec. 1914 to Nov. 1915 and April to Nov. 1916, and in France Nov. 1915 to March 1916 and Nov. 1916 to Nov. 1917, Killed in action at Cambrai Nov. 27, 1917.

RALPH HOSEGOOD.

Articled to F. J. Harris, of Bristol. Joined Sept. 5, 1914, as Private, 12th Batt. Gloucestershire Regt. (Bristol's Own). Gazetted 2nd Lieut. in same Regt. March 29, 1915, and later became officer in 95th Trench Mortar Battery. Once mentioned in Dispatches. Served at Home Sept. 1914 to Nov. 1915, and in France Nov. 1915 to July 1916. Killed in action at Longueval July 23, 1916. Buried in Dantzig Alley Cemetery at Mametz.

JOHN FAYRER HOSKEN.

Admitted April 1903. Member of Walbrook & Hosken, of 4 St. Paul's Churchyard, E.C. Joined Nov. 11, 1915, Railway Transport Establishment, as Lieut. (graded as Staff Lieut. 2nd Class), Railway Transport Officer (graded as Staff Lieut. 1st Class 1916, promoted Staff Capt. Dec. 1918. Served in France Dec. 1915 to Jan. 1919.

SYDNEY LORY HOSKING.

Admitted March 1904. Member of Hosking & Berkeley, of 35 Lincoln's Inn Fields, W.C. Mobilised Aug. 1914, as Capt., 7th (City of London) Batt. London Regt. (T.), promoted Major 1915, Lieut.-Col. 1917. Twice mentioned in Dispatches. Served at Home 1914 to 1916 and 1918 and 1919, and in France 1917 and 1918. Gassed April 17, 1918.

GEORGE FINCH HOTBLACK.

Admitted May 1908. Member of Waltons & Co., of 101 Leadenhall Street, E.C. Served as Staff Lieut., XXII Corps Heavy Artillery.

FRANK BOYD HOTCHEN.

Articled to H. C. Lings, of Manchester. Joined Sept. 7, 1914, as Private, 20th Batt. Royal Fusiliers. Gazetted 2nd Lieut. East Lancashire Regt. Jan. 25, 1917, promoted Lieut. July 1918, Capt. Nov. 1918, attached to Royal Engineers. Served in France Nov. 1915 to Aug. 1916 and March 1917 to July 1919.

ARTHUR THEODORE HOUGHTON.

Admitted Dec. 1904. Member of Houghton, Myres & Reveley, of Preston. Joined Aug. 5, 1914, as 2nd Lieut., 4th Batt. Loyal North Lancashire Regt., promoted Lieut. Oct. 1915, Temp. Capt. Jan. 1916, Substantive Capt. June 1916. Awarded the M.C. Served in France and Belgium 1915 to 1917. Wounded at Festubert June 14, 1915, and at Vancelette Farm Nov. 30, 1917.

CECIL GILBERT HOUGHTON.

Admitted June 1905. Member of Gilbert Houghton & Son, of 63 Finsbury Pavement, E.C. Joined Oct. 1914, as Private, Inns of Court O.T.C., and attained the rank of Sergeant. Commissioned as 2nd Lieut. in same Regt May 2, 1916, subsequently promoted Lieut. and A/Capt. Served at Hom and in France.

NOËL HOUGHTON.

Admitted Feb. 1908. Member of Gilbert Houghton & Sons, of 63 Finsbur Pavement, E.C. Enlisted Aug. 1914, as Private, Inns of Court O.T.C. Com missioned June 1915, Temp. Major Dec. 1915, A/Lieut.-Col. in command o 16th Batt. Notts and Derby Regt. (Sherwood Foresters) 1917. Specia mention in Dispatches. Served in France. Killed in action Sept. 13, 1917.

ALEC GUY HOULDER.

Admitted Feb. 1905, practising at 6 Lloyd's Avenue, E.C. Served a Major, 2nd (Reserve) City of London Batt. Royal Fusiliers.

WILSON ALFRED LAWRENCE HOULDER.

Admitted April 1912, practising at 27 Chancery Lane, W.C. Joinec Jan. 17, 1916, as Driver, Royal Army Service Corps. Gazetted 2nd Lieut in same Regt. Feb. 29, 1916, promoted Lieut. Aug. 1917, attached to Nortl Stafford Regt. Jan. 1918. Served at Home Jan. to Sept. 1916 and Oct. 191 to March 1919, and in France Sept. 1916 to Oct. 1917.

EDWARD BICKNELL HOULSTON.

Admitted Dec. 1904. Managing Clerk with Parson, Lee & Co., of 24 Lim Street, E.C. Mobilised Aug. 1914, as Sergeant, 16th Batt. County of Londo Regt. (Queen's Westminster Rifles), and attained the rank of Company-Sergeant Major in May 1915. Gazetted Lieut. Royal Army Ordnance Departmen March 19, 1916, promoted A/Capt. May 1918. Served at Home Aug. to Oct 1914; and in France and Belgium Nov. 1914 to June 1919.

CHARLES FREDERICK HOUSE.

Articled to W. H. House, of Sevenoaks. Served as Private, Royal Wes Kent Regt.

ALFRED CYRIL HOWARD.

Admitted June 1914. Clerk with Harold Salt, of Bournemouth. Joinec Sept. 28, 1914, as Private, 1/7 Batt. Hampshire Regt. Commissioned a 2nd Lieut. 3rd Batt. Hampshire Regt. Jan. 31, 1917, and subsequently pro moted Lieut. Awarded the M.C. Served at Home, India and Egypt, Franc and Salonica.

CHARLES MALCOLM HOWARD.

Admitted Oct. 1912. Member of Charles Howard & Co., of Manchester Joined Aug. 1914, as Private, The Rifle Brigade. Gazetted 2nd Lieut. Machin Gun Corps Dec. 1914, promoted Lieut., Capt., and subsequently Major Awarded the M.C. Served in France and Egypt. Gassed and wounded.

HENRY WILFRID HOWARD SMITH HOWARD.

Articled to J. B. Pearman, of 10 Norfolk Street, W.C. Joined May 13 1915, as Private, Inns of Court O.T.C. Gazetted 2nd Lieut. Royal Sussex Regt. Aug. 21, 1915, promoted Lieut. July 1917. Served in Egypt, Palestin

Jan. 1916 to June 1918, and in France June to Sept. 1918. Wounded at 1st Battle of Gaza March 26, 1917.

JULIAN ARTHUR HOWARD-WATSON.
Admitted Nov. 1902, practising at Liverpool. Joined in 1915 as Driver, Royal Army Service Corps. Subsequently commissioned in same Regt., and attained the rank of Temp. Capt. and Courts-Martial Officer to Army of the Black Sea.

BENJAMIN EDWARD HOWE.
Admitted Nov. 1911. Of Port Talbot. Joined Dec. 31, 1915, as 2nd Lieut., 4th Batt. The Welch Regt. (T.), subsequently promoted Lieut. Served in Egypt and Palestine.

PHILIP HOWE.
Articled to Albert Howe, of Sheffield. Joined Sept. 1914, as Private, 12th Batt. York and Lancaster Regt. Gazetted 2nd Lieut. 10th Batt. West Yorkshire Regt. Nov. 2, 1914, promoted Lieut. May 1916, Capt. June 1917. Awarded the M.C. Served in France. Wounded Aug. 2, 1915, July 1, 1916, and May 2, 1918.

OWEN BULMER HOWELL.
Admitted Nov. 1906. Member of Neish, Howell & Haldane, of 47 Watling Street, E.C. Joined July 1916, as 2nd Lieut., Royal Flying Corps, acted as Pilot Instructor and as Temp. Flight Commander, transferred to Royal Naval Air Service as Sub-Lieut. June 1917, and to Royal Air Force as Lieut. April 1918. Served at Home, and on Anti-Submarine work in Home Waters.

VERNON HOWELL.
Articled to W. Howell, of Llanelly. Joined Nov. 30, 1914, as 2nd Lieut., 15th Batt. The Welch Regt., promoted Lieut. July 1915, Capt. 1917. Served at Home $1\frac{1}{2}$ years, France 2 years, and in India July 1918 to Feb. 1919 with 26th Punjabis, and Feb. to Dec. 1919 with 87th Punjabis in Mesopotamia. Wounded July 27, 1917.

WILLIAM JENNINGS HOWEY.
Admitted June 1917, practising at 3 Gray's Inn Square, W.C. Joined Royal Flying Corps Sept. 1916 as 2nd Class Air-Mechanic, appointed 1st Air-Mechanic June 1917, promoted Corporal June 1918. Served in France 1916 to 1919.

JOHN LESLIE DESPARD HOWITT.
Articled to A. G. Hawkins, of Colchester. Served as 2nd Lieut., 10th Batt. Essex Regt., promoted Lieut. Feb. 1917.

CHARLES WILFRED HOWLETT.
Articled to F. R. Howlett, of Maidstone. Joined Sept. 1914 as Private, Public School Corps. Gazetted 2nd Lieut. 9th Batt. King's Own Yorkshire Light Infantry 1915. Served in France Sept. 1915 to July 1916. Killed in action at Battle of the Somme July 1, 1916.

THOMAS FREDERICK HOWSE.

Admitted Jan. 1902. Member of King, Hughes & Howse, of Maidstone. Joined July 5, 1918, as Private, 28th Batt. County of London Regt. (Artists Rifles). Gazetted 2nd Lieut. Royal West Kent Regt. Feb. 3, 1919. Served at Home.

THOMAS ASPDEN HOWSON.

Admitted Feb. 1910. Of Blackburn, Lancs. Mobilised Aug. 1914 as 2nd Lieut., Royal Field Artillery (T.F.), promoted Lieut. Aug. 1914, Temp. Capt. April 1915, Capt. June 1916. Once mentioned in Dispatches. Served at Home, and in France and Belgium.

HARRY HOYLE.

Articled to Alex Wright, of Bacup. Joined Royal Flying Corps July 27, 1916, as a 2nd Air-Mechanic, promoted 1st Air-Mechanic Dec. 1917. Served in France Aug. 1916 to Jan. 1919.

HENRY HOYLE.

Admitted Feb. 1901, practising at Bacup. Served as 2nd Air-Mechanic, No. 5 Squadron, Royal Flying Corps.

JOHN CLEON HUBBARD.

Admitted Dec. 1913. Member of Hopper & Hubbard, of Holsworthy, Devon. Joined July 16, 1915, as 2nd Class Air-Mechanic, Royal Flying Corps, appointed 1st Class Air-Mechanic Oct. 1915, promoted Sergeant Dec. 1915, Flight Sergeant May 1916. Served at Home.

LEONARD HUBBARD.

Admitted Nov. 1901, practising at 59 Chancery Lane, W.C. Joined and commissioned Oct. 7, 1914, as Lieut., Royal Army Service Corps, promoted Capt. June 1917. Served in France and Salonica.

HAROLD ROBERT HUDLESTON.

Admitted July 1908. Member of the Solicitor's Staff, London and North-Western Railway Company, Euston Station, N.W. Joined April 22, 1915, as Private, Inns of Court O.T.C. Gazetted 2nd Lieut. and attached to 14th Batt. Middlesex Regt. June 23, 1915. Served in France. Killed in action in Battle of Somme, France, July 1, 1916.

ALLAN HARRISON HUDSON.

Articled to Arthur Briggs, of Stockport. Served as 2nd Lieut., 9th Batt. Manchester Regt. Died June 14, 1915, of wounds received in action at the Dardanelles.

ERNEST WALTER HUDSON.

Admitted Feb. 1902. Member of Watson, Burton & Corder, of Newcastle-upon-Tyne. Joined March 1915, as 2nd Lieut., 1/1 Northumbrian Brigade Royal Field Artillery (T.), promoted Lieut. Oct. 1915. Served in France and Flanders.

FRANK HUDSON.

Admitted Jan. 1907. Member of Roberts, Riley, Creeke, & Hudson, of Burnley and Manchester. Enlisted May 1916, as Private, Border Regt. Gazetted 2nd Lieut. Border Regt. March 1917, transferred to the 12th Batt.

Manchester Regt. Nov. 1917. Served in France May 1917 to Oct. 1918. Killed in action at Neuvilly, France, Oct. 12, 1918.

NORMAN HUDSON.

Articled to T. G. Baynes, of Dartford, Kent. Joined Jan. 24, 1916, as Private, 23rd Batt. Royal Fusiliers. Served in France. Wounded and taken prisoner at Miraumont Feb. 17, 1917. Leg since amputated.

NOEL HUGH-JONES.

Articled to Llewellyn Hugh-Jones, of Wrexham. Mobilised Aug. 1914, as Lieut., 4th Batt. Royal Welch Fusiliers (T.), crossed to France Nov. 1914, severely wounded June 1915. Obtained Cadetship at Wellington College, Madras, 1916; torpedoed in Mediterranean, awarded Medal of Royal Humane Society for gallantry on that occasion. As Capt. 53rd Sikhs F.F. attached 2/151 Indian Infantry F.F. Served in Palestine 1918. Awarded M.C.

ALLAN GIBSON HUGHES.

Admitted Aug. 1912. Member of H. W. Hughes & Son, of Shrewsbury. Mobilised Aug. 1914, as Lieut., 4th Batt. King's Shropshire Light Infantry, promoted Capt. 1916., A.D.C. to General F. Ventris 1915 to 1917, and additional duties of G.S.O. III. Served in the East, France, and Belgium. Wounded Dec. 30, 1917.

DAVID WYNFORD HUGHES.

Articled to Thomas Hughes, of Ebbw Vale. Joined Nov. 12, 1915, as Private, 3rd Batt. Monmouthshire Regt., promoted Lance-Corporal Feb. 1916. Gazetted 2nd Lieut. Nov. 12, 1916, promoted Lieut. May 1918. Served at Home and in France. Wounded Jan. 1917.

EDMUND JOHN HUGHES.

Admitted Nov. 1906, practising at Aberdare. Joined Sept. 30, 1915, as Private, Inns of Court O.T.C. Discharged Inns of Court May 1916 medically unfit. Joined The Welch Regt., as Private, July 1917. Gazetted 2nd Lieut. Labour Corps Feb. 22, 1918, promoted A/Lieut. April 1918. Served at Home as Commandant Prisoners of War Camp.

EDWARD GEORGE VICTOR HUGHES.

Articled to T. F. Howse, of Maidstone. Joined Sept. 18, 1914, as Private, 19th Batt. Royal Fusiliers. Gazetted 2nd Lieut. The Queen's Own Royal West Kent Regt. Jan. 9, 1915, promoted Lieut. June 1916, Capt. Nov. 1917. Twice mentioned in Dispatches. Awarded M.C. Served in France.

ERIC YORATH HUGHES.

Articled to Evan Davies, of Cardiff. Served as 2nd Lieut., 2nd Welsh Brigade Royal Field Artillery, promoted Lieut. June 1916.

ERNEST CHARLES HUGHES.

Admitted May 1914, of Northwich. Served with the 11th Batt. Cheshire Regt.

GEOFFREY LEONARD HUGHES.

Articled to R. H. Rotherham, of Coventry. Joined Sept. 1914, as Private, 3rd City of Birmingham Batt. Royal Warwickshire Regt., transferred to Royal Sussex Regt. 1915, to 19th Batt. Royal Fusiliers 1915, to 24th Batt.

Royal Fusiliers 1916, attaining rank Lance-Sergeant. Served in France. Reported missing, believed killed, at Beaumont Hamel Nov. 13, 1916, since presumed to have been killed on that date.

GEORGE EDWARD HUGHES.

Admitted Oct. 1910, practising at Bournemouth prior to War. Joined Nov. 23, 1914, as 2nd Lieut., East Surrey Regt. (T.F.), promoted Temp. Capt. Dec. 1915, seconded 70th Provisional Batt. (T.F.) 1915, to 17th Batt. Essex Regt. 1916, and to Inland Waterways and Docks, Royal Engineers, 1917. Served at Home.

GEORGE OSWALD HUGHES.

Admitted Dec. 1906. Member of Hooson & Hughes, of Wrexham. Joined May 29, 1915, as Private, 131st Field Ambulance, 38th (Welsh) Division, and subsequently promoted Sergeant. Served in France and Flanders Dec. 1915 to Feb. 1919.

HUGH BURGESS HUGHES.

Admitted Nov. 1910. Managing Clerk with Ellis, Peirs & Co., of 17 Albemarle Street, W. Joined Nov. 4, 1915, as Cadet, London University O.T.C. Gazetted 2nd Lieut. Royal Field Artillery (Special Reserve) Jan. 14, 1916, promoted A/Lieut. Nov. 1916, Substantive Lieut. (Special Reserve) July 1917. Served in France and Belgium June 1916 to April 1917.

JOHN ARTHUR HUGHES.

Admitted Feb. 1884, practising at Barry, near Cardiff. Served as Lieut.-Col., in Recruiting Staff, and County Director for Glamorgan V.A.D. Resigned commission on Recruiting Staff owing to close of Recruiting Office Jan. 1918. Awarded C.B.E.

JOHN ARTHUR HUGHES.

Admitted July 1909, practised at Conway. Served as 2nd Lieut., 4th (Denbighshire) Batt. Royal Welch Fusiliers in France. Killed in action Jan. 27, 1915.

JOHN HENRY GLYNNE HUGHES.

Admitted Nov. 1898, practising at Ammanford. Served with Royal Air Force.

LEWIS REGINALD HUGHES.

Articled to A. J. Hughes, of Aberystwyth. Served in France as 2nd Lieut., 4th Batt. North Staffordshire Regt., attached to the 2nd Batt. Royal Scots Fusiliers. Died of wounds received in action on May 17, 1915.

PERCY BARTLETT HUGHES.

Admitted Nov. 1912. Member of Percy Hughes & Roberts, of Birkenhead. Joined Oct. 1915, as Private, Inns of Court O.T.C. Commissioned as 2nd Lieut. Westmorland and Cumberland Yeomanry Nov. 1919, subsequently promoted Lieut. Served at Home 1915 to 1916, and afterwards in France.

SAM HUGHES.

Articled to Jagger & Clement Jones, of Wrexham. Enlisted, as Private, 15th Batt. Royal Welch Fusiliers. Gazetted 2nd Lieut. The Welch Regt. Served in France. Killed in action at Ypres, Nov. 8, 1917.

THOMAS ARTHUR HUGHES.

Admitted Dec. 1907, practising at Colwyn Bay, North Wales. Joined March 1, 1915, as Private, 17th Batt. Royal Welch Fusiliers. Commissioned in same Regt. May 1, 1915, promoted Capt. April 1916. Served in France Aug. 1916 to March 1918. Wounded March 10, 1918.

THOMAS JOHN HUGHES.

Articled to F. M. Radcliffe, of Liverpool. Joined Sept. 22, 1915, as Voluntary Ambulance Driver, British Red Cross Society. Awarded Croce di Guerra (Italian Military Cross). Served in France Sept. to Oct. 1915, and in Italy Oct. 1915 to March 1919.

WILLIAM HUGHES.

Admitted Jan. 1902. Member of Hogan & Hughes, of 7 Arthur Street, E.C. Joined in 1915, as a Private, 28th Batt. County of London Regt. (Artists Rifles). Went to France in the spring of 1916, and received a commission as 2nd Lieut. Bedfordshire Regt. Awarded the M.C. Dangerously wounded near Ovillers July 3, 1918. Died from wounds Sept. 14, 1918.

WILLIAM EDWIN HUGHES-NARBOROUGH.

Admitted Oct. 1906. Member of Hughes-Narborough & Thomas, of "Effingham House," Arundel Street, Strand, W.C. Joined in 1917, as 1st Air Mechanic, Royal Naval Air Service, subsequently promoted Aero Engine Instructor (Staff) Aero Engine School. Served at Home.

CHARLES KENELM HULBERT.

Admitted Jan. 1902. Member of Pye-Smith & Hulbert, of Salisbury. Joined April 8, 1915, as 2nd Lieut., promoted Lieut. 85th Provisional Batt. (T.) June 1915, A/Capt. 7th Batt. Wiltshire Regt. Oct. 1916, Temp. Capt March 1917, Temp. Major Sept. 1917. Awarded the M.C. and Bar. Served at Home and in Egypt, Salonica, and France.

ERNEST GRAHAM JOHNSTON HUMBERT.

Admitted Jan. 1913. Managing Clerk with R. S. Taylor, Son & Humbert, of 4 Field Court, Gray's Inn, W.C. Joined Aug. 4, 1914, as Private, Inns of Court O.T.C. Granted commission Oct. 1914, posted to 9th Batt. Royal Berkshire Regt. Oct. 1914, promoted Lieut. Jan. 1915, attached 2nd Batt. Hampshire Regt. May 1915. Served at Gallipoli. Died of wounds June 8, 1915.

OWEN JOHNSTON HUMBERT.

Admitted Dec. 1910. Member of R. S. Taylor, Son & Humbert, of 4 Field Court, Gray's Inn, W.C. Joined June 1, 1916, as Private, Royal Army Service Corps. Gazetted 2nd Lieut. Royal Army Service Corps July 10, 1916, attached 142nd Siege Battery Royal Garrison Artillery, attached 4th Siege Battery Feb. 1917, attached XVIII. Corps Headquarters Aug. 1917, posted to 33rd Auxiliary Petrol Company Sept. 1917; promoted Lieut. Jan. 1918, Adjutant 5th Army Troops Mechanical Transport Company March 1918. Served in France 1916 to 1919.

CYRIL MITFORD HUMBLE-CROFTS.

Admitted Feb. 1905. Solicitor to The National Cash Register Company, Tottenham Court Road, W.C. Joined Sept. 1914, as Private, Hon. Artillery

Company. Gazetted as 2nd Lieut. Hon. Artillery Company Dec. 1914, Capt. 13th Batt. Royal Sussex Regt. Feb. 1915. Served in France March to June 1916. Killed in action at Richebourg l'Avoué, France, June 30, 1916.

BRUCE HUMFREY.

Articled to H. Scott Tucker, of 2 Laurence Pountney Hill, E.C. Joined in Oct. 1914, as Private, 2nd (Public Schools) Batt. Royal Fusiliers, subsequently gazetted Lieut. 1st Garrison Batt. Manchester Regt. Served in India.

WILLIAM MURRAY HUMPHREY.

Admitted Nov. 1901, practising at Sunderland. Joined Dec. 3, 1915, as Private, Seaforth Highlanders, promoted Lance-Corporal Jan. 1917, Corporal Sept. 1917, Sergeant 43rd Royal Fusiliers June 1918, Company-Quartermaster-Sergeant Dec. 1918. Awarded the M.S.M. Served in France.

DUDLEY FRANCIS HUMPHREYS.

Articled to R. H. Humphreys, of Giltspur Chambers Holborn Viaduct, E.C. Joined Aug. 3, 1914, as Private, 28th Batt. County of London Regt. (Artists Rifles). Gazetted 2nd Lieut. 2nd Batt. Queen's Royal West Surrey Regt. Dec. 15, 1914. Served at Home and in France. Killed at Festubert May 16, 1915.

GWILYM VAUGHAN HUMPHREYS.

Articled to Robert Davies, of Denbigh. Joined Jan. 10, 1917, as Private, Royal Welch Fusiliers, afterwards transferred to King's Liverpool Regt. Labour Batt. Served at Home.

REGINALD PERCY HUMPHREYS.

Articled to J. W. Alsop, of Liverpool. Served as 2nd Lieut., 7th Batt. King's Liverpool Regt. (T.)

GERALD NORMAN HUNNYBUN.

Admitted Aug. 1911. Of Huntingdon. Joined Sept. 1914, as 2nd Lieut., 9th Batt. Yorkshire Regt., and subsequently promoted Adjutant, Lieut., and Major. Twice mentioned in Dispatches. Awarded the M.C. Served in France and Italy. Killed Oct. 23, 1918.

KENNETH HUNNYBUN.

Admitted March 1911. Member of Hunnybun & Sons, of Huntingdon. Served as Capt., Huntingdonshire Cyclist Batt. (T.), promoted Major June 1916. Mentioned in Dispatches. Awarded the D.S.O.

MARTIN GERALD WOODLEY HUNNYBUN.

Admitted April 1904. Member of Hunnybun & Sons, of Huntingdon. Served as Lance-Corporal, Huntingdonshire Cyclist Batt. (T.). Gazetted Lieut. 9th Batt. Argyll and Sutherland Highlanders July 1917.

CHARLES ANTHONY HUNT.

Admitted May 1902. Chief Assistant Solicitor, Metropolitan Water Board, 2 South Place, E.C. Joined June 14, 1917, as Private, Inns of Court O.T.C. Gazetted 2nd Lieut. Labour Corps Dec. 16, 1917. Served in France and at Home.

EDGAR WALLER HUNT.

Admitted Dec. 1912. Member of Dixon & Hunt, of 4 Verulam Buildings, Gray's Inn, W.C. Joined Feb. 1916, as Private, Hertfordshire Yeomanry. Gazetted 2nd Lieut. Westminster Dragoons (attached Queen's Own Oxfordshire Hussars). Wounded in France Sept. 3, 1918.

HARRY HUNT.

Admitted June 1905, practising at Woking. Joined May 16, 1916, as Staff-Sergeant, Royal Army Service Corps Forage Department. Served at Home.

JACK HUNT.

Admitted Oct. 1912, practising at Peterborough. Joined Jan. 1, 1917, as Private, 5th T.R.B. (Infantry), promoted Lance-Corporal 2/6 West Yorkshire Regt. (T.) April 1917. Gazetted 2nd Lieut. 4th Batt. Lincolnshire Regt. (T). Jan. 3, 1918. Served at Home Jan. to April 1917 and July 1917 to March 1919, and in France April to July 1917.

JOSEPH HUNT.

Admitted Jan. 1904. Member of Fowle & Hunt, of Northallerton. Joined Nov. 4, 1914, as 2nd Lieut. 2/4 Batt. Loyal North Lancashire Regt., subsequently promoted Lieut. and Capt. Served at Home and in France.

ROBERT LANCELOT GIBBS HUNT.

Articled to John Hunt, of Banbury. Gazetted 2nd Lieut. 6th Batt. Oxford and Bucks Light Infantry Sept. 12, 1914, promoted Lieut. Feb. 1915, Capt. Aug. 1916. Served in France. Wounded at Ypres April 1916. Killed at Gueudecourt Oct. 7, 1916.

WALTER JOHN HUNT.

Admitted April 1898, practising at Pershore, Worcestershire. Mobilised Aug. 1914, as Capt., 8th Batt. Worcestershire Regt., promoted Major June 1916. Served at Home and in France.

GERALD WILLIAM HUNTBACH.

Admitted April 1914. Member of W. M. Huntbach, of Hanley. Mobilised Aug. 1914, as Lieut., 4th Batt. King's Shropshire Light Infantry (T.F.), promoted Capt. Oct. 1914, transferred to Machine Gun Corps (Motors) Aug. 1915, to Tank Corps Dec. 1916, promoted to Temp. Major Jan. 1917. Served at Home Aug. 1914 to Feb. 1916, and in France Feb. to Oct. 1916 and Aug. 1917 to April 1919. Wounded at Cambrai Nov. 20, 1917.

WILLIAM HUNTBACH.

Admitted Feb. 1886, practising at Hanley. Served as Major, 4th Batt. King's Shropshire Light Infantry.

ARTHUR JOHN HUNTER.

Articled to E. L. Chapman, of 44 Bloomsbury Square, W.C. Served as Lance-Corporal, 14th Batt. County of London Regt. (London Scottish).

RICHARD JOCELYN HUNTER.

Admitted Nov. 1912. Member of Hunter & Haynes, of 5 New Square, Lincoln's Inn, W.C. Served as Capt., London Regt. Wounded Aug. 24, 1918. Died before reaching Clearing Station.

WILLIAM STUART HUNTER.

Admitted May 1913. Managing Clerk with H. T. Kearsey, of Grimsby. Joined Dec. 1915, as 2nd Lieut., 8th Batt. Lincolnshire Regt. Killed in action July 31, 1919.

WENSLEY BARCLAY HUNTON.

Admitted Dec. 1894. Member of W. B. & C. Hunton, of Richmond, Yorks. Rejoined Aug. 31, 1914, with rank of Capt. the Special Reserve of the A.P.W.O. Yorkshire Regt., Temp. Major March to Oct. 1915, promoted Substantive Major June 1918. Served at Home, Flanders, and Bermuda.

WILLIAM HUNTRISS.

Admitted April 1911. Member of Huntriss & Huntriss, of Halifax. Joined Sept. 1914 Public Schools and University Corps. Gazetted Lieut. 3rd Batt. Duke of Wellington's West Riding Regt., afterwards attached to Gold Coast Regt. Served in France and East Africa. Wounded in France. Died at Coomassie of pneumonia Oct. 23, 1916.

HUGH SWANN HURRELL.

Articled to H. F. J. Banham, of Royston, Herts. Served as 2nd Lieut., Kent Cyclist Batt.

JOHN NORMAN HURRELL.

Admitted Oct. 1908, practising at Kingsbridge, Devon. Joined Sept. 18, 1914, as 2nd Lieut., 1/7 (C.) Batt. Devon Regt., promoted Lieut. June 1916, attached 2/8 Batt. Worcestershire Regt. May 1916, attached 61st Medium Trench Mortars Aug. 1916, and subsequently posted to Y Battery 61st Medium Trench Mortars. Served at Home and in France. Taken prisoner at St. Quentin March 21, 1918.

NORMAN CECIL HURST.

Articled to F. H. Stapley, of Eastbourne. Joined Aug. 28, 1915, as 2nd Lieut., Sussex Royal Garrison Artillery and attached to 164th Siege Battery, promoted to Lieut. June 1916, A/Major June 1917, promoted A/Capt. and 2nd in command of 323rd Siege Battery April 1918, appointed A/Major of 323rd Siege Battery May 4 to 11, 1918, remained A/Capt. May 1918 to April 1919. Served at Home Aug. 1915 to Sept. 1916, and in France Sept. 1916 to April 1919.

CHARLES JOHN HUSKINSON.

Admitted Aug. 1888. Member of Larken & Co., of Lincoln and Newark. Mobilised Aug. 1914 as Col. in command of 8th Batt. Sherwood Foresters and went to France as Lieut.-Col. in 1914, promoted Colonel in 1918. Twice mentioned in Dispatches. Awarded O.B.E. (Military). Served in France.

WILLIAM GORDON HUTCHENCE.

Admitted Nov. 1909, practised at Saltburn-by-the-Sea. Served as Capt., 18th (Service) Batt. Durham Light Infantry, promoted Major Jan. 1917.

ANTHONY CHRISTOPHER CAMPBELL HUTCHINSON.

Admitted Dec. 1908, practised at 18 Austin Friars, E.C. Joined Sept. 1914, as 2nd Lieut., 5th Batt. Royal Fusiliers, promoted Lieut. 1915, Capt. 1916 when he transferred to the Regular Army, A/Major Oct. 1916. Served in the Serbian retreat and in Salonica and was given command of a Machine Gun Company. Joined the Egyptian Expeditionary Force Sept. 1917, and served in Palestine. Contracted influenza which developed into double pneumonia. Died Nov. 18, 1918.

ARTHUR ST. CLARE HUTCHINSON.

Admitted July 1909. Of Croydon. Served as 2nd Lieut., 4th Batt. South Wales Borderers.

EDGAR FRANCIS HUTCHINSON.

Admitted March 1914. Member of M. W. and E. F. Hutchinson, of Middlesbrough. Joined Nov. 1914, as Private, Inns of Court O.T.C. Commissioned as 2nd Lieut. 4th Batt. Yorkshire Regt. (T.) March 1915. Served in France. Killed in action at Ypres May 24, 1915.

HANLEY HUTCHINSON.

Admitted Oct. 1913, practised at Ripon. Joined Sept. 1914, as Lieut., 5th Batt. West Yorkshire Regt., subsequently appointed Machine Gun Officer to Brigade. Served in France. Wounded Aug. 31, 1917, died Sept. 1, 1917.

MILES WILLIAM HUTCHINSON.

Admitted Feb. 1903. Member of M. W. and E. F. Hutchinson, of Middlesbrough. Joined May 4, 1917, as Private, 83rd Training Reserve Batt. Yorkshire Regt., transferred to 3rd Batt. Duke of Wellington's West Riding Regt. July 1917, and to 19th Officers Cadet Batt. Nov. 1917. Gazetted 2nd Lieut. 2nd Batt. Notts and Derby Regt. (Sherwood Foresters) May 1918. Served at Home and in France.

NOEL WILFRID HUTCHINSON.

Admitted April 1914. Managing Clerk with Crossman, Prichard & Co., of 16 Theobald's Road, Gray's Inn, W.C. Joined Sept. 4, 1914, as Private, 28th Batt. County of London Regt. (Artists Rifles). Commissioned 2nd Lieut. Royal Militia, Isle of Jersey, Feb. 9, 1915, seconded to Royal Army Service Corps (M.T.) Dec. 1915, promoted Temp. Lieut. June 1916, appointed Adjutant Royal Army Service Corps, London District, with acting rank of Capt. Aug. 1918. Served at Home and in Jersey.

ALFRED HUTLEY.

Admitted April 1899, practising at Leeds. Served with the Legion of Frontiersmen (Leeds District).

ARTHUR MILES HUTTON.

Admitted March 1909. Managing Clerk with Whites & Co., of 28 Budge Row, E.C. Mobilised Aug. 4, 1914, as Private, 28th Batt. County of London Regt. (Artists Rifles), promoted Lance-Corporal Feb. 1915. Commissioned 2nd Lieut. Royal Army Service Corps Aug. 15, 1915, promoted Lieut. June 1916, appointed A/Capt. Oct. 1918. Served at Home till Sept. 1915, Dardanelles Oct. 1915 to Feb. 1916, Egypt Feb. 1916 to Feb. 1918 and April to Aug. 1919, Palestine Feb. 1918 to April 1919.

HAROLD EDWARD HYDE.

Articled to C. J. Bayspool Porter, of 2 Wardrobe Place, Doctors' Commons, E.C. Joined Aug. 1915, as Private, 1/4 Batt. London Regt. (Royal Fusiliers), and subsequently promoted Lance-Corporal. Awarded the M.M. Served at Home, Malta, Cairo, Dardanelles, and France. Killed in action Sept. 9, 1916.

JOHN BEAN HYDE.

Admitted May 1911. Member of Watson, Atkinson & Hyde, of Liverpool. Served as Private, Royal Army Service Corps.

LEONARD PERCY I'ANSON.

Admitted Feb. 1901, practised at Middlesbrough. Mobilised Aug. 1914, as Lieut., 4th Batt. (T.) Yorkshire Regt. ("Green Howards"). Served in France. Killed at the Battle of St. Julien, near Ypres, Apri 27, 1915, within a few days of landing.

JOHN HUGH WILLIAMS IDRIS.

Admitted Feb. 1914. Managing Clerk with R. E. H. Fisher, of 21 Old Buildings, Lincoln's Inn, W.C. Joined Oct. 1914, as Private, Inns of Court O.T.C., subsequently promoted Corporal. Gazetted 2nd Lieut. 19th Batt. London Regt. May 28, 1915, promoted A/Lieut. Aug. 1915 and A/Capt. 1916, transferred to 6th Batt. London Regt. as Lieut. June 1917, and promoted A/Capt. 1918. Awarded the M.C. Served at Home, France and Belgium, and Germany.

FREDERICK JOHN ILES.

Admitted March 1898, practised at Bristol. Served as Private, Bristol Batt. Gloucestershire Regt.

GEOFFREY INCE.

Articled to J. Donaldson Harward, of Stourbridge. Joined June 28, 1917, as Gunner, Royal Garrison Artillery and posted to 6th Siege Battery, promoted Bombardier Oct. 1917. Served in France Jan. 1918, in Italy Feb. to Nov. 1918.

JOHN OSCAR INCE.

Admitted July 1899. Member of Ince, Colt, Ince & Roscoe, of St. Benet Chambers, Fenchurch Street, E.C. Served as Able Seaman, Royal Naval Volunteer Reserve (Anti-Aircraft Corps).

ALFRED EDWARD INDERWICK.

Admitted May 1911. Of 31 Budge Row, Cannon Street, E.C. Served as Private, 695th Coy. (M.T.) Royal Army Service Corps.

DONALD GORDON INESON.

Admitted Dec. 1914. Managing Clerk with Scholefield, Taylor & Maggs, of Batley, Yorks. Joined Nov. 1915, as Cadet, Leeds University O.T.C. Gazetted 2nd Lieut. 5th Batt. York and Lancaster Regt. Jan. 29, 1916. Served in France. Discharged May 31, 1917, on account of gas poisoning.

CHARLES WILLIAM INGHAM.

Admitted Oct. 1914. Managing Clerk with Thomas Hidderley, of Stockport. Joined 1916 Royal Naval Volunteer Reserve (Wireless Section), subsequently Petty Officer Telegraphist. Served in English Channel and around Scottish Coast.

PERCIVAL ARTHUR INGHAM.
Articled to N. L. Fleming, of Bradford. Joined Dec. 27, 1916, as Private, 6th Batt. Duke of Wellington's West Riding Regt., remained on Staff work at Recruiting Office the whole time.

JOHN EDWARD INGHAM.
Admitted March 1907. Of Halifax. Served as Gunner, Royal Field Artillery.

REGINALD THOMAS INGHAM.
Admitted Jan. 1916, practising at Clitheroe. Joined Nov. 1917, as Gunner, Royal Garrison Artillery. Served at Home and in France.

WILLIAM HENRY INGHAM.
Admitted Aug. 1905, practising at Halifax. Joined Aug. 2, 1916, as Gunner, Royal Garrison Artillery. Gazetted 2nd Lieut. Royal Garrison Artillery Aug. 4, 1918. Served at Home.

NORMAN MURRAY INGLEDEW.
Admitted Feb. 1903. Member of Ingledew & Sons, of Cardiff. Joined Oct. 27, 1914, as 2nd Lieut., 7th (Cyclist) Batt. The Welch Regt. (T.), promoted Lieut. March 1915, A/Capt. July 1915, Temp. Capt. 15th (Pioneer) Batt. Loyal North Lancashire Regt. July 1918. Served at Home and in France.

CECIL GEORGE INGLIS.
Articled to W. G. Thomas, of Ellesmere. Joined Sept. 1, 1914, as Private, 1st Batt. King's Liverpool Regt. Gazetted 2nd Lieut. June 2, 1916. Served in France. Invalided out March 4, 1918.

STANLEY INGLIS.
Admitted Oct. 1913, practised at Stockton-on-Tees. Joined May 1916, as Private, Cameron Highlanders. Served in France and Flanders. Killed in action near Kemmel April 25, 1918.

FREDERICK JOHN MILLAR INGOLDBY.
Admitted Aug. 1909. Member of Wilson, Bell, Ingoldby & Son, of Louth. Mobilised Aug. 1914, as Lieut., 5th (T.) Batt. Lincolnshire Regt., promoted Capt. Oct. 1914, Major Dec. 1917. Served in England Aug. 1914 to Feb. 1915 and July 1915 to Jan. 1919, France and Belgium Feb. to July 1915. Wounded at Zillibeke July 14, 1915.

HUMPHREY INGOLDBY.
Articled to F. J. Ingoldby, of Louth. Served as 2nd Lieut., 1st Batt. Lincolnshire Regt., promoted Lieut. April 1916. Mentioned in Dispatches.

ARTHUR IRVINE INGRAM.
Admitted Feb. 1912. Member of Thring, Sheldon & Ingram, of Bath. Joined Oct. 31, 1914, as 2nd Lieut., 2/4 Batt. Somerset Light Infantry, A/Capt. 1916 to 1918, Adjutant 1915 to 1918, Temp. Major April 1918, promoted Capt. July 1918. Served in India, Burma, Palestine, Egypt, and Sudan.

JOHN HAMPDEN INSKIP.
Admitted Sept. 1905. Member of James Inskip & Son, of Bristol. Served in Royal Flying Corps.

LESLIE INSKIPP.

Articled to F. W. Morgan, of Hastings. Joined Oct. 1914, as Private, Hon. Artillery Company. Killed in action in France March 12, 1915.

FREDERICK MITCHELL IREDALE.

Admitted Dec. 1898. Member of Cohen & Cohen, of 2 Finsbury Circus, E.C. Served as Capt., Royal Air Force.

WILLIAM MORLEY IRONS.

Articled to William Irons, J.P., of Sheffield. Joined April 14, 1916, Sheffield University O.T.C. Granted a commission as Lieut. 3rd Batt. York and Lancaster Regt. Sept. 24, 1917, and at once sent out to France. Killed in action at Neuve Eglise April 13, 1918.

PAGET GEORGE IRVINE.

Admitted Nov. 1901, practised at Bristol. Joined Sept. 18, 1914, as Lieut., 1/6 Batt. Gloucestershire Regt., promoted Capt. Aug. 1915. Served in France March to Nov. 1915. Killed in action at Hebuterne, France, Nov. 30, 1915.

SAMUEL IRWIN.

Articled to E. C. Pearson, of Manchester. Joined Sept. 8, 1914, as Private, 20th Batt. Royal Fusiliers (U.P.S.) Gazetted 2nd Lieut. Manchester Regt. about March 1919. Served in France Nov. 1915 to June 1918.

EDWARD SWINTON WODEHOUSE ISAAC.

Admitted May 1897. Member of C. O. Humphreys & Son, of 4 and 5 Warwick Court, Gray's Inn, W.C. Joined Sept. 28, 1914, as Private, Essex Yeomanry. Gazetted 2nd Lieut. Royal Army Service Corps Sept. 2, 1915, promoted Lieut. May 1917. Served in France Dec. 1914 to April 1919.

GEORGE GOWER ISAAC.

Admitted Jan. 1899. Member of Hartland, Isaac, Watkins & Lewis, of Swansea. Served as Major, South Wales Royal Army Service Corps (T.) Died of pneumonia Aug. 1, 1916.

CYRIL BICKFORD ISARD.

Articled to his father A. J. Isard, of 41 Moorgate Street, E.C. Served as Capt., 10th Batt. London Regt. Killed in action.

JAMES ISHERWOOD.

Admitted July 1884, practising at Heywood, and Bury. Served as Lieut.-Col. 5th Batt. Lancashire Fusiliers. Mentioned in Dispatches and awarded C.B.

JOHN ISMAY.

Admitted June 1907, practised at Newcastle-upon-Tyne. Served as Private, 21st Batt. Royal Fusiliers.

ALFRED HUBERT IVENS.

Admitted Jan. 1899, practising at Yarmouth, Isle of Wight Joined in Melbourne in 1914, as Private, 3rd Brigade Australian Army Service Corps, and subsequently promoted Corporal. Served at Home, Gallipoli, Egypt, France, and Belgium.

FRANCIS BURDETT IVENS.

Admitted April 1905. Formerly of 34 and 35 High Holborn, and for some years at Iposi, Fed. Malay States. Joined in 1916, as Private, 28th Batt. County of London Regt. (Artists Rifles). Gazetted 1st Lieut. Scots Guards. Once mentioned in Dispatches. Served at Home, France, etc., and in West Africa.

KENNETH HILL IVES.

Admitted June 1914. Of Leeds. Joined Aug. 1914, as 2nd Lieut., 8th Batt. Prince of Wales' West Yorkshire Regt. Died of pneumonia at York Military Hospital Dec. 9, 1914.

JAMES ALBERT IVESON.

Articled to Harry Wray, of Hull. Joined July 26, 1915, as Private, Inns of Court O.T.C. Gazetted 2nd Lieut. Royal Garrison Artillery (T.) Nov. 1915, Lieut. June 1916, A/Capt. June 1918. Awarded the M.C. Served in France and Belgium March 1916 to Nov. 1918. Wounded Nov. 2, 1917.

HAROLD JACKS.

Admitted Oct. 1913, practised at South Shields, and Jarrow. Mobilised Aug. 1914 with the 7th Batt. Durham Light Infantry. Went to France April 1915 and wounded at 2nd Battle of Ypres. Received appointment on General Staff of Northern Command, York, and afterwards Staff Capt. to 208th (Reserve) Infantry Brigade, Doncaster, subsequently appointed to 4th Nigeria Regt. and on the Staff of the West African Frontier Force. Died at Lagos, Nigeria, Jan. 27, 1919.

ALBERT JACKSON.

Admitted March 1912. Member of J. T. Jackson & Co., of Oldham. Served as 2nd Lieut., Garr. Batt. Royal Welch Fusiliers.

ARTHUR HARDING JACKSON.

Admitted Nov. 1908. Member of Jackson & Jackson, of Sheffield. Served as 2nd Lieut., York and Lancashire Regt.

BASIL JACKSON.

Admitted July 1905. Member of Jacksons & Monk, of Middlesbrough. Mobilised Aug. 1914, as Capt., 4th Batt. A.P.W.O. Yorkshire Regt. (T.), promoted Major April 1915, Staff Capt. Aug. 1914 to Aug. 1916, Brigade Major 142nd Infantry Brigade Aug. 1916 to Jan. 1917, attached British Mission to Portuguese Expeditionary Force Jan. to Dec. 1917, G.S.O. VII. Corps Dec. 1917 to Nov. 1918. Twice mentioned in Dispatches. Awarded the D.S.O., T.D., and Ancient Order of Aviz of Portugal. Served in France and at Home. Wounded April 22, 1915.

CHARLES JAMES JACKSON.

Admitted April 1884, practising at Norwich. Served as Capt., 10th Batt. Norfolk Regt.

EVELYN WILLAN JACKSON.

Admitted Oct. 1905. Managing Clerk with Sharman, Jackson & Archer, of Wellingborough. Joined Sept. 29, 1914, as Lieut., T.F. Reserve (General

List), commission cancelled 1916 owing to medical unfitness. Gazetted 2nd Lieut. 152nd Labour Company Aug. 1917, promoted Lieut. Feb. 1919 Served in Belgium and France Oct. 1917 to Dec. 1918, and at Home.

FRANCIS JAMES GIDLOW JACKSON.

Admitted Nov. 1912. Member of Denham & Jackson, of Manchester. Mobilised August 1914, as 2nd Lieut., 2nd East Lancashire Brigade Royal Field Artillery (T.), promoted Temp. Lieut. Nov. 1914, Substantive Lieut. June 1916, Capt. March 1918. Awarded the M.C. Served in Egypt 1914, Gallipoli 1915, Sinai 1916, France and Belgium 1917 to 1919.

FRANCIS LEONARD HUNTER JACKSON.

Admitted Aug. 1913, practised at Ilkeston. Joined March 1915 as Seaman, Public Schools Batt. Royal Naval Division. Promoted Sub-Lieut. Royal Naval Volunteer Reserve June 1915 (Howe Batt. Royal Naval Division), promoted Lieut. June 1917. Served at Gallipoli Aug. 1915 until Evacuation, France May 1916 to Oct. 1917. Killed in action at Passchendaele Oct. 26, 1917.

FREDERICK GEORGE JACKSON.

Admitted Jan. 1898, practising at Leeds. Joined July 24, 1917, as Private, 105th (Service) Coy. Royal Army Ordnance Corps. Served at Home.

HAROLD HEYWOOD JACKSON.

Admitted July 1909, practising at Wigan, Lancashire. Joined Feb. 1915, as Cadet, Manchester University O.T.C. Gazetted 2nd Lieut. 9th Batt. King's Liverpool Regt. (T.) Dec. 1915, promoted Temp. Capt. March 1916. Served in France. Wounded July 31, 1917.

HAROLD WARTERS JACKSON.

Admitted Dec. 1904. Member of Jackson & Jackson, of Sheffield. Served as Private, Inns of Court O.T.C.

HERBERT EDMUND JACKSON.

Articled to W. N. Jackson, of Salisbury. Joined Sept. 4, 1914, as Private, 1/4 Batt. Wiltshire Regt. Obtained commission in same Regt. June 1917. Served in India, Egypt, Palestine, Sudan. Wounded at 3rd Battle of Gaza Nov. 17, 1917.

HOWARD MURRAY JACKSON.

Articled to A. O. Warren, of 4 Great James Street, W.C. Served as Trooper, Royal Bucks Hussars.

IVOR JACKSON.

Admitted Nov. 1910. Member of A. M. Jackson & Co., of Hull. Joined Aug. 29, 1914, as Lieut., 10th (Service) Batt. East Yorkshire Regt., promoted Capt. Dec. 1914, Adjutant Nov. 1914 to Sept. 1917, Courts-Martial Officer Canadian Corps Aug. to Sept. 1917, transferred to General List on appointment as Staff Captain Sept. 1917, Staff Capt. 137th Infantry Brigade, 46th (North Midland) Division (T.), Sept. 1917 to Oct. 1918. Awarded the M.C. Served at Home Aug. 1914 to Nov. 1915 and from Dec. 1918, Egypt Dec. 1915 to March 1916, and France March 1916 to Dec. 1918. Wounded June 21 1918, and Oct. 2, 1918.

JOHN GEORGE JACKSON.
Admitted Feb. 1913, practising at Plymouth. Joined July 1915 Inns of Court O.T.C., commissioned July 3, 1916, The Welch Regt. (T.), attached 2nd Batt. Manchester Regt., subsequently promoted Capt. Wounded on Western Front Dec. 1, 1916.

THOMAS JACKSON.
Articled to Reuben Cohen, of Stockton-on-Tees. Served as Private, Royal Army Medical Corps (T.).

VINCENT HARRY ORWELL JACKSON.
Articled to Frank Collis, of Stoke-on-Trent. Served as Private, 2nd Batt. North Staffordshire Regt. Subsequently gazetted 2nd Lieut. in same Regt.

WILLIAM JACKSON.
Admitted Nov. 1895. Member of Oliver Jones, Billson & Co., of Liverpool. Joined Oct. 1914, as Private, Royal Fusiliers (Sportsman's Batt.), transferred to Inns of Court O.T.C. Dec. 1914. Gazetted 2nd Lieut. 6th Batt. Notts and Derby Regt. March 1915, promoted Lieut. July 1917. Served at Home Oct. 1914 to July 1917, and in France July 1917 to Dec. 1918.

JOHN REGINALD JACOB.
Admitted Dec. 1896, practising at Abergavenny. Mobilised Aug. 1914, as Capt., 3rd Batt. Monmouthshire Regt., promoted Major Nov. 1915. Served at Home.

WILLIAM GEORGE JACOBSON.
Admitted April 1912. Managing Clerk with Messrs. Browne, Son & Williams, of Nottingham. Joined Dec. 14, 1915, as Gunner, Royal Garrison Artillery, promoted Bombardier March 1916, Sergeant Nov. 1916. Served at Home Dec. 1915 to May 1916, and in France May 1916 to Feb. 1919.

WALTER GEORGE JACOMB-HOOD.
Admitted Nov. 1901. Member of Norgate & Hood, of Dereham, Norfolk. Joined Nov. 10, 1914, as 2nd Lieut., 6th Batt. Norfolk Regt., promoted Lieut. Dec. 1914, A/Capt. April 1915, Lieut. 6th Batt. Somerset Light Infantry June 1918. Served at Home Nov. 1914 to July 1918, and in France Aug. 1918 to Feb. 1919.

HENRY HARRIS JAGO.
Articled to W. H. Jago, of Plymouth. Joined Sept. 1914 as Private in Public Schools Batt. Gazetted 2nd Lieut. 3rd Batt. Devonshire Regt. July 1915, promoted A/Capt. and subsequently A/Major. Awarded the D.S.O. and M.C. with Bar. Served in France. Killed in action April 25, 1918.

ALYN REGINALD JAMES.
Articled to R. P. James, of Wrexham. Joined as Motor Dispatch Rider, attached to Denbighshire Yeomanry. Obtained commission in Denbighshire Yeomanry and attained the rank of Capt., subsequently attached Royal Flying Corps. Missing and afterwards reported killed near Amiens on March 24, 1918, whilst leading his flight.

ARTHUR PERKINS JAMES.

Admitted Jan. 1881, practising at Cardiff. Served as Col. Commanding 5th (Reserve) Batt. The Welch Regt. (T.).

CHARLES HERBERT JAMES.

Articled to W. J. Vaughan, of Fishguard. Served as Trooper, Pembrokeshire Yeomanry.

CYRIL HAMMOND JAMES.

Articled to F. Lawson Lewis, of Eastbourne. Joined Dec. 7, 1914, as 2nd Lieut., 4th Batt. Royal Sussex Regt., promoted Lieut. May 1916, Capt. May 1917. Served in France.

DAVID WATKIN JAMES.

Admitted Dec. 1901, practising at Tonypandy. Served as Private, Royal Army Service Corps (M.T.).

EDWARD CUTHBERT ALINGTON JAMES.

Admitted Feb. 1911, practising at East Retford. Served as 2nd Lieut., 8th Batt. Notts and Derbyshire Regt. (Sherwood Foresters) (T.), subsequently attained the rank of Capt. Mentioned in Dispatches.

ENOCH LEWIS JAMES.

Admitted June 1912. Managing Clerk with Morgan, Bruce & Nicholas, of Pontypridd, Glam. Joined Nov. 1915 Inns of Court O.T.C. Gazetted 2nd Lieut. Royal Welch Fusiliers Nov. 1916. Served in France. Killed in action in France Feb. 18, 1917.

GWILYM CHRISTOPHER BOWRING JAMES.

Admitted May 1909. Member of Gwilym James, Charles & Davies, of Merthyr Tydfil. Joined Sept. 1916 Inns of Court O.T.C. Gazetted 2nd Lieut. 3rd Batt., attached 2nd Batt., South Wales Borderers. Served in France. Died in No. 21 Casualty Clearing Station, France, Nov. 23, 1917, from wounds received in action.

HAROLD GWYNNE JAMES.

Admitted Oct. 1914. Member of Gwynne James & Son, of Hereford. Served as Lieut., Welsh Division Royal Army Service Corps (T.), promoted Capt. 30th Divisional Supply Column Royal Army Service Corps June 1916. Mentioned in Dispatches.

HENRY JAMES.

Admitted June 1910. Assistant Solicitor Halifax Corporation. Joined the Middlesex Regt. and attained the rank of Lance-Sergeant. Served in France. Reported missing Aug. 18, 1916.

HERBERT VICTOR JAMES.

Admitted July 1912. Managing Clerk with W. T. James, of Eastbourne. Joined Aug. 30, 1914, as Private, Universities and Public Schools Brigade (18th Royal Fusiliers). Gazetted 2nd Lieut. Royal Flying Corps July 7, 1916, transferred to 3rd Royal Sussex Regt. June 1917, promoted Capt., transferred to General List, and appointed Courts-Martial Officer Oct. 1917. Served in France.

JOHN EGBERT JAMES.

Admitted March 1898. Managing Clerk with Travers Smith, Braithwaite & Co., of 4 Throgmorton Avenue, E.C. Joined June 1916, as 2nd Lieut., Royal Garrison Artillery (Special Reserve), subsequently promoted Lieut. Served at Home.

JOHN PERCIVAL JAMIESON.

Admitted Feb. 1913, practised at Whetstone. Served as 2nd Lieut., 4th Batt. Middlesex Regt., promoted Lieut. Sept. 1918. Mentioned in Dispatches. Awarded the D.S.O.

WILLIAM HUSKISSON VYVYAN JAQUES.

Admitted April 1915. Member of Jaques & Co., of 8 Ely Place, E.C. Served as Private, 5th (City of London) Batt. London Regt. (London Rifle Brigade).

GEORGE FREDERICK JERVAULX JARVIS.

Admitted May 1907. Managing Clerk with M. J. Jarvis, of 4 Finsbury Square, E.C. Mobilised Aug. 4, 1914, as Farrier-Sergeant, Hon. Artillery Company. Obtained commission 5th Reserve Cavalry (20th Hussars) Oct. 28, 1916. Awarded the M.C. Served in Egypt and in France. Killed France Sept. 28, 1918.

HORACE EUSTACE GEORGE JARVIS.

Articled to Charles Bowen, of 25 Ely Place, E.C. Served as Able Seaman, H.M.S. *Achates*.

MATTHEW JERVOISE JARVIS.

Admitted July 1893, practising at 4 Finsbury Square, E.C. Mobilised Aug. 4, 1914, as Quartermaster-Sergeant " A " Battery Horse Artillery, Hon. Artillery Company. Raised 2/A Battery and promoted (Acting) Camp Quartermaster. Awarded the Territorial Force Efficiency Medal. Served at Home.

REGINALD FREDERIC TUDOR JASPER.

Articled to Thomas Smith, of 9 John Street, Bedford Row, W.C. Joined Sept. 8, 1914, as Private, 28th Batt. County of London Regt. (Artists Rifles). Gazetted 2nd Lieut. July 24, 1915, promoted Lieut. Jan. 1917. Served at Home, France, and Belgium. Wounded at Battle of the Somme July 1, 1916.

JOHN WILLIAM JEAKES.

Admitted Jan. 1916. Member of Hickson, Moir & Jeakes, of 52 New Broad Street, E.C. Joined Sept. 1914, as Private, 10th Batt. Royal Fusiliers. Gazetted 2nd Lieut. Jan. 27, 1915, attached 9th Batt. Royal Berkshire Regt. Feb. 1915, promoted Lieut. Oct. 1915, attached to 1st Batt. in France Oct. 1915, and subsequently to 6th Batt. Served in France Oct. 1915 to Feb. 1917 and Aug. to Oct. 1917. Severely wounded Feb. 25, 1917. Killed in action near Poelcappelle, Flanders, Oct. 12, 1917.

GERALD MARK JEANS.

Admitted Feb. 1913, practising at 50 Bedford Row, W.C. Joined Nov. 8, 1916, as Private, Inns of Court O.T.C. Gazetted 2nd Lieut. Wiltshire Regt.

Aug. 1, 1917. Served in Belgium and France. Wounded on Ypres-Comines Canal April 26, 1918, on La Bassée Canal Aug. 18, 1918, near Valenciennes Nov. 4, 1918.

FRANK ARTHUR JEFFCOATE.

Articled to W. E. Lester, of Nuneaton. Joined Sept. 6, 1914, as Private, 7th Batt. Oxford and Bucks Light Infantry, promoted Sergeant Sept. 1916. Gazetted 2nd Lieut. Machine Gun Corps Sept. 26, 1917. Served at Home Sept. 1914 to Sept. 1915 and March to Nov. 1917, in France Sept. to Nov. 1915, Salonica Nov. 1915 to Jan. 1917, and in Mesopotamia Nov. 1917 to March 1919.

HERBERT ATHELSTAN JEFFERY.

Admitted Jan. 1908. Managing Clerk with Herbert J. Jeffery, of Bradford. Joined British Red Cross Society May 1, 1915, as Registrar to No. 4 Red Cross Hospital, B.E.F., transferred to No. 2 Red Cross Hospital as Quartermaster Dec. 1915, transferred to Headquarters for special duty Feb. 1919, appointed Deputy Commandant of Orderlies Headquarters June 1919, appointed Secretary to the Deputy Commissioner Sept. 9, 1919, appointed Deputy Demobilisation Officer (for France) Nov. 1919. Awarded M.B.E. Served in France throughout.

ERIC WEBB JEFFREYS.

Articled to L. Moore, of Newport, Mon. Joined Sept. 3, 1914, as Private, Public Schools Brigade, 21st Batt. Royal Fusiliers. Gazetted 2nd Lieut. 2nd Batt. The Welch Regt., Jan. 7, 1915, promoted Lieut. June 1915, Capt. Aug. 1915, acted as Major in France with The Welch Regt., as Instructor in Tactics with No. 16 O.C.B. 1917, transferred to Royal Flying Corps as Capt. and Flying Officer 1918. Served at Home and in France. Twice wounded.

FRANCIS BERNARD JEFFRIES.

Articled to Herbert Jeffries, of Birmingham. Joined June 3, 1918, as Cadet, Royal Air Force. Gazetted 2nd Lieut. Royal Air Force, Aug. 8, 1918. Served at Home.

HAROLD JOHN FOTHERINGHAM JEFFRIES.

Admitted Jan. 12, 1911. Member of Wartnaby, Jeffries & Son, of Market Harborough. Mobilised Aug. 4, 1914, as Capt., 5th Batt. Leicestershire Regt. (T.), promoted Major Sept. 1915. Served in France from Feb. 1915. Killed in action at Hooge Sept. 26, 1915.

HERBERT WILLIAM JELF.

Admitted June 1908. Member of Taylor, Hoare & Jelf, of 12 Norfolk Street, Strand, W.C. Joined June 8, 1916, as Sub.-Lieut., Royal Naval Volunteer Reserve. Served afloat with Grand Fleet (10th Cruiser Squadron and 9th Cruiser Squadron) and on Detached Service.

CYRIL DONALD THOMAS JENKINS.

Articled to Richard Jenkins, of Swansea. Joined March 1915, as 2nd Lieut., 3rd Batt. Royal Welch Fusiliers. Served in Gallipoli. Wounded and afterwards attached to Royal Flying Corps. Killed Oct. 2, 1916.

DAVID JENKINS.

Articled to T. A. Rees, of Merthyr Tydfil, Glam. Joined Oct. 1915, as Private, Welch Guards. Obtained commission in Royal Welch Fusiliers April 1917 and attached South Wales Borderers 1918 as Lieut. Served in France. Wounded at Pilkem, Ypres, July 31, 1917. Torpedoed SS. *Leinster* Oct. 10, 1918.

EDWARD BASIL TERENCE JENKINS.

Articled to R. H. Bentley, of 232 Strand, W.C. Joined Sept. 6, 1914, as Private, Inns of Court O.T.C., promoted Corporal 1915. Subsequently gazetted Lieut. Royal Fusiliers. Served in France. Wounded Somme 1916. Discharged unfit, Oct. 1918.

JOHN HENRY JENKINS.

Admitted May 1906, practising at Carnarvon. Joined June 1, 1915, as 2nd Lieut., 2/6 Batt. Royal Welch Fusiliers, promoted Capt. May 1917. Served in Gallipoli, Egypt, and Palestine throughout the campaign. Wounded at Gaza March 26, 1917.

MARTIN GWYN JENKINS.

Admitted April 1907, practising at Aberavon. Mobilised Aug. 1, 1914, as Lieut., Glamorgan Royal Horse Artillery, and promoted Major in March 1919. Awarded the T.D. Served on the Western Front with the 35th Division 1917, 1918, and 1919.

GEORGE WELLS JENNINGS.

Admitted May 1911. Member of G. W. Jennings & Son, of Bishop Auckland. Served as 2nd Lieut., Royal Field Artillery, promoted Lieut. 1916.

RICHARD WILLIAM JENNINGS.

Admitted July 1914, practised at Bristol. Enlisted Sept. 1914 and gazetted 2nd Lieut. Worcestershire Regt. shortly afterwards, subsequently promoted Lieut. Once mentioned in Dispatches. Died of wounds July 3, 1916.

SIDNEY AUGUSTUS JENNINGS.

Admitted Feb. 1912. Managing Clerk with Walter A. Jennings, of 152 Kentish Town Road, N.W. Joined Aug. 1914, as Rifleman, 12th Batt. County of London Regt., transferred to Inns of Court O.T.C. as Private Jan. 1916. Gazetted 2nd Lieut. Royal Garrison Artillery Nov. 1916, promoted Lieut. May 1917. Served in France and Belgium.

CLIFFORD MORGAN JEREMY.

Articled to W. R. Davies, of Pontypridd. Joined Aug. 1918, as Private, 53rd Batt. The Welch Regt., promoted Lance-Corporal Feb. 1919, Corporal June 1919, Sergeant Aug. 1919, transferred to 52nd Batt. The Welch Regt. Sept. 1919. Served at Home (Ireland) and Germany.

ADRIAN JEROME SMITH JEROME.

Admitted July 1903. Member of Gunner, Wilson & Jerome, of Newport, and Shanklin, I. of W. Joined Dec. 1, 1915, as 2nd Lieut., General List, and subsequently promoted Lieut.

ARTHUR REGINALD FRANKENSTEIN ZACHARIAS JESSEL.

Admitted Dec. 1911, practising at Oxford. Served as Cadet, Oxford University O.T.C. Gazetted 2nd Lieut. 8th (Service) Batt. Northamptonshire Regt.

ROBERT WILFRED FAIREY JESSON.

Admitted Feb. 1913. Managing Clerk with Hepherd & Winstanley, of Southampton. Joined Aug. 6, 1914, Inns of Court O.T.C. Gazetted 2nd Lieut. 5th Batt. Wiltshire Regt. Aug. 28, 1914, promoted Lieut. Oct. 1914, Capt. March 1915, A/Major while second in command of Batt. Sept. 1916. Once mentioned in Dispatches. Served at Gallipoli 1915. Wounded Aug. 9, 1915, returned to Regt. Oct. 1915, invalided home frostbite Dec. 1915, went to Mesopotamia July 1916. Killed in action Feb. 22, 1917, in Mesopotamia, outside Kut.

THOMAS EDWARD JESSON.

Admitted May 1906, practising at Ashby-de-la-Zouch. Served as Capt., 5th Batt. Leicestershire Regt.

JOSEPH WILFRID JESSOP.

Admitted Dec. 1911, practising at Birmingham. Joined Jan. 31, 1916, as Private, Inns of Court O.T.C. Gazetted 2nd Lieut. Royal Warwickshire Regt. March 28, 1917, transferred to Machine Gun Corps March 1918, promoted Lieut. Sept. 1918. Served at Home Jan. 1916 to May 1917 and Dec. 1917 to Sept. 1918, and in France, Belgium, and Germany May to Dec. 1917 and Sept. 1918 to Jan. 1919. Wounded at Battle of Cambrai Dec. 4, 1917.

JAMES GORDON JEUDWINE.

Admitted Nov. 1904. Member of Powell, Jarvis & Jeudwine, of Newtown, North Wales. Joined June 12, 1916, as Gunner, Royal Garrison Artillery. Gazetted 2nd Lieut. Aug. 1917, promoted Lieut. Feb. 1919. Served in France and Belgium 1916 to 1918.

FRANK NORMAN JEWELL.

Articled to Leonard Warner, of Fareham. Served as Lieut., 9th (Cyclist) Batt. Hampshire Regt., promoted Capt. Sept. 1914.

HERBERT BRITT JOBBINGS.

Admitted June 1914. Member of J. W. Stead & Jobbings, of Leeds. Joined Nov. 17, 1916, as Private, Royal Army Service Corps, and posted for service with Director-General of Transportation, General Headquarters, transferred to Royal Engineers May 1917 and promoted Corporal. Commissioned in France and posted as 2nd Lieut. to 60th Labour Company Nov. 14, 1917. Awarded Special Russian Red Cross by Czarina. Served in England and France.

GEORGE WILLIAM JOBLING.

Articled to T. B. Nowell of Burnley. Mobilised Aug. 1914, as Gunner, 1st East Lancashire Brigade Royal Field Artillery (T.), subsequently Signaller with 6th Reserve Brigade. Served in Egypt, Gallipoli, 1915 to 1916, Syria, France, and Belgium. Wounded at Ypres Sept. 1917.

DAVID MOY JOHN.

Articled to A. E. Crowther, of Cardiff. Served as Private, 21st (Service) Batt. Royal Fusiliers.

HUBERT EDWARD JOHN.

Admitted April 1912, practising at Llanelly. Mobilised Aug. 1914, as Lieut., 4th Batt. The Welch Regt. (T.), promoted Capt. Oct. 1914. Awarded the M.C. Served in Gallipoli Aug. to Dec. 1915, Egypt Jan. to Dec. 1916, and Palestine Jan. to March 1917. Wounded at 1st Battle of Gaza March 26, 1917.

FRANCIS TREMENHEERE JOHNS.

Admitted Feb. 1914. Managing Clerk with Francis A. Johns, of Ringwood. Joined Aug. 5, 1914, as Lance-Corporal, 9th Batt. Hampshire Regt. Gazetted 2nd Lieut. Dorset Royal Garrison Artillery (T.) Oct. 8, 1915, promoted Lieut. June 1916. Served at Home and with B.E.F.

HERBERT DAVID JOHNS.

Admitted Dec. 1911, practising at Milford Haven. Mobilised Aug. 1914, as 2nd Lieut., Pembrokeshire Royal Garrison Artillery (T.), promoted Lieut. June 1916, Capt. Dec. 1916, Major Sept. 1917. Once mentioned in Dispatches. Awarded the M.C. Served in France Dec. 1916 to March 1919.

ALBERT JOHN JOHNSON.

Articled to J. F. Jones, of 30 Great St. Helen's, E.C. Served as Private, 5th Batt. East Kent Regt. (The Buffs).

ARTHUR AINSLIE JOHNSON.

Admitted June 1912, practising at Newcastle-upon-Tyne. Joined 1914, as 2nd Lieut., Northumberland Fusiliers, promoted Lieut. Dec. 1914, Capt. April 1915, appointed Staff Capt. Aug. 1915, appointed Deputy Assistant Adjutant-General Aug. 1917, promoted Major May 1918. Three times mentioned in Dispatches. Awarded O.B.E. (Military Division). Served in France 1915 to 1919.

BASIL HENRY JOHNSON.

Articled to Sir H. J. Johnson, of 101 Leadenhall Street, E.C. Served as 2nd Lieut., 1st Batt. Hertfordshire Regt. (T.), promoted Lieut. July 1916.

CHARLES HENRY JOHNSON.

Admitted Aug. 1906, practising at Manchester. Served as Signaller, Royal Field Artillery.

CHARLES VILLIERS JOHNSON.

Admitted March 1892, practising at Brighton. Mobilised Aug. 1914, as Capt., 6th Batt. Royal Sussex Regt., promoted Major Nov. 1914. Awarded the T.D. Served on the East Coast of England and in Ireland.

CONINGSBY SAMUEL JOHNSON.

Admitted May 1908, practising at Reading. Joined April 26, 1915, as Private, Inns of Court O.T.C., promoted to Sergeant Sept. 1915. Commissioned 2nd Lieut. in same Regt. April 1916, transferred as 2nd Lieut. to Royal Field Artillery Oct. 1916, promoted Lieut. April 1918. Awarded the M.C. Served in France.

CYRIL BENTON JOHNSON.

Articled to W. P. Norton, of 57½ Old Broad Street, E.C. Mobilised Aug. 5, 1914, as Lieut., 6th Batt. Notts and Derbyshire Regt. (Sherwood Foresters), promoted Capt. May 1916, and subsequently to Lieut.-Col. Once mentioned in Dispatches. Wounded July 1916. Killed Sept. 21, 1917.

DENYS BILLINGHURST JOHNSON.

Articled to W. P. Johnson, of Midhurst, Sussex. Gazetted Dec. 7, 1914, as 2nd Lieut., 2/4 Batt. Royal Sussex Regt., promoted Lieut. Sept. 1917, transferred 10th Reserve Batt. Suffolk Regt. March 1916 and to 11th Batt. Suffolk Regt. Aug. 1916. Awarded the M.C. Served in France.

ERNEST STAPLEY HEMING JOHNSON.

Admitted Feb. 1907, practising at 19 Great Winchester Street, E.C. Mobilised Aug. 1914, as Private, Hon. Artillery Company and attained rank of Sergeant in 1915. Commissioned in Royal Army Ordnance Corps Nov. 1916, promoted to Capt. 1918. Served in France.

FRANCIS KINLOCH MURRAY JOHNSON.

Admitted June 1910. Managing Clerk with Budd, Johnson & Jecks, of 24 Austin Friars, E.C. Mobilised with Inns of Court O.T.C. Gazetted Sept. 1914 2nd Lieut. King's Dragoon Guards, subsequently Staff Capt. Embarkation Staff, Bombay. Served in France and India. Wounded at Hooge, near Ypres, May 1915.

FRANK BIRLEY JOHNSON.

Admitted Oct. 1914. Formerly of Nottingham. Served as Capt., 13th Batt. Notts and Derbyshire Regt. (Sherwood Foresters).

FREDERIC DAVID KEENE JOHNSON.

Admitted March 1905. Member of Johnson & Son, of Newcastle, Staffs. Joined March 31, 1917, as Private, Royal Army Service Corps (M.T.). Served at Home.

GEORGE JOHNSON.

Admitted April 1909, practising at Jarrow. Joined Feb. 5, 1917, as 2nd Class Air Mechanic, Royal Flying Corps. Gazetted 2nd Lieut. Royal Air Force Nov. 1917, promoted Capt. April 1918. Served at Home and with Anti-Submarine Operations Unit in conjunction with Royal Navy.

GEORGE GEOFFREY FLOYD JOHNSON.

Articled to Frank Johnson, of Bradford. Mobilised Aug. 1914 as 2nd Lieut. in the Special Reserve (Essex Regt.), afterwards invalided and attached to King's African Rifles. Served in France and Africa.

JOHN ALFRED JOHNSON.

Admitted Aug. 1886. Member of Price, Johnson & Jackson, of Wigan. Served as Lieut., 9th Batt. King's Liverpool Regt.

LUTHER VINCENT BURGOYNE JOHNSON.

Articled to O. H. Cochrane, of Middlesbrough. Mobilised Aug. 1914, as Lieut., 8th Batt. Durham Light Infantry (T.), promoted Capt. Sept. 1914. Served in France. Killed at Grafenstaffel Ridge, N.E. of Ypres, April 25, 1915.

MONTAGUE KEMMIS JOHNSON.

Articled to H. W. Johnson, of 24 Austin Friars, E.C. Joined Aug. 29, 1914, as 2nd Lieut., 1st Batt. London Regt. (T.), transferred to Royal Garrison Artillery (T.) Nov. 1915, promoted Lieut. June 8, 1916. Served in Malta and in France.

PHILIP JOHNSON.

Admitted Feb. 1906. Member of Day & Yewdall, of Leeds. Joined Dec. 20, 1915, as Lieut., Royal Army Ordnance Corps, promoted Capt. June 1917, Major May 1918. Served at Home Dec. 1915 to April 1917, and in France April 1917 to Feb. 1919.

REGINALD EGERTON JOHNSON.

Articled to C. R. Johnson, of 10 New Square, Lincoln's Inn, W.C. Joined Sept. 5, 1914, as Private in The Rifle Brigade. Commissioned as 2nd Lieut. Somerset Light Infantry Oct. 20, 1914, promoted Lieut. Jan. 1915, joined Royal Flying Corps Aug. 1916, graduated as Pilot Dec. 1916, made Staff Capt. (Air Ministry) in the Royal Air Force June 1918. Served at Home and in France. Wounded May 24, 1917.

SAMUEL CLEMENT JOHNSON.

Admitted Jan, 1905. Of Ealing. Served as Lieut., Royal Field Artillery. Died Feb. 8, 1919, after illness contracted on active service.

SIDNEY MIDLANE JOHNSON.

Admitted Feb. 1910. Secretary of County Councils' Assoc., of 84 Eccleston Square, S.W. Joined Aug. 4, 1914, as Private, Hon. Artillery Company. Served in France and Belgium. Wounded at Kemmel Jan. 29, 1915. Discharged July 15, 1915.

SYDNEY HARCOURT JOHNSON.

Admitted Oct. 1908, practising at Liverpool. Served as Lieut., 5th Batt. King's Liverpool Regt.

THOMAS GEORGE JOHNSON.

Articled to A. J. Willett, of Warrington,. Joined Aug. 4, 1914, as Trooper, Duke of Lancaster's Own Imperial Yeomanry. Gazetted 2nd Lieut. and Signal Officer 9th Batt. Royal Inniskilling Fusiliers Dec. 11, 1914, promoted Lieut. July 1916, appointed Adjutant and Assistant Commandant 36th Division School of Instruction with rank of Capt. Nov. 1916, rejoined 9th Batt. Royal Inniskilling Fusiliers as Bombing Officer in 1917, afterwards transferred to Oswestry and attached to 3rd Batt. as Assistant Brigade Gas Officer, sailed for India Sept. 1918, joined 30th Lancers at Peshawar and appointed Signal Officer to the Regiment. Served in France and India.

THOMAS ROSCOE JOHNSON.

Articled to R. H. Armstrong, of Liverpool. Joined Sept. 1914, as Private, 17th Batt. King's Liverpool Regt., promoted to be Lewis-Gunner Aug. 1916. Served at Home and in France. Reported as missing since Oct 12, 1916, and afterwards ascertained to have been killed in action on that date.

WILLIAM GODFREY EARLAM JOHNSON.

Articled to Thomas Ellis, of Wigan. Mobilised Aug. 1914, as Lieut., 5th Batt. Manchester Regt., promoted Temp. Capt. June 1915, Capt. Aug. 1915.

Served in Egypt Sept. 1914 to May 1915, Gallipoli May to June 1915, Palestine April 1916 to Feb. 1917, and in France Feb. to Oct. 1917. Died of wounds Oct. 13, 1917.

HOWARD RICHMOND JOHNSTON.

Articled to W. W. A. Tree, of Worcester. Joined Sept. 15, 1914, as Private, 21st Batt. Royal Fusiliers. Commissioned 2nd Lieut. King's Own Royal Lancaster Regt. July 7, 1916, promoted Lieut. Jan. 1918, A/Capt. Oct. 1918. Once mentioned in Dispatches. Awarded the D.S.O. Served in France. Wounded at Ypres Sept. 26, 1917.

JAMES JOHNSTONE.

Admitted Dec. 1898, practising at 36 Basinghall Street, E.C. Served as Trooper, 2nd Batt. King Edward's Horse.

WILLIAM McCALL JOHNSTONE.

Articled to Samuel Williams, of Nottingham. Mobilised Aug. 1914, as Gunner, Notts Royal Horse Artillery. Gazetted 2nd Lieut. Royal Field Artillery March 17, 1915. Served at Home Aug. 1914 to Jan. 1916, and in France Jan. to Feb. 1916. Killed in action Feb. 13, 1916.

ARCHIBALD HENRY JOLLIFFE.

Articled to H. A. Pritchard, of Leicester. Joined Oct. 26, 1914, as 2nd Lieut., 1/5 Batt. Cheshire Regt., promoted Lieut. April 1916, A/Capt. June 1917. Awarded the M.C. Served in France. Wounded April 28, 1915, and May 8, 1917.

GEORGE WILLIAM ERNEST JOLLY.

Admitted Oct. 1913, practising at Hove, Sussex. Joined July 26, 1916, as Trooper, The Sussex Yeomanry, transferred as Private to 4th (Reserve) Batt. Royal Sussex Regt. Jan. 1917, and to Garrison Officers Cadet Batt., Cambridge, as Cadet Feb. 1917. Gazetted as 2nd Lieut. 1st (Reserve) Garrison Batt. Suffolk Regt. April 14, 1917, promoted Lieut. Oct. 1918 when appointed Secretary British Customs Commission, British Salonica Force, transferred to 3rd Suffolk Regt. May 1919. Served at Home and Salonica.

LOUIS NATHANIEL JONAS.

Admitted April 1913. Of 79 Shaftesbury Avenue, W.C. Joined Dec. 1915, as Private, 28th Batt. County of London Regt. (Artists Rifles). Gazetted 2nd Lieut. and posted to 8th Batt. The Queen's Regt. May 2, 1917, promoted Lieut. Nov. 1918. Served in France. Wounded Aug. 1, 1917, lost left eye.

ALBERT VICTOR JONES.

Admitted Oct. 1912. Managing Clerk with William Sturges & Co., of Caxton House, Westminster. Joined Aug. 1914, as Private, Hon. Artillery Company. Killed in action near Wulverghem, Belgium, Nov. 25, 1914.

ALLAN GWYNNE JONES.

Articled to Sir William Joynson-Hicks, M.P., of Lennox House, Norfolk Street, Strand, W.C. Joined Nov. 2, 1914, as Private, Public Schools Batt. Royal Fusiliers, and subsequently gazetted Lieut. Welch Guards. Once mentioned in Dispatches. Awarded the D.S.O. Served in France. Wounded Sept. 4, 1915, and July 31, 1917.

ARTHUR JONES.

Articled to Batesons, Warr & Welmshurst, of Liverpool. Served as 2nd Lieut., 7th Batt. King's Liverpool Regt. (T.).

ARTHUR VERNON JONES.

Articled to J. D. H. Osborn, of Colwyn Bay. Enlisted Sept. 1914 in the 13th Batt. Royal Welch Fusiliers. Gazetted 2nd Lieut. 13th Batt. Royal Welch Fusiliers Oct. 25, 1914, promoted Lieut. Aug. 1915, Capt. Feb. 1917, Adjutant July 1916 to April 1917. Acted Staff Capt. and Brigade Major 113th Infantry Brigade at various periods, attached to 113th Brigade Headquarters and Headquarters 38th (Welsh) Division for Staff course April 1917 to Jan. 1918, attached Headquarters XV. Corps Jan. to March 1918, acted General Staff Officer III. 38th (Welsh) Division May 1918 to Aug. 1918, appointed General Staff Officer III. 38th (Welsh) Division Oct. 1918 to Dec. 1918 when he was promoted to Quartermaster; General's Staff; General Headquarters. Once mentioned in Dispatches. Served in France Dec. 1915 to Feb. 1919. Died of pneumonia at No. 20 General Hospital, Camiers, Feb. 16, 1919. Buried at Etaples.

BARRY ST. PATRICK JONES.

Admitted March 1910. Managing Clerk with R. Sheriton Holmes, of Newcastle-upon-Tyne. Joined Aug. 1914, as Private, Northumberland Fusiliers. Commissioned as 2nd Lieut. 16th Batt. Northumberland Fusiliers 1914, promoted Capt. in Durham Light Infantry 1915. Served in France.

CECIL BUCKINGHAM JONES.

Articled to W. E. Hough, of Runcorn, Cheshire. Joined Sept. 4, 1916, as Private, Royal Army Service Corps (M.T.), promoted Lance-Corporal, became Cadet in 24th Officers Cadet Batt. Tank Corps July 1918, and subsequently granted commission. Served at Home.

CHARLES EDWARD TUDOR JONES.

Articled to H. W. Michelmore, of Exeter. Mobilised Aug. 4, 1914, as 2nd Lieut., 7th Batt. Devonshire Regt. Subsequently obtained a Regular Commission and proceeded to Royal Military Academy, Sandhurst. From thence posted to East Lancashire Regt. and promoted Lieut. and afterwards to Capt., subsequently attached to Royal Flying Corps as Observer. Served at Home and France. Killed Dec. 15, 1915. Shot down over German Lines by Immelman, near Valenciennes, and buried by the Germans with full military honours.

CYRIL GORDON JONES.

Admitted June 1908. Member of Jones & Son, of Colchester. Joined Oct. 1915, as 2nd Lieut., Royal Flying Corps, promoted Capt. April 1918. Once mentioned in Dispatches. Served in France July 1916 to Dec. 1917. Wounded Dec. 8, 1917.

CYRIL OSWALD JONES.

Admitted Dec. 1904, practising at Wrexham. Served as Lieut., 4th (Reserve) Batt. Royal Welch Fusiliers.

DONALD APPLEFORD JONES.

Admitted Dec. 1906. Member of William Dawes & Co., of Rye, Sussex. Joined Aug. 11, 1914, as Private, 5th Batt. Royal Sussex Regt., transferred to Royal Army Service Corps Jan. 1915, promoted to Staff Sergt.-Major May 1917. Awarded M.S.M. Served at Home.

EDMUND STANLEY JONES.

Admitted Dec. 1901, practising at Malton, Yorkshire. Joined Sept. 5, 1914, as Temp. Capt., 4th Batt. Yorkshire Regt. (T.), Substantive Capt. June 1916, also acted at D.A.P.M. in the Eastern Command. Served at Home.

EDWARD EARLE JONES.

Articled to A. P. Whitwell, of Darlington. Joined Jan. 1915 Inns of Court O.T.C. Commissioned as 2nd Lieut. 4th Batt. Yorkshire Regt. Feb. 13, 1915. Served in France. Severely wounded at Hooge May 24, 1915. Died Aug. 1, 1916, of wounds received near Remy the previous day.

EDWARD OLIVER JONES.

Articled to James Porter, of Conway. Joined April 1915, as Private, Inns of Court O.T.C. Granted a commission as 2nd Lieut. 6th Batt. Royal Welch Fusiliers (T.) Nov. 9, 1915, promoted Temp. Lieut. July 1916, granted substantive rank of Lieut. July 1917, attached to 19th Batt. The Queen's Royal West Surrey Regt. Aug. 1917 to Feb. 1918, to 4th (Reserve) Royal Welch Fusiliers Feb. to April 1918, and to 1/4 Batt. of same Regt. April 1918 to Jan. 1919. Served at Home and in France.

ERIC ARTHUR GODDARD JONES.

Admitted Feb. 1910. Member of Douglas & Goddard Jones, of 10 Old Jewry Chambers, E.C. Joined April 13, 1916, as Private, 10th Batt. Royal Sussex Regt. Served in France and Belgium Sept. 1916 to end of 1918.

FEATHERSTONE LEWIS JONES.

Articled to A. L. Jones, of Rhyl. Joined Aug. 14, 1914, as Trooper, Denbighshire Hussars (Yeomanry). Gazetted 2nd Lieut. Lancashire Fusiliers Dec. 9, 1914, transferred to the East Lancashire Regt. March 1915. Served in France June to Nov. 1915. Discharged Nov. 15, 1915.

FELIX ERNEST JONES.

Admitted April 1912, practised at 37 Norfolk Street, Strand, W.C. Joined May 1915 as Private, Inns of Court O.T.C., and promoted Company Quartermaster-Sergeant July 1915. Gazetted 2nd Lieut. 1/4 Batt. Oxford and Bucks Light Infantry Dec. 1915, promoted Lieut. July 1917. Awarded the M.C. Served at Home May 1915 to March 1916, France March 1916 to July 1916 (wounded), Home July 1916 to Feb. 1917, Flanders Feb. to Aug. 1917. Killed in action at St. Julien, near Ypres, Aug. 16, 1917.

GLENDOWER JONES.

Articled to G. H. Hindley, of Liverpool. Served as Private, 4th Batt. Manchester Regt.

HAROLD MOUAT JONES.

Admitted Dec. 1898. Member of Jutsum & Jones, of 11 Queen Victoria Street, E.C. Joined Dec. 1915, as Private, 28th Batt. County of London Regt. (Artists Rifles). Commissioned as 2nd Lieut. Royal Army Ordnance Corps May 30, 1916, promoted Lieut. Aug. 1916. Served at Home till Feb. 1917 and afterwards in Egypt.

HENRY GILMAN JONES.

Admitted March 1905, practising at Salford, Lancs. Joined Feb. 28, 1917, as Private, Inns of Court O.T.C. Gazetted 2nd Lieut. Royal Army Service Corps Oct. 28, 1917, promoted Lieut. April 1919. Served at Home Feb. to Nov. 1917, in France and Flanders Nov. 1917 to April 1919, and in Germany April to Dec. 1919.

HENRY VAUGHAN EDWARDS JONES.

Articled to J. C. Woods, of Swansea. Mobilised Aug. 4, 1914, as 2nd Lieut., 7th Batt. The Welch Regt. (T.), promoted Lieut. Oct. 1914, Capt. Dec. 1914. Once mentioned in Dispatches. Awarded the M.C. Served in France.

HERBERT EDWARD JONES.

Admitted July 1913. Assistant Secretary, Law Society, London, W.C. Joined Sept. 1915, as 2nd Lieut., Royal Sussex Regt., promoted Lieut. June 1916, A/Capt. and Second in Command Oct. 1916, A/Staff Capt. 116th Infantry Brigade Sept. 1917. Twice mentioned in Dispatches. Awarded the M.C. Served in France March 1916 to Oct. 1918. Wounded Sept. 1918.

HERBERT JAMES HILEY JONES.

Admitted Oct. 1913, practising at Portsmouth. Joined Aug. 1916, as Gunner, Hon. Artillery Company, appointed Battery Artificer Jan. 1918. Served in Belgium and France. Wounded March 27, 1918.

HUGH BIRD JONES.

Articled to J. H. Pierce, of Wrexham, N. Wales. Mobilised Aug. 5, 1914, as Signaller, 4th Royal Welch Fusiliers, promoted Corporal Nov. 1914, Sergeant Jan. 1915, discharged time-expired Feb. 1916, voluntarily re-enlisted in Motor Machine Gun Service July 1916 as a Gunner, promoted Corporal Sept. 1916, C.Q.M.S. Nov. 1916. Commissioned 2nd Lieut Tank Corps Nov. 1917. Resigned on account of ill-health caused by wounds Aug. 29, 1919. Served at Home and in France. Wounded on Amiens Front Aug. 5, 1918, left leg amputated.

HUGH MYDDELTON JONES.

Admitted Jan. 1911. Of 7 Mark Lane, E.C. Mobilised Aug. 5, 1914, as Sergeant, "B" Battery Hon. Artillery Company. Commissioned 2nd Lieut. Royal Field Artillery June 28, 1917, appointed Adjutant and A/Capt. July 1918. Served at Home, Egypt, Aden, Palestine, and Syria.

HUMPHREY LLEWELLYN JONES.

Articled to F. Llewellyn-Jones, of Mold. Served as 2nd Lieut., Royal Welch Fusiliers.

ILLBYD RHYS GIFFORD JONES.

Articled to David Davies, of Cardigan. Mobilised Aug. 4, 1914, as 2nd Lieut., 4th Batt. The Welch Regt. (T.), promoted Temp. Lieut. Nov. 1914, Temp. Capt. and Substantive Lieut. July 1915, Substantive Capt. Oct. 1916, attached to Royal Flying Corps as Flying Officer (Observer) Dec. 1917 to Dec. 1918. Served at Home Aug. 1914 to July 1915 and May 1916 to May 1917, Gallipoli and Egypt July 1915 to May 1916, France May to Dec. 1917, and Italy March to June 1918.

IVOR WILLIAM JONES.

Admitted Oct. 1904. Member of William Jones & Son, of Cardiff. Joined Oct. 5, 1914, as Private, The Welch Regt. Subsequently gazetted Lieut. The Welch Regt. Served in France.

IVOR WYN JONES.

Articled to Edward Jones, of Blaenau Festiniog. Joined Oct. 1915, as 2nd Lieut., 7th Royal Welch Fusiliers, subsequently promoted Lieut. and attached to 24th Batt. London Regt. Served in France. Died at Poperinghe from wounds received on June 7, 1917. Buried at Military Cemetery in Reeny, near Poperinghe.

JOHN EUSTACE JONES.

Admitted April 1898. Member of Walker, Smith & Way, of Chester. Joined Nov. 12, 1915, as 2nd Lieut., Royal Army Service Corps, promoted Temp. Lieut. July 1917, A/Lieut. June 1916 to June 1917, A/Capt. June 1917 to Jan. 1918, Temp. Capt. Jan. 1918. Twice mentioned in Dispatches. Served at Home.

JOHN LLOYD JONES.

Articled to M. J. Greener, of 52 Bedford Row, W.C. Joined Aug. 1914, as Private, 28th Batt. County of London Regt. (Artists Rifles), became Lance-Corporal, then obtained commission as Lieut. in 2nd Batt. Yorkshire Regt. about May 1915, rising to Capt. Twice mentioned in Dispatches. Awarded the M.C. Served in France. Wounded Aug. 1915. Died from septic pneumonia while home on leave March 11, 1916.

LAWRENCE JONES.

Admitted June 1897. Member of Lawrence, Jones & Co., of 4 St. Mary Axe, E.C. Joined Aug. 1914, as Lieut., Royal Army Service Corps, promoted Capt. March 1915. Served in France 1915 to 1916. Discharged Aug. 1916.

LEONARD HOWSON JONES.

Admitted July 1912. Member of Kent & Jones, of Longton. Served as Private, 5th Batt. North Staffordshire Regt.

MORRIS VERNON JONES.

Admitted May 1911. Member of Jones, Paterson, Henry & Co., of Liverpool. Joined Sept. 1, 1914, as Private, 10th Batt. King's Liverpool Regt. (Liverpool Scottish). Gazetted 2nd Lieut. May 1915, promoted Lieut. May 1916. Served in France Nov. 1914 to June 1915, Gallipoli Aug. to Dec. 1915, Egypt Dec. 1915 to Aug. 1917, and Palestine Aug. 1917 to Nov. 1918. Wounded Gallipoli Aug. 10, 1915, Palestine Oct. 27, 1917.

OSMAN WYNNE JONES.

Admitted Sept. 1900, practising at Liverpool. Served as Lance-Corporal, 243rd Coy. Royal Army Service Corps.

OWEN MORRIS JONES.

Admitted July 1917. Of Portmadoc. Joined Oct. 1915, as Private, Inns of Court O.T.C. Gazetted 2nd Lieut. Royal Welch Fusiliers Dec. 21, 1916, promoted Lieut. June 1918. Served in France Jan. 1917 to Oct. 1918. Killed at Poix de Noir, near Forest Le Cateau, France, Oct. 31, 1918.

PAUL ESMOND RUSSELL JONES.

Articled to T. B. Jones, of Newport, Mon. Mobilised Aug. 1914, as 2nd Lieut., 4th Welsh Brigade Royal Field Artillery (T.), promoted A/Capt. July 1917, Staff Capt. Royal Artillery Aug. 1917, 3rd (Lahore) D.A.C. Aug. 1918, Staff Capt. Feb. 1919. Once mentioned in Dispatches. Awarded Order of the Nile (4th Class). Served at Home 1914 to 1915, France 1915, Egypt 1916 and 1919, Palestine 1916, 1917, and 1918.

REES ARTHUR JONES.

Admitted Oct. 1906, practising at Swansea. Joined Dec. 15, 1915, as Sub.-Lieut. Royal Naval Volunteer Reserve for service with Royal Naval Division. Invalided out of Service Feb. 3, 1916. Rejoined and commissioned as Assistant-Paymaster Royal Naval Volunteer Reserve Dec. 2, 1916, granted new commission Lieut. Oct. 17, 1917. Served as Executive Officer for South-Western District for Arming Merchant Ships, Devonport to Fishguard, including the Bristol Channel.

THEODORE TUDOR FREDERICK JONES.

Articled to Daniel Perkins, of Port Talbot. Joined Aug. 29, 1916, as Private, Royal Army Service Corps (M.T.), Served in France Nov. 1916 to March 1919.

THOMAS BAKER JONES.

Admitted Feb. 1886. Member of Hornby & Baker Jones, of Newport, Mon. Joined Oct. 12, 1915, as Capt., 1st Batt. Monmouthshire Regt. (T.), subsequently seconded to 4th Batt. Resigned Oct. 26, 1917. Served at Home.

THOMAS CLIFFORD JONES.

Articled to W. Britton Seldon, of Bideford, and afterwards with the B. & A. Tobacco Co. Joined April 13, 1916, as Private, 5th Batt. County of London Regt. (London Rifle Brigade). Killed in action on the Somme about Oct. 10, 1916.

THOMAS DANIEL JONES.

Admitted Feb. 1913. Member of Marchant, Harries & Jones, of Aberdare. Joined Oct. 24, 1916, as Private, Royal Naval Air Service and Royal Air Force. Served at Home.

THOMAS ROBERT JONES.

Articled to J. R. Jones, of Bala, N. Wales. Joined Oct. 1915, as Private, Inns of Court. Commissioned to Royal Welch Fusiliers Sept. 5, 1916, subsequently Lieut. in King's African Rifles. Served at Home, France, and East Africa.

THORNTON BURNETT JONES.

Admitted June 1906, practised at Liverpool. Served as Private, 6th (Cyclist) Batt. Norfolk Regt.

TREVOR JOHN JONES.

Admitted April 1914. Managing Clerk with T. C. Smith, of Berwick-on-Tweed. Joined June 16, 1915, as 2nd Lieut., Brecknockshire Batt. South Wales Borderers (T.), attached 4th (Service) Batt. Oct. 1917, promoted Lieut. July 1917, A/Capt. Jan. 1919. Served in India March 1916 to Oct. 1917, and in Mesopotamia and Kurdistan Oct. 1917 to April 1919.

WILLIAM JONES.

Articled to E. W. Davies, M.P., of Carnarvon. Joined Dec. 6, 1915, a Private, 21st Batt. Royal Welch Fusiliers. Gazetted 2nd Lieut. 3rd Bat Manchester Regt. Aug. 1, 1917. Served at Home and in France.

WILLIAM BRAMWELL JONES.

Admitted Jan. 1898, practising at Llanelly. Served as Major, 4th Bat The Welch Regt.

WILLIAM EDWARD GLYN JONES.

Admitted Oct. 1909, practised at Swansea. Served as Private, Sportsman Batt. Royal Fusiliers.

WILLIAM HOLDEN JONES.

Admitted April 1914. Managing Clerk with Richard Hankinson & Son of Manchester. Enlisted May 6, 1915, as Private, Royal Army Service Corp (M.T.) and attained the rank of Company Sergeant-Major. Gazetted 2nd Lieut in same Regt. July 1918. Served at Home and in France.

WILLIAM JAMES JONES.

Admitted Sept. 1878, practising at Haverfordwest. Served as Lieut.-Col 4th Batt. The Welch Regt.

WILLIAM JAMES JONES.

Articled to J. W. Cocks, of Liverpool. Joined Aug. 31, 1914, as Private, 6t Batt. King's Liverpool Regt. Gazetted Lieut. in same Regt. Nov. 13, 1914 Served in France May 1915 to June 1916. Killed in action June 28, 1916.

WILLIAM SYDNEY JONES.

Articled to W. H. Watts, of 45 Lincoln's Inn Fields, W.C. Joined Sept. 2 1914, as 2nd Lieut., 10th Batt. London Regt., promoted Lieut. June 1915 Capt. July 1916, Adjutant 1916 to 1917, Staff Capt. 1918 to 1919. Served in France.

WILLIAM CRAUFORD JORDAN.

Admitted Aug. 1906. Member of Wiltshire, Son & Jordan, of Grea Yarmouth. Joined Dec. 23, 1914, as 2nd Lieut., 2/5 Batt. Suffolk Regt. promoted Substantive Lieut. June 1916, A/Capt. Nov. 1915 to Feb. 1918 attached 2/4 Batt. Royal Berkshire Regt. April 1918 to Jan. 1919. Served a Home and in France.

FRED ALMA JORDON.

Admitted Oct. 1908, practising at Doncaster. Served as Private, Wes Yorkshire Regt.

CHRISTOPHER HENRY JOSE.

Admitted Aug. 1905, practised at Bristol. Served as Lieut., Ammunition Column 1st Home Counties Royal Field Artillery, promoted Capt. June 1916 and subsequently Major.

WALTER JOHN JOSEPH.

Admitted Nov. 1890. Member of Joseph, Steward & Pretty, of Norwich and Pretty, Joseph & Steward, of Ipswich. Joined Aug. 1, 1917, as Cadet Royal Army Service Corps. Gazetted Lieut. in Royal Army Service Corps.

WILLIAM FRANKLIN GEORGE JOSEPH.

Admitted April 1908. Managing Clerk with Tamplin, Tayler & Joseph, of 165 Fenchurch Street, E.C. Joined Oct. 1914, as Private, Inns of Court O.T.C. Gazetted 2nd Lieut. Royal Berkshire Regt. March 1915. Served in France Sept. 1915 to May 1918. Killed in action May 27, 1918.

JOHN JOSSELYN.

Admitted April 1896. Member of Josselyn & Sons, Ipswich; and John Josselyn, London. Mobilised Aug. 1914, as Capt., 6th Batt. Suffolk Regt., promoted Major Nov. 1914, Brigade Major Jan. 1915 to May 1916, Lieut.-Col. 2/5 Batt. West Yorkshire Regt. May 1916 to Dec. 1917, attached to Staff Southern Command March to May 1918, joined North Russian Expeditionary Force May 25, 1918 (as Lieut.-Col.), commanded a Russian Battalion on Kem Front, Murmansk Railway June and July 1918, commanded original Dvina River and Vaga River Expedition Aug. to Oct. 1918 (as Temp. Colonel), President Claims Commission, North Russia, from Jan. 1919 (Temp. Colonel). Four times mentioned in Dispatches. Awarded C.M.G., D.S.O., O.B.E., T.D., Croix de Guerre (French), St. Anne, 2nd Class, with swords (Russian). Served at Home 1914 to 1916, France 1916 to 1917, North Russia 1918 to 1919, and Home, attached War Office, 1919 to 1920. Wounded near Hindenburg Line at Croisilles 1917.

ARTHUR HERBERT JOTCHAM.

Admitted April 1912, practising at Wotton-under-Edge, and Dursley. Joined Sept. 1, 1916, as Gunner, Royal Garrison Artillery. Commissioned 2nd Lieut. Royal Garrison Artillery July 7, 1917, promoted Lieut. Jan. 1919. Served in France Aug. 1917 to Aug. 1918.

COLIN JOSEPH PATRICK CADWALLADUR JOWETT.

Articled to G. C. Rallison, of Bristol. Mobilised Aug. 1914, as 2nd Lieut., 6th Batt. Gloucestershire Regt. (T.), promoted Lieut. Oct. 1914, Capt. May 1915. Served at Home.

JOHN RAYMOND JOYNSON.

Articled to J. H. Joynson, of Liverpool. Served as Private, 6th Batt, King's Liverpool Regt. (T.).

JAMES CRITCHLEY JUBB.

Admitted April 1909, practised at Leeds. Joined Oct. 1914, as 2nd Lieut., 4th (Reserve) Batt. King's Own Yorkshire Light Infantry, promoted Lieut. Sept. 1915. Served in France. Reported missing July 23, 1916, and afterwards presumed to have died on that date.

HARRY BURFORD JUDGE.

Admitted April 1913, practising at 317 High Holborn, W.C. Joined April 7, 1915, as 2nd Lieut., King's Own Yorkshire Light Infantry, and subsequently promoted A/Capt. Served at Home 1915, France 1915 to 1916 and in 1918, and Macedonia 1916 to 1918. Once wounded.

ARTHUR DUDLEY JULIUS.

Articled to A. O. Julius, of 8 Old Jewry, E.C. Served as Private, 1st (Public Schools) Batt. Royal Fusiliers.

ALEXANDER OCHTERLONY JUPP.
Admitted Aug. 1908. Of Swindon. Joined Jan. 21, 1917, as Lieut., General List, Recruiting Staff. Served at Home.

EMIL JULIUS KAFKA. (Enlisted under the name of Emile Julius Knight).
Admitted Nov. 1908. Formerly of 22 Montpelier Square, W. Served as Private, 31st Batt. Middlesex Regt.

TOM DE SHURLAND KAINS.
Admitted Nov. 1913. Of Exeter. Served as Private, 4th (Public Schools) Batt. Royal Fusiliers.

CHARLES JOHN HERMANN KAPPELL.
Admitted April 1906, practising at Neath, Glam. Served as Private, The Welch Regt.

FREDERICK WYLIE KAY.
Articled to T. Wylie Kay, of Blackpool. Joined May 12, 1915, as 2nd Lieut., 3rd Batt. Loyal North Lancashire Regt., promoted Lieut. July 1917, Capt. July 1917. Served at Home May to Dec. 1915, Egypt and Sinai Dec. 1915 to Feb. 1917, and in France and Belgium March to Sept. 1917. Wounded Ypres Sept. 6, 1917.

WILLIAM ASTELL KAYE.
Admitted July 1898. Member of Kekewich, Smith & Kaye, of 2 Suffolk Lane, Cannon Street, E.C. Served as Able Seaman, Royal Naval Volunteer Reserve (Anti-Aircraft Corps).

JOHN HENRY KEARNS.
Admitted Dec, 1906, practising at 128 Seymour Place, Bryanston Square, W. Joined Nov. 14, 1916, as Private, Royal Fusiliers, subsequently transferred to Army Pay Corps with rank of Corporal. Served at Home.

ARTHUR STANLEY KEARTON.
Articled to J. D. B. Lewis, of Mansion House Chambers, E.C. Joined Nov. 1916, as Cadet, 28th Batt. County of London Regt. (Artists Rifles). Gazetted 2nd Lieut. 3rd Batt. Royal Welch Fusiliers Dec. 1917, attached 25th Batt. King's Liverpool Regt. May 1918. Served in France.

REGINALD TOM KEEN.
Admitted Oct. 1906. Member of Bourne & Keen, of Southam, Warwickshire. Joined April 1915, as 2nd Lieut., 8th Batt. Worcestershire Regt., promoted Lieut. Aug. 1915, subsequently A/Capt. attached Headquarter Staff Tees Garrison, O.C. Physical Training and Bayonet Training. Awarded the M.C. Served at Home and in France. Wounded Nov. 5 and 6, 1916.

CHARLES KEENE.
Admitted June 1917. Managing Clerk with A. R. Chamberlayne, of 45 Parliament Street, Westminster, S.W. Joined Oct. 3, 1918, as Private, Royal Army Service Corps. Served at Home.

THOMAS MANN KEENE.
Admitted May 1891. Member of Keene & Kelly, of Mold. Served as Major, 5th Batt. Royal Welch Fusiliers, promoted Lieut.-Col. June 1916. Mentioned in Dispatches and awarded O.B.E.

JOSEPH IBBOTSON KEER.
Admitted Nov. 1912. Member of Ernest Wilson & Keer, of Sheffield. Gazetted 2nd Lieut. 10th Batt. Lancashire Fusiliers Sept. 3, 1914, promoted Lieut. Feb. 1915, Capt. Dec. 1915, A/Major Aug. 1918, Temp. Major Oct. 1918, transferred to Machine Gun Corps (Infantry) July 1916, (Motors) Sept. 1916, (Heavy) or Tank Corps Nov. 1916, and served with Tank Corps until Sept. 1919. Served in France July 1915 to July 1916, July 1917 to Jan. 1918 and Oct. to Nov. 1918, and in Germany (Army of Occupation) April to Sept. 1919. Wounded July 1915.

RICHARD ERNEST CLAYTON KEIGHLEY.
Articled to Herbert Woodhouse, of Hull. Commissioned 2nd Lieut., East Riding Royal Garrison Artillery March 16, 1915, promoted Lieut. June 1916, A/Capt. March 1917. Served in France. Killed in action in France Aug. 1, 1917.

GERALD KEITH.
Admitted Nov. 1902. Member of G. and G. Keith, of 18 Southampton Street, Holborn, W.C. Joined Dec. 3, 1915, as Lieut., Royal Army Ordnance Department, promoted Capt. Sept. 1917. Three times mentioned in Secretary of State's List. Awarded O.B.E. (Military). Served at Home.

WILLIAM HENRY KELLEY.
Articled to Joseph Cockshutt, of Preston. Joined Nov. 1914, as Capt., 5th Batt. South Lancashire Regt., transferred Royal Air Force with rank of Capt. April 1917. Served in France. Wounded twice. Discharged May 1918.

CLAUDE CLIFTON KELLY.
Admitted July 1905. Member of Kelly & Son, of Ross, Herefordshire. Gazetted Aug. 25, 1914, as 2nd Lieut., 2/1 Batt. Herefordshire Regt., promoted Lieut. May 1915, A/Capt. March 1916. Served at Home and in France. Taken prisoner at St. Quentin.

HUGH CYRIL KELLY.
Admitted Feb. 1911. Member of Gamlin & Kelly, of Rhyl. Joined Aug. 1, 1915, as Rifleman, 18th Batt. King's Royal Rifles. Gazetted 2nd Lieut. 5th Batt. Royal Welch Fusiliers Sept. 1915, promoted Lieut. Jan. 1917. Served at Home and in France.

NORMAN LUCIUS KELLY.
Admitted Dec. 1910, practised at Worplesdon. Served as 2nd Lieut., 2nd Batt. Monmouthshire Regt., promoted Lieut. July 1918.

ROBERT STEWART KELLY.
Admitted Nov. 1897. Member of Keene & Kelly, of Mold. Served as Capt. 16th (Service) Batt. Royal Welch Fusiliers.

CECIL HERBERT KEMP.

Admitted Oct. 1908. Chief Assistant Solicitor to the Birmingham Corporation. Enlisted Nov. 1, 1915, as Gunner, Royal Field Artillery. Commissioned as 2nd Lieut. in same Regt. Aug. 1917, posted to 12th Battery 7th Division Oct. 1917. Served in France and Italy. Gassed during the Austrian attack in Italy June 15, 1918.

WILLIAM ROBERT KEMPSON.

Articled to W. F. Hansell, of Norwich and Cromer. Mobilised Aug. 1914, as Lieut., 1st East Anglian Brigade Royal Field Artillery, attached Royal Naval Air Service (East Indies and Egypt Squadron, Port Said) Feb. 1917, seconded to Royal Flying Corps and qualified as Observer, promoted Capt. June 1916. Once mentioned in Dispatches. Awarded Croix de Guerre (French Division de Syrie). Served in England Aug. 1914 to Oct. 1915, France Nov. 1915 to Feb. 1916, Egypt, Palestine, and Mediterranean and Red Sea March 1916 to Feb. 1919.

HAROLD KENDALL.

Admitted April 1914, practised at Leeds. Served as Corporal, Army Pay Corps.

PERCY DALE KENDALL.

Admitted Feb. 1904. Member of Banks, Kendall & Taylor, of Liverpool. Joined Aug. 4, 1914, as Private, 10th Batt. King's Liverpool Regt. (T.) (Liverpool Scottish). Commissioned 2nd Lieut. in same Batt. and Regt. Oct. 14, 1914, promoted Lieut. Jan. 1915. Served in France and Belgium. Killed in action Jan. 25, 1915. Buried at Kemmel, Belgium.

HADEN MOSTYN KENDRICK.

Admitted Dec. 1913. Member of H. Haden Kendrick & Son, of Wolverhampton. Joined Sept. 1914, as Private, 5th Batt. South Staffordshire Regt. Gazetted 2nd Lieut. in same Batt. and Regt. March 1915, attached Royal Flying Corps July 1916. Served in France. Killed in aeroplane accident Sept. 18, 1916.

THOMAS LUSON KENDRICK.

Admitted March 1914. Of Taunton. Joined 1/1 Kent Cyclist Batt. as Lieut., Aug. 1914, promoted Temp. Capt. Dec. 1914, Permanent Capt. June 1916. Served at Home Aug. 1914 to Feb. 1916, and in India Feb. 1916 to Nov. 1919.

LEONARD MARK KENNAWAY.

Admitted April 1903, practising at Teignmouth and Newton Abbot. Joined Sept. 1, 1914, as Private, 9th Batt. Devonshire Regt. Served at Home. Invalided out April 1, 1915.

CHARLES COURTENAY MARSHALL KENNEDY.

Admitted Dec. 1907. Managing Clerk with Foyer & Co., of 26 Essex Street, Strand, W.C. Mobilised Aug. 1914, as Capt., 1st Batt. Hertfordshire Regt., Camp Commandant 54th Division Oct. 1914, G.S.O. III. Oct. 1914 to July 1915, promoted Brigade Major 151st Infantry Brigade (50th Division) July 1917, appointed G.S.O. II., 32nd Division, Jan. 1918, G.S.O. II., VI. Corps July 1918. Once mentioned in Dispatches. Awarded the M.C. Served in Gallipoli, Egypt, France.

DOUGLAS WYBURN KENNEDY.

Admitted May 1905, practising in Solicitor's Department, London County Council. Joined Nov. 8, 1915, as 2nd Lieut., Royal Army Service Corps (M.T.). Served in France and Belgium. Discharged Feb. 8, 1917.

JOHN KENNEDY.

Admitted Feb. 1914. Of 25 Abingdon Street, S.W. Served as 2nd Lieut., Royal Army Service Corps.

WILLIAM KENNEDY.

Admitted Feb. 1907. Member of L. W. Kennedy & Glover, of Ormskirk. Joined Dec. 16, 1914, as Private, 17th Batt. King's Liverpool Regt., transferred to Inns of Court O.T.C. Sept. 1915. Gazetted 2nd Lieut. 21st Batt. King's Liverpool Regt. Jan. 20, 1916, transferred to 67th Training Reserve Batt. Sept. 1916, and promoted Lieut., appointed A/Adjutant Feb. 1917, transferred to 19th Batt. King's Liverpool Regt. Dec. 1917. Served at Home and in France. Gassed Jan. 3, 1918.

IVOR CHARLES KENSHOLE.

Admitted Jan. 1914. Member of Kensholes & Prosser, of Aberdare, Glam. Gazetted Oct. 1914 2nd Lieut. 5th Batt. The Welch Regt. (T.), seconded to 20th Batt. Cheshire Regt., and finished as Substantive Capt. 5th Batt. The Welch Regt. Served in France June 1916 to July 1917.

FREDERIC EDWIN KENT.

Admitted Nov. 1888, practising at Liverpool. Served as Col. Commanding West Lancashire Royal Artillery.

HUGH BULKELEY KENT.

Admitted Aug. 1886, practising at Liverpool. Mobilized Aug. 1914, as Capt., Royal Garrison Artillery, and served at Home until Sept. 1915.

WILLIAM HENRY KENT.

Admitted Nov. 1911, practising at 11 Gray's Inn Place, W.C. Served as Corporal, No. 4 Coy. (Reserve Batt.) Hon. Artillery Company.

WILLIAM JOHN KENT.

Admitted May 1899. Member of Kent & Jones, of Longton. Served as Major, 2nd North Midland Brigade Royal Field Artillery.

EDGAR KENTISH.

Admitted Jan. 1908. Managing Clerk with Paines, Blyth & Husdath, of 14 St. Helen's Place, E.C. Joined July 12, 1917, as Private, Inns of Court O.T.C., transferred to Royal Air Service as Corporal Dec. 1917. Served at Home.

WILLIAM KENTISH.

Admitted April 1908. Member of James, Barton & Kentish, of Birmingham. Joined Sept. 5, 1914, as Private, 14th Batt. Royal Warwickshire Regt. Gazetted 2nd Lieut. 8th Batt. Royal Warwickshire Regt. June 20, 1915, promoted Temp. Lieut. Nov. 1915, Temp. Capt. May 1916, reverted to substantive rank of 2nd Lieut. Jan. 1917, promoted Lieut. July 1917, A/Capt. with 10th Batt. Feb. to Nov. 1918, and with 3rd Batt. Nov. 1918 to Feb. 1919. Served at Home and in France. Wounded at Cambrai Oct. 21, 1918.

BERTIE TRAYTON KENWARD.

Admitted May 1906, practising at 9 Staple Inn, London. Joined Sept. 1916, as 2nd Lieut., Royal Army Service Corps (M.T.), promoted Lieut. April 1918. Served at Home 1916 to 1917, and in France 1917, 1918 and 1919.

GEOFFREY KENYON.

Admitted Feb. 1909. Member of Kenyon & Son, of Thorne. Joined May 1916, as Private, 8th Batt. Royal Fusiliers, subsequently promoted Lance-Corporal. Served in France. Killed Oct. 7, 1916.

GRANVILLE MONTAGUE KENYON.

Admitted Nov. 1896, practising at 3 Pancras Lane, Queen Street, E.C. Served as Capt., 2nd London Divisional Royal Army Service Corps.

HAROLD GODFREY KENYON.

Admitted Jan. 1906. Member of Kenyon & Son, of Thorne and Doncaster, and also of 2 South Square, Gray's Inn, W.C. Mobilised Aug. 1914, as Capt., 9th Batt. Middlesex Regt., promoted Major Nov. 1914. Gazetted Capt. Royal Field Artillery Feb. 1917, promoted Major Jan. 1918. Served in France. Wounded March 21, 1918, and April 29, 1918.

WILSON KENYON.

Articled to J. H. Field, of Huddersfield. Joined Jan. 15, 1915, as Private, 1/5 Batt. Duke of Wellington's West Riding Regt. Gazetted 2nd Lieut. in same Regt. May 29, 1917, promoted Lieut. Nov. 1918, seconded Machine Gun Corps June 1918. Served two years in France and Belgium.

MALCOLM COLIN KERR.

Admitted Oct. 1911. Of Manchester. Joined June 6, 1916, as Gunner, Royal Field Artillery, and subsequently promoted to Bombardier.

WILLIAM HENRY MYDDLETON KERSEY.

Articled to S. Cozens-Hardy, of Norwich. Joined Feb. 1915, as 2nd Lieut., Essex and Suffolk Royal Garrison Artillery (T.), promoted Lieut. 1916, Capt. 1917. Served at Home till Sept. 1916 on Anti-Aircraft work, and subsequently with 166th Siege Battery in Belgium and France. Killed near Ypres Oct. 17, 1917.

GEOFFREY GOODIER KERSHAW.

Admitted Feb. 1911, practising with Grundy, Kershaw, Samson & Co., of Manchester. Joined Aug. 31, 1914, as Private, 1/6 Batt. Manchester Regt. (T.). Gazetted 2nd Lieut. in same Regt. April 25, 1915, promoted Lieut. June 1915, Capt. Aug. 1918. Twice mentioned in Dispatches. Awarded the M.C. Served in Egypt Sept. 1914 to April 1915, and June 1916 to March 1917, in Gallipoli April to Aug. 1915, and in France March 1917 to Feb. 1919. Wounded Aug. 7, 1915.

LIONEL KERWOOD.

Admitted Jan. 1908. Member of Alfred Kerwood & Son, of Birmingham. Mobilised Aug. 1914 with the 8th Batt. Worcestershire Regt., promoted Major, and subsequently attached to 13th Batt. Cheshire Regt. Killed in action on the Somme Oct. 21, 1917.

PHILIP MALCOLM KERWOOD.

Articled to his father Alfred Kerwood, of Redditch. Mobilised, as Lieut., 8th Batt. Worcestershire Regt. Killed in action in Flanders June 25, 1915.

JOHN BERTRAM KEVILL.

Admitted Nov. 1909, practising at Chorley, Lancs. Joined Aug. 1914, as Trooper, Duke of Lancaster's Yeomanry. Subsequently Capt. Royal Field Artillery. Twice mentioned in Dispatches. Awarded the M.C. Served in Egypt to Jan. 1915 and subsequently in France.

FRANCIS HENRY KIDD.

Admitted Nov. 1909. Member of R. and R. F. Kidd, of North Shields. Joined Sept. 27, 1914, as Capt. Tynemouth Royal Garrison Artillery (T.F.), promoted Major. Served at Home Sept. 1914 to June 1916, India July to Nov. 1916, Mesopotamia Nov. 1916 to April 1918, and in Salonica May to Aug. 1918.

ARTHUR CYRIL KIDSON.

Articled to A. F. Kidson, of Folkestone. Joined Nov. 9, 1917, as Private, No. 8 Officer Cadet Batt. Gazetted 2nd Lieut. 4th (Reserve) Batt. East Kent Regt. (Buffs) May 1, 1918, transferred to 7th Batt. Oct. 1918. Served in France.

HENRY ARNOLD KILNER.

Admitted July 1904, practising at Oldham. Joined June 1915, as 2nd Lieut., 1/10 Batt. Manchester Regt., promoted Lieut. Oct. 1917, seconded to Tank Corps Nov. 1917, A/Capt. Tank Corps Aug. 1918 to Jan. 1919. Once mentioned in Dispatches. Awarded the M.C. Served at Home June 1915 to Jan. 1916, Sinai Peninsula Feb. 1916 to March 1917, and France March 1917 to Jan. 1919. Wounded April 1918.

WILLIAM HAROLD KIMPTON.

Admitted May 1903, practising at Birmingham. Mobilised in Aug. 1914, and served with Royal Army Medical Corps until June 1916, when transferred to Royal Army Service Corps (South Midland Division) as Lieut., promoted Capt. Feb. 1918. Served in France.

AUSTIN MICHAEL KING.

Admitted Feb. 1897. Member of Stone, Thomas & King, of Bath. Served with French Red Cross in France July to Sept. 1915. Joined Royal Army Service Corps March 1916. Commissioned as 2nd Lieut. in same Regt. May 1, 1916, promoted Lieut. Nov. 1917. Served in France June 1916 to March 1919.

BERNARD ELLIS KING.

Articled to A. E. King, of Cambridge. Joined Oct. 1914, as Private, 28th Batt. County of London Regt. (Artists Rifles). Gazetted 2nd Lieut. Norfolk Regt. Nov. 1914, promoted Lieut. July 1916. Given commission in Regular Army, promoted A/Capt. July 1917. Once mentioned in Dispatches. Awarded the M.C. Served in Egypt and Palestine. Wounded at Gaza April 1917.

CHARLES FRANCIS KING.

Admitted April 1914. Member of George C. Carter & Co., of 3 Arundel Street, Strand, W.C. Mobilised Aug. 1914, as Private, Inns of Court O.T.C. Commissioned as 2nd Lieut. 9th Batt. Cheshire Regt. Sept. 11, 1914, promoted Temp. Lieut. Dec. 1914, Temp. Capt. July 1916, A/Major Jan. 1917, A/Lieut.-Col. March 1917, reverted A/Major July 1917, promoted Temp. Lieut.-Col. and transferred to 9th Batt. The Welch Regt. (in command) Oct. 1917, transferred to 9th Batt. Cheshire Regt. (in command) Oct. 1918. Twice mentioned in Dispatches. Awarded the D.S.O. and Bar and the M.C. Served in France. Wounded Aug. 1915, July 1916, and March 1918.

DAVID KING.

Admitted Feb. 1915. Member of Ungoed-Thomas & King, of Carmarthen. Joined April 1916 as Private, Royal Welch Fusiliers (2nd London Welch). Gazetted 2nd Lieut. Royal Welch Fusiliers early 1917. Served in France. Killed in action at Pilkem Ridge, Flanders, July 30, 1917.

EDGAR BLAKE KING.

Admitted Feb. 1905, practised at 145 Fleet Street, E.C. Served as 2nd Lieut., 3rd Wessex Brigade Royal Field Artillery.

FRITZ HUBERT KING.

Articled to H. H. Scott, of Gloucester. Joined Jan. 6, 1915, as Private, Royal Army Ordnance Corps, subsequently promoted Corporal. Gazetted 2nd Lieut. Gloucestershire Regt. March 3, 1919. Served in France June to Dec. 1915, and in Balkans Dec. 1915 to June 1918.

GEOFFREY STUART KING.

Articled to J. A. Forward, of Chard. Joined Aug. 8, 1914, as Private, West Somerset Yeomanry. Commissioned 2nd Lieut. West Somerset Yeomanry Oct. 6, 1914, seconded to Machine Gun Corps March 1917, promoted Capt. Aug. 1917, Temp. Major Feb. 1918. Awarded the M.C. Served in France 1917 to 1919. Wounded March 1918.

GUY STANDISH KING.

Admitted May 1906, practising at 10 Little College Street, Westminster, S.W. Served as 2nd Lieut., Royal Garrison Artillery.

HAROLD KING.

Admitted June 1912. Assistant County Solicitor to the North Riding of Yorkshire County Council. Joined Dec. 1915, as 2nd Lieut., Border Regt., transferred to Royal Field Artillery May 1917. Served in France and Belgium. Gassed and nephritis March 1918. Discharged Sept. 1918.

HARRY TREVOR KING.

Admitted Aug. 1912, practising at Bury. Served as Trooper, Derbyshire Yeomanry (Reserve Regt.).

JOHN SKELTON CLARKE KING.

Admitted June 1912, practised at Brighton. Enlisted in the 4th Batt. Oxford and Bucks Light Infantry and attained the rank of Sergeant. Awarded the D.C.M. Gazetted 2nd Lieut. Oxford and Bucks Light Infantry Nov. 1915. Killed in action May 3, 1916.

REGINALD HENRY KING.

Admitted Oct. 1907. With Bridgman & Co., of 4 College Hill, E.C. Joined Sept. 18, 1916, as Cadet. Gazetted 2nd Lieut. Royal Army Service Corps Oct. 26, 1916, promoted Lieut. Oct. 1918, A/Capt. Feb. 1919, retaining rank until June 1920. Served with North Russian Expeditionary Force. Taken prisoner on mutiny of Russian White Guards of the Onega River Column and handed over to Bolsheviks on July 20, 1919, taken to Moscow and kept in a common gaol with ordinary criminals for eight months. Released March 28, 1920.

RICHARD HENRY KING.

Admitted Oct. 1906, practised at Mansfield. Joined May 8, 1916, as Cadet, Nottingham University College O.T.C. Gazetted Temp. 2nd Lieut. 3rd Batt. Notts and Derby Regt. (Sherwood Foresters) Jan. 25, 1917, and afterwards attached to 12th Batt. Served at Home May 1916 to March 1917 and in France March to June 1917. Killed in action near Ypres June 27, 1917.

THOMAS CHARLES KING.

Articled to R. H. King, of 10 Ironmonger Lane, E.C. Joined as Private, University of London O.T.C., afterwards Corporal 28th Batt. County of London Regt. (Artists Rifles).

RICHARD ROBERT KINGSBURY.

Admitted Aug. 1909. Member of Kingsbury & Turner, of 369 and 371 Brixton Road, S.W. Joined Sept. 7, 1917, as Private, 2/28 Batt. County of London Regt. (Artists Rifles), promoted Lance-Corporal in 1918. Served at Home.

THOMAS KINGSBURY.

Admitted Oct. 1910. Member of Kingsbury & Turner, of 369 and 371 Brixton Road, S.W. Joined Dec. 2, 1914, as Rifleman, 5th City of London Batt. London Regt. (London Rifle Brigade), and subsequently promoted Sergeant. Awarded the D.C.M. Served in France. Wounded at Passchendaele, Belgium, Sept. 20, 1917.

GERALD MONTAGUE KINGSFORD.

Admitted Oct. 1908. Member of Kingsford, Arrowsmith & Wightwich, of Canterbury. Mobilised Aug. 1914, as Capt., 4th Batt. East Kent Regt. (The Buffs), promoted Major June 1916, attached to 4th Batt. The Queen's Own Royal West Kent Regt. as Lieut.-Col. Aug. 1919. Served at Home, India, Aden, North-West Frontier, Baluchistan, and Derajat District.

GUY THORNHILL KINGSFORD.

Admitted Dec. 1906. Of Sekondi, Gold Coast Colony. Served as Major, 1st London Division Royal Engineers. Mentioned in Dispatches. Awarded D.S.O.

FRANK ALFORD KINGSWELL.

Admitted June 1907, practised at Wakefield. Obtained commission in The Queen's Own Yorkshire Dragoons, subsequently promoted Lieut. and attached to The Rifle Brigade. Killed in action March 23, 1918.

SIDNEY HURLSTON KIRBY.

Articled to F. T. Dorman, of 23 Essex Street, W.C. Served as 2nd Lieut., 7th (Reserve) Batt. Royal Warwickshire Regt, promoted Lieut. Aug. 1918.

HAROLD KIRKCONNEL.

Admitted July 1899. Managing Clerk with W. F. & W. Willoughby, of Daventry. Joined Feb. 1915, as Private, Grenadier Guards. Gazetted 2nd Lieut. Cheshire Regt. Oct. 21, 1915, transferred to Royal Welch Fusiliers April 1916, promoted Lieut. July 1917. Served in France.

LAWRENCE JOSHUA KIRKHAM.

Admitted Oct. 1906, practising at Sheffield. Joined Dec. 11, 1916, as Private, Royal Army Service Corps (M.T.). Gazetted 2nd Lieut. Royal Army Service Corps (M.T.) Dec. 18, 1917. Served in France Jan. to Oct. 1917 and Dec. 1917 to April 1919.

ERNEST ROYALTON KISCH.

Admitted Dec. 1911. Member of Adler & Perowne, of 46 and 47 London Wall, E.C. Joined Dec. 1914, as 2nd Lieut., 13th Batt. London Regt., promoted Lieut. June 1915, Capt. June 1916. Awarded the M.C. Served at Home 1914 to 1916, France June to Dec. 1916, Salonica Dec. 1916 to June 1917, Palestine June 1917 to March 1919.

EUSTACE NUGENT KITCAT.

Articled to W. H. Hunt, of Lennox House, Norfolk Street, Strand. Joined June 11, 1915, as Private, 28th Batt. County of London Regt. (Artists Rifles). Gazetted 2nd Lieut. in 2/7 Batt. West Yorkshire Regt. (Leeds Rifles) Nov. 14, 1915, promoted Lieut. June 1916. Served in France Jan. 1917 to Feb. 1918. Wounded Sept. 21, 1917.

EDWARD BAGEHOT KITE.

Admitted April 1898. Member of G. H. Kite & Sons and W. Poole & Kites, of Taunton, and North Curry. Served as Major, 5th Batt. Somerset Light Infantry.

HERBERT TRENCHARD KITE.

Admitted Feb. 1909. Member of G. H. Kite & Sons and W. Poole & Kites, of Taunton and North Curry. Served as Capt., 5th (Reserve) Batt. Somerset Light Infantry.

HENRY LANE KITSON.

Admitted Aug. 1897. Member of Kitson & Trotman, of Beaminster, Dorset. Mobilised Aug. 1914, as Capt., 1st V.B. Dorset Regt., promoted Major Oct. 1914, Lieut.-Col. May 1917. Served in India and Mesopotamia.

WALTER KINLOCH KITSON.

Admitted Feb. 1904. Member of Kitsons, Hutchings, Easterbrook & Co., of Torquay. Served as Lieut., 5th (Reserve) Batt. Devonshire Regt.

ARTHUR HAROLD LASCELLES KNAPP.

Admitted Jan. 1913, practising at 1 King's Bench Walk, Temple, E.C. Joined the Army Reserve Class B, Dec. 11, 1915, transferred as Gunner to Royal Marine Artillery March 1916. Served with Grand Fleet (H.M.S. *Barham*, Flagship 5th Battle Squadron).

GEORGE CREASY KNEE.

Admitted Oct. 1906. Deputy Town Clerk of Hull. Joined Nov. 1914, as 2nd Lieut., 4th Batt. East Yorkshire Regt., promoted Lieut. Jan. 1915, Capt. April 1915, attached to 8th Batt. in France. Killed by shell at Arras May 3, 1917.

GEORGE BROOK KNIGHT.

Admitted Nov. 1902, practising at Farnborough, Hants. Served as Capt., 7th Batt. Duke of Cornwall's Light Infantry.

JOHN HALL KNIGHT.

Admitted Aug. 1888. Member of Knight & Sons, of Newcastle-under-Lyme, Staffs. Mobilised Aug. 4, 1914, as Lieut.-Col. and Hon. Col., 5th Batt. North Staffordshire Regt. Mentioned in Dispatches. Served in France. Killed at attack on Hohenzollern Redoubt Oct. 13, 1915.

JOHN HENRY KNIGHT.

Admitted Feb. 1909, practising at Bath. Joined Aug. 20, 1916, and became a Cadet. Wounded June 3, 1917.

JOSEPH KNIGHT.

Admitted March 1906, practising at Southampton. Mobilised Aug. 4, 1914, as Capt., Royal Artillery (T.F.), promoted Major June 1915. Served in France and Belgium 1916 to 1919.

PERCY NORMAN KNIGHT.

Articled to J. W. Tilling, of Devonshire Chambers, 146 Bishopsgate, E.C. Joined Aug. 31, 1914, as Rifleman, 16th Batt. London Regt. (Queen's Westminster Rifles). Gazetted 2nd Lieut. 10th Batt. London Regt. Nov. 14, 1914, promoted Lieut. July 1916, Capt. Nov. 1917, attached to 162nd Company Machine Gun Corps and promoted A/Major March 1918. Served at Home Aug. 1914 to Sept. 1915, Gallipoli Sept. to Nov. 1915, Egypt Nov. 1915 to Nov. 1917, Palestine and Syria Nov. 1917 to Aug. 1919.

WILLIAM BERNARD KNIGHT.

Admitted Nov. 1908. Member of Colman & Knight, of 11 Gray's Inn Square, W.C. Served as 2nd Lieut., 4th Batt. North Staffordshire Regt., attached to 1st Batt. Bedfordshire Regt. Killed in action on Hill 60, near Ypres, April 21, 1915.

HERBERT WHEATLEY KNOCKER.

Admitted Feb. 1901. Member of Knocker, Knocker & Co., of Sevenoaks. Served as Capt., West Riding Regt.

ROGER BIRKBECK KNOTT.

Admitted Aug. 1912, practising at 36 Bedford Row, W.C. Served as 2nd Lieut., Salford Batt. Royal Fusiliers, subsequently attained the rank of Major. Mentioned in Dispatches. Awarded the M.C.

ARTHUR KNOWLES.

Admitted May 1906. Member of F. Knowles & Son, of Hyde, Cheshire. Joined Aug. 7, 1916, as Private, Royal Army Service Corps (M.T.). Served in Macedonia.

EDGAR LAWTON KNOWLES.

Articled to Arthur Knowles, of Hyde. Joined April 14, 1916, as Private, Royal Army Service Corps (M.T.). Served at Home.

FRANK HENRY KNOWLES.

Admitted May 1911, practised at York. Joined Aug. 1914, as Capt., 5th Batt. West Yorkshire Regt. Served in France. Killed in action at Bullecourt May 3, 1917.

GEOFFREY KNOWLES.

Admitted Nov. 1911, practising at Leeds. Joined Aug. 1914 Leeds University O.T.C. Gazetted 2nd Lieut. Royal Field Artillery Oct. 1915, promoted Lieut. July 1917. Once mentioned in Dispatches. Awarded the M.C. Served in France and Belgium. Wounded Nov. 7, 1914.

HEDLEY KNOWLES.

Articled to M. R. Knowles, of Skipton, Yorks. Mobilised Aug. 1914, as 2nd Lieut., 1/6 Batt. Duke of Wellington's West Riding Regt., promoted Lieut. Dec. 1914. Served in France. Killed May 30, 1915.

WILLIAM DOUDNEY KNOWLES.

Admitted Oct. 1911, practising at Liverpool. Served as 2nd Lieut., 5th Batt. South Lancashire Regt. (T.), subsequently attained the rank of Capt.

HENRY RICHARD KNOYLE.

Articled to W. M. Knoyle, of Glanamman, Carmarthenshire. Joined Dec. 3, 1915, as Private, 27th Batt. Royal Fusiliers, transferred to 32nd Batt. and afterwards to 3rd Batt. Served in France May 1916 to March 1917 and June to Oct. 1918, and Salonica Nov. 1917 to May 1918. Wounded at Le Catelet, France, Oct. 3, 1918.

CHARLES EDWARD KUFEKE.

Articled to J. G. Alexander, of Liverpool. Served as Private, 3rd (City) Batt. King's Liverpool Regt.

KENNETH KUSEL.

Admitted July 1905, practising at Liverpool. Served as Private, 797th Area Employment Company.

CECIL JOHN FAIRFAX KYNASTON.

Admitted May 1904. Managing Clerk with Thomas Eggar & Co., of Brighton; and Winchester House, E.C. Joined June 1917, as 2nd Lieut., Royal Flying Corps, promoted Lieut. Royal Air Force Sept. 1918. Served at Home.

ARTHUR VENABLES KYRKE.

Admitted June 1878. Member of Canning & Kyrke, of Chard, Somerset. Commanded 11th Batt. Somerset Light Infantry (commission dated Dec. 18, 1914), Lieut.-Col., attached to Staff of X. Corps, B.E.F., May 1917. Retired Aug. 26, 1918. Served at Home (Eastern Coast Defence), and France and Flanders. Lost left eye (by accident) on duty on Active Service.

CYRIL DUNMAN LACEY.
Admitted April 1906. Member of Lacey & Son, of Bournemouth. Joined Sept. 1914, as Private, 16th Batt. Middlesex Regt. Commissioned as 2nd Lieut. 9th Batt. King's Royal Rifle Corps Dec. 30, 1914, promoted Lieut. June 1915, Capt. Aug. 1916, Major Dec. 1916. Four times mentioned in Dispatches. Awarded the M.C. Served at Home and in France, also with Military Mission to Siberia, commanding Batt. in Anglo-Russian Brigade. Twice wounded.

GEORGE NELSON LACEY.
Admitted Dec. 1910. Managing Clerk with Light & Fulton, of 1 Laurence Pountney Hill, E.C. Joined Dec. 29, 1917, as Cadet, 22nd (Garrison) Officer Cadet Batt. Gazetted 2nd Lieut. Labour Corps May 19, 1918, promoted Lieut. Nov. 1919. Served at Home.

CHARLES CLARENCE LADDS.
Articled to W. H. Sturton, of Peterborough. Joined Aug. 27, 1918, as Hydrophone Operator, Royal Naval Volunteer Reserve. Served at Home.

JOHN ERIC LADNER.
Admitted Nov. 1905. Of London. Served as Private, 18th Batt. Royal Fusiliers.

JOHN LAING.
Admitted Dec. 1896, practising at Bamburgh, Northumberland. Joined Feb. 11, 1915, as Capt., 2/1 Batt. Northumberland Fusiliers (2nd Tyneside Scottish). Served in France.

WILLIAM FREDERICK LAING.
Articled to L. S. Iliff, of Sunderland. Joined Sept. 5, 1914, as Private, 7th Batt. Durham Light Infantry. Gazetted 2nd Lieut. in same Regt. March 5, 1915, promoted Lieut. Nov. 1915, Capt. and Adjutant Jan. 1916. Awarded the M.C. Served in France. Wounded at Arras April 11, 1917. Taken prisoner at Chemin des Dames May 27, 1918.

ROBERT EDWARD ALGERNON LAIRD.
Articled to Austen Whetham, of Bridport. Joined Dec. 1, 1915, as Rifleman, 5th City of London Batt. London Regt. (London Rifle Brigade), subsequently transferred to 17th Batt. King's Royal Rifle Corps. Served in France. Killed Oct. 15, 1916.

ARTHUR BERNARD MARSHALL LAKE.
Articled to L. S. Cleaver, of Liverpool. Served as Lieut., 5th Batt. Cheshire Regt., subsequently promoted Capt.

HAROLD WALTER LAKE.
Admitted April 1909, practising at Bury St. Edmunds. Joined Jan. 5, 1917, as 2nd Lieut., Coldstream Guards, subsequently promoted Lieut. Awarded the M.C. Served in France.

WILLIAM WALTON LAKE.
Admitted March 1911. Member of W. J. Lake & Son, 61 Carey Street, Lincoln's Inn, W.C. Joined Aug. 7, 1916, as Gunner, Royal Field Artillery

(T.F.), and attained the rank of Sergeant. Gazetted 2nd Lieut. in same Regt. Feb. 1918, and Lieut. Aug. 1919. Served at Home.

LIONEL VICTOR POLLOCK LALONDE.

Articled to John Hodge, of Weston-super-Mare. Joined Sept. 1914, as Trooper, Royal Gloucestershire Hussars. Gazetted 2nd Lieut. 9th Batt. Somerset Light Infantry April 1915, and afterwards transferred to 45th Coy. Machine Gun Corps. Served in France. Died March 31, 1916, from pneumonia contracted whilst in trenches.

LEONARD WILLIAM HENRY LAMAISON.

Admitted April 1900. Member of Powell, Burt & Lamaison, of 28 and 29 St. Swithin's Lane, E.C. Joined Sept. 1914 Inns of Court O.T.C. Subsequently gazetted 2nd Lieut. Royal Warwickshire Regt., promoted Lieut. 1916. Served in France. Killed in action near Laventie July 2, 1916.

ARTHUR FREDERICK THURLOW LAMB.

Articled to J. A. Grundy, of Manchester. Gazetted 2nd Lieut. 6th (Service) Batt. York and Lancaster Regt. Aug. 25, 1914, promoted Lieut. Feb. 1915, Capt. Jan. 1916. Served in Gallipoli (Suvla Bay) July 1915 to Jan. 1916, Egypt Jan. to June 1916, France July to Dec. 1916 and Jan. to March 1918. Wounded near Cambrai March 21, 1918.

ARTHUR JOHN LAMB.

Admitted Dec. 1913. Member of Dennes, Lamb and Drysdale, of Southend. Joined Dec. 13, 1914, as Private, Hon. Artillery Company, and attained rank of Bombardier. Gazetted 2nd Lieut. 6th London Brigade Royal Field Artillery Aug. 1, 1915, promoted Lieut. June 1916, Capt. July 1917, Brigade Signal Officer 140th Brigade, 41st Division, Aug. 1918 to Jan. 1919, Classification Officer Signal Classification Board, Eastern Command Headquarters. Served at Home and in France.

BRUCE LAMB.

Admitted May 1900, practising at Andover. Mobilised Aug. 1914, as Capt., Royal Wiltshire Yeomanry, promoted Major 1915, 2nd in command 1918. Served at Home.

ERIC CHARLES EDWARD LAMB.

Admitted Feb. 1900, practising at 9 & 10 King Street, Cheapside, E.C. Joined March 17, 1917, as Gunner, Royal Horse Artillery. Gazetted 2nd Lieut. Dec. 1, 1917, and posted to 11th Divisional Train Jan. 6, 1918. Served in France.

JOHN ELLIOT LAMB.

Admitted Aug. 1901, practising at Caistor, Lincolnshire. Mobilised Aug. 1914 as Major commanding 1st North Midland (Reserve) Brigade Royal Field Artillery. Served at Home.

JOSEPH LAMB.

Articled to G. K. Taylor, of Liverpool. Served as Private, 10th Batt. King's Liverpool Regt. (Liverpool Scottish) (T.).

ALEC SYDNEY LAMBERT.
Articled to H. W. Fawcett, of Bridlington. Joined Aug. 12, 1915, as 2nd Lieut., 3/5 Batt. Yorkshire Regt. (T.F.), transferred to East Riding Royal Garrison Artillery (T.F.) Oct. 1916, promoted Lieut. April 1918, A/Capt. March 1919. Awarded the M.C. Served at Home and in France.

BASIL SYLVESTER LAMBERT.
Admitted May 1908, practised at Brighton. Served as Gunner, 86th Siege Battery Royal Garrison Artillery.

DUDLEY DAVIES LAMBERT.
Admitted Jan. 1907. With Chamberlain & Johnson, of Llandudno. Joined July 12, 1915, as 2nd Lieut., 6th Batt. Royal Welch Fusiliers (T.), promoted Temp. Lieut. April 1916, Temp. Capt. July 1916 to July 1917, Substantive Lieut. July 1917, Temp. Capt. and Judicial Officer (Class FF) Nov. 1918, employed under Occupied Enemy Territory Administration, Palestine (South), as President of the Court of First Instance, Jerusalem. Served in Palestine 1917, 1918, 1919.

ERIC TOM LAMBERT.
Admitted Sept. 1903, of Bombay. Served as Capt., Bombay Artillery.

FRANCIS JOHN LAMBERT.
Admitted Feb. 1909, practising at Gateshead-upon-Tyne. Mobilised Aug. 1914, as Capt., 9th Batt. Durham Light Infantry, promoted Staff Capt. and Brigade Major 190th Brigade. Awarded the O.B.E. (Military Division). Served at Home and in Ireland.

GEOFFREY FONTAINE LAMBERT.
Articled to C. B. Hepworth, of Coventry House, South Place, Finsbury, E.C. Joined Sept. 1914, as Private, Inns of Court O.T.C. Obtained commission as 2nd Lieut. Hertfordshire Regt. Feb. 1915. Served at Home Sept. 1914 to July 1915 and in France July 1915 to April 1916. Wounded near Festubert April 1, 1916, and died at British Red Cross Hospital No. 2, Rouen, France, April 15, 1916.

JOHN BERNARD WATSON LAMBERT.
Member of Lamberts, of Malvern. Joined Nov. 22, 1915, as 2nd Lieut., Royal Army Service Corps (M.T.). Served in France.

NORMAN FORSTER LAMBERT.
Admitted Dec. 1912. Member of Lambert & Lambert, of Gateshead-upon-Tyne. Mobilised Aug. 1914, as 2nd Lieut., 9th Batt. Durham Light Infantry, promoted Temp. Capt. April 1915, Substantive Capt. June 1916. Served in France and Belgium from April 1915.

THOMAS LAMBERT.
Admitted Nov. 1900, practising at Gateshead. Mobilised Aug. 1914, as Capt., 9th Batt. Durham Light Infantry, subsequently appointed O.C. 9th Batt. Durham Light Infantry Depot. Served at Home. Discharged July 24, 1917.

WILLIAM ASHCROFT LAMBERT.

Admitted May 1908, practising at Sheffield. Joined Sept. 1, 1918, as Private, Inns of Court O.T.C. Served at Home.

LAWRENCE LAMONBY.

Admitted Feb. 1908. Member of Lamonby & Lamonby, of Penrith. Served as Capt., 4th Batt. Border Regt., promoted Major July 1917. Mentioned in Dispatches. Awarded D.S.O.

CHARLES FRANK LAMPARD.

Admitted Nov. 1902, practising at 6 Gray's Inn Square, W.C. Joined 1914, as Lance-Sergeant, 9th (Service) Batt. Norfolk Regt. Gazetted 2nd Lieut. 10th Batt. Norfolk Regt., promoted Lieut. April 1917.

ARTHUR JAMES LAMPORT.

Admitted Feb. 1909. Of Southampton. Served as Trooper, Hants Yeomanry (Carabineers).

CHARLES EDWARD LANCASTER.

Articled to R. Lancaster, of Loughborough, and Coalville. Joined Sept. 1914, as Private, University and Public Schools Corps. Gazetted 2nd Lieut. 1st Batt. Leicestershire Regt. (Regular Army) about Sept. 1916. Served in France Oct. 1915 to March 1918. Killed in action March 21, 1918.

WILLIAM HENRY LAND.

Admitted Nov. 1883. Of Halifax. Served as Colonel commanding 4th (Reserve) Batt. West Riding Regt.

FRANCIS PALMER LANDON.

Admitted July 1899. Member of E. F. & H. Landon, of 53 New Broad Street, London, E.C. Joined Jan. 1915 Royal Army Service Corps O.T.C., and subsequently gazetted 2nd Lieut., promoted Lieut. April 1915, Capt. Feb. 1916, Major June 1917. Served at Home 1915, 1918, and 1919, and in France 1916 and 1917.

JOSEPH HERBERT ARTHUR LANDON.

Admitted Nov. 1910, practised at 53 New Broad Street, E.C. Served as Capt. Royal Flying Corps, and as Major 4th Batt. Essex Regt. Mentioned in Dispatches. Awarded the D.S.O.

HECTOR ALAN LANE.

Admitted Nov. 1911. With Sisson & Delay, of Singapore. Gazetted Lieut. 1st Batt. East Lancashire Regt. on outbreak of War, and went to Flanders April 1915. Killed in action near Ypres May 13, 1915.

JOHN DUNN LANE.

Articled to W. G. Earengey, of Cheltenham. Joined Sept. 1914, as Private, Gloucestershire Regt., promoted Corporal Oct. 1916. Gazetted 2nd Lieut. Machine Gun Corps May 28, 1917, promoted Lieut. Nov. 1918. Awarded the D.C.M. Served in France March 1915 to Jan. 1917 and Oct. 1917 to July 1918. Wounded Aug. 1916.

JOHN KIRKLAND LANE.

Admitted April 1910, practising at Southwell, Notts. Mobilised Aug. 1914, as Lieut., 8th Batt. Sherwood Foresters (Notts and Derby Regt.), promoted

Capt. Nov. 1914, Temp. Major May 1916, attached Northumberland Fusiliers Dec. 1917. Served 2 years in France and Belgium, and remainder of time at Home. Wounded May 1915.

WILLIAM ARTHUR POWLETT LANE.

Admitted Feb. 1902. Of 14 Carlyle Square, Chelsea, S.W. Served as Lieut., Royal Naval Volunteer Reserve, 2nd Reserve Batt. Royal Naval Division.

JOSEPH CHARLTON LANE-CLAYPON.

Admitted Dec. 1905, practising at Mercers Hall, Ironmonger Lane, E.C. Joined Nov. 23, 1914, as Private, 28th Batt. County of London Regt. (Artists Rifles). Gazetted Temp. 2nd Lieut. 7th Batt. Leicestershire Regt. Dec. 5, 1915, transferred to General List (Intelligence Corps) March 1917, promoted Temp. Lieut. July 1917. Wounded on Western Front July 15, 1916.

ERNEST PHILIP HENRY LANG.

Admitted Nov. 1905. Of Hong Kong. Served as Lieut., 1/1 Batt. Monmouthshire Regt.

EDWARD HENNAH LANGHAM.

Admitted Feb. 1900. Member of Langham, Son & Douglas, of Hastings, and 10 New Court, Lincoln's Inn, W.C. Mobilised Aug. 1914, as Major, 5th (Cinque Ports) Batt. Royal Sussex Regt., 2nd in Command of Batt. Feb. 1915, on Staff of VIII. Corps, France and Belgium, 1916 and 1917. Once mentioned in Dispatches. Served in France and Belgium 1915 to 1919. Wounded at Battle of Festubert May 9, 1915.

FREDERICK GEORGE LANGHAM.

Admitted July 1888. Member of Langham, Son & Douglas, of 10 New Court, Lincoln's Inn, W.C. Served as Lieut.-Col. commanding 5th Batt. (Cinque Ports) Royal Sussex Regt. Mentioned in Dispatches. Awarded C.M.G.

COLIN KENDALL LANGLEY.

Admitted May 1914, practising at Birmingham. Served as Private, Hon. Artillery Company.

CYRIL OWEN LANGLEY.

Admitted Dec. 1903. Member of Fowler, Langley & Wright, of Wolverhampton. Mobilised Aug. 5, 1914, as 2nd Lieut., 6th Batt. South Staffordshire Regt., promoted Capt. and Adjutant Sept. 1914, Brigade-Major 2/1 Staffordshire Infantry Brigade May 1915, Staff Capt. 176th Infantry Brigade, 59th Division, B.E.F., Feb. 1916, Staff Capt. Headquarters No. 12 District, Sept. 1917. Once mentioned in Dispatches. Served at Home 1914 and 1915, in France 1916 and 1917, and in Ireland 1916, 1917, 1918, and 1919.

FRANCIS EDMUND LANGLEY.

Admitted 1875. Of 76A High Street, St. John's Wood, N.W. Served as Capt., 8th (Service) Batt. The Queen's Royal West Surrey Regt.

WILLIAM HUMPHRIES LANGLEY-SMITH.

Articled to W. H. Langley-Smith, of Gloucester. Joined Sept. 11, 1916, as Private, 2/5 Batt. Norfolk Regt., appointed Lance-Corporal Nov. 1916 but reverted to Private at own request Feb. 1917, clerk to Headquarter Staff 208th Infantry Brigade March to Oct. 1917, transferred to Royal Army Service Corps (M.T.) Oct. 1917. Served at Home Sept. 1916 to Jan. 1918 and Nov. to Dec. 1919, in India Jan. to Oct. 1918 and July to Nov. 1919, and in Persia Oct. 1918 to July 1919.

JOSEPH LAWRENCE LANGTON.

Articled to J. D. Langton, of 2 Paper Buildings, Temple, E.C. Joined Oct. 1916, as Sub.-Lieut., Royal Naval Air Service, promoted Lieut. Royal Air Force April 1918. Served with Grand Fleet, H.M.S. *Furious*.

ERIC ALLPORT LANKESTER.

Admitted March 1893, practising at 10 Charles Street, St. James's Square, S.W. Rejoined Hon. Artillery Company as Capt., Aug. 5, 1914, promoted Major Nov. 1916. Three times mentioned in Dispatches. Served at Home Aug. to Sept. 1914 and in July 1915, France and Belgium Sept. 1914 to July 1915, and afterwards in America. Wounded at Hooge June 16, 1915.

OWEN HECKFORD LAPTHORN.

Articled to L. N. Blake, of Portsmouth. Joined July 1, 1915, as Cadet, Inns of Court O.T.C. Gazetted 2nd Lieut. Royal Field Artillery (Special Reserve) Aug. 12, 1916. Served in Flanders (Ypres Salient). Killed in action near Zillebeke May 28, 1917.

ALBERT JAMES LARCOMBE.

Articled to Horace Garland, of 165 Queen Victoria Street, E.C. Joined Nov. 6, 1915, as Private, Royal Army Medical Corps. Served in France.

GERALD CHARLES WILLIAM LARGE.

Admitted Jan. 1911, practising at Coventry. Served as Lieut., 7th Batt. Royal Warwickshire Regt.

EDMUND LARKEN.

Admitted Aug. 1900. Member of Toynbee, Larken, Mason & Co.; and Larken & Co., of Lincoln, and Newark. Mobilised Aug. 1914, as Capt., Lincolnshire Yeomanry, promoted Major 1915, Temp. Lieut.-Col. July 1917, Headquarter Staff at Northern Command, York, Feb. to Sept. 1916, G.H.Q. France to June 1919. Five times mentioned in Dispatches including special mention by name in body of Sir D. Haig's Final Dispatch. Awarded O.B.E. and C.B.E. Served at Home and France.

ARDERNE MERE LATHAM.

Admitted Oct. 1898. Member of Stubbs & Latham, of Finsbury Pavement, E.C. Mobilised Aug. 1914, as Capt., Royal Field Artillery, appointed to 15th D.A.C. June 1915, as Capt., posted to 16th D.A.C. Feb. 1916, commanded No. 1 Section, which in Feb. 1917 became the 77th Army Brigade Ammunition Column. Served in France.

HAROLD LATHAM.

Articled to W. H. Tyrer, Town Clerk of Wigan. Joined Feb. 1915, as Corporal, Royal Engineers. Served in France and Belgium July 1915 to Oct. 1918. Died from wounds Oct. 7, 1918.

FARQUHAR WILLIAM FORBES LATHOM.
Admitted Feb. 1904, practising at Luton, Bedfordshire. Joined Sept. 17, 1914, as Capt., 2/5 Batt. Bedfordshire Regt., promoted Major July 1915, Major (Second in Command) 4th Batt. Bedfordshire Regt. Oct. to Dec. 1917, Major (Second in Command) 1/28 Batt. County of London Regt. (Artists Rifles) Dec. 1917 to March 1918. Awarded the M.C. Served at Home Sept. 1914 to Oct. 1917, and in France Oct. 1919 to March 1918. Wounded at Ypres, near Cambrai, March 24, 1918.

HENRY LATTEY.
Admitted April 1882, practising at 138 Leadenhall Street, E.C. Joined Sept. 9, 1914, as Company Sergeant-Major, Corps of School of Musketry, Bisley. Gazetted Lieut. Oct. 1915, promoted Capt. Jan. 1916. Served at Home Sept. 1914 to June 1916, and in France June 1916 to Sept. 1918. Discharged Sept. 1918.

HENRY PATRICK TABOR LATTEY.
Admitted Feb. 1909. Managing Clerk with Payne & Co., of Bombay, India. Joined April 30, 1915, as 2nd Lieut., Indian Army Reserve of Officers, attached 7th Gurkha Rifles, promoted Lieut. April 1916, Capt. April 1919. Served in Mesopotamia Sept. 1915 to Feb. 1916, and July 1916 to Feb. 1917, and on Indian Frontier March 1918. Wounded at Ctesiphon Nov. 22, 1915, and at Advance on Bagdad Jan. 16, 1917.

EDWARD OSBORN LAUDERDALE.
Admitted Feb. 1913. Managing Clerk with Dunderdale & Dehn, of 85 London Wall, E.C. Joined Sept. 3, 1914, as Private, 19th Batt. Royal Fusiliers. Gazetted 2nd Lieut. The Welch Regt. May 12, 1915, subsequently promoted Lieut. and A/Capt., A/Staff Capt. 58th Infantry Brigade. Served at Home Sept. 1914 to Dec. 1916, and in France Dec. 1916 to April 1919.

FRANK ASHLEY LAVENDER.
Admitted Dec. 1907, practised at Wolverhampton, and Walsall. Gazetted 2nd Lieut. South Staffordshire Regt. Nov. 1915, and went to the front June 1916. Killed in action March 14, 1917.

FRANKLIN LAVENDER.
Articled to E. Griffiths, of Bishop's Castle. Joined Aug. 24, 1914, as Private, Hon. Artillery Company (Infantry). Gazetted 2nd Lieut. 10th Bedfordshire Regt. Oct. 7, 1915, transferred to Machine Gun Corps March 1916, promoted Lieut. May 1917. Served in France Sept. 1914 to June 1915 and Aug. 1916 to Oct. 1917. Wounded at Ypres June 9, 1915.

EDGAR LAVERACK.
Articled to E. A. Laverack, of Hull. Joined Sept. 10, 1914, as 2nd Lieut., 4th Batt. East Yorkshire Regt. (T.), promoted Lieut. June 1916, Capt. July 1916. Once mentioned in Dispatches. Served at Home Sept. 1914 to May 1915 and April 1916 to April 1917, and in France May 1915 to April 1916 and April 1917 to May 1918. Taken prisoner at Chemin des Dames, May 28, 1918.

NEVILLE ALFRED GWYNN LAVINGTON.

Admitted April 1907. Member of Titley, Long & Lavington, of Bath. Joined Oct. 11, 1915, as Private, Royal Army Service Corps (M.T.). Gazetted 2nd Lieut. in same Regt. Dec. 1915, promoted Lieut. July 1917. Served in France and Italy (2 years overseas).

HENRY TIFFING LAWDEN.

Admitted Oct. 1913, practising at 28 John Street, Bedford Row, W.C. Mobilised Aug. 1914, as Private, Hon. Artillery Company (Machine Gun Section). At Royal Military College, Sandhurst, Dec. 1914 to May 1915. Gazetted 2nd Lieut. Royal Scots Fusiliers and Machine Gun Corps May 1915, promoted Lieut. April 1916, A/Capt. Jan. 1919. Awarded the M.C. Served in France May 1915 to Aug. 1916 and May 1918 to Feb. 1919. In Palestine Nov. 1917 to May 1918, and in India from Feb. 1920. Wounded Dec. 13, 1914, and July 23, 1916.

CHARLES AIKIN LAWFORD.

Admitted April 1903. Managing Clerk with Rooper & Whately, of 17 Lincoln's Inn Fields. Joined May 1915, as 2nd Lieut., 10th Batt. South Staffordshire Regt., promoted Lieut. May 1916, Capt. Nov. 1917, Staff Capt. 22nd Infantry Brigade. Three times mentioned in Dispatches. Awarded M.C. and Italian Croce di Guerra. Served at Home 1915 to 1916, France 1916 to 1917, and Italy 1917 to 1919.

HERBERT MARTIN BENSON LAWFORD.

Admitted Oct. 1911. Member of Longueville & Co., of Oswestry. Obtained commission in Royal Fusiliers on outbreak of War, and promoted Capt. June 1915. Wounded March 1916 and returned to front in Sept. 1916. Reported missing Oct. 7, 1916, and subsequently officially reported killed in action on that day.

SIR ALEXANDER WALDEMAR LAWRENCE, BART.

Admitted Aug. 1902, practised at 3 King's Bench Walk, E.C. Served as Able Seaman, Royal Naval Volunteer Reserve (Anti-Aircraft Corps).

ARTHUR LAWRENCE.

Admitted April 1909. Member of Wm. Lawrence, of Millom. Joined March 1917, as Private, Royal Army Ordnance Corps, promoted Armourer Staff-Sergeant 4th Batt. Hampshire Regt. Awarded the Russian Albert Medal. Served in Ireland.

CHARLES PHILIP LAWRENCE.

Articled to the late E. K. Blyth, of 112 Gresham House, Old Broad Street, E.C., and employed after passing final in office of Public Trustee. Joined as Private, the Ceylon Contingent which arrived in Egypt in Nov. 1914. Gazetted 2nd Lieut. 27th Punjabis (Indian Army) Feb. 1915. Served in Egypt, France, and Mesopotamia. Wounded April 17, 1916. Died of wounds on April 29, 1916, whilst in Hospital Ship *Varela* on the way to Bombay, and was buried at sea.

CLEMENT GEORGE LAWRENCE.

Admitted May 1914, practised at 11 Red Lion Square, W.C. Served as Private, 28th Batt. County of London Regt. (Artists Rifles).

IDWAL THOMAS LAWRENCE.

Articled to George David, of Cardiff. Served as Lieut., 18th Batt. The Welch Regt., promoted Capt. Nov. 1917. Mentioned in Dispatches. Awarded the M.C.

JOHN NARBETH LAWRENCE.

Admitted Oct. 1911, practising at Pembroke Dock. Joined Jan. 4, 1917, as Private, 28th Batt. County of London Regt. (Artists Rifles). Gazetted 2nd Lieut. 17th Batt. Royal Welch Fusiliers August 1, 1917, promoted Lieut. Feb. 1919. Served at Home Jan. to Sept. 1917, in France Sept. 1917 to Aug. 1918, and in Ireland Dec. 1918 to March 1919. Wounded Aug. 22, 1918.

SAMUEL JAMES LAWRY.

Admitted Feb. 1899, practising at Plymouth. Joined Dec. 18, 1914, as 2nd Lieut., Devon Royal Garrison Artillery (T.), promoted Lieut. June 1915, A/Capt. Aug. 1916. Served in France 2½ years.

WILLIAM DENNIS LAWRY.

Admitted Aug. 1896, practising at Penzance. Served as Capt., 4th Batt. Duke of Cornwall's Light Infantry.

ALEXANDER HENRY DRUMMOND LAWSON.

Admitted Nov. 1899. Member of Lawson, Coppock & Hart, of Manchester, Joined Nov. 1915, as Private, 17th Lancers. Gazetted 2nd Lieut. 10th Reserve Regiment of Cavalry Dec. 21, 1916, promoted Capt. and Adjutant South Irish Horse Dec. 1917. Served in France.

JOHN HARDY LAWTON.

Articled to J. H. Hallsworth, of Oldham. Joined Dec. 2, 1914, as 2nd Lieut. 7th Batt. Duke of Wellington's West Riding Regt., promoted Lieut. June 1916, A/Capt. Aug. to Sept. 1916, Capt. June 1918. Served in France and Belgium.

FRANK LAXON.

Admitted Jan. 1908, practised at Coventry. Joined as Private, 9th Batt. Royal Scots (Edinburgh), subsequently promoted Lance-Corporal.

MATTHEW HENRY LAXTON.

Admitted May 1913. Member of Warren G. Laxton & Son, of Bristol. Mobilised Aug. 1914, as Lieut., 6th Batt. Gloucestershire Regt. (T.), promoted Temp. Capt. June 1915, Substantive Capt. July 1916. Served in France.

HARRY LAYCOCK.

Admitted Jan. 16, 1905. Member of Waterworth & Laycock, of Keighley. Joined Sept. 18, 1916, as Gunner, Royal Field Artillery. Served in France.

JOHN LAYCOCK.

Admitted Aug. 1911, practised at Runcorn. Joined Sept. 7, 1914, as Private. Gazetted 2nd Lieut. 9th Batt. Yorkshire Regt. Dec. 11, 1914, and subsequently attained the rank of A/Major Royal Engineers. Mentioned in Dispatches and awarded the M.C.

ALAN LAYFIELD.

Admitted April 1912, practising at Liverpool. Joined Nov. 5, 1914, as Private, 20th Batt. King's Liverpool Regt., and attained the rank of Sergeant.

Gazetted 2nd Lieut. in same Regt. Oct. 26, 1915, promoted Lieut. Feb. 1917, A/Capt. July 1917, Staff Capt. 237th Infantry Brigade, July 1919. Once mentioned in Dispatches. Awarded the M.C. Served in France and Russia (Murman Coast). Wounded at Battle of Somme July 23, 1916, and at Battle of Ypres July 31, 1917.

GEORGE REGINALD STUART LAYNG.

Articled to Winterbotham, Gurney & Co., of Cheltenham. Joined Sept. 1914, as Lieut., 10th Batt. Gloucestershire Regt., attached to 1st Trench Mortar Battery. Served in France. Wounded at Bazintin-le-Petit Aug. 18, 1916, dying four hours later. Buried at Warloy, near Albert.

BERNARD CECIL LAYTON.

Admitted Oct. 1908. Member of Laytons, of 29 Budge Row, E.C. Served as Corporal, 18th Batt. Royal Fusiliers. Gazetted Lieut. 4th Batt. Grenadier Guards Sept. 1915.

EDWARD THOMAS LEA.

Admitted April 1896, practising at 52 Queen Victoria Street, E.C. Mobilised Aug. 1914, as Lieut.-Col., 4th London (Howitzer) Brigade Royal Field Artillery, and took Brigade overseas, but had to return after a short stay, having passed the age limit for Command.

GEORGE HARRY LEA.

Admitted April 1914, practising at Stoke-on-Trent. Joined July 15, 1917, as Gunner, Royal Garrison Artillery. Served in France Dec. 1917 to Oct. 1918. Wounded at Cambrai Oct. 11, 1918.

WILLIAM ELMER LEA.

Articled to William Lea, of 317 High Holborn, W.C. Enlisted Nov. 6, 1914, as Private, 2/28 Batt. County of London Regt. (Artists Rifles), transferred to 2/13 Batt. London Regt. in June 1916. Gazetted 2nd Lieut. 20th Batt. London Regt. Dec. 19, 1916, attached 2/5 Batt. East Lancashire Regt. Feb. to Oct. 1917, attached to Kite Balloon Section of Royal Air Force Sept. 1918 to Feb. 1919, promoted Lieut. June 1918. Served in France June to Aug. 1916 and March to Oct. 1917. Wounded at Passchendaele Oct. 9, 1917.

EDMUND LEACH.

Articled to Edwin Berry, Esq., of Liverpool. Joined Nov. 3, 1915, as Cadet Manchester University O.T.C., posted to 1st Officer Cadet Batt. as Cadet July 1916. Gazetted 2nd Lieut. Machine Gun Corps, Dec. 29, 1916, promoted Lieut. June 1918. Served in France March 1917 to April 1918. Wounded at Avuloy Wood March 27, 1918.

ROLAND WALTER HARRISON LEACH.

Admitted March 1911. Of 10 Serjeant's Inn, W.C. Served as Trooper, East African Rifles.

FRANCIS JOHN GRAHAM LEADBITTER.

Admitted Dec. 1904. Member of Flux, Leadbitter & Neighbour, of 21 Great St. Helen's, E.C. Joined Jan. 1916 Inns of Court O.T.C. Commissioned 2nd Lieut. 11th Batt. King's Royal Rifle Corps Nov. 1916. Served in France, Jan. to March 1917. Killed near Ginchy March 5, 1917.

SYDNEY LEADER.

Admitted May 1895, practising at 76 Newgate Street, E.C., and Antwerp, Belgium. Enlisted Oct. 21, 1914, in 14th Supply Coy. 18th London Regt. and attained rank of A/Staff-Sergeant at Internment Camp, Alexandra Palace. Commissioned 2nd Lieut. 13th Batt. County of London Regt. (Kensingtons) Oct. 5, 1915, and attached Intelligence A., 4th Army, Jan. 28, 1916, promoted Lieut. Jan. 1917, Temp. Capt. July 1917, graded G.S.O. 3 Feb. 21, 1918, as Head Censor 4th Army. Served in England Oct. 1914 to Oct. 1915, and in France Oct. 1915 to Jan. 1919. Once mentioned in Dispatches.

ALFRED ERIC PIOZZI LEAK.

Articled to Oliver Leak, of Barnoldswick. Served as Private, Royal Field Artillery.

REGINALD LEAK.

Articled to C. Newton Pratt, of Manchester. Joined Sept. 1914, as Private, 6th Batt. Manchester Regt. Gazetted 2nd Lieut. 6th Batt. Lancashire Fusiliers Dec. 1914. Served at Home and in Gallipoli. Wounded at Cape Helles, Gallipoli, Aug. 7, 1915, and died at sea from result of wounds Aug. 26, 1915. Buried at sea.

CLAUDE GUY LEATHAM.

Admitted Nov. 1911. Member of Claude Leatham & Co., of Wakefield, Pontefract, and Castleford. Joined in 1915, as 2nd Lieut., 60th Rifles (King's Royal Rifle Corps), and subsequently promoted Capt. Appointed to Staff of Lieut.-General Sir Thomas Morland, K.C.B., K.C.M.G., etc., commanding XIII. Corps, 1918. Once mentioned in Dispatches. Awarded the M.C. and Bar. Served in France, Belgium, and Italy. Wounded twice.

ANTHONY HEDLEY LEATHART.

Admitted April 1906. Member of Lee & Pembertons, of 44 Lincoln's Inn Fields. Joined Sept. 1914, as 2nd. Lieut., 250th (Northumbrian) Brigade Royal Field Artillery (T.), promoted Lieut. June 1916, A/Capt. June 1917, A/Major June 1918. Once mentioned in Dispatches. Awarded the M.C. and Croix de Guerre (French). Served in France April 1915 to Jan. 1919. Wounded twice.

FRANCIS HOLDSWORTH LEATHER.

Admitted Nov. 1888, practising at Weobley, and Hereford. Mobilised Aug. 4, 1914, as Lieut.-Col., Royal Army Service Corps 53rd (Welsh) Divisional Train, promoted Col. Aug. 1918. Commanded 53rd (Welsh) Divisional Train, XI Divisional Train, O.C. Royal Army Service Corps Independent Force. Four times mentioned in Dispatches. Awarded D.S.O. Served at Home and France and Belgium.

REGINALD LEATHER.

Admitted June 1915. Of Coventry. Served as Driver, "A" Battery, Hon. Artillery Company.

JOHN BARKER LEAVER.

Articled to Alfred Varley, of Colne, Lancs. Joined Sept. 1915, as Cadet, Royal Army Service Corps. Gazetted 2nd Lieut. and subsequently promoted Capt. Served in India and East Persia.

JAMES ASHHURST LE BRASSEUR.

Admitted Feb. 1912. Member of Le Brasseur & Oakley, of 40 Carey Street, W.C. Served as Private, 2nd (Service) Batt. Hon. Artillery Company.

GEORGE WILLIAM LEDWARD.

Admitted Nov. 1913. Managing Clerk with Partridge & Wilson, of Bury St. Edmund's. Mobilised Aug. 1914, as Capt., 5th Batt. Suffolk Regt. (T.). Served at Home and at Gallipoli. Killed at Gallipoli Aug. 12, 1915.

JOCELYN CHARLES LEDWARD.

Admitted April 1914. Member of Beachcroft, Hay & Ledward, of 9 Theobald's Road, W.C. Joined Sept. 1914, as Private, Inns of Court O.T.C. Gazetted 2nd Lieut. Jan. 21, 1915, attached No. 14 Officer Cadet Batt. April 1916, promoted Lieut., attached 4th Reserve Batt. Leicestershire Regt. Oct. 1917, promoted Capt. and attached 1/4 Batt. Leicestershire Regt. May 1918. Served in France May to Oct. 1918. Wounded near Bohain, France, Oct. 10, 1918.

ALAN TREVELYAN LEE.

Articled to G. T. Lee, of Derby. Served as Sub.-Lieut., Royal Naval Air Service.

ARTHUR NEALE LEE.

Admitted July 1903, practised at Nottingham. Served as Capt., 7th Batt. Notts and Derbyshire Regt. (Sherwood Foresters), subsequently Brigade Major 1st Sherwood Foresters Brigade. Mentioned in Dispatches. Awarded the D.S.O. and O.B.E.

HENRY CHARLES CYRIL LEE.

Articled to A. E. Withy, of Bath. Joined April 22, 1915, as Private, Inns of Court O.T.C., and attained the rank of Company Quartermaster-Sergeant. Served at Home.

JOHN KENNETH LEE.

Admitted Oct. 1915, practising at Barnsley. Joined Dec. 9, 1915, as Private, Royal Army Service Corps, and attained the rank of Staff Sergeant-Major. Served in France.

WILLIAM FREDERICK LEE.

Admitted July 1905, practised at Brampton. Served as Capt., Border Regt.

WILLIAM ROBERT CHARLES PAUL FREEMAN LEE.

Articled to J. Parker Ayres, of 61 Carey Street, W.C. Joined the Inns of Court O.T.C. shortly before outbreak of War. Gazetted 2nd Lieut. Royal Fusiliers and subsequently attached 2nd Batt. Royal Welch Fusiliers. Served in France. Killed in action July 10, 1915.

ERIC YORKE TORKINGTON LEECH.

Articled to R. A. Losey, of Leicester. Joined Aug. 11, 1914, as Private, 4th Batt. Leicestershire Regt. Discharged as medically unfit Sept. 1914. Rejoined May 1915 as Private 2/28 Batt. London Regt. (Artists Rifles), transferred to 2/13 London Regt. (Kensingtons) June 1916. Served at

Home to June 1916, France June to Nov. 1916, Serbia Nov. 1916 to Aug. 1917, and in Egypt and Palestine Sept. 1917 to Jan. 1919.

JAMES LEES.

Admitted June 1906. Member of Weston, Grover & Lees, of Manchester. Joined Sept. 5, 1914, as Private, 16th (Public Schools) Batt. Middlesex Regt. Gazetted Lieut. Royal Army Service Corps (M.T.) May 19, 1915, promoted Capt. June 1916. Served at Home, in France, Egypt, Palestine, and the Balkans.

WILLIAM DONALD LEES.

Admitted June 1905. Member of Lees, Smith & Tetlow, of 3 Berners Street, W. Served as Cadet, 22nd (Garrison) Officers Cadet Batt.

FRANK EMIL LEFFMAN.

Admitted Oct. 1911. Practising at 17 Tower Royal, Cannon Street, E.C. Served as Sergeant, Inns of Court O.T.C.

ANTHONY LANGLOIS MASSY LEFROY.

Admitted July 1906. Managing Clerk with Holloway, Blount & Duke, of 24 Lincoln's Inn Fields, W.C. Joined Inns of Court O.T.C. Oct. 1914. Commissioned as 2nd Lieut. 3/4 Batt. Devonshire Regt. (T.) March 24, 1915, transferred to 2/4 Batt. April 1916, promoted Lieut. July 1917, Temp. Capt. Feb. 1918, Temp. Major May 1919. Served at Home Oct. 1914 to March 1916, and in India April 1916 to 1920.

GEORGE FREDERICK LEFROY.

Admitted Jan. 1908. Member of Seldon & Lefroy, of Barnstaple. Served as Capt., 37th Division Royal Artillery.

REGINALD ROY LEHMANN.

Articled to W. B. Glasier, of 47 Essex Street, Strand. Joined Sept. 1914, as Private, 1/6 Batt. Seaforth Highlanders. Served in France. Killed in action at Festubert June 16, 1915.

EDGAR NOBLETT LEIGH.

Admitted April 1915. Managing Clerk with Robert Ferguson, of Blackburn. Joined July 17, 1917, as Third Writer, Royal Navy. Served at Home, H.M.S. *Research.*

JOHN NEWHILL LELEN.

Admitted Oct. 1908. Practised at Torquay. Served as Private, Sportsman's Batt. Royal Fusiliers. Subsequently gazetted 2nd Lieut. 9th (Service) Batt. Lincolnshire Regt.

SYDNEY CURTIS LEMAN.

Articled to G. C. Leman, of 44 Bloomsbury Square, W.C. Joined Aug. 1914, as Private, 2/14 Batt. County of London Regt. (London Scottish). Gazetted 2nd Lieut. 8th (S.B.) Oxford and Bucks Light Infantry (Pioneers) Oct. 10, 1914, promoted Lieut. Nov. 1914. Once mentioned in Dispatches. Served in France Sept. to Nov. 1915, Salonica Nov. 1915 to Sept. 1918, and with Army of Occupation in Bulgaria Sept. 1918 to Jan. 1919.

WILLIAM ERNEST LEMAN.

Articled to Frederick Steward, of Southend-on-Sea. Served as 2nd Lieut., Essex and Suffolk Royal Garrison Artillery.

WILLIAM GASPARD LE MARCHANT.

Admitted May 1901. Member of E. Cave & Co., of 86 Hatton Garden, E.C. Enlisted Jan. 5, 1915, in 24th Batt. Royal Fusiliers. Gazetted 2nd Lieut. 6th Batt. King's Royal Rifle Corps Sept. 1, 1915, promoted Lieut. July 1917. Served at Home and in France 1916 and 1917. Invalided out of the Service and placed on the Retired List Jan. 15, 1918.

HUBERT FRANCIS AUGUSTINE LE MESURIER.

Articled to F. E. V. R. Roberts, of Liverpool. Joined the Inns of Court O.T.C. Oct. 1, 1914. Gazetted 2nd Lieut. Cheshire Regt. Dec. 1, 1914, promoted Capt. June 1915, Major July 1917. Awarded the M.C. Served in France. Wounded May 1917 and March 24, 1918. Taken prisoner March 24, 1918.

HERBERT GALLIENNE LEMMON.

Admitted Feb. 1904. Practising at Abergavenny, Mon. Joined Dec. 16, 1916, Royal Horse and Royal Field Artillery. Gazetted 2nd Lieut. Jan. 13, 1917, promoted Lieut. July 1918. Served at Home.

FRANK DONALD LENTON.

Articled to Robert Epton, of Lincoln. Joined 1914, as Private, Hon. Artillery Company. Served in France. Wounded at Locre March 24, 1915, and died as the result of wounds at Bailleul Hospital March 26, 1915.

JAMES ALOYSIUS LEONARDT.

Articled to S. S. Guest, of Birmingham. Joined June 3, 1918, as Ordinary Seaman, Royal Naval Volunteer Reserve, and subsequently promoted to Ordinary Telegraphist. Served at Home.

ALGERNON LESSER.

Admitted July 1894. Practised at 20 Wormwood Street, E.C. Served as Capt., 13th Batt. County of London Regt. (Kensington).

WALTER EDWIN LESTER.

Admitted July 1905. Member of Palmer & Lester, of Nuneaton. Served as Corporal, Royal Air Force.

ARNOLD LETHERBY.

Admitted Oct. 1914. Formerly with Shelley & Johns, of Plymouth. Enlisted Nov. 1915, as Private, 3/5 Batt. Devonshire Regt. and subsequently promoted Lance-Corporal, transferred to No. 5 Officer Cadet Batt. (Cambridge) April 1916. Gazetted 2nd Lieut. 3/4 Batt. Duke of Cornwall's Light Infantry April 23, 1916, promoted Lieut. March 1918. Served in England Nov. 1915 to Sept. 1916, France Sept. 1916 to Dec. 1917, and Ireland June 1918 to May 1919. Wounded at Masnières, near Cambrai, Nov. 30, 1917.

MALCOLM HENRY IKIN LETTS.

Admitted April 1905. Practising at 8 Bartlett's Buildings, E.C. Joined April 1917, as Lieut., General List. Served at Home.

LESLIE SPRY LEVERTON.

Articled to P. T. Pearce, of Plymouth. Joined June 15, 1915, as 2nd Lieut., 5th Batt. Duke of Cornwall's Light Infantry, promoted Lieut. June 1917. Awarded the M.C. and Bar. Served in France and Flanders May 1916 to April 1918, and with Army of Black Sea Sept. to Dec. 1919. Wounded March 28, 1918.

RICHARD HENRY LEVETT.

Admitted Feb. 1906. Member of Buss & Levett, of Tunbridge Wells. Joined Jan. 19, 1915, Inns of Court O.T.C. Commissioned as 2nd Lieut. 9th Batt. Royal West Kent Regt. May 23, 1915, attached 3rd Batt., acted as Assistant Adjutant Christmas 1915 to May 1916, and from May to Aug. 1916 was Acting Adjutant to the Regt. Served at Home. Died of blood poisoning at Chatham Aug. 20, 1916.

HARRY LEVI.

Admitted July 1911. Practised at Manchester. Served as 2nd Lieut., Royal Fusiliers. Killed in action Nov. 30, 1917.

CARL NORTON LEVIN.

Admitted April 1914. Of Newcastle-upon-Tyne. Joined Sept. 7, 1914, as Private, 9th (Service) Batt. Northumberland Fusiliers. Received commission in 21st Batt. Northumberland Fusiliers (Tyneside Scottish) April 1915, promoted Capt. Oct. 1915 and thence, until killed, Commanded the 102nd Light Trench Mortar Battery. Awarded the M.C. Served in France over 2 years. Killed in action near Croisilles March 21, 1918.

BERTRAM ARTHUR LEVINSON.

Admitted May 1910. Member of Bartlett & Gluckstein, of 199 Piccadilly, W. Joined Jan. 1917 as Sapper, Royal Engineers (London Electrical Engineers), transferred to Cadet Officers Training School Jan. 1918. Commissioned 2nd Lieut. Royal Garrison Artillery July 31, 1916. Served at Home.

HYAM MOSES LEVY.

Admitted Feb. 1909. Member of Chamberlain, Johnson & Levy, of 30 Essex Street, W.C. Joined Aug. 10, 1914, as Driver, Hon. Artillery Company, and attained the rank of Sergeant. Gazetted 2nd Lieut. in same Regt. Nov. 1915, promoted Lieut. 1917. Served in Egypt 1916 and in Salonica and Palestine 1917. Contracted malaria typhoid in Palestine Nov. 1917.

ALFRED WILLIAM LEWIS.

Admitted Nov. 1901. Practising at Rhyl. Joined Nov. 29, 1915, as Private, Royal Army Service Corps. Served at Home.

BERNARD LEWIS.

Admitted Dec. 1879. Practising at Penyffordd, Flintshire. Mobilised Aug. 1914 as Major, Flintshire National Reserve. Served as O.C. 1/5 and 3/5 Royal Welch Fusiliers and transferred to Royal Defence Corps. Always on Home Service.

BRINLEY RICHARD LEWIS.

Articled to T. W. James, of Swansea. Joined Oct. 1914, as Trooper, Glamorganshire Yeomanry. Gazetted 2nd Lieut. Royal Field Artillery May

1915, promoted Lieut. 1916, Major Nov. 1916. Once mentioned in Dispatches. Served in France Dec. 1915 to April 1917. Killed in action at Ypres April 2, 1917.

CONRAD ESDAILE TYRRELL LEWIS.
Admitted April 1911. Practising at Albany Court Yard, Piccadilly, W. Joined 1914, as Private, 12th (Public Schools) Batt. Middlesex Regt. and subsequently gazetted 2nd Lieut. 6th Batt. Royal Irish Fusiliers.

EDWARD MILTON LEWIS.
Admitted Feb. 1913. Managing Clerk with N. Strickland & Fletcher, of Bristol. Joined March 8, 1915, as Private, Royal Army Service Corps, promoted Corporal Dec. 1915. Awarded Ginchy Diamond 16th (Irish) Division. Served in France. Discharged April 18, 1918.

ERIC VAUGHAN LEWIS.
Admitted Aug. 1906. Managing Clerk with Davies, Sanders & Co., of Chesterfield. Joined Aug. 1914, as Private, 23rd Batt. County of London Regt. Served in France. Killed in action May 26, 1915.

FRANCIS BALL LEWIS.
Admitted Oct. 1887. Practising at 3 Bucklersbury, E.C. Joined Sept. 1914, as Corporal, 17th Batt. Royal Fusiliers. Joined 21st Batt. Northumberland Fusiliers as Major in Jan. 1915. Died of pneumonia while serving with the 19th Batt. King's Royal Rifle Corps at Home March 30, 1917.

FREDERICK GUSTAV LEWIS.
Admitted Sept. 1899. Practising at 16 Berners Street. Mobilised Aug. 1914, as Lieut.-Col., 13th Kensington Batt. London Regt., Brigadier-General 142nd Infantry Brigade Aug. 1915, promoted Substantive Colonel, Brigadier-General 166th Infantry Brigade, April 1917, Section Commander Tees Garrison Oct. 1918, Hon. Colonel 13th Kensington Batt. London Regt. Nov. 1918, Deputy Director of Mobilisation, War Office, Jan. 1919, Member Reorganisation of After War Army Committee Nov. 1919. Seven times mentioned in Dispatches. Awarded C.B., C.M.G., and T.D. Served in France Nov. 1914 to May 1915, July 1915 to Dec. 1916, and April to Dec. 1917.

GERALD PATTERSON LEWIS.
Admitted Dec. 1912. Practised at Bristol. Served as Private, Bristol University O.T.C.

GUILFORD EDWARD LEWIS.
Admitted June 1886. Practising at 14 South Square, Gray's Inn, W.C. Joined April 16, 1917 as Lieut., General List Intelligence Staff. Served at Home. Relinquished commission Jan. 25, 1918.

HORACE GEORGE CRAWFORD TYRRELL LEWIS.
Articled to E. T. Lewis, of 2 and 3 Albany Court Yard, Piccadilly, W. Mobilised Aug. 1914, as 2nd Lieut., 15th Batt. County of London Regt. (Civil Service Rifles), promoted Lieut. Oct. 1914, Capt. Nov. 1915, appointed G.S.O. III., III. Corps Nov. 1916. Twice mentioned in Dispatches. Served in France March 1915 to Feb. 1919.

LAURENCE REDDROP LEWIS.

Admitted Aug. 1905. Managing Clerk with Davies, Sanders & Co., of Chesterfield. Joined Aug. 1914, as Private, 18th Batt. Royal Fusiliers. Gazetted 2nd Lieut. 11th Batt. South Wales Borderers Feb. 1915, promoted Capt. Oct. 1915. Served in France Nov. 1915 to July 1916. Killed in action July 12, 1916.

REGINALD STROTHER LEWIS.

Admitted March 1910, practising at Aberdare, S. Wales. Joined Oct. 26, 1914, as 2nd Lieut., Royal Field Artillery, promoted Lieut. Oct. 1914, A/Capt. Dec. 1917. Served in France 1916 to 1919.

STUART HERMON LEWIS.

Admitted June 1912. Of Solicitor's Department, London County Council, Strand, W.C. Joined Sept. 26, 1914, as 2nd Lieut. (S.R. of Officers), The Queen's Own Royal West Kent Regt., promoted Capt. 1915, later attached to 1st Batt. Northamptonshire Regt., finally Staff Capt. to Headquarters XXIII. Corps. Twice mentioned in Dispatches. Served in France. Wounded at the Battle of Loos Sept. 27, 1915.

WILLIAM OWEN LEWIS.

Articled to W. Clothier, of Liverpool. Served as 2nd Lieut., 4th Batt. Royal Welch Fusiliers. Killed.

ROBERT HENRY LEWIS-MANNING.

Articled to William Kenshole, of Aberdare. Joined Nov. 28, 1915, as Private, 14th Batt. County of London Regt. (London Scottish), transferred to Tank Corps Jan. 1917. Served at Home, in France, Belgium, and in Ireland. Wounded Nov. 1917.

WILLIAM PLUMPTON LEWIS.

Admitted Feb. 1912. Of Cardiff. Served as Lieut., 3rd Batt. The Welch Regt., attached 2/1 Batt. Pembroke Yeomanry.

ARTHUR THEWLIS LEWTHWAITE.

Admitted July 1902. Practising at 3 Duncan Street, Islington, N. Mobilised Aug. 3, 1914, as Lieut., 11th Batt. County of London Regt., promoted Capt. Aug. 1914. Served at Home Aug. 1914 to July 1915, Gallipoli July to Dec. 1915, Egypt (Canal Zone) Dec. 1915 to Feb. 1917, and Palestine Feb. 1917 to March 1919.

EDMUND THOMAS MALLOCK LIAS.

Articled to W. S. Sharpe, of 12 New Court, Lincoln's Inn, W.C. Served as Private, 2nd Mounted Divisional Signal Squadron Royal Engineers (T.).

GEORGE JAMES LIDDLE.

Admitted Oct. 1889. Practising at 24 and 25 Great Tower Street, E.C. Embodied at the outbreak of War, as Capt., 1st London Brigade Royal Field Artillery (T.). Served at Home in command of a Territorial Force Depôt.

JOHN CUTHBERT LIDGETT.

Admitted Oct. 1911. Managing Clerk with Slack, Monro, Saw & Co., of 0 Queen Street, E.C. Joined Feb. 17, 1916, as Private, 28th Batt. County of

London Regt. (Artists Rifles). Gazetted 2nd Lieut. 3rd Batt. South Lancashire Regt. Dec. 19, 1916, transferred to 11th Batt. and promoted Lieut. July 1917. Served in France. Killed in action near Ham March 24, 1918.

HERBERT SEPPINGS LIDIARD.

Admitted May 1914. Practising at 7 Great James Street, W.C. Served as 2nd Lieut., 3rd (City of London) Batt. Royal Fusiliers, promoted Capt. April 1917. Mentioned in Dispatches and awarded the M.C.

RICHARD JOHN ABRAHAM LIDIARD.

Articled to his father, Herbert Lidiard, of 7 Great James Street, W.C. Gazetted Sept. 1914 2nd Lieut. 3rd City of London Batt. Royal Fusiliers. Killed in action in France July 1, 1916.

REUBEN LIEBERMAN.

Articled to A. E. Carr, of Leeds. Joined May 1916, as Private, West Yorkshire Regt., transferred to Labour Corps Feb. 1917, promoted Sergeant April 1917. Awarded the M.S.M. Served at Home and in France (2 years).

DONALD OWEN LIGHT.

Articled to G. M. Light, of 1 Laurence Pountney Hill, E.C. Joined Feb. 17, 1915, as 2nd Lieut., Royal Army Service Corps, promoted Lieut. May 1915, Capt. Dec. 1915, attached to Middlesex Regt. 1917. Once mentioned in Dispatches. Served in France Nov. 1917 to April 1918. Wounded and taken prisoner at Bois Grenier April 9, 1918.

OWEN FULLER LIGHT.

Articled to Sir T. A. Bramsdon, Kt., M.P., of Portsmouth. Joined Jan. 14, 1915, as Sapper, Hampshire (Fortress) Royal Engineers (T.), promoted Corporal 1916. Commissioned 2nd Lieut. Hants Royal Garrison Artillery (T.) Jan. 6, 1918. Served at Home and in France. Wounded at Ribeauville, France, Nov. 4, 1918.

WILFRID PETRE LIGHTBODY.

Articled to J. A. H. Hooker, of 20 Victoria Street, Westminster. Joined Dec. 1914, as 2nd Lieut., 9th Batt. Norfolk Regt., promoted Lieut. March 1915. Served at Home and in France. Killed Sept. 26, 1915.

JOSEPH BENEDICT BRADLEY LIGHTBOUND.

Articled to C. A. M. Lightbound, of 26 Great St. Helen's, E.C., and Liverpool. Joined July 1, 1915, as 2nd Lieut., 8th (Irish) Batt. King's Liverpool Regt., and subsequently promoted Lieut., attached to 12th Batt. Dec. 1916 to March 1917. Served in France.

JOHN EDWARD LIGHTBURN.

Admitted May 1914, practising at Wigan. Served as Lieut., 5th Batt. Manchester Regt.

GEORGE LIONEL SPENCER LIGHTFOOT.

Articled to E. W. Lightfoot, of Carlisle. Joined Oct. 27, 1914, as 2nd Lieut., 10th Batt. Border Regt., transferred to 5th Batt. Wiltshire Regt. March 1916, transferred to Royal Air Force April 1918, promoted Lieut. Aug. 1917. Served in Gallipoli and Egypt 1915 and 1918, and Mesopotamia 1916,

1917, and 1918. Wounded at Beit Aiessa April 27, 1916, during the attempt to relieve General Townshend in Kut.

STANLEY LIGHTMAN.

Admitted Oct. 1915, practising at Leeds. Served as Acting Paymaster, Northern Command, York, Nov. 1915 to end of War.

BERTRAM EDWARD LILLEY.

Admitted Jan. 1909, practised at 35 Bedford Row, W.C. Served as Lieut., Royal Army Service Corps.

CONRAD IVAN LILLINGTON.

Articled to G. C. Woods, of 6 Lancaster Place, Strand, W.C. Joined Aug. 22, 1914, as Private, 4th Batt. Somerset Light Infantry. Gazetted Lieut. in same Regt. Oct. 7, 1914. Served at Home, in India, and in Mesopotamia. Killed in action at Es Sinn, Mesopotamia, March 8, 1916, in an attempt to relieve Kut.

WILLIAM HAROLD LILLINGTON.

Admitted July 1912. Practised at Carmarthen. Served as 2nd Lieut., 10th Batt. South Wales Borderers.

WILLIAM CARTER LINAY.

Admitted Feb. 1911. Managing Clerk with Ford, Lloyd, Bartlett & Michelmore, of 38 Bloomsbury Square, W.C. Mobilised 1914, as Trooper, 3rd County of London Yeomanry. Gazetted 2nd Lieut. Royal Army Service Corps April 1, 1915, promoted Lieut. Aug. 1915, Capt. Sept. 1917, transferred to Notts & Derby Regt. (Sherwood Foresters) Oct. 1917. Served at Home Aug. 1914 to April 1915, and in France April 1915 to Feb. 1919.

THOMAS GRENVILLE LINDLEY.

Articled to Alexander Pollock, of 6 Lincoln's Inn Fields, W.C. Joined Sept. 1914, as Private, 1/20 Batt. County of London Regt. (T.). Gazetted 2nd Lieut. July 1917 and attached to 10th Batt. London Regt. Killed in action near Ypres Sept. 24, 1917.

ROLLO CHRISTISON LINDSAY.

Admitted Aug. 1912. Member of Field & Sons, of Liverpool. Joined Aug, 5, 1914, as Private, 10th Batt. King's Liverpool Regt. (Liverpool Scottish). Gazetted 2nd Lieut. March 1915, promoted Lieut. April 1915. Served in Belgium. Wounded June 16, 1915. Gazetted out on account of wounds Dec. 3, 1916.

WILLIAM FREDERICK LINDSELL.

Admitted March 1912, practising at Manchester. Served as Capt., th Batt. Cheshire Regt. (T.).

ROBERT CHALONER LINDSEY-BRABAZON.

Articled to T. A. L. Whittington, of Neath. Enlisted Sept. 7, 1914, in th Batt. King's Shropshire Light Infantry. Granted commission 6th Batt. he Welch Regt. Dec. 4, 1914, promoted Lieut. July 1916, Capt. Aug. 1916, djutant March 1916 to June 1919. Twice mentioned in Dispatches. Awarded ıe M.C. Served in France.

FREDERICK THORP LINELL.

Admitted Dec. 1904. Member of Holmes, Son & Pott, of Capel House, New Broad Street, E.C. Joined Jan 8, 1917, as Private, Royal Army Service Corps (M.T.). Served at Home and in France.

HUBERT FREDERIC LING.

Admitted June 1909. Member of F. G. Ling & Son, of Framlingham. Mobilised Aug. 1914, as Lieut., 4th Batt. Suffolk Regt. (T.), promoted Capt. March 1915, Major April 1918. Awarded the M.C. Served in France 3 years and at Home 2 years. Wounded Aug. 1916.

CLAUDE FRANK LINGARD.

Articled to F. C. Lingard, of 4 New London Street, E.C. Joined Aug. 30, 1914, as 2nd Lieut., Royal Engineers (Signals), promoted Lieut. July 1915, Temp. Capt. 1916. Served in France May to June 1915 and Aug. to Sept. 1915, in East Africa Dec. 1915 to Dec. 1916, and in Serbia June 1917 to Dec. 1918. Wounded in France June 7 and Sept. 27, 1915, in East Africa April and Sept. 1916.

JOHN REGINALD LINGARD.

Admitted Oct. 1912. Member of Lingards & Hamp, of Manchester. Served as Lieut., Manchester Regt., attached Lancashire Fusiliers. Reported wounded in the advance from Suvla Bay, Gallipoli, Aug. 21, 1915, and afterwards reported wounded and missing and subsequently presumed to have died.

HAROLD CRONSHAW LINGS.

Admitted Oct. 1905, practising at Manchester. Mobilised Aug. 4, 1914, as Capt., 8th Batt. Manchester Regt., promoted Major July 1916. Twice mentioned in Dispatches. Awarded the D.S.O. Served in Egypt 1914 and 1916, Gallipoli 1915, France 1917. Wounded June 4, 1915, and Oct. 2, 1917.

GEORGE LINTER.

Articled to S. V. Farrington, of Brighton. Joined Aug. 10, 1914, as Gunner, Sussex Royal Garrison Artillery (T.), and attained the rank of Sergeant 1917. Commissioned 2nd Lieut. Royal Garrison Artillery Feb. 18, 1918, and posted to No. 1 Siege Artillery Reserve Brigade, Shoreham. Awarded the M.M. Served at Home Aug. 1914 to Nov. 1916 and June 1917 to June 1919, and in France Nov. 1916 to June 1917.

FREDERICK LINTON.

Admitted Nov. 1899. Member of Woodcock, Stobart & Co., of Wigan. Joined June 1918, as Private, Royal Air Force. Served at Home.

ROBERT ERNEST BENTHAM LISLE.

Admitted June 1901. Member of Appleby & Lisle, of Newcastle-upon-Tyne. Joined Oct. 8, 1914, as 2nd Lieut., 8th Batt. Durham Light Infantry, subsequently promoted to Lieut., Capt., and Major. Served in France. Killed in action March 30, 1918.

GEORGE LISTER.

Admitted Jan. 1911. Member of Mitcheson, Wharton & Lister, of Heckmondwike. Joined 1914, as Private, 5th Batt. West Riding Regt. Gazetted 2nd Lieut. 2nd Batt. East Yorkshire Regt. Awarded the M.B.E.

HERBERT DIXON LISTER.

Admitted July 1909, practised at Llandilo. Served as Sergeant, 4th (Reserve) Batt. The Welch Regt.

RICHMOND HOLME LITTLE.

Articled to H. M. A. Ward, of Harwich, Essex. Joined June 1915, as 2nd Lieut., 3rd Batt. Essex Regt., promoted Lieut. July 1917, Capt. March 1918. Served in Labour Corps after return from France. Served in France and at Home.

JOHN ROBERT LIVERSAGE.

Admitted Oct. 1908, practising at Prestwich. Served as Private, 23rd Batt. King's Liverpool Regt.

ALAN GEORGE HILTON LIVESEY.

Articled to F. K. Bull, of 6 Old Jewry, E.C. Joined at commencement of War, as 2nd Lieut., Loyal North Lancashire Regt. Served in France. Killed in action at Loos Sept. 27, 1915.

JOHN WILLIAM LIVESEY.

Admitted Oct. 1911, practising at Bootle, Lancs. Served as Private, Royal Army Ordnance Corps.

MOSTYN CLEWES LLEWELLIN.

Admitted Nov. 1902. Member of Llewellin & Co., of Newport, Mon. Served as Capt., 1st Batt. Monmouthshire Regt. Taken prisoner and interned in Holland.

EDWARD ALFRED ROBERT LLEWELLYN.

Admitted Feb. 1914, practising at 8 Lammas Park Gardens, Ealing, W. Joined Nov. 1914, as Private, 2/5 London Field Ambulance Royal Army Medical Corps. Commissioned as 2nd Lieut. Herefordshire Regt. May 1915, promoted Temp. Capt. July 1916, attached to Contract Dept. of the War Office 1917, appointed Military Magistrate in Egypt Nov. 1919. Served at Home, in Gallipoli, and in Egypt.

FRED LLEWELLYN.

Admitted Aug. 1912, practised at Tunstall. Served as Major, 8th (Service) Batt. Oxford & Bucks Light Infantry.

HAROLD ALFRED LLEWELLYN.

Articled to G. C. Downing, of Cardiff. Enlisted in the 7th Batt. Welch Cyclists shortly after the outbreak of War and soon afterwards transferred to the Cardiff "Pals" Batt. Gazetted 2nd Lieut. Royal Welch Fusiliers Dec. 1914, promoted Lieut. Oct. 1915, transferred to the South Wales Borderers. Accidentally killed June 14, 1916.

HERBERT LORD LLEWELLYN.

Admitted June 1891, practising at 4 & 5 Norfolk Street, Strand, W.C. Joined Oct. 18, 1914, as Lieut., 10th Batt. Northumberland Fusiliers, promoted Capt. Dec. 1914, Major Aug. 1916. Served in France.

RUPERT ARTHUR LLEWELLYN.

Admitted Feb. 1899, practising at Stoke-on-Trent, Staffs. Joined Oct. 7, 1914, as Capt., East Lancashire Regt. Served in France and at Home. Wounded Sept. 27, 1915.

WILLIAM EUSTACE LLEWELLYN.

Admitted April 1914. Managing Clerk with J. Moy Evans, of Swansea. Joined Nov. 8, 1915, as Private, Inns of Court O.T.C. Gazetted Lieut. Royal Marines Nov. 22, 1916. Served in France. Taken prisoner at Arras April 28, 1917.

ALBERT VICTOR LLOYD.

Admitted Aug. 1910, practised at Cardiff. Served as Lieut. in Mesopotamia.

ARTHUR LLOYD.

Admitted June 1914. Managing Clerk with Whittington & David, of Neath. Joined Nov. 1916, as Driver, Royal Horse Artillery. Granted commission as 2nd Lieut. Royal Garrison Artillery May 29, 1917, promoted Capt. and Adjutant 68th Brigade in France Sept. 1918. Served at Home Nov. 1916 to July 1917, and in France July 1917 to March 1919.

DAVID HOWARD LLOYD.

Admitted Oct. 1917. Member of Rustons & Lloyd, of Newmarket. Joined Oct. 1915, as Private, 28th Batt. County of London Regt. (Artists Rifles). Commissioned as 2nd Lieut. 1st Batt. Monmouthshire Regt. (T.F.) July 1916. Served in France. Wounded Easter 1917 (including gas and shell shock). Discharged Aug. 1917.

EDMUND COMMELINE LLOYD.

Admitted March 1912. Managing Clerk with Thurstons & Jolly, of Thornbury, Glos. Joined Oct. 10, 1914, as 2nd Lieut., Royal Field Artillery (Special Reserve), promoted Lieut. July 1915, A/Capt. and Adjutant Jan. 1919. Served in France. Wounded, causing amputation of right arm, Dec. 19, 1915.

GEOFFREY POPPLETON LLOYD.

Admitted Oct. 13, 1913. Member of Lloyd & Son, of Leominster. Joined Sept. 2, 1914, as 2nd Lieut., 1st Batt. Herefordshire Regt., promoted Lieut. June 1916. Served in Dardanelles Campaign July to Sept. 1915 (Suvla Bay), with Egyptian Expeditionary Force April to Dec. 1916 (Egypt and Sinai Desert), and with British Expeditionary Force Dec. 1917 to March 1918 (France). Captured at Lagnicourt, France, March 21, 1918; prisoner at Rastratt, Karlsruhe, Mainz, till Nov. 24, 1918.

GEORGE LLEWELLYN LLOYD.

Admitted Oct. 1899. Member of Lloyd & Pratt, of Newport, Mon. Served as 2nd Lieut., Royal Horse Artillery.

LIONEL ROBERT LLOYD.

Admitted Sept. 1905. Member of R. & C. B. Jenkins & Lloyd, of Swansea. Joined Feb. 3, 1915, as 2nd Lieut., South Wales Borderers (T.), promoted Lieut. July 1916. Served at Home, France, and Belgium.

RICHARD GLYN LLOYD.

Articled to John Furniss, of Liverpool. Enlisted 1914, as Private, 1st (City) Batt. King's Liverpool Regt., and subsequently gazetted Temp. Lieut. in same Regt. Awarded the M.C. Reported missing and subsequently presumed to be killed April 1916.

THOMAS HENRY LLOYD.

Admitted Feb. 1905. Member of Corsellis & Berney, of Lincoln's Inn Fields, Wandsworth, and Balham. Joined Sept. 1914, as Capt., 11th (Service) Batt. Royal Warwickshire Regt., promoted Major in France Dec. 1915. Awarded the O.B.E. (Military Division), seconded for Duty with the Ministry of Munitions, Labour Supply Department, 1918. Served in France 1915 to 1916, England 1917.

WILLIAM ROYSTON LLOYD.

Articled to W. M. Lloyd, of 26 Wormwood Street, E.C. and Walthamstow. Served as Private, 7th (City of London) Batt. London Regt. Died in France on June 27, 1915, while on Active Service.

ALDBOROUGH RUPERT CAULFIELD LLOYD-WILLIAMS.

Admitted July 1906, pracised at Walton-on-Thames. Served with Public Schools Batt. Middlesex Regt. Gazetted Lieut. Lancashire Fusiliers July 1916.

AUBREY DUNCAN LOCK.

Admitted Feb. 1901. Of Birmingham. Served as Private, Royal Army Service Corps.

FREDERICK ROBERT LOCK.

Admitted Sept. 1887, practising at Liverpool. Served as Lieut.-Col., 5th (Reserve) Batt. King's Liverpool Regt.

HENRY OSMOND LOCKE.

Admitted Dec. 1901. Member of Lock, Reed & Lock, of Dorchester. Mobilised Aug. 4, 1914, as Capt., 4th Batt. Dorset Regt., promoted Major June 1916. Awarded the T.D. Served at Home Aug. to Oct. 1914, India Nov. 1914 to Feb. 1916, Mesopotamia Feb. to July 1916, and in Palestine and Egypt Aug. 1917 to June 1919.

GARSTANG BRADSTOCK LOCKETT.

Articled to G. G. Smith, of Liverpool. Joined Oct. 25, 1916, as 2nd Lieut., Cheshire Yeomanry. On going to France in Jan. 1917 attached to 1st Batt. Cheshire Regt. as 2nd Lieut., afterwards promoted Lieut. and Capt. Awarded the M.C. Served at Home, in France, and in Italy. Died from wounds received in action on Nov. 4, 1918.

ROBERT KERR LOCKETT.

Admitted March 1902. Member of Evans, Lockett & Co., of Liverpool. Served as 2nd Lieut., Lancashire Hussars (T.), subsequently Major 12th Batt. Tank Corps.

HENRY KING LOCKHART.

Admitted Oct. 1907. Member of L. C. & H. K. Lockhart, of Hexham. Joined Jan. 3, 1915, as Private, Motor Cyclist Section, Royal Engineers, promoted Lance-Corporal shortly afterwards. Served at Home. Accidentally killed whilst training at Borden Camp, near Hitchin, June 19, 1915.

THOMAS EDGAR LOCKING.

Admitted Aug. 1911. Managing Clerk with Locking, Holdich & Locking, of Hull. Joined Nov. 1914, as 2nd Lieut., East Riding Royal Garrison Artillery (T.), promoted Lieut. June 1917. Served at Home and in France. Wounded at Sanctuary Wood, Hooge, Nov. 29, 1917. Died of wounds at Base Hospital, Wimereux, Jan. 20, 1918.

ALAN PARKER LOCKWOOD.

Articled to J. K. Parker, of Sheffield. Joined Sept. 3, 1914, as Private, 12th Batt. York and Lancaster Regt. Granted commission as 2nd Lieut. 2/6 Batt. Notts and Derby Regt. (Sherwood Foresters) Sept. 3, 1915. Awarded the M.C. Served in France. Wounded, lost right arm, April 1917.

JAMES HORACE LOCKWOOD.

Admitted Dec. 1912. Member of Windybank, Samuell & Lawrence, 28 & 29 St. Swithin's Lane, E.C. Served as Capt., Royal Field Artillery. Gassed Sept. 1916. Accidentally injured June 1918.

JOHN CUTTS LOCKWOOD.

Admitted June 1914. Of Chipping Norton. Served as 2nd Lieut., 4th Batt. Essex Regt.

LESLIE KING LODGE.

Admitted Dec. 1913. Of Portsmouth. Served as Gunner, Hampshire Royal Garrison Artillery, afterwards as Private, Inns of Court O.T.C., and subsequently gazetted Lieut. Royal Garrison Artillery.

PHILIP LOFTS.

Admitted Feb. 1894. Member of Lowe & Co., of 2 Temple Gardens, E.C. Joined Sept. 1914, as Private, Hertfordshire Yeomanry. Gazetted 2nd Lieut. Hertfordshire Yeomanry July 1915, promoted Lieut. July 1917. Served in England and in Egypt.

GEORGE BERNARD LOMAS-WALKER.

Admitted Feb. 1903. Member of Booth, Wade, Farr & Lomas-Walker, of Leeds. Served as Assistant Paymaster, Northern Command, afterwards as Major (Field Cashier) Army Pay Dept., France.

ALFRED JAMES LONG.

Articled to William Shakespeare, of Birmingham. Served as 2nd Lieut., 3rd Batt. North Staffordshire Regt.

ERNEST WILLIAM LONG.

Admitted Dec. 1903. Practising at 44 Bedford Row, W.C. Mobilised Aug. 1914, as Capt., 1/25 Batt. London Regt., seconded Machine Gun Corps (Senior Tactical Instructor, Armoured Motor Service, India) June 1908. Served at Home and India, with Waziristan Field Force May to Aug. 1917.

CYRIL MURGATROYD LONGBOTHAM.

Articled to L. H. Longbotham, of Halifax. Served as Lieut. in the Indian Army (72nd Punjabis) when War declared, and subsequently promoted Capt. Once mentioned in Dispatches. Served in France March 1915, India 1916 to 1917, Tomaliland 1918. Died in Switzerland of tuberculosis contracted on Service.

WILLIAM LEWES JENNINGS LONGBOURNE.

Admitted Dec. 1912. Of 7 Lincoln's Inn Fields, W.C. Served as 2nd Lieut., 5th Batt. The Queen's Royal West Surrey Regt. Killed in action at Gallipoli Aug. 9, 1915.

FREDERICK CECIL LONGDEN.

Admitted Oct. 1913. Managing Clerk with Longden, Mann & Longden, of Sunderland. Mobilised Aug. 1914, as 2nd Lieut., 4th Batt. Durham Light Infantry, attached 2nd Batt. Northumberland Fusiliers 1915, promoted A/Capt. 15th Batt. Durham Light Infantry 1918. Served in France and Belgium. Once dangerously wounded. Killed in action at Miraumont, on the Ancre, Aug. 24, 1918.

JAMES MORLEY LONGDEN.

Admitted Aug. 1898. Member of Longden, Mann & Longden, of Sunderland. Joined Nov. 10, 1914, as Capt., 18th (County) Batt. Durham Light Infantry, promoted Major and 2nd in Command 21st Reserve Batt. 1915 and 13th Batt. 1917, Lieut.-Col. in command of 12th Batt. Nov. 1917, G.H.Q., Italy, April 1918. Served at Home 1914 to 1917, in France 1917, and in Italy 1917 to 1918. Invalided Aug. 1918.

SIR CHARLES ELTON LONGMORE, K.C.B.

Admitted July 1879. Member of Longmores, of Hertford. Rejoined Aug. 1914, as Colonel, and raised and commanded 2/1 Batt. Hertfordshire Regt. Twice mentioned to Secretary of State for valuable services in connection with War. Served at Home. Retired May 1916.

JOHN ALEXANDER LONGMORE.

Articled to P. R. Longmore, of Hertford. Joined Aug. 8, 1917, as Private, Coldstream Guards. Gazetted 2nd Lieut. Coldstream Guards Nov. 28, 1917, promoted Lieut. May 1919. Served at Home Aug. 1917 to Feb. 1918 and March to May 1919, and in France and Germany Sept. 1918 to March 1919.

PHILIP ELTON LONGMORE.

Admitted Feb. 1911, practising at Hertford, Herts. Mobilised Aug. 5, 1914, as Capt., Hertfordshire Regt, promoted Major June 1916, D.A.A.G. 2nd Army Feb. 1916 to Nov. 1917. Twice mentioned in Dispatches. Awarded Cavalier of the Order of St. Maurice and Lazaus, Italy. Served in France Nov. 1914 to Nov. 1917 and March 1918 to July 1919, and in Italy Nov. 1917 to March 1918. Wounded at Givenchy April 22, 1915.

GEORGE EDMUND LONGRIGG.

Admitted Feb. 1903. Member of Macdonald & Longrigg, of Bath. Mobilised Aug. 4, 1914, as Lieut., North Somerset Yeomanry, promoted Capt. Jan. 1915. Served in Flanders Oct. 1914 to June 1915, and at Home June 1915 to Feb. 1919. Wounded at Ypres May 1915.

CEDRIC LLEWELLYN LONGSTAFF.

Admitted Dec. 1901, practised at Lichfield. Mobilised Aug. 1914, as Capt., 6th Batt. North Staffordshire Regt., promoted Major in May 1916. Awarded the T.D. Served at Home and in France and Flanders. Reverted to T.F. Reserve Jan. 26, 1918.

VICTOR CHARLES HAMILTON LONGSTAFFE.

Admitted Oct. 1912. Member of Dod, Longstaffe, Son & Fenwick, of 6 Berners Street, W. Served as Sub-Lieut., Royal Naval Volunteer Reserve, Royal Naval Air Service.

JOHN LONGTON.

Articled to H. J. Longton, of Warrington. Served as Cadet, Sandhurst College.

JOHN FREDERICK LONSDALE.

Admitted Aug. 1900. Member of Lonsdale & Everidge, of 1 Adam Street, Adelphi, W.C. Joined June 1918, as Private, Inns of Court O.T.C., afterwards with 22nd (Garrison) Officers Cadet Corps, Cambridge, and subsequently gazetted 2nd Lieut. Middlesex Regt.

GILBERT HENRY LORD.

Admitted April 1904. Member of Lord & Gunn, of 4 Dove Court, Old Jewry, E.C. Joined Dec. 1, 1915, as Private, 28th Batt. County of London Regt. (Artists Rifles). Gazetted 2nd Lieut. 5th Batt. The King's Own Royal Lancaster Regt. July 11, 1916, promoted Lieut. Jan. 1918. Once mentioned in Dispatches. Awarded the M.C. Served in France and Belgium. Wounded at 3rd Battle of Ypres Aug. 2, 1917.

WILLIAM HAWORTH LORD.

Articled to W. P. Kay, of Darwen. Served in Royal Army Service Corps.

JOHN TREVELYAN LOUCH.

Admitted Feb. 1914. Member of W. H. Belcher & Co., of Newbury, Berks. Served as Lieut., Wessex (Reserve) Divisional Train, Royal Army Service Corps (T)., subsequently promoted Capt.

HENRY DODDINGTON LOVEDAY.

Admitted Aug. 1904. Managing Clerk with Stockton, Sons & Fortescue, of Banbury. Joined Nov. 1914, as Private, 4th Batt. Oxford and Bucks Light Infantry. Served in France. Killed in action Aug. 1916.

ARTHUR JAMES LOVELACE.

Admitted Nov. 1903. Clerk to Kenneth Brown, Baker & Baker, of Lennox House, Norfolk Street, Strand, W.C. Joined June 19, 1916, as 2nd Air-Mechanic (Fitter), Royal Flying Corps, subsequently promoted 1st Air-Craftsman. Served at Home and in Egypt.

THOMAS WHITE LOVELACE.

Admitted Nov. 1909. Managing Clerk with Burt & Evans, of Ross, Herefordshire. Joined Oct. 11, 1915, as 2nd Lieut., 2/2 Wessex (Howitzer) Brigade Royal Field Artillery (T.F.), promoted Lieut. June 1916, attached 20th Battery Royal Field Artillery Feb. 1917, Hon. Capt. and A.D.C. to Lieut.-Governor of Bihar and Orissa, India, Aug. 1917 to March 1918. Served at Home Oct. 1915 to May 1916, India May 1916 to Jan. 1917 and May 1917 to April 1918, Mesopotamia Jan. to May 1917. Concussion from shell explosion March 14, 1917. Wounded April 21, 1917.

BERTRAM LOVELL.

Articled to Edward Lovell, of Gravesend. Joined Feb. 10, 1916, as Private, 28th Batt. County of London Regt. (Artists Rifles). Gazetted 2nd Lieut. Tank Corps Nov. 24, 1916, promoted Lieut. May 1918, A/Capt. Aug. 1918 to April 1919. Awarded the M.C. Served at Home, France, Belgium, and Germany. Wounded July 31, 1917.

EDWARD WYCHERLEY LOVELL.

Admitted July 1902. Member of Edward Lovell & Son, of Gravesend. Joined July 19, 1916, as Private, The Queen's Own Royal West Kent Regt., and subsequently promoted Corporal. Awarded the M.M. Served at Home and in France. Wounded at Avelny Wood, Somme, June 30, 1918, and discharged from wounds Sept. 20, 1918.

JOHN SPENCER LOVELL.

Admitted Dec. 1895. Member of Lovell & White, of 5 Thavies Inn, E.C. Joined Dec. 1915, as 2nd Lieut., Royal Garrison Artillery (Special Reserve), promoted A/Capt. March 1917. Served in France and Belgium. Wounded Aug. 14, 1917, and Nov. 2, 1918.

HOWARD ST. JOHN LOW.

Articled to V. H. Low, of 12 Bread Street, Cheapside, E.C. Mobilised Aug. 1914, as Private, 28th Batt. County of London Regt. (Artists Rifles). Served at Home and in France 1914 to 1915. Discharged May 20, 1915, "being no longer fit physically for War service." Died Sept. 21, 1917.

ARTHUR HOLDEN LOWE.

Admitted Oct. 1912. Of 1 Frederick's Place, Old Jewry, E.C. Served as Capt., 8th Batt. Oxford and Bucks Light Infantry.

CHARLES CONYERS LOWE.

Admitted Nov. 3, 1908. Member of Stapleton & Son of Stamford. Joined Nov. 1, 1915, as Private, Inns of Court O.T.C. Gazetted 2nd Lieut. Machine Gun Corps Sept. 26, 1916, promoted Lieut. March 1918. Served in France March 1917 to Jan. 1919.

NORMAN DOSSON LOWLESS.

Admitted July 1905. Member of Lowless & Lowless, of Pembroke. Served as Capt., 4th Batt. The Welch Regt.

ERNEST ALFRED LOWNDES.

Admitted July 1902. Member of Lowndes & Son, of 15 George Street, Mansion House, E.C. Joined Oct. 10, 1914, as Private, Inns of Court O.T.C. Gazetted Lieut. King's Own Yorkshire Light Infantry Dec. 20, 1914, promoted Capt. Jan. 1915. Served at Home and in France. Discharged Oct. 1917 on account of injuries received on Active Service.

WILLIAM HENRY LOWNDES.

Admitted Jan. 1909. Member of Lightfoot & Lowndes, of Thame, Oxon. Joined Aug. 11, 1917, as Paymaster Sub-Lieut., Royal Naval Volunteer Reserve, H.M.S. *Crescent*, appointed on Staff of Commander-in-Chief Coast of Scotland, about Dec. 1917 as Assistant Duty Staff Officer. Served with H.M.S. *Crescent* and at Rosyth.

ARCHIBALD LOY.

Articled to C. A. White, of Barnsley. Joined Oct. 30, 1916, as 3rd Writer, in H.M. Navy, promoted Paymaster Sub-Lieut. Royal Naval Volunteer Reserve Oct. 2, 1917. Served in Home waters Nov. 1916 to Oct. 1917, and on Staff of Commander-in-Chief North America and West Indies Station Nov. 1917 to March 1919.

ALFRED EYRE OWEN LUCAS.

Admitted Oct. 1913. Of Bombay. Served as Private, Bombay Volunteer Rifles.

EDWARD LUCAS.

Admitted Jan. 1913. Member of Lucas & Lucas, of Sheffield. Joined Oct. 1914, as 2nd Lieut., 4th Batt. York and Lancaster Regt., promoted Lieut. March 1915, Temp. Capt. June 1915, Capt. June 1916, A/Major three times. Awarded the M.C. and French Croix de Guerre with Gold Star. Served at Home Oct. 1914 to Jan. 1917, and in France Jan. 1917 to Jan. 1919.

GEORGE FREDERICK LUCAS.

Admitted Aug. 1903. Member of Lucas, Hutchinson & Meek, of Darlington. Joined Aug. 1914, as Lieut., 4th Batt. Yorkshire Regt., promoted Capt. Aug. 1915, transferred to Royal Flying Corps Sept. 1916. Once mentioned in Dispatches. Served in France 1915 to 1916. Wounded at Ypres, May 1915.

WILLIAM HERBERT LUCAS.

Articled to H. N. Lucas, of Sheffield. Joined Aug. 5, 1914, Inns of Court O.T.C. Gazetted 2nd Lieut. 8th Batt. North Staffordshire Regt. Sept. 8, 1914, promoted Lieut. June 1915. Served at Home until July 1915, and subsequently in France. Killed in action Jan. 21, 1916.

ERIC WILLIAM HARRY LUCK.

Admitted Feb. 1911, practising at Chester. Joined Sept. 10, 1914, as 2nd Lieut., 5th Batt. Cheshire Regt., promoted Capt. June 1916. Served at Home and in Egypt.

PERCY LUDBROOK.

Admitted April 1907. Managing Clerk with Oliver & Nutt, of 14 Coleman Street, E.C. Joined Sept. 1, 1914, as Private, 28th Batt. County of London Regt. (Artists Rifles), promoted Lance-Corporal May 1915. Gazetted 2nd Lieut. 7th Batt. London Regt. Sept. 22, 1915, promoted Lieut. Feb. 1917, posted to 18th Batt. April to May 1918, and to 19th Batt. May 1918 to May 1919, A/Capt. Sept. 1916 to March 1917, Aug. to Nov. 1917 and Aug. 1918 to May 1919. Served at Home and in France.

FRANK LUDLAM.

Articled to A. E. C. Ludlam, of Sheffield. Joined Sept. 5, 1914, as Trooper, Queen's Own Yorkshire Dragoons. Obtained commission in Royal Field Artillery as 2nd Lieut. Oct. 17, 1914, and joined " B " Battery 107th Brigade, promoted Lieut. Sept. 1915, Capt. April 1917, Major March 1918. Awarded the M.C. Served in France Aug. 1915 to Aug. 1916 and Sept. 1917 to Feb. 1919. Wounded at Guillemont, Somme, Aug. 22, 1916.

LEONARD GORDON SUTTON LUDLOW.

Articled to H. S. Ludlow, of 7 Broad Court Chambers, Bow Street, W.C. Served as 2nd Lieut., 4th Batt. King's Own Yorkshire Light Infantry.

JOSEPH WILLIAM LUMB.

Admitted Aug. 1906, practised at Barnoldswick, near Skipton. Joined Jan. 5, 1917, as Private, Inns of Court O.T.C. Gazetted 2nd Lieut. 1/4 Batt.

Duke of Wellington's West Riding Regt. Sept. 1917. Awarded the M.C. Served in France. Wounded Oct. 18, 1918, and died Oct. 30, 1918. Interred at Etaples Military Cemetery, France.

SAM LUMB.

Admitted Dec. 1912, practised at Halifax. Served as Private, Notts and Derby Regt. (Sherwood Foresters). Died Nov. 2, 1917, of wounds received in action.

ARCHIBALD BASIL LUMLEY.

Articled to Claude Lumley & Co., of 130 Strand, W.C. Joined Nov. 12, 1914, Inns of Court O.T.C., and subsequently promoted Corporal. Served at Home. Discharged June 6, 1916.

ARTHUR GORBUTT LUNT.

Admitted June 1913. Member of Shield & Mackarness, of Petersfield and Alresford, Hants; and London. Joined Feb. 5, 1917, as Driver, Royal Horse Artillery. Gazetted 2nd Lieut. Royal Garrison Artillery July 31, 1917. Served at Home and in France.

GILBERT LUPTON.

Articled to D. F. Hart, of Manchester. Served as Corporal, Duke of Lancaster's Own Yeomanry.

HAROLD BROWNRIGG LUPTON.

Admitted Sept. 1907. Of Chorley. Served as Private, Stretcher Bearer Company.

ALLAN AYLMER LUXMOORE.

Admitted June 1906. Member of Wilsons, Ornsby & Cadle, of Durham. Joined Aug. 4, 1916, as Lieut., Northumberland Fusiliers, promoted Capt. Feb. 1917 Served at Home.

GEORGE HENRY HUDSON LYALL.

Admitted May 1897. Member of Gush, Phillips, Walters & Williams, of 3 Finsbury Circus, E.C. Joined April 1918 Royal Air Force. Gazetted Lieut. May 1918, Capt. Aug. 1918, Staff-Capt. Sept. 1918. Once mentioned in Dispatches. Awarded the M.B.E. (Military Division). Served at Home and with British Peace Delegation, Paris, during 1919.

CHARLES RADFIRTH LYMN.

Articled to F. C. Lymn, of Matlock. Joined Sept. 4, 1914, as Private, 4th Batt. University and Public School Corps (21st) (Service) Batt. Royal Fusiliers. Gazetted 2nd Lieut. 2nd Batt. Lincolnshire Regt. Sept. 1916, transferred as Sub-Lieut. to Royal Naval Volunteer Reserve Nov. 1916 and attached Royal Naval Air Service, Airship Section (Meteorological Officer), promoted Lieut. June 1917, Capt. Royal Air Force Aug. 1918. Served at Home Sept. 1914 to Nov. 1915 and May 1916 to April 1919, and in France Nov. 1915 to May 1916.

ROBERT FRANCIS LYNE.

Admitted July 1906. Member of Lyne & Co., of Newport, Mon. Joined Sept. 30, 1914, as 2nd Lieut., 1/4 Welsh Brigade Royal Field Artillery (T.), promoted Lieut. June 1916, A/Capt. July 1918, Temp. Capt. March 1919.

Once mentioned in Dispatches. Served in Gallipoli July to Dec. 1915, and in Egypt and Palestine Dec. 1915 to July 1919.

ALGERNON JASPER LYON.

Admitted Nov. 1877. Member of Lyon & Son, of Cambridge. Served in France with 40th Div. B.E.F. from June 17, 1917, as a Town Major with rank of Colonel.

ABRAHAM MONTAGU LYONS.

Articled to Williams & Son, of Lincoln. Joined Oct. 23, 1914, as Lieut., Durham Light Infantry, transferred to General List of Officers Nov. 1915, employed as a Recruiting Officer for the London Recruiting District Nov. 1915 to March 1916, reported to Durham Light Infantry in Sept. 1916. Invalided on account of ill-health Sept. 1916. Served in England.

CECIL HYNES LYSON.

Articled to A. W. Weldon, of 27 Chancery Lane, W.C. Joined 1914, as Cadet, University of London O.T.C. Subsequently gazetted Lieut. Royal Army Ordnance Dept.

LUMLEY FITZGERALD LYSTER.

Articled to F. H. Edwards, of Liverpool. Served as 2nd Lieut., Royal Army Medical Corps, promoted Lieut. Aug. 1917.

GEORGE HALL LYSTER-TODD.

Admitted April 1910. Of 14 Hart Street, W.C. Joined April 1916, as Assistant Paymaster, Royal Naval Volunteer Reserve. Discharged as unfit for Active Service April 1917. Joined the British Red Cross Society in July and went to Le Havre, where worked as a Searcher in the Wounded and Missing Department. Served at Home, Scapa Flow on H.M.S. *Cyclops*, and then in Le Havre, France. Died from tuberculosis at Avon, near Fontainebleau, France, Oct. 12, 1919.

SANDYS STUART MACASKIE.

Admitted Feb. 1913. Member of Guedella, Jacobson & Spyer, of Winchester House, Old Broad Street, E.C.; and Austin Friars House, E.C. Served as 2nd Lieut., 1st Batt. County of London Yeomanry (Middlesex Hussars), promoted Capt. June 1916.

GEORGE CECIL GORDON MACAULAY.

Articled to A. H. Redfearn, of Heckmondwike. Joined Sept. 19, 1914, Public School Batt., attached 12th Batt. Middlesex Regt. Gazetted 2nd Lieut. 3rd Batt. East Yorkshire Regt. Feb. 8, 1915, promoted Lieut. 60th Trench Mortar Battery March 1916. Served in France Aug. 1915 to Sept. 1916 and Nov. 1916 to May 1917. Wounded on the Somme, Sept. 16, 1916. Killed at Bailleul, near Arras, May 2, 1917.

ALEXANDER HAMILTON McBEAN.

Admitted Nov. 1900. Member of R. A. Willcock, Taylor & Co., of Wolverhampton. Served as Capt., 6th Batt. South Staffordshire Regt.

WALTER McBRIDE

Admitted Dec. 1911. Member of McBride & Co., 150 Southampton Row, W.C. Served as Capt., 9th Batt. London Regt.

COLIN McCARRAHER.

Articled to G. A. Waller, of Southampton. Joined May 5, 1915, as Private, 28th Batt. County of London Regt. (Artists Rifles). Commissioned 2nd Lieut. 4th (Hallamshire) Batt. York and Lancaster Regt. Sept. 24, 1915. Served in France. Wounded on the Somme July 21, 1916. Discharged on account of wounds July 1, 1917.

THADDEUS FRANCIS McCARTHY.

Articled to R. A. Loseby, of Leicester. Joined Dec. 1915 as Private, 28th Batt. County of London Regt. (Artists Rifles). Gazetted 2nd Lieut. Loyal North Lancashire Regt. Sept. 1916, promoted Lieut. March 1918. Awarded the M.C. Served in France. Wounded Aug. 10, 1917. Killed in action at Bailleul, France, April 14, 1918.

JOHN PONSONBY McCLELLAN.

Admitted May 1909. Managing Clerk with Linklater & Co., of 2 Bond Court, E.C. Mobilised Aug. 5, 1914, as Lance-Corporal, 1/14 Batt. County of London Regt. (London Scottish) and attained the rank of Sergeant. Served in France and Belgium Sept. 1914 to Oct. 1915. Wounded at Hulluch Oct. 13, 1915. Discharged as result of wounds Feb. 28, 1918.

GEORGE McCONNELL.

Admitted Nov. 1902, practising at North Shields. Joined June 13, 1916, as Sapper, Royal Engineers (Tyne Electrical Engineers) (T.). Commissioned 2nd Lieut. June 12, 1917, promoted Lieut. Dec. 1918. Served at Home.

THOMAS ROBERT McCREADY.

Articled to Edgcombe Stevens, of Plymouth. Joined March 13, 1915, as 2nd Lieut., Royal Marines, promoted Lieut. Nov. 1915, Capt. Nov. 1916, Major Aug. 1917. Lieut.-Col. Dec. 1917, seconded Machine Gun Corps for services with Royal Naval Division Dec. 1917. Three times mentioned in Dispatches. Awarded the D.S.O. and M.C. Served in Gallipoli July to Nov. 1915, and in France, Belgium, and Germany Aug. 1916 to Nov. 1919. Wounded Aug. 10, 1915, June 7, 1916, and Jan. 3, 1918.

HENRY GOURLAY CRICHTON McCREATH.

Admitted June 1909, practising at Newcastle-upon-Tyne. Served as Capt., Border Regt.

REGINALD McDONALD.

Admitted Aug. 1905, practising at Devonport. Joined June 19, 1918, as Driver, Royal Army Service Corps (M.T.). Commissioned as 2nd Lieut. in same Regt. Oct. 14, 1918. Served in France.

RONALD BRUCE McDONALD.

Admitted Dec. 1908. Member of Joynson-Hicks, Hunt-Cardew & McDonald, of Lennox House, Norfolk Street, Strand, W.C. Joined Dec. 15, 1915, as Private, Royal Army Service Corps (M.T.). Gazetted 2nd Lieut.

June 19, 1916, promoted Lieut. Dec. 1917, Capt. May 1918. Once mentioned in Dispatches. Served at Home and in Italy.

ARTHUR CURTEISS MACE.
Articled to A. J. Ellis, of Maidstone. Served as Private, 3rd (Public Schools) Batt. Royal Fusiliers.

JOSEPH MUNN MACE.
Admitted April 1883, practising at Tenterden. Mobilised Aug. 4, 1914, as Col. in command of 1/5 Batt. East Kent Regt. (The Buffs). Twice mentioned in Dispatches. Served in Mesopotamia. Wounded at Sheik Saad Jan. 7, 1916.

LAWRENCE JOSEPH McEVOY.
Admitted March 1910, practising at Blackburn. Served as Private, Royal Army Medical Corps.

NORMAN HOWARD STANLEY MACFADZEAN.
Admitted Jan. 1904, practising at Sunderland. Joined Feb. 3, 1917, as Private, Hon. Artillery Company. Served in France and Belgium April to Nov. 1917, Italy Dec. 1917 to Dec. 1918, and with Army of Occupation in Austria Dec. 1918 to Jan. 1919.

CYRIL SKELTON McFALL.
Articled to Arthur Porter, of Romford, Essex. Joined Dec. 11, 1915, as Private, 3rd Batt. Essex Regt. Served at Home.

JAMES ALEXANDER McFARLANE.
Articled to W. L. Holden, of Liverpool. Served as Capt., Railway Transport Officer, West Lancs. Division (T.)

JAMES MACFIE.
Admitted Jan. 1892. Member of Barrow, Smith & Macfie, of Manchester. Joined June 4, 1915, as Lieut., Manchester Regt. (T.), promoted to Major Indian Army Reserve of Officers, and appointed Deputy Judge Advocate-General to Baluchistan Expeditionary Force. Assistant Judge Advocate-General Southern Command, India. Served in India and Afghanistan.

JOSEPH CHARLES McGRATH.
Admitted Aug. 1901, practising at Wakefield. Joined Feb. 1915, as 2nd Lieut., 161st Brigade Royal Field Artillery, promoted Lieut. July 1915 when appointed Adjutant to 175th Brigade, promoted Capt. and Staff Capt. General Staff Oct. 1915. Once mentioned in Dispatches. Served in France 3 years.

HUGH WELLS MACHELL.
Admitted Sept. 1902, practising at Workington. Joined 1917, as Paymaster, Royal Naval Volunteer Reserve. Served at Home at Admiralty, and in Mediterranean, Adriatic, and Sea of Marmora.

HUGH JOHN TURNLY McILVEEN.
Admitted April 1902, practising at Lewes. Joined Dec. 6, 1915, as Lieut., Royal Army Service Corps, subsequently promoted Capt. Served at Home.

JOHN MACILVENNA.

Admitted Feb. 1908, practising at Newcastle-upon-Tyne. Joined Nov. 22, 1915, as Lieut., Royal Army Veterinary Corps, promoted Capt. Nov. 1916, Major (Deputy Assistant Director of Veterinary Services, General Headquarters E.E.F.) Jan. 1919. Twice mentioned in Dispatches. Awarded O.B.E. (Military Division). Served in Egypt, Syria, and Palestine.

ARTHUR ARNOLD McILWAINE.

Articled to Edward Wilson, of Newport, and Shanklin, Isle of Wight. Joined Sept. 1914, as Private, 3rd Batt. Hampshire Regt. Subsequently gazetted 2nd Lieut. Loyal North Lancashire Regt. Killed in France March 4, 1916.

RONALD CHARLES MACINTOSH.

Articled to A. C. Macintosh, of Cardiff. Joined Aug. 6, 1914, as Gunner, Royal Field Artillery, promoted to Sergeant. Served in France, Egypt, and Palestine 1915 to 1919.

DAVID MACIVER.

Admitted Jan. 1901. Member of Cameron, Maciver & Davie, of Liverpool. Joined Nov. 1917, as Private, 3rd Batt. King's Liverpool Regt. Gazetted 2nd Lieut. Labour Corps Feb. 1918, transferred 9th (Russian) Labour Batt. June 1918. Served at Home.

JOHN BICKERTON McKAIG.

Admitted April 1910. Managing Clerk with Weightman, Pedder & Co., of Liverpool. Mobilised Aug. 1914, as Capt., 6th Batt. The King's Liverpool Regt., promoted Major Aug. 1916, Lieut.-Col. Sept. 1916 and commanded 6th Rifle Batt. King's Liverpool Regt. from Sept. 1916 to end of War. Four times mentioned in Dispatches. Awarded the D.S.O. and Bar. Served in France and Belgium Feb. 1915 to June 1919.

ALEXADNER WILLIAM MACKAY.

Articled to C. O. Jones, of Holyhead. Joined Oct. 1915, as 2nd Lieut., 26th Batt. Royal Fusiliers (Bankers). Promoted Lieut. and Adjutant Jan. 1916, Capt. and Adjutant June 1917. Awarded the M.C. Served in France from spring 1916 to Sept. 1917. Died of wounds Sept. 28, 1917.

DONALD PALEY MACKAY.

Admitted May 1909. Member of Russell & Mackay, of York. Mobilised Aug. 1914, as Capt. 1/5 Batt. West Yorkshire Regt., and subsequently promoted Major. Served in France April 1915 to Oct. 1917. Killed in action at Passchendaele Oct. 9, 1917.

ANDREW NEILL MACKEAN.

Articled to F. W. Owen, of 58 Lombard Street, E.C. Mobilised Aug. 1914, as Private, Hon. Artillery Company. Gazetted 2nd Lieut. Royal Garrison Artillery (S.R.) Oct. 28, 1915, and subsequently promoted Capt. Once mentioned in Dispatches. Awarded the M.C. Served in France Sept. 1914 to April 1915 and June 1916 to Jan. 1919.

FREDERICK JOHN McKENZIE.

Admitted Feb. 1879, practised at Sunderland. Served as Lieut.-Col., (General Service) Regular Army.

GEORGE ARCHIBALD MACKENZIE.

Admitted Dec. 1907, practising at 108A Cannon Street, E.C. Joined Sept. 2, 1914, as Private, 18th (1st Public Schools) Batt., Royal Fusiliers. Gazetted 2nd Lieut. Royal Field Artillery Jan. 1, 1915, promoted Lieut. Nov. 1915. Served in France July 1915 to Jan. 1917. Services subsequently lent to Foreign Office. Served British Legation, Athens, 1917 to 1918.

HAROLD EDGAR McKENZIE.

Admitted Oct. 13, 1909, practising at Southport, Lancs. Joined Dec. 1, 1915, as 2nd Lieut., 4th East Lancs. Brigade Royal Field Artillery. Promoted Lieut. June 1917. Served in France Sept. 1916 to Dec. 1917. Injured in action at Ronssoy.

JOHN LANDSEER MACKENZIE.

Admitted April 1913. Managing Clerk with W. Silverwood Cope, of 3 New Court, Lincoln's Inn, W.C. Joined Oct. 1914, as Private, Royal West Surrey Regt., transferred to Royal Sussex Regt. Served at Home, in Egypt, and on Western Front, and with the Army of Occupation, the Rhine.

WILLIAM FREDERICK MACKETT.

Articled to F. A. P. Sylvester, of Trowbridge, Wilts. Joined Sept. 1, 1914, as Private, 1/4 Batt. Wiltshire Regt. (T.), promoted Lance-Corporal Sept. 1914, attached 2nd Batt. Dorset Regt. May 1915, transferred to Royal Engineers Jan. 1917, and attained rank of Company Sergeant-Major. Granted a G.S. commission and attached to Royal Engineers (I.W.T.) Aug. 25, 1917, promoted Lieut. Feb. 1919. Twice mentioned in Dispatches. Served at Home Sept. to Oct. 1914, India Oct. 1914 to May 1915, and in Mesopotamia May 1915 to Jan. 1919. Wounded at Ctesiphon Nov. 24, 1915.

MILBURN VINCENT MACKEY.

Admitted April 1914. Of Rochester. Served as Private, Inns of Court O.T.C.

GEORGE VINCENT MACKRELL.

Admitted Oct. 1913. Member of T. K. Greenwood and Mackrell, of Bradford. Joined Dec. 6, 1915, as Motor Cyclist Pioneer, Royal Engineers, promoted Motor Cyclist Corporal May 1916. Served in France. Wounded in Somme offensive March 24, 1918.

OSCAR WHITTICK MACKRILL.

Admitted Feb. 1909. Member of Mackrill & Cooper, of Hull. Joined May 1916, as Air-Mechanic (Driver), Royal Naval Air Service. Served at Home and in France.

DOUGLAS MACLAREN.

Admitted Sept. 1903, practising at Carlisle. Mobilised in Aug. 1914, as Capt., 11th Batt. Border Regt. and subsequently attached 25th Batt. King's Liverpool Regt. Served at Home and in France.

FRANCIS MALCOLM McLAREN.

Articled to T. W. Thompson, of Newcastle-upon-Tyne. Mobilised Aug. 1914, as 2nd Lieut., 6th Batt. Northumberland Fusiliers (T.), promoted Lieut. May 1915, Capt. Sept. 1917. Served in France and Belgium.

ALAN STEWART MACLAUCHLAN.

Admitted Jan. 1911, practising at Southampton. Joined Sept. 1914, as Private, 7th City of London Batt. London Regt. Gazetted 2nd Lieut. Hants Royal Garrison Artillery (T.) March 26, 1915, promoted Lieut. 1916. Served at Home Anti-Aircraft Unit 1916, and in France Jan. to March 1915 and 1917 to 1918. Killed at Arras March 28, 1918.

JOHN STUART McLELLAN.

Admitted Feb. 1898, practised at Rochester. Served as Lieut., The Rifle Brigade, promoted Capt. Oct. 1918.

ALAN FRANCIS MACLURE.

Admitted Nov. 1897. Member of Crofton, Craven & Co., of Manchester. Mobilised Aug. 4, 1914, as Lieut.-Col., 7th Batt Lancashire Fusiliers. Served in Egypt and Gallipoli. Wounded at Gallipoli May 1915 and placed on Reserve May 1916.

JOHN MAXWELL McMASTER.

Admitted Feb. 1882, practising at Liverpool. Served as Lieut.-Col. (Hon. Col.), 5th Batt. King's Liverpool Regt. (T.) Mentioned in Dispatches. Awarded C.M.G.

JOHN MELROSE MACMILLAN.

Admitted June 1906, practising at Wadebridge, Cornwall. Joined Oct. 1914, as Lieut., Supernumerary Coy. Duke of Cornwall's Light Infantry, transferred to Royal Defence Corps April 1916, promoted Capt. July 1917. Served at Home.

WILLIAM JOHN McMILLIN.

Admitted Feb. 1909, practising at Liverpool. Mobilised Aug. 1914, as Capt., 9th Batt. King's Liverpool Regt. Served at Home. Invalided out Oct. 15, 1916.

ARTHUR DE FREYNE MACMIN.

Articled to J. Macmin, of 15 Dowgate Hill, Cannon Street, E.C. Joined Oct. 1914, as Private, 13th Batt. County of London Regt., promoted Corporal Dec. 1914. Gazetted 2nd Lieut. Feb. 1915, promoted Lieut. June 1916, Capt. July 1917, attached Machine Gun Corps June 1918. Served at Home and in France.

DONALD SCOTT ANDERSON McMURTRIE.

Articled to J. H. Inskip, of Bristol. Served as 2nd Lieut., 6th Batt. Gloucestershire Regt. and subsequently transferred to South Midland Royal Engineers.

BRIAN CAMERON MACNAMARA.

Articled to C. H. Rundell, of 9 John Street, W.C. Served as Private, Inns of Court O.T.C.

HENRY CHARLES MACNAMARA.

Admitted Feb. 1914, practised at Hull. Served as Capt., 2nd Northumbrian Brigade Royal Field Artillery.

DOUGLAS RAMSAY McNAUGHT.

Articled to Samuel Garrett, of St. Michael's Rectory, Cornhill, E.C. Joined Inns of Court O.T.C. July 1915, and obtained commission as 2nd Lieut. 8th Batt. Gordon Highlanders Aug. 1915. Served in France April 1916 to Jan. 1917. Invalided home Jan. 1917. Accidentally killed March 27, 1917, while conducting operations at Porton Range, Salisbury Plain.

DONALD ROBERT McNISH.

Admitted Dec. 1906. Practised at Nottingham. Served as Lance-Corporal.

ALISTER MACNIVEN.

Articled to A. D. Brooks, of Birmingham. Served with 7th Batt. Queen's Own Cameron Highlanders.

GERALD EDWARD CAMPBELL MACONCHY.

Admitted Feb. 1901, practising at Arundel Street, W.C. Joined Oct. 25, 1918, as 2nd Lieut., Royal Air Force. Served at Home.

AGNEW MAIN MACPHAIL.

Articled to David Main, of Carlisle. Joined Aug. 15, 1914, as 2nd Lieut., 3rd Batt. Royal Berkshire Regt., promoted to Lieut. March 1915, Capt. Dec. 1915, attached to 1st Batt. King's Shropshire Light Infantry April to June 1915. Awarded M.B.E. Served at Home and in France. Wounded at Ypres June 6, 1915.

ERNEST FRANK McQUEEN.

Admitted Aug. 1905, practising at 45 Bloomsbury Square, W.C. Joined Aug. 10, 1914, as Private, Hon. Artillery Company (Infantry), promoted A/Corporal Feb. 1915. Recommended for commission in the field May 1915, but wounded before appointment. Served in Flanders Sept. 1914 to June 1915. Severely wounded at Ypres June 10, 1915. Discharged Dec. 12, 1915.

NORMAN McQUEEN.

Admitted Jan. 1906, practising at 5 Argyle Place, W. Served as Lieut., 10th Batt. Argyll and Sutherland Highlanders, promoted Capt. Oct. 1915. Mentioned in Dispatches. Awarded D.S.O. and Bar. Brevet Major June 1919.

HUBERT FRANKLIN MADDERS.

Member of Sharpe, Pritchard & Co., of 12 New Court, Carey Street, W.C. Joined Dec. 1915, as 2nd Lieut., Royal Field Artillery. Served in France. Killed near Authville, in the Battle of the Somme, July 1, 1916.

LIONEL CUTHBERT MADDISON.

Articled to R. W. Cooper, of Newcastle-upon-Tyne. Served as 2nd Lieut., 15th Batt. Northumberland Fusiliers.

FRANK MADGETT.

Admitted Sept. 1907, practising at 218 Strand, W.C. Joined Sept. 17, 1915, as 2nd Lieut., Royal Field Artillery. Promoted Lieut. April 1916, Adjutant April 1916, Capt. June 1917, Staff Capt. 1918 to 1919, Brigade Major 1919. Once mentioned in Dispatches. Served at Home and in France.

GEORGE EDWARD HINDLEY MAGGS.

Admitted May 1885. Member of Scholefield, Taylor & Maggs, of Batley. Mobilised Aug. 1914, as Capt., 4th Batt. King's Own Yorkshire Light Infantry, promoted Major July 1915, Brigade Major 187th Infantry Brigade, 62nd Division, Feb. to Sept. 1915. Once mentioned in Dispatches. Served at Home (England and Ireland).

JOHN GEORGE MAHAFFY.

Admitted May 1911, practising at Manchester. Served as 2nd Lieut., Royal Irish Regt.

WILLIAM ARTHUR MAHANY.

Admitted Oct. 1904, practising at Plymouth. Joined Nov. 1916, as 3rd Writer, Royal Navy. Served in the Grand Fleet and at Devonport.

HEATHFIELD MACMAHON MAHON.

Admited Feb. 1903. Member of Hyde, Mahon & Pascall, of 33 Ely Place, Holborn, E.C. Joined June 6, 1916, as Gunner, Royal Garrison Artillery. Gazetted 2nd Lieut. Dec, 20, 1916, promoted Lieut. June 1918. Served at Home June 1916 to May 1917 and in France May 1917 to Jan. 1919.

DAVID MAIN.

Admitted Aug. 1884. Member of Blackburn & Main, practising at Carlisle. Served at Home from May 15, 1915, as Major (Lieut.-Col. and Hon. Col. retired) Royal Field Artillery (T.). Once mentioned in Dispatches.

FRANCIS HENRY MAINPRICE.

Articled to W. E. M. Mainprice, of Manchester. Joined Nov. 4, 1914, as 2nd Lieut., 7th Batt. Lancashire Fusiliers, promoted Lieut. 1915, Capt. 1917. Once mentioned in Dispatches. Awarded the M.C. Served at Gallipoli Oct. 1915 to Jan. 1916, Sinai Desert, Jan. 1916 to Feb. 1917, and in France Feb. 1917 to April 1918. Wounded April 5, 1918, left arm amputated.

ALEXANDER WOOD MAITLAND.

Articled to Percy S. Howarth, of Bury. Joined Oct. 1915, as Private, Inns of Court O.T.C. Gazetted 2nd Lieut. Royal Field Artillery June 9, 1917, promoted Lieut. Nov. 1918. Once mentioned in Dispatches. Awarded the M.C. Served in France. Wounded at Sandemont Sept. 17, 1918.

JOHN PELHAM BLANCHARD MAITLAND.

Admitted Sept. 1905. Member of Maitland & Son, of Wakefield. Joined the Army soon after the outbreak of War and subsequently gazetted 2nd Lieut. 11th Batt. King's Own Yorkshire Light Infantry. Attained the rank of Capt. Died of pneumonia at Military Hospital, Harrogate, Aug. 2, 1915.

HUGH JOHN MAITLAND-JONES.

Articled to M. R. Richards, of Llanelly. Served as Trooper, Montgomeryshire Yeomanry.

MAURICE MICHAEL MAIZELS.

Admitted July 1916, practising at Bradford, Yorks. Joined Nov. 6, 1916, as Ordinary Seaman, Royal Naval Volunteer Reserve, afterwards Telegraphist. Served in Home Waters, H.M.T. *Roche Castle*.

RONALD EVERITT MAJOR.
Admitted July 1914. Of Liverpool. Served as 2nd Lieut., 4th Batt. Royal Welch Fusiliers (T.).

MATTHEW JAMES MANNIA MAKALUA.
Articled to A. W. Weldon, of 27 Chancery Lane, W.C. Joined in 1914, as Private, 28th Batt. County of London Regt. (Artists Rifles). Gazetted Lieut. 3rd South Down Batt. Royal Sussex Regt. and subsequently promoted Major. Awarded O.B.E. and Croix de Guerre.

JOHN RAYMOND MALLALIEU.
Articled to John Watson, of Liverpool. Joined Feb. 23, 1915, as 2nd Lieut., 14th Batt. Cheshire Regt., promoted Lieut. May 1917, transferred to 9th Batt. Dec. 1915, attached 2nd Batt. Oct. 1918. Awarded the M.C. Served in France Dec. 1915 to July 1916 and May 1917 to March 1918, and in Salonica Sept. 1918 to Feb. 1919. Wounded July 1916 and March 1918.

GEORGE MALPAS.
Articled to Edward Hobbs, of Portsmouth, and afterwards Managing Clerk with Hubert A. Way, of Southsea. Joined Jan. 21, 1916, as Driver, Royal Marine Artillery. Served in France.

EDWARD MARTIN MAMMATT.
Admitted April 1912. Member of Owen & Mammatt, of Birmingham. Served as 2nd Lieut., 6th Batt. Leicestershire Regt., promoted Lieut. Feb. 1918.

FREDERICK WILLIAM MANDER.
Admitted May, 1903. Member of C. J. Mander & Sons, of 7 New Square, Lincoln's Inn, W.C. Joined O.T.C., Royal Army Service Corps (M.T.) March 12, 1917. Granted commission as 2nd Lieut. May 7, 1917. Served at Home 6 months and in France 13 months.

HARRY ILIFFE MANDER.
Admitted Dec. 1897, practising at Coventry. Joined July 18, 1918, as Private, 13th Batt. Somerset Light Infantry. Served at Home.

JOHN STEELE MANDNELL.
Admitted Jan. 1898. Of 8 Coleman Street, E.C. Served with 1st Batt. Border Regt.

EDWARD ASHBURNER MANISTY.
Admitted July 1898. Member of Nicholl Manisty & Co., of 1 Howard Street, Strand, W.C. Joined Nov. 1914, as Major, Lincolnshire Yeomanry. Served at Home. Retired May 6, 1917.

FRANCIS CYRIL CHURCHILL MANLEY.
Articled to F. C. Manley, of Hull. Joined Sept. 1914, as 2nd Lieut., 4th Batt. East Yorkshire Regt. and was afterwards with the Royal Engineers (T.), then Royal Field Artillery Reserve of Officers, "C" Battery, 167th Brigade, 33rd Division, then transferred as Observer to Royal Air Force, 52nd Squadron. Served in France. Accidentally killed at Throwley Aerodrome, Kent, Aug. 11, 1918.

FREDERICK JAMES MANN.

Articled to F. W. Mann, of Bank Buildings, Kingsway, W.C. Joined 1914, as Sergt., 3rd Batt. Northamptonshire Regt. Gazetted 2nd Lieut. 7th Batt. Dorsetshire Regt., promoted Capt. May 1918. Mentioned in Dispatches and awarded the M.C.

LESLIE JOHN MANN.

Articled to F. J. Mann, of 17 Essex Street, Strand, W.C. Mobilised Aug. 4, 1914, as Private, 1st Batt. Hon. Artillery Company (Infantry). Granted temp. commission as 2nd Lieut. Royal Army Service Corps Feb. 1915, granted commission as 2nd Lieut. in Regular Army (Permanent) Nov. 1915, gazetted as Flying Officer (Pilot) and seconded to Royal Flying Corps Jan. 1916, promoted Lieut. (Substantive rank) Sept. 1916, appointed Acting Flight Commander April 1918, gazetted Temp. Capt. Royal Air Force Dec. 1918. Twice mentioned in Dispatches. Awarded the M.C. Served in France Sept. 1914 to Jan. 1915, Home Jan. 1915 to Feb. 1916, N.W.F. India Feb. to Oct. 1916, Egypt Oct. 1916 to Jan. 1917, India Jan. 1917 to Oct. 1918, Aden and Arabia Oct. 1917 to May 1918. Wounded while flying over Turkish lines near Aden May 1918.

PHILIP DALLA MANN.

Articled to W. D. Mann, of Sunderland. Joined Sept. 1914, as Private, 16th Batt. Middlesex Regt. Gazetted 2nd Lieut. Durham Light Infantry Jan. 1915, promoted A/Capt. General List, attached to 151st Trench Mortar Battery. Served in France Aug. 1915 to Nov. 1916.

CHARLES IORWERTH MANSEL-HOWE.

Articled to Stanley Hoare, of 7 Wilmington Square, W.C. Served in the 28th Batt. County of London Regt. (Artists Rifles). Gazetted 2nd Lieut. 21st Batt. London Regt, promoted Lieut. Killed in action Aug. 9, 1918.

HERBERT CHARLES MANSFIELD.

Admitted Oct. 1909, practising at Leicester. Joined Nov. 22, 1915, as Private, Inns of Court O.T.C. Served at Home. Discharged Sept. 26, 1916.

GEORGE ARTHUR MANT.

Articled to Walter Bartlett, of 24 Bedford Row, W.C. Joined Sept. 22, 1914, as 2nd Lieut., 9th Batt. Royal Sussex Regt., promoted Lieut. Nov. 1914, Capt. Sept. 1916, transferred to Suffolk Regt. March 1916. Served at Home Sept. 1914 to April 1916 and Jan. to May 1918, and in France April 1916 to Jan. 1918. Discharged May 28, 1918.

EDWARD JOHN STANLEY MAPLES.

Articled to H. S. Maples, of Spalding. Joined Oct. 1914, as 2nd Lieut., 4th Batt. Lincolnshire Regt., promoted Lieut. Feb. 1915, Capt. Oct. 1915. Awarded M.C. Served at Home Oct. 1914 to July 1915, and in France July 1915 to June. 1917. Wounded Ypres Salient July 1915 and in Lens Sector June 1917. Resigned owing to wounds July 1918.

FREDERICK CHAUNCY MAPLES.

Admitted Nov. 1901. Member of Maples, Teesdale & Co., of 6 Frederick's Place, Old Jewry, E.C. Served as Lieut., Royal Field Artillery.

KENNETH JAMES MAPLES.

Admitted July 1903. Solicitor to Great Western Railway, Paddington. Mobilised Aug. 1914, as Capt., 3rd Batt. South Staffordshire Regt., attached as Capt. to 2nd Batt. in France March 1915. Served at Plymouth till March 1915, and later in France. Killed at Festubert, France, May 16, 1915.

FRANK PERCIVAL MARCH.

Admitted Aug. 1910, practising at Portsmouth. Served as 2nd Lieut., 9th (Service) Batt. South Lancashire Regt., promoted Lieut. May 1917.

ARTHUR REGINALD MARCHANT.

Admitted July 1904, practising at 23 St. Swithin's Lane, E.C. Joined April 27, 1917, as Private, 28th Batt. County of London Regt. (Artists Rifles). Gazetted 2nd Lieut. Royal Army Service Corps Sept. 30, 1917. Served in France Oct. 1917 to March 1919.

ERNEST WILLIAM MARCHANT.

Admitted July 1913. Member of Emery, Emery & Marchant, of Ramsgate and Broadstairs. Joined Sept. 3, 1914, as Private, 18th Batt. Royal Fusiliers (Public Schools Brigade). Gazetted 2nd Lieut. 14th Batt. Middlesex Regt. Jan. 30, 1915, promoted Lieut. May 1915. Served in France. Wounded and taken prisoner at Serre, France, Nov. 13, 1916. Repatriated Dec. 13, 1918.

ROBERT PERCY MARCHANT.

Admitted April 1912, practising at Mansfield, Notts. Joined Sept. 16, 1914, as Private, Public Schools Batt. Royal Fusiliers, promoted Sergeant Oct. 1914. Gazetted 2nd Lieut. and posted to 28th Batt. Middlesex Regt. Aug. 5, 1916, transferred to Royal Army Service Corps Nov. 1917, promoted Lieut. Feb. 1918. Once mentioned in Dispatches. Served in France Nov. 1915 to March 1916 and Jan. 1917 to Jan. 1919.

WILLIAM FRANCIS MARCHANT.

Admitted Nov. 1898. Member of Marchant, Newington & Tipper, of 27 College Street, Cannon Street, E.C.; and Deptford. Served as Capt., 20th (Reserve) Batt. County of London Regt. Mentioned in Dispatches and awarded the O.B.E.

WILLIAM MATTHEW MARCHANT.

Admitted Dec. 1909, practising at 4 King's Bench Walk, E.C. Served as Lance-Corporal, Royal Army Service Corps.

FREDERICK NICHOLS MARCY.

Admitted Sept. 1903. Of 45 Oxford Terrace, W. Served as Private, Inns of Court O.T.C.

AUBYN JACK MARGARY.

Admitted Dec. 1909. Managing Clerk with Lovell, Son & Pitfield, of 3 Gray's Inn Square W.C. Joined March 10, 1917, as Gunner, Royal Garrison Artillery. Gazetted 2nd Lieut. Royal Garrison Artillery April 8, 1918. Served at Salonica Aug. 1918 to May 1919, and at Constantinople May to June 1919.

KEITH FREELING MARKBY.

Articled to Thomas Markby, of 57 Coleman Street, E.C. Served as Private, 18th (Service) Batt. Royal Fusiliers.

CHARLES CORNWELL MARKHAM.

Articled to C. A. Markham, of Northampton. Joined Dec. 28, 1915, as Driver, "3 B" Battery, Hon. Artillery Company. Drafted to "1 B" Battery Ammunition Column April 1917. Served in England, Egypt, Palestine, Syria.

CHRISTOPHER ALEXANDER MARKHAM.

Admitted Aug. 1887. Member of J. & C. Markham, of Northampton. Mobilised Aug. 1914, as Major, 6th (Service) Batt. Northamptonshire Regt. Performed duty at the Depôt Royal Fusiliers Regiment, Hounslow, March to Sept. 1915, Recruiting Officer, Kettering, Northamptonshire, Sept. 1915 to March 1916, then served at the Depôt Northamptonshire Regt., Northampton, until retirement. Retired April 17, 1918.

GEORGE WOODFINE MARKS.

Articled to A. H. Collingwood, of Carlisle. Mobilised Aug. 5, 1914, as 2nd Lieut., Royal Field Artillery, promoted Lieut. Aug. 1914, Temp. Capt. Oct. 1915, Substantive Capt. June 1916. Served in Egypt 1915 to 1917, including the Gallipoli Campaign and the advance across the Sinai Peninsula, and in France and Belgium Feb. 1917 to April 1919. Wounded at Cape Helles Sept. 1915.

HENRY NEVILLE MARKS.

Admitted Nov. 1911. Employed as Assistant Solicitor to the Carlisle Corporation. Mobilised Aug. 1914, as Lieut., Royal Field Artillery, promoted Temp. Capt. Oct. 1915, Permanent Capt. June, 1916. Served in Egypt May 1915 to Jan. 1917, including 6 months on Gallipoli and the advance across the Sinai Peninsula, and in France and Belgium Feb. 1917 to Feb. 1919.

REGINALD WILLIAM MARLEY.

Admitted March 1914. Of 19 Holborn Viaduct, E.C.; and Watford. Served as 2nd Lieut., 5th (Reserve) Batt. Border Regt.

DOUGLAS HERON MARRABLE.

Admitted Feb. 1882, practised at Dorchester. Served as Lieut., Territorial Reserve of Officers, Musketry Officer 51st Infantry Brigade. Retired with rank of Capt.

NEVILLE FRECKELTON MARRIOTT.

Articled to Richard Marriott, of Nottingham. Joined Aug. 25, 1914, as Private, Royal Fusiliers (4th Public Schools Battalion). Gazetted 2nd Lieut. 9th Batt. Lincolnshire Regt. Sept. 28, 1914, promoted to Lieut. Aug. 1915, transferred to Machine Gun Corps Dec. 1915, promoted Capt. May 1918, and Adjutant Nov. 1918. Twice mentioned in Dispatches. Awarded the M.C. Served in France March 1916 to April 1919.

RICHARD JOHN MARRIOTT.

Admitted Sept. 1905. With the Public Trustee, Cornwall House, Stamford Street, E.C. Joined April 9, 1915, as Private, 28th (North-West) Batt. Canadian Infantry. Served in France and Belgium. Wounded at Hill 60 (Ypres) July 7, 1916.

CHARLES ALBERT MARRIS.

Admitted Nov. 1897. Member of Marris & Marris, of Worksop. Served as 2nd Air-Mechanic, Royal Air Force.

HAROLD COLQUHOUN MARRIS.
Admitted May 1906. Member of Rice, Waite & Marris, of Boston, Lincs. Served as 2nd Lieut., 4th Batt. Lincolnshire Regt., promoted Capt. June 1916.

HAROLD HOLDEN MARSDEN.
Articled to Henry Crellin, of Blackburn. Served as 2nd Lieut., Royal Field Artillery.

THOMAS MARSDEN.
Admitted Dec. 1907, practising at Blackburn. Served as Private, Royal Army Ordnance Corps.

ARTHUR PERCIVAL MARSH.
Admitted April 1911. Managing Clerk with Vizard, Oldham, Crowder & Cash, of 51 Lincoln's Inn Fields, W.C. Mobilised Aug. 1914, as Lieut. 5th Batt. Leicestershire Regt., promoted Capt. Feb. 1915. Served in France and at Home. Wounded at Ypres July 1, 1915.

DUNCAN MARSH.
Admitted Nov. 1911, practising at Northwich, Cheshire. Joined Sept. 22, 1914, as 2nd Lieut., 6th Batt. Hampshire Regt., promoted Lieut. Jan. 1915, Capt. Jan. 1916. Served at Home.

JOHN ROWLAND MARSH.
Admitted Jan. 1913. Member of Richardson, Marsh & Co., of Liverpool. Mobilised Aug. 1914, as Lieut. 2nd Lancs. Battery (Heavy Battery) Royal Garrison Artillery, promoted Capt. Nov. 1914. Served at Home till 1915, in France 1916 to 1918, and afterwards in Germany.

ROBERT BARKLEY MARSH.
Articled to Hugh Bellingham, of Swansea. Joined Oct. 1914, as Private, 5th Batt. Somersetshire Light Infantry. Subsequently gazetted 2nd Lieut. in same Regt., and attained rank of Capt. Served in India.

ROBERT PRESTON MARSH.
Admitted Jan. 1913. Member of Marsh & Son, of Rotherham. Served as Capt., 5th Batt. York and Lancaster Regt. Mentioned in Dispatches.

ALFRED TURNER MARSHALL.
Admitted Feb. 1907, practised at Herne Bay. Joined Cambridge University O.T.C. May 1916. Gazetted 2nd Lieut. 5th Batt. Suffolk Regt. Jan. 1917, ordered to India with draft April 1917, and attached for service to 1/7 Batt. Hampshire Regt. Served with Aden Field Force 1918, and promoted Lieut. July 1918. Invalided to England Jan. 1919.

ARTHUR WILLIAM MONTAGUE MARSHALL.
Admitted Sept. 1894. Member of Gerald & Arthur Marshall, of 10 New Square, Lincoln's Inn, W.C. Served as Chief Petty Officer, Royal Naval Volunteer Reserve (Anti-Aircraft Corps).

CHARLES BENNETT MARSHALL.
Admitted Feb. 1902. Member of Lewin, Gregory & Anderson, of 2 Millbank House, Westminster, S.W. Joined Dec. 1, 1914, as Lieut., Royal Field Artillery, promoted Staff Capt. and Temp. Capt. June 1915, Temp. Major and

D.A.A.G. June 1917. Three times mentioned in Dispatches. Awarded the M.C. Served at Home Dec. 1914 to Sept. 1915, France Sept. to Dec. 1915, Macedonia Dec. 1915 to Dec. 1918.

CLAUDE WILLIAM MARSHALL.

Admitted July 1907. Member of Marshall & Son, of Ipswich. Joined March 1, 1915, as Private, Inns of Court O.T.C. Gazetted 2nd Lieut. 14th Batt. The Rifle Brigade June 18, 1915, promoted Lieut. 1917. Served at Home and in France. Wounded March 9, 1916, at Ypres; Aug. 31, 1916, Somme; July 25, 1917, Ypres.

EDWARD RALPH MARSHALL.

Admitted April 1913. Member of George M. Seabroke & Son, of Rugby. Joined Aug. 1916, as Private, Royal Warwickshire Regt. Gazetted 2nd Lieut. Coldstream Guards Nov. 16, 1916, promoted Lieut. May 1917. Served in France.

GEORGE RAYMOND MARSHALL.

Articled to J. G. Marshall, of Sunderland. Served as Private, Durham Light Infantry.

GEORGE SIMS MARSHALL.

Admitted July 1907. Member of T. D. Marshall, Hall & Co., of South Shields. Joined Feb. 1915, as 2nd Lieut., 9th Batt. Durham Light Infantry, promoted Capt. May 1916, Major and D.A.A.G. (Legal) Nov. 1919. Once mentioned in Dispatches. Served at Home, Salonica, and Constantinople.

HENRY GEORGE MARSHALL.

Admitted Dec. 1912. Of 8 New Square, Lincoln's Inn, W.C. Served in Inns of Court O.T.C.

JOHN MARSHALL.

Admitted Dec. 1903, practising at 30 Fleet Street, E.C. Joined March 27, 1915, as Private, 3/1 Essex Yeomanry, transferred 3rd Batt. Hon. Artillery Company (Infantry) as Private Oct. 1915. Gazetted 2nd Lieut. Royal Army Service Corps March 28, 1918, promoted Lieut. Sept. 1919. Served at Home March 1915 to March 1916, in France and Belgium March 1916 to Dec. 1917, in Macedonia and with Black Sea Army May 1918 to Oct. 1919.

JOHN STEAD STANLEY MARSHALL.

Admitted April 1900, practising at 26 Theobald's Road, Gray's Inn, W.C. Joined June 30, 1916, as Cadet. Gazetted 2nd Lieut. Royal Garrison Artillery (S.R.) Aug. 22, 1916, promoted Lieut. Feb. 1918. Served at Home and in France.

JOHN THEOBALD MARSHALL.

Articled to Cornelius Marshall, of Manchester. Served as Lieut., 14th Batt. Manchester Regt., attached 1st Batt. Prince of Wales' Own Yorkshire Regt.

JOHN WOODALL MARSHALL.

Articled to Edward Clarke, of Newcastle-upon-Tyne. On outbreak of War joined 2nd Regt. La Legion Etrangère (French Foreign Legion) and served with that until Feb. 1915, when transferred to British Army. Gazetted 2nd Lieut.

Northumberland Fusiliers, and subsequently promoted Lieut. Awarded the M.C. Killed in action July 1916.

ROLAND MARSHALL.
Admitted Dec. 1913, practising at 17 Tower Royal, Cannon Street, E.C.; and Liverpool. Served as Sergeant, Lancashire Hussars. Gazetted Lieut. Royal Field Artillery.

WILLIAM MARSHALL.
Admitted Dec. 1891, practising at 49 Dover Street, W. Served as Official Searcher for the Red Cross.

WILLIAM MARSHALL.
Admitted Nov. 1913, practised at Durham. Joined 1914, as Lieut., 8th Batt. Durham Light Infantry. Served at Home and in France. Killed at 2nd Battle of Ypres April 27, 1915.

WILLIAM SKINNER MARSHALL.
Admitted Nov. 1901, practising at Nottingham. Joined Aug. 11, 1914, as Capt., 7th (Robin Hood) Batt. Notts and Derby Regt. (Sherwood Foresters). Served at Home.

DONALD MILLWARD MARSTON.
Articled to H. T. Weyman, of Ludlow. Served as Lieut., 4th Batt. King's Shropshire Light Infantry.

EDMUND RICHARD MARSTON.
Admitted Dec. 1890. Member of Marston & Sons, of Ludlow. Joined Aug. 14, 1914, as Recruiting Officer at Ludlow, with the rank of Temp. Capt. Served at Home. Retired Sept. 1, 1917.

HENRY JOHN MARSTON.
Admitted June 1906, practising at Poole, Dorset. Served as 2nd Lieut., Royal Garrison Artillery.

JOHN ARTHUR MARSTON.
Admitted Nov. 1908. Member of Garrard, Wolfe & Co., 13 Suffolk Street, Pall Mall East, S.W. Joined June 8, 1916, as Private, Suffolk Regt., promoted Corporal Aug. 1916 and Sergeant Dec. 1916. Gazetted 2nd Lieut. 3rd (Reserve) Garrison Batt. Royal Welch Fusiliers Dec. 16, 1917, attached 23rd Batt. Cheshire Regt. April 1918. Served at Home, Ireland, and France.

JOHN BEALE MARSTON.
Articled to J. B. Marston, of Mold. Served as Capt., 5th Batt. Royal Welch Fusiliers (T.).

RICHARD WHISTON MARTELL.
Admitted Dec. 1905, practising at 6 King's Bench Walk, E.C. Served as Lieut., Royal Field Artillery, promoted Capt. June 1916. Mentioned in Dispatches.

ARTHUR EDWIN MARTIN.
Articled to J. C. Woods, of Swansea. Joined April 7, 1916, as Private, Pembroke Yeomanry. Gazetted 2nd Lieut. in same Regt. April 26, 1917,

promoted Lieut. Oct. 26, 1918, and attached 1st Batt. King's Shropshire Light Infantry. Served in France. Wounded at Dickebusch July 17, 1918.

CECIL HAGUE MARTIN.

Articled to J. G. Martin, of Nottingham. Joined Nov. 1914, as Driver, 2/1 North Midland Field Ambulance. Gazetted 2nd Lieut. Royal Army Service Corps, March 25, 1915, promoted Lieut. Sept. 1915, Capt. May, 1918. Served in France.

FRANK DOUGLAS MARTIN.

Admitted Nov. 1911. Clerk with Martin & Sons, of Nottingham. Joined Sept. 23, 1914, as 2nd Lieut., Notts and Derby Regt. (Sherwood Foresters), promoted Lieut. Oct. 1914, Capt. May 1918. Served in France and Belgium, Oct. 1915 to 1920. Wounded at Authuille Wood, near Albert, France, July 1, 1916.

HUBERT JOSEPH BAYNES MARTIN.

Admitted Dec. 1911. Managing Clerk with Webster & Watson, of Newton Abbot. Joined Dec. 5, 1914, as Private, 18th (Service) Batt. Royal Fusiliers. Gazetted 2nd Lieut. 1st Garrison Batt. East Kent Regt. (The Buffs) Sept. 11, 1916, promoted Lieut. March 1918, transferred to 2/1 West Kent Yeomanry Aug. 1918. Served in France and at Home.

HUBERT SINCLAIR MARTIN.

Admitted Dec. 1913, practising at Great Yarmouth. Served as Capt., 1st East Anglian Brigade, Royal Field Artillery, promoted Major June 1916. Mentioned in Dispatches.

JAMES FLETCHER MARTIN.

Articled to William Martin, of 20 Budge Row, E.C. Joined Sept. 7, 1914, as Private, Hon. Artillery Company (Infantry), promoted Lance-Corporal March 1916, Corporal June 1916, and Sergeant Nov. 1916. Served in France and Belgium, and with Army of Occupation.

JAMES GODFREY MARTIN.

Admitted Jan. 1898. Member of Martin & Haslett, of 7 Philpot Lane, E.C. Joined Oct. 12, 1914, as Private, 23rd (1st Sportsman's) Batt. Royal Fusiliers. Gazetted Temp. Lieut. July 3, 1915, and posted to 11th (Service) Batt. Royal Warwickshire Regt., transferred to 12th (Reserve) Batt. Aug. 1915, promoted Temp. Capt. June 1916, Temp. Major Nov. 1917 and transferred to North Staffordshire Regt. and appointed Second in Command of the 8th (Service) Batt., temporarily commanded 1/4 Batt. King's Shropshire Light Infantry March 1918, and the 9th Batt. Cheshire Regt. April 1918. Once mentioned in Dispatches (Special). Awarded D.S.O., M.C., and Croix de Guerre (French) (Gold Star). Served in France and Flanders. Wounded at Hill 60 Oct. 1917 and at Bligny June 1918.

JOHN KINGSLEY LUNN MARTIN.

Admitted June 1906, practised at Stockton-on-Tees. Mobilised Aug. 1914, as Capt., Durham Light Infantry, being attached to the 17th Batt., and afterwards the 10th Batt. Served at Home, Montserrat, and in France. Killed at Hooge Aug. 1, 1915.

JOHN LANCELOT MARTIN.

Admitted 1905, practising at Reading, Berks. Joined July 2, 1915, as 2nd Lieut., Territorial Force Reserve (General List), 2nd Lieut. 21st Batt. The Rifle Brigade Sept. 1915, attached No. 3 Armoured Train July 1916, promoted Temp. Lieut. Oct. 1916, Lieut. July 1917, attached Headquarters Alexandria District 1917 to 1918, attached Special Intelligence 1918, appointed D.A.C., Chief Censor's Staff, 1919. Served in Egypt 1916, 1917, and 1918, and in France 1919.

LESLIE COMMERFORD MARTIN.

Admitted Nov. 1911. Member of Martin & Son, of Gravesend. Joined Sept. 2, 1916, as Aircraftsman 2nd Grade, Royal Naval Air Service. Promoted Aircraftsman 1st Grade, Aug. 1917, subsequently 1st Private (motor-boat deckhand) Royal Air Force April 1918. Served at Home.

OSWALD NORMAN MARTIN.

Admitted Oct. 1913. Member of Griffiths & Martin, of Hay, Hereford. Served as Private, 14th Batt. County of London Regt. (London Scottish).

WILLIAM HARROD MARTIN.

Articled to H. J. Martin, of 29 Queen Street, E.C. Joined Sept. 1914, as Private, 16th Batt. County of London Regt. (Queen's Westminster Rifles). Gazetted 2nd Lieut. 24th Batt. County of London Regt. (The Queen's) Aug. 1915. Served in France Jan. to May 1915, July to Aug. 1915, and May to Sept. 1916. Wounded May and Aug. 1915. Killed in action at High Wood, France, Sept. 14, 1916.

WILLIAM JAMES ROYLE MARTIN.

Articled to W. H. Martin, of 18 Ironmonger Lane, E.C. Served as 2nd Lieut., 11th (Service) Batt. Royal Fusiliers, promoted Lieut. March 1916. Awarded the M.C.

ERNEST MARTINEAU.

Admitted Jan. 1886. Member of Ryland, Martineau & Co., of Birmingham. Mobilised Aug. 5, 1914, as Lieut-Col. Commanding 6th Batt. Royal Warwickshire Regt., transferred to Command of 83rd Provisional Batt. July 1915, transferred to T.F. Reserve Sept. 1916, appointed Hon. Col. 6th Batt. Royal Warwickshire Regt. Feb. 1917. Once mentioned in Dispatches. Also once brought to notice of Secretary of State. Awarded C.M.G. Served at Home and in France.

WILFRID MARTINEAU.

Articled to H. B. Carslake, of Birmingham. Served as Lieut., 6th Batt. Royal Warwickshire Regt., promoted Capt. June 1916. Mentioned in Dispatches and awarded the M.C.

CHARLES JOHN BEECH MASEFIELD

Admitted Oct. 1905. Member of Blagg, Son & Masefield, of Cheadle, Staffs. Joined July 26, 1915, as 2nd Lieut., 5th Batt. North Staffordshire Regt. (T.), promoted Lieut. Feb. 1916, A/Capt. May 1917. Awarded the M.C. Served in France and at Home. Fatally wounded and taken prisoner at Lens July 1, 1917, and died in German Field Hospital at Le Forest on the following day.

CHARLES EDWIN MASON.

Articled to C. B. Hill, of Norwich. Served as Private, 8th Batt. Norfolk Regt. Killed in action in France Jan. 29, 1916.

DANIEL JOHNSTON MASON.

Admitted July 1898, practising at Workington and Whitehaven. Mobilised Aug. 1914, as Major, The Cumberland Royal Field Artillery, promoted Lieut.-Col. 210th Brigade, 42nd Division (T.) Dec. 1917. Once mentioned in Dispatches. Awarded D.S.O. and T.D. Served in England Aug. 1914 to May 1915, Egypt May to June 1915, Gallipoli (Cape Helles) June 1915 to Jan. 1916, Egypt and Sinai Peninsula June 1916 to March 1917, France and Belgium March 1917 to April 1919.

ERNEST EDWIN MASON.

Admitted Feb. 1916, practising at Manchester. Served as Private, General Staff Intelligence, 3rd Army Headquarters.

HERBERT MASON.

Admitted Aug. 1889. Member of Lindsay, Greenfield & Mason, of 11 Ironmonger Lane, E.C. Joined Dec. 20, 1914, as Private 24th (Service) Batt. Royal Fusiliers (2nd Sportsman's). Gazetted Lieut. Royal Naval Volunteer Reserve July 20, 1915, attached R.N.A.S. (Armoured Car Division), promoted Capt. Royal Air Force April 1918. Served in France Nov. 1916 to Feb. 1918, and at Home Feb. 1918 to Jan. 1919.

JAMES ERNEST MASON.

Admitted May 1899. Member of Amery, Parkes & Co., of 18 Fleet Street, E.C. Joined June 4, 1915, as Lieut., Royal Army Service Corps, promoted Capt. Dec. 1915, Major June 1917, Lieut.-Col. Sept. 1918. Once mentioned in Dispatches. Awarded O.B.E. Served at Home.

JOHN MELLARD MASON.

Admitted April 1915. Member of Sherratt, Nelson & Mason, of Burslem and Kidsgrove. Joined Nov. 1, 1915, as 2nd Lieut., 3/5 Batt. North Staffordshire Regt., promoted Lieut. Oct. 1917. Served in Egypt 1916, Salonica 1917, and in Malta 1918.

JOHN RICHARD MASON.

Admitted Feb. 1900. Member of Mason & Co., of 115 High Holborn, W.C. Joined May 1917, as Sub.-Lieut., Royal Naval Volunteer Reserve, promoted Lieut. June 1918. Served at Home.

LOUIS MASON.

Admitted Aug. 1885, practising at Maidstone. Served as Lieut., Royal Naval Volunteer Reserve.

MAURICE LUDLAM MASON.

Admitted Feb. 1906. Member of Dixon & Mason, of Pewsey, Wilts. Joined 1916 Officers Cadet Unit and subsequently gazetted 2nd Lieut. and attached to 69th Siege Battery Royal Garrison Artillery, promoted Lieut. Aug. 1918. Awarded the Chevalier de l'Ordre de la Couronne (Belgium) also Croix de Guerre (1917). Served in France and Belgium whole of 1917 and 1918, and on the Rhine.

NORMAN MASON.

Articled to A. G. Inglis, of Liverpool. Served as Private, Royal Army Service Corps.

WILLIAM JOSEPH MASON,

Admitted Nov. 1909. Member of W. M. Mason & Son, of 76 Finsbury Pavement, E.C. Mobilised Aug. 1914 with City of London Yeomanry (Roughriders) and served as Private and Lance-Corporal. Gazetted 2nd Lieut. Oxfordshire Yeomanry (Queen's Own Oxfordshire Hussars) Aug. 24, 1917, promoted Lieut. Feb. 1919. Served in Egypt April to Aug. 1915 and Dec. 1915 to Nov. 1916, Gallipoli (Suvla Bay) Aug. to Dec. 1915, Balkans Nov. 1916 to Feb. 1917, and in France Oct. 1917 to Sept. 1918. Wounded at Frières Wood March 23, 1918.

HENRY THORNTON MASSER.

Admitted Oct. 1915. Member of J. T. Masser & Co., of Nottingham. Joined Feb. 2, 1916, as Private, Royal Army Service Corps (M.T.) Gazetted 2nd Lieut. April 1917, promoted Lieut. Oct. 1918. Once mentioned in Dispatches. Served in Mesopotamia and at Home.

GEORGE EDWARD MASSEY.

Admitted Dec. 1907. Member of Shaen, Roscoe, Massey & Co., of 8 Bedford Row, W.C. Joined Jan. 1, 1917, as Gunner, Royal Horse Artillery. Commissioned 2nd Lieut. Jan. 30, 1918, and joined 3rd Batt East Kent Regt. (The Buffs) Feb. 1918, attached G.H.Q. Constantinople Jan. 1919, appointed Courts-Martial Officer and Temp. Capt. G.H.Q. Constantinople Feb. 1919. Served at Home, Salonica, Macedonia, and Turkey.

EDWARD TOURNOUR MASTER.

Admitted Feb. 1904. Member of Hussey & Master, of 11 Stone Buildings, Lincoln's Inn, W.C. Joined Aug. 25, 1915, as 2nd Lieut. (Temp. Lieut.) 3/7 Batt. Prince of Wales' Own West Yorkshire Regt., promoted Temp. Capt. Jan. 1916, Substantive Lieut. June 1916, A/Capt. Jan. 1919. Served at Home Aug. 1915 to May 1917, and in France May 1917 to March 1919.

CHARLES WALTON MASTERS.

Admitted Dec. 1913. Managing Clerk with J. P. Foster & Cateaux, of Cairo, and Alexandria, Egypt. Joined Aug. 4, 1914, as Private, 6th Batt. Gloucestershire Regt. Commissioned 2nd Lieut. 10th Batt. Northumberland Fusiliers Jan. 9, 1915, promoted Lieut. Nov. 1916, Capt. (General List) Nov. 1918. Served in France 1915 to 1918. Wounded Sept, 18, 1918.

ALFRED WARTON MATCHAM.

Admitted Jan. 1909. Of 17 Faraday Mansions, Queen's Club Gardens, W. Served as Lieut., 2nd Essex Battery, 2nd East Anglian Brigade, Royal Field Artillery, subsequently promoted Capt.

NOEL EDWARD MATHER.

Admitted Oct. 1913, practised at Chesterfield and Newcastle-upon-Tyne. Served as 2nd Lieut., Northumberland Fusiliers. Killed in action near Ypres April 27, 1915.

MAURICE ARTHUR MATHEW.

Admitted Feb. 1913. Member of Sparkes, Pope, Thomas & Mathew, of Crediton and Exeter. Joined Oct. 16, 1916, as Private, 2/1 Batt. Hertfordshire Regt. Promoted Sergt. May 1917. Gazetted 2nd Lieut. Royal Garrison Artillery Feb. 1919. Served at Home.

DOUGLASS MATHEWS.

Admitted Dec. 1894. Member of Wood & Sons, of 31 Poultry, E.C. Mobilised Aug. 1914, as Capt., 12th (Reserve) Batt. County of London Regt., and subsequently promoted Major. Served at Home.

WILFRID CLARKSON MATHEWS.

Admitted Nov. 1905. Practised at 110 Cannon Street, E.C. Served as 2nd Lieut., Kent Fortress Engineers (T.), promoted Lieut. June 1916.

FRANCIS EDWARD LLOYD MATHIAS-THOMAS.

Admitted Oct. 1908, practising at Tenby. Mobilised Aug. 1914, as Lieut., Royal Garrison Artillery, promoted Capt. 1915. Served at Home.

FREDERICK GEORGE LESLIE MATHISON.

Articled to W. H. Mathison, of Birkenhead. Served as Dispatch Rider, Royal Naval Volunteer Reserve (Anti-Aircraft Corps).

ARTHUR DONALD TAYLOR MATTHEWS.

Articled to F. G. Bradford, of Yeovil. Served as Private, 5th Batt. Somerset Light Infantry (T.). Killed in action.

ARTHUR JACOB MATTHEWS.

Articled to J. C. Wood, of Swindon. Joined Sept. 1914 as Trooper, Royal Wiltshire Yeomanry. Discharged medically unfit for Service March 1915.

CYRIL VINCENT MATTHEWS.

Admitted March 1914, practising at Wolverhampton. Joined April 11, 1916, as Private, 6th Batt Royal Fusiliers, and subsequently promoted to Corporal. Commissioned 2nd Lieut. 1st Garrison Batt. Suffolk Regt. April 26, 1917, attached 2nd City of London Yeomanry Sept. 1917 to March 1918, and to 12th Batt. Suffolk Regt. March 1918 to March 1919, promoted Lieut. Oct. 1915. Served at Home and France and Belgium. Wounded Oct. 23, 1918.

FRANCIS REGINALD MATTHEWS.

Admitted June 1916. Managing Clerk with Trower, Still & Co., of 5 New Square, Lincoln's Inn, W.C. Joined Oct. 6, 1917, as Asst. Paymaster, Royal Naval Volunteer Reserve, H.M.S. *President* for duty in Convoy Section, Admiralty. Served at Admiralty Oct. 1917 to Aug. 1918, and on Convoy Escort Duty Aug. to Nov. 1918 (West Coast Africa Convoys).

GEORGE LIPSCOMBE MATTHEWS.

Admitted April 1880, practising at 26 Cannon Street E.C. Mobilised Aug. 1914, as Major, 4th Batt. East Kent Regt. (The Buffs). Awarded T.D. Served in India and Aden 1914 to 1918. Retired April 1918.

MARMADUKE CAPPER MATTHEWS.

Admitted Nov. 1887. Member of G. F. Hudson, Matthews & Co., of 32 Queen Victoria Street, E.C. Mobilised Aug. 1914 as Major and Hon. Lieut.-Col., attached to General Staff 25th Division. Served at Home (Musketry Training Staff).

SYDNEY EDGAR MATTHEWS.

Articled to A. W. Easterling, of Bangor, N. Wales. Joined April 13, 1915, as Private, Royal Army Service Corps, and attained the rank of Warrant Officer. Served at Home.

WILLIAM HENRY MATTHEWS.

Admitted Jan. 1915. Managing Clerk with Botterell & Roche, of 24 St. Mary Axe, E.C. Joined as Private, Inns of Court O.T.C. and subsequently gazetted Temp. 2nd Lieut. Royal Garrison Artillery. Served in France. Killed in action Sept. 28, 1918.

WILLIAM MONKMAN MAUD.

Admitted Nov. 1904, practised at Guildford. Served as 2nd Lieut., The Queen's Royal West Surrey Regt. Promoted Capt. Aug. 1916.

ARTHUR PERCY LEES MAUDE.

Admitted March 1910, practising at Wath-on-Dearne. Served as Private, Royal Army Medical Corps.

HENRY OWEN HAMER MAUDE.

Admitted Sept. 1907. Member of Maude & Tunnicliffe, of Arundel House, Arundel Street, W.C. Served as 2nd Lieut., 1st Home Counties Royal Field Artillery, promoted Lieut. June 1916.

GEORGE HYSLOP MAUGHAN.

Admitted Aug. 1911. Managing Clerk with Walter Topham, of Harrogate. Joined May 1914, as Private, 5th Batt. West Yorkshire Regt. (T.). Gazetted 2nd Lieut. 4th East Lancashire Royal Field Artillery Feb. 24, 1915, promoted Lieut. June 1916. Served at Home Aug. 1914 to Dec. 1915, Egypt Jan. 1916 to March 1917, Salonica April 1917 to Aug. 1918 and Nov. 1919 to April 1920, France Sept. to Oct. 1918, and at Constantinople April to Oct. 1920.

ALLAN MAW.

Admitted April 1914. Member of Ascroft, Maw & Shimeld, of Oldham, Lancs. Joined Sept. 5, 1914, as 2nd Lieut., 10th Batt. Manchester Regt. (T.), promoted Lieut. Aug. 1915, Capt. June 1916. Served at Gallipoli 1915, and in France (attached 2/5 Batt. Lancashire Fusiliers) 1916. Wounded at Ginchy, on the Somme, Sept. 9, 1916.

WILLIAM GEORGE CANNEY MAW.

Admitted Aug. 1910. Managing Clerk with W. Wilkinson, of Bishop Auckland. Joined Dec. 7, 1914, as Lieut., Durham Light Infantry. Served at Home 1914 to 1915 and 1916 to 1919, and in France 1915. Wounded and gassed Ypres Salient Dec. 19, 1915.

EDWIN GEORGE MAWBY.

Admitted Jan. 1902. Member of Mawby, Mawby & Morris, of 6 and 7 Queen Street, Cheapside, E.C. Joined Aug. 1914, as Trooper, The Westminster Dragoons. Gazetted Lieut. Welch Guards in 1915. Served in Egypt and in France. Killed at the Battle of Loos Sept. 27, 1915.

ERNEST WILLIAM MAWDSLEY.

Admitted Nov. 1910. Member of Mawdsley & Hadfield, of Southport. Joined Sept. 1, 1914, as Private, 18th Batt. King's Liverpool Regt. Gazetted 2nd Lieut. 19th Manchester Regt. Feb. 22, 1915, subsequently Capt. 21st Trench Mortar Battery May 1917. Served in France Nov. 1915 to Oct. 1917 and in U.S.A. as member of British Military Mission Nov. 1917 to Nov. 1918. Wounded July 10, 1916.

ARTHUR JEFFERAY MAWER.

Admitted March 1889, practising at Wells, Somerset. Joined Dec. 27, 1914, as Capt., Territorial Force Reserve. Served at Home. Resigned Oct. 24, 1918.

EDWARD STANLEY MAWER.

Admitted Jan. 1913. Formerly of High Wycombe. Joined Aug. 1914, as Gunner, Hon. Artillery Company (Mounted Section), promoted Bombardier 1916. Gazetted 2nd Lieut. Royal Field Artillery 1916, promoted Lieut. 1918, A/Capt. 1919. Served in Egypt 1915, Gallipoli Aug. to Dec. 1915, Mesopotamia 1916 to 1918, India 1918 to 1919.

ALFRED ERNEST MAWN.

Articled to Joseph Hood, M.P., of 7 Millbank, S.W. Joined Oct. 6, 1914, as Private, Inns of Court O.T.C., and attained rank of Sergeant. Gazetted 2nd Lieut. Royal Army Ordnance Corps May 25, 1916, promoted Lieut. Aug. 1916. Served in France April 1917 to Jan. 1918, and at Home.

JOHN MAWSON.

Articled to R. W. Buchanan, of Ripon. Joined Nov. 1914, as Motor Driver in British Red Cross Society. Joined Feb. 1916 as Air-Mechanic Royal Flying Corps. Served at Home and in Serbia May to Dec. 1915. Died of pneumonia April 6, 1916.

JOSEPH LANDT MAWSON.

Articled to Joseph Mawson, of Durham. Joined June 1917, as Private, Royal Army Service Corps (M.T.). Commissioned in same Regt. Feb. 4, 1918. Served practically whole period in France and Belgium. Went into hospital with shell shock Sept. 1918, and invalided out Feb. 1919.

REGINALD STUART MAXWELL.

Articled to J. A. Maxwell, of 52 Bishopsgate, E.C. Served as 2nd Lieut. 8th (Service) Batt. East Yorkshire Regt. Awarded the M.C.

CHARLES HENRY MAY.

Admitted Feb. 1913. Of 49 Lincoln's Inn Fields, W.C. Served as 2nd Lieut., 7th Batt. Royal Sussex Regt., attached Motor Machine Gun Service, promoted Capt. Nov. 1917. Mentioned in Dispatches and awarded the M.C.

HENRY ALLAN ROUGHTON MAY.

Admitted Nov. 1885. Member of Minet, May & Co., of 5 Dowgate Hill, Cannon Street, E.C. Mobilised Aug. 1914, and served as Lieut.-Col. Commanding 28th Batt. County of London Regt. (Artists Rifles). Once mentioned in Dispatches. Awarded C.B. and Brevet Colonel. Served in France Oct. 1914 to Dec. 1915, and at Home 1916 to 1919.

RICHARD TRELAWNY MAY.

Articled to C. W. How, of 49 Lincoln's Inn Fields, W.C. Joined Inns of Court O.T.C. on outbreak of War, and shortly afterwards gazetted 2nd Lieut. Royal Sussex Regt., attained rank of Capt. Once mentioned in Dispatches. Killed in action July 7, 1916.

CHARLES GARDE MAYBURY.

Articled to P. N. Binns, of Bedford. Joined Aug. 6, 1914, as Sapper, Royal Engineers, promoted Lance-Corporal Sept. 1915. Gazetted 2nd Lieut. Royal Engineers Oct. 26, 1917. Served in France Dec. 1914 to April 1919.

FRANK BERTRAM MAYER.

Admitted Jan. 1907. Member of Mayer & Nelson, of Burslem. Joined Sept. 9, 1914, as Private, 5th Batt. North Staffordshire Regt. Gazetted 2nd Lieut. in same Regt. Nov. 6, 1914, and promoted Lieut. April 1915. Served at Home and in France. Killed in action at Loos Oct. 13, 1915.

THOMAS RICHARD MAYHEW.

Articled to R. C. Mayhew, of Lowestoft. Served as Private, Public Schools Batt. Middlesex Regt.

SAMUEL TOMKINS MAYNARD.

Admitted Oct. 1891. Member of Maynard & Smith, of Brighton and Burgess Hill. Mobilised Aug. 1914, as Major, Royal Army Service Corps (T.), promoted Lieut.-Col. June 1916. Twice brought to notice of Secretary of State for War. Awarded the T.D. Served at Home. Commanded 67th Divisional Train 1914 to 1915, A.D.B.O. Eastern Command July 1915 to July 1919.

CHARLES WILLIAM MAYO.

Admitted Dec. 1903. Member of C. W. Mayo & Thomas, of Eastbourne. Joined Nov. 30, 1914, as Lieut., 13th Batt. Royal Sussex Regt., promoted Capt. May 1915, transferred to 2nd Batt. Jan. 1919. Served at Home Nov. 1914 to Feb. 1915, France March 1915 to Jan. 1919, and Germany Jan. to April 1919. Wounded March 25, 1918.

CHRISTOPHER MEAD.

Admitted Oct. 1913. Member of Mead & Co., of 2 King's Bench Walk, Temple, E.C. Obtained commission as 2nd Lieut. 4th Batt. East Surrey Regt. and later attached to 2nd Batt. Wounded July 1915. Killed in action in France Sept. 28, 1915.

HENRY GIFFORD MEAD.

Admitted April 1899. Member of Mead & Sons, of 116 Jermyn Street, St. James's, S.W. Mobilised Aug. 1914, as Major, 7th London Brigade Royal Field Artillery (T.), and subsequently promoted Lieut.-Col. Once mentioned in Dispatches. Served in France March 1915 to Dec. 1916, Salonica Dec. 1916 to May 1917, Palestine May 1917 to March 1919.

PHILIP CLEMENT MEAD.

Admitted Dec. 1898. Managing Clerk with Longmores, of Hertford. Joined Oct. 12, 1914, Royal Naval Air Service (A.A.C.), transferred to Royal Naval Volunteer Reserve 1916. Served at Home. Discharged April 1918.

WILLIAM MEADOWS.

Admitted Jan. 1899, practised at Manchester. Served as 2nd Lieut., Cheshire Regt.

SAMUEL BERTIE MEADS.

Articled to E. L. Manning, of Nottingham. Joined Nov. 15, 1915, as Trooper, Derbyshire Imperial Yeomanry. Transferred Sept. 1916 to 14th Batt. Durham Light Infantry as Private. Attached to Intelligence Office, XIX. Corps Headquarters Aug. 1917. Transferred Oct. 1917 to 277th Area Employment Company Labour Corps, but continued service in the Intelligence Office. Served at Home until Sept. 1916 and in France and Belgium Sept. 1916 to Dec. 1918. Slightly wounded at Loos April 6, 1917.

GEORGE VICKERMAN MEAL.

Articled to A. H. Williams, of 276 Camberwell New Road, S.E. Joined Oct. 16, 1914, as Private, 19th Batt. Royal Fusiliers. Obtained commission as 2nd Lieut. Machine Gun Corps Aug. 5, 1916, promoted Lieut. Feb. 5, 1918. Served in France Nov. 1915 to March 1916, at Salonica Jan. to June 1917, and in Palestine July 1917 to June 1919.

EDWARD FREDERIC MEDCALF.

Admitted Nov. 1907. Managing Clerk with Deacon & Co., of 9 Great St. Helen's, E.C. Joined Dec. 1, 1914, as 2nd Lieut., 8th Batt. Oxford and Bucks Light Infantry, promoted Lieut. May 1915, Capt. Sept. 1915, Major July 1917. Once mentioned in Dispatches. Awarded Greek Military Cross. Served at Home and in France and Serbia.

JOHN PERCIVAL MEDLEY.

Admitted Dec. 1906. Member of Medley, Drawbridge & Co., of Scarborough. Joined Sept. 9, 1914, as Adjutant, Scarborough Volunteers, subsequently Capt. Second in Command 4th Batt. A.P.W.O. Yorkshire Regt. (V.).

GEORGE PROBART MEDLICOTT.

Admitted March 1910. Member of Geo. H. Medlicott & Son, of Kingliton, Radnorshire. Joined Sept. 14, 1914, 28th Batt. County of London Regt. (Artists Rifles). Gazetted 2nd Lieut. in Intelligence Service (Censor Staff) General List Jan. 10, 1916, transferred Royal Garrison Artillery (270th Siege Battery) Oct. 1916, promoted Lieut. July 1917, appointed A/Captain (Adjutant 3rd Brigade Royal Garrison Artillery) Aug. 1917. Once mentioned in Dispatches. Awarded French Croix de Guerre (à l'ordre Brigade). Served at Home Sept. 1914 to Jan. 1915, and in France Jan. 1915 to May 1919.

HERBERT MEDWIN.

Admitted Jan. 1913, practising at 7 New Square, Lincoln's Inn, W.C. Joined Sept. 8, 1916, as Aircraftsman, Royal Naval Air Service, promoted

Petty Officer Royal Naval Air Service Aug. 1917, Sergeant Clerk Royal Air Force April 1918. Served at Home.

HAROLD JAMES MEE.

Admitted Feb. 1899, practising at Mortlake. Served as Private, 9th Batt. County of London Regt. (Queen Victoria's Rifles).

ERNEST ANTHONY MEEK.

Articled to G. F. Lucas, of Darlington. Joined Jan. 29, 1914, as 2nd Lieut., 5th Batt. Durham Light Infantry (T.), promoted Substantive Lieut. Aug. 1915, Capt. June 1916. Once mentioned in Dispatches. Awarded the M.C. Served in France 3½ years. Wounded May 29, 1918.

RAYMOND MEEKE,

Admitted Sept. 1907, practising at Sheffield. Joined Dec. 4, 1914, as Sub-Lieut., Royal Naval Volunteer Reserve, subsequently transferred to Royal Garrison Artillery and attained the rank of Major. Awarded the French Croix de Guerre. Served in France.

CLAUDE MEESON.

Admitted Oct. 1913. Of Battlebridge, Essex. Joined Sept. 16, 1914, as Private, 19th Batt. Royal Fusiliers. Gazetted 2nd Lieut. Machine Gun Corps Sept. 26, 1916, promoted Lieut. March 1918. Served in France.

RICHARD RONALD HORNSEY MEGGESON.

Admitted Dec. 18, 1913. Of Chelmsford. Joined Sept. 24, 1914, as Private, Hon. Artillery Company (Infantry). Gazetted 2nd Lieut. Royal Garrison Artillery (S.R.) Sept. 14, 1916, promoted Lieut. March 1918, A/Capt. Oct. 1918. Served at Home and in France and Belguim April 1915 to June 1916 and Oct. 1916 to Feb. 1919.

JOSEPH BLOOM MEGGITT.

Admitted April 1897, practising at Mansfield, Notts. Joined June 17, 1918, as 3rd Air-Mechanic, Royal Air Force. Served at Home.

WILLIAM EWART MEIKLE.

Admitted Dec. 1907. Member of Reed, Ryder & Meikle, of North Shields. Joined June 1, 1915, as 2nd Lieut., 9th Batt. Durham Light Infantry (T.), promoted Lieut. Nov. 1917, A/Capt. Oct. 1918. Awarded the M.C. Served in France 2 years. Wounded at Butte de Warlincourt Nov. 4, 1916.

CECIL BEVEN MELLENFIELD.

Admitted Jan. 1906. Managing Clerk with Nisbet, Daw & Nisbet, of 35 Lincoln's Inn Fields, W.C. Joined Oct. 1914, as Private, 5th Batt. Middlesex Regt. and attained the rank of Corporal. Gazetted 2nd Lieut. South Lancashire Regt. April 1, 1915. Served in France and Flanders Oct. 1915 to Oct. 1916. Killed in action Oct. 23, 1916. Buried where he fell.

JOHN GEORGE MELLISH.

Articled to R. T. Walter, of Ilminster. Joined June 11, 1915, as 2nd Lieut., 8th Batt. Wiltshire Regt. Transferred to 5th Batt., and subsequently became a Machine Gun Officer. Served on Gallipoli Peninsula, then in Mesopotamia 1916 and 1917. Wounded April 4, 1916, and in Jan. and Feb. 1917. Killed in action before Bagdad March 10, 1917.

EDWARD ERIC MELLOR.
Articled to R. O. Mellor, of Oldham. Joined Sept. 1914, as Private, 20th Batt. Royal Fusiliers (Public Schools). Served in France. Killed at High Wood (Somme) July 20, 1916.

ERNEST MELLOR.
Admitted April 1911. Member of Docker, Hosgood & Co., of Birmingham. Joined June 1915, as Gunner, Royal Garrison Artillery. Gazetted 2nd Lieut. Royal Garrison Artillery (S.R.) Discharged Nov. 30, 1918. Served in France.

GEORGE RUPERT MELLOR.
Admitted Nov. 1901. Member of Vaudrey Osborne & Mellor, of Manchester. Joined Jan. 6, 1915, as Capt., 10th Batt. South Lancashire Regt., transferred to 1st Garrison Batt. King's Liverpool Regt. Aug. 1915, attached 1/11 Batt. London Regt. July to Oct. 1917, and 3rd Batt. South Lancashire Regt. Aug. 1918 to Jan. 1919. Served in Egypt and Palestine.

JOHN SYDNEY MELLOR.
Articled to F. H. Jones, of 8 Coleman Street, E.C. Served with 16th Batt. County of London Regt. (Queen's Westminsters).

PERCY MELLOR.
Articled to Joseph Griffith, of Newcastle, Staffs. Served as 2nd Lieut., North Staffordshire Regt. Sept. 1914 to Oct. 13, 1915, when reported wounded and missing. Subsequently presumed to have died.

PERCY BERNULF DE CLEGG MELLOR.
Admitted Jan. 1888, practising at Brierley Hill, Staffs. Joined with British Red Cross Society 1915. Officer in charge of Wounded and Missing Department at Le Havre and Rouen. Served in France. Resigned Dec. 1916.

REGINALD ERNEST MELLY.
Admitted October 1911. Managing Clerk with Dixon & Coles, of Wakefield. Joined Sept. 2, 1914, as Private, King's Liverpool Regt. Gazetted 2nd Lieut. in same Regt. Feb. 15, 1915, promoted Lieut. May 1915. Served in France 1915, 1916. Killed in action on the Somme July 30, 1916.

CHARLES MELVILLE MELVILLE.
Admitted Dec. 1911, practising at 40 Bedford Row, W.C. Served as 2nd Lieut., 13th Batt. Royal Fusiliers. Awarded the M.C.

WILLIAM HENRY WOOD MENZIES.
Admitted Jan. 1901, practising at Manchester. Joined May 1916, as Private, 2/6 Batt. Cheshire Regt. and afterwards promoted Lance-Corporal. Granted Commission and posted to 1/7 Batt. Cheshire Regt. and then attached 102nd Light Trench Mortar Battery, subsequently promoted Lieut. Awarded the M.C. Served at Home and in Palestine and France.

THOMAS MILBOURN MERCER.
Articled to T. Luya, of Liverpool. Served as Trooper, King Edward's Horse.

LEONARD ARTHUR DE LACEY MEREDITH.

Admitted Aug. 1914. Of 133 Westbourne Terrace, W. Served as 2nd Lieut., 3rd Batt. Gloucestershire Regt.

BERNARD MERIVALE.

Admitted Oct. 1906. Formerly member of Nelson, Eddisons & Lupton, of Leeds. Served as 2nd Lieut., 8th (City of London) Batt. London Regt. (Post Office Rifles), promoted Capt. March 1917.

JOHN WILLIAM MERIVALE.

Admitted Oct. 1912. Of Newcastle-upon-Tyne. Mobilised Aug. 1914, as Lieut., 7th Batt. Northumberland Fusiliers, promoted Capt. 1915. Once mentioned in Dispatches. Served in France 1915 to 1916. Wounded April 1915. Killed in action Sept. 15, 1916.

EDWARD LEWIS MERRETT.

Admitted May 1915. Of 3 and 4 Lincoln's Inn Fields, W.C. Served as Lieut. (A/Capt.), Royal Army Service Corps.

LAWRENCE BRUCE MERRICK.

Admitted June 1909. Of Putney. Served with 1st Cavalry Cadet Squadron.

WILLIAM MERRICK.

Admitted May 1895. Member of Powell, Rogers & Merrick, of 17 Essex Street, Strand, W.C. Serving on Aug. 4, 1914, as Senior Major and Second in Command 6th Batt. East Surrey Regt., promoted Temp. Lieut.-Col. commanding 2/6 Batt. East Surrey Regt. Jan. 1915, promoted Substantive Lieut.-Col. June 1916. Served at Home and in France and Belgium 1916, 1917, and 1918.

MARK MARSHALL MERRIMAN.

Admitted Jan. 1903. Member of Merrimans, of 3 Mitre Court, Temple, E.C. Gazetted 2nd Lieut. Royal Flying Corps Jan. 1, 1917 (Equipment Officer), subsequently promoted Capt. (Administrative, Royal Air Force).

WALTER MERRITT.

Admitted Jan. 1907, practising at 21 St. Helen's Place, E.C. Joined Feb. 15, 1915, Inns of Court O.T.C. Gazetted Lieut. Royal Army Ordnance Corps May 25th, 1915, promoted Temp. Capt. Nov. 1918. Served in France.

FRANK MELHUISH MERSON.

Admitted July 1905, practising at 9 Essex Street, Strand, W.C. Mobilised as Sergeant, Hon. Artillery Company, Aug. 5, 1914. Gazetted 2nd Lieut. in same Regt. Aug. 26, 1914, promoted Lieut. Dec. 1914, Capt. June 1916, A/Major Oct. 1918. Awarded the M.C. Served in France Sept. 1914 to Jan. 1915, June to Sept. 1915, and May to Nov. 1916. Wounded outside Beaucourt, Battle of the Ancre, Nov. 13, 1916.

FREDERIC WILLIAM METCALFE.

Admitted Nov. 1913. Assistant Clerk in the House of Commons. Joined Aug. 15, 1914, as 2nd Lieut., The Rifle Brigade (Special Reserve), promoted Lieut. July 1915, Capt. Jan. 1917. Served in France and Belgium. Wounded in 2nd Battle of Ypres April 1915.

OSWALD KILLINGBECK METCALFE.
Admitted June 1917. Lecturer in Public and Common Law at Sheffield University. Joined Sept. 18, 1917, as Sapper, Royal Engineers Signals. Served in North Russia, Murmansk Front.

PERCY HULBERT GELDART METCALFE.
Articled to J. G. Metcalfe, of 10 New Square, Lincoln's Inn, W.C. Joined Aug. 1914, as Private, 28th Batt. County of London Regt. (Artists Rifles). Obtained Commission in Dorset Yeomanry Feb. 1915, permanent Commission 4th Dragoon Guards, Regular Army, Oct. 3, 1916. Served at Home, Mudros, and Egypt.

PERCY KYNASTON METCALFE.
Admitted Dec. 1905. Member of Gasquet, Metcalfe & Walton, of 92 Great Tower Street, E.C. Served as Lieut., Royal Army Service Corps, promoted Capt. Feb. 1917. Awarded M.B.E.

HUGH MOWBRAY MEYLER.
Admitted Feb. 1898. Member of Sheppard & Meyler, of Taunton. Joined Sept. 16, 1914, as Capt., 5th Batt. Middlesex Regt., transferred to Border Regt. Oct. 1915, and to Royal Flying Corps March 1916, promoted Major June 1917, Lieut.-Colonel Nov. 1917. Twice mentioned in Dispatches. Awarded the M.C., D.S.O., Croix de Chevalier of the Order of Leopold (Belgian) and Belgian Croix de Guerre. Served in France, Belgium, and Germany. Gassed June 1915, wounded Oct. 1917, injured in parachute descent in Belgium Sept. 1918.

FRANK LEE MICHELL.
Articled to E. Michell, of Wellington, Somerset. Joined Dec. 13, 1917, as Gunner, Royal Field Artillery. Gazetted 2nd Lieut. Royal Garrison Artillery June 24, 1918. Served in France and Germany.

HENRY THEODORE MICHELMORE.
Admitted Feb. 1913. Member of Michelmores, of Exeter. Mobilised Aug. 1914, as Capt., Royal Field Artillery (T.), promoted Major June 1916. Once mentioned in Dispatches. Awarded the M.C. and Bar. Served in India 1914 to 1916, Mesopotamia 1916 to 1917, and France 1917 to 1919. Wounded at Arras March 28, 1918.

HENRY WILLIAM MICHELMORE.
Admitted Nov. 1887. Member of Michelmores, of Exeter. Served as Commandant of a Red Cross Detachment and O.C. of a Red Cross Temporary Hospital.

JEFFERY EDWARDS MORTON MICHELMORE.
Admitted July 1905. Member of Ford, Lloyd, Bartlett & Michelmore, of 38 Bloomsbury Square, W.C. Joined Sept. 21, 1914, as 2nd Lieut., 6th Batt. East Surrey Regt., promoted Lieut. June 1915, A/Capt. March 1916. Served in France. Killed in action at Fleurbaix April 9, 1918.

WILLIAM GODWIN MICHELMORE.
Articled to H. W. Michelmore, of Exeter. Mobilised Aug. 4, 1914, as Capt., Wessex Divisional Signal Company Royal Engineers (T.F.), promoted Major March 1917. Commanding 58th Divisional Signal Coy., subsequently

Commanding 19th Divisional Signal Coy., and afterwards Commanding Lancashire Divisional Signal Coy., Army of the Rhine. Once mentioned in Dispatches. Awarded the D.S.O. and M.C. Served in France. Wounded at 3rd Battle of Ypres Oct. 24, 1917.

ALFRED MICHELSON.

Admitted Aug. 1903. Member of Hasties, of 65 Lincoln's Inn Fields, W.C. Serving at outbreak of War as Colour Sergeant Inns of Court O.T.C. Gazetted 2nd Lieut. Special List Sept. 8, 1914, and attached as Interpreter to 59th Scinde Rifles (F.F.) Indian Expeditionary Force. Attached Indian Corps Headquarters July 1915, attached to XI. Corps Headquarters, in command of Labour Corps Nov. 1915, transferred to Intelligence Corps March 1916, promoted Lieut. May 1916, attached General Staff as Garrison Intelligence Officer Chatham, with Temp. rank of Capt. Jan. 1917, rejoined Intelligence Corps Sept. 1918, substantive rank of Capt. Nov. 1918. Seconded for service under the Foreign Office with the Inter-Allied Rhineland High Commission Jan. 1920. Served at Home, France, Belgium, and Germany.

JOHN MIDDLEBROOK.

Articled to E. H. Middlebrook, of Leeds. Served as Private, 2nd West Yorkshire Field Ambulance (Reserve) Royal Army Medical Corps (T.).

KENNETH MIDDLEMISS.

Articled to C. H. Pearce, of Hull. Joined Aug. 4, 1914, as Private, East Riding Yeomanry. Gazetted as 2nd Lieut. 4th Batt. East Yorkshire Regt. Jan. 19, 1917, promoted Lieut. July 1918. Awarded the M.C. Served in Egypt Oct. 1915 to July 1916, France and Belgium Feb. 1917 to Nov. 1918. Wounded May 1917, Nov. 1917, Nov. 4, 1918.

ALAN LOMAS MIDDLETON.

Articled to Gilbert Middleton, of Leeds. Served as Lieut., 1st West Riding Brigade, Royal Field Artillery. (T.), promoted Capt. June 1916.

HENRY DUBS MIDDLETON.

Admitted Oct. 1906. Member of Middleton & Sons, of Leeds. Served as Capt., Royal Field Artillery.

JOHN LEAM MIDDLETON.

Articled to W. E. Wakerley, of Chesterfield. Joined Sept. 10, 1914, as Private, 12th Batt. York and Lancaster Regt. Gazetted 2nd Lieut. Sept. 18, 1914, promoted Lieut. Nov. 1914, Capt. July 1916, transferred to Royal Flying Corps May 1917, promoted Flight Commander No. 40 Squadron July 1918. Awarded the D.F.C. Served at Home, Egypt, France, and Salonica. Wounded at Neuve Chapelle Aug. 1916.

THOMAS ARTHUR MIDGLEY.

Admitted Sept. 1907. Member of Wilson, Lambert & Midgley, of 30 Bedford Row, W.C. Served as Private, 14th (Reserve) Batt. County of London Regt. (London Scottish).

THOMAS ALAN MILBURN.

Admitted July 1905. Member of Milburn & Co., of Workington, Cumberland. Mobilised Aug. 1914, as Major, 5th Batt. Border Regt., and subsequently promoted to Lieut.-Colonel. Once mentioned in Dispatches. Awarded O.B.E. and T.D. Served in France and Belgium Oct. 1914 to Aug. 1915 and at Home Aug. 1915 to May 1919.

WILLIAM MARTIN MILBURN.

Admitted May 1908. Member of R. Milburn & Son, of Brampton, Cumberland. Joined Nov. 1915, as Corporal Dispatch Rider, Royal Engineers (Signal Service). Served at Home, and in Mesopotamia and India 1916 to 1919. Once wounded.

EDGAR CHARLES MILEHAM.

Admitted March 1902. Member of Rooper & Whateley, of 17 Lincoln's Inn Fields, W.C. Served as Lieut., Royal Garrison Artillery.

ALFRED CROSFIELD VERNOR MILES.

Articled to E. Vernor Miles, of 30 Theobald's Road, Bedford Row, W.C. Joined Aug. 1914, as Private, 28th Batt. County of London Regt. (Artists Rifles). Gazetted 2nd Lieut. 2nd Batt. The Welch Regt. April 1915. Served in France Oct. 1914 to Aug. 1915. Killed in action near Cambrin Aug. 24, 1915.

FREDERICK STUART MILES.

Articled to A. S. Miles, of Tenbury. Joined June 27, 1916, as 2nd Air-Mechanic, Royal Flying Corps, promoted 1st Air-Mechanic Dec. 1916, Corporal June 1917, Sergeant March 1918. Served in France 2½ years.

EDGAR MILLAR.

Admitted Oct. 1904. Member of W. R. Millar & Sons, of 22 St. Thomas Street, London Bridge, S.E. Joined Jan. 1917, as Private, Royal Fusiliers, appointed Acting Paymaster to Royal Horse and Royal Field Artillery (T.) Nov. 1917. Served at Home.

WILLIAM MILLAR.

Articled to W. R. Millar, jun., of 22 St. Thomas Street, London Bridge, S.E. Joined Sept. 12, 1914, as Private, 2/1 Batt. City of London Regt. (Royal Fusiliers) (T.) transferred to Heavy Branch Machine Gun Corps (Tank Corps) March 1917. Appointed A/Lance-Corporal on being appointed Machine Gun Instructor Oct. 1918. Served at Malta Feb. to Aug. 1915, Gallipoli Sept. to Dec. 1915, Egypt Jan. to April 1916, France April to July 1916 and May 1917 to March 1918. Wounded at Maricourt (Somme) March 25, 1918.

HAROLD LEWIS HOLLAND MILLARD.

Admitted June 1900. Member of Donaldson & Birkinshaw, of Singapore, Straits Settlements. Left Singapore in Nov. 1914 and appointed Capt. 7th Batt. Northamptonshire Regt. Sent to Gallipoli May 1915 and attached to 1st Batt. Border Regt. Promoted Major Oct 28, 1916. Once mentioned in Dispatches. Served at Home and in Gallipoli, Egypt, and France. Killed near Bethune April 12, 1917.

WILLIAM KELSON JAMES MILLARD.

Admitted Sept. 1915. Of Cheltenham. Served as 2nd Lieut., 7th Batt. Gloucestershire Regt.

ARTHUR EDWARD MILLER.

Admitted Feb. 1913. Clerk with Dickinson, Miller & Turnbull. Joined Aug. 9, 1914, as Dispatch Rider, Tyne Garrison Headquarters Staff. Gazetted 2nd Lieut. Tynemouth Royal Garrison Artillery March 14, 1915, promoted Lieut. June 1916, A/Capt. March 1918. Served in Macedonia and at Home.

ARTHUR HUGH LIDDELL MILLER.

Admitted Nov. 1908. Managing Clerk with Shaen, Roscoe, Massey & Co., of 6–8 Ludgate Hill, E.C. Joined March 2, 1916, as Private, Royal Fusiliers. Served at Home.

ARTHUR JOHN MILLER.

Articled to A. J. M. Duncan, of 21 Leadenhall Street, E.C. Joined June 28, 1917, as Private, Royal Army Service Corps (Remounts). Served at Home. Discharged physically unfit Nov. 6, 1917.

HENRY WILLIAM MILLER.

Admitted Feb. 1893. Of Ipswich. Served as Major, 3rd East Anglian Brigade Royal Field Artillery.

JOHN ERIC HALL MILLER.

Articled to R. T. Guthrie, of Blyth, Northumberland. Joined Durham University O.T.C. as a Cadet Dec. 1914. Gazetted as 2nd Lieut. 1st Batt. Northumberland Fusiliers May 3, 1915. Served at Home and in Flanders. Killed at Ypres Jan. 11, 1916.

MATTHEW ROWLATT MILLER.

Admitted Jan. 1914. Of Southsea. Served as Capt., 6th Batt. Hampshire Regt. (T.).

REGINALD TAVERNER MILLER.

Articled to T. B. Miller, of 12 Savile Row, W. Served as 2nd Lieut., Manchester Regt., and subsequently promoted Capt. Mentioned in Dispatches.

THOMAS PEACOCK MILLER.

Admitted May 1914, practised at Newcastle-upon-Tyne as one of the staff of Thomas Gee & Co. Served as Lieut., Lancashire Fusiliers. Killed in action in France March 27, 1918.

GEORGE MILLHOUSE.

Articled to G. B. Black, of Scarborough. Joined May 12, 1915, as 2nd Lieut., Yorkshire Regt., promoted Lieut. May 1917. Served at Home May 1915 to April 1916 and Sept. 1918 to April 1919, France and Belgium April 1916 to Nov. 1917, Italy Nov. 1917 to Sept. 1918. Wounded in Contalmaison on Somme July 30, 1916.

GEORGE HOGG MILLONS.

Admitted March 1895. Member of Millons & Newcombe, of Newcastle-upon-Tyne. Joined Dec. 18, 1914, as Lieut., 5th Batt. Northumberland Fusiliers, transferred to Royal Defence Corps April 1916, promoted Capt. Nov. 3, 1916, transferred T.F. Reserve (General List) Oct. 1919. Served at Home.

FRANCIS RICHARD MILLS.

Admitted Oct. 1904. Of 91A Linden Garden, W. Joined Oct. 19, 1914, as Private, 21st Batt. Royal Fusiliers, promoted Sergeant March 1915. Gazetted

2nd Lieut. Nov. 1916 in same Regt., promoted Lieut. May 1918. Served in France 1915 to 1919. Wounded at Cambrin Jan. 15, 1916.

GEORGE HERBERT MILLS.

Articled to J. M. B. Turner, of Bournemouth. Joined Dec. 1, 1916, as Private, Coldstream Guards, promoted Lance-Corporal April 1917. Served in France and Belgium July 1917 to Nov. 1918, and with Army of Occupation Dec. 1918 to Feb. 1919.

KENNETH LE GAI MILLS.

Articled to D. R. Locking, of Hull. Joined Oct. 21, 1915, as Private, 28th Batt. County of London Regt. (Artists Rifles). Gazetted 2nd Lieut. Royal Flying Corps Feb. 4, 1917. Served at Home and in France. Killed in France Nov. 11, 1917.

THOMAS PIERCY MILLS.

Admitted April 1908. Member of Rider, Heaton, Meredith & Mills, of 8 New Square, Lincoln's Inn, W.C. Served as Capt., 1st (City of London) Batt. Royal Fusiliers.

ALEXANDER NICOL MILNE.

Admitted Feb. 1910. Managing Clerk with Taylor, Kirkman & Co., of Manchester. Joined Aug. 1914, as Private, 6th Batt. Manchester Regt. Gazetted 2nd Lieut. in same Regt. April 1915, promoted Capt. Aug. 1915. Once mentioned in Dispatches. Served in Gallipoli. Killed in Gallipoli Aug. 7, 1915.

DAVID BARRETT MILNE.

Admitted July 1900. Member of Rivers & Milne, of 88 Gracechurch Street, E.C. Joined June 1916, as Hon. Lieut., Army Canteen Committee. Gazetted 2nd Lieut. Royal Army Service Corps March 1917, commanding 405th Siege Battery (R.G.A.) Ammunition Column, transferred to No. 19 Ammunition Sub-Park Oct. 1917, promoted Lieut. Sept. 1918. Served at Home June 1916 to March 1917, and in France March 1917 to Feb. 1919.

RALPH KNOWLES MILNE.

Admitted Nov. 1904. Member of Edwin Berry & Co., of Liverpool. Joined Aug. 4, 1914, as Sapper, West Lancashire Divisional Signal Company Royal Engineers, commissioned in same Regt. Sept. 4, 1915, promoted A/Capt. March 1918. Once mentioned in Dispatches. Awarded the M.C. Served in France July 1916 to June 1919. Wounded June 1917, March 1918.

THOMAS BAXTER MILNE.

Admitted Aug. 1909. Assistant Solicitor Corporation of Brighton. Mobilised Aug. 4, 1914, as Private, 14th Batt. County of London Regt. (London Scottish). Commissioned 2nd Lieut. Royal Field Artillery (T.) Jan. 25, 1915, promoted Lieut. July 1916, appointed Temp. Capt. June 1915, Temp. Major May 1916, reverted to A/Capt. March 1917, appointed A/Major June to July 1918, and afterwards A/Capt. Once mentioned in Dispatches. Awarded Belgian Croix de Guerre. Served in France 1914, 1916, and 1917 to 1919. Wounded Nov. 2, 1914.

JAMES MILNER.

Admitted Jan. 1911. Member of J. H. Milner & Son, of Leeds. Mobilised Aug. 1914, as Capt. and Adjutant, West Riding Division Royal Army Service Corps, also served as Capt. 2nd Batt. Devonshire Regt. Once mentioned in Dispatches. Awarded M.C. Served at Home Aug. 1914 to April 1915 and Dec. 1918 to Nov. 1919, and in France April 1915 to Dec. 1918. Wounded and taken prisoner at Chemin des Dames May 27, 1918.

HAROLD AUBREY MILTON.

Admitted Dec. 1907, practising at 9 Staple Inn, W.C. Joined Aug. 17, 1914, Public Schools O.T.C. Gazetted 2nd Lieut. 21st Batt. London Regt. Sept. 23, 1914, promoted Lieut. May 1915, Capt. Nov. 1915, transferred to 2/23 Batt. London Regt., A/Major Oct. 1918, A/Lieut.-Col. Nov. 1918. Twice mentioned in Dispatches. Awarded the M.C. and Croix de Guerre (French). Served in France May to Nov. 1916 and May 1918 to Nov. 1919. Salonica Nov. 1916 to June 1917, and Palestine June 1917 to May 1918.

JAMES CLYMO MILTON.

Admitted April 1895, practising at Chorley, Lancs. Rejoined Sept. 1914, as Capt., East Lancashire Regt., promoted Major Jan. 15, 1915, appointed Instructor on Staff, No. 3 Officer Cadet Batt. Aug. 1916, subsequently employed at War Office and appointed General Staff Officer A.G. 3 (L.). Mentioned for valuable services during this War. Awarded the M.B.E. Served at Home 1914 to 1915, Egypt and Sinai Peninsula 1916, and France 1916. Invalided Home June 7, 1916.

THOMAS ST. MICHAEL MILTON.

Admitted Sept. 1905. Member of J. P. & T. St. M. Milton, of Penzance. Joined July 1917, as Private, Royal Army Ordnance Corps. Gazetted 2nd Lieut. Devonshire Regt. Aug. 1918 and attached 6th Batt. Dorsetshire Regt. Served at Home and in France. Wounded at Poix-du-Nord, France, Oct. 28, 1918.

ROLAND MINOR.

Articled to H. W. Minor, of Manchester. Joined Sept. 1914, as Private, Public Schools Batt. Gazetted 2nd Lieut. King's Own Royal Lancaster Regt. May 26, 1915. Served at Home and France. Killed in Somme offensive July 1, 1916.

THOMAS CHARLES WYNNE MINSHALL.

Admitted July 1913. Member of Minshall, Parry-Jones & Pugh, of Oswestry. Mobilised Aug. 1914 with 4th Batt. Royal Welch Fusiliers (T.) and attained the rank of Capt. Served in France. Killed in action near Contalmaison March 25, 1918.

GEORGE BOTTERELL MINSHULL.

Articled to L. A. Blackmore, of Ilfracombe. Joined Feb. 8, 1918, as Private, Devonshire Regt., transferred to Royal Air Force Cadet Corps Oct. 1918, remained until the Cadet Schools were disbanded in Dec. 1918, when returned to original unit. Served at Home.

FRANK MISKIN.

Admitted Dec. 1911. Member of Bracher & Son, of Maidstone. Joined Jan. 1915, as Private, Inns of Court O.T.C. Gazetted 2nd Lieut. 9th Batt. Royal West Kent Regt. Feb. 1915, Capt. 22nd Batt. Middlesex Regt. Nov. 1915, Capt. 12th Batt. Suffolk Regt. April 1916, Major 12th Batt. Suffolk Regt. Aug. 1917, Lieut.-Col. 13th Batt. Yorkshire Regt. March 1918. Awarded the M.C. Served in France.

ALBERT JEFFERY MITCHELL.

Admitted May 1907, practising at 35 Lincoln's Inn Fields, W.C. Served as Private, Hon. Artillery Company.

EDMUND BASCOMBE MITCHELL.

Admitted Nov. 1902. Member of Mitchell, Lucas & Mitchell, of 4 Romford Road, Stratford, E. Joined May 1916 as Gunner. Served in France and Belgium. Injured Aug. 1916.

ERNEST HARRY MITCHELL.

Admitted Dec. 1906, practised at 85 The Grove, Stratford, E. Served as Corporal, 5th (City of London) Batt. London Regt. (London Rifle Brigade). Gazetted 2nd Lieut. Royal Army Service Corps, promoted Capt. June 1917. Mentioned in Dispatches.

GEORGE MITCHELL.

Admitted July 1910. Practised at Halifax. Joined Jan. 1915 as Private, Queen's Own Yorkshire Dragoons, drafted to 2nd Batt. Duke of Cornwall's Light Infantry Sept. 1916 and sent to Salonica. Killed Sept. 13, 1918. Buried at the Karasouli Military Cemetery, Greece.

HAROLD CHARLES BARNES MITCHELL.

Admitted Dec. 1908. Of Bombay. Served as Capt. 1st Batt. Hertfordshire Regt., attached to Bombay Volunteer Rifles, promoted Major June 1916.

ROBERT MOGER.

Admitted Sept. 1905. Assistant Solicitor to the Bath Corporation. Mobilised Aug. 4, 1914, as Capt., 4th Batt. Somersetshire Light Infantry. Served in India Nov. 1914 to Jan. 1916, and in Mesopotamia Jan. to April 1916. Wounded at Beib Aisha April 1916. Invalided out Oct. 1917.

WILLIAM MOGER.

Admitted Nov. 1911. Member of F H. & R. A. Moger, of Bath. Mobilised Aug. 1914, as Lieut., 4th Batt. Somersetshire Light Infantry, promoted Capt. June 1916 and attached 1st Batt. The Yorkshire Regt. Served in Mesopotamia 1916, India 1914, 1915, 1917, and 1918, and Afghanistan 1919.

SCOTT TREVOR MOILLIETT.

Articled to T. W. Williams, of Bristol. Served as 2nd Lieut., 2nd Batt. The Welch Regt.

GERALD CHAMBERLAIN MOLE.

Admitted April 1914. Managing Clerk with Mole, Rosling & Vernon, of Reigate, Surrey. Joined Sept. 16, 1914, as Private, 16th Batt. Middlesex

Regt. Commissioned as 2nd Lieut. 3rd Batt. Royal Sussex Regt. June 1915, attached to 9th Batt., promoted Lieut. July 1917, attached to 3rd Corps School Dec. 1917. Served in France June 1916 to Dec. 1918.

FRANCIS GUY MONCKTON.

Articled to H. Monckton, of Maidstone. Joined Sept. 30, 1914, as 2nd Lieut., Royal Army Service Corps (T.). Seconded to Tank Corps as Capt. Jan. 1917. Served in France.

GEORGE CHESTER TANCRED MONEY.

Admitted Dec. 1910. Member of Hunt & Money, of 24 Haymarket, S.W. Joined March 1, 1915, as 2nd Lieut., Royal Army Service Corps, promoted Lieut. 1916, Capt. 1918. Once mentioned in Dispatches. Served in France.

RANDALL HERBERT MONIER-WILLIAMS.

Articled to M. F. Monier-Williams, of 6 & 7 Great Tower Street, E.C. Joined Aug. 10, 1914, as Private, 5th Batt. East Surrey Regt. Injured while in training. Invalided out June 30, 1915. Employed M.I.I.C. War Office June 1915 to April 1919. Commissioned Lieut. Royal Naval Volunteer Reserve April 1917. Served at Home and in United States.

GEORGE EDWARD MONKLAND.

Articled to F. G. Monkland, of 1 Frederick's Place, E.C. Joined Nov. 1914 as 2nd Lieut., 2/7 Batt. Black Watch (R.H.), promoted Lieut. May 1915, with 1/7 Batt. from Jan. 1917. Served in France. Wounded at the Chemical Works at Roeux, near Arras, April 23, 1917. Discharged May 1918.

CHARLES PHETHEAN MONKS.

Admitted April 1912. Member of J. Phethean, of Monks & Co., of Bolton. Joined Oct. 1914, as 2nd Lieut., Royal Field Artillery, promoted Lieut. Nov. 1914. Served in France Jan. to June 1915. Killed in action at Hooge June 1915.

FREDERIC ROBERT D'OYLEY MONRO.

Admitted Nov. 1902. Member of Monro, Law & Co., of 70 Queen Street, E.C. Joined May 1916 as Cadet. Gazetted 2nd Lieut. Royal Garrison Artillery Aug. 11, 1916, promoted Lieut. Feb. 1918. Served in France Jan. 1917 to Dec. 1918.

RICHARD HEADLEY MONTAGU.

Admitted July 1907. Member of Montagu, Mileham & Montagu, of 5 and 6 Bucklersbury, E.C. Gazetted 2nd Lieut. Isle of Wight Rifles (Princess Beatrice's Batt.) Hampshire Regt. Jan. 1915, promoted Lieut. a few months later, and became Bombing Instructor, gave that appointment up to go to France. Served in Flanders. Killed by a bomb on Sept. 21, 1917. Buried the next day near Bodmin Copse.

GEORGE ALBERT BANNERMAN MONTAGUE.

Admitted July 1910. Member of Latchams & Montague, of Bristol. Joined Aug. 20, 1914, as Private, 1/6 Batt. Gloucestershire Regt., and attained the rank of Sergeant. Gazetted 2nd Lieut. Feb. 1916. Served in France March 1915 to July 1916. Wounded July 6, 1916. Discharged in consequence of wounds April 3, 1917.

HASTINGS SETON MONTGOMERIE.

Admitted Aug. 1897, practising at 1 South Square, Gray's Inn, W.C. Mobilised Aug. 1914, as Major, 9th Batt. Middlesex Regt. Served in India and Salonica.

PERCY ALFRED MOODIE.

Admitted Dec. 1906. Member of Moodie & Sons, of 2 Basinghall Avenue, E.C. Joined Aug. 1914, as Private, 14th Batt. County of London Regt. (London Scottish). Gazetted Lieut. in Royal Fusiliers Jan. 1915, transferred to Royal Flying Corps Dec. 1915, promoted Flight Commander Feb. 1917, Staff Capt. Feb. 1919. Served at Home during 1916 and in France.

CHARLES SYDNEY MOORE.

Admitted April 1910, practising at St. Leonard's-on-Sea. Joined Jan. 15, 1918, as 2nd Lieut. (Inland Waterways and Docks) Royal Engineers, and later transferred to 3rd Batt. Essex Regt. Served in France and with the Army of Occupation in Germany.

DONALD GWYTHER MOORE.

Admitted Jan. 1913 of Plymouth. Served as Cadet, O.T.C.

EDWARD DUKE MOORE.

Admitted Oct. 1904, practising at 7 King Street, Cheapside, E.C. Mobilised Aug. 1914, as Capt., Inns of Court O.T.C. (T.), transferred as Capt. to East Riding Yeomanry Oct. 1914, promoted Temp. Major April 1915, Major June 1916, Temp. Lient.-Col. Dec. 1917, subsequently appointed 2nd in Command as Major of 102nd (Lincoln and East Riding Yeomanry) Batt. Machine Gun Corps. Twice mentioned in Dispatches. Awarded D.S.O. and T.D. Served at Home until Oct. 1915, Egypt and Palestine Oct. 1915 to May 1918, and France May 1918 to March 1919.

EDWARD HAYDEN MOORE.

Articled to Robert Brown, of Newcastle-upon-Tyne. Joined Aug. 1914, as 2nd Lieut., York and Lancaster Regt. Went to France 1915. Wounded and mentioned in Dispatches. Promoted Capt. 1916. Awarded the M.C. Died of wounds April 25, 1917.

GEORGE WILLIAM MOORE.

Articled to C. J. Band, of Coventry. Joined Nov. 1914, as 2nd Lieut., 13th Batt. Royal Warwickshire Regt, promoted Lieut. Feb. 1915 and transferred to 9th Batt. Served in Gallipoli (Suvla Bay) Sept. to Dec. 1915. Wounded (frostbite, lost right leg and part of left foot, Dec. 4, 1916).

HUGH STIRLING MOORE.

Admitted Oct. 1914. Of Nottingham. Joined Oct. 1914, as Private, Royal Fusiliers (Public Schools Batt.). Gazetted 2nd Lieut. Notts and Derby Regt. Aug. 1, 1916, and attached to Leicestershire Regt. Twice mentioned in Dispatches. Served in France. Killed in action at Polygon Wood Oct. 1, 1917.

JOHN MOORE.

Articled to H. D. Bateson, of Liverpool. Served as Private, 10th Batt. King's Liverpool Regt. (Liverpool Scottish) (T.).

LEONARD WILLIAM MOORE.

Admitted April 1902. Member of Clutton & Moore, of Bristol. Joined June 16, 1916, as Private, 1st (Garrison) Batt. Worcestershire Regt. Gazetted 2nd Lieut. Royal Army Ordnance Corps March 15, 1917, promoted Lieut. June 15, 1917. Served at Home June to Sept. 1916, and in France Sept. 1916 to April 1919.

MAURICE MOORE.

Admitted Feb. 1890, practising at Sunderland. Joined Aug. 1914, as Capt., Northern Cyclist Batt., C.O. Divisional Cyclist Companies, subsequently Lieut.-Col. 2/4 Batt. Northumberland Fusiliers. Twice mentioned in Dispatches. Served at Home.

ROBERT BROWN MOORE.

Articled to J. B. Paynter, of Yeovil. Joined Sept. 22, 1914, as 2nd Lieut., 5th Batt. Somerset Light Infantry. Promoted Capt. Oct. 1917. Served in India 1914 to 1917, and in Palestine April 1917 to Jan. 1919.

STANLEY SPENCER MOORE.

Admitted Dec. 1909, practising at 6 Finsbury Square, E.C. Mobilised Aug. 4, 1914, as Private, Hong Kong Defence Corps, and subsequently served as Volunteer Ambulance Driver with the French Army, transferred to 28th Batt. County of London Regt. (Artists Rifles) July 1918, and to Royal Air Force Sept. 1918. Served in Hong Kong and France.

THOMAS MOORE.

Admitted Feb. 1914. Member of Moore & Sons, of Yeovil. Joined Sept. 16, 1914, as 2nd Lieut., 1/5 Batt. Somerset Light Infantry, promoted Lieut. Feb. 1916, Capt. June 1917. Served in India Oct. 1914 to April 1917, and in Egypt and Palestine April 1917 to June 1919. Wounded in attack and taking of Rafa Village April 9, 1918.

THOMAS ERIC LYNDON MOORE.

Articled to A. A. Newman, of Newport, Mon. Mobilised Aug. 1914, as Lieut., 4th Welsh Brigade Royal Field Artillery, promoted Capt. 1916. Served in Egypt and Palestine.

TOM MOORE.

Articled to George Baron, of Bacup. Joined Dec. 2, 1915, as Private, Royal Fusiliers. Appointed Lance-Corporal July 1918, Corporal Jan. 1919. Served at Home to Aug. 1916 and Dec. 1917 to Feb. 1919, and in France Aug. 1916 to Dec. 1917.

JOHN MOORE-BAYLEY.

Admitted Sept. 1907. Member of Moore-Bayley & Co., of Birmingham. Joined April 2, 1917, as Private, Inns of Court O.T.C. Served at Home.

GRAHAM MOORE-WILLIAMS.

Admitted Dec. 1907. Solicitor on the Staff of the Ministry of Munitions. Joined Aug. 18, 1914, as Private, Public Schools Batt. (Middlesex Regt.). Gazetted 2nd Lieut. 3rd Batt. The King's Own Royal Lancaster Regt. (Special Reserve) Feb. 22, 1915, promoted Lieut. July 1916, Capt. 1917. Served in

France 1915 and 1916. Wounded at Battle of Loos Sept. 28, 1915, and twice at Battle of Serre Nov. 13, 1916.

ROWLAND EDWARD MOORHOUSE.

Articled to E. P. Moorhouse, of 14 Bedford Street, Covent Garden, W.C. Joined University of London O.T.C., Sept. 1916, appointed to No. 20 O.C. Batt., Crookham, June 1917. Gazetted 2nd Lieut. 9th Batt. Middlesex Regt. Sept. 22, 1917, and subsequently attached 23rd (Service) Batt. Served in Italy Dec. 1917 to Feb. 1918, in France Feb. and March 1918, and in Belgium April 1918. Reported missing, believed killed, April 1918, and subsequently reported killed near Weiltje, Ypres, April 19, 1918.

WILLIAM MILES MORANT.

Admitted Oct. 1913. Solicitor on staff of Sir Charles W. Matthews, K.C.B., etc., Director of Public Prosecutions, Whitehall, S.W. Joined 1914, as 2nd Lieut., 7th Batt. Durham Light Infantry, promoted Capt. Nov. 1915. Served in France. Killed in action at Merville, France, April 11, 1918.

PERCIVAL JOHN HOSKING MORCOM.

Articled to John Shelly, of Plymouth. Joined Dec. 1915, as 2nd Lieut., Duke of Cornwall's Light Infantry, promoted Lieut. June 1917. Served in France Aug. 1916 to April 1918. Killed at Merville April 11, 1918.

ADRIAN CHARLES MOREING.

Articled to J. B. Birkbeck, of 20 Copthall Avenue, E.C. Mobilised Aug. 1914, as Lieut., 3rd Batt. London Regt., promoted Temp. Capt. April 1915, Capt. June 1916, seconded for duty as Law Officer attached to Headquarters Southern Command Nov. 1916. Served at Home Aug. 1914 and May 1915 to Nov. 1918, Malta Sept. to Dec. 1914, and in France Jan. to May 1915.

RAYMOND LAURENCE MORETON.

Admitted April 1910, practising at 12 Serjeant's Inn, Temple, E.C. Joined March 5, 1915, as Private, Inns of Court, O.T.C. Gazetted 2nd Lieut. 11th Batt. London Regt. (Finsbury Rifles) May 15, 1915. Served at Home March to Sept. 1915, Gallipoli Oct. to Dec. 1915, and Egypt Dec. 1915 to March 1916. Invalided out May 11, 1916.

ARNOLD JOHN MORGAN.

Admitted Sept. 1912. Member of James Morgan & Co., of Cardiff. Served in Motor Cycle Corps, Royal Engineers.

ARTHUR CROKE MORGAN.

Admitted Nov. 1903. Member of Park, Nelson & Co., of 11 Essex Street, Strand. Joined May 1916 as Cadet. Gazetted 2nd Lieut. Royal Garrison Artillery July 7, 1916, promoted Lieut. Jan. 1918. Served at Home.

CHARLES CAREY MORGAN.

Admitted Oct. 1910. Of 33 Old Broad Street, E.C. Served as Capt., 337th Siege Battery Royal Garrison Artillery.

CYRIL FRANK MORGAN.

Admitted May 1908. Member of Foyster, Waddington & Morgan, of Manchester. Joined Dec. 18, 1915, as 2nd Lieut., Royal Field Artillery, promoted Lieut. July 1917, A/Capt. March 1918, Capt. and Adjutant Dec. 1918. Awarded the M.C. Served in Belgium and France 1916 to 1919.

DANIEL OWEN MORGAN.

Articled to John Evans, of Llandyssul. Served as Private, No. 2 Coy., The Welch Regt.

DAVID HUGHES MORGAN.

Admitted Nov. 1899. Of Penally, South Wales. Rejoined Aug. 1914, as Capt., South Wales Borderers, and subsequently promoted Major. Received the honour of Knighthood. Served at Home as Commandant of Musketry Camp, Penally, Pembrokeshire.

EDWARD LESLIE MORGAN.

Articled to S. H. Jarvis, of Newtown, North Wales. Joined as Private, Inns of Court O.T.C. Gazetted 2nd Lieut. Special Reserve of Officers Oct. 28, 1916, posted to Royal Field Artillery. Served in France May to Nov. 1917. Died of gas poisoning in Belgium Nov. 9, 1917.

EDWARD STANLEY PARKER MORGAN.

Admitted April 1915. Member of Taylor, Willcocks & Co., 240 Lavender Hill, S.W.; and 218 Strand, W.C. Joined Nov. 9, 1914, as Private, 2/3 Wessex Field Ambulance. Subsequently gazetted 2nd Lieut. Royal Garrison Artillery. Served in France Dec. 1916 to July 1918.

EVAN BERNARD MORGAN.

Articled to O. W. Owen, of Liverpool. Joined Oct. 1914, as Prob. Flight Sub-Lieut., Royal Naval Air Service. Gazetted 2nd Lieut. 5th Batt. Cheshire Regt. (T.) Jan. 1915, promoted Lieut. Royal Engineers (T.) March 1918. Served in France March to Aug. 1915 and April to Aug. 1916, and in Palestine May to Nov. 1917. Wounded July 1918.

GEORGE BERNARD MORGAN.

Articled to A. W. Heaton, of Birmingham. Served as 2nd Lieut., Royal Field Artillery, promoted Lieut. Oct. 1916.

GEORGE ELTON MORGAN.

Admitted Aug. 1911, practised at Wrexham. Joined Jan. 1916, as Private, Royal Welch Fusiliers. Gazetted 2nd Lieut. The Welch Regt. May 1917. Served in France and Belgium. Killed in action near Langemarck Aug. 15, 1917.

HENRY ROBERT MORGAN.

Admitted July 1890, practising at King's Lynn. Mobilised as Major, 5th Batt. Norfolk Regt. Served for first 2 years of War.

HUGH PENRITH MORGAN.

Articled to G. H. Morgan, of Shrewsbury. Mobilised Aug. 5, 1914, as 2nd Lieut., 1/1 Shropshire Royal Horse Artillery, promoted Lieut. Oct. 1914, Capt. June 1916, A/Major 28th Battery Royal Field Artillery Nov. 1918. Awarded the M.C. Served in France and Belgium.

ISAAC DAVID MORGAN.

Admitted May 1910, practising at Aberdare. Served as Private, E Coy., 1st Labour Batt.

JOHN RHYS MORGAN.

Admitted Sept. 1907, practising at Maesteg, Glamorganshire. Joined April 11th, 1917, as Private, King's Shropshire Light Infantry, transferred to Army Pay Corps June 1917, promoted Corporal April 1918. Served at Home.

JOHN WALTER REES MORGAN.

Articled to L. R. Morgan, of Neath. Joined Oct. 8, 1914, as Private, 1st Sportsman's Batt. Royal Fusiliers. Gazetted 2nd Lieut. 4th Batt. Royal Dublin Fusiliers April 1915. Served in France July 1915 to July 1916. Killed at Beaumont Hamel July 1, 1916.

LLEWELLYN REES MORGAN.

Admitted May 1908, practising at Neath. Joined May 1, 1918, as Private, 2/28 Batt. County of London Regt. (Artists Rifles). Served at Home.

OSCAR TREHARNE MORGAN.

Admitted April 1903. Deputy Town Clerk, Newport, Mon. Joined June 1915, as 2nd Lieut. and subsequently promoted Lieut. Served at Home. Resigned Oct. 1917.

OWEN MORGAN.

Admitted March 1910. Member of Samuel Wright, Morgan & Co., of Bradford and Shipley. Joined Sept. 21, 1914, as Private, 16th (Service) Batt. West Yorkshire Regt. Gazetted Temp. Lieut. in same Regt. Sept. 23, 1914. Served in Egypt Dec. 1915 to March 1916, and in France March to June 1916. Wounded June 10, 1916. Invalided out Nov. 1916.

THOMAS EYTON MORGAN.

Articled to Hugh Hughes, of Aberystwyth. Joined Nov. 1915, as Gunner, Royal Horse and Royal Field Artillery. Gazetted 2nd Lieut. Royal Garrison Artillery July 7, 1916, promoted Lieut. Jan. 1918. Served at Home owing to injury contracted on Service.

THOMAS HENRY MORGAN.

Admitted Nov. 1900. Member of T. H. Morgan & Co., of Colwyn Bay. Joined Dec. 1, 1914, as Capt. and Adjutant, 10th Service Batt. South Wales Borderers, promoted Major June 1915, A/Lieut.-Col. commanding 11th South Wales Borderers Oct. 1917. Twice mentioned in Dispatches. Awarded the O.B.E. (Military Division). Served in France and Belgium.

WILLIAM MORGAN.

Admitted Dec. 1904. Member of Samuel Wright, Morgan & Co., of Bradford and Shipley. Joined May 1916, as Private, Army Cyclist Corps. Gazetted Temp. 2nd Lieut. West Yorkshire Regt., and Temp. 2nd Lieut. Machine Gun Corps. Served in France 1917 to 1918. Died of wounds July 23, 1918.

DAVID MORLEY.

Articled to J. W. Mills, of Beverley. Joined Dec. 16, 1914, as Private, Argyll and Sutherland Highlanders, and subsequently promoted Corporal. Gazetted 2nd Lieut. 4th Batt. East Yorkshire Regt., and attached to 13th Batt. Dec. 1916. Served in France, Salonica, and France. Killed June 16, 1917.

FREDERICK BRYAN MORLEY.

Articled to H. V. Vaughan, of Builth Wells, Breconshire. Joined Nov. 8, 1915, as Rifleman, 9th Batt. County of London Regt. (Queen Victoria's Rifles). Gazetted 2nd Lieut. 5th Batt. King's Royal Rifle Corps Oct. 26, 1916, promoted A/Capt. 9th Batt. Sept. 1917, Substantive Capt. Oct. 1918. Served in France. Gassed at Polderhoek Chateau Oct. 1917.

JOHN ALFRED MORLEY.

Admitted Jan. 1909. Member of Pierron & Morley, of Hammersmith Road, W. Joined July 10, 1916, as Private, 28th Batt. County of London Regt. (Artists Rifles). Gazetted 2nd Lieut. Royal Army Ordnance Corps Jan. 1917, promoted Lieut. April 1917. Served at Home.

RICHARD JAMES MORLEY.

Articled to James Morley, of 38 Lincoln's Inn Fields, W.C. Served as 2nd Lieut., Machine Gun Corps.

GEOFFREY WILMOT MORRICE.

Admitted Feb. 1911. Of 3 and 4 Clement's Inn, W.C. Served as 2nd Lieut., Wessex Divisional Train, Royal Army Service Corps, promoted Lieut. July 1917. Mentioned in Dispatches.

ARCHIBALD JAMES MORRIS.

Articled to E. H. W. Holt, of 9 Mincing Lane, E.C. Joined Sept. 1914, as Private, 14th Batt. County of London Regt. (London Scottish), and attained the rank of Sergeant. Served in France March 1915 to June 1916. Killed at Hebuterne, France, June 15, 1916.

ARCHIBALD JOHN MORRIS.

Admitted Dec. 1913. Managing Clerk with Lewis C. Thomas, of Neath. Joined Dec. 1915, as Private, Royal Welch Fusiliers, promoted Lance-Corporal April 1916, Sergeant Oct. 1916. Gazetted 2nd Lieut. South Wales Borderers May 1917, promoted Lieut. Nov. 1918, and subsequently A/Capt. Once mentioned in Dispatches. Awarded the M.B.E. (Military Division). Served in Belgium and France 1916 to 1917, and in Salonica 1917 to 1919.

CHARLES EDMUND MORRIS.

Admitted Nov. 1914. Of Milford Haven. Served as 2nd Lieut., Pembrokeshire Royal Garrison Artillery (T.), and subsequently attained the rank of Major. Mentioned in Dispatches.

FREDERICK MORRIS.

Articled to William Morris, of 17 Throgmorton Avenue, E.C. Joined Oct. 21, 1914, as 2nd Lieut., Scottish Horse, and attached to South Notts Hussars. Subsequently promoted to Lieut. Served at Suvla Bay, Egypt, and Salonica, Drowned by the torpedoing of the transport *Leasowe Castle* May 27, 1918.

GEORGE PARKER MORRIS.

Articled to L. C. Evans, of Salford. Joined Aug. 12, 1914, as 2nd Lieut., 16th Batt. Manchester Regt., promoted Lieut. Jan. 1915, transferred to Machine Gun Corps Nov. 1916, promoted Capt. Nov. 1917, Major May 1918. Served at Home and in France. Wounded July 1, 1916.

HAROLD SPENCER MORRIS.
Admitted June 1910. Member of J. F. Morris & Son, of Carmarthen. Served as Lieut., 15th (Service) Batt. The Welch Regt.

HARRY MORRIS.
Articled to R. F. Payne, of Sheffield. Served as Private, Sheffield Batt. York and Lancaster Regt.

HENRY MATTHEW MORRIS.
Articled to T. R. Thompson, of Cardiff. Joined Aug. 15, 1914, as 2nd Lieut., 4th Batt. Manchester Regt., promoted Lieut. June 1915, Capt. Jan. 1917, attached 2nd Manchester Regt. May 1915 to Nov. 1916, Staff Capt. 14th Infantry Brigade Nov. 1916 to March 1917. Served in France May 1915 to March 1917, and in India April 1917 to Jan. 1918.

HOWARD MORRIS.
Admitted Feb. 1907, practising at 52 Bedford Row, W.C. Joined July 26, 1915, as 2nd Lieut., Royal Army Service Corps, promoted Lieut. March 1916, Capt. May 1918. Once mentioned in Dispatches. Awarded the M.C. Served in France Aug. 1915 to Nov. 1919.

HUMPHREY WILLIAM MORRIS.
Admitted Oct. 1907. Member of H. C. Morris, Woolsey, Morris & Kennedy, of 2 Walbrook, E.C. Joined Dec. 10, 1914, as Lieut., Royal Naval Volunteer Reserve (Auxiliary Patrol Section). Served as C.O. in Motor Launches Jan. 1916 to Dec. 1918.

JOHN CONWAY MORRIS.
Articled to T. W. Trevor, of Bangor. Served as Private, 4th (Public Schools) Batt. Royal Fusiliers.

JOHN ERNEST MORRIS.
Admitted Oct. 1904, practising at Cardiff. Served as 2nd Lieut., Royal Welch Fusiliers.

JOHN EDWARD PHILIPPS MORRIS.
Admitted April 1909. Managing Clerk with Wade & Son, of Newport, Mon. Joined Aug. 5, 1916, as Private, 5th Batt. Royal Fusiliers, transferred to 1st (H.S.) Garrison Batt. The Buffs Sept. 1916, attached Staff of Dover Garrison Headquarters Oct. 1916, promoted Lance-Corporal June 1917, employed as Courts-Martial Clerk for the Garrison. Served at Home.

LYNDON HENRY MORRIS.
Admitted March 1913. Of Shrewsbury. Served as Capt., 4th Batt. King's Shropshire Light Infantry and as Adjutant in the Far East from Oct. 1914 to Oct. 1916, returned to France and served as Capt. in 1st Batt., afterwards served in Ireland, returned to 1st Batt. King's Shropshire Light Infantry and commanded that Batt. as Lieut.-Col. during closing stages of War, and during the March into Germany following the Armistice. Awarded the M.C. Served in Burma, Straits Settlements, China, and France. Wounded at Cambrai Nov. 20, 1917.

RAYMOND EARDLEY MORRIS.

Admitted Oct. 1907, practising at Weston-super-Mare. Joined Dec. 23, 1914, as Lieut., Gloucestershire Regt., transferred to Scottish Rifles and promoted Capt. Feb. 1917. Served in Mesopotamia. Invalided Aug. 21, 1918.

ROBERT PARRY MORRIS.

Articled to M. E. Nee, of Carnarvon. Joined Dec. 7, 1914, as Private, 16th Batt. Royal Welch Fusiliers, transferred to Welsh Royal Garrison Artillery Feb. 1915, promoted Lieut. and subsequently Capt. Awarded the M.C. Served in France. Twice wounded. Killed in action Oct. 27, 1917.

WILLIAM FRANCIS MORRIS.

Admitted Feb. 1900. Member of Munton, Morris & Co., of Temple Chambers, E.C. Embodied Aug. 1914, as Major, Second in Command 1/21 Batt. London Regiment, promoted Temp. Lieut.-Col. Commanding 1915, appointed Claims Officer 47th Divisional Staff 1915, President No. 2 Area Quartering Committee Scottish Command 1919. Awarded the T.D. Served in France 1914 to 1916, and at Home 1916 to 1919.

ERIC JOHN MORRISH.

Articled to H. B. James, of Leeds. Joined Sept. 8, 1914, as Cadet, Leeds University O.T.C. Gazetted 2nd Lieut. 7th Batt. East Yorkshire Regt. Nov. 26, 1914. Served in France. Wounded Sept. 26, 1915.

DOUGLAS CHARLES ADEY MORRISON.

Admitted Dec. 1904. Member of Morrison & Masters, of Swindon. Mobilised Aug. 1914, as Capt., 4th Batt. Wiltshire Regt. (T.), promoted Major 1918. Served in India and at Home.

GERARD HUMPHREY MORRISON.

Articled to C. A. Coward, of 30 Mincing Lane, E.C. Mobilised Aug. 1914, as 2nd Lieut., 5th City of London Batt. London Regt. (London Rifle Brigade), landed in France on Nov. 5, 1914, as Lieut., promoted Capt. shortly before death. Killed near Ploegsteert Wood March 31, 1915.

WILLIAM ALEXANDER RUSSELL MORRISON.

Articled to Walter Molineux, of Newcastle-upon-Tyne. Served as Private, King's Royal Rifle Corps. Killed in action Sept. 15, 1916.

GUY RALLISON MORRISS.

Admitted April 1914. Practising with Davidson & Morriss, of 40 & 42 Queen Victoria Street, E.C. Joined Nov. 8, 1915, as 2nd Lieut., Royal Army Service Corps, promoted Lieut. July 1917, Capt. Dec. 1917. Served in Egypt and Palestine.

FRANCIS ALFRED VIVIAN MORSE.

Admitted July 1903. Practising at 79 Queen Street, Cheapside, E.C. Served as Able Seaman, Royal Naval Volunteer Reserve (Anti-Aircraft Corps). Gazetted 2nd Lieut. London Electrical Engineers, Royal Engineers (T.), promoted Lieut. June 1916.

PERCY LAPPER MORSE.

Admitted May 1910. Member of Grover & Morse, of 27 Queen Victoria Street, E.C. Joined 1916, as Private, King's Royal Rifle Corps. Granted a Commission in 1/4 Batt. Gloucestershire Regt. June 1917. Served in France and Flanders. Wounded Oct. 8, 1917. Died in hospital, No. 8 Rouen, Nov. 20, 1917.

GALBRAITH MORTEN.

Articled to J. G. Morten, of 99 Newgate Street, E.C. Joined Aug. 1914, as Private, 28th Batt. County of London Regt. (Artists Rifles). Gazetted 2nd Lieut. 1st Batt. King's Liverpool Regt. Feb. 1915. Served in France. Killed in action May 15–16, 1915.

HAMISH MACPHERSON MORTEN.

Articled to J. G. Morten, of 99 Newgate Street, E.C. Joined Nov. 28, 1915, as Private, 28th Batt. County of London Regt. (Artists Rifles). Subsequently commissioned and promoted Lieut.

JAMES MORTON.

Admitted Nov. 1901. Practising at Sheffield. Served as Corporal, 62nd Signal Coy., Royal Engineers.

JAMES FAIRFAX AMPHLETT MORTON.

Articled to J. A. Morton, of Kidderminster. Served as 2nd Lieut., 6th Batt. King's Royal Rifle Corps.

PERCIVAL CLARE MORTON.

Admitted Aug. 1908. Chief Assistant Solicitor, Halifax Corporation. Joined June 5, 1916, as Private, 27th Batt. Royal Fusiliers. Subsequently gazetted 2nd Lieut. York and Lancaster Regt. Served in France. Taken prisoner April 12, 1918. Died of wounds April 13, 1918.

ERNEST HEDLEY HATTERSLEY MOSBY.

Articled to William Dust, of Sheffield. Served as Private, Royal Marines.

JOHN MOSER.

Admitted May 1913. Clerk with Milne, Moser & Sons, of Kendal. Joined Canadian Engineers, as Sapper, Aug. 4, 1914, proceeded to England and France, evacuated from France sick, and was returned to Canada and discharged March 1916. Granted commission in Canadian Army Pay Corps April 1916 till resignation in April 1919, rank on resignation Hon. Capt. Served in Canada, England, and France, and afterwards in Canada.

GODFREY MOSLEY.

Admitted Aug. 1891, practising at Derby. Mobilised Aug. 1914 as Lieut.-Col. Commanding 5th Batt. (Sherwood Foresters) Notts and Derby Regt. Served at Home 1914 to 1915, and in France 1915. Transferred to Territorial Reserve Sept. 1915.

ISSAAC HENRY MOSLEY.

Admitted April 1910. Formerly Managing Clerk with Sanderson, Adkin, Lee & Eddis, of 46 Queen Victoria Street, E.C. Joined Sept. 5, 1914, as Private, Hon. Artillery Company. Gazetted 2nd Lieut. Hon. Artillery Company Aug. 5, 1915, promoted Lieut. July 1917, A/Capt. Feb. 1917. Awarded the M.C. Served in France Sept. 1915 to April 1919.

FREDERICK BLUNDELL MOSS BLUNDELL.

Admitted Dec. 1897. Member of Moss, Lowe & Co., of Hull. Mobilised Aug. 4, 1914, as Lieut.-Col., 2nd Northumbrian Brigade, Royal Field Artillery

(T.), promoted Col. Aug. 1918. Five times mentioned in Dispatches. Awarded C.M.G., D.S.O., and T.D. Served at Home Aug. 1914 to April 1915, and in France April 1915 to May 1918. Taken prisoner on the Aisne May 28, 1918.

SYDNEY HUGH MOSSE.
Admitted March 1913. Practising at 171 Queen Victoria Street, E.C. Served as Lance-Corporal, 28th Batt. County of London Regt. (Artists Rifles).

KENNETH MOSSMAN.
Admitted Feb. 1908. Managing Clerk with Davenport, Cunliffe & Blake, of 48 Chancery Lane, W.C. Mobilised Aug. 1914, as Private, 1st Batt. Hon. Artillery Company, promoted Sergeant Dec. 1914. Gazetted 2nd Lieut. 4th Batt. Worcestershire Regt. May 1916, transferred Royal Engineers as Lieut. Dec. 1917. Served in France and attached British Military Mission U.S.A. three months. Wounded Ancre July 1916.

GEORGE HOLMES MOSSOP.
Articled to T. F. Gaskell, of Liverpool. Joined March 25, 1916, as Rifleman, 2/6 (Rifle Batt.) King's Liverpool Regt., transferred to Labour Corps June 1918. Served in France. Gassed at Armentières July 29, 1917.

LIONEL GORDON MOTE.
Admitted June 1909. Member of E. and J. Mote, of 1 South Square, Gray's Inn, W.C. Served as Private, 6th (Cyclist) Batt. Royal Sussex Regt., subsequently promoted Lance-Corporal.

HARRY MOTTERSHEAD.
Articled to F. A. Daniel, of Macclesfield. Joined Sept. 3, 1917, as Temp. Assistant in Casualty Section of the Department of the Accountant-General of the Navy, Admiralty.

FRANCIS JOSEPH MOTTRAM.
Admitted June 1905, practising at Stafford and Hanley. Served as Major and Adjutant, Ammunition Column, North Midland Brigade, Royal Field Artillery.

ERNEST HILL MOTUM.
Admitted July 1901. Assistant Solicitor to the Town Clerk of Newcastle-upon-Tyne. Joined Aug. 1914, as 2nd Lieut., 8th Batt. Durham Light Infantry, promoted Capt. July 1916. Once mentioned in Dispatches. Served in France and Belgium. Wounded April 26, 1915, and Feb. 8, 1916.

JOHN ISAAC MOULTON.
Admitted Jan. 1903. Member of Dunning, Kay & Armstrong, of Leeds. Joined June 1916, as Private, 3rd Batt. East Yorkshire Regt., promoted Lance-Corporal July 1916. Served in France Sept. 1917 to Feb. 1919.

OSCAR PERCY MOUNT.
Admitted Oct. 1910. Of Colombo, Ceylon. Served as 2nd Lieut., Royal Field Artillery.

BERNARD MOUNTAIN.

Admitted Oct. 1908. Of Grimsby. Joined Dec. 11, 1916, as Lieut., Royal Army Medical Corps, promoted Capt. Dec. 1917. Served in Mesopotamia May 1917 to May 1918.

HAROLD MOUNTAIN.

Admitted Sept. 1905. Member of Bates & Mountain, of Grimsby. Served as Major, North Midland Brigade, Royal Field Artillery (T.).

WALTER EDMUND IRVINE MOURILYAN.

Admitted Jan. 1899, practising at Richmond, Surrey. Joined April 1915, as A.B., Anti-Aircraft Corps, Royal Naval Volunteer Reserve. Served at Home. Discharged Jan. 1917.

JOHN HEWITT MOWLL.

Admitted Oct. 1913. Clerk with Mowll & Mowll, of Dover. Mobilised Aug. 1914, as Lieut., Cinque Ports Royal Engineers, promoted Substantive Capt. Dec. 1914. Served at Dover (Harbour Defences).

CLARENCE EDWIN MOXON.

Articled to E. H. Foster, of Leeds. Joined Leeds University O.T.C. Dec. 1914 as Cadet. Gazetted 2nd Lieut. 2nd West Riding Brigade Royal Field Artillery Feb. 22, 1915, promoted Lieut. Dec. 1916. Served in France. Resigned Dec. 22, 1917.

JOHN EVELYN MOXON.

Admitted Feb. 1913. Managing Clerk with Cutts & Son, of Bognor. Joined Aug. 29, 1914, as Private, 5th Batt. Gloucestershire Regt. Served in France March 1915 to Nov. 1917, and in Italy Dec. 1917 to Dec. 1918.

REGINALD ARTHUR WITHERS MOYLAN-JONES.

Admitted Feb. 1911. Managing Clerk with Birt & Son, of Southwark, S.E. Joined Sept. 1914, as Private, 28th Batt. County of London Regt. (Artists Rifles), subsequently promoted Sergeant and appointed Sergeant-Instructor on Staff of Machine Gun School, B.E.F. Served in France.

AUGUSTUS MOZLEY-STARK.

Admitted Nov. 1884, practising at 24 Pelham Street, South Kensington. Served as A/Paymaster to Royal Field Artillery at Woolwich Sept. 1915 to March 1917, later in the Legal Branch Ministry of Munitions, and until Armistice at Navy and Army Canteen Board (Solicitor's Branch).

ROBERT MUCKLE.

Admitted Sept. 1915. Member of Criddle & Ord, of Newcastle-upon-Tyne. Joined April 13, 1917, as Private, 2/28 Batt. County of London Regt. (Artists Rifles), afterwards Cadet O.C.B. Cambridge, and subsequently 2nd Lieut. 36th Batt. Northumberland Fusiliers. Served at Home.

GORDON DENNE MUGGERIDGE.

Admitted May 1903. Member of Martineau & Reid, of 2 Raymond Buildings, Gray's Inn, W.C. Joined Feb. 1916, as Naval Instructor, Royal Navy. Title of rank changed in 1918 to "Instructor Lieutenant." Served with British Adriatic Squadron, Mediterranean (H.M.S. *Queen*), June 1916 to Feb. 1917, with 1st Battle Cruiser Squadron, North Sea (H.M.S. *Tiger*), Feb. 1917 to March 1918. During remainder of time employed on shore at Royal Naval College, Greenwich, and at Royal Air Force Station, Eastchurch.

JOHN HENRY MULCAHY.

Admitted May 1910. Member of Mulcahy & Waugh, of Blaydon-on-Tyne. Joined Feb. 12, 1917, as Private, Durham Light Infantry, subsequently transferred to 444th Home Service Employment Company. Served at Home.

HARRY GEORGE MUMFORD.

Admitted March 1897, practised at Friars House, New Broad Street, E.C. Served as Lieut., 20th Batt. County of London Regt., promoted Capt. June 1916. Awarded M.B.E.

JOE DOUGLAS MUNBY.

Admitted Jan. 1909. Member of Tasker Hart & Munby, of Scarborough. Joined July 5, 1917, as Private, Inns of Court O.T.C. Gazetted 2nd Lieut. Royal Army Service Corps April 27, 1918. Served in France and Belgium and on the Rhine.

EDWIN GEORGE STANISLAUS MUNDAY.

Articled to Alfred Howard, of 10 Clifford's Inn, E.C. Enlisted Oct. 1914 in 7th Batt. London Regt., promoted Corporal at Loos 1915. Wounded (with loss of big toes, left arm permanently crippled, and 17 additional wounds) Nov. 6, 1915, and invalided out of Army and pensioned July 1916. Subsequently obtained commission as 2nd Lieut. 3rd Batt. (attached 13th Batt.) Essex Regt. Nov. 9, 1916. Served in France. Killed in action Feb. 20, 1917.

RALPH MUNDAY.

Admitted May 1910. Of Putney. Served as Trooper, 3rd Batt. County of London Yeomanry (Sharpshooters). Subsequently gazetted Lieut. 9th Batt. Notts and Derbyshire Regt. (Sherwood Foresters). Awarded M.C.

HENRY WADSWORTH MUNK.

Admitted Feb. 1903. Assistant Solicitor with Capron & Co., of Savile Place, W. Granted commission as Lieut. in Royal Naval Volunteer Reserve Sept. 27, 1915.

HECTOR CAMERON MUNRO.

Admitted Feb. 1911, practising at Exeter. Joined July 26, 1917, as Private, Royal Army Medical Corps, promoted Lance-Corporal Nov. 1917. Served at Home.

LAURENCE GEORGE HENSMAN MUNSEY.

Admitted Dec. 1912. Assistant Solicitor Essex County Council. Joined Nov. 29, 1915, Inns of Court O.T.C. Appointed to commission as 2nd Lieut. Royal Army Ordnance Corps April 27, 1916, promoted Lieut. July 1916. Served at Home Nov. 1915 to Nov. 1916, and at Salonica Nov. 1916 to Feb. 1919.

AUSTIN EDWARD SCOTT MURRAY.

Admitted March 1907. Of 7 Bloomsbury Square, W.C. Joined Sept. 1914, as 2nd Lieut., 7th Batt. Norfolk Regt., promoted Lieut. Sept. 1914, Capt. Dec. 1914, Major Nov. 1918. Twice mentioned in Dispatches. Awarded the M.C. Served in France.

BERNARD ALLEYNE MURRAY.

Articled to J. E. Corbould, of 1 Henrietta Street, Cavendish Square, W. Mobilised Aug. 1914, as Private, Inns of Court O.T.C. Gazetted 2nd Lieut. 1/1 Notts (Sherwood Rangers) Yeomanry Sept 13, 1914, promoted Lieut. June 1916, seconded to Signal Service Royal Engineers to command 7th Mounted Brigade Signal Troop (subsequently renamed 14th Cavalry Brigade Signal Troop Royal Engineers) May 1917, promoted Capt. April 1918. Awarded the M.C. Served in Egypt Aug. to Oct. 1915, at Salonica Oct. 1915 to June 1917, and in Palestine and Syria July 1917 to July 1919.

EDWARD DOUGLAS MURRAY.

Admitted Nov. 1907. Member of Winter, Bothamley & Co., of 16 Bedford Row, W.C. Joined Sept. 4, 1914, as Private, 28th Batt. County of London Regt. (Artists Rifles). Gazetted Lieut. Royal Highlanders (The Black Watch) Jan. 27, 1915. Served in France. Died July 20, 1916, of wounds received in action on previous day.

FREDERICK STANLEY MURRAY.

Admitted Aug. 1914. Of Plymouth. Joined June 17, 1915, as 2nd Lieut., 3rd Batt. North Staffordshire Regt., promoted Lieut. May 1916 and then appointed Adjutant. Volunteered and was selected for service in East Africa, May 1917, attached to King's African Rifles. Wounded on the Makondi Plateau Nov. 17, 1917, and died in the Field Hospital.

JAMES WALTER MURRAY.

Admitted Nov. 1908. Member of Bradshaw & Murray, of Barrow-in-Furness. Joined Aug. 1914, as Private, 16th Batt. Middlesex Regt. Gazetted Lieut. 3rd Batt. Border Regt., attached Nigeria Regt., W.A.F.F., June 1915 to Nov. 1918. Served in Cameroon Campaign.

JOHN EDWARD MUSGRAVE.

Admitted Nov. 1911. Member of Waugh & Musgraves, of Cockermouth. Joined Sept. 24, 1914, as Private, 21st (Service) Batt. Royal Fusiliers, promoted Sergeant and Company Sergeant-Major Oct. 1914. Gazetted 2nd Lieut. Jan. 1, 1915, promoted Capt. March 1915, transferred to Royal Engineers and appointed Adjutant April 1916. Once mentioned in Dispatches. Served at Home Sept. 1914 to Oct. 1915 and May 1918 to Jan. 1919, and in France Oct. 1915 to May 1918.

SYDNEY ASHURST MUSSON.

Admitted Feb. 1897, practising at 21 Bedford Row, W.C. Joined Oct. 29, 1914, as Private, Army Pay Corps, promoted Lance-Corporal Dec. 1914, Corporal April 1915, Sergeant June 1915. Commissioned 2nd Lieut. Royal Army Service Corps July 29, 1917. Served at Home Oct. 1914 to April 1917, in France Aug. 1917 to Aug. 1918, and in Spain Sept. 1918 to Feb. 1919.

ERNEST ALEX MYER.

Admitted March 1897. Member of Hermann H. Myer & Co., of 46 and 47 London Wall, E.C. Mobilised Aug. 1914, as Major, 6th City of London Rifles. Served in France. Killed in action April 3, 1915.

HENRY DENNIS MYER.

Admitted Dec. 1914. Member of Montagu Mileham, Solomon & Myer, of 5 and 6 Bucklersbury, E.C. Mobilised Aug. 1914, as Lieut., 6th Batt. City of London Rifles, promoted Capt. Sept. 1914, Major June 1916, attached 4th Batt. North Staffordshire Regt. May 1917 to March 1918, and to 40th Batt. Royal Fusiliers March 1918 to May 1919. Served in France and Flanders March to Oct. 1915 and Oct. 1917 to March 1918, and in Egypt and Palestine Aug. 1918 to May 1919. Wounded, Loos, Sept. 25, 1915.

ARTHUR FRANCIS MYERS.

Articled to C. H. L. Emanuel, of 23 Finsbury Square, E.C. Mobilised Aug. 1914, as Trooper, 3rd County of London Yeomanry (Sharpshooters). Gazetted 2nd Lieut. 10th Special Reserve of Cavalry Sept. 6, 1916, transferred to 4th Queen's Own Hussars Feb. 1917, promoted Lieut. March 1918. Served at Home Aug. 1914 to April 1915, Egypt April 1915 to Feb. 1916, and in France Feb. 1917 to March 1918. Killed in action at Moreuil March 31, 1918.

HENRY JOHN MYERS.

Admitted Dec. 1907, practised at Folkestone and Hythe. Joined Feb. 28, 1917, as Private, 14th Batt. County of London Regt. (London Scottish). Gazetted 2nd Lieut. Royal Army Service Corps July 1917, A/Capt. Sept. 1918 to July 1919. Served in France and at Home. Died of pneumonia Feb. 19, 1919.

JONAS LOUIS MYERS.

Articled to Harry Myers, of 25 Wormwood Street, E.C. Joined Aug. 4, 1914, as Gunner, "B" Batt. Hon. Artillery Company. Gazetted 2nd Lieut. Royal Field Artillery Jan. 1917, promoted Lieut. June 1918. Served in Eastern Campaign March 1915 to Aug. 1916, and on Western Front Feb. 1917 to Feb. 1919. Wounded Sept. 1918.

TRAFFORD NADIN.

Admitted July 1903. Member of Gadsby, Coxon & Nadin, of Derby. Joined Sept. 5, 1914, as 2nd Lieut., 2/5 Batt. Notts and Derby Regt. (Sherwood Foresters), promoted Capt. and Adjutant 1915. Served in the Irish Rebellion and in France. Wounded March 21, 1918. Died of pneumonia following wounds June 8, 1918.

FRANK WILLIAM NALDER.

Articled to H. R. Wansbrough, of Bristol. Served as Motor Cyclist, British Red Cross Society. Subsequently gazetted 2nd Lieut. 4th Batt. Somerset Light Infantry. Promoted Lieut. July 1917.

JOHN VIVIAN NANCARROW.

Admitted Jan. 1910, practised at Middlesbrough. Mobilised Aug. 1914, as Capt., 4th Batt. Yorkshire Regt. (T.), sent to Flanders in April 1915. Killed at Fortuyn, near St. Julien, April 24, 1915.

ANDREW NANCE.
Admitted May 1908, practising at Reading. Joined Dec. 6, 1916, as Stoker, Royal Navy. Served at Home and at East Indian Stations.

SIR WILLIAM LENNOX NAPIER, BART.
Admitted Sept. 1902, practised at Mowbray House, Norfolk Street, W.C. Served as Temp. Major, 4th Batt. South Wales Borderers. Killed in action at Gallipoli Aug. 13, 1915.

RAMSAY LLEWELYN IVES NARES.
Admitted Aug. 1913. Managing Clerk with Francis & Crookenden, of 23 Lincoln's Inn Fields, W.C. Joined Sept. 2, 1914, as Lieut., Royal Fusiliers, promoted Capt. July 1917, afterwards A.D.C. to G.O.C. 28th Division. Twice mentioned in Dispatches. Awarded the M.B.E. Served in France Sept. to Oct. 1915, and with Salonica Force Nov. 1915 to Feb. 1919.

HERBERT MASON NASH.
Articled to J. R. Nash, of Farnham, Surrey. Joined Nov. 29, 1915, as Private, 28th Batt. County of London Regt. (Artists Rifles). Commissioned to Royal Garrison Artillery Dec. 18, 1916, promoted Lieut. June 1918. Served in Palestine.

LESLIE CHESSBOROUGH FLEETWOOD NASH.
Admitted Feb. 1909. Member of Wood, Nash, Hewett & Riddett, of 6 Raymond Buildings, Gray's Inn, W.C. Joined Sept. 22, 1914, as 2nd Lieut., 10th (Service) Batt. The Rifle Brigade, promoted Lieut. Oct. 1914, Capt. Nov. 1914, Major Dec. 1918. Served in France. Gassed Sept. 1918.

HARRY LOUIS NATHAN.
Admitted April 1913. Member of Herbert Oppenheimer, Nathan & Vandyk, of 1 Finsbury Square, E.C. Mobilised Aug. 4, 1914, as Lieut., 1st (City of London) Batt. Royal Fusiliers, promoted Temp. Capt. Jan. 1915, Temp. Lieut.-Col. Nov. 1915, Temp. Major Jan. 1916, Permanent Capt. and Temp. Major June 1916. Served at Home, Malta, Egypt, Gallipoli, and France. Wounded July 1916 at Vimy Ridge. Invalided Sept. 1917 on account of wounds received in action.

HUGH PARKER NAUNTON.
Articled to A. W. Timbrell, of 44 King William Street, E.C. Served as 2nd Lieut., 8th Batt. Suffolk Regt., and subsequently attained the rank of Capt. 9th Batt. East Surrey Regt. Mentioned in Dispatches. Awarded D.S.O.

JAMES NAYLOR.
Articled to Herbert Boocock, of Halifax. Joined May 6, 1916, as Gunner, Royal Field Artillery. Gazetted 2nd Lieut. Royal Field Artillery Oct. 1917, and attached 147th (Army) Brigade. Served in France.

JOHN NEAL.
Admitted Oct. 1913. Member of Arthur Neal & Co., and Arthur Neal & Son, of Sheffield and London. Joined Aug. 11, 1914, as Cadet O.T.C., transferred Jan. 1915 Royal Naval Volunteer Reserve. Gazetted 2nd Lieut.

Royal Garrison Artillery Feb. 6, 1915, promoted Lieut. Nov. 1915, Capt Sept. 1917, A/Major Nov. 1916. Awarded the M.C. Served at Home and in France.

CHARLES GOODALL NEALE.

Admitted Dec. 1900, practising at 1 Queen Victoria Street, E.C. Served as Private, Royal Garrison Artillery.

EDWIN MARRAT NEAVE.

Articled to Edwin Parkes, of Eccles. Joined Sept. 5, 1914, as Private, 20th Batt. Royal Fusiliers (3rd Public Schools Batt.). Served in France.

EGLIN NEEDHAM.

Articled to Frederick Lang, of Manchester. Gazetted Dec. 23, 1914, as Temp. 2nd Lieut. 11th Batt. East Surrey Regiment, transferred to Machine Gun Corps Nov. 1915, promoted Temp. Lieut. July 1916, A/Capt. June 1917, A/Major Feb. 1918. Served in France. Wounded at La Boiselle July 1, 1916.

HAROLD JOHN COOKE NEOBARD.

Admitted April 1912, practising at Reading, Berks. Joined Sept. 4, 1914, as Private, 2/28 Batt. County of London Regt. (Artists Rifles). Gazetted 2nd Lieut. 7th (Service) Batt. Royal Berkshire Regt. Nov. 1914, promoted Lieut. Jan. 1915, Temp. Capt. on appointment as Liaison Officer with the French Armée d'Orient and graded as G.S.O.III. on the Staff of G.O.C. in C. British Expeditionary Force, Salonica, and Army of the Black Sea Nov. 1916 (General List), Substantive Capt. May 1918, subsequently worked as G.S.O.III., Operations G.H.Q. Constantinople Army of the Black Sea. Awarded O.B.E. and Chevalier of the Legion of Honour. Served at Home Sept. 1914 to Sept. 1915, France Sept. to Nov. 1915, Macedonia Nov. 1915 to Dec. 1918, Turkey-in-Europe Dec. 1918 to Sept. 1919.

WILLIAM PERCY NESS-WALKER.

Admitted Nov. 1908, practised at Whitby. Mobilised Aug. 1914, as Capt., North Riding Battery, 2nd Northumbrian Brigade, Royal Field Artillery (T.), promoted Major June 1918. Awarded the M.C. Served in France. Killed Dec. 30, 1917.

NOEL WILFRID NEVE.

Articled to W. H. House, of Sevenoaks. Served as Cadet, University of London O.T.C.

WALTER GREGORY NEVE.

Articled to his father, Arthur H. Neve, of Tonbridge. Joined March 1915, as Private, Inns of Court O.T.C., and subsequently gazetted 2nd Lieut. 2nd Batt. East Kent Regt. (The Buffs). Killed in action Balkan Front (Salonica Force) Aug. 25, 1917.

CLIVE NEVILL.

Articled to Leonard Nevill, of 35 Bucklersbury, E.C. Served as Private, 28th Batt. Royal Fusiliers. Went to France Aug. 1916. Killed in action Oct. 7, 1916.

ROBERT NEVILL.
Articled to his father, Robert Nevill, of Tamworth. Joined Dec. 1915, as 2nd Lieut., South Lancashire Regt., promoted Capt. Sept. 1916. Awarded the M.C. and Bar. Served in France. Killed in action at Nieppe April 10, 1918.

MAURICE MICHAEL JOHN NEVILLE.
Admitted Dec. 1908. Member of G. & O. New & Neville, of Evesham. Mobilised Aug. 5, 1914, as Lieut., Worcestershire Regt., promoted Capt. July 1916, boarded permanently unfit for Infantry and joined Royal Army Service Corps as Lieut. Sept. 1916, attached 220th Siege Battery Royal Garrison Artillery, promoted A/Capt. March 1917. Once mentioned in Dispatches. Awarded O.B.E. (Military Division). Served at Home and in France.

FRANK OSSIAN WALTER NEW.
Articled to W. J. New, of Melton Mowbray. Gazetted Aug. 25, 1914, as Temp. 2nd Lieut., 6th Batt. Leicestershire Regt., promoted Temp. Lieut. March 1915, Temp. Capt. Dec. 1918. Served in France 1915, 1916, and 1918. Wounded June 30, 1916, and Oct. 23, 1918.

LESLIE PENRY NEW.
Articled to W. W. Marks, of Bedford. Served as Lieut., 5th (Reserve) Batt. Bedfordshire Regt.

OLIVER CURTIS NEW.
Articled to W. H. Hadfield, of Stockport. Joined July 25, 1916, as Private, 5th City of London Batt. London Regt. (London Rifle Brigade), transferred to 4th Batt. Machine Gun Corps Oct. 1916, subsequently promoted Lance-Corporal. Served in France Nov. 1916 to April 1918. Missing, presumed killed, April 10–12, 1918. Last seen near Estaires in charge of gun.

THOMAS GLADSTONE NEW.
Admitted Nov. 1907. Managing Clerk with Beale & Co., of Birmingham. Mobilised Aug. 4, 1916, as Sapper, Royal Engineers (Railway Operating Division), promoted Sergeant Nov. 25, 1916, served on Staff of A.D. Light Railways First Army, B.E.F. Awarded the M.S.M. Served in France Nov. 1916 to Feb. 1919.

ROBERT EDWIN NEWBERY.
Admitted April 1911. Member of Dale & Newbery, of Staines. Joined Nov. 13, 1916, as Private, Inns of Court O.T.C., promoted Lance-Corporal Dec. 1916, transferred to Machine Gun Corps March 1917. Commissioned 2nd Lieut. Aug. 26, 1917, promoted Lieut. May 1918. Awarded the M.C. Served in France Oct. 1917 to March 1919.

BERTRAM CLARKE NEWBOLD.
Admitted Sept. 1900, practising at Burton-on-Trent. Joined Dec. 1, 1914, as Lance-Sergeant, 1st King Edward's Horse. Gazetted 2nd Lieut. 1/6 Batt. North Staffordshire Regt. (T.), promoted Lieut. Sept 1916. Served in France.

JACK NEWBOULT.
Articled to Alfred Bates, of Morecambe. Joined Sept. 1, 1914, as Private, 1/5 Batt. The King's Own Royal Lancaster Regt., and attained the rank of

Sergeant. Commissioned as 2nd Lieut. in same Regt. Sept. 26, 1917, promoted Lieut. March 1919. Served in England Sept. 1914 to Feb. 1915 and April to Dec. 1917, France Feb. 1915 to April 1917 and Dec. 1917 to March 1918, and with Army of Black Sea Oct. 1918 to Sept. 1919. Wounded at Ypres April 23, 1915.

MATTHEW BANKS NEWELL.

Admitted Feb. 1914, practised at Manchester. Joined 1914, as Private, Manchester University O.T.C. Gazetted 2nd Lieut. Cheshire Regt. Dec. 19, 1914. Served at Gallipoli 1915, and in Mesopotamia 1916. Killed in action April 4–5, 1916.

ROBERT AUGUSTUS NEWILL.

Admitted Feb. 1886, practising at Wellington, Salop. Mobilised Aug. 1914, as Major, Shropshire Royal Horse Artillery, transferred T.F. Reserve 1916. Once mentioned in Dispatches. Served at Home and 14 days in France.

ROBERT DANIEL NEWILL.

Admitted May 1914. Of Wellington, Salop. Joined Dec. 1, 1911, as 2nd Lieut. 1/1 Shropshire Royal Horse Artillery (T.), promoted Lieut. April 1914, Temp. Capt. May 1915, Substantive Capt. June 1916, transferred to "A" Battery, 290th Brigade, Royal Field Artillery, Sept. 1916, posted No. 8 Reserve Brigade Royal Horse Artillery, Bulford, July 1917, commanded and formed combined R.A. Training Depôts, Jubbulpore, India, March 1918 till disbanded Sept. 1919, Staff Capt. Jubbulpore Brigade (5th [Mhow] Division) Oct. 1919 to March 1920. Served at Home Aug. 1914 to Jan. 1917, France from Jan. to June 1917, India from March 1918 to March 1920.

HERBERT ARCHER HAYES NEWINGTON.

Admitted July 1903. Member of Marchant & Newington, of 27 College Street, E.C. Mobilised Aug. 4, 1914, as Lieut., 14th Batt. County of London Regt. (London Scottish), promoted Capt. June 1916, appointed A.M.L.O. Aug. 1915, D.A.Q.M.G. Boulogne Dec. 1915, D.A.Q.M.G. H.Q. Lines of Communication Feb. 1917, Assistant Director of Labour, G.H.Q. (Temp. Lieut.-Col.) June 1917, Deputy Controller of Labour G.H.Q. Feb. 1918, Labour Commandant XVII. Corps (Temp. Col.) Oct. 1918, and finally commanded Cambrai sub-area. Five times mentioned in Dispatches. Awarded D.S.O. and Brevet Majority. Served in France.

NORMAN GEORGE NEWINGTON.

Admitted Feb. 1901. Of the Board of Trade, S.W. Served as Private, 9th Batt. Royal Fusiliers.

NORMAN CHESTER NEWLAND.

Admitted Nov. 1911. Managing Clerk with J. D. Adey, of Newport, Mon. Joined Sept. 13, 1914, as 2nd Lieut., 1st Batt. Monmouthshire Regt. (T.). Served in France. Wounded and taken prisoner at 2nd battle of Ypres May 8, 1915, and died in German Military Hospital at Roulers May 30, 1915.

ALBERT GORDON NEWMAN.

Articled to A. A. Newman, of Newport, Mon. Joined Sept. 9, 1914, as 2nd Lieut., 3rd Batt. Monmouthshire Regt., promoted Lieut. Dec. 1914,

Temp. Capt. Sept. 1915, Perm. Capt. June 1916, attached to King's Royal Rifle Corps March 1917, to Liverpool Regt. June 1917, and to 2nd Batt. Monmouthshire Regt. May 1918. Once mentioned in Dispatches. Served in France 2½ years. Wounded June 1918.

CYRIL JAMES NEWMAN.

Articled to J. H. Bate, of Wrexham, North Wales. Joined Nov. 25, 1914, as Private, 16th Batt. Royal Welch Fusiliers. Gazetted 2nd Lieut. in same Regt. Jan. 1, 1915, promoted Lieut. Aug. 1915, A/Capt. April 1918, reverted to Lieut. October 1918, A/Capt. Sept. to Nov. 1919, attached to Assyrian Batt. Served at Home Nov. 1914 to Feb. 1916, in India Feb. 1916 to Sept. 1918, and in Mesopotamia Sept. 1918 to Oct. 1919.

DOUGLAS NEWMAN.

Articled to Frederick Last, of 17 Sackville Street, Piccadilly, W. Joined Nov. 23, 1914, as Private, Inns of Court O.T.C., commissioned 1/6 Batt. Suffolk Regt. March 16, 1915, and disembodied from T.F. as Capt. Served at Home and in France. Wounded Aug. 28, 1918.

TREVOR CLYDE NEWMAN.

Admitted Oct. 1905, practising at 22 Southampton Street, Bloomsbury, W.C. Served as Able Seaman, Royal Naval Volunteer Reserve (Anti-Aircraft Corps).

WILLIAM HILL NEWSON.

Articled to N. T. Davidson, of 10 and 11 Lime Street, E.C. Embodied as Private in Inns of Court O.T.C. Aug. 4, 1914, and attained rank of Sergeant, commissioned as 2nd Lieut. 6th Batt. Gordon Highlanders, T.F., Nov. 14, 1914, promoted Lieut. April 1915, Capt. June 1915, appointed Adjutant Sept. 1915, appointed 2nd in Command of 7th Batt. with acting rank of Major Oct. 1917, posted as 2nd in Command 52nd (Graduated) Batt. Royal Sussex Regt. June 1918, rejoined 6/7 Batt. Gordon Highlanders as Capt. Dec. 1918. Once mentioned in Dispatches. Awarded the M.C. Served in France and at Home. Wounded June 3, 1915, at Givenchy.

CECIL NEWSTEAD.

Articled to E. C. Newstead, of Ottley. Joined Sept. 8, 1914, as Gunner, Royal Field Artillery (T.). Served in France April 1915 to March 1916.

CHARLES EDWARD NEWTON.

Admitted April 1900. Member of Wedlake, Letts & Birds, of 11 Serjeant's Inn, Temple, E.C. Mobilised as Sergeant, 28th Batt. County of London Regt. (Artists Rifles). Gazetted Lieut. Oct. 1914, Capt. 1915. Once mentioned in Dispatches. Awarded Brevet Majority. Served at Home.

EDGAR HENRY NEWTON.

Articled to Walter Scott, of 25 College Hill, E.C. Mobilised Aug. 4, 1914, as Capt., Royal Army Service Corps and appointed Brigade Supply Officer 1st London Division, appointed D.P.O.S. Sussex Oct. 1914, promoted Major June 1915, appointed D.P.O.S. Norfolk Oct. 1915, and D.P.O.S. Yorkshire March 1916, appointed on H.Q. Staff Southern Area Forage Committee as Administrative Officer Machinery Services Dec. 1917, Senior Supply Officer

57th Division B.E.F. France July 1918, appointed on D.D.S.T. Staff 5th Army H.Q. B.E.F. France to superintend feeding of Belgian civilians in occupied territory Oct. 1918. Once mentioned in Dispatches.

FRANK NEWTON.

Admitted Jan. 1911. Member of F. Newton & Son, of Stockport. Joined Aug. 29, 1916, as Sapper, Royal Engineers. Served at Home. Discharged Jan. 7, 1918.

FRANK LESLIE NEWTON.

Articled to H. W. Knocker, of Sevenoaks. Served as Private, Inns of Court O.T.C.

HUBERT WHITE NEWTON.

Admitted Nov. 1902, practising at 37 Queen Victoria Street, E.C. Joined Sept. 15, 1916, as Private, 1/6 (Cyclist) Batt. Norfolk Regt., drafted to 12th (Yeo.) Batt. Norfolk Regt. Oct. 1917. Served at Home Sept. 1916 to Oct. 1917, in Palestine Oct. 1917 to April 1918, and in France May 1918 to Feb. 1919.

REGINALD ARTHUR NEWTON.

Admitted Dec. 1908, practising at 40 Claremont Road, Cricklewood, N.W. Joined Sept. 15, 1914, as 2nd Lieut. Royal Army Service Corps (M.T.), promoted Lieut. March 1915, Capt. Feb. 1916. Served in France.

THOMAS GLYN NICHOLAS.

Articled to D. W. Jones, of Merthyr Tydfil. Joined July 1915, as 2nd Lieut., 12th Batt. The Welch Regt., promoted Lieut. July 1916, and attached to 14th Batt. Once mentioned in Dispatches. Served in France. Killed in action near Ypres Feb. 19, 1917.

CHARLES RICE ILTYD NICHOLL.

Admitted Jan. 1907. Member of Nicholl, Manisty & Co., of 1 Howard Street, Strand, W.C. Mobilised Aug. 4, 1914, as Major, Queen's Own Oxfordshire Hussars (Yeomanry T.F.), and subsequently promoted Lieut.-Col. Once mentioned in Dispatches. Served in France Sept. 1914 to July 1915 and Jan. 1917 to March 1919.

DUDLEY NICHOLLS.

Admitted Dec. 1911, practising at 106 Cambridge Street, Warwick Square, S.W. Served as Lieut., 13th Batt. Royal Warwickshire Regt.

ERNEST JAMES NICHOLLS.

Admitted Feb. 1903. Member of J. Nicholls & Son, of 12 Old Jewry Chambers, E.C. Joined London University O.T.C. 1914. Commissioned as 2nd Lieut. March 31, 1915, and gazetted to 11th Batt. Loyal North Lancashire Regt. Served in France, attached to 8th Batt. March 1916 to May 1916. Killed in action at Vimy Ridge May 22, 1916. Buried in Military Cemetery at Ecouvres, near Mont St. Eloy, Arras.

GEORGE LAWSON NICHOLLS.

Admitted Feb. 1915, practising at 106 Cambridge Street, Warwick Square, S.W. Served as Capt., Royal Air Force.

BASIL GEORGE NICHOLS.

Articled to G. A. Nichols, of 233 Lavender Hill, S.W. Joined May, 1915, as Private, Inns of Court O.T.C. Gazetted 2nd Lieut. Royal Field Artillery (T.F.) Oct. 27, 1915, promoted Lieut. June 1916, attached Royal Flying Corps Balloon Observer Oct. 1916. Served in France and Italy. Wounded in Italy Dec. 31, 1918.

SIDNEY KENNETH NICHOLS.

Admitted Aug. 1911. Managing Clerk with De la Chapelle & Co., of 34 and 36 Gresham Street, E.C. Joined Sept. 1, 1914, as Private, 18th Batt. Royal Fusiliers. Gazetted 2nd Lieut. Yorkshire Regt Feb. 1, 1915, promoted Lieut. March 1916, Capt. July 1916, and Adjutant Staff Capt. 69th Inf. Bde. Dec. 1916, Staff Capt. War Office Feb. 1919 to Jan. 1920. Three times mentioned in Dispatches. Awarded the M.C. Served at Home Sept. 1914 to Aug. 1915 and Oct. 1918 to Jan. 1920, in France Aug. 1915 to Nov. 1917, and in Italy Nov. 1917 to Oct. 1918.

ARTHUR HARRY NICHOLSON.

Articled to H. S. Badger, of Liverpool. Served as Temp. 2nd Lieut., 19th (Service) Batt. Manchester Regt. Died of wounds April 9, 1917.

CUTHBERT FREER NICHOLSON.

Admitted Nov. 1914. Of Huddersfield. Served as Gunner, 3A Battery Hon. Artillery Company.

GEOFFREY NICHOLSON.

Articled to J. H. Nicholson, of Hexham. Served as Private, Inns of Court O.T.C.

JOSEPH ARTHUR NICHOLSON.

Admitted Dec. 1900. Member of Johnson & Nicholson, of Lowestoft. Joined Nov. 1916, as Private, Inns of Court O.T.C., transferred as Gunner to Royal Garrison Artillery June 1917. Gazetted 2nd Lieut. Royal Garrison Artillery (S.R.) Sept. 1, 1917. Served in France.

MONTAGU NICHOLSON.

Admitted Oct. 1906, practising at Doncaster. Served as Driver, Royal Engineers.

ROBERT LEONARD ST. CLARE NICHOLSON.

Admitted Nov. 1901. Member of Nicholson & Gasquoine, of Chester and Prestatyn. Served as Capt., 7th Batt. Cheshire Regt. Territorial Force Reserve.

ROBERT WILLIAM NICHOLSON.

Admitted Nov. 1912. Managing Clerk with Dees & Thompson, of Newcastle-upon-Tyne. Rejoined 6th Batt. Northumberland Fusiliers on Aug. 22, 1914, as Lieut., promoted Temp. Capt. July 1915, Substantive Capt. June 1916. Served at Home and in France. Wounded April 26, 1915, Jan. 20, 1916, and April 11, 1916.

THEODORE NICHOLSON.

Articled to J. S. Nicholson, of Sunderland. Joined April 15, 1915, as Cadet, Durham University O.T.C. Gazetted 2nd Lieut. Royal Field Artillery

Sept. 28, 1915, promoted Lieut. June 1916, A/Capt. Nov. 1917. Once mentioned in Dispatches. Served in France and Belgium Feb. 1916 to Sept. 1918. Wounded Sept. 1, 1918.

THOMAS EDWARD NICHOLSON.

Admitted Nov. 1913. With Septimus Ward, of Newcastle-upon-Tyne. Joined Aug. 1914, as Private, 16th Batt. Northumberland Fusiliers. Gazetted 2nd Lieut. 25th Batt. Northumberland Fusiliers (2nd Tyneside Irish) Feb. 15, 1915, promoted Lieut. Sept. 1915. Served in France. Killed in action at La Boisselle July 1, 1916, whilst in charge of the Machine Gun Section of his Batt.

ROBERT ODDIE NICKSON.

Admitted Nov. 1901, practising at Blackpool. Served as 2nd Lieut., Royal Garrison Artillery.

DOUGLAS HAROLD NIELD.

Articled to C. E. Nield, of Liverpool. Joined Sept. 1914, as Trooper, King Edward's Horse, transferred to 1st Motor Machine Gun Battery as a Gunner Oct. 1914, transferred to Royal Army Service Corps (M.T.) as a Dispatch-Rider Dec. 1914. Served in France Dec. 1914 to May 1919.

RALPH KENNETH TAYLOR NIGHTINGALE.

Articled to Frank Taylor, of 198 Upper Richmond Road, Putney, S.W. Mobilised Aug. 5, 1914, as Lieut., 4th Batt. Lancashire Fusiliers (Special Reserve), promoted Lieut. Oct. 1913, Capt. Oct. 1914, A/Major Jan. 1916, whilst in command of 9th (S.) Batt. Lancashire Fusiliers, Adjutant March 1916 to July 1917, Staff Capt. 33rd Inf. Bde. July 1917 to Feb. 1919. Once mentioned in Dispatches. Awarded the M.C. Served at Home Aug. to Nov. 1914 and June to Nov. 1915, France Nov. 1914 to May 1915 and July 1916 to Feb. 1919, Egypt, Imbros, and Mudros Nov. 1915 to July 1916. Wounded (gas) at Ypres May 2, 1915.

ERNEST NIXON.

Articled to George Wilkinson, of Newcastle-upon-Tyne. Gazetted 2nd Lieut. 7th Batt. Northumberland Fusiliers Oct. 19, 1914, promoted Temp. Lieut. March 1915, Temp. Capt. March to June 1915 and Nov. 1915 to March 1917, Substantive Lieut. Feb. 1916, Acting Capt. Nov. 1917 to Jan. 1918 and Feb. 1918 to Feb 1919 Once mentioned in Dispatches. Served at Home and in France and Belgium. Wounded June 18, 1915, and Nov. 21, 1916.

CYRIL HUBERT MAYER NIXSON.

Admitted April 1909. Assistant in Solicitors' Dept., G.N.R., King's Cross Station, N. Gazetted July 31, 1915, as 2nd Lieut., Herefordshire Regt., promoted Lieut. July 1917, attached 1st Batt. Royal Warwickshire Regt. Dec. 1917, A/Capt. while O.C. Egyptian Servants School, Helwich, March to Nov. 1918. Served with Egyptian Expeditionary Force.

ARCHIBALD FRANCIS NOBLE.

Admitted Oct. 1908. Member of Adams, Howker & Noble, of Bank Chambers, Tower Bridge Road, S.E. Joined Aug. 1914, as Lieut., 10th Batt. Cheshire Regt., promoted Capt. and Adjutant Dec. 1914. Once mentioned in Dispatches. Served in France. Killed in action at Vimy Ridge May 21, 1916.

HERBERT LOVIS NOEL-COX.

Admitted Feb. 1886, practising at 9 John Street, Adelphi, Strand, W.C. Served as Medical Officer at County of London War Hospital, Epsom, Aug. 1915 to May 1917 and at the Military Hospital, Belmont, Surrey, May 1917 to Jan. 1919.

ARTHUR CHARLES NOON.

Admitted Feb. 1913. Managing Clerk with C. T. Price, of 9 Bush Lane, E.C. Joined Sept. 16, 1914, as Private, University and Public Schools Corps. Gazetted 2nd Lieut. 3rd Batt. Devonshire Regt. May 1915, promoted Lieut. July 1917, A/Capt. Aug. 1918. Served in France and Palestine. Wounded in July 1916, and Sept. 1918.

CHARLES LOUIS NORDON.

Admitted Oct. 1904. Member of Charles Nordon & Co., of 56 Moorgate Street, E.C. Joined Oct. 19, 1917, as Private, Inns of Court O.T.C.

DUNCAN NORMAN.

Articled to G. W. Pritchard, of 2, 3, and 4 Billiter Avenue, E.C. Joined Aug. 4, 1914, West Lancashire Divisional Royal Engineers, and gazetted 2nd Lieut. Aug. 22, 1914, promoted Lieut. and A/Capt., O.C. Signals XIX. Corps Aug. 1918 to Feb. 1919. Awarded the M.C., the Chevalier of the Order of Leopold (Belgian), and the Croix de Guerre (Belgian). Served in France.

HAROLD EDWARD FRANCIS NORRIS.

Admitted Feb. 1905, practising at 23 Bedford Row, W.C. Served as Lieut., 1st Home Counties Div., Royal Army Service Corps, promoted Capt. Jan. 1918.

JOHN PERCIVAL FOXLEY NORRIS.

Admitted April 1914. Of Capel House, New Broad Street, E.C. Served as Lieut., 3rd Batt. Cheshire Regt., promoted Capt. Aug. 1916.

ROBERT NORRIS.

Admitted June 1909. Member of Norris & Sons, of Liverpool. Served as Lieut., 4th (Reserve) Batt. Cheshire Regt.

WILLIAM ERIC NORRIS.

Articled to C. H. Norris, of Burslem. Joined April 10, 1916, as Private, Montgomeryshire Yeomanry, transferred to Officer Cadet Batt. Oct. 1916. Granted Commission in Montgomeryshire Yeomanry Mar. 28, 1917, transferred to 17th Batt. The Welch Regt., and went to France Dec. 1917. Killed in France Jan. 14, 1918.

WILLIAM JAMES GEORGE NORRIS.

Admitted May 1909, practising at Savoy Court, Strand, W.C. Served as Lieut., 12th (Service) Batt. West Yorkshire Regt.

DOUGLAS HORACE GILBERT NORTHCOTE.

Articled to J. H. Welfare, of 60 Coleman Street, E.C. Served as 2nd Lieut., The Buffs (East Kent Regt.). Reported on Mar. 14, 1915, as killed in action, subsequently reported missing, believed killed.

OTHO STUART IRWIN NORTHCOTE.

Articled to Harvey Clifton, of 4 New Court, Lincoln's Inn, W.C. Mobilised Aug. 1914, as Private, Inns of Court O.T.C. Gazetted 2nd Lieut. Suffolk Regt. Sept. 10, 1914, promoted Lieut. Feb. 1915, Capt. Aug. 1917. Served at Home and in France. Wounded at La Boisselle Oct. 5, 1915, at Passchendaele Sept. 30, 1917, at Cambrai Nov. 20, 1917. Discharged unfit Aug. 25, 1918.

ROLAND THOMAS SOUTHMEAD NORTHWAY.

Admitted Jan. 1894, practising at Broadstone, nr. Wimborne, Dorset. Joined June 28, 1918, as Gunner, Royal Garrison Artillery. Served at Home.

THOMAS NOTTIDGE.

Admitted July 1909, practising at 7 Queen Anne's Gate, Westminster, S.W. Joined 1914 Inns of Court O.T.C., subsequently gazetted 2nd Lieut. 5th (Reserve) Regt. of Cavalry, transferred to Berkshire Yeomanry, promoted Lieut. July 1917.

ARTHUR JOSHUA NUNN.

Admitted March 1904, practising at Cheltenham. Joined June 29, 1915, as Private, 5th Batt. The Welch Regt., promoted Lance-Corporal 1915, Corporal 1916, Sergeant 1918, and transferred to Royal Army Ordnance Corps. Served at Home June 1915 to April 1917, and in France April 1917 to April 1919.

ALLAN VAUGHAN NUTT.

Admitted Dec. 1908, practising at Derby. Joined Sept. 1914, as Private, 21st (S.) Batt. Royal Fusiliers (Public Schools Batt.). Gazetted 2nd Lieut. 14th Batt. York and Lancaster Regt. Jan. 16, 1915, promoted Lieut. April 1915, Capt. May 1915, Adjutant Sept. 1915, Major (2nd in Command) Feb. 1917, A/Lieut.-Col. 13th Batt. April 1918. Attached 15th Batt. West Yorks Regt. as A/Lieut.-Col. June to July 1918, when rejoined 13th Batt. York and Lancaster Regt. as Second in Command, A/Lieut.-Col. in command 15th Batt. West Yorks Regt. Sept. to Oct. 1918. Three times mentioned in Dispatches. Awarded the D.S.O. and Bar. Served in Egypt July to March 1916, and in France March 1916 to Oct. 1918. Wounded near Armentières Oct. 6, 1918.

ERNEST NUTTALL.

Admitted Oct. 1910. Member of Craven & Nuttall, of Todmorden. Joined May 29, 1916, as Gunner, Royal Garrison Artillery, promoted Bombardier Aug. 1916, Corporal April 1918. Served in Mesopotamia.

REGINALD JOHN CHARLES NUTT-HAMBLIN.

Admitted Feb. 1903, practising at Bristol. Served as Gunner, Royal Garrison Artillery.

FREDERICK HARRY NYE.

Admitted July 1906. Member of Nye & Clewer, of Brighton. Served as Sub.-Lieut., Royal Naval Volunteer Reserve.

EDWARD RALPH OAKDEN.

Articled to J. W. Briggs, of Nottingham. Gazetted Lieut. 10th Batt. Notts and Derby Regt. (Sherwood Foresters) Sept. 1914, promoted Capt. July

1915. Served in France and Belgium. Wounded Aug. 1915, returned to France March 1916. Shot in the face and both eyes destroyed in the attack at Fencourt July 2, 1916. Died March 22, 1917, as a result of wound.

CECIL OAKES.
Admitted Nov. 1907, practising at Liverpool. Joined Sept. 1914, as Private, 21st (P.S.) Batt. Royal Fusiliers. Gazetted 2nd Lieut. 5th Batt. Cheshire Regt. Nov. 1914, promoted Temp. Capt. Feb. 1915, Temp. Major April 1916. Served at Home and in France. Wounded at Menin Oct. 14, 1918.

ROBERT EDWIN OAKLEY.
Articled to S. J. Ellis, of 27 Lincoln's Inn Fields; and Watford. Joined Sept. 7, 1914, as Private, 21st Batt. Royal Fusiliers. Gazetted 2nd Lieut. Bedfordshire Regt. Feb. 1915, promoted Lieut. Aug. 1915. Awarded the M.C. Served in France Aug. 1916 to March 1919.

MAURICE BARRY O'BRIEN.
Admitted Oct. 1906. Member of Martin & Barry O'Brien, of 68 Victoria Street, Westminster, S.W. Served as Sergeant, Inns of Court O.T.C.

WILFRID PHILIP ODDIE.
Articled to G. M. Schmidt, of 37 Norfolk Street, W.C. Joined as Private, 5th Batt. East Surrey Regt., subsequently gazetted 2nd Lieut. Indian Army Reserve of Officers. Awarded M.C. and Bar.

ARTHUR WILLIAM ODGERS.
Admitted Nov. 1897. Member of Cannon Brookes & Odgers, of Norfolk House, Norfolk Street, W.C. Joined Sept. 1914, as Capt., 8th Batt. Worcestershire Regt. Appointed Adjutant No. 5 Infantry Base Depôt May 1917, Adjutant No. 2 Medical Board Base Depôt Dec. 1917. Served in France May 1916 to Feb. 1919.

JOHN COLEMAN O'DONOHOE.
Articled to W. H. Lane, of 56 Gresham Street, E.C. Served as 2nd Lieut., 6th Batt. Royal Irish Fusiliers.

GERALD BAILDON OERTON.
Admitted April 1913, practising at Torrington. Served as Capt., 6th Batt. Devonshire Regt., and subsequently promoted Major.

THOMAS OERTON.
Admitted Feb. 1908, practising at Bideford, North Devon. Joined Aug. 1914, as Private, 14th Batt. Royal Warwickshire Regt. Commissioned as 2nd Lieut. 3rd Batt. Devonshire Regt. March 25, 1915, and was attached Base Headquarters, Rouen, Jan. 1917. Became Assistant Military Landing Officer (graded and paid as Staff Captain) May 1917. Employed on Court Martial and Discipline work, acting as assistant D.A.A.G. Returned to 2nd Batt. Devonshire Regt. May 1918, and subsequently held rank of Lieut. 3rd Batt. (Special Reserve). Once mentioned in Dispatches. Served at Home Aug. 1914 to July 1915 and Dec. 1915 to Jan. 1917, and in France July to

Dec. 1915 and Jan. 1917 to May 1918. Wounded Nov. 1915. Taken prisoner at Chemin des Dames May 27, 1918.

GEORGE HERBERT OGDEN.

Articled to J. A. Brierley, of Oldham. Joined June 14, 1917, as Private, Royal Army Service Corps. Served in Salonica.

JOHN STANLEY OGDEN.

Articled to J. H. Ogden, of Manchester. Joined Sept. 4, 1914, as Private, 3rd Public School Batt. Royal Fusiliers. Gazetted 2nd Lieut. 3rd Batt. Loyal North Lancashire Regt. Aug. 12, 1915, promoted Lieut. 7th Batt. July 1916, appointed Adjutant April 1917, promoted A/Capt. Sept. 1917, Temp. Capt. Dec. 1917, Lieut. 3rd (Special Reserve) Batt. Feb. 1918. Served in France June 1916 to Feb. 1918.

ALAN FREEMAN WALKER OGILVIE.

Admitted May 1899, practising at 37 and 39 Essex Street, W.C. Served in Army Pay Corps.

JAMES NORWOOD OGLETHORPE.

Admitted Aug. 1912. Of Millom. Served as Private, 2nd Batt. Hon. Artillery Coy. (Infantry).

JOHN ATKINSON OGLETHORPE.

Articled to J. Wilson, of Workington, Cumberland. Joined Aug. 1914, as Private, 4th Batt. Border Regt. Commissioned as 2nd Lieut. in Indian Army Reserve of Officers Feb. 1, 1917, and attached to 2/32 Sikh Pioneers, promoted Lieut. Feb. 1918, A/Capt. and Adjutant Depôt 2/32 Sikh Pioneers Feb. to May 1918, Lieut. 1/32 Sikh Pioneers May to Dec. 1918, A/Capt. and Instructor in charge of Indian Section School of Musketry and Bayonet Training M.E.F., Baghdad, Dec. 1918 to April 1919. Attached to Special Batt. in India during Indian Riots and Afghan War April to June 1919. Staff British Military Base Depôt Baluchistan Force (Afghan War) June to Oct. 1919. Served at Home, Burma, India, Mesopotamia, and North West Frontier of India (Afghan War).

RALPH STUART OGLETHORPE.

Articled to J. E. Oglethorpe, of Lancaster. Joined Aug. 1915, as 2nd Lieut., 11th Batt. The King's Own Royal Lancaster Regt., promoted Lieut. Jan. 1916, Adjutant July 1916. Transferred to 1/50 Kumaon Rifles, Indian Army Jan. 1918. Mentioned for services in Palestine. Served at Home, in France May 1915 to March 1916, India Jan. to May 1918, and in Egypt and Palestine from July 1918.

GEORGE OKELL.

Admitted Nov. 1899, practising at Ross, Herefordshire. Joined Feb. 1915, as Private, Inns of Court O.T.C. Gazetted 2nd Lieut. 15th Batt. The Welch Regt. July 1915, promoted Lieut. Jan. 1917. Served in France. Wounded July 31, 1917.

GEORGE HAROLD O'KELL.

Admitted April 1906, practising at Sheffield. Served as Capt., 9th Batt. Manchester Regt.

HERBERT ROOKE OLDFIELD.
Admitted July 1881. Member of Oldfields, of 13 Walbrook, E.C. Served as 2nd Lieut., Royal Air Force, Q7, from April to Dec. 1918, and promoted Hon. Capt. Dec. 9, 1918. Served at Home (Administrative Department).

JOHN ANTHONY THOMAS OLDFIELD.
Admitted May 1907, practising at Rhyl. Joined March 16, 1917, as Gunner, Royal Field Artillery. Served in France Dec. 1917 to Aug. 1919.

PERCY BERTRAM BOYD OLDFIELD.
Admitted Aug. 1914. With Oldfields, of 13 Walbrook, E.C. Joined Feb. 7, 1915, as 2nd Lieut., 5th City of London Batt. London Regt. (London Rifle Brigade), promoted Lieut. June 1916, Capt. Aug. 1917, Instructor 16th Officer Cadet Batt. Jan. 1917 to Feb. 1919. Served in France April 1915 to July 1916. Wounded July 1, 1916.

WILLIAM BROMLEY OLDFIELD.
Articled to Albert Oldfield, of Macclesfield. Served as Trooper, Cheshire Yeomanry.

ERNEST FITZJOHN OLDHAM.
Admitted March 1892. Member of Vizard, Oldham, Crowder & Cash, of 51 Lincoln's Inn Fields, W.C.; and 5 Little College Street, S.W. Served as Chief Petty Officer, Royal Naval Air Service (Anti-Aircraft Corps).

MONTAGUE TOPLADY OLDING.
Admitted March 1903. Managing Clerk with Rochester, Pusey & Co., of 90 Cannon Street, E.C. Joined July 28, 1916, as Private, Royal Fusiliers. Transferred to 31st Infantry Training Reserve Nov. 1916, and to 16th Batt. Royal West Surrey Regt. Dec. 1916. Served at Home. Discharged Feb. 12, 1917, with tuberculosis.

CHARLES FREDERICK OLIVER.
Admitted Jan. 1892, practising at Leicester. Served as Lieut.-Col., 4th (Reserve) Batt. Leicestershire Regt.

CHARLES FREDERICK OLIVER.
Articled to G. A. Lightfoot, of Carlisle. Served as Private, 4th Batt. Border Regt.

COLIN MORGAN OLIVER.
Admitted Oct. 1911. Member of Hempsons, of 33 Henrietta Street, Strand, W.C. Mobilised Aug. 4, 1914, as Capt., 5th Batt. Suffolk Regt., promoted Temp. Major Aug. 1915, Substantive Major June 1916. Appointed Staff Capt. G.H.Q. E.E.F. Dec. 1917, Headquarters Force in Egypt May 1918, and Northern Command Nov. 1918. Served in Gallipoli Aug. to Dec. 1915, in Palestine 1917 to 1918, and at Home.

JOHN MILNER OLIVER.
Admitted May 1909. Member of Tatham, Worthington & Co., of Manchester. Joined Sept. 1914, as 2nd Lieut., 16th Batt. Manchester Regt., and subsequently promoted Lieut. Served in France. Killed on the Somme (Trones Wood) July 7, 1916.

RODERIC MAGRATH OLIVER.

Admitted Nov. 1908. Member of Oliver & Lyall, of 52 Cornhill, E.C. Joined Oct. 1914, as 2nd Lieut., 5th Batt. East Kent Regt. (The Buffs), and subsequently promoted Lieut. and Adjutant. Transferred to Household Batt. (Household Cavalry) Oct. 1916, and to 2nd Batt. Grenadier Guards. Served at Home till Oct. 1916, and afterwards in France. Killed in action at St. Leger, near Arras, France, Aug. 27, 1918.

JOHN WILLIAM ARTHUR OLLARD.

Articled to K. de H. Ollard, of Wisbech and March. Mobilised Aug. 4, 1914, as 2nd Lieut., Cambridgeshire Regt., promoted Capt. 1915, and A/Major (2nd in Command) Northamptonshire Regt. 1917. Once mentioned in Dispatches. Served in France 1915.

KENNETH DE HAVILLAND OLLARD.

Admitted Nov. 1907, practising at Wisbech, Cambs. Gazetted Oct. 3, 1914, as Lieut., T.F. Reserve. Served at Home as Appeal Military Representative Cambs and Hunts Appeal Tribunals.

GEORGE HENRY OLLEY.

Admitted March 1902, practising at Liverpool. Served as Private, Royal Irish (Signal Section).

HAROLD MANATON OMMANEY.

Admitted July 1912. Member of Sutton, Ommaney & Oliver, of 3 and 4 Great Winchester Street, E.C. Served as Able Seaman, Royal Naval Volunteer Reserve.

HENRY SIGISMUND OPPÉ.

Admitted Nov. 1908. Member of Drummond, White-Cooper & Phillips, of Shanghai. Joined March 1905, as Lieut., 11th (R.) Batt. Alexandra, Princess of Wales' Own Yorkshire Regt. Attached 6th Batt. Yorkshire Regt. Sept. 1915. Served at the Dardanelles. Killed in action at Suvla Bay Nov. 6, 1915.

WATKIN OPPENHEIM.

Admitted April 1897. Member of Oppenheim, Son & Ross, of Liverpool. Served as Major, West Lancashire Division Royal Engineers (T.). Mentioned in Dispatches.

ALBERT MARTIN OPPENHEIMER.

Admitted Dec. 1894. Of 10 Copthall Avenue, E.C. Joined Aug. 4, 1914, as First Commissioner, St. John Ambulance and British Red Cross Society. Awarded the Crown of Italy. Served in France and Belgium.

GEORGE FREDERICK ORCHARD.

Admitted Nov. 1913. Member of F. H. H. Orchard & Son, of Exeter. Served as 2nd Lieut., 4th Batt. Devonshire Regt., promoted Lieut. June 1916.

JAMES WILLIAM ORCHARD.

Admitted Nov. 1896. Member of F. H. H. Orchard & Son, of Exeter. Mobilised as Lieut., 4th Batt. Devonshire Regt., subsequently received substantive rank of Capt. and Staff Capt. G.S. India. Served in India and Mesopotamia.

ROBERT HENRY ORME.

Admitted Oct. 1909, practising at Ampthill. Served as Private, 5th Batt. Bedfordshire Regt.

BENJAMIN ORMEROD.

Admitted July 1913, practising at Blackburn. Served as 2nd Lieut., 4th Batt. East Lancashire Regt., and subsequently promoted Capt.

GEORGE RILEY ORMEROD.

Admitted June 1909, practising at Accrington, Lancs. Joined June 21, 1917, as Petty Officer, Royal Naval Volunteer Reserve. Served at Home (Ireland).

WALTER SELWYN ORPEN.

Articled to J. W. Greene, of Bury St. Edmunds. Gazetted Sept. 1914 2nd Lieut. North Staffordshire Regt. Went to the Front June 1915, attached to the Lancashire Fusiliers. Killed in action July 6, 1916.

FRANK WILLIAM ORR.

Admitted April 1904, practising at 13 Bedford Row, W.C. Joined June 14, 1916, as Cadet. Gazetted 2nd Lieut. Royal Garrison Artillery Aug. 22, 1916, promoted Lieut. Feb. 1918, A/Capt. and Adjutant Oct. 1917. Served at Home.

KEITH FAULKNER ANDREW ORRELL.

Articled to J. A. Orrell, of Manchester. Joined Aug. 7, 1915, as 2nd Lieut., 6th Batt. South Lancashire Regt. Served in Mesopotamia. Killed in action in Mesopotamia Jan. 13, 1917.

WILLIAM JOHN ORTON.

Articled to W. L. J. Orton, of Coventry. Joined July 27, 1917, as Private, 28th Batt. County of London Regt. (Artists Rifles), promoted Corporal Feb. 1919. Awarded the M.M. Served in France 1918.

GERALD OSBORNE.

Admitted Dec. 1907. Managing Clerk with Robinson & Wilkins, of 58 Russell Square, W.C. Joined Aug. 1915, as Petty Officer, Royal Naval Air Service. Gazetted 2nd Lieut. Machine Gun Corps March 25, 1917, promoted Lieut. Sept. 1918. Served in France.

HAROLD JOHN OSBORNE.

Articled to J. C. Moberly, of Southampton. Mobilised Aug. 1914, as 2nd Lieut., 4th Batt. Hampshire Regt., promoted Lieut. Sept. 1914. Once mentioned in Dispatches. Served at Home Aug. to Oct. 1914, India Nov. 1914 to March 1915, and in Mesopotomia March to Aug. 1915. Wounded in action Nasiriyeh, Mesopotamia, July 25, 1915. Died of wounds received in action Aug. 4, 1915.

JOHN OSBORNE.

Admitted Nov. 1910, practised at Rochdale. Served as Sergeant, 7th Batt. King's Own Scottish Borderers.

THOMAS ARCHER WINDSOR OTHER.

Admitted Sept. 1905, practising at Bournemouth. Joined Sept. 28, 1916, as Sub-Lieut., Royal Naval Volunteer Reserve, subsequently promoted Lieut. Served in North Sea and on West Coast of Ireland.

LESLIE DEAN OVERELL.

Admitted Dec. 1912. Member of Overell & Son, of Leamington Spa. Mobilised Aug. 1914, as Capt., 7th Batt. Royal Warwickshire Regt., promoted Major Sept. 1918. Served at Home and in France. Severely wounded at Cambrai Dec. 3, 1917.

ERNEST HADDON OWEN.

Admitted Oct. 1909. Member of Haddon Owen & Son, of Louth. Joined Aug. 15, 1914, as 2nd Lieut., 3rd Batt. Lincolnshire Regt., attached 1st Batt. South Wales Borderers Nov. 1914, promoted Lieut. Dec. 1914. Served in France. Killed in action at Festubert Dec. 21, 1914.

GERALD CAMPBELL OWEN.

Admitted Dec. 1909. Member of Faithfull, Owen, Blair & Wright, of Dacre House, Victoria Street, Westminster, S.W. Commissioned Dec. 28, 1915, as 2nd Lieut., 9th Batt. Royal Scots Fusiliers, promoted Lieut. Jan. 1918, Capt. Staff Class FF (Intelligence Corps) March 1918. Served in India, Oct. 1916 to Feb. 1917, and in Mesopotamia Feb. to Nov. 1917.

HENRY LEFTWYCH HADDON OWEN.

Admitted May 1912. Member of Bartlett & Sons, of Sherborne. Joined August 1914, as 2nd Lieut., Dorsetshire Regt., seconded to Royal Flying Corps 1916, Squadron Commander June 1918. Awarded the A.F.C. Served in India and in France. Wounded April 1917.

ROWLAND HELY OWEN.

Articled to his father, Hely Owen, of Huddersfield. Mobilised Aug. 4, 1914, as Lieut., 2nd Batt. Duke of Wellington's West Riding Regt., and landed in France Aug. 15, 1914. Wounded at 1st Battle of Ypres Nov. 7, 1914. Killed in action at Hill 60 April 18, 1915.

SACKVILLE HERBERT EDWARD GREGG OWEN.

Admitted Feb. 1906, practising at Narberth. Served as 2nd Lieut., Pembrokeshire Yeomanry.

WILLIS LEE OXLEY.

Admitted April 1904, practising at Sheffield. Joined Dec. 1917, as Technical Officer, Royal Air Force, subsequently gazetted 2nd Lieut. Served at Home.

JOSEPH OXSPRING.

Articled to J. G. Chambers, of Sheffield. Served as A.B., Royal Naval Volunteer Reserve (Anti-Aircraft Corps).

CYRIL WILLIAM GREGORY VANCE PACKMAN.

Articled to Philip Sprinz, of 76 Finsbury Pavement, E.C. Joined Aug. 3, 1914, as Private, 1/16 Batt. City of London Regt. (Queen's Westminster Rifles). Gazetted 2nd Lieut. Seaforth Highlanders July 30, 1915. Invalided April 1916, 2nd Lieut. Royal Army Service Corps (M.T.) Oct. 30, 1916, promoted Lieut. April 1918. Served in France Nov. 1914 to July 1915, and Dec. 1916 to Aug. 1918.

JAMES GORDON REAY PACY.

Articled to J. F. Burnicle, of Sunderland. Gazetted 2nd Lieut. Durham Light Infantry (Special Reserve of Officers) Sept. 27, 1915, promoted Lieut. July 1, 1917. Awarded M.C. Served in France and at Home. Wounded on the Somme Sept. 25, 1916.

HAROLD AUGUSTUS PADLEY.

Articled to G. E. B. Padley, of Lincoln. Joined 1914, as 2nd Lieut., 6th Batt. Lincolnshire Regt.

ALFRED CECIL DUDLEY PAGE.

Articled to J. F. Stops, of Northampton. Joined Sept. 15, 1914, as Private, 7th Batt. Northamptonshire Regt. Gazetted 2nd Lieut. 5th Batt. Northamptonshire Regt. April 20, 1915, and appointed Recruiting Officer. Served at Home Sept. 1914 to Nov. 1915, and in France Nov. 1915 to April 1916, and July to Aug. 1916. Wounded April 4, 1916. Killed Aug. 18, 1916.

HAROLD ASTON PAGE.

Admitted Dec. 1910. Member of S. W. Page & Son, of Wolverhampton. Served as Lieut., 6th Batt. South Staffordshire Regt. (T.), promoted Capt. June 1916.

RAYMUND CHARLES PAGE.

Admitted Nov. 1901. Member of S. W. Page & Sons, of Wolverhampton. Joined May 1916, as Gunner, Royal Garrison Artillery. Gazetted 2nd Lieut. 1st Garrison Batt. King's Own Yorkshire Light Infantry April 15, 1917. Served in France with 8th Batt. South Staffordshire Regt. Died Sept. 24, 1918.

STANLEY CLARENCE MARTEL PAGE.

Articled to F. J. Maw, of 12 Norfolk Street, Strand, W.C. Joined June 13, 1916, as Private, 28th Batt. County of London Regt. (Artists Rifles). Gazetted 2nd Lieut. Royal Field Artillery (Special Reserve) Feb. 11, 1917, promoted Lieut. Aug. 1918. Served in Belgium and France March 1917 to Jan. 1919. Wounded at Ypres, August 1918.

WILLIAM WALTER KEIGHLEY PAGE.

Admitted Dec. 1902. Of Calcutta. Served as Lieut., 10th Batt. Bedfordshire Regt. Awarded the M.C.

OLIVER DAYRELL PAGET PAGET-COOKE.

Articled to Sir Henry Paget-Cooke, of 11 Old Square, W.C. Joined Sept. 3, 1914, as Private, 28th Batt. County of London Regt. (Artists Rifles). Gazetted 2nd Lieut. Royal Army Service Corps April 15, 1915, transferred to Grenadier Guards Dec. 1917. Served at Home and in France. Wounded at Bienvillers, France, April 24, 1918.

EDWARD PAICE.

Admitted March 1910. Managing Clerk with Rider, Heaton & Co., of 8 New Square, Lincoln's Inn, W.C. Joined June 1917, as Private, Devonshire Regt., transferred to Army Pay Corps July 1917, promoted Corporal July 1918. Served at Home.

GRYLLS PHILLIPS PAIGE.

Admitted Dec. 1904. Member of Grylls & Paige, of Redruth. Mobilised Aug. 1914, as Capt., 4th Batt. Duke of Cornwall's Light Infantry, served as A/Major June 1918 to June 1919, with two short periods (about 8 weeks) A/Lieut.-Col., Station Staff Officer Bareilly, India, Aug. 1915 to Jan. 1916. Adjutant 1/4 Batt. Duke of Cornwall's Light Infantry Oct. 1916 to June 1918. Once mentioned in Dispatches. Served in India Oct. 1914 to Jan. 1916, Aden Jan. 1916 to Feb. 1917, and in Egypt and Palestine Feb. 1917 to June 1919.

ARTHUR RICHARD PAIN.

Admitted July 1903, practising at Marlborough, Wilts. Joined Sept. 2, 1914, as Private, 1st (P.S.) Batt. Royal Fusiliers. Gazetted Temp. Lieut. Somerset Light Infantry Nov. 14, 1914. Served in Gallipoli.

LEONARD ALFRED GREVIS PAINE.

Admitted July 1917, practising at Tooley Street, S.E. Gazetted 2nd Lieut. 2/1 City of London Brigade, Royal Field Artillery (T.) March 12, 1915, promoted Lieut. June 1916. Served in France to Dec. 1916, and afterwards at Home as Military Representative on Tribunal of Recruiting Staff.

GERALD RICHARD PALING.

Articled to J. E. Dell, of Brighton. Joined Dec. 6, 1915, as Private, Royal Fusiliers (Public Schools Batt.), subsequently promoted A/Sergeant. Served in France July to Nov. 1916. Wounded at Beaumont Hamel Nov. 13, 1916. Discharged May 5, 1917.

CHARLES COURTNEY PALMER.

Admitted Dec. 1908. Member of Simpson, Palmer & Winder, of 1 Southwark Street, S.E. Joined Nov. 22, 1915, as Private, Inns of Court O.T.C., promoted Lance-Corporal May 1916, Corporal July 1916. Gazetted 2nd Lieut. Royal Marines Oct. 1916, promoted Lieut. Oct. 1917. Served at Home and in France. Wounded in France Feb. 6, 1917. Loss of right eye.

PTOLEMEY WESTON PARDY.

Articled to S. A. Butt, of 2 Walbrook, E.C. Served as Private, 16th Batt. County of London Regt. (Queen's Westminsters).

LEONARD FARMER PARIS.

Admitted Dec. 1908. Member of Paris, Smith & Randall, of Southampton. Joined Hampshire Royal Garrison Artillery (T.) in Sept. 1916, subsequently commissioned as 2nd Lieut. in same Regt. Served at Home.

CHARLES ERNEST PARISH.

Admitted Sept. 1900, practised at Birmingham. Joined Sept. 1914, as Private, 15th Batt. Royal Warwickshire Regt. Served in France and Flanders. Killed near High Wood July 23, 1916.

JOHN BERNARD ANDERSON PARISH.

Admitted May 1911. Member of Hickson & Parish of 134 Fleet Street, E.C. Mobilised Aug. 1914, as 2nd Lieut., 2nd London Brigade, Royal Field Artillery (T.), promoted Lieut. Dec. 1914, A/Capt. April 1915, Substantive Capt. June 1916. Served at Home and in France.

SYDNEY CHRISTIAN PARISH.

Admitted Feb. 1905. Member of Sanders, Locker & Parish, of Birmingham. Joined Dec. 1916, as Private, 1st Infantry Batt. Hon. Artillery Company, subsequently promoted Corporal. Served in France 1917 to 1918. Injured Oct. 1918.

ALBERT BARTON PARK.

Articled to G. H. Millons, of Newcastle-upon-Tyne, subsequently Clerk with Childs, Harling, Reid & Wilson, 3 Southampton Street, Bloomsbury Square, W.C. Joined Nov. 17, 1915, as Cadet, 28th Batt. County of London Regt. (Artists Rifles). Gazetted 2nd Lieut. 5th Batt. King's Own Royal Lancaster Regt. July 11, 1916, promoted Lieut. Jan. 1918, attached to 1/4 Batt. in France. Served in France Sept. 1916 to Nov. 1918.

LESLIE PARK.

Articled to J. C. Heald, of Wigan. Joined Feb. 2, 1915, as Private, Inns of Court O.T.C. Gazetted 2nd Lieut. 3rd Batt. Dorset Regt. June 2, 1915, promoted Lieut. July 1917, transferred to Indian Army Reserve of Officers Feb. 1918 to April 1919. Served in France 1915, and in India 1918. Wounded Oct. 13, 1915.

ARTHUR PARKER.

Admitted Oct. 1905, practising at Blackpool. Served as Private, 3rd (Public Schools) Batt. Royal Fusiliers.

EDWIN CHARLES LEWIS PARKER.

Admitted March 1897, practising at Salisbury. Joined April 1915, as Lieut., Royal Army Service Corps (M.T.), promoted Capt. Aug. 1915, Major, Aug. 1917. Three times mentioned in Dispatches. Awarded O.B.E. (Military). Served at Home, Mesopotamia, and Persia.

GEORGE BERTHOLD PARKER.

Admitted Nov. 1900. Member of Richardson & Parker, of Scarborough. Joined Sept. 1916 British Red Cross Society. Served in Mesopotamia.

GEORGE LESLIE PARKER.

Admitted Dec. 1908. Of St. Leonard's-on-Sea. Mobilised Aug. 1914, as Lieut., 95th Coy. Royal Garrison Artillery, promoted Capt. Aug. 1916, A/Major Dec. 1916. Once mentioned in Dispatches. Served in Bermuda, France, Belgium, and at Home.

HAROLD PARKER.

Admitted Feb. 1904. Member of Forshaw, Parker & Co., of Preston, Lancs. Mobilised Aug. 1914, as Capt., 4th Batt. Loyal North Lancashire Regt., promoted Temp. Major Oct. 1915, Staff Course, Cambridge, May to June 1917, Brigade Major 1st London Reserve Brigade July 1917 to April 1918, Substantive Major Feb. 1918, A/Brigade Major 29th Division April 1918, Brigade Major 31st Division June 1918, and 42nd Division Oct. 1918. Twice mentioned in Dispatches. Awarded the D.S.O. Served in France. Gassed June 1915, wounded Aug. 14, 1916, and injured June 17, 1918.

HUGH ALGERNON PARKER.

Admitted Dec. 1903. Member of Royds, Rawstorne & Co., of 46 Bedford Square, W.C. Joined May 1915, as Lieut., Lincolnshire Yeomanry, promoted

Temp. Capt. Aug. 1916, Substantive Capt. June 1917. Once mentioned in Dispatches. Served in England May 1915 to March 1917, and in France March 1917 to April 1919.

JAMES STANLEY PARKER.

Articled to W. E. Farr, of Leeds. Served in Leeds University O.T.C.

JOHN ANTHONY PARKER.

Admitted Nov. 1907. Member of Parkers & Hammond, of Friars House, New Broad Street, E.C. Joined March 27, 1916, as Private, Royal Army Service Corps. Gazetted 2nd Lieut. Royal Army Ordnance Corps Oct. 16, 1916, promoted Lieut. Jan. 1917. Served at Home.

REGINALD FRANK PARKER.

Admitted April 1903. Member of Sharpe, Pritchard & Co., of 12 New Court, Carey Street, W.C.; and Parliament Mansions, Victoria Street, S.W. Joined Oct. 1914, as Private, Inns of Court, O.T.C., promoted Sergeant Nov. 1914. Gazetted Lieut. 21st Batt. Manchester Regt. Jan. 1915, promoted Capt. Feb. 1915, Staff Capt. (General List) Oct. 1916. Three times mentioned in Dispatches. Awarded M.C. and O.B.E. (Military Division). Served at Home Oct. 1914 to Oct. 1915, France Oct. 1915 to Dec. 1917, and Italy Dec. 1917 to March 1919.

TREVOR JAMES MORDAUNT BARON PARKER.

Articled to Moses Thomas, of Aberavon. Joined Oct. 4, 1915, as Private, Royal Army Service Corps (M.T.). Commissioned in same Regt. Feb. 4, 1918, promoted Lieut. Aug. 1919. Served in France Feb. 1916 to Oct. 1919.

WILFRID WATSON PARKER.

Admitted March 1894. Member of Parker & Hollebone, of 35 Bloomsbury Square, W.C. Joined Sept. 1914, as Capt., Queen Victoria's Rifles, appointed Brigade Musketry Officer Dec. 1914. Awarded M.B.E. (Military) and T.D. Served at Home.

WILLIAM TAYLOR PARKES.

Admitted July 1902. Member of Amery, Parkes & Co., of 18 Fleet Street, E.C. Joined May 14, 1916, as Private, Heavy Branch Machine Gun Corps, transferred to Tank Corps as Corporal Dec. 1916. Gazetted 2nd Lieut. Tank Corps Aug. 1917, promoted Lieut. Feb. 1919. Awarded the M.C. Served in France. Wounded Sept. 28, 1918.

FREDERICK PARKIN.

Admitted Aug. 1885. Member of Hearle-Cock & Parkin, of Truro. Recalled for service Aug. 5, 1914, and formed and commanded Depôt 4th Batt. Duke of Cornwall's Light Infantry from that date to Feb. 1917, transferred to Territorial Force Reserve Feb. 1917. Awarded the T.D. Served at Home.

GEORGE MONTAGU PARKIN.

Articled to Trower, Still, Parkin & Keeling, of 5 New Square, W.C. Served as Lieut., 2nd North Midland Brigade, Royal Field Artillery, promoted Capt. June 1916. Mentioned in Dispatches. Awarded the M.C.

SYDNEY PARKINSON.

Admitted May 1914, practising at Wigan. Joined Nov. 1916, as Private, Royal Army Ordnance Corps (attached Royal Artillery), promoted Corporal Jan. 1918. Served in France.

THOMAS CLIFTON PARKINSON.

Admitted April 1912. Member of Parkinson, Slack & Needham, of Manchester. Served as 2nd Lieut., 7th Batt. Lancashire Fusiliers (T.), and subsequently promoted Lieut.

DENIS FILLINGHAM PARR.

Articled to George Parr, of Nottingham. Gazetted 2nd Lieut. 9th Batt. Notts and Derby Regt. (Sherwood Foresters) Sept. 1914. Reported missing July 7, 1916, and subsequently officially reported to have died on that date.

CHARLES OWAIN ST. JOHN PARRY.

Articled to J. H. S. Butt, of 4 Trafalgar Square W.C. Joined Oct. 22, 1914, as Private, 2/5 Batt. The Queen's Royal West Surrey Regt. Gazetted 2nd Lieut. 3rd Batt. The Queen's April 30, 1915, seconded to Labour Corps May 1917, promoted Lieut. Oct. 1917. Served at Home and in France.

HENRY OWEN PARRY.

Admitted June 1900, practising at Criccieth. Served as Private, Machine Gun Corps.

JOHN SAMUEL PARRY.

Admitted March 1903, practising at Wrexham. Served as Gunner, Royal Garrison Artillery.

WILLIAM HENRY LIDDON PARRY.

Articled to G. A. Double, of 91 Fore Street, E.C. Joined 2nd Sept. 1914, as Private, 21st Batt. Royal Fusiliers. Subsequently gazetted 2nd Lieut. 24th Batt. Royal Fusiliers. Served in France. Died Nov. 29, 1916, of wounds received in action Nov. 13, 1916.

ALFRED CYRIL PARSONS.

Articled to J. W. W. Mathew, of Exeter. Joined Sept. 1914, as Private, 19th (Service) Batt. Royal Fusiliers, and subsequently promoted Corporal. Gazetted 2nd Lieut. Somerset Light Infantry Aug. 5, 1916, promoted Lieut. 1918, and afterwards Capt. Served in France Nov. 1915 to April 1916, Sept. 1916, and Nov. 1917 to March 1918. Wounded at Goudecourt Sept. 1916. Killed March 29, 1918.

GODFREY VALENTINE HOPE PARSONS.

Articled to Donald Maclean, of Cardiff. Served as 2nd Lieut., 2nd Welsh Brigade, Royal Field Artillery (T.), promoted Lieut. June 1916.

HENRY ALEXANDER PARSONS.

Admitted Sept. 1903. Member of Lee-Roberts & Parsons, of Bedford. Served as Gunner, Essex and Suffolk Royal Garrison Artillery.

HERBERT PARSONS.

Admitted March 1885, practising at 17 Heathfield Park, Willesden Green, N.W. Joined Oct. 21, 1914, as Sergeant, 18th Batt. County of London Regt.

(London Irish), transferred to 23rd Batt. The Rifle Brigade Dec. 1915, to 13th Batt. Royal Defence Corps July 1917. Served at Home Oct. 1914 to Jan. 1916 and June to Dec. 1917, and in India Jan. 1916 to June 1917. Discharged by special order of War Office to take up post as Deputy Assistant Censor Dec. 8, 1917.

JOHN STANLEY PARSONS.

Articled to John Parsons, of Leicester. Mobilised Aug. 1914, as Lieut., 4th Batt. Leicestershire Regt., transferred to Signals, Royal Engineers, Jan. 1916, and promoted Temp. Capt., promoted Temp. Major Jan. 1917. Twice mentioned in Dispatches. Awarded D.S.O. Served in France and Belgium 1915, and 1917 to 1919.

STANLEY PARSONS.

Admitted Jan 1906, practising at St. Blazey, Par, Cornwall. Joined Aug. 1, 1918, as Private, Royal Air Force. Served at Home.

WILLIAM LANSBURY PARSONS.

Admitted April 1900, practising at Brixham, South Devon. Joined Nov. 23, 1914, as Lieut., Army Ordnance Department, afterwards Royal Army Ordnance Corps, promoted A/Capt. Sept. 1916, Temp. Capt. Oct. 1917, Temp. Major Oct. 1917, A/Lieut.-Col. Dec. 1918. Once mentioned in Dispatches. Served at Home.

ERNEST GEORGE PARTON.

Admitted Feb. 1905. Member of Drake, Son & Parton, of 24 Rood Lane, E.C. Served as 2nd Lieut., 13th Batt. County of London Regt., promoted Capt. June 1916.

ROBERT HENRY PARTRIDGE.

Articled to his father, F. H. Partridge, of King's Lynn. Gazetted 2nd Lieut. 5th Batt. Norfolk Regt. (T.) Nov. 18, 1914, promoted Lieut. 1916. Served at Gallipoli, Egypt, Palestine. Died at Gaza Sept. 4, 1917.

THOMAS HERBERT PARTRIDGE.

Admitted April 1909. Member of Gillespie & Co., of Walsall. Served as A/Paymaster, Army Pay Department.

ARCHIBALD BESLEY PASMORE.

Admitted April 1912. Managing Clerk with Hicklin, Washington & Pasmore, of 1 Trinity Square, Southwark, S.E. Mobilised Aug. 1914, as Sergeant, Westminster Dragoons Yeomanry. Discharged time expired Feb. 1916. Joined Royal Horse and Royal Field Artillery April 1916. Commissioned 2nd Lieut. (S.R.) July 7, 1916, promoted Lieut. (S.R.) Jan. 1918. Served in Egypt Sept. 1914 to Aug 1915, and Nov. 1915 to Jan. 1916, Gallipoli Aug. to Nov. 1915, France July to Sept. 1916, Home Sept. 1916 to June 1917, Mesopotamia June 1917 to April 1918, and Palestine April 1918 to July 1919. Wounded on the Somme Sept 15, 1916, during attack on Les Bœufs and Goudecourt.

WILLIAM HAYMEN PASSBY.

Admitted Aug. 1909, practising at Rochester and Chatham. Mobilised Aug. 1914, as Capt., Kent Royal Garrison Artillery (T.), promoted Major

Sept. 1914, A/Lieut.-Col. Royal Artillery as C.R.A. China Command July 1917. Mentioned for valuable services rendered in connection with the War. Served at Home July 1914 to Jan. 1916 and July to Oct. 1919, in France Jan. to July 1916, and in Hong Kong May 1917 to July 1919. Wounded at Ypres June 24, 1916.

KENELM GRANBY PASSMAN.

Articled to C. H. Passman, of Leamington Spa. Joined Dec. 1914, as Private, Royal Warwickshire Regt. Subsequently gazetted Lieut. Suffolk Regt. Served in France. Killed in action Aug. 30, 1918.

JOHN CRISP PATERSON.

Articled to Sir Frank Crisp, of 17 Throgmorton Avenue, E.C. Joined Oct. 1914, as Private, Hon. Artillery Company. Gazetted 2nd Lieut. 3rd Batt. Devonshire Regt. Aug. 26, 1915, promoted Lieut. July 1917. Served in France 1916. Wounded on the Somme Sept. 6, 1916.

SAMUEL PATEY.

Admitted Nov. 1895. Member of H. W. & S. Patey, of 42 Finsbury Square, S.E. Joined July 1918 Inns of Court O.T.C., transferred to Royal Garrison Artillery as Cadet Oct. 1918. Gazetted Temp. 2nd Lieut. Royal Garrison Artillery April 1919. Served at Home.

FRANK PATTESON.

Admitted July 1902, practising at 303 High Holborn, W.C. Joined March 7, 1917, as Rifleman, 16th Batt. County of London Regt. (Queen's Westminster Rifles). Gazetted 2nd Lieut. Scots Guards May 28, 1918. Served at Home and in France and Cologne.

GEORGE NORMAN PATTINSON.

Admitted Dec. 1913, practising at Windermere. Joined Red Cross Aug. 1915. Commissioned Lieut. Royal Army Service Corps (attached 1st Heavy Artillery Brigade) June 19, 1916, promoted A/Capt. June 1917. Served in France.

JAMES PHILIP PAULL.

Admitted May 1886, practising at Truro, Cornwall. Rejoined Royal Engineers as Capt. and Hon. Major Oct. 13, 1914. Served at Home and in France.

RICHARD GEORGE PAVER-CROW.

Admitted Aug. 1903. Member of Titley & Paver-Crow, of Harrogate. Joined British Red Cross Society in France May 18, 1915. Joined Cavalry Squadron Inns of Court O.T.C. as Trooper, Jan. 19, 1916. Granted commission of 2nd Lieut. Royal Army Service Corps June 5, 1916, promoted Lieut. Dec. 1917. Served in France May to Nov. 1915 and Nov. 1917 to April 1919, and in Serbia July to Nov. 1916.

JAMES HAWKINS PAWLYN.

Admitted Nov. 1908, practising at 59 Strand, W.C. Served as Private, Royal Army Ordnance Corps.

ROBERT HENRY PAWSON.

Admitted March 1911. Managing Clerk with Belk, Cochrane & Belk, of Middlesbrough. Joined Jan. 1915, as Private, 4th Batt. Yorkshire Regt.

Gazetted Sub-Lieut. Royal Naval Volunteer Reserve Nelson Batt. Dec. 15, 1916, subsequently amalgamated with Drake Batt. Served in France. Reported wounded and missing, afterwards killed, March 25, 1918.

CLARENCE ALFRED PAYNE.

Admitted Dec. 1916, practising at Bradford. Served as Private, 26th Batt. Durham Light Infantry.

FREDERICK CHARLES PAYNE.

Admitted March 1901. Member of Payne & Payne, of Hull. Joined Oct. 1, 1917, as Private, King's Own Yorkshire Light Infantry. Gazetted 2nd Lieut. Labour Corps Dec. 16, 1917, promoted Capt. and appointed Staff Capt. Royal Air Force April 1918. Once mentioned in Dispatches. Served at Home.

JOHN ANNESLEY PAYNE.

Admitted Nov. 1915. Managing Clerk with Ruston, Clark & Ruston, of 14 Norfolk Street, Strand; and Brentford. Joined Nov. 1915, as 2nd Lieut., Royal Army Service Corps, promoted Lieut. 1917. Served in France.

ROBERT ALEXANDER PAYNE.

Admitted Feb. 1904, practising at Sutton, Surrey. Served as Private, 29th Batt. (Canadians) The Bombers.

ROBERT HARRY PAYNE.

Admitted Feb. 1891, practising at Manchester. Joined Nov. 1914, as Lieut., The Queen's Royal West Surrey Regt., Transport Officer to 1st Batt. South Wales Borderers April 1916 to May 1917. Served in France. Resigned commission Nov. 15, 1917.

SYDNEY PAYNE.

Admitted Aug. 1899, practising at Leicester. Joined Aug. 1916, as Gunner, Royal Garrison Artillery. Gazetted 2nd Lieut. Royal Garrison Artillery (S.R.) Dec. 1917, promoted Lieut. June 1919. Served in France.

EDWIN COLEMAN PAYNTER.

Admitted July 1906, practised at Alnwick. Served as Lieut., Royal Field Artillery.

GEOFFREY LITTLEWOOD PEACE.

Articled to J. W. Littlewood, of Wellington, Shropshire. Mobilised Aug. 1914, as 2nd Lieut., 4th Batt. King's Shropshire Light Infantry (T.), promoted Lieut. Nov. 1914, Capt. Aug. 1918. Once mentioned in Dispatches. Served in Burma Oct. 1914 to Feb. 1915, Malay States Feb. 1915 to April 1917, and in France June 1917 to Sept. 1918. Wounded Dec. 1917.

DAVID FRANCIS PEACOCK.

Admitted Feb. 1914. Managing Clerk with Rawnsley & Peacock, of Bradford, Yorks. Joined Sept. 7, 1914, as Private, 1/6 Batt. Duke of Wellington's West Riding Regt., promoted Lance-Corporal Dec. 1914. Gazetted 2nd Lieut. in same unit Jan. 20, 1915, promoted Lieut. Jan. 1916, Temp. Capt. Oct. 1916, reverted to Lieut. July 1917, Assistant Adjutant May to Nov. 1918, Acting Adjutant Nov. 1918 to March 1919, Capt. and Adjutant March and April 1919. Served in France and Belgium. Invalided Home with gas and trench fever Jan. 1916.

COLIN PEAKE.

Admitted Dec. 1913. Managing Clerk with Peake, Bird, Collins & Co., of 6 Bedford Row, W.C. Mobilised Aug. 1914, as Lieut., Leicestershire (Prince Albert's Own) Yeomanry. Served in France. Killed in action near Ypres May 13, 1915.

GEOFFREY COPSON PEAKE.

Admitted Nov. 1905. Member of Bond, Barwick & Peake, of Leeds. Mobilised Aug. 1914, as Capt., Royal Field Artillery (T.), promoted Major July 1916. Served in France 1915, 1916, and 1917, and in Egypt Feb. to Aug. 1916. Wounded at Passchendaele Nov. 10, 1917.

GEORGE ALAN PEAKE.

Articled to H. R. Peake, of 2 Clement's Inn, Strand, W.C. Served as Capt., 8th (Reserve) Batt. Middlesex Regt.

HENRY ARTHUR WYATT PEAKE.

Articled to H. A. Peake, of Sleaford. Joined Aug. 4, 1914, Inns of Court O.T.C. Gazetted 2nd Lieut. 3rd Batt. Essex Regt. Aug. 16, 1914, promoted Capt. May 1916. Served in France Dec. 1914 to June 1915 and May to July 1916, attached to 2nd and 9th Batts. Wounded June 9, 1915. Missing July 3, 1916, near Oilliers, in advance on Somme, and subsequently reported killed in action on that day.

HUGH ROSINDELL PEAKE.

Admitted June 1877, practising at 231 Strand, W.C. Served as Colonel, 8th Batt. Middlesex Regt. (Recruiting Staff).

LEWIS GEORGE PEAKE.

Admitted Oct. 1914. Member of Mullis & Peake, of Romford, Essex. Joined Aug. 9, 1916, as Gunner, Royal Garrison Artillery, and attained the rank of Sergeant. Served at Home.

ARTHUR CARLTON PEARCE.

Articled to Arthur Pearce, of 58 West Smithfield, E.C. Joined Aug. 28, 1914, as Private, Public Schools Corps, transferred to Inns of Court O.T.C. Sept. 1914. Gazetted 2nd Lieut. Royal Army Service Corps Nov. 10, 1914, promoted Lieut. Aug. 1915, transferred to 3rd Batt. Notts and Derby Regt. Sherwood Foresters) Sept 1917, A/Capt. 1918. Served in France Sept. 1915 to July 1918. Killed near Béthune July 22, 1918.

ARTHUR CECIL PEARCE.

Admitted Dec. 1909. Of the Public Trustee Office. Served as Sergeant, 2nd London Clearing Hospital, Royal Army Medical Corps (T.).

CYRIL HARVEY PEARCE.

Admitted July 1902. Member of Middlemiss, Pearce & Miller, of Hull. Mobilised Aug. 1914, as Major, 5th Batt. Yorkshire Regt., subsequently promoted Lieut.-Col. Awarded C.B.E. Served in France and Belgium 1915, 1916, and 1917. Wounded July 1917.

JOHN PEARCE.

Articled to F. B. Wyatt, of South Molton, Devon. Mobilised Aug. 1914, as Capt., 6th Batt. Devonshire Regt. (T.), and promoted Major in June 1916. Served in India Oct. 1914 to Dec. 1915, in Mesopotamia Dec. 1915 to Oct. 1916, and in France Jan. to July 1918.

JULIAN PHILLIPS PEARCE.

Articled to F. C. Pearce, of 70 Gracechurch Street, E.C. Joined Aug. 1914, as 2nd Lieut., attached to 2nd Batt. Essex Regt., promoted Lieut. 1915, Capt. Jan. 1916. Served in Mons Retreat and Battle of Aisne. Taken prisoner Nov. 1914, sent to Crefeld Swarmsted, Holtzminden.

WALTER KENNEDY PEARCE.

Articled to A. W. Pearce, of Southampton. Mobilised Aug. 1914, as Lieut., 5th Batt. Hampshire Regt., and promoted Capt. June 1916. Served at Home and in India.

GERALD DOUGLAS PEARCE-JONES.

Articled to A. Pearce-Jones, of 33 John Street, Bedford Row, W.C. Joined Aug. 22, 1914, as Volunteer Motor Driver, and joined 1st Divisional Train, attached 2nd Infantry Brigade. Commissioned 2nd Lieut. Royal Field Artillery (S R.) April 10, 1915, promoted Temp. Lieut. Nov. 1915, A/Capt. May 1917, Permanent Lieut. June 1917, A/Major Aug. 1918. Served at Home May to Sept. 1915, in France Aug. 1914 to May 1915 and Sept. 1915 to Jan. 1916, and at Salonica Jan. 1916 to April 1919.

ANDRÉ MELLARD PEARKES.

Admitted Jan. 1913. Managing Clerk with Sedgwick, Turner, Sworder & Wilson, of Watford. Mobilised Aug 1914 with 28th Batt. County of London Regt. (Artists Rifles). Gazetted 2nd Lieut. 9th Batt. West Yorkshire Regt. Sept. 17, 1914, promoted Lieut. Dec. 1914, and Capt. March 1915. Served in Gallipoli, and took part in the Suvla Bay operations. Killed in action in Gallipoli Aug. 9, 1915.

LESLIE VINCENT PEARKES.

Articled to A. E. Pearkes, of 21 College Hill, Cannon Street, E.C. Joined Nov. 12, 1915, as Sub-Lieut., Royal Naval Volunteer Reserve (attached Royal Naval Air Service), promoted Flight-Lieut. March 1917, Capt. Royal Air Force April 1918. Once mentioned in Dispatches. Awarded the French Croix de Guerre with Palms Served with French Army at Verdun March 1916 to July 1917, on Submarine Patrols Aug. 1917 to April 1918, and Night Flying Defence of London April to Nov. 1918. Wounded in aerial fight over Saarbrücken Nov. 11, 1916, and sustained concussion of the brain whilst night flying at Eastchurch Oct. 4, 1918.

PEARMAN BEEBEE PEARMAN-SMITH.

Admitted April 1914. Member of S. Pearman-Smith & Sons, of Walsall. Served in 4th (Public Schools) Batt. Royal Fusiliers.

ALFRED PEARSON.

Articled to Alfred Pearson, of Manchester. Joined Manchester University O.T.C. Oct. 1915. Gazetted 2nd Lieut. 6th Batt. Lancashire Fusiliers July 20,

1916, promoted Lieut. Jan. 1918. Served in France Jan. to May 1917 and July 1918 to Jan. 1919. Wounded April 15, 1917, May 17, 1917, and Aug. 11, 1918.

FRANK PEARSON.

Admitted July 1894 Practised at Kirkby Lonsdale and Ingleton. Joined March 12, 1917, as Capt., Loyal North Lancashire Regt. Served at Home. Died of pneumonia contracted while on Active Service Feb. 5, 1918.

FRANK SHAKESPEARE PEARSON.

Admitted Aug. 1889. Member of Thomas Guest & Pearson of Birmingham. Lieut.-Col. South Midland Royal Army Service Corps. Died, the result of a fall from his horse while on military duty, Sept. 5, 1916.

HAROLD FELLOWS PEARSON.

Admitted April 1903. Member of Janson, Cobb, Pearson & Co., of College Hill, E.C. Joined Dec. 21, 1914, as Private, Inns of Court O.T.C. Obtained commission in the Middlesex Regt. and attained the rank of Capt. Awarded the M.C. Served in France. Wounded March 24, 1918.

HUGH WATSON PEARSON.

Admitted Feb. 1914. Member of Pearsons & Russell, of Malton, Yorks. Mobilised Aug. 1914, as Lieut., East Riding Yeomanry, promoted Capt. in June 1916, attached to Machine Gun Corps in May 1918 and promoted A/Major in Sept. 1918. Served at Home 1914 to 1915, in Egypt 1915 to 1916, Palestine 1917 to 1918, and in France 1918 to 1919.

ROBERT TUTE PEARSON.

Admitted Aug. 1913. Member of Pearsons and Russell, of Helmsley, Yorks. Served as Lieut., West Riding Division, Royal Army Service Corps, promoted Capt. June 1916. Mentioned in Dispatches. Awarded the M.C.

THOMAS HOWEL PEARSON.

Admitted Aug. 1911. Managing Clerk with Chamberlayne, Hacking & Co., of 45 Parliament Street, Westminster, S.W. Joined Aug. 1914, as Private, 1/2 County of London Yeomanry (Westminster Dragoons). Gazetted 2nd Lieut. 3/1 West Kent Yeomanry Nov. 28, 1916, promoted Lieut. May 1918, attached to Royal Air Force Jan. to Oct. 1918, and to Royal West Kent Regt. Oct. 1918 to March 1919. Served at Home Aug. to Sept. 1914 and June 1916 to Nov. 1918, in Egypt and Gallipoli Sept. 1914 to June 1916, and in France Nov. 1918 to March 1919.

THOMAS ROYSTON PEARSON.

Articled to P. W. Allen, of Nottingham. Served as 2nd Lieut., South Notts Yeomanry.

WILLIAM ALFRED PEARSON.

Admitted Nov. 1883, practising at York. Rejoined as Capt., on Declaration of War, for General Service Abroad and posted to the 2/5 Batt. West Yorkshire Regt. Served at Home.

WILLIAM GAREUCINRES PEARSON.

Admitted Jan. 1907. Member of H. G. Pearson & Son, of Barrow-in-Furness. Mobilised Aug. 4, 1914, as Capt., 4th Batt. King's Own Royal Lancaster Regt. (T.). Gazetted Major June 1916. Served in France.

Wounded and taken prisoner at Festubert June 15, 1915, transferred to Switzerland Dec. 1916 and to England Sept. 1917. Retired through ill-health contracted during the War Dec. 1917.

WILLIAM GEORGE FREDERICK PEARSON.

Admitted Aug. 1905, practising with Thorpe, Meadows & Pearson, of Hastings. Joined Dec. 5, 1915, as Private, 28th Batt. County of London Regt. (Artists Rifles). Gazetted 2nd Lieut. Sept. 18, 1917, promoted Lieut. March 1919. Awarded the M.C. Served in France.

ROBERT EUSTACE PEART.

Admitted Oct. 1914, of Tottenham. Served as Private, 28th Batt. County of London Regt. (Artists Rifles). Died in France Oct. 26, 1916, as the result of an accidental gunshot wound whilst training for a commission.

KENNETH PECK.

Admitted Aug. 1914, practising at Southport. Joined July 1917, as Private, Inns of Court O.T.C. Gazetted 2nd Lieut. King's Liverpool Regt. May 1918. Served in France.

SAMUEL WILTON PEED.

Admitted April 1893, formerly practising at Cambridge. Joined Oct. 1914, as Private, Howitzer Battery Field Artillery, New Zealand Expeditionary Force, and attained the rank of Sergeant. Died at Cairo, Egypt, of pneumonia March 21, 1915.

FREDERICK WILLIAM PEET.

Articled to James Reynolds, of 70 Basinghall Street, E.C. Joined June 1915, as Private, Hon. Artillery Company, and attained the rank of Sergeant. Killed in action in France Dec. 1, 1916.

JAMES THOROUGOOD PEET.

Admitted Oct. 1911. Managing Clerk with Cattarns & Harris, of 22 Billiter Street, E.C. Joined Sept. 5, 1914, as Private, 19th Batt. King's Liverpool Regt. Gazetted Temp. 2nd Lieut. 19th Batt. the Lancashire Fusiliers July 5, 1915, promoted Temp. Lieut. March 1915, Temp. Capt. April 1915. Served at Home and in France.

WILFRID JOHN PEGGE.

Admitted Oct. 1913. Member of Wilding, Bonney & Pegge, of Manchester. Served as Lieut., King's Liverpool Regt. Mentioned in Dispatches. Awarded M.C.

HUGH JOHN CHEVALLIER PEIRS.

Admitted Nov. 1912. Member of Ellis, Peirs & Co., of 17 Albemarle Street, W. Rejoined Sept. 1914, as Capt., 8th Batt. The Queen's, promoted Major 1915, T/Lieut.-Col. 1918. Five times mentioned in Dispatches. Awarded D.S.O. and 2 Bars, and C.M.G. Served in France and Belgium 1915 to 1918. Wounded Aug. 1916, April 1918, and Oct. 1918.

CHARLES LEIGH PEMBERTON.

Articled to F. S. Whittingham, of Stroud. Served as Private, 18th (Service) Batt. Royal Fusiliers.

ROGER BUSICK PEMBERTON.
Articled to H. A. Whately, of 44 Lincoln's Inn Fields, W.C. Joined Sept. 18, 1914, as 2nd Lieut., 7th Batt. Oxfordshire and Buckinghamshire Light Infantry, promoted Lieut. Nov. 1914, Capt. Oct. 1916, gazetted General Staff Officer III. 28th Division Jan. 1918. Served at Home Sept. 1914 to Sept. 1915, and Jan. to June 1919, in France Sept. to Dec. 1915, and Salonica Dec. 1915 to Dec. 1918.

WILLIAM HARRIS PEMBERTON.
Articled to C. H. Wimshurst, of Liverpool. Served as Capt., Royal Army Service Corps. Mentioned in Dispatches.

JOHN GILBERT PEMBROOK.
Admitted Dec. 1911, practised at Canterbury. Served as 2nd Lieut., 1st Batt. Kent Cyclist Corps, promoted Lieut. July 1917.

JOHN PENNINGTON.
Admitted Oct. 1911. Member of Wright, Beckett & Pennington, of Manchester. Served as 2nd Lieut., King's Liverpool Regt.

ALBERT EDWARD PENNY.
Admitted Nov. 1903, practising at Harlesden, N.W. Joined May 21, 1915, as 2nd Lieut., 7th Batt. Middlesex Regt., and subsequently promoted Lieut. Served in France. Wounded Aug. 8, 1916.

ARTHUR RAYMOND PENNY.
Admitted Nov. 1913. Of Tiverton, Devon. Joined Aug. 7, 1914, as Lance-Corporal 1/1 West Somerset Yeomanry. Gazetted 2nd Lieut. 7th Batt. (Reserve) Dorset Regt. June 10, 1915, transferred to Army Cyclist Corps Oct. 1915, promoted Lieut. (XVII. Corps) Cyclist Batt. July 1917. Served in France April 1916 to Oct. 1919.

THOMAS EDWARD PENNY.
Admitted April 1908. Member of Penny & Son, of Berkhamsted, Herts. Joined Oct. 14, 1915, as Private, Inns of Court O.T.C. Gazetted 2nd Lieut. 1st Batt. Hertfordshire Regt. April 22, 1916, promoted Lieut. Oct. 1917. Served in France and Belgium. Wounded Ypres Oct. 28, 1917. Gazetted out on account of wounds received in action.

LESLIE ERNEST PEPPIATT.
Admitted July 1913, practising at 10 Lincoln's Inn Fields, W.C. Joined Aug. 10, 1914, as Private, Inns of Court O.T.C. Gazetted 2nd Lieut. 7th Batt. London Regt. Sept. 7, 1914, promoted Temp. Lieut. Oct. 1914, Temp. Capt and Adjutant April 1915, Capt. June 1916, A/Major May 1917 to Jan. 1918. Twice mentioned in Dispatches. Awarded the M.C. and Bar. Served at Home and in France. Wounded March 21 and Aug. 31, 1918.

ANDREW FRANCIS PERCIVAL.
Admitted Aug. 1911. Member of Percival & Son, of Peterborough. Joined April 1916, as Gunner, Royal Garrison Artillery. Gazetted 2nd Lieut. Royal Garrison Artillery Dec. 18, 1916, promoted Lieut. June 1918. Served in France.

JOHN LAKEMAN PERCIVAL.

Articled to W. E. Hart, of Sheffield. Joined Sept. 5, 1914, as 2nd Lieut., 6th Batt. Notts & Derby Regt. (Sherwood Foresters), promoted Lieut. Jan. 1915, A/Capt. July 1916, Capt. April 1918, A/Major July to Sept. 1918. Awarded the M.C. Served in France Feb. 1915 to Nov. 1918. Wounded Oct. 13, 1915, Jan. 9, 1917, April 12, 1918, June 21, 1918, and Sept. 10, 1918.

REGINALD GRANT PERCIVAL.

Articled to Alfred Hutchison, of 6 Stone Buildings, Lincoln's Inn, W.C. Joined Sept. 26, 1914, as Driver, Hon. Artillery Company. Gazetted 2nd Lieut. Royal Garrison Artillery (S.R.) Sept. 26, 1916, promoted Lieut. March 1918. Served at Home Sept. 1914 to April 1915 and May to Oct. 1916, in Egypt April 1915 to May 1916, and in France Oct. 1916 to Jan. 1919.

HAMLYN HORWOOD PERHAM.

Admitted July 1897. Member of Perham & Sons, of Bristol. Joined Oct. 1914, as Private, Sportsman's Batt. Royal Fusiliers. Died of meningitis Feb. 20, 1915.

FREDERICK WILLIAM PERKINS.

Admitted March 1914, practising at 139 Oxford Street, W. Joined Jan. 22, 1917, as Private, Inns of Court O.T.C. Commissioned as 2nd Lieut. Royal Garrison Artillery Dec. 2, 1917. Served in France.

HUBERT BARRY PERKINS.

Admitted Dec. 1909, practised at 16 Great James Street, W.C. Served as 2nd Lieut., 1st Batt. Monmouthshire Regt.

WILLIAM JACKSON PERKINS.

Admitted Aug. 1881, practising at Guildford. Served from Sept. 15, 1914, as Lieut.-Col. and Hon. Col. 2/5 Batt. The Queen's. Twice mentioned in Dispatches. Awarded C.M.G. Served at Home.

WILLIAM JACKSON PERKINS, Jun.

Articled to W. J. Perkins, of Guildford. Embodied Aug. 4, 1914, as Lieut., 5th Batt. The Queen's, promoted Capt. June 1916, A/Major Jan. 1918 to Aug. 1919. Twice mentioned in Dispatches. Awarded the M.C. and O.B.E. Served at Home Aug. 1914 to Jan. 1915, in France Jan. to Oct. 1915, in Egypt and Salonica Dec. 1915 to Dec. 1918, and at the Dardanelles Dec. 1918 to Aug. 1919.

GEORGE ARTHUR CHATER PERKS.

Admitted July 1905, practising at Norwich. Commissioned Nov. 13, 1916, as 2nd Lieut. 2/6 Batt. Norfolk Regt., attached to 92nd Punjabis, Indian Army Reserve of Officers as Lieut. Dec. 1917. Served in England and India.

ARTHUR VIVIAN PERRY.

Admitted Jan. 1913, practising at Hankow, China. Joined Dec. 26, 1915, as Private, Royal Army Service Corps (M.T.). Gazetted 2nd Lieut. in same Regt. Jan. 24, 1916, promoted Lieut. Oct. 1916, Capt. May 1918. Once mentioned in Dispatches. Served in France Jan. 1916 to March 1919. Returned to China June 1919.

ISAAC GEOFFREY BATTEN PERRY.
Admitted Oct. 1908. Member of Waltons & Co., of 101 Leadenhall Street, E.C. Served as Capt., 11th Batt. London Regt.

JOHN CYRIL PERRY.
Admitted Nov. 1913. Managing Clerk with Parson, Lee & Co., of 24 Lime Street, E.C. Joined Sept. 3, 1914, as Rifleman, 9th Batt. London Regt. (Queen Victoria's Rifles), promoted Lance-Corporal Oct. 1914, A/Sergeant Jan. 1915. Commissioned 2nd Lieut. Royal Garrison Artillery (T.) Jan. 27, 1915, promoted Lieut. June 1916, Capt. and Adjutant June 1918. Served in France and at Home. Wounded at Les Bœufs Nov. 4, 1916.

FREDERIC GORDON PETCH.
Articled to Frank Hay, of 9 Lincoln's Inn Fields, W.C. Joined Nov. 16, 1914, as Private, Royal Army Medical Corps, promoted Corporal Dec. 1914. Gazetted 2nd Lieut. Royal Garrison Artillery Jan. 31, 1916, promoted Lieut. July 1916, Staff Lieut. (H.Q. V. Corps Heavy Artillery) April 1918, Temp Capt. (Staff) June 1918. Awarded the M.C. Served in France March 1915 to Jan. 1916 and Feb. 1917 to March 1919, and draft conducting to Hong Kong and back July to Nov. 1916. Remainder of time at Home.

APSLEY KENELM PETER.
Admitted Dec. 1908. Member of Peter, Peter & Sons, of Holsworthy. Joined 1914, as Lieut., 6th Batt. Devonshire Regt. (T.) and attained the rank of Capt.

GERALD PETER.
Admitted April 1909. Member of Peter, Peter & Sons, of Launceston, Holsworthy, and Bude. Joined Aug. 4, 1917, as Private, 2/28 Batt. County of London Regt. (Artists Rifles). Subsequently gazetted 2nd Lieut. Royal Garrison Artillery. Served at Home.

REGINALD ARTHUR PETER.
Admitted Dec. 1903, practising at Looe, Cornwall. Joined Aug. 5, 1914, as Capt., Cornwall Royal Garrison Artillery (T.), Adjutant Oct. 1914 to Nov. 1916, promoted Major Nov. 1916. Twice mentioned in Dispatches. Served at Home.

STUART LUTTRELL PETER.
Articled to Gerald Peter, of Launceston, Cornwall. Joined Aug. 1914, as Private, 1/5 Batt. Duke of Cornwall's Light Infantry (T.). Gazetted 2nd Lieut. Aug. 28, 1914, promoted Lieut. May 1917, Capt. April 1918. Served in India Dec. 1914 to Dec. 1916, and in Egypt and Palestine Jan. 1917 to Jan. 1919.

GERARD PETERS.
Admitted Aug. 1914. Clerk with Collyer, Bristow & Co., of 4 Bedford Row, W.C. Joined Oct. 1915, as Private, Inns of Court O.T.C. Gazetted 2nd Lieut. 6th Batt. Gloucestershire Regt. Sept. 5, 1916. Served in France. Died in action near Chemlnes, in France, Feb. 24, 1917.

JOHN CECIL PETERS.
Admitted April 1910. Member of E. J. & A. Peters, of York. Mobilised Aug. 4, 1914, as Lieut., 5th Batt. Prince of Wales' Own West Yorkshire

Regt. (T.), subsequently promoted Capt. Twice mentioned in Dispatches. Awarded the M.C. Served in France. Discharged unfit for Military Service Jan. 1917.

SYDNEY CONRAD PETERS.

Admitted Nov. 1888, practising at Hove, Sussex. Served as Lieut.-Col., 6th Batt. Hampshire Regt.

HENRY ALOYSIUS PETRE.

Admitted Nov. 1906. Managing Clerk with Blount, Lynch & Petre, of 48 Albemarle Street, W. Mobilised Aug. 1914, as Lieut., Australian Flying Corps, promoted Capt. Nov. 1915, Major Sept. 1916, transferred to Royal Flying Corps Feb. 1918, to Royal Air Force April 1918. Five times mentioned in Dispatches. Awarded the D.S.O. and M.C. Served in Mesopotamia and at Home.

CHARLES EDWARD PETTIT.

Admitted March 1896. Member of Pettit & Westlake, of 13 Granville Place, Oxford Street, W. Mobilised Aug 3, 1914, as Capt., "B" Battery Hon. Artillery Company, promoted Major and seconded to Command 2/1 Warwick Royal Horse Artillery June 1916. Once mentioned in Dispatches. Served in Egypt and Aden Hinterland April 1915 to April 1916, and in France June to Nov. 1917, remainder of time at Home. Severely wounded N.E. of Ypres Oct. 4, 1917.

HAROLD SHARP PETTITT.

Articled to Arthur Pettitt, of Leeds. Joined June 25, 1917, as Ord. Seaman, Royal Naval Volunteer Reserve. Appointed Telegraphist Oct. 1917. Served in the North Sea, English Channel, and North and South Atlantic Oceans.

RICHARD STATHERS PETTY.

Admitted March 1912, practising at York. Joined April 1916, as Gunner, Royal Garrison Artillery, promoted Lance-Bombardier Feb. 1918. Served in France, Belgium, and Germany Jan. 1917 to Jan. 1919.

THOMAS HENRY PEVERELL.

Admitted April 1913. Employed with Downing, Handcock, Middleton and Lewis, of 22 Gt. St. Helen's. E.C. Joined Sept. 8, 1914, as 2nd Lieut., Intelligence Corps (Special List), promoted Lieut. and posted to 4th Batt. Seaforth Highlanders April 1915, promoted Capt. May 1916, Adjutant Sept. 1916 to Nov. 1917. Awarded the D.S.O. and M.C. Served in France Sept. 1914 to Nov. 1917. Wounded Oct. 13, 1915, and Nov. 22, 1917 (lost a leg). Captured by Germans Nov. 22, 1917, and exchanged and repatriated May 1918.

AXEL CHRISTIAN PHARO.

Admitted Oct. 1911. Member of Stones, Morris & Morris, of 41 Moorgate Street, E.C. Joined Sept. 24, 1914, as 2nd Lieut. General List. attached Royal Horse Guards, transferred to Royal Army Service Corps Dec. 1914, promoted Temp Lieut. Feb. 1915, Temp. Capt. April 1917. Served in Belgium Oct. to Dec. 1914, and in France Dec. 1914 to Feb. 1917.

EDMUND JULIAN PHELPS.
Admitted Dec. 1907, practising at 110 Cannon Street, E.C. Served as Private, Public Schools Batt. Middlesex Regt.

MURRAY NEWTON PHELPS.
Admitted Aug. 1896. Member of Phelps & Keeling, of Birmingham. Rejoined Aug. 4, 1914. Gazetted Capt. 6th Batt. Royal Warwickshire Regt. (T.), Assistant Provost-Marshal of 61st Division Aug. 15, 1914. Once mentioned in Dispatches. Awarded T.D. and Officier de l'Etoile Noire (French). Served in France and Flanders May 1916 to Nov. 1918.

CHARLES MURRAY PHILIPPS.
Admitted March 1910, practising at Blackpool. Joined May 19, 1916, as Gunner-Driver, 9th Battery Royal Field Artillery, subsequently promoted Bombardier, then transferred to Royal Garrison Artillery. Served in France. Discharged Sept. 18, 1918.

ARTHUR AUSTIN PHILLIPS.
Articled to William Maddocks, of Coventry. Served as Gunner, Warwickshire Royal Horse Artillery.

CECIL AUGUSTUS PHILLIPS.
Articled to Griffith Saunders, of Llanelly. Joined Aug. 4, 1914, as 2nd Lieut., 4th Batt. The Welch Regt., promoted Lieut. 1915, Capt. Aug. 1915, Adjutant 1916, Major and C.O. of 4th and 5th Batts. The Welch Regt. 1918. Three times mentioned in Dispatches. Awarded the M.C. and Bar. Served in Gallipoli, Egypt, and Palestine.

CHARLES KEITH PHILLIPS.
Admitted Nov. 1911, practising at 60 Haymarket, S.W. Joined Feb. 2, 1915, as 2nd Lieut., 15th Batt. Royal Irish Rifles, promoted Lieut. Oct. 1915, Staff Capt. Headquarters 2nd Army Feb. 1917, transferred to General List, D.A.A.G. G.H.Q. British Forces in Italy, and promoted Major. Once mentioned in Dispatches. Awarded the O.B.E. Served in France Oct. 1915 to Nov. 1917, and in Italy Dec. 1917 to Jan. 1919.

CHARLES KENDALL PHILLIPS.
Admitted June 1914, practised at Harrogate. Served as 2nd Lieut., 5th Batt. Prince of Wales Own West Yorkshire Regt., promoted Capt. Jan. 1918. Mentioned in Dispatches. Awarded the M.C.

CYRIL ST. JOHN PHILLIPS.
Articled to Henry Reed, of Sheffield. Served as 2nd Lieut., 2nd Batt. Duke of Wellington's West Riding Regt.

FRANK JUSTICE PHILLIPS.
Admitted Dec. 1910, practised at Birmingham. Served as Sergeant, Royal Engineers. Killed in action 1916.

GORDON TUCKER PHILLIPS.
Admitted Nov. 1902, practising at Oxford. Served as Capt., 6th Batt. Royal Welch Fusiliers.

HENRY GEORGE PHILLIPS.

Admitted Aug. 1892, practising at Plymouth. Joined April 5, 1916, as Private, Royal Army Service Corps (Motor Lorry Driver). Served in France.

HERBERT ASHLEY PHILLIPS.

Admitted Nov. 1900, practised at Chippenham. Served as Capt., 4th Batt. Wiltshire Regt., promoted Major June 1916.

JENKIN LEWIS PHILLIPS.

Admitted April 1901, practising at Cardiff. Joined Sept. 20, 1916, as Private, Royal Army Service Corps (M.T.). Served at Home (5 months), and in France and Belgium (2 years).

JOHN TREVELYAN PHILLIPS.

Articled to T. W. E. Phillips, of Tredegar, Mon. Joined March 1915. Gazetted 2nd Lieut. 3rd Batt. Monmouthshire Regt. (T.F.) April 19, 1915, promoted Lieut. March 1916, Capt. April 1916, seconded as Capt. Royal Engineers Jan. to Sept. 1918. Served in France and Germany.

JOSEPH ALEXANDER PHILLIPS.

Admitted May 1912. Assistant Solicitor Inland Revenue, Somerset House. Served as Lieut., 13th Batt. King's Liverpool Regt. Reported wounded and missing, and subsequently officially presumed killed in action on May 3, 1917.

PERCY HEPBURN PHILLIPS.

Articled to J. C. Phillips, of 14 Coleman Street, E.C. Served as Lieut., 11th Batt. County of London Regt. (Finsbury Rifles), promoted Capt. June 1916. Mentioned in Dispatches.

WALTER CLIFFORD PHILLIPS.

Admitted Aug. 1880, practising at Newport, Mon. Regazetted Oct. 20, 1914, to command as A/Lieut.-Col. 2/4 Welsh Brigade Royal Field Artillery, vacated appointment June 22, 1916. Appointed Permanent President Quartering Committee, Western Command, 2nd Area, Feb. 1917, Conducting Officer special mission *re* missing operating in North France and Belgium July 1919. Served at Home, France, and Belgium.

WILLIAM DAVID PHILLIPS.

Admitted Sept. 1890, practising at Aberdare, Glamorgan. Mobilised with 5th Batt. The Welch Regt. (T.F), as Major and 2nd in Command, promoted Lieut.-Col. Dec. 1915. Once mentioned in Dispatches. Awarded the T.D. Served in France.

WILLIAM ENGLAND PHILLIPS.

Articled to A. G. S. Robertson, of Bath. Mobilised Aug. 1914, as Lieut., 1/4 Batt. Somerset Light Infantry, promoted Capt. Feb. 1916, Major March 1919. Once mentioned in Dispatches. Served on North-West Frontier of India 1915, and in Mesopotamia Feb. 1916 to Nov. 1918. Wounded at Beit Ailssa April 17, 1916.

WILLIAM GODFREY PHILLIPS.

Admitted Jan. 1908, practising at Stamford. Served as Corporal, Brigade Signal Station.

WILLIAM MALLAM PHILLIPS.

Admitted Aug. 1909. Member of Langley, Stevens & Phillips, of Lincoln. Mobilised Aug. 1914, as Capt., 4th Batt. Lincolnshire Regt. (T.), promoted Major (and attached 1/5 Batt. King's Own Royal Lancaster Regt.) 1918. Once mentioned in Dispatches. Served at Home, Irish Rebellion, and in France. Wounded April 10, 1918.

RALEGH BULLER PHILLPOTTS.

Admitted July 1907. Member of Linklaters & Paines, of 2 Bond Court, E.C. Joined Aug. 5, 1914, as Lieut., Royal 1st Devon Yeomanry, promoted Capt. Dec. 1915, Staff Capt. Levant Base Force Jan. 1916. Served at Home, Gallipoli, and in Egypt. Placed on T.F. Reserve June 30, 1916.

WILLIAM PHILPOT.

Admitted Nov. 1905, practised at Doncaster. Served as 2nd Lieut., West Riding Brigade Royal Field Artillery, promoted Lieut. June 1916.

GEORGE BEVAN PICKERING.

Articled to C. S. Bache, of West Bromwich. Joined Oct. 1, 1917, as Private, West Yorkshire Regt. Served at Home.

ANTHONY FREDERICK INGHAM PICKFORD.

Admitted March 1907. Assistant Solicitor to Manchester Corporation. Joined Nov. 1915, as 2nd Lieut., Royal Army Service Corps (Supply and Horse Transport), promoted Lieut. May 1917, Capt. May 1918. Served at Home and in France.

HARRY THORNTON PICKLES.

Admitted July 1914. Of Manchester. Joined Sept. 18, 1914, as Private, 10th Batt. Duke of Wellington's West Riding Regt. Gazetted 2nd Lieut. in same Regt. Feb. 1915. Served at Home Sept. 1914 to Feb. 1916, and in France till April 1916. Killed by shell shock April 26, 1916.

ALAN ROACH PIERSON.

Admitted Oct. 1912. Of the Solicitors' Department, H.M. Customs and Excise. Joined Sept. 1914, as Private, Inns of Court O.T.C. Gazetted Lieut. Royal Army Ordnance Corps Feb. 1915, promoted Capt. Feb. 1916, Major May 1918.

STANLEY PIESSE.

Admitted April 1902. Of 15 Old Jewry Chambers, E.C. Joined June 1916, as Cadet, Royal Garrison Artillery. Gazetted 2nd Lieut. Aug. 11, 1916, promoted Capt. Jan. 1917. Served at Home.

ARTHUR PERCIVAL VERNON PIGOT.

Articled to Henry Greenall, of Warrington, Lancs. Gazetted 2nd Lieut. 3rd Batt. South Lancashire Regt. Aug. 15, 1914, promoted Lieut. May 1915, Capt. Sept. 1915, A/Major Dec. 1918, attached 2nd Batt. Loyal North Lancashire Regt. Dec. 1914 to Dec. 1916, and to 2nd Batt. South Lancashire Regt. May 1918 to June 1919. Served in East Africa Dec. 1914 to Dec. 1916, at Home Aug. to Dec. 1914 and Dec. 1916 to May 1918, and in France May 1918 to June 1919. Wounded Dec. 16, 1916.

ALBERT HORACE PILBROW.

Admitted Nov. 1908, practising at 328 Camberwell New Road, S.E. Joined April 1917 as Private, subsequently Lieut. 197th Labour Company.

LESLIE LEONARD PILKINGTON.

Admitted July 1914. Managing Clerk with Lycett, Jepson, Birley & Co., of Manchester. Joined Nov. 15, 1916, as Private, Notts and Derby Regt. (Sherwood Foresters), promoted Corporal April 1917, transferred to Army Reserve July 1918 on appointment as Official of Ministry of National Service, Nottingham.

ROBERT LAWRENCE PILLMAN.

Articled to A. E. Leonard, of Bank Buildings, Ludgate Circus, E.C. Joined Aug. 1914, as Private, 10th Batt. Royal Fusiliers. Gazetted 2nd Lieut. 10th Batt. Royal West Kent Regt. July 10, 1915, promoted Lieut. Oct. 1915, Capt. 1916. Served in France. Died July 8, 1916, from wounds received in action near Armentières.

JOHN ROBERT PINDER.

Admitted Oct. 1890, practising at Derby. Rejoined Oct. 1, 1914, as Major, 5th Batt. Notts and Derby Regt. (Sherwood Foresters). Assisted to raise and train 2/5 Batt. and was Second in Command until June 1915, Second in Command of 21st Batt. June 1915 to Sept. 1917, at Headquarters of the Humber Garrison Sept. 1917 to March 1918, and with the Derbyshire Cyclist Regt. March to Oct. 1918. Served at Home.

VICTOR PINNINGTON.

Articled to C. S. Shortt, of Newcastle-upon-Tyne. Served as 2nd Lieut., 2nd Batt. Northumberland Fusiliers (Tyneside Scottish).

CHARLES BERNARD PINNOCK.

Admitted June 1902, practising at Portsmouth. Joined Sept. 1914, as 2nd Lieut., 6th Batt. Hampshire Regt., promoted Substantive Lieut. July 1916, Temp. Capt. Oct. 1915, relinquished rank Dec. 1916. A/Capt. whilst employed on Central Quartering Committee, Tyne Garrison. Served at Home.

ROY PINSENT.

Admitted Aug 1909. Member of Pinsent & Co., of Birmingham. Joined Jan 4, 1916, as 2nd Lieut., Royal Engineers Signals, promoted Lieut. July 1917. Served in Egypt 1916 to 1917, and in Palestine and Syria 1917 to 1919.

CHARLES ARTHUR MATTHEWS PIPER.

Articled to C. A. Piper, of 13 Vincent Square, Westminster. Mobilised Aug. 4, 1914, as Private, 5th City of London Batt. London Regt. Served in France and Flanders. Killed in action May 13, 1915.

HENRY EDMUND GORDON PIPER.

Articled to C. A. Piper, of 13 Vincent Square, Westminster, S.W. Joined June 15, 1916, as Private, Royal Army Service Corps (M.T.). Gazetted 2nd Lieut. in same Regt. Oct. 23, 1916, promoted Lieut. April 1918. Served at Home and in France.

GEORGE CECIL LYNE PIRKIS.
Admitted July 1904. Member of Batchelor, Batchelor & Pirkis, of Outer Temple, Strand, W.C. Served as Private, Inns of Court O.T.C., subsequently gazetted 2nd Lieut. 11th (Reserve) Batt. York and Lancaster Regt., promoted Capt. Nov. 1917.

ARTHUR ALEXANDER PITCAIRN.
Admitted Dec. 1902. Member of Wootton & Son, of 65 London Wall, E.C. Joined Nov. 1915 Inns of Court O.T.C. Gazetted 2nd Lieut. 1/4 Batt. Seaforth Highlanders Feb. 1917, subsequently promoted Lieut. and Capt. Served in France.

STANLEY ARTHUR PITMAN.
Articled to W. J. Pitman, of 11 & 12 Finsbury Square, E.C. Served as Gunner, "A" Battery Hon. Artillery Company.

BEAVAN WILLIAM PITT.
Articled to T. L. Shoosmith, of Northampton. Joined May 1916, as 2nd Lieut., Royal Flying Corps. Served in France. Killed in action while flying May 10, 1917.

GORDON HENRY PITT.
Articled to A. H. Bentley, of 10 Billiter Square, E.C. Served as 2nd Lieut., Nottinghamshire Yeomanry (Sherwood Rangers), promoted Capt. Dec. 1917. Mentioned in Dispatches.

SYDNEY HEWITT PITT.
Articled to Sydney Pitt, of 16 St. Andrew Street, Holborn Circus, E C. Joined Sept. 1, 1914, as 2nd Lieut., Royal Field Artillery, promoted Lieut. Dec. 1915, A/Capt. April to Dec. 1917. Once mentioned in Dispatches. Awarded the M.C. Served in France Dec. 1914 to Feb. 1916, and Salonica Feb. 1916 to May 1918.

WILLIAM ALFRED PITT, Jun.
Admitted Aug. 1902. Member of W. A. Pitt & Son, of Bristol. Joined Sept. 20, 1915, as 2nd Lieut., 11th Batt. Gloucestershire Regt., afterwards attached to 7th Batt. Served in Mesopotamia, Kut, Bagdad, afterwards at Belgaum and Bangalore, in India.

CHARLES SEYMOUR PITTIS.
Articled to A. Y. Young-James, of Newport, Isle of Wight. Mobilised Aug. 1914, as 2nd Lieut., 8th Batt. Hampshire Regt. (T.F.), promoted Lieut. Aug. 1914, Temp. Capt. Sept. 1915, Capt. July 1916. Twice mentioned in Dispatches. Awarded the M.C. Served at Gallipoli, Suvla Bay landing Aug. 1915, Egypt and Palestine July 1916 to April 1917. Killed at Gaza April 19, 1917.

CHARLES HUBERT PLACKETT.
Admitted Nov. 1910. Member of Harland & Plackett, of Leeds. Served as Lieut., 4th Batt. King's Own Yorkshire Light Infantry, promoted Capt. June 1916.

CHARLES STANLEY PLANT.

Articled to H. A. E. Plant, of Preston. Served as Trooper, Cheshire Yeomanry.

EDMUND HUBERT PLANT.

Admitted Nov. 1907, practised at Swansea. Served as Lieut., 7th (Cyclist) Batt. The Welch Regt. and attained the rank of Capt.

GEORGE GOSLING PLANT.

Admitted April 1898. Member of Steavenson, Sons & Plant, of Darlington. Served as Capt. and Adjutant, 5th (Reserve) Batt. Durham Light Infantry.

HARVEY FORSHAW PLANT.

Admitted April 1912. Managing Clerk with Rawle, Johnstone & Co., of 1 Bedford Row, W.C. Mobilised Aug. 5, 1914, as Lieut., Royal Field Artillery, promoted Capt. Oct. 1914, Major March 1917. Once mentioned in Dispatches. Awarded the M.C. Served at Home 1 year, and in France 3 years. Wounded April 9, 1918.

WILLIAM JAMES PLANT.

Admitted April 1912. Managing Clerk with Plant, Abbott & Plants, of Preston and Poulton-le-Fylde. Joined Aug. 8, 1914, as Private, 3rd Batt. Loyal North Lancashire Regt. Gazetted 2nd Lieut. in same Regt. Feb. 27, 1915, promoted Lieut. Aug. 1915, Temp. Capt. April 1917. Served in France Aug. to Oct. 1914, Feb. to May 1916, and April to Nov. 1917, and the remainder of time at Home. Wounded Oct. 1914.

EDWARD ARTHUR PLATT.

Admitted July 1914. Of 5 Chester Terrace, Regent's Park, N.W. Served as Private, 28th Batt. County of London Regt. (Artists Rifles).

WALTER LESLIE PLATTS.

Admitted July 1908, practising at Hull. Joined 1915, as Sub-Lieut., Royal Naval Volunteer Reserve, promoted Lieut. Jan. 1917. Served in Anti-Submarine campaign as Commanding Officer of various vessels.

GILBERT PLAYER.

Admitted April 1899. Of Sunderland. At outbreak of War purchased (with two friends) and lent to the Admiralty, Motor Yacht *Yvonne*, and served in Royal Navy with this boat, patrolling E. Coast 1914 to 1915. When patrol work was taken over by Torpedo-boat destroyers, commissioned as 2nd Lieut. in 21st Batt. Durham Light Infantry. Served in France with 18th (County) Batt. Durham Light Infantry. Died of wounds in France July 30, 1916.

JOHN CHRISTOPHER PLEWS.

Articled to W. H. Kingswell, of Wakefield. Served as 2nd Lieut., 4th Batt. King's Own Yorkshire Light Infantry, promoted Capt. June 1916.

CUTHBERT HERBERT POLL.

Articled to Claude Stratford, of Norwich. Joined Sept. 27, 1914, as Trooper, Eastern Mounted (Norfolk Yeomanry) Brigade. Gazetted 2nd Lieut., 2/6 Cyclist) Batt. Norfolk Regt. Jan. 25, 1917, promoted Lieut. July 1918. Served at Home, Gallipoli, and Egypt.

WALTER HUNGERFORD POLLEN.

Articled to L. L. Yeatman, of 37 Norfolk Street, W.C. Served as Lieut., 4th Batt. Scottish Rifles (Cameron Highlanders). Awarded the M.C.

JAMES BURTON POLLITT.

Admitted Aug. 1884, formerly practising at Manchester. Served as Col., 7th Batt. Manchester Regt.

CHARLES FREDERICK POLLOCK.

Admitted Dec. 1887. Member of Harrison, Pollock & Harrison, of Vernon House, Bloomsbury Square, W.C. Served as Flight Lieut., Royal Naval Air Service, subsequently became Lieut.-Col. in the Royal Air Force. Served in France. Awarded O.B.E. and A.F.C.

EVELYN HAY POLLOCK.

Admitted March 1885. Of Hambledon, Hants. Served as Lieut.-Col., commanding Wessex (Reserve) Divisional Train, Royal Army Service Corps (T.). Awarded O.B.E.

VIVIAN ARTHUR POLLOCK.

Admitted Feb. 1904. Formerly member of Pollock & Co., of 6 Lincoln's Inn Fields, W.C. Served as Capt., 11th Batt. Durham Light Infantry.

ARTHUR GEORGE POOLE.

Articled to Burges & Sloan, of Bristol. Gazetted 2nd Lieut. 12th Batt. Gloucestershire Regt. 1914, subsequently attained the rank of Capt. and attached 6th Batt. Went to France in 1915. Severely wounded Oct. 1917. Once mentioned in Dispatches. Died of pneumonia Nov. 23, 1918.

GILBERT SANDFORD POOLE.

Admitted May 1907. Member of Hugh R. Poole & Son, of South Petherton, Somerset. Mobilised Aug. 1914, as Lieut., West Somerset Yeomanry, promoted Capt. Sept. 1914, Major March 1915, Lieut.-Col. Nov. 1918, attached 12th (West Somerset Yeomanry) Batt. Somerset Light Infantry. Once mentioned in Dispatches. Awarded the D.S.O. Served at Home Aug. 1914 to Sept. 1915, Gallipoli Oct. to Nov. 1915, Egypt and Palestine May 1916 to May 1918, and in France and Belgium Jan. to Dec. 1918.

WILLIAM JOHN ROWLAND ERNEST POOLE.

Articled to J. W. Render, J.P., of Harrogate. Joined Sept. 2, 1914, as Private, 2/5 Batt. West Yorkshire Regt. and attained rank of Sergeant. Gazetted 2nd Lieut. York and Lancashire Regt. July 1915. Served in France. Wounded July 1916. Killed in action Oct. 9, 1917.

JOHN WIGNALL POOLEY.

Articled to A. E. Habgood, of Bristol. Commissioned July 22, 1915, as 2nd Lieut., 4th Batt. Gloucestershire Regt., seconded Machine Gun Corps. March 1916, promoted Lieut. Feb. 1917, A/Capt. Nov. 1918. Served in France. Wounded at Ypres Sept. 11, 1916.

ROGER ALVIN POORE.

Admitted July 1896. Of 6 Southwick Crescent, W. Served as Major, Royal Welch Fusiliers. Killed in action Sept. 26, 1917.

CYRIL MONTAGU POPE.

Articled to R. B. Pope, of Brighton. Mobilised Aug. 1914, as Lieut. 2nd Batt. Worcestershire Regt. Served in France Aug. to Oct. 1914. Died of Wounds Oct. 24, 1914.

EDWARD ALEXANDER POPE.

Admitted July 1898, practised at Dorchester. Mobilised Aug. 1914, as Major, 3rd Batt. The Welch Regt. Raised and commanded 12th Batt. South Wales Borderers and served with them in France. Wounded April 1917. Returned to England and took command of 3rd Batt. The Welch Regt. Nov. 1917. Awarded the D.S.O. Invalided out of Army March 1919. Died of disease contracted on Active Service April 9, 1919.

ERIC HAMILTON POPE.

Articled to W. Stuckey, of Brighton. Mobilised Aug. 4, 1914 as 2nd Lieut., 6th Batt. Royal Sussex Regt., promoted Lieut. May 1914, Capt. March 1915. Served at Home Aug. 1914 to Oct. 1917, Palestine Oct. 1917 to April 1918, France April to Sept. 1918, and in Ireland Oct. 1918 to March 1919.

HORACE OCTAVIUS KELWAY POPE.

Articled to H. K. Pope, of Southampton. Served with 4th (Public Schools) Batt. Royal Fusiliers. Subsequently gazetted 2nd Lieut. 16th Batt. Middlesex Regt., promoted Lieut. July 1917.

PHILIP GLADSTONE POPE.

Admitted March 1911. Of Exeter. Joined Dec. 1915, as 2nd Lieut., Royal Field Artillery, and subsequently promoted Lieut., Adjutant 35th Brigade Oct. 1916. Killed near Passchendaele Oct. 16, 1917.

SEYMOUR FELL POPE.

Admitted Dec. 1904. Member of Sparkes, Pope & Thomas, of Crediton, Devon. Joined Oct. 1, 1914. Gazetted 1st Lieut. 2/6 Devon Regt. June 1, 1916, promoted Capt. March 1918, Major Feb. 1918, D.A.Q.M.G. Base Headquarters, Basra, Mesopotamia, Oct. 1916 to Aug. 1918, D.A.Q.M.G. Refugee Camp, Baquba, Mesopotamia, Aug. 1918 to Feb. 1919. Three times mentioned in Dispatches. Awarded O.B.E. Served at Home Oct. to Dec. 1914, in India Jan. 1915 to Sept. 1916, and in Mesopotamia Sept. 1916 to Feb. 1919.

BERNARD EYRE POPPLETON.

Admitted Oct. 1911, practising at Castleford. Mobilised Aug. 1914, as Capt., 5th Batt. King's Own Yorkshire Light Infantry. Appointed O.C. 89th Territorial Force Depôt, Doncaster, June 1916, transferred to 4th Batt. King's Own Yorkshire Light Infantry Oct 1916. Served at Home Aug. 1914 to Jan. 1917, and in France Jan. 1917 to Feb. 1919.

HERBERT WALTER PORT.

Admitted March 1907. Member of Fillmer & Port, of Brighton. Joined Jan. 24, 1917, as Gunner, Royal Garrison Artillery. Gazetted 2nd Lieut. Labour Corps Feb. 24, 1918. Served in France.

FREDERICK ERNEST GILCHRIST PORTER.

Articled to W. J. R. Gaze, of 13 Suffolk Street, Pall Mall, S.W. Joined Sept. 1914, as Private, Inns of Court O.T.C. Subsequently gazetted 2nd Lieut.

7th Batt. Loyal North Lancashire Regt. and attained the rank of Capt. Served in France 1915 and 1916. Wounded on the Somme Nov. 2, 1916. Died at Warloy, near Albert, Nov. 3, 1916.

JOHN COPESTAKE PORTER.

Admitted April 1899. Member of Ward, Bowie, Porter & Co., of 7 King Street, E.C. Served as Lieut., Remounts, France.

ROBERT HORNBY PORTER.

Admitted Jan. 1909. Of Elland. Joined May 27, 1915, as 2nd Lieut., 3/4 Batt. West Riding Regt. (T.), promoted Lieut. Jan. 1917, A/Capt. July to Nov. 1917 and May to Nov. 1918. Served in France Jan. 1917 to Feb. 1918 and Oct. to Nov. 1918, and in Ireland March to Oct. 1918. Wounded at Fresnoy Nov. 4, 1918.

RODERICK SPICER RUSSELL PORTER.

Admitted Dec. 1911. With the Public Trustee until 1913 and then went to Rangoon, Burma. Joined Nov. 20, 1914, as 2nd Lieut., Indian Army Reserve of Officers. Attached for training to Durham Light Infantry Dec. 1914 and to 124th Baluchi Light Infantry Jan. 1915. Attached for service to 101st Grenadiers April 1915 and to 130th King George's Own Baluchis June 1915 to June 1916, promoted Lieut. Killed in action near Mkalarns, East Africa, June 9, 1916.

ROYDEN SPENCER BAYSPOOL PORTER.

Admitted Feb. 1912, practised at 2 Wardrobe Place, Doctors' Commons, E.C. Joined 1914, as Private, 2nd Batt. Hon. Artillery Company, subsequently gazetted 2nd Lieut. Hon. Artillery Company. Died Feb. 6, 1917, in a hospital abroad.

THOMAS BRANDAM PORTER.

Articled to T. S. Porter, of Bedford. Served as Corporal, West Anglian Royal Engineers.

HERBERT MARTIN RIXSEN POTHECARY.

Admitted May 1905. Member of Balderston, Warren & Pothecary, of 32 Bedford Row, W.C. Served as Private, 28th Batt. County of London Regt. (Artists Rifles) and subsequently gazetted Lieut. Prince of Wales' Own West Yorkshire Regt. Mentioned in Dispatches. Awarded the M.C.

WALTER FRANK POTHECARY.

Admitted May 1905, practising at 1 Gresham Buildings, Basinghall Street, E.C. Mobilised Aug. 1914, as Lance-Corporal, 5th City of London Batt. London Regt. (London Rifle Brigade) and attained rank of Sergeant. Commissioned to 5th Batt. Hampshire Regt. (T.) April 1915. Appointed Adjutant June 1915, promoted Capt. 1916, T/Major Commandant Southern Command Bombing School, Lyndhurst, Feb. 1917 to Nov. 1919. Awarded the D.C.M. and Brevet Majority. Served in France and at Home.

ARTHUR CYRIL POTTER.

Articled to Charles S. Preston, of 12 Lincoln's Inn Fields, W.C. Joined 25th Batt. County of London (Cyclists) Regt. Aug. 4, 1914. Granted commission as 2nd Lieut. 4th Batt. Royal Warwickshire Regt. Nov. 11, 1914, seconded to

Machine Gun Corps Dec. 1915, promoted Lieut. July 1916, A/Capt. March 1918. Served in France April 1915 to April 1917, and in Egypt and Palestine Nov. 1917 to Feb. 1919. Wounded July 1, 1916.

JOHN RANDALL POTTER.

Admitted July 1901, practising at 3 Bucklersbury, E.C. Joined Aug. 3, 1915, as Lieut., Royal Naval Volunteer Reserve, attached to Royal Naval Air Service, promoted Lieut.-Commander Dec. 1916. Transferred to Royal Air Force April 1918 with rank of Major. Served at Home.

LAWRENCE PETCHELL POTTER.

Admitted Dec. 1911, practising at Broad Street House, E.C. Joined May 25, 1916, as Gunner, Royal Garrison Artillery. Posted to 336th Siege Battery Jan. 1917. Served in France May 1917 to Dec. 1918.

CHARLES POTTS.

Articled to Hubert Potts, of Chester. Joined Feb. 1916, as Private, Inns of Court O.T.C. Gazetted 2nd Lieut. 4th Batt. Cheshire Regt. March 1917. Went to France April 1917, attached 11th Batt. Cheshire Regt. Wounded June 7, 1917, at Battle of Messines Ridge, and died in France on June 11, 1917.

CYRIL ASHFORD POTTS.

Admitted Sept. 1905. Of Broseley, Salop. Joined Sept. 4, 1914, as Private, 1/6 Batt. South Staffordshire Regt. Gazetted 2nd Lieut. March 11, 1915, promoted Lieut. June 1916, A/Capt. Nov. 1916. Awarded the M.C. Served in France March 1915 to April 1919.

HAROLD GARNOCK POTTS.

Admitted Feb. 1908, practised at Broseley. Served as Lance-Corporal, Royal Army Service Corps (M.T.) Died Feb. 6, 1916.

ALLEN LESLIE POUND.

Admitted Nov. 1911. Member of Broxholm & Pound, of 62 Oxford Street, W. Joined Nov. 1916, as Private, Inns of Court O.T.C. Gazetted 2nd Lieut. Royal Fusiliers May 30, 1917, promoted Lieut. Nov. 1918.

BENJAMIN WILLIAM POUNDER.

Articled to Sir Robert Fox, Town Clerk of Leeds. Joined Nov. 1914, as 2nd Lieut., 2/5 Batt. West Riding Regt., and subsequently promoted Lieut. Served in France and Belgium. Killed in action at Passchendaele Oct. 9, 1917.

CHARLES SWAN POWELL.

Admitted Feb. 1910. Member of Williams & Powell, of 276 Camberwell New Road, S.E. Joined London University O.T.C. Sept. 1914. Gazetted 2nd Lieut. 6th Batt. Leicestershire Regt. Nov. 27, 1914. Served in France July 1915 to July 1916. Killed at Bazentin-le-petit (Somme) July 14, 1916.

JAMES LESLIE GROVE POWELL.

Admitted in 1874. Member of Powell, Rogers & Merrick, of 17 Essex Street, W.C. Served as Col. Commanding 6th (Reserve) Batt. East Surrey Regt.

JOHN GEOFFREY NELSON POWELL.

Articled to F. N. Powell, of Llanelly. Gazetted Oct. 3, 1914, as 2nd Lieut., Welsh Field Company, Royal Engineers (T.), promoted Lieut. June 1916.

Once mentioned in Dispatches. Awarded the M.C. Served at Home Oct. 1914 to Oct. 1915, at Suvla Bay Oct. to Dec. 1915, in Egypt Dec. 1915 to 1917, and in Palestine 1917 to 1919.

OWEN MARKHAM POWELL.

Admitted Dec. 1886. Member of Longbourne, Stevens & Powell, of 7 Lincoln's Inn Fields. Mobilised with T.F. Reserve and served as Capt. 24th Batt. The Rifle Brigade. Transferred to T.F. Reserve Dec. 1916. Served at Home and in India.

SCOTT POWELL.

Admitted May 1912. Managing Clerk with Nicholson, Patterson & Freeland, of 46 Queen Anne's Gate, Westminster, S.W. Joined Aug. 1914, as Private, Inns of Court O.T.C., and shortly afterwards gazetted 2nd Lieut. Royal Welch Fusiliers. Attained the rank of Temp. Capt. Once mentioned in Dispatches. Served at Home, at the Dardanelles, in Egypt, and in Mesopotamia. Killed in action April 5, 1916.

WILLIAM NEILSON POWELL.

Articled to J. S. Corbett, of Cardiff. Served as 2nd Lieut., 3rd Wessex Brigade, Royal Field Artillery.

BASIL ROY POWER.

Admitted Jan. 1914, practising at 4 College Hill, Cannon Street, E.C. Served as 2nd Lieut., London Rifle Brigade.

EDWARD PAULET POWLES.

Admitted April 1892. Member of Wiley & Powles, of 30 Duke Street, S.W. Served as Lieut., 14th Batt. The Rifle Brigade.

HENRY POWNALL.

Articled to Harold Hyde, of Ashton-under-Lyne. Joined March 1916, as Private, Hon. Artillery Company (Infantry). Gazetted 2nd Lieut. Hon. Artillery Company Jan. 25, 1917, promoted Lieut. July 1918. Served in France April to Nov. 1917, and in Italy Nov. 1917 to Dec. 1918.

ATHERTON RICHARD NORMAN POWYS.

Admitted April 1912, practising at 6 Lincoln's Inn Fields, W.C. Joined July 28, 1917, as Private, Inns of Court, O.T.C. Gazetted 2nd Lieut. Royal Garrison Artillery (T.) Feb. 1919. Served at Home.

CHARLES LANGFORD POYSER.

Admitted May 1903, in practice with Watson, Burton & Corder, of Newcastle-upon-Tyne. Joined May 1916, as Private, Inns of Court, O.T.C.. Subsequently gazetted Lieut. Royal Garrison Artillery (S.R.)

FREDERICK WILLIAM POZZI.

Articled to W. T. Jones, of Bangor. Joined Nov. 6, 1915, as Private, 28th Batt. County of London Regt. (Artists Rifles). Gazetted 2nd Lieut. 3/6 Batt. Royal Welch Fusiliers July 10, 1916, promoted Lieut. Feb. 1918. Served in France. Wounded Dec. 25, 1917, and April 19, 1918.

JACOB PRAG.

Admitted May 1911, practising at 20 High Holborn, W.C. Served as Lance-Corporal, 3rd Batt. Wiltshire Regt.

BASIL HENRY PRANCE.

Admitted April 1915. Of Plymouth. Joined Sept. 29, 1915, as 2nd Lieut., 7th Batt. Devonshire Regt., promoted Lieut. March 1917, transferred to 1st Batt. May 2, 1917. Served in France and Italy. Wounded May 31, 1918.

LUTHER HENRY ALLEN PRATT.

Admitted Feb. 1899, practising at Cardiff. Joined May 7, 1917, as Sapper, Royal Engineers. Commissioned as 2nd Lieut. General List, attached I.W. & D. Royal Engineers Oct. 1917. Served at Home.

PHILIP SOUTHWELL PREESTON.

Admitted Oct. 1906. Managing Clerk with Cunnington, Son & Orfeur, of Braintree, Essex. Joined Aug. 1, 1916, as 2nd Lieut., Royal Field Artillery, promoted Lieut. Feb. 1918. Served in France. Killed in action near Cayeux March 28, 1918.

MACKENZIE WILSON PRENTIS.

Admitted Jan. 1907. Practising at 12 Gray's Inn Square, W.C. Joined Sept. 4, 1914, as Private, Royal Fusiliers. Served in France. Wounded at Ypres July 31, 1917. Invalided out of Service March 1, 1918.

GERALD STANLEY PRESSWELL.

Admitted April 1908. Managing Clerk with S. Ernest Crosse, of Exeter. Joined Jan. 16, 1915, as Private, 15th Batt. Royal Welch Fusiliers, and attained the rank of Sergeant. Gazetted 2nd Lieut. Labour Corps April 14, 1918. Served at Home Jan. to Dec. 1915, and in France and Belgium Dec. 1915 to Feb. 1919.

ARTHUR MONTAGU PRESTON.

Admitted Feb. 1911. Of Hong Kong. Served as Lieut., 4th Batt. Cheshire Regt., attached Hong Kong Volunteer Corps, promoted Capt. Aug. 1918.

FRANCIS NOEL DYKES PRESTON.

Admitted Feb. 1912. Deputy Town Clerk of Doncaster. Joined Hon. Artillery Company (Infantry) April 16, 1917, as Private. Served in France and Belgium July 1917 to Jan. 1918.

IVOR KERRISON PRESTON.

Admitted Nov. 1907. Member of Preston & Francis, of Bournemouth. Joined Oct. 3, 1916, as Private, 28th Batt. County of London Regt. (Artists Rifles). Gazetted 2nd Lieut. Royal Garrison Artillery Dec. 1917. Served in France 1916, 1917, and 1918.

RICHARD JAMES PRESTON.

Articled to A. W. Preston, of Norwich. Commissioned as 2nd Lieut. 2/6 Batt. Norfolk Regt. Nov. 4, 1914, promoted Lieut. June 1915, Capt. Jan. 1916, seconded to 2/5 Batt. King's Own Yorkshire Light Infantry July 1916, returned to 2/6 Batt. Norfolk Regt. Oct. 1918, attached 2/4 Batt. Border Regt. Nov. 1918. Served in France 1917. Wounded Feb. 21, 1917.

ARTHUR PERCY PRICE.

Admitted June 1914. Member of Darnell & Price, of Northampton. Joined Oct. 1916, as Private, 28th Batt. County of London Regt. (Artists Rifles).

Gazetted 2nd Lieut. 8th Batt. West Yorkshire Regt. (Leeds Rifles) June 1917. Served in France.

ARTHUR REES PRICE.

Admitted May 1906. Member of Kendall, Price & Francis, of 61 Carey Street, Lincoln's Inn, W.C. Joined Inns of Court O.T.C. Aug. 1914. Gazetted 2nd Lieut. 2/5 Batt. Devonshire Regt. Dec. 3, 1914, promoted Lieut. June 1916, Staff Capt. (Temp. Capt.) General Headquarters, E.E.F., Aug. 1917. Once mentioned in Dispatches. Served in Egypt and Palestine Sept. 1915 to 1919.

CHARLES FREDERICK TEMPEST PRICE.

Articled to Thomas Brownson, of Hyde. Served as Private, 1st (City) Batt. Manchester Regt.

CHARLES WILLIAM MACKAY PRICE.

Admitted Feb. 1893, practising at 10 Lincoln's Inn Fields, W.C. Joined Sept. 1914 7th Batt. The Queen's Royal West Surrey Regt., promoted Major June 1916. Once mentioned in Dispatches. Served at Home and in France.

CLIFFORD JAMES PRICE.

Admitted June 1914. Managing Clerk with Braund & Hill, of 6 Gray's Inn Square, W.C. Joined Nov. 13, 1916, as Private, Inns of Court O.T.C. Gazetted Sub-Lieut. Royal Naval Volunteer Reserve, Royal Naval Division, June 1917. Served in France.

EDMOND LONG PRICE.

Admitted Nov. 1902, practising at Talley. Served as Lieut., Pembroke Yeomanry.

HUBERT DAVENPORT PRICE.

Admitted Oct. 1911. Member of Price, Atkins & Price, of Birmingham. Served as 2nd Lieut., Worcestershire Yeomanry. Mentioned in Dispatches. Awarded M.C.

IDRIS THOMAS PRICE.

Admitted May 1909. Member of Phillips & Price, of Porth. Joined May 1916, as Ordinary Seaman, Royal Naval Division (63rd) Anson Batt., subsequently promoted to Petty Officer, Anson Batt. Served in France. Discharged Nov. 1, 1918.

JAMES HODGSON PRICE.

Articled to J. W. Broughton, of Accrington. Joined Jan. 15, 1915, as Trooper, Duke of Lancaster's Own Yeomanry, and attained the rank of Assistant Quartermaster-Sergeant. Served in Serbia (Salonica) and at Home. Wounded Sept. 1917.

JOHN EDWARDS NESBITT PRICE.

Admitted July 1910, practising at Newent, Glos. Joined Dec 21, 1914, as Private, Royal Army Ordnance Corps. Served in France July 1915 to Dec. 1918.

LIONEL LEWIS PRICE.

Admitted Dec. 1912. Formerly of Hanover Street, W. Joined Nov. 1914, as Private, Inns of Court O.T.C. Subsequently gazetted Lieut. Royal Welch Fusiliers. Invalided out of Army in 1916.

THOMAS RALPH PLUMER PRICE.

Admitted Nov. 1907, practising at Southampton. Served as 2nd Lieut., Hampshire Royal Garrison Artillery (T.), promoted Lieut. June 1916.

WALTER HUGH PRICE.

Admitted Oct. 1911. Member of Samuel Price & Sons, of Worcester House, Walbrook, E.C. Joined May 9, 1916, as Sub-Lieut., Royal Naval Volunteer Reserve, promoted Lieut. May 1917. Served first at Peterhead on Motor Patrol Boat, then to Halifax, Nova Scotia, in command of "Q" or Mystery Boat, then to Dover Patrol in command Motor Patrol Boat, and in the Zeebrugge April 1918, and in final attack on Ostend. Died of double pneumonia at Dover arising from the two Naval engagements July 2, 1919.

WILLIAM EWART PRICE.

Articled to Arthur Smith, of Wigan. Joined Feb. 21, 1916, as Private, 10th Batt. South Lancashire Regt., promoted Lance-Corporal April 1916, Corporal July 1916, Company Quartermaster-Sergeant Nov. 1916, Company Sergeant-Major May 1918, transferred to Cheshire Regt. Jan. 1918, and to Black Watch Feb. 1918. Served at Home and in France.

JOHN BERNARD PRICE-HUGHES.

Admitted March 1911, practising at Barry, near Cardiff. Served as Lieut., Glamorgan (Fortress) Royal Engineers, promoted Capt. June 1916.

JOHN PRICHARD.

Articled to J. P. Prichard, of Cardiff. Joined Aug. 1914, as Lieut., Royal Field Artillery, promoted Capt. 1915, Major 1917. Three times mentioned in Dispatches. Served in Gallipoli 1915, Egypt 1916, Mesopotamia 1916, 1917, and 1918, India and Afghanistan 1918 and 1919. Wounded in 1918.

THOMAS PREECE PRICHARD.

Admitted Dec. 1904. Member of Davies & Prichard, of Cardiff. Joined 1916 as Private, Royal Army Service Corps. Subsequently gazetted Lieut. Royal Air Force. Served at Home.

BERNARD CECIL PRIDE.

Admitted Jan. 1916, practised in Solicitor's Office, Euston Station, N.W. Served as Private, Suffolk Regt.

HENRY SYDNEY PRIDEAUX.

Admitted Dec. 1908, practising at Truro, Cornwall. Joined Oct. 11, 1915, as 2nd Lieut., Duke of Cornwall's Light Infantry, promoted Lieut. June 1917. Served in France. Shell shock and trench fever May 1917.

ROBERT FLEMYNG PRIDEAUX.

Admitted May 1901, practising at Shrewsbury. Joined Dec. 8, 1915, as Private, Inns of Court O.T.C. Gazetted 2nd Lieut. Hants Royal Garrison Artillery (T.) Feb. 1, 1917, promoted Lieut. Aug. 1918. Served in England and India.

HENRY PRIDHAM.

Admitted June 1910, practising at Plymouth. Mobilised Aug. 1914 and served as Capt., 5th (Prince of Wales') Batt. Devonshire Regt. Served in

India Oct. 1914 to March 1917, and in Egypt and Palestine April 1917 to Jan. 1919. Wounded at El Teb, north-west of Jerusalem, Nov. 23, 1917.

WILLIAM PRIESTLY.

Admitted Aug. 1896, practising at Sunderland. Served as Major, 7th Batt. Durham Light Infantry.

STEPHEN PRIESTMAN.

Admitted Dec. 1912. Member of Thos. Priestman & Sons, of Hull. Joined June 1917, as Private, Royal Army Ordnance Corps, and subsequently promoted Corporal. Served at Home 1917 to Oct. 1918, and in Salonica Oct. 1918 to May 1919.

ARTHUR VENN PRIOR.

Admitted Jan. 1907. Member of Lethbridge, Money & Prior, of 25 Abingdon Street, S.W. Joined Oct. 1914, as Assistant Paymaster, Royal Naval Volunteer Reserve for service with Royal Naval Division, promoted Paymaster Jan. 1916 (rank subsequently named Paymaster Lieutenant-Commander), Claims Officer of 63rd Royal Naval Division in France June 1916 to Jan. 1919. Served at Home Oct. 1914 to Feb. 1916, in Mediterranean Feb. to May 1916, and in France and Belgium May 1916 to Jan. 1919.

BASIL CYPRIAN PRIOR.

Admitted Nov. 1909. Member of Asher Prior & Son, of Colchester, Essex. Joined April 21, 1915, as 2nd Lieut., 2/5 Batt. Essex Regt., promoted Lieut. June 1916. Served in France with the 10th Batt.

BERNARD HENRY LEATHES PRIOR.

Admitted Feb. 1902. Member of Pickering & Co., of 4 Stone Buildings, Lincoln's Inn, W.C. Mobilised Aug. 4, 1914, as Lieut.-Col. Commanding 6th Batt. Norfolk Regt., promoted Colonel Aug. 1918. Seven times mentioned in Dispatches. Awarded D.S.O. and Bar. Served at Home 1914 to 1916, and in France 1916 to 1919. Wounded Oct. 1916, Dec. 1916, Jan. and March 1918.

CHARLES BOLINGBROKE LEATHES PRIOR.

Admitted April 1906, practising at East Dereham, Norfolk. Joined Nov. 3, 1914, as Lieut., 6th Batt. Norfolk Regt, gazetted Capt. and served as A/Major whilst attached to Royal North Devon Hussars. Served in France April to Nov. 1917, and in Italy Nov. 1917 to Jan. 1918.

PERCY NEVILLE PRIOR.

Admitted July 1909, practised at Oxford. Served as Lance-Corporal, 13th Batt. Warwickshire Regt.

THOMAS MACDONALD PRITCHARD.

Admitted Aug. 1908. Member of Pritchard, Englefield & Co., of Painters' Hall, Little Trinity Lane, E.C. Joined Sept. 1914, as Private, 18th (Service) Batt. Royal Fusiliers. Gazetted 2nd Lieut. Machine Gun Corps Sept. 1916 and subsequently promoted Lieut. Once mentioned in Dispatches. Served in France. Wounded Jan. 1916.

THEODORE BEAL PRITCHETT.

Articled to F. H. Pepper, of Birmingham. Mobilised Aug. 1914, as Lieut., 5th South Midland Brigade Royal Field Artillery, promoted Capt. Nov. 1914,

A/Major Sept. 1916, Substantive Major Feb. 1918. Awarded the M.C. Served in France. Wounded July 1916.

ALFRED KYME PROCTER.

Articled to Alfred Procter, of York. Mobilised Aug. 1914, as 2nd Lieut., West Riding Division Transport and Supply Column, Royal Army Service Corps, attained the rank of Capt. in July 1915. Served at Home. Discharged medically unfit May 26, 1916.

RAWSTHORNE PROCTER.

Admitted Feb. 1904, practising at Pinner's Hall, Old Broad Street, E.C. Obtained commission as Sub-Lieut. Royal Naval Volunteer Reserve April 1916, promoted Lieut. April 1917. Once mentioned in Dispatches. Awarded the D.S.C. Served in Home, French, and Belgian waters.

VICTOR CHARLES PROCTER.

Articled to A. D. Jenkins, of Guildford. Served as Private, Inns of Court O.T.C.

FREDERICK PROCTOR.

Articled to Southern & Fullalove, of Burnley. Joined Aug 7, 1914, as 2nd Lieut., 5th Batt. East Lancashire Regt., promoted Temp. Lieut. June 1915, Permanent Lieut. March 1916, Temp. Capt. April 1917, Permanent Capt. Aug. 1917. Served in Egypt Sept. 1914 to May 1915, at Gallipoli May to June 1915, and in France Oct. 1917 to Jan. 1918. Wounded at Gallipoli June 6, 1915, and in France Jan. 1, 1918.

HENRY ARTHUR BERNARD PROCTOR.

Articled to Sidney Field, of Liverpool Served as 2nd Lieut., Montgomeryshire Yeomanry, promoted Lieut. July 1917.

WILLIAM PROCTOR.

Articled to William Proctor, of Manchester. Joined May 20, 1916, as Private, 6th Batt. Manchester Regt., and promoted Lance-Corporal Dec. 1916. Gazetted 2nd Lieut. 1/6 Batt. Lancashire Fusiliers April 28, 1917, transferred to 1/7 Batt. July 1918, promoted Lieut. Oct. 1918. Served in France June 1917 to Jan. 1919.

REGINALD PROUDFOOT.

Admitted May 1907. Of Southampton. Joined Sept. 23, 1914, as Private, Inns of Court, O.T.C. Gazetted Temp. Lieut. Army Ordnance Dept. (now Royal Army Ordnance Corps) June 4, 1915, A/Capt. June 1917, Temp. Capt. March 1919. Once mentioned in respect of service at Home. Served at Home.

ALFRED OWEN CHALLENOR PRYCE.

Admitted June 1907, practised at Abingdon, Berks. Joined Dec. 30, 1914, as Ordinary Seaman, Royal Naval Volunteer Reserve, rated Able Bodied April 1915. Discharged from Royal Naval Volunteer Reserve Sept. 1916, on appointment as 2nd Lieut. 5th (Reserve) Batt. Scottish Rifles (Cameronians), promoted Lieut. 1918. Served at Gallipoli, in Ireland, and in France. Wounded in Gallipoli Oct. 13, 1915. Killed in action at Metven, in Flanders, April 14, 1918.

EDWARD CALCOTT PRYCE.

Admitted April 1914. Member of Arthur Taylor & Co., of 1 Queen Victoria Street, E.C. Mobilised Aug. 1914, as 2nd Lieut. Royal Field Artillery, promoted Lieut. Dec. 1914, A/Capt. May 1916, Substantive Capt. April 1918. Once mentioned in Dispatches. Served at Home Aug. 1914 to Nov. 1915, France Nov. 1915 to Feb. 1916, Egypt and Palestine Feb. 1916 to Jan. 1919.

CYRIL HERBERT PRYOR.

Admitted Jan. 1893. Member of Savory, Pryor & Blagden, of Outer Temple, 222 Strand, W.C. Joined Nov. 1916 and served as Capt. Infantry. War mentions for valuable services.

WALTER ERNEST PUCKERING.

Admitted Oct. 1917. Member of J. Edmund Jones, of York and Pocklington. Joined Dec. 7, 1917, as Private, Inns of Court O.T.C., afterwards Cadet No. 22 Officer Cadet Battalion, Christ's College, Cambridge. Served at Home. Discharged Oct. 1, 1918.

CYRIL HENRY WALLACE PUGH.

Articled to H. J. Wallace Pugh, of Oswestry. Joined Sept. 17, 1914, as Private, 21st Batt. Royal Fusiliers. Gazetted 2nd Lieut. 3rd Batt. King's Shropshire Light Infantry (Special Reserve) Aug. 5, 1916, promoted Lieut. Feb. 1918, A/Capt. 6th Batt. Feb. 1919. Awarded the M.C. Served in France Nov. 1915 to Sept. 1919. Wounded Feb. 11, 1917, and Nov. 25, 1917.

MAURICE HENRY PUGH.

Admitted Nov. 1909. Member of Hepherd, Winstanley & Pugh, of Southampton. Joined Jan. 17, 1918, as Private, Inns of Court O.T.C. Subsequently gazetted 2nd Lieut. Royal Garrison Artillery. Served at Home.

MERVYN PHIPPEN PUGH.

Articled to J. Ratcliffe, of Reading. Joined Aug. 1914, as Private, 19th (Public Schools) Batt. Royal Fusiliers. Gazetted 2nd Lieut. Royal Berkshire Regt. Feb. 26, 1915, promoted Lieut. Sept. 1915, A/Capt. May 1917 to May 1919, A/Major Oct. 1918 to Feb. 1919. Once mentioned in Dispatches. Awarded the M.C. and D.S.O. Served in France Oct. 1915 to June 1916 and Jan. 1917 to May 1919, and at Home. Wounded at Vimy Ridge June 1, 1916.

CHARLES MAXWELL PULLAN.

Articled to John Adgie, of Leeds. Joined the University of Leeds O.T.C., and gazetted 2nd Lieut. Royal Field Artillery. Killed in action March 22, 1917.

MAURICE PULLIBLANK.

Admitted Jan. 1905, practising at Merthyr Tydfil. Joined April 28, 1917, as 3rd Air-Mechanic, Royal Flying Corps, promoted 2nd Air-Mechanic May 1918, 1st Air-Mechanic Aug. 1918, subsequently rated as L.A.C. Royal Air Force. Served at Home.

GERALD COZENS PULLMAN.

Admitted June 1913. Member of Nicholson, Graham & Jones, of 24 Coleman Street, E.C. Mobilised Aug. 1914, as Lieut., 6th Batt. East Surrey

Regt. (T.), promoted Capt. Aug. 1914, Temp. Major Dec. 1918, Staff Capt. Aden Infantry Brigade March 1917 to Dec. 1918, Deputy Assistant Adjutant-General Aden Field Force Dec. 1918 to May 1919. Twice mentioned in Dispatches. Awarded O.B.E. (Military Division). Served in India Oct. 1914 to March 1917, and in Aden March 1917 to April 1919.

WILLIAM RICHARD PUMFREY.

Admitted Jan. 1907. Member of Henry Pumfrey & Son, of 14 Paternoster Row, E.C. Joined May 5, 1917, as Cadet. Gazetted 2nd Lieut. Royal Army Service Corps (M.T.) July 2, 1917, promoted Lieut. Jan. 1919. Served in France, and with Army of Occupation, Germany.

ARNOLD PUMPHREY.

Admitted June 1914. Of Sunderland. Joined Sept. 1, 1914, as Private, 5th City of London Batt. London Regt. (London Rifle Brigade). Gazetted 2nd Lieut. 20th Batt. Durham Light Infantry Oct. 7, 1915, promoted Lieut. Jan. 1916, Capt. April 1916, and shortly afterwards given command of a Company. Once mentioned in Dispatches. Awarded the D.S.O. Served in France and Flanders. Wounded at Ploegsteert 1914, again on the Somme 1916, and gassed at Ypres 1915. Killed at Tower Hamlets, near Ypres, Sept. 21, 1917.

JAMES SEPTIMUS PUNCHARD.

Admitted Nov. 1898. Member of Talbot, Rheam & Punchard, of Milnthorpe. Joined Aug. 25, 1915, as 1st Lieut., King's Own Royal Lancaster Regt. Served in France. Wounded Aug. 1916. Died, as result of wounds and gas, April 2, 1919.

THOMAS WOODS PURDY.

Admitted June 1900. Of Aylsham. Mobilised Aug. 1914 as Capt., 1/5 Batt. Norfolk Regt., attained the rank of Major in Nov. 1915, Temp. Lieut.-Col. April to Oct. 1916. Once mentioned in Dispatches for services in England. Served in Gallipoli Peninsula Aug. 1915, in Egypt Oct. 1916, and 1918 and 1919, and in Palestine March to Oct. 1917. Wounded at Suvla Bay Aug. 1, 1915.

HAROLD ROBERT PYBUS.

Articled to Robert Pybus, of Newcastle-upon-Tyne. Joined Aug. 15, 1914, as 2nd Lieut., 4th Batt. Durham Light Infantry, promoted Lieut. Aug. 1915. Served at Home Aug. 1914 to Aug. 1915, and in France and Flanders until Oct. 1915. Wounded in Flanders in Oct. 1915. Killed in motor-bicycle accident while on duty with his regiment at Seaham Harbour, Durham, July 24, 1916.

HUGH PYBUS.

Admitted July 1910. Member of Gibson, Pybus & Pybus, of Newcastle-upon-Tyne. Mobilised Aug. 4, 1914, as Lieut., 1st Northumbrian Brigade Royal Field Artillery (T.), promoted A/Capt. June 1915, Capt. June 1916, A/Major May 1918. Served at Home Aug. 1914 to March 1915, in France April 1915 to Aug. 1916, and in India Nov. 1917 to Nov. 1919.

JOHN MILBURN PYBUS.

Admitted Nov. 1903. Member of W. Mark Pybus & Sons, of Newcastle-upon-Tyne. Joined Nov. 1914, as 2nd. Lieut., Royal Army Service Corps, promoted Lieut. Feb. 1915, Capt. April 1915. Once mentioned in Dispatches. Served in France.

TALBOT EDWARD BAINES PYE-SMITH.

Admitted Aug. 1912, practising at 3 Portsmouth Street, Lincoln's Inn Fields, W.C. Mobilised Aug. 1914, as Lieut. 4th Batt. Wiltshire Regt., promoted Capt. June 1916. Once mentioned in Dispatches. Served at Home Aug. to Oct. 1914, in India Nov. 1914 to Sept. 1917, and in Egypt and Palestine Sept. 1917 to June 1919.

GEORGE PYKE.

Admitted April 1910. Managing Clerk with Pyke, Franklin & Gould, of 63 Lincoln's Inn Fields, W.C. Mobilised Aug. 1914, as Trooper, 2nd County of London Yeomanry, served as Lance-Corporal whilst on Active Service in Egypt. Granted commission and posted to British West Indies Regt. April 9, 1916. Served in Gallipoli and in Egypt. Died on Active Service in Egypt April 17, 1916.

ROBERT LANDER PYMAN.

Admitted Jan. 1909. Member of Wallace, Pyman & Co., of 35 Basinghall Street, E.C. Joined Dec. 15, 1916, as Private, Inns of Court O.T.C., subsequently Gunner, Royal Garrison Artillery. Served at Home.

WILLIAM McDONALD QUENET.

Articled to Mark Storey, of Sunderland. Joined April 1916, as Private, 3rd Batt. Durham Light Infantry. Served in France.

PERCY MILCREST QUIGGIN.

Admitted June 1914. Member of J. M. Quiggin & Son, of Liverpool. Joined Aug. 7, 1914, as Private, 10th (Scottish) Batt. King's Liverpool Regt. Commissioned 2nd Lieut. Lancashire and Cheshire Royal Garrison Artillery Sept. 1915, promoted Lieut. June 1916, A/Capt. April 1917 and A/Major Oct. 1918. Awarded the M.C. Served in France.

JOHN QUINN.

Admitted July 1902. Member of John Quinn, Monkhouse, Dixon & Quinn, of Liverpool. Served as Gunner, Royal Field Artillery.

JOHN DOUGLAS HENDERSON RADCLIFFE.

Admitted Jan. 1912. Member of Radcliffes & Hood, of 28 Old Queen Street, Westminster, S.W. Joined Aug. 1914, as Private, Inns of Court O.T.C. Gazetted 2nd Lieut. 7th (1st Service) Batt. King's Royal Rifle Corps, and attained the rank of Capt. Served in France and Flanders. Killed in action July 30, 1915.

OSWALD ALFRED RADLEY.

Admitted Nov. 1911. Assistant Solicitor to Town Clerk, Leeds. Joined Oct. 2, 1914, as 2nd Lieut., 1/7 Batt. Cheshire Regt., promoted Lieut. Jan. 1915, Capt. July, 1916, Brigade Machine Gun Officer 159th Infantry Brigade Aug.

to Oct. 1915, A.P.M. Musa Matrah May to Aug. 1915, Staff Capt. Roma Feb. to April 1917, Staff Capt. 232nd Infantry Brigade April 1917 to Oc 1918, Staff Capt. Palestine L. of C. Nov. 1918 to June 1919. Once mention in Dispatches. Awarded the M.C. Served in England Oct. 1914 to Ju 1915, Gallipoli Aug. to Dec. 1915, Egypt Dec. 1915 to Nov. 1916, Sinai ar Palestine Nov. 1916 to June 1919. Wounded Sept. 19, 1918.

FREDERICK MONRO RAIKES.

Admitted March 1900. Member of Wilkinson, Raikes & Son, of 3 Nicholas Lane, E.C. Joined Sept. 1915, as 2nd Lieut., Brecknockshire Bat South Wales Borderers, subsequently promoted Lieut. in Machine Gun Corp Served in Mesopotamia. Killed shortly before the recapture of Kut Feb. 2 1917.

WALTER HUGH RALEY.

Articled to Joseph Raley, of Barnsley. Joined Aug. 1914, as 2nd Lieut 5th Batt. York and Lancaster Regt. Served in France. Killed in actic May 14, 1915.

WILLIAM EMSLEY RALEY.

Admitted Dec. 1881. Member of Raley & Sons, of Barnsley. Mobilise Aug. 1914, as Major, 13th Batt. York and Lancaster Regt., promoted Lieut Col., 14th Batt. Jan. 1915, Lieut.-Col. 15th Batt. Sept. 1915. Once mentione for valuable services. Awarded O.B.E. (Military Division). Served at Hom Resigned, owing to ill-health, Sept. 1, 1916.

WILLIAM HENRY GEORGE RALEY.

Admitted Oct. 1908. Managing Clerk with Raley & Sons, of Barnsle Mobilised Aug. 1914, as Capt., 3rd Batt. Yorkshire Regt. Once mentione in Dispatches. Served in France. Killed in action at Givenchy, La Bassé June 17, 1915.

WILLETT RAM.

Admitted Feb. 1897. Member of Cross, Ram & Son, of Haleswort Suffolk. Joined June 8, 1916, as Private, Northamptonshire Regt. Grante commission in Royal Army Service Corps (M.T.) Jan. 5, 1917. Served i Serbia, Turkey, etc.

HAROLD JOHN RAMSBOTHAM.

Admitted Oct. 1908, practising at Lyme Regis, Dorset. Joined Jul 20, 1917, as Private, Royal Army Ordnance Corps. Served in France.

RICHARD RAMSBOTTOM.

Admitted Oct. 1910, practised at Accrington. Served as Lieut., Lancashi Fusiliers.

ARTHUR AMHERST RAMSDEN.

Admitted Aug. 1911, practised at Bath. Served as Private, 9th Bat Somerset Light Infantry. Killed in action Sept. 3, 1916.

ARTHUR MAXWELL RAMSDEN.

Articled to William Ramsden, of Huddersfield. Joined Sept. 18, 191 as Private, 15th Batt. West Yorkshire Regt. Gazetted 2nd Lieut. 8th Bat West Yorkshire Regt. Feb. 1915, A/Capt. Dec. 1916, promoted Lieut. Jul

1917, A/Capt. Oct. 1917 and Nov. 1918. Served at Home Sept. 1914 to July 1915 and July 1917 to Nov. 1918, and in France July 1915 to July 1917 and Nov. 1918 to April 1919. Wounded July 1916 and July 1917.

JAMES HILDEBRAND RAMSDEN.

Admitted Sept. 1905. Member of Ramsden-Tagore & Co., of 5 The Albany Courtyard, Piccadilly, W. Joined Dec. 1915, as Lieut., Royal Naval Volunteer Reserve. Served with Intelligence Division, Downs Boarding Flotilla.

ARTHUR HILDEBRAND RAMSDEN-TAGORE.

Admitted July 1890. Member of Ramsden-Tagore & Co., of 5 The Albany Courtyard, Piccadilly, W. Joined Nov. 3, 1914, as Temp. Lieut., Royal Naval Volunteer Reserve. Served at Moray Firth (Cromarty Command) in Motor Drifters *Pursuit* and *Ivanhoe* 1914 to Oct. 1915, Lowestoft M.L. 23 Dec. 1915 to June 1916, Mediterranean, Gallipoli (Italy) and Adriatic M.L. 168 June 1916 to Aug. 1917, Lowestoft M.L. 125th Hydrophone Flotilla Oct. 1917 to Jan. 1919.

WALTER JAMES RAMSEY.

Admitted May 1914. Of Jarrow. Served as Capt., Royal Army Service Corps.

REGINALD RUPERT RAMUZ.

Admitted Dec. 1907, practising at Southend-on-Sea. Joined March 17, 1917, as Private, Royal Army Service Corps (M.T.). Served in Egypt, Palestine, and Syria.

GEORGE ST. JOHN RANDS.

Articled to G. W. Rands, of Northampton. Joined Aug. 1914, as Private, 19th Batt. Royal Fusiliers. Gazetted 2nd Lieut. 1/4 Batt. Northamptonshire Regt. Oct. 8, 1914, and subsequently promoted Lieut. Served in the Near East.

ROBERT GEORGE RAPER.

Admitted July 1902. Member of Raper & Son, of Battle, Sussex. Served as Capt., 8th Batt. South Staffordshire Regt. and promoted Major May 1915. Killed in action July 2, 1916.

JOHN CECIL RASH.

Admitted Nov. 1912, practised at Diss, Norfolk. Served as Trooper, Suffolk Yeomanry. Gazetted Lieut. 4th Batt. Suffolk Regt. July 1917. Mentioned in Dispatches.

LAURENCE PERCY RATCLIFFE.

Articled to H. B. Ratcliffe, of Bradford. Joined Sept. 4, 1915, as Ord. Seaman, Royal Naval Volunteer Reserve. Granted commission as Sub-Lieut. Royal Naval Volunteer Reserve Jan. 15, 1918. Served with Grand Fleet, Dover Patrol, and on Belgian Coast.

ARTHUR RATCLIFFE-ELLIS.

Admitted June 1899. Member of Peace & Ellis, of Wigan. Served as Capt., 5th (Reserve) Batt. Manchester Regt., promoted Major June 1916.

JAMES SAMUEL RICHARD DOKE RAWCLIFFE.

Admitted Feb. 1910. Assistant Solicitor with Town Clerk of Hastings. Joined Dec. 1916, as 2nd Class Air-Mechanic, Royal Air Force, promoted 1st

Class Air-Mechanic Oct. 1917, Corporal Feb. 1918. Served in France Jan. 1917 to Dec. 1918.

FREDERICK RENSHAW RAWES.

Admitted Feb. 1903. Of Penrith, Cumberland. Joined Inns of Court O.T.C. Jan. 1916 as Private. Gazetted 2nd Lieut. Manchester Regt. Nov. 22, 1916. Served in France. Wounded in Battle of Arras April 9, 1917. Gazetted out of Army on account of ill-health Feb. 23, 1918.

THOMAS FREDERICK RAWLE.

Admitted Aug. 1909. Member of Rawle, Johnstone & Co., of 1 Bedford Row, W.C. Served as Private, Inns of Court O.T.C., and subsequently gazetted 2nd Lieut. South Wales Borderers, promoted Lieut. Dec. 1916. Awarded M.C.

JAMES PERCY SALMON RAWLINGS.

Admitted April 1899, practising at Great Broughton. Served as Private, Durham Light Infantry.

HOWARD ST. GEORGE RAWLINS.

Admitted May 1903. Member of Sewell & Rawlins, of Cirencester, Glos. Joined March 3, 1915, as 2nd Lieut., Royal Army Service Corps, promoted Lieut. Sept. 1915, Capt. Aug. 1917. Once mentioned in Dispatches. Awarded O.B.E. Served at Salonica.

HUGH PENROSE CARDOZO RAWLINS.

Admitted Oct. 1904. Member of Rawlins & Rawlins, of Bournemouth. Joined 1916, as Private, Hon. Artillery Company. Gazetted 2nd Lieut. 10th Batt. King's Own Yorkshire Light Infantry 1916. Served in France and Belgium. Killed 3rd Battle of Ypres, Polygon Wood, Oct. 4, 1917.

CHARLES CECIL RAWLINSON.

Admitted Feb. 1903. Member of Cecil J. Rawlinson & Son, of 47 New Broad Street, E.C. Joined Jan. 1915, as Able Seaman, Royal Naval Air Service Anti-Aircraft Corps, promoted Chief Petty Officer July 1915. Gazetted 2nd Lieut. Royal Garrison Artillery (Special Reserve) May 17, 1916, promoted Lieut. Nov. 1917. Served at Home Jan. 1915 to June 1916, and in France June 1916 to Dec. 1918.

CURWEN VAUGHAN RAWLINSON.

Articled to G. W. P. Mellor, of 45 Lincoln's Inn Fields, W.C. Joined Oct. 1914, as 2nd Lieut., 3rd Batt. Dorset Regt., attached 1st Batt. Served in Flanders. Killed in action May 22, 1915.

GEORGE TENNANT RAWNSLEY

Articled to F. G. Peacock, of Bradford. Served as Private, Inns of Court O.T.C.

RICHARD GALPINE RAWORTH.

Articled to E. Raworth, of Harrogate. Mobilised Aug. 1914, as 2nd Lieut., Northern Signal Coys., Royal Engineers (T.), promoted Lieut. Nov. 1914, A/Capt. Aug. 1917 to July 1918, Capt. Sept. 1919. Once mentioned in Dispatches. Served with Egyptian Expeditionary Force.

ALFRED COOPER RAWSON.

Admitted Nov. 1901, practising at 188 Strand, W.C. Joined Oct. 1915, as Sub-Lieut., Royal Naval Volunteer Reserve, Royal Naval Division, promoted Lieut. and subsequently Lieut.-Commander. Served at Home.

HENRY FOSTER RAWSON.

Admitted April 1909, practised at Bradford. Served as Private, Royal Army Service Corps (M.T.).

ARTHUR EDMUND RAY.

Admitted Nov. 1886, practising at Northampton. Served as Major, 4th Batt. Northamptonshire Regt.

JACK EMERSON RAY.

Articled to L. S. Holmes, of Liverpool. Joined Aug. 23, 1914, as Paymaster Sub-Lieut., Royal Naval Volunteer Reserve, promoted to Paymaster Lieut.-Commander Dec. 1914. Served at Home.

MONTAGUE JAMES RAYMOND.

Admitted March, 1894, practising at Wimborne, Dorset. Mobilised as Major, Commanding Dorset Royal Garrison Artillery (T.). Once mentioned in Dispatches. Awarded the T.D. Served at Home.

CECIL LANGTON RAYMOND-BARKER.

Articled to E. M. Johnson, of 9 New Square, Lincoln's Inn. Joined at outbreak of War, as Private, 28th Batt. County of London Regt. (Artists Rifles). Gazetted 2nd Lieut. 2nd Batt. Royal Scots Fusiliers Nov. 1914, posted to 12th Batt. The Rifle Brigade July 1915. Served in France Oct. 1914 to Dec. 1914 and July to Sept. 1915. Killed in action at the Battle of Loos Sept. 25, 1915.

EDWIN RAYMOND-BOND.

Admitted Oct. 1913. Deputy Clerk to Justices for City of Cardiff. Joined March 1915, as 2nd Lieut., 18th Batt. The Welch Regt., promoted Lieut. Oct. 1915, transferred to Royal Flying Corps Nov. 1915, promoted Capt. Aug. 1916, Major (Technical) Royal Air Force Aug. 1917, A/Lieut.-Col. Aug. 1918. Served at Home and at Salonica.

JOHN WILLIAM RAYNER.

Articled to Thomas Dodds, of Newcastle-upon-Tyne. Served in Durham University O.T.C.

LESLIE KING RAYNER.

Admitted Feb. 1912. Of Bank Chambers, 329 High Holborn, W.C. Joined Aug. 1914, as Private, Hon. Artillery Company, and attained the rank of Sergeant. Subsequently gazetted 2nd Lieut. 13th Batt. Royal Sussex Regt. and promoted to Temp. Capt. Served at Home and in France. Wounded July 1916. Killed near Ypres April 18, 1917.

WILFRID RAYWOOD.

Admitted Dec. 1909, practising at Bournemouth. Commissioned as 2nd Lieut. 3/7th Batt. Hampshire Regt. Nov. 30, 1915. Served in India April 1916 to Sept. 1917, and in Mesopotamia Sept. 1917 to March 1919.

ARTHUR JOHN STRATFOLD READ.

Articled to J. S. Stooke-Vaughan, of 31 Great James Street, Bedford Row, W.C. Joined 1914, as Trooper, Royal Bucks Hussars. Served at Gallipoli, Egypt, and Palestine. Killed in action in Palestine Nov. 15, 1917.

PHILIP AUSTIN OTTLEY READ.

Admitted April 1907, practised at Manchester. Served as Capt., 5th Batt. Loyal North Lancashire Regt., promoted Major June 1916. Mentioned in Dispatches and awarded O.B.E.

RICHARD ODDEN READ.

Admitted Nov. 1903. Conveyancing Clerk with Boodle, Hatfield & Co., of 53 Davies Street, Berkeley Square, W. Joined Jan. 10, 1917, as Private, Hon. Artillery Company (Infantry). Served in France and Italy.

WILLIAM PARSONS READE.

Admitted Sept. 1899. Member of H. L. & W. P. Reade of Congleton, Cheshire. Mobilised Aug. 5, 1914, as Capt., 7th Batt. Cheshire Regt., appointed Adjutant Oct. 1914, promoted Temp. Major May 1915, Substantive Major Dec. 1915, Temp. Lieut.-Col. Dec. 1915 to Aug. 1916. Once mentioned in Dispatches. Served at Home Aug. 1914 to July 1915 and Sept. 1916 to May 1917, at Gallipoli Aug. to Dec. 1915, in Egypt Dec. 1915 to Aug. 1916, and in France and Flanders May 1917 to May 1919.

GEORGE EDWARD HAROLD READER.

Admitted April 1910, practised at 35 Coleman Street, E.C. Served as Lieut., Royal Army Ordnance Dept.

HAROLD CYPRIAN READER.

Admitted Nov. 1908, practised at Blyth. Served as Lieut., Tynemouth Royal Garrison Artillery (T.), promoted Capt. June 1916.

CHARLES EDWARD HAY RECKITT.

Articled to G. H. Young, of 23 East Arbour Street, E. Joined Aug. 4, 1914, as Private, 28th Batt. County of London Regt. (Artists Rifles) and subsequently became A/Capt. and Adjutant Royal Engineers. Twice mentioned in Dispatches. Awarded O.B.E. (Military Division). Wounded in France July 10, 1915.

FREDERICK ADAM CORRIE REDDEN.

Admitted April 1902, practising at 17 Victoria Street, S.W. Rejoined Sept. 29, 1914, as Sergeant, Inns of Court O.T.C., promoted Company Quartermaster-Sergeant. March 1915. Gazetted 2nd Lieut. 1/9 (Reserve) Batt. Worcestershire Regt. Nov. 19, 1917. Served at Home Sept. 1914 to March 1918, and in France March 1918 to April 1919.

ARTHUR REDFERN.

Articled to Edwyn Holt, of Manchester. Served as Private, 3rd Batt. Lancashire Fusiliers.

SYDNEY ERNEST REDFERN.

Admitted June 1905. Member of Ball and Redfern, of 10 Gray's Inn Place, W.C. Joined Sept. 1914, as 2nd Lieut., Royal Field Artillery (T.), promoted Lieut. 1915, A/Capt. March 1918. Once mentioned in Dispatches. Awarded M.C. Served at Home Sept. 1914 to Oct. 1915, and in France and Belgium Oct. 1915 to Jan. 1919. Wounded at Battle of the Somme Sept. 17, 1916, and at Hooge, Battle of Ypres, Aug. 4, 1917.

THOMAS HOWARD REDFERN.

Admitted Dec. 1900. Member of Pettit Walton & Co., of 11 New Square, Lincoln's Inn, W.C.; Leighton Buzzard, Beds; and Fenny Stratford, Bucks. Joined Sept. 1914, as Corporal, 5th Batt. The Rifle Brigade (Prince Consort's Own). Gazetted Lieut. 9th (Service) Batt. East Yorkshire Regt. Feb. 5, 1915, promoted Capt. Sept. 1915, Adjutant of 9th (2nd Reserve) Batt. June 1915 to July 1917, Posting Officer 7th Recruit Distribution Batt. Training Reserve Dec. 1917 to Jan. 1919. Served in France July to Sept. 1917.

HENRY GORDON REDMAN.

Admitted May 1908, practised at Devizes. Served as Lieut., 4th Batt. Wiltshire Regt., promoted Capt. May 1917. Mentioned in Dispatches and awarded O.B.E.

EDWARD TURBERVILLE BERNARD REECE.

Admitted May 1906, practising at Cardiff. Joined May 3, 1917, as Private, 28th Batt. County of London Regt. (Artists Rifles), transferred as Corporal to Royal Flying Corps Oct. 1917 and Instructor in Machine Gunnery. Served at Home.

GERALD REECE.

Articled to H. G. Vassall, of Bristol. Served as Cadet, Bristol University O.T.C.

JOHN WYNNE PAYNTER REECE.

Admitted Feb. 1911, practising at Abergele. Served as Lieut., Royal Welch Fusiliers.

ANDREW GORDON REED.

Admitted March 1907. Member of Howell, Yearsley & Reed, of Welshpool. Joined Aug. 5, 1914, as Lieut., 7th Batt. Royal Welch Fusiliers, promoted Capt. July 1915. Served at Gallipoli. Killed at Suvla Bay Aug. 10, 1915.

DANE BARON REED.

Articled to E. E. Baron Reed, of 1 Guildhall Chambers, E.C. Obtained commission in the Middlesex Regt. shortly after the outbreak of War, and promoted Lieut., Adjutant, and Capt. Killed in action Aug. 18, 1916.

ETHELBERT WREFORD REED.

Admitted Nov. 1901. Of 4 Bedford Row, W.C. Served as 2nd Lieut., 170th Siege Battery, Royal Garrison Artillery.

GUY REED.

Admitted Feb. 1910, practised at 1 Guildhall Chambers, E.C. Joined the Public Schools Batt. Royal Fusiliers, as Private, soon after outbreak of War, and shortly afterwards received commission in Bedfordshire Regt., promoted Lieut. Died Aug. 23, 1918, of wounds received in action the previous day.

PAUL MAURICE REED.

Articled to T. M. Reed, of Bridgwater. Joined Aug. 1914, as Private, Somerset Light Infantry. Gazetted 2nd Lieut. 8th Batt. Somerset Light Infantry Dec. 1914, attached to Royal Flying Corps Nov. 1915. Served at Home and subsequently in Egypt. Died of pneumonia in 1st Australian (Heliopolis) General Hospital on Dec. 27, 1915, and buried in Old Cairo Cemetery.

WALTER REED.

Admitted March 1894, practising at Hull. Joined July 1917 as Officer Cadet. Gazetted 2nd Lieut. Northern Command Discharge Centre Nov. 18, 1917. Served at Home.

ALBERT LLOYD REES.

Articled to Thomas Phillips, of Llandovery. Joined Aug. 1914, as Sergt., Pembrokeshire Yeomanry. Gazetted 2nd Lieut. 18th Batt. Royal Welch Fusiliers and attained the rank of Capt. Killed in action Nov. 1917.

DAVID EDMUNDS REES.

Articled to J. C. Edmunds, of Llandilo. Joined May 31, 1915, Inns of Court O.T.C. Gazetted 2nd Lieut. 8th Batt. Northamptonshire Regt. June 13, 1915, relinquished commission in 1916, and in 1917 joined Royal Flying Corps as 2nd Air-Mechanic Wireless Operator.

JOHN THOMAS TUDOR REES.

Admitted July 1907, practised at Cardiff. Served as 2nd Lieut., 3rd Batt. The Welch Regt.

JUSTIN DAVID REYNOLDS REES.

Admitted April 1910, practised at Merthyr Tydfil. Served as Private, Welsh Field Ambulance, Royal Army Medical Corps, and subsequently promoted Lance-Corporal.

TREVOR JONES REES.

Articled to A. W. Andrews, of Swansea. Joined Aug. 1914, as Private, 7th Batt. The Welch Regt. Gazetted 2nd Lieut. Aug. 28, 1915, Lieut. July 1917, Capt. Sept. 1918. Served in France and Egypt. Wounded near St. Quentin May 1917.

WILLIAM FOSTER REEVE.

Admitted Dec. 1903. Member of H. Clifford Gosnell & Reeve, of Finsbury House, E.C. Served as Private, Hon. Artillery Company (Infantry).

WILLIAM VEVERS REEVE.

Admitted Nov. 1901, practising at 35 Coleman Street, E.C. Joined Jan. 17, 1917, as Private, Royal Army Ordnance Corps, promoted Lance-Corporal May 1918, A/Sergeant Sept. 1918. Served in France.

RICHARD MERVYN EDMUND REEVES.

Admitted Aug. 1912, practising at Bristol. Joined Aug. 4, 1914, as Private, 1st. Batt. Hon. Artillery Company. Gazetted 2nd Lieut. 3rd Batt. Leicestershire Regt. Feb. 9, 1915, promoted Lieut. Sept. 1915, Capt. Oct. 1915. Served in France and Belgium Sept. 1914 to Jan. 1915, and Gallipoli April to June 1915. Wounded at Gallipoli June 18, 1915.

ROBERT GILBERT BROOMAN REGGE.

Articled to S. H. Ackroyd, of 1 Broad Street Place, E.C. Joined Sept. 1, 1914, as Private, Royal Army Service Corps (M.T.) East Anglian Division. Gazetted 2nd Lieut. 9th (Service) Batt. Yorkshire Regt. Jan. 1, 1915. Resigned commission Sept. 1915 on account of heart trouble contracted on Service. Applied Red Cross and obtained position as unpaid Dispatch Rider Dec. 1915, and on eve of embarkation refused permission to proceed by Red Cross doctors' orders owing to heart trouble. Received commission in Royal Naval Volunteer Reserve Oct. 11, 1917, as Sub-Lieut. On sea in drifter 6 months.

GEORGE RODHOUSE REID.

Admitted April 1898. Member of Childs, Harding, Reid and Wilson, of 3 Southampton Street, W.C. Served as Lieut., Royal Naval Volunteer Reserve.

HUGH SPENCER RELPH.

Admitted Feb. 1912, of Alberta. Served as Lieut., 9th Batt. 1st Canadian Expeditionary Force.

JAMES HUGH RENDELL.

Admitted Nov. 1910. Member of Church, Rendell, Bird & Co. of 9 Bedford Row, W.C. Served as 2nd Lieut., Royal Army Service Corps.

CLARENCE HENRY RENNEY.

Admitted Nov. 1912. Managing Clerk with Davis, Lloyds & Wilson, of Newport, Mon. Joined June 26, 1915, as 2nd Lieut., 1st Northumbrian Brigade, Royal Field Artillery (T.), promoted Lieut. June 1916, A/Capt. Feb. 1919, A/Major Feb. 1919. Served in France Nov. 1915 to July 1919.

MORGAN BOWES RENNIE.

Articled to S. N. Young, of 76 Cheapside, E.C. Served as Private, Royal Army Medical Corps (T.).

HENRY FRANCIS RENNOLDSON.

Admitted Oct. 1912. Member of J. H. & H. F. Rennoldson, of South Shields. Served as Lieut., 4th Northumbrian (Howitzer) Brigade, Royal Field Artillery, promoted Capt. June 1916. Mentioned in Dispatches.

ELWYN GEORGE RENTON.

Admitted March 1911. Member of Carr & Renton, of Harrogate. Joined Oct. 9, 1915, as 2nd Lieut., Royal Army Service Corps, promoted Lieut. April 1916. Served in India. Died of pneumonia at Lahore May 29, 1918.

CECIL ABBOTT REYNOLDS.

Admitted Nov. 1905, practising at 83–91 Great Titchfield Street, W. Joined Aug. 7, 1917, as Lieut., Royal Naval Volunteer Reserve. Served at Coast of Ireland Station (additional for service with S.N.O. Berehaven).

CHARLES EDWARD REYNOLDS.

Articled to Nathaniel Reynolds, of 7 Arundel Street, Strand, W.C. Joined Sept. 1914, as 2nd Lieut., 2/21 Batt. London Regt., promoted Lieut. 1916, transferred to Royal Air Force March 1917. Served in France, Salonica, and Egypt. Killed on returning from a raid Oct. 23, 1918.

DAVID REYNOLDS.

Articled to Nathaniel Reynolds, of 7 Arundel Street, Strand, W.C. Joined Sept. 1, 1914, as Private, 28th Batt. County of London Regt. (Artists Rifles). Gazetted 2nd Lieut. 1st Batt. East Lancashire Regt. July 10, 1915, promoted Lieut. Jan. 1916, A/Capt. July 1916 to 1919. Served in France 1914 to 1919.

FRANCIS GODFREY BAYLIE REYNOLDS.

Articled to Sydney Brain, of Reading. Served as 2nd Lieut., Bucks Batt. Oxford and Bucks Light Infantry, promoted Capt. June 1916.

HUGH REYNOLDS.

Admitted Jan. 1906. Member of Reynolds & Son, of 7 Arundel Street, Strand, W.C. Joined Aug. 25, 1914, as Private, Hon. Artillery Company. Gazetted 2nd Lieut. Duke of Cornwall's Light Infantry Nov. 7, 1915, promoted Lieut. July 1917. Served in France Dec. 1914 to Nov. 1916 and Sept. to Oct. 1917. Wounded Oct. 1917.

JAMES REYNOLDS.

Articled to F. W. Biddle, of 22 Aldermanbury, E.C. Joined as Private, 5th City of London Batt. London Regt. (London Rifle Brigade). Served in France. Killed in action at Hill 60 May 2, 1915.

ALFRED VIOTTI RHODES.

Articled to Walter Reed, of Hull. Joined Sept. 1, 1914, as Private, 10th Batt. East Yorkshire Regt. Gazetted 2nd Lieut. in same Regt. May 18, 1915, promoted Lieut. Nov. 1916, Capt. July 1917, transferred to Tank Corps as Capt. Dec. 1917. Awarded the M.C. Served at Home Sept. 1914 to Dec. 1915, in Egypt Dec. 1915 to Feb. 1916, in France March 1916 to April 1919, and in Germany April to Dec. 1919.

ARTHUR RHODES.

Articled to F. S. Rhodes, of Manchester. Joined Sept. 17, 1914, as 2nd Lieut., 7th Batt Durham Light Infantry. Served in Flanders. Reported missing, and subsequently presumed killed, May 24, 1915.

WILLIAM ATKINSON RHODES.

Admitted Dec. 1908, practised at Reading. Served as Corporal, 171st Labour Company.

GEORGE CHARLES DUDLEY RICE.

Admitted March 1900, practised at 3 Great St. Helen's, E.C. Served as Major, 12th Batt. Royal Fusiliers.

ARTHUR PIERRE RICHARDS.

Articled to H. W. Richards, of 26 Lincoln's Inn Fields, W.C. Served as Lieut., 14th Batt. Durham Light Infantry.

EDWARD STUART RICHARDS.

Admitted July 1909, practised at Granville House, Arundel Street, W.C. Served as Capt., 13th (Wirral) Batt. Cheshire Regt.

ERNEST HAMILTON RICHARDS.

Articled to J. T. Phoenix, of Cardiff. Joined Aug. 6, 1914, as Private, Welsh Divisional Signal Coy., Royal Engineers. Gazetted 2nd Lieut. 18th Batt.

The Welch Regt. April 1915, promoted Lieut. June 1915, Capt. Sept. 1915. Served at Home, and in France and Italy.

FRANK LEONARD RICHARDS.

Articled to F. J. Simpson, of Higham Ferrers. Joined Oct. 1914, as Private, Royal Fusiliers. Died of pneumonia contracted on service Dec. 11, 1914.

GORDON BRINLEY RICHARDS.

Admitted March 1911. Member of Jennings, Chater & Richards, of 40 Chancery Lane, W.C. Joined Oct. 1914, as Private, Inns of Court O.T.C. Gazetted 2nd Lieut. 1st Batt. London Regt. (T.) Nov. 1914, promoted Lieut. April 1915, transferred to Royal Army Service Corps March 1916, gazetted Capt. Oct. 1918. Awarded Chevalier de l'Ordre de la Couronne, Croix de Guerre (Belge). Served at Home and France.

GWILYM IVOR RICHARDS.

Articled to Edward Lewis, of Cardiff. Joined July 26, 1916, as Gunner, 2/2 Coy. Glamorgan Royal Garrison Artillery. Served as Gunner on H.M. Patrol *Sylvia* Bristol Channel Examination Service; France and Belgium. Wounded in action April 6, 1918, at Courcelles à Bois.

JOHN EUGENE RICHARDS.

Admitted Nov. 1908. Clerk with Thorpe & Perry, of Nottingham, Joined April 30, 1915, as 2nd Lieut., 3rd Batt. Notts and Derby Regt. (Sherwood Foresters), promoted Lieut. Jan. 1916, A/Capt. Oct. 1917, Adjutant Oct. 1917 to May 1919. Once mentioned in Dispatches. Served at Home and in France. Wounded, Somme, Sept. 26, 1916.

JOHN WILLIAM RICHARDS.

Admitted Jan. 1910. Member of Sterns, of 41 The Broadway, Stratford, E. Joined Inns of Court O.T.C. Received commission as 2nd Lieut. Royal Marine Light Infantry Aug. 30, 1915, afterwards promoted Lieut. Served at Salonica, Eastern Mediterranean, and in France. Killed in action at Beaumont Hamel Nov. 13, 1916.

MAURICE JOHN RICHARDS.

Articled to H. G. Vassall, of Bristol. Joined May 8, 1915, as 2nd Lieut., Royal Field Artillery (T.), promoted Lieut. June 1916. Awarded the M.C. Served in France. Wounded Aug. 16 and Dec. 3, 1917.

NESTOR ERNEST RICHARDS.

Articled to G. F. Forsdike, of Cardiff. Served as 2nd Lieut., 8th Batt South Wales Borderers.

RICHARD WATKIN RICHARDS.

Admitted March 1911. Member of C. Richards & Sons, of Llangollen, Served as 2nd Lieut., 4th Batt. Royal Welch Fusiliers. Mentioned in Dispatches and awarded M.C.

WALTER EDWARD RICHARDS.

Articled to G. E. Hart, of Uckfield. Joined April 1917, as Rifleman, 9th (Reserve) Batt. London Regt. (Queen Victoria's Rifles), transferred as Gunner to 1st (Reserve) Brigade, Royal Field Artillery, Aug. 1917. Gazetted 2nd Lieut.

3rd Batt. Royal Sussex Regt. June 26, 1918. Served in France. Wounded Sept. 20, 1918. Died, as the result of wounds, Dec. 11, 1918.

WILLIAM JOHN RICHARDS.

Admitted July 1915. Of Tonypandy. Joined Aug. 22, 1915, as 2nd Lieut., The Welch Regt., promoted Lieut. July 1917. Served at Home Aug. 1915 to June 1916, and in France June 1916 to Oct. 1918. Died of wounds at Etucourt-Ytres Oct. 12, 1918.

ARTHUR JOHN BUCHANNAN RICHARDSON.

Articled to William Richardson, of Guisborough, Yorks. Joined June 1913, as 2nd Lieut., 4th Batt. Yorkshire Regt. Died of cerebro-spinal meningitis contracted on service Jan. 4, 1915.

EWART RICHARDSON.

Admitted Feb. 1904, practised at Middlesbrough. Joined July 1915, as 2nd Lieut., 4th Batt. Yorkshire Regt. Served in France May to Sept. 1916. Killed in action near Martinpuich Sept. 26, 1916.

FRANK ARNOLD RICHARDSON.

Admitted March 1904, practising at Aspatria. Served as 2nd Lieut., 170th Siege Battery.

GUY BERNARD RICHARDSON.

Admitted Nov. 1910, practised at Bradford. Served as Able Seaman, Hawke Batt. 63rd Royal Naval Division. Killed in action Feb. 4, 1917, after serving in Gallipoli.

JAMES HENRY RICHARDSON.

Admitted April 1906, practising at Birmingham. Served as Private, 29th Batt. Royal Fusiliers.

JOHN SHERBROOKE RICHARDSON.

Admitted Dec. 1901. Member of Carnell & Richardson, of Sevenoaks. Joined June 2, 1916, as Private, 16th Batt. County of London Regt. (Queen's Westminster Rifles). Gazetted 2nd Lieut. Northumberland Fusiliers Feb. 1917. Served in France. Killed during the attack on Vimy Ridge April 9, 1917.

JOHN WATSON RICHARDSON.

Admited Jan. 1907. Member of Sorby, Hall & Richardson, of Sheffield. Joined Sept. 1914, as 2nd Lieut., York and Lancaster Regt., promoted Capt. Dec. 1914, Major June 1916. Served in France. Killed in action at Bullecourt May 3, 1917.

PERCIVAL BLYTHE RICHARDSON.

Admitted May 1898. Member of Richardson & Mitchell, of Sheffield. Joined Sept. 1914, as Lieut., York and Lancaster Regt., subsequently promoted Capt. Machine Gun Corps. Served in France. Died of trench fever at Abbeyville, France, March 9, 1918.

SYDNEY OWEN BELLERBY RICHARDSON.

Admitted April 1912, practised at Birmingham. Served as 2nd Lieut., 8th Batt. Royal Warwickshire Regt., subsequently promoted Capt.

WILLIAM EWEN RICHARDSON.

Admitted Dec. 1909, practising at 113 Stapleton Hall Road, Stroud Green, London, N. Joined June 11, 1915, as Private, Sportsman's Batt. 24th Batt. Royal Fusiliers. Served at Home. Discharged March 30, 1916.

EDWARD HAROLD RICHES.

Admitted Nov. 1907, practising at 85 Gracechurch Street, E.C. Joined June 1915, as 2nd Lieut., Royal Field Artillery, promoted Lieut. Sept. 1916, Capt. Oct. 1917, Major Oct. 1917. Served in France. Wounded at Passchendaele Dec. 18, 1917.

THOMAS HERBERT RICHMOND.

Admitted Oct. 1908. Of Kendal, and afterwards with Orr, Dignam & Co., of Calcutta. Joined Aug. 1914, as Lieut., 1/4 Batt. Border Regt., exchanged into 3rd Batt. King's Own Yorkshire Light Infantry Sept. 1914 and promoted Capt. Served in France Sept. to Oct. 1914. Wounded at the 1st Battle of Ypres Oct. 28, 1914. Died at Boulogne Nov. 1, 1914.

HENRY JAMES RICKETTS.

Admitted April 1906. Member of W. T. Ricketts & Son, of 103 King's Cross Road, W.C. Joined Aug. 1914, as Private, 17th Batt. Royal Fusiliers. Gazetted 2nd Lieut. in same Regt. Nov. 1914, promoted Lieut. Nov. 1915, Capt. Nov. 1916, Major Jan. 1918. Once mentioned in Dispatches. Awarded the M.C. Served in France. Wounded 1916 and 1917.

RICHARD CECIL HEWAT RIDDEL.

Articled to John H. Inskip, of Bristol. Joined Bristol University O.T.C. Sept. 1914. Gazetted 2nd Lieut. 2/5 Batt. Somerset Light Infantry Dec. 11, 1914, promoted Lieut Jan. 1915, transferred to 2/76 Punjabis, Indian Army, Nov. 1918 as A/Capt. and Company Commander, Full Capt. Sept. 1919. Served in India. Killed in action at Abnoi Pass Jan. 14, 1920.

ARTHUR ELLIOTT RIDDETT.

Admitted Sept. 1899. Member of Wood, Nash, Hewett & Riddett, of 6 Raymond Buildings, Glay's Inn, W.C. Joined June 30, 1917, as Officer Cadet. Gazetted 2nd Lieut. Royal Garrison Artillery Nov. 1, 1917. Served at Home (Coast Defence).

NORMAN LOCK RIDDETT.

Admitted Aug. 1910. Managing Clerk with J. Scott Duckers, of Chancery Lane, W.C. Joined Aug. 26, 1914, as Private, City of London Batt. 10th Royal Fusiliers. Gazetted 2nd Lieut. Special Reserve of Officers East Surrey Regt. Nov. 22, 1916. Served in France July 1915 to May 1916 and Dec. 1916 to Oct. 1917. Killed in action near Poelcapelle Oct. 12, 1917.

HENRY ALFRED RIDDLE.

Admitted Feb. 1904, practised at 3 Finsbury Circus, E.C. Served as 2nd Lieut., 2nd (Public Schools) Batt. Royal Fusiliers.

JOHN GEORGE EDMUND RIDEAL.

Admitted Feb. 1910. Member of Rideal & Son, of Barnsley. Mobilised Aug. 1914, as Lieut., York and Lancaster Regt. (T.), promoted Capt. in Sept.

1914, appointed Brigade Machine Gun Officer to the 1/3 West Riding Infantry Brigade (T.), afterwards known as 148th Infantry Brigade Sept. 1914. seconded as Brigade Machine Gun Officer to 148th Infantry Brigade Headquarters April 1915, formed the 148th Brigade Machine Gun Company (afterwards known as 148th Coy. Machine Gun Corps), on Active Service in France, and seconded and appointed O.C. in Feb. 1916, O.C. 63rd Coy. Machine Gun Corps, 37th Division, Aug. to Sept. 1917, appointed Divisional Machine Gun Officer to the 37th Division Headquarters Sept. 1917, and Second in Command to the 37th Batt. Machine Gun Corps Feb. 1918. Three times mentioned in Dispatches. Awarded the D.S.O. Served at Home Aug. 1914 to April 1915, and in France April 1915 to April 1917 and Aug. 1917 to Feb. 1919.

GEORGE THOMAS RIDGE.

Articled to A. Pengilly, of Weymouth. Gazetted Nov. 4, 1915, as 2nd Lieut., 3rd Batt. Dorsetshire Regt., posted to 1st Batt. Somerset Light Infantry Aug. 1916, transferred to 3rd Batt. June 1917, promoted Lieut. July 1917. Awarded the M.C. Served at Home Nov. 1915 to Aug. 1916, and in France and Belgium Aug. 1916 to July 1919.

THOMAS RIDGWAY.

Admitted Oct. 1904, practising at Warrington. Joined Aug. 1914, as 2nd Lieut., 4th Batt. South Lancashire Regt., promoted Capt. Dec. 1914, Adjutant June 1917, Major April 1918, Lieut.-Col. April 1918. Twice mentioned in Dispatches. Awarded M.C. and Bar and D.S.O. Served in France and Belgium.

FRANCIS JAMES RIDLER.

Admitted June 1909. Managing Clerk to Arthur E. Eves & Jones, of 7 Mark Lane, E.C. Joined Jan. 10, 1917, as Private, Inns of Court O.T.C., and subsequently gazetted 2nd Lieut. Royal Garrison Artillery. Served in France Oct. 1917 to Feb. 1919.

LANCELOT EDWIN RIDLEY.

Articled to E. P. Ridley, of Ipswich. Joined as 2nd Lieut., 4th Batt Royal Berkshire Regt., and subsequently promoted Lieut. and Adjutant. Served in France. Killed in action on Somme Aug. 1916.

THOMAS MATTHEW RIDLEY.

Admitted April 1900. Member of Ridley & Reay-Smith, of Newcastle-upon-Tyne. Joined Dec. 7, 1915, as Gunner, Royal Garrison Artillery. Served in France, Flanders, and Belgium. Wounded Aug. 1918.

WOOLLASTON, JOHN RIGBEY.

Admitted April 1901. Member of James Rigbey, Son & Brown, of Birmingham. Joined June 1916, as 2nd Lieut., Royal Army Service Corps. Served in France July 1916 to Feb. 1919.

HERBERT PARROTT RIGBY.

Admitted April 1903. Member of H. P. & R. S. Rigby, of Middlewich, Winsford, and Sandbach. Mobilised Aug. 3, 1914, as Capt., 1/7 Batt. Cheshire Regt. (T.), acted as Military Representative for Cheshire Appeal Tribunal 4th (Reserve) Cheshire Regt. (T.) and Legal Adviser and Courts-Martial Officer

XXIII. Corps. Awarded T.D. Served in Gallipoli 1915 and at Home 1916 to 1919. Severely wounded at Suvla Bay Aug. 10, 1915.

WILLIAM PERCY RIGDEN.

Admitted Feb. 1901, practising at 33 Chancery Lane, W.C. Mobilised Aug. 1914, as Lieut.-Col., 1st (Reserve) Home Counties Brigade, Royal Field Artillery, subsequently attached General Headquarters British Army on the Rhine. Once mentioned in Dispatches. Awarded O.B.E. Served at Home, in France, and in Germany.

SAMUEL RIGG.

Admitted March 1910. Member of Rigg & Strong, Wigton, Cumberland. Mobilised Aug. 1914, as Lieut., 5th Batt. Border Regt., and attained the rank of Major. Once mentioned in Dispatches. Served in France Oct. 1914 to March 1918. Reported wounded and missing March 25, 1918, since been officially presumed to have died on or after that date.

ALBERT VICTOR RILEY.

Admitted 1912. Managing clerk with Frank Johnson, of Bradford. Joined Oct. 11, 1914, as 2nd Lieut., Royal Field Artillery, promoted Lieut. April 1916. Served in France. Killed in action Aug. 20, 1917.

PENNINGTON RILEY.

Admitted Dec. 1903, practising at Liverpool. Joined Aug. 5, 1914, as Rifleman, 5th Batt. King's Liverpool Regt. Gazetted 2nd Lieut. in same Regt. Sept. 1914, promoted Lieut. Jan. 1916, Capt. June 1916. Served in France July 1915 to April 1916 and Aug. 1918 to Jan. 1919.

ARTHUR MITCHELL RIMER.

Articled to John Durham, of Kingston-on-Thames. Joined Sept. 1914, as Private, 10th Batt. Royal Fusiliers. Wounded in the advance on Pozières July 15, 1916. Died in Kitchener Hospital, Brighton, July 23, 1916.

ALLAN WILLIAM RIPPON.

Admitted July 1912. Managing clerk with Kenneth Brown, Baker, Baker & Co., of Lennox House, Norfolk Street, W.C. Joined Oct. 17, 1917, as 2nd Lieut., Royal Flying Corps, promoted Capt. Royal Air Force (Staff Officer III.) April 1918. Served at Home.

ARTHUR PRESTON RISING.

Admitted April 1899. Member of Worship, Rising & Frederick, of Great Yarmouth. Joined March 25, 1916, as Lieut., No. 3 Observer Coy., Royal Defence Corps, transferred as Lieut. to 462nd Protection Coy., Royal Defence Corps, Oct. 1918. Served at Home.

GEORGE SOUTHERN RITCHIE.

Admitted April 1902. Member of Southern, Fullalove & Ritchie, of Burnley. Joined Oct. 6, 1914, as Private, 21st Batt. Royal Fusiliers. Gazetted 2nd Lieut. Machine Gun Corps Aug. 5, 1916, promoted Lieut. Tank Corps Feb. 1918, Capt. Oct. 1918. Awarded the M.C. Served in France Nov. 1915 to March 1916, and May 1917 to Jan. 1919.

JOHN DOUGLAS RITCHIE.

Admitted Feb. 1908. Town Clerk of Burnley. Joined Nov. 1915, as 2nd Lieut., 4th Batt. Gordon Highlanders (T.), seconded to Tank Corps

Aug. 1917, gazetted Lieut. in 4th Gordon Highlanders July 1917, A/Capt. in Tank Corps March 1918. Awarded the M.C. Served at Home and in France. Wounded at Beaumont Hamel Nov. 18, 1916.

ROBERT RITSON.

Admitted Dec. 1907, practising at Southampton, and Eastleigh, Hants. Joined Jan. 31, 1915, as Sub-Lieut., Royal Naval Volunteer Reserve in Royal Naval Division, transferred to Army as Lieut. Machine Gun Corps July 14, 1917, promoted Temp. Capt. Nov. 1917. Served in Gallipoli May 1915 to Jan. 1916, and in France May 1916 to Feb. 1917, May to Sept. 1917, and Aug. 1918 to Feb. 1919. Wounded in France Feb. 17, 1917.

ERNEST PERCY RIVAZ.

Admitted April 1904. With Ellis, Peirs & Co., of 17 Albemarle Street, W. Served as Lieut., Royal Army Service Corps.

HENRY GIBSON RIVINGTON.

Admitted Nov. 1900. Member of Gibson & Weldon, of 27 Chancery Lane, W.C. Joined Aug. 23, 1918, as Private, Inns of Court O.T.C. Served at Home.

REGINALD THURSTON RIVINGTON.

Admitted Nov. 1907. Member of Rivington & Son, of 1 Fenchurch Buildings, E.C. Joined June 20, 1916, as Pioneer, Royal Engineers. Gazetted 2nd Lieut. Royal Army Service Corps April 12, 1917, promoted Lieut. Oct. 1918. Served at Home June to Nov. 1916, and in France, Belgium, and on the Rhine Nov. 1916 to Oct. 1919.

EDWARD ELVY ROBB.

Admitted Feb. 1894. Member of Elvy Robb & Welch, of 19 Bedford Row, W.C. Served as Capt., Royal Flying Corps, and subsequently as Major Royal Air Force.

ALAN DIXON ROBERTS.

Articled to Harold McGowan, of Newcastle-upon-Tyne. Served as Private, Public Schools Batt. Royal Fusiliers.

BERTRAM SANTELLE ROBERTS.

Admitted Oct. 1908. Member of Bayley & Roberts, of Durham. Joined Oct. 1, 1914, as Temp. 2nd Lieut., 18th (Service) Batt. Durham Light Infantry, subsequently promoted Lieut. and Capt. Served at Home.

DOUGLAS LESLIE ROBERTS.

Articled to John Roberts, of Narberth, S. Wales. Joined Nov. 11, 1915, as Private, Inns of Court O.T.C. Gazetted 2nd Lieut. Royal Field Artillery Nov. 11, 1916, and promoted Lieut. 18 months later. Served in France. Gassed twice, at Ypres and Passchendaele Ridge, June and Dec. 1917.

ELFORD HARDING ROBERTS.

Admitted April 1905, practised at Shotton, Flintshire. Served as Capt., 5th Batt. Royal Welch Fusiliers.

ENOS HERBERT GLYNNE ROBERTS.

Admitted Oct. 1913. Managing Clerk with Messrs. Rigby & Herron, of Liverpool. Joined Nov. 11, 1914, as 2nd Lieut., 9th Batt. King's Liverpool

Regt. (T.), promoted A/Lieut. April 1916, A/Capt. Nov. 1916, Substantive Lieut. June 1917, Substantive Capt. Oct. 1917. Awarded the M.C. and Bar. Served in France and Belgium Oct. 1915 to April 1919, and with Rhine Army of Occupation April to Oct. 1919.

ERNEST WOOLLEY ROBERTS.

Admitted July 1909. Member of Chapman, Roberts & Beck, of Manchester. Joined Aug. 6, 1914, as 2nd Lieut., 7th Batt. Lancashire Fusiliers. Served in Egypt and Gallipoli. Killed in action at the Dardanelles June 6, 1915.

HAROLD LESLIE ROBERTS.

Admitted March 1913, practising at Neath and Briton Ferry. Joined Nov. 29, 1915, as Gunner, Royal Field Artillery. Served in France, Salonica, and South Russia with Army of Black Sea.

HENRY SHERIFF ROBERTS.

Admitted Jan. 1912. Of Chester. Mobilised Aug. 1914, as Capt., Royal Welch Fusiliers, appointed to Depôt Cheshire Regt. Oct. 1914, to 11th Batt. Lancashire Fusiliers Feb. 1915, and transferred to 17th Batt. Royal Welch Fusiliers Aug. 1915. Served in France and Flanders. Severely wounded at Laventie April 1916. Killed in action at Langemarck Aug. 27, 1917.

HUGH OLIVER ROBERTS.

Admitted Oct. 1904. Deputy Clerk to the Justices for the City and County of Newcastle-upon-Tyne. Joined Sept. 4, 1914, as Lieut., 6th Batt. Northumberland Fusiliers, promoted Capt. Nov. 1915, transferred to 20th Batt. The Rifle Brigade Sept. 1915, attached to 2/10 Batt. Middlesex Regt. June 1917, rejoined 20th Batt. The Rifle Brigade Dec. 1917. Once mentioned in Dispatches. Served at Home Sept. 1914 to Jan. 1916, and in Egypt and Palestine Jan. 1916 to Feb. 1919. Wounded at Beersheba Nov. 6, 1917.

JAMES REGINALD HOWARD ROBERTS.

Admitted May 1913. Assistant Solicitor to the Corporation of Stoke-on-Trent. Joined Aug. 1914, as Private, 1st Denbighshire Hussars Yeomanry, promoted Lance-Corporal Oct. 1915. Commissioned 2nd Lieut. Duke of Lancaster's Own Yeomanry Dec. 1915, promoted Lieut. July, 1917, attached 24th Batt. Royal Welch Fusiliers Nov. 1917, rejoined Duke of Lancaster's Own Yeomanry Jan. 1918, seconded as Signal Officer to 54th Batt. Machine Gun Corps March 1918. Served at Home 1914 to 1915, Irish Rebellion 1916, in France 1916 to 1917, and in Egypt, Palestine, and Syria 1917 to 1919. Injured June 1917.

JOSEPH ROBERTS.

Admitted June 1913. Member of Percy Hughes & Roberts, of Birkenhead. Joined Oct. 1915, as Private, Inns of Court O.T.C. Commissioned 2nd Lieut. Oct. 1, 1916, Royal Field Artillery, A/Capt. June 1917, promoted Lieut. (A/Capt.) March 1918. Served at Home 1915 and 1916, and afterwards in France.

KENNETH FARQUHARSON ROBERTS.

Articled to W. F. Wakeford, of 27 Abingdon Street, Westminster. Joined Sept. 1914, as Private, Inns of Court O.T.C., and attained rank of Corporal. Commissioned Lieut. Royal Army Ordnance Dept. Jan. 22, 1915, promoted

Capt. March 1915, Major June 1918. Once mentioned in Dispatches. Served in France and India.

RALPH JENNINGS ROBERTS.

Articled to G. L. Stokes, of Tenby. Served as 2nd Lieut., 9th Batt. South Wales Borderers.

RICHARD ROBERTS.

Admitted Jan. 1906, practising at Wrexham. Served as Capt., 4th Batt. Royal Welch Fusiliers, and attained the rank of Major.

RICHARD JOHN SAMUEL ROBERTS.

Articled to Harold Greenwood, of Llanelly. Joined Jan. 12, 1918, H.M.S. *Research* as Paymaster Sub-Lieut., Royal Naval Volunteer Reserve. Served at Home.

RUPERT WYNNE ROBERTS.

Admitted Jan. 1915, practising at Denbigh. Joined May 4, 1917, as Gunner, Royal Field Artillery. Served in France.

VINCENT ALLEN ROBERTS.

Admitted May 1916. Clerk with Alex. Wright & Co., of Bacup. Joined July 20, 1916, Royal Flying Corps, subsequently Royal Air Force. Served in France.

WILLIAM LAWTON ROBERTS.

Articled to Arthur Godlee, of Birmingham. Joined as Private, 15th Batt. Royal Warwickshire Regt. Served in France. Died from wounds July 30, 1916.

WILLIAM NORMAN ROBERTS.

Admitted Aug. 1904, practised at Leeds. Served as Capt., Royal Army Service Corps.

WALTER GREENWOOD ROBERTSHAW.

Articled to B. H. Richardson, of Brighouse. Joined Oct. 16, 1914, as Private, 2/4 Batt. Duke of Wellington's West Riding Regt., promoted Sergeant Nov. 1914, transferred to 62nd Divisional Train Royal Army Service Corps July 1916. Once mentioned in Dispatches. Awarded the M.S.M. Served at Home, and in France, Belgium, and Germany.

ADAM ROBERTSON.

Articled to Stephen Peckover, of Leeds. Joined Sept. 1914, as Private, Grenadier Guards. Gazetted Temp. 2nd Lieut. Northumberland Fusiliers Nov. 1915. Served at Home. Died in England Feb. 2, 1917, whilst in the Army.

NORMAN ROBERTSON.

Admitted Nov. 1904, practised at Cardiff. Served as Assist. Paymaster, Royal Naval Volunteer Reserve.

NORMAN CAIRNS ROBERTSON.

Articled to Frank Kinder, of 25 Lincoln's Inn Fields, W.C. Joined Sept. 1914 Inns of Court O.T.C Obtained commission in 2nd Batt. Hampshire Regt. and attained rank of Capt. Served in France. Taken prisoner about April 1917. Died after an operation June 20, 1917, at Hanover whilst prisoner.

GILBERT LEONARD ROBEY.
Admitted May 1919, practising at Plymouth. Served as Lieut., IX. Corps School, B.E.F.

HERBERT WILLIAM HENRY ROBINS.
Admitted July 1907, practising at 35 Outer Temple, Strand, W.C. Joined Dec. 28, 1914, as Pioneer, Signal Service, Royal Engineers, and attained the rank of Staff Sergeant. Gazetted 2nd Lieut. Royal Army Service Corps June 22, 1918.

ARTHUR JOHN DIXON ROBINSON.
Admitted Jan. 1914. Clerk with Robinson & Sons, of Blackburn. Mobilised Aug. 1914, as Lieut., 1/4 Batt. East Lancashire Regt., promoted Capt. Nov. 1915. Once mentioned in Dispatches. Awarded the M.C. Served at Home, Egypt, Gallipoli, and France. Wounded at Gallipoli June 6, 1915, and in France Aug. 25, 1917.

BELTRAN FORD ROBINSON.
Admitted May 1910. Managing Clerk with Bromley & Hyde, of Ashton-under-Lyne. Joined Oct. 6, 1914, as 2nd Lieut., 9th Batt. Manchester Regt., promoted Lieut. Nov. 1914, Capt. Aug. 1915. Served in Gallipoli 1915, Egypt (Sinai) 1916, and in France and Belgium 1917.

BERTRAM LANGHORNE ROBINSON.
Admitted Feb. 1899. Member of Proud, Robinson & Roddam, of Bishop Auckland. Joined Oct. 1914, as 2nd Lieut., Royal Army Service Corps (T.), and subsequently promoted Capt. Served in France about 2 years. Invalided Home and died Sept. 6, 1917.

CHARLES ROBINSON.
Admitted April 1897. Member of Robinson & Sons, of Watton, Norfolk. Served as Lieut., 5th Batt. Norfolk Regt.

CHARLES KEITH ROBINSON.
Articled to Charles Robinson, of 1 Lancaster Place, Strand, W.C. Mobilised 1914, as 2nd Lieut., 9th Batt Middlesex Regt., promoted Lieut. Aug. 1914, Temp. Capt. Oct. 1914, Perm. Capt. June 1916, transferred as A/Brigade Major 225th Brigade Oct. 1915 to April 1916, attached Royal Flying Corps as Adjutant Oct. 1916, transferred to Flying Branch Nov. 1916. Served at Home and in France.

EDWARD NORMAN ROBINSON.
Articled to E. W. Dawes, of Middlesbrough. Joined Feb. 14, 1916, as Private, 4th Batt. Yorkshire Regt. Gazetted 2nd Lieut. 13th Batt. Yorkshire Regt. Dec. 19, 1916, promoted Lieut. June 1918. Once mentioned in Dispatches. Served in France, Belgium, and North Russia. Wounded Nov. 25, 1917.

FRANCIS GEORGE ROBINSON.
Admitted June 1901, practising at Ilkeston, Heanor, and Nottingham. Joined Oct. 6, 1914, as 2nd Lieut., 5th Batt. Notts and Derby Regt. (Sherwood Foresters), promoted Lieut. June 1915, Temp. Capt. June 1916, A/Capt. 1917, Capt. T.F. Reserve June 1918. Served in France and Flanders.

FREDERICK DIXON ROBINSON.

Admitted July 1883. Member of Robinson & Sons, of Blackburn and Clitheroe. Mobilised as Lieut.-Col. in Command of 4th Batt. East Lancashire Regt. on outbreak of the War. Once mentioned in Dispatches. Served in Egypt and Gallipoli. Placed on T.F. Reserve Aug. 1917.

FREDERICK VIVASH ROBINSON.

Admitted Nov. 1912, practising at 7 St. John's Hill, Clapham Junction, S.W. Joined Feb. 1917, as Private, Royal Army Service Corps. Gazetted 2nd Lieut. Royal Field Artillery June 1918. Served in France.

GEOFFREY NICHOLAS ROBINSON.

Articled to F. D. Robinson, of Blackburn. Mobilised Aug. 1914, as 2nd Lieut., 4th Batt. East Lancashire Regt. (T.), promoted Lieut. Nov. 1914, Capt. March 1917. Once mentioned in Dispatches. Served in Egypt Sept. 1914 to April 1915 and Feb. 1916 to March 1917, at Gallipoli May 1915 to Jan. 1916, in France March to Sept. 1917, and at Home Sept. 1917 to Jan. 1919. Wounded (gas poisoning) at Passchendaele Sept. 1917.

GEORGE ROBINSON.

Admitted Aug. 1908, practising at Middlesbrough. Joined April 26, 1916, as Gunner, transferred to 3rd Field Survey Batt. Royal Engineers as Sapper April 1917. Served in France Sept. 1916 to Jan. 1919.

GLEESON EDWARD ROBINSON.

Admitted Dec. 1904, formerly practising at 170 Strand, W.C. Served as 2nd Lieut., 179th Brigade, Royal Field Artillery, promoted Lieut. July 1917, Mentioned in Dispatches and awarded M.C. and Bar.

HORACE VICTOR GEORGE ROBINSON.

Articled to H. J. Brown, of Warwick. Joined Inns of Court O.T.C. Oct. 1915. Gazetted 2nd Lieut. 7th Batt. Worcestershire Regt. Nov. 27, 1916. Served in France. Reported missing, and subsequently presumed to have been killed, Oct. 24, 1917.

HUGH MUSCHAMP ROBINSON.

Admitted June 1907. Managing Clerk with Radcliffes & Hood, of 28 Old Queen Street, S.W. Rejoined Nov. 8, 1914, as Ordinary Seaman, Royal Naval Division, promoted Able-Bodied Seaman, Hawke Batt. Royal Naval Division Feb. 1915. Gazetted 2nd Lieut. Royal Garrison Artillery (Special Reserve) Oct. 1, 1916, promoted Lieut. April 1918. Served on Gallipoli Peninsula May to Aug. 1915, and in France May 1917 to April 1919.

JOHN CYRIL CHARLES HENRY ROBINSON.

Admitted Nov. 1912, practised at Burnley. Served as Capt., 5th Batt. East Lancashire Regt. Went to Egypt Sept. 1914, and transferred to France March 1917. Killed in action June 2, 1917.

JOHN EDGAR ROBINSON.

Articled to D. F. Hart, of Manchester. Joined Dec. 11, 1915, as Private, promoted Lance-Corporal April 1916, Corporal Aug. 1916. Served at Salonica. Wounded Sept. 15, 1916. Discharged April 17, 1917.

JOHN HENRY ROBINSON.

Admitted Dec. 1913. Member of Clay & Robinson, of Retford, Worksop, and Sheffield. Joined Oct. 1914, as Trooper, Sherwood Rangers Imperial Yeomanry, and promoted Lance-Corporal and Dispatch Rider. Gazetted 2nd Lieut. 4th Batt. Somerset Light Infantry Jan. 1917, and then attached to 2/6 Batt. North Staffordshire Regt. Served at Home and in France. Killed in action at Cambrai Nov. 30, 1917.

JOHN WILFRID ROBINSON.

Articled to J. A. Baty, of Hexham. Joined Aug. 4, 1914, 4th Batt. Northumberland Fusiliers (T.). Gazetted 2nd Lieut. in same Regt. Sept. 14, 1914, promoted Lieut. July 1916, Capt. Oct. 1916. Served in France April 1915 to Nov. 1916. Twice wounded. Killed in action at Butte of Warlencourt Nov. 14, 1916.

JOSEPH WILLIAM ROBINSON.

Admitted Feb. 1914. Managing Clerk with J. Burniston, of Goole. Mobilised 1914, as Lieut., 5th Border Regt., promoted Temp. Capt. July 1915, Capt. Jan. 1917. Once mentioned in Dispatches. Served in Belgium and France Oct. 1914 to Oct. 1916. Invalided out of Service July 10, 1917.

PERCY DOUGLAS ROBINSON.

Admitted Jan. 1912, practised at Harrogate. Joined 1914, as 2nd Lieut., 9th Batt. Northumberland Fusiliers, promoted Lieut. 1915, Capt. 1916. Served in France. Killed in action at Battle of the Somme 1916.

SIDNEY ROBINSON.

Articled to R. B. Jackson, of Ulverston. Joined April 20, 1918, as Assistant Paymaster, Royal Navy Volunteer Reserve. Title changed to Paymaster Sub-Lieut. Served on Staff of Admiral Northern Patrol in the Orkneys May to Aug. 1918, and in Egypt with Senior British Naval Officer, Suez Canal, Sept. 1918 to May 1919.

SIDNEY HERBERT ROBINSON.

Articled to T. W. Robinson, of Birmingham. Mobilised Aug. 1914, as 2nd Lieut., Royal Field Artillery (T.), promoted Lieut. Sept. 1914, Capt. Sept. 1917. Once mentioned in Dispatches. Awarded M.C. Served in France. Wounded Nov. 1916. Discharged on account of wounds Dec. 12, 1917.

THOMAS CHAMBERS ROBINSON.

Admitted March 1899. Member of Robinson & Sons, of Blackburn. Mobilised Aug. 5, 1914, as Capt., 4th Batt. East Lancashire Regt. (T.), appointed Staff Capt. 126th East Lancs. Infantry Brigade Aug. 1914 to Oct. 19, 1916, promoted Major July 1915. Appointed D.A.A.G. to Desert Column, E.E.F., Oct. 1916 to June 1917, A.A. and Q.M.G. to Yeomanry Mounted Division E.E.F. June 1917 to Aug. 1919. Twice mentioned in Dispatches. Awarded the D.S.O., T.D., and Order of the Nile. Served in Egypt Sept. 1914 to May 1915, Gallipoli May to Dec. 1915, and in Palestine, Syria, etc., Jan. 1916 to Aug. 1919.

GORDON BLEWS ROBOTHAM.

Articled to W. B. Robotham, of Derby. Joined Oct. 6, 1914, as 2nd Lieut., 5th Batt. Notts and Derby Regt. (Sherwood Foresters), transferred to Royal Air Force March 1916, promoted Lieut. June 1916, Capt. July 1917. Once mentioned in Dispatches. Awarded the D.F.C. Served in France May to Aug. 1915 and May 1916 to Nov. 1919. Wounded July 17, 1915.

EDWARD MOORE ROBSON.

Admitted Oct. 1912. Managing Clerk wth Rider, Heaton & Co., of 8 New Square, Lincoln's Inn, W.C. Joined 1914, as 2nd Lieut., 5th Batt. Yorkshire Regt. (T.), subsequently promoted Lieut. and Capt. Awarded the M.C. Served at Home and in France and Belgium (went overseas July 1915). Twice wounded. Killed in action April 11, 1918.

FREDERICK WILLIAM ROBSON.

Admitted Aug. 1909, practised at Pocklington. Mobilised Aug. 1914, as Capt., 5th Batt. Yorkshire Regt., and subsequently promoted to Lieut.-Col., appointed to the command of 6th Batt. Durham Light Infantry 1917. Three times mentioned in Dispatches. Awarded the D.S.O. Served at Home and in France and Belgium (went overseas April 1915). Slightly wounded in Battle of St. Julien April 1915. Killed in action March 28, 1918.

NORMAN SPOTTISWOODE ROBSON.

Articled to J. H. Youll, of Newcastle-upon-Tyne. Gazetted Dec. 23, 1915, as 2nd Lieut., promoted Lieut. June 1917. Served in Infantry and Royal Flying Corps. Served in France. Wounded Nov. 14, 1916.

STANLEY ROBSON.

Admitted July 1910. Member of Underwood & Robson, of Hull. Joined Nov. 16, 1915, as Rifleman, King's Royal Rifle Corps. Gazetted 2nd Lieut. 4th Batt. East Yorkshire Regt. (T.) May 29, 1917. Served in France. Wounded at Battle of the Somme Sept. 15, 1916. Killed near Albert March 31, 1918.

WILLIAM NEWBY ROBSON.

Admitted Nov. 1909, practising at Sunderland. Joined Sept. 1916, as Private, Royal Army Service Corps (M.T.), employed as Heavy Lorry Driver. Gazetted 2nd Lieut. Royal Army Service Corps Feb. 23, 1917, promoted Lieut. Aug. 23, 1918, A/Capt. May to June 1918. Served in Palestine April 1917 to March 1919. Torpedoed April 15, 1917, whilst proceeding to Egypt in H.M.T. *Arcadian*.

CHARLES HUBERT ROCHE.

Admitted Dec. 1887, practising at Daventry. Joined Sept. 24, 1914, as Trooper, Lovat's Scouts. Gazetted Lieut. Royal Army Service Corps Jan. 12, 1915, promoted Capt. Dec. 1917. Served at Home and in France June 1916 to March 1919.

WILLIAM HENRY RODD.

Articled to R. R. Rodd & Son, of East Stonehouse, Plymouth, Devon. Joined March 17, 1917, as Sub-Lieut., Royal Naval Volunteer Reserve, attached Royal Naval Air Service, promoted Lieut. Jan. 1918, promoted Capt. Royal Air Force, April 1908. Served at Dunkirk (France), Dover, and Torquay.

HUME BUCKLEY RODERICK.

Admitted Nov. 1910. Member of Roderick and Richards, of Llanelly. Mobilised Aug. 1914, as Capt., 4th Batt. The Welch Regt. (T.), transferred to Welch Guards Aug. 1917 with rank of Lieut., and subsequently appointed A/Capt. Served in Egypt and in France. Killed in action at Cambrai Dec. 1, 1917.

ARTHUR CHRISTOPHER RODWELL.

Admtted Feb. 1906, Member of Keen, Rogers & Co., of 59 Carter Lane, Doctors' Commons, E.C. Joined Dec. 6, 1916, as Private, Inns of Court O.T.C. Gazetted 2nd Lieut. 241st Siege Battery Royal Garrison Artillery Sept. 1, 1917, attached to H.Q. 30th Brigade March 1918, promoted Lieut. March 1919. Served in France.

FRANCIS JOHN RODWELL.

Admitted April 1909, practising at Halesworth, Suffolk. Mobilised Aug. 4, 1914, as Capt., 4th Batt. Suffolk Regt., promoted Major Oct. 1916. Awarded O.B.E. Served at Home Aug. to Nov. 1914 and March 1915 to May 1919, and in France Nov. 1914 to March 1915. Wounded at Battle of Neuve Chapelle March 11, 1915.

JAMES CAULFIELD ROE.

Admitted Feb. 1898, practising at 24 Lawrence Lane, E.C. Served as Lieut., 1st Batt. Lincolnshire Yeomanry.

ALEXANDER BOYD ROEBUCK.

Admitted March 1914. Member of Oddie & Roebuck, of Blackburn and Nelson. Joined Sept. 1, 1914, as 2nd Lieut., 4th Batt. East Lancashire Regt. (T.), promoted Lieut. Dec. 1914, Substantive Capt. 1917. Served at Home, Gallipoli, Egypt, France, and Belgium. Wounded at Ypres Sept. 3, 1917.

ALFRED DENYS STRICKLAND ROGERS.

Admitted Feb. 1909. Managing Clerk with Stanton, Atkinson & Bird, of Newcastle-upon-Tyne. Mobilised Aug. 4, 1914, as Capt., 6th Batt. Northumberland Fusiliers, promoted Major July 1916. Served at Home Aug. 1914 to May 1917, and in Flanders May 1917 to June 1918. Wounded May 27, 1918.

EDWARD AMBROSE GORDON ROGERS.

Admitted Oct. 1909. Member of Reginald Rogers & Son, of Falmouth. Joined Aug. 4, 1914, as Capt., Cornwall Royal Garrison Artillery (T.). Served at Home (was *en route* for service abroad with 93rd Siege Battery). Died at the Helena Hospital, Shorncliffe, as a result of collision with a motor, April 9, 1916.

JOHN PERCIVAL ROGERS.

Articled to John Rogers, of Falmouth. Joined Dec. 5, 1915, as 2nd Lieut., 1st Batt. Herefordshire Regt., promoted Lieut. July 1917. Served at Home Dec. 1915 to Sept. 1917 and Sept. 1918 to Jan. 1919, in Palestine and Egypt Sept. 1917 to June 1918, and in France June to Sept. 1918. Wounded at Anata Dec. 28, 1917, and at Parcy Tigny July 23, 1918.

PHILIP MORTON ROGERS.

Articled to R. H. Wilson, of Bury St. Edmunds. Joined Nov. 20, 1914, as Private, Royal Army Service Corps (M.T.). Gazetted 2nd Lieut. Royal

Flying Corps Dec. 6, 1917, promoted Lieut. Royal Air Force April 1918. Served at Home Nov. 1914 to Sept. 1916, and Salonica and Egypt Sept. 1916 to Aug. 1919.

SYDNEY ROGERS.

Admitted Dec. 1898, practising at Brondesbury, N.W. Served as Capt., 2/3 Scottish Horse.

WILLIAM JAMES ALEXANDER ROGERS.

Articled to Charles Rogers, of 89 Chancery Lane, W.C. Served as Trooper, Legion of Frontiersmen.

WILFRED CHORLEY ROGERSON.

Articled to Alfred Pearson, of Manchester. Joined Dec. 1915, as 2nd Air-Mechanic, Royal Flying Corps, promoted 1st Air-Mechanic Feb. 1916. Commissioned as 2nd Lieut. Royal Army Service Corps (M.T.) Sept. 1916, promoted Lieut. July 1918. Served in France and at Home.

ARTHUR GILBERT ROLLASON.

Articled to his father, A. A. Rollason, of Birmingham. Mobilised Aug. 1914, as Lieut., Worcestershire Regt., promoted Capt. April 1915. Served at Home and in France. Died from wounds (after an operation) in Field Hospital, Doullens, France, July 30, 1915, buried Louvencourt Cemetery, France.

EDWARD HOWARD ROLLINSON.

Articled to Wm. Rollinson, of 147 Cannon Street, E.C. Joined 1916, as Private, 2/28 Batt. County of London Regt. Gazetted 2nd Lieut. Norfolk Regt. Aug 29, 1917, appointed Staff Lieut. Nov. 1918. Served with Egyptian Expeditionary Force.

WILLIAM STUART ROLLO.

Admitted May 1909. Member of R. J. Jones, Sephton, Rollo & Farmer, of Liverpool. Joined Aug. 4, 1914, as 2nd Lieut., Royal Engineers, promoted Capt. 1914. Once mentioned in Dispatches. Awarded M.C. Served in France and Belgium 1914 to 1919.

JESSEL ANIDJAR ROMAIN.

Articled to A. A. Romain, of 132 Seymour Place, Bryanston Square, W. Joined Sept. 1914, as Private, Hon. Artillery Company (Infantry). Gazetted 2nd Lieut. Bedfordshire Regt. Oct. 7, 1915, promoted Lieut. July 1916. Served at Home and in France. Wounded at Gouvelle, Arras, in April 1917.

FREDERICK ROMER.

Admitted Jan. 1879. Member of Romer & Skan, of 4 Copthall Chambers, E.C. Joined Nov. 8, 1914, as Lieut., Royal Naval Volunteer Reserve. Awarded O.B.E. Served at Admiralty.

HAROLD GEORGE ROMER.

Admitted July 1911, practising at 20 Copthall Avenue, E.C. Joined Aug. 1914, as Private, Inns of Court O.T.C. Gazetted Lieut. 22nd Batt. County of London Regt. (Queen's) Sept. 1914, promoted Capt. May 1915. Served in France. Resigned March 1918.

CHARLES KEITH JAGO ROOKE.

Admitted April 1891. Member of Freeman & Son, of 30A George Street, Hanover Square, W. Served as Corporal, 12th Infantry Batt. Tasmanian Expeditionary Force. Officially assumed killed in action April 25, 1915.

WALLACE MORTIMER ROOKE.

Articled to Kenneth Macdonald, of Bath. Mobilised Aug. 1914, as Lieut., Royal Wiltshire Yeomanry, attached 2nd Batt. Wiltshire Regt. in France 1915, promoted Capt. June 1916. Once mentioned in Dispatches. Served in France. Died of pneumonia contracted on Service Oct. 8, 1918.

LIONEL CHARLES TURNER ROOM.

Admitted Aug. 1906. Member of Watson, Sons & Room, of 12 Bouverie Street, E.C., and Hammersmith. Joined Jan. 1915, as 2nd Lieut., Royal Marine Light Infantry, promoted Lieut. Sept. 1915, Capt. March 1917. Once mentioned in Dispatches. Served in Gallipoli Campaign 1915, and on Special Service in Ægean 1916 to 1918.

JOHN ROPER.

Admitted Nov. 1909. Member of John J. Roper, of Bridport, Dorset. Mobilised Aug. 1914, as Lieut., 4th Batt. Dorsetshire Regt., promoted Capt. Oct. 1914. Served at Home Aug. to Oct. 1914, in India Nov. 1914 to Feb. 1916 and July 1916 to April 1919, and in Mesopotamia Feb. to July 1916.

WILLIAM ROSCOE.

Admitted Oct. 1913. Managing Clerk with Bircham & Co., 50 Old Broad Street. Mobilised Aug. 5, 1914, as Private, 28th Batt. County of London Regt. (Artists Rifles). Gazetted Temp. 2nd Lieut. 2nd Batt. South Lancashire Regt. Jan. 27, 1915, attached Machine Gun Corps Jan. 1916, promoted Temp. Lieut. Feb. 1916, Temp. Capt. Oct. 1916, appointed Assistant Instructor (Machine Gun Training Centre) Jan. 1917, promoted A/Major April 1918. Once mentioned in Dispatches. Awarded the M.C. Served in Belgium and France Oct. 1914 to Sept. 1916 and June to Dec. 1918. Wounded June 22, 1915.

ARTHUR RAYMOND ROSE.

Articled to J. G. B. Porter, of 2 Wardrobe Place, Doctors' Commons. Joined Sept. 1914, as Private, 16th Batt. London Regt. (Queen's Westminster Rifles). Gazetted 2nd Lieut. 2/5 Batt. King's Own Yorkshire Light Infantry Sept. 30, 1915, promoted Lieut. July 1917. Awarded the M.C. Served in Flanders, France, and Germany.

DONALD HOULT ROSE.

Articled to T. L. Maughan, of Newcastle-upon-Tyne. Served as Temp. Warrant Telegraphist, Royal Naval Reserve, to H.M.S. *Glasgow* for Falkland Islands Wireless Telegraph Station.

ERIC DUDLEY ROSE.

Admitted May 1914, practised at Stoke Newington, N. Joined Aug. 8, 1914, 1st Batt. Hon. Artillery Company, and went into action Nov. 1914.

Obtained commission in London Regt. Nov. 1915, promoted to Capt. Served in France and Salonica. Killed in action March 30, 1918.

HARCOURT GEORGE SAINTE CROIX ROSE.

Admitted April 1908. Member of Norton, Rose & Co., of 57½ Old Broad Street, E.C. Served as Lieut., 1st (Reserve) Batt. Hertfordshire Regt.

HARRY CECIL ROSE.

Admitted Aug. 1908, practising at Faringdon, Berks. Joined Aug. 1914, as 2nd Lieut., Royal Army Service Corps, promoted Major Feb. 1917. Twice mentioned in Dispatches. Served in Egypt and Salonica.

PHILIP VIVIAN ROSE.

Solicitor to the London, Brighton & South Coast Railway. Joined at the outbreak of War and appointed Staff Capt. 63rd Infantry Brigade. Served at Home and in France. Wounded at Loos (where taken prisoner) and remained in Germany for 17 months, when sent Home. Died April 25, 1917, of wounds received in Loos Battle.

REGINALD GEORGE ROSE.

Articled to J. A. Aldred, of 43-46 Southampton Buildings, W.C. Joined Nov. 7, 1914, Inns of Court O.T.C. Gazetted 2nd Lieut. Essex Regt. March 1915, transferred to 9th Essex Regt. March 1916. Served at Home and in France. Wounded Mouquet Farm Sept. 1916. Invalided from Service June 1917.

JOHN BRENCHLEY ROSHER.

Admitted July 1914. Member of Rashleigh, Turner, Mann & Rosher, of 63 Lincoln's Inn Fields, W.C. Joined Aug. 5, 1914, as Private, 28th Batt. County of London Regt. (Artists Rifles). Gazetted 2nd Lieut. 10th Batt. Durham Light Infantry Sept. 1914, promoted Lieut. Nov. 1914, Capt. Sept. 1915, Major July 1916, Lieut.-Col. July 1917, Lieut.-Col. 6th Batt. Machine Gun Corps March 1918. Four times mentioned in Dispatches. Awarded D.S.O. and Bar and M.C. Served in France 1915 to 1919. Wounded Sept. 1915 (Ypres) and Aug. 1916 (Somme).

ARTHUR WILLIAM ROSS.

Admitted April 1912, practising at 12 Coleman Street, E.C. Served as 2nd Lieut., 10th Batt. County of London Regt., promoted Capt. July 1917.

CHARLES GORDON ROSS.

Admitted July 1910. Member of Cardew, Smith & Ross, of 25 Bedford Row, W.C. Joined Sept. 26, 1914, as 2nd Lieut., 17th Batt. County of London Regt. (T.), promoted Temp. Lieut. June 1915, Temp. Capt. Dec. 1915, Substantive Capt. June 1916, A/Major July 1918. Once mentioned in Dispatches. Awarded the M.C. Served in France and Flanders June to Dec. 1916 and June to Oct. 1918, in Salonica Dec. 1916 to Feb. 1917, and in Palestine Jan. to June 1918.

JOHN ALEXANDER ROSS.

Admitted May 1907. Of the Solicitor's Department, Great Northern Railway. Joined as 2nd Lieut., 17th Batt. London Regt. Served in France. Killed at Loos, France, Oct. 16, 1915.

JOHN HENRY ROSS.

Articled to George Wheeldon, of Southport. Joined Sept. 3, 1914, as Private, 7th Batt. King's Liverpool Regt. Served in France. Wounded June 21, 1915. Discharged Feb. 15, 1916.

WILLIAM FREDERICK ROSSITER.

Admitted Aug. 1904, practising at Weston-super-Mare. Joined July 2, 1916, as Private, 3rd Batt. Royal Warwickshire Regt. Gazetted 2nd Lieut. Royal Army Service Corps, promoted Lieut. June 1919. Served in France and Belgium. Wounded May 5, 1917.

WILFRED STEWART ROTHERA.

Admitted Jan. 1904. Member of Rothera & Sons, of Nottingham. Gazetted Oct. 1915 as 2nd Lieut. 8th Batt. West Yorkshire Regt. (Leeds Rifles), subsequently promoted Lieut. Served in France. Gassed Nov. 1917.

LESLIE JOSEPH ROW.

Articled to his father, Charles Row, of Norwich. Joined Aug. 1914, as Private, Norfolk Cyclist Corps, and subsequently gazetted 2nd Lieut. 1st Batt. Norfolk Regt. Served at Home and in France. Killed in action at Arras June 2, 1916.

JOHN CHEETHAM SELWYN ROWBOTHAM.

Articled to Edward Rowbotham, of Oldham. Served as 2nd Lieut., 10th (Reserve) Batt. Manchester Regt (T.), promoted Capt. June 1916. Mentioned in Dispatches and awarded M.C.

CECIL DENTON ROWE.

Articled to Thos. Hewitt, of 158 Leadenhall Street, E.C. Joined Dec. 1915, as Rifleman, King's Royal Rifle Corps. Obtained commission as 2nd Lieut. Royal Fusiliers May 1917. Served at Home and in France. Wounded and taken prisoner near Ytres, south of Cambrai, March 23, 1918.

JOHN SOUTHAM ROWE.

Articled to H. E. Tudor, of 27 Chancery Lane, W.C. Joined Nov. 20, 1915, as Private, 28th Batt. County of London Regt. (Artists Rifles). Gazetted 2nd Lieut. Royal Garrison Artillery (S.R.) Dec. 17, 1917. Once mentioned in Dispatches. Served at Home Nov. 1915 to Jan. 1916 and May to Dec. 1917, and in France Feb. 1916 to May 1917 and Jan. 1918 to April 1919.

STEPHEN GILBY ROWE.

Articled to William Rowe, of Redruth, Cornwall. Joined April 15, 1915, as Trooper, 2/3 Scottish Horse. Gazetted 2nd Lieut. 9th Batt. Duke of Cornwall's Light Infantry July 24, 1915, promoted Lieut. July 1917, attached to 2/21 Punjabis Feb. 1918, promoted A/Capt. (Depôt Adjutant) Aug. 1918. Served in France May 1916 to Nov. 1917, and in India Feb. 1918 to Feb. 1919.

CYRIL MALCOLM SPENSER ROWLAND.

Admitted Dec. 1902, practising at Bournemouth. Gazetted Jan. 15, 1917, Temp. Lieut. General List., attached D.G.R. and E. Jan. 1917, O.C Graves Regt. Unit 17, on Sections south of Arras to Boves, to July 1918, detached to G.H.Q., South, for special duty south of Soissons and Rheims, with 15th, 34th, 51st, and 62nd Divisions July 1918, A/Capt. Nov. 18, 1918, whilst employed under D.A.D.G.R. and E. 4th Army, later transferred to D.A.D.G.R. and E. 3rd Army. Served in France.

FRANK ROWLAND.

Admitted Feb. 1912. Practising at Birmingham. Served as Capt., 6th London Field Ambulance, Royal Army Medical Corps (T.).

GLYN VENMORE ROWLAND.

Articled to C. A. Jones, of Carnarvon, N. Wales. Joined Aug. 29, 1914, as 2nd Lieut., Welsh (Carnarvon) Royal Garrison Artillery, promoted Lieut April 1915, Capt. April 1916. Served in France and Belgium.

ARTHUR WILLIAM ROWLANDS.

Articled to C. H. Wimshurst, of Liverpool. Joined Oct. 1914, as Private, 10th Batt. King's Liverpool Regt. (Liverpool Scottish), and in 1915 granted commission in Royal Army Service Corps while in France, promoted Lieut., transferred to Royal Flying Corps, and served as an Observer for 6 months. Killed in Lincolnshire Aug. 15, 1917, while landing his machine at night.

WILLIAM JAMES ROWLES.

Articled to J. F. Fearon, of Woking. Joined May 1915, as Sub-Lieut., Royal Naval Volunteer Reserve, Royal Naval Division, subsequently promoted Lieut. Served afloat at Scapa, and at Northern Base, Ireland.

RICHARD SIDNEY ROWSE.

Admitted July 1905, practised at Redruth. Served as 2nd Lieut., 5th Batt. Duke of Cornwall's Light Infantry. Died Sept. 2, 1915, whilst drilling his men at the military camp at Tavistock.

EDMUND ROYDS.

Admitted July 1882. Member of Royds, Rawstorne & Co., of 46 Bedford Square, W.C. Served as Major, Lincolnshire Yeomanry.

CLAUDE RANDALL ROYLE.

Admitted Feb. 1911, practising at Scarborough. Served as Private, 21st (Service) Batt. King's Royal Rifle Corps.

ERNEST RUPERT ROYLE.

Admitted April 1905, practising at Wembley. Joined Nov. 1915, as Lieut., Gen. List Staff, promoted Capt. July 1916. Once mentioned in Dispatches. Awarded O.B.E. (Military Division). Served at Home on Recruiting Staff 1915 to 1917, and subsequently at the Ministry of National Service.

VERNON PETER ROYLE.

Admitted Oct. 1910, practised at 33 Walbrook, E.C. Served as 2nd Lieut., Royal Army Ordnance Dept.

SAMUEL LEWIS ROZELAAR.

Articled to George Vandamm, of Devonshire Chambers, Bishopsgate, E.C. Joined Sept. 1, 1914, as Private, Public School Brigade. Received commission in Royal Berkshire Regt. Nov. 19, 1914, A/Capt. Trench Mortar

Battery (Command) July 1916. Served in France, Belgium, and Dublin. Wounded at Chaulnes March 25, 1918. Drowned on Irish Mail Steamer *Leinster*, which was torpedoed Oct. 10, 1918, on his way again to France.

RONALD FRANCIS RUBINSTEIN.
Articled to S. J. Rubinstein, of 56 Raymond Buildings, Gray's Inn. Joined June 25, 1915, as Private, 28th Batt. County of London Regt. (Artists Rifles). Gazetted 2nd Lieut. 5th Batt. Gloucestershire Regt. Nov. 1, 1915, promoted A/Capt. Oct. 1917. Served in France Aug. 1916 to Oct. 1917, and in Italy Oct. 1917 to June 1918. Captured by Austrians Asiago Plateau June 15, 1918. Released Nov. 3, 1918.

WILLIAM ERNEST RUCK.
Admitted May 1880. Served as Hon. Lieut.-Col., 1st V.B. Hampshire Regt. Served at Home in Royal Defence Corps.

NOEL BATEMAN RUDD.
Admitted April 1912. Assistant Solicitor to the Corporation of Norwich. Joined Dec. 2, 1914, as Private, Inns of Court O.T.C. Commissioned 2nd Lieut. 2/4 Batt. Norfolk Regt. Feb. 25, 1915, promoted Temp. Lieut. June 1915, Temp. Capt. Sept. 1915, reverted to Lieut. (Substantive) on transfer to Indian Army Reserve Officers Sept. 1917, A/Capt. attached 1/48 Pioneers July 1918. Served at Home 1914 to 1917, India 1917 to 1918, Mesopotamia and Persia 1918 to 1919, and North-West Frontier 1919.

LEO GERALD RUDDIN.
Articled to A. R. Moon, of Manchester. Joined Manchester University O.T.C., as Cadet, Oct. 1914. Gazetted 2nd Lieut. 6th Batt. Cheshire Regt. Feb. 1915, promoted Lieut. Dec. 1915, Capt. Jan. 1917. Awarded the M.C. Served in France and Belgium. Wounded at St. Julien, Ypres, July 31, 1917.

HORACE GOWING RUDDOCK.
Admitted Sept. 1907. Member of Harmer, Ruddock & Son, of Great Yarmouth. Mobilised Aug. 1914, as Capt., 1st East Anglian Brigade Royal Field Artillery, promoted Major June 1916. Served in France, Egypt, and Sudan.

THOMAS RUDDOCK.
Articled to Arnold H. Miller, Town Clerk of Norwich. Joined about April 1915 as Private in the O.T.C. Subsequently gazetted Lieut. 4th Batt. East Kent Regt., afterwards attached 7th (Service) Batt. Served in France. Killed in action in France Aug. 7, 1918. Buried Querrieux British Cemetery, Querrieux.

REGINALD FRANCIS RUGG.
Articled to H. B. Lawford, of 12 New Court, Carey Street, W.C. Joined Sept. 1, 1914, as Rifleman, 9th Batt. County of London Regt. (Queen Victoria's Rifles). Gazetted 2nd Lieut. Royal Welch Fusiliers (Special Reserve) March 6, 1915, promoted Lieut. June 1915, Capt. Oct. 1915. Served in France and Belgium.

THOMAS RUMNEY.

Articled to W. V. Hamilton, of Manchester. Mobilised Aug. 4, 1914, as Lieut., 2nd East Lancs. Brigade Royal Field Artillery (T.), transferred to Regular Army 1914, lent to Foreign Office 1917 to 1918, attached Royal Flying Corps and Royal Air Force 1918 to Oct. 1919. Served with Indian Expeditionary Force, Sinai, Sept. 1914 to Sept. 1915, at Home to Jan. 1917, and in Greece (Foreign Office Diplomatic Service) to Dec. 1917, and at Home and at Aden Jan. 1918 to Oct. 1919.

LESLIE ERIC RUNDELL.

Articled to C. H. Rundell, of 9 John Street, Bedford Row, W.C. Mobilised Aug. 1914, as Private, 28th Batt. County of London Regt. (Artists Rifles). Commissioned to 7th Batt. London Regt. Nov. 1914, and subsequently promoted Capt. and A/Major, appointed Staff Capt. Once mentioned in Dispatches. Awarded the M.C. and Bar. Served at Home and in France. Died of wounds Dec. 11, 1917, after having been previously wounded 3 times.

WILFRED OATES RUSHTON.

Articled to William Drysdale, of Liverpool. Joined Jan. 25, 1915, as Private, Inns of Court O.T.C. Gazetted 2nd Lieut. 18th Batt. Lancashire Fusiliers April 20, 1915, promoted Lieut. June 1916. Appointed Staff Capt. Headquarters 104th Infantry Brigade Nov. 1917, promoted Substantive Capt. May 1918, appointed Staff Capt. Headquarters Northern Command, York, Nov. 1918. Awarded the M.C. Served in France Jan. 1916 to Oct. 1918. Wounded Aug. 29, 1916, on Somme, and Nov. 29, 1917, Houthulst Forest.

CHARLES ANDREW SUTHERTON RUSS.

Admitted Feb. 1909. Managing Clerk with Maddocks, Ogden & Co., of Coventry. Served as 2nd Lieut., Royal Garrison Artillery. Served at Hong Kong 1915 to 1917, at Home 1918, and in Malta 1918.

DAVID LESLIE RUSSELL.

Articled to Ernest Humbert, of 4 Field Court, Gray's Inn, W.C. Mobilised August 1914, as Lieut., 8th City of London Regt. (T.) (Post Office Rifles), promoted Capt. Dec. 1914. Served at Home and in France. Killed in action at Festubert May 24, 1915.

GEOFFREY GEORGE RUSSELL.

Admitted Nov. 1904, practising at 27 Bolton Street, Piccadilly, W. Served as 2nd Lieut., 4th East Anglian Brigade, Royal Field Artillery (T.).

HENRY HARTLEY RUSSELL.

Admitted Nov. 1902, practised at Bucklebury, Berks. Served as 2nd Lieut., 9th Batt. Royal Berkshire Regt.

VINCENT RUSSELL.

Admitted Oct. 1912, practising at Derby. Joined 1916, as Private, and subsequently became Corporal. Served in France and Belgium 1917, Italy 1917 to 1918, and with Army of Occupation in Austria 1918 to 1919.

WILLIAM TAYLOR RUSSELL.

Articled to William Russell, of Bolton. Served as 2nd Lieut., Loyal North Lancashire Regt.

WILLIAM RICHARD RUSSILL.

Admitted Jan. 1908. Managing Clerk with W. A. G. Davidson & Co., of 40 Chancery Lane, W.C.; and Acton, W. Joined Oct. 7, 1918, as 3rd Clerk, Royal Air Force. Served at Home.

CARTERET ANDERSON RUST.

Admitted Sept. 1902, practising at 1 Lincoln's Inn Fields, London, W.C. Joined Oct. 30, 1916, as Private, Royal Fusiliers, transferred to Army Pay Corps about Feb. 1917 and promoted to Lance-Sergeant. Served at Home.

BASIL DONALD RUSTOM.

Admitted Nov. 1912. Managing Clerk with Tanner & Clarke, of Bristol. Joined Aug. 7, 1914, as Private, Army Pay Corps, promoted A/Sergeant Aug. 1915, transferred to Infantry 1916, and to Machine Gun Corps 1917. Served at Home and in France.

CECIL HAROLD SOWERBY RUSTON.

Admitted Feb. 1909. Member of A. Harold Ruston & Son, of Chatteris. Joined April 1916 Cambridge University O.T.C., and subsequently gazetted 2nd Lieut. East Kent Regt. (The Buffs). Served in France Dec. 1916 to April 1918. Killed in action at Villers-Brettoneux, near Amiens, April 4, 1918.

FREDERICK VYVYAN RUSTON.

Admitted Feb. 1904. Member of Ruston, Clark & Ruston, of 14 Norfolk Street, Strand, W.C. Joined Sept. 8, 1917, as 2nd Lieut., Royal Flying Corps. Served in France.

RONALD SOWERBY RUSTON.

Articled to A. A. Ruston, of Newmarket. Joined Oct. 21, 1914, as 2nd Lieut., 5th Batt. Suffolk Regt., seconded to 1/1 East Anglian Division Cyclist Company (T.) April 1915, subsequently seconded to the Army Cyclist Corps and served with the 54th Divisional Company, Army Cyclist Corps, promoted Lieut. June 1916, Capt. June 1916. Served at Home Oct. 1914 to July 1915, in Gallipoli July to Dec. 1915, and in Egypt, Palestine, and Syria Dec. 1915 to May 1919.

CHARLES RANDALL RUTHERFORD.

Admitted April 1895. Member of Edmonds and Rutherford, of 19 Great Winchester Street, E.C. Served as Lieut., Royal Army Service Corps.

GODFREY LAIRD RUTHERFORD.

Articled to C. J. Archer, of Stockton-on-Tees. Joined Sept. 15, 1914, as 2nd Lieut., 5th Batt. Durham Light Infantry (T.), promoted Substantive Lieut. July 1916, Substantive Capt. May 1918. Once mentioned in Dispatches. Awarded the M.C. Served at Home Sept. 1914 to April 1915 and May 1915 to Jan. 1916, and in France April to May 1915 and Jan 1916 to Dec. 1918. Wounded at Sanctuary Wood, near Ypres, May 15, 1915.

JOHN HUGHES RUTHERFORD.

Admitted May 1909. Member of Rutherfords, of Liverpool. Joined Jan. 22, 1915, as 2nd Lieut., Infantry, promoted Temp. Capt. Wounded

Salonica March 1918. Served in France Sept. to Oct. 1915 and June to Nov. 1918, and at Salonica Nov. 1915 to June 1918.

LAURENCE EDGAR RUTHERFORD.

Admitted Nov. 1914. Of Liverpool. Served as Capt., 7th Batt. King's Liverpool Regt.

MARK RUTHERFORD.

Admitted April 1907. Member of Postlethwaite & Rutherford, of Leeds. Enlisted 1916 in the Scots Guards and served 14 months in the ranks. Subsequently gazetted 2nd Lieut. Tank Corps, promoted to Capt. Killed in action July 23, 1918.

CLARENCE LESLIE RUTTER.

Articled to C. E. Rutter, of Wincanton, Somerset. Joined Friends' Ambulance Unit Sept. 2, 1914, and the Royal Naval Volunteer Reserve as Ord. Telegraphist Feb. 1916, subsequently rated Telegraphist. Served in France and Belgium Oct. 1914 to Dec. 1915, and with Channel Patrol out of Portland 1916, with North Sea Patrol out of Cromarty 1916 to Jan 1918.

WILLIAM ERNEST OSWALD RUTTER.

Admitted April 1911, practising at Ellesmere, Salop. Joined Sept. 1915, as 2nd Lieut., 4th Batt. Royal Welch Fusiliers, subsequently promoted Lieut. (A/Capt.) and attached 23rd Batt. Served at Home.

WILLIAM FARLEY RUTTER.

Admitted April 1911. Member of Rutter & Rutter, of Shaftesbury and Gillingham (Dorset) and Wincanton and Mere (Wilts.) Joined Nov. 1915, as Orderly, the Friends' Ambulance Unit of the British Red Cross Society, promoted Corporal Dec. 1915, Sergeant April 1916, Quartermaster-Sergeant Oct. 1916. Served on No. 17 Ambulance Train and then on No. 16 Ambulance Train in France. Nov. 1915 to Jan. 1919.

FRANK GIBBS RYE.

Admitted April 1901. Member of Rye and Eyre, of 13 Golden Square, W. Served as Lieut., Royal Garrison Artillery.

FRANK HENRY RYLAND.

Articled to F. T. Ryland, of Windsor. Joined Oct. 13, 1915, as Private, 5th (Reserve) Batt. Coldstream Guards, promoted Lance-Corporal Jan. 1916. Gazetted 2nd Lieut. 3rd Batt. Royal Berkshire Regt. Aug. 1, 1917, promoted Lieut. Feb. 1919. Served in France Aug. 1916 to Feb. 1917, Oct. to Nov. 1917, and Aug. 1918 to Jan. 1919.

HENRY MONTAGU RYLAND.

Admitted Dec. 1901. Member of Woodcock, Ryland, & Parker, of 15 Bloomsbury Square, W.C. Joined Sept. 28, 1914, as Capt., 7th Batt. London Regt., subsequently Capt., Staff Officer (3rd Class) Royal Air Force.

HAROLD BERTRAM RYLANDS.

Articled to R. A. Edgar, of Manchester. Joined Dec. 1914, as 2nd Lieut., 16th Batt. Royal Lancashire Fusiliers, and subsequently promoted Lieut.

Served at Home and in France. Killed in action at Beaumont Hamel Nov. 23, 1916.

REGINALD VICTOR RYLANDS.
Articled to R. A. Edgar, of Manchester. Mobilised Aug. 1914, as Lieut., 7th Batt. Manchester Regt., promoted Capt. Sept. 1914. Served at Home, Sudan, Egypt, and Gallipoli. Killed at Gallipoli May 29, 1915.

BERNARD CHARLES SADLER.
Admitted March 1905. Member of Richardson, Sadlers & Callard, of 3 St. James's Street, S.W. Joined May 1916, as Private, Royal Army Ordnance Corps, subsequently transferred to Royal Irish Rifles and promoted Corporal. Served in France. Died of wounds received in France May 5, 1918.

HUGH ROBSON SADLER.
Admitted Dec. 1897. Member of Richardson, Sadlers & Callard, of 3 St. James's Street, S.W. Joined Nov. 27, 1915, as Lieut., Royal Army Service Corps, transferred to Gen. List and appointed Staff Capt. Malta Command Feb. 1916. Once mentioned in Dispatches. Served at Home, Malta, and Salonica attached G.H.Q. and XII. Corps.

ROBERT TOWERS SAFFELL.
Admitted April 1916, practised at Thanet House, Temple Bar, W.C. Served as 2nd Lieut., Royal Field Artillery.

THOMAS WALTER SAINT.
Admitted Jan. 1911. Member of H. B. Wedlake, Saint & Co., of Bank Chambers, Finsbury Park, N. Served as Air-Mechanic, Royal Air Force.

HERBERT WHITMORE ST. GEORGE.
Articled to H. E. Loynes, of Wells. Mobilised Aug. 1914, as 2nd Lieut., 5th Batt. Norfolk Regt. (T.), promoted Lieut. Jan. 1915, Capt. May 1917. Served at Home Aug. 1914 to Sept 1915 and Sept. 1917 to Jan. 1919, at Gallipoli Sept. to Dec. 1915, and in Egypt and Palestine Dec. 1915 to Aug. 1917. Wounded at Gaza, Palestine, April 19, 1917.

FREDERIC WILLIAM REED SALE.
Admitted Nov. 1894. Member of Horwood & James, of Aylesbury. Served as Capt., 11th (Lonsdale) Batt. Border Regt.

RICHARD CRAWFORD SALE.
Articled to his father, W. T. Sale, of Leominster. Mobilised Aug. 1914, as Capt., 1st Batt. Herefordshire Regt. Once mentioned in Dispatches. Served at the Dardanelles, in Egypt, and in Palestine. Killed in action in the attack on Gaza March 26, 1917.

RICHARD LAUDER SALE.
Admitted Oct. 1912. Managing Clerk with Alfred Sale, of Atherstone. Joined May 1915 Inns of Court O.T.C. Gazetted 2nd Lieut. Royal Horse Guards Oct. 1915, promoted Lieut. 1917. Served in France Jan. 1916 to Jan. 1918. Died of wounds received in raid on enemy's lines Jan. 15, 1918.

JOHN JAMES SALISBURY.

Admitted Nov. 1898, practising at Bristol. Joined Aug. 27, 1917, as Aircraftsman, Royal Naval Air Service, promoted Leading Aircraftsman Sept. 1918. Served at Home.

HAROLD GEOFFREY SALT.

Admitted April 1907. Member of Salt & Sons, of Shrewsbury. Joined May 31, 1916, as Private, 2/5 Batt. East Kent Regt. (The Buffs). Gazetted 2nd Lieut. Royal Army Service Corps March 1918 and attached Camel Transport Coy. Served at Home May 1916 to May 1918, and in Palestine and Egypt May 1918 to March 1919.

FREDERICK GURNEY SALTER.

Admitted Jan. 1905. With the Official Solicitor, Royal Courts of Justice, Strand, W.C. Joined Sept. 2, 1914, as Private, 19th (Universities and Public Schools) Batt. Royal Fusiliers. Gazetted 2nd Lieut. 5th Batt. The Rifle Brigade May 28, 1915, promoted Lieut. July 1917, attached to War Office July 1916 to May 1918, when transferred to the Ministry of National Service (Legal Branch of the Recruiting Department). Served in France and at Home. Wounded at Fleurbaix, near Armentières, Jan. 14, 1916. Leg subsequently amputated.

JOHN THELWALL SALUSBURY.

Admitted Aug. 1908. Member of Salusbury & Woodhouse, of Leicester. Attested Leicestershire Regt. Dec. 1915, transferred to 28th Batt. County of London Regt. (Artists Rifles) May 1916. Gazetted 2nd Lieut. Royal Garrison Artillery (S.R.) Dec. 4, 1916, promoted Lieut. June 1918. Once mentioned in Dispatches. Served in France, Flanders, and Italy.

JOHN DELAHAYE SAMPSON.

Admitted Jan. 1914. Practising at Oldbury, Worcs. Joined Nov. 1914, as 2nd Lieut., 15th Batt. The Welch Regt., promoted Lieut. May 1915, Capt. May 1917. Awarded the M.C. Served in France 1915 to 1919.

PERCY VERNON MONTAGU SAMPSON.

Admitted Aug. 1902, practising at 1 Queen Street Place, Cannon Street, E.C. Served as Corporal, Royal Army Veterinary Corps, on Staff of Assistant Director of Veterinary Services.

SAMUEL JOHN MARTON SAMPSON.

Admitted Oct. 1908. Member of Greene & Greene, of Bury St. Edmunds. Mobilised Aug. 1914, as Capt., 9th Batt. London Regt. (Queen Victoria's Rifles), promoted Major July 15, 1915, temporarily commanded various Battalions of the London Regiment in France Aug. to Oct. 1918. Once mentioned in Dispatches. Awarded the M.C. and T.D. Served in France. Wounded in 2nd Battle of the Somme on Hill 60 April 19, 1915.

FELIX RUMNEY SAMSON.

Admitted April 1911. Of 6 Austin Friars, E.C. Served as Lieut., Royal Naval Volunteer Reserve, attached Royal Naval Air Service.

ALBERT HENRIQUES SAMUEL.

Admitted Feb. 1904, practised at 10 John Street, Adelphi, W.C. Served as A/Corporal, Royal Flying Corps.

REGINALD EVAN SAMUEL.

Admitted Oct. 1914, practising at Porth, Glam. Joined Feb. 13, 1915, as Private, 1st Welsh Casualty Clearing Station, 53rd Division, promoted Corporal July 1915, A/Lance-Sergeant. Feb. 1917, Sergeant., sub. rank, Aug. 1918. Served in Gallipoli July to Dec. 1915, in Egypt Dec. 1915 to Dec. 1916, and Sinai Peninsula and Palestine Jan. 1916 to Feb. 1919.

WILFRID GILBERT SAMUEL.

Articled to G. E. Samuel, of 5 & 6 Great Winchester Street, E.C. Joined Sept. 1, 1914, as Private, Universities and Public Schools Batt. Royal Fusiliers. Commissioned as 2nd Lieut. 6th Batt. Suffolk Regt. May 1915, promoted Lieut. April 1916, Capt. Dec. 1916, Adjutant 1917, attached to 2nd Batt. Bedfordshire Regt. Aug. 1918 as Lieut. Served in France June to Sept. 1918. Killed at Roussoy, near Cambrai, Sept. 21, 1918.

ALBERT LEWIN SAMUELL.

Admitted Feb. 1903. Member of Windybank, Samuell & Laurence, of 28-29 St. Swithin's Lane, E.C. Joined Nov. 8, 1916, and posted to Royal Fusiliers for service in Army Pay Corps, transferred to Class W Reserve to take up appointment as an Acting Paymaster in Army Pay Department March 1917. Served at Home.

FRANK STAINTON SANDBACH.

Admitted May 1912. Managing Clerk with Slater, Heelis & Co., of Manchester. Joined O.T.C. April 1916. Gazetted 2nd Lieut. 2nd East Lancashire Royal Field Artillery (T.) March 1917. Served in France June to July 1917. Killed in action July 29, 1917.

SYDNEY ROBERT SANDEMAN.

Admitted Dec. 1912. Member of Boulton, Sons & Sandeman, of 21A Northampton Square, E.C. Served as Lieut., Royal Garrison Artillery. Reported wounded and missing April 22, 1915, subsequently presumed to have died on that day.

JOHN FURSE SANDERS.

Admitted Feb. 1902, practising at South Molton, Devon. Joined Sept. 6, 1914. Gazetted 2nd Lieut. Devonshire Regt. Sept. 6, 1914, promoted Lieut. Oct. 1914, Capt. April 1917. Served at Home as Courts-Martial Officer. Resigned Feb. 15, 1918.

ROWLAND FREDERICK JOHN SANDERS.

Articled to C. E. Woolston, of Wellingborough. Joined Aug. 11, 1916, Royal Garrison Artillery. Gazetted 2nd Lieut. (Special Reserve) Royal Garrison Artillery June 10, 1917, promoted Lieut. Dec. 1918. Served on Western Front Oct. 1917 to March 1919, and with Army of the Rhine March to June 1919.

WILLIAM LACEY SANDERS.

Admitted Nov. 1906. Member of Wontner & Sons, of 40 Bedford Row, W.C. Joined Aug. 28, 1914, as Private, 10th Batt. Royal Fusiliers. Subsequently commissioned in King's Royal Rifle Corps and attained the rank of

Capt. Awarded Belgian Croix de Guerre. Wounded Sept. 15, 1916, and March 21, 1918. Served in France.

THOMAS LANCELOT SANDERSON.

Articled to J. T. Sanderson, of Lancaster. Joined Sept. 1, 1918, as Cadet, Household Brigade, Officers Cadet Batt. (Coldstream Guards). Served at Home. Died at the Military Hospital, High Barnet, Dec. 9, 1918.

PERCY ALEXANDER SANDFORD.

Admitted April 1898, practising at Gravesend. Served as 2nd Lieut., Royal Marines, promoted A/Capt. June 1918.

HENRY GILBERT SANDIFORD.

Articled to Percy Maylam, of Canterbury. Joined Sept. 2, 1914, as Driver, Royal Army Service Corps, and attained the rank of Sergeant. Gazetted 2nd Lieut. Royal Field Artillery Oct. 1, 1917, subsequently Lieut. April 1919. Served at Home and in France.

JOHN EDGAR SANGER.

Admitted Dec. 1913, practising at Salisbury. Joined Aug. 25, 1916, as Pioneer (Motor Cyclist), Signal Service Royal Engineers, promoted M.C./Corporal Jan. 1917. Served in Mesopotamia and Persia.

CHARLES EDWARD SANKEY.

Articled to H. T. Box, of Cardiff. Joined Sept. 18, 1914, as Rifleman, The Rifle Brigade (Prince Consort's Own). Gazetted 2nd Lieut. 17th Batt. The Welch Regt. Nov. 16, 1914, promoted Lieut. June 1915, Capt. Sept. 1915, Adjutant June 1916. Served at Home Sept. 1914 to July 1917, and in France July 1917 to Feb. 1918. Resigned July 12, 1918.

GEOFFREY BARHAM SANKEY.

Admitted Dec. 1911, practised at Canterbury and Margate. Served as Lieut., Kent Cyclist Batt. and subsequently promoted Capt.

WILLIAM JAMES SATCHELL.

Admitted Feb. 1911. Managing Clerk with Murray, Hutchins & Co., of 11 Birchin Lane, E.C. Joined Nov. 16, 1914, as 2nd Lieut., 2/1 Huntingdonshire Cyclist Batt., promoted Temp. Lieut. June 1915, Substantive Lieut. June 1916, Temp. Capt. Oct. 1916, Substantive Capt. March 1917, Adjutant Aug. 1917 to Feb. 1919, attached 3rd Batt. Bedfordshire Regt. Feb. to July 1919. Served at Home 1914 to 1919, and in Egypt 1919.

PERCY HENRY SATCHWELL.

Admitted May 1904. Member of William Webb & Son, of Morpeth. Served as Lance-Corporal, 7th Batt. Northumberland Fusiliers and subsequently gazetted 2nd Lieut. 22nd (Service) Batt. Northumberland Fusiliers (3rd Tyneside Scottish).

REGINALD EDWARD SATTERTHWAITE.

Admitted April 1914, practising at 4 Throgmorton Avenue, E.C. Mobilised Aug. 1914, as Capt. and Adjutant, 5th Batt. Royal West Kent Regt. Proceeded to India in 1914, served on Staff in India 1916, subsequently appointed Brigade Major 11th Infantry Brigade, Quetta. Served in Afghan War.

FRANCIS WILLIAM SAUNDERS.
Articled to A. M. King, of Bath. Served as 2nd Lieut., 4th Batt. Wiltshire Regt. Promoted Lieut. July 1917.

HENRY JAMES HUZZEY SAUNDERS.
Admitted Feb. 1918, practising at Wantage. Served as Lieut., Royal Fusiliers. Mentioned in Dispatches.

HUGH ABERCROMBIE CHILDERS SAUNDERS.
Admitted March 1906, practised at Exeter. Served as Private, 4th Batt. Devonshire Regt.

JAMES JOHN SAUNDERS.
Articled to R. A. Logan, of Dorchester. Served as Lieut., Dorset Royal Garrison Artillery (T.). Mentioned in Dispatches.

ALBERT SAVILLE.
Admitted May 1911, practised at 8 Warwick Court, Gray's Inn, W.C. Served as 2nd Lieut., 5th (Reserve) Batt. King's Loyal North Lancashire Regt., promoted Capt. June 1916.

MAURICE JEFFERY SAVORY.
Articled to E. J. C. Savory, of 61 Carey Street, Lincoln's Inn, W.C. Joined Sept. 1914, as 2nd Lieut., 9th Batt. Duke of Wellington's West Riding Regt., promoted Lieut. Nov. 1914, Capt. Jan. 1916. Served in France July 1915 to April 1916 and Jan. to Feb. 1917. Severely wounded April 26, 1916. Died of wounds Feb. 3, 1917.

WILLIAM DAVID SAVOURS.
Articled to J. A. Hughes, of Barry Dock. Served as Trooper, Glamorganshire Yeomanry (Reserve).

HAROLD SAXON.
Admitted Jan. 1907. Member of Sharratt and Saxon, of Manchester. Served as Private, Lancashire Fusiliers.

GEORGE DEVEREUX BASSET SCALE.
Admitted Dec. 1911. Assisted his father, Robert Scale, of Maesteg, Glam. Joined on outbreak of War in Vancouver, B.C., as Private, and came to England with first Canadian Contingent. Transferred to 10th Batt. Royal Welch Fusiliers as 2nd Lieut. in 1915, promoted Lieut. 1915, Capt. 1916. Served in France. Killed in action in France July 20, 1916.

WILFRED STANLEY SCAMMEL.
Articled to J. C. Glyde, of Bristol. Served as 2nd Lieut., 10th Batt. Worcestershire Regt., promoted Capt. April 1918. Mentioned in Dispatches and awarded M.C.

ISAAC HINTON SCARTH.
Articled to William Richardson, of Guisborough. Joined May 4, 1915, as 2nd Lieut., 4th Batt. Yorkshire Regt., promoted Lieut. April 1917. Served in France and Belgium. Killed at Wancourt April 23, 1917.

MORTIMER EDWARD HAROLD SCHIFF.

Admitted Aug. 1914. Managing Clerk with Stephenson, Harwood & Co., of 31 Lombard Street, E.C. Joined April 1915, as Private, Inns of Court O.T.C. Gazetted 2nd Lieut. 12th Batt. Suffolk Regt. Dec. 1915, promoted Lieut, March 1916, Capt. May 1917. Served in France. Reported missing Sept. 25, 1917, and since presumed to have been killed on that day.

JOHN JAMES SCHOFIELD.

Admitted June 1913. Member of Wilson & Schofield, of Castleford. Joined Sept. 1914, as Private, 16th Batt. West Yorkshire Regt. Gazetted 2nd Lieut. 3rd Dorsetshire Regt. (S.R.) Aug. 1915, promoted Capt. and Adjutant of Bristol Vol. Regt. April 1917, Capt. 6th Batt. Dorset Regt. Feb. 1918. Served in France. Wounded during Somme battle July 1916 and in Aug. 1918.

FRANK SCHOLEFIELD.

Admitted Oct. 1909, practised at Penistone. Served as Lieut., 10th Batt. Manchester Regt., promoted Capt. June 1916.

WILLIAM THACKERY SCHOLES.

Admitted Feb. 1911, practising at Leeds. Served as 2nd Lieut., West Riding Regt., promoted Lieut. July 1917.

HAROLD SCHOLFIELD.

Admitted June 1907. Managing Clerk with Ernest I. White, of Bath. Joined June 10, 1916, as Private, 13th Batt. Devonshire Regt., promoted Lance-Corporal July 1916, attached to 6th Batt. Worcestershire Regt. Sept. 1916, to 1st Batt. 1916, and to Royal Engineers (Transportation Branch), Jan. 1918. Served in France Dec. 1916 to March 1919.

RICHARD DENHAM SCHOLFIELD.

Articled to L. C. Evans, of Salford. Served as 2nd Lieut., 6th Batt. King's Own Royal Lancaster Regt. Killed in action at the Dardanelles Aug. 10, 1915.

BERNARD ALBERT SCHOOLING.

Admitted Feb. 1911. In the Solicitors' Department of the Prudential Assurance Co., Ltd., Holborn, E.C. Joined July 1915, as Rifleman, 5th City of London Batt. London Regt. (London Rifle Brigade). Gazetted 2nd Lieut. Royal North Devon Hussars Nov. 1916, promoted Lieut. May 1918, attached the Devonshire Regt. March 1918. Served at Home and in France. Wounded Oct. 1918.

ROBERT SCHULZ.

Articled to A. F. Forster, of 28 Lincoln's Inn Fields, W.C. Served as 2nd Lieut., 4th Batt. East Kent Regt. (The Buffs).

MACKAY JOHN GRAHAM SCOBIE, C.B.

Admitted —— 1875, practising at Hereford. Joined as Lieut.-Col. Raised, and commanded from Nov. 12, 1914, to Nov. 1915, 15th Batt. The Welch Regt. Lieut.-Col. General List Nov. 1915 to May 1916. Served at Home.

FREDERICK WILLIAM SCORAH.
Admitted Aug. 1907. Member of Arthur Neal & Co., of Sheffield. Joined Aug. 1916, as Gunner, Royal Garrison Artillery. Gazetted 2nd Lieut. Royal Garrison Artillery Feb. 23, 1917, promoted Lieut. Aug. 1918. Awarded the M.C. Served in France. Wounded at Passchendaele Oct. 20, 1918.

CHARLES REYNOLDS SCORER.
Admitted July 1899. Member of Burton, Scorers & White, of Lincoln. Mobilised Aug. 4, 1914, as Capt., 4th Batt. Lincolnshire Regt. Served in France. Wounded at Monchy, on the Somme, Aug. 6, 1916. Resigned March 28, 1918.

ALBERT WALTER SCOTT.
Articled to H. A. Scott, of 7 Staple Inn, Holborn, W.C. Joined Sept. 1914 as Cadet, London University O.T.C. Gazetted 2nd Lieut. Durham Light Infantry March 1915, promoted Lieut. July 1916, A/Capt. Nov. 1917. Once mentioned in Dispatches. Served in India and Mesopotamia.

CHARLES EDWARD SCOTT.
Admitted Nov. 1889. Member of Wade Tetley, Wade & Scott, of Bradford. Mobilised Aug. 1914, as Major, 6th Batt. West Yorkshire Regt. (T.), promoted A/Lieut.-Col. July 1916. Once mentioned in Dispatches. Served at Home and in France. Wounded July 24, 1916. Died Aug. 9, 1916.

ERNEST GRUGEON SCOTT.
Admitted Jan. 1906, practising at Finsbury House, Blomfield Street, E.C. Joined Aug. 1, 1916, as Private, Royal Army Service Corps (M.T.). Gazetted 2nd Lieut. in same Regt. Dec. 4, 1916, promoted Lieut. July 1918. Served in France 1916 to 1919.

GEOFFREY LACY SCOTT.
Admitted Nov. 1909. Of Calcutta. Served as Capt., 5th (Service) Batt., Suffolk Regt.

GEORGE REGINALD SCOTT.
Admitted Feb. 1903, practised at Leeds. Served as Lieut., 9th Batt. East Yorkshire Regt., and attained the rank of Major. Mentioned in Dispatches.

HENRY COOPER SCOTT.
Admitted Oct. 1906. Member of Munby & Scott, of York. Mobilised Aug. 4, 1914, as Capt., 5th Batt. West Yorkshire Regt., promoted Major commanding X. Corps Cyclist Batt. June 1916, Lieut.-Col. 5th West Yorkshire Regt. May 1918. Served in France April 1915 to Jan. 1917, and at Home March 1917 to Feb. 1919.

INVER LYLE SCOTT.
Admitted Dec. 1909. Managing Clerk with Bewes & Dickinson, of Stonehouse, Plymouth. Granted Temp. Commission as Paymaster Sub-Lieut. Royal Naval Volunteer Reserve July 13, 1919, attached to Mediterranean Naval Staff Office, Malta.

JOHN CHRISTOPHER SCOTT.
Articled to Edward Fletcher, of Leeds. Mobilised Aug. 5, 1914, as 2nd Lieut., Royal Field Artillery, promoted Lieut. July 1, 1916, Capt. April 1918.

Served on Home Defence Aug. 1914 to April 1915, and in France and Flanders April 1915 to July 1919.

ROBERT HAMILTON SCOTT.

Admitted July 1909. Managing Clerk with King, Wigg & Brightman, of 11 Queen Victoria Street, E.C. Mobilised Aug. 1914, as Private, Hon. Artillery Company (Infantry). Commissioned in 1st Batt. Royal Scots Fusiliers April 1915, promoted A/Capt. 1918, attached 9th Brigade Headquarters. Once mentioned in Dispatches. Served in France.

RONALD JOCELYN LESLIE SCOTT.

Articled to William May, of 18 Austin Friars, E.C. Mobilised Aug. 1914, as Private, 28th Batt. County of London Regt. (Artists Rifles). Gazetted 2nd Lieut. 10th Batt. Black Watch Oct. 1914, promoted Lieut. Indian Army July 1917, Capt. 1/152 Punjabis (I.A.) Nov. 1917. Served in France 1915 to 1916, India (Burma) 1917 to 1918, and in Palestine 1918 to 1919.

THEODORE JAMES SCOTT.

Admitted Nov. 1905, practised at 75 Cornhill, E.C. Joined Dec. 1916, as Private, 35th Training Reserve Batt. Died of influenza Jan. 26, 1917.

WALTER GILBERT SCOTT.

Admitted June 1903. Member of Morgan, Scott & Scott, of Cardiff. Joined Aug. 1914, as Private, The Welch Regt. Gazetted Capt. and Adjutant The Welch Regt. 1915, Major Royal Flying Corps 1917, attached General Staff Air Ministry. Served at Home.

WILLIAM ALLAN SCOTT.

Admitted Oct. 1915. Managing Clerk with Field, Roscoe & Co., 36 Lincoln's Inn Fields, W.C. Joined July 5, 1916, as Flight Sub-Lieut. Royal Naval Air Service, promoted Flight Lieut. Sept. 1917, Flight Commander March 1918, Capt. Royal Air Force April 1918. Awarded the D.S.C. and D.F.C. Served in France May 1917 to Oct. 1918.

WILLIAM EMILEY OSCAR SCOTT.

Admitted Aug. 1905. Member of W. E. O. Scott & Son, of South Shields. Joined 1915, as 2nd Lieut., 9th Batt. Durham Light Infantry. Served in France. Killed in action Sept. 29, 1916.

GEOFFREY CAMERON SCRIMGEOUR.

Admitted Nov. 1912, practising at Preston, Lancs. Joined Aug. 10, 1914, as 2nd Lieut., Royal Field Artillery (T.), promoted Lieut. June 1915, A/Capt. Oct. 1916, A/Major May 1918, Capt. Oct. 1918. Once mentioned in Dispatches. Awarded D.S.O. and M.C. and Bar. Served in France Sept. 1915 to end of War. Wounded Oct. 1915.

WILLIAM VAUGHAN SCULTHORPE.

Articled to J. J. Dodd, of 11 New Square, Lincoln's Inn, W.C. Joined Aug. 6, 1915, as Private, West Kent Regt. Gazetted 2nd Lieut. 22nd Batt. London Regt. (Queen's) Nov. 2, 1915. Killed in action in Flanders June 8, 1917.

CLAUDE SEABROKE.

Admitted July 1903. Member of G. M. Seabroke & Son, of Rugby. Mobilised Aug. 4, 1914, as Capt., 7th Batt. Royal Warwickshire Regt., promoted

Substantive Major Aug. 29, 1914, subsequently attached 2nd Batt. Loyal North Lancashire Regt. Awarded the T.D. Served at Home, Egypt, Palestine, France, and Belgium.

CHARLES BROWETT SEAGER.

Admitted Dec. 1912. Of 46 Parliament Street, S.W. Served as Private, 13th Batt. London Regt. (T.).

JOHN EDWARD SEAGER.

Admitted Jan. 1909, practised at Chelmsford. Served as Sergeant, 28th Batt. County of London Regt. (Artists Rifles).

WILLIAM CAVENDISH SEARLE.

Articled to T. A. Kirkham, of 38 Bedford Row, W.C. Served as 2nd Lieut., 9th Batt. Bedfordshire Regt., promoted Capt. Feb. 1917.

GEORGE SCOTT SEAWARD.

Admitted May 1912, of East Sheen. Served as 2nd Lieut., 6th (Reserve) Batt. East Surrey Regt.

JOHN SEDDON.

Admitted Feb. 1907, practising at Farnworth. Joined Aug. 1, 1916, as Private, Royal Army Service Corps (M.T.). Served in France and Belgium.

JOHN ROBINSON SEDGWICK.

Admitted Nov. 1905, practised at 18 Finsbury Square, E.C. Served as Lance-Corporal, 16th Batt. County of London Regt. (Queen's Westminsters).

JOSEPH SEED.

Admitted March 1904, practising at Blackpool. Served as Capt., 4th (Reserve) Batt. Loyal North Lancashire Regt.

LAWRENCE ARTHUR SEELEY.

Articled to A. U. Seeley, of 2 South Square, W.C. Served as 2nd Lieut., East Surrey Regt. (T.), promoted Lieut. July 1917.

JAMES HAROLD SELFE.

Admitted July 1911. Managing Clerk with Ticehurst, McIlquham & Wyatt, of Cheltenham. Joined Sept. 7, 1914, as Private, 5th Batt. The Queen's Own Royal West Kent Regt., and attained rank of Company Sergeant-Major. Obtained commission in same Regt. Dec. 1915 and subsequently appointed Capt. and Adjutant. Awarded the M.C. Served at Home and in France.

HARRY OLIVER SELWAY.

Admitted Aug. 1914, practised at Stourbridge. Enlisted 1914 in 7th Batt. Worcestershire Regt. (T.), and subsequently promoted Lance-Corporal. Died at the Anglo-American Hospital, Wimereux, France, Dec. 9, 1915.

LIONEL FRANK SESSIONS.

Articled to J. P. Winterbotham, of Cheltenham. Joined Nov. 1915, British Red Cross Society. Awarded Italian Bronze and Silver Medal. Served in Italy. Lost left leg above knee Sept. 4, 1917.

CLAUD CREWE TREFUSIS RAMSAY WILMOT SETON.

Admitted April 1910. Member of Shelton & Co., of 3 New Court, Lincoln's Inn, W.C., and Wolverhampton. Joined Sept. 5, 1914, as Private, Staffordshire Yeomanry. Gazetted 2nd Lieut. Machine Gun Corps (motors) Sept. 25, 1915, promoted A/Capt. Commanding 12th Light Armoured Motor Battery May 1916. Served on the Staff of the Occupied Enemy Territory Administration from Dec. 1918. Twice mentioned in Dispatches. Awarded the M.C. Served in Egypt and Palestine. Wounded 2nd Battle of Es Salt, Palestine, May 1, 1918.

ALGERNON PERCY SEWELL.

Admitted June 1905. Managing Clerk with Stenning, Knocker & Thompson, of Headcorn, Kent. Joined Dec. 13, 1915, as Dresser in Hospital Ship *Letitia*, I.M.S. Gazetted 2nd Lieut. Royal Garrison Artillery (S.R.) Aug. 22, 1916, promoted Lieut. Feb. 1918, A/Capt. and Adjutant July 1918. Twice mentioned in Dispatches. Served in Mediterranean Dec. 1915 to March 1916, and at Home July 1916 to May 1919.

CECIL HAROLD SEWELL.

Articled to his father, H. B. Sewell, of Greenwich. Joined Nov. 1914, as Private, Public Schools Batt. (Royal Fusiliers). Gazetted 2nd Lieut. Royal West Kent Regt. (Reserve of Officers), Sept. 1916, and shortly afterwards transferred to the heavy branch Machine Gun Corps, and to the Tank Corps on its formation, promoted Lieut. Awarded the V.C. Served in France. Killed in action Aug. 29, 1918.

EDWARD OWEN SEWELL.

Articled to Charles Gardner, of 80 Cheapside, E.C. Joined Aug. 3, 1914, as Private, Inns of Court O.T.C. Gazetted Temp. 2nd Lieut. South Lancashire Regt. Sept. 12, 1914, promoted Temp. Lieut. Nov. 1914, Temp. Capt. Dec. 1914, appointed Staff Capt. 56th Infantry Brigade Jan. 1916, Brigade Major Aug. 1916, appointed G.S.O. II. to 8th Division July 1918, promoted Temp. Major May 1918. Three times mentioned in Dispatches. Awarded M.C. and Bar and Croix de Guerre avec Palme (French). Served in France 1915 to 1919. Wounded March 14, 1916, Jan. 29, 1917, and March 24, 1918.

HARRY KEMP SEWELL.

Admitted April 1908. Member of H. B. Sewell & Son, of Greenwich, and 4 Walbrook, E.C. Mobilised Aug. 1914, as Sergeant, West Kent Yeomanry and shortly afterwards granted a commission in the Royal Field Artillery and posted to the Meerut Division of the Indian Expeditionary Force in France. Went to Mesopotamia for the relief of General Townshend. Wounded and invalided to Bombay and sent Home. Died Aug. 20, 1917.

DARRACOTT SEYMOUR.

Admitted May 1910, practised at Eastleigh, Hants. Joined as Private, 6th (Reserve) Batt. Hampshire Regt. (T.) and subsequently gazetted 2nd Lieut. 9th (Service) Batt. Royal Sussex Regt.

HOWARD SEYS-PHILLIPS.

Articled to E. P. Beale, of Birmingham. Joined Sept. 28, 1914, as Temp. Lieut., 5th Batt. Bedfordshire Regt (T.), promoted Temp. Capt. July 1915, Substantive Capt. June 1916, Adjutant June 1918 to June 1919, with 7th Batt. Aug. 1917 to May 1918, and with 2nd Batt. May 1918 to June 1919. Awarded

French Croix de Guerre with Silver Star. Served at Home Sept. 1914 to Aug. 1917, and in France Aug. 1917 to June 1919.

KENNETH GEORGE SHACKLES.

Articled to W. E. Barton, of Hull. Joined Sept. 1914, as Private, 10th Batt. East Yorkshire Regt. Granted a commission as 2nd Lieut. 4th Batt. East Yorkshire Regt. Jan. 1917. Served in Egypt and France. Killed near Arras May 11, 1917.

PHILIP FRANK SHACKLOCK.

Articled to H. S. Shacklock, of Sutton-in-Ashfield, Notts. Joined June 1915, as Private, 2/8 Batt. Notts and Derby Regt. (Sherwood Foresters) and attained the rank of Sergeant. Served at Home, Irish Rebellion, and in France. Died in France Oct. 10, 1917, of wounds received in action Sept. 28, 1917.

BERNARD LOUIS SHAFFER.

Articled to Charles Howard, of Manchester. Joined Jan. 24, 1916, as Private, Hon. Artillery Company (Infantry). Served in France and Belgium.

HENRY ISAAC SHAFTOE.

Admitted June 1908. Member of J. A. Shaftoe & Son, of York. Joined May 31, 1915, as 2nd Lieut., Prince of Wales' Own West Yorkshire Regt., promoted Lieut. June 1916, A/Capt. March 1918 to Dec. 1919, Adjutant 3/5 Batt. May to Sept. 1916, and 7th Reserve Batt. Sept. 1916 to Sept. 1917. Served at Home May 1915 to Nov. 1917, in France and Flanders Nov. 1917 to Feb. 1919, and in Germany Feb. to Nov. 1919.

HENRY SHAPCOTT.

Admitted Nov. 1909, practised at Blackpool. Served as 2nd Lieut., 1st Lancashire Battery Royal Garrison Artillery, promoted Lieut. June 1916, and subsequently A/Capt. Mentioned in Dispatches and Awarded M.C.

HEREWARD REID SHARMAN.

Admitted June 1897. Member of Reid Sharman & Co., of 52 Bedford Row, W.C. Served as Cadet, Royal Army Service Corps (M.T.).

JOHN CHARLES LANCELOT SHADWELL SHARMAN.

Admitted July 1915, practising at 8 Great Eastern Road, Stratford, E., and 7 York Buildings, Adelphi, W.C. Joined Nov. 1915, as Trooper, 1st Life Guards (Household Cavalry). Served at Home. Discharged permanently unfit May 25, 1917.

ALFRED GOODWIN SHARP.

Articled to Sir Kingsley Wood, of 15 Walbrook, E.C. Joined Sept. 18, 1914, as Private, 2/2 Batt. London Regt. (Royal Fusiliers). Received commission as 2nd Lieut. in the 4th Batt. London Regt. (Royal Fusiliers) Jan. 16, 1915. Served in Malta Dec. 1914 to May 1915, and in France Aug. to Sept. 1915 and July to Sept. 1916. Wounded in France Sept. 1916. Discharged May 5, 1917, owing to ill-health contracted on Active Service.

AUBREY TEMPLE SHARP.

Admitted Feb. 1914. Member of Sharp & Lancaster, of Coalville. Mobilised Aug. 1914, as Lieut., 5th Batt. Leicestershire Regt., promoted Capt. April 1915, seconded Machine Gun Corps July 1916, Major Feb. 1918. Once mentioned in Dispatches. Awarded O.B.E. (Military Division). Served in France and Flanders. Injured Aug. 1915 at Ypres.

HUBERT CHALLEN SHARP.

Admitted Jan. 1913, practising at Moreton-in-Marsh, Gloucestershire. Joined Sept. 18, 1916, as 2nd Lieut., Royal Flying Corps, promoted Lieut. Royal Air Force June 1918. Served at Home Sept. 1916 to Feb. 1918, and in Italy Feb. 1918 to Feb. 1919.

STEPHEN OSWALD SHARP.

Articled J. H. Cockburn, of Rotherham. Joined Sept. 11, 1914, as Private, 12th Batt. York and Lancaster Regt. Gazetted Lieut. in same Regt. Nov. 20, 1914. Killed in action in Battle of Somme July 1, 1916.

REGINALD LAWFORD SHARPE.

Admitted Dec. 1912. Managing Clerk with Sharpe, Pritchard & Co., of 12 New Court, Carey Street, W.C. Mobilised Aug. 1914, as Lance-Corporal, Inns of Court O.T.C. Gazetted 2nd Lieut. 1st Batt. London Regt. Sept. 28, 1914, promoted Temp. Lieut. March 1915, Temp. Capt. April 1915, Lieut. May 1916, Capt. July 1916. Served at Malta Feb. to July 1915, at Gallipoli July 1915 to Jan. 1916, in Egypt Jan. to April 1916, and in France April to Sept. 1916 and Dec. 1917 to May 1918. Wounded at Gallipoli Oct. 4, 1915.

WILLIAM SEAFORD SHARPE.

Admitted Jan. 1904. Member of Sharpe, Pritchard & Co., of 12 New Court, Carey Street, W.C. Joined Dec. 10, 1914, as Private, Inns of Court O.T.C. Gazetted 2nd Lieut. 1st Batt. London Regt. (Royal Fusiliers) Feb. 14, 1915, promoted Lieut. April 1915, Capt. Sept. 1918. Served at Home and at Malta, Egypt, Gallipoli, and France. Wounded near Bullecourt June 16, 1917.

FRANK DEEKS SHARPLES.

Articled to E. L. Billson, of Liverpool. Served as 2nd Lieut., West Lancashire Division, Royal Army Service Corps, promoted Lieut. June 1916. Mentioned in Dispatches. Awarded O.B.E.

RICHARD SHARPLES.

Admitted Aug. 1878. Member of Sharples & Sons, of Accrington. Served as Lieut.-Col., commanding 11th (Service) Batt. East Lancashire Regt.

RICHARD EDGAR SHARPLES.

Admitted Nov. 1911. Member of Sharples & Sons, of Accrington. Served as Private, Royal Army Service Corps (M.T.) and subsequently promoted Corporal.

WILLIAM EDMUND SHARPLES.

Admitted May 1894. Member of Sharples & Sons, of Accrington. Served as Major, 5th Batt. East Lancashire Regt., promoted Lieut.-Col. May 1915.

BASIL SHARPLEY.

Admitted May 1911. Member of Sharpley & Son, of Louth. Served as 2nd Lieut., 1st North Midland Brigade Royal Field Artillery, promoted Lieut. June 1916.

FRANCIS JOSEPH MARSHALL SHAW.

Articled to Frank Marshall, of Newcastle-upon-Tyne. Enlisted Sept. 15, 1914, in Public School Batt., selected for Sandhurst Nov. 1914. Commissioned 2nd Lieut. 3rd Batt. Notts and Derby Regt. (Sherwood Foresters), April 16, 1915. Served in France Dec. 1915 to July 1916. Killed in action at La Boiselle, France, July 5, 1916.

FREDERICK ADOLPH SHAW.

Admitted Dec. 1911. Member of Wordsworth, Russell & Shaw, of 72 Gresham House, E.C. Served as Lieut., Royal Army Service Corps.

HARRY FREDERICK SHAW.

Articled to W. H. Brightman, of 11 Queen Victoria Street, E.C. Joined Aug. 10, 1914, as Private, 1st Batt. Hon. Artillery Company (Infantry). Gazetted 2nd Lieut. 22nd Batt. Middlesex Regt. Oct. 1915, transferred to 12th Batt. Suffolk Regt. April 1916, promoted Lieut. July 1917. Served in France and at Home. Wounded at Loos Aug. 12, 1916. Loss of right eye.

HUGH WYBERGH SHAW.

Admitted Nov. 1910. Member of Shaw & Son, of 40 Chancery Lane, W.C. Served as Capt., Kent Cyclist Batt.

NORMAN HENRY SHEARD.

Admitted Feb. 1911, practising at Manchester. Served as 2nd Lieut., 7th Batt. Lancashire Fusiliers.

WALTER WEST SHEARMAN.

Articled to J. W. Botsford, of Cardiff. Served as Private, 21st (Service) Batt. Royal Fusiliers.

ERROLL DAVID SHEARN.

Admitted Aug. 1913. Managing Clerk with Simmons & Simmons, of 18 Finch Lane, E.C. Joined Aug. 1914, as Private, 20th (Service) Batt. Royal Fusiliers. Gazetted 2nd Lieut. Hampshire Regt. May 20, 1915, promoted Lieut. Jan. 1916, Capt. May 1918, transferred to Royal Air Force. Once mentioned in Dispatches. Served in France. Wounded July 1, 1916.

THOMAS ANGRAVE HOMER SHEERS.

Admitted Aug. 1902. Solicitor in Education Department, Essex County Council, Chelmsford. Joined Jan. 8, 1917, as Private, 1/8 (Cyclist) Batt. Essex Regt. Served in England and Ireland.

LANCELOT HULL SHEFFIELD.

Admitted Jan. 1905. Formerly member of Sheffield, Son & Powell, of 52 Lime Street, E.C., and subsequently of Victoria, B.C. Joined the Canadian Naval Volunteers, and was on the Cruiser *Rainbow* till after the naval battle at Falkland Islands, subsequently discharged, and in Jan. 1915 joined Inns of Court O.T.C. Gazetted 2nd Lieut. 3rd Batt. Dorset Regt. June 1915, and attained the rank of Capt. Served with H.M.S. *Rainbow* on Pacific Aug. 1914 till Dec. 1914, and in Mesopotamia Jan. 1916 to March 1917. Killed in action March 25, 1917.

REGINALD ELEY SHELDON.

Articled to W. J. Board, of Nottingham. Joined June 1916 Nottingham University O.T.C. Subsequently gazetted 2nd Lieut. 7th Batt. Notts and Derby Regt. (Sherwood Foresters). Served in France. Wounded at Neuve Eglise April 13, 1918. Died at Red Cross Hospital (No. 8), Boulogne, April 15, 1918.

CHARLES EDGAR SHELLY.

Articled to R. A. Reay-Nadin, of Sutton Coldfield. Joined July 1915, as Private, Inns of Court O.T.C. Commissioned 2nd Lieut. 8th Batt. (P.W.O.) West Yorkshire Regt. (T.F.) (Leeds Rifles) Nov. 12, 1915, promoted Lieut. July 1916, seconded for service with Indian Army Reserve of Officers Feb. 1918, and attached to 1/117 Mahrattas, appointed Adjutant of Depôt 1/117 Mahrattas Sept. 1918 until May 1919 with acting rank of Capt., promoted Capt. Nov. 1919. Served in France and Belgium July 1916 to Feb. 1918, and in India March 1918 to Aug. 1919. Wounded at Nieuport, Belgium, July 20, 1917.

JOHN PARKER SHELTON.

Admitted Feb. 1911. Of Canada; and Tottenham, N. Served as 2nd Lieut., 8th Batt. Hampshire Regt.

HERBERT JOHN CAMPBELL SHEPARD.

Admitted Aug. 1904, practising at Tredegar. Joined Aug. 31, 1916, as Lieut., Labour Batt. Served in France Oct. 1916 to Jan. 1919.

CHARLES BURNEY SHEPHERD.

Admitted Nov. 1902. Member of Marris & Shepherd, of 27 Chancery Lane, W.C. Joined May 31, 1916, as Trooper, Pembroke Yeomanry. Gazetted 2nd Lieut. Royal Army Service Corps Nov. 10, 1916, promoted Lieut. May 1918. Served at Home May to Nov. 1916, and in Belgium and France Nov. 1916 to Dec. 1918.

NORMAN ROBINSON SHEPHERD.

Admitted Dec. 1906. Member of Graham, Shepherd & Sons, of Sunderland. Joined Sept. 6, 1914, as Private, 7th Batt. Durham Light Infantry. Gazetted 2nd Lieut. in same Regt. March 5, 1915, promoted Lieut. Aug. 1915, Capt. Oct. 1916. Served in France July 1915 to Nov. 1916. Killed near the Butte de Walencourt Nov. 4, 1916.

FREDERIC CHARLES SHEPPARD.

Admitted Jan. 1905. Member of Sheppard & Son, of Battle, Sussex. Joined Jan. 28, 1918, as Lieut., Royal Naval Volunteer Reserve, subsequently Capt. Royal Air Force. Served at Home.

STUART MORTON WINTER SHEPPARD.

Articled to H. B. Sheppard, of Taunton. Served as 2nd Lieut., 7th Batt. Norfolk Regt., and subsequently 2nd Lieut. 12th (Service) Batt. Lancashire Fusiliers.

WILLIAM STEPHENSON SHEPTON.

Articled to J. L. Wheatley, of Cardiff. Served as Gunner, Glamorganshire Royal Garrison Artillery (T.).

ALFRED SHERMAN.

Articled to J. F. Griffith, of 10 St. Swithin's Lane, E.C. Served as Private, 9th Batt. Royal Scots.

CHARLES ERNEST SHERWIN.

Admitted Oct. 1912, practised at Portsmouth. Served as 2nd Lieut., Hants (Fortress) Royal Engineers, promoted Capt. June 1916. Mentioned in Dispatches. Awarded the M.C.

GEORGE GERARD SHIEL.

Admitted Nov. 1910. Managing Clerk with Dawson & Co., of 2 New Square, Lincoln's Inn, W.C. Joined Aug. 4, 1914, as Private, 1st Batt. Hon. Artillery Company. Gazetted 2nd Lieut. 3rd Northumberland Fusiliers (S.R.) April 18, 1915, promoted Lieut. Oct. 1915, A/Capt. 2nd Batt. Oct. 1915, A/Major Machine Gun Corps Dec. 1916. Three times mentioned in Dispatches. Awarded the M.C. Served in France Sept. 1914 to March 1915 and from Oct. to Nov. 1915, in Egypt Nov. 1915, and at Salonica Nov. 1915 to 1919.

ARTHUR ROBERT SHIELD.

Admitted March 1900, practised at Austin Friars House, E.C. Served as Bombardier, Hon. Artillery Company.

CLEMENT RIDLEY SHIELD.

Admitted June 1912, of Alresford, Hants. Obtained commission in 4th Batt. Highland Light Infantry Sept. 1914, and afterwards appointed Staff Capt. Took part in fighting at Ypres, and sent to the Staff College in France, and subsequently appointed to a Divisional Staff. Once mentioned in Dispatches. Awarded the M.C. Killed Oct. 7, 1916.

GEORGE EUSTACE RIDLEY SHIELD.

Admitted Feb. 1906. Member of Shield & Mackarness, of 7 Union Court, Old Broad Street, E.C. Served as 2nd Lieut., 4th Batt. Devonshire Regt., promoted Capt. June 1916.

JOHN STANLEY MARSH SHINGLER.

Articled to W. E. O. Rutter, of Ellesmere, Salop. Joined Oct. 1914, as 2nd Lieut., 4th Batt. Royal Welch Fusiliers, and subsequently promoted Lieut. Awarded the M.C. Served in France. Killed June 1918.

FRANCIS LESLIE SHORT.

Articled to E. M. Johnson, of 9 New Square, Lincoln's Inn, W.C. Given a commission as 2nd Lieut., 3rd Batt. Royal West Kent Regt. Aug. 1914, and shortly afterwards made Regimental Signalling Officer. Took a draft of the King's Royal Rifle Corps to France 1915, served for a short time with the East Kent Regt. (The Buffs), and then joined the 1st Batt. of his own Regt., appointed Transport Officer and acted in that capacity until invalided home in June 1915. Later appointed Signalling Officer to the Thames Section, promoted Lieut. March and Capt. Dec. 1915. Died in London June 3, 1916, as a result of illness contracted on Active Service.

GEORGE ERNEST SHRIMPTON.

Admitted Dec. 1906. Member of Radcliffes & Hood, of 28 Old Queen Street, S.W. Joined May 14, 1917, as Private, Inns of Court O.T.C. Gazetted

2nd Lieut. 3rd Batt. Devonshire Regt. Feb. 1918, attached Machine Gun Corps July 1918. Served in Belgium.

JAMES LISTER SHUTE.

Articled to Thomas Cross, of Birmingham. Served as 2nd Lieut., 3rd Batt. Royal Warwickshire Regt., promoted Capt. April 1917. Mentioned in Dispatches. Awarded the M.C.

ARTHUR ELLIOT SHUTER.

Admitted Jan. 1900. Member of Dawes & Sons, of 2 Birchin Lane, E.C. Mobilised Aug. 1914, as Lieut., 5th County of London Royal Field Artillery, promoted Temp. Capt. Aug. 1915, Substantive Capt. Aug. 1916, transferred to 6th Reserve Brigade Dec. 1916 and to 419th Battery Oct. 1917, promoted A/Major Dec. 1917, Major and invalided out Feb. 1919. Served in France. Wounded, High Wood, Somme, Sept. 20, 1916.

CHARLES OCTAVIUS SICH.

Admitted April 1908. Member of Tansley, Hall & Sich, of 46 Lincoln's Inn Fields, W.C. Joined March 5, 1915, as Capt., 8th Batt. Middlesex Regt. (T.), attached 4th Batt. Somersetshire Light Infantry from Oct. 1917 to May 1918 and to 13th Batt. Somersetshire Light Infantry May 1918 to April 1919. Served at Home.

GERALD SIDEBOTHAM.

Articled to J. J. Sidebotham, of Manchester. Gazetted Aug. 1914, as 2nd Lieut., 1/4 Batt. Cheshire Regt., promoted Lieut. 1915, A/Capt. from Feb. 1916. Served in Gallipoli (Suvla Bay), Egypt, and Palestine. Wounded at Suvla Bay Aug. 9, 1916. Killed in Palestine March 9, 1918.

LAWRENCE SILBURN.

Articled to C. S. Shortt, of Newcastle-upon-Tyne. Commissioned as 2nd Lieut. Northumbrian Divisional Train (T.F.) Nov. 30, 1914, promoted A/Lieut. and Capt. Royal Army Service Corps (T.), and seconded to Durham Light Infantry in 1917 as permanent Lieut. Served in France 1915 to 1917 and in 1918. Wounded and captured on St. Quentin Sector Sept. 24, 1918.

THOMAS FRANK SILL.

Admitted Jan. 1910. Member of A. H. Sill & Son, of Middlesbrough. Served as Gunner, 4th Battery 1st (Reserve) Brigade Royal Field Artillery.

ARTHUR HENRY SILLEM.

Articled to H. Martin Holman, of St. Michael's Rectory, Cornhill, E.C. Joined Aug. 1914, as Private, University Public Schools Brigade. Gazetted 2nd Lieut. 4th Batt. North Staffordshire Regt. May 1915, and subsequently promoted Lieut. Served in France. Killed near Bapaume, March 24, 1918.

GEORGE REGINALD SILLS.

Admitted July 1898. Member of Hebb & Sills, of Lincoln. Joined Aug. 4, 1914, as Capt., 4th Batt. Lincolnshire Regt. (T.F.), promoted Major Sept. 1916. Served in France July to Dec. 1916. Resigned Aug. 7, 1918, on account of ill-health.

HUGH FLETCHER SILVERWOOD.
Articled to Charles Asplin, of Grays, Essex. Mobilised Aug. 1914, as 2nd Lieut., 6th Batt. Essex Regt., and attained the rank of Capt, A/Major for 8 months in 1916. Served in Gallipoli, Egypt, and Palestine. Killed in Battle of Gaza March 27, 1917.

JOHN LEA SIMCOX.
Admitted April 1913. Member of T. & J. W. Simcox, of Birmingham. Joined Aug. 28, 1914, as 2nd Lieut., 5th Batt. Royal Warwickshire Regt., promoted Lieut. June 1915, Capt. July 1915. Served in France. Wounded (accidentally) March 1916. Invalided out June 1916 owing to ill-health caused by wounds.

JOSEPH BRUCE SIMMONS.
Admitted Dec. 1904, practising at Reading. Joined March 1, 1918, as Private, Royal Army Ordnance Corps. Served at Home.

PERCY COLEMAN SIMMONS.
Admitted June 1896. Member of Simmons & Simmons, of 18 Finch Lane, E.C. Joined May 22, 1917, as Lieut., appointed Staff Lieut. Dec. 1917, Staff Capt. Royal Air Force April 1918, and Staff Major May 1918. Once mentioned in Dispatches. Served at Home.

ALFRED THOMAS SIMPSON.
Admitted Nov. 1881. Member of Stone & Simpson, of Tunbridge Wells. Mobilised as Col. commanding 4th (Reserve) Batt. Royal West Kent Regt. Once mentioned in Dispatches. Served in Gallipoli 1915, Egypt 1916, and in France 1917. Wounded at Gallipoli Aug. 1915. Transferred to Reserve Aug. 1918.

ARTHUR ERNEST SIMPSON.
Admitted Dec. 1897, formerly practised in London. Served as Lieut., Royal Army Service Corps. Accidentally shot by sentry at Torquay Jan. 24, 1915.

FRANCIS JOSEPH SIMPSON.
Admitted Feb. 1897. Member of Simpson & Mason, of Higham Ferrers. Joined Sept. 1914, as Lieut., National Reserve, Northamptonshire Regt., promoted Capt. March 1917, and on leaving Brigade Staff, Felixstowe Section, promoted Major (General List) July 1918. Served on Intelligence Staff at Home and Assist. Competent Military Authority No. 27 Area Northern Command and No. 4 Area Southern Command.

GEOFFREY BARNSLEY SIMPSON.
Articled to E. O. Simpson, of Leeds. Joined Sept. 14, 1914, as 2nd Lieut., 7th Batt. York and Lancaster Regt, promoted Lieut. Jan. 1915, Capt. March 1915. Served in France. Died of wounds Nov. 12, 1915.

GEORGE COLVILLE SIMPSON.
Admitted Nov. 1910, practised at Sheffield. Served as 2nd Lieut., 13th Division, Royal Field Artillery, promoted Lieut. July 1917.

GERALD HEMPLOE SIMPSON.
Admitted Feb. 1903. Member of Simpson & Scott, of Chesham, Bucks. Joined July 22, 1914, as 2nd Lieut., Bucks Batt. Oxford and Bucks Light In-

fantry, promoted Temp. Lieut. Sept. 1914, Temp. Capt. May 1915, Substantive Capt. Oct. 1915, transferred to South Midland Royal Engineers July 1916, rejoined Oxford and Bucks Light Infantry Jan. 1919. Served at Home.

HERBERT SIMPSON.

Admitted Dec. 1892. Member of Herbert Simpson & Bennett, of Leicester. Joined Sept. 15, 1914, as Capt., 4th Batt. Leicestershire Regt. Served at Home.

MAURICE ROWTON SIMPSON.

Articled to H. G. Bennett, of Leicester. Joined Oct. 10, 1916, as Private, Royal Army Service Corps (M.T.). Gazetted 2nd Lieut. Royal Field Artillery June 17, 1918. Served in England and in France.

ODO LOUIS DAVID MACKAY SIMPSON.

Admitted April 1909, formerly practised at 3 Arundel Street, W.C., and afterwards at Alberta. Enlisted with a Canadian Regt. and wounded in 1916. Received commission in Notts and Derby Regt. (Sherwood Foresters) and promoted Lieut. Killed by a sniper July 1918.

ROBERT ARTHUR ABBS SIMPSON.

Admitted Nov. 1901. Of Barnsley. Served as Lieut., Northumberland Fusiliers. Killed in action.

VIVIAN SUMNER SIMPSON.

Admitted Oct. 1906. Member of George J. Simpson & Sons, of Sheffield. Joined Sept. 1914, as Private, 12th (Sheffield City Batt.) York and Lancaster Regt., subsequently gazetted 2nd Lieut. in same Regt. and attained the rank of Capt. Twice mentioned in Dispatches. Awarded the M.C. Served in France. Killed in action at Vieux Berguin April 13, 1918.

GEORGE STANLEY SINNOTT.

Admitted March 1894. Member of James Sinnott & Son, of Bristol. Joined Nov. 17, 1914, as Major and Hon. Lieut.-Col., Royal Defence Corps. Once mentioned in Dispatches. Served at Home.

EDWARD RALPH SEROCOLD SKEELS.

Admitted April 1892, practising at 55 Chancery Lane, W.C. Joined Aug. 30, 1915, as Lieut., Army Pay Department, promoted Capt. July 1919. Served in France Aug. 1915 to Oct. 1919, and in Italy Oct. to Dec. 1919.

ALAN JOHN SKELTON.

Articled to Skelton & Co., of Manchester. Joined Oct. 17, 1917, as Cadet, Royal Field Artillery. Gazetted 2nd Lieut. Royal Field Artillery March 21, 1918. Served in France. Wounded at Oppy Wood, near Arras, Aug. 27, 1918.

FREDERICK OSWALD SKIDMORE.

Articled to E. B. Thorneycroft, of Wolverhampton. Mobilised Aug. 4, 1914, as Trooper, Staffordshire Yeomanry. Gazetted 2nd Lieut. 4th Batt. South Staffordshire Regt. Nov. 18, 1914, transferred to 2nd Batt. King's Own Yorkshire Light Infantry Oct. 1915, seconded to Tank Corps Jan. 1917, promoted Lieut. May 1917, A/Capt. Oct 1918, Temp. Capt. May 1919. Once mentioned in Dispatches. Served in France and at Home. Wounded July 1, 1916, and Nov. 4, 1917.

CHARLES BLACKETT SKINNER.

Admitted Dec. 1892, practised at 10 Queen Street, E.C. Served as Capt., 17th (Service) Batt. Royal Fusiliers.

EDWARD HOWARD SKINNER.

Admitted Nov. 1911. Managing Clerk with H. L. Staffurth, of Bognor. Joined Aug. 1914 6th Batt. Somersetshire Light Infantry. Gazetted 2nd Lieut. 1st Batt. Devonshire Regt. July 1915. Served in France. Killed in action on the Somme Sept. 25, 1916.

THOMAS ARNOLD SKINNER.

Admitted March 1901, practised at Sheffield. Joined June 1915, as 2nd Lieut., 7th Batt. King's Own Scottish Borderers. Served in France. Twice wounded. Fatally wounded at the 2nd Battle of the Somme July 28, 1917, and died at Rouen Aug. 10, 1917.

WALTER VIVIAN DOUGLAS SKRINE.

Articled to A. V. Lloyd-Jones, of 2 Gresham Buildings, E.C. Joined Aug. 1915, as 2nd Lieut., 3/4 Batt. York and Lancaster Regt., subsequently promoted Lieut. and attached 187th Trench Mortar Battery. Once mentioned in Dispatches. Awarded the M.C. and Bar. Served in France Jan. 1917 to 1919.

EDWARD SIDEBOTTOM SLACK.

Admitted Sept. 1907. Member of Parkinson, Slack & Needham, of Manchester. Served as Private, 6th Batt. Manchester Regt. and subsequently gazetted 2nd Lieut. in same Regt.

FRANK SLADE.

Articled to J. A. Batley, of Leeds. Joined Aug. 5, 1914, as Corporal, Royal Army Medical Corps (T.) and attained rank of Sergeant. Gazetted 2nd Lieut. Royal Garrison Artillery (S.R.) April 1, 1917, promoted Lieut. Sept. 1918. Served in France Oct. 1914 to Nov. 1916, and in East Africa July 1917 to Jan. 1919.

MEAD SLADE.

Articled to W. W. Reed, of Dorchester. Joined in 1914, as Trooper, Dorset Imperial Yeomanry. Transferred to Indian Army and commissioned Nov. 1915 and posted to 74th Pioneers, A/Capt. 1918. Served at Home, in India, Burma, and Mesopotamia.

PERCIVAL CLAUDE AVERY SLADE.

Admitted Sept. 1905. Member of Slade & Son, of Wallingford, Berks. Joined Sept. 19, 1914, as 2nd Lieut., Royal Berkshire Regt., promoted Lieut. Jan. 1915, Capt. and Adjutant Royal Defence Corps Jan. 1917, attached Staff Headquarters Southern Command. Served at Home.

ROBERT BLACKMORE SLADE.

Admitted March 1914. Member of J. R. Slade & Son, of Swanage. Joined Aug. 28, 1914, as 2nd Lieut., Dorset Royal Garrison Artillery (T.), promoted Temp. Lieut. April 1915, Lieut. June 1916, A/Capt. Dec. 1916 to April 1917, A/Major April 1917 to July 1918, attached to 123rd Siege Battery April 1916 to July 1918. Once mentioned in Dispatches. Served at Home

Aug. 1914 to July 1916, and in France July 1916 to July 1918. Killed in action in France July 10, 1918.

ST. BARBE RUSSELL SLADEN.

Admitted Aug. 1895. Member of St. Barbe Sladen & Wing, of 9 Queen Anne's Gate, Westminster, S.W. Mobilised Aug. 1914, as Major and second in Command, 5th Batt. The Queen's Royal West Surrey Regt., and in June 1915 given Command of the 2/5 Batt., promoted Lieut.-Col. Aug. 1915, attached to the 1st Batt. Oct. 1917, and in Dec. 1917 given Command of that Batt. Served in India 1914 to June 1915, and in France Oct. 1917 to March 1918. Killed on Passchendaele Ridge while acting as Brigadier 19th Brigade March 12, 1918, and buried at Ypres on the following day.

JOHN CYRUS SLATER.

Admitted Feb. 1903. Member of Eardley, Holt, Lightly & Slater, of 32 St. James's Place, S.W. Joined March 1915, as Private, 5th City of London Batt. London Regt. (London Rifle Brigade). Gazetted 2nd Lieut. in same Regt. Oct. 5, 1916. Served in France. Died of pneumonia at Camiers Hospital July 7, 1917.

PERCIVAL JAMES SLATER.

Articled to Slater & Co., of Darlaston. Mobilised Aug. 1914, as 2nd Lieut., Unattached List, T.F., posted to 6th Batt. South Staffordshire Regt. Sept. 1914, promoted Lieut. May 1915, Capt. June 1916, attached Royal Flying Corps Oct. 1917. Once mentioned in Dispatches. Awarded D.F.C. Served in France. Wounded Oct. 13, 1915.

THOMAS WEYMARK SLATER.

Articled to C. J. Slater, of 19 Walbrook, E.C. Joined June 18, 1915, as Rifleman, 1/6 Batt. County of London Regt. (Queen's Westminsters). Served in France. Wounded Sept. 15, 1916, Battle of Somme. Invalided out Jan. 10, 1917.

WILLIAM SLATER.

Admitted Dec. 1913. Member of Little & Slater, of Blackburn. Joined Sept. 4, 1914, as Trooper, 11th Hussars, subsequently gazetted 2nd Lieut. Royal Field Artillery.

STUART BERTRAM SLEEMAN.

Admitted June 1912, practised at Bristol. Served as Lieut., 6th Batt. Devonshire Regt.

GEORGE NICHOLAS SLINGER.

Articled to G. N. Slinger, of Accrington. Enlisted Dec. 1914, as Gunner. Accrington and Burnley Howitzer Brigade (afterwards 158th Brigade) Royal Field Artillery and attained the rank of Bombardier. Gazetted 2nd Lieut. in same Regt. April 5, 1915, joined 159th Brigade Sept. 1916. Once mentioned in Dispatches. Served at Home until Jan. 1916, and subsequently up to date of death in France. Killed near Arras Nov. 28, 1916.

GEORGE NICHOLAS SLINGER.

Admitted Aug. 1889, practising at Accrington, Lancashire. Joined Sept. 11, 1914, as Capt., 11th Batt. East Lancashire Regt. promoted Major

Oct. 1914 and appointed Second in Command of Batt. May 1915, appointed to Command Depôt 11th Batt. East Lancashire Regt. Sept. 1915 to March 1916, Temp. Commanded 12th (Reserve) Batt., appointed Second in Command of 12th Batt. and remained with that unit until Sept. 1916, attached to Headquarters Staff (Prees Heath Centre) as Legal Adviser and Courts-Martial Officer Sept. 1916 to May 1919. Served at Home, with exception of a short period in France in Jan. 1916.

JOHN HENRY SLINGSBY.

Admitted March 1903, practising at Nuneaton. Joined Dec. 20, 1917, as 2nd Lieut., Royal Flying Corps, promoted Capt. Royal Air Force Oct. 1918. Served at Home.

CUTHBERT HANNINGTON SLOAN.

Admitted Nov. 1913. Managing Clerk with C. J. Parker, of Temple Chambers, W.C. Joined Sept. 1914, as Private, 28th Batt. County of London Regt. (Artists Rifles) and appointed Quartermaster-Sergeant Instructor Machine Gun School, G.H.Q., France, 1916. Gazetted 2nd Lieut. Machine Gun Corps 1917, promoted Lieut. 1919. Served in France.

HAROLD LAURENCE SLOCOCK.

Admitted Nov. 1904. Member of Cripps & Shone, of Marlow, Bucks. Joined April 12, 1915, as Lieut., Royal Army Service Corps, promoted Capt. Feb. 1917. Served at Home, and in France, Salonica, and Egypt.

FERDINAND WILLIAM SMALLPEICE.

Admitted Feb. 1901. Member of Smallpeice & Co., of Guildford. Served as Major, 5th Batt. The Queen's Royal West Surrey Regt.

HAROLD NEVIL SMART.

Admitted June 1907. Member of Rehder & Higgs, of 29 Mincing Lane, E.C. Mobilised Aug. 1914 with Royal Naval Volunteer Reserve and appointed Assistant Paymaster Dec. 1914, Staff Paymaster Oct. 1916, Commander Royal Navy April 1918, Lieut. (A/Lieut.-Commander) April 1918, Naval Transport Officer (1st Grade) April 1918. Twice mentioned in Dispatches. Awarded C.M.G. and Russian Order of St. Anne. Served in North Sea, Mediterranean, Dardanelles, N. Russia, and Admiralty.

LOVEL FRANCIS SMEATHMAN.

Admitted July 1910. Member of Lovel Smeathman & Son., of Hemel Hempstead, Herts. Mobilised Aug. 1914, as Lieut., 1st Batt. Hertfordshire Regt., promoted Capt. Oct. 1914, Major Dec. 1915, and Lieut.-Col. May 1916, attached to and Commanding 9th Royal Welch Fusiliers Oct. 1916. Four times mentioned in Dispatches. Awarded the D.S.O. and M.C. Served in France Nov. 1914 to 1919. Wounded Sept. 25, 1915, and Nov. 8, 1918.

HUGH LIONEL SMEDLEY.

Admitted Jan. 1908, practising at Solicitors' Office, Waterloo Station. S.E. Joined Aug. 30, 1914, as Private, 15th Batt. London Regt. (Civil Service Rifles). Commissioned 2nd Lieut. 11th Royal Fusiliers June 27, 1917, promoted A/Capt. Sept. 1918, and Lieut. Dec. 1918. Awarded M.C. and M.M. Served in France. Wounded March 23, 1918.

GEORGE MILMAN SMERDON.

Admitted March 1914, practising at 40 Chancery Lane, W.C. Joined April 16, 1917, as Private, Royal Engineers, promoted Sergeant 1918. Served at Home.

ALAN MONTAGUE SMITH.

Admitted May 1912. Member of A. G. Smith & Son, of Melksham, Wilts. Joined Sept. 3, 1914, as Private, 1/4 Batt. Wiltshire Regt. Obtained commission in June 1918, and gazetted to 1/4 Batt. Duke of Cornwall's Light Infantry, attached to 38th Batt. Royal Fusiliers. Served in India Oct. 1914 to Nov. 1915 and April 1916 to Sept. 1917, in Mesopotamia Nov. 1915 to April 1916, and in Palestine Oct. 1917 to Feb. 1919.

ALAN MORTEN TWEEDY SMITH.

Articled to R. Tweedy Smith, of 89 Chancery Lane. W.C. Mobilised Aug. 1914 with 28th Batt. County of London Regt. (Artists Rifles). Gazetted 2nd Lieut. 1st Batt. Royal West Surrey Regt. Jan. 1915. Once mentioned in Dispatches. Served in France 1914 and 1915. Killed in an attack on the Hohenzollern Redoubt, at Loos, Oct. 13, 1915.

ALBANY GORDON SMITH.

Articled to C. S. Bigg, of Leicester. Joined June 11, 1916, as Cadet, Nottingham University O.T.C. Gazetted 2nd Lieut. South Notts Yeomanry (T.) Aug. 28, 1917, attached to 5th Batt. Notts and Derby Regt. April 1918 subsequently gazetted Lieut. Served at Home.

ALEXANDER NOEL SMITH.

Articled to T. C. Smith, of Berwick-on-Tweed. Joined Sept. 1914, as Private, 4th Batt. Royal Scots. Gazetted 2nd Lieut. 7th Batt. Northumberland Fusiliers Feb. 1915, promoted Temp. Lieut. 1915, Temp. Capt. 1916. Served in France 1916. Died at Boulogne Sept. 26, 1916, from wounds received in action Sept. 15, 1916.

ALFRED CECIL DENISON SMITH.

Admitted Oct. 1913. Member of Senior & Barratt, of Wakefield. Joined Sept. 7, 1914, as Private, 4th (City) Batt. Manchester Regt. Received commission as 2nd Lieut. in 9th Batt. East Yorkshire Regt. Feb. 8, 1915, promoted Lieut. July 1917. Awarded the M.C. Served in France and Belgium, attached to 7th Batt. Wounded near Gouzeaucourt Sept. 18, 1918.

ALFRED ELLIOTT SIDNEY SMITH.

Admitted July 1899. Member of Capon & Elliott Smith, of 29 Bedford Row, W.C. Joined May 8, 1915, as Lieut., Royal Army Service Corps. Served in France Oct. 1916 to April 1917.

ALFRED ERNEST STANLEY SMITH.

Admitted June 1906. Member of Lees, Smith & Tetlow, of 3 Berners Street, Oxford Street, W. Joined March 27, 1917, as Rifleman, 5th City of London Batt. London Regt. (London Rifle Brigade). Gazetted 2nd Lieut. 6th Batt. London Regt. (City of London Rifles) Oct. 18, 1917. Awarded the M.C. Served in France. Wounded Aug. 9, 1918.

ALFRED PARTON SMITH.
Articled to W. A. Gibb, of Birmingham. Joined Jan. 4, 1917, as Sapper, Royal Engineers, promoted Lance-Corporal July 1917, Corporal Jan. 1918, Sergeant June 1918. Served at Home.

ALFRED WILLIAM SMITH.
Admitted Oct. 1910. Managing Clerk with Pinsent & Co., of Birmingham. Joined Dec. 12, 1914, as Private, South Wales Mounted Brigade Field Ambulance, Royal Army Medical Corps (T.), promoted Corporal Aug. 1915, Sergeant Dec. 1915, Quartermaster-Sergeant Jan. 1916. Served at Home Dec. 1914 to June 1917, and in Salonica June 1917 to April 1919.

ALGERNON SMITH.
Admitted July 1912. Member of White, Smith & Co., of Barnsley. Served as Private, Lancashire Fusiliers.

ARTHUR KIRKE SMITH.
Admitted Nov. 1902. Member of Little & Co., of Bombay. Joined March 16, 1916, as 2nd Lieut., Indian Army Reserve of Officers (Cavalry). Served in Mesopotamia.

BASIL MARCH SMITH.
Articled to Middleton Smith, of Whitby, Yorkshire. Joined Aug. 18, 1915, as Private, Hon. Artillery Company. Commissioned as 2nd Lieut. Royal Field Artillery Feb. 20, 1917, promoted Lieut. Aug. 1918. Served in Greece, Serbia, and Bulgaria.

BERNARD CLIVE SMITH.
Articled to Moody & Woolley, of Derby. Served as 2nd Lieut., 3rd Batt. Notts and Derby Regt. (Sherwood Foresters).

CECIL PLUMBE SMITH.
Admitted Nov. 1896. Member of Walker, Smith & Way, of Chester. Joined June 7, 1915, as Lieut., 2nd Batt. Cheshire Regt., attached to East Lancashire and South Lancashire Regts. Served at Home. Resigned Aug. 1916.

CHARLES WILLIAM SMITH.
Admitted Oct. 1909. Member of C. A. Piper & Smith, of 13 Vincent Square, Westminster, S.W. Served as Gunner, Royal Horse Artillery, and subsequently gazetted 2nd Lieut. Royal Garrison Artillery.

CLAUDE SOUTTER SMITH.
Articled to B. S. Smith, of Birmingham. Joined Nov. 13, 1914, as 2nd Lieut., 59th Divisional Signal Coy. Royal Engineers (T.), promoted Lieut. July 1916. Served at Home and Ireland 1914 to Feb. 1917, and in France, Belgium and Germany Feb. 1917 to Feb. 1919.

DAVID DUNCAN SMITH.
Admitted Feb. 1911, practising at 6 Austin Friars, E.C. Served as Lieut., 4th Batt. West Riding Regt.

EDWARD SMITH.
Articled to W. G. Bate, of 35 Bedford Row, W.C. Joined June 1915, as Private, 28th Batt. County of London Regt. (Artists Rifles). Gazetted 2nd

Lieut. 21st Batt. London Regt. (First Surrey Rifles) Dec. 1915. Served in France. Discharged on account of ill-health June 30, 1916.

EDWARD ARTHUR LAST SMITH.

Admitted April 1907. Member of Ridsdale & Son, of 5 Gray's Inn Square, W.C. Served as Capt., Royal Welch Fusiliers, attached 51st Batt. The Welch Regt.

EDWARD CASTLEMAN SMITH.

Admitted April 1884, practised at Blandford. Served as Lieut.-Col. commanding 3rd Batt. Dorset Regt.

FREDERIC NORMAN SMITH.

Admitted April 1908. Assistant Solicitor Birkenhead Corporation. Joined May 2, 1915, as Private, Inns of Court O.T.C. Gazetted 2nd Lieut. Royal Army Service Corps July 1915. Served in England, Ireland, and Gallipoli (Anzac).

GEORGE GARNER SMITH.

Admitted Nov. 1892. Member of Evans, Lockett & Co., of Liverpool. Served with Section Sanitaire Anglaise, Convoi Automobile, France.

GERALD HOWARD SMITH.

Admitted Dec. 1909. Member of Underhill, Thorneycroft & Smith, and Neve, Thorneycroft & Co., of Wolverhampton. Received commission in the South Staffordshire Regt. in Oct. 1914 and proceeded to the Front in March 1915, promoted Lieut. Once mentioned in Dispatches. Awarded the M.C. Died March 29, 1916, of wounds received in action.

GILBERTSON SMITH.

Admitted April 1890. Member of Miller & Smiths, of 3 Salter's Hall Court, E.C. Raised the 2/25 Cyclist Batt. London Regt. in Aug. 1914 and commanded it till disbandment. Lieut.-Col., promoted Colonel Sept. 1915. Served at Home.

GRAHAM SMITH.

Articled to J. K. Torkington, of 307 High Holborn, W.C. Joined Nov. 29, 1915, as Private, Inns of Court O.T.C. Gazetted 2nd Lieut. 5th Batt. Suffolk Regt. Dec. 1916, promoted Lieut. June 1918, attached 11th Batt. Jan. 1917. Served at Home and in France. Wounded April 28, 1917.

GRAHAM GOULD SMITH.

Admitted July 1914. Of Bedford. Joined July 1915, as Private, Inns of Court O.T.C. Gazetted 2nd Lieut. 1/4 Batt. Oxford and Bucks Light Infantry and attained rank of Capt. Once mentioned in Dispatches. Served in France.

HARRY EDGAR SMITH.

Articled to A. W. Stanton, of 108A Cannon Street, E.C. Served as Private, 28th Batt. County of London Regt. (Artists Rifles).

HENRY CHARLES JOHN RUSSELL SMITH.

Admitted Aug. 1904. Managing Clerk with Vizard, Oldham, Crowder & Cash, of 51 Lincoln's Inn Fields, W.C. Joined Cadet School Royal Army

Service Corps (M.T.) Dec. 1916. Commissioned in same Regt. Feb. 1917, promoted Lieut. Aug. 1918. Served in Palestine, Gaza, and Syria.

HERBERT GEORGE SMITH.

Admitted May 1899, practising at Liverpool. Joined June 21, 1916, as Private, 28th Batt. County of London Regt. (Artists Rifles). Gazetted 2nd Lieut. Royal Army Ordnance Corps Nov. 25, 1916, promoted Lieut. Feb. 1917, Major and Deputy Assistant Director of Ordnance Services Sept. 1918. Served at Home.

HORACE MILNER ALDERSON SMITH.

Admitted Dec. 1909. Member of Ayrton & Alderson Smith, of Liverpool. Joined Feb. 12, 1916, as Private, 14th Batt. County of London Regt. (London Scottish). Gazetted 2nd Lieut. in same Batt. Jan. 1917, promoted Lieut. July 1918. Served in France March to April 1917 and June to Oct. 1918, and in Palestine Nov. 1917 to June 1918. Wounded near Wervicq Oct. 14, 1918.

JEFFERY PETER FREDERICK HANWORTH SMITH.

Admitted Nov. 1912, practised at 222 Strand, W.C. Served as 2nd Lieut. Royal Army Service Corps.

JOHN ALEXANDER HAY SMITH.

Articled to T. G. Cowan, of 18 Austin Friars, E.C. Joined Aug. 1914, as Lieut., 11th Batt. Royal Scots. Served in France. Killed at Festubert Aug. 14, 1915.

JOHN CARRINGTON SMITH.

Articled to Arthur Lees, of Ashton-under-Lyne. Joined Jan. 26, 1916, as Private, 28th Batt. County of London Regt. (Artists Rifles). Gazetted 2nd Lieut. 3rd Batt. South Lancashire Regt. Sept. 26, 1916. Served in France 1916 to 1917 and at Home 1918 to 1919.

JOHN EDWARD SMITH.

Articled to Thomas Smith, of Halifax. Joined July 1, 1916, as Private, 18th (Queen Mary's Own) Hussars. Gazetted 2nd Lieut. 5th Reserve Cavalry Regt. July 8, 1917. Served at Home. Invalided and gazetted out on account of sickness April 15, 1918.

JOHN HENRY SMITH.

Admitted Nov. 1904. Member of Pearce, Foster & Smith, of 70 Gracechurch Street, S.E. Served as 2nd Lieut.

LEONARD DANVERS SMITH.

Admitted Nov. 1913. Managing Clerk with Bircham & Co., of 50 Old Broad Street, E.C. Joined April 1916, as Sapper, London Electrical Engineers. Served at Home.

NEVILLE HAYWOOD SMITH.

Admitted April 1909, practising at Ipswich. Joined June 23, 1915, as 2nd Lieut., 4th Batt. Suffolk Regt., promoted Lieut. Jan. 1917. Served in France. Wounded on the Somme July 15, 1916.

NORMAN DOUGLAS SMITH.

Admitted Oct. 1909, practised at 31 Basinghall Street, E.C. Served as Private, Hon. Artillery Company.

OSWALD FRYER SMITH.
Admitted Oct. 1911. Member of T. J. Smith & Son, of Liverpool. Served as Sub-Lieut., Royal Naval Volunteer Reserve.

PHILIP GATTY SMITH.
Admitted Sept. 1900. Member of Smith, Smith & Fielding, of Sheffield. Mobilised Aug. 1914, as Major, Queen's Own Yorkshire Dragoons. Served in France and Belgium July 1915 to April 1916 and at Home Aug. 1914 to July 1915 and April 1916 to Nov. 1919. Wounded by gassing near Bailleul April 1916 and subsequently unfit for foreign service.

REGINALD RUSSELL SMITH.
Admitted May 1913. Managing Clerk with Ball, Smith & Playne, of Stroud, Glos. Joined Sept. 18, 1914, as Private, 19th (Public Schools) Batt. Royal Fusiliers. Discharged medically unfit Nov. 1914. Joined 5th Batt. Middlesex Regt. as Private, Feb. 1916, transferred to 1st Home Service Batt. Royal West Kent Regt. April 1916. Gazetted 2nd Lieut. Royal Garrison Artillery (S.R.) Sept. 1, 1917 and served in London Anti-Aircraft Defences Dec. 1917 to Oct. 1918. Served at Home.

SAMUEL ARTHUR SMITH.
Admitted May 1905. Member of Smith, Youatt & Smith, of Manchester. Joined Aug. 26, 1916, as Air-Mechanic, Royal Flying Corps, promoted to 1st Class Air-Mechanic Jan. 1917, Corporal April 1917, Sergeant May 1917, Flight Sergeant Sept. 1918. Once mentioned in Dispatches. Served in France and Belgium Sept. 1916 to April 1918, and at Home May 1918 to March 1919.

SAMUEL PERCY SMITH.
Admitted Nov. 1913. Member of S. Pearman Smith & Sons, of Walsall. Joined Aug. 1914, as 2nd Lieut., 5th Batt. South Staffordshire Regt., and subsequently promoted Lieut. and Capt. Served in France. Killed at Gommecourt Feb. 28, 1917.

THOMAS JAMES THOMPSON SMITH.
Admitted July 1910. Member of T. J. Smith & Son, of Liverpool. Served in the Royal Navy.

THOMAS OSWALD SMITH.
Admitted Jan. 1912, practised at Bolton. Served as Lieut., 5th Batt. Loyal North Lancashire Regt., promoted Capt. June 1916. Mentioned in Dispatches and awarded the D.S.O.

TURBERVILLE SMITH.
Admitted April 1907, practising at Uxbridge. Joined Dec. 16, 1916, as Cadet O.T.C. Gazetted 2nd Lieut. Royal Army Service Corps (M.T.) Feb. 23, 1917, promoted Lieut. Aug. 1918. Awarded the M.C. Served in France.

VERE HERBERT SMITH.
Articled to J. E. Huxtable, of 14 St. Helen's Place, E.C. Joined Aug. 15, 1914, as 2nd Lieut., 5th Batt. The Rifle Brigade, transferred to 3rd Batt. in France. Served at Home till Feb. 1915 and in France Feb. to March 1915. Killed at Armentières March 21, 1915.

VIVIAN SMITH.

Articled to W. S. Burton, of Newcastle-upon-Tyne. Joined Dec. 16, 1914, as 2nd Lieut., Northumberland Fusiliers, transferred to Royal Flying Corps May 28, 1917. Served in France. Wounded June 4, 1916. Wounded and taken prisoner May 28, 1917, shot about 17 miles E. of Douai. Prisoner until Dec. 13, 1918.

VIVIAN ARTHUR SMITH.

Admitted Oct. 1908. Managing Clerk with Bircham & Co., of 50 Old Broad Street, E.C. Joined Sept. 3, 1914, as Rifleman, 2/21 Batt. County of London Regt. (1st Surrey Rifles). Served at Home. Discharged March 1915. Suffered from heart-strain finally resulting in death in Jan. 1917.

WILLIAM FRANCIS SMITH.

Admitted Aug. 1903, practising at 158 Aldersgate Street, E.C. Joined Aug. 4, 1916, as Private, Royal Fusiliers, transferred to 10th Batt. Royal West Surrey Regt., attached to 213th Infantry Brigade Headquarters May 1917 to March 1918, transferred to 3rd Royal Sussex Regt. and attached to 51st (Grad.) Batt. Royal Sussex May to Nov. 1918, attained rank of Lance-Corporal. Served at Home.

WILLIAM MACKENZIE SMITH.

Admitted Feb. 1893. Member of Smith, Smith & Fielding, of Sheffield. Mobilised Aug. 1914 as Lieut.-Col. Commanding Queen's Own Yorkshire Dragoons, promoted Col. Aug. 1918. Once mentioned in Dispatches. Awarded the D.S.O. Served at Home Aug. 1914 to July 1915, and in France and Belgium July 1915 to April 1919.

WYNDHAM ALEXANDER SMITH.

Admitted Feb. 1910. Member of Baker & Smith, of Upton-on-Severn and Tewkesbury. Joined 1915, as 2nd Lieut., Royal Gloucestershire Hussars. Served in Egypt. Killed in action at Katia, in the Sinai Peninsula, April 26, 1916.

JAMES RUPERT SMITH-SAVILLE.

Articled to Sir Lewis Beard, of Blackburn, Lancs. Joined Dec 6, 1916, as Private, Inns of Court O.T.C. Gazetted 2nd Lieut. 4th East Lancashire Regt. (T.) Aug. 29, 1917, subsequently promoted Lieut. March 1919. Served in France. Wounded Oct. 10, 1918, at Le Cateau.

EDWARD PERCY SMYTH.

Admitted July 1901. Member of Latham, New & Smyth, of Melton Mowbray and Leicester. Joined May 5, 1916, as Lieut., Royal Naval Volunteer Reserve, attached Royal Naval Air Service (Tech.), transferred to Royal Air Force as Capt. April 1918 and promoted to A/Major. Served at Home as Head Inspector of Airship Envelopes, R.N. Airship Fabric Works, Shepherd's Bush, London.

BERTRAM CECIL KEITH SNAGG.

Admitted Feb. 1899, practised at Newcastle-upon-Tyne and Gateshead. Served as Capt., Royal Marines. Died in the Naval Hospital at Chatham Feb. 27, 1919.

JOHN ROBERT SNAPE.

Admitted Dec. 1905, practising at Maesteg, Glam. Joined March 15, 1917, as Private, Welch Guards. Gazetted 2nd Lieut. 14th Batt. The Welch Regt. June 20, 1918. Served at Home and in France.

LESLIE NINIAN LLEWELLYN SNAPE.

Admitted Oct. 1913. Member of Snape & Snape, of Maesteg, and Bridgend, Glam. Joined Sept. 4, 1914, as Trooper, 4th (Queen's Own) Hussars, promoted Sergeant 12th Cavalry Reserve Nov. 1914, and Sergeant 2nd Batt. Royal Irish Regt. April 1915. Served in Ireland to April 1915, and in France May 1915 to July 1916. Killed in action at Mametz Wood July 4, 1916.

SIDNEY FRANK SNAPE.

Articled to Herbert Johnson, of Coventry. Joined July 23, 1915, as Private, Inns of Court O.T.C. Gazetted 2nd Lieut. 2/5th Royal Warwickshire Regt. Nov. 15, 1915, promoted Lieut. July 1917. Served in France. Wounded on the Ypres-St. Julien Road Aug. 24, 1917, right leg eventually amputated above the knee.

NOEL VIVIAN SNELL.

Articled to J. B. Snell, of 1 and 2 George Street, Mansion House, E.C. Joined Sept. 5, 1914, as Sapper, Royal Engineers (Wireless Signals). Gazetted 2nd Lieut. Royal Engineers (Wireless) June 3, 1917, promoted Lieut. Dec. 1918, A/Capt. Feb, 1919. Served in Gallipoli May to Dec. 1915, Egypt and Sinai Jan. to Oct. 1916, and at Home.

ARTHUR SNOW.

Admitted Dec. 1900. Member of James & Snow, of Exeter. Served as Capt., 3rd Batt. Devonshire Regt.

JOHN STANLEY SNOWBALL.

Articled to E. J. Birdsall, of Scarborough. Joined Nov. 22, 1914, as Private, Inns of Court O.T.C. Gazetted 2nd Lieut. 6th South Staffordshire Regt. Feb. 19, 1915, seconded 137th Machine Gun Coy. March 1916, promoted Lieut. June 1916, A/Capt. No. 2 Machine Gun Coy. Feb. 1918, A/Major "B" Coy., 1st Batt. Machine Gun Corps March 1918. Once mentioned in Dispatches. Awarded the M.C. Served at Home Nov. 1914 to Oct. 1915, and in France and Germany Oct. 1915 to March 1919.

HENRY FREDERICK SNOWDON.

Admitted March 1908. Member of Appleton, Son & Snowdon, of Leeds. Joined Sept. 24, 1914, as Private, 15th Batt. West Yorkshire Regt. Gazetted 2nd Lieut. 2/1 (City of London) Batt. Royal Fusiliers Nov. 13, 1914, promoted A/Capt. Jan. 1915, and Temp. Lieut. 8th Batt. City of London (Post Office Rifles) June 1916. Served in Malta and the Dardanelles Jan. to Dec. 1915, and in France June to Oct. 1916. Killed in action Oct. 6, 1916.

JOHN HAROLD SOADY.

Admitted July 1911, practising at Hull. Mobilised Aug. 1913, as 2nd Lieut., East Riding Royal Garrison Artillery (T.), promoted Lieut. March 1915, A/Capt. Oct. 1917, Substantive Capt. Feb. 1919. Served at Home Aug. 1914 to March 1916, France and Belgium March 1916 to Feb. 1919, and with Rhine Army from Feb. 1919.

MERVYN HENRY SOAMES.

Admitted Jan. 1906. Member of Soames & Thompson, of 12 Coleman Street, E.C. Served as Capt. 5th (City of London) Batt. London Regt. (London Rifle Brigade).

FREDERICK ALBERT SOBEY.

Articled to R. A. Reay-Nadin, of Sutton Coldfield. Served as Private, Birmingham University O.T.C.

LESLIE SODDY.

Articled to H. W. Fovargue, of Eastbourne. Joined Jan. 1916, as Private, Inns of Court O.T.C. Subsequently gazetted Lieut. Royal Garrison Artillery (S.R.). Served with 270th Siege Battery in France. Wounded at Langemarcke Aug. 1917.

HERBERT SOLOMON.

Admitted July 1913. Managing Clerk with Alsop, Stevens, Crooks & Co., of Liverpool. Joined Feb. 1915, as Private, 17th (Service) Batt. King's Liverpool Regt. Gazetted 2nd Lieut. Feb. 26, 1917, promoted Lieut. Aug. 1918 Lancashire and Cheshire Royal Garrison Artillery. Served in France.

PHINEAS SAMUEL SOLOMON.

Admitted Nov. 1900. Member of Michael Abrahams, Sons & Co., of 5 Tokenhouse Yard, E.C.; and Paris. Joined April 24, 1917, as 3rd Class Air-Mechanic Royal Flying Corps, promoted 2nd Class Air-Mechanic Aug. 1917, transferred to Royal Air Force April 1918. Served in Belgium and France May 1917 to July 1918.

ROBERT BERNARD SOLOMON.

Admitted Aug. 1912. Member of Montagu Mileham & Co., of 5 and 6 Bucklersbury, E.C. Mobilised Aug. 1914, as Driver, Hon. Artillery Company, and attained the rank of Sergeant-Major. Obtained commission Oct. 1915. Served as A/Staff Capt. and subsequently as A/Major in charge of C/173rd Brigade Royal Field Artillery. Three times mentioned in Dispatches. Awarded the M.C. and French Croix de Guerre with Gold Star. Served in France and Flanders.

JOHN PERCY SOMERS.

Admitted Nov. 1898. Member of Chandler, Somers & Boulton, of 8 New Court, Lincoln's Inn, W.C. Gazetted Lieut. Territorial Force Reserve as an Instructor at N.R.A. School of Musketry Sept. 14, 1914, promoted Capt. Feb. 1915, Temp. Major Dec. 1915, Brevet Major Jan. 1918. Once mentioned in Dispatches. Awarded the O.B.E. Served during whole War at N.R.A. School of Musketry, Bisley Camp.

JOHN ROBERT SOMERS-SMITH.

Admitted July 1913. Of 5 Kensington Square Mansion, Young Street, W. Mobilised as Lieut., 5th Batt. County of London Regt. (London Rifle Brigade), and afterwards promoted Capt. Awarded the M.C. at the 2nd Battle of Ypres. Killed in action July 1, 1916.

STAFFORD EDWARD SOMERVILLE.

Admitted Dec. 1879, practising at Doncaster. Re-engaged Aug. 6, 1914, as Colonel, 5th Batt. King's Own Yorkshire Light Infantry, and served as Recruiting Officer at Doncaster.

STAFFORD DUDLEY SOMERVILLE.

Articled to S. E. Somerville, of Doncaster. Mobilised Aug. 1914, as Lieut., 5th Batt. King's Own Yorkshire Light Infantry, promoted Temp. Capt. Jan. 1915, Lieut. 1st Batt. May 1916. Served in France and Belgium. Killed at Battle of the Somme July, 5, 1916.

WILLIAM ARTHUR SOUTHALL.

Articled to G. L. Welford, of Manchester. Joined May 3, 1916, as Private, 28th (Reserve) Batt. Royal Fusiliers, and subsequently with the 12th and 24th Batts. Served in France. Wounded near Souchez April 17, 1917.

WILLIAM DOBSON SOULSBY.

Admitted Feb. 1910, practised at Blyth, Northumberland. Joined April 4, 1917, as Private, 5th (City of London) Batt. London Regt. (London Rifle Brigade). Gazetted 2nd Lieut. 6th Batt. London Regt. Feb. 29, 1918. Served in France. Killed near Peronne, Aug. 31, 1918.

WILLIAM ARTHUR SOUTHALL.

Articled to G. L. Welford, of Manchester. Served as Private, 28th (Reserve) Batt. Royal Fusiliers.

GUY SOUTHERN.

Admitted Oct. 1910. With Southern, Fullalove & Ritchie, of Burnley. Joined Nov. 20, 1915, as 2nd Lieut., 4th Batt. Gordon Highlanders, promoted Lieut. July 1917, seconded to Royal Air Force Aug. 1918, A/Capt. Nov. 1918. Served at Home 1915 to 1916 and 1916 to 1919, and in France and Belgium 1916.

NORMAN SOUTHERN.

Admitted June 1910, practising at Newcastle-upon-Tyne. Mobilised Aug. 1914, as Lieut., 3rd Northumberland Battery Royal Field Artillery (T.), promoted A/Capt. Nov. 1914, Substantive Capt. July 1916, A/Major 36th Battery 33rd Brigade, R.F.A. (8th Division), Dec. 1917 to May 1918. Awarded the M.C. Served in France and Belgium. Slightly wounded (Ypres Salient) Jan. 1916. Taken prisoner while serving with 8th Division on the Aisne May 27, 1918.

COMPTON SOUTHGATE.

Articled to J. T. Southgate, of 18 Ironmonger Lane, E.C. Served as 2nd Lieut., 14th Batt. Northumberland Fusiliers, promoted Capt. Jan. 1915. Mentioned in Dispatches and awarded the M.C.

ALFRED HENRY SOUTHRON.

Admitted March 1908. Managing Clerk with Jeffreys & Powell, of Brecon. Joined Dec. 30, 1915, as 2nd Lieut., Brecknockshire Batt. South Wales Borderers, promoted Lieut. July 1917, Temp. Capt. whilst Staff Capt 5th (MHOW) Division, India; July 1918 to Aug. 1919, Temp. Major whilst Deputy

Assistant Quartermaster General 5th (MHOW) Division, India, Aug. to Oct. 1919. Served in India Nov. 1916 to Nov. 1919.

JAMES HERBERT SOWERBY.

Admitted May 1909. Managing Clerk with Stuckey, Son & Pope, of Brighton. Joined Aug. 1914, as Private, 10th Batt. Royal Fusiliers. Served in France. Missing near Pozières July 15, 1916. Body found and buried Aug. 1917.

GEORGE HENRY JOSEPH SOWTER.

Admitted Oct. 1906. Member of Sowter & Son, of Brigg, and Scunthorpe, Lincolnshire. Mobilised Aug. 1914, as Lieut.; 5th Batt. Lincolnshire Regt., promoted Capt. Oct. 1914. Served in France and Belgium Jan. to Oct. 1915. Killed at the Hohenzollern Redoubt Oct. 13, 1915.

DONALD HARRY SPAIN.

Admitted Dec. 1910. Managing Clerk with Cotching & Son, of Horsham. Joined March 1, 1915, as Private, Royal Army Service Corps (M.T.). Commissioned to the Royal Army Service Corps Oct. 29, 1916, attached to Labour Corps 1917, promoted Capt. Royal Army Service Corps, A/Asst. Cont. of Labour, Rouen, Oct. 1918. Served in France March 1915 to May 1919.

ARTHUR PECHEY SPANTON.

Admitted Nov. 1914, practised at 15 New Broad Street, E.C. Joined July 1915, as Private, Hon. Artillery Company. Served in France Nov. 1915 to Nov. 1916. Killed in action Nov. 1, 1916.

JOHN WOODFIELD SPANTON.

Admitted Feb. 1902, practised at Leicester. Joined Sept. 1914, as Private, 4th Public Schools and University Corps. Gazetted 2nd Lieut. 6th Batt. The Rifle Brigade, afterwards with the 13th Batt. Once mentioned in Dispatches. Served in France. Wounded at Gavrelle April 26, 1917. Died from after effects June 13, 1917.

ALFRED JOHN SPARK.

Articled to Alfred Appleby, of Newcastle-upon-Tyne. Joined Nov. 17, 1915, as Private, Inns of Court O.T.C. Gazetted 2nd Lieut. Royal Field Artillery Aug. 6, 1916, promoted Temp. Capt. Jan. 1918. Once mentioned in Dispatches. Served in India, Mesopotamia, Persia, and Russia.

REGINALD BRABANT SPARKES.

Admitted April 1903, practising at Crosby Buildings, Crosby Square, E.C. Joined Aug. 22, 1914, as Private, 10th Batt. Royal Fusiliers. Gazetted 2nd Lieut. 5th Batt. The Queen's Royal West Surrey Regt. March 26, 1915, promoted Lieut. Aug. 1915, Capt. Dec. 1916. Once mentioned in Dispatches. Awarded the M.C. Served at Home and in France. Wounded at Omiécourt, France, March 26, 1918.

ERIC SPARKS.

Articled to William Sparks, of 32 Walbrook, E.C. Served as 2nd Lieut. 3rd (Southdown) Batt. Royal Sussex Regt., promoted Capt. April 1917. Mentioned in Dispatches.

FREDERICK JAMES SPARKS.

Admitted Dec. 1903. Deputy Town Clerk, Portsmouth. Joined Aug. 16, 1914, as Capt., 4th Batt. Wiltshire Regt. Served in India. Resigned Sept. 26, 1916.

LIONEL CUTHBERT LANGDON SPARKS.

Admitted May 1911, practising at 63 and 64 Chancery Lane, W.C. Served as Private, 2nd Batt. Dorsetshire Regt.

ARTHUR EDWARD SPARLING.

Admitted Dec. 1904. Member of Sparling & Son, of Colchester. Joined Sept. 1914, as 2nd Lieut., 8th (Reserve) Cyclist Batt. Essex Regt, promoted Lieut. Jan. 1915. Served at Home. Died from pneumonia Feb. 18, 1915.

CYRIL WELLESLEY SPARROW.

Admitted July 1906, practising at 3 St. Helen's Place, E.C. Joined Sept. 15, 1914, as Private, Public Schools Batt. (16th Service Batt.) Middlesex Regt. Gazetted 2nd Lieut. 3rd (Special Reserve) Batt. King's Shropshire Light Infantry June 8, 1915, promoted Lieut. July 1, 1917, Assistant to the Controller of Iron and Steel Production, Ministry of Munitions, London, Jan. 1917 to Feb. 1919. Served at Home.

WILLIAM AUSTIN SPARROW.

Admitted April 1906, practising at Bath. Joined Dec. 27, 1916, as Private, Gloucestershire Regt., posted to Army Pay Office, Warwick, Jan. 1917, promoted Lance-Corporal April 1917 and Corporal Jan. 1918, transferred to 1st (Garrison) Batt. Worcestershire Regt. April 1918, to 5th Batt. July 1918, and to 1st Batt. Oct. 1918, promoted A/Lance-Sergeant Dec. 1918. Served at Home, France, and Belgium.

HERBERT OTTO SPATZ.

Articled to C. G. Dehn, of 85 London Wall, E.C. Joined Sept. 3, 1914, as Private, 18th Batt. Royal Fusiliers. Gazetted 2nd Lieut. Middlesex Regt. Sept. 26, 1916, promoted Lieut. March 1918. Awarded the M.C. Served in France, Flanders, and Italy.

HENRY LAWRENCE SPEAR.

Admitted April 1904, practising at Plymouth. Joined Jan. 3, 1917, as A/Paymaster, Army Pay Department.

JAMES HABERSHAM SPEEDING.

Admitted Feb. 1895. Member of Wilford, Speeding & Waller, of Sunderland. Served as Capt., Royal Garrison Artillery, promoted Major June 1916. Mentioned in Dispatches. Awarded D.S.O.

DAVID EWART SPEIGHT.

Admitted April 1902. Member of Armitage & Speight, of Leeds. Joined the O.T.C. Sept. 1914. Gazetted 2nd Lieut. Royal Engineers Feb. 19, 1915, promoted Lieut. June 1915, Capt. Sept. 1915, Major Feb. 1918. Once mentioned in Dispatches. Awarded the M.C., Chevalier de l'ordre Leopold, and Croix de Guerre (Belgian). Served at Home Sept. 1914 to Dec. 1915, in Egypt Dec. 1915 to Feb. 1916, and in France Feb. 1916 to March 1919.

CHARLES EDWARD SPENCER.

Admitted Dec. 1911, practising at Monument Station Buildings, E.C. Joined Jan. 1917, as Private, Inns of Court O.T.C. Gazetted 2nd Lieut. Royal Garrison Artillery Sept. 2, 1917, appointed to 63rd Siege Battery Oct. 1917, promoted Lieut. March 1919, appointed to Headquarters 72nd (Army) Brigade March 1919. Served in France Oct. 1917 to July 1919.

GERALD THEODOSIUS LEIGH SPENCER.

Admitted Feb. 1909. Managing Clerk with Stone, Thomas & King, of Bath. Joined Sept. 10, 1914, as Private, 14th Batt. Royal Warwickshire Regt. Gazetted 2nd Lieut. in same Regt. Dec. 2, 1914, promoted Lieut. Jan. 1915, Capt. May 1919, Adjutant 14th Batt. Royal Warwickshire Regt. June 1915 to Aug. 1917, Company Commander 51st Batt. Devonshire Regt. Aug. 1917 to Nov. 1918, Education Officer to Batt. Jan. to May 1919 and to 3rd Southern Infantry Brigade May to Nov. 1919. Awarded O.B.E. (Military Division). Served at Home Sept. 1914 to Nov. 1915 and Aug. 1916 to April 1919, in France Nov. 1915 to Aug. 1916, and in Germany April to Nov. 1919.

HAROLD JOHN SPENCER.

Admitted June 1914, practising at Nottingham. Served with 2nd Batt. (Robin Hood's) Notts and Derby Regt. (Sherwood Foresters).

RICHARD BASSET SPENCER.

Admitted April 1909. Member of R. H. Spencer & Son, of Tredegar. Joined Oct. 1, 1914, as 2nd Lieut., 3rd Batt. Monmouthshire Regt. (T.), promoted Temp. Lieut. Oct. 1915, Temp. Capt. May 1916, Permanent Lieut. June 1916, A/Capt. Dec. 1917 to March 1918, attached 1st (Reserve) Batt. April 1917 to March 1918, to 87th Infantry Brigade Headquarters as Asst. Staff Capt. March to May 1918, and to 1/2 Batt. Monmouthshire Regt. May 1918 to April 1919. Served at Home, and in France, Belgium, and Germany.

LEOPOLD SPERO.

Articled to Dudley Evans, of 14 Stratford Place, W. Served with London University O.T.C.

ARTHUR CHARLES NEWTON SPICER.

Articled to P. L. H. Canning, of 26 Craven Street, W.C. Joined Sept. 2, 1914, as Private, University and Public Schools Brigade. Gazetted 2nd Lieut. 7th Batt. South Staffordshire Regt. Nov. 1914, and Lieut. Royal Air Force Feb. 1918. Served in Gallipoli. Wounded Aug. 1915.

HERBERT GEORGE SPILLER.

Admitted July 1904, practised at Taunton. Joined Sept. 6, 1917, as Private, 28th Batt. County of London Regt. (Artists Rifles). Served in France. Died of disease contracted whilst on Active Service May 7, 1920.

CECIL COOPER SPINK.

Articled to his father, F. W. Spink, of Hull. Served as 2nd Leut., 10th (Service) Batt. East Yorkshire Regt. Killed in action in France June 4, 1916.

EDWARD HOLT SPINK.

Admitted Nov. 1913, practised at Pontefract. Served as Private, 1st Batt. Royal Fusiliers.

HAROLD SPINK.

Articled to Richardson & Parker, of Scarborough. Joined Aug. 17, 1915, as Junior Reserve Attendant, Royal Naval Aux. Sick Berth Reserve, promoted to Senior Reserve Attendant June 1916. Served at Home and in Home Waters.

SYDNEY COOPER SPINK.

Articled to Grant McLean, of Brighton. Served as Sub-Lieut., Royal Naval Volunteer Reserve.

RONALD HENRY SPINNEY.

Admitted March 1910, formerly Town Clerk's Assistant, Wednesbury; and afterwards of Java. Joined March 1915, as Private, 28th Batt. County of London Regt. (Artists Rifles). Gazetted 2nd Lieut. Coldstream Guards June 30, 1915, subsequently promoted Lieut. Served in France and Belgium. Wounded June 27, 1916. Died of wounds in hospital at Abeele, near Poperinghe, July 2, 1916.

GUY LEOPOLD SPOONER.

Admitted Aug. 1899, practising at Plymouth. Joined Oct. 6, 1914, as Sub-Lieut., Royal Naval Reserve. Gazetted 2nd Lieut. Devonshire Regt. June 16, 1916, subsequently Brigade Musketry Officer 227th Brigade, and Staff Capt. 68th Division. Served in North Sea, and in Belgium and France.

ARTHUR SPOTTISWOODE.

Articled to Arthur Whitehead, of 29 Spring Gardens, S.W. Joined Sept. 14, 1914, as Private, 16th Batt. Middlesex Regt. and attained the rank of Sergeant. Gazetted Temp. 2nd Lieut. 1914, Temp. Lieut. 1915, Temp. Capt. 1915, A/Major 1918, served with 16th, 24th, 2nd, and 19th Batts. Middlesex Regt. and 26th Batt. Royal Fusiliers. Awarded the M.C. and Bar. Served in France, Belgium, and Germany July 1916 to May 1917 and June 1918 to Feb. 1919.

GILBERT EDWIN SPRAKE.

Admitted April 1910. Member of D. L. Sprake & Son, of Accrington. Mobilised Aug. 1914, as Lieut., 5th Batt. East Lancashire Regt. (T.). Served in Egypt Sept. 1914 to May 1915. Killed in action at the Dardanelles June 7, 1915.

THOMAS EDGE SPROSTON.

Admitted Dec. 1910, practising at Newcastle-under-Lyme. Mobilised Aug. 1914, as 2nd Lieut., North Midland Royal Garrison Artillery (T.), promoted Lieut. Jan. 1915, Capt. June 1717. Served in France. Invalided out April 23, 1918.

FREDERICK WILLIAM SPROTT.

Admitted Oct. 1912. Of Bombay. Served as 2nd Lieut., Indian Reserve of Officers (attached 92nd Punjabis). Died at Amara, in Mespotamia, Aug. 25, 1916.

ALWYN HOLBERTON SQUARE.

Admitted Dec. 1909. Member of Clarke, Clarke & Square, of 28 Bolton Street, Piccadilly, W. Served as Driver, "A" Battery, Hon. Artillery Company. Gazetted 2nd Lieut. 127th Battery Royal Field Artillery, promoted Capt. Feb. 1918. Mentioned in Dispatches. Awarded M.C.

EDWARD ELLIOT SQUARE.
Admitted July 1896. Member of Elliot Square & Geake, of Plymouth. Joined June 20, 1918, as Gunner, Royal Garrison Artillery, promoted Lance-Bombardier Sept. 1918. Served at Home.

SIDNEY ELLIOT SQUARE.
Admitted Nov. 1899. Of Bodmin, Cornwall. Joined June 1916, as Gunner, Royal Garrison Artillery. Served in German East Africa 2 years.

CHARLES STEPHENSON SQUIRES.
Admitted March 1914. Member of Merrimans, of 3 Mitre Court, Temple, E.C. Joined Aug. 5, 1914, as Private, Inns of Court O.T.C.

CHARLES NOBLE STACEY.
Articled to J. H. Milton, of 9 Staple Inn, W.C. Served as Lieut., 7th Batt. Middlesex Regt. Killed in action in France May 10, 1915.

HERBERT LEONARD STACEY.
Admitted Jan. 1906, practised at Liverpool. Served as 2nd Lieut., 7th Batt. King's Liverpool Regt. (T.). Died of wounds July 31, 1917.

JAMES OLIVER STACEY.
Admitted Nov. 1902. Member of Macdonald & Stacey, of 2 Norfolk Street, W.C. Served as Private, Royal Air Force.

JOHN ATHERFOLD STACEY.
Admitted Jan. 1905, practising at Manchester. Joined May 23, 1915, as Gunner, Royal Field Artillery, transferred to Royal Garrison Artillery Jan. 1918. Served with Heavy Trench Mortars May 1916 to June 1918. Served in Egypt Dec. 1915 to Feb. 1916 and in France March 1916 to June 1918. Wounded at Chocques (Béthune) June 16, 1918.

CHARLES ERIC STADDON.
Admitted April 1913. Joined May 1915, as Private, Inns of Court O.T.C. Gazetted 2nd Lieut. 2/5 Batt. The Queen's Own Royal West Kent Regt. (T.) Sept. 18, 1915, promoted Lieut. July 1917, Capt. Aug. 1918. Served in India 1917, Mesopotamia 1917 to 1919, and in Afghanistan 1919.

HARRY KENNETH STADDON.
Articled to G. C. Bantoft, of Ipswich. Joined Nov. 15, 1914, as Private, 1st (Reserve) East Anglian Field Ambulance (T.). Gazetted 2nd Lieut., 2/6 (Cyclist) Batt. Suffolk Regt. (T.) Feb. 12, 1915, promoted Lieut. Dec. 1915, promoted A/Capt. 4th Batt. Oct. 1917. Once mentioned in Dispatches. Served at Home and in France.

HUBERT LANGLEY STAFFORD.
Admitted Jan. 1914, practising at Newcastle-upon-Tyne. Served as Lieut., 5th Batt. Northumberland Fusiliers (T.), promoted Capt. Feb. 1915.

GEORGE STAINTON.
Admitted Nov. 1899, practising at Whitstable, Kent. Joined Jan. 5, 1916, as Lieut. and Quartermaster, Royal Army Medical Corps, transferred to

General List Nov. 1918 and appointed Staff Lieut. (2nd Class), subsequently promoted Capt. Jan. 1919, Staff Lieut. (1st Class) March 1919.

GEOFFREY WILLIAM STALLARD.

Articled to A. W. Stallard, of 27 Old Jewry, E.C. Served as Flight Officer, Royal Naval Air Service.

RICHARD HENRY STALLARD.

Articled to J. H. Thursfield, of Kidderminster. Served as Lieut., 8th (Reserve) Batt. Worcestershire Regt., promoted Capt. March 1918. Mentioned in Dispatches and awarded M.C. and Bar.

PERCIVAL VERE STALLON.

Admitted Dec. 1903. Member of Percy Robinson & Co., of 15 Great Marlborough Street, W. Gazetted 2nd Lieut. 3rd Batt. The Welch Regt. Aug. 5, 1916, subsequently promoted Lieut. Awarded the M.C.

SIDNEY ROBERT STAMMERS.

Articled to S. J. R. Stammers, of 52 Coleman Street, E.C. Joined Inns of Court O.T.C. as Private, Aug. 14, 1914. Gazetted 2nd Lieut. West Yorkshire Regt. Sept. 21, 1914, transferred to Motor Machine Gun Service Dec. 1914, promoted Lieut. March 1915, transferred to Royal Flying Corps Nov. 1915, promoted Capt. Jan. 1916, Flight Commander Oct. 1916 and A/Squadron Commander Nov. 1918. Once mentioned in Dispatches. Awarded the A.F.C. Served in France March 1915 to May 1916 and July 1917 to March 1918.

WILLIAM ARTHUR EDMUND STAMP.

Admitted Nov. 1901. Member of Dunning, Rundle & Stamp, of Honiton and Ottery St. Mary. Joined Aug. 4, 1914, as Capt., 4th Batt. Devonshire Regt. Once mentioned in Dispatches. Served at Home Aug. to Oct. 1914, in India Oct. 1914 to Feb. 1916, and in Mesopotamia Feb. 1916 to Feb. 1919. Wounded West of Hai, in Mesopotamia, Jan. 29, 1917.

HERBERT CLAUDE STANFORD.

Admitted April 1914. Of Weybridge. Joined Aug. 10, 1914, and gazetted 2nd Lieut. 7th Batt. Suffolk Regt. Sept. 1914, promoted Lieut. Dec. 1914, Capt. March 1916, transferred to General List March 1917. Awarded the M.C. Served in France and Belgium.

JAMES GORDON STANIER.

Admitted April 1908. Of Victoria, British Columbia. Served as Private, 4th Field Ambulance, Canadian Army Medical Corps.

GEOFFREY STANILAND.

Admitted Aug. 1903. Member of Allisons & Staniland, of Louth. Joined Sept. 29, 1914, as 2nd Lieut., 1/4 Batt. Lincolnshire Regt. Served in France. Killed in action April 13, 1915.

MEABURN STANILAND.

Admitted May 1903. Member of Staniland & Son, of Boston, Lincs. Mobilised Aug. 1914, as Capt., 4th Batt. Lincolnshire Regt. (T.). Served in France. Killed in action July 29, 1915.

FRANCIS OLIVER STANSFIELD.

Articled to Josiah Longland, of Warrington. Joined Sept. 4, 1914, as Private, 19th Batt. King's Liverpool Regt. and attained the rank of Sergeant. Gazetted 2nd Lieut. 18th Batt. Lancashire Fusiliers June 19, 1916, promoted Lieut. Dec. 1917, transferred to King's African Rifles Feb. 1918. Served in France Nov. 1915 to July 1916, and in East Africa Feb. 1918 to March 1919. Wounded at Battle of Somme (Trones Wood) July 22, 1916.

CLAUDE WILFRID STANTON.

Articled to his father, J. W. Stanton, of Chepstow. Served as Capt., 1st Batt. Monmouthshire Regt. Killed in action near Ypres May 8, 1915.

HORACE MILLS ALDERSON STANTON.

Articled to Richard Wade, of Market Deeping, Lincs. Joined June 10, 1915, as Private, Inns of Court O.T.C. Gazetted 2nd Lieut. Royal Field Artillery (Special Reserve) June 17, 1916, promoted Lieut. Dec. 1917. Served in Ireland June to July 1916, India Sept. to Dec. 1916, Mesopotamia Jan 1917 to July 1918, Persia July to Sept. 1918, Turkestan Sept. to Nov. 1918, Caucasus Nov. 1918 to April 1919.

JOHN STANTON.

Admitted Feb. 1911. Member of Stanton & Sons, of Chorley, Lancs. Served as 2nd Lieut., Royal Army Service Corps (M.T.), promoted Lieut., Nov. 1917.

REGINALD WALKER STAPLETON.

Admitted March 1912. Member of J. A. Stapleton & Son, of Dewsbury. Served as 2nd Lieut., York and Lancaster Regt., promoted Lieut. Sept. 1918.

HENRY MILES STAPYLTON-SMITH.

Admitted June 1915, practising with H. G. Stapylton-Smith, of Bexhill, Sussex. Joined Oct. 25, 1915, as Private, Royal Army Service Corps (M.T.). Gazetted 2nd Lieut. in same Regt. April 26, 1917, promoted Lieut. Oct. 1918. Once mentioned in dispatches. Served at Home Oct. to Dec. 1915, and in France, Belgium, and Germany Dec. 1915 to June 1919.

JOHN CHARLES STARKIE.

Admitted Nov. 1909. Member of Wallis & Starkie, of Doncaster. Joined Aug. 12, 1916, as Driver, Hon. Artillery Company. Killed in action July 20, 1917.

HUGH SHEARDOWN STAVELEY.

Articled to Geo. L. Shackles, of Hull. Joined Oct. 1914, as Private, 11th Batt. East Yorkshire Regt., subsequently granted a commission as 2nd Lieut. in the same Regt. Served at Home and in France. Killed in action at Oppy Ridge May 3, 1917.

JOHN WALTER STEAD.

Admitted April 1886, practising at Leeds. Raised the 15th Batt. West Yorkshire Regt. (The Leeds Pals) and commanded them on mobilisation, afterwards commanded the 11th Batt. King's Own Yorkshire Light Infantry. Served at Home and in France 1914 to 1916.

GRAHAM STRANG STEEL.

Admitted July 1900. Member of Morley, Shirreff & Co., of 53 Gresham House, Old Broad Street, E.C. Served as Capt., Royal Air Force.

ARNOLD FRANCIS STEELE.

Articled to W. M. Willcocks, of 218 Strand, W.C. Joined Sept. 9, 1915, as Private, British Red Cross Society. Promoted Officer 4th Class Dec. 1916, Officer 3rd Class June 1918, Adjutant No. 4 Branch Dec. 1916 to April 1919. Once mentioned in Dispatches. Served in France.

ERIC STEELE.

Articled to Harmer Steele, of 21 College Hill, E.C. Served as 2nd Lieut., 18th Batt. County of London Regt. (London Irish Rifles).

HUGH RUTHERFORD CLUNNY BIDEN STEELE.

Admitted April 1902, practising at Westminster. Joined March 1, 1915, as Private, Inns of Court O.T.C., and attained the rank of Sergeant. Subsequently Capt. Royal Berkshire Regt.

LESLIE FAWCETT STEMP.

Articled to White & Leman, of Bank Buildings, Ludgate Circus, E.C. Joined Aug. 4, 1915, as Cadet, University of London O.T.C., subsequently Lieut., A/Capt., and A/Major. Prisoner in Germany May 27 to Dec. 13, 1918.

BERNARD CLEMENT STENNING.

Admitted April 1905, practised at 64 Cannon Street, E.C., and Leatherhead. Joined 1916 as Private, King's Royal Rifle Corps. Gazetted 2nd Lieut. East Surrey Regt. Dec. 1916. Served in France. Died July 26, 1917, from wounds received the same day.

LESSEL PALMER STEPHEN.

Admitted May 1897, formerly practising at 18 & 19 Ironmonger Lane, E.C. Joined 1915 as Lieut., Royal Army Service Corps, and subsequently promoted A/Capt.

EDWARD WILLIAM STEPHENS.

Articled to Guy Tassell, of Faversham. Joined Oct. 1914 as 2nd Lieut., 4th Batt. Royal West Kent Regt., and attained the rank of Capt. Served in France.

HAROLD EDRIC STEPHENS.

Admitted Oct. 1911. Practising at 38 Lincoln's Inn Fields, W.C. Joined Inns of Court O.T.C. Aug. 1914. Commissioned 2nd Lieut. 6th Batt. Oxford & Bucks Light Infantry Sept. 12, 1914, promoted Lieut. Nov. 1914, Capt. Feb. 1915. Served at Home, and in France and Belgium. Wounded March 6, 1916.

JOHN HERRING STEPHENS.

Admitted Jan. 1903, practised at Winchcomb, Glos. Served as Lieut., Royal Engineers. Mentioned in Dispatches.

CHARLES HAROLD SIMPSON STEPHENSON.

Admitted March 1907. Member of Mee & Co., of Retford. Joined Nov. 25, 1915, as 2nd Lieut., 8th Batt. Notts and Derby Regt. (Sherwood Foresters), subsequently promoted Lieut. Once mentioned in Dispatches. Served at Home and in France. Wounded near Le Touret, Béthune, Sept. 5, 1918.

HARRY STEPHENSON.

Admitted June 1899, practising at Leeds. Joined Sept. 6, 1916, as Gunner, Royal Garrison Artillery. Gazetted 2nd Lieut. Royal Garrison Artillery June 6, 1917, promoted Lieut. Dec. 1918. Served with 298th, 335th and 92nd Siege Batteries. Served in Belgium and France.

PAUL STEPHENSON.

Admitted March 1905, practised at Paignton. Served as 2nd Lieut. 6th (Reserve) Batt. Notts and Derby Regt. (Sherwood Foresters), promoted Lieut. Jan. 1918.

CHARLES ARRAGON STEVENS.

Admitted Dec. 1898, practising at Bristol. Served as Lance-Corporal, Bristol University O.T.C.

FRANK BENTHAM STEVENS.

Admitted Jan. 1906. Member of Stevens & Son, of Brighton. Joined April 10, 1916, as Private, Sussex Yeomanry, transferred to Royal Flying Corps (Balloons) July 1916. Gazetted 2nd Lieut. (General List) Sept. 1, 1916, appointed Balloon Officer Sept. 1916, promoted Lieut. and Balloon Commander April 1917, awarded Observer's Wing May 1917, promoted Capt. and Balloon Company Commander Dec. 1917. Served at Home April to Oct. 1916 and Dec. 1917 to Oct. 1918, and in France Oct. 1916 to Dec. 1917 and Oct. 1918 to Jan. 1919.

GEORGE ERIC STEVENS.

Admitted Oct. 1912. Managing Clerk with Stevens & Son, of Brighton. Joined Sept. 1914, as Private, University and Public Schools Corps, subsequently Stretcher Bearer in 20th Batt. Royal Fusiliers. Served in France. Killed in action near Cambrin, Pas de Calais, France, March 13, 1916.

GEORGE SOUTHALL STEVENS.

Admitted Feb. 1906. Managing Clerk with Stevens, Miller & Jones, of Norwich. Joined Sept. 1914, as Private, 2/4 Batt. Norfolk Regt. (T.). Gazetted 2nd Lieut. in same Regt. July 1915, promoted Lieut. 1917. Served in France Oct. 1916 to May 1918 with 2nd Batt. Manchester Regt., and subsequently with the 32nd Trench Mortar Battery. Gassed at Nieuport 1917.

HAROLD CHARLES GILBARD STEVENS.

Articled to G. D. Docker, of Dorchester, Dorset. Joined Feb. 12, 1915, as 2nd Lieut., 10th Batt. Manchester Regt., promoted Lieut. June 1916, Staff Dec. 1917 to Aug. 1919. Served in France 1916 to 1917.

JOHN JULIEN CHURCH STEVENS.

Articled to R. A. Stevens, of 32 Victoria Street, Westminster, S.W. Joined Aug. 15, 1915, as Private, in 28th Batt. County of London Regt. (Artists Rifles). Granted commission as 2nd Lieut. in 5th Batt. South Staffordshire Regt. Nov. 27, 1915, promoted Lieut. July 1917. Served in Irish Rebellion April 1916, and in France Aug. to Oct. 1916. Wounded Sept. 30, 1916.

FREDERICK LEOPOLD STEWARD.

Admitted Dec. 1910, practising as Manby & Steward, at Wolverhampton. Joined Aug. 8, 1914, as Private, 8th Batt. Worcestershire Regt. (T.) and attained the rank of Lance-Sergeant. Gazetted 2nd Lieut. 6th Batt. South Staffordshire Regt. (T.) March 1, 1915, promoted Lieut. and subsequently appointed Appeal National Service Representative, M.N.S., Wolverhampton. Served at Home and in France. Wounded April 25, 1915. Demobilised May 1, 1918.

GERRARD BULWER STEWARD.

Admitted Feb. 1907. Member of Steward & Rouse, of Ipswich. Joined Sept. 17, 1914, as Capt., Suffolk Regt., promoted Major Jan. 1918. Once mentioned in Dispatches. Awarded the M.C. Served in France. Injured, permanently, in horse accident at Ypres.

RUSSELL GODFREY STEWARD.

Admitted March 1895. Member of Pretty, Joseph & Steward, of Ipswich. Joined Sept. 7, 1914, as 2nd Lieut., Norfolk Regt., subsequently promoted Capt. and Temp. Major, Adjutant 3/4 Batt. Suffolk Regt. June 1915 to March 1916, Headquarter Staff 64th (Highland) Division March 1916 to May 1919.

BERTRAND STEWART.

Admitted Oct. 1897. Member of Markby, Stewart & Co., of 57 Coleman Street, E.C. Mobilised Aug. 1914, as Capt., West Kent Yeomanry. Served with the Cavalry Division of the B.E.F. on the Staff of the General. Killed in action Sept. 16, 1914.

DOUGLAS MARTIN STEWART.

Admitted Feb. 1912. Of York. Served as Private, 38th Divisional Train, Royal Army Service Corps.

EDWARD STEWART.

Admitted Feb. 1882. Of Alton, Hants. Joined Aug. 5, 1914, as Private, 1/4 Batt. Hampshire Regt., and attained the rank of A/Sergeant. Served in India and Mesopotamia. Discharged July 28, 1916.

FRANCIS JOHN STEWART.

Admitted Nov. 1907. Member of F. Stewart & Son, of 25 Laurence Pountney Lane, E.C. Joined Sept. 22, 1916, as Private, 28th Batt. County of London Regt. (Artists Rifles). Gazetted 2nd Lieut. Royal Garrison Artillery March 12, 1917, A/Capt. and Adjutant Sept. 1917 to May 1918, promoted Lieut. Sept. 1918. Served at Home and in France.

ROBERT STROTHER STEWART.

Admitted Nov. 1905, formerly practising at Newcastle-upon-Tyne. Served as 2nd Lieut., Tynemouth Royal Garrison Artillery, promoted Lieut. June 1916.

JOSEPH EDWARD DANTHORPE STICKNEY.

Admitted Aug. 1903, practising at Hull. Joined June 1915 as 2nd Lieut., 4th Batt. East Yorkshire Regt., promoted Capt. 4th Batt. York and Lancaster Regt. July 1916, A/Major March to Aug. 1917 and March 1918 to March 1919. Twice mentioned in Dispatches. Awarded the D.S.O. and M.C. and Bar. Served in France. Wounded July 29, 1917.

ERNEST ARTHUR STIEBEL.

Admitted Sept. 1902, practised at Lennox House, Norfolk Street, W.C. Joined Nov. 1, 1915, as Private, Inns of Court O.T.C. Died Aug. 24, 1917, from illness contracted during training in O.T.C.

FREDERIC WILLIAM CHEERE STILEMAN.

Admitted March 1913. Member of Stileman & Underwood, of 7 Bedford Row, W.C. Joined Aug. 1914, as Private, Hon. Artillery Company. Given a commission as Capt. in the 11th Batt. Gloucestershire Regt. Jan. 1915. Served at Home Aug. 1914 to July 1916 and in France July 13 to 23, 1916. Reported missing as on July 23, 1916, and assumed to have been killed on that day.

EDGAR WATSON STILES.

Admitted Jan. 1904, practised at Berwick-upon-Tweed. Joined July 1915, as 2nd Lieut., 7th Batt. Northumberland Fusiliers (T.F.), and afterwards promoted Lieut. Served latterly with 149th Trench Mortar Battery. Once mentioned in Dispatches. Served in France and Belgium. Died of wounds at St. Omer, France, April 13, 1918.

HENRY JOHN EDWIN STINSON.

Admitted Dec. 1912. Member of Peachey & Co., Arundel House, Arundel Street, Strand, W.C. Joined Aug. 1914, as Private, Inns of Court O.T.C. Subsequently commissioned in Royal Garrison Artillery and attained rank of Major 111th Heavy Battery. Awarded M.C. and Bar. Served in France.

ARTHUR WILLIAM SINCLAIR STOCKDALE.

Admitted June 1913. Of 102 Albion House, New Oxford Street, W.C.; and Sunderland. Joined Sept. 4, 1914, as Private, 7th Batt. Durham Light Infantry. Gazetted 2nd Lieut. in same Regt. Feb. 9, 1915. Served in France April to May 1915. Killed at 2nd Battle of Ypres May 24, 1915.

FRANK STOCKDALE.

Articled to J. H. Stockdale, of Wednesbury, Staffs. Joined Sept. 1914, as Private, 16th Batt. Royal Warwickshire Regt. Gazetted 2nd Lieut. Jan. 1915, promoted Lieut. April 1916, transferred to Royal Welch Fusiliers and gazetted Capt. Aug. 1917. Once mentioned in Dispatches. Served in France Nov. 1915 to Sept. 1916 and in Salonica Jan. 1917 to Sept. 1918. Wounded in the Doïran Offensive on Sept. 18, 1918, and died the next day.

GUY NELSON STOCKDALE.

Articled to Charles Lupton, of Leeds. Mobilised Aug. 1914, as 2nd Lieut., 1st Batt. West Yorkshire Regt., promoted Lieut. March 1915, Capt. Jan. 1917, A/Major June 1917, transferred as 2nd in Command to 11th Batt. Essex Regt. March 1918. Awarded the M.C. and Bar. Served in France Sept. 1914 to Aug. 1915, and May 1916 to March 1918. Wounded Feb. 6, 1915. Missing and later presumed killed near Morchies March 21, 1918.

GORDON LIST TRELAWNEY STOCKER.

Admitted Dec. 1913. Member of Brown, Briggs & Co., of Stockport. Served as Lieut., Royal Army Service Corps.

ARTHUR STOCKTON.

Admitted Jan. 1891. Member of Stockton, Sons & Fortescue, of Banbury. Mobilised Aug. 1914, as Lieut.-Col., 4th Batt. Oxford and Bucks Light Infantry. Served at Home.

JAMES GODFREY STOCKTON.

Articled to A. E. Eves, of 7 Mark Lane, E.C. Mobilised Aug. 5, 1914, with Inns of Court O.T.C. Commissioned 2nd Lieut. Oxford and Bucks Light Infantry Sept. 3, 1914, promoted Lieut. July 1915, Capt. June 1917. Served in France May 1916 to Aug. 1917. Killed in action Aug. 22, 1917.

ILLTYD HENRY STOCKWOOD.

Articled to S. H. Stockwood, of Bridgend. Served as 2nd Lieut., 4th Batt. South Wales Borderers.

JOHN ARTHUR STOCKWOOD.

Admitted March 1903, practised at Bridgend, South Wales. Joined Aug. 1914, as Private, 10th Batt. The Rifle Brigade, and subsequently promoted to Sergeant. Served in France. Killed at Guillemont Sept. 3, 1916.

RALPH CYRIL STODDARD.

Articled to W. M. Wilson, of Alfreton. Joined Oct. 20, 1914, as 2nd Lieut., 10th Batt. South Lancashire Regt., transferred to Royal Flying Corps as Flight Lieut. Oct. 1915. Served in France. Killed while flying near Grandecourt July 3, 1916.

ADRIAN BEATSON STOKES.

Admitted Sept. 1890, practised at Southwark and Hove. Served as Private, 6th (Cyclist) Batt. Royal Sussex Regt.

REGINALD ALEXANDER STOKES.

Admitted Dec. 1913, practised at Hong Kong. Joined March 10, 1915, as Temp. 2nd Lieut. 9th Batt. King's Own Yorkshire Light Infantry, promoted Lieut. Sept. 1916. Served in France 1915 to 1917. Killed near La Bassée Feb. 24, 1917.

THOMAS ADRIAN OWEN STOKES.

Admitted Nov. 1896. Member of Breese, Jones & Casson, of Portmadoc. Joined Sept. 1918, as Private, Duke of Lancaster's Own Yeomanry. Served at Home (Ireland).

WILLIAM RUSSELL STOKES.

Articled to G. Stokes, of 21 Great St. Helen's, E.C. Joined Aug. 8, 1914, as Private, Hon. Artillery Company. Obtained commission as 2nd Lieut. 9th Batt. King's Own Yorkshire Light Infantry Feb. 10, 1915, transferred to Machine Gun Corps Sept. 1916, promoted Lieut. Sept. 1916. Served in France. Wounded April 13, 1918.

ARNOLD STONE.

Admitted July 1912. Managing Clerk with Evan Barlow, of Leicester. Mobilised Aug. 1914, as Lieut., 5th Batt. Notts and Derby Regt. (T.), promoted Capt. 1915, gazetted to permanent rank as Capt. 1917. Served in France

May 1915 to April 1917. Reported missing April 29, 1917, and since presumed to have been killed that day.

ARTHUR STONE.

Admitted Jan. 1903. Member of Stones, Morris & Stone, of 41 Moorgate Street, E.C. Served as Lieut.-Col., Lancashire Fusiliers. Awarded the D.S.O. Killed in action Oct. 2, 1918.

FRANCIS LE STRANGE STONE.

Admitted April 1910. Member of Stones, Morris & Stone, of 41 Moorgate Street, E.C. Served as 2nd Lieut., 3rd (King's Own) Hussars, promoted Lieut. Sept. 1916. Mentioned in Dispatches. Awarded the M.C.

FREDERICK ARTHUR STONE.

Admitted July 1, 1914. Managing Clerk with F. S. Wingent, Solicitors' Department, Hearts of Oak Benefit Society, Euston Road, N.W. Joined May 9, 1917, as Gunner, Royal Horse Artillery, transferred to Royal Garrison Artillery April 1918 and promoted Bombardier March 1919. Served in France, Germany, and at Home.

ROLAND STONE.

Admitted Oct. 1904, practised at Derby. Served as 2nd Lieut., Notts and Derby Regt. (Sherwood Foresters), promoted Lieut. Sept. 1918.

GERALD TOWELL STONEHAM.

Articled to F. W. Stoneham, of 150–151 Fenchurch Street, E.C. Joined Sept. 3, 1914, as Private, 28th Batt. County of London Regt. (Artists Rifles). Gazetted 2nd Lieut. Nov. 28, 1914, and posted to 8th Batt. The Queen's Own Royal West Kent Regt., promoted Lieut. Oct. 1915, transferred to Royal Flying Corps Aug. 1916, gazetted Flying Officer Observer Aug. 1917, transferred to Royal Air Force April 1918, transferred to Administrative (from Flying) Branch Feb. 1919. Served in Flanders and France Oct. 1915 to March 1916, and in Aerial Defence of London May 1917 to June 1919. Sustained compound fracture of right leg in aeroplane crash Aug. 5, 1918.

MARK STOREY.

Admitted April 1906. Member of James Storey & Sons, of Sunderland. Held the rank (Permanent) of Lieut. 7th Batt. Durham Light Infantry (T.F.) at the outbreak of War, promoted Capt. (Permanent) Aug. 1914, gazetted Adjutant Aug. 1915, promoted Major (Permanent) June 1916, seconded for duty June 1917 with The Rifle Brigade (A/Adjutant June 1917 to Aug. 1918), Second in Command Aug. 1918 to Feb. 1919. Once mentioned in Dispatches. Served at Home.

JAMES PARKER STORRS.

Articled to Robert Innes, of Manchester. Joined May 1915, as Lieut., 6th Batt. Cheshire Regt., and afterwards transferred to 13th Batt. Served in France. Died of wounds Aug. 8, 1917.

EDWARD HENRY HUSSEY STOTT.

Articled to G. F. Stott, of Leeds. Joined May 3, 1916, as Private, 24th Reserve Batt. Middlesex Regt. Received Commission in Machine Gun Corps

March 25, 1917. Served at Home and in France. Killed in action Sept. 3, 1917.

HUGH OSWALD DOUGLAS STOWELL.

Admitted Nov. 1910. Of Brighton. Served as Lance-Corporal, Middlesex Regt. Killed in action May 12, 1917.

WILLIAM ROSCOE STRAHAN.

Articled to R. M. Wood, of 9 New Square, Lincoln's Inn, W.C. Joined Sept. 25, 1914, as Private, Inns of Court O.T.C. Gazetted 2nd Lieut. 18th Batt. London Regt. (London Irish Rifles) June 3, 1915, promoted Lieut. and Adjutant May 1916, Lieut. (Permanent) 1917, Capt. (Permanent) Sept. 1918. Served at Home Sept. 1914 to Nov. 1915 and Aug. 1917 to March 1919, and in France Nov. 1915 to Aug. 1917.

FRANK CECIL GEORGE STRATTON.

Admitted May 1910. Managing Clerk with Anderson & Co., of 17 Ironmonger Lane, E.C. Mobilised Aug. 4, 1914, as Capt., 9th Batt. Middlesex Regt., promoted Major 1918. Once mentioned in Dispatches. Served at Home Aug. to Oct. 1914, India Dec. 1914 to Oct. 1917, and Mesopotamia Oct. 1917 to 1919.

GEORGE FREDERIC STORRS STRATTON.

Admitted Dec. 1907. Member of Strattons, of Newport, Isle of Wight. Joined Dec. 14, 1914, as 2nd Lieut., 2/8 Batt. Hampshire Regt., promoted Temp. Lieut. Jan. 1916, Substantive Lieut. June 1916, Substantive Capt. April 1916. Once mentioned in Dispatches. Served at Home.

ALBERT HAROLD OCTAVIUS STREATFEILD.

Admitted Oct. 1904. Managing Clerk with E. F. Turner & Sons, of 115 Leadenhall Street, E.C. Mobilised Aug. 1914, as 2nd Lieut., 5th (Cinque Ports) Batt. Royal Sussex Regt., promoted Lieut. Sept. 1914, Capt. Dec. 1914. Served in France June 1915 to Jan. 1919.

WILLIAM GEORGE STREET.

Admitted Nov. 1913, practising at 12 Queen Street, Cheapside, E.C. Served as Sergeant, 9th Batt. County of London Regt. (Queen Victoria's Rifles).

DAVID LOUIS STRELLETT.

Admitted Nov. 1915, practising at 66 Whitcomb Street, W.C. Served as Private, Connaught Rangers.

MICHAEL JOHN STRETCH.

Admitted May 1913. Of Hanley. Served with Royal Naval Air Service.

EDWARD TALFOURD STRICK.

Admitted April 1906. Member of Strick & Bellingham, of Swansea. Joined Nov. 3, 1914, as 2nd Lieut., 2/6 Batt. The Welch Regt., promoted Capt. Jan. 3, 1915. Served at Home. Died June 19, 1915, of sickness or disease contracted whilst serving.

HERBERT SLADE STRICKLAND.

Admitted April 1909, practised at Hastings and Eastbourne. Joined June 6, 1915, as Sub-Lieut., Nelson Batt. Royal Naval Volunteer Reserve, subsequently transferred to Hawke Batt. Served at Lemnos and in France. Killed in action at Issy, France, Sept. 3, 1918.

HAROLD WALKER STRINGER.

Admitted Dec. 1892, practising at New Milton, Hants. Joined Dec. 1914, as Private, Royal Fusiliers. Served in France. Injured at Givenchy Dec. 1915.

PHILIP AUSTIN SELBORNE STRINGER.

Articled to G. R. Stringer, of 74–78 High Road, Kilburn, N.W. Joined Aug. 1914, as Private, 19th Batt. Royal Fusiliers. Gazetted 2nd Lieut. 5th Batt. Essex Regt. March 1915, promoted Lieut. June 1916, Capt. Sept. 1916. Served at Home and in France.

JULIAN STRODE.

Admitted Feb. 1906. Member of Morice Strode & Son, of 8 Serjeant's Inn, E.C. Joined Sept. 1, 1914, as Private, 28th Batt. County of London Regt. (Artists Rifles), promoted A/Sergeant 1916, and attached General Staff G.H.Q. France, Sergeant June 1918. Twice mentioned in Dispatches. Awarded the M.S.M. Served in France March 1915 to Dec. 1918.

THOMAS LANCELOT WILLIAM STROTHER.

Admitted Nov. 1911, practised at Harrogate. Served as Sergeant, 21st (Service) Batt. Royal Fusiliers.

DOUGLAS AIKENHEAD STROUD.

Admitted Jan. 1900. Of Wallington, Surrey. Joined Nov. 18, 1915, as Private, Inns of Court O.T.C. Gazetted 2nd Lieut. 8th City of London Batt. London Regt. (T.) (Post Office Rifles) July 30, 1916, promoted Lieut. Royal Army Service Corps Jan. 30, 1918. Served in France. Wounded at Bullecourt June 2, 1917.

ROBERT SPURRELL DACRE STUART.

Articled to R. E. Stuart, of Stroud, Glos. Served as Lieut., 5th Batt. Gloucestershire Regt., promoted Capt. March 1917.

THOMAS DUNCAN HENLOCK STUBBS.

Admitted March 1895. Member of Lucas, Hutchinson & Meek, of Middlesbrough. Mobilised as Major, Northumbrian (North Riding) Royal Garrison Artillery and subsequently with the 189th Heavy Battery, the 32nd Siege Battery, the 509th Siege Battery, and Second in Command of 4th Siege Artillery Brigade, Aldershot. Once mentioned in Dispatches. Awarded the T.D. Served in Belgium April 1915 to July 1916 and April to Oct. 1917, and at Home Aug. 1914 to April 1915, July 1916 to April 1917, and Oct. 1917 to April 1919. Twice invalided home.

GEORGE ROBERT STUBINGTON.

Admitted Nov. 1905, practised at Nottingham. Served as Lieut., 7th Batt. Notts and Derby Regt. (Sherwood Foresters) (T.), and attained the rank of Capt.

WILLIAM OWEN CECIL STUCHBERY.

Admitted Oct. 1914, practising at Maidenhead. Served as Trooper, 2nd Life Guards.

WILSON STUCKEY.

Admitted Aug. 1878, practising at Brighton. Rejoined in 1914, as Major, 4th (Reserve) Batt. Sussex Regt., and subsequently in the Royal Defence Corps. Served at Home.

WILFRED HENRY STYER.

Admitted Feb. 1913, practised at Reading. Joined Aug. 8, 1914, as 2nd Lieut., 19th Batt. London Regt. (T.), subsequently nominated 2nd Lieut. 4th Batt. Royal Fusiliers (Regulars). Served in France. Accidentally wounded at School at Blandaque, St. Omer, Oct. 26, from which he died in hospital Nov. 3, 1916.

CORNELIUS VINCENT SUCKLING.

Admitted Nov. 1905. Member of Robinson & Suckling, of Portsmouth. Mobilised Aug. 1914, as Lieut., 1/5 Batt. Royal Warwickshire Regt. (T.), promoted Capt. 1915. Served in France. Killed in action at the Battle of the Somme July 16, 1916.

ARTHUR SUGDEN.

Admitted Nov. 1909, practising at 2 Thames House, Queen Street Place, E.C. Served as Lieut., Royal Army Service Corps (M.T.).

THOMAS EDWARD SUGDEN.

Admitted Aug. 1911, practising at Keighley, Yorkshire. Joined April 1, 1917, as Driver, Hon. Artillery Company. Served in Palestine and Syria.

ARTHUR NEVILLE SUGGIT.

Admitted April 1910. Formerly member of Tetlow, Suggit & Co., of 3 Berners Street, Oxford Street, W., now at The Public Trustee Office, Kingsway, W.C. Joined Sept. 1914, as Private, 4th University and Public Schools Batt., afterwards the 21st Batt. Royal Fusiliers, promoted Corporal April 1915. Commissioned July 1916, 2nd Lieut. Norfolk Regt., 2nd Lieut. 9th Batt. Gloucestershire Regt. April 1917, promoted A/Capt. and Adjutant Feb. 1918. Once mentioned in Dispatches. Served at Home Sept. 1914 to Nov. 1915, France Nov. 1915 to April 1916, Home April 1916 to April 1917, Salonica April 1917 to July 1918, France July to Nov. 1918, Home Nov. 1918 to Jan. 1919. Wounded at Cambrin Jan. 1916.

DUDLEY LEYCESTER SUMMERHAYS.

Articled to T. C. Summerhays, of Eastcheap Buildings, Eastcheap, E.C. Enlisted as Private 5th Batt. East Surrey Regt. on outbreak of War, and afterwards obtained commission as 2nd Lieut. 9th Batt. County of London Regt. (Queen Victoria's Rifles). Killed in action on Hill 60 on April 21, 1915.

REGINALD SHERRIFF SUMMERHAYS.

Admitted Jan. 1905. Member of T. C. Summerhays & Son, of Eastcheap Buildings, London, E.C. Joined April 1, 1917, as Cadet, and subsequently gazetted Lieut. Royal Army Service Corps. Appointed in July 1918 (owing to injuries received on service) Legal Adviser to Controller Aircraft Production, Ministry of Munitions of War. Served at Home.

HERBERT WALKER SUMMERSON.

Admitted Feb. 1912, practised at Darlington. Joined Dec. 1915, as Private, 28th Batt. Royal Fusiliers. Gazetted 2nd Lieut. in 9th Batt. Loyal North Lancashire Regt. Sept. 1917. Served in France. Died of wounds June 5, 1918.

LIONEL RANDOLPH COLERIDGE SUMNER.

Articled to R. P. Sumner, of Gloucester. Joined Aug. 5, 1914, as Lieut., 1/5 Batt. Gloucestershire Regt., promoted Capt. June 1915, A/Major June 1918 and Jan. to Aug. 1919. Once mentioned in Dispatches. Awarded the M.C. Served at Home and in France. Wounded on the Somme Jan. 23, 1916, and gassed at Ypres Sept. 29, 1917.

AUBONE ALFRED SURTEES.

Admitted Feb. 1891, practising at 2 Bond Court, Walbrook, E.C. Served as Capt., 9th Batt. Northumberland Fusiliers.

JOHN EWALD SUTCLIFFE.

Admitted April 1910. Member of Eastwoods, Sutcliffes, Sager & Gledhill, of Todmorden and Hebden Bridge. Gazetted Capt. 2/6 Batt. Lancashire Fusiliers Oct. 10, 1914. Served in France. Wounded April 13, 1917. Resigned Dec. 14, 1917, on account of wounds received in action.

JOSEPH HEDLEY SUTCLIFFE.

Admitted Aug. 1911. Managing Clerk with Basil S. Briggs, of Wakefield. Joined Oct. 1914, as Private, Inns of Court O.T.C. Gazetted 2nd Lieut. 7th Batt. Essex Regt. March 8, 1915, promoted Lieut. Sept. 1915, Capt. June 1916. Served at Home owing to breakdown in health. Two years as an Education Officer 1917 to 1919.

NORMAN WARDEN SUTCLIFFE.

Articled to H. D. Sutcliffe, of Manchester. Served as Lance-Corporal, 6th Batt. Manchester Regt.

ROBERT SUTCLIFFE.

Admitted April 1904. Member of Sutcliffe & Trenholme, of Bradford. Enlisted on outbreak of War in the Public Schools Batt. Middlesex Regt. Gazetted 2nd Lieut. West Yorkshire Regt. in Oct. 1914, promoted Lieut. Served in Egypt. Died at sea of wounds received in action on July 1, 1916.

JOHN JAMES SUTHERLAND.

Admitted April 1899, practising at Gateshead. Joined June 9, 1916, as Private, Royal Fusiliers, promoted Lance-Corporal July 1916. Served in France.

ALFRED WALTER SUTTON.

Admitted Dec. 1913, practised at Newcastle-upon-Tyne. Served as 2nd Lieut., 8th Batt. Durham Light Infantry, promoted Lieut. June 1916. Mentioned in Dispatches.

CHARLES GEORGE SUTTON.

Admitted May 1909, practising at Coventry. Mobilised Aug. 1914 with 7th Batt. Royal Warwickshire Regt. (T.), promoted Capt. Aug. 1914. Served in

Flanders and France Feb. to Nov. 1915, and at Home Aug. 1914 to Feb. 1915 and Nov. 1915 to Jan. 1919. Injured by horse accident March 1916 when Staff Capt. 3/1 Warwick Infantry Brigade.

JOHN GALLIENNE SWAINSON.

Admitted April 1904. Member of Swainson, Satterthwaite & Swainson, of Lancaster. Joined Feb. 1917, as Private, 5th Batt. King's Own Royal Lancaster Regt. Gazetted 2nd Lieut. Royal Army Service Corps Dec. 1917. Served at Home Feb. to Dec. 1917, and in France Dec. 1917 to Jan. 1919.

THOMAS SWALE.

Admitted April 1915. Managing Clerk with F. J. & C. Poole, of Widnes, Lancs. Joined Sept. 24, 1915, as Corporal Despatch Rider, Signal Section, Royal Engineers. Served in France, Belgium, and Germany March 1916 to Jan. 1919.

FRANCIS BENJAMIN SWALLOW.

Admitted Oct. 1905. Of Clarence Road, Clapham Park, S.W. Served as Private, London Regt.

HAROLD EDWARD SWALLOW.

Admitted Dec. 1910. Member of Lees & Co., of Westminster. Joined Dec. 7, 1915, as Cadet, Royal Field Artillery. Gazetted 2nd Lieut. Royal Field Artillery July 14, 1916, promoted Lieut. Jan. 1918, Capt. April 1918, Major Oct. 1918. Served at Home and in France.

LEONARD SWALLOW.

Articled to A. D. Jenkins, Town Clerk, of Guildford. Joined Nov. 16, 1914, as Corporal, 5th Batt. The Queen's Royal West Surrey Regt., transferred to Hon. Artillery Company March 1915, and attained the rank of Company Sergeant-Major. Served at Home and in France. Killed in action at Beaumont Hamel Nov. 13, 1916.

JOHN HAROLD SWAN.

Articled to Percy Corder, of Newcastle-upon-Tyne. Served as 2nd Lieut., 5th Batt. Northumberland Fusiliers, promoted Capt. June 1916. Mentioned in Dispatches and awarded the M.C.

FREDERICK BERTRAND SWANWICK.

Admitted April 1912. Of Chesterfield. Served as 2nd Lieut., Derbyshire Yeomanry, promoted Capt. Dec. 1917.

EDGAR SWARBRICK.

Admitted April 1912, practising at 16 George Street, Westminster, S.W. Served as Private, Royal Army Service Corps (M.T.).

EDGAR JOHN SWAYNE.

Admitted July 1886. Member of Gold, Edwards & Co., of Denbigh. Gazetted to command 2/4 Royal Welch Fusiliers Oct. 10, 1914, appointed to command 47th Provisional Batt. June 1915, and to 23rd Batt. Royal Welch Fusiliers Jan. 1917, transferred to T.F. Reserve as Lieut.-Col. May 30, 1917. Served at Home.

GERALD HERBERT LESLIE SWEET.

Articled to J. L. Sweet, of 2 Bedford Row, W.C. Mobilised Aug. 4, 1914, as Private, 1st Batt. Hon. Artillery Company. Commissioned 2nd Lieut.

2nd Batt. Northumberland Fusiliers Feb. 14, 1915, transferred to Royal Flying Corps March 1917, and to Royal Air Force April 1918, promoted Capt. May 1917, Major Aug. 1918. Once mentioned in Dispatches. Served in France Sept. 1914 to April 1915 and Aug. to Oct. 1915, and at Home March 1917 to May 1919. Wounded at Ypres April 25, 1915, and at Loos Oct. 30, 1915.

JOHN LAXON LESLIE SWEET.

Articled to J. L. Sweet, of 2 Bedford Row, W.C. Joined 48th Highlanders of Canada at outbreak of War. Came to England with 1st Division, went to France Jan. 1915, given commission in 2nd Batt. Royal Scots Fusiliers March 1915. Recommended for D.S.O. 1915. Served in France. Killed near Givenchy June 16, 1915.

HERBERT SWINNERTON.

Admitted Dec. 1904. Member of Thompson & Debenhams, of London and St. Albans. Mobilised Aug. 1914, as Capt., 1/25 Batt. London Regt., promoted Major June 1916, Camp Commandant Headquarters North-West Frontier Force July to Oct. 1919, Deputy Assistant Adjutant Northern Command, India, Nov. 1919 to May 1920. Served at Home, in India, and in Afghan War.

HERBERT LIVINGSTON SWIRE.

Articled to C. J. Davis, of Glossop. Joined Sept. 7, 1914, as Private, 12th Batt. King's Royal Rifle Corps. Gazetted 2nd Lieut. 11th Batt. Notts and Derby Regt. (Sherwood Foresters) Sept. 26, 1917, promoted Lieut. March 1919. Awarded the M.C. and Italian Silver Medal for Valour. Served in France July 1915 to April 1917 and Aug. to Oct. 1918, and in Italy Dec. 1917 to Aug. 1918. Wounded at Guisancourt Oct. 5, 1918.

ARTHUR HOVEY CHARLESWORTH SYKES.

Articled to H. A. Sanders, of Chesterfield. Served as 2nd Lieut., 9th (Service) Batt. West Riding Regt.

BERNAL SYKES.

Admitted Feb. 1910, practised at Halifax. Served as 2nd Lieut., 7th (Reserve) Batt. West Riding Regt., promoted Lieut. June 1916.

GERALD EDWARDS SYKES.

Admitted April 1908, practising at Hull. Joined Aug. 18, 1915, as 2nd Lieut., East Riding Royal Garrison Artillery, seconded to Royal Garrison Artillery (Siege) 1916, promoted Lieut. June 1916, with 457th Siege Battery 1916 to 1917 and 450th Siege Battery 1917 to 1918, attached to General Headquarters British Rhine Army at Cologne, as Courts-Martial Officer, with Temp. rank of Capt. Dec. 1918. Served in France and Belgium and with Army of Occupation of the Rhine. Gassed near Lens July 1918.

REGINALD SYKES.

Admitted Oct. 1911, practised at Manchester. Served as Corporal, 9th Batt. King's Royal Rifle Corps. Killed in action Sept. 15, 1916.

CHARLES WILLIAM SYMES.

Admitted Dec. 1907, practised at Blandford. Served as Capt., 4th Batt. Dorset Regt. Died in Mesopotamia Oct. 9, 1915.

GEOFFREY GEORGE HETLEY SYMES.

Articled to G. P. Symes, of Weymouth. Mobilised Aug. 1914, as 2nd Lieut., Dorset Royal Garrison Artillery (T.F.), promoted Lieut. April 1915, attached "B" A.A. Battery. Served at Home Aug. 1914 to Jan. 1917, and in France Jan. 1917 to April 1919.

JOHN SYMES.

Admitted Aug. 1902, practising at Crediton, Devon. Joined Oct. 9, 1914, as 2nd Lieut., 6th Batt. Devonshire Regt., promoted Temp. Capt. July 1915, appointed a Courts-Martial Officer Oct. 1917 and attached to XXII. Corps Headquarters Jan. 1918. Once mentioned in Dispatches. Awarded the O.B.E. (Military). Served at Home 2 years, and in France 2 years and 5 months. Wounded at Bullecourt May 6, 1917.

ARTHUR GEORGE SYMONDS.

Admitted Dec. 1883. Member of Symonds & Sons, of Dorchester, Dorset. Mobilised Aug. 1914, as Major, 4th Batt. Dorset Regt. (T.). Served in India Nov. 1914 to Feb. 1916 and July 1916 to May 1918, and in Mesopotamia Feb. to July 1916.

CHRISTOPHER BARKER SYMONDS.

Admitted Oct. 1887, practised at Wirksworth. Served as Major, Royal Army Service Corps.

DANIEL GEORGE SYMONDS.

Admitted Feb. 1911. Managing Clerk with Symonds & Sons, of Dorchester. Mobilised Aug. 1914, as Lieut., 4th Batt. Dorset Regt. (T.), promoted Capt. 1914, A/Major at various times. Twice mentioned in Dispatches. Served in Mesopotamia.

JOHN DUDLEY BARKER SYMONDS.

Articled to C. B. Symonds, of Wirksworth. Served as 2nd Lieut., 6th Batt. Notts and Derby Regt. (Sherwood Foresters), promoted Capt. Dec. 1917.

WILLIAM FREDERICK JOHN SYMONDS.

Admitted Feb. 1892. Member of Nash, Field & Co., of 12 Queen Street, Cheapside, E.C. Mobilised Aug. 1914, as Major, 2/22 London Regt., subsequently Lieut.-Col. 2nd Batt. South Staffordshire Regt., 12th Batt. London Regt. and 11th Batt. London Regt. Awarded the D.S.O. Served at Home and in France. Killed in action in France April 24, 1918.

RICHARD HERBERT SYMONDS-TAYLER.

Admitted Dec. 1894. Member of Humfrys & Symonds, of Hereford. Mobilised Aug. 1914, as Major, King's Shropshire Light Infantry, transferred to the Herefordshire Regt. Dec. 1914, promoted Lieut.-Col. Jan. 1916, transferred to 4th (Reserve) Batt. Shropshire Light Infantry July 1917. Once mentioned in Dispatches. Served at Home. Resigned July 1918.

FREDERICK NOBLE SYMS.

Admitted March 1904, practised at Newcastle-upon-Tyne. Served as Lieut., 5th Batt. Northumberland Fusiliers, promoted Capt. March 1916. Mentioned in Dispatches.

THOMAS HENRY WARCUP TACON.
Admitted May 1912, practising at Eye, Suffolk. Joined Sept. 1914, as 2nd Lieut., Royal Field Artillery, promoted Temp. Lieut. Aug. 1915, Temp. Capt. March 1916, A/Major Sept. 1917, Temp. Major Feb. 1918. Once mentioned in Dispatches. Awarded the M.C. Served in France.

HAROLD TWEEDALE TAIT.
Admitted July 1906. One of the Solicitor-Assistants to London and North Western Railway Company, Euston Station. Gazetted Capt. and Group Adjutant, Middlesex Volunteer Regt. Nov. 15, 1916. Appointed full time paid Group Adjutant Oct. 1918. Served at Home.

JOHN EDWARD LIGHTFOOT TALBOT.
Articled to T. W. Williams, of Bristol. Joined Nov. 1, 1914, as Private, Gloucestershire Regt. Gazetted 2nd Lieut. Indian Army June 5, 1918, attached Political Department I.A. Aug. 1918, promoted Capt. Nov. 1918. Served in Gallipoli 1915, in Egypt 1916, and in Mesopotamia 1916 to 1918.

RUPERT KERSHAW TALBOT.
Articled to George Whittington, of Leeds. Joined Sept. 16, 1914, as 2nd Lieut., 11th Batt. West Yorkshire Regt., promoted Lieut. Dec. 1914, Capt. Jan. 1916, joined 3rd Batt. Nov. 1916. Served in France. Wounded in attack on Contalmaison July 5, 1916.

HUGH TALLENTS.
Admitted Dec. 1909. Member of Tallents & Co., of Newark-upon-Trent. Mobilised Aug. 1914, as Capt., Nottinghamshire (Sherwood Rangers) Yeomanry, promoted Major 1916. Twice mentioned in Dispatches. Awarded the D.S.O. Served in Gallipoli, Egypt, Salonica, and Palestine.

ERNEST WILLIAM TAME.
Admitted June 1913. Assistant Solicitor with Town Clerk of Bristol. Mobilised Aug. 4, 1914, as Capt., 1/6 Batt. Gloucestershire Regt. Served at Home Aug. 1914 to March 1915, in France March 1915 to Nov. 1917, and in Italy Nov. 1917 to Jan. 1919.

ARTHUR REGINALD TANFIELD.
Admitted Feb. 1914. Member of Tanfield & Tanfield, of Dudley. Joined Sept. 9, 1914, as Private. Gazetted 2nd Lieut. Worcestershire Regt. June 1915, promoted Lieut. Jan. 1916. Served in France. Wounded Sept. 9, 1916. Discharged on account of ill-health caused by wounds March 24, 1918.

LAURENCE EDGAR TANNER.
Articled to E. R. Tanner, of Bristol. Served as 2nd Lieut., 4th (City of Bristol) Batt. Gloucestershire Regt.

PHILIP FRANK TANNER.
Admitted Aug. 1898, practising at West Southbourne, Bournemouth, Hants. Joined April 14, 1917, as 2nd Lieut., 4th Batt. Dorset Regt. (T.F.), promoted Lieut. Oct. 1918, attached to 11th Batt. Somerset Light Infantry during whole period of service. Served at Home and in France and Belgium.

FREDERIC BARON TANQUERAY.

Admitted March 1914, practised at Woburn, Beds. Joined Sept. 1914, as Private, 16th Batt. Middlesex Regt. Gazetted 2nd Lieut. in same Regt. 1915. Served in France. Killed in action near Beaumont Hamel July 1, 1916.

WILLIAM MONRO TAPP.

Admitted July 1884, practising at 27 South Molton Street, W. Served as Motor Driver, attached to the Belgian Army.

CLAUD EDWARD TARBET.

Admitted July 1908. Managing Clerk with Garnett, Tarbet & Co., of Liverpool. Joined Sept. 10, 1914, as Rifleman, 6th Batt. Liverpool Regt. Gazetted 2nd Lieut., Chinese Labour Corps March 3, 1918. Served in France and Belgium.

MONTAGUE TARBET.

Articled to W. H. Tarbet, of Exeter. Joined Sept. 1914, as Private, 20th Batt. Royal Fusiliers. Commissioned as 2nd Lieut. Dorset Regt. Jan. 1915, transferred to Royal Air Force as A/Adjutant Aug. 1918. Attained rank of A/Capt. Served in France July to Dec. 1915 and Aug. 1916 to April 1917. Once wounded. Left fore-arm amputated.

FRANCIS NATHANIEL TARR.

Articled to William Simpson, of Leicester. Mobilised Aug. 1914, as Lieut., 4th Batt. Leicestershire Regt. Machine Gun Officer to the Batt., appointed A/Adjutant. Served in France to July 1915. Killed near Ypres July 18, 1915.

GEOFFREY NOWILL TASKER.

Admitted Nov. 1908, practising at Sheffield. Joined Nov. 7, 1917, as Private, Royal Army Service Corps (M.T.). Served in France.

CAUTLEY TATHAM.

Admitted Oct. 1912, practised at 11 Queen Victoria Street, E.C. Mobilised Aug. 1914, as Corporal, Hon. Artillery Company. Gazetted 2nd Lieut. in same Regt., Sept. 16, 1914, promoted Lieut. Jan. 1915, Temp. Capt. May 1915. Served in France. Wounded at the Battle of Hooge June 16, 1915. Died of wounds at Bailleul June 18, 1915.

CECIL FRANCIS TATHAM.

Admitted Oct. 1914. Managing Clerk with Freshfields & Leese, of 31 Old Jewry, E.C. Joined Oct. 1915, as 2nd Lieut., Royal Army Service Corps, promoted Lieut. July 1917, transferred to The Queen's Regt. (8th Batt.) Aug. 1917, A/Capt. Feb. 1919. Served at Home Oct. 1915 to July 1916, and in France July 1916 to March 1919.

HAROLD LEWIS TATHAM.

Admitted Feb. 1906. Member of B. & F. Tolhurst, of Gravesend, Kent. Joined April 1917, as Private, Hon. Artillery Company. Gazetted 2nd Lieut. Welch Guards Feb. 27, 1918. Served in France.

RALPH PERCEVAL TATHAM.

Admitted Dec. 1906. Member of Tatham & Procter, of 36 Lincoln's Inn Fields, W.C. Joined May 1916, as Private, 28th Batt. County of London Regt.

(Artists Rifles). Gazetted 2nd Lieut. Royal Army Service Corps June 1917, promoted Lieut. Dec. 1918. Served in France.

ALBERT CECIL TAYLOR.
Admitted July 1912. Managing Clerk with Dod, Longstaffe, Son & Fenwick, of 16 Berners Street, W. Joined Sept. 1914, as Private, University and Public Schools Batt. Royal Fusiliers. Gazetted 2nd Lieut. 3rd Batt. Suffolk Regt. May 20, 1915. Served at Home and in France. Killed at Battle of Somme, Delville Wood, July 20, 1916.

ALFRED MILES TAYLOR.
Admitted Jan. 1900, practising at Bromley, Kent. Joined Sept. 2, 1915, as Private, Inns of Court O.T.C. Gazetted 2nd Lieut. Notts and Derby Regt. (Sherwood Foresters) Jan. 4, 1916, promoted Lieut. July 1917. Served at Home, in Ireland (Rebellion of Easter 1916), and in France.

ALFRED WILLIAM TAYLOR.
Admitted Feb. 1910. Member of Taylor & Capes, of Doncaster. Served as Capt., 5th Batt. King's Own Yorkshire Light Infantry. Awarded the M.C. and O.B.E.

ARNOLD FRED TAYLOR.
Articled to F. B. Darling, of 7 New Square, Lincoln's Inn, W.C. Joined March 21, 1917, as Capt., General List, attached for duty as Adjutant to 3rd V.B. Duke of Cambridge's Own (Middlesex Regt.). Served at Home.

ARTHUR GILBERT TAYLOR.
Admitted Feb. 1913, practising at Manchester. Joined June 14, 1915, as Sapper, East Lancashire Divisional Engineers (T.F.). Commissioned 2nd Lieut. in same Regt. Aug. 17, 1915, promoted Lieut. June 1916, A/Capt. Feb. 1918. Once mentioned in Dispatches. Served at Home June 1915 to Oct. 1917, and in Palestine Oct. 1917 to July 1919.

ARTHUR TURNER TAYLOR.
Admitted April 1913. Of 115 Leadenhall Street, E.C. Served as 2nd Lieut., 2nd (City of London) Batt. Royal Fusiliers. Mentioned in Dispatches and awarded M.C.

BERTRAM GLEDHILL TAYLOR.
Articled to T. A. Davison, of Castleford. Served as Private, West Riding Division, Royal Army Service Corps.

BRYON SAMUEL WILLIAM TAYLOR.
Articled to T. A. Matthews, of Hereford. Joined Jan. 1917, as Private, Inns of Court O.T.C. Gazetted 2nd Lieut. Royal Flying Corps July 1917, promoted Lieut. Royal Air Force April 1918. Once mentioned in Dispatches. Awarded the D.F.C. Served at Home and in France.

CECIL GEORGE TAYLOR.
Admitted Aug. 1899, practising at Lowestoft. Joined Sept. 30, 1914, as Capt. in Corps of the School of Musketry, promoted Major Sept. 1918. Once mentioned in Dispatches. Awarded the O.B.E. (Military). Served at Home and in France.

CHARLES HERBERT TAYLOR.

Admitted Nov. 1911. Member of Sewell & Taylor, of Carlisle. Joined Sept. 9, 1914, as Private, 1/4 Batt. Border Regt., subsequently promoted Sergeant and Staff Colour Sergeant (Deputy Examiner in Military Accounts, Temporary Civilian Officer) Dec. 1918. Served in India.

CHARLES HILLSBOROUGH RIMINGTON TAYLOR.

Admitted April 1902, practising at 226 Kentish Town Road, N.W. Mobilised Aug. 4, 1914, as Major, 4th Batt. Essex Regt., promoted Lieut.-Col. 1918, Col. 1919. Three times mentioned in Dispatches. Awarded the O.B.E. (Military) and T.D. Served in Gallipoli, Egypt, and France.

CHARLES PAUL TAYLOR.

Admitted Feb. 1907. Member of Crossman & Co., of Thornbury, Glos.; and Bristol. Joined July 18, 1916, as Private, Royal Army Service Corps, attached 138th S.B. Royal Garrison Artillery, promoted Corporal Jan. 1917, C.Q.M.S. June 1918. Served at Home and in Macedonia with British Salonica Forces.

EDWARD MALLALIEU BROOKE TAYLOR.

Articled to H. C. B. Taylor, of Bakewell, Derbyshire. Mobilised Aug. 1914, as Lieut., 6th Batt. Notts and Derby Regt. (Sherwood Foresters) (T.), promoted Capt. Aug. 1914, G.S.O. III., 46th Division, Dec. 1917, Brigade Major 10th Infantry Brigade Aug. 1918. Twice mentioned in Dispatches. Awarded the M.C. Served in France and Belgium. Wounded May 1915.

EDWARD STEWARDSON TAYLOR.

Admitted June 1912. Member of G. Taylor & Son, of Scarborough. Served as Capt., 5th (Reserve) Batt. Yorkshire Regt.

ERIC TAYLOR.

Articled to C. R. Evans, of Bristol. Mobilised Aug. 1914, as Lieut., 4th (City of Bristol) Batt. Gloucestershire Regt. (T.F.), promoted Capt. Oct. 1914. Served in France. Invalided out July 22, 1918.

ERNEST TAYLOR.

Admitted Nov. 1911, practised at Halifax. Served as 2nd Lieut., 4th Batt. Duke of Wellington's West Riding Regt. Died 1915 of wounds received in action.

ERNEST HENRY TAYLOR.

Admitted Jan. 1911, practising at Rochdale. Joined Jan. 6, 1915, as Private, Royal Army Service Corps (M.T.), and subsequently transferred to Inns of Court O.T.C. Gazetted Lieut. 5th Batt. Loyal North Lancashire Regt., and attached Royal Engineers Signals. Served at Home, in France and Belgium, and with Army of Occupation. Wounded June 1, 1916, and Aug. 9, 1916.

ERNEST OLIVER TAYLOR.

Articled to E. S. Taylor, of Birmingham. Joined Sept. 1, 1914, as Private, 14th Batt. (1st City of Birmingham) Royal Warwickshire Regt. Gazetted 2nd Lieut. 13th Batt. Royal Warwickshire Regt. Dec. 4, 1914, promoted Lieut. Aug. 1915, Capt. Machine Gun Corps Nov. 1916, transferred to Army Signal Service Royal Engineers July 1917. Served in Egypt and Palestine.

GEOFFREY CHARLES RIMINGTON TAYLOR.

Admitted Oct. 1905, practised at 63 New Broad Street, E.C. Served as Capt., 8th (Reserve) Cyclist Batt. Essex Regt.

GERALD KYFFIN TAYLOR.

Admitted Dec. 1884. Member of Snowball, Kyffin Taylor & Pruddah, of Liverpool. Joined Jan. 10, 1915, as Colonel, Royal Artillery, promoted Hon. Brigadier-General in Aug. 1917. Awarded C.B.E. Served at Home. Retired Jan. 6, 1916.

HAROLD ISAAC TAYLOR.

Admitted March 1903. Member of Iliffe, Sweet & Co., of 2 Bedford Row, W.C. Served as Rifleman, 12th Batt. London Regt.

HARRY ALFRED TAYLOR.

Admitted Aug. 1894. Member of Stooke-Vaughan, Taylor & White, of 31 Great James Street, Bedford Row, W.C. Joined the Sportsman's Batt., as Private, March 1916 and afterwards transferred to the East Kent Regt. (The Buffs). Served at Home and in France. Died of wounds May 7, 1917.

HERBERT TAYLOR.

Admitted Nov. 1888. Member of R. A. Willcock, Taylor & Co., of Wolverhampton. Served as Lieut.-Col., 6th Batt. South Staffordshire Regt. Once mentioned in Dispatches. Awarded the T.D. Served in Irish Rebellion and in Belgium.

HERBERT BROOKE TAYLOR.

Admitted July 1878. Member of Brooke Taylor & Co., of Bakewell. Recalled Sept. 6, 1914, for special service on Staff of 45th Regimental District and given rank of Lieut.-Col., transferred to Recruiting Staff, 45th Recruiting Area, ranking as Major Aug. 1915, Head of School of Instruction No. 6 District for Recruiting Officers 1916 to 1917, sent to Ministry of National Service as Assistant Director of Recruiting for Derbyshire Nov. 1, 1917, retired June 13, 1918. Once mentioned in Dispatches. Awarded M.B.E. and C.B.E. (Military). Served at Home.

HERBERT CLIFFORD BROOKE TAYLOR.

Admitted June 1909. Member of Brooke, Taylor & Co., of Bakewell. Mobilised Aug. 1914, as Capt., 6th Batt. Notts and Derby Regt. (Sherwood Foresters), promoted Major May 1918. Served in France and at Home.

JAMES ARTHUR ATKINSON TAYLOR.

Admitted Feb. 1910, practising at Bolton. Joined April 23, 1917, as Gunner, Royal Field Artillery. Gazetted 2nd Lieut. May 31, 1918. Served in France.

JOHN TAYLOR.

Admitted Nov. 1913, practising at Halifax. Served as 2nd Lieut., 5th Batt. West Yorkshire Regt., promoted Lieut. June 1917.

JOHN NORMAN TAYLOR.

Admitted July 1908. Of Calcutta. Served as Sergeant, Calcutta Light Horse.

JOSIAH TAYLOR.

Articled to Sydney Taylor, of Buxton. Joined Aug. 1914 as Cadet Corporal. Gazetted 2nd Lieut. 6th Batt. Notts and Derby Regt. (Sherwood Foresters) Nov. 1914, promoted Temp. Lieut. June 1915, Lieut. June 1916, seconded as Lieut. to Royal Engineers (Signal Service) Aug. 1915. Twice mentioned in Dispatches. Served in France. Wounded July 1, 1917.

LEOFRIC TAYLOR.

Admitted Oct. 1904, practising at Manchester. Served as Private, 3rd (Public Schools) Batt. Royal Fusiliers.

LEONARD MAINWARING TAYLOR.

Admitted Feb. 1908. Member of Scholefield, Taylor & Maggs, of Batley, Yorks. Mobilised Aug. 1914, as Capt., 4th Batt. King's Own Yorkshire Light Infantry, Adjutant Sept. to Oct. 1914, Staff Capt. 148th Infantry Brigade, 49th Division, Nov. 1915 to Aug. 1916, Brigade Major Aug. 1916 to June 1917, promoted Major July 1917, Brigade Major 8th (Reserve) Infantry Brigade July 1917 to Feb. 1918, attached 8th Infantry Brigade, 3rd Division, March 1918, Brigade Major 10th Infantry Brigade, 4th Division, April to Aug. 1918, G.S.O. II., 6th Division, Aug. 1918 to March 1919 and to Midland Division June to Sept. 1919. Five times mentioned in Dispatches. Awarded the D.S.O., the M.C., and the Croix de Guerre (French). Served at Home Aug. 1914 to March 1915 and July 1917 to Feb. 1918, and in France and Germany March 1915 to July 1917 and Feb. 1918 to Sept. 1919.

PERCY JAMES TAYLOR.

Admitted Aug. 1897, practising at Southport. Served as Hon. Lieut., 7th Batt. King's Liverpool Regt.

PERCY WELLINGTON TAYLOR.

Admitted Dec. 1895, practising at 21 Panton Street, S.W. Joined Aug. 8, 1914, as Trooper, King Edward's Horse. Gazetted 2nd Lieut. in Royal Army Service Corps March 11, 1915, promoted Lieut. Aug. 1915, appointed Courts Martial Officer with rank of Capt. Aug. 1919. Served in Belgium and France March 1915 to Feb. 1920.

RAYMOND SEATON TAYLOR.

Admitted April 1907. Member of Seaton Taylor & Co., of 5 Gray's Inn Square, W.C. Joined Dec. 8, 1915, as Private, Hon. Artillery Company. Served in France and at Home. Gassed at St. Julien Oct. 1917. Discharged unfit for service Dec. 10, 1918.

RICHARD EARNSHAW TAYLOR.

Articled to A. W. Drury, of Goole. Served as Private, 8th Batt. King's Own Yorkshire Light Infantry.

RICHARD STEPHENS TAYLOR.

Admitted Nov. 1893. Member of R. S. Taylor, Son & Humbert, of 4 Field Court, Gray's Inn, W.C. Joined Sept. 1914, as Capt., Territorial Force Reserve, transferred to East Kent Regt. (The Buffs) March 1915, and to East Surrey Regt. Oct. 1915, promoted Major Oct. 1915. Served in France May 1916 to Jan. 1919.

ROBERT TAYLOR.
Admitted Oct. 1908, practised at Huddersfield. Served as Capt., 7th Batt. Duke of Wellington's West Riding Regt. (T.), promoted Major June 1916.

ROBERT EMERY TAYLOR.
Admitted Feb. 1907. Member of Stileman, Underwood & Taylor, of 7 Bedford Row, W.C. Joined Sept. 2, 1914, as Private, 19th Batt. Royal Fusiliers. Gazetted 2nd Lieut. 6th Batt. Middlesex Regt. April 1915, promoted Lieut. July 1917, Staff Capt. 189th Infantry Brigade Royal Naval Division April 1918. Once mentioned in Dispatches. Awarded the M.C. Served at Home Sept. 1914 to May 1916, and in France and Belgium May 1916 to July 1919.

ROLAND ORMSBY TAYLOR.
Admitted June 1913, formerly practising at Swadlincote, Derbyshire, and subsequently Assistant Solicitor to the Metropolitan Railway, London. Joined Sept. 1, 1914, as 2nd Lieut., The King's Own Royal Lancaster Regt., promoted Lieut. July 1917. Afterwards attached General Headquarters 1st Echelon Egyptian Expeditionary Force (1919) as Assistant to Deputy Judge-Advocate General. Served in Salonica, Serbia, Egypt, and Palestine.

SANCROFT GRIMWOOD TAYLOR.
Admitted Feb. 1902. Member of Taylor, Simpson & Mosley, of Derby. Served as Wireless Telegraphist.

THOMAS RALPH TAYLOR.
Admitted Jan. 1911. Member of Standring, Taylor & Co., of Rochdale. Joined Sept. 1914, as Private, University and Public Schools Batt. Gazetted 2nd Lieut. 6th Batt. Lancashire Fusiliers Oct. 26, 1914. Served at Gallipoli. Wounded June 10, 1915. Killed in action at the Vineyard on the Krithia Road Aug. 7, 1915.

WALTER JAMES TAYLOR.
Admitted Feb. 1900. Member of Wansbroughs, Robinson, Taylcr & Taylor, of Bristol. Served as Corporal, 4th (Reserve) Batt. Somerset Light Infantry, subsequently gazetted Lieut. in the same Regt.

WILLIAM JAMES WINTER TAYLOR.
Admitted Nov. 1901. Member of Rutland & Taylor, of High Wycombe. Joined Dec. 1915, as Driver, Royal Army Service Corps. Commissioned 2nd Lieut. 6th Batt. Oxford and Bucks Light Infantry July 1917, attached Labour Corps and granted rank of A/Capt. Aug. 1918. Served in France 1916 to 1919.

WILLIAM JOSEPH TAYLOR.
Admitted July 1905. Member of W. J. & J. G. Taylor, of Cambridge. Joined Sept. 1916, as Private, 28th Batt. County of London Regt. (Artists Rifles), and subsequently gazetted 2nd Lieut. Hunts Cyclist Batt. Awarded the Belgium Croix de Guerre. Served in France Nov. 1916 to Feb. 1918.

WILLIAM KINGSLEY TAYLOR.
Admitted Jan. 1909. Of Sunderland. Served as Lieut., 7th Batt. Durham Light Infantry.

CYRIL HENRY TAYNTON.

Admitted May 1907, practising at Gloucester. Joined Oct. 1915, as 2nd Lieut., 3/1 South Midland Brigade Royal Field Artillery (T.F.), promoted Lieut. 1917. Served in France. Wounded at Battle of Somme Sept. 1916.

FRED WHITELEY TEAL.

Admitted Nov. 1911, practising at Halifax. Joined Nov. 27, 1916, as Private, Inns of Court O.T.C., and subsequently gazetted 2nd Lieut. 5th Batt. Norfolk Regt. Served in France. Wounded at Sambre-vise Canal Oct. 27, 1918.

RALPH GRENVILLE TEARLE.

Admitted March 1907, practising at Luton. Joined Sept. 25, 1916, as Private, Bedfordshire Regt., attached to Army Pay Corps, transferred to Middlesex Regt. Aug. 1917 and to Machine Gun Corps Oct. 1917. Served in France.

RICHARD HARRY RIDING TEE.

Admitted Feb. 1913. Solicitor to the Willesden Council. Joined Dec. 29, 1915, as Able Seaman, Royal Naval Volunteer Reserve, Anti-Aircraft section. Served at Home. Discharged Jan. 1917.

GEORGE CYRIL TEEBAY.

Articled to P. J. McKnight, of Hanley, Stoke-on-Trent. Joined Sept. 9, 1914, as Gunner, "B" Battery, 54th Brigade Royal Field Artillery. Served in Ireland Sept. 1914 to June 1915, Egypt July to Oct. 1915, Serbia Oct. to Dec. 1915, and Macedonia Dec. 1915 to June 1918. Wounded May 25, 1917.

HUGH TEESDALE.

Admitted April 1912. Member of Maples, Teesdale & Co., of 6 Fredericks Place, E.C. Joined Jan. 1916, as Private, Inns of Court O.T.C. Gazetted 2nd Lieut. Inns of Court O.T.C. Sept. 1916, Lieut. (Technical) Royal Air Force 1918. Served at Home.

HENRY ADAM TELFER.

Articled to W. Telfer Leviansky, of 90 and 91 Queen Street, Cheapside, E.C. Joined Sept. 1914, as Private, Public Schools Batt., and subsequently gazetted 2nd Lieut. 9th Batt. King's Own Yorkshire Light Infantry, promoted Lieut. 1916 and A/Capt. May 1916. Joined Trench Mortar Battery 1916. Served in France Nov. 1915 to July 1916. Killed in action July 1, 1916.

HILTON ROBERTS TELFORD.

Articled to F. E. Forster, of Newcastle-upon-Tyne. Joined Aug. 4, 1914, as Trooper, Northumberland Hussars. Commissioned as 2nd Lieut. 21st Northumberland Fusiliers (2nd Tyneside Scottish) Jan. 1915, Transport Officer Lieut. July 1915, Capt. 1917. Served in France. Wounded at Villerette Sept. 8, 1917. Died Sept. 9, 1917. Buried in New British Cemetery, Tincourt.

CLIFFORD JAMES TEMPERLEY.

Articled to H. Temperley, of Newcastle-upon-Tyne. Joined Aug. 4, 1914, as Lance-Corporal, Northern Cyclist Batt. Gazetted 2nd Lieut. Nov. 25, 1914, transferred to Royal Flying Corps as Flying Officer April 1915, promoted

Lieut. July 1916, Capt. Aug. 1917, Staff Capt. (S.O. 1st Class) Aug. 1918, Adjutant Dec. 1918. Served at Home and in France. Wounded Oct. 28, 1917 (shot down out of control).

HAROLD KENYON TEMPERLEY.

Articled to Henry Temperley, of Newcastle-upon-Tyne. Joined March 27, 1915, as 2nd Lieut., 6th Batt. (T.) Northumberland Fusiliers, afterwards attached to 1/7 Batt., promoted Lieut. June 1916. Once mentioned in Dispatches. Served at Home March 1915 to May 1917, and in France and Flanders May 1917 to Oct. 1917. Killed in action at Houthulst Forest Oct. 26, 1917.

ROBERT TEMPERLEY.

Admitted Oct. 1904. Member of Botterell, Roche & Temperley, of Newcastle-upon-Tyne. Served as Major, 19th (Service) Batt. Northumberland Fusiliers. Awarded O.B.E.

NORMAN TEMPEST.

Articled to Walter Tempest, of Leeds. Joined Nov. 1915, as Corporal, Royal Engineers. Commissioned as 2nd Lieut. in Royal Garrison Artillery July 7, 1917, promoted Lieut. Jan. 1919. Awarded the Italian Croce di Guerra. Served at Home and in France, Belgium, and Italy.

WILLIAM TEMPLE.

Admitted Aug. 1895. Member of Temple & Geoghegan, of Felixstowe. Mobilised Aug. 1914, as 2nd Lieut., 3rd Batt. Suffolk Regt., promoted Capt. Seconded in 1915 for service with Railway Traffic Establishment, Temp. Major whilst holding the appointment, Deputy Assistant Director Railway Traffic since June 1917, and subsequently President de la Commission Regulatrice Alliée Baltic Plebiscite Area and Danzig. Served in France Aug. 1914 to Jan. 1919, with British Army of the Rhine Jan. 1919 to Jan. 1920, and in Baltic Plebiscite Area Jan. 1920.

THOMAS JOHN WEMBRIDGE TEMPLEMAN.

Admitted April 1908. Member of Dunn & Baker, of Exeter, Crediton, Okehampton, &c. Joined June 16, 1916, as Sub-Lieut., Royal Naval Volunteer Reserve, promoted Lieut. June 1917, in command of M.L. 46, Naval Base, Brightlingsea, Essex. Served in North Sea.

CLAUD ROMAKO À BECKETT TERRELL.

Admitted Aug. 1910. With Drew & Napier, Singapore, S.S., 1911. Joined Jan. 12, 1916, as 2nd Lieut., Royal Field Artillery (Special Reserve), attached to No. 6 Battery and attained the rank of Capt., transferred to 460th Battery Howitzer Brigade, and later attached to 15th Brigade Royal Horse Artillery. Awarded the M.C. Served in France. Wounded June 8, 1917. Died June 10, 1917.

LAWRENCE BRETON TERRY.

Articled to Lee, Musgrove & Co., of Birmingham. Served as Corporal, Special Reserve (Motor Cyclist Section) Royal Engineers.

JOHN CHARLES DODSWORTH TETLEY.

Admitted April 1911. Member of Jenkins, Baker, Reynolds & Co., of 38 Old Jewry, E.C. Joined Sept. 1914, as Private, 28th Batt. County of

London Regt. (Artists Rifles), obtained Commission in same Regt. Nov. 1914, and rose to Capt., transferred to Grenadier Guards Oct. 1916 as Lieut., and subsequently given a Company. Served at Home and in France. Killed Oct. 9, 1917.

ROBERT HENRY TETLEY.

Admitted Oct. 1889, practising at 50 Jermyn Street, S.W. Joined Oct. 1915 as Private, Royal Army Service Corps (M.T.) Gazetted 2nd Lieut. Nov. 1916. Served in France. Gazetted out Aug. 1917.

WILLIAM GERALD TETLEY.

Articled to W. E. Tetley, of Bradford. Served as Lieut., 6th Batt. West Yorkshire Regt. (T.), promoted Capt. June 1916.

WILLIAM THAIRLWALL.

Admitted Nov. 1911. Managing Clerk with Read & Eastwood, of Blackburn, Lancs. Joined July 10, 1915, as Private, Royal Army Medical Corps, and attained the rank of A/Staff Sergeant. Once mentioned in Dispatches. Served with Salonica Army Nov. 1915 to April 1919, and with Allied Corps, Constantinople, May to Sept. 1919.

GEORGE ROBIN THATCHER.

Admitted May 1909. Member of Geo. Thatcher & Son, of 32 Essex Street, Strand, W.C. Joined Jan. 1915, as Able Seaman, Royal Naval Volunteer Reserve. Gazetted 2nd Lieut. Royal Garrison Artillery Jan. 17, 1916, promoted Lieut. July 1917. Awarded the M.C. Served in France. Killed in action April 1, 1918.

RAYMOND VALENTINE THATCHER.

Articled to R. Attenborough, of Thavies Inn, E.C. Served as Private, 16th Batt. County of London Regt. (Queen's Westminster Rifles), attached to 60th Rifles.

STANLEY CECIL THEOPHILUS.

Admitted Aug. 1911. Member of Soames, Edwards & Jones, of Lennox House, Norfolk Street, Strand, W.C. Joined Aug. 1914, as Private, 1st Batt. Hon. Artillery Company. Gazetted Lieut. The Rifle Brigade March 1915, A/Capt. and O.C. 60th Trench Mortar Battery June 1916, Temp. Capt. Tank Corps Nov. 1917. Awarded the M.C. Served in France Sept. 1914 to Feb. 1917, March to Nov. 1916, and Dec. 1917 to March 1919.

RAYMOND SAMUEL THICKNESSE.

Articled to F. J. K. Hull, of 5 Little College Street, Westminster, S.W. Joined Aug. 1914, as Private, University and Public Schools Corps (Royal Fusiliers). Obtained Commission in Lancashire Fusiliers Aug. 1916. Served in France and Belgium. Killed in action on the Passchendaele Ridge Oct. 9, 1917.

JOHN EGREMONT THIMBLEBY.

Admitted June 1912. Clerk with Thimbleby & Son, of Spilsby. Joined 1914, as 2nd Lieut., 2/5 Batt. Lincolnshire Regt. Served in England. Accidentally killed in a motor cycle collision at St. Albans Aug. 29, 1915.

ARTHUR LATIMER THOMAS.

Articled to E. R. Tanner, of Bristol. Joined British Red Cross Society and served at No. 1 Red Cross (Duchess of Westminster's) Hospital, Le Touquet, France, March to Aug. 1915. Joined Royal Army Medical Corps as Private, Sept. 23, 1915, served at 2nd Southern General Hospital and at No. 3 British General Hospital, Mesopotamia, June 1917 to June 1919.

BERNARD THOMAS.

Admitted Jan. 1900. Managing Clerk with Capron & Co., of 7 Savile Place, W. Joined March 12, 1916, as Assistant Paymaster, Royal Naval Volunteer Reserve, promoted to acting rank of Paymaster Lieut. March 1918. Served in light cruiser *Phaeton*, 1st Light Cruiser Squadron of Grand Fleet, acted as Secretary to Senior Officer British Baltic Force.

CHARLES THOMAS.

Articled to W. J. Everett, of Pontypool. Served as Private, 4th (Cyclist) Batt. The Welch Regt.

CHARLES CLIFFORD THOMAS.

Articled to C. V. Thomas, of Camborne, Cornwall. Mobilised Aug. 1914, as Lieut., 4th Batt. Duke of Cornwall's Light Infantry, promoted Capt. June 1, 1916. Once mentioned in Dispatches. Served in India Nov. 1914 to Jan. 1916, in Aden Jan. 1916 to Feb. 1917, and in Palestine Feb. 1917 to Aug. 1919.

CHARLES GORDON THOMAS.

Admitted April 1909, practised at Eastbourne. Served as Ambulance Driver.

CHARLES LESLIE THOMAS.

Articled to L. C. Thomas, of Neath. Joined Oct. 5, 1915, as Private, Inns of Court O.T.C. Gazetted 2nd Lieut. Machine Gun Corps Feb. 1917, promoted Lieut. Aug. 1918. Served at Home and in France. Wounded May 29, 1917.

CLARENCE THOMAS.

Articled to C. M. C. Dahne, of Swansea. Joined Glamorgan Yeomanry as Trooper in Aug. 1914, and promoted Corporal and Sergeant. Gazetted 2nd Lieut. and subsequently promoted Lieut., eventually transferred to Royal Army Service Corps. Served in France.

DAVID WILLIAMS EVAN THOMAS.

Admitted Nov. 1889. Member of D. W. E. & M. F. Thomas, of Brecon, S. Wales. Mobilised Aug. 1914, as Major, Brecknockshire Batt. South Wales Borderers, attained rank of Lieut.-Col. in 1916 (Aug.), in command of 1st Brecknockshire Batt. South Wales Borderers. Served in Aden 1914 to Aug. 1915 and in India 1915 to Jan. 1919.

ELLIOTT CREWDSON THOMAS.

Admitted Dec. 1900. Managing Clerk with Bridges, Sawtell & Co., of 23 Red Lion Square, W.C. Joined Dec. 24, 1914, as Capt., Suffolk Regt. Railway Transport Officer (General List) Dec. 1917. Served at Home and in Italy.

EVAN BEVAN THOMAS.

Admitted Oct. 1906, practising at Ferndale, Glam. Served as 2nd Air-Mechanic, Royal Flying Corps.

FRANCIS BERNARD VIVIAN THOMAS.

Articled to J. V. Thomas, of Penzance. Gazetted 2nd Lieut. 4th Batt. Duke of Cornwall's Light Infantry April 1915, promoted Lieut. March 1916. Killed in action Sept. 22, 1916.

FREDERICK DUNBAR THOMAS.

Admitted Aug. 1918. Member of Howlett & Whitehead, of Maidstone. Mobilised Aug. 4, 1914, as Lieut., 1st London Brigade Royal Field Artillery (T.), promoted Capt. April 1915, Major Dec. 1916, Lieut.-Col. Oct. 1918. With 298th (Army) Brigade Royal Field Artillery June 1916 to March 1919. Twice mentioned in Dispatches. Awarded the M.C. Served at Home Aug. 1914 to Sept. 1915 and May 1916 to March 1917, and in France Oct. 1915 to May 1916 and March 1917 to March 1919. Wounded June 9, 1917.

GRIFFITH JAMES CARADOC THOMAS.

Admitted Nov. 1900, practising at Manchester. Joined Jan. 18, 1915, as Gunner, Royal Field Artillery, attained rank of Sergeant. Served at Home and in France.

HUGH GARETH THOMAS.

Articled to H. H. Thompson, of Cheltenham. Mobilised Aug. 4, 1914, as Private, 1/5 Batt. Gloucestershire Regt. Gazetted 2nd Lieut. 8th Batt. Gloucestershire Regt. Sept. 19, 1915. Served in France May to Sept. 1915 and Jan. to July 1916. Killed at the Battle of the Somme at Bazentin-le-Petit July 31, 1916.

JOHN ANTRON THOMAS.

Articled to A. R. Thomas, of Helston, Cornwall. Mobilised Aug. 1914, as 2nd Lieut., 5th Batt. Duke of Cornwall's Light Infantry, promoted Capt. in April 1916. Served at Home Aug. 1914 to May 1916 and Dec. 1917 to Jan. 1919, and in France May 1916 to July 1917. Contracted fever May 1917.

JOHN HUGH THOMAS.

Articled to C. O. Jones, of Holyhead. Enlisted Dec. 1915, as Private, 21st Batt. Royal Welch Fusiliers. Subsequently obtained commission and attained the rank of Lieut. in the 3rd, attached 15th, Batt. The Welch Regt. Served in France. Wounded at Pilkem Ridge, near Ypres, Aug. 2, 1917.

JOHN PAGE THOMAS.

Articled to D. W. James, of Penygraig. Joined Sept. 15, 1914, as Private, University and Public Schools Corps (20th Batt. Royal Fusiliers). Served in France. Wounded at High Wood 1916. Discharged Feb. 1918.

KENNETH GALBRAITH THOMAS.

Admitted June 1914, Assistant Solicitor to Town Clerk of Burnley. Joined Aug. 21, 1914, as 2nd Lieut., 5th Batt. East Lancashire Regt. (T.), attained the rank of Capt. Once mentioned in Dispatches.

KENNETT RUFF THOMAS.

Articled to C. R. Thomas, of Maidenhead. Joined Feb. 28, 1917, as Rifleman, 16th Batt. County of London Regt. (Queen's Westminster Rifles). Gazetted 2nd Lieut. Royal Flying Corps Nov. 30, 1917, promoted Lieut. Royal Air Force April 1918. Served at Home and in France and Germany.

MOLYNEUX FREDERICK THOMAS.

Admitted Dec. 1890, practising at Brecon, S. Wales. Joined Aug. 5, 1914, as Lieut., 1/1 Brecknockshire Batt. South Wales Borderers, promoted Capt. June 1916. Served in Aden and India.

OLIVER STEPHEN THOMAS.

Articled to Moses Thomas, of Aberavon, Port Talbot. Joined Nov. 13, 1915, as Corporal, 16th Batt. The Welch Regt. (Cardiff City Batt.). Subsequently gazetted 2nd Lieut. Tank Corps. Served in France March 1916 to Feb. 1918.

OWEN BAYLIS THOMAS.

Admitted Nov. 1885, practising at 59 Chancery Lane, W.C. Joined Dec. 2, 1914, as Lieut., National Reserve, transferred to 2/5 Batt. Royal West Kent Regt. May 1915, and to Royal Defence Corps May 1916, promoted Capt. Feb. 1919. Served at Home.

PETER DAVID THOMAS.

Admitted Dec. 1894. Member of Peter Thomas & Clark, of 1 Bush Lane, E.C. Mobilised Aug. 1914, as Lieut., 6th Batt. The Welch Regt., promoted Capt. June 1915 and Brevet Major Jan. 1919, Organising Secretary for Minister of Munitions Yorkshire Area July 1915 to March 1919. Twice mentioned in Dispatches. Awarded C.B.E., M.V.O., and Cavaliere of the Crown of Italy. Served at Home Aug. to Oct. 1914, and in France Oct. 1914 to June 1915.

RICHARD VERNON THOMAS.

Articled to G. M. Riley, of Halifax. Joined Oct. 27, 1914, as Private, 4th Batt. West Riding Regt., promoted Lance-Corporal March 1915, Corporal April 1917, and Sergeant April 1918. Served at Home, France, and Belgium.

STEPHEN WALTER THOMAS.

Admitted Oct. 1895, practised at Swansea. Served as Capt. 5th Batt. The Welch Regt. (T.).

THOMAS PRICE THOMAS.

Admitted Feb. 1901, practising at Ystrad Mynach, Cardiff. Joined June 25, 1918, as Private, 28th Batt. County of London Regt. (Artists Rifles). Gazetted 2nd Lieut. The Welch Regt. 1919. Served at Home.

WILLIAM OLIVER THOMAS.

Articled to T. R. Evans, of Holyhead. Joined Sept. 5, 1914, as Private, Royal Anglesey Royal Engineers. Gazetted 2nd Lieut. Royal Welch Fusiliers, March 1915, transferred to Royal Flying Corps July 1917, promoted Lieut. Aug. 1917, Capt. and Wing Adjutant Jan. 1918. Awarded the M.C. Served in Belgium and France.

ALAN BRODRICK THOMPSON.

Admitted June 1914. Managing Clerk with Griffith & Co., of Newcastle-upon-Tyne. Mobilised Aug. 1914, as Lieut., 6th Batt. Northumberland Fusiliers,

A/Staff Capt. 3/1 Northumbrian Division 1915–1916, Northumbrian Reserve Brigade 1916–1918, Hornsea Demob. Sub-Area 1918, A/Brigade Major Eastern Reserve Brigade, 1919. Mentioned for valuable services in connection with the War. Served in France and Belgium April to May 1915 and remainder of time at Home. Wounded in 2nd Battle of Ypres, near St. Julien, April 26, 1915. Buried in dug-out.

ALBERT EDWARD THOMPSON.

Articled to C. S. Hays, of Heckmondwike, Yorks. Joined Jan. 12, 1916, as Driver, "2/A" Battery, Hon. Artillery Company, Gunner April 1918, Lewis Gun Instructor June 1918. Served in England Jan. 1916 to June 1917, in France and Belgium June 1917 to Nov. 1918, and in Germany Nov. 1918 to May 1919.

ALEXANDER THOMPSON.

Articled to Vincent Thompson, of Newcastle-upon-Tyne. Served as Private, 9th Batt. Northumberland Fusiliers.

BARRY CORT THOMPSON.

Admitted Jan. 1902. Member of Henry Thompson & Sons, of Grantham. Mobilised Aug. 1914, as Capt. 4th Batt. Lincolnshire Regt. (T.) and attained the rank of Major. Resigned commission on account of ill-health Feb. 12, 1918. Served in France 1915.

EDMUND CUTHBERT THOMPSON.

Admitted May 1902. Member of Hedley & Thompson, of Sunderland. Joined Aug. 15, 1916, as Lieut., General List, transferred to Royal Flying Corps Dec. 1917 and to Royal Air Force April 1918. Served at Home.

EDWARD REDFERN THOMPSON.

Admitted Oct. 1913. Member of Redfern, Son & Thompson, of Manchester. Joined Sept. 7, 1914, as Private, 20th Batt. Royal Fusiliers. Subsequently commissioned and attained the rank of Major 12th Batt. Manchester Regt. Awarded the M.C. Served in France. Wounded July 7, 1916, and Sept. 18, 1917.

FREDERICK CHARLES THOMPSON.

Admitted April 1896, practised at York. Mobilised Aug. 1914, as Capt., 5th Batt. West Yorkshire Regt. (T.), promoted Major 1915. Once mentioned in Dispatches. Served in France April 1915 to July 1916. Reported missing at the Battle of the Somme July 2, 1916, and believed to have been killed that day.

GEOFFREY JOHN THOMPSON.

Articled to G. J. Fowler, of 13 Bedford Row, W.C. Joined Aug. 5, 1914, as Private, Inns of Court O.T.C. Gazetted 2nd Lieut. 10th Batt. Essex Regt. Sept. 18, 1914, promoted Lieut. Nov. 1914, A/Capt. Nov. 1916 to March 1917, Capt. Dec. 1918. Awarded the M.C. Served at Home Sept. 1914 to July 1915, and in France July 1915 to Jan. 1919.

GEORGE THOMPSON.

Admitted Dec. 1905. Member of Greenway, Sons & Thompson, of Plymouth. Served as Lieut., Devonshire Royal Garrison Artillery. Died at the Military Hospital, Devonport, Jan. 16, 1915.

HAROLD GORDON THOMPSON.

Admitted April 1904, practised at 19 Laurence Pountney Lane, E.C. Served as Capt., Royal Army Service Corps.

HERBERT GARTHWAITE THOMPSON.

Admitted Oct. 1910. Member of Neve, Thompson & Jevons, of Tonbridge, and Southborough, Kent. Joined Nov. 20, 1914, as Temp. Paymaster Sub-Lieut. Royal Naval Reserve, promoted to Temp. A/Paymaster and then to Temp. Paymaster. Served mostly afloat in North Atlantic with Blockading Squadron (10th Cruiser Squadron).

HOWARD PARKER THOMPSON.

Admitted April 1902. Managing Clerk with Snow, Fox & Higginson, of 7 Great St. Thomas Apostle, E.C. Joined March 15, 1917, as Private, Royal Army Service Corps. Served at Home.

JOHN THOMPSON.

Admitted Dec. 1903, practising at Felixstowe. Joined Nov. 13, 1916, as Private, East Yorkshire Regt., transferred to Durham Light Infantry Jan. 1917. Served at Home.

JOHN CECIL CASTER THOMPSON.

Admitted Feb. 1907. Managing Clerk with Blundell, Baker & Co., of 16 Sergeant's Inn, Fleet Street, E.C. Joined Aug. 1914, as Private, 28th Batt. County of London Regt. (Artists Rifles). Gazetted 2nd Lieut. Scots Guards Jan. 1, 1915, promoted Lieut. Jan. 1916 (after reported missing). Served in France. Reported missing, believed killed Jan. 31, 1915.

JOHN WILLIAM HOWARD THOMPSON.

Admitted July 1883. Member of Gustavus Thompson & Sons, of Devereux Chambers, E.C. Served as Capt., 11th (Service) Batt. Devonshire Regt.

JOSEPH INDERMAUR THOMPSON.

Admitted Nov. 1900, practising at 2 South Square, Gray's Inn, W.C. Joined Feb. 9, 1917, as 2nd Lieut., Royal Flying Corps, subsequently attained the rank of Capt. Served in England and Scotland.

KENNETH HERBERT THOMPSON.

Admitted June 1905. Member of Stanley Attenborough & Co., of 18 Piccadilly, W. Joined June 25, 1916, as Gunner, Royal Field Artillery. Gazetted 2nd Lieut. 2nd Batt. West Yorkshire Regt. June 25, 1917, promoted Lieut. Dec. 1918. Awarded the M.C. and Bar. Served in France.

MAYNARD FALCON THOMPSON.

Articled to W. T. Highet, of Workington. Served as Lieut., 4th East Lancashire Brigade, Royal Field Artillery (T.), promoted Capt. June 1916. Mentioned in Dispatches.

OLIVER THOMPSON.

Articled to A. P. Williamson, of Retford. Joined Sept. 9, 1914, as Private, Nottinghamshire (Sherwood Rangers) Yeomanry, promoted Sergeant 1917. Served in Gallipoli 1915, Salonica 1916, and Palestine 1917. Wounded and taken prisoner by Turks on Tata Ridge Nov. 30, 1917.

PERCY LANGHORN THOMPSON.

Admitted May 1911, practised at Carlisle. Joined May 1, 1915, as Private, 16th Batt. Middlesex Regt. (Public Schools Batt.). Subsequently gazetted 2nd Lieut. Durham Light Infantry. Served in France. Killed in action June 12, 1917.

REGINALD PAUL THOMPSON.

Admitted May 1911, practised at Cardiff. Joined Sept. 4, 1914, as Private, 21st (Service) Batt. Royal Fusiliers. Gazetted 2nd Lieut. 3rd (Special Reserve) Batt. Somerset Light Infantry May 20, 1915. Served at Home Sept. 1914 to July 1916, and in France and Belgium July to Aug. 1916. Killed in action near Ypres Aug. 9, 1916.

RICHARD HENRY VAUGHAN THOMPSON.

Admitted Feb. 1909. Member of Beachcroft, Thompson & Co., of 9 Theobald's Road, W.C. Joined Aug. 1914 Inns of Court O.T.C. Obtained commission and attached to 11th (Service) Batt. Royal Fusiliers Sept. 1914, subsequently promoted Capt. Served in France July 1915 to Sept. 1916. Killed in action Sept. 26, 1916.

RONALD WILFRED THOMPSON.

Articled to W. D. Soulsby, of Blyth, Northumberland. Joined Nov. 1914, as Private, 1/1 Northern Cyclist Batt. and promoted Lance-Corporal Dec. 1914. Gazetted 2nd Lieut. in same Batt. June 1915, promoted Lieut. July 1916, attached to The Welch Regt. Aug. 1918. Served at Home and in France. Wounded Sept. 1918.

STANLEY PICKARD THOMPSON.

Admitted Feb. 1914, practising at Hornsea, E. Yorks. Joined Sept. 10, 1915, as 2nd Lieut., 4th Batt. East Yorkshire Regt., promoted Lieut. Nov. 1917. Served at Home.

VICTOR HERBERT THOMPSON.

Admitted Oct. 1909, practised at Birmingham. Served with 1st Batt. Royal Warwickshire Regt.

WILLIAM EDWIN THOMPSON.

Admitted Feb. 1904. Managing Clerk with Henry Thompson & Sons, of Grantham. Joined Jan. 1916, as Private, 28th Batt. County of London Regt. (Artists Rifles), promoted Corporal 1918. Served in France.

GEORGE WILFRED RUSSELL THOMSON.

Articled to J. A. White, of Stevenage House, Holborn Viaduct, E.C. Served as Private.

JOHN LESLIE THOMSON.

Admitted Dec. 1911. With Royal Indemnity Co., 84 William Street, New York, U.S.A. Given a commission in the Governor-General's Foot Guards 1915, and subsequently joined the Canadian Expeditionary Force as Lieut. Served in France May to July 1916. Shot by sniper July 19, 1916.

SPENCER THOMSON.

Admitted Jan. 1914. Managing Clerk with Pontifex, Pitt & Co., 16 St. Andrew Street, Holborn Circus, E.C. Gazetted 2nd Lieut. Royal Fusiliers Sept. 1914, promoted Lieut. Dec. 1914, Capt. March 1916, attached to 14th

Batt. and afterwards transferred to 2nd Batt. Awarded the M.C. Served at Gallipoli, in Egypt, and in France. Killed in action at Monchy April 24, 1917.

WILLIAM ROBINSON KETCHEN THOMSON.

Admitted Jan. 1909, practised at Gateshead. Joined Nov. 1916, as 2nd Lieut., Royal Garrison Artillery. Served in France. Killed Oct. 16, 1917.

GEORGE HERBERT THORN.

Admitted Dec. 1901, practised at Mayfield, Sussex. Served as Private, 3rd Batt. Royal Sussex Regt.

ALFRED HENRY THORN-PUDSEY.

Admitted H. 1888. Member of Thorn-Pudsey & Derry, of Iron Bridge, Shropshire. Rejoined Aug. 11, 1914, as Capt., Recruiting Officer of the 53rd Area. Served at Home.

ARTHUR HENRY THORNBACK.

Admitted Nov. 1900. Member of Waller & Thornback, of Southampton. Mobilised as 2nd Lieut., Hampshire Royal Garrison Artillery, subsequently attained the rank of Capt. Served at Home Aug. 1914 to Nov. 1917, and in India Nov. 1917 to Sept. 1919.

HAROLD UNDERHILL HATTON THORNE.

Admitted March 1904, practised at Reading. Mobilised Aug. 1914, as Capt., Royal Berkshire Regt. and went to the Front March 1915, promoted Major and was temporarily Second in Command of a Battalion of the King's Own Scottish Borderers, subsequently promoted Lieut.-Col. and given command of a Battalion of the Royal Scots. Killed in action April 9, 1917.

JOHN PARRY THORNE.

Admitted Dec. 1910, practised at 170 Strand, W.C. Served as Private, 5th (Reserve) Batt. South Staffordshire Regt. (T.).

HENRY LANGTON THORNHILL.

Admitted April 1899, practising at Euston Station N.W. Joined Jan. 1915, as Capt., Royal Engineers, promoted Major 1916. Served in France.

PERCY ROBERT THORNLEY.

Articled to Fraser Sutton, of Manchester. Joined Sept. 4, 1914, as Private, 20th Batt. Royal Fusiliers, promoted Lance-Corporal April 1917, Corporal Dec. 1917. Served in France 1915 to 1918, and in Germany 1918 to 1919. Wounded in High Wood (Somme) July 20, 1916.

PHILIP REGINALD THORNTON.

Admitted Dec. 1905. Member of Hughes, Bartlett & Thornton, of 115 High Holborn, W.C. Joined Nov. 13, 1914, as 2nd Lieut., Wiltshire Regt., promoted Lieut. Jan. 1915, transferred to Machine Gun Corps Dec. 1915, promoted Capt. Sept. 1916, transferred to Tank Corps Nov. 1916, promoted A/Major Jan. 1917. Served in France and at Home. Wounded at Neuve Chapelle March 1915.

WILLIAM CLIFFORD THORNTON

Admitted April 1913. Managing Clerk with Iveson, Macaulay & Redfearn, of Heckmondwike. Joined Nov. 1914, as 2nd Lieut., West Riding Regt., promoted Lieut. April 1915. Served at Home. Resigned Sept. 1915.

HENRY WILLIAM THORNTON-JONES.

Articled to J. G. Jones, of Bangor. Joined Nov. 1915, as Private, 22nd Batt. Royal Welch Fusiliers, and attained the rank of Sergeant. Gazetted 2nd Lieut. The Welch Regt. and subsequently promoted Lieut. Served at Home and in France.

WILLIAM JOHN CREENY THOROLD.

Admitted Nov. 1903. Member of Woolsey, Sayer & Thorold, of Norwich. Joined May 1, 1916, as Private, 26th (Bankers') Batt. Royal Fusiliers. Gazetted 2nd Lieut. Royal Army Service Corps April 30, 1917, promoted Lieut. Oct. 1918. Served at Home, in Belgium and France, and with Army of Occupation in Germany.

COLLINGWOOD FORSTER THORP.

Admitted Oct. 1904. Member of Dickson, Archer & Thorp, of Alnwick. Served as Lieut., 15th Batt. Northumberland Fusiliers.

ROBERT GORDON THORP.

Admitted April 1908. Member of Whitford & Thorp, of 28 Budge Row, E.C. Joined March 31, 1917, Inns of Court O.T.C., subsequently gazetted 2nd Lieut. 51st Batt. Bedfordshire Regt. Served at Home and in Germany.

EDWARD ALWYN THRALL.

Admitted Aug. 1909. Member of Coulter, Hancock & Thrall, of Truro. Joined May 27, 1918, as Private, Royal Army Ordnance Corps, attained rank of Corporal. Served at Home.

HERBERT EDWARD THRELFALL.

Admitted Oct. 1910. Of Blackburn. Served as Lance-Corporal, 11th Hussars, 12th (Reserve) Cavalry Regt.

RAYMOND MELVILLE THRUPP.

Admitted Aug. 1912, practised at 8 Bloomsbury Square, W.C. Served as Private, 28th Batt. County of London Regt. (Artists Rifles). Gazetted 2nd Lieut. 1st Batt. Notts and Derby Regt. (Sherwood Foresters).

JOHN HORACE THURSFIELD.

Admitted April 1905, practising at Kidderminster. Mobilised as Capt., 6th Batt. South Staffordshire Regt. (T.), subsequently attained the rank of Major (A/Lieut.-Col.). Awarded the M.C. Served in France. Wounded at Passchendaele, Sept. 26, 1917, and at Cambrai, Dec. 6, 1917.

WILLIAM HEATH THURSFIELD.

Admitted July 1897. Managing Clerk with Lawrance, Webster, Messer & Nicholls, of 14 Old Jewry Chambers, E.C. Joined June 30, 1917, as Cadet. Gazetted 2nd Lieut. Royal Army Service Corps Aug. 26, 1917. Served in France.

FRANK THWAITE.

Admitted July 1904, practising at 20 Gamage Buildings, Holborn, E.C. Joined Dec. 6, 1916, as Private, Inns of Court O.T.C. Gazetted 2nd Lieut. 3rd Batt. Royal Warwickshire Regt. Aug. 1, 1917, transferred to Machine Gun Corps April 1918, gazetted Lieut. Feb. 1919. Served in France

Aug. to Nov. 1917 and Aug. 1918 to June 1919, and in Italy Nov. 1917 to April 1918.

GEORGE FARQUHARSON TICEHURST.

Admitted Dec. 10, 1903. Member of Ticehuist, McIlquham & Wyatt, of Cheltenham. Joined June 3, 1915, as Private, 3rd Batt. Gloucestershire Regt., and promoted Lance-Corporal Aug. 1915. Gazetted 2nd Lieut. (Special Reserve) Sept. 15, 1915, promoted Lieut. July 1917. Served in France. Wounded May 8, 1917.

PAUL BURRELL TIDDEMAN.

Admitted July 1908, practising at 61 Moorgate Street, E.C. Joined Dec. 9, 1915, as Private, Royal Army Service Corps (M.T.), promoted Sergeant Aug. 1917. Served in France and Belgium and with Army of Occupation in Geimany Aug. 1916 to March 1919.

GEORGE HENRY RICHARDS TILDESLEY.

Admitted Dec. 1914, practised at Beaumaris. Served as 2nd Lieut., 3rd Batt. Royal Welch Fusiliers.

JOHN EDWARD TILLETT.

Articled to A. A. Padley, of Market Rasen. Served as Lieut., 3rd Special Reserve, attached 1st Batt. Lincolnshire Regt. Killed in action Oct. 8, 1918.

WILFRID SIDNEY TILLETT.

Admitted Feb. 1902. Member of W. H. Tillett & Co., of Norwich. Joined Sept. 20, 1916, as Private, 2/5 Batt. Yorkshire Regt., transferred to 14th Batt. Suffolk Regt. 1918. Served at Home.

JOHN TILLY.

Admitted Oct. 1911. Managing Clerk with Turnbull & Tilly, of West Hartlepool. Enlisted Sept. 15, 1914, as Private, 21st (Service) Batt. Royal Fusiliers. Gazetted 2nd Lieut. 8th Batt. Yorkshire Regt. Sept. 22, 1914, promoted Lieut. Jan. 1915, Capt. July 1916. Awarded the M.C. Served in France 1915, 1916, 1917, and in Italy 1918. Wounded Nov. 22, 1915, and Aug. 5, 1916. Killed in action at Asiago, Italy, June 8, 1918.

WILLIAM TILLY.

Admitted Aug. 1900. Member of Johnson & Tilly, of Lancaster & Morecambe. Served as Capt., 5th Batt. King's Own Royal Lancaster Regt.

WILBERFORCE ONSLOW TIMES.

Articled to Sir Charles Longmore, K.C.B., of Hertford. Mobilised Aug. 1914, as Lieut., Hertfordshire Regt., promoted Capt. June 1915, transferred to Bedfordshire Regt. Jan. 1915, Temp. Major March 1918, Staff Capt. 188th Infantry Brigade May 1916 to Feb. 1918, D.A.A.G. 23rd Division Feb. 1918 to May. 1919. Three times mentioned in Dispatches. Awarded the M.C. Served in France and Belgium Nov. 1914 to June 1919. Once wounded.

THOMAS BUCKLEY TIMMINS.

Admitted July 1902. Member of Timmins & Timmins, of Bath. Mobilised Aug. 1914, as Capt., 4th Batt. Somerset Light Infantry, subsequently Major 6th Batt. Devonshire Regt. Served in India and Mesopotamia.

JOHN HUMPHREY TINDAL.

Articled to Edward Meade-King, of Bristol. Joined Dec. 1914, as Gunner, 1/127 (Bristol) Heavy Battery Royal Garrison Artillery. Served in German East Africa. Died of fever in Africa Feb. 15, 1917.

RICHARD FREDERICK TINDALL.

Articled to Courtenay Stevens, of 42 Bedford Row, W.C. Joined Aug. 1914, as 2nd Lieut., 3rd Batt., attached 2nd Batt., Lincolnshire Regt., subsequently promoted Lieut. Killed in action in France Sept. 25, 1915.

KIRTON TINDLE.

Articled to J. S. Tindle, of South Shields. Joined March 1, 1917, as 2nd Lieut., Durham Light Infantry. Served in France April 1917 to March 1918. Reported as missing March 26, 1918, and afterwards presumed to have been killed on that date.

GEORGE GWINNETTE NOBLE TINSON.

Admitted Dec. 1912, practised at Swansea. Served as 2nd Lieut. 6th (Service) Batt. King's Own Royal Lancaster Regt., promoted Lieut. June 1916. Mentioned in Dispatches and awarded the M.C.

GEORGE TIZZARD.

Admitted May 1910. Member of Seldon, Lefroy & Tizzard, of Barnstaple. Joined Sept. 9, 1914, as Private, 1/6 Batt. Devonshire Regt., promoted Lance-Corporal Jan. 1915. Gazetted 2nd Lieut. in same Regt. Dec. 1915. Served in India Nov. 1914 to Dec. 1915, and in Mesopotamia Dec. 1915 to March 1916. Killed in action at Deijailah, Mesopotamia, March 8, 1916.

EDWIN LEWIS TODD.

Admitted July 1906, practising at Sunderland. Joined Nov. 1915, as Cadet, Durham University O.T.C., transferred as Private to 21st (Reserve) Batt. Durham Light Infantry Feb. 1916. Gazetted 2nd Lieut. 3rd (Reserve) Batt. P.W.O. West Yorkshire Regt. Oct. 24, 1916, transferred to 10th (Service) Batt. Dec. 1916, attached 2/1 Regt. P.W.O. Yorkshire Hussars March 1918, promoted Lieut. April 1918. Served at Home Nov. 1915 to Dec. 1916 and March to April 1918, in France and Belgium Dec. 1916 to Feb. 1918, and in Ireland May 1918 to Feb. 1919. Wounded at Arras May 4, 1917.

JOHN GEORGE TODD.

Member of Maughan & Hall, of Newcastle-upon-Tyne. Joined Aug. 1914. as Private, Public Schools Batt. Subsequently obtained commission in 4th Batt. Tyneside Scottish (23rd Northumberland Fusiliers) and attained the rank of Capt. Killed in action at La Boiselle July 1, 1916.

THOMAS TOFT.

Admitted Aug. 1899. Member of Watson, Chorley & Toft, of Kendal. Joined Aug. 10, 1916, as Gunner, Royal Garrison Artillery. Gazetted 2nd Lieut. Royal Garrison Artillery, and later A/Capt. Army Pay Department. Served in Flanders, France, and Egypt.

ALFRED BUCKLAND TOLHURST.

Admitted Aug. 1911, practised at 44 Bedford Row, W.C. Joined May 13, 1916, as Rifleman, 5th City of London Batt. London Regt. (London Rifle Brigade). Served in France. Killed in action near Arras April 7, 1917.

ALFRED WILFRED TOLHURST.

Articled to F. J. Tolhurst, of Gravesend and Southend-on-Sea. Joined March 1917, as Cadet, Cambridge University O.T.C., and subsequently gazetted Temp. 2nd Lieut. Royal Flying Corps. Served at Home. Accidentally killed whilst flying Oct. 6, 1917.

BERNARD JOSEPH TOLHURST.

Articled to F. J. Tolhurst, of Gravesend. Served as 2nd Lieut., 12th Batt. Duke of Wellington's West Riding Regt.

CLAUD CHARLES TOLHURST.

Articled to J. T. Freer, of Tonbridge, Kent. Joined March 30, 1916, as Trooper, 2/1 Queen's Own West Kent Imperial Yeomanry, transferred to Royal West Kent Regt. Nov. 1916 and to the Observation Section of the Royal Engineers March 1918. Served in France Dec. 1916 to Jan. 1919. Wounded Aug. 1917.

EDWARD NORTHCOTE TOLLER.

Admitted March 1909. Member of Toller & Son, of Kettering. Joined Sept. 11, 1914, as Private, 20th Batt. Royal Fusiliers (University and Public Schools Corps), promoted to Sergeant-Major Oct. 1914. Gazetted 2nd Lieut. 20th Batt. Royal Fusiliers Jan. 1915, lent to 180th Royal Engineers in charge of listening galleries Jan. to April 1916, returned to 20th Royal Fusiliers as Lieut. April 1916, promoted Capt. May 1916. Served in England Sept. 1914 to Nov. 1915 and in France Nov. 1915 to July 1916. Killed in action at High Wood July 20, 1916.

THOMAS ERIC TOLLER.

Admitted March 1909. Member of Toller, Burgess & Pochin, of Leicester. Joined Nov. 30, 1914, as 2nd Lieut., 10th Batt. Leicestershire Regt., attached East Lancashire Regt. Oct. 1915, and to 126th Infantry Brigade (Assistant Staff Capt.) Dec. 1915, transferred Royal Munster Fusiliers Sept. 1916, promoted Lieut. Nov. 1916, and Capt. June 1917. Once mentioned in Dispatches. Served at Home Nov. 1914 to Sept. 1915, Gallipoli Sept. to Dec. 1915, Suez Canal Defences Jan. to June 1916, Macedonia Aug. 1916 to Sept. 1917, Palestine Sept. 1917 to May 1918, and in France June to Nov. 1918.

FRANK OLIPHANT TOMKINS.

Admitted Feb. 1895. Member of Thorowgood, Tabor & Hardcastle, of 11 Copthall Court, E.C. Joined Oct. 6, 1914, as Private, 23rd Batt. Royal Fusiliers. Obtained a commission as 2nd Lieut. Royal Army Service Corps July 23, 1916, promoted Lieut. Jan. 1918. Served in France.

FRANK SAVILL TOMKINS.

Admitted Oct. 1908, practised at 3 Raymond Buildings, Gray's Inn. Joined the Inns of Court O.T.C. in Sept. 1914 and subsequently obtained a commission in the 7th Batt. Gloucestershire Regt., promoted Lieut. March 1915. Killed in action at the Dardanelles Aug. 8, 1915.

FRANCIS MARTIN TOMKINSON.

Admitted Feb. 1907. Member of Evershed & Tomkinson, of Birmingham. Mobilised Aug. 1914, as Lieut., 7th Batt. Worcestershire Regt., promoted Capt. Aug. 1914, Temp. Major July 1915, Temp. Lieut.-Col. Feb. 1916, reverted to Temp. Major 1916, promoted A/Lieut.-Col. Dec. 1916. Six times mentioned in Dispatches. Awarded D.S.O. and Bar, Officer of Legion of Honour (France), Croce di Guerra (Italy), to be Brevet Lieut.-Col. on promotion to Major. Served in France March 1915 to Nov. 1917, and in Italy Nov. 1917 to April 1919.

HARRY CECIL HERBERT SEYMOUR TOMKINSON.

Admitted May 1910. Member of Pedley, Timperley & Tomkinson, of Crewe. Served as 2nd Lieut. Royal Air Force. Died of pneumonia Nov. 2, 1918.

MORTON JAMES BARING TOMLIN.

Admitted Aug. 1887. Member of Tomlin & Dinwiddy, of 8 Old Burlington Street, W. Mobilised Aug. 1914 as Lieut.-Col. Commanding 21st Batt. County of London Regt. (First Surrey Rifles). Once mentioned in Dispatches. Awarded O.B.E., Military Order of Savoy (Italian)—Cavalier. Served at Home and in Flanders.

CLARENCE SAMUEL TOMLINSON.

Admitted March 1909, practising at Folkestone. Served as Lieut. Ammunition Column.

ERNEST HOSKINS TOMLINSON.

Admitted Feb. 1904, practised at Burton-on-Trent. Served as Capt., 6th Batt. North Staffordshire Regt., promoted Major May 1916.

CHARLES HENRY TOMLISON.

Admitted April 1910, practising at Congleton. Joined June 3, 1916, as Gunner, Royal Garrison Artillery, subsequently commissioned in same Regt. and attained the rank of Lieut.

CUTHBERT BLAGDEN TOMPKINS.

Articled to F. B. Tompkins, of Chichester. Joined Dec. 3, 1914, as Ordinary Seaman (Public Schools Batt.) Royal Naval Volunteer Reserve. Gazetted Nov. 27, 1915, as Sub-Lieut. Royal Naval Volunteer Reserve with Hawke Batt. Royal Naval Division. Served at Home Dec. 1914 to May 1915 and April 1918 to Jan. 1919, at Gallipoli and Ægean Islands May 1915 to May 1916, and in France May 1916 to March 1917 and May 1917 to April 1918. Wounded at Mesnil-sur-Ancre April 12, 1918.

OSCAR BERRY TOMPKINS.

Admitted April 1910. Member of Berry Tompkins & Co., of 4 Great James Street, Bedford Row, W.C. Joined Sept. 1, 1914, as Private, 9th Batt. County of London Regt. (Queen Victoria's Rifles), subsequently gazetted Lieut. Machine Gun Corps. Served in France. Wounded at Ypres May 9, 1915.

GEORGE EDWARD TOMPSON.

Admitted Nov. 1908, practising at Colchester. Rejoined 5th Batt. Essex Regt. at mobilisation as 2nd Lieut., promoted Lieut. Nov. 1914, Temp. Capt. July 1915 to June 1916, Capt. June 1916, Staff Officer to British Base Commandant, Beirout, Syria, Nov. 1918. Once mentioned in Dispatches. Served in Egypt, Palestine, and Syria.

JAMES WYNDHAM TOMSON.

Admitted Feb. 1905. Managing Clerk with Baileys, Shaw & Gillett, of 5 Berners Street, London, W. Joined Dec. 1914 Inns of Court O.T.C. Gazetted 2nd Lieut. 5th Batt. Leicestershire Regt. and subsequently promoted Lieut. and Capt. Once mentioned in Dispatches. Served in France. Killed at St. Quentin Sept. 24, 1918.

JOHN TONGE.

Admitted Jan. 1886, practised at Grimsby. Served as Lieut.-Col. Royal Field Artillery. Awarded the C.M.G. Killed in action in France April 19, 1917.

GEORGE HENRY TONKS.

Admitted Feb. 1915, practising at Willenhall. Joined May 22, 1916, as Private, Royal Army Service Corps, transferred from Horse Transport to Supply Branch Dec. 1916. Served in France as Supply Clerk and afterwards attached General Headquarters, Intelligence Dept., and subsequently at Cologne as Clerk on Staff of the Military Governor.

FRANK HENRY TOONE.

Admitted Feb. 1899. Member of C. W. & F. H. Toone, of Loughborough. Joined March 31, 1917, as Gunner, Royal Garrison Artillery, subsequently promoted Sergeant. Served in Palestine Aug. 1917 to March 1918, and in France March to Aug. 1918.

ERIC ADOLPHUS BLAGBURN TOOTH.

Articled to Adolphus Tooth, of 37 Lincoln's Inn Fields, W.C. Served as Flight Sub-Lieut., Royal Naval Air Service.

GERALD EDWARD GUY TOOTH.

Articled to Adolphus Tooth, of 37 Lincoln's Inn Fields, W.C. Joined Oct. 28, 1914, as Private, Inns of Court O.T.C. Gazetted 2nd Lieut. Leicestershire Regt. Nov. 28, 1914, promoted Lieut. Feb. 1915, gazetted Adjutant Jan. 1916, promoted Capt. July 1916, gazetted G.S.O. III. 21st Divisional Headquarters June 1918. Awarded the M.C. and Bar and Croix de Guerre. Served in France July 1915 to April 1919.

CECIL WOTTON TOOVEY.

Articled to John Toovey, of 10 & 11 Lime Street, E.C. Mobilised Aug. 1914, as 2nd Lieut., 2/9 Batt. Middlesex Regt., and subsequently promoted Lieut., attached to the 82nd Punjabis in 1915, was subsequently gazetted to the Regular Indian Army and attained the rank of Capt. Once mentioned in Dispatches. Served at Home, India, and Mesopotamia.

ERNEST KRUGER TOPHAM.

Admitted April 1907, practised at Bradford. Served as Acting Paymaster, Army Pay Department.

ALEXANDER ROSS TOPPING.

Articled to H. J. Stileman, of 16 Southampton Street, Bloomsbury Square, W.C. Joined June 26, 1917, as Gunner, Royal Garrison Artillery, transferred to Army Pay Corps Nov. 1917, promoted Corporal and later A/Sergeant.

THOMAS EDWARD TOPPING.

Admitted Aug. 1894, practising at Blackpool. Mobilised Aug. 1914, as Major, 2nd West Lancashire Brigade Royal Field Artillery, subsequently attained the rank of Brig.-Gen. Five times mentioned in Dispatches. Awarded C.B., C.M.G., and D.S.O. Served in France.

MAURICE JULIAN TOSSWILL.

Admitted Jan. 1903. Member of Dymond, Findeisen & Tosswill, of Torquay. Joined Nov. 9, 1914, as 2nd Lieut., 2/7 Batt. Devonshire Regt., promoted Temp. Capt. Oct. 1915. Served at Home.

JOHN GORDON TOVEY.

Articled to H. W. Grimes, of Gloucester. Joined July 13, 1915, Royal Engineers. Gazetted 2nd Lieut. 61st Divisional Train Royal Army Service Corps Feb. 14, 1915, gazetted Temp. Lieut. June 1915, Lieut. July 1917. Once mentioned in Dispatches. Awarded the M.C. Served in France and Belgium.

WILLIAM HOLLAND TOWLSON.

Admitted May 1912. Managing Clerk with C. &. W. Kenshole, of Aberdare, South Wales. Joined June 1916, as Private, Royal Welch Fusiliers, and afterwards promoted Lance-Corporal. Obtained commission as 2nd Lieut. Jan. 1917, appointed to 122nd Machine Gun Corps. Served in France March to Sept. 1917. Wounded at Hollebeck July 31, 1917. Died at Lady Murray's Hospital, Le Trėport, Sept. 28, 1917.

CHARLES AUBREY TOWN.

Admitted July 1910. With Scatcherd, Hopkins & Brighouse, of Leeds. Joined Sept. 20, 1914, as Private, Leeds Pals Batt. (15th Batt. West Yorkshire Regt.). Gazetted 2nd Lieut. 11th Batt. West Yorkshire Regt., attached 13th Batt., promoted Lieut. April 1917, Capt. June 1917. Once mentioned in Dispatches. Awarded the M.C. Served in France. Twice wounded. Killed in action Sept. 20, 1917.

FRANCIS EDWARD STEAVENSON TOWNSEND.

Articled to H. G. Steavenson, Town Clerk, of Darlington. Joined Aug. 1914, as 2nd Lieut., 5th Batt. Durham Light Infantry, promoted Lieut. July 1915. Served in France April 1915 to Sept. 1916. Wounded on the Somme Sept. 16, 1916, and died at Abbeville Sept. 30, 1916.

FREDERICK OCTAVIUS TOWNSEND.

Admitted Oct. 1894, practising at Abingdon. Served as Sergeant, 132nd Heavy Battery Royal Garrison Artillery.

GEOFFREY TOWNSEND.

Admitted March 1904, practising at Rawtenstall. Served as Major, 5th Batt. East Lancashire Regt.

EDMUND NEVILLE TRAPPES-LOMAX.
Admitted April 1906. Of Canada. Served as Lance-Corporal, 30th Batt. Canadian Expeditionary Force.

HAROLD PAGET TRAVERS.
Admitted Sept. 1897, practised at 26 Budge Row, E.C. Served as Major, 22nd Batt. London Regt.

GARNET WETHEY TREASURE.
Articled to Frank Treasure, of Gloucester. Joined Nov. 30, 1915, as Private, 5th City of London Batt. London Regt. (London Rifle Brigade). Served in France. Wounded at Dickebusche Aug. 7, 1917.

WARREN FRANCIS TREE.
Admitted Oct. 1909. Member of Tree & Son, of Worcester. Joined Sept. 1914, as 2nd Lieut., 10th Batt. Worcestershire Regt., promoted Lieut. 1915, Capt. July 1916. Served in France. Wounded Oct. 1915. Killed in action at Bazentin-le-Petit, France, July 22, 1916.

FRANCIS CHARLES ALFRED EDWARD TREGONING.
Articled to C. H. Peter, of Launceston. Served as Lance-Corporal, Duke of Cornwall's Light Infantry.

FRANK WILLIAM TREHEARNE.
Admitted April 1904. Member of Leslie Hardy & Trehearne, of 17 Bedford Row, W.C. Joined Dec. 10, 1915, as Gunner, Royal Horse Artillery, promoted A/Bombardier Sept. 1918. Served at Home.

REGINALD BLAIR TRENFIELD.
Articled to J. W. Trenfield, of Chipping Sodbury, near Bristol. Mobilised Aug. 5, 1914, with the Royal Gloucestershire Hussars Yeomanry. Gazetted 2nd Lieut. in Royal Army Service Corps May 25, 1915, promoted Lieut. Sept. 1915, Capt. Sept. 1916. Served in France Aug. 1915 to Dec. 1916 and in Salonica Jan. 1917 to Feb. 1919.

ALFRED ERNEST YATES TRESTRAIL.
Admitted Dec. 1900. Managing Clerk with Armitage, Sykes & Hinchcliffe, of Huddersfield. Joined Oct. 27, 1914, as Capt., 14th Batt. Cheshire Regt., promoted Temp. Major Feb. 1915, A/Lieut.-Col. March 1919. Served with the 14th, 10th, 3rd, and 15th Batt. Cheshire Regt. Once mentioned in Dispatches. Awarded the D.S.O. Served in France June to Dec. 1916 and March 1918 to May 1919. Wounded June 3, 1918.

CHARLES TUDOR TREVOR.
Admitted Feb. 1901, practising at Guisborough. Joined Aug. 4, 1915, as Gunner, Royal Field Artillery, Motor Machine Gun Service. Gazetted 2nd Lieut. Northumbrian (North Riding) Royal Garrison Artillery (T.), Nov. 15, 1915, promoted Lieut. June 1917, attached 91st Heavy Battery, 10th Heavy Battery and "X" Battery 2nd Reserve Brigade Heavy Artillery Training Centre. Served in Egypt and Palestine.

ARNOLD JAMES TRINDER.
Admitted Dec. 1902. Member of Trinder, Capron & Co., of 156 Leadenhall Street, E.C. Joined Oct. 1914, as Private, 28th Batt. County of London Regt.

(Artists Rifles). Gazetted 2nd Lieut. 3rd Batt. Northumberland Fusiliers May 1915. Served in France and Flanders. Killed at Hooge, Flanders, June 16, 1915.

WALTER ARNOLD TROATH.

Articled to H. W. M. Aldridge, of Bournemouth. Joined Nov. 15, 1915, as Cyclist, 3/9 (Cyclists) Hampshire Regt., transferred as Private to 5th (Reserve) Batt. Sept. 1916. Gazetted 2nd Lieut. 4th (Reserve) Batt. Dorsetshire Regt. Aug. 29, 1917, promoted Lieut. March 1919. Served at Home Nov. 1915 to Jan. 1918 and June to July 1919, and in India Jan. 1918 to June 1919.

STUART ERNEST TROTTER.

Admitted Jan. 1912. Member of Trotter & Patteson, of 64 Victoria Street, S.W. Joined Dec. 28, 1915, as Private, 28th Batt. County of London Regt. (Artists Rifles). Gazetted 2nd Lieut. 16th Batt. County of London Regt. (Queen's Westminster Rifles) July 11, 1916, promoted Lieut. Jan. 1917, A/Capt. May to Sept. 1918. Served in France. Wounded at Battle of Arras April 14, 1917.

ALEC GEORGE TROUGHTON.

Admitted Jan. 1912. Managing Clerk with Holman, Fenwick & Willan, of 1 Lloyds Avenue, E.C. Commissioned as Sub-Lieut. Royal Naval Volunteer Reserve (Auxiliary Patrol) March 3, 1916, promoted Sub-Lieut. in Command Nov. 1916, Lieut. in Command of "H.M.M.L. 376" March 1917. Served at Sea from May 1916 to Feb. 1919, including patrol, &c., off West Irish Coast.

LIONEL HOLMES WOOD TROUGHTON.

Admitted Aug. 1907, practised at Gravesend. Served as Private, Public Schools Batt. Royal Fusiliers, and subsequently gazetted 2nd Lieut. 10th (Service) Batt. The Rifle Brigade. Awarded the M.C.

WILLIAM GOSSELIN TROWER.

Articled to Sir Walter Trower, of 5 New Square, Lincoln's Inn, W.C. Mobilised Aug. 1914, as 2nd Lieut., 1/2 East Anglian Brigade Royal Field Artillery (T.), promoted A/Capt. May 1915, Capt. 1918. Once mentioned in Dispatches. Served in France Nov. 1915 to Feb. 1916, and in Egypt and Palestine Feb. 1916 to Feb. 1919.

RICHARD HAROLD TRUDGETT.

Admitted Dec. 1904, practising at 46 Queen Victoria Street, E.C. Joined Sept. 1914, as Private, Hon. Artillery Company. Gazetted 2nd Lieut. Royal Army Ordnance Corps Dec. 1917, promoted Lieut. June 1918. Served at Home Sept. 1914 to Dec. 1916, and in France Dec. 1916 to June 1919.

STEPHEN ALFRED HERMAN TRUMPLER.

Admitted Oct. 1905. Member of Bloxam, Ellison & Co., of 1 Lincoln's Inn Fields, W.C. Joined Dec. 4, 1915, as 2nd Lieut., Royal Army Service Corps, subsequently promoted Lieut. Served in England Dec. 1915 to April 1917, and in Macedonia, Serbia, and Bulgaria April 1917 to Jan. 1919.

ALWYNE LAYBOURNE TRUNDLE.
Articled to H. V. Scott, of York. Served as 2nd Lieut., 1st West Riding Brigade Royal Field Artillery (T.), promoted Lieut. July 1917, A/Major Jan. 1919. Awarded Croix de Guerre.

EDGAR LAWRENCE NEWALL TUCK.
Admitted Feb. 1912. Managing Clerk with Godden, Holme & Ward, of 34 Old Jewry, E.C. Joined Jan. 25, 1915, as Private, Royal Army Medical Corps (T.), 2nd London District, promoted Corporal March 1915, Sergeant April 1915. Granted commission in Labour Corps July 15, 1917, attached to 17th Batt. Worcestershire Regt. May 1918. Adjutant XV. Corps Signal School Aug. 1918 to Jan. 1919, promoted Lieut. Jan. 1919. Served at Home Jan 1915 to May 1918, and in France May 1918 to Feb. 1919.

ALFRED TUCKER.
Admitted Nov. 1909. Member of Farr, Lomas-Walker & Tucker, of Doncaster. Mobilised Aug. 1914, as Capt., 5th Batt. King's Own Yorkshire Light Infantry (T.). Served at Home Aug. 1914 to April 1915, and in France April to Aug. 1915. Killed at Hooge, near Ypres, Aug. 8, 1915.

GEOFFREY SOMERVILLE PITTS TUCKER.
Admitted Nov. 1911, practising at Barnstaple. Served as 2nd Lieut., 9th Batt. Cheshire Regt.

JAMES PARKE TUCKER.
Articled to H. V. I. Watts, of Newton Abbot. Joined Sept. 1914, as Private, Royal Fusiliers (Public Schools Batt.). Obtained commission in 3rd Batt. Notts and Derby Regt. (Sherwood Foresters) Jan. 1915. Attached to 1st Batt. July 1916 and subsequently to 10th Batt., promoted A/Capt. Dec. 1916, and Temp. Capt. March 1917. Served in Belgium and France. Killed in action at Monchy-le-Preux, near Arras, April 23, 1917.

ROBERT EDWARD TUCKER.
Admitted Oct. 1886. Member of Tucker & Son, of Ashburton, Devon. Joined Oct. 3, 1914, as Lieut.-Col. 2/5 Batt. Devonshire Regt., commanded Batt. in Egypt Nov. 1915 to June 1916, commanded 16th Essex Regt. Oct. 1916 to March 1917, Staff appointment in France June 1917 to June 1918. Served in Egypt and France and at Home.

GERALD TUDOR.
Articled to W. L. Yorath, of Cardiff. Joined Sept. 2, 1914, as Private, 1/1 Brecknock Batt. South Wales Borderers. Gazetted Temp. 2nd Lieut. 12th Batt. Royal Welch Fusiliers Nov. 16, 1915, attached 19th Batt. Cheshire Regt. May 1916, promoted Temp. Lieut. May 26, 1916, attached Labour Corps May 1917, promoted Temp. Capt. Sept. 1917, graded as Staff Capt., Assistant Labour Commandant, Army Headquarters, Feb. 1918. Three times mentioned in Dispatches. Awarded O.B.E. Served at Home Sept. to Oct. 1914, Nov. 1915 to April 1916, and Jan. to Feb. 1919, at Aden Nov. 1914 to July 1915, in India July to Oct. 1915, and in France May 1916 to Dec. 1918.

ALEXANDER RICHARD TUEARSLY-TUNBRIDGE.

Admitted June 1912, practising at Feltham. Served as Private, 14th Batt. County of London Regt. (London Scottish). Gazetted 2nd Lieut. 8th Batt. King's Liverpool Regt.

BERTRAM TUFF.

Admitted July 1908. Member of Arnold Day & Tuff, of Rochester, Kent. Joined Dec. 21, 1914, as Sub.-Lieut., Royal Naval Volunteer Reserve, promoted Lieut. Aug. 1917. Served at Home.

FRANK NOEL TUFF.

Articled to Bertram Tuff, of Rochester. Joined June 1, 1915, as 2nd Lieut., Royal East Kent Mounted Rifles. Served at Home and Gallipoli. Died at Malta Nov. 5, 1915, of wounds received at Gallipoli on Oct. 23, 1915.

ALBERT EDWARD TUNALEY.

Admitted Oct. 1910, practised at Manchester. Served as 2nd Lieut., 13th Batt. Lancashire Fusiliers.

EDWARD WILLLIAM TUNBRIDGE.

Admitted Jan. 1908. Member of Tunbridge & Co., of Birmingham. Joined Dec. 1915, as 2nd Lieut., 2/4 South Midland (Howitzer) Brigade Royal Field Artillery, promoted Lieut. June 1917. Served in France May 1916 to Feb. 1919.

WILLIAM STEPHEN TUNBRIDGE.

Admitted July 1882. Member of Tunbridge & Co., of Birmingham. Mobilised Aug. 4, 1914, as Major, 3rd Worcester Battery Royal Field Artillery, Lieut.-Col. 24th South Midland (Howitzer) Brigade Royal Field Artillery April 1915. Mentioned for valuable services connected with the War. Served at Home. Transferred to Territorial Force Reserve Dec. 21, 1915.

GERALD ENGLAND TUNNICLIFFE.

Admitted May 1914. Member of Maude & Tunnicliffe, of Arundel House, Arundel Street, W.C. Joined Sept. 1, 1914, as 2nd Lieut., 2/13 (Kensington) Batt. London Regt. (T.), promoted Lieut. Dec. 1914, Capt. July 1915, seconded to 105th Provisional Batt. and appointed Adutant July 1915, subsequently transferred to 107th Provisional Batt., 31st Batt. London Regt., and 17th Batt. Gloucestershire Regt. Employed at, and attached to, Judge Advocate-General's Office Aug. 1917 to Oct. 1919. Served at Home.

CHARLES HENRY TURKINGTON.

Admitted Oct. 1909., practising at Wolverhampton. Joined Sept. 1, 1914, as Private, University and Public Schools Batt. Royal Fusiliers. Gazetted 2nd Lieut. 9th Batt. North Staffordshire Regt. Dec. 9, 1914, promoted Lieut. Jan. 1917, Capt. June 1917. Served in Gallipoli Aug. to Nov. 1915, in Mesopotamia Feb. 1916 to July 1918, and in Russia Aug. 1918 to Feb. 1919. Wounded in Mesopotamia April 5, 1916.

ALAN WILLIAM TURNBULL.

Articled to J. H. Sprott, of Shrewsbury. Joined Sept. 28, 1914, as 2nd Lieut., 8th Batt. Seaforth Highlanders. Commissioned as 2nd Lieut. in same Batt. Sept. 28, 1914, promoted Lieut. July 1916, A/Capt. Aug. 1916,

Capt. Sept. 1916, appointed Adjutant Feb. 1917, promoted Major April 1918, A/Lieut.-Col. Jan. 1919. Once mentioned in Dispatches. Awarded the M.C. Served in France July to Oct. 1915 and April 1916 to July 1919. Wounded Sept. 25, 1915, and Oct. 30, 1918.

DONALD TURNBULL.

Admitted Nov. 1916, practised at Leeds. Served as Private, Royal Army Service Corps.

JOHN TURNBULL.

Admitted Feb. 1886, practising at Durham. Served as Lieut.-Col. Commanding 8th (Service) Batt. Durham Light Infantry. Three times mentioned in Dispatches.

JOHN OSWIN TURNBULL.

Articled to F. C. Vaughan, of Cardiff. Served as 2nd Lieut., 3rd Batt. The Welch Regt.

WILLIAM ANDREW TURNBULL.

Admitted May 1902. Member of Turnbull & Sons, of Scarborough. Joined Sept. 1914, as Private, 5th Batt. Yorkshire Regt. (T.). Subsequnetly gazetted 2nd Lieut. in same Regt. Wounded at Hooge 1915. Killed in action July 17, 1916.

ALBERT ERNEST TURNER.

Admitted Oct. 1912, practised at Lincoln. Served as Private, 15th County of London Batt. London Regt. (Civil Service Rifles). Killed in action in France Oct. 5, 1916.

ARTHUR TURNER.

Admitted Feb. 1877, practised at Birmingham. Served as Lieut.-Col., North Midland Division Royal Engineers. In charge of Military Administrative Centre at Smethwick. Died Aug. 11, 1915.

ARTHUR BROOKE TURNER.

Admitted July 1913, practising at Birmingham. Served as Aide-de-Camp, South Midland Division 6th Batt. Royal Warwickshire Regt. Awarded M.C.

CECIL PHILIP TURNER.

Admitted Jan. 1902. Member of Cree & Turner, of 109 Jermyn Street, St. James's, S.W. Joined May 16, 1918, as Mechanic 2nd Class, Royal Navy. Served at Home.

CHARLES FRANK TURNER.

Articled to F. W. Bromley, of Ashton-under-Lyne. Joined July 8, 1915, as Private, 21st Batt. Royal Fusiliers, attached to Royal Engineers Jan. 1916 to Sept. 1917. Served in France. Reported missing between Sept. 20 and 23, 1917, and subsequently reported to have been killed in action between those dates. Buried near Gheluvelt, south-east of Ypres.

CYRIL TURNER.

Admitted Oct. 1908, practising at Dunedin House, Basinghall Avenue, E.C. Joined Aug. 28, 1914, as Private, Hon. Artillery Company, and attained the rank of Company Quartermaster-Sergeant. Wounded in Belgium April and May 1915. Relegated to Reserve Nov. 1916.

FREDERICK BENTLEY TURNER.

Admitted June 1908, practising at 1 and 2 Milk Street, Cheapside, E.C. Served as 2nd Lieut., 143rd Labour Company.

GEORGE McDOUGALL TURNER.

Articled to J. H. Turner, of York. Served as 2nd Lieut., 5th Batt. Yorkshire Regt.

GEORGE PERRIOR TURNER.

Admitted Feb. 1906, practised at Southampton. Joined Oct. 1914 Inns of Court O.T.C. Gazetted 2nd Lieut. Hampshire Regt. and went to the Front in March 1916. Killed in action June 30, 1916, whilst in command of a Trench Mortar Battery.

HAROLD KEYNES TURNER.

Articled to J. B. Purchase, of 14 Regent Street, W. Served as Private, 28th Batt. County of London Regt. (Artists Rifles), and subsequently gazetted 2nd Lieut. Shropshire Light Infantry. Mentioned in Dispatches. Awarded the M.C.

HENRY ELLIOT TURNER.

Admitted Oct. 1908, practising at Bristol. Enlisted as Motor Cyclist, Royal Engineers Sept. 14, 1914, promoted Sergeant 1915. Granted commission in Royal Engineers Jan. 1916. Twice mentioned in Dispatches. Awarded the M.C. Served in France Oct. 1914 to Oct. 1915 and June 1916 to Jan. 1919.

JAMES ALGERNON TURNER.

Admitted June 1907, practising at Dunedin House, Basinghall Street, E.C. Joined Sept. 5, 1914, as Private, Hon. Artillery Company. Served in France. Wounded at Hooge Sept. 1915.

JOHN CLEMENCE TURNER.

Articled to G. H. Turner, of 369 Brixton Road, S.W. Mobilised Aug. 1914 as Private, 5th City of London Batt. London Regt. (London Rifle Brigade), attained the rank of Regimental Quartermaster-Sergeant. Awarded the M.S.M. Served in France.

JOHN HERBERT TURNER.

Articled to E. G. C. Chapman, of Dulverton. Served as Trooper, Royal North Somerset Yeomanry.

JOHN REGINALD TURNER.

Articled to J. M. B. Turner, of Bournemouth. Mobilised Aug. 1914, as Lieut., 3rd Batt. Dorsetshire Regt. and drafted to 1st Batt. Served in France Aug. to Oct. 1914. Killed in action at Pont Fixe, near Festubert, Oct. 13, 1914.

LEONARD VANE TURNER.

Admitted Oct. 1913. Clerk with Sole, Turner & Knight, of 69 Aldermanbury, E.C. Mobilised Aug. 5, 1914, as Private, 14th Batt. County of London Regt. (London Scottish). Served in France Sept. to Dec. 1914. Killed in action Dec. 21, 1914.

MICHAEL HOWARD TURNER.

Admitted Dec. 1913. Of Toronto. Served as Private, 6th Fort Carrys "C" Coy., Canadian Contingent.

MONTAGU TREVOR TURNER.

Admitted April 1908. Member of C. & M Turner, of 199 Piccadilly, W. Served with 2nd Batt. Royal Sussex Regt. Sept. 1914 to Feb. 1915, promoted Capt. Feb. 1915, appointed Assistant Provost Marshal 39th Division Aug. 1915, Assistant Provost Marshal VI. Corps, with the temporary rank of Major Oct. 1917 to April 1919. Twice mentioned in Dispatches. Awarded O.B.E. and M.C. Served in France and Belgium and with Army of Occupation in Germany.

REGINALD STANLEY TURNER.

Articled to G. W. Barrows, of Nottingham. Joined Sept. 29, 1914, as Private, 10th Batt. Notts and Derby Regt. (Sherwood Foresters), promoted Lance-Corporal July 1915. Served in Flanders. Killed in action Aug. 27, 1915.

STANLEY TURNER.

Admitted Nov. 1908, practising at Rochdale. Joined Dec. 10, 1915, as Sapper, Royal Engineers, transferred to Tank Corps Dec. 1917 and promoted Sergeant. Served in France.

WILLIAM VICTOR TURNER.

Articled to G. H. Dawes, of Pinners Hall, E.C. Joined Nov. 27, 1914, as 2nd Lieut., 16th Batt. Royal Fusiliers. Served at Gallipoli, Cape Helles, and Suvla Bay. Wounded Gallipoli Aug. 21, 1915. Relinquished commission on account of ill-health caused by wounds March 3, 1917.

CECIL WILLIAM TURTON.

Articled to H. Montague Williams, of Brighton. Mobilised Aug. 1914, as 2nd Lieut., 1/6 Cyclist Batt. Royal Sussex Regt., promoted Lieut. Oct. 1915. Served at Home. Accidentally killed Feb. 4, 1916.

CYRIL BARNETT TUSON.

Articled to H. T. Barnett, of 2 Camomile Street, Bishopsgate, E.C. Joined Aug. 4, 1914, as Private, Inns of Court O.T.C. (Cavalry). Gazetted 2nd Lieut. 7th London Brigade Royal Field Artillery Sept. 24, 1914, promoted Lieut. 235th Brigade June 1916. Served in France March 1915 to Oct. 1916 and April 1917 to May 1918.

GUY LUNTLEY TUTIN.

Articled to his father, George Tutin, of Nottingham. Served as Lieut., 3rd Batt. Notts and Derby Regt. (Sherwood Foresters). Died at Brook War Hospital, Woolwich, Jan. 27, 1919.

ALAN TWEEDALE.

Admitted Feb. 1908. Member of Tweedale, Sons & Lees, of Oldham. Enlisted as Private Public Schools Batt. Middlesex Regt. Sept. 1914. Obtained commission as 2nd Lieut. 10th Batt. Manchester Regt. (T.F.) June 1915, promoted Lieut. June 1917. Served in Gallipoli, Egypt, France, Belgium, and at Home.

ARTHUR CLEMENT TWEEDY.

Admitted April 1889, practising at Monmouth. Mobilised Aug. 1914 with Royal Garrison Artillery (T.F.) and attained the rank of Major. Served at Home (Severn Defences and Sheerness).

ALBERT EDWIN TWORT.

Admitted Oct. 1914. Managing Clerk with Freshfield & Sons, of Old Jewry, E.C. Joined Jan. 1916, as Private, The Queen's Royal West Surrey Regt., became Signaller and lent to Royal Irish Rifles. Served in France. Died from wounds in hospital at Avesnes Dec. 19, 1916.

CHARLES NOEL WALKER TYACKE.

Admitted Nov. 1907. Member of J. Walker Tyacke & Son, of Helston, Cornwall. Joined Aug. 1914, as 2nd Lieut., Duke of Cornwall's Light Infantry, promoted Capt. 1915. Served in France. Killed at Verlaines, near St. Quentin, March 23, 1918.

ARTHUR TYLER.

Admitted Dec. 1911, practised at 23 Rood Lane, E.C. Served as 2nd Lieut., Royal Army Service Corps, promoted Capt. May 1918. Mentioned in Dispatches and awarded M.C.

CECIL ULLYOTT.

Admitted May 1914, practised at Hull. Joined Jan. 1916, as Private, Inns of Court O.T.C. Gazetted 2nd Lieut. 5th (Cyclist) Batt. East Yorkshire Regt. Nov. 1916, promoted Lieut. April 1918. Served in France and at Home. Killed in action near Grandecourt Aug. 23, 1918.

HAROLD HENRY UNDERWOOD.

Articled to Thomas Ottaway, of St. Albans. Joined Oct. 8, 1914, as 2nd Lieut., 2/4 Batt. Northamptonshire Regt., promoted Capt. Dec. 1916. Served at Gallipoli, in Egypt, and in Palestine. Killed at Battle of Gaza April 17, 1917.

JOHN MIDDLETON UNDERWOOD.

Articled to C. C. Underwood, of 13 Holles Street, Cavendish Square, W. Joined Aug. 27, 1914, as Driver, Royal Field Artillery (T.). Gazetted 2nd Lieut. Royal Field Artillery June 19, 1915. Served in Flanders and France. Killed in action between Ginchy and Marval, France, Nov. 10, 1916.

JOHN WILLIAM UNDERWOOD.

Admitted Oct. 4, 1907, practising at Dukinfield. Mobilised Aug. 4, 1914, as Lieut., 6th Batt. Cheshire Regt., promoted Capt. Nov. 1914. Served at Home.

CHARLES HENRY UNSWORTH.

Articled to C. H. Unsworth, of Warrington. Joined June 1916, as Private, 10th Batt. King's Liverpool Regt. (Liverpool Scottish), promoted Corporal Nov. 1917. Served at Home and in France.

ARTHUR UPTON.

Admitted March 1914, practising at Birmingham. Joined the Army Sept. 10, 1914, and wounded in action July 22, 1916. Discharged March 15, 1917.

CECIL CHARLES UPTON.

Admitted Dec. 1901, practising at Romford, Essex. Joined March 2, 1916, as Gunner, Royal Garrison Artillery. Served in France and Belgium.

JOHN ALBERIC EVERARD UPTON.

Articled to John St. Clair Upton, of Market Drayton. Joined Sept 7, 1914, as Private, 16th Service (Public Schools) Batt. Middlesex Regt., and subsequently promoted Corporal. Gazetted 2nd Lieut. 3rd Batt. King's Shropshire Light Infantry June 5, 1915. Served in France April to Aug. 1916. Died Aug. 20, 1916, of wounds received in action on Aug. 18, 1916, near Guillemont, France.

ARTHUR URBAN.

Admitted March 1912. Managing Clerk with Sir Robert Vaughan Gower, of Tunbridge Wells. Joined May 1915, as Private, Inns of Court O.T.C. Gazetted 2nd Lieut. 9th Batt. East Surrey Regt. Served in France. Killed Sept. 2, 1916.

PAUL URBAN.

Admitted Aug. 1914, practised at Donnington House, Norfolk Street, W.C. Served as Private, Hon. Artillery Company.

ERNEST HENRY BROADBENT USHER.

Articled to C. Loriston Clarke, of Bristol. Mobilised Aug. 1914, as Gunner, Gloucestershire Royal Field Artillery (T.). Gazetted 2nd Lieut. Royal Field Artillery (S.R.) April 3, 1915, gazetted 2nd Lieut. Royal Field Artillery (regular permanent commission) Jan. 3, 1916, promoted Lieut. July 1917, A/Capt. Jan. 1917, A/Major April 1918. Awarded the M.C. Served at Home Aug. 1914 to June 1915, in France June 1915 to Sept. 1918, and subsequently in Army of Black Sea and Egypt. Wounded Sept. 13, 1918.

JOHN CLERE VAISEY.

Admitted Sept. 1905. Managing Clerk with Cameron Kemm & Co., of Gresham House, London, E.C. Joined Sept. 2, 1914, as Private, Public Schools Brigade (19th Service Batt. Royal Fusiliers), transferred to 22nd (Service) Batt. Royal Fusiliers April 1916 as Lance-Corporal. Awarded the M.M. Served in France Nov. 1915 to Nov. 1916. Wounded Dec. 3, 1915. Invalided out Feb. 17, 1917.

ROLAND MADDISON VAISEY.

Admitted May 1909. Member of A. W. Vaisey & Son, of Devereux Chambers, Temple, W.C.; Tring; and Berkhamstead. Obtained a commission in the Royal Field Artillery in July 1916 and attained the rank of Capt. Killed in action Sept. 7, 1918.

JOHN VALE.

Articled to Alfred Anstey, of Exeter. Joined Jan. 9, 1915, as Private, 16th Batt. Middlesex Regt. Gazetted 2nd Lieut. Sept. 25, 1915, and transferred to Dorsetshire Regt., promoted Lieut. 1916. Once mentioned in Dispatches. Awarded the M.C. Served in France. Gassed, shell-shock Sept. 27, 1916.

FRANK LOUIS VANDERPUMP.

Admitted Dec. 1912, practising at 53 King William Street, E.C. Served as Private, Hon. Artillery Company, and subsequently gazetted 2nd Lieut. South Wales Borderers, promoted Lieut. March 1916. Mentioned in Dispatches. Awarded the M.C.

HENRY JOHN VAN DRUTEN.

Articled to C. L. Norden, of 56 Moorgate Street, E.C. Joined March 25, 1915, as Private, Inns of Court O.T.C. Subsequently commissioned and attained the rank of Capt. in Middlesex Regt. Wounded at Miraumont, Ancre, Feb. 17, 1917. Served in France.

ARTHUR VANDYK.

Admitted Nov. 1914. Member of Herbert Oppenheimer, Nathan & Vandyk, of 1 Finsbury Square, E.C. Joined Dec. 22, 1914, as 2nd Lieut., 12th (S.) Batt. Royal Fusiliers, promoted Lieut. 24th Batt. London Regt. (The Queen's), subsequently transferred to Royal Air Force. Served in France. Wounded on the Somme Sept. 1916.

EUSTACE HAZZEL VANT.

Admitted Feb. 1913, practising at Settle, Yorks. Served as Capt., 4th (Reserve) Batt. Loyal North Lancashire Regt.

ERIC JOHN VARDON.

Articled to P. J. Vardon, of 12 Savile Row, London, W. Joined Sept. 28, 1914, as 2nd Lieut., 2/5 Batt. East Surrey Regt., promoted Temp. Lieut. Dec. 1914, Temp. Capt. and Adjutant July 1915, A/Capt. and Adjutant 16th Queen's (Royal West Surrey) Regt. Jan. 1918, Temp. Major and D.A.A. and Q.M.G. May 1919. Once mentioned in Dispatches. Awarded M.B.E. (Military), 3rd Class St. Anne and 2nd Class St. Stanislas (Russian). Served at Home and in North Russia.

JOHN KENNETH VARVILL.

Articled to J. K. Wright, of Nottingham. Served as 2nd Lieut. 6th (Service) Batt. East Lancashire Regt., and attained the rank of Capt. Mentioned in Dispatches. Awarded the M.C.

HUBERT HARRIS DE COURCY VAUGHAN.

Admitted June 1904, practised at Berkeley, Glos. Served as 2nd Lieut., Queen's Own Oxfordshire Hussars, promoted Lieut. July 1917.

JOHN FREDERICK VAUGHAN.

Admitted Feb. 1914, practising at Willenhall, Staffs. Joined May 1918 as Clerk in Royal Air Force. Served at Royal Air Force Depôt, Blandford, Dorset.

ALFRED JULIAN VAUX.

Admitted May 1899. Managing Clerk with Corsellis & Berney, of 64 East Hill, Wandsworth, S.W. Joined Sept. 2, 1914, as Private, 9th Batt. County of London Regt., subsequently commissioned and attained the rank of Capt. Royal Berkshire Regt. Served in France.

FRANCIS GEORGE VAUX.

Admitted Feb. 1914. Managing Clerk with Lucas & Wyllys, of Great Yarmouth. Joined Aug. 4, 1914, as Private, Norfolk Yeomanry. Gazetted 2nd Lieut. 5th Batt. Durham Light Infantry May 28, 1915, promoted Lieut. Sept. 1917. Served at Home Aug. 1914 to June 1916, and in France June 1916 to Feb. 1919.

ARTHUR CHARLES THOMAS VEASEY.

Admitted Nov. 1904. Member of Morris, Veasey & Co., of 40 King Street, Cheapside, E.C. Joined Aug. 8, 1914, as 2nd Lieut., 8th Batt. Hampshire Regt., promoted Capt. and Adjutant Dec. 1914, Major May 1915, commanded Batt. in Gallipoli Aug. and Sept. 1915. Three times mentioned in Dispatches. Served at Home and Gallipoli.

THOMAS HUBERT VEASEY.

Admitted April 1909, practising at Baldock, Herts. Joined Sept. 19, 1914, as 2nd Lieut., 11th Batt. Worcestershire Regt., promoted Lieut. Dec. 1914, Capt. July 1915, Major Aug. 1918, transferred to General List Jan. 1915, Staff Capt. 78th Infantry Brigade Jan. 1915 to Aug. 1917, D.A.A.G. G.H.Q. British Salonica Force Aug. 1917 to March 1919, D.A.A.G. Army of the Black Sea March to Aug. 1919. Twice mentioned in Dispatches. Awarded the M.C. and Serbian Order of White Eagle, 4th Class. Served at Home Sept. 1914 to Sept. 1915, in France Sept. to Nov. 1915, with British Salonica Force Nov. 1915 to March 1919, and with Army of Black Sea March to Aug. 1919.

JOHN LEWES HOLE VELLACOTT.

Admitted March 1902. Member of Crosse, Wyatt & Vellacott, of Barnstaple. Served as Lieut., Duke of Wellington's West Riding Regt.

ALFRED ERNEST VENABLES.

Admitted Jan. 1902, practised at 18 Austin Friars, E.C. Joined the Royal Flying Corps in May 1916. Killed whilst flying in April 1917.

CHARLES EDGCOMBE VENNING.

Admitted May 1903. Member of Borlase & Venning, of Penzance. Joined Sept. 3, 1914, as Private, Royal 1st Devon Yeomanry. Gazetted Lieut. Oct. 1914, Capt. Dec. 1914, Temp. Major Jan. 1916. Served at Home Sept. 1914 to Dec. 1916, and in France Dec. 1916 to March 1919.

JOHN VENNING.

Admitted June 1906. Member of Bird & Bird, of 5 Gray's Inn Square, W.C. Joined Aug. 4, 1914, as Private, Inns of Court O.T.C. Gazetted 2nd Lieut. 1st Batt. London Regt. Sept. 1914, promoted Lieut. May 1915, Capt. Nov. 1915, A/Major Nov. 1917. Once mentioned in Dispatches. Awarded the M.C. Served at Home and in France. Wounded Sept. 11, 1918.

DOUGLAS GEORGE VERNEY.

Admitted Nov. 1912, practising at Southend-on-Sea. Joined Feb. 28, 1916, as Sapper, London Electrical Engineers, Royal Engineers (T.), and attained the rank of Corporal. Served at Home.

THOMAS MELLARD VERNON.

Admitted Feb. 1902, practising at Guiseley and Otley. Joined Sept. 4, 1916, as Ordinary Seaman, Royal Naval Volunteer Reserve, promoted A.B. Jan. 1918. Employed as a Gunner on defensively armed merchant ships and made voyages to the United States, Canada, and France.

FREDERICK HERBERT VERRALL.

Admitted Jan. 1910. Member of Verrall & Sons, of Worthing. Joined the Royal Naval Volunteer Reserve in March 1916, and attained the rank of Leading Telegraphist.

WILLIAM JAMES EGERTON VERRALL.

Admitted Feb. 1903. Member of Verrall & Sons, of Worthing. Joined April 20, 1917, as Private, Inns of Court O.T.C., and subsequently gazetted 2nd Lieut. 1st (Reserve) Batt. Worcestershire Regt.

GUY NAUNTON VERTUE.

Admitted Nov. 1913. Member of Vertue, Son & Churcher, of 19 Hanover Square, W. Joined March 1917, as Private, Royal Army Ordnance Corps. Served at Home.

GEORGE ALFRED TURNER VIALS.

Admitted April 1911, practising at Northampton. Joined May 1915 Inns of Court O.T.C. Gazetted 2nd Lieut. 4th Batt. Duke of Wellington's West Riding Regt. May 28, 1915, promoted Lieut. 1917. Served at Home.

GEORGE CECIL VICARY.

Admitted May 1905, practising at Lymington, Hants. Joined March 1916, as Gunner, Royal Garrison Artillery and attained the rank of Corporal. Gazetted 2nd Lieut. Royal Garrison Artillery Jan. 1916, promoted Lieut. June 1918. Served in France and Italy.

GEORGE EDWARD VICARY.

Admitted April 1889, practising at Warminster, Wilts. Mobilised as Capt. 1/4 Batt. Wiltshire Regt. (T.). Served in India.

JOHN VICARY.

Articled to G. D. Woollcombe, of Newton Abbot. Served as 2nd Lieut., Gloucestershire Regt., and promoted Lieut. Dec. 1916. Twice mentioned in Dispatches. Awarded the M.C. and two Bars.

CYRIL HAMPTON VICK.

Admitted Dec. 1910, practising at 27 Copthall Avenue, London Wall, E.C. Joined March 1915, as 2nd Lieut., Gloucestershire Regt., promoted Temp. Capt. Aug. 1916, A/Major The Queen's Own Worcestershire Hussars Jan. 1919, transferred to Worcestershire Regt. Dec. 1915 and to The Queen's Own Worcestershire Hussars March 1918. Served in France. Gassed at Gavrelle April 1917.

HENRY REGINALD VICKERS.

Admitted Jan. 1905. Member of Henry Vickers, Son & Brown, of Sheffield. Served as Capt., West Riding Divisional Royal Field Artillery.

STANSFELD VICKERS.

Admitted Jan. 1907, practising at Paignton. Mobilised Aug. 1914, as Capt., 2nd Devon Battery 4th Wessex Brigade Royal Field Artillery (T.), promoted Temp. Major Aug. 1914, Substantive Major June 1916. Once mentioned in Dispatches. Awarded the D.S.O. Served in India Oct. 1914 to March 1917, in France June 1917 to Sept. 1918, and in Egypt Aug. to Oct. 1919. Wounded at Ronsoy Sept. 21, 1918.

WILLIAM HENRY VICKRESS.

Admitted July 1902. Member of Hasties, of 65 Lincoln's Inn Fields, W.C. Joined Dec. 1914 as Lieut., Royal Army Service Corps, and attained rank of Major. Awarded the D.S.O.

BENJAMIN WILLIAM VIGO.

Admitted Aug. 1906. Member of Soames & Vigo, of Ely Place, E.C. Served with British Red Cross Society as Hon. Lieut. 1917, and Hon. Capt. Sept. 1918. Once mentioned in Dispatches. Awarded M.B.E. Served at Home 1915 and in Mesopotamia 1916 to 1919.

GEOFFREY VINALL.

Admitted July 1902. Member of Isaac Vinall & Sons, of Lewes. Joined Nov. 16, 1915, as Private, 26th Batt. Royal Fusiliers, transferred to 31st Batt. Royal Fusiliers June 1916. Served at Home. Discharged Jan. 4, 1917.

HUGH JOHN VINALL.

Admitted March 1897. Member of Isaac Vinall & Sons, of Lewes. Joined Aug. 27, 1917, as Private, Royal Army Service Corps and posted to 64th Railhead Supply Detachment. Once mentioned in Dispatches. Served at Home Aug. to Sept. 1917, in France Sept. to Nov. 1917, and in Italy Nov. 1917 to Jan. 1919.

CHARLES WORSLEY VINCENT.

Admitted June 1898, practising at Ryde, I. of W. Joined Aug. 12, 1914, as Lieut. and Quartermaster, 8th Batt. Hampshire Regt., promoted Capt. Dec. 1914, Major April 1917. Once mentioned in Dispatches. Served in Palestine. Wounded in second Battle of Gaza April 19, 1917.

HENRY EDWARD VINCENT.

Articled to F. H. Trethowan, of Salisbury, Joined Nov. 23, 1915, as Private, Inns of Court O.T.C. Gazetted 2nd Lieut. 15th Batt. Cheshire Regt. Oct. 25, 1916, promoted Capt. and Adjutant April 1918. Once mentioned in Dispatches. Awarded the M.C. Served in France and Flanders Nov. 1916 to April 1919.

WILLIAM MORRIS VINCENT.

Admitted Oct. 1914. Member of Vincent & Vincent, of 20 Budge Row, E.C. Joined Sept. 1914, as Private, Inns of Court O.T.C. Gazetted 2nd Lieut. 8th Batt. Suffolk Regt. Dec. 1914. Served in Egypt, attached to 4th Batt. Essex Regt. Killed at the Battle of Gaza March 26, 1917.

ERIC VINE.

Admitted Oct. 1911. Of 10 Old Jewry Chambers, E.C. Served as Private, 28th Batt. County of London Regt. (Artists Rifles).

WILFRID GEORGE VINT.

Admitted May 1911. Member of Vint, Hill & Killick, of Bradford. Joined March 27, 1916, as Private, 3rd Batt. Duke of Wellington's West Riding Regt. Served in France. Killed in action at Beaucourt Dec. 8, 1916.

JOHN TREWREN VIZARD.

Admitted Jan. 1906. Member of Vizard & Son, of Monmouth. Joined Feb. 22, 1915, as 2nd Lieut., Glamorgan Royal Garrison Artillery (T.), promoted Lieut. Nov. 1915, seconded to 315th Siege Battery Jan. 1917, promoted A/Capt. Oct. 1917. Awarded the Italian Bronze Medal " al valore." Served in Italy April 1917 to Dec. 1918.

GORDON PHILLIPS VOSS.

Admitted April 1910. Managing Clerk with R. Voss & Son, of 173 Bethnal Green Road, E. Mobilised Aug. 4, 1914, as Private, 28th Batt. County of London Regt. (Artists Rifles), and subsequently Sergeant Instructor Machine Guns, G.H.Q. School, France. Gazetted 2nd Lieut. No. 5 Battery Motor Machine Gun Service Oct. 29, 1915, promoted Lieut. Tank Corps Nov. 1916, and Capt. Oct. 1918. Awarded the M.C. and Bar. Served at Home, in France, and in the United States of America.

FRANCIS MINCHIN VOULES.

Admitted Dec. 1890. Of 65 Bishopsgate, E.C. Knight of Grace of the Order of St. John of Jerusalem. Appointed Commissioner for Holland for the British Red Cross Society Nov. 1917, and as such had charge of the occupation, employment, instruction, and general welfare work of the British Prisoners of War interned in Holland, subsequently assisted in the repatriation of the Prisoners of War. Visited Berlin in Dec. 1918 to arrange the transport of our Prisoners from Germany, and afterwards had charge of the Russian Prisoners of War in the X. and VII. Corps in Germany from Jan. to July 1919. Awarded the C.B.E.

CECIL WILLIAM GRENVILLE VOWLES.

Articled to G. S. Sinnott, of Bristol. Served as Private, 6th Batt. Gloucestershire Regt., and subsequently gazetted 2nd Lieut. South Midland Royal Engineers.

HENRY HAYES VOWLES.

Admitted Dec. 1900, practising at Dursley, Glos. Joined Sept. 12, 1914, as Private, 12th Batt. Gloucestershire Regt. Gazetted 2nd Lieut. 13th Batt. Gloucestershire Regt. May 14, 1915, promoted Lieut. July 1916, Capt. July 1917, transferred to 3rd Batt. Nov. 1918. Served in France March 1916 to June 1918.

GASTON FREDERICK BAYARD WACE.

Admitted Feb. 1913. Of St. Albans. Joined March 1916, as Voluntary Driver, British Red Cross. Gazetted 2nd Lieut. General Staff Intelligence Section 2nd Echelon Egyptian Exped. Force Dec. 1917. Served in Egypt.

HENRY EDWARD WACE.

Admitted April 1914. With Ernest Bevir & Son, Devereux Chambers, Temple. Mobilised Aug. 1914, as Lieut., 4th Batt. King's Shropshire Light Infantry (T.), promoted Capt. Oct. 1914. Once mentioned in Dispatches. Served at Home and in Burma, Singapore, South Africa, and France. Killed in action April 14, 1918.

HENRY LANCELOT WADDINGTON.

Articled to E. J. Birdsall, of Scarborough. Joined Aug. 14, 1915, as Private, Royal Army Service Corps (M.T.). Gazetted 2nd Lieut. Royal Flying Corps Nov. 22, 1916, promoted Lieut. Aug. 1917, Capt. Royal Air Force Oct. 1918. Served in France and Belgium.

JOHN EVELYN ALEXANDER WADDINGTON.

Articled to Evelyn Waddington, of Usk, Monmouthshire. Joined Oct. 14, 1914, as 2nd Lieut., 2nd Batt. Monmouthshire Regt., promoted Lieut. Aug. 1915, Capt. Aug. 1916, reverted to Lieut. 1917. Served at Home and France.

ARTHUR CAMPBELL WADE.

Admitted Aug. 1895. Member of Carleton Holmes, Fell & Wade, of 12 Bedford Row. Joined Nov. 1914, as A.B., Royal Naval Volunteer Reserve. Gazetted Sub-Lieut. Royal Naval Volunteer Reserve March 10, 1915, promoted Lieut. Nov. 1915, Lieut.-Commander Jan. 1918, Major Royal Air Force April 1918. Served at Home and in France.

HENRY OSWALD WADE.

Admitted Dec. 1894. Member of Wade, Tetley, Wade & Scott, of Bradford, Yorks. Mobilised as Lieut.-Col. 6th Batt. West Yorkshire Regt. (T.), promoted Colonel Aug. 1918. Twice mentioned in Dispatches. Awarded the D.S.O. Served in France and Belgium. Wounded July 1, 1916.

HUGH ROBERT WADE.

Articled to C. A. Wade, of Henfield, Sussex. Mobilised Aug. 1914, as Lieut., 1st Home Counties Brigade Royal Field Artillery (T.F.), promoted Temp. Capt. Aug. 1915 (Permanent Capt. June 1916), A/Major Dec. 1916, A/Lieut.-Col. Oct. 1918. Once mentioned in Dispatches. Served in India 1914 to 1915, Mesopotamia 1915 to 1916, India 1916 to 1917, Mesopotamia 1917 to 1919.

JOHN SEYMOUR WADE.

Admitted Jan. 1910, practising at Suffolk House, Laurence Pountney Hill, E.C. Joined Aug. 14, 1917, as Private, 15th Batt. London Regt., and subsequently received hon. commission as 2nd Lieut. Royal Air Force. Served at Home.

PERCY JACKSON WADE.

Admitted Nov. 1905. Deputy Town Clerk, Middleton. Joined Sept. 1914, as Private, Manchester Regt. Served in France. Killed in the Battle of the Somme July 1, 1916.

HENRY HARMAN WADESON.

Admitted Oct. 1913. Managing Clerk with Hayter, Simpson & Fisher, of Cockermouth and Keswick. Joined 1914, as Lieut., Hampshire Regt., transferred to Reserve of Indian Officers as Lieut. in 55th Punjabi Native Border Rifles 1915, promoted Capt. Served in North-West Frontier, India, and East African campaign.

ROBERT EDGAR WADSWORTH.

Admitted Jan. 1909, practising at Leeds. Joined Nov. 6, 1916, as Private, 25th (Works) Batt. Durham Light Infantry, attached Forage Dept. Royal Army Service Corps, promoted Sergeant Feb. 1917. Served at Home as Confidential Clerk to D.P.O.S., Cheshire, Forage Dept. Royal Army Service Corps.

WILLIE WADSWORTH.

Articled to W. Bailey, of Halifax. Joined July 1, 1916, as Private, 11th Reserve Cavalry (18th Hussars), transferred to Machine Gun Corps (Cavalry) Feb. 1917. Served in France and in Mesopotamia.

ARTHUR WAINWRIGHT.

Admitted Jan. 1904. Member of Wainwright, Woolfe & Browne, of Grimsby. Served as Private, 5th Batt. East Yorkshire Regt. (T.), subsequently transferred to Royal Army Service Corps and attained the rank of Corporal. Served in Egypt.

MONTAGUE STEPHEN WAKEFIELD.

Articled to Edward Boase, of Penzance. Obtained a commission in the Notts and Derby Regt. (Sherwood Foresters) in Jan. 1915, and promoted Lieut. Sept. 1915. Served in France. Killed in action Nov. 20, 1917.

HENRY HOWARD WALFORD.

Admitted Feb. 1914. Member of Munton, Morris, King & Co., of Temple Avenue, E.C. Joined May 7, 1915, as 2nd Lieut., Royal Army Service Corps (T.), promoted Lieut. July 1917, Capt. Jan. 1919, Staff Headquarters, London District, Oct. 1917 to Jan. 1920. Served at Home.

CHARLES SHELBORNE WALKER.

Admitted Oct. 1899. Member of Walker & Son, of Doncaster. Served as Capt., 2nd West Riding Brigade Royal Field Artillery.

CHARLES VALENTINE WALKER.

Admitted Aug. 1912. Of the Solicitors' Dept. H.M. Customs and Excise. Joined May 1918, as Private, 28th Batt. County of London Regt. (Artists Rifles). Gazetted 2nd Lieut. King's Royal Rifle Corps March 1919.

CHARLES VIVIAN WALKER.

Admitted Oct. 1912. Member of Bromley & Walker, of Leeds. Joined Aug. 22, 1914, as Corporal, Leeds University O.T.C. Gazetted Lieut. King's Own Yorkshire Light Infantry Dec. 10, 1914, promoted Temp. Capt. June 1916 to command a Machine Gun Company overseas, Capt. Nov. 1917. Once mentioned in Dispatches. Served in France June 1916 to Aug. 1917.

EDWARD WALKER.

Admitted Aug. 1903, practising at Birmingham. Served as 2nd Lieut., South Midland Division Royal Army Service Corps.

EDWARD LOUIS HAVILAND WALKER.

Admitted Oct. 1909, practising at 59 Strand, W.C. Joined Oct. 29, 1915, as Private, Inns of Court O.T.C. Commissioned Nov. 11, 1916, in Royal

Garrison Artillery, posted to 1/1 Lowland Heavy Battery Jan. 1917. Served in France Jan. 1917 to March 1919. Wounded June 2, 1917, gassed Sept. 1918.

GEORGE HALLIWELL WALKER.

Articled to J. H. Hall, of Bolton. Joined Nov. 2, 1915, as Cadet, Manchester University O.T.C. Gazetted 2nd Lieut. 8th Batt. Manchester Regt. Aug. 4, 1916, promoted Lieut. Feb. 1918. Served at Home and in France. Wounded March 27, 1918 (France).

GEORGE LOUIS WALKER.

Admitted Feb. 1902. Member of Lamb, Kyffin Taylor & Walker, of Liverpool. Mobilised Aug. 4, 1914, as Major commanding 2nd West Lancashire Brigade Royal Field Artillery (T.), promoted Lieut.-Col. in June 1916. Commanding 47th Brigade Nov. to Dec. 1917, 178th Brigade Sept. to Nov. 1918, 78th Brigade Jan. to April 1919 and 51st Brigade April to Oct. 1919. Three times mentioned in Dispatches. Awarded the T.D. Served at Home Sept. 1916 to Oct. 1917, and Jan. to Oct. 1918, in France Sept. 1914 to Sept. 1916, Oct. to Dec. 1917, Sept. 1918 to April 1919, and on the Rhine April to Oct. 1919. Wounded Aug. 15, 1916.

GEORGE ROLLO SELBORNE WALKER.

Articled to C. S. T. Neumann, of Bradford. Joined Aug. 8, 1914, as 2nd Lieut., 6th Batt. Prince of Wales's Own West Yorkshire Regt., promoted Temp. Capt. Nov. 1914, Capt. June 1916. Served in France. Wounded in the Battle of the Somme July 21, 1916, and in the Battle of Cambrai Nov. 22, 1917. Invalided from service on account of wounds June 20, 1918.

HAROLD WALKER.

Admitted Feb. 1906. Member of Winskell & Walker, of South Shields. Joined Sept. 22, 1916, as Gunner, Royal Garrison Artillery, promoted Bombardier Jan. 1918. Served in France.

JOHN WICKHAM WALKER.

Admitted Feb. 1913. Member of Walker & Son, of Bawtry, Yorkshire. Mobilised Aug. 1914, as Capt., 5th Batt. King's Own Yorkshire Light Infantry. Once mentioned in Dispatches. Served in France and Flanders. Killed in action near Thiepval, France, July 5, 1916.

JOSEPH WALKER.

Admitted Dec. 1899. Member of Hall, Walker & Norton, of Huddersfield. Joined Oct. 1914, as 2nd Lieut., 5th Batt. Duke of Wellington's West Riding Regt., promoted Capt. Oct. 1915. Once mentioned in Dispatches. Awarded the O.B.E. Served in France. Wounded May 1917.

MILES WALKER.

Articled to Roberts & Andrew, of Exeter. Served as 2nd Lieut., Royal Army Service Corps.

MILES RAINIFORTH WALKER.

Admitted Nov. 1906. Managing Clerk with Stuart & Tull, of Gray's Inn, W.C. Joined Jan. 31, 1917, as Gunner, Royal Garrison Artillery (Anti-Aircraft Section). Served in France. Died at 52nd Stationary Hospital, Le Havre, France, Feb. 6, 1919.

RAINFORTH ARMITAGE WALKER.

Admitted Jan. 1909. Managing Clerk with Frederick Walker & Co., of 68 Coleman Street, E.C. Joined Aug. 1914, as Private, 10th Batt. Royal Fusiliers. Gazetted 2nd Lieut. 8th Batt. Royal West Kent Regt. 1915, promoted Lieut. 1917. Served in France. Wounded Oct. 1918.

RICHARD WALKER.

Articled to Alfred Platts, of Bingley. Joined March 3, 1915, as Private, 62nd Division Royal Field Artillery, afterwards promoted to Sergeant. Served in France. Killed April 4, 1917.

THOMAS HENRY WALKER.

Admitted March 1904, practising at Peterborough. Mobilised 1914, as Major, Royal Field Artillery, Staff (Brigade Major R.A. 53rd Division, and Staff Officer to G.O.C., R.A., XX. Corps) March to Nov. 1917, A/Lieut.-Col. commanding 265th Brigade Royal Field Artillery 1917 to 1919, promoted Lieut.-Col. Oct. 1918, granted Regular Commission in Royal Horse and Field Artillery as Major Nov. 1918 with seniority from May 1915. Once mentioned in Dispatches. Awarded the D.S.O. Served in France 1915 to 1916, and in Egypt and Palestine 1916 to 1919.

VICTOR KYNASTON WALKER.

Articled to P. K. Metcalfe, of 92 Great Tower Street, E.C. Served as Private, 5th City of London Batt. London Regt. (London Rifle Brigade).

WILLIAM EATON GUY WALKER.

Articled to C. H. Williams, of Nottingham. Mobilised Aug. 1914 with 7th Batt. Notts and Derby Regt. (Sherwood Foresters) and attained the rank of Capt. Served in France. Killed in action July 2, 1916.

GEOFFREY CRESSWELL WALL.

Admitted Nov. 1908. Formerly of Bristol. Served as 2nd Lieut., 60th Rifles.

HARRY WALL.

Admitted Dec. 1907, practising at Keighley. Joined Dec. 1915, as Private, Inns of Court, eventually Lieut. 2/8 Batt. Worcestershire Regt. Served at Home and in France. Wounded April 1918.

JOHN WALL.

Admitted Oct. 1911. Member of Wall & Son, of Wigan. Mobilised Aug. 1914, as Lieut., 5th Batt. Manchester Regt., promoted Capt. June 1915. Served in Egypt Sept. 1914 to May 1915, with Med. Exped. Force May to July 1915, Egyptian Exped. Force April 1916 to March 1917, British Exped. Force March 1917 to March 1918, and at Home March 1918 to Jan. 1919.

GEORGE FREDERICK WALLACE.

Admitted May 1909, practising at 27 Essex Street, Strand, W.C. Served as Corporal, Royal Air Force.

JOHN PITCAIRN WALLACE.

Admitted Nov. 1909, formerly of Romford. Served with the Seaforth Highlanders.

THOMAS WALLACE.
Admitted May 1911. Of Cardiff. Joined Sept. 10, 1914, as Private. Gazetted 2nd Lieut. 17th Batt. The Welch Regt. Jan. 10, 1915, promoted Lieut. June 1915, Capt. Nov. 1915. Awarded the M.C. Served in France May to Aug. 1916 and Jan. to July 1917, and at Salonica July 1918 to Oct. 1919. Wounded May 31, 1916, July 10, 1917, and Sept. 18, 1918.

ARTHUR HORACE WALLER.
Admitted Nov. 1902. Managing Clerk with Buss, Bretherton, & Murton-Neale, of Tunbridge Wells. Joined May 28, 1915, as Private, West Kent Yeomanry, and attained the rank of Sergeant. Served at Home.

GUY CHARLES WALLINGTON.
Admitted Jan. 1906. Member of Seaton Taylor & Co., of 5 Gray's Inn Square, W.C. Joined June 6, 1916, as Private, 13th Batt. London Regt., commissioned 2nd Lieut. in same Batt. Jan. 24, 1917, promoted Lieut. July 1917. Served in France.

ARTHUR WALLIS.
Articled to the late H. R. Leigh, of Horwich. Joined Nov. 19, 1915, as Sapper, Royal Engineers. Gazetted 2nd Lieut. Loyal North Lancashire Regt. June 30, 1918. Served in France July to Oct. 1918. Wounded Oct. 1, 1918. Died in hospital Oct. 2, 1918.

GEORGE LLOYD WALLIS.
Admitted July 1910. Managing Clerk with E. L. Wallis, of Hereford. Mobilised Aug. 5, 1914, as Trooper, Berkshire Yeomanry. Gazetted 2nd Lieut. 1st Batt. Herefordshire Regt. May 9, 1915, promoted Lieut. June 1916. Served at Home Aug. 1914 to March 1915, June to Nov. 1915, and Oct. 1916 to April 1919, in Egypt April to June 1915 and with the Med. and Egyptian Exped. Forces Nov. 1915 to Oct. 1916. Wounded at Romani, Sinai Peninsula, Egypt, Aug. 4, 1916.

NOEL VEDER WALLIS.
Admitted April 1908, practised at 14 Philpot Lane, E.C. Served as 2nd Lieut., Cheshire Regt. Killed in action April 10, 1917.

OWEN BERNARD WALLIS.
Admitted Oct. 1913. Managing Clerk with Meredith & Mills, of 8 New Square, Lincoln's Inn, W.C. Mobilised Aug. 4, 1914, as Lieut., 1st Batt. Herefordshire Regt., promoted Capt. June 1916, appointed Courts-Martial Officer, Dublin District, Aug. 1919. Served at Home Aug. 1914 to July 1915, Oct. 1916 to Sept. 1917, and March 1918 to March 1919, with Med. and Egyptian Exped. Forces July 1915 to Oct. 1916, and in France Sept. 1917 to March 1918. Wounded at Suvla Bay Aug. 9, 1915, and at Lebucquière, France, March 23, 1918.

LEO BERNARD WALLWORK.
Articled to Henry Langton, of Chorley, Lancs. Joined July 3, 1915, as Private, Royal Army Service Corps, subsequently promoted to Corporal. Served at Remount Depôt, Lathom Park, Ormskirk, Lancs.

ARNOLD BRUNSDON WALMSLEY.

Admitted July 1898. Member of Walmsley & Stansbury, of 222 Strand, W.C. Joined June 1916, as Sapper, Royal Engineers, subsequently promoted to Lance-Corporal. Served at Home and in France. Discharged medically unfit Jan. 1918.

HORATIO SPENCER WALPOLE.

Admitted Oct. 1909. Member of Dangerfield, Blythe & Co., of 26 Craven Street, Charing Cross, W.C. Joined Jan. 1916, as Private, Inns of Court O.T.C. Gazetted 2nd Lieut. and subsequently Lieut. Coldstream Guards. Served at Home and in France. Wounded on the Somme July 1917. Killed near Arras April 9, 1918.

JAMES DERMOT WALSH.

Articled to W. F. O. Edmonds, of 13 Clifford's Inn, E.C. Joined Dec. 27, 1916, as Gunner, Royal Garrison Artillery. Served at Home.

SAXON WALSHAW.

Admitted Aug. 1903. Member of Walshaws, of Halifax. Joined Aug. 10, 1916, as Ordinary Seaman, Royal Navy, promoted A.B. May 1917. Served at Home.

FREDERICK RUSSELL DOGGETT WALTER.

Articled to B. Cozens-Hardy, of Norwich. Joined Oct. 10, 1914, as Private, 2/4 Batt. Norfolk Regt., promoted Sergeant July 1916, transferred to Depôt Norfolk Regt. Sept. 1918. Once mentioned in Dispatches. Served at Home.

ALFRED WALTERS.

Admitted Dec. 1888, practising at Camborne, Cornwall. Mobilised 1914, as Capt., 4th Batt. Duke of Cornwall's Light Infantry, promoted Major Dec. 1914, Lieut.-Col. and second in command Labour Corps Record Office, Nottingham, Feb. 1919. Mentioned for special work. Awarded the O.B.E. and T.D. Served at Home.

DONALD ALFRED HAYES WALTERS.

Articled to Thurstan Peter, of Redruth, Cornwall. Joined July 16, 1917, as Private, Duke of Cornwall's Light Infantry. Gazetted 2nd Lieut. Devonshire Regt. April 7, 1918, and seconded to the 15th Batt., and subsequently attached to 3rd Batt. Served at Home.

LESLIE HADFIELD WALTERS.

Articled to H. B. Shepheard, of 4 Broad Street Place, E.C. Joined Sept. 1915 as Cadet, Inns of Court O.T.C. Gazetted 2nd Lieut. 5th Batt. Suffolk Regt. July 1916. Served in France Oct. 1916 to Feb. 1917. Killed in action Feb. 17, 1917.

SYDNEY EVELYN WALTERS.

Articled to Henry Walters, of Stone, Staffordshire. Joined Sept. 10, 1916, as Private, 28th Batt. County of London Regt. (Artists Rifles), transferred to Machine Gun Corps Sept. 1917, obtained commission as 2nd Lieut. in Tank Corps March 28, 1918. Joined 9th Tank Batt. Sept. 1918. Awarded the M.C. Served in France 1916, 1917, and 1918.

THOMAS DEVALL WALTHALL.
Admitted May 1909. Member of Currie & Walthall, of Birmingham. Served as Capt., 1/5 Batt. South Staffordshire Regt.

WILLIAM LEES PERCIVAL WALTON.
Articled to A. H. Worthington, of Manchester. Mobilised Aug. 1914, as Private, 1/6 Batt. Manchester Regt. Gazetted 2nd Lieut. Machine Gun Corps Dec. 29, 1916. Served at Gallipoli and in France. Killed at Cambrai Nov. 30, 1917.

GILBERT DYKE WANSBROUGH.
Admitted Dec. 1914. Managing Clerk with Wansbroughs & Co., of Bristol. Joined Oct. 1914, as 2nd Lieut., 4th Batt. Gloucestershire Regt., promoted Lieut. June 1915, Capt. June 1917. Served in France 1916 to 1917, and in Italy 1917 to 1918.

REGINALD WALTER WANSBROUGH.
Admitted Oct. 1911. Member of Wansbroughs, Robinson, Tayler & Taylor, of Bristol. Served as Motor Dispatch Rider, Royal Engineers, and subsequently as Lieut. Tank Corps.

RICHARD ERNEST WARBURTON.
Admitted Nov. 1899, practising at Liverpool. Joined July 1917, as Sapper, Royal Engineers, promoted Corporal Oct. 1917. Served at Home and Overseas. In France Feb. to Dec. 1918.

ARTHUR HAROLD WARD.
Admitted Jan. 1906. Member of A. E. Ward & Son, of Exeter. Joined Oct. 4, 1916, as Private, Hon. Artillery Company (Infantry), promoted Lance-Corporal July 1916. Served at Home and in France, Belgium, Italy, and Austria.

CECIL WELLESLEY WARD.
Admitted May 1906. Member of Cowling & Swift, of York. Joined 1915, as 2nd Lieut., Royal Field Artillery. Served in Flanders. Killed in action in Flanders Sept. 12, 1917.

DAVID ERNEST WARD.
Articled to J. C. Porter, of 7 King Street, E.C. Served as Lieut., 7th (City of London) Batt. London Regt., promoted Capt. June 1916.

FRANCIS WELSFORD WARD.
Admitted Dec. 1912. Of Bristol. Mobilised Aug. 5, 1914, as 2nd Lieut., 1/4 Batt. Gloucestershire Regt., promoted Lieut. 1915 and Capt. 1916. Served in Flanders 1915. Returned to England invalided. Military Representative to the Appeal Tribunal for Hampshire and Isle of Wight. Served again in Flanders in 1917. Killed in action near Belcapelle Oct. 9, 1917.

FRANK STANLEY WARD.
Admitted June 1901. Member of Westhorp, Cobbold & Ward, of Ipswich. Served as Capt., 3rd East Anglian (Howitzer) Brigade Royal Field Artillery (T.), promoted Major June 1916.

GEORGE STEPHEN WARD.

Articled to James Beaumont, of Leeds. Joined Sept. 25, 1914, as 2nd Lieut., West Yorkshire Regt., promoted Lieut. Jan. 1915, Capt. July 1916, Adjutant July 1916, transferred General List (New Armies) July 1917. Served in Egypt Dec. 1915 to Feb. 1916, France Feb. 1916 to Dec. 1916 and at Home Dec. 1916 to Sept. 1919. Invalided to England Dec. 18, 1916.

HAROLD MATHIAS ARTHUR WARD.

Admitted April 1910. Member of Ward, Hugh-Jones & Ward, of Harwich. Mobilised July 1914, as Capt., Essex and Suffolk Artillery (T.), promoted Major Royal Garrison Artillery June 1916. Twice mentioned in Dispatches. Awarded the D.S.O. and T.D. Served at Home on Staff 1914 to 1916, in France 1916 to 1918, and in Germany 1918 to 1919.

HERBERT CHARLES WARD.

Articled to John Ward, of Folkestone. Joined Nov. 25, 1914, as Private, 2nd Home Counties Field Ambulance, Royal Army Medical Corps, promoted Sergeant Dec. 1914, A/Staff-Sergeant Sept. 1915, with 52nd General Hospital Jan. 1919 and 159th Field Ambulance Aug. 1919, A.D.M.S. Staff "Syren" Force, North Russia, Aug. 1919. Served in Salonica, Serbia, Bulgaria, Macedonia Jan. 1917 to April 1919, and in North Russia Aug. to Oct. 1919.

JOHN PERCIVAL WARD.

Admitted Sept. 1907. Member of Toulmin, Ward & Co., of Liverpool. Mobilised Aug. 8, 1914, as Capt., Cheshire Field Coy., Royal Engineers and Adjutant for Welsh Divisional Royal Engineers, attached to 442nd Glamorgan Field Coy., Jan. 1916, to 438th Cheshire Field Coy. Nov., 1916, promoted A/Major Dec. 1916. Once mentioned in Dispatches. Awarded the M.C. Served at Home Aug. 1914 to July 1915 and Sept. 1915 to Nov. 1916, at Gallipoli July to Sept. 1915, and in France Nov. 1916 to Jan. 1919.

OCTAVIUS WHITTARD WARD.

Admitted Nov. 1907. Member of Hole, Seldon & Ward, of Bideford. Joined Nov. 19, 1914, as Private, 19th Batt. Royal Fusiliers. Commissioned 2nd Lieut. 3rd Batt. Royal Sussex Regt. May 9, 1915, promoted Lieut. July 1917, Staff Lieut. (I.B.) July 1918. Served at Home 1914 to June 1916 and April 1917 to April 1919, and in France and Belgium June 1916 to April 1917.

RICHARD WARD.

Admitted Jan. 1904. Member of Bulmer, Lawson & Ward, of Leeds. Joined Aug. 16, 1915, as Private, Inns of Court O.T.C. Gazetted 2nd Lieut. 1/7 Batt. West Yorkshire Regt. Nov. 15, 1915, promoted Lieut. June 1916. Served in France and Belgium March 1916 to March 1919.

THOMAS GEOFFREY MOORE WARD.

Articled to T. P. Wray, of Chesterfield. Joined June 12, 1915, as 2nd Lieut., 14th Batt. Notts and Derby Regt. (Sherwood Foresters), transferred to 8th Batt. Leicestershire Regt. Sept. 1916, promoted Lieut. July 1917. Served in France 1916 to 1918. Wounded on Somme Sept. 25, 1916.

HAROLD WARD-JONES.

Articled to Harold Pemberton, of Liverpool. Joined Sept. 4, 1914, as Private, 19th Batt. King's Liverpool Regt. Gazetted 2nd Lieut. 19th Batt. Royal Welch Fusiliers April 19, 1915, promoted Lieut. 1916, transferred to Indian Army in 1918 and subsequently posted to 2/27 Punjabis. Served at Home and in France and India.

ROBERT FOX WARDLE.

Admitted Feb. 1905. Member of Tomlinson, Wardle & Hartopp, of 222 Strand, W.C. Served as Lieut., 6th Batt. North Staffordshire Regt., and subsequently promoted Capt., transferred to Royal Army Service Corps and attained the rank of Temp. Major.

FRANK WARDLEY.

Admitted June 1912. With Fernandes & Greaves, of Wakefield. Mobilised 1914, as 2nd Lieut., 4th Batt. King's Own Yorkshire Light Infantry (T.), promoted Lieut. Sept. 1915, Capt. June 1916, Staff Capt., Dieppe, May 1917 to Nov. 1918. Served in France April to July 1915 and March to Dec. 1918, and at Home Dec. 1918 to May 1919.

FRANCIS HENRY WARE.

Admitted April 1898, practised at 7 Queen Street Place, E.C. Joined Nov. 12, 1914, as Capt. 13th (Princess Louise's Kensington) Batt. London Regt. Served in France. Killed at the Battle of the Somme July 1, 1916.

INNES NOËL WARE.

Articled to C. C. Lucas, of York. Mobilised Aug. 1914, as 2nd Lieut., West Riding Heavy Battery Royal Garrison Artillery, subsequently attained the rank of Staff Lieut. Served at Home Aug. 1914 to May 1915, and in France and Germany May 1915 to March 1919. Wounded Aug. 1918.

WILLIAM ROBERT ALEXANDER WAREING.

Articled to G. W. Pritchard, of 2, 3, and 4 Billiter Avenue, E.C. Joined Aug. 20, 1914, as Temp. 2nd Lieut., 11th (Service) Batt. King's Liverpool Regt., Infantry, subsequently turned into Pioneers, promoted Temp. Lieut. July 1916, Temp. A/Capt. July 1917. Awarded the M.C. Served on the Western Front May 1915 to March 1918. Wounded at Elverdinghe, near Ypres, Jan. 14, 1916. Killed in action at Flavy le Martel, near St. Quentin, France, March 23, 1918.

WILLIAM HENRY WARHURST.

Articled to J. W. Jackson, of Grimsby. Joined Dec. 7, 1915, as Private, Inns of Court O.T.C. Gazetted Sub-Lieut. Royal Naval Volunteer Reserve Nov. 22, 1916, attached Hawke Batt. 63rd (Royal Naval) Division. Served in France. Wounded March 23, 1918.

GEORGE EDWARD DUDLEY WARMINGTON.

Admitted Sept. 1900, practising at Bank Chambers, Tooley Street, S.E. Joined March 1, 1915, as 2nd Lieut., Durham Light Infantry. Gazetted Capt. June 1915. Served in France and Flanders.

LOUIS CRISPIN WARMINGTON.

Admitted July 1910. Joined Sept. 3, 1914, as Private, 9th Batt. Royal Fusiliers. Gazetted Lieut. 18th Batt. Durham Light Infantry Sept. 24, 1914, promoted Capt. Oct. 1917 and appointed Courts-Martial Officer. Once mentioned in Dispatches. Served in Egypt 1915 and in France 1916 to 1919.

ARCHIBALD WARNER.

Admitted Jan. 1910. Managing Clerk with Bennett & Ferris, of 68 Coleman Street, E.C. Joined June 4, 1915, as Private, 28th Batt. County of London Regt. (Artists Rifles). Gazetted 2nd Lieut. 5th City of London Batt. London Regt. (London Rifle Brigade) Oct. 28, 1915. Served in France. Killed July 1, 1916.

CHARLES EDWARD WARNER.

Admitted Nov. 1886, practising at Tonbridge, Kent. Served as Lieut.-Col. commanding 2/1 Kent Cyclist Batt. Awarded O.B.E. (Military Division). Served at Home.

GERALD HEWETT WARNER.

Admitted June 1910. Member of Warner & Son, of Fareham, Hants. Mobilised Aug. 1914, as Capt., Wessex (Hants) Royal Garrison Artillery, subsequently attained the rank of Major. Once mentioned in Dispatches. Served in France.

KENNETH CHARLES HARMAN WARNER.

Articled to C. E. Warner, of Tonbridge, Kent. Mobilised Aug. 1914, as Capt., Kent Cyclist Batt., promoted Major June 1916, Adjutant Dec. 1914 to June 1917, A/Lieut.-Col. Sept. to Oct. 1918, second in command of 7th York and Lancaster Regt. June 1918 to Feb. 1919. Once mentioned in Dispatches. Awarded the D.S.O. Served at Home and in France.

CHARLES GORDON WARREN.

Articled to E. C. Rawlings, of 2 Walbrook, E.C.; and afterwards Managing Clerk with Batchelor & Batchelor, of 15 Outer Temple, W.C., and Greenwich. Joined Aug. 6, 1914, as Private, 20th Batt. London Regt. Gazetted 2nd Lieut. 21st Batt. London Regt. Nov. 1917. Served in France. Killed in action at Bullecourt Aug. 28, 1918.

JOHN CROSBY WARREN.

Articled to J. C. Warren, of Nottingham. Mobilised Aug. 1914, as 2nd Lieut., 7th Batt. Notts and Derby Regt. (Sherwood Foresters) (Robin Hood's) (T.F.), promoted Lieut. Oct. 1915, Temp. Capt. July 1915, Capt. June 1916, Temp. Major Sept. 1917. Twice mentioned in Dispatches. Awarded the M.C. Served in England Aug. 1914 to Feb. 1915, and in France Feb. 1915 to Feb. 1916, when invalided home, in England (chiefly at Crookham and Aldershot, Instruction Officer O.T.C.) till Sept. 1917, when returned to France. Killed March 21, 1918.

REGINALD GEOFFREY WARREN.

Admitted April 1909. Member of Warrens, of 5 Bedford Square, W.C. Embodied Aug. 4, 1914, as Capt., 9th Batt. London Regt., Adjutant May 1915 to May 1916, promoted Major June 1916, Company Commander No. 16

Officer Cadet Batt. March to Oct. 1917, Deputy Assistant Quartermaster General XXIII. Corps April 1918, D.A.Q.M.G. Headquarters Southern Command May 1918 to June 1919, D.A.Q.M.G. Murmansk, North Russia, July to Nov. 1919. Once mentioned in Dispatches. Awarded Order of St. Stanislas 2nd Class (Russian). Served at Home, France 1914 to 1915, North Russia 1919.

JOHN EDWARD HOLDICH WARTNABY.

Admitted Dec. 1910, practising with E. F. Knapp-Fisher at Chapter Clerks' Office, Westminster Abbey. Joined Oct. 1914, as 2nd Lieut., Royal Field Artillery, promoted Lieut. Dec. 1915, Capt. Sept. 1916. Twice mentioned in Dispatches. Served in France. Wounded Sept. 1916.

ROBERT INNYS BAKER WARTON.

Admitted Aug. 1902, practised at Vancouver and Prince Rupert Island. Enlisted as a Sapper in the Canadian Engineers on the outbreak of War and came to England with the first Canadian Contingent. Killed in action near Ypres April 23, 1915.

WILLIAM LEWIS WASBROUGH.

Articled to E. T. M. Teesdale, of 6 Fredericks Place, Old Jewry, E.C. Served as 2nd Lieut., 1st Batt. Loyal North Lancashire Regt. Killed in action on Sept. 26 or 27, 1915.

WILLIAM JAMES FRASER WASHINGTON.

Admitted June 1916, practising at Morecambe. Joined Royal Naval Air Service in Sept. 1917 as A.C. 2, subsequently became Corporal in Royal Air Force.

ROBERT BERNARD WATERER.

Articled to A. J. Corner, of Hereford. Served as Corporal Dispatch Rider, Western Army Troops Signal Company Royal Engineers.

THOMAS FRANCIS WATERHOUSE.

Admitted July 1887. Member of Waterhouse & Son, of Wolverhampton. Served as Lieut.-Col. commanding 6th Batt. South Staffordshire Regt. Mentioned in Dispatches. Awarded the D.S.O. and T.D.

LAWRENCE ALOYSIUS WATKIN.

Articled to J. W. Watkin, of Railway Approach, London Bridge, S.E. Joined Sept. 14, 1914, as Private, 19th Batt. Royal Fusiliers (University and Public Schools Brigade). Gazetted 2nd Lieut. 11th Batt. Suffolk Regt. April 3, 1915, transferred to Machine Gun Corps Dec. 1915, promoted Lieut. Dec. 1916. Served in France and Belgium May 1916 to June 1917, otherwise at Home. Wounded at Messines June 7, 1917.

DAVID WILLIAM WATKINS.

Articled to J. J. Lewis, of Swansea. Served as Private, 21st Batt. Royal Welch Fusiliers.

ERNEST WATKINS.

Admitted June 1914. Managing Clerk with Howell, Yearsley & Reed, of Welshpool. Joined Nov. 15, 1915, as Private, Montgomeryshire Yeomanry. Served in Ireland. Died at Dublin March 5, 1916.

ERNEST VAUGHAN WATKINS.

Admitted Dec. 1912. Joined Sept. 1914, as Private, 21st (P.S.) Batt. Royal Fusiliers. Gazetted 2nd Lieut. The Welch Regt. 1917. Served in France and Mesopotamia.

HUBERT HOLMES WATKINS.

Admitted Feb. 1910. Member of Watkins & Co., of Pontypool. Joined Oct. 24, 1914, as Lieut., 2nd Batt. Monmouthshire Regt., attached West Yorkshire Regt. Oct. 1917 to March 1918, joined South Wales Borderers in Dec. 1918, attained the rank of Capt. Served in France.

ILTYD EDWIN MAITLAND WATKINS.

Articled to J. M. Watkins, of Usk. Mobilised Aug. 4, 1914, as Capt., 2nd Batt. Monmouthshire Regt. (T.). Served at Home Aug. 1914 to Feb. 1915 and in Belgium Feb. to May 1915. Killed near Ypres May 7, 1915.

SYDNEY WATKINS.

Admitted Jan. 1908. Member of Aneurin O. Evans & Co., of Denbigh. Served as Lieut., Royal Army Service Corps (M.T.).

VIVIAN HOLMES WATKINS.

Admitted Nov. 1913. Assistant Solicitor to J. L. Wheatley, Town Clerk of Cardiff. Mobilised Aug. 1914, as Capt., 2nd Batt. Monmouthshire Regt. (T.). Served in France. Died of wounds Feb. 20, 1915.

HENRY RICHARD WATLING.

Admitted Sept. 1907. Of 35 Cromwell Road, S.W. Served as Lieut., 16th Batt. P.W.O. West Yorkshire Regt. Mentioned in Dispatches.

CYRIL WILLIAM WATMOUGH.

Admitted May 1912. Managing Clerk with Druces & Attlee, of 10 Billiter Square, London, E.C. Joined March 17, 1917, as Private, 29th Batt. Middlesex Regt. Gazetted 2nd Lieut. Royal Army Service Corps June 1918. Served at Home.

VALENTINE HOWELL WATNEY.

Admitted April 1911. Managing Clerk with Burton, Yeates & Hart, of 23 Surrey Street, W.C. Received commission as 2nd Lieut., 7th Batt. Royal Berkshire Regt. Dec. 28, 1914, transferred to Machine Gun Corps Jan. 1916, promoted Lieut. July 1916. Served in France July to Nov. 1916. Wounded at Beaumont Hamel Nov. 15, 1916. Died of wounds, in London, Feb. 3, 1917.

ARTHUR JAMES WATSON.

Articled to W. P. Kay, of Darwen. Joined Nov. 4, 1914, as Private, 11th Coy. Royal Army Medical Corps, promoted Corporal Oct. 1915, Gazetted 2nd Lieut. 3/4 Batt. East Lancashire Regt. Dec. 21, 1915, transferred to 2/4 Batt. South Lancashire Regt. Sept. 1917, promoted Lieut. July 1917. Served at Home Nov. 1914 to Feb. 1917 and Nov. 1917 to April 1918, and in France Feb. to Nov. 1917 and April 1918 to Feb. 1919.

CHARLES BAILEY WATSON.

Admitted June 1902. Assistant Solicitor Surrey County Council, Kingston-on-Thames. Joined Nov. 26, 1915, as Private, 29th Batt. Royal Fusiliers, promoted A/Sergeant 1917 and transferred to 11th Batt. Served in France. Discharged Oct. 31, 1917.

CLEMENT GOODMAN WATSON.

Admitted Nov. 1904. Member of Burgess & Watson, of Market Harborough. Served as 2nd Lieut., Royal Army Service Corps (M.T.).

THE HON. DAVID KENNETH WATSON.

Admitted Nov. 1901. Member of Webster & Watson, of Newton Abbot. Joined Oct. 14, 1914, as 2nd Lieut., 7th Batt. Devonshire Regt. (T.), promoted Temp. Capt. March 1915, Substantive Capt. June 1918, attached 6th Batt. Wiltshire Regt. Served at Home and in France.

DOUGLAS STATHAM WATSON.

Admitted Feb. 1900. Member of Barham & Watson, of Bridgwater, and Burnham-on-Sea, Somerset. Mobilised Aug. 1914, as Capt., 1/5 Batt. Somerset Light Infantry, promoted Major 1916. Once mentioned in Dispatches. Awarded D.S.O. and T.D. Served in India and Palestine.

FRANCIS WILLIAM WATSON.

Articled to F. T. Langley, of Wolverhampton. Joined Dec. 2, 1914, as 2nd Lieut., 296th Brigade Royal Field Artillery, promoted Lieut. June 1915, A/Capt. and Adjutant May 1917. Awarded the M.C. and Bar. Served in France. Gassed at Essarts (Somme) April 5, 1918.

HARRY CRAWFORD WATSON.

Admitted Sept. 1887. Member of W. J. and H. C. Watson, of Barnard Castle. Mobilised Aug. 1914, as Lieut.-Col., 6th Batt. Durham Light Infantry. Mentioned for valuable services and promoted to Brevet Col. Served in Flanders and at Home.

JAMES WATSON.

Admitted May 1906. Member of Watson, Carrick & Sons, of Hull. Mobilised 1914, as Lieut., 2nd Northumbrian Brigade, Royal Field Artillery promoted Capt. Aug. 1914, Major June 1916. Served in England Aug. 1914 to April 1915, and in France and Belgium April 1915 to Dec. 1916. Relegated to Territorial Force Reserve July 1918.

JOHN PEIRSON WATSON.

Admitted Feb. 1906. Member of H. & J. P. Watson, of Middlesbrough. Joined Dec. 11, 1915, as Private, Middlesex Regt. Gazetted 2nd Lieut. April 26, 1917, and appointed to East Yorkshire Regt. May 1917. Served in Belgium and France 1916 and 1917. Reported wounded and missing July 29, 1917, subsequently presumed killed.

LAWRENCE CECIL WATSON.

Admitted Dec. 1905. Member of Watson & Watson, of Darlington. Joined Dec. 1915 as Private, Inns of Court O.T.C. Gazetted 2nd Lieut. 6th Batt. Durham Light Infantry March 1, 1917, promoted Lieut. Sept. 1918. Served in France. Wounded near Estaires April 9, 1918.

MAURICE MURRAY WATSON.

Articled to A. Horne, of 55 Gracechurch Street, E.C. Joined Nov. 8, 1914, as Private, Inns of Court O.T.C. Gazetted 2nd Lieut. 11th Batt. South

Staffordshire Regt. March 17, 1915, promoted Lieut. 7th Batt. July 1917, Capt. Sept. 1918, attached 6th Batt. Manchester Regt. Sept. to Nov. 1915. Served in Gallipoli 1915, France 1917 to 1919.

ROBERT WATSON.

Admitted Jan. 1903, practising at Newcastle-upon-Tyne. Served as Private, 4th (Public Schools) Batt. Royal Fusiliers.

THOMAS CLIFFORD WATSON.

Admitted Jan. 1914. Member of Watson, Esam & Barber, of Sheffield. Served as Gunner, Royal Garrison Artillery.

ALFRED GORDON WATTS.

Articled to E. J. Neale, of Brighton. Joined Nov. 29, 1915, as Private, Inns of Court O.T.C. Commissioned as 2nd Lieut. Royal Garrison Artillery (Special Reserve) Nov. 9, 1916, promoted Lieut. May 1918, A/Capt. Nov. 1918. Served at Home Nov. 1915 to April 1917, and in France April 1917 to Jan. 1919.

ARCHIBALD WODEHOUSE WATTS.

Admitted June 1913. Managing Clerk with Walmsley & Stansbury, of 222 Strand, W.C. Joined Dec. 14, 1915, as 2nd Lieut., 4th Batt. East Yorkshire Regt., transferred to 26th Batt. Liverpool Regt. Aug. 1916. Discharged June 30, 1917. Served at Home with Army, in France with Y.M.C.A. 1915, and in France and Belgium with Church Army 1918 to 1919.

DUDLEY HALDANE WATTS.

Admitted Feb. 1913. Managing Clerk with Kerby, Son & Karuth, of 10 & 11 Austin Friars, E.C. Joined Sept. 1914 Inns of Court O.T.C. Gazetted 2nd Lieut. Queen's Own Royal West Kent Regt. Nov 1914. Served in Flanders. Reported wounded and missing at battle of Loos Sept. 25–26, 1915, and subsequently presumed to have been killed in action.

FRANCIS MAPLETON IREMONGER WATTS.

Articled to Francis Watts, of Newton Abbot. Joined Feb. 17, 1915, as 2nd Lieut., Worcestershire Regt, promoted Lieut. Aug. 1915, seconded to the Royal Flying Corps Sept. 1915, Temp. Capt. Jan. 1918 to May 1919, seconded to Royal Air Force April 1918. Awarded the M.B.E. Served in France March to April 1915 and Jan. to Dec. 1916, and in Mesopotamia Jan. 1918 to Aug. 1919, otherwise at Home. Wounded March 22, 1915.

HAROLD VAUGHAN IREMONGER WATTS.

Admitted Oct. 1906. Member of Watts, Woollcombe & Watts, of Newton Abbot. Joined Oct. 18, 1914, as 2nd Lieut., 1/7 Batt. Devonshire Regt., promoted Temp. Capt. Jan. 1915, formed and commanded 1/1 Wessex Divisional Cyclist Company Oct. 1915, granted Captaincy Wessex Divisional Cyclist Company July 1916, joined 2nd Batt. Devonshire Regt. July 1917. Served at Home Oct. 1914 to March 1917, and in France March to Aug. 1917. Died of wounds Aug. 11, 1917.

ISAAC SEYMOUR WATTS.

Admitted Feb. 1910. Member of Reginald Bell & Co., of 3–7 Southampton Street, Strand, W.C. Served as Lieut., Royal Army Service Corps.

LESLIE NORMAN WATTS.

Admitted Dec. 1907. Member of Emmerson & Co., of Sandwich, and Deal, Kent. Joined Feb. 1917, as 2nd Lieut., General List, promoted Lieut. Aug. 1918. Served at Home.

WALTER FREDERICK WATTS.

Admitted Nov. 1913, practising at Ilfracombe. Served as Sergeant, Royal Army Service Corps (M.T.).

THOMAS HENRY WAUGH.

Admitted Sept. 1910. Member of Mulcahy & Waugh, of Blaydon-on-Tyne. Joined Sept. 17, 1915, as 2nd Lieut., 9th Batt. Durham Light Infantry (T.), promoted Lieut. June 1916, Capt. Dec. 1917. Served at Home Sept. 1915 to Aug. 1917, and in France Aug. 1917 to April 1919.

CHARLES NEWBY WAWN.

Admitted June 1907, practising at Bishop Auckland, and Ferry Hill, Durham. Mobilised as 2nd Lieut. 6th Batt. Durham Light Infantry, promoted Lieut. Nov. 1914, and attached Royal Engineers Sept. 1917. Served in France 2 years.

ERNEST EDWARD BRUCE WAY.

Articled to E. W. Way, of Southsea. Joined Sept. 22, 1914, as 2nd Lieut., 6th Batt. Hampshire Regt. (T.), promoted Lieut. July 1916, attached 17th Batt. Jan. 1916 to Nov. 1918 and to 51st Batt. Nov. 1918 to April 1919. Served at Home 1914 to 1919, and with Army of Occupation, Germany, 1919.

ERNEST WILLIAM WAY.

Admitted Dec. 1890. Member of W. A. Way & Son, of Southsea. Served as Capt., 6th Batt. Hampshire Regt. (T.).

LESLIE BOLITHO WAY.

Admitted Oct. 1912, practising at Portsmouth. Joined May 12, 1915, as Temp. 2nd Lieut., Durham Light Infantry, subsequently promoted Lieut.

CLARE WAYMAN.

Articled to C. E. S. Whitford, of 28 Budge Row, E.C. Joined Nov. 14, 1914, as 2nd Lieut., 9th Batt. Suffolk Regt., promoted Lieut. Sept. 1916, Capt. Sept. 1917, transferred to Labour Corps March 1917 on account of wounds received in action. Served in France Aug. 1915 to Sept. 1916, and March 1917 to June 1918, in England remainder of time. Wounded on the Somme Sept. 13, 1916.

CHARLES WEBB.

Admitted April 1911. Member of William Webb & Son, of Morpeth. Joined Dec. 4, 1915, as Motor Cyclist Pioneer, Royal Engineers (Signal Service), subsequently promoted Motor Cyclist Corporal and attached 3rd Army Wireless Company Advanced Directing Station, and 3rd Army Signal Company as Dispatch Rider. Awarded the M.S.M. Served in France Sept. 1916 to March 1919.

EDWARD SIDNEY WEBB.

Admitted July 1903, practising at Birmingham. Joined Oct. 15, 1915, as 2nd Lieut., 4th Batt. Oxford and Bucks Light Infantry, subsequently promoted Lieut. and attached to Labour Corps. Served at Home. Invalided out March 26, 1918.

FRANCIS FREDERICK CHARLES WEBB.

Admitted Dec. 1902, practising at 12 Abchurch Lane, E.C. Joined Nov. 3, 1914, as Private, School of Musketry, promoted Staff Sergeant Nov. 1914. Gazetted 2nd Lieut. Suffolk Regt. Jan. 27, 1916, promoted Lieut. July 1917, Capt. Sept. 1918 General List. Served at Home.

FRANK BURNS WEBB.

Articled to Samuel Bishop, of Manchester. Served as 2nd Lieut., 3rd Batt. King's Own Royal Lancaster Regt., attached 4th Batt. Lincolnshire Regt.

HENRY LUMLEY WEBB.

Admitted March 1884. Of 6 Clement's Inn, W.C. Served as Major, 13th (Reserve) Batt. County of London Regt., and subsequently promoted Lieut.-Col.

WALTER THOMAS WEBB.

Admitted Nov. 1904. Member of W. Webb & Sons, of Suffolk House, Laurence Pountney Hill, Cannon Street, E.C. Joined Oct. 1914, as Private, 16th Batt. Middlesex Regt. Gazetted 2nd Lieut. 4th Batt. East Surrey Regt. May 21, 1915, promoted Lieut. July 1917. Served at Home Oct. 1914 to Jan. 1917 and July 1917 to Oct. 1918, and in France and Belgium Jan. to July 1917 and Oct. 1918 to March 1919.

WILFRED WILLIAM WEBB.

Admitted Nov. 1901. Member of W. Webb & Sons, of Suffolk House, E.C. Joined Dec. 10, 1915, as Rifleman, The Rifle Brigade, transferred as Private to King's Own Royal Lancaster Regt. Nov. 1916, promoted Corporal June 1917, Sergeant May 1918, posted to 816th (Div.) Employment Company June 1918. Once mentioned in Dispatches. Served with British Salonica Force in Macedonia, Serbia, &c., Nov. 1916 to March 1919.

STANLEY WEBB-JOHNSON.

Admitted May 1911. Member of Hasties, of 65 Lincoln's Inn Fields, W.C. Mobilised Aug. 4, 1914, and sent to India with 1/6 Batt. East Surrey Regt. and attained the rank of Capt. Served with the Aden Field Force as Brigade Machine Gun Officer 1916 to 1917. Subsequently returned to India and appointed Staff Officer to the Inspector of Infantry and afterwards Instructor at the Officers' School of Instruction.

FREDERICK HERBERT EDWIN WEBBER.

Admitted Dec. 1909. Member of Webber & Coffin, of Portsmouth. Mobilised Aug. 1914, as Lieut., Royal Engineers (T.), promoted Temp. Capt. Jan. 1915, Capt. June 1916. Served at Home from March 1916 to Feb. 1918, employed on revision of Scottish Naval Base Defences and construction of permanent defence works.

BERNARD PERCY WEBSTER.

Articled to M. Arnold, of Watford. Joined Nov. 14, 1914, as Private, Royal Fusiliers. Gazetted 2nd Lieut. Royal Fusiliers Sept. 26, 1916, promoted Lieut. Aug. 1917, A/Capt. Sept. 1918. Once mentioned in Dispatches. Served in France. Wounded Feb. 17, 1917, and Oct. 1918.

FRED WEBSTER.

Articled to Sir Robert E. Fox, Town Clerk, of Leeds. Joined Nov. 1915, as Cadet, Leeds University O.T.C. Gazetted 2nd Lieut. Royal Garrison Artillery July 19, 1916, promoted A/Lieut. July 1917, A/Capt. and Adjutant Aug. 1917 to Dec. 1918, with 172nd Siege Battery Aug. 1916 to March 1917, and 8th Brigade R.G.A. March 1917 to Dec. 1918. Once mentioned in Dispatches. Served in France Sept. 1916 to Dec. 1918.

JOHN RICHARD WEBSTER.

Admitted May 1907. Managing Clerk with Francis & Crookenden, of 23 Lincoln's Inn Fields, W.C. Joined Sept. 14, 1914, as 2nd Lieut., 4th Batt. City of London Regt. (Royal Fusiliers), promoted Lieut. July 1915, Adjutant Oct. 1915, Capt. May 1916. Served at Home, Malta, Gallipoli, Egypt, Flanders, and France. Killed in action in France Sept. 9, 1916.

REGINALD EVERARD ADOLPHE WEBSTER.

Admitted Feb. 1914. Formerly of 4 Lincoln's Inn Fields, W.C. Joined Aug. 3, 1914, as Private, 1st Batt. Hon. Artillery Company. Gazetted 2nd Lieut. 2nd Batt. Oxford and Bucks Light Infantry Jan. 23, 1916, promoted Temp. Capt. Nov. 1916. Served in France and Belgium Sept. 1914 to Nov. 1916. Wounded at Beaumont Hamel Nov. 19, 1916.

ALFRED OWEN WEBSTER WEBSTER-JONES.

Admitted Nov. 1906, practised at Hastings. Joined Sept. 1914, as Private, University Public Schools Batt. (20th Batt. Royal Fusiliers). Gazetted 2nd Lieut. Oxford and Bucks Light Infantry May 1915, promoted Lieut. Oct. 1916. Served at Home and in France. Killed at Beaumont Hamel Nov. 13, 1916.

ARTHUR HAROLD MANNERS WEDDELL.

Admitted Dec. 1902. Member of J. C. and R. Weddell, of Berwick-on-Tweed. Served as Capt., 7th Batt. Northumberland Fusiliers (T.), subsequently promoted Major and employed at Ministry of Labour.

JOHN RICHARD BAGGALLAY WEEDING.

Admitted Dec. 1906. Member of the Staff of the Surrey County Council at Kingston. Joined Aug. 10, 1914, as Mechanic, Royal Flying Corps. Gazetted 2nd Lieut. The Welch Regt. Oct. 1914. Once mentioned in Dispatches. Served in France Aug. to Dec. 1914. Killed in action near Festubert Dec. 22, 1914.

PERCY PENKIVIL WEEKES.

Admitted Aug. 1907. Member of Weekes & Son, of Plymouth. Joined Jan. 1917 as Private, Royal Army Service Corps (M.T.). Served seven months in France, remainder of time at Home.

HARRY WEEKS.

Admitted Oct. 1913. Managing Clerk with Baldwin, Weeks & Baldwin, of Clitheroe. Joined April 5, 1917, as Gunner, Royal Garrison Artillery, acted as Observer and Battery Commander's Assistant. Served in France Aug. 1917 to Jan. 1919.

WILLIAM EDWARD WEEKS.

Articled to J. L. Thompson, of Brighton. Served as 2nd Lieut., Royal Sussex Regt. Awarded the M.C.

HUGH NEVILLE WEGG.

Admitted Oct. 1908. Practised at 5 Bedford Row, W.C. Enlisted Sept. 2, 1914, in 16th Batt. Middlesex Regt., and attained the rank of Sergeant. Gazetted 2nd Lieut. in same Regt. Jan. 1915, promoted Lieut. March 1915, Capt. March 1916. Served in France. Killed in action near Peronne Mar. 25, 1918.

JOHN WEIGHTMAN.

Managing Clerk with Weightman, Pedder & Co., of Liverpool. Joined Oct. 1914, as Hon. 2nd Lieut., Royal Marines, gazetted Sub-Lieut. Armoured Car Division Nov. 1914. Served with Royal Naval Division at Dunkirk and Belgium Oct. to Nov. 1914, and in Gallipoli March to June 1915. Killed near Cape Helles, Gallipoli, June 4, 1915.

WILLIAM WEISS.

Admitted July 1911, practising at 36/37 Queen Street, E.C. Joined April 1917, as Private, Royal Army Ordnance Corps. Served in France May 1917 to Sept. 1918, and in India Oct. 1918 to March 1919.

ERIC STANLEY WELCH.

Articled to M. B. Clappe, of Pinner's Hall, E.C. Joined Nov. 5, 1914, as 2nd Lieut. 8th Batt. Royal West Kent Regt. Appointed Instructor, Eastern Command N.C.O.'s School of Instruction, June 1916, promoted Lieut. July 1917. Served in France. Wounded in Zouave Wood, Ypres, Jan. 12, 1916.

GEORGE JAMES CULLUM WELCH.

Articled to F. E. Robb, of 19 Bedford Row, W.C. Joined Jan. 11, 1915, as Cadet, University of London O.T.C. Gazetted 2nd Lieut. 3rd Batt. Royal Berkshire Regt. (S.R.) April 11, 1915, promoted Lieut. May 1916, posted to 6th Batt. Sept. 1916, Temp. Capt. March 1917, G.S.O. III. 18th Division July 1918 to Sept. 1918, A/Capt. attached 8th Batt. East Surrey Regt. Nov. 1918. Awarded M.C. Served at Home and in France. Wounded Oct. 2, 1916, and Sept. 30, 1918.

JOHN WELCH.

Admitted Jan. 1910, practising at Lancaster. Joined O.T.C. Jan. 1915. Commissioned as 2nd Lieut. 4th (T.) Batt. King's Own Royal Lancaster Regt. June 13, 1915, promoted Capt. July 1917. Served in France Jan. to Aug. 1916, and May 1917 to April 1919. Wounded during Battle of Somme Aug. 8, 1916.

CHARLES GEORGE WELD.

Admitted Dec. 1903. Managing Clerk with Frere, Cholmeley & Co., of 28 Lincoln's Inn Fields, W.C. Joined Dec. 1914, as 2nd Lieut., 11th Batt. Worcestershire Regt., promoted Lieut. Feb. 1917, A/Capt. July to Dec. 1917. Served in France and Belgium 1915 to 1916, 1917, and 1918. Wounded at Bazentin-le-Petit July 22, 1916.

HUGH EDWARD WELD.

Articled to his father H. C. Weld, of 1 Lancaster Place, Strand, W.C. Enlisted as Private in 28th Batt. County of London Regt. (Artists Rifles) in Aug. 1914 and proceeded to France with the 1st Batt. in Oct. Gazetted 2nd Lieut. Jan. 1, 1915, and attached to the Scots Guards. Reported missing Jan. 25, 1915, and subsequently reported killed in action near Cuinchy, La Bassée.

GILBERT TREVOR WELLINGTON.

Admitted Aug. 1904. Member of Wellington & Clifford, of Gloucester. Joined May 31, 1916, as Private, 3/1 Batt. Royal Gloucestershire Hussars Yeomanry. Gazetted 2nd Lieut. Reserve of Officers (Cavalry) Dec. 21, 1916, and attached 9th (subsequently 2nd) Reserve Cavalry Regt., attached 3rd County of London Yeomanry July 1917, transferred Machine Gun Corps April 1918, attached 103rd (City and 3rd County of London Yeomanry) Batt. Machine Gun Corps May 1918, promoted Lieut. June 1918. Served at Home and in Ireland; and in Egypt, Palestine, and France.

BERNARD NORMAN WELLS.

Admitted Feb. 1900. Member of Watson, Watson & Wells, of Barnard Castle. Served as Lieut., Royal Army Ordnance Department.

CHARLES ALEXANDER WELLS.

Admitted Nov. 1906. Of 20 Oakwood Court, Kensington, W. Joined Aug. 4, 1914, as Lieut., 3rd Batt. Hampshire Regt., promoted Capt. Feb. 1915, Brevet Major June 1918, Staff April 1917 to July 1919. Twice mentioned in Dispatches. Awarded the O.B.E. Served in France June 1915 to July 1919.

HALLIFAX VYVYAN WELLS.

Admitted Feb. 1900. Member of H. H. Wells & Sons, of 17 Paternoster Row, E.C. Served as Private, Royal Army Service Corps (M.T.).

JOHN BARTHROPPE WELMAN.

Articled to F. P. Welman, of 9 Southampton Street, Bloomsbury, W.C. Served with the Hon. Artillery Company, and subsequently as 2nd Lieut. Royal Field Artillery, attached to Royal Flying Corps.

CHARLES ELIOT WEST.

Admitted Nov. 1897, practising at Swanage, Dorset. Joined June 3, 1918, as 2nd Lieut., Royal Army Service Corps, attached to War Office.

GILBERT LEWIS WEST.

Admitted Dec. 1905. Member of Bull & Bull, of 3 Stone Buildings, Lincoln's Inn, W.C. Served as Private, Inns of Court O.T.C.

JOHN FREDERICK WEST.

Admitted Dec. 1911, practising at Oxford and Reading. Served as 2nd Lieut., Royal Garrison Artillery, promoted Lieut. Oct. 1918.

HAROLD WESTBROOK.

Articled to Josiah Longland, of Warrington. Served as Private, Royal Army Medical Corps.

OSWALD WESTERN.

Admitted Oct. 1914. Managing Clerk with Western & Sons, of 35 Essex Street, W.C. Mobilised Sept. 1914, as Private, Hon. Artillery Company (Infantry). Gazetted 2nd Lieut. Royal Garrison Artillery Dec. 10, 1916, and posted to 323rd Siege Battery, promoted Lieut. June 1918. Served in France. Wounded at Pilchem, near Ypres, Aug. 2, 1917.

ARTHUR REGINALD ASTLEY WESTON.

Articled to W. E. P. Burges, of Bristol. Commissioned from London University O.T.C. as 2nd Lieut., Royal Field Artillery (Special Reserve) Nov. 17, 1915, promoted Lieut. July 1917, A/Capt. Feb. 1919, Adjutant 14th Brigade Royal Horse Artillery. Once mentioned in Dispatches. Served at Home Nov. 1915 to March 1916, in France March 1916 to Nov. 1917 and April to Nov. 1918, Italy Nov. 1917 to April 1918, and in Germany Nov. 1918 to June 1919.

HERBERT WESTRON.

Admitted July 1904. Of Canterbury. Joined Sept. 1914, as Private, Royal Fusiliers (Public Schools Brigade), promoted Sergeant 1917, subsequently received commission (Temp.). Served in France and Belgium.

HAROLD ASHWELL WESTROPE.

Admitted Feb. 1911, practised at Hull. Served as 2nd Lieut., 4th (Reserve) Batt. East Yorkshire Regt. Mentioned in Dispatches.

EDWARD LIONEL HAVERSHAM WHALL.

Admitted Feb. 1911. Managing Clerk with J. S. and C. A. Whall, of Worksop. Joined Nov. 15, 1915, as Private, Norfolk Regt. Gazetted 2nd Lieut. 18th Batt. King's Royal Rifle Corps April 1917. Served at Home and in France. Killed in action Sept. 20, 1917.

AUBREY FITZGERALD WHARTON.

Articled to J. H. T. Wharton, of Southampton. Joined Aug. 1914, as Lieut., 5th Batt. Hampshire Regt., promoted Capt. Oct. 1914. Served in India and Burma 1914 to 1919, and Afghan Campaign 1919.

FRANK HAMMOND WHARTON.

Articled to H. W. Lydall, of 37 John Street, Bedford Row, W.C. Gazetted 2nd Lieut. 3rd (attached 1st) Batt. Loyal North Lancashire Regt. Oct. 14, 1914. Served in France. Killed at the Battle of Loos Sept. 25, 1915.

NORMAN WHARTON.

Admitted Aug. 1900. Member of Wilkinson, Wharton & Brown, of Scarborough and Whitby. Joined Nov. 12, 1915, as Private, 21st Batt. King's Royal Rifle Corps. Obtained commission in Durham Light Infantry Jan. 25, 1917, promoted Lieut. July 1918. Served in France April to Aug. 1916 and March to Nov. 1917. Gassed Nov. 3, 1917.

ELLIS GEORGE WHATELY.

Admitted Nov. 1909. Member of Rooper & Whately, of 17 Lincoln's Inn Fields, W.C. Joined Sept. 1914, as Private, Universities and Public Schools Batt. Gazetted 2nd Lieut. Hertfordshire Regt. Oct. 1914, promoted Lieut. Jan. 1916, Capt. June 1917 (Staff Capt. 6th Infantry Brigade), Major

(D.A.A.G. 41st Division) July 1917, Brevet Major Oct. 1917. Four times mentioned in Dispatches. Awarded the M.C., Brevet Major, Croix de Guerre (Belgian). Served in France, Belgium, and Italy.

CLAUDE WHATLEY.

Admitted Nov. 1908. Member of Whatley & Son, of 27 Lincoln's Inn Fields, W.C. Joined Sept. 15, 1914, as Temp. Lieut., Royal Army Service Corps, promoted Temp. Capt. Feb. 1915, Temp. Major May 1919. Once mentioned in Dispatches. Awarded Order of St. Anne (Russian). Served at Home and in France and North Russia.

RICHARD ARUNDELL WHATTEN.

Articled to R. J. Mullings, of Cirencester. Served as Private, Public Schools Batt. Royal Fusiliers.

HUBERT ASHCOMBE WHEATCROFT.

Admitted Nov. 1902. Member of Corbin, Greener & Cook, of 52 Bedford Row, W.C. Rejoined March 27, 1915, Notts and Derby Mounted Brigade Royal Army Service Corps, promoted Capt. Aug. 1915. Served at Home.

EDWARD RICHARD WHEATLY.

Admitted April 1904. Member of Wells, Geething & Stanley, of Hull. Joined July 1916, as Private, Royal Field Artillery. Gazetted 2nd Lieut. Royal Field Artillery April 1917. Served in France. Killed at Poperinghe Oct. 11, 1917.

FREDERICK THOMAS WILLIAM WHEELER.

Articled to F. A. Holman, of 1 Lloyds Avenue, E.C. Joined Nov. 1915, as Private, 5th City of London Batt. London Regt. (London Rifle Brigade). Served in Flanders. Killed in action Oct. 3, 1916.

WYNN POWELL WHELDON.

Admitted Jan. 1907, practising at 63 Queen Victoria Street, E.C. Enlisted Sept. 1914 Inns of Court O.T.C. Commissioned in 14th Batt. Royal Welch Fusiliers Dec. 7, 1914, promoted Capt. July 1915, Major July 1916, 2nd in Command July 1916 to Nov. 1918. Once mentioned in Dispatches. Awarded the D.S.O. Served in France Dec. 1915 to Nov. 1918. Wounded Nov. 7, 1918.

JOHN SNOW WHELPTON.

Admitted Jan. 1912, practising at Hull. Served as Private, Inns of Court O.T.C. Gazetted 2nd Lieut. 4th Batt. East Yorkshire Regt., promoted Lieut. July 1918.

KENNETH WHETSTONE.

Admitted Dec. 1906, practising at Southwold, Suffolk. Joined June 7, 1915, as 2nd Lieut., Royal Army Service Corps, promoted Lieut. May 1916, Capt. June 1917. Served in France July 1915 to Nov. 1916, and afterwards at Home.

WILLIAM REGINALD HARVEY WHISTON.

Admitted June 1893. Member of Whiston & Sons, of Derby. Served as Major, 5th (Reserve) Batt. Notts and Derby Regt. (Sherwood Foresters), and subsequently promoted Lieut.-Col.

CEDRIC HUGH WHITAKER.

Articled to G. H. Freeman, of 23 Bedford Row, W.C. Served as Lieut., 40th Divisional Train Royal Army Service Corps, promoted Temp. Capt. June 1917.

ARTHUR KEMP WHITBURN.

Articled to E. G. Bretherton, of Tunbridge Wells. Joined Sept. 1, 1914, as Private, 1/4 Batt. Queen's Own (Royal West Kent Regt.), transferred to Indian Ordnance Department Dec. 1916, and promoted Sergeant. Served in India, Baluchistan March to May 1918, North-West Frontier (Kohat Kurram Valley) June to Oct. 1919.

JOHN HERBERT WHITCOMBE.

Admitted Nov. 1906. Managing Clerk with Slater, Heelis & Co., of Manchester. Joined Nov. 17, 1917, as Private, Army Pay Corps, promoted Corporal Nov. 1918. Served at Home.

ROBERT HENRY WHITCOMBE.

Admitted March 1887, practising at Bewdley. Mobilised Aug. 4, 1914, as Major, 48th (South Midland) Divisional Train Royal Army Service Corps. Twice mentioned in Dispatches. Awarded the D.S.O. Served in France from March 23, 1915, to Feb. 8, 1917.

HAROLD FORBES WHITE.

Admitted Sept. 1907. Member of White & Leonard, of Bank Buildings, Ludgate Hill, E.C. Joined Nov. 5, 1914, as 2nd Lieut., Royal Army Service Corps (T.F.), subsequently Capt. S.S.O. North Russian Expeditionary Force Served in France and North Russia.

HENRY HEWLETT EALES WHITE.

Admitted Dec. 1911. Managing Clerk with Pritchard & Sons, of 2 Billiter Avenue, E.C. Mobilised Aug. 4, 1914, as Private, 14th Batt. County of London Regt. (London Scottish). Gazetted 2nd Lieut. Royal Scots Fusiliers Sept. 12, 1914, promoted Lieut. Nov. 1914, Capt. Jan. 1915. Served in France May 1915 to Sept. 1915, wounded Sept. 1915. Reported wounded and missing, Battle of Loos, Sept. 27, 1915, and subsequently presumed (officially) killed in action.

HOWARD BELMONT WHITE.

Admitted July 1906. Member of H. Brunel White & Son, of Carmarthen, South Wales. Gazetted 2nd Lieut. 1/4 Batt. The Welch Regt. (T.) Dec. 8, 1914, promoted Lieut. June 1916, A/Capt. April 1917 to Oct. 1918, Capt. Oct. 1918. Awarded M.C. Served in Gallipoli 1915, Western Desert of Egypt (Senussi Campaign) 1916, Sinai Peninsula, Palestine, 1917 to 1919.

LOWELL ALDERSEY WHITE.

Admitted Jan. 1912, practising at 9 Bush Lane, Cannon Street, E.C. Mobillsed 1914, as Capt., 7th Batt. Middlesex Regt. Served at Gibraltar and at Home. Resigned May 1916.

MAURICE WHITE.

Articled to J. W. Parkes, of 22 Bedford Row, W.C. Served as 2nd Lieut., Indian Reserve of Officers.

MONTAGUE ADELBERT FREDERICK HAMILTON WHITE.

Admitted June 1915. Member of Bailey & White, of Lowestoft and Beccles. Joined July 1916, as Gunner, Royal Garrison Artillery, Glamorgan. Commissioned Sept. 1917 in Royal Garrison Artillery, and posted to 284th Siege Battery Nov. 1917 to Dec. 1918. Served at Home and in France.

NOEL BLANCO WHITE.

Admitted Jan. 1912. Member of T. & N. Blanco White, of 10 Bedford Row, W.C. Served as Private, Hon. Artillery Company. Subsequently gazetted 2nd Lieut. General List and attained the rank of Capt. Mentioned in Dispatches. Awarded the D.S.O. and M.C.

REGINALD FRANKLAND WHITE.

Admitted July 1913, practising at Whitby. Served as Private, Hon. Artillery Company (Infantry).

REGINALD LEWIS WHITE.

Articled to Richard King, of Temple Chambers, Temple Avenue, E.C. Served as Private, Inns of Court O.T.C.

SIDNEY HAMPDEN WHITE.

Articled to S. White, of 23 Leadenhall Street, E.C. Served as Capt., 10th Batt. Middlesex Regt., and subsequently promoted Major. Served in India.

BASIL HAMILTON WHITEFORD.

Admitted Nov. 1899. Member of Whiteford & Bennett, of Plymouth. Joined Oct. 1914, as Private, 18th Service Batt. Royal Fusiliers (Public Schools). Gazetted 2nd Lieut. 11th Batt. Devonshire Regt. July 1916, promoted Lieut. Royal Berkshire Regt. Jan. 1918. Served in France Nov. 1915 to March 1916. Rest of service at Home.

ARTHUR WHITEHEAD.

Admitted Dec. 1909. Member of Arthur Whitehead & Son, of Salisbury. Joined Oct. 16, 1916, as Private, Royal Army Service Corps. Gazetted 2nd Lieut. Nov. 1916, promoted Lieut. May 1918. Served in France Dec. 1916 to May 1919.

HUGH CHRISTOPHER WHITEHEAD.

Admitted June 1914. Member of Burch, Whitehead & Davidsons, of 6 Bolton Street, Piccadilly, W. Served as Capt., Dorset Yeomanry.

JAMES LOY WHITEHEAD.

Admitted April 1907. Member of J. D. Whitehead & Son, of Pickering, Yorks. Joined Nov. 11, 1914, as Capt., 6th Batt. A.P.W.O. Yorkshire Regt., transferred to 11th Batt. Jan. 1915. Served at Home and in France.

JOHN WHITEHEAD.

Admitted Feb. 1904, practising at Preston. Served as Private, 3/4 Batt. Loyal North Lancashire Regt.

JOHN WHITEHEAD.

Admitted Oct. 1910. Deputy Town Clerk, Tynemouth. Joined Sept. 15, 1914, as Private, 1/4 Batt. Border Regt. Gazetted 2nd Lieut. same Batt.

Oct. 29, 1914, promoted Lieut. June 1916, Capt. Sept. 1917. Served in Burma and India.

REGINALD HENRY HUGHES WHITEHEAD.

Admitted July 1904. Member of Henry John Whitehead & Son, of Cambridge. Mobilised Aug. 1914, as Corporal, Suffolk Hussars. Gazetted 2nd Lieut. Leicestershire Royal Horse Artillery Aug. 26, 1914, and subsequently promoted Capt., was in command of 19th Brigade Royal Horse Artillery Ammunition Column. Acted as Prosecutor at Courts Martial at Aleppo and also as Judge Advocate. Awarded M.C. Served at Home and in Egypt.

LEOPOLD SHILSON WHITEHORN.

Admitted Nov. 1908. Member of Whitehorns, of Banbury (Oxon) and Winslow (Bucks). Joined Feb. 9, 1916, as Private, 29th Batt. Royal Fusiliers, promoted Lance-Corporal Aug. 1916. Served in France July to Oct. 1916. Wounded in attack at Grandecourt, near Bapaume, Somme, on Oct. 7, 1916, and taken prisoner, remaining in Germany hands at Lager Parchim i/M till Oct. 21, 1917, when interned in Switzerland on account of wounds.

WILLIAM JOSEPH WHITEHORN.

Admitted Jan. 1906. Member of Whitehorns, of Banbury, Oxon. Joined Sept. 18, 1914, as Private, 19th (Public Schools) Batt. Royal Fusiliers. Granted a commission as 2nd Lieut. 7th (Service) Batt. South Wales Borderers Feb. 1915, promoted Lieut. June 1918. Served in Serbia (Salonica Expedition) Jan. 1916 to Sept. 1918. Reported missing near Jumeaux, Macedonia, Sept. 18, 1918, and subsequently presumed (by War Office) killed on that date.

JOHN HUBERT WHITEHOUSE.

Articled to J. B. Lazenby, of Newcastle-upon-Tyne. Served as Lieut., Royal Army Service Corps.

CHRISTOPHER HORSLEY WHITELEGGE.

Admitted Jan. 1912. Clerk with Great Western Railway Company, Paddington Station, W. Joined May 25, 1915, as Temp. 2nd Lieut., Royal Army Service Corps, promoted Temp. Lieut. Feb. 1916, Temp. Capt. Sept. 1918. Served in France and Belgium July 1915 to Jan. 1918.

GERARD TARVER WHITELEY.

Admitted Oct. 1898, practising at Town Hall Chambers, High Street, Southwark, S.E. Rejoined Nov. 3, 1914, as Capt., 23rd Batt. Cheshire Regt. Served at Home. Resigned March 1918.

ANTHONY ADAMSON WHITESIDE.

Admitted Sept. 1907, practising at Douglas, Isle of Man. Joined March 8, 1916, as Private, 26th Batt. Royal Fusiliers. Gazetted 2nd Lieut. 3rd King's Own Yorkshire Light Infantry March 29, 1917, promoted Capt. and appointed Courts Martial Officer to the Tay Defences April 1918. Served in France May 1917 to Jan. 1918.

HAROLD OXENDALE WHITESIDE.

Articled to Edward Whiteside, of Blackpool. Joined Aug. 1, 1915, as Private, 19th (Reserve) Batt. Royal Irish Rifles, subsequently gazetted 2nd Lieut. 10th Batt. Royal Irish Rifles. Served at Home and in France.

GEORGE ARTHUR WHITFIELD.

Admitted July 1904. Member of Whitfield, Byrne & Dean, of 22 Surrey Street, W.C. Joined April 1918, as Private, Inns of Court O.T.C., and subsequently a Cadet at 22nd Garrison Officer Cadet Batt., Cambridge. Served at Home.

JAMES GIBSON WHITFIELD.

Admitted Nov. 1901. Member of Taunton & Whitfield, of Birmingham. Joined Oct. 19, 1914, as Lieut , Royal Warwickshire Regt. (T.F.), promoted Capt. and Adjutant Feb. 1916, Major (Commandant) Divisional Reception Camp, B.E.F., July 1918 to Jan. 1919. Served in France 1916 and 1918.

JOHN LAWRENCE WHITFIELD.

Admitted Dec. 1906. Member of John Whitfield & Son, of Chorley, Lancs. Served as Capt., 4th Batt. Loyal North Lancashire Regt. (T.). Died at Boulogne June 23, 1915, of wounds received in action on June 15.

CHARLES EDWARD WHITFORD.

Admitted Dec. 1894. Member of Whitford & Sons, of St. Columb, Cornwall. Mobilised Aug. 1914, as Capt., Duke of Cornwall's Light Infantry, and subsequently promoted Major. Awarded the T.D. Served at Home. Transferred to Territorial Force Reserve May 1917.

JOHN SAMUEL WHITHAM.

Articled to G. E. H. Maggs, of Batley. Joined Aug. 11, 1914, as Cadet, Leeds University O.T.C. Gazetted 2nd Lieut. 8th Batt. West Yorkshire Regt. Oct. 7, 1914, promoted Lieut. Feb. 1915, transferred to Royal Army Service Corps (M.T.) April 1916, promoted Capt. Jan. 1918. Twice mentioned in Dispatches. Served at Home Aug. 1914 to June 1916, and in France and Flanders June 1916 to Jan. 1919.

FREDERICK CHARLES WHITING.

Articled to A. Rendall, of Yeovil. Served as 2nd Lieut., 8th Batt. Wiltshire Regt., and attained the rank of Capt.

EDWARD NATHAN WHITLEY.

Admitted May 1899. Member of Hirst, Whitley & Akeroyd, of Halifax. Embodied as Major 2nd West Riding Brigade Royal Field Artillery (T.) at outbreak of War, promoted Lieut.-Col. Aug. 1914, appointed Brigadier-General commanding Royal Artillery 47th Division B.E.F. March 1917, promoted Colonel Aug. 1918, relinquished appointment as Brigadier-General Royal Artillery March 1919. Seven times mentioned in Dispatches. Awarded the C.B., C.M.G., and D.S.O. Served in France April 1915 to March 1919.

JOHN BEACH WHITMORE.

Articled to H. Bradshaw, of 116 Fore Street, E.C. Served as Capt., 16th Batt. County of London Regt. (Queen's Westminster Rifles). Awarded the T.D.

ARTHUR WHITTAKER.

Admitted Nov. 1914. Assistant Solicitor with the Town Clerk of Burnley. Joined Sept. 27, 1915, as 2nd Lieut., Lancashire and Cheshire Royal Garrison Artillery, promoted Lieut. July 1916, A/Capt. March 1917. Served in France

1917, and in Salonica 1918 to 1919. Wounded Sept. 30, 1917, gassed Oct. 30, 1917.

FRANCIS WHITTAKER.

Articled to J. H. Billinge, of Manchester. Joined Aug. 31, 1914, as Private, The Rifle Brigade. Gazetted 2nd Lieut. 2/8 Batt. Lancashire Fusiliers June 18, 1915, promoted Temp. Lieut. Nov. 1915, Lieut. July 1917, A/Capt. Labour Corps Jan. 1918, Temp. Capt. July 1918, Temp. Capt. in Army and Staff Capt. Dec. 1918, Temp. Major and Deputy Assistant Adjutant General Oct. 1919. Served in France Dec. 1914 to Jan. 1915 and Feb. 1917 to Jan. 1920, remainder at Home.

JOHN WHITTAM.

Admitted May 1912. Of County Hall, Spring Gardens, S.W. Served as Private, 4th Batt. Seaforth Highlanders (T.).

ALFRED ROLFE WHITTINGHAM.

Articled to A. E. Whittingham, of Nantwich, Cheshire. Joined Dec. 9, 1915, as Private, 15th Batt. London Regt. (Civil Service Rifles), transferred to 179th Light Trench Mortar Battery 60th Division June 1916. Served in France June to Dec. 1916, Macedonia Dec. 1916 to June 1917, Palestine June 1917 to March, 1919.

JOHN HERBERT WHITTINGHAM.

Articled to Herbert Whittingham, of Bolton, Lancs. Joined Feb. 1915, as Private, Manchester University O.T.C. Gazetted 2nd Lieut. 2/3 East Lancashire Brigade Royal Field Artillery (T.) Jan. 4, 1916, promoted Lieut. June 1917. Served at Home and in France.

CECIL HENRY WHITTINGTON.

Admitted April 1901, practising at Queen Anne's Chambers, Westminster, S.W. Joined the Royal Flying Corps in April 1916, and subsequently attained the rank of Brigadier-General. Awarded C.M.G., C.B.E.

ROBERT HUGH WHITTINGTON.

Admitted Feb. 1899. Member of Fuller, Whittington and Fielding, of Bath. Joined Royal Flying Corps in May 1916, attained the rank of Capt.

WALTER JAMES WHITTON.

Admitted Nov. 1909. Managing Clerk with C. V. Young & Cowper, of 65 Stoke Newington Road, N. Joined Jan. 16, 1915, as Rifleman, 16th Batt. County of London Regt. (Queen's Westminster Rifles), subsequently promoted Sergeant. Served in France June to Nov. 1916 and June 1918 to Feb. 1919, at Salonica Nov. 1916 to June 1917, and in Palestine June 1917 to June 1918. Wounded in Palestine Feb. 22, 1918.

CHARLES EDWARD WHITWORTH.

Admitted April 1914. Of Nottingham. Joined Sept. 1914, as Private, Lincolnshire Regt. Gazetted 2nd Lieut. 6th Batt. (Princess Alexandra's Own) Yorkshire Regt. March 1915. Once mentioned in Dispatches. Served at Gallipoli. Reported wounded and missing and subsequently presumed to have died of wounds Aug. 22, 1915.

ROBERT HENRY WHITWORTH.

Admitted Dec. 1909, practising at 124 Chancery Lane, W.C. Joined Feb. 20, 1915, as Lieut., Royal Army Service Corps, promoted Capt. Aug. 1916. Mentioned for Home Service. Served at Home.

JOSEPH BAZALGETTE WICKHAM.

Articled to Ellis & Ellis, of 10, Little College Street, Westminster, S.W. Served as Lieut., 4th Dragoon Guards.

SAMUEL WICKINS.

Admitted Feb. 1902, lately practising at 9 Quality Court, W.C. Joined Sept. 1914 as Lieut. in Highland Light Infantry, promoted Capt. Nov. 1914, Major May 1918. Served at Home and in France. Wounded seriously Battle of Loos Sept. 1915.

CHARLES RICHARD WIGAN.

Articled to Charles Wigan, of Norfolk House, Victoria Embankment, W.C. Joined Aug. 5, 1914, as 2nd Lieut., 1/5th Batt. The Queen's Royal West Surrey Regt., promoted Lieut. March 1915, Capt. June 1916. Appointed A.D.C. to G.O.C. 15th (Indian) Division Oct. 1918. Awarded M.C. Served in India Dec. 1914 to Dec. 1915, and in Mesopotamia Dec. 1915 to May 1919.

NORMAN HAIG WIGHTWICK.

Admitted Aug. 1904. Member of Kingsford, Arrowsmith & Wightwick, of Canterbury. Joined Nov. 19, 1914, as Lieut., Territorial Force Reserve, General List. Gazetted 2nd Lieut. Royal East Kent Yeomanry April 6, 1915, promoted Lieut. June 1916, Capt. March 1918. Served at Home.

HAROLD HARTLEY WILBERFORCE.

Admitted Dec. 1907. Member of J. T. Ware & Wilberforce, of York. Mobilised Aug. 1914 as Capt., West Riding Division Royal Army Service Corps, promoted Temp. Major Aug. 1914, Temp. Lieut.-Col. Feb. 1916, Major (Substantive) 1918. Commanding 62nd Divisional Train March 1916 to March 1919. Twice mentioned in Dispatches. Awarded the D.S.O. and Croix de Guerre (French). Served at Home; and in France, Belgium, and Germany.

ARTHUR HERBERT WILD.

Articled to J. I. T. Ferens, of Hull. Joined Sept. 2, 1914, as Private, 10th Batt. East Yorkshire Regt. Gazetted 2nd Lieut. 13th Batt. East Yorkshire Regt. Nov. 10, 1914, transferred to 14th Batt. Dec. 1915 and to 15th Batt. May 1916, promoted Lieut. July 1917, attached to 9th Batt. Northamptonshire Regt. March to Oct. 1918, and part of that time acted as Commandant of Brigade Signal School. Once mentioned in Dispatches. Served in France Aug. 1916 to March 1918 and Oct. 1918 to Jan. 1919.

FREDERIC JAMES WILD.

Articled to H. W. Chell, of Bury, Lancashire. Joined Oct. 29, 1915, as Temp. 2nd Lieut., 10th (Reserve) Batt. East Lancashire Regt., promoted Temp. Lieut. July 1917, Temp. Staff Lieut. (2nd Class) April 1919. Served at Home Oct. 1915 to July 1916, and in France July 1916 to March 1917. Wounded and taken prisoner near Achiet-le-Petit March 8, 1917.

ARCHIE RAYMOND WILKINS.

Admitted Feb. 1910. Member of Sayers & Wilkins, of Hove. Served as 2nd Lieut., 3rd Batt. (attached 1st Batt.) Manchester Regt. Killed in action in Mesopotamia on March 8, 1916.

ERNEST AUGUSTUS WILKINS.

Admitted Dec. 1905. Member of Wilkins, Son & Thompson, of Uttoxeter. Joined Sept. 3, 1914, as Private, 7/10 Batt. Royal Fusiliers (Stockbrokers). Commissioned 2nd Lieut. Royal Field Artillery Jan. 20, 1915, promoted Lieut. July 1917. Served in Gallipoli, Egypt, India, and Salonica.

ERNEST WILLIAM WILKINS.

Admitted Feb. 1900. Member of G. A. & E. W. Wilkins, of Ashby-de-la-Zouch, Leicestershire. Joined June 5, 1917, as Lieut., Royal Naval Volunteer Reserve, subsequently Capt. Royal Air Force. Served at Home.

LAWRENCE ARNOLD WILKINS.

Articled to Robert Barber, of Nottingham. Joined Dec. 10, 1914, as 2nd Lieut., 2/4 Batt. York and Lancaster Regt. (T.), promoted Lieut. June 1917, and Capt. July 1918. Served in Flanders and France Sept. 1915 to Aug. 1918. Killed in action at Ervillers, north-west of Bapaume, Aug. 25, 1918.

ROBERT BIRD MANNING WILKINS.

Admitted April 1909, practised at 4 Great James Street, Bedford Row, W.C. Served as Driver, Royal Field Artillery. Subsequently gazetted 2nd Lieut. in same Regt. and promoted Lieut. June 1919.

VERNON SPENCER WILKINS.

Articled to S. E. Wilkins, of Aylesbury. Enlisted Feb. 1915, as Private, 5th City of London Batt. London Regt. (London Rifle Brigade) and went to France. Invalided home 1916, and afterwards gazetted 2nd Lieut. 4th Batt. Oxford and Bucks Light Infantry, and returned to France, subsequently wounded and returned home. Rejoined his Batt. in Italy, again invalided home, and in Aug. 1918 transferred to 4th Batt. in France. Died of influenza Nov. 11, 1918.

CHARLES WILKINSON.

Admitted March 1914. With John Storey & Son, of Leicester. Joined June 1915, as 2nd Lieut., Royal Field Artillery, transferred to Royal Air Force March 1918, and subsequently promoted Lieut. Awarded the M.C. Died Nov. 21, 1918, of pneumonia following influenza, whilst on leave from France.

CHARLES LEYBURN WILKINSON.

Admitted May 1911, practised at Newcastle-upon-Tyne. Mobilised Aug. 1914, as Lieut., 1st Northumbrian Brigade Royal Field Artillery, promoted Capt. Aug. 1914, Major Oct. 1914. Once mentioned in Dispatches. Awarded the D.S.O. Served in France 1915 to 1918. Wounded spring of 1916 and April 6, 1918, and died from wounds April 7, 1918.

GEORGE EDWARD WILKINSON.

Admitted Oct. 1906. Member of Wilkinson & Marshall, of Newcastle-upon-Tyne. Served as 2nd Lieut., 6th Batt. Northumberland Fusiliers (T.), and attained the rank of Capt., also as Major Machine Gun Corps. Mentioned in Dispatches. Awarded the M.C.

JOHN MUSGRAVE WILKINSON.

Articled to A. T. Simpson, of Tunbridge Wells. Joined Sept. 2, 1914, as Private, Royal Fusiliers. Gazetted 2nd Lieut. Royal Army Service Corps Jan. 28, 1915, promoted Lieut. Aug. 1916. Served in Salonica Aug. 1916 to Dec. 1917.

NOEL READ ELLERSHAW WILKINSON.

Admitted Dec. 1911. Member of M. C. Hill & Wilkinson, of Newcastle-upon-Tyne. Served as Lieut., Royal Army Service Corps, and attained the rank of Temp. Capt. Awarded the O.B.E.

WILLIAM WILKINSON.

Admitted Jan. 1888, practising at Bishop Auckland. Mobilised Aug. 1914 as Major, and raised and commanded the 2/6 Batt. Durham Light Infantry. Placed on T.F. Reserve July 1915 owing to ill-health contracted on Service. Served at Home.

WILLIAM DURHAM WILKINSON.

Admitted Dec. 1895. Member of Wilkinson & Son, of 47 Bloomsbury Square, W.C. Joined Sept. 13, 1914, as Private, 16th (S.) Batt. Middlesex Regt. Gazetted Lieut. 17th (S.) Batt. Middlesex Regt. Jan. 25, 1915, promoted Capt. July 1915, 2nd in command 52nd Graduated Batt. July 1916, Personal Assistant to Controller Priority Department, Ministry of Munitions, Sept. 1918. Awarded O.B.E. (Military). Served in France Nov. 1915 to July 1916.

ROGER HUSSEY WILLCOCKS.

Admitted Aug. 1913. Member of Bridgman & Co., of 4 College Hill, E.C. Joined Aug. 1914, as Driver, "A" Battery Hon Artillery Company. Gazetted 2nd Lieut. Hon. Artillery Company Oct. 1915, transferred to Royal Field Artillery (T.) Jan. 1916, promoted Lieut. June 1916. Once mentioned in Dispatches. Served at Home Aug. 1914 to Oct. 1915, Egypt (Sinai Peninsula) Oct. 1915 to Dec. 1916, Salonica (Struma Valley) Dec. 1916 to March 1918. Demobilised March 1918.

EDWARD ARCHIBALD WILLETT.

Admitted July 1902. Member of Latter & Willett, of Bromley, Kent. Joined Oct. 1914, as Private, 1st Sportsman's Batt. Royal Fusiliers. Served at Home. Died in Camp at Romford, Essex, of cerebro-spinal meningitis on Feb. 9, 1915.

JOHN WICKHAM WILLETT.

Admitted May 1915. Managing Clerk with Latter & Willett, of Bromley, Kent. Joined Sept. 13, 1914, as Private, 16th Batt. Middlesex Regt. Gazetted 2nd Lieut. 2/12 Batt. London Regt. July 27, 1915, promoted Lieut. 1916. Served in France. Wounded April 5, 1917.

CHARLES NORMAN BERESFORD WILLEY.

Articled to A. N. F. Goodman, of Devonport and Plymouth. Joined May 5, 1915, as 2nd Lieut., 2/5 Batt. (Prince of Wales's Own) Devonshire Regt. (T.), transferred to Devon Royal Garrison Artillery Oct. 1915. Gazetted

Temp. Lieut. Oct. 1916, Lieut. as from June 1916. Subsequently proceeded overseas as O.C. 108th A.A. Sections. Joined 'D.' A.A. Battery, 1st Army, B.E.F. France, subsequently Adjutant and Orderly Officer at Headquarters Central A.A. Group, B.E.F. France. Served at Home May 1915 to May 1917, and in France May 1917 to Dec. 1918.

THOMAS ARTHUR WILLEY.

Articled to Arthur Willey, of Leeds. Served as 2nd Lieut., West Yorkshire Regt.

ALBERT HENRY WILLIAMS.

Admitted Dec. 1886, practising at Edinburgh Lodge, Howick Place, Westminster, S.W. Gazetted Lieut. General List July 12, 1916, gazetted Capt. Sept. 1917. Received letter of thanks from G.O.C. London District. Awarded O.B.E. (Military Division). Served at Home, attached Headquarters London District.

ARCHARD TREVOR WILLIAMS.

Admitted Nov. 1908. Managing Clerk with the late W. Maurice Williams, of Leicester. Mobilised Aug. 1914, as Capt., Lincolnshire and Leicester Coy. Royal Army Service Corps, promoted Temp. Major Oct. 1915, Major June 1916. Served with 46th (North Midland) Division to Nov. 1915, and subsequently with the 59th, 58th, and 34th Divisional Trains. O.C. Ripon Sub-District Royal Army Service Corps Nov. 1919. Twice mentioned in Dispatches. Awarded O.B.E. Served at Home till Feb. 26, 1915, France, Flanders, and Germany till Aug. 1919.

ARTHUR JONES WILLIAMS.

Admitted May 1910. Member of Tofield & Williams, of Sheffield. Joined Sheffield University O.T.C. May 29, 1916. Enlisted in 2/28 Batt. County of London Regt. (Artists Rifles) June 6, 1916. Commissioned 2nd Lieut. 3rd Batt. The Welch Regt. Feb. 27, 1917. Served in Palestine May to Nov. 1917. Killed in action in Palestine Nov. 3, 1917.

ARTHUR MONTAGU WILLIAMS.

Admitted July 1906. Member of Browne, Son & Williams, of Nottingham. Mobilised Aug. 1914, as Lieut., 7th Batt. Notts and Derby Regt. (Sherwood Foresters). Killed in action in France June 1915.

ARTHUR RHYS WILLIAMS.

Admitted March 1915. Member of Rees Williams & Son, of Aberdare. Joined Dec. 13, 1916, as Private, Royal Welch Fusiliers, transferred to 15th Batt. South Lancashire Regt. Jan. 1917, promoted C.Q.M.S. Sept. 1918. Served at Home.

AUBREY BRANSBY WILLIAMS.

Admitted June 1901. Member of Williams & Williams, of Swansea. Served as Lieut., 18th Batt. Royal Welch Fusiliers.

CHARLES JAMES WILLIAMS.

Admitted April 1913. Of 36 Theobald's Road, W.C. Joined the Inns of Court O.T.C. Aug. 1914, and gazetted to 8th Batt. Bedfordshire Regt., promoted Lieut. Feb. 1915. Died in Flanders Dec. 19, 1915, from the effects of wounds and gas poisoning.

DAVID HAROLD WILLIAMS.

Admitted Oct. 1908, practising at Gorseinon, Glam. Mobilised Aug. 1914, as 2nd Lieut., 6th Batt. The Welch Regt., and attained the rank of Capt., subsequently attached to Ministry of National Service.

DOUGLAS WILLIAMS.

Admitted Oct. 1913, practised at Sheffield. Served as 2nd Lieut., King's Own Yorkshire Light Infantry. Died July 1916 of wounds received in action.

DOUGLAS LIONEL GWYNNE WILLIAMS.

Articled to W. M. Williams, of Leicester. Served as 2nd Lieut., North Midland Divisional Cyclists, promoted Lieut. July 1917, A/Capt. Courts Martial Officer Jan. 1919.

DYSON BROCK WILLIAMS.

Admitted June 1911. Member of Williams & Williams, of Swansea. Joined Oct. 3, 1914, as Lieut., 14th (Swansea) Batt. The Welch Regt., promoted Capt. and Adjutant Nov. 1914, Major May 1915, 2nd in Command Jan. 1916, Lieut.-Col. Aug. 1918. Once mentioned in Dispatches. Awarded the D.S.O. Served in France 1915 to 1919. Once wounded.

EDWARD HERBERT WILLIAMS.

Admitted Feb. 1913, practised at Coventry. Served as Lieut., 9th Batt. South Wales Borderers. Killed in action 1916.

FREKE BULKELEY WILLIAMS.

Articled to Bircham & Co., of 46 Parliament Street, S.W. Served as 2nd Lieut., 23rd Batt. County of London Regt.

GEORGE WILLIAMS.

Admitted July 1912. Member of Kingsley Wood & Co., of 15 Walbrook, E.C. Served as Lieut., Royal Air Force.

GEORGE EDGAR PROPERT WILLIAMS.

Articled to R. T. P. Williams, of Haverfordwest. Served as Private, Public Schools Batt. Royal Fusiliers.

GODFRY EDGAR MOSTYN WILLIAMS.

Articled to S. B. Williams, of Broadstairs. Served as Corporal, Royal Army Medical Corps.

GUY WILLIAMS.

Admitted Jan. 1909. Member of Luya & Williams, of Liverpool. Served as Seaman, Royal Naval Volunteer Reserve.

HAROLD JAMES WILLIAMS.

Admitted Oct. 1896, practised at Lewisham. Served as Private, 32nd Batt. Middlesex Regt., and subsequently as Sergeant, Education Staff, attached 52nd (Grad.) Batt. Manchester Regt.

HENRY WILLIAM DAVIES WILLIAMS.

Admitted April 1908. Managing Clerk with Eaton Evans & Williams, of Haverfordwest and Milford Haven. Mobilised Aug. 1914, as 2nd Lieut., 4th

Batt. The Welch Regt., promoted Lieut. Feb. 1915, Capt. Sept. 1916. Served in Gallipoli and at Home. Wounded at Suvla Bay Landing Aug. 10, 1915.

HUGH CAMERON WILLIAMS.

Articled to J. F. McIntyre, of Birkbeck Chambers, Holborn, W.C. Served as 2nd Lieut., The Queen's Royal West Surrey Regt., promoted Lieut. July 1917, A/Capt. Feb. 1918.

HUGH HAMMERTON WILLIAMS.

Admitted Nov. 1910. Managing Clerk with Rawle, Johnstone & Co., of 1 Bedford Row, London, W.C. Joined Nov. 1914, as A.B., Royal Naval Volunteer Reserve, promoted Chief Petty Officer May 1915, transferred with commission (2nd Lieut. Royal Garrison Artillery, S.R.) July 1916. Appointed Adjutant A.A. Defences, Tees Garrison, and A/Lieut. June 1917, promoted Lieut. Jan. 1918, appointed A/Capt. and to the command of 23rd A.A. Coy. Middlesbrough July 1918. Twice mentioned in Dispatches. Served afloat June to Nov. 1915 on Belgian Coast with the Monitors of Dover Patrol bombarding, and afterwards at Home.

HUGH LLWYD HARRIES WILLIAMS.

Articled to W. L. Williams, of Fishguard. Joined May 17, 1916, as Gunner, Royal Field Artillery. Gazetted 2nd Lieut. Royal Field Artillery (S.R.) April 8, 1917, promoted Lieut. Oct. 1918, seconded to I. W. & D. Royal Engineers Aug. 1918. Served in France Sept. 1917 to April 1918. Wounded at Ypres Oct. 7, 1917, wounded and gassed at Vermelles April 18, 1918.

IVOR LLEWELLYN WILLIAMS.

Admitted May 1913. Managing Clerk with John Moxon, of Newport, Mon. Joined Sept. 10, 1914, as Private, Monmouthshire Regt. Gazetted 2nd Lieut. Cambridgeshire Regt. June 10, 1915, promoted Lieut. Sept. 1916, Capt. April 1917. Served in France Sept. 1915 to May 1916. Wounded May 10, 1916.

JOHN WILLIAMS.

Admitted April 1907. Member of T. W. Henwood & Co., of Carnarvon. Joined Oct. 6, 1914, as Private, 13th Batt. Royal Welch Fusiliers, and attained rank of Company Sergeant-Major. Commissioned 2nd Lieut. 16th Batt. Royal Welch Fusiliers Jan. 22, 1915, promoted Lieut. April 1915, Capt. July 1915, transferred to 12th Batt. July 1915, and to 17th Batt. Sept. 1916, attached Headquarters 38th Division March 1917 to April 1919. Served in France and Belgium.

JOHN COLLINGWOOD WILLIAMS.

Admitted Jan. 1914, practising at Bristol. Served as 2nd Lieut., Tyneside Scottish Batt. Northumberland Fusiliers.

JOHN GRIFFITH WILLIAMS.

Admitted Oct. 1908, practised at Bargoed, Glam. Served as 2nd Lieut., Brecknockshire Batt. South Wales Borderers (T.).

JOHN LIAS CECIL WILLIAMS.

Articled to J. C. F. Barfield, of 1 West Street, E.C. Joined Nov. 1914, as Private, Inns of Court O.T.C. Gazetted 2nd Lieut. Royal Welch Fusiliers

Jan. 5, 1915, promoted Lieut. June 1915, Capt. Oct. 1917. Served in France. Wounded at Mametz Wood, Battle of the Somme, July 1916, gassed at Nieuport, Belgian Coast, Aug. 1917, shell-shock at Passchendaele Village, Belgium, Dec. 1917.

JOHN LLOYD VAUGHAN SEYMOUR WILLIAMS.

Admitted Dec. 1890. Member of Lawrence & Co., of Bristol. Served as Lieut.-Col., South Midland Divisional Royal Engineers. Mentioned in Dispatches. Awarded the T.D.

JOHN RICHARD WILLIAMS.

Articled to J. D. H. Osborn, of Colwyn Bay. Joined Feb. 7, 1916, as Private, 4th (Reserve) Batt. Royal Welch Fusiliers, and attained the rank of Corporal. Gazetted 2nd Lieut. 6th Batt. Royal Welch Fusiliers June 27, 1917, posted to 2nd Batt. Sept. 1917, transferred to Royal Air Force and posted to 16th Squadron April 1918, promoted Lieut. Dec. 1918. Served in France Sept. 7, 1917, to Jan 26, 1919.

JOSEPH EDWARD WILLIAMS.

Articled to R. H. Chapman, of Manchester. Joined Dec. 18, 1917, as Private, 53rd (Y.S.) Batt. King's Liverpool Regt. Died in hospital near Rhyl Feb. 5, 1918.

LESLIE WILLIAMS.

Admitted June 1906, practising at Llanelly. Joined Aug. 26, 1915, as 2nd Lieut., 2/8 Batt. Durham Light Infantry. Invalided out Nov. 19, 1915. Rejoined as Private 3rd Reserve Garrison Batt. Royal Welch Fusiliers April 1918, afterwards Private 18th Batt. The Welch Regt. Served in France.

LESLIE CARADOC WILLIAMS.

Articled to F. Llewellyn-Jones, of Mold. Enlisted on outbreak of War as Trooper, Cheshire Yeomanry, and gazetted 2nd Lieut. Royal Field Artillery in Aug. 1915. Killed in action Aug. 27, 1917.

MEREDYTH ROBERT OWEN WILLIAMS.

Articled to R. E. Cooke, of Luton, Beds. Joined Sept. 1915 Inns of Court O.T.C. Gazetted Temp. 2nd Lieut. Northumberland Fusiliers May 1916. Served in France July 1916 to March 1917. Killed in action near Arras March 14, 1917.

NICHOLAS THOMAS WILLIAMS.

Articled to C. V. Thomas, of Camborne, Cornwall. Joined Dec. 10, 1914, as 2nd Lieut., 2/5 Batt. Devonshire Regt., promoted Lieut. Dec. 1915, attached 1/6 Batt. May 1916, attached Burma Rifles 1917, rejoined 1/6 Batt. Devonshire Regt. 1918. Served at Home 1914 to Sept. 1915, Egypt 1915, Mesopotamia 1916, India 1917 to 1918.

OWEN HENRY MOULSDALE WILLIAMS.

Admitted April 1907, practising at Llangefin, Anglesey. Joined Royal Garrison Artillery May 1, 1916, and subsequently promoted Bombardier 183rd Siege Battery Royal Garrison Artillery. Posted to 67th Siege Battery in France and later transferred to Corps of M.F.P. (employed as Courts-Martial

Clerk to the A.P.M. at Le Havre Base March 1917 to Jan. 1919). Served in France Nov. 1916 to Feb. 1919.

RICHARD EDMUND WILLIAMS.

Admitted May 1907, practising at Ebbw Vale, Mon. Joined Nov. 4, 1915, as Private, Royal Army Medical Corps (T.), promoted A/Corporal on two occasions and reduced to Private on transfer to another unit. Served at Home.

ROBERT WILLIAMS.

Admitted Nov. 1914. Member of Parfitt, Cresswell & Williams, of 567/9 Fulham Road, S.W. Joined Oct. 1915, as Private, Inns of Court O.T.C. Gazetted 2nd Lieut. Royal Welch Fusiliers Aug. 5, 1916, promoted Lieut. Feb. 1918. Awarded the M.C. Served in France. Wounded at Ypres Feb. 18, 1917.

ROGER FRITZ DAHNE WILLIAMS.

Admitted Oct. 1910, practising at Swansea. Served as Private, Sportsman's Batt. Royal Fusiliers.

ROLAND VAUGHAN WILLIAMS.

Articled to A. H. Williams, of 276 Camberwell New Road, S.E. Joined Sept. 15, 1915, as Private, 28th Batt. County of London Regt. (Artists Rifles). Gazetted 2nd Lieut. Royal Flying Corps Jan. 25, 1917. Served in France. Killed in action while flying near Bapaume June 5, 1917. Buried in English Military Cemetery, Beugney.

RONALD GUS WILLIAMS.

Admitted June 1910. Joined May 10, 1915, as Private, Inns of Court O.T.C. Gazetted 2nd Lieut. The Welch Regt. Nov. 5, 1915, promoted Lieut. Nov. 1916, transferred to Machine Gun Corps Feb. 21, 1916. Twice mentioned in Dispatches. Served in France and Italy May 1916 to Jan. 1919.

ROWLAND CHARSLEY WILLIAMS.

Admitted April 1898, practising at 79 Lombard Street, E.C. Enlisted April 17, 1915, as Private, 3rd Batt. Essex Regt., promoted Lance-Corporal Aug. 1915, Corporal Dec. 1915, Sergeant Oct. 1916. Served at Home.

SAMUEL ROGER THOMAS ANTON MONTAGU WILLIAMS.

Admitted Sept. 1907, practised at Tunbridge Wells. Mobilised Aug. 1914, as Lieut., South Eastern Mounted Brigade Field Ambulance Royal Army Medical Corps, and afterwards transferred to the Royal East Kent Mounted Rifles. Died of wounds Oct. 25, 1915.

THOMAS WILLIAMS.

Articled to T. Millward, of Pentre, Glam. Joined Oct. 13, 1914, as Private, 2/7 Batt. (Cyclists) The Welch Regt., promoted Corporal Dec. 1914, Sergeant Jan. 1915. Gazetted 2nd Lieut. 11th Batt. South Wales Borderers May 31, 1915, transferred Army Cyclist Corps July 1915, promoted Lieut. Oct. 1916, Capt. Jan. 1917. Served in France Nov. 1915 to Nov. 1917 and Nov. 1918 to April 1919, and Italy Nov. 1917 to Feb. 1918.

THOMAS DAWKING WILLIAMS.

Admitted Nov. 1907, practising at Nelson and Llancaiach, Glam. Joined Nov. 4, 1914, as 2nd Lieut., Royal Field Artillery, promoted Lieut. and Adjutant

Jan. 1916. Served in Belgium and France Dec. 1915 to Aug. 1917, and at Home Aug. 1917 to June 1919.

THOMAS LESLIE WILLIAMS.

Articled to W. H. Borlase, of Penzance. Served as 2nd Lieut., 4th (Reserve) Batt. Duke of Cornwall's Light Infantry, promoted Lieut. July 1917.

WILLIAM EMERSON WILLIAMS.

Admitted Nov. 1909, practising at Aberdare. Joined Jan. 2, 1916, as Private, Royal Army Service Corps (M.T.). Served in France.

WILLIAM OWEN WILLIAMS.

Articled to J. Evans Thomas, of Liverpool. Joined Sept. 1915 Liverpool University O.T.C. Commissioned as 2nd Lieut. to 12th Batt. Royal Welch Fusiliers Jan. 29, 1916, transferred to 23rd Batt. The Welch Regt. Aug. 1916, promoted Lieut. July 1917. Served at Home Sept. 1915 to Aug. 1916, Salonica Aug. 1916 to Feb. 1919, Constantinople Feb. to Aug. 1919.

CORNELIUS WILLIAMSON.

Admitted July 1911, practised at Harrogate. Served as 2nd Lieut., South Wales Borderers.

DAVID ARNOT WILLIAMSON.

Admitted Aug. 1914. Of Newcastle-upon-Tyne. Served as 2nd Lieut., Tyne Electrical Engineers, and attained the rank of Capt.

GEORGE HAROLD WILLIAMSON.

Admitted April 1913, practising at Derby. Joined 1914, as Private, 4th Public Schools Batt. Royal Fusiliers. Subsequently gazetted 2nd Lieut. 5th Batt. Notts and Derby Regt. (Sherwood Foresters), promoted Lieut. June 1916. Mentioned in Dispatches. Awarded the M.C.

JAMES EDWARD WILLIAMSON.

Admitted April 1905. Member of Williamson, Hill & Co., of 13 Sherborne Lane, E.C. Joined May 13, 1916, as Private, 2/5 Batt. East Kent Regt. (The Buffs). Gazetted 2nd Lieut. 9th Batt. Middlesex Regt. May 31, 1917, subsequently promoted Lieut. Served in France Sept. to Oct. 1917. Wounded near Poelcapelle, Ypres Salient, Oct. 4, 1917.

JOHN MAURICE WILLIAMSON.

Articled to L. C. Cholmeley, of 28 Lincoln's Inn Fields. Joined Aug. 6, 1914, as Private, 28th Batt. County of London Regt. (Artists Rifles). Gazetted 2nd Lieut. 2nd Batt. Gordon Highlanders March 1915. Killed in action near Festubert May 17, 1915.

CHARLES FREDERICK WILLIS.

Admitted July 1905. Member of Willis & Willis, of Rotherham. Served as Major, York and Lancaster Regt. Killed in action March 8, 1918.

JOHN EDWIN WILLIS.

Admitted Oct. 1910, practised at 14 Queen Street, Cheapside, E.C. Enlisted Dec. 1914, as Private, 25th (Cyclist) Batt. London Regt., and in April 1915 received commission as Sub-Lieut. in the Royal Naval Volunteer Reserve

(Royal Naval Division attached Machine Gun Corps). Served through the Gallipoli campaign, at Salonica, and in France. Died April 22, 1917, of wounds received in action on April 19.

JOHN GALBRAITH WILLIS.

Articled to E. Huntsman, of Nottingham. Served as 2nd Lieut., Royal Army Service Corps (T.).

VIVIAN VERE WILLIS.

Admitted April 1912. Member of W. G. & V. Willis, of Leighton Buzzard. Served as Trooper, 2nd King Edward's Horse and subsequently as 2nd Lieut. Tank Corps.

EDWARD WILLIS-FLEMING.

Articled to C. C. Gill, of Bath. Joined Dec. 6, 1915, as Private, Inns of Court O.T.C. (Squadron). Commissioned in Leicester Yeomanry (T.) June 1917, and attached for service in France to 11th Hussars. Served at Home 2 years and in France 1½ years.

PHILIP HENRY WILLMOT.

Admitted Dec. 1885, practising at West Bromwich, Staffs. Joined Jan. 23, 1917. Gazetted Capt. 1st Volunteer Batt. South Staffordshire Regt., appointed Officer Commanding 33rd Special Service Company June 1918, attached 2/1 Huntingdonshire Cyclist Batt. June to Sept. 1918, appointed second in command 1st Volunteer Batt. South Staffordshire Regt. Sept. 1918. Served at Home.

FREDERICK WILLIAM WILLMOTT.

Admitted Sept. 1912. Member of C. P. Clarke & Co., of Taunton. Joined April 3, 1915, as 2nd Lieut., 11th Batt. East Yorkshire Regt., promoted Capt. Jan. 1917, Staff Capt. Oct. 1917 to March 1919. Awarded the M.B.E. Served in Egypt and France. Wounded in France Aug. 27, 1916, loss of left eye.

MAURICE GORDON WILLMOTT.

Articled to W. P. Davies, of 60 Uxbridge Road, W. Served as Capt., 17th Batt. King's Royal Rifle Corps. Mentioned in Dispatches. Awarded the M.C.

FREDERICK WILLOUGHBY.

Admitted Aug. 1884. Member of W., F. & W. Willoughby, of Daventry. Mobilised Aug. 1914, as Junior Major, 4th Batt. Northamptonshire Regt., second in command 2/4 Batt. Nov. 1914, Commanding 2/4 Batt. Dec. 1915, posted to the T.F. Reserve Sept. 1918. Twice mentioned in Dispatches and appointed Deputy Lieut. for the County of Northampton. Awarded O.B.E. (Military Division).

GEORGE CLARKSON WILLOUGHBY.

Articled to Alexander Crossman (junior) of 16 Theobalds Road, Gray's Inn, W.C. Joined Feb. 3, 1915, as Private, 12th Batt. London Regt. (T.F.) Gazetted 2nd Lieut. Oct. 11, 1915, promoted Lieut. July 1917, A/Capt. Feb. 1919, transferred to 19th Batt. The Queen's Royal West Surrey Regt. March to Oct. 1918. Served at Home Feb. 1915 to Feb. 1917 and Feb. to Oct. 1918, and with British Exped. Force Feb. 1917 to Feb. 1918 and Oct. 1918 to April 1919. Accidentally wounded by rifle grenade April 29, 1917.

ROLAND MOFFATT PEROWNE WILLOUGHBY.

Admitted Nov. 1899, practising at Mowbray House, Norfolk Street, W.C. Rejoined Nov. 1914, as Major, 9th Batt. County of London Regt. (Queen Victoria's Rifles). Served at Home, and conducted a draft to France. Raised, and subsequently Second in Command of draft-finding unit of regiment until establishment of the general training reserve in Aug. 1916 ; then to Recruiting Officer's duties (Recruiting Officer in Wilts, later Munition Area Recruiting Officer for Wilts) until 1918 ; thereafter O.C. Regimental Depôt.

ALBAN NOEL WILLS.

Admitted Oct. 1909, practised at Doncaster. Served as Capt., King's Own Yorkshire Light Infantry. Died of wounds March 7, 1918.

ALFRED LESLIE WILLS.

Articled to Alfred Wills, of 21 Leadenhall Street, E.C. Passed from Sandhurst as 2nd Lieut. 4th Batt. Worcestershire Regt. Feb. 1915, promoted Lieut. 1916. Served in Gallipoli and in France. Once severely wounded. Killed at Monchy le Preaut April 23, 1917.

FREDERICK WILLS.

Articled to J. W. Robson, of Manchester. Joined Oct. 1914, as Private, O.T.C. Commissioned Jan. 1, 1916, in Royal Garrison Artillery, promoted Lieut. July 1917, Capt. Aug. 1917. Served in France.

THOMAS WILLS.

Articled to Thomas Wills, sen., of Bath. Joined Sept. 29, 1916, as Private, Royal Army Service Corps. Served in France.

CHRISTOPHER WILLSON.

Admitted Nov. 1893. Of Hong Kong. Served as Lieut., Hong Kong Royal Garrison Artillery. Subsequently transferred to Royal Field Artillery and attained the rank of Major. Served in France and as Commander Royal Artillery Depôt, Archangel, North Russia. Once mentioned in Dispatches. Awarded the O.B.E.

CHARLES ALEXANDER WILMOT.

Admitted March 1899. Member of Charles Wilmot & Co., of 7 New Court, Lincoln's Inn, W.C. Served as 2nd Lieut., Royal Air Force.

DOUGLAS ALFRED THEODORE WILMOT.

Admitted May 1903. Managing Clerk to Henderson, Buckle & Goodman, of 5 Philpot Lane, E.C. Joined Jan. 1915, as Private, 28th Batt. County of London Regt. (Artists Rifles). Commissioned 2nd Lieut. Oxford and Bucks Light Infantry May 12, 1915, promoted Lieut. July 1916, Capt. Aug. 1918. Served in France April to May 1915, Home May to Dec. 1915, Mesopotamia Dec. 1915 to May 1919, Afghanistan May to Sept. 1919.

GEORGE ARTHUR WILMOT.

Admitted March 1890, practised at 5 and 6 Clement's Inn, W.C. Served as Capt., 4th Batt. Royal Warwickshire Regt. Awarded the M.C.

ROBERT CONINGSBY WILMOT.

Admitted Nov. 1909. Managing Clerk with Rider, Heaton, Meredith & Mills, of 8 New Square, Lincoln's Inn, W.C. Enlisted in the Public Schools Corps at the beginning of the War, subsequently obtained commission in the 10th Batt. Notts and Derby Regt. (Sherwood Foresters) and attained the rank of Capt. Served in France. Severely wounded Aug. 25, 1915. Killed Oct. 29, 1917.

ALBERT GEORGE ERNEST WILSON.

Admitted Oct. 1896, practised at Nottingham. Joined Aug. 1915, as Private, Hon. Artillery Company. Served in France. Killed May 3, 1917.

ALEXANDER BERNARD WILSON.

Admitted Feb. 1904. Member of Whale & Wates, of 71 Powis Street, Woolwich, and 107 Cannon Street, E.C. Joined Oct. 1916, as Private, 3rd Batt. Royal West Kent Regt. Commissioned 2nd Lieut. Royal Army Ordnance Corps April 1917, promoted Lieut. July 1917, Capt. Dec. 1918. Served at Home.

ALFRED WILSON.

Admitted Feb. 1913. Managing Clerk with E. S. Spencer, of East Retford. Joined Feb. 7, 1917, as Private, Royal Army Service Corps, transferred to Army Pay Corps Aug. 1917. Served at Home.

BASSETT FITZ-GERALD WILSON.

Admitted Nov. 1913. Member of Mackrell, Maton, Godlee & Quincey, of 21 Cannon Street, E.C. Joined Aug. 1914, as Private, Inns of Court O.T.C. Gazetted 2nd Lieut. 11th Batt. King's Royal Rifle Corps Oct. 1914, promoted Lieut. Nov. 1914, Capt. April 1915, Staff Capt. 59th Brigade (General List) March 1916, attached 9th Batt. King's Royal Rifle Corps Oct. 1917, and to Headquarters 32nd Division Nov. 1917, appointed Staff Capt. Liaison Officer to 2nd American Corps March 1918. Twice mentioned in Dispatches. Awarded the M.C. Served in France.

BRERETON KNYVET WILSON.

Admitted Sept. 1891. Member of Bignold, Pollard & Wilson, of Norwich. Joined April 1915, as Private, Royal Army Service Corps (M.T.), and attained the rank of Sergeant. Gazetted Lieut. Dec. 1915, promoted Capt. Sept· 1918. Served in France and at Home.

CECIL EUSTACE WILSON.

Articled to W. H. Herbert, of 10 Cork Street, W. Joined 1914, as Private, 28th Batt. County of London Regt. (Artists Rifles), afterwards gazetted 2nd Lieut. Royal Flying Corps. Killed in action April 16, 1917.

CHARLES JOSEPH CLAYTON WILSON.

Admitted Dec. 1903. Member of Beor & Wilson, of Swansea. Joined Dec. 1, 1915, as 2nd Lieut., 4th Batt. Shropshire Light Infantry, promoted Lieut. July 1917. Served at Home.

CHRISTOPHER MUNKHOUSE WILSON.

Admitted May 1914. Managing Clerk with Wilson & Sons, of Salisbury. Mobilised Aug. 1914, as Lieut., 4th Batt. Wiltshire Regt. (T.), seconded to

Royal Engineers Signals Aug. 1914, promoted Capt. June 1915, Major Feb. 1917. Once mentioned in Dispatches. Served in France.

ERNEST EDWARD WILSON.

Admitted Nov. 1915. Member of Ince, Colt, Ince & Roscoe, of St. Benet Chambers, Fenchurch Street, E.C. Joined Dec. 8, 1915, as Private, Inns of Court O.T.C. Discharged Sept. 1916 owing to injuries received during training.

GEOFFREY FRANCIS EDWARD WILSON.

Articled to H. D. Wilson, of Lancaster. Mobilised Aug. 1914, as 2nd Lieut., Royal Field Artillery, promoted Lieut. March 1915, Capt. June 1916, appointed Adjutant 1917. Served in France and Belgium.

GEORGE WILSON.

Admitted Oct. 1911. Member of Graham, White, Llewellin & Wilson, of Launceston. Joined Jan. 25, 1915, as Corporal, Royal Engineers (Dispatch Rider). Gazetted Temp. 2nd Lieut. Army Cyclist Corps July 24, 1915, promoted Temp. Lieut. Jan. 1916, Adjutant May 1916, Temp. Capt. Aug. 1917, Staff Capt. Reinforcements, Rouen (and transferred to General List) July 1918. Served in France Sept. 1915 to Feb. 1919.

GRAHAM WILSON.

Articled to Stanley Wilson, of Tynemouth. Joined May 1, 1915, as Private, Royal Marines (Submarine Miners), promoted Sergeant Jan. 1916, Chief Petty Officer Royal Naval Volunteer Reserve Jan. 1917. Gazetted Sub-Lieut. April 1918. Served at Home and in Trawlers—English Channel, Adriatic, Ægean, &c.

HAROLD GRAHAM WILSON.

Admitted June 1908. Member of Frankish, Kingdon & Wilson, of Hull. Mobilised with 5th Batt. Lincolnshire Regt. (T.F.) on outbreak of War with rank of Capt., promoted Temp. Major July 1915, Substantive Major June 1916, Lieut.-Col. March 1918. Twice mentioned in Dispatches. Awarded D.S.O. and T.D. Served in France from Feb. 1915. Wounded at Hohenzollern Redoubt, Loos, Oct. 13, 1915.

HERBERT DUCKWORTH WILSON.

Admitted May 1891. Member of Holden & Wilson, of Lancaster. Mobilised Aug. 1914, as Major, 2nd West Lancashire Brigade Royal Field Artillery. Gazetted Lieut.-Col. March 1918. Twice mentioned in Dispatches. Awarded D.S.O. and T.D. Served in France and Belgium. Wounded Jan. 10, 1917, March 31, 1917, and April 18, 1918.

JOHN WILSON.

Admitted Jan. 1909, practising at Newcastle-upon-Tyne. Joined Sept. 9, 1918, as 3rd Clerk, Royal Air Force, subsequently Aircraftsman 1st Class. Served in France.

JOHN ALAN WILSON.

Articled to Thomas B. R. Wilson, of Newport, Mon. Joined Oct. 4, 1914, as Lieut., 1st Batt. Monmouthshire Regt., promoted Capt. June 1916. Served at Home, France, Belgium, and with Army of the Rhine. Wounded May 8, 1915, and Sept. 6, 1917.

JOSEPH WILSON.

Admitted Feb. 1914, practising at Bootle. Joined Jan. 1916 London University O.T.C. Commissioned Lieut. Royal Field Artillery Reserve Brigade, 189th Heavy Battery and 156th Siege Battery Sept. 16, 1916. Awarded M.C. Served in France and Belgium. Once wounded.

KENNETH FORSHAW WILSON.

Admitted Jan. 1907. Member of Laces & Co., of Liverpool. Joined Aug. 31, 1914, as Private, 10th (Scottish) Batt. King's Liverpool Regt. Received commission as 2nd Lieut. Nov. 1914, promoted Lieut. Dec. 1914, Capt. June 1916, Adjutant to 14th Batt. South Lancashire Regt. Nov. 1916 to Jan. 1919. Served at Home.

REGINALD MORICE WILSON.

Articled to R. A. Wilson, of Salisbury. Served as Corporal, Wessex Divisional Signalling Company Royal Engineers.

THOMAS WILSON.

Member of Partridge & Wilson, of Bury St. Edmunds. Mobilised Aug. 1914, as Lieut., 6th (Cyclist) Batt. Suffolk Regt., promoted Capt. Aug. 1914, attached 2/16 Batt. London Regt. (Queen's Westminster Rifles) March 1916, A/Major second in command Aug. 1917 to June 1918, attached 1st Garrison Batt. Royal Warwickshire Regt. June 1918, then Adjutant and Quartermaster School of Instruction El-Arish, E.E.F. Awarded M.C. Served on East Coast Aug. 1914 to March 1916, in Ireland April to May 1916, France June to Nov. 1916, Salonica Nov. 1916 to June 1917, E.E.F. June 1917 to Jan. 1919. Wounded in France Sept. 28, 1916, and in Jerusalem Dec. 8, 1917.

KENNETH ARTHUR WILSON-BARKWORTH.

Admitted May 1911, practised at Hull. Served as Capt., 4th Batt. East Yorkshire Regt. (T.). Awarded the M.C. Killed in action in France Oct. 25, 1917.

HAROLD WILTON.

Admitted March 1913. With Ballantyne, Clifford & Hett, of Dock House, Billiter Street, E. Rejoined Royal Field Artillery (T.F.) as Capt. Aug. 1914. Died in India Dec. 1914.

HENRY PLEYDELL WILTON.

Admitted May 1889, practising at Sandown, Isle of Wight. Mobilised Aug. 1914, as Major, 8th Batt. Hampshire Regt., transferred to 8th Batt. Essex Regt. Dec. 1914, Draft-Conducting Officer 1916, President of Sub-Area Quartering Committee, Canterbury, 1917 to 1919, Assistant Area Commandant, East Kent, 1918 to 1919. Awarded T.D.

FRANK HENRY CUFAUDE WILTSHIRE.

Admitted April 1908, practising as Town Clerk of Birmingham. Joined Dec. 14, 1914, and gazetted 2nd Lieut. 2/1 Batt. the London Regt. (T.), promoted Lieut. April 1915, Capt. Feb. 1916, reverted to Lieut. June 1916, promoted Capt. June 1917. Once mentioned in Dispatches. Awarded the M.C. Served in Malta Jan. to Aug. 1915, Gallipoli Aug. 1915 to Jan.

1916, Egypt Jan. 1916 to April 1916, France April 1916 to Aug. 1918. Wounded at Croisilles Aug. 20, 1918.

PERCY WILTSHIRE.

Admitted Nov. 1894. Member of Wiltshire, Sons & Jordan, of Great Yarmouth. Mobilised Aug. 1914 with the 1st East Anglian Brigade Royal Field Artillery (T.), and attained the rank of Major. Killed in action in France April 25, 1917.

FRANCIS KNOWLES WINDEATT.

Admitted April 1898. Member of Windeatt & Windeatt, of Totnes, Devon. Mobilised Aug. 1914, as Major, 5th Batt. Devonshire Regt., promoted Lieut.-Col. in command Sept. 1917, appointed Military Magistrate, Jerusalem, May 1918. Twice mentioned in Dispatches. Awarded T.D. Served in India 1914 to 1916, Palestine 1917 and 1918.

GEORGE EDGCOMBE WINDEATT.

Admitted July 1902. Member of Windeatt & Windeatt, of Totnes. Mobilised Aug. 1914, as Capt., 5th Batt. Devonshire Regt., transferred to 6th Batt. Devonshire Regt. (T.) as Major March 1916. Once mentioned in Dispatches. Awarded O.B.E. (Military Division) and T.D. Served in France.

JOHN WINDEATT.

Admitted Nov. 2, 1900. Managing Clerk with Windeatt & Windeatt, of Totnes, Devon. Mobilised Aug. 1914 as Capt., 5th Batt. Devonshire Regt., held acting rank of Major and Lieut.-Col. at different times in 1917 to 1918, promoted Major Nov. 1918. Awarded M.C. and Bar., T.D., and Order of the Nile (4th Class). Served in India, Egypt, Palestine, and France.

WILLIAM HENRY WINDER.

Admitted July 1909, practising at Lancaster. Joined Aug. 1914 1/5 Batt. King's Own Royal Lancaster Regt. Discharged after thirty days' service owing to physical injury. Served at Home.

WALTER EDWARD WINDSOR.

Admitted Dec. 1888. Member of Windsor & Brown, of 228 Bishopsgate, E.C. Served as Capt., 153rd Heavy Battery Royal Garrison Artillery.

LAWRENCE ARTHUR WINGFIELD.

Articled to G. A. Wingfield, of 74 Cheapside, E.C. Joined June 22, 1915, as Private, Inns of Court O.T.C. Gazetted 2nd Lieut. 6th Batt. (Special Reserve) Royal Fusiliers Aug. 26, 1915. Seconded to Royal Flying Corps Sept. 1915, promoted Flying Officer Dec. 1915, Lieut. Flying Officer Feb. 1918, temp. commission Royal Air Force, Lieut. April 1918. Awarded D.F.C. Served in France Jan. to July 1916. Taken prisoner July 1, 1916. Escaped and returned to England Oct. 4 to Oct. 22, 1917.

WILLIAM HUGH WINN-JONES.

Admitted Aug. 1912. Member of Winn-Jones & Co., of 43 St. Mary Axe, E.C. Joined Nov. 19, 1914, as Private in the Infantry, subsequently commissioned and attained the rank of Temp. Capt.

GERALD HARCOURT WINNETT.

Admitted Feb. 1910. Managing Clerk with William C. Dawson & Loncaster, of Hull. Joined July 29, 1915, as Private, 18th Batt. Royal Fusiliers. Gazetted 2nd Lieut. Labour Corps Aug. 15, 1917, promoted Lieut. Feb. 1916. Served in France Nov. 1915 to Aug. 1919.

HOWARD WINNETT.

Admitted Jan. 15, 1901. Member of Hatten, Winnett & Hatten, of Gravesend, Kent. Joined Oct. 1914 as Private, 18th Batt. Royal Fusiliers. Received commission as 2nd Lieut. in 3rd Batt. South Staffordshire Regt. July 16, 1915, promoted Lieut. July 1917, served with 2nd Batt. Lincolnshire Regt. and 2nd and 1/6 Batt. South Staffordshire Regt. Served in France 1916, 1917, and 1918.

GEORGE BYRON WINSOR.

Admitted Nov. 1913, practising at 13 Copthall Avenue, E.C. Mobilised Aug. 1914, as Private, 16th Batt. County of London Regt. (Queen's Westminsters.) Gazetted 2nd Lieut. 17th Batt. County of London Regt. 1917, and subsequently promoted Capt. Served in Egypt and France. Wounded in Egypt.

JOHN GEORGE WINTER.

Articled to William Glossop, of Chesterfield. Served as Cadet, Sheffield University O.T.C., and subsequently gazetted 2nd Lieut. South Staffordshire Regt.

JOHN WILLIAM WINTER.

Articled to W. H. Back, of Norwich. Joined Sept. 1, 1914, as Private, 19th Batt. Royal Fusiliers (Public Schools). Gazetted 2nd Lieut. Norfolk Regt. Dec. 30, 1914, promoted Lieut. Nov. 1915, transferred to Royal Flying Corps April 1917, and became Flying Officer Observer, promoted Capt. in Royal Air Force Nov. 1918. Served at Home 1914 to 1915, N.W. Frontier India Nov. 1915 to Oct. 1917, and Aden Nov. and Dec. 1917.

FREDERICK PAGE WINTERBOTHAM.

Admitted April 1911. Member of Waterhouse & Co., of 10 and 12 Bishopsgate, E.C. and 1 New Court, W.C. Joined Oct. 25, 1915, as 2nd Lieut., Royal Garrison Artillery, and attached to various Anti-Aircraft Batteries, promoted Lieut. July 1917. Once mentioned in Dispatches. Served in France and Belgium April 1916 to April 1919.

JAMES PERCIVAL WINTERBOTHAM.

Admitted Jan. 1909. Member of Winterbotham, Gurney & Co., of Cheltenham. Joined 1914 as Private, Public Schools Batt. Royal Fusiliers. Subsequently gazetted 2nd Lieut. Gloucestershire Regt. and attained the rank of Capt. Mentioned in Dispatches. Awarded the M.C.

WILLIAM WINTERBOTHAM.

Admitted March 1904. Member of Waterhouse & Co., of 10 and 12 Bishopsgate, E.C. and 1 New Court, Lincoln's Inn, W.C. Served as Lieut., Royal Garrison Artillery.

HAROLD CARL WINTLE.
Admitted Dec. 1911, practising at Bristol. Served as Sergeant, Royal Gloucestershire Hussars Yeomanry, and subsequently as Lieut. 2nd Reserve Regt. of Cavalry.

LOUIS WISE.
Admitted Dec. 1900. Member of Wise & Wise, of Manchester. Joined Aug. 9, 1915, as 2nd Lieut., Royal Field Artillery (T.), promoted Lieut. June 1916. Served in France 1916 and 1917.

WILLIAM HENRY WISE.
Admitted Aug. 1887. Assistant Solicitor, Bristol Corporation. Mobilised Aug. 1914 as Major, Royal Field Artillery (T.), promoted Lieut.-Col. June 1917, posted to Territorial Force Reserve Aug. 24, 1917. Once mentioned in Dispatches. Served in France and Belgium.

PERCY WOLF.
Admitted April 1901. Deputy Town Clerk of Blackburn. Mobilised Aug. 1914 as Lieut., 4th Batt. East Lancashire Regt. (T.) and subsequently promoted Capt. Served in Egypt and Gallipoli. Killed in action June 4, 1915.

JOSEPH RICHARDSON WOLFENDEN.
Articled to Wilfrid Clothier, of Liverpool. Joined May 10, 1915, as 2nd Lieut., 9th Batt. King's Own Scottish Borderers. Gazetted out June 1915. Commissioned June 19, 1915, as 2nd Lieut. West Lancashire Army Service Corps (T.), subsequently transferred (Dec. 1916) to 47th (London) Divisional Train, Royal Army Service Corps, promoted Lieut. July 1917, attached 3rd Batt. Border Regt. Jan. 1919. Served in France, Belgium, and at Home. Wounded at Messines June 1917.

ARTHUR HENRY WOOD.
Articled to C. F. Entwistle, of Manchester. Joined Nov. 17, 1915, as Private, Royal Army Medical Corps. Served in France.

BRIAN ROBERT PHILLIP WOOD.
Articled to R. S. Wood, of High Wycombe, Bucks. Joined Aug. 1914 as Private, 7th City of London Batt. London Regt. Gazetted 2nd Lieut. in same Batt. Jan. 1915. Once mentioned in Dispatches. Served in France. Killed at Mazingarbe July 2, 1915.

CARL SUTCLIFFE WOOD.
Admitted Dec. 1913. Member of Wharton, Wilde & Wood, of Manchester. Served as 2nd Lieut., 7th (Reserve) Batt. Manchester Regt. (T.), promoted Lieut. Nov. 1916.

CHARLES BERTRAM WOOD.
Admitted Dec. 1913. Of Pickering, Yorks. Joined 1915 as 2nd Lieut., Rifle Brigade. Served in France. Died of wounds Nov. 5, 1917.

CHARLES HERBERT WOOD.
Admitted June 1909, practising at Preston. Served as 2nd Lieut., 1st East Lancashire Brigade Royal Field Artillery.

DUBRIC WOOD.

Admitted Oct. 1911. Member of Frederic Wood & Son, of Wrington, near Bristol. Joined Aug. 8, 1914, as M/C Corporal, Royal Engineers, subsequently gazetted Lieut. Royal Engineers (Signals). Served in France $2\frac{1}{2}$ years.

EDWARD CHARLES WOOD.

Admitted June 1906. Managing Clerk with H. R. Hodder, of 76 Finsbury Pavement, E.C. Joined Aug. 8, 1918, as Sapper, Royal Engineers. Served at Home.

EDWARD HAMILTON WOOD.

Articled to R. R. Tredgold, of 71 Lincoln's Inn Fields, W.C. Joined May 15, 1915, as 2nd Lieut., 14th Batt. The Duke of Cambridge's Own (Middlesex) Regt., promoted Lieut. Aug. 1917, attached to 6th Batt. May 1915 to June 1916, to 2/4 Batt. Oxford and Bucks Light Infantry June to Nov. 1916, and to 24th Recruit Distribution Batt. Training Reserve Nov. 1917 to Jan. 1919 as Assistant Posting Officer. Served at Home and in France. Wounded 1916, gassed 1917.

FREDERICK GEORGE WILLIAM WOOD.

Admitted Aug. 1882, practised at Brandon, Suffolk. Served as Major, 4th Batt. Norfolk Regt.

GEOFFREY DAYRELL WOOD.

Articled to A. M. Walker, of 3 Raymond Buildings, Gray's Inn, W.C. Joined Aug. 5, 1914, as 2nd Lieut., 7th Batt. Suffolk Regt., and subsequently promoted Lieut. Served in France June to Oct. 1915. Killed near Loos at Hohenzollern Redoubt Oct. 13, 1915.

HENRY STANLEY WOOD.

Admitted Dec. 1912. Member of Morgan, Wright, Horner, Sampson & Wood, of Bradford. Joined Jan. 10, 1916, as Private, Inns of Court O.T.C. Gazetted 2nd Lieut. 7th Batt. West Riding Regt. Jan. 1917, promoted Lieut. Aug. 1918. Served in France.

ROBERT BRAITHWAITE WOOD.

Admitted March 1907. Managing Clerk with J. J. Newcombe, of Okehampton. Joined Aug. 1916 as Gunner, Royal Field Artillery. Commissioned 2nd Lieut. Royal Garrison Artillery (S.R.) June 24, 1917, promoted Lieut. Dec. 1918. Served at Home.

RONALD MAXWELL WOOD.

Articled to H. W. Badger, of York. Mobilised as 2nd Lieut. 5th Batt. Prince of Wales' Own (West Yorkshire Regt.) (T.) August 1914, promoted Substantive Lieut. April 1916, Capt. Nov. 1916, seconded to Machine Gun Corps Feb. 1917, and promoted Temp. Major Feb. 1918, reverted to Capt. 5th Batt. Prince of Wales' Own (West Yorkshire Regt.) (T.) Dec. 1918. Served at Home Aug. 1914 to April 1915 and Dec. 1916 to Dec. 1918, and in France and Flanders April to Dec. 1915 and March to Nov. 1916.

RUPERT WOOD.

Admitted Oct. 1911, practising at Ashton-under-Lyne. Joined Oct. 20, 1916, as 3rd Writer, H.M.S. *Victory*, joined H.M.S. *Venerable* June 1918.

Served in Home waters, attached at various times to the following naval bases—Portsmouth, Portland, Falmouth, and Rosyth.

SYDNEY GEORGE WOOD.

Admitted Oct. 1913, practising at 6 Stone Buildings, Lincoln's Inn, W.C. Joined Sept. 8, 1914, 28th Batt. County of London Regt. (Artists Rifles). Gazetted 2nd Lieut. 1/7 Northumberland Fusiliers (T.) Dec. 3, 1915, promoted Lieut July 1917 Awarded the M.C. Served in France and Belgium and at Home. Wounded (gassed) at the Battle of the Aisne May 27, 1918.

THOMAS BASIL WOOD.

Articled to O. B. Giles, of Boston, Lincs. Joined Oct. 1914, as 2nd Lieut., 4th Batt. Lincolnshire Regt. Served in France. Killed in action at Hohenzollern Redoubt Oct. 13, 1915.

TREVOR LEY CODNER WOOD.

Admitted April 1905. Member of Winter, Bothamley, Wood & Murray, of 16 Bedford Row, W.C. Served with the 28th Batt. County of London Regt. (Artists Rifles) and subsequently as Capt. 5th Batt. London Regt. (T.F.R.).

VERNON SPENCER WOOD.

Admitted March 1905. Member of Wood & Lord, of Manchester. Joined Oct. 1915 as 2nd Lieut., Royal Army Service Corps, promoted A/Lieut. Oct. 1916, A/Capt. June 1917, Substantive Lieut. July 1917, Substantive Capt. Jan. 1918. Once mentioned in Dispatches. Served at Home.

CYRIL FRANK WOODBRIDGE.

Admitted Dec. 1914. Member of Woodbridge & Sons, of 5 Serjeant's Inn, Fleet Street, E.C. Joined Aug. 4, 1914, as 2nd Lieut., Royal Field Artillery, promoted Lieut. Feb. 1916, Capt. Dec. 1916, Major Feb. 1919. Once mentioned in Dispatches. Awarded the M.C. Served at Gallipoli April to Aug. 1915, Serbia Oct. to Dec. 1915, Salonica Jan. 1916 to Aug. 1917, Palestine Sept. 1917 to end, Egyptian Revolution March 1919 to June 1919.

EDGAR THOMAS WOODBRIDGE.

Admitted Feb. 1898. Member of Woodbridge & Sons, of 7 New Square, Lincoln's Inn, W.C., and Uxbridge. Joined July 16, 1918, as Private, Inns of Court O.T.C., subsequently became a Cadet in Royal Garrison Artillery. Served at Home.

STEPHEN ANTHONY RUSTON WOODBRIDGE.

Admitted Jan. 1913. Managing Clerk with Charles & Dayrell, of 67 Moorgate Street, E.C. Joined Sept. 1914 as Private, Inns of Court O.T.C., promoted Corporal Nov. 1914. Gazetted 2nd Lieut. Royal Warwickshire Regt. Nov. 27, 1914, promoted Capt. Aug. 1916. Served in France July 1915 to Aug. 1916. Fatally wounded while on patrol duty Aug. 17, 1916. Died, London hospital, Sept. 15 1916.

ALFRED TAYLOR WOODCOCK.

Articled to J. H. Payne, of Hull. Joined Nov. 1915 as Rifleman, 21st King's Royal (Yeoman) Rifles. Gazetted 2nd Lieut. 4th Batt. East Yorkshire

Regt. (T.). Served at Home and in France. Wounded and shell shock Nov. 1917. Wounded in lungs and taken prisoner, Forest of Nieppe, April 12, 1918. Died of wounds, Cologne hospital, June 4, 1918.

FREDERIC ARTHUR WOODCOCK.

Admitted Nov. 1901. Member of Samuel Woodcock & Sons, of Bury, Lancashire. Mobilised Aug. 1914 as Major, 5th Batt. Lancashire Fusiliers, promoted Lieut.-Col. 1915. Served in Egypt 1914 to 1915, Gallipoli 1915, Sinai Peninsula 1916, Home 1917 to 1919.

FREDERICK WOODCOCK.

Articled to F. A. Woodcock, of Manchester. Joined Aug. 2, 1915, as 2nd Lieut., Royal Garrison Artillery, promoted Lieut. 1917, joined Royal Flying Corps April 1917, served as Observation Officer till Jan. 1918, when came home to train as pilot, promoted Capt. and Flight Commander Aug. 1918. Awarded the M.C. Served in France Nov. 1915 to Jan. 1918 and June to Oct. 1918. Killed in action in France Oct. 31, 1918.

JOHN BURRELL HOLME WOODCOCK.

Admitted June 1911. Managing Clerk with J. J. Williamson, of Deal. Mobilised as Lieut., 1st Batt. Pembrokeshire Yeomanry, promoted Capt. Nov. 1914, Major Aug. 1916. Twice mentioned in Dispatches. Awarded D.S.O. Served in Egypt and Palestine Sept. 1916 to April 1918, and in France May 1918 to July 1919.

FRANK MESSENGER WOODGATE.

Admitted March 1907, practising at 59 Gracechurch Street, E.C. Served as Private, 16th Batt. Royal Sussex Regt., in Egypt.

GILES MUSGRAVE GORDON WOODGATE.

Admitted Aug. 1909. Member of Fraser & Woodgate, of Wisbech. Rejoined Nov. 1916 as Private, Royal Army Ordnance Corps. Gazetted 2nd Lieut. in same Regt. Nov. 1917, promoted Lieut. Feb. 1918, attached G.H.Q., France (Q.M.G. Branch) June 1918, transferred to General List and promoted Temp. Capt. March 1919, Staff Capt. (G.H.Q., France) March 1919. Served in France and Flanders.

JOHN WILLIAM WOODHEAD.

Admitted Dec. 1909, practised at Otley. Joined Sept. 17, 1914, as 2nd Lieut., 2/6 Batt. Duke of Wellington's West Yorkshire Regt., promoted Lieut. Feb. 1915, Capt. Feb. 1917. Served at Home on the Staff of the War Office, Directorate of Lands, London, from Aug. 11, 1916. Died from pneumonia Nov. 27, 1918.

GERALD HERBERT WOODHOUSE.

Articled to Herbert Woodhouse, of Hull. Mobilised Aug. 4, 1914, as Lieut. in East Riding of Yorkshire Yeomanry. Appointed Adjutant of 2/1 Regt., with temporary rank of Capt. Sept. 1914, promoted Temp. Major April 1916, Substantive Capt. June 1916, relinquished Adjutancy Jan. 1917 on becoming second in command of Regt., posted to 1st Reserve Cavalry Regt.

Aug. 1917, and relinquished temporary rank of Major, posted to 1/1 East Riding of Yorkshire Yeomanry Nov. 1917, seconded as Staff Capt. on General Staff Intelligence, G.H.Q., E.E.F., June 1918. Served at Home Aug. 1914 to Oct. 1917, and in Palestine Oct. 1917 to May 1919.

LESLIE WOODHOUSE.

Articled to H. V. I. Watts, of Newton Abbot. Served as Private, Public Schools Batt. Royal Fusiliers.

RALPH MANTELL WOODHOUSE.

Articled to W. M. Woodhouse, of 3 South Square, Gray's Inn, W.C. Joined Oct. 18, 1914, as 2nd Lieut., 4th Batt. Dorset Regt., promoted Temp. Lieut. Jan. 1915, Temp. Capt. Sept. 1915, reverted to 2nd Lieut. Dec. 1915, promoted A/Lieut. May 1916, A/Capt. Jan. 1917, reverted to Lieut. Oct. 1917, promoted A/Capt. May 1918, reverted to Lieut. Aug. 1918. Served at Home 1914 to 1915, India Dec. 1915 to Feb. 1916, Mesopotamia Feb. to Sept. 1916, Palestine Dec. 1917 to Nov. 1918, Egypt Nov. 1918 to Sept. 1919.

GEOFFREY EDWARD WOODROFFE.

Articled to W. A. Ashby, of 39 Eastcheap, E.C. Joined Nov. 9, 1914, as Private, 28th Batt. County of London Regt. (Artists Rifles). Gazetted 2nd Lieut. in same Regt. July 10, 1916, promoted Lieut. Jan. 1918. Served in France. Wounded at Passchendaele Oct. 30, 1917.

KENNETH DERRY WOODROFFE.

Articled to C. J. Woodroffe, of 39 Eastcheap, E.C. Joined Sept. 4, 1914, as Private, 28th Batt. County of London Regt. (Artists Rifles). Gazetted 2nd Lieut. 2nd Batt. Northumberland Fusiliers July 24, 1915, promoted Lieut. July 1917. Served at Home Sept. 1914 to Jan. 1915, France Jan. to Oct. 1915, Macedonia Oct. 1915 to June 1918, France June 1918 to April 1919.

SYDNEY MELSON WOODROW.

Admitted May 1905. Member of Sir Thos. Wright, Son & Aysom, of Leicester. Joined July 17, 1915, as 2nd Lieut., Royal Field Artillery, promoted Lieut. July 1917. Served in France. Wounded on the Somme July 23, 1916, and at Passchendaele, Nov. 10, 1917.

ERNEST REGINALD WOODWARK.

Admitted Feb. 1907. Member of Sadler & Woodwark, of Lynn. Mobilised Aug. 1914, as Lieut., 1/5 Batt. Norfolk Regt. (T.), promoted Capt. Oct. 1914. Served at Gallipoli. Killed Aug. 12, 1915.

CHARLES STANLEY WOOLDRIDGE.

Admitted April 1913. Managing Clerk with Chadwick, Son & Nicholson, of Dewsbury. Joined Jan. 17, 1917, Inns of Court O.T.C. Gazetted 2nd Lieut. 3rd Batt. Devonshire Regt. Oct. 31, 1917, promoted A/Capt. Oct. 2, 1918, with 1st Batt. Jan. 1918 to Jan. 1919. Once mentioned in Dispatches. Awarded M.C. Served at Home Jan. 1917 to Jan. 1918, Italy Jan. to April 1918, France April to Dec. 1918. Wounded April 28, 1918.

LEONARD GORDON WOOLDRIDGE.

Articled to E. J. Stannard, of 19 Eastcheap, E.C. Served as Private, University and Public Schools Batt.

ALEXANDER SUSMAN WOOLF.

Articled to William Sutton, of Newcastle-upon-Tyne. Joined Oct. 16, 1915, as 2nd Lieut., Army Cyclist Corps, promoted Lieut. July 1917, attached 18th Corps Headquarters Aug. 1917. Once mentioned in Dispatches. Served at Home 1915, and in France and Belgium 1916 to 1919.

WALTER RICHARD MORTIMER WOOLF.

Admitted Dec. 1910. Member of Templer Down, Hogg & Woolf, of 31 Lombard Street, E.C. Joined Feb. 1915 as 2nd Lieut., 2nd Batt. Border Regt. Served in France. Wounded at Loos Sept. 25, 1915, and died on the following day.

RONALD WOOLFENDEN.

Articled to R. S. H. Woolfenden, of Denton, Lancs. Joined Sept. 5, 1914, as Private, 20th (Public Schools) Batt. Royal Fusiliers. Awarded the M.M. Served in France. Killed on the Somme Aug. 18, 1916. Buried Dasurs Cemetery, near Corbie, on Somme.

HUMPHREY WILLIAM WOOLLCOMBE.

Articled to J. Y. Woollcombe, of Plymouth. Mobilised as Lieut., Royal Engineers (T.), appointed Adjutant with acting rank of Capt. June 1917 to Oct. 1918. Served in Gibraltar Dec. 1914 to March 1915, and in France June 1915 to Dec. 1918.

SIR CHARLES AUGUSTUS WOOLLEY.

Admitted April 1883. Member of A. C. Woolley & Bevis, of Brighton. Rejoined and gazetted on Nov. 13, 1914, with rank of Major and Hon. Lieut.-Col. 6th (Cyclist) Batt. Royal Sussex Regt., and appointed to command the Depôt, and was in command of No. 26 T.F. Depôt, Brighton. Received the honour of Knighthood. Served at Home.

CHARLES HUMPHREY WOOLRYCH.

Admitted Dec. 1910. Of 5 New Square, Lincoln's Inn, W.C. Served as 2nd Lieut., 1st London Brigade Royal Field Artillery (T.), promoted Lieut. June 1916.

THOMAS HOLMES WOOSEY.

Admitted June 1906, practising at Cardiff. Joined March 1, 1915, as Private, Hon. Artillery Company. Gazetted 2nd Lieut. South Wales Borderers Oct. 1, 1916, promoted Lieut. Feb. 1916, Capt. Sept. 1916, held the appointment of Adjutant to the Batt. Feb. 1916 to April 1918. Once mentioned in Dispatches. Served in France.

CHARLES EARNSHAW WOOSNAM.

Admitted Aug. 1910. Member of Cottrell & Son, of Birmingham. Served as Lieut., Royal Army Service Corps, attached to the Highland Division, and attained the rank of Temp. Capt. Awarded the O.B.E.

FRANK STANLEY WOOTTON.

Admitted July 1906. Member of Wood & Wootton, of 13 Fish Street Hill, E.C. Joined Aug. 26, 1916, as Private, 5th City of London Batt. London Regt. (London Rifle Brigade). Served in France. Killed in action May 5, 1917.

ALAN FLETCHER WORDEN.

Admitted Aug. 1912. Member of Worden & Worden, of Southport. Joined Sept. 7, 1914, as Private, 7th Batt. King's Liverpool Regt. Gazetted 2nd Lieut. 7th Batt. Lancashire Fusiliers July 20, 1916, promoted Lieut. Jan. 1918. Awarded the M.C. Served at Home and in France. Wounded at Athies, near Arras, May 4, 1917.

LEONARD WORDEN.

Admitted March 1912. Deputy Town Clerk, County Borough of Smethwick. Joined Jan. 5, 1915, as Private, 15th (Service) Batt. Royal Warwickshire Regt. and attained rank of A/Company Quartermaster-Sergeant. Subsequently gazetted Lieut. Duke of Cornwall's Light Infantry, attached Supply and Transport Corps. Served at Home, and in India and Aden.

THOMAS HOWARD WORDSWORTH.

Articled to E. B. Kite, of Taunton. Joined June 14, 1915, as 2nd Lieut., Sussex Royal Garrison Artillery (T.), subsequently promoted Lieut. Served in France March to April 1916 and Dec. 1917 to Jan. 1919 with 481st Siege Battery.

JOHN FORTESCUE WORSLEY.

Admitted Dec. 1913. Member of Morgan & Co., of Calcutta. Joined July 1915 as 2nd Lieut., Grenadier Guards, and subsequently promoted Lieut. Served in France. Killed at Fontaine Notre Dame in Battle of Cambrai Nov. 27, 1917.

FREDERICK WORTHINGTON.

Articled to J. W. Jackson, of Grimsby. Served as Capt., Lincolnshire Regt. Wounded on the Somme July 1916. Killed in action April 28, 1917.

WALTER WORTHINGTON.

Admitted June 1893, practising at Hull. Joined Sept. 14, 1914, as Capt., 12th (Service) Batt. East Yorkshire Regt., transferred to 1st Garrison Batt. East Yorkshire Regt. Oct. 1915, attached to King's Own Yorkshire Light Infantry in Sept. 1917. Served at Home and in India from Feb. 1916 to Sept. 1917.

GERALD LASCELLES WOULFE.

Admitted Nov. 1912. Member of Wakeford, May, Woulfe & Gwyther, of 37 Bloomsbury Square, W.C. Joined Sept. 1914 as 2nd Lieut., Northamptonshire Regt. Served in France 1915 to 1916. Killed at the Battle of the Somme July 14, 1916.

MARC EUGENE TOWNSEND WRATISLAW.

Admitted Dec. 1899, practising at Rugby. Joined Dec. 1916 as Lieut., Special List, attached Southern Command as Assistant Recruiting Officer, promoted Capt. Appeal Military Representative July 1917, transferred to Ministry of National Service May 1918, resigned Sept. 1918, transferred to Royal Army Service Corps (M.T.) Oct. 1918. Served at Home.

KENNETH CHRISTOPHER GEORGE WRAY.

Articled to Herbert Hatton, of Warrington. Joined Aug. 26, 1914, as 2nd Lieut., 4th Batt. South Lancashire Regt., and attained the rank of Capt. Served in France and Belgium Feb. 1915 to Aug. 1916. Killed in the Battle of the Somme Aug. 9, 1916.

THOMAS PERCY WRAY.

Admitted Dec. 1908, practising at Chesterfield. Joined Aug. 27, 1917, as A.C.2, Royal Naval Air Service, promoted A.C.1 Feb. 1918. Served at Home.

TOM NORMAN WRENCH.

Articled to A. J. Wardle, of Liverpool. Joined Aug. 11, 1916, as Private, Royal Army Service Corps (M.T.). Granted commission in same Regt. March 25, 1917, promoted Lieut. Sept. 1918. Served at Home Aug. 1916 to April 1917, in France April 1917 to April 1919, and in Germany April to Oct. 1919.

JOHN HARRIS WRENTMORE.

Admitted July 1886. Member of Wrentmore & Son, of 29 Bedford Row, W.C. Mobilised Aug. 1914 as Sergeant, 28th Batt. County of London Regt. (Artists Rifles) and attained rank of Company Sergeant-Major. Gazetted Lieut. T.F. Reserve Sept. 1916, Assistant Recruiting Officer and Military Representative until Nov. 1917, transferred to National Service, London Region Headquarters Staff. Served at Home.

ARTHUR ERNEST WRIGHT.

Admitted Sept. 1891. Member of Wright, Son & Aysom, of Leicester. Mobilised Aug. 4, 1914, as Lieut.-Col. Royal Army Service Corps (T.). Once mentioned in Dispatches. Awarded the T.D. Served at Home.

ARTHUR VERNON WRIGHT.

Admitted Jan. 1908. Member of Day & Wright, of Bristol and Clevedon. Joined March 18, 1916, as Private, 1/4 Batt. Royal Berkshire Regt., and subsequently promoted Lance-Corporal. Killed in action in France Aug. 14, 1916.

CYRIL FREDERICK WRIGHT.

Articled to T. A. Wright, of Leicester. Joined Aug. 30, 1914, as Private, 4th Batt. Leicestershire Regt. Subsequently commissioned and attained the rank of Capt. Awarded M.C. Served two years in France. Twice wounded, at Ypres Sept. 1915 and at Lens June 1917.

DONALD HODGSON WRIGHT.

Articled to R. C. Haworth, of Manchester. Joined Sept. 1914 as Private, 20th (Public Schools) Batt. Royal Fusiliers. Killed in action July 20, 1916.

EDMUND LANCELOT WRIGHT.

Admitted April 1907, practised at Hitchin. Served as Capt., Somerset Light Infantry. Died of wounds July 1916.

EDWARD MARTIN WRIGHT.

Articled to Alexander Wright, of Bacup. Joined Sept. 1914 as 2nd Lieut., 5th Batt. East Lancashire Regt., promoted Lieut. 1915, Capt. 1916. Served at Home and in France. Killed at Mouchy le Preux, near Arras, April 10, 1917.

EDWIN ERNEST STANLEY WRIGHT.

Admitted Nov. 1902. Member of Blyth, Dutton, Hartley & Blyth, of 112 Gresham House, E.C. Joined Jan. 31, 1916, as Private, Inns of Court O.T.C. and attained the rank of Sergeant. Gazetted 2nd Lieut. Royal Sussex Regt. Feb. 1919. Served at Home.

EDWIN GEORGE CHAPMAN WRIGHT.

Admitted April 1912. Member of Dean, Son & Wright, of Liverpool. Served as 2nd Lieut., 8th (Irish) Batt. King's Liverpool Regt. (T.), promoted Lieut. July 1917.

EGERTON LOWNDES WRIGHT.

Admitted Oct. 1912. Member of Wilson, Wright & Davies, of Manchester and Preston. Joined Sept. 1914 as 2nd Lieut., Bucks Batt. Oxford and Bucks Light Infantry, promoted Lieut. Sept. 1914, Capt. June 1915, Adjutant Jan. 1916, G.S.O. III. with 7th Army Corps Feb. 1916, and afterwards with 11th Division, Brigade Major 6th Infantry Brigade Dec. 1916. Twice mentioned in Dispatches. Awarded the M.C. Served in France and Belgium March 1915 to May 1918. Killed in action May 11, 1918.

GEOFFREY LOWNDES WRIGHT.

Articled to M. F. Davies, of Manchester. Served in the Royal Field Artillery and attained the rank of Major. Awarded the M.C.

HENRY NEWCOME WRIGHT.

Admitted March 1909. Member of Stephens & Wright, of St. Austell. Joined Sept. 1914 as 2nd Lieut., King's Own Yorkshire Light Infantry, promoted Lieut. Yorkshire Regt. Oct. 1914, Capt. Cyclist Corps Jan. 1916. Served in France July 1915 to Jan. 1918.

HORACE LEAF WRIGHT.

Admitted July 1901. Member of Roche & Wright, of Daventry. Mobilised Aug. 4, 1914, as Capt. 4th Batt. Northamptonshire Regt. (T.F.), promoted Major June 1916, attached to Headquarters 162nd Infantry Brigade Aug. 1914 to Aug. 1915, second in command 1/4 Batt. Northamptonshire Regt. June 1916 to Oct. 1916, Staff Capt. 162nd Infantry Brigade Oct. 1916 to March 1917, Brigade Major March to Sept. 1917, G.S.O. II. 21st Corps Sept. 1917 to Jan. 1918, G.S.O. II. G.H.Q., E.E.F. Jan. 1918 to May 1919. Twice mentioned in Dispatches. Awarded O.B.E. (Military Division) and Order of the Nile (4th Class). Served in Gallipoli July to Sept. 1915, and in Egypt,

Palestine, and Syria March 1916 to May 1919. Wounded at Gallipoli Aug. 15, 1915.

PETER WRIGHT.

Admitted Oct. 1914. Member of Wright, Becket, Wright & Co., of Liverpool. Joined Aug. 1914 Inns of Court O.T.C. Gazetted 2nd Lieut. Royal Field Artillery and subsequently promoted Lieut., Capt., and Major. Awarded the M.C. Served in France and Belgium. Killed in action Jan. 11, 1918.

ROBERT WRIGHT.

Admitted Sept. 1907. Of Market Rasen. Served as Major, Lincolnshire Yeomanry. Was in the S.S. *Mercia* when it was attacked and was then severely wounded. Killed in action 1917.

WILLIAM GIRVAN WRIGHT.

Articled to W. H. Hastings, of Sidmouth. Served as 2nd Lieut., 9th Batt. Argyll and Sutherland Highlanders, and attained the rank of Capt. Mentioned in Dispatches. Awarded the M.C. and Bar.

JOSEPH WURZAL.

Admitted Jan. 1916, practising at Leeds. Joined July 6, 1916, as Private, Royal Air Force, promoted Sergeant April 1917. Served at Home July 1916 to Oct. 1917, in France and Belgium Oct. 1917 to Nov. 1918, and in Italy Nov. 1918 to Feb. 1919.

GEORGE MONTAGU GRIFFITH WYATT.

Admitted April 1910. Managing Clerk with Waltons & Co., of 101 Leadenhall Street, E.C. Mobilised Aug. 1914, as Lieut., 12th Batt. County of London Regt., promoted Temp. Capt. Sept. 1914, and subsequently A/Major. Once mentioned in Dispatches. Served in France and Belgium Dec. 1914 to May 1915, April to July 1916 and Sept. 1918 to March 1919. Wounded May 5, 1915, and July 1916.

WILLIAM HERBERT WYATT.

Admitted July 1913, Managing Clerk with Bird & Bird, of 5 Gray's Inn Square, W.C. Joined Aug. 1914 as Private, 28th Batt. County of London Regt. (Artists Rifles). Gazetted 2nd Lieut. 1st Batt. East Yorkshire Regt. May 1915. Served in France Oct. 1914 to May 1916. Killed near Fricourt May 4, 1916.

JOHN THEODORE WYKES.

Admitted Dec. 1889. Member of Wykes & Francis, of Derby. Served as Capt., 5th (Reserve) Batt. Notts and Derby Regt. (Sherwood Foresters).

ARTHUR WYLDE.

Admitted July 1913, practised at 35 Ludgate Hill, E.C., and Norwood, S.E. Served as Driver, 2nd London Divisional Train Royal Army Service Corps.

WALTER NELSON WYLES.

Admitted June 1912. Member of Breeze & Wyles, of 4 Walbrook, E.C. Served as Corporal, Royal Garrison Artillery.

JAMES LESLIE WYNN-EVANS.

Articled to O. W. Owen, of Liverpool. Joined Sept. 1915 as Private, Inns of Court O.T.C. Gazetted 2nd Lieut. 11th Batt. London Regt. (Finsbury Rifles) Jan. 1916, promoted Lieut. July 1917, seconded to 163rd Machine Gun Company May 1918. Served in Egypt and Palestine June 1916 to Jan. 1919.

ARTHUR MEREDYTH WYNNE.

Articled to C. J. Archer, of Stockton-on-Tees. Served as 2nd Lieut., Royal Flying Corps. Awarded the A.F.C.

ARTHUR GERALD VAVASOUR YATES.

Admitted Nov. 1912. Of Macclesfield. Joined Aug. 1914 as Private, 28th Batt. County of London Regt. (Artists Rifles). Obtained commission as 2nd Lieut. 16th Batt. County of London Regt. (Queen's Westminster Rifles) July 20, 1915. Served at Home and in France. Killed near Gommecourt July 1, 1916.

JAMES YATES.

Admitted Dec. 1906. Member of March, Pearson & Yates, of Manchester. Commissioned Sub.-Lieut. Royal Navy Oct. 1915, attached to Staff Experimental and Testing Section, Kite Balloons; Jan. 1916, promoted Lieut. Royal Navy Oct. 1917, attached Royal Naval Air Service, transferred to Royal Air Force April 1918 as (Hon.) Capt. Flying, promoted Capt. Royal Air Force Technical Feb. 1919 (dated Oct. 1917). Served at Home.

JAMES YATES.

Admitted Nov. 1913. Member of James Yates & Son, of Southport. Joined Sept. 1914 as Private, 7th Batt. King's Liverpool Regt. Gazetted 2nd Lieut. April 7, 1915, and posted to 16th Batt. King's Liverpool Regt., transferred to 6th Batt. South Lancashire Regt. as Lieut. June 1917. Served in Mesopotamia Nov. 1916 to March 1919.

RICHARD YATES.

Admitted July 1910. Member of John & Richard Yates, of Blackburn. Served as Capt., 1st East Lancashire Brigade Royal Field Artillery (T.). Mentioned in Dispatches.

WILLIAM WALTER YATES.

Admitted Feb. 1905. Member of Barlow, Barlow & Lyde, of 165 Fenchurch Street, E.C. Joined Jan. 4, 1918, as 2nd Lieut., Royal Army Service Corps (M.T.). Served in France May 1918 to April 1919.

IAN DAVID YEAMAN.

Admitted April 1911. Managing Clerk with Rickerby & Co., of Cheltenham. Joined Sept. 9, 1914, as Private, 2/5 Batt. Gloucestershire Regt. Gazetted 2nd Lieut. Royal Field Artillery April 13, 1915, promoted Lieut. July 1916, attached Royal Engineers (Signal Service) Sept. 1917. Served in France Jan. 1916 to April 1918. Wounded at La Rolanderie, near Armentières, April 9, 1918.

JOSEPH YEARSLEY.
Articled to P. C. Kelly, of Liverpool. Joined July 27, 1915, as Driver, Royal Field Artillery. Served at Home 4 months, in France and Belgium 3 years, and in Germany 4 months.

WILLIAM WALLACE YEEND.
Articled to A. S. F. Pruen, of Cheltenham. Joined April 17, 1917, as Private, Cameron Highlanders, transferred to Argyll and Sutherland Highlanders Dec. 1917. Gazetted 2nd Lieut. Seaforth Highlanders Sept. 1918. Served in France.

GLYNNE LOUGHER YORATH.
Articled to F. N. Jones, of Cardiff. Joined Sept. 2, 1914, as Private, Brecknock Batt. South Wales Borderers. Gazetted 2nd Lieut. in same Regt. Nov. 20, 1915, promoted Lieut. July 1917. Served at Aden Oct. 1914 to Aug. 1915, in India Aug. to Nov. 1915, at Home Nov. 1915, and afterwards in France. Killed at Bourlon Wood Nov. 23, 1917.

WILLIAM CHARTRES YOULL.
Admitted Nov. 1900. Member of Chartres & Youll, of Newcastle-on-Tyne. Served as Private, Inns of Court O.T.C., and subsequently gazetted 2nd Lieut. 4th Batt. Northumberland Fusiliers, promoted Lieut. July 1918.

COLIN TURNER YOUNG.
Articled to T. P. Young, of 29 Mark Lane, E.C. Joined Aug. 4, 1914, Inns of Court O.T.C., subsequently obtained commission in Duke of Wellington's West Riding Regt. and attained the rank of Capt. Once mentioned in Dispatches. Wounded severely, Hill 60, April 15, 1915. Killed near St. Quentin April 25, 1917.

EDWIN FRITZ YOUNG.
Admitted Dec. 1901. Member of E. W. Hobbs & Young, of Lewes and Brighton. Joined Dec. 28, 1915, as Orderly, British Red Cross Hospital, Netley, Hants, Corporal Wardmaster British Red Cross Hospital May 1916, Pay Sergeant British Red Cross Hospital Nov. 1916, transferred to Somerset Light Infantry as Private May 1918. Served at Home, Ireland, France and Belgium.

HENRY GEORGE MELVIN YOUNG.
Admitted Nov. 1911. Member of W. W. Young, Son & Ward of 24 Ely Place, Holborn, E.C. Gazetted 2nd Lieut., 4th Batt. Queen's Royal West Surrey Regt. Oct. 29, 1914, promoted Capt. July 1915.

JAMES YOUNG.
Admitted Nov. 1903, practising at Southend-on-Sea. Joined May 1916 as Private, 20th Hussars. Gazetted 2nd Lieut. Royal Army Ordnance Department, afterwards Royal Army Ordnance Corps Sept. 1917, promoted Lieut. Dec. 1917. Served at Home.

JOHN ARTHUR YOUNG.

Admitted April 1907. Member of William Johnston & Co., of Stockport. Joined 1914 as Private, Public School Batt. Royal Fusiliers, joined Inns of Court O.T.C. Feb. 1915. Gazetted 2nd Lieut. York and Lancaster Regt. 1915, transferred to 17th Batt. Notts and Derby Regt. (Sherwood Foresters) 1916, promoted Capt. Oct. 1917. Served in France. Killed in action Oct. 3, 1917.

ROBERT WILLIAM YOUNG.

Admitted Oct. 1914, practised at Evesham. Served as Private, Royal Army Ordnance Corps.

ALEXANDER YOUNG YOUNG-JAMES.

Admitted Nov. 1908, practised at Newport and Cowes, Isle of Wight. Mobilised Aug. 1914, as 2nd Lieut., 1/8 Batt. Hampshire Regt. Isle of Wight Rifles (T.). Served at Gallipoli. Reported missing, believed killed, Aug. 12, 1915. Death on that date subsequently presumed.

Printed at THE BALLANTYNE PRESS
SPOTTISWOODE, BALLANTYNE & CO. LTD.
Colchester, London & Eton, England

www.ingramcontent.com/pod-product-compliance
Ingram Content Group UK Ltd.
Pitfield, Milton Keynes, MK11 3LW, UK
UKHW050950290926
15470UKWH00005B/1738

9 781847 341198